MODERN AUDITING & ASSURANCE SERVICES

6TH EDITION

T0342497

Philomena Leung

Paul Coram

Barry J. Cooper

Peter Richardson

WILEY

Sixth edition published 2015
by John Wiley & Sons Australia, Ltd
42 McDougall Street, Milton Qld 4064

Typeset in 10.5/12 pt Minion Pro Regular

© John Wiley & Sons Australia, Ltd 2011, 2015

The moral rights of the authors have been asserted.

National Library of Australia
Cataloguing-in-Publication entry

Title:	Modern auditing & assurance services/ Philomena Leung; Paul Coram; Barry Cooper; Peter Richardson.
Edition:	6th ed.
ISBN:	9781118615249 (pbk.)
Notes:	Includes index.
Subjects:	Auditing — Textbooks.
Other Authors/Contributors:	Leung, Philomena, author. Coram, Paul, author. Cooper, Barry J., author. Richardson, Peter, author.
Dewey Number:	657.45

Cover and internal design images: © Digital Vision

Typeset in India by diacriTech

Printed in China by
Printplus Limited

10 9 8 7 6 5 4 3

ABOUT THE AUTHORS

Philomena Leung is Professor and Head of the Department of Accounting and Corporate Governance at Macquarie University, Sydney. She has had extensive teaching experience at tertiary and postgraduate levels for over 30 years, specialising in auditing, ethics and corporate governance. Prior to undertaking the role at Macquarie University, Philomena held senior academic positions at Hong Kong Polytechnic University and in Australia at Victoria University, RMIT University and Deakin University. Her PhD in accounting ethics and her KPMG auditing experience from Hong Kong provide an insight into issues relevant to the accounting and auditing profession. Philomena has written for a number of academic and professional journals in the areas of auditing, corporate governance, ethics, internal auditing and accounting education. She has received a number of research grants and has led and co-authored many research projects in the areas of ethics education, internal auditing and professional issues. Philomena has spoken at many conferences and seminars and is a sought-after speaker for national and international forums and media interviews. She is actively involved in the auditing profession, bridging between academia and practice. Philomena believes in supporting the development and reshaping of the profession in Australia and internationally.

Paul Coram is Professor of Accounting and Head of the School of Accounting and Finance at the University of Adelaide. Paul has a Masters in Accounting from the University of Western Australia and a PhD from the Australian National University. He worked as an auditor and became a Chartered Accountant with one of the Big Four firms in Australia, also gaining work experience as an auditor in London. He is actively involved with the Institute of Chartered Accountants and has been a member for over 20 years. Paul has postgraduate qualifications in education and was the inaugural winner of the Pearson Education Accounting Lecturer of the Year Award in 2001. Paul complements his teaching with research in auditing, and has a particular interest in the areas of audit quality and the value of assurance services. He has presented and published his research in Australia and internationally, and serves on the editorial board of the leading auditing journal, *Auditing: A Journal of Practice and Theory*.

Barry J Cooper is Professor of Accounting and Interim Head of the School of Accounting, Economics and Finance at Deakin University, Melbourne. He has a Bachelor of Commerce and a Master of Education from Melbourne University, a PhD from RMIT University, is a Fellow of CPA Australia and the Association of Chartered Certified Accountants (ACCA), and is a past global president of ACCA. After gaining experience as an auditor, Barry joined RMIT University in 1972 where he taught auditing and financial accounting. In 1987, he joined Hong Kong Polytechnic University and was Head of the Department of Accountancy for 4 years. After returning to Melbourne, he was appointed Head of Accountancy at RMIT University until late 1997, when he took leave and joined CPA Australia as National Director — Member Services. During his time at CPA Australia, Barry was responsible for the operations of the CPA divisions throughout Australia and Asia. After returning to RMIT, Barry later joined Deakin University and is currently Head of the School of Accounting, Economics and Finance at Deakin University. During his academic career, Barry has undertaken a number of research projects in the areas of auditing, ethics and accounting education, presented at numerous conferences, published a number of articles in professional and academic journals, and co-authored several books.

Peter D Richardson is a manager with a public sector organisation as well as a teacher of financial reporting and auditing to students preparing for the exams of the ICAA and CPA Australia. He has a Bachelor of Commerce (Hons) and is a member of the Institute of Chartered Accountants in England and Wales. After spending 10 years working for various private accounting firms in the United Kingdom, Peter joined BPP Professional Education, a UK-based public company which, among other things, teaches students strategies for passing their UK professional accounting exams. After 6 years with BPP in the United Kingdom, Peter relocated to Singapore as Managing Director of the local BPP subsidiary, where he was responsible for setting up a BPP school. In 2006 he moved to Australia and joined Deakin University as a lecturer in accounting and auditing.

BRIEF CONTENTS

part 1 **THE AUDITING AND ASSURANCE ENVIRONMENT   2**

  1 An overview of auditing   4
  2 Governance and the auditor   44
  3 Professional ethics, independence and audit quality   94
  4 Other assurance engagements and quality standards   162
  5 The auditor's legal liability   202

part 2 **AUDIT PLANNING   246**

  6 Overview of the audit of financial reports   248
  7 The auditor's report   280
  8 Client evaluation and planning the audit   314
  9 Audit risk assessment   366
  10 Materiality and audit evidence   414

part 3 **AUDIT TESTING METHODOLOGY   452**

  11 Tests of controls   454
  12 Designing substantive procedures   488
  13 Audit sampling   526

part 4 **AUDITING TRANSACTIONS AND BALANCES   566**

  14 Auditing sales and receivables   568
  15 Auditing purchases, payables and payroll   618
  16 Auditing inventories and property, plant and equipment   664
  17 Auditing cash and investments   708

part 5 **COMPLETING THE AUDIT   756**

  18 Completing the audit   758

CONTENTS

Preface xii

Abbreviations xviii

How to use this book xix

Acknowledgements xxii

part 1 THE AUDITING AND ASSURANCE ENVIRONMENT 2

1 An overview of auditing 4

1.1 Auditing fundamentals 6
   1.1.1 What is an audit? 6
   1.1.2 What does an audit provide? 8
   1.1.3 Why is there a demand for audits? 8
   1.1.4 Who provides audits? 13
1.2 What is assurance? 14
1.3 The auditing environment 15
   1.3.1 The accounting profession 15
   1.3.2 Case law 18
   1.3.3 The early 2000s — challenges and changes 19
   1.3.4 Regulation and other oversight 21
1.4 Auditing standards 24
   1.4.1 Australian auditing standards 25
   1.4.2 International auditing standards 27
   1.4.3 The Clarity project 27
1.5 Does the audit meet the demands of users? 28
   1.5.1 Who are the users of audits? 28
   1.5.2 Do audits provide good value? 29
   1.5.3 The audit expectation gap 30

2 Governance and the auditor 44

2.1 What is governance? 47
   2.1.1 Enterprise governance: a framework 48
2.2 The auditor and governance 49
   2.2.1 Overall objectives of the auditor 49
   2.2.2 The role of the auditor in enterprise governance 50
   2.2.3 Corporate governance (conformance) and the auditing function 51
   2.2.4 Business governance (performance) and auditing and assurance services 52
   2.2.5 The audit trinity concept 53
2.3 Issues in governance 55
   2.3.1 Risk management and internal control 55
   2.3.2 Financial misstatements — earnings management 59

2.4 Internal and operational auditing in the governance process 60
   2.4.1 Internal auditing 60
   2.4.2 Operational auditing 64
   2.4.3 The widening role of internal audit 65
2.5 Enhancing accountability through the audit committee 67
   2.5.1 The role and objectives of the audit committee 67
2.6 Governance in the public sector 71
   2.6.1 The requirements of public accountability 71
   2.6.2 Parliamentary committees 72
   2.6.3 The auditor-general and the Australian National Audit Office 73
   2.6.4 Audit mandates 74
   2.6.5 Financial statement audits 75
   2.6.6 Performance auditing 76
   2.6.7 Performance engagements 78

3 Professional ethics, independence and audit quality 94

3.1 The role of the professional accountant 97
   3.1.1 The concept of a profession 97
   3.1.2 The duties of a professional accountant 99
3.2 Professional ethics and the accountant 100
   3.2.1 An understanding of ethics and ethical issues 100
   3.2.2 Professional ethics for accountants 103
   3.2.3 The *Code of Ethics for Professional Accountants* 104
3.3 Professional independence 110
   3.3.1 Statutory provisions enhancing auditors' independence 111
   3.3.2 Independence of mind and in appearance 114
   3.3.3 Independence for audit and review engagements — a conceptual approach 115
   3.3.4 Other current recommendations for enhancing independence 123
   3.3.5 Monitoring auditor independence 124
3.4 Corporate collapses and reforms 125
   3.4.1 Accounting crises and corporate collapses 125
   3.4.2 The ASIC surveillance program 130
   3.4.3 The spate of reforms 131
3.5 Audit quality 135
   3.5.1 Technical competence 135

3.5.2 Ethical competence — the significance of ethical values in auditing 137

3.5.3 Quality controls in auditing firms 140

3.6 Professional discipline 147

3.6.1 Disciplinary procedures 148

---

4 Other assurance engagements and quality standards 162

4.1 Assurance engagement standards 165

4.1.1 The assurance engagement framework 165

4.1.2 Categories of assurance engagements 168

4.2 Assurance engagements involving historical financial information 173

4.2.1 Audits of historical financial information 173

4.2.2 Review engagements relating to financial reports and other historical financial information 175

4.3 Assurance engagements other than audits or reviews of historical financial information 177

4.4 Examples of assurance engagements other than those relating to historical financial information 179

4.4.1 Compliance engagements 180

4.4.2 Performance engagements 180

4.4.3 Prospective financial information 180

4.4.4 Effectiveness of control procedures 181

4.4.5 Sustainability assurance reports 181

4.4.6 Forensic auditing engagements 187

4.4.7 Continuous audit 189

4.5 Quality management and the assurance practitioner 190

4.5.1 The ISO standards 191

4.5.2 Total quality management and the assurance practitioner 193

---

5 The auditor's legal liability 202

5.1 The legal environment 204

5.1.1 The litigation crisis 205

5.1.2 The professional standards legislation 207

5.1.3 The impact of the CLERP 9 Act 208

5.2 Liability to shareholders and auditees 209

5.2.1 Due care 209

5.2.2 Negligence 214

5.2.3 Privity of contract 215

5.2.4 Causal relationship 217

5.2.5 Contributory negligence 218

5.2.6 Damages 219

5.3 Liability to third parties 220

5.3.1 Proximity 222

5.3.2 Avoidance of litigation 231

5.4 Competition and consumer legislation 233

5.5 The global financial crisis (GFC) and potential liabilities for auditors 234

---

part 2 AUDIT PLANNING 246

---

6 Overview of the audit of financial reports 248

6.1 The appointment of an independent auditor 250

6.1.1 Principles of the appointment of auditors 250

6.1.2 The removal and resignation of auditors 251

6.1.3 The registration of auditors 251

6.2 Duties of an independent auditor 253

6.2.1 The duty to use reasonable care and skill 253

6.2.2 The duty to be independent 253

6.2.3 Statutory duties to report to members and to ASIC 253

6.2.4 Professional duties 255

6.3 Auditing standards 256

6.3.1 The standard-setting framework 256

6.3.2 The development and importance of auditing standards 257

6.4 Independent auditor relationships 261

6.4.1 Shareholders 261

6.4.2 The board of directors and audit committee 261

6.4.3 Internal auditors 263

6.4.4 Management 263

6.5 Management and the auditor — responsibilities 264

6.5.1 The relationship between accounting and auditing 264

6.5.2 The division of responsibility 266

6.6 Benefits and limitations of an audit 266

6.6.1 Benefits 267

6.6.2 Limitations 268

6.7 An overview of the audit process 269

---

7 The auditor's report 280

7.1 Standards of reporting 282

7.1.1 Financial statements 283

7.1.2 Accounting standards 284

7.1.3 Relevant statutory and other requirements 284

7.2 The auditor's report and communication with management 285
   7.2.1 Forming an opinion 285
   7.2.2 Expression of opinion 286
   7.2.3 Unmodified auditor's report 286
   7.2.4 Modified auditor's report 293
   7.2.5 Circumstances to modify 294
   7.2.6 Form and content of modifications 297
   7.2.7 Emphasis of matter and other matter in the independent auditor's report 298
7.3 Other reporting considerations for corporate entities 301
   7.3.1 Reporting on consolidated statements 301
   7.3.2 Comparatives 301
   7.3.3 Initial engagements (opening balances) 302
   7.3.4 Half-year statements 303

8 Client evaluation and planning the audit 314

8.1 Acceptance and continuance of client relationships 317
   8.1.1 Client evaluation 318
   8.1.2 Ethical and legal considerations 320
8.2 Audit engagement letters 323
8.3 Steps in planning an audit 326
8.4 Understanding the entity and its environment 327
   8.4.1 Industry, regulatory and other external factors 328
   8.4.2 The nature of the entity, including its selection and application of accounting policies 329
   8.4.3 The entity's objectives, strategies and related business risks 331
   8.4.4 Measurement and review of the entity's financial performance 333
8.5 Analytical procedures in planning 333
8.6 Consideration of fraud risk in planning 334
   8.6.1 Fraudulent financial reporting 337
   8.6.2 Misappropriation of assets 342
   8.6.3 Auditing for fraud 344
8.7 Audit documentation 346
   8.7.1 The purpose and function of working papers 346
   8.7.2 Working paper files 347
   8.7.3 Preparing working papers 351
   8.7.4 Reviewing working papers 352
   8.7.5 Ownership and custody of working papers 352

9 Audit risk assessment 366

9.1 Risk assessment and financial statement assertions 368
   9.1.1 Management's financial statement assertions 368
9.2 Business risk assessment 372
9.3 Risk assessment procedures 373
   9.3.1 Enquiries 373
   9.3.2 Analytical procedures 374
   9.3.3 Observations and inspections 374
9.4 Internal control 375
   9.4.1 The importance of internal control 375
   9.4.2 Internal control system 377
   9.4.3 Limitations of control 386
9.5 Understanding internal control 387
   9.5.1 What to understand about internal control 387
   9.5.2 Procedures to obtain an understanding 388
   9.5.3 Documenting the understanding 389
9.6 Preliminary assessment of control risk 397
   9.6.1 The purpose of the preliminary assessment 397
   9.6.2 The process of assessing control risk 397
9.7 Audit risk 399
   9.7.1 Audit risk components 400
   9.7.2 The relationships among risk components 401

10 Materiality and audit evidence 414

10.1 Materiality 417
   10.1.1 The concept of materiality 417
   10.1.2 Preliminary judgements about materiality 418
   10.1.3 Materiality for the financial report as a whole 419
   10.1.4 Materiality for particular classes of transactions, account balances or disclosures 422
   10.1.5 The relationship between materiality and audit evidence 422
10.2 Audit strategies 423
   10.2.1 Developing the audit strategy 423
   10.2.2 The relationship between strategies and transaction classes 426
10.3 Audit evidence 426
   10.3.1 Auditor's objectives as responses to assessed risks 426

10.3.2 The nature of audit evidence 427

10.3.3 The auditing standard applying to evidence 428

10.3.4 Types of corroborating information 431

10.4 **Auditing procedures 435**

10.4.1 Types of auditing procedures 436

10.4.2 The relationships among auditing procedures, types of evidence and assertions 438

10.4.3 Classification of auditing procedures 440

10.4.4 Evaluation of evidence obtained 441

part 3 **AUDIT TESTING METHODOLOGY 452**

11 **Tests of controls 454**

11.1 **Control risk assessment and audit strategy 456**

11.1.1 Assessing the control risk 456

11.1.2 Audit strategy 457

11.2 **Tests of controls 460**

11.2.1 Designing tests 461

11.2.2 Audit programs for tests of controls 462

11.3 **Using internal auditors 464**

11.3.1 Coordination with internal auditors 464

11.4 **Final assessment of control risk 465**

11.4.1 Documenting the assessed level of control risk 465

11.5 **Communication of internal control matters 466**

11.6 **Types of controls in an information technology environment 468**

11.7 **Computer-assisted audit techniques 470**

11.7.1 Test data 470

11.7.2 Integrated test facility 471

11.7.3 Parallel simulation 471

11.7.4 Continuous monitoring of online real-time systems 472

11.7.5 Assessing and testing IT controls 473

12 **Designing substantive procedures 488**

12.1 **Assessing the risk of material misstatement 490**

12.1.1 The type of potential misstatement 491

12.1.2 The magnitude of potential misstatements 492

12.1.3 The likelihood of material misstatement 493

12.2 **Determining detection risk 493**

12.2.1 Predominantly substantive approach 495

12.3 **Designing substantive procedures 495**

12.3.1 Nature 496

12.3.2 Timing 502

12.3.3 Extent 503

12.3.4 Computer-assisted audit techniques as substantive procedures 503

12.3.5 Audit risk and choice of substantive procedures 506

12.4 **Developing audit programs for substantive procedures 507**

12.4.1 Framework for developing audit programs 507

12.4.2 Audit programs in initial engagements 509

12.4.3 Assertions, audit objectives and substantive procedures 509

12.4.4 Illustrative audit program 509

12.5 **Special considerations when designing substantive procedures 512**

12.5.1 Income statement accounts 512

12.5.2 Accounts involving accounting estimates including fair value accounting estimates and related disclosures 513

12.5.3 Fair value accounting estimates and related disclosures 514

12.5.4 Related parties 514

12.5.5 Specific considerations for inventory and segment information 515

12.5.6 External confirmations 515

13 **Audit sampling 526**

13.1 **Basic concepts of sampling 528**

13.1.1 Sampling risk and non-sampling risk 529

13.1.2 Statistical and non-statistical sampling 531

13.1.3 Types of testing 532

13.2 **Use of samples for audit tests 533**

13.2.1 Planning the sample 534

13.2.2 Selecting and testing the sample 538

13.2.3 Evaluating the results 542

13.3 **Statistical sampling techniques 544**

13.3.1 Attribute sampling plans 544

13.3.2 Variable sampling plans 544

13.3.3 Probability-proportional-to-size sampling 545

13.3.4 Choice of statistical sampling method 545

13.4 Non-statistical sampling techniques 546

    13.4.1 Why use non-statistical sampling? 546

    13.4.2 Formal and informal non-statistical sampling 547

part 4   AUDITING TRANSACTIONS AND BALANCES   566

14   Auditing sales and receivables   568

14.1 Brief summary of audit procedures 570

14.2 Audit objectives 571

14.3 Sales, cash receipts and sales adjustment transactions 573

    14.3.1 Credit sales transactions 575

    14.3.2 Cash receipts transactions 578

    14.3.3 Sales adjustment transactions 581

14.4 Developing the audit plan 581

    14.4.1 Understanding the entity and the identification of inherent risks 582

    14.4.2 Internal control components 584

    14.4.3 Assessment of control risk 585

    14.4.4 Tests of operating effectiveness 587

    14.4.5 Final assessment 591

14.5 Substantive procedures 592

    14.5.1 Determining detection risk 592

    14.5.2 Designing substantive procedures 594

15   Auditing purchases, payables and payroll   618

15.1 Brief summary of audit procedures 620

15.2 Audit objectives 621

15.3 Purchase, payment and purchase adjustment transactions 623

    15.3.1 Purchase transactions 625

    15.3.2 Payment transactions 628

15.4 Payroll transactions 630

15.5 Developing the audit plan 634

    15.5.1 Understanding the entity and the identification of inherent risks 635

    15.5.2 Internal control environment 636

    15.5.3 Assessment of control risk 637

    15.5.4 Final assessment 643

15.6 Substantive procedures 643

    15.6.1 Determining detection risk 644

    15.6.2 Designing substantive procedures 645

16   Auditing inventories and property, plant and equipment   664

16.1 Brief summary of audit procedures 666

16.2 Inventory 667

    16.2.1 Audit objectives 668

    16.2.2 Recording inventory transactions 669

    16.2.3 Developing the audit plan 673

    16.2.4 Substantive procedures for inventories 678

16.3 Property, plant and equipment 687

    16.3.1 Audit objectives 688

    16.3.2 Developing the audit plan 689

    16.3.3 Substantive procedures for property, plant and equipment 690

17   Auditing cash and investments   708

17.1 Brief summary of audit procedures 710

17.2 Cash 712

    17.2.1 Audit objectives 712

    17.2.2 Developing the audit plan 713

    17.2.3 Substantive procedures for cash balances 715

    17.2.4 Other issues 728

17.3 Investments 732

    17.3.1 Audit objectives 732

    17.3.2 Developing the audit plan 733

    17.3.3 Substantive procedures for investments 736

    17.3.4 Substantive procedures for consolidated financial statements 740

part 5   COMPLETING THE AUDIT   756

18   Completing the audit   758

18.1 Completing the fieldwork 762

    18.1.1 Undertaking a review of subsequent events 762

    18.1.2 Considering the appropriateness of the going concern assumption 766

    18.1.3 Reviewing for contingent liabilities 768

    18.1.4 Written representations 771

    18.1.5 Performing analytical procedures 774

18.2 Evaluating the findings 777

    18.2.1 Making the final assessment of materiality and audit risk 777

    18.2.2 Undertaking the technical review of the financial statements 779

    18.2.3 Undertaking the final review(s) of working papers 779

    18.2.4 Formulating an opinion and drafting the auditor's report 780

18.3 Communicating with the entity 781

    18.3.1 Communication of audit matters with those charged with governance 781

    18.3.2 Communicating matters with the audit committee 783

Glossary 801

Index 811

*M*odern Auditing & Assurance Services, 6th edition, is written for courses in auditing and assurance at undergraduate, postgraduate and professional levels. The practice of auditing is explained in the context of auditing theory, concepts and current practice, with appropriate reference to the Australian auditing standards and the respective international standards on auditing.

Auditors play a vital role in the current economic environment, with increasing responsibility for ensuring market integrity. The development of auditing practice reflects how the accounting profession responds to the complex demands of information, competition, corporate failures and technology. Auditing continues to evolve in response to the changing business and regulatory landscape to maintain its relevance and importance. This book is a comprehensive guide to the development and practice of audits of a financial report, with an authoritative insight into the fundamental role of auditors, the influences on audits, and related issues.

Significant changes from the previous edition

This textbook has been further revised with new and contemporary developments since the last edition. The major changes are noted below.

Recent auditing topics embedded within the chapters

- Audit Quality — readers will appreciate that audit quality is a concept that underpins most of this text. The recent exposure draft issued by the International Auditing and Assurance Standards Board (IAASB) in relation to the Audit Quality Framework Paper is a consequence of various debates highlighted within this text. While the topic is being further developed at the time of writing, readers should appreciate that the topic continues to be an issue at the forefront of the profession. Audit quality includes the extent of applying professional judgement and scepticism in undertaking the audit engagement. Audit quality is discussed in chapters 3 and 4 and is referred to throughout the text.
- The role, purpose and the market for the audit profession — this topic is referred to in chapters 1 and 2, as the global audit profession critically re-evaluates the effectiveness of the audit market and its regulation.
- Ethics and corporate governance — professional ethics as defined in detail in APES 110 has reinforced the concept of the public interest. Discussions on professional ethics and the related topic of corporate governance are paramount to auditing and assurance services. The latest ASX corporate governance principles, the overriding principle of the public interest, and the requirements for the auditor to be proactive in dealing with auditing issues by meeting with the audit committee members, are discussed in chapters 1, 3 and 18.
- Scepticism — the importance of the attribute of scepticism to auditors' judgements has increased significantly in recent years. More consideration of this attribute in planning and evaluation of evidence are included in chapters 8 and 10.
- Internal controls — COSO produced a new framework on internal control in 2013 and relevant changes from this new framework have been included in chapters 9 and 11.
- Latest developments in regulatory regimes and audit expectations — this text is deliberate in providing a well-rounded view of what the auditors do, in addition to performing the technical functions. The expectations of the auditors in relation to the aftermath of the

global financial crisis, and the latest legal and regulatory changes such as those provided in the competition and consumer laws, are discussed in chapter 5.

- Audit reporting — the auditing profession has more recently re-examined the nature and extent of the audit report, and the language and presentation of the audit report to members. The topic of completing the audit is discussed in chapter 18, with details of means to communicate audit findings to various stakeholders. The key changes in the chapter include the explanation on matters relating to the going concern of the audit client. The IAASB has proposed to significantly reform the content of a standard audit report. This is contained in its 2013 Exposure Draft *Reporting on Audited Financial Statements: Proposed New and Revised International Standards on Auditing*. Chapter 7 on the auditor's report contains an extensive Professional Environment that outlines the main changes that are proposed in the ED. However, as a new standard is not planned to be released until late 2014 (after publication of this text) we could not include these changes in the main body of the chapter.
- Professional environment vignettes have been revised and updated throughout the text. These chapter vignettes present relevant, topical audit issues and/or events that relate the audit processes presented in the chapter to the business world.
- There has been a major revision to the end of chapter materials. In making these changes we have also utilised recent materials from the Institute of Chartered Accountants in Australia and the Association of Chartered Certified Accountants — we thank both of these organisations for their support.

Organisation

How to use this book. This feature helps readers see at a glance how they can make best use of the key features of this text.

Chapter openers. The chapter openers present a summarised account of the main elements in each chapter, the learning outcomes and the relevant professional statements, thus providing readers with a broad contextual base from which to approach each chapter. Each chapter contains an easy-to-read scene setter that provides a lively 'entrée' to the topic. Lecturers can use these scene setters to provoke class debate.

Learning objectives. The learning objectives are linked to the relevant section of the text by the restatement of the objective in the margin.

Learning checks. The learning checks are presented in a number of blocks in each chapter, summarising the major points covered. These checks reinforce student learning and provide a basis for revision.

Professional environment vignettes. In each chapter, professional environment vignettes highlight changes and some contextual information in the professional audit environment. These vignettes keep students up to date with recent trends, new developments and changes in technology that affect auditing and assurance services.

Glossary. The key terms, bolded in the text and listed at the end of each chapter, are defined in a glossary at the end of the book. This enables readers to clarify quickly the meaning of technical or unusual terms throughout the text.

Content

Part 1: The auditing and assurance environment

Part 1 provides insight into the major issues affecting the auditing and assurance environment. It takes the reader on a comprehensive journey to appreciate the development of the role of auditors, the legislative and regulatory regimes and current changes to the role of an auditor. This part of the text will give students an understanding of fundamental aspects of the auditing and assurance environment and insight into parts of the auditor's role and function that are directly relevant and of interest to audit partners as well as leaders in business and government.

Chapter 1 'An overview of auditing' sets the scene. It provides answers to fundamental questions about auditing including what an audit is, what auditors provide, why audits exist and their role in the capital markets and society. It also considers the environment within which auditors operate and the standards that they operate under. Finally, the chapter considers the important question of whether audits meet the demands of users.

Chapter 2 'Governance and the auditor' is a new chapter that introduces the overarching framework of enterprise governance and how auditing contributes to its key aspects of business and corporate governance. The overall objectives of the auditor relating to financial reporting, communication with those charged with governance, and risks and controls are explained with a view to establishing the reader's appreciation of the growing spectrum of assurance and value-adding activities that an auditor undertakes. The auditor needs to appreciate the risks of financial misstatements and the governance processes that safeguard the extent of earnings management. Other governance processes such as internal auditing, operational auditing and performance auditing are discussed. The chapter also covers accountability and governance processes in the public sector, and the role of an audit committee in supporting corporate governance. Chapter 2 combines the previous chapter 18 with details on the public sector, but focuses on governance to provide the broader framework of auditing.

Chapter 3 'Professional ethics, independence and audit quality' discusses the importance of professional ethics and independence in the role undertaken by the auditor. In particular, the chapter explains the conceptual principles underlying the *Code of Ethics for Professional Accountants* and describes the regulatory and conceptual framework of professional independence and the key guidelines for auditors. Corporate collapses are discussed in the context of the challenges these present to the auditing profession and the consequent regulatory reforms that often result. Finally, the chapter focuses on the issue of audit quality and the processes that the auditor must adopt to ensure that quality standards are met.

Chapter 4 'Other assurance engagements and quality standards' discusses assurance engagements other than the audit of an annual financial report. It starts by considering what is and what is not an assurance engagement by looking at the criteria that must be met. The chapter then considers a range of assurance services relating to historical and future financial information and other assurance engagements including compliance and performance engagements, sustainability reports and assurance on a greenhouse gas statement, including reference to the NGERs Act. It also highlights the international benchmark of quality standards that many international audit and assurance engagements will be measured against. These benchmarks include the ISO standards and total quality management standards.

Chapter 5 'The auditor's legal liability', discusses the legal environment and the auditor's liability to shareholders and auditees. The question of potential liability to third parties is also considered. As all professionals are covered by competition laws, partnerships, audit companies or sole practitioners and their associations have become subject to the competition provisions of the Trade Practices Act and the competition codes, and the issues that are of relevance to auditors are highlighted. Finally, the global financial crisis and the potential liabilities for auditors are examined.

Part 2: Audit planning

Part 2 examines the crucial evaluations and decisions associated with the audit planning process. Proper planning is important to ensure that the audit is conducted in an effective and efficient manner and to highlight key risk areas early in the audit process.

Chapter 6 'Overview of the audit of financial statements' provides an overview of the appointment of the independent auditor, the responsibilities and duties of auditors, and consideration in more detail of the audit standard setting process. This chapter also explains the important relationships that auditors have with some key stakeholders and the benefits and limitations of an audit.

Chapter 7 'The auditor's report' discusses the latest auditing standards regarding modifications. The chapter provides details on the updated information relating to the standards of reporting, the auditor's communication with management and some other reporting considerations. There is also an extensive Professional Environment that outlines the significant changes to the auditor's report that are currently under consideration by standard setters.

Chapter 8 'Client evaluation and planning the audit' reflects the ethical and legal requirements an auditor should consider before accepting an engagement. It also considers the steps in planning the audit as well as the important requirement of the auditor to understand the entity and its environment as part of the audit-planning process. The enhanced requirements for auditors to consider fraud in planning are also discussed in this chapter.

Chapter 9 'Audit risk assessment' explains how the understanding of the entity and its environment influences the auditor's risk assessment and how risk assessments should be framed in terms of management's financial statement assertions. This chapter also discusses the importance of auditors undertaking a broader business risk assessment of their clients, as well as the nature of internal control and risks related to internal control. Finally, the chapter concludes with a discussion on the nature of audit risk.

Chapter 10 'Materiality and audit evidence' looks at materiality in detail, with explanations of the relevant audit strategies and procedures. The important aspect of ensuring appropriate and sufficient audit evidence is explained. The nature of audit evidence, with the respective assertions, is discussed with a view to providing students with an appreciation of how reliability is assessed. Materiality is a judgement and the method to collect and assess audit evidence is the key technique in arriving at the audit opinion.

Part 3: Audit testing methodology

Chapter 11 'Tests of controls' explains the link between the control risk assessment and audit strategy. It explains how auditors test controls and the importance of communicating control deficiencies found to management. The chapter then considers the types of controls in an information technology environment and how auditors can perform tests of controls in these environments.

Chapter 12 'Designing substantive procedures' discusses the consideration given to assessing the risk of material misstatement before performing appropriate substantive procedures. This includes evaluation of the type, magnitude and likelihood of potential misstatements. Reference is made in the scene setter and the professional environment vignettes to recent corporate events where the quality of auditors' substantive work has been questioned.

Chapter 13 'Audit sampling' looks at sampling from an overall principles approach rather than in-depth detail of statistical techniques, with more details in the appendixes. Research showing why haphazard sampling is bias prone is considered in a professional environment feature.

Part 4: Auditing transactions and balances

Chapter 14 'Auditing sales and receivables' includes issues associated with overstatement of sales by corporations and the need to protect both companies and their customers when using electronic funds transfers.

Chapter 15 'Auditing purchases, payables and payroll' illustrates transactions in computer information systems and how payables can be manipulated to suit corporate goals.

Chapter 16 'Auditing inventories and property, plant and equipment' deals with the audit of inventories and considers the audit of property, plant and equipment.

Chapter 17 'Auditing cash and investments' emphasises the risk of fraud in the main text and in both of the professional environment vignettes. The section on investments reflects current changes in technology, financial instruments and audit standards. For example, it includes a discussion on the audit implications of the Clearing House Electronic Subregister System used to process and record most listed shares.

Part 5: Completing the audit

Chapter 18 'Completing the audit' summarises the responsibilities of the auditor in respect of completing the fieldwork, evaluating the findings and communicating with the client regarding the audit. It incorporates the changes to the accounting standard on events after the end of the reporting period, which categorises these events as 'adjusting' and 'non-adjusting' events. It also reflects ASA 260 *Communication with Those Charged with Governance* (ISA 260), which emphasises that audit communication should be with those charged with governance rather than with executive management. The scene setter highlights the importance of continuing solvency of client companies that might lead to a judgement for a qualified audit report in the Westpoint Group case.

End-of-chapter questions

The end-of-chapter questions have been revised following individual chapter changes. Each chapter contains ten multiple-choice questions to help readers assess their understanding of the concepts. These are followed by review questions. More practical issues are then examined in the professional application questions and case studies. The final question, a research-based exercise, provides opportunities for readers to investigate interesting areas. The end-of-chapter material provides ample opportunities for self-study and can be used for assignments, seminars and in the classroom.

Writing a textbook is a team effort. We would like to thank a number of our colleagues for their input, interest and constructive advice during various editions of the text and we would especially like to thank the excellent editorial, production and management team at John Wiley & Sons Australia, Ltd.

Philomena Leung, Paul Coram, Barry Cooper and *Peter Richardson*
August 2014

ABBREVIATIONS

AAA	American Accounting Association	CLERP 9 Act	*Corporate Law Economic Reform Program Act* 2004
AARF	Australian Accounting Research Foundation		
AASB	Australian Accounting Standards Board	COSO	Committee of Sponsoring Organizations (of the Treadway Commission)
ACCA	Association of Chartered Certified Accountants	CPA	certified practising accountant
AGM	annual general meeting	CPA Australia	formerly the Australian Society of Certified Practising Accountants
AGS	auditing guidance statement (Australia)		
AICPA	American Institute of Certified Public Accountants	EFT	electronic funds transfer
		FRC	Financial Reporting Council
ANAO	Australian National Audit Office	GAAP	generally accepted accounting principles (US)
APESB	Accounting Professional and Ethical Standards Board	IAASB	International Auditing and Assurance Standards Board
APS	miscellaneous professional statement (Australian)	IAPS	international auditing practice statement
		IASB	International Accounting Standards Board
ASIC	Australian Securities and Investments Commission	ICAA	Institute of Chartered Accountants in Australia
ASX	Australian Securities Exchange	IFAC	International Federation of Accountants
AUASB	Auditing and Assurance Standards Board	IIA	Institute of Internal Auditors
CAAT	computer-assisted audit technique	ISA	international standard on auditing
CALDB	Companies Auditors and Liquidators Disciplinary Board	ISAE	international standard of assurance engagements
CEO	chief executive officer	ISO	International Organization for Standardization
CFO	chief financial officer	JCPAA	Joint Committee of Public Accounts and Audit
CIA	certified internal auditor	LJ	Lord Justice
CIS	computer information system	PY	Professional Year
CJ	Chief Justice	SCARF	systems control audit review file
CLERP 9	Corporate Law Economic Reform Program Paper No. 9	SEC	Securities and Exchange Commission
		VFM audit	value-for-money audit

HOW TO USE THIS BOOK

Modern Auditing & Assurance Services 6th edition has been designed with you — the student — in mind. The design is our attempt to provide you with a book that both communicates the subject matter and facilitates learning. We have tried to accomplish these goals through the following elements.

The **overview** provides a brief summary of the topics, processes and procedures developed within the chapter.

Learning objectives are clearly stated and linked to subsequent discussion in the chapter.

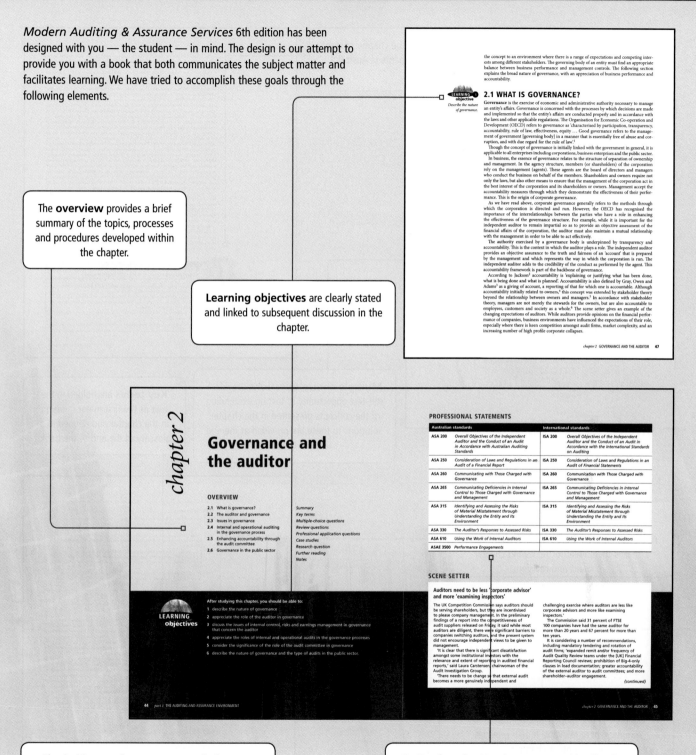

The double-page **chapter opener** displays, at a glance, the chapter content and regulatory framework, expected learning outcomes and chapter scene setter.

The list of **professional statements** identifies the Australian and international regulatory context and the issues discussed in each chapter.

Professional environment boxes amplify and apply the chapter content and profile current, topical industry issues and developments in Australia and internationally.

The Institute of Internal Auditors (IIA) was incorporated in New York in 1941 and is now a worldwide organisation, with local chapters in over 100 countries. It is administered through regional groupings. National institutes have also been formed in some countries. In Australia, the first chapter of the IIA was established in Sydney in 1952. A national institute, the Institute of Internal Auditors–Australia, was formed in 1986. It currently has seven chapters and a sub-branch, and is one element in the IIA's South Pacific region, which includes New Zealand, Papua New Guinea and the South Pacific islands. The IIA administered its first certified internal auditor's examination in 1972.

In 2002, the IIA's Board of Regents launched a global research study to define the knowledge, skills and abilities required of a global internal auditor in order to develop a 'common body of knowledge' for the certified internal auditor examination. For the first time in its history, the IIA electronically gathered data via a survey conducted in eight languages. The survey concluded in January 2003 with nearly 2000 responses (40% from North America and 60% from other countries). Nearly two-thirds of respondents held positions of audit manager and above. Respondents also represented all industries and mirrored that of the IIA membership profile. The latest Common Body of Knowledge (CBOK) survey that was published was in 2006 and the results of the survey supported the existing syllabus content with modifications. It identified that the key common body of knowledge for internal auditors is in governance, risk and control. The skills of business analysis, information technology and business management required to effectively conduct internal audit engagements are acknowledged. The syllabuses have been modified based on the findings. The latest CBOK study in 2010 found that the core competencies of an internal auditor include communication skills, problem identification and solution skills, and keeping up to date with industry and regulatory changes and professional standards. Understanding the business was ranked as the most important overall technical skill in both the 2006 and 2010 surveys.

To become a certified internal auditor (CIA), a person must pass the examination and have a minimum of 2 years experience as an internal auditor (or equivalent). Auditing experience in public accounting qualifies as work experience in internal auditing. To retain the CIA certificate, the person must comply with the IIA's standards and code of ethics. IIA Australia has recently launched its graduate certificate in internal auditing and provides learners with a comprehensive set of knowledge and skills for a career in internal auditing.

The objective of internal auditing is to help members of an organisation to effectively discharge their responsibilities. In meeting this objective, internal auditing provides analyses, appraisals, recommendations, counsel and information concerning the activities that have been audited. The objectives of internal auditing include risk management and promotion of effective governance and control throughout the organisation at a reasonable cost.

PROFESSIONAL ENVIRONMENT
New guidance could add teeth to internal audit

Small companies should benefit from revised internal audit standards. They could make the chief audit executive a whole lot more popular, too.
Internal auditors will have a louder voice in their company come January 1, 2013 — that's when new revisions to internal auditor standards drawn up by the Institute of Internal Auditors (IIA) will go into effect.
. . . The IIA's standards are technically best practices, since the IIA has no regulatory authority to actually enforce them.

Source: K Hoffelder, New guidance could add teeth to internal audit', CFO.com, 24 October 2012.

MULTIPLE-CHOICE questions

2.1 Which of the following statements is incorrect?
A. Enterprise governance can be applied to both corporations and other business entities, including the public sector.
B. Enterprise governance is a concept of business performance within the organisation with which only the board of directors should comply.
C. Enterprise governance encompasses conformance and performance and is an overall concept that includes corporate governance processes.
D. Internal control and risk management processes are part of enterprise governance.

2.2 The audit trinity concept refers to:
A. Governance, management and audit.
B. Conformance, performance, assurance.
C. Past, current and future approaches.
D. External audit, internal audit, audit committee.

2.3 The auditor-general must report on an exception basis if:
A. Records have not been made available for inspection.
B. Records have been retained for at least 10 years.
C. Proper accounting records have been kept.
D. All the necessary information and explanations were obtained.

2.4 The key benefit to management of an internal audit function is that it:
A. Provides assurance to management that fraudulent activities will be detected.
B. Reduces external audit costs.
C. Aids management in the areas of risk management, control and governance processes.
D. Provides assurance to management that the organisation is complying with its legal requirements.

2.5 The Institute of Internal Auditors states that:
A. Internal auditing provides a disciplined approach to evaluating risks, controls and governance processes.
B. Internal auditing should concentrate on an advisory and consultancy role for management.
C. Internal auditing's role is to support the external audit requirements.
D. All internal audit personnel should be certified internal auditors.

2.6 Which of the following statements best describes the appropriate relationship between internal and external auditors?
A. The internal auditor often competes with the external auditor for audit assignments.
B. The internal auditor's work should supplement the work of the external auditor.
C. There should be proper coordination of the work of the internal and external auditors.
D. There should be complete independence between the work of the internal and the external auditors.

2.7 The approach that has been suggested for operational audits is the:
(i) Risk-based audit approach
(ii) Value-for-money audit approach
(iii) Process audit approach.
A. (i) and (ii) only.
B. (i) and (iii) only.
C. (ii) and (iii) only.
D. (i), (ii) and (iii).

Multiple-choice questions provide a self-test opportunity to test understanding of the concepts presented in the chapter. Solutions to these are provided at the end of the chapter.

Key terms are bolded in the text at the first major mention in the chapter and defined in a glossary at the end of the book.

Learning checks identify and reinforce the key issues raised, and occur at the end of each main section. Their simple checklist format makes them ideal for reviewing chapter content and revision.

Learning check

Do you know ...

2.4 ☐ Audit committees perform an important role in corporate governance. They comprise non-executive directors who can provide independent oversight over the financial reporting and auditing function of the organisation.

2.5 ☐ Detailed guidelines of the role of audit committees are contained in the ASX corporate governance principles and all the ASX top 300 companies must have an independent audit committee.

2.6 ☐ The public sector has a tiered system of accountability and governance. Many public sector organisations also apply corporate governance principles and the Australian National Audit Office publishes detailed guidelines on the governance and accountability requirements for the public sector.

2.7 ☐ The auditor-general and the Australian National Audit Office work closely together to ensure proper reporting through audits of financial reports and performance audits carried out to ensure not only compliance but also efficiency and effectiveness.

SUMMARY

Governance is a broad concept that signifies the authority to govern. Such authority is underpinned by transparency and accountability in the way in which such an entity is operated. Enterprise governance encompasses corporate governance and business performance. It promotes significant aspects of governance — conformance and performance — for organisations, and can be applied to business entities, the public sector and not-for-profit organisations. Auditing plays a vital role in enterprise governance, providing assurance for the accountability processes and ensuring certain standards of conformance.

Many auditing and assurance functions are undertaken by internal auditors. Internal auditing, a fast-growing profession that assumes a significant role in the current audit reform, is also undergoing rapid development and change. Internal auditing is now referred to as a key function which combines the roles of internal control, risk management and corporate governance. The accountability of internal auditors is largely through an effective audit committee. Audit committees enhance the effectiveness of corporate and business governance through their link with the board, management and the auditors (both internal and external). The accountability of the public sector, on the other hand, lies with the auditor-general and the work of the Australian National Audit Office. The A-G adopts the AUASB standards. The ANAO also publishes detailed work plans and better audit practice guides.

KEY TERMS

agencies, p. 72	enterprise risk management, p. 55
audit mandates, p. 74	governance, p. 47
audit trinity, p. 53	internal auditing, p. 60
conformance, p. 48	operational auditing, p. 64
corporate governance, p. 51	performance, p. 48
earnings management, p. 59	performance audits, p. 76
enterprise governance, p. 48	risk management, p. 55

The **summary** outlines the core issues explored in the chapter and reinforces key points. Where relevant, it also provides links to other chapters.

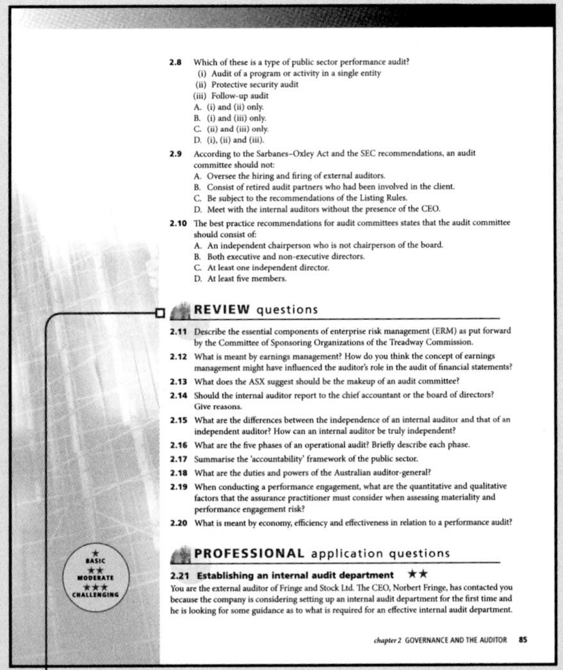

2.8 Which of these is a type of public sector performance audit?
(i) Audit of a program or activity in a single entity
(ii) Protective security audit
(iii) Follow-up audit
A. (i) and (ii) only.
B. (i) and (iii) only.
C. (ii) and (iii) only.
D. (i), (ii) and (iii).

2.9 According to the Sarbanes–Oxley Act and the SEC recommendations, an audit committee should not:
A. Oversee the hiring and firing of external auditors.
B. Consist of retired audit partners who had been involved in the client.
C. Be subject to the recommendations of the Listing Rules.
D. Meet with the internal auditors without the presence of the CEO.

2.10 The best practice recommendations for audit committees states that the audit committee should consist of:
A. An independent chairperson who is not chairperson of the board.
B. Both executive and non-executive directors.
C. At least one independent director.
D. At least five members.

REVIEW questions

2.11 Describe the essential components of enterprise risk management (ERM) as put forward by the Committee of Sponsoring Organizations of the Treadway Commission.
2.12 What is meant by earnings management? How do you think the concept of earnings management might have influenced the auditor's role in the audit of financial statements?
2.13 What does the ASX suggest should be the makeup of an audit committee?
2.14 Should the internal auditor report to the chief accountant or the board of directors? Give reasons.
2.15 What are the differences between the independence of an internal auditor and that of an independent auditor? How can an internal auditor be truly independent?
2.16 What are the five phases of an operational audit? Briefly describe each phase.
2.17 Summarise the 'accountability' framework of the public sector.
2.18 What are the duties and powers of the Australian auditor-general?
2.19 When conducting a performance engagement, what are the quantitative and qualitative factors that the assurance practitioner must consider when assessing materiality and performance engagement risk?
2.20 What is meant by economy, efficiency and effectiveness in relation to a performance audit?

★ BASIC
★★ MODERATE
★★★ CHALLENGING

PROFESSIONAL application questions

2.21 Establishing an internal audit department ★★
You are the external auditor of Fringe and Stock Ltd. The CEO, Norbert Fringe, has contacted you because the company is considering setting up an internal audit department for the first time and he is looking for some guidance as to what is required for an effective internal audit department.

chapter 2 GOVERNANCE AND THE AUDITOR **85**

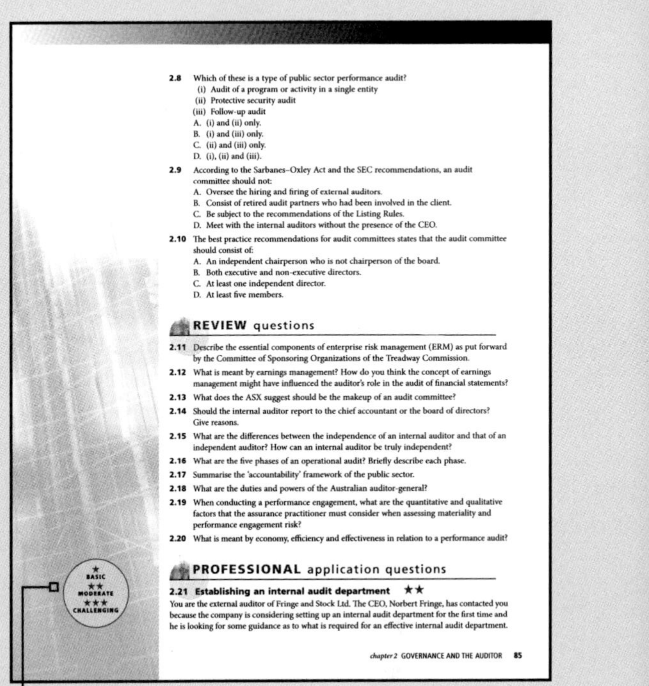

2.8 Which of these is a type of public sector performance audit?
(i) Audit of a program or activity in a single entity
(ii) Protective security audit
(iii) Follow-up audit
A. (i) and (ii) only.
B. (i) and (iii) only.
C. (ii) and (iii) only.
D. (i), (ii) and (iii).

2.9 According to the Sarbanes–Oxley Act and the SEC recommendations, an audit committee should not:
A. Oversee the hiring and firing of external auditors.
B. Consist of retired audit partners who had been involved in the client.
C. Be subject to the recommendations of the Listing Rules.
D. Meet with the internal auditors without the presence of the CEO.

2.10 The best practice recommendations for audit committees states that the audit committee should consist of:
A. An independent chairperson who is not chairperson of the board.
B. Both executive and non-executive directors.
C. At least one independent director.
D. At least five members.

REVIEW questions

2.11 Describe the essential components of enterprise risk management (ERM) as put forward by the Committee of Sponsoring Organizations of the Treadway Commission.
2.12 What is meant by earnings management? How do you think the concept of earnings management might have influenced the auditor's role in the audit of financial statements?
2.13 What does the ASX suggest should be the makeup of an audit committee?
2.14 Should the internal auditor report to the chief accountant or the board of directors? Give reasons.
2.15 What are the differences between the independence of an internal auditor and that of an independent auditor? How can an internal auditor be truly independent?
2.16 What are the five phases of an operational audit? Briefly describe each phase.
2.17 Summarise the 'accountability' framework of the public sector.
2.18 What are the duties and powers of the Australian auditor-general?
2.19 When conducting a performance engagement, what are the quantitative and qualitative factors that the assurance practitioner must consider when assessing materiality and performance engagement risk?
2.20 What is meant by economy, efficiency and effectiveness in relation to a performance audit?

★ BASIC
★★ MODERATE
★★★ CHALLENGING

PROFESSIONAL application questions

2.21 Establishing an internal audit department ★★
You are the external auditor of Fringe and Stock Ltd. The CEO, Norbert Fringe, has contacted you because the company is considering setting up an internal audit department for the first time and he is looking for some guidance as to what is required for an effective internal audit department.

chapter 2 GOVERNANCE AND THE AUDITOR **85**

Review questions test your understanding of the material presented in the chapter and encourage considered comment.

Professional application questions reflect 'real world' auditing scenarios and are graded according to difficulty. The questions are designed to develop professional skills in analysing, interpreting, evaluating, communicating and reporting audit information.

Case studies, graded according to difficulty, encourage detailed evaluation of the audit scenario presented. These challenging exercises are ideal for group discussion and build professional communication skills.

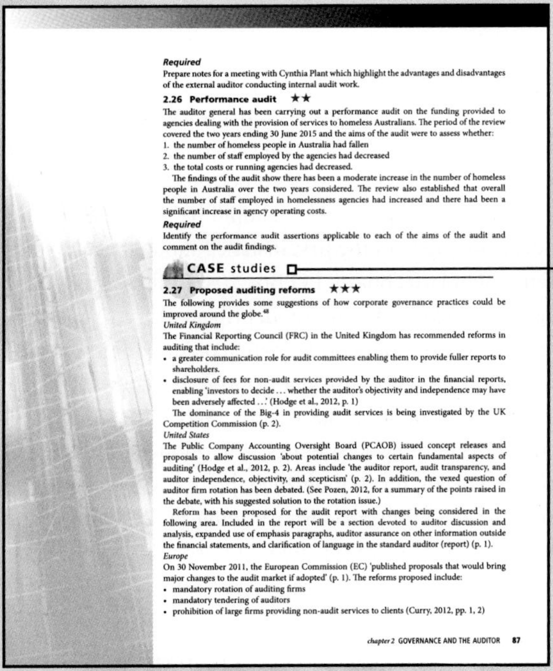

Required
Prepare notes for a meeting with Cynthia Plant which highlight the advantages and disadvantages of the external auditor conducting internal audit work.

2.26 Performance audit ★★
The auditor general has been carrying out a performance audit on the funding provided to agencies dealing with the provision of services to homeless Australians. The period of the review covered the two years ending 30 June 2015 and the aims of the audit were to assess whether:
1. the number of homeless people in Australia had fallen
2. the number of staff employed by the agencies had decreased
3. the total costs or running agencies had decreased.

The findings of the audit show there has been a moderate increase in the number of homeless people in Australia over the two years considered. The review also established that overall the number of staff employed in homelessness agencies had increased and there had been a significant increase in agency operating costs.

Required
Identify the performance audit assertions applicable to each of the aims of the audit and comment on the audit findings.

CASE studies

2.27 Proposed auditing reforms ★★★
The following provides some suggestions of how corporate governance practices could be improved around the globe.[48]

United Kingdom
The Financial Reporting Council (FRC) in the United Kingdom has recommended reforms in auditing that include:
- a greater communication role for audit committees enabling them to provide fuller reports to shareholders.
- disclosure of fees for non-audit services provided by the auditor in the financial reports, enabling 'investors to decide . . . whether the auditor's objectivity and independence may have been adversely affected . . .' (Hodge et al., 2012, p. 1)

The dominance of the Big-4 in providing audit services is being investigated by the UK Competition Commission (p. 2).

United States
The Public Company Accounting Oversight Board (PCAOB) issued concept releases and proposals to allow discussion 'about potential changes to certain fundamental aspects of auditing' (Hodge et al., 2012, p. 2). Areas include 'the auditor report, audit transparency, and auditor independence, objectivity, and scepticism' (p. 2). In addition, the vexed question of auditor firm rotation has been debated. (See Pozen, 2012, for a summary of the points raised in the debate, with his suggested solution to the rotation issue.)

Reform has been proposed for the audit report with changes being considered in the following area. Included in the report will be a section devoted to auditor discussion and analysis, expanded use of emphasis paragraphs, auditor assurance on other information outside the financial statements, and clarification of language in the standard auditor (report) (p. 1).

Europe
On 30 November 2011, the European Commission (EC) 'published proposals that would bring major changes to the audit market if adopted' (p. 1). The reforms proposed include:
- mandatory rotation of auditing firms
- mandatory tendering of auditors
- prohibition of large firms providing non-audit services to clients (Curry, 2012, pp. 1, 2)

chapter 2 GOVERNANCE AND THE AUDITOR **87**

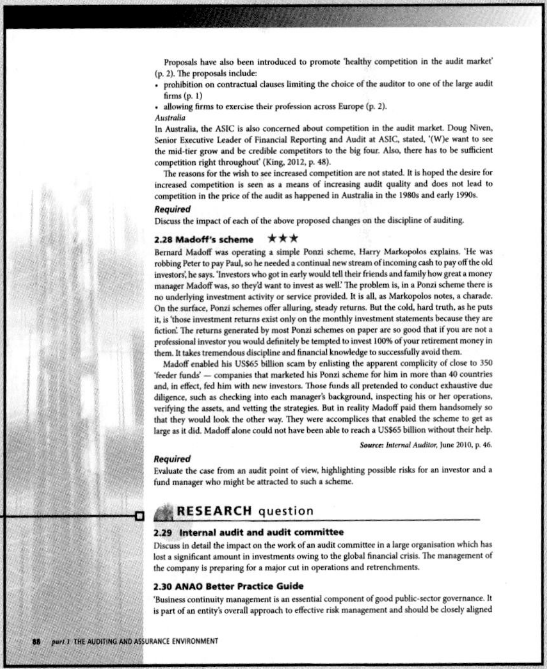

Proposals have also been introduced to promote 'healthy competition in the audit market' (p. 2). The proposals include:
- prohibition on contractual clauses limiting the choice of the auditor to one of the large audit firms (p. 1)
- allowing firms to exercise their profession across Europe (p. 2).

Australia
In Australia, the ASIC is also concerned about competition in the audit market. Doug Niven, Senior Executive Leader of Financial Reporting and Audit at ASIC, stated, '(W)e want to see the mid-tier grow and be credible competitors to the big four. Also, there has to be sufficient competition right throughout' (King, 2012, p. 48).

The reasons for the wish to see increased competition are not stated. It is hoped the desire for increased competition is seen as a means of increasing audit quality and does not lead to competition in the price of the audit as happened in Australia in the 1980s and early 1990s.

Required
Discuss the impact of each of the above proposed changes on the discipline of auditing.

2.28 Madoff's scheme ★★★
Bernard Madoff was operating a simple Ponzi scheme, Harry Markopolos explains. 'He was robbing Peter to pay Paul, so he needed a continual new stream of incoming cash to pay off the old investors', he says. 'Investors who got in early would tell their friends and family how great a money manager Madoff was, so they'd want to invest as well.' The problem is, in a Ponzi scheme there is no underlying investment activity or service provided. It is all, as Markopolos notes, a charade. On the surface, Ponzi schemes offer alluring, steady returns. But the cold, hard truth, as he puts it, is 'those investment returns exist only on the monthly investment statements because they are fiction'. The returns generated by most Ponzi schemes on paper are so good that if you are not a professional investor you would definitely be tempted to invest 100% of your retirement money in them. It takes tremendous discipline and financial knowledge to successfully avoid them.

Madoff enabled his US$65 billion scam by enlisting the apparent complicity of close to 350 'feeder funds' — companies that marketed his Ponzi scheme for him in more than 40 countries and, in effect, fed him with new investors. Those funds all pretended to conduct exhaustive due diligence, such as checking into each manager's background, inspecting his or her operations, verifying the assets, and vetting the strategies. But in reality Madoff paid them handsomely so that they would look the other way. They were accomplices that enabled the scheme to get as large as it did. Madoff alone could not have been able to reach a US$65 billion without their help.

Source: *Internal Auditor*, June 2010, p. 46.

Required
Evaluate the case from an audit point of view, highlighting possible risks for an investor and a fund manager who might be attracted to such a scheme.

RESEARCH question

2.29 Internal audit and audit committee
Discuss in detail the impact on the work of an audit committee in a large organisation which has lost a significant amount in investments owing to the global financial crisis. The management of the company is preparing for a major cut in operations and retrenchments.

2.30 ANAO Better Practice Guide
'Business continuity management is an essential component of good public-sector governance. It is part of an entity's overall approach to effective risk management and should be closely aligned

88 *part 1* THE AUDITING AND ASSURANCE ENVIRONMENT

The **research question** takes you beyond the text encouraging you to complete various research-based activities.

ACKNOWLEDGEMENTS

The authors and publisher would like to thank the following copyright holders, organisations and individuals for their permission to reproduce copyright material in this book.

Images

• Department of the Treasury: **24** Originally from webpage 'Strengthening the Financial Reporting Framework', © Commonwealth of Australia 2013. • Taylor & Francis Group (UK): **31** Adapted from B. Porter, 'An empirical study of the audit expectation-performance gap', *Accounting & Business Research*, vol. 24, no. 93, p. 50, 1993, Taylor & Francis Group, www.informaworld.com. • Competition Commission UK: **46** 'Figure 1 — Key auditor interactions and relationships' from Audit Market Investigation Issues Statement, 2011 © Competition Commission UK. • IFAC: **49** This figure is from 'Enterprise Governance: Getting the Balance Right' of the Professional Accountants in Business Committee, published by the International Federation of Accountants (IFAC) in February 2004 and is used with permission of IFAC. • Emerald Group Publishing Ltd: **54** From Porter, B. 'The Audit Trinity: the key to securing corporate accountability', *Managerial Auditing Journal*, vol. 24, no. 2, 2009, Fig. 3, pp. 156–82 © Emerald Group Publishing Limited. • American Institute of CPAs: **57** 'Relationship of Objectives and Components' from Enterprise Risk Management, Integrated Framework, Executive Summary, September 2004, p. 5 © 2004 by the Committee of Sponsoring Organizations of the Treadway Commission; permission via AICPA. • Australian National Audit Office: **77** From 'Guidelines for the Conduct of Performance Audits', November 2013, p. 5 © Australian National Audit Office (www.anao.gov.au). • AUASB: **171–2, 257** © 2014 Auditing and Assurance Standards Board (AUASB). The text, graphics and layout of this publication are protected by Australian copyright law and the comparable law of other countries. No part of the publication may be reproduced, stored or transmitted in any form or by any means without the prior written permission of the AUASB except as permitted by law. For reproduction or publication permission should be sought in writing from the Auditing and Assurance Standards Board. Requests in the first instance should be addressed to the Executive Director, Auditing and Assurance Standards Board, PO Box 204, Collins Street West, Melbourne, Victoria, 8007; **776** From 'Going Concern Issues In Financial Reporting. A Guide For Companies And Directors', published by the Auditing and Assurance Standards Board and Australian Institute of Company Directors, 2009 © 2014 Auditing and Assurance Standards Board (AUASB). The text, graphics and layout of this publication are protected by Australian copyright law and the comparable law of other countries. No part of the publication may be reproduced, stored or transmitted in any form or by any means without the prior written permission of the AUASB except as permitted by law. For reproduction or publication permission should be sought in writing from the Auditing and Assurance Standards Board. Requests in the first instance should be addressed to the Executive Director, Auditing and Assurance Standards Board, PO Box 204, Collins Street West, Melbourne, Victoria, 8007. • © KPMG: **189** Fig. 12 from 'A Survey of fraud, bribery and corruption in Australia and New Zealand 2012'; **335–6** From 'A Survey of fraud, bribery and corruption in Australia and New Zealand 2012', pp. 4–5. • Julie Clarke: **215** From www.australiancontractlaw.com © Dr Julie Clarke, School of Law, Deakin University. • American Accounting Association: **340** Fig. 1 from p. 239 of 'Earnings Management: Reconciling the views of Accounting Academics, Practitioners, and Regulators' by Dechow and Skinner, *Accounting Horizons*, vol. 14, no. 2, June 2000, pp. 235–50 © American Accounting Association. • © John Wiley & Sons, Inc.: **463** From 'Modern Auditing' by W. Boynton and R. Johnson, 2007, p. 493; **471** From 'Modern Auditing' by W. Boynton and R. Johnson, 2007, p. 479.

Text

• © Australian Securities & Investments Commission: **5** Media Release '12-301MR ASIC's audit inspection findings for 2011–12', 4 December 2012; **206–7** Media Release '13-156MR Wickham auditor removed from industry', 27 June 2013; **416** Media Release '12-301MR ASIC's audit inspection findings for 2011–12', 4 December 2012. Reproduced with permission. • © European Union: **20** Press Release 'Restoring confidence in financial statements: the European Commission aims at a higher quality, dynamic and open audit market', MEMO/11/856, 1995–2013. • AUASB: **25–6, 26** © 2014 Auditing and Assurance Standards Board (AUASB). The text, graphics and layout of this publication are protected by Australian copyright law and the comparable law of other countries. No part of the publication may be reproduced, stored or transmitted in any form or by any means without the prior written permission of the AUASB except as permitted by law. For reproduction or publication permission should be sought in writing from the Auditing and Assurance Standards Board. Requests in the first instance should be addressed to the Executive Director, Auditing and Assurance Standards Board, PO Box 204, Collins Street West, Melbourne, Victoria, 8007; **49, 63, 79, 259–60, 721–3** © Commonwealth of Australia 2014. All legislation herein is reproduced by permission but does not purport to be the official or authorised version. It is subject to Commonwealth of Australia copyright. The Copyright Act 1968 permits certain reproduction and publication of Commonwealth legislation. In particular, s. 182A of the Act enables a complete copy to be made by or on behalf of a particular person. For reproduction or publication beyond that permitted by the Act, permission should be sought in writing from the Commonwealth available from the Auditing and Assurance Standards Board. Requests in the first instance should be addressed to the Executive Director, Auditing and Assurance Standards Board, PO Box 204, Collins Street West, Melbourne, Victoria, 8007; **262, 783–4** From *Audit Committees. A Guide to Good Practice*, Second Edition, jointly published by the Auditing and Assurance Standards Board, Australian Institute of Company Directors and The Institute of Internal Auditors — Australia, August 2012 © 2014 Auditing and Assurance Standards Board (AUASB). The text, graphics and layout of this publication are protected by Australian copyright law and the comparable law of other countries. No part of the publication may be reproduced, stored or transmitted in any form or by any means without the prior written permission of the AUASB except as permitted by law. For reproduction or publication permission should be sought in writing from the Auditing and Assurance Standards Board. Requests in the first instance should be addressed to the Executive Director, Auditing and Assurance Standards Board, PO Box 204, Collins Street West, Melbourne, Victoria, 8007; **775** From 'Going Concern Issues In Financial Reporting. A Guide For Companies And Directors', published by the Auditing and Assurance Standards Board and Australian Institute of Company Directors, 2009 © 2014 Auditing and Assurance Standards Board (AUASB). The text, graphics and layout of this publication are protected by Australian copyright law and the comparable law of other countries. No part of the publication may be reproduced, stored or transmitted in any form or by any means without the prior written permission of the AUASB except as permitted by law. For reproduction or publication permission should be sought in writing from the Auditing and Assurance Standards Board. Requests in the first instance should be addressed to the Executive Director, Auditing and Assurance Standards Board, PO Box 204, Collins Street West, Melbourne, Victoria, 8007. • Institute of Chartered Accountants Australia (ICAA): **33** 'US improves Audit committee communication', dated 7 June 2013, provided courtesy of the Institute of Chartered Accountants Australia; **255** From 'Adding value — a new look audit report' by Andrew Stringer, *Charter*, August 2012; **341** From 'The must have skills of an auditor' by Leon Gettler, *Charter*, October 2012; **399** From 'The risk-based audit approach' by Susan Fraser, *Charter*, December 2011; **241** Taken or adapted from the Professional Year Program of the ICAA — 1998, Advanced Audit Module; **241–2** Taken or adapted from the Professional Year Program of the ICAA — 1996, Advanced Audit Module; **274–5** Taken or adapted from the Professional Year Program of the ICAA — 1998, Accounting 2 Module; **309** Taken or adapted from the Professional Year Program of the ICAA — 1996, Advanced Audit Module; **311** Taken or adapted from the Professional Year Program of the ICAA — 1998, Advanced Audit

Module; **363** Taken or adapted from the Professional Year Program of the ICAA — 1999, Advanced Audit Module; **407** Taken or adapted from the Professional Year Program of the ICAA — 2008, Audit and Assurance Module; **411–12** Taken or adapted from the Professional Year Program of the ICAA — 1996, Accounting 2 Module.; **445–6** Taken or adapted from the Professional Year Program of the ICAA — 1998, Advanced Audit Module; **446–7** Taken or adapted from the Professional Year Program of the ICAA — 1997, Advanced Audit Module; **448–9** Taken or adapted from the Professional Year Program of the ICAA — 1999, Advanced Auditing Module; **481** Taken or adapted from the Professional Year Program of the ICAA — 1999, Advanced Audit Module; **482** Taken or adapted from the Professional Year Program of the ICAA — 2008, Audit and Assurance Module; **484** Taken or adapted from the Professional Year Program of the ICAA — 1999, Advanced Audit Module; **559–60** Taken or adapted from the Professional Year Program of the ICAA — 1996, Accounting 2 Module; **561** Taken or adapted from the Professional Year Program of the ICAA — 1996, Advanced Audit Module; **562–3** Taken or adapted from the Professional Year Program of the ICAA — 1996, Accounting 2 Module; **609–10** Taken or adapted from the Professional Year Program of the ICAA — 1999, Accounting 2 Module; **612** Taken or adapted from the Professional Year Program of the ICAA — 1997, Accounting 2 Module; **656–7** Taken or adapted from the Professional Year Program of the ICAA — 1999, Accounting 2 Module; **657** Taken or adapted from the Professional Year Program of the ICAA — 1997, Accounting 2 Module; **657–8** Taken or adapted from the 2006 Auditing Supplementary Exam of the ICAA; **659–60** Taken or adapted from the Professional Year Program of the ICAA — 1999, Advanced Audit Module; **702** Taken or adapted from the Professional Year Program of the ICAA — 1999, Advanced Audit Module; **702–3** Taken or adapted from the Professional Year Program of the ICAA — 1999, Accounting 2 Module; **750–1** Taken or adapted from the Professional Year Program of the ICAA — 1997, Advanced Audit Module; **793** Taken or adapted from the Professional Year Program of the ICAA — 2000, Accounting 2 Module; **795–6** Taken or adapted from the Professional Year Program of the ICAA — 1999, Advanced Audit Module; **796–7** Taken or adapted from the Professional Year Program of the ICAA — 2000, Accounting 2 Module; **797–8** Taken or adapted from the Professional Year Program of the ICAA — 1999, Accounting 2 Module; **798–9** Taken or adapted from the Professional Year Programme of the ICAA — 1999, Advanced Audit Module. Provided courtesy of the Institute of Charted Accountants Australia. • John Wiley & Sons Australia: **87** From 'Current Affairs in Auditing — June 2012' by Rod Johnson © John Wiley & Sons, Australia; **619** From Moroney, Campbell and Hamilton, 2011, 'Auditing: A Practical Approach', John Wiley & Sons Australia, pp. 101–2; **772–3** From Appendix 2, pp. 578–9 of 'ASA 580 Written Representations Auditing & Assurance Handbook 2010', ICAA, published by John Wiley & Sons Australia. • Institute of Internal Auditors: **88** 'Madoff's scheme' from 'Fighting the good fight' by Russell Jackson, Internal Auditor, June 2010, p.46, reprinted with permission from the June 2010 issue of Internal Auditor (IA), published by The Institute of Internal Auditors, Inc., www.theiia.org. • © Commonwealth of Australia: **123** © Report of the HIH Royal Commission — Vol I: The failure of HIH: A Corporate Collapse and its Lessons. Source: Licensed from the Commonwealth of Australia under Creative Commons Attribution 3.0 Australia Licence. • Copyright Agency Limited: © Fairfax Media **137** 'More sceptical accountants wanted' by P. Durkin, *Australian Financial Review*, 5 November 2012; **164–5** 'Integrated reporting brings legal worries' by S. Drummond, *Australian Financial Review*, 17 April 2013; **203** 'Auditors need legal defence to act as early warning system' by S. Drummond, *Australian Financial Review*, 15 May 2013; **264** 'Wanted: Professional Sceptics' by P. Durkin, *Australian Financial Review*, 5 November 2012; **45–6** 'UK Regulator says auditor incentives serve wrong customer' by S. Drummond, *Australian Financial Review*, 25 February 2013; **489–90** 'Accounting board bends rules for deciding asset values' by B. Appelbaum and Z. Goldfarb, *The Age*, 4 April 2009; **569** 'Lehman ordered to pay councils millions' by Eric Johnston, *The Age*, 21 September 2012; **759–60** 'IAASB shake-up has auditors on the hop' by A. King, Australian Financial Review, 1 August 2013; **81–2** 'NSW government CFO standards '20 years old'' by S. Drummond, *Australian Financial Review*, 31 October 2012; **95–6** 'PwC: Australia not like the UK on tax avoidance' by K. Walsh, *Australian Financial Review*, 16 May 2013; © News Limited **665** 'Sims shares slashed after $60m British inventory fraud' by S. Tasker, *The Australian*, 22 January 2013. • Ernst & Young: **185** Reproduced with permission from Santos Limited and Ernst & Young. • © KPMG Australia: **188** From the 'Forensic Fraud and Misconduct Survey 2010, Australia and New Zealand', p. 17. • © Dr Julie Clarke: **215** From www.australiancontractlaw.com, School of Law, Deakin University. • © Qantas Airways Limited: **277**. • IFAC: **288–93** This figure and text are extracts from Exposure Draft 'Reporting on Audited Financial Statements: Proposed New And Revised International Standards on Auditing (ISAs)', published by The International Auditing and Assurance Standards Board (IAASB) of the International Federation of Accountants (IFAC) in July 2013 and are used with permission of IFAC; **467** This text is an extract from 'Evaluating and Improving Internal Controls in Organizations: Executive Summary' published by the International Federation of Accountants (IFAC) in April 2013 and is used with permission of IFAC. • © American Institute of Certified Public Accountants (AICPA): **310** Copyright 1961–1994. All rights reserved. Used with permission; **401** From Audit Guide: Consideration of the Internal Control Structure in a Financial Statement Audit, 1990, pp. 117–18; **466** From Audit Guide: Consideration of the Internal Control Structure in a Financial Statement Audit, 1990, p. 145; **613–14** Copyright 1961–1994. All rights reserved. Used with permission. • Elsevier: **315–16** From K Trotman and W Wright, 'Triangulation of audit evidence in fraud risk assessments', *Accounting, Organizations and Society*, vol. 37, no. 1, pp. 41–53, 2012 © Elsevier B.V. http://dx.doi.org/10.1016/j.aos.2013.07.002. • ACCA: **332** Fig. 2 from article 'risky business' by Connie Richardson, *Student Accountant*, September 2006, p. 46. This figure first appeared in Student Accountant, ACCA's magazine for trainees www.accaglobal. com; **408** Adapted from ACCA 1999 Audit Framework (UK Stream), Module C, Certificate stage; **408** Adapted from ACCA 2007, Audit & Internal Review exam; **479** Adapted from ACCA June 2006 and December 2006, Audit & Internal Review Exam papers; **481** Adapted from ACCA June 2006 and December 2006, Audit & Internal Review Exam papers; **482** Adapted from ACCA June 2006 and December 2006, Audit & Internal Review Exam papers; **483–4** Adapted from ACCA Audit and Assurance (International), Paper F8 (INT), June 2008; **613** Adapted from ACCA Audit Framework, Paper 6(U), December 1998; **658** Adapted from ACCA Audit Framework, Paper 6, December 1995; **658–9** Adapted from ACCA Audit Framework, Paper 6, December 1997; **660–2** Adapted from ACCA Audit Framework, Paper 6, June 1996; **701–2** Adapted from ACCA Audit Framework, Paper 6(U), December 1998; **703–4** Adapted from ACCA Audit Framework, Paper 6, December 1995; **704** Adapted from ACCA Audit Framework, Paper 6, June 1997; **704–5** Adapted from ACCA June 2006 and December 2006, Audit & Internal Review Exam papers; **749–50** Adapted from ACCA Audit Framework, Paper 6, December 1997; **751** Adapted from ACCA Audit Framework, Paper 6, June 1996; **751–2** Adapted from ACCA Audit Framework, Paper 6, December 1997; **752** Adapted from ACCA Audit Framework, Paper 3.4, December 1991. • CPA Journal: **383** 'Auditing in the cloud: Challenges and opportunities' by Christina Nicolaou, Andreas Nicolaou, and George Nicolaou, The CPA Journal, January 2012, copyright 2012, with permission from the New York State Society of Certified Public Accountants; **541–2** Excerpts from 'How Reliable is Haphazard Sampling?' by Thomas W Hall, Terri L Herron and Bethane Jo Pierce, reprinted from The CPA Journal, January 2006, copyright 2006, with permission from the New York State Society of Certified Public Accountants. • © American Accounting Association: **475** From 'An Investigation of Factors Influencing the Use of Computer-Related Audit Procedures' by Jarvin, Bierstaker and Lowe, *Journal of Information Systems*, vol. 23, no. 1, Spring 2009, pp. 97–118. • © Worrells Solvency & Forensic Accountants: **580–1** Fact Sheet 'Point of Sale Fraud — Stealing Cash Receipts'; **674–5** Fact Sheet 'Stock Fraud — Inventory Records Fraud'.

• Philip Keeffe: **628** From article 'Be wary of fake invoice fraud' by Phil Keeffe, 29 April 2010, via www.suite101.com. • Smart Company: **633–4** 'Clive Peeters hit by $20 million employee fraud — how you can avoid getting stung' by James Thomson, 12 August 2009. This article first appeared on SmartCompany.com.au. • John Wiley & Sons, Inc.: **716** from 'Essentials of Corporate Fraud' by Tracy Coenen, 2008, pp. 72–84 © John Wiley & Sons, Inc. • © Barry Fish: **730–1** 'How safe is your money? Top 10 tips to prevent cash register fraud and theft', 18 September 2009, sourced via www.articlesbase.com. • CPA Australia: **785** 'Tips for auditors in the global financial crisis' © 2010. Reproduced with the permission of CPA Australia Ltd.

Every effort has been made to trace the ownership of copyright material. Information that will enable the publisher to rectify any error or omission in subsequent editions will be welcome. In such cases, please contact the Permissions Section of John Wiley & Sons Australia, Ltd.

part 1

THE AUDITING AND ASSURANCE ENVIRONMENT

1   An overview of auditing

2   Governance and the auditor

3   Professional ethics, independence and audit quality

4   Other assurance engagements and quality standards

5   The auditor's legal liability

chapter 1

An overview of auditing

OVERVIEW

1.1 Auditing fundamentals

1.2 What is assurance?

1.3 The auditing environment

1.4 Auditing standards

1.5 Does the audit meet the demands of users?

Summary

Key terms

Multiple-choice questions

Review questions

Professional application questions

Case study

Research question

Further reading

Notes

LEARNING objectives

After studying this chapter, you should be able to:

1 explain what an audit is, what it provides, and why it is demanded

2 describe how assurance relates to auditing

3 discuss the importance of the profession, case law and regulation to auditing

4 explain the importance of national and international auditing standards

5 evaluate whether audits meet the demands of users.

PROFESSIONAL STATEMENTS

Australian standards		International standards	
Foreword to AUASB Pronouncements[1]		—	
ASA 200	Overall Objectives of the Independent Auditor and the Conduct of an Audit in Accordance with Australian Auditing Standards	ISA 200	Overall Objective of the Independent Auditor and the Conduct of an Audit in Accordance with International Standards on Auditing
ASA 700	Forming an Opinion and Reporting on a Financial Report	ISA 700	Forming an Opinion and Reporting on Financial Statements

SCENE SETTER

ASIC's audit inspection findings

ASIC Chairman Greg Medcraft has described as 'disappointing' the results of ASIC's audit inspection report, which shows a decline in audit quality.

The report for the 18 months to 30 June 2012 covered inspections of 20 Australian audit firms and found 18% of the 602 audit areas reviewed did not perform all of the procedures necessary to obtain reasonable assurance that the audited financial report was not materially misstated. The figure for the previous 18 months was 14%.

While the financial reports audited may not have been materially misstated, the auditor had not obtained reasonable assurance that the financial report as a whole was free of material misstatement.

'Auditors are gatekeepers that play a critical role in ensuring that Australian investors can be confident and informed,' Mr Medcraft said.

'These results are disappointing. Audit firms need to increase their efforts to improve audit quality and the consistency of audit execution.'

ASIC will work with firms and the audit profession more generally on how they can improve audit quality. We will monitor the implementation and execution of any plans to improve audit quality, and their effectiveness.

ASIC has identified three areas needing improvement:
- the sufficiency and appropriateness of audit evidence obtained by the auditor
- the level of professional scepticism exercised by auditors, and
- the extent of reliance that can be placed on the work of other auditors and experts.

The audit areas reviewed included impairment of assets, going concern assessments, and other significant areas involving significant estimates or judgements. ASIC's audit inspection program aims to promote high-quality external audits of financial reports of listed and other public interest entities in Australia. High-quality audits are an important contributor to financial report quality and market confidence.

Audit quality comes down to three key points:
- the likelihood of material misstatement
- the likelihood that the audit detects misstatement, and
- whether the auditor does anything about it.

ASIC publishes its public audit inspection reports every 18 months to inform all audit firms, the investing public, companies, audit committees and other interested stakeholders in the financial reporting chain, of findings and areas of focus.

Source: Australian Securities and Investments Commission, *12–301MR ASIC's audit inspection findings for 2011–12,* 4 December 2012.

The objective of this chapter is to give you an understanding of some key **auditing** concepts and to introduce topics of importance that will be discussed in more detail later in the text. The chapter starts by addressing what an **audit** actually is, what auditors provide, why audits exist, and the role they fulfil in the capital market and society. These are very important questions and important concepts that anyone studying auditing should understand. These issues frame the exposition of many of the other topics in this book. This is followed by a brief discussion of the broader concept of **assurance**, which is discussed in more detail in chapter 4. The environment within which auditors operate is then considered. There is also consideration of the organisations and laws and **regulations** within which auditors operate. The accounting profession is then discussed as well as a brief examination of the early impact of case law. This is followed by a discussion of the significant crises and changes that occurred in the early 2000s and more recently the global financial crisis (GFC) across many jurisdictions, and some of the effects of these crises are discussed in more detail in chapter 5. The next section provides consideration of the most important regulation that auditors deal with, which is the **auditing standards**. The standards and standard-setting bodies are introduced as well as the interrelationship with international auditing standards, and the Clarity[2] project. Finally, we examine how well the audit function performs when examined by the users of these reports. There is evidence that it is useful, but there are also ongoing issues such as the **audit expectation gap** which continues to pose a challenge for the auditing profession.

<blockquote></blockquote>

LEARNING 1 objective

Explain what an audit is, what it provides, and why it is demanded.

1.1 AUDITING FUNDAMENTALS

Across the globe, auditors can be found everywhere business is conducted. However, what do most people know about auditors and the audit function? The answer is probably not that much! This chapter, as an introduction to this book, will provide answers to some fundamental questions such as:

- What is an audit?
- What does an audit provide?
- Why is there a demand for audits?
- Who provides audits?

Core roles of auditors include supporting the stability of capital markets and assisting in ensuring accountability for the government sector. This book will improve your understanding of auditing and assurance in a broad sense, but will also give you a much more detailed understanding about the audit of a financial report which is the most common type of audit. This will help you understand how audits of financial statements are a crucial part of business and **corporate governance**. The focus of the following discussion (and a significant part of the book) therefore will be on the independent financial report audit. It should be noted that many of the principles of auditing in a financial report context also apply to other types of audits and assurance services (discussed in chapters 2 and 4).

1.1.1 What is an audit?

A definition of what the audit provides is in the audit standard ASA 200 *Overall Objectives of the Independent Auditor and the Conduct of an Audit in Accordance with Australian Auditing Standards* (ISA 200), where it states the objective of a **financial report audit** is for the auditor to express an opinion about whether the financial report is prepared in all material respects in accordance with an applicable financial reporting framework. In the case of most general purpose frameworks, that opinion is on whether the financial report is presented fairly, in all material respects, or gives a true and fair view in accordance with the framework. An audit conducted in accordance with Australian auditing standards and relevant ethical requirements enables the auditor to form that opinion (ASA 200.3; ISA 200.3).

A seminal work by Mautz and Sharaf[3] examined some of the general concepts of auditing such as evidence, due care, disclosure and independence, to develop a theory of auditing. In concluding, based on their review of the history and development of auditing, they stated:

> ... the purpose of an audit still seems to be to provide certain interested parties with an attestation of the reliability of certain information supplied by those entrusted with the property of others.[4]

These definitions clarify what an audit provides, but do not define what it actually is. This is better outlined in the report of the Committee on Basic Auditing Concepts of the American Accounting Association which defines auditing as:

> A systematic process of objectively obtaining and evaluating evidence regarding assertions about economic actions and events to ascertain the degree of correspondence between those assertions and established criteria and communicating the results to interested users.[5]

In summary, the auditor is setting out to achieve enhanced **credibility** of information disclosed to increase **reliability** for the users of the financial statements. Accounting is a representation of the economic situation of an entity for a period, which managers are required to represent to users. These representations by managers are known as **assertions** about the economic actions and events of the entity. The auditor's task is to obtain **evidence** to validate these assertions and ensure economic events are appropriately communicated to users.

Figure 1.1 shows how auditing fits into the reporting framework. As depicted, you can see that the audit is an integral part of the financial reporting process. Auditing is not adding any extra financial disclosure to users, but is providing credibility to the disclosures made by management to users of the financial statements. This raises the question as to why organisations are prepared to pay to have an external party audit their accounts to provide assurance on the information disclosed. The easy answer to this in many developed economies for most large corporations is simply because it is required by government regulation. However, there is more to it than this, and it is discussed in the next section.

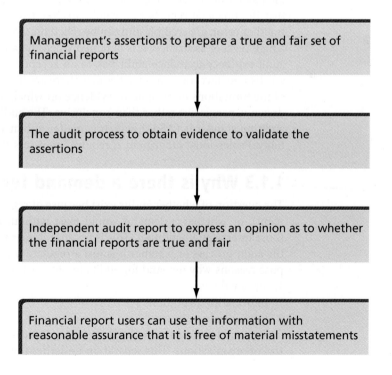

FIGURE 1.1:
Structure of an audit

1.1.2 What does an audit provide?

A brief summary of *some* of the important points outlined in an audit report are as follows (more discussion and examples of audit reports are in chapter 7) and are outlined in ASA 700 *Forming an Opinion and Reporting on a Financial Report* (ISA 700 as amended by ASA 2011-1).

Auditor's Responsibility

- The auditor's responsibility is to express an *opinion* on the financial report.
- The auditor's report shall state that the audit was conducted in accordance with Australian auditing standards.
- An audit should be described. This includes stating that the auditor has performed procedures to obtain *evidence* about the amounts and disclosures in the financial report. The procedures will vary dependent on the auditor's assessment of the *risks of material misstatement*.
- The auditor's report shall state that the auditor believes that *sufficient and appropriate audit evidence* has been obtained to form an opinion.

Auditor's Opinion

- Where the financial reporting framework is a fair presentation framework, which is generally the case for a general purpose financial report, the auditor forms an opinion on whether the financial report *presents fairly*, in all material respects (or represents a *true and fair view*), in accordance with the applicable financial reporting framework (the accounting standards in accordance with the Australian Accounting Standards Boards and *Corporations Act 2001*).
- Where the financial reporting framework is a compliance framework, the auditor forms an opinion on whether the financial report is prepared, in all material respects, in accordance the framework.

The auditor is giving an opinion not an absolute guarantee. The assessments of '**presents fairly**' or 'a **true and fair view**' are both based on the condition that immaterial misstatements may not be detected. Therefore the auditor is providing a reasonable level of assurance that the financial reports as a whole are free from material misstatement, whether due to fraud or error, are credible and can be relied on. ASA 200 states that **reasonable assurance** is a high level of assurance. It is obtained when the auditor has received sufficient appropriate audit evidence to reduce audit risk to an acceptably low level. Reasonable assurance is not an absolute level of assurance because there are limitations of an audit. The auditor is aware of the limitations of most audit evidence on which s/he draws conclusions and the opinion drawn is persuasive rather than conclusive. The auditor's work is directed by the Australian auditing standards (ASAs), which is made explicit in the discussion on auditor's responsibility. Professional judgement is required to assess the risks of material misstatement.

1.1.3 Why is there a demand for audits?

The question of whether audits exist because of regulatory mandate (i.e. required by government), or whether a demand would exist without this mandate, is an important one for those interested in auditing. This is because it goes to the core of whether there is a value to the audit process or whether it is just a regulatory cost. There are three theories which propose reasons why demand for audits might exist without regulatory mandate:

1. agency theory
2. information hypothesis
3. insurance hypothesis.

Demand for audits has existed ever since there has been separation of ownership and control of organisations. This separation underlies the first reason for a demand for auditing.

Agency theory

The separation of ownership and control of organisations has resulted in an **information asymmetry** problem for the owners of the organisation — also known as an agency problem. Jensen and Meckling[6] described an agency relationship as:

> ... a contract under which one or more persons engage another person to perform some service on their behalf which involves delegating some decision-making authority to the agent.

The owners entrust managers to run the company on their behalf; however, the problem is that the managers do not necessarily have the same incentives as the owners of the company. **Agency theory** is based on the assumption that each party will act in his or her self-interest. Management are engaged to run the company on the behalf of owners, but will probably be trying to maximise their own resource consumption. The owners know that the managers do not have the same incentives as they do and they will assume that managers are acting in their own interests. Managers have a large amount of control as to how decisions are made in companies and there are many ways in which they might act in their own interests to the detriment of shareholders. It may be, for example, that managers might enjoy first-class travel, dining and accommodation, which may be more than is necessary for their company duties. However, on a more significant (sometimes possibly illegal) note, they might manipulate earnings in the short term to earn bonuses, which would not be in the long-term interest of the company.

As a logical consequence of this agency problem, owners will 'price protect' themselves on the assumption that managers are acting for themselves. This could be observed by a reduction in demand for company shares or remuneration packages for managers that make assumptions as to their behaviour. These types of actions obviously cause a problem for managers because even if they are acting in the best interests of the organisation, the owners will be penalising them on the assumption they are not. The agency problem is why managers produce financial reports for shareholders to try to alleviate their concerns. However, there is still a risk that this information may be biased. For this reason, it is in the best interest of *both parties* to obtain the services of an independent auditor to check the financial reports prepared by management and provide reasonable assurance that it is true and fair to the users of the financial reports. In developing agency theory, Jensen and Meckling[7] hypothesised that an audit by someone independent of the manager reduces the incentive problems that arise when the firm manager does not own all of the residual claims on the firm. They proposed that an audit is a monitoring activity that will increase the value of the firm when there are agency problems. Following these arguments, regulation would not appear to be necessary to observe audits occurring.

Watts and Zimmerman[8] examined historical records and found the function of an 'audit' role existing in one form or another without legislative mandate over the past 1000 years in the United Kingdom. The Industrial Revolution in the mid nineteenth century signalled a major expansion of audit demand. This is because up until that time most businesses were small and the owner of the business was also the manager. For these entities, there were no agency problems. The Industrial Revolution meant that some businesses became significantly larger and it was impossible for the owner to also be the manager as other shareholders were needed to raise capital; and the size and complexity of the businesses meant that more professional managers were needed to manage the businesses on behalf of the owners. This separation of ownership and management meant that there was an agency problem. The owners wanted to maximise their profits and the managers wanted to maximise their personal utility which was not necessarily aligned with the owners. This meant that there was a need to obtain an audit. The role for an auditor to provide assurance on the reliability of the financial statements produced by management was seen as valuable to reduce the information asymmetry between these two parties. From their extensive review of historical records, Watts and Zimmerman concluded a couple of important points:

> The survival of the bonding and auditing practices from the Ipswich merchant guild in 1200 to the British joint stock banks of 1836 ... is consistent with the existence of agency problems and the use of bonding and monitoring to reduce agency costs.
>
> Overall, the evidence suggests that the existence of the independent audit is not the direct result of government fiat.[9]

The posting of a **bond** by agents occurred in some of the early organisations. This meant that a sum of money was posted as a bond to provide security for fraudulent or other inappropriate behaviour to protect the principals' capital. It was to achieve the same objective as auditing to help ensure that the managers acted in the best interests of shareholders. The agency relationship is represented in figure 1.2.

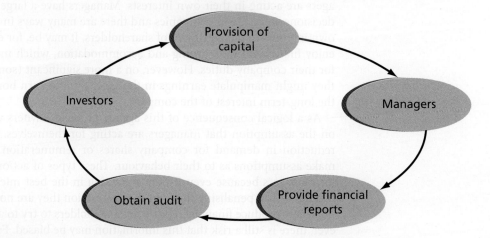

FIGURE 1.2:
The agency relationship

Obtaining a car loan

Assume you are a young university student, who does some part-time work. Think about a situation where you might want to apply for a loan to buy a new car. If you approach a bank to try to get a loan, what sort of questions would the bank want to ask you? It could be assumed that they would be interested in the following if they provided you with a loan:
- Will the capital (loan) they provide you to buy the car be secure?
- Will they continue to receive the interest on the capital from you?
- What happens if you stop paying?

Although it is a different situation to shareholders and managers of companies, there are similarities. The concerns that the bank has about how you will use the capital that they have entrusted to you by providing a loan are similar to the concerns that shareholders will have by entrusting managers to run companies that are built on the capital that they provide. Both the bank and the shareholders will want to ensure that their capital is safe. There are a couple of things that the bank will ask for to provide them with some comfort that they will receive their capital and interest back from you in relation to the loan.
- They will want to obtain evidence regarding the income you say you earn from your part-time job. For this reason, they might want to confirm with your employer that you work for them and they also might want to sight a few pay slips. This will provide them with some evidence that you do actually have the job that you say you have and that the amount you earn is as much as you stated.

- They will also want to obtain evidence of the existence of other assets you say you have. If this includes deposits at another financial institution, they will want copies of the bank statements to provide evidence that these amounts exist.
- The bank will also want some sort of security in case you lose your job and cannot pay, or, alternatively, just decide to not continue paying. They will probably take security over the car itself; however, that is of limited value due to the fact that cars depreciate very quickly and also there will be transaction costs in selling the car. For this reason, they will probably also want a guarantor. This is someone who agrees that they will pay the bank if you default. If you are young, this may be your parents.

These three actions that are taken by the bank are similar to some of the actions that might be observed in the relationship between shareholders and managers. The first two examples are obtaining evidence about the fact that you are working, the amount you earn (confirming income) and the amount of your assets. This is similar to obtaining an audit. An audit confirms assertions that the managers make about the financial statements on matters such as the net assets and net income of the company owned by the shareholders. Early audits were actually done by committees of shareholders (principals) until there were too many shareholders and companies became too large. In this case, the principal is the bank and it is relatively easy for them to evaluate this evidence. The third example is more related to bonding, where financial assets are available in case of default. This was observed in early agency relationships where managers put up capital as a 'bond' to be available for the owners in cases of fraud.

Like the relationship between shareholders and managers, the relationship between you and the bank is not one based on trust. They do not trust you with their money! They want to take all steps necessary to ensure that their funds are secure and they will assume that you act in your own self interest. In truth, your motivations are also not necessarily always directed at the bank's best interests! You might want to spend your money on other things besides paying them back. You might get so annoyed with your job that you want to quit — thereby also making it very difficult for you to pay the bank back. The bank knows you have these incentives and takes actions to protect itself accordingly.

Agency theory is an economic way of explaining these interrelationships and motivations. An audit is theoretically expected in agency relationships, and it has been what is consistently observed — indicating that it is a good mechanism for mitigating the agency problems in a firm.

As well as the agency rationale for auditing, Wallace[10] noted a couple of other reasons for a demand for auditing: the information hypothesis and the insurance hypothesis.

Information hypothesis

According to the **information hypothesis**, the audit improves the quality of information, which provides benefits through the reduction of risk, improvements of decisions, and the increase in profits. Investors will demand this information because it is useful for decision making and will assist them in assessing the risks and returns associated with their investments. The audit will reduce estimation risk (i.e. the uncertainty associated with the realisation of future cash flows). There will also be value within the firm to assist in improving financial data for internal decision making; it can detect errors and motivate employees to exercise more care in preparing records in anticipation of an audit.

There is some overlap between the information hypothesis and agency theory. Information that is useful in monitoring an agent's performance is also useful for making investment decisions. However, the focus of the agency demand for auditing is more related to the stewardship role of accounting — which is more an examination of what has happened. The focus of the information hypothesis is more towards the decision usefulness role of accounting. It is also a demand for auditing that comes from a greater number of users of financial information from both within and outside of the firm. However, it should be noted that the information hypothesis is certainly the major reason for the demand for assurance services discussed later in this chapter and in more detail in chapter 4.

Insurance hypothesis

The **insurance hypothesis** was suggested as creating additional demand for auditing and appealed to two different groups. The first related to investors and creditors who might demand an audit to show that they are being prudent to insure against losses. As described by Wallace:[11]

> The ability to shift financial responsibility for reported data to an auditor lowers the expected loss from litigation or related settlements to managers, creditors, and other professionals involved in the securities market. As potential litigation awards increase, this insurance demand for an audit from managers and professional participants in financial activities can be expected to grow.

Historically, this was certainly the case. Auditors were seen as the ones with 'deep pockets', (i.e. the ones left standing after a corporate collapse with a good amount of available funds). They were a good option to make a claim for funds to recover losses by investors and, therefore, a useful source of a potential claim if things went wrong. The difficulty with this is that it may have contributed to the litigation crisis for the auditing profession (see discussion in chapter 5). Since this litigation crisis, it would be fair to say auditors would not want to consider any demand for their services to stem from 'insurance' reasons. The economics of this are also in the auditor's favour as audit fees are a very small proportion of company revenue and assets.[12] It would be unreasonable for anyone to assume a significant insurance component with such an unbalanced cost/benefit trade-off. The other reason it is unlikely that this is a major reason for a demand in auditing in Australia is due to the significant changes in the legal environment, which have reduced the legal exposure for auditors (see chapter 5).

The second group to benefit from the insurance aspect of auditing includes a diverse set of regulators who can potentially insulate themselves from criticism by directing blame at the auditors. This was clearly illustrated in some of the reactions to the **corporate collapses** in Australia in the early 2000s of One.Tel, Harris Scarfe, and HIH Insurance, and more recently in the Centro case. An example of this was a headline on the front page of *The Australian* titled 'Heat's on auditor for HIH crash'.[13] Certainly, the Royal Commission into HIH also made a number of criticisms about the auditors. However, the focus on auditors also conveniently deflected criticism of the Australian Prudential Regulation Authority, which also had oversight responsibilities in relation to HIH. It is probably fair to say that this aspect of the insurance hypothesis, which benefits government regulators and politicians, still exists today. Some examples include the collapse of Westpoint Corporation in 2006 that resulted in the Australian Securities and Investments Commission (ASIC) imposing bans on three auditors,[14] and the collapse of ABC Learning in 2008, which has focused attention on the regulators and the auditors, as stated by the following commentator, 'ASIC won't be the only one in the doghouse. The roles of the auditors won't be ignored and the repercussions may go well beyond ABC Learning'.[15]

In the Centro (2012) case, ASIC accepted an enforceable undertaking from the former Centro auditor (a Melbourne partner of PwC). The enforceable undertaking prevents the auditor from practising as a registered auditor from the date of the decision to 30 June 2015. It follows ASIC's investigation into the 2007 financial reports of Centro Properties Group. The financial report failed to properly classify as current interest-bearing liabilities of A$1.514 billion, which were disclosed as non-current. Other failures included failure to disclose a substantial guarantee to lenders, failure of the auditor to obtain sufficient appropriate audit evidence, and failure to ensure that the auditing procedures were adequate and that, allegedly, the discrepancies were communicated to those charged with governance. The actions of the Centro case have brought about a substantially increased understanding of the existing duties of directors and auditors in the preparation, approval and audit of financial reports. There is no doubt now that auditors must obtain reasonable assurance that a financial report is not materially misstated.[16]

Regulation

There are a number of factors that create a demand for audits irrespective of whether they are regulated or not. However, in most jurisdictions there is regulation and it has existed for a long time. In 1844 the Joint Stock Companies Registration and Regulation Act (UK) was the first regulation to provide for an audit to examine the accounts of a company. The annual presentation of the balance sheet to the shareholders and the carrying out of a statutory audit were made mandatory in 1900 under the Companies Act 1862 (UK). The majority of large corporate entities around the world do require audits by government authority. However, this is due to the importance of reliability of financial information in the markets and also is a broader public policy issue for governments. Further, it is not just the corporate sector that sees the value in mandating an audit function to increase the credibility and reliability of financial information. In the Australian environment, all of the following bodies are required to have an annual audit:

- companies, registered schemes and disclosing entities (except small proprietary companies)
- commonwealth and state government departments, statutory authorities, government companies and business undertakings, and municipalities
- not-for-profit organisations, including educational institutions.

The fact that such a range of organisations are mandated to have an audit does suggest the importance of the role. However, the historical observation of audits shows it is intrinsically necessary in commercial interactions, and by its continued existence it shows that this process of an audit has been an efficient and effective monitoring mechanism. It should be of some comfort to auditors that even in a world without these legal requirements, we would expect to see a good number of audits still occurring anyway.

As noted in the preceding discussion, audits have existed in one form or another for a thousand years and for most of this time there was no legislative mandate. The most widely accepted reason for a demand for auditing is due to agency theory. Generally, agency theory relates to financial statement audits. Financial statement audits are the main focus of this text and are also discussed in more detail in chapter 6. There are a number of other costs and benefits associated with auditing which are also discussed further in chapter 6.

Auditing services are not limited to financial report audits. They have been changing rapidly over the past twenty years in response and to the complexities of economic and technological advancements in corporations and most recently to growing public expectations of **accountability**. The auditing profession has also responded to demands for other types of services in developing an assurance framework, with auditing being part of the assurance services that firms provide, discussed later in this chapter and in chapter 4.

1.1.4 Who provides audits?

Financial report audits are provided by **external auditors** (also referred to as independent auditors), who are either individual practitioners or members of public accounting firms who render professional auditing services to clients. By virtue of their education, training and experience, independent auditors are qualified to perform the types of audits described in this chapter. However, they can also provide many other assurance services. The clients of independent auditors may include profit-making business enterprises, not-for-profit organisations, government agencies and individuals.

Like members of the medical and legal professions, independent auditors work on a fee for service basis. There are similarities between the role of an independent auditor in a public accounting firm and that of a solicitor who is a member of a law firm. However, there is also a major difference — the auditor is expected to be independent of the client in carrying out an audit and reporting the results, whereas the solicitor is expected to be an advocate for the client in rendering legal services (as well as to the court).

Audit **independence** involves both conceptual and technical considerations (see chapter 2). It is enough to say at this point that an auditor, to be independent, should be without bias in respect of the client under audit and should appear to be objective to those relying on the results of the audit.

Only independent auditors registered with ASIC can perform an audit of reporting entities in Australia. The purpose of registration is to set minimum standards of competence, integrity and accountability. Various state Acts also stipulate that only a registered company auditor may audit real estate agents' trust accounts, solicitors' trust accounts, and so on. The criteria for registration of auditors are stipulated in s. 1280 of the Corporations Act, which prescribes that a person applying for registration must be:

- ordinarily resident in Australia
- a member of the Institute of Chartered Accountants in Australia or CPA Australia or another approved body
- a graduate or have obtained a diploma from a prescribed university or other prescribed institution in Australia and must have passed the examinations in such subjects as the university or other institution certifies to ASIC to represent a course of study in accountancy (including auditing) of not less than 3 years duration and in commercial law (including company law) of not less than 2 years duration, or who has other equivalent qualifications acceptable to ASIC.

In addition, the person must have sufficient experience in auditing and must be a fit and proper person to be registered as an auditor.

LEARNING objective 2

Describe how assurance relates to auditing.

1.2 WHAT IS ASSURANCE?

An audit is an **assurance engagement**. Assurance is a broad term to describe any situation where information is prepared by one party and then attested to its accuracy by another party. This describes an audit but it is a broader term than 'audit' which usually relates to a financial report audit and implies a reasonable level of assurance. As noted earlier in the chapter, what is considered 'reasonable assurance' by the auditing standards is considered to be a 'high' level of assurance.

Assurance engagements relate to a much broader set of potential engagements that may be financial or non-financial, and the level of assurance provided can vary according to the particular engagement. Chapter 4 discusses in more detail some of the various types of assurance engagements that can be provided. Figure 1.3 is a simple illustration of the relationship between assurance engagements and the financial report audit.

The Australian auditing standards define an assurance engagement as 'an engagement in which an assurance practitioner expresses a conclusion designed to enhance the degree of confidence of the intended users other than the responsible party about the outcome of the evaluation or measurement of a subject matter against criteria'.[17]

Assurance engagement

Financial report audit

FIGURE 1.3:
The relationship between
auditing and assurance

The financial report audit is a very significant type of assurance service, as it is still the major source of revenue for accounting firms in the assurance domain. This book will focus on the audit of financial reports as it is the major service that is provided and it is inextricably linked to the production of financial reports. The market may change in the future as users start to demand some of the other types of assurance services discussed in chapter 4. However, provision of assurance services is an area where accounting firms will have competition from other providers, whereas accounting firms have a mandated monopoly on the provision of financial report audits.

LEARNING 3 objective

Discuss the importance of the profession, case law and regulation to auditing.

1.3 THE AUDITING ENVIRONMENT

Auditors operate in a complex environment that is subject to a number of important influences, such as the requirements of their own profession, case law and regulation. This section will explain these influences and how they affect auditing and also illustrate how they have changed in relative importance over the years.

1.3.1 The accounting profession

The accounting profession emerged in conjunction with the rapid growth of auditing in the nineteenth century. The first professional society of accountants was formed in Scotland in 1854 and in England in 1870.[18] In Australia, the first professional body was the Adelaide Society of Accountants in 1884.[19] Interestingly, in the United Kingdom, these bodies were created to provide information on the accountant's reputation, not for auditing, but for bankruptcies. This decision to allow accountants to work in this field was not universally applauded. As noted by Watts and Zimmerman, one judge remarked in 1875:[20]

> The whole affairs in bankruptcy have been handed over to an ignorant set of men called accountants, which was one of the greatest abuses ever introduced into the law.

A side effect of this development was that the accounting professional societies began to establish brand names. This was particularly important given that there was an increase in the demand for auditing services at this time. The fact that the accounting professional bodies had been established and began to set and monitor standards of conduct, thereby developing their competence and integrity, meant that their 'brand' became more valuable. It was a logical progression for the accounting profession to become the major provider of audit services. The value of their brand and reputation meant that the quality and independence of the audit function provided by their members could be certified at a relatively low cost to demanders of audited financial statements. More consideration of the concept of the 'accounting profession' is considered in chapter 3.

Developments in the UK influenced Australia significantly and accounting professional associations began to appear in the 1880s. Accounting bodies have been instrumental in the development of audit practice over the years by:

- developing standards of practice through research and issuance of standards, professional education, and the establishment of rules of conduct for members
- ensuring professional conduct and effective self-regulation of quality of service
- maintaining standards of qualifications through accredited courses, examinations and practical experience for accountants seeking to become members.

The last 15 years have seen a significant change in the role of the accounting profession in Australia and also internationally. This has been, in part, a response to some of the corporate scandals of the early 2000s when a lot of trust was lost in the accounting profession (discussed in section 1.3.3). The main regulatory changes are noted in section 1.3.4 of this chapter. The responsibility for accounting and auditing standard setting for companies that report under the Corporations Act is now under government control. The regulation of accountants involved in the corporate reporting world is now mainly performed by ASIC. The accounting profession's main ongoing responsibilities are associated with maintaining standards of qualification, ongoing professional development and ethical standard setting.

In Australia, the use of the term 'accountant' is not regulated. However, s. 88B of the Corporations Act defines 'qualified accountant' as follows:

(1) For the purposes of this Act, a *qualified accountant* is a person covered by a declaration in force under subsection (2).
(2) ASIC may, in writing, declare that all members of a specified professional body, or all persons in a specified class of members of a specified professional body, are qualified accountants for the purposes of this Act.
(3) ASIC may, in writing, vary or revoke a declaration made under subsection (2).

Professional bodies

The three main professional accounting bodies in Australia are the Institute of Chartered Accountants in Australia (ICAA), CPA Australia, and the Institute of Public Accountants (IPA). Membership is necessary to represent oneself as a professional accountant in the Australian environment. It is also necessary to satisfy the registration qualification for auditors and liquidators, and is a requirement for those conducting an audit under various state Acts in Australia. These professional bodies provide a broad range of services to their respective members and are involved in local and international standard setting.

The Institute of Chartered Accountants in Australia

The ICAA was constituted by Royal Charter in 1928. It was formed through a merger of various state accounting professional bodies that dated back to the 1880s. It now operates under a Supplemental Royal Charter granted by the Governor General in 2005. The primary membership base of the ICAA has traditionally been members in public practice. However, more recently, the ICAA has also encouraged commerce and industry to participate in the training of chartered accountants (CA). In 2012, the ICAA had about 60 000 members, with more than 12 000 graduates enrolled in the CA program. About 38% of its members work in public practice, 35% in commerce and 12% work overseas.[21] The ICAA is also a member of the Global Accounting Alliance (GAA), which is an international accounting coalition with membership of 785 000 people over 165 countries.[22]

The services that the ICAA provides to its members include professional and technical standards and continuing professional education, including the education of future members through the CA program. The ICAA maintains a library, information service and bookshop for its members. Its publications include a monthly journal (*Charter*) and *Members' Handbook*.

The ICAA's strategic plan in 2012–13 included the following core purpose:

Through its leadership, the Institute enhances and promotes the reputation and role of Chartered Accountants, both individually and collectively, and ensures the highest professional quality of its current and future members, for the benefit of the business community and the public interest.[23]

CPA Australia

The Australian Society of Accountants was established in 1952. As with the ICAA, it comprised antecedent bodies that dated back to the nineteenth century. In 1990, the name was changed to the Australian Society of Certified Practising Accountants and then to CPA Australia in 2000. In 2011, CPA Australia had approximately 139 000 members. Approximately 18% of its members are engaged in public practice, 32% in the corporate sector and 19% in small to medium-sized enterprises.[24]

CPA Australia celebrated 125 years in 2011 and in its annual report it highlighted the goal to maximise CPA Australia's share of people who aspire to build a career on professional accounting skills. CPA Australia publishes *InTheBlack*, a magazine for its members, which states that:

Our core services to members include education, training, technical support and advocacy. Staff and members work together with local and international bodies to represent the views and concerns of the profession to governments, regulators, industries, academia and the general public.

Our international presence continues to grow in terms of representation on international bodies and influence in the profession globally. In areas of financial reporting, taxation and corporate governance we are thought leaders in Australia and internationally.[25]

In line with the strategy mentioned above, CPA Australia has developed new CPA pathways articulations with a number of tuition providers that allow entry into the CPA programs from a non-Australian university accounting degree.

The Institute of Public Accountants

The Institute of Public Accountants is a professional organisation for accountants recognised for their practical and hands-on skills and broad understanding of the total business environment. They have more than 24 000 members and students.

Practice entities

The public accounting profession comprises firms of a large variation in size that may operate internationally, nationally, regionally or locally. From the perspective of the practice entities that have the most impact on auditing, the '**Big Four**' (Deloitte, Ernst & Young, KPMG and PricewaterhouseCoopers) are dominant both economically and politically. Following the collapse of Arthur Andersen in 2002, there were some concerns about the dominance of these four major players. However, there has been significant growth in the 'second tier' accounting firms since this time. In part, this has been helped by more stringent independence requirements that have been introduced, which has resulted in some limitations in the work that the Big Four can bid for. There are a number of 'second tier' firms that have grown in size and influence over the past ten years, including BDO, Grant Thornton, Nexia, Pitcher Partners, PKF, Moore Stephens, RSM Bird Cameron and WHK. Mergers of smaller firms occurred from time to time. In 2012, for example, Grant Thornton Australia acquired the BDO NSW and Victoria practice for $60 million and expanded its global income and network.[26]

1.3.2 Case law

Case law has been an important influence on what an auditor does and what an auditor reports since the late nineteenth century. The growth in the auditing function meant that there were more users of the audited financial reports. Increased size of companies and greater numbers of users meant that the likelihood that cases would come before the courts increased. Auditing in the early days was associated with detection of **fraud**, checking all or most transactions, and trust in management's assertions. However, the growing complexity, greater separation of owners from managers and increasing size of businesses, meant that this type of auditing could not continue. One of the first major cases that addressed some of these emerging issues for the auditing profession at the time was *Kingston Cotton Mill Co.* (1896) 2 Ch. 279, where Lopes delivered the following passage that still has *some* relevance today:

> It is the duty of an auditor to bring to bear on the work he has to perform that skill, care and caution that a reasonably competent, careful and cautious auditor would use. What is reasonable skill, care and caution must depend on the particular circumstances of each case. An auditor is not bound to be a detective, or, as was said, to approach his work with suspicion or with a foregone conclusion that there is something wrong ... He is a watchdog, but not a bloodhound ... If there is anything calculated to excite suspicion, he should probe it to the bottom but, in the absence of anything of that kind, he is only bound to be reasonably cautious and careful ... Auditors must not be made responsible for not tracking out ingenious and carefully laid schemes of fraud, where there is nothing to arouse their suspicion.

The emphasis of **reasonable skill and care** was a downgrading of the perceptions of auditor responsibility up to this time. It meant that the concepts of risk, materiality and sampling could be developed in the knowledge that the auditor was not attempting to provide absolute assurance on a set of financial statements. The term 'reasonable assurance' is still in the current audit opinion. This legal judgement also outlined that the audit role was not to detect fraud — which continues to be a source of comfort to the audit profession! Fraud is difficult to detect because it differs from error in that there is an intention to hide it, thereby making it harder to find than standard 'errors'. This judgement lessened the auditors' responsibility in this area and some have suggested since that it went too far.

Fraud was also addressed in the major Australian case of *Pacific Acceptance Corporation v. Forsyth* (1970) 92 WN NSW (29). Moffit J noted that the auditors should pay due regard to the possibility of fraud and actively investigate the possibility of fraud if suspicious circumstances exist. Moffit J also addressed the concept of 'reasonable skill and care' and that it calls for changed standards to meet changed business conditions or changed understanding of the dangers.

The rigour, extent and detail in the current auditing standards as well as their legal mandate (discussed later in this chapter) means that following the auditing standards is the best option for an auditor in ensuring that the audit is undertaken with 'reasonable skill and care'. In relation to fraud, the responsibilities for auditors in this area have increased significantly in recent years, as discussed later in this book (see chapter 8).

The important cases affecting auditors are discussed in more detail in chapter 5. However, in recent years, greater regulation (particularly in relation to independence) and the expanded number and extent of auditing standards (which are also mandated under the Corporations Act) have had more influence on audit practice than case law. The balance of importance appears to have shifted to regulation. There have also been changes that have reduced auditors' potential liability through the courts (see chapter 5), which have also affected the relative importance of case law compared to regulation.

1.3.3 The early 2000s — challenges and changes

The early 2000s were marked by some major corporate collapses as well as corporate frauds. For example, in the United States the collapse of Enron and exposure of fraudulent accounting, which was then followed by the major fraud in WorldCom, ultimately resulted in the collapse of one of the 'Big 5' accounting firms, Arthur Andersen. There was significant regulatory change in the United States after these corporate problems through the passage of the Sarbanes–Oxley Act (2002). In Australia, there were also corporate collapses in the early 2000s with the most notable being HIH Insurance. HIH was a leading Australian insurance group that went into liquidation in March 2001 and was also audited by Arthur Andersen. This was such a significant event it resulted in a Royal Commission and some of the recommendations were incorporated into the Corporate Law Economic Reform Program (CLERP) 9, which forever changed the regulatory landscape in Australia (discussed in the next section of this chapter). Some main changes of CLERP 9 were to expand the requirements on independence for auditors and also the creation of the Financial Reporting Council (FRC), which had a significant effect on the role of the accounting profession in the regulatory landscape. No longer would the accounting profession in Australia be responsible for the setting of auditing standards. Some of the corporate collapses and their legal ramifications are discussed in more detail in chapter 5.

These accounting problems seemed to illustrate to the public and governments that the auditors were not sufficiently monitoring and reporting on problems within some major corporations. De Angelo provided an important definition of **audit quality** that states it is the 'market-assessed joint probability that a given auditor will both (a) discover the breach in the client's accounting system, and (b) report the breach'.[27] It requires that auditors have the ability to pick up errors or irregularities and then they have the independence to do something about it.

The regulatory changes in Australia clearly focused on the second part of this definition. One particular issue that was highlighted related to the very large non-audit fees that were being earned by the auditing firms at that time. Many observers questioned how the auditor could be independent when they were earning such large fees from **non-audit services**. There is an argument that any fees earned by the audit firm from the client create an economic dependency. However, non-audit fees were seen as particularly problematic because of the following reasons: (a) they are generally more profitable than fees charged for the audit; (b) in the 1990s many auditing firms marketed these services very heavily, such that the audit appeared to be a 'secondary' consideration for the firms; and (c) most importantly, the public and government saw these fees as being inextricably linked to the perceived problems of independence that were observed in the early 1990s.

Another side effect of the problems of the early 2000s was actually a good thing for auditors! The attention to the audit function and the prominence given to it actually raised its importance in the business sector and within the wider community. It is not often that auditors make the front page of a newspaper![28] This profile and focus of importance of auditing in corporate governance meant that auditors could expend more time on the audit role and have that time appropriately reflected in fees. This was illustrated by the significant increases in audit fees, with four years of double-digit fee increases from 2002.[29] This contrasts to much of the 1990s, where auditing was seen by accounting firms as a loss leader to get access to the lucrative non-audit fees available from clients (this was no longer the case post 2002).

In the United States, the system was in a greater state of shock because of the significance of their corporate collapses. The scandal of Enron led the US regulators to make some significant changes to address the problems that they perceived with auditing (particularly in relation to independence) and corporate governance. The Sarbanes–Oxley Act made it illegal to provide certain non-audit services to audit clients and changed the regulation of the auditing profession. The Act created a new Public Company Accounting Oversight Board (PCAOB) with the authority to establish auditing standards, **quality control** standards, and independence standards for auditors of public companies. It also gave the PCAOB the authority to inspect the work of auditors.

Section 404 of the Sarbanes–Oxley Act was also a major change that significantly affected the work of both company management and auditors. The management of companies are required to disclose in their annual report the adequacy of their internal control structures and procedures for financial reporting and the auditors are required to provide assurance and report on these issues. This part of the Sarbanes–Oxley Act was costly to companies and has been one of the more controversial regulatory changes for some time. It should be noted that the changes as per Section 404 have not been followed in any other major jurisdictions although the effect of them has been felt in other jurisdictions because of the number of large US multinational companies.

The changes in Australia through the passage of CLERP 9 (discussed in the next section) were significant but not as extensive as the Sarbanes–Oxley changes.

Given the blame directed at auditors during the corporate problems of the early 2000s, one might have expected a similar reaction towards auditors in the aftermath of the global financial crisis (GFC) of 2007–08. Interestingly, this has not yet occurred to any great extent in the United States or Australia, but has had major consequences in Europe as the following Professional Environment extract demonstrates.

PROFESSIONAL ENVIRONMENT

Restoring confidence in financial statements: the European Commission aims at a higher quality, dynamic and open audit market

The 2008 financial crisis highlighted considerable shortcomings in the European audit system. Audits of some large financial institutions just before, during and since the crisis resulted in 'clean' audit reports despite the serious intrinsic weaknesses in the financial health of the institutions concerned. Recent inspection reports by national supervisors have also criticised the quality of audits.

Under the proposals adopted today by the European Commission, this situation is to change by clarifying the role of the auditors and introducing more stringent rules for the audit sector aimed in particular at strengthening the independence of auditors as well as greater diversity into the current highly-concentrated audit market. Furthermore, the Commission is also proposing to create a Single Market for statutory audit services allowing auditors to exercise their profession freely and easily across Europe, once licensed in one Member State. There are also proposals for a strengthened and more coordinated approach to the supervision of auditors in the EU. Taken together, all the measures should enhance the quality of statutory audits in the EU and restore confidence in audited financial statements, in particular those of banks, insurers and large listed companies.

Internal Market and Services Commissioner Michel Barnier said:

Investor confidence in audit has been shaken by the crisis and I believe changes in this sector are necessary: we need to restore confidence in the financial statements of companies. Today's proposals address the current weaknesses in the EU audit market, by eliminating conflicts of interest, ensuring independence and robust supervision and by facilitating more diversity in what is an overly concentrated market, especially at the top-end.

Source: European Commission, *Restoring confidence in financial statements: the European Commission aims at a higher quality, dynamic and open audit market*, press release, Brussels, 30 November 2011.

1.3.4 Regulation and other oversight

The Corporate Law Economic Reform Program Paper No. 9 (CLERP 9) was enacted as the *Corporate Law Economic Reform Program (Audit Reform and Corporate Disclosure) Act 2004*. The Bill was a response to the Ramsay Report about auditor independence and also incorporated some of the recommendations from the HIH Royal Commission. It made a number of changes in the law in relation to regulation of auditing (particularly in relation to independence) and corporate governance. However, the Bill did not replicate the Sarbanes–Oxley Act in the United States which takes a very rules-based approach. Even though it has specific requirements, it would be fair to say that CLERP 9 is more of a principles-based approach compared to the Sarbanes–Oxley Act. The following are some of the main changes under CLERP 9 found in Part 2M.4 of the Corporations Act.

Audit independence

This is the area that received the most criticism in the United States and in Australia. A few of the main changes are presented below.

- *Non-audit services.* These services were not prohibited in Australia as they were in the United States. However, more detailed disclosures of the types of non-audit services were included in requirements of CLERP 9, as well as a requirement for a statement by directors that they are satisfied the provision of non-audit services did not affect audit independence and the reasons they were satisfied in relation to this issue (s. 300 (11B)(b) of the Corporations Act). Not surprisingly, the effect of this and the general 'negative' climate in relation to auditors undertaking non-audit services has meant that the amount of these services purchased by companies has dropped off significantly. Audit firms have also responded to these changes by 'spinning-off' their consulting arms that provided the non-audit services into separate organisations. For example, in 2002 PricewaterhouseCoopers spun off its consulting activities into a separate entity that it called 'Monday'; unsurprisingly, the name was not a hit! In late 2002 PricewaterhouseCoopers sold the business to IBM.
- *Audit partner rotation.* There is a perception that if an audit partner stays with the client for a long period of time, he or she will become too familiar with the client and it will impair independence. This was certainly perceived as a problem in the development of CLERP 9 and initially there was some consideration that this problem could be mitigated by a requirement that the audit firm rotate. This was opposed by larger accounting firms as they would clearly have the most to lose if large clients had to rotate firms. Eventually the Bill opted for audit partner rotation instead, and the requirement is now that a person who plays a significant role in an audit in 5 out of 7 years must rotate (s. 324DA).
- *Auditor working for the client.* This issue was brought to prominence from the relationships observed between Arthur Andersen and HIH Insurance and highlighted in the HIH Royal Commission. A number of audit partners had left Arthur Andersen to take senior positions at HIH. This certainly raised questions about the level of familiarity between the two organisations and therefore the ability to remain independent. The Bill prohibits a member of an audit firm, or director of an audit company who was a professional member of an audit team, from becoming an officer of an audit client until two years from the date of ceasing with the audit firm.

Quality-related changes

The main focus on the changes affecting auditors related to audit independence. There were some changes that did affect audit quality. Two of the main ones were as follows.

- *The role of the Financial Reporting Council.* The role was broadened to include oversight of the Australian Auditing and Assurance Standards Board (AUASB). The auditing standards issued by the AUASB also now have the force of law. This greater government control of the audit standard-setting process, along with the auditing standards having the force of law, is considered to be a way of improving audit quality. Historically, this is a major change because it has almost completely removed the accounting profession from an area where it previously had sole responsibility.

- *Annual general meetings.* The shareholders are permitted to submit questions to the auditors before the AGM. The auditor must also attend the AGM and there should be a reasonable opportunity for the shareholders to ask questions of the auditor and for the auditor to respond. This new requirement is indirectly related to audit quality as it increases the accountability of the auditors. It is an important change because there is very little communication between the auditors and the shareholders and this change provides an important link between the two.

There are many other changes that were put into legislation through CLERP 9. More details of the CLERP 9 changes are contained in the ASIC and Corporations Act websites noted below.

Australian Securities and Investments Commission (ASIC)

ASIC regulates the corporate, markets and financial services sector in Australia. The activities overseen by ASIC include the advising on, selling of, and disclosure of financial products and services to consumers so they have adequate information and are treated fairly with adequate avenues for redress. ASIC is set up under the *Australian Securities and Investments Commission Act 2001* (ASIC Act) and carries out most of its work under the Corporations Act.

ASIC is accountable to the Australian Parliament through the Attorney-General. Its objectives (s. 1(2)) are:

- to maintain, facilitate and improve the performance of companies, the securities markets and the futures markets
- to promote the informed and confident participation of investors and consumers in the financial system
- to achieve uniformity of administration of the Corporations Act throughout Australia
- to administer the laws that confer functions and powers on it effectively and with a minimum of procedural requirements
- to receive, process and store — efficiently and quickly — the information given to ASIC under the laws
- to ensure that the documents are available for public access
- to take action to enforce and give effect to national scheme law.

Of particular interest to auditors is the expanded role of ASIC in recent years to be responsible for reviewing the quality of audit work performed. A recent review of this work did not show a great result for auditors as described in the Professional Environment below. Further discussion on audit quality is in chapter 3. The ASIC website can be found at www.asic.gov.au.

The Corporations Act and other Australian legislation can be found at the official government website, www.comlaw.gov.au, and also at www.austlii.edu.au, the website maintained by the University of Technology, Sydney and University of New South Wales faculties of law. Important sections of the Corporations Act are noted throughout this textbook. Further discussion on the Corporations Act as it pertains to the conduct of the audit and auditor appointment and removal is contained in chapter 6.

The Companies Auditors and Liquidators Disciplinary Board (CALDB)

The CALDB is a statutory body established in 1990 under the ASIC Act. It hears applications from ASIC to determine whether auditors or liquidators have breached the Corporations

Act, and has the power to impose a penalty if it determines that a registered auditor or liquidator has failed to carry out duties properly, or is not a fit and proper person to be registered. Penalties include the cancellation or suspension of registration, an imposition of restrictions on conduct, or an admonition.

CALDB members are appointed by the Treasurer based on the requirements of the ASIC Act 2001 and have a breadth of knowledge and experience encompassing the law, accounting and business.

The Australian Securities Exchange (ASX)

The ASX is also an important participant in the market but is *not a regulator*. The ASX describes itself as 'a regulated commercial organisation that monitors specific aspects of the businesses of other organisations'.[30]

To list on the ASX there are a number of Listing Rules designed to protect investors. The Listing Rules are enforceable against listed entities under the requirements of the Corporations Act. Listing Rules create obligations that are additional and complementary to the statutory obligations under the Corporations Act. The ASX became a public company in 1998 and operates as the main national securities exchange for equities, derivatives and fixed-interest securities. It facilitates capital raisings and trading for listed companies settlement and capital matching, and provides comprehensive market data and information to a range of users. A couple of areas where there are enhanced requirements under the Listing Rules are firstly in Listing Rule 4.10.3 where it requires a statement of the extent to which an entity has followed the best practice recommendations of the ASX Corporate Governance Council; and secondly in relation to continuous disclosure where Listing Rule 3.1 notes that once a company becomes aware of any information that a reasonable person would expect to have a material effect on the price or value of its securities, it should inform the market. The ASX maintains the integrity of the capital market and its website can be located at www.asx.com.au.

Do you know ...

1.1 ☐ The objective of a financial report audit is for the auditor to express an opinion about whether the financial report is prepared in all material respects in accordance with a financial reporting framework.

1.2 ☐ Agency theory is the main theory that explains why audits exist, which is primarily due to the information asymmetry between shareholders and managers.

1.3 ☐ There is significant evidence that audits would be demanded without regulatory mandate. However, most financial report audits in Australia are currently performed to comply with Corporations Act requirements.

1.4 ☐ The accounting profession has been a significant part of the growth and importance of audit services over the past century. Recently, due to the corporate crises of the early 2000s, some of the profession's role has been taken over by government bodies, such as the Australian Securities and Investments Commission (ASIC).

1.5 ☐ Major changes to enhance independence for auditors were enacted by CLERP 9 in 2004. These changes related to non-audit services; audit partner rotation; auditor working for the client; and others.

1.6 ☐ ASIC has a significant role in regulation of auditors. This includes enforcing and administrating the Corporations Act and reviewing audit work performed.

1.4 AUDITING STANDARDS

Auditing standards are of crucial importance to clarify auditors' responsibilities. The audit standard-setting process was originally controlled by the accounting profession through the Australian Accounting Research Foundation (AARF), which was founded in 1966. In recent years this has changed due to the implementation of CLERP 9 (2004). First, standard setting now comes under the control of the Auditing and Assurance Standards Board (AUASB) which is under the oversight of the Financial Reporting Council. Second, auditing standards now have the force of law under the Corporations Act, s. 336. These were significant changes for the auditing environment in Australia.

The legal mandate of auditing standards adds considerable weight to their importance to auditors and also to the standard setters in determining what is appropriate. Australia is one of the very few jurisdictions in the world to have legally enforceable auditing standards. However, the Australian accounting profession does not think the extra costs associated with these changes have increased audit quality or public confidence.[31] The new structure of accounting and auditing standard setting is shown in figure 1.4.

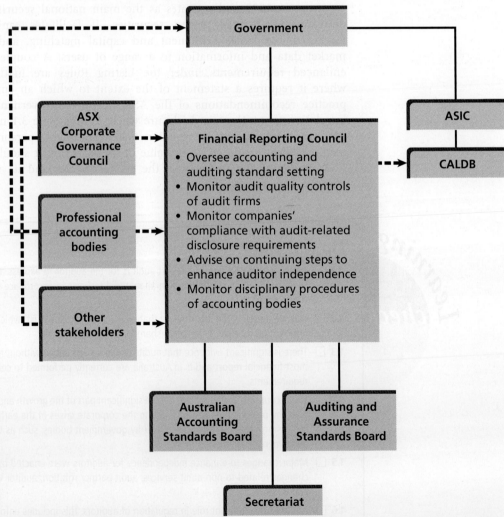

FIGURE 1.4:
Oversight structure of financial reporting in Australia

Source: Australian Government Department of the Treasury, *Reform Proposals: Expanded Financial Reporting Council,* www.treasury.gov.au.

1.4.1 Australian auditing standards

Australian auditing standards are overseen by two bodies: the Financial Reporting Council (FRC) and the Australian Auditing and Assurance Standards Board (AUASB). The primary role of the FRC is to set the strategic direction for the AUASB and the primary role of the AUASB is to develop high-quality auditing and assurance standards.

Financial Reporting Council

The FRC is a statutory body under the ASIC Act. Its objectives are to set accounting and auditing standards in the Australian environment and as part of this they also promote the continued adoption of international best practice accounting and auditing standards. The other major objective relates to auditor independence. There are significant monitoring responsibilities in this area to ensure that audits are conducted with appropriate levels of independence. This includes evaluating the systems and processes used by auditors to ensure compliance with auditor independence requirements and the systems and processes used by professional accounting bodies for planning and performing quality assurance reviews. The importance of this part of the role underpins the key attribute of independence and the perceived failing of this part of the audit function in the early 2000s.

The ASIC Audit Inspection findings reported in the scene setter on page 5 highlights that audit quality is more than just compliance with Auditing Standards. The Professional Environment below shows the need for professional judgement and scepticism in performing financial report audits.

PROFESSIONAL ENVIRONMENT
Professional scepticism in an audit of a financial report

*A*ustralia continues to experience a prolonged period of economic uncertainty and with that comes associated challenges for firms and participants in capital markets. Against this backdrop, the value of an independent audit is heightened as it enhances the degree of user confidence in financial reports.

Many entities today face difficult economic conditions that give rise to financial reporting challenges such as the assessment of going concern, the determination of fair values and the choice of approach to accounting estimates. Furthermore, today's financial reporting requirements seek to address information that is ever more relevant to users. As a result of this challenging environment, more judgement and increased subjectivity is involved in management's accounting and reporting decisions. These developments highlight the importance of auditors exhibiting a sceptical mindset, especially in areas of financial reporting that are complex or involve estimation.

The inspection programs of the Australian Securities and Investments Commission (ASIC) have raised concerns about whether professional scepticism is being applied properly in practice. ASIC's findings provoke questions about whether auditors: respond appropriately to unreliable audit evidence; seek to corroborate evidence rather than challenge it; and adequately demonstrate in the audit working papers how professional scepticism has been applied. ASIC refers to key areas of audit judgement where the level of professional scepticism exercised or evidenced in the audit fi les needs to be improved, particularly: fair value measurement of assets; impairment calculations; and going concern assessments.

Importantly, audit committees play a significant influencing role and commonly seek to foster appropriate professional scepticism in the external audit. Auditors, in turn, should demonstrate the value of their audit by seeking to convince audit committees that they have properly exercised professional scepticism in the conduct of the audit.

The need for professional scepticism in an audit cannot be overemphasised. Scepticism is an essential attitude that enhances the auditor's ability to exercise professional judgement in identifying and responding to conditions that may indicate possible misstatement. Professional scepticism includes a critical assessment of audit evidence. It also means remaining alert for evidence that contradicts other audit evidence or that brings into question the reliability of information obtained from management and those charged with governance. The consistent application of professional scepticism is imperative for auditors to draw appropriate conclusions in the conduct of their work.

The Auditing and Assurance Standards Board (AUASB) takes this opportunity to emphasise to both auditors and others, the important and fundamental role that professional scepticism has to play in the audits of financial reports. So too, it is opportune to remind audit firms of their role in education, mentoring and inspiring partners and staff to cultivate a sceptical mindset, recognising that it is a vital ingredient in performing high quality audit engagements.

Source: M Kelsall, 'Professional scepticism in an audit of a financial report'
AUASB Bulletin, August 2012.

Auditing and Assurance Standards Board

The AUASB's mission is to develop, in the **public interest**, high-quality auditing and assurance standards and related guidance to enhance the relevance, reliability and timeliness of information provided to users of audit and assurance services. These auditing standards now have the force of law under s. 336 of the Corporations Act. The Minister (Federal Treasurer) appoints the Chair of the AUASB and the FRC appoints the other members of the AUASB. The FRC is required to issue the strategic direction to the AUASB. The strategic direction is as follows.[32]

(a) The AUASB should develop Australian Auditing Standards that have a clear public interest focus and are of the highest quality.
(b) The AUASB should use, as appropriate, International Standards on Auditing (ISAs) of the International Auditing and Assurance Standards Board (IAASB) as a base from which to develop Australian Auditing Standards.
(c) The AUASB should make such amendments to ISAs as necessary to accommodate and ensure that Auditing Standards both exhibit and conform to the Australian regulatory environment and statutory requirements, including amendments as necessary for Australian Auditing Standards to have the force of law and be capable of enforcement under the requirements of the *Corporations Act 2001*.
(d) The process of developing Australian Auditing Standards should include monitoring and reviewing auditing and assurance standards issued by other standard setting organisations in other national jurisdictions and considering other matters relevant to achieving the objectives of Part 12 of the ASIC Act. Consequently, where appropriate and considered to be in the public interest and necessary to producing standards of high quality, the AUASB should incorporate additional requirements in its Australian Auditing Standards.
(e) The AUASB should continue to develop auditing and assurance standards other than for historical financial information as well as developing and issuing other guidance on auditing and assurance matters, and may participate in audit research that is conducive to, and which significantly benefits, the standard setting activities of the AUASB.

As noted in point (b) the AUASB should use, as appropriate, international standards as a base to develop Australian auditing standards. In each Australian auditing standard there is a conformity paragraph which explains the relationship of an AUASB standard with its equivalent international standard. If there are any differences they should be noted in this paragraph.

The AUASB also issues Standards on Review Engagements (ASREs), Standards on Assurance Engagements (ASAEs), and Standards on Related Services (ASRSs).

1.4.2 International auditing standards

International auditing standards are issued by the International Auditing and Assurance Standards Board, which is a standard-setting body that operates under the auspices of the International Federation of Accountants. The International Federation of Accountants was founded in 1977 and is a worldwide organisation for the accounting profession that comprises 159 members and associates in 124 countries and jurisdictions. The International Auditing and Assurance Standards Board sets standards (International Standards on Auditing (ISAs)) and its goal is as follows:

> The IAASB's goal is to serve the public interest by setting high quality auditing, assurance, quality control and related services standards and by facilitating the convergence of international and national standards, thereby enhancing the quality and uniformity of practice throughout the world and strengthening public confidence in the global auditing and assurance profession.[33]

As noted in the aforementioned goal, as well as the setting of standards, convergence of standards is something that is a core part of the IAASB's objectives. The AUASB is also committed to convergence of international and national standards.

Other pronouncements by the IAASB include: International Standards on Assurance Engagements; International Standards on Related Services; International Standards on Quality Control; and International Auditing Practice Statements. More information can be found at their website, www.ifac.org.

1.4.3 The Clarity project

The Clarity project was begun by the IAASB in 2004, with the objective (as the title suggests) of improving the clarity of auditing standards. The process involved redrafting of all ISAs in accordance with the new Clarity conventions, and developing Clarity conventions by which all future standards would be drafted. In October 2007 the AUASB announced that the existing Australian auditing standards would be also revised and redrafted based on the new Clarity ISAs. The AUASB issued a statement in November 2008 on the drafting policies and rules for the new Clarity ASAs and noted that they would only be amended from the ISAs due to one of three possible reasons:[34]

1. where the auditing standard must address Australian legal and/or regulatory requirements (e.g. references to the *Corporations Act 2001*)
2. where the auditing standard must comply with Australian legislative instrument requirements (e.g. use of Australian spellings)
3. where the auditing standard needs to address 'additional public interests' matters, (e.g. changes that, in the AUASB's view, add value in the Australian context, such as maintaining ASA Requirements and Explanatory Guidance).

The complete suite of new ASA Clarity standards was issued at the end of October 2009, to be legally binding from 1 January 2010. The main changes to the format of the ASAs from these changes are as follows.

- The mandatory requirements are now in the first part of each standard, which now includes an overall objective in each ASA. Bold typeset is no longer used to denote mandatory requirements. The implementation guidance follows the mandatory requirements and is differentiated by paragraphs prefixed with an 'A'.
- The mandatory components are formatted as follows: Application, Operative Date, Objective(s), Definition(s), and Requirement(s).

The new Clarity suite of standards comprises 41 standards, compared to the previous 35. These new standards are discussed in chapter 6.

1.5 DOES THE AUDIT MEET THE DEMANDS OF USERS?

This chapter has presented a number of points about the role of auditors. The question then from all of this is: Does the audit deliver what users want? This is a difficult question to answer. Audits are to a certain extent 'protected' by a high degree of confidentiality. It is very difficult to peruse an auditor's working papers and therefore it is difficult to assess the quality of the audit function. This issue is why companies, when engaging auditors, use surrogates to assess audit quality, such as the brand name of the auditor. This provides the companies with a way to send a 'signal' to the market about their auditor's quality. For example, research shows that firms with higher agency costs (greater separation between owners and managers) choose larger 'brand name' auditors.[35] Outlined on the following pages is a discussion of this difficult issue.

1.5.1 Who are the users of audits?

The audit is primarily designed for the shareholders of a company. In reading an audit report this fact will usually be clear in the title. This is because an audit is essentially to mitigate information asymmetry due to agency problems. It is also reflected in the case law through the *Caparo Industries Pty Ltd v. Dickman & Others* (1990) 1 All ER 568 case which emphasised that the auditors owed a duty of care to the shareholders as a group (see chapter 5).

However, the groups that might potentially use the audited financial reports are much more extensive than simply the current shareholders as a group. Figure 1.5 illustrates the number and variety of parties that might be interested in the audited reports of a public company.

FIGURE 1.5:
Users of audit reports

As auditing is mandated by government regulation it cannot just completely ignore the fact that there are a diverse range of users of the audit report. To maintain its position as a provider of audit services to the market the audit profession must manage the expectations of this very diverse group of users. If a lesson is to be learnt from the significant regulatory response to the corporate collapses of the early 2000s, it is that auditors also need to consider the expectations of their work from broader groups — even if they do not have direct legal liability to these groups. However, the auditor must ultimately remember that despite these various users, the importance of current shareholders is paramount in terms of an auditor's legal liability. This is an important point to clarify because among the above groups their objectives might not always be aligned. Some examples are as follows.

- Current shareholders might have different interests and needs to future shareholders. This is particularly pertinent when there is the possibility of a company takeover.
- Shareholders might have a different view on how profits might be distributed than employees.
- Shareholders might have a different preference for the risk profile of investment choices by the firm compared to bankers and creditors.

There are a large number of possible users and the reality is that the auditor cannot be all things to all people. In summary, the current shareholders are the paramount user group.

1.5.2 Do audits provide good value?

Assessing the value of an audit is a difficult issue. It can be examined in a number of ways, for example: how often audits are associated with company failure; whether they get the audit report correct; how much they cost; or whether they provide economic value in the market.

An article by Jere Francis argued that audit failure is very infrequent.[36] By examining the number of lawsuits in the United States against auditors as a measure of 'failure', between 1960 and 1995 there were only 28 lawsuits per year on average. This implies an annual audit failure rate of 0.28%. The number of successful lawsuits is even smaller at about 50% of this figure. He then examined business failure rates, Accounting and Auditing Enforcement Releases (AAERs), and earnings restatements. His conclusion was that all of this ex post evidence points to a very low failure rate of much less than 1% annually. Overall, this certainly appears to be a very successful outcome for auditing.

In examining audit fees in the United States, Francis noted that for the largest 5500 US public listed companies, audit fees represented 0.04% of sales. His conclusion from all of this is that auditing is a relative 'bargain'. Indeed, in looking at this cost and with consideration of the number of 'failures' it would seem reasonable to describe auditing as successful.

The difficulty with an analysis of this type is that it is associating company success with auditor success and because most companies do continue without failing or being the subject of litigation, making this association will make the audit function look good. The method of measurement also does not pick up if the audit has been deficiently performed but no problems have been externally observed — which is very difficult to do. So yes, in terms of the fees, it would appear that the audit process is not an overly costly one. However, in terms of measuring 'success' on the surface it certainly looks like the audit process has been valuable and successful. The difficulty in evaluating this is because we do not know what has occurred behind the scenes, and whether the financial statements do indeed reflect the economic reality of the entity.

The value of auditing can also be measured by looking to the market. Studies have shown that the market places a stock price premium on independently audited information[37] and also reduced interest rates on audited information.[38] These observations are consistent with some of the theories for why we would expect to see a demand for auditing even if it was not regulated as discussed earlier in this chapter.

Another observable way of evaluating audit quality is to examine whether they get their audit reports right. As noted by Francis, getting an audit report wrong is due to two different types of errors: false negatives and false positives. A false negative is where there has been a clean audit report and in actual fact there should have been a going concern qualification issued. A study found that only 30% of bankruptcies are preceded by a going concern audit report, suggesting 70% have a false negative audit report.[39] A false positive is where a going concern report is issued for a firm that does not subsequently fail. A study found that six out of seven or about 85% are false positives.[40] Overall, the evidence here suggests that auditors are not particularly accurate in their reporting choices, they are conservative (high level of false positives) but also fail to get it right when a problem does subsequently occur (high level of false negatives).

In a more recent article by Timothy Fogarty and John Rigsby[41], the authors provide a reflective analysis of the development of the new audit approach in the early 2000s whereby audit was sold as a private sector good. The authors argued that the social purposes of the audit as a public interest good are less likely to be converted by the firms to ones that can be commercially exploited. There is, however, a vast amount of lack of understanding about auditing and its contextual factors.

An attempt to improve the communication between the auditors and the audit committee of companies, and thus the quality of the audit report, has been made recently in the United States. The Public Company Accounting Oversight Board (PCAOB) has adopted a new auditing standard aimed at enhancing the relevance and timeliness of the communications between the auditor and the audit committee on significant financial reporting and auditing matters. See the Professional Environment vignette on page 33.

In summary, there is some good news for auditors from an economic market-based perspective, but the results are not so good when looking at their performance on audit reports. However, in the market for public opinion, the news is worse and this is generally described as the 'audit expectation gap'. This is discussed below.

1.5.3 The audit expectation gap

The audit expectation gap has been a public issue for the auditing profession since the early 1970s.[42] The audit expectation gap comprises the difference between what financial statement users believe the audit provides and what an audit actually does provide. This has been an ongoing problem for the audit profession because what underpins the value of the audit is the perceived credibility of the audit function. Auditing is a difficult service in which to observe actual quality because all that is produced for users is a homogenous report. From a user perspective the underlying extent or quality of work behind the audit report is not completely clear from perusal of the report.

A good definition of the audit expectation gap was provided by Porter in 1993.[43] She described it as 'the audit expectation–performance gap'. This indicates that the gap has two major components:

1. a gap between what society expects auditors to achieve and what they can be reasonably expected to accomplish ('reasonableness gap')
2. a gap between what society can reasonably expect auditors to accomplish and what they are perceived to achieve ('performance gap'). The performance gap comprises deficient performance and deficient standards.

These gaps are illustrated in figure 1.6.

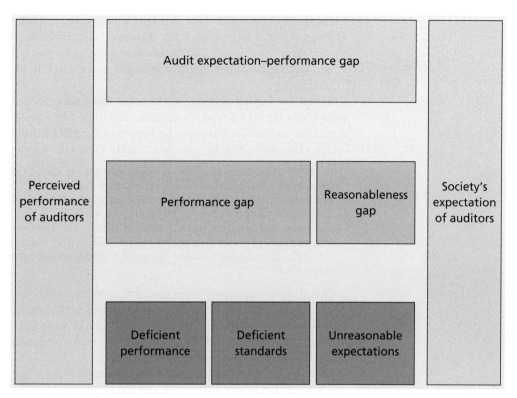

FIGURE 1.6:
Structure of the audit expectation–performance gap

Source: Adapted from B Porter, 'An empirical study of the audit expectation–performance gap', *Accounting and Business Research* 24(93), 1993, p. 50.

The usefulness of this definition is that it acknowledged the gap was more than just a problem relating to the users of financial reports, and that the performance of auditors was also deficient. However, it also shows how difficult it would be to remove this gap. It requires a comprehensive approach of improving performance, improving standards, and education of users about what are reasonable expectations. The difficulty of reducing the audit expectation gap was acknowledged by a report of the Institute of Chartered Accountants in 2003 called 'Financial report audit: Meeting the market expectations'.[44] This report noted that attempts to reduce the audit expectation gap by only trying to manage community expectations had largely failed. It also suggested that there is a need to expand the role of auditors to meet market expectations. The three key areas where they felt that changes could be made to address the 'deficient standards' component of figure 1.6 were as follows.

1. *Reporting internal control.* Reporting on **internal control** has not been taken on in the Australian environment — unlike in the United States with the Sarbanes–Oxley Act (discussed earlier in this chapter). In fact, the most recent iteration of the audit report actually includes a specific disclaimer on the issue of reporting on internal controls.

2. *Detection of fraud.* This has been an area where auditors have expanded their responsibilities in recent years through the development of ASA 240 *The Auditor's Responsibilities Relating to Fraud in an Audit of a Financial Report* (ISA 240) (discussed further in chapter 8). However, it is still not seen as the core objective of an audit and the only responsibility that still exists in relation to fraud is *material* fraud. This is different to the market's expectation as stated by the Chairman of the FRC, Jeff Lucy:

> I would say there is, in fact, now a clear market expectation to this effect — that is, that auditors are bloodhounds not just watchdogs. Simply put, the market expects auditors to pick up instances of fraud.[45]

3. *Evaluation of going concern.* Current auditors' responsibilities include a consideration of going concern (see chapter 18). However, they make no positive assurance about what they do in this regard. Despite not commenting on this issue, the fact is that users think auditors are guaranteeing the ongoing financial viability of a firm, which is not currently true.

Except for further changes to the audit standard on fraud, not much was done on the areas where the ICAA report recommended improvements to 'reduce' the gap. At about the same time as the ICAA report, the Report of the HIH Royal Commission by Justice Owen in 2003 also addressed the issue of the audit expectation gap:

> In recent years there has been considerable debate about the nature and scope of audit services and the so-called 'audit expectation gap', namely the difference between what auditors actually do when they conduct an audit and what shareholders and others think auditors do, or should do, in conducting the audit.
>
> My experience ... has been that audit reports are uninformative about the nature and scope of audit services performed by the auditor. The terms of the standard audit report are quite formulaic and would not assist a reader to understand the nature and scope of the audit.[46]

This is quite a criticism about the communicative value of the audit document, certainly coming from a lawyer. A report commissioned by the International Auditing and Assurance Standards Board and American Institute of Certified Public Accountants Auditing Standards Board reported the results of interviews of financial analysts and focus groups with a range of financial statement users.

The conclusion of the report was that the audit reports are not very informative to users of financial statements. It concludes as follows:

> Overall, our findings suggest that this lack of interest in the audit report content is a joint function of confusion on the part of both auditors and users about the intended message of an auditor's report and homogeneity of the content of the that report.[47]

It is true that there are areas in the performance of the audit work where improvements could be made and there is also the possibility of improvements in how this could be communicated (see Professional Environment opposite which is a follow-up to the aforementioned study). However, education of the investing public and other stakeholders about what an audit provides is also an important step.

The proposed changes in the Professional Environment are to improve communication with users about what an auditor already does. This is therefore attempting to deal with the 'reasonableness gap' in figure 1.6. However, there is no indication that any of these changes are going to be enacted.

The long history of the audit expectation gap and the lack of dealing with some of its key aspects are an ongoing problem for the auditing profession. The audit expectation gap continues to exist due to many different factors, including the complexity of the audit environment, global business practices, and the increasing demand by stakeholders for accountability and assurances.

Houghton, Jubb and Kend[48] further offered their views concerning the variability of judgements in relation to identifying the level of audit materiality, a concept frequently used in deciding on the implications of an error or discrepancy found by auditors, and the necessary work that requires the auditor to seek further evidence or to draw the attention of users of the financial report. It is, therefore, probably not unreasonable to suggest the significant additional government regulation of auditing that occurred after the corporate collapses of the early 2000s were, in part, due to the audit expectation gap. For the audit function as it currently exists to have a strong and prosperous future, all aspects of the audit expectation gap need to be addressed.

In 2012 the profession introduced changes to the Audit Report, with an emphasis to enable better communication. At the time of updating, the audit report changes are receiving comments from the audit community.[49]

Learning
check

Do you know ...

1.7 ☐ The Auditing and Assurance Standards Board develops auditing standards for the Australian auditing environment under the guidance of the Financial Reporting Council and with consideration of the standards issued by the International Auditing and Assurance Standards Board.

1.8 ☐ The financial report audit has many potential users. The auditor should be aware that there are a diverse range of users who may be interested in the audit report.

1.9 ☐ From an economic perspective, there is reasonable evidence that audits provide good value.

1.10 ☐ The audit expectation gap comprises the difference between what financial statement users believe the audit provides and what an audit actually does provide.

SUMMARY

The audit function has successfully operated as a monitoring mechanism to deal with the agency problem for hundreds and even thousands of years. The fact that it has lasted so long shows the success of the audit function. The provision of assurance by auditors has been a way of adding to the credibility and reliability of information, which adds value to the information disclosed. Historically, the accounting profession has been a crucial part of accreditation, standard setting, and regulation of auditing professionals. Auditing standards are the guiding principles for auditors, and these have developed significantly over the past thirty years and have also become internationalised.

More recently, the number of corporate collapses of the early 2000s and the concerns arising from the global financial crisis in 2007–08 has seen a change in the regulatory environment for auditors. Governments around the world saw the corporate collapses as being evidence of some fundamental problems for the auditing profession as well as for corporate governance. One response in Australia was for the government to take over responsibility for audit standards and make them legally mandated.

Ultimately, the success of auditing is also to do with how it is perceived by its key stakeholders. From a legal perspective, the main group to whom auditors owe a duty of care are current shareholders of the company they are auditing. There is evidence that the audit does provide reasonable value from a market-based perspective. However, it is difficult to assess the success or otherwise of the auditing function in this way. Auditors provide assurance on publicly disclosed information so the potential users of their services are therefore broad. There are many different views on what an audit does or should provide and this creates the foundation of the 'audit expectation gap'. As the value of the audit is conditional on users seeing it as a 'value adding' service, it will be important for the accounting profession and regulators to deal with this expectation gap. However, the audit function served by a strong accounting profession has served a valuable role in society for many years and has shown to be adaptable to changing circumstances. There is no reason to believe that this will not happen in the future as the audit continues to evolve to meet the changing demands of users.

KEY TERMS

accountability, p. 13

agency theory, p. 9

assertion, p. 7

assurance, p. 6

assurance engagement, p. 14

audit, p. 6

audit expectation gap, p. 6

audit quality, p. 19

auditing, p. 6

auditing standards, p. 6

Big Four, p. 17

bond, p. 10

case law, p. 18

corporate collapses, p. 12

corporate governance, p. 6

credibility, p. 7

evidence, p. 7

external auditors, p. 13

financial report audit, p. 6

fraud, p. 18

independence, p. 14

information asymmetry, p. 9

information hypothesis, p. 11

insurance hypothesis, p. 12

internal control, p. 31

non-audit services, p. 19

presents fairly, p. 8

public interest, p. 26

quality control, p. 20

reasonable assurance, p. 8

reasonable skill and care, p. 18

regulation, p. 6

reliability, p. 7

true and fair view, p. 8

MULTIPLE-CHOICE questions

1.1 What does an auditor do?
   A. Provide a guarantee on the ongoing viability of a company.
   B. Provide an independent opinion on the financial report.
   C. Help management to produce the financial report.
   D. Ensure that the financial report contains no fraud or error.

1.2 What best describes the 'agency problem' that results in a demand for audits?
   A. Shareholders act in their own interests and not in the interests of the company.
   B. Banks have different information expectations to shareholders.
   C. Managers act first in the interests of shareholders to the detriment of creditors.
   D. Managers act in their own interests rather than the interests of shareholders.

1.3 Regulators' use of the audit function to insulate themselves from blame in a corporate failure most relates to which reason for a demand for auditing?
   A. Insurance hypothesis.
   B. Agency theory.
   C. Information hypothesis.
   D. The audit expectation gap.

1.4 Additional to those criteria that concern the financial report audit of a company, the auditor of a listed company must consider the following:
   A. Ethical standards issued by the professional bodies.
   B. Accounting standards.
   C. The Corporations Act.
   D. The ASX Listing Rules.

1.5 The key reason for the radical audit reforms over the past decade is:
   A. The disparity of revenues and practices between the big firms and the smaller accounting practices.
   B. The inability of auditors to meet their liability claims.
   C. The alleged accounting fraud and audit failures related to major corporate collapses.
   D. The recommendations of the Companies Auditors and Liquidators Disciplinary Board.

1.6 The purpose of the surveillance program undertaken by ASIC is to:
   A. Obtain evidence on the negligence of auditors and accountants.
   B. Develop a complete framework of creative accounting mechanisms.
   C. Evaluate the adequacy of compliance with respect to financial reporting.
   D. Ensure dividends are not paid from financial reports that have been misstated.

1.7 The main objective of CLERP 9 was to:
   A. Ensure Australia's legal provisions are as close as possible to the US legislation.
   B. Strengthen the financial reporting process so as to ensure the integrity of the capital market.
   C. Limit the liability issues of the audit and legal profession.
   D. Minimise possible conflicts of interest in the auditing profession.

1.8 A financial report audit provides which level of assurance?
   A. A high level of assurance.
   B. An acceptable level of assurance.
   C. A moderate level of assurance.
   D. A minimum level of assurance.

1.9 Who are the primary financial report users that auditors need to be concerned about?
A. Managers of the audited firm.
B. Banks who provide capital to the firm.
C. The general public.
D. Shareholders of the firm.

1.10 Why does the expectation gap as defined by Porter (1993) still exist in current times?
A. There are more naive users of financial reports who do not understand the nature of audit.
B. Mergers and failures of audit firms.
C. An increasing amount of auditing standards to be studied.
D. The increasing complexity of financial report audits and the increasing level of expectations of users.

REVIEW questions

1.11 Describe the nature of an audit.

1.12 What does an independent auditor do during a financial report audit?

1.13 Explain how agency theory results in a demand for auditing.

1.14 How has the accounting profession's role changed in recent years? What does the accounting profession currently have responsibility for?

1.15 How has case law affected auditing practice?

1.16 There were a number of major corporate collapses in the early 2000s. What was the main Australian regulatory response to these problems?

1.17 How have corporate collapses influenced the role of auditing in recent years?

1.18 What role does ASIC have in the regulation of auditors?

1.19 What role does the ASX play in the financial report audit of a listed company?

1.20 What are the current implications of the audit expectation gap? Can it be reduced?

★
BASIC
★★
MODERATE
★★★
CHALLENGING

PROFESSIONAL application questions

1.21 Is audit failure the same as a corporate failure?

Below is an extract of a letter written by Lee White (General Manager of Leadership and Quality — Institute of Chartered Accountants in Australia) which was published in the *Australian Financial Review*.

> Your 'Regulator to crack down on auditors' (June 2) article implies that the external auditing process should safeguard against corporate collapses. Moreover, it suggests the quality of financial reporting and auditing in Australia is less than satisfactory. This is incorrect. Some do see audit as a guarantee to prevent poor management behaviour, bad business decisions or ultimately corporate failure. It is none of these. An audit enhances the accountability or corporate stewardship to its shareholders. Let's be clear — a corporate failure does not equate to audit failure.

Required

Describe what Lee White means when he refers to what an audit does.

1.22 Level of assurance ★

Auditors perform audit attestation to enhance the credibility of the financial report. However, it is quite impossible for the auditors to provide an absolute assurance regarding the subject matter on which they express their opinion.

Required
(a) Why is it impossible for an auditor to provide absolute assurance regarding subject matter on which they express their opinion?
(b) Explain what type of assurance an auditor should provide in a financial report audit.

1.23 Organisations associated with the profession ★

Several private and public sector organisations are associated with the public accounting profession. The following are functions pertaining to these organisations:
1. Issue certificates of public practice to members.
2. Promulgate accounting standards and statements of accounting concepts.
3. Promulgate auditing standards and audit guidance statements.
4. Regulate the distribution and trading of securities offered for public sale.
5. Establish a code of professional ethics.
6. Impose mandatory continuing education on members.
7. Issue statements of auditing standards.
8. Take punitive action against an independent auditor.
9. Establish accounting principles for state and local government entities.
10. Establish quality control standards for audit work.
11. Undertake investigation of perceived breaches of the Corporations Act.
12. Provide timely guidance on urgent financial reporting issues.

Required
Indicate the organisation(s) associated with each activity.

1.24 Audit objectives ★★

You have obtained employment in the accounting firm of Bing Lee and Partners as an audit assistant. You have heard that the firm is not very modern in its approach. On your first day at work, Mr Tom Lee, Bing Lee's son who is also an audit manager, calls you into his office and tells you that the audit is solely to provide assurance on the assets of the firm. The auditor must focus on this as their primary duty. He also states that the auditor's main role is to support management in ensuring that they properly communicate the financial situation of the firm to users of the financial statements — whoever they might be.

Required
Comment on the audit manager's view of auditing.

1.25 Review of auditing ★★

In December 2012, ASIC released its Audit inspection program report for 2011–12,[50] one conclusion in that report was that there had not been any improvement in audit quality since the last report. The following is included in the Executive summary of that report:

> We found that, in 18% of the 602 key audit areas that we reviewed across 117 audit files over firms of all sizes, auditors did not obtain sufficient appropriate audit evidence, exercise sufficient scepticism, or otherwise comply with auditing standards in a significant audit area. While the financial reports audited may not have been materially misstated, in these instances, the auditor had not obtained reasonable assurance that the financial report as a whole was free of material misstatement.

Required
Discuss the advantages and disadvantages of the responsibility of reviewing audit work being undertaken by ASIC rather than the audit profession.

1.26 Value of auditing ★★

You are the managing director of a start-up company in Australia that is developing an innovative product that will revolutionise heating and cooling for homes in Australia by a unique environmentally friendly system. The company has high expectations of growth and its market research suggests the product will be very well received. The company was financed by several wealthy businesspeople and has only borrowed a moderate amount from a large Australian bank. At this point in time there is no legal mandate for an audit and none of the key stakeholders have insisted that one be obtained.

Required
Would you obtain an audit for this company? Explain the reasons for your decision.

1.27 Expectation gap ★★

You are an audit senior in an accounting firm and you asked the audit partner about the 'audit expectation gap'. The audit partner provided his opinion on the issue as follows:

> There is a so called 'audit expectation gap', and it is associated with unreasonable expectations of users. They want all fraud found, and a guarantee that the company will continue forever! This is quite unreasonable and not what the audit is designed to do! Perhaps we could do more on these issues, but it would be more work, cost more, and I doubt whether the companies would be prepared to pay anyway.

Required
Discuss the views of the audit partner.

1.28 Independence and reliability ★★★

Independence has always been a fundamental aspect of the accountancy profession. A commentary in 2003 suggested the following:

> ... the public interest will be best served by reprioritising professional and ethical objectives to establish *reliability* in fact and appearance as the cornerstone of the profession, rather than relationship-based *independence* in fact and appearance.[51]

Required
Based on the series of accounting crises and corporate collapses in the early 2000s, discuss the importance of maintaining independence (and reliability) by an auditor. What do you think of the above comment?

 CASE study

1.29 Carla's Coffee Pty Ltd ★★★

Carla has developed a business of roasting coffee beans in the inner northern suburbs of Melbourne since 1995. This business has relied on supplying high-quality, fair-trade organic coffee to many of the small cafés in Melbourne. As the number of these cafés has grown and as there has been a growth in demand for organic coffee generally, her business has expanded. The business operates out of a small warehouse in Northcote in Melbourne. In the past five years, Carla has considerably expanded her operations and is now supplying a couple of the major supermarket chains in Australia. The business is very profitable and the balance sheet is strong. During the growth period the company actually bought a few cafés, which have so far performed well, and also provide a guaranteed customer base for her coffee.

Carla obtained a moderate loan from Northpac Banking Corporation to assist in funding her expansion. This loan is secured over the company assets. The company recently purchased a much larger warehouse in Preston with the funds from the loan. They plan to move operations to that location in the next financial year. Carla's personal contacts have been instrumental in the growth of the business.

Carla has decided though that it is time to do other things. She would like to sell the business and will depart as Chairman of the Board and Chief Executive Officer. The financial statements have been prepared by Wendy, the Chief Financial Officer. Carla decides to approach a dozen potential investors to offer shares in her business and she gives them a copy of the latest set of financial statements prepared by Wendy. The latest financial statement shows strong growth over the past five years and in particular the current year's performance was very good — resulting in a bonus to the Chief Financial Officer. A number of the senior people in the company were given shares by Carla (including Wendy) and most of them are also considering selling out as well.

There was a recent press report in *The Age* that suggested that the coffee used by Carla's Coffee was picked by child labour in Colombia working under terrible conditions. This breaches the rules of the fair-trade certification and the publicity is causing some of Carla's customers to rethink their relationship with Carla's Coffee.

Either or both of the following sets of questions can be answered after reading the above case.

Required

(a) Who are the various parties with an interest in Carla's Coffees? Outline what you think their interests, motivations and concerns would be.

(b) Who would demand an audit of Carla's Coffee? Why would they want an audit?

Required

(a) Assume you have been appointed as an auditor for Carla's Coffee. On what items in the financial report would you be focusing your main attention to provide users with an opinion that the financial report represents a 'true and fair' view of the economic performance of Carla's Coffee?

(b) Would you have any particular concerns if it was the 'dozen potential investors' who had engaged you to undertake the audit?

(c) What other aspects of the above case would concern you as an auditor and why?

RESEARCH question

1.30 Auditing and the global financial crisis

In the report 'Audit Quality in Australia', released by the Treasury in March 2010, the following was noted:

> Treasury proposes to encourage focused discussion with key stakeholders including ASIC, the FRC, the Auditing and Assurance Standards Board (AUASB), the major audit firms and the professional accounting bodies on strategies to minimise identified audit expectation gaps. Treasury is of the view that any proposals to change the current standard audit report would need to be subjected to rigorous cost/benefit analysis to ensure that the risks associated with any changes do not negate the potential benefits. In that context, Treasury is concerned that because of the wide disparity between the sophistication of retail and more sophisticated investors in terms of their understanding of financial statements and audit reports, any changes to the standard audit report may have the perverse effect of introducing confusion among some users, leading to a widening of the expectations gap.

Required

(a) Find recent research on the 'audit expectation gap'. Is changing the audit report the only problem associated with this 'gap'?

(b) Does research suggest that the audit report should stay the same because changing it would lead to confusion among users?

FURTHER READING

ASX Corporate Governance Principles and Recommendations, September 2007, www.asx.com.au.

Australian Securities and Investments Commission (ASIC), *Audit Inspection Program Public Report for 2008–09*, ASIC, Canberra, 2010.

C Cullinan, 'Enron as a symptom of audit process breakdown: Can the Sarbanes–Oxley Act cure the disease?', *Critical Perspectives on Accounting* 15, 2004, pp. 853–64.

JR Francis, 'What do we know about audit quality?', *The British Accounting Review* 36, 2004, pp. 345–68.

Institute of Chartered Accountants in England and Wales (ICAEW), *Agency Theory and the Role of Audit*, ICAE, London, 2005.

Institute of Chartered Accountants in England and Wales (ICAEW), *Audit Purpose*, ICAEW, London, 2006.

RK Mautz & HA Sharaf, *The Philosophy of Auditing*, American Accounting Association, Madison, Wisconsin, 1961.

Treasury, Commonwealth of Australia, *Audit Quality in Australia — A Strategic Review*, Treasury: Canberra, 2010.

J Turner, T Mock, P Coram & G Gray, 'Improving transparency and relevance of auditor communications with financial statement users', *Current Issues in Auditing* 4, 2010, pp. A1–A8.

I Fraser & C Pong, 'The future of the external audit function', *Managerial Auditing Journal*, 2009, pp. 104–13.

P Sikka, S Filling & P Liew, 'The audit crunch: reforming auditing', *Managerial Auditing Journal*, 2009, pp. 135–55.

NOTES

1. The *Foreword to the AUASB Pronouncements* was published in April 2006. This gives the AUASB the authority to publish auditing and assurance standards that have legal backing. It also detailed, in paragraphs 19–21, its relationship with the International Auditing and Assurance Standards Board.

2. The Clarity Project involved the International Auditing and Assurance Standards Board (IAASB) reviewing and reissuing all its standards to improve the clarity of wording and implementing new drafting conventions, which make the standards easier to apply consistently. The complete set of revised clarified international auditing standards (ISAs) was published early in 2009, effective for audits of financial statements for periods beginning on, or after, 15 December 2009. Given Australia's international harmonisation commitments, the Australian Auditing and Assurance Standards Board (AUASB) has adopted this work and, where necessary, adapted it to local conditions. It has also completed its own 'Clarity Project' in 2009. The complete suite of revised standards was issued as legally binding ASA auditing standards at the end of October 2009 and become operative for periods beginning on or after 1 January 2010.

3. RK Mautz & HA Sharaf, *The Philosophy of Auditing*, American Accounting Association, Madison, Wisconsin, 1961.

4. ibid., p. 243.

5. American Accounting Association, Committee on Basic Auditing Concepts, *A Statement of Basic Auditing Concepts*, Sarasota, FL, AAA, 1973.

6. MC Jensen & WH Meckling, 'Theory of the firm: managerial behaviour, agency costs and ownership structure', *Journal of Financial Economics* 3, 1976, pp. 305–60.

7. ibid.

8. RL Watts & JL Zimmerman, 'Agency problems, auditing and the theory of the firm: Some evidence', *Journal of Law and Economics* 26, 1983, pp. 613–33.

9. ibid., p. 633.

10. WA Wallace, *The Economic Role of the Audit in Free and Regulated Markets: a Review*, Touche Ross & Co. New York, 1980.

11. ibid.

12. JR Francis, 'What do we know about audit quality?', *The British Accounting Review* 36, 2004, pp. 345–68.

13. *The Australian*, 30 January 2002, p. 1.

14. *The Sydney Morning Herald*, 18 August 2009.

15. *The Sydney Morning Herald*, 2 January 2009.

16. On 19 October 2009, ASIC commenced civil penalty proceedings against current and former officers of Centro. On 27 June 2011, Justice Middleton handed down his liability decision and on 31 August 2011, Justice Middleton handed down his penalty decision (11–188MR ASIC). On 19 June 2012 a A$200 million settlement of representative class actions brought against Centro and PwC was approved by the Federal Court.

17. Auditing and Assurance Standards Board (AUASB) 2010, Definitions, www.auasb.gov.au, viewed 16 September.

18. RL Watts & JL Zimmerman op. cit., p. 631.

19. R Linn, *Power, Progress and Profit: A History of the Australian Accounting Profession*, Australian Society of Certified Practising Accountants, Melbourne, 1996.

20. ibid., p. 631.

21. ICAA, *Annual Report 2012*, 2012, www.charteredaccountants.com.au.

22. Global Accounting Alliance, 2013, www.globalaccountingalliance.com.

23. ICAA, *Strategic Plan, 2012*, www.charteredaccountants.com.au.

24. CPA Australia, *Annual Report, 2011*, www.cpaaustralia.com.au.

25. CPA Australia, 'About us', *InTheBlack*, http://www.itbdigital.com/about-us.

26. S Drummond, 'Grant Thornton deal a boost', *Australian Financial Review*, 18 July 2012.

27. LE DeAngelo, 'Auditor size and audit quality', *Journal of Accounting and Economics* 3, 1981, p. 186.

28. *The Australian*, 30 January 2002, p. 1.

29. *The Australian Financial Review*, 6 March 2006, p. 1.

30. Money Management, 'Australian Securities Exchange, profile', 25 July 2010, www.money management.com.au, viewed 15 September 2010.

31. A Hecimovic, N Martinov-Bennie & P Roebuck, 'The force of law: Australian Auditing Standards and their impact on the auditing profession', *Australian Accounting Review* 19, 2009, pp. 1–10.

32. Auditing and Assurances Standards Board, 'AUASB corporate plan 1 July 2009 to 30 June 2012', 2009, pp. 12–13.

33. International Federation of Accountants, 'An overview of the IAASB's role and standard-setting process', www.ifac.org.

34. Auditing and Assurance Standards Board, 'Redrafting ASAs — Drafting policies and rules', AUASB, 2008, www.auasb.gov.au.

35. JR Francis & ER Wilson, 'Auditor changes: A joint test of theories relating to agency costs and auditor differentiation', *The Accounting Review* 63, 1988, pp. 663–82.

36. JR Francis, 'What do we know about audit quality?' *The British Accounting Review* 36, 2004, pp. 345–68.

37. M Willenborg, 'Empirical analysis of the economic demand for auditing in the initial public offerings market', *Journal of Accounting Research* 37, 1999, pp. 225–39.

38. DW Blackwell, TR Noland & DB Winters, 'The value of auditor assurance: Evidence from loan pricing', *Journal of Accounting Research* 36, 1998, pp. 57–70.

39. J Carcello & Z Palmrose, 'Auditor litigation and modified reporting on bankrupt clients', *Journal of Accounting Research*, 1994, pp. 1–30.

40. J Francis & J Krishnan, 'Evidence on auditor risk-management strategies before and after the private securities litigation reform act of 1995', *Asia-Pacific Journal of Accounting and Economics*, 2002, pp. 135–57.

41. TJ Fogarty & JT Rigsby, 'A reflective analysis of the 'new audit' and the public interest – The revolutionary innovation that never came', *Journal of Accounting & Organizational Change*, vol. 6, no. 3, 2010, pp. 300–29.

42. CD Liggio, 'The expectation gap: The accountants legal Waterloo', *Journal of Contemporary Business* 3, 1974, pp. 27–44.

43. B Porter, 'An empirical study of the audit expectation–performance gap', *Accounting and Business Research* 24, 1993, pp. 49–68.

44. ICAA, *Financial Report Audit: Meeting the Market Expectations*, 2003, www.charteredaccountants.com.au.

45. Australian Securities and Investments Commission (ASIC), Speech by Chairman Jeff Lucy, March 2004.

46. The HIH Royal Commission Report, *The Failure of HIH: A Critical Assessment*, vol. 1, Australian Treasury, April 2003.

47. T Mock, J Turner, G Gray & P Coram, '*The unqualified auditor's report: A study of user perceptions, effects on user decisions and decision processes, and directions for future research*', sponsored by the Auditing Standards Board and the International Auditing and Assurance Standards Board, 2004.

48. KA Houghton, C Jubb & M Kend, 'Materiality in the context of audit: the real expectation gap', *Managerial Auditing Journal*, vol. 26, no. 6, 2011, pp. 482–500.

49. In June 2012, the International Auditing and Assurance Standards Board (IAASB) released *Invitation to Comment (ITC): Improving the Auditor's Report*. A podcast was published for readers to ascertain the contexts of the recommendations. The proposal represents a major shift in auditor reporting. The podcast by Aeve Baldwin and published via CPA Australia is available at http://www.itbdigital.com/opinion/2012/10/30/mind-the-expectation-gap-what-auditors-need-to-know-about-reporting-changes.

50. Australian Securities and Investments Commission, *REPORT 317: Audit inspection program report for 2011–12*, December 2012, www.ifiar.org.

51. M Taylor, F DeZoort, E Munn & M Thomas, 'A proposed framework emphasising auditor reliability over auditor independence', *Accounting Horizons* 17(3), 2003, p. 257.

Answers to multiple-choice questions

1.1 *B*   1.2 *D*   1.3 *A*   1.4 *D*   1.5 *C*   1.6 *C*   1.7 *B*   1.8 *A*   1.9 *D*   1.10 *D*

chapter 2

Governance and the auditor

OVERVIEW

2.1 What is governance?

2.2 The auditor and governance

2.3 Issues in governance

2.4 Internal and operational auditing in the governance process

2.5 Enhancing accountability through the audit committee

2.6 Governance in the public sector

Summary

Key terms

Multiple-choice questions

Review questions

Professional application questions

Case studies

Research question

Further reading

Notes

LEARNING objectives

After studying this chapter, you should be able to:

1 describe the nature of governance

2 appreciate the role of the auditor in governance

3 discuss the issues of internal control, risks and earnings management in governance that concern the auditor

4 appreciate the roles of internal and operational audits in the governance processes

5 consider the significance of the role of the audit committee in governance

6 describe the nature of governance and the type of audits in the public sector.

PROFESSIONAL STATEMENTS

Australian standards		International standards	
ASA 200	Overall Objectives of the Independent Auditor and the Conduct of an Audit in Accordance with Australian Auditing Standards	ISA 200	Overall Objectives of the Independent Auditor and the Conduct of an Audit in Accordance with the International Standards on Auditing
ASA 250	Consideration of Laws and Regulations in an Audit of a Financial Report	ISA 250	Consideration of Laws and Regulations in an Audit of Financial Statements
ASA 260	Communicating with Those Charged with Governance	ISA 260	Communication with Those Charged with Governance
ASA 265	Communicating Deficiencies in Internal Control to Those Charged with Governance and Management	ISA 265	Communicating Deficiencies in Internal Control to Those Charged with Governance and Management
ASA 315	Identifying and Assessing the Risks of Material Misstatement through Understanding the Entity and Its Environment	ISA 315	Identifying and Assessing the Risks of Material Misstatement through Understanding the Entity and Its Environment
ASA 330	The Auditor's Responses to Assessed Risks	ISA 330	The Auditor's Responses to Assessed Risks
ASA 610	Using the Work of Internal Auditors	ISA 610	Using the Work of Internal Auditors
ASAE 3500	Performance Engagements		

SCENE SETTER

Auditors need to be less 'corporate advisor' and more 'examining inspectors'

The UK Competition Commission says auditors should be serving shareholders, but they are incentivised to please company management. In the preliminary findings of a report into the competitiveness of audit suppliers released on Friday, it said while most auditors are diligent, there were significant barriers to companies switching auditors, and the present system did not encourage independent views to be given to management.

'It is clear that there is significant dissatisfaction amongst some institutional investors with the relevance and extent of reporting in audited financial reports,' said Laura Carstensen, chairwoman of the Audit Investigation Group.

'There needs to be change so that external audit becomes a more genuinely independent and challenging exercise where auditors are less like corporate advisors and more like examining inspectors.'

The Commission said 31 percent of FTSE 100 companies have had the same auditor for more than 20 years and 67 percent for more than ten years.

It is considering a number of recommendations, including mandatory tendering and rotation of audit firms; 'expanded remit and/or frequency of Audit Quality Review teams under the [UK] Financial Reporting Council reviews; prohibition of Big-4-only clauses in load documentation; greater accountability of the external auditor to audit committees; and more shareholder–auditor engagement.

(continued)

The Commission also looked at whether the Big-4 accounting firms engage in 'tacit collusion', bundle audit and non-audit services together to raise barriers to expansion to other firms; undercut mid-tier firms with low prices; or that they can exercise 'undue influence over the formation of regulation or on regulatory bodies through their extensive alumni networks'.

But it said it could not find sufficient evidence to support these claims.

The Institute of Chartered Accountants in Australia (ICAA) agreed with the UK Commission's plans to strengthen the role of the audit committee.

Source: S Drummond, 'UK Regulator says auditor incentives serve wrong customer', *Australian Financial Review*, 25 February 2013.

In the most recent statutory audit services market investigation (2013) undertaken by the Competition Commission in the United Kingdom the investigators revisited the purpose of audits. The issue facing shareholders is that although they are the owners of a company, it is management who run the company (the principal–agent relationship). The shareholders tend to have much less information than management and they rely on independent assurance such as that which can be provided by an auditor. Using this assumption, the Commission investigated how well auditors represented shareholders' interests and the extent to which competition was focused on meeting management rather than shareholder demand, leading to lack of appropriate scepticism on the part of the auditors and unmet demand for better information as regards the audit process from shareholders. The complexity of the shareholder–management–auditor relationship can be depicted as shown in figure 2.1.

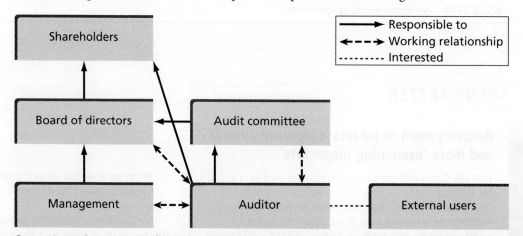

FIGURE 2.1:
Key auditor interactions and relationships

Source: Issues Statement, Audit Market Investigation, Competition Commission, United Kingdom, 22 February 2013, p. 10.

Figure 2.1 shows that auditors work closely with a company's board of directors and its management, though the latter's incentives may not be aligned with those of the shareholders to whom the auditor owes a duty of care. The audit committee also has an oversight role with respect to the auditor but ultimately reports to the board of directors. Lastly, external users such as lenders and potential investors are also interested in the audit report of a company. These interactions highlight the complexity of the audit process and its relationship with the governance of the company. These relationships are essential to effective corporate governance.

The term 'corporate governance' has been widely used in recent times. This chapter introduces you to the concept of 'governance', which is applicable to all entities, including corporations and the public sector. The complexity of governing an enterprise involves applying the concept to an environment where there is a range of expectations and competing interests among different stakeholders. The governing body of an entity must find an appropriate balance between business performance and management controls. The following section explains the broad nature of governance, with an appreciation of business performance and accountability.

LEARNING **1** objective

Describe the nature of governance.

2.1 WHAT IS GOVERNANCE?

Governance is the exercise of economic and administrative authority necessary to manage an entity's affairs. Governance is concerned with the processes by which decisions are made and implemented so that the entity's affairs are conducted properly and in accordance with the laws and other applicable regulations. The Organisation for Economic Co-operation and Development (OECD) refers to governance as 'characterised by participation, transparency, accountability, rule of law, effectiveness, equity … Good governance refers to the management of government [governing body] in a manner that is essentially free of abuse and corruption, and with due regard for the rule of law'.[1]

Though the concept of governance is initially linked with the government in general, it is applicable to all enterprises including corporations, business enterprises and the public sector.

In business, the essence of governance relates to the structure of separation of ownership and management. In the agency structure, members (or shareholders) of the corporation rely on the management (agents). These agents are the board of directors and managers who conduct the business on behalf of the members. Shareholders and owners require not only the laws, but also other means to ensure that the management of the corporation act in the best interest of the corporation and its shareholders or owners. Management accept the accountability measures through which they demonstrate the effectiveness of their performance. This is the origin of corporate governance.

As we have read above, corporate governance generally refers to the methods through which the corporation is directed and run. However, the OECD has recognised the importance of the interrelationships between the parties who have a role in enhancing the effectiveness of the governance structure. For example, while it is important for the independent auditor to remain impartial so as to provide an objective assessment of the financial affairs of the corporation, the auditor must also maintain a mutual relationship with the management in order to be able to act effectively.

The authority exercised by a governance body is underpinned by transparency and accountability. This is the context in which the auditor plays a role. The independent auditor provides an objective assurance to the truth and fairness of an 'account' that is prepared by the management and which represents the way in which the corporation is run. The independent auditor adds to the credibility of the conduct as performed by the agent. This accountability framework is part of the backbone of governance.

According to Jackson[2] accountability is 'explaining or justifying what has been done, what is being done and what is planned'. Accountability is also defined by Gray, Owen and Adams[3] as a giving of account, a reporting of that for which one is accountable. Although accountability initially related to owners,[4] this concept was extended by stakeholder theory beyond the relationship between owners and managers.[5] In accordance with stakeholder theory, managers are not merely the stewards for the owners, but are also accountable to employees, customers and society as a whole.[6] The scene setter gives an example of the changing expectations of auditors. While auditors provide opinions on the financial performance of companies, business environments have influenced the expectations of their role, especially where there is keen competition amongst audit firms, market complexity, and an increasing number of high profile corporate collapses.

2.1.1 Enterprise governance: a framework

To encompass the governance concept and recognise the performance requirements, the concept of enterprise governance provides an umbrella framework that combines different aspects of accountability. **Enterprise governance** is a framework that covers both the corporate governance regime and the business governance perspectives of an organisation. The joint Chartered Institute of Management Accountants (CIMA) and International Federation of Accountants (IFAC) *Enterprise Governance: Getting the Balance Right* quoted a definition of enterprise governance as:

> ... the set of responsibilities and practices exercised by the board and executive management with the goal of providing strategic direction, ensuring the objectives are achieved, ascertaining that risks are managed appropriately, and verifying that the organisation's resources are used responsibly.[7]

The definition assumes the dual role of directors in both monitoring (conformance) and strategy (performance), and acknowledges the inherent tension between governance and value creation. It also helps to illustrate the multiple roles of the accountant and auditor. It is also argued that the enterprise governance model is capable of accommodating different governance models across the world.

This concept of enterprise governance is appropriate for the purpose of demonstrating the role of audit and assurance services. We describe this aspect of the framework in detail in this section.

Enterprise governance incorporates corporate governance responsibilities and the contribution to value creation and business success. It comprises the corporate governance concept of **conformance** and accountability, and the strategic direction concept of **performance** and value creation of an organisation or enterprise. Enterprise governance is perceived as a model that can be applied to corporations, not-for-profit organisations and the public sector.

Figure 2.2 shows that enterprise governance is premised on the entire accountability framework of an organisation. The conformance aspect, based mainly on corporate governance best practice, covers issues such as:

- the roles of the chair of the board and top management (e.g. the CEO's responsibility to ensure accountability and independence)
- the composition, skills base, remuneration and training of the board and its committees — roles of non-executive directors and audit, nomination and remuneration committees
- the adequacy and reasonableness of compensation schemes for executives
- internal control structures, risk management and the role of internal audit
- the financial reporting and disclosure regime
- the independence of the audit function and the reporting mechanisms.

It should be noted that the term 'enterprise governance' is not commonly known while 'corporate governance' is generally applied in a broad manner. In the executive summary of the Directorate for Financial and Enterprise Affairs' *Corporate Governance and the Financial Crisis*, issued in February 2010, the OECD Steering Group found that corporate governance weaknesses in remuneration, risk management, board practices and the exercise of shareholder rights had played a role in the development of the global financial crisis. Nevertheless, the group believe that the *OECD Principles of Corporate Governance* (2004) provide a good basis to adequately address the key concerns and encourage and support companies using agreed international and national standards. This chapter covers the concepts of governance, which, more technically, implies enterprise governance, and includes both corporate and business governance.

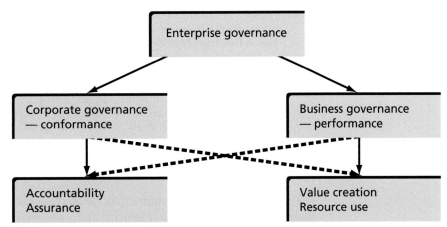

FIGURE 2.2:
The enterprise governance framework

Source: Adapted from CIMA/IFAC, *Enterprise Governance: Getting the Balance Right* (p. 10), Copyright © February 2004 by IFAC. All rights reserved.

LEARNING 2 objective

Appreciate the role of the auditor in governance.

2.2 THE AUDITOR AND GOVERNANCE

While the independent auditor acts as an external disinterested assurer of financial reports, some enterprises and corporations practise internal governance through the internal auditor and the establishment of the audit committee. In this section of the chapter, we will discuss the governance role of the external and internal auditor, the audit committee and those charged with these responsibilities in the public sector.

2.2.1 Overall objectives of the auditor

In chapter 1, we learn about the types of audit and assurance services that are performed by an auditor. In general an auditor is a qualified professional who performs audits, reviews and assurance services in a competent and objective manner in accordance with a set of criteria which include applicable laws, professional pronouncements and other quality control procedures.

ASA 200 *Overall Objectives of the Independent Auditor and the Conduct of an Audit in Accordance with Australian Auditing Standards*, paragraph 11 (ISA 200.11) states the following:

In conducting an audit of a financial report, the overall objectives of the auditor are:
(a) To obtain reasonable assurance about whether the financial report as a whole is free from material misstatement, whether due to fraud or error, thereby enabling the auditor to express an opinion on whether the financial report is prepared, in all material respects, in accordance with an applicable financial reporting framework; and
(b) To report on the financial report, and communicate as required by the Australian Auditing Standards, in accordance with the auditor's findings.

For the purposes of an audit undertaken in accordance with the Australian auditing standards, ASA 200 paragraph Aus 13.4 (ISA 200.13) states that management and those charged with governance have the following responsibilities:

(i) For the preparation of a financial report in accordance with the applicable financial reporting framework, including where relevant, their fair presentation;

(ii) For such internal control as management and, where appropriate, those charged with governance determine is necessary to enable the preparation of a financial report that is free from material misstatement, whether due to fraud or error; and

(iii) To provide the auditor with:
  (a) Access to all information, of which management and, where appropriate, those charged with governance are aware that is relevant to the preparation of a financial report such as records, documentation and other matters;
  (b) Additional information that the auditor may request from management and, where appropriate, those charged with governance, for the purpose of the audit; and
  (c) Unrestricted access to persons within the entity from whom the auditor determines it necessary to obtain audit evidence.

The auditing standards require that, in carrying out financial report audits, the auditor should work with the management and, wherever appropriate, those charged with governance. In particular, the following standards provide some examples of the auditor's interactions with those charged with governance.

- ASA 250 *Consideration of Laws and Regulations in an Audit of a Financial Report* (ISA 250) requires the auditor to consider in detail the laws and regulations in an audit of a financial report. The auditor must enquire of the management and those charged with governance whether the entity is in compliance with the laws and regulations. Written representations and information regarding non-compliance are needed to ensure that the auditor may report as appropriate.

- ASA 260 *Communication with Those Charged with Governance* (ISA 260) specifically discusses the communication necessary to occur between the auditor and those charged with governance of an entity. It provides a list of matters such as problems in relation to internal control and non-compliance of which the auditor must ensure each member of the governance body is fully aware.

- ASA 265 *Communicating Deficiencies in Internal Control to Those Charged with Governance and Management* (ISA 265) requires the auditor to communicate deficiencies in internal control to those charged with governance. The auditor must obtain sufficient audit evidence to ensure that the deficiencies are documented and properly communicated to the governance body of the entity.

- ASA 315 *Identifying and Assessing the Risks of Material Misstatement through Understanding the Entity and Its Environment* (ISA 315) refers to the identification and assessment of risks of material misstatements through understanding the environment of the entity. The auditor communicates with the governance body and relevant members of the management to assess the risks of material misstatements.

- ASA 330 *The Auditor's Responses to Assessed Risks* (ISA 330) follows ASA 315 (ISA 315) which deals with the auditor's responses to assessed risks and approaches to the audit plan in a manner to ensure such risks are considered in the nature and extent of obtaining audit evidence.

Thus, it is important to understand that the effectiveness of an auditor's assurance engagement is very much a function of the relationship between the auditor and the management, and the governance body of the enterprise or corporation.

2.2.2 The role of the auditor in enterprise governance

The conformance aspect of enterprise governance is directly related to the role of the auditor, in that the audit function provides the assurance of verifiability, compliance and accountability of the organisation. As the conformance aspect is also concerned with historical matters, it corresponds with the underlying concept in the *International Framework for Assurance Engagements* covered in chapter 1.

The main role of the external auditor is to give an independent opinion on the truth and fairness of the financial statements of the organisation. Depending on the jurisdiction in which the organisation is based, the external auditor may also be required to ensure that the organisation and the board of directors have complied with all relevant legislation and regulations. In fulfilling this role, the external auditor works closely with those charged with the governance of the organisation, in particular the audit committee where one exists. The legal and other developments in corporate governance, such as the *Corporate Law Economic Reform Program Act 2004* (CLERP 9), the Australian Securities Exchange (ASX) Corporate Governance Council's *Corporate Governance Principles and Recommendations*, and guidelines concerning non-executive directors and audit committees, are all aimed at ensuring the effectiveness of accountability processes.

On the other hand, the performance dimension refers to the different tools and practices that are applied to enhance the value of the organisation. The performance aspect includes setting appropriate strategic directions; comprehending and managing risk and the key drivers of performance; and decision-making processes. Auditing and assurance services include those assurance services that deal with historical financial information. The different types of assurance services that use the expertise and experience of auditors and professional accounting firms can also add significant value to the organisation. Moreover, the identification of risks and the assessment of risk management processes overlap the corporate governance and strategic areas of the organisation.

2.2.3 Corporate governance (conformance) and the auditing function

Corporate governance has been defined by mainstream accounting and finance literature as the range of control mechanisms that protect and enhance the interests of shareholders of business enterprises. However, recent developments and debates on corporate governance recognise the value of enhancing the relationship between the corporation and that of the wider community and stakeholders. Corporate governance is the framework of rules, relationships, systems and processes within and by which authority is exercised and controlled in corporations. It encompasses the structure, the systems and the relationships among parties such as the board of directors, management (including key officers), auditors, regulators, shareholders and the public. It influences how the objectives of the company are set and achieved, how risk is monitored and assessed, and how performance is optimised. Effective corporate governance structures encourage companies to create value, through entrepreneurial activity, innovation, development and exploration, and provide accountability and control systems commensurate with the risks involved. The principles of corporate governance were highlighted in the ASX Corporate Governance Council's *Corporate Governance Principles and Recommendations*.[8]

The OECD revised its corporate governance principles to strengthen three main areas highlighted in a discussion document which reviewed the improvements needed in auditing:

1. to ensure the basis for an effective corporate governance framework through the promotion of transparency and efficient markets, legal and regulatory requirements, division of responsibilities among different government authorities to ensure the public interest is served, and the provision of supervisory and enforcement authorities

2. to ensure equitable treatment of shareholders by enhancing their rights and authorities and clarifying the role of institutional investors in a fiduciary capacity
3. to deal with conflicts of interest with the principles covering disclosures; the role of providers of corporate information such as rating agencies; the duties of the auditors and their accountability to shareholders; and the protection of minority shareholders' rights.

Baker and Owsen argued that the role of auditing need not be constrained within the narrow bounds of investor decision making, but should be viewed in relation to the wider needs of various stakeholder groups and society generally. They based their arguments on a concept that audited financial reports should render assurance that:

- the financial statements are right
- the company will not fail
- there has been no fraud
- the company has acted within the law
- the company has been competently managed
- the company has adopted a responsible attitude to environmental and societal matters.[9]

The above concept highlights some of the broader expectations of stakeholders regarding the auditor's role, but it is important to realise that the auditor can only provide a reasonable assurance regarding the financial report. The financial report audit is governed by the Australian auditing standards and the laws and regulations that are applicable. Further, the auditor does not guarantee in relation to the company's going concern, or in relation to fraud. These aspects will be discussed later in this book.

It was argued that corporate governance mechanisms such as the *OECD Principles of Corporate Governance* (originally published in 1999, but updated in 2004) were steps in the right direction. However, according to Baker and Owsen, the proposals concentrate mainly on protecting shareholder interests; they do not pay enough attention to the interests of other stakeholders and society generally. Moreover, they do not focus on the role that auditing could play in corporate governance, along the lines suggested in this section of the chapter. The authors perceived that more research should be devoted to how the role of auditing in corporate governance might be increased for the benefit of all stakeholders and society generally.

2.2.4 Business governance (performance) and auditing and assurance services

Although the role of monitoring performance is mainly the responsibility of the board, the application of tools, techniques and practices directly involves the accountant and some of the assurance services provided in assisting management and the board. For example, the following assurance services add value to the organisation.

- Due diligence audits and assurances investigate the value of strategic initiatives such as mergers and acquisitions, prospectuses and investment decisions.
- Forensic and probity (ethics) audits provide assurance on the risk of frauds and ethical failures which might lead to loss of property for the organisation.
- Social auditing identifies risks, processes and performances in relation to social and environmental issues faced by the organisation.
- Performance audits carried out in the public sector enhance the value-added nature of operations and ensure they are effectively and efficiently carried out.

In the current environment, accountants and auditors — the traditional gatekeepers of the financial reporting regime — play a significant role in strengthening both corporate and business governance.

Their roles can be summarised as follows.

- They provide assurance of the integrity and reliability of the *internal control and risk management* systems of clients.
- They ensure an awareness of, and use relevant measures to detect, possible financial misstatements (such as *earnings management* practices).
- They ensure *audit independence* through safeguards and professional development programs.
- They enhance *audit quality* control processes.
- They actively practise the *code of conduct*.
- They monitor the development of and adherence to *auditing standards* nationally and internationally.

2.2.5 The audit trinity concept

Porter claims that the **audit trinity** is the key to securing corporate accountability.[10] She refers to the external audit, internal audit and the audit committee as the tripartite. The audit function is to perform some defined duties that complement and interlock with those of the other members. For example, traditionally external auditors have focused their attention on financial information.

In the past decade or so, the responsibilities of auditors have primarily remained concerned with financial information. However, the auditing standards have become more exacting and explicit. Auditors have to assess their auditee's status as a going concern, and detect and report on corporate fraud and other illegal acts. They also have to ascertain the consistency of other information and ensure there are no material misstatements in the financial information that was audited. ASA 700 *Forming an Opinion and Reporting on a Financial Report*, (ISA 700) requires an independent auditor to report on general purpose financial statements, with an additional responsibility that they report on other legal and regulatory requirements. Some external auditors also have the responsibility to report on the company's corporate responsibility reports.

On the other hand, the role of internal auditors has also been broadened to include a wide range of corporate governance and accountability matters. Internal auditors are not only responsible for the effective and efficient operation of the company's internal financial controls, they are also charged with:[11]

- overseeing the company's entire internal control system
- ensuring all the risks faced by the company are identified in a timely manner and effectively managed
- the development and implementation of the company's code of conduct
- ensuring that corporate fraud and other illegal acts are detected promptly and reported to an appropriate level of management or governing body
- the conduct of internal environmental audits and the audit of environmental management systems as required.

As important as the external and internal auditors are, the broadening role of the audit committee has been the key element in most of the corporate governance pronouncements. Audit committees are expected to oversee both the internal audit and external audit functions, ensuring that their work is properly coordinated; review the company's financial matters and the related governance practices, including the code of conduct; monitor compliance; and address internal control weaknesses, environmental issues and risk management. The audit trinity concept is reproduced in figure 2.3 (overleaf).

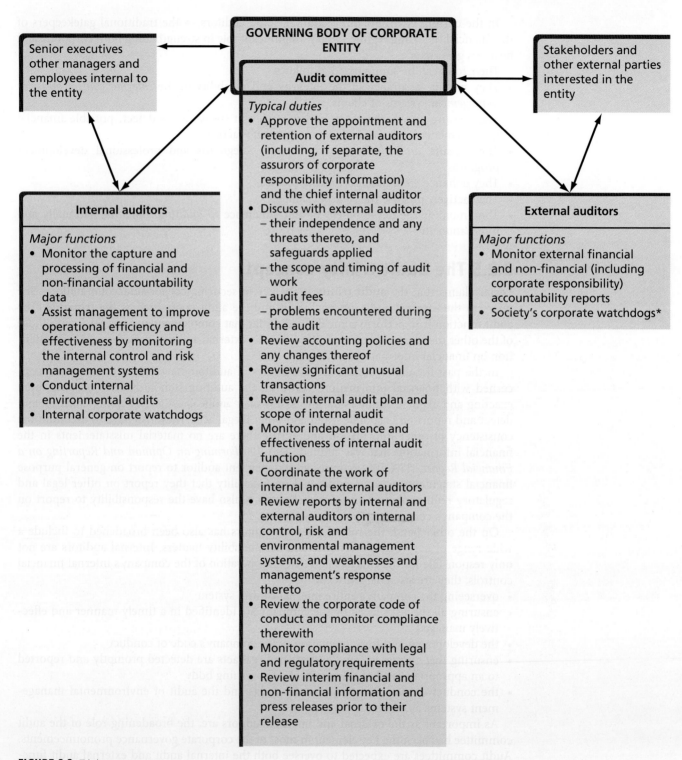

GOVERNING BODY OF CORPORATE ENTITY

Audit committee

Typical duties
- Approve the appointment and retention of external auditors (including, if separate, the assurors of corporate responsibility information) and the chief internal auditor
- Discuss with external auditors
  – their independence and any threats thereto, and safeguards applied
  – the scope and timing of audit work
  – audit fees
  – problems encountered during the audit
- Review accounting policies and any changes thereof
- Review significant unusual transactions
- Review internal audit plan and scope of internal audit
- Monitor independence and effectiveness of internal audit function
- Coordinate the work of internal and external auditors
- Review reports by internal and external auditors on internal control, risk and environmental management systems, and weaknesses and management's response thereto
- Review the corporate code of conduct and monitor compliance therewith
- Monitor compliance with legal and regulatory requirements
- Review interim financial and non-financial information and press releases prior to their release

Senior executives other managers and employees internal to the entity

Stakeholders and other external parties interested in the entity

Internal auditors

Major functions
- Monitor the capture and processing of financial and non-financial accountability data
- Assist management to improve operational efficiency and effectiveness by monitoring the internal control and risk management systems
- Conduct internal environmental audits
- Internal corporate watchdogs

External auditors

Major functions
- Monitor external financial and non-financial (including corporate responsibility) accountability reports
- Society's corporate watchdogs*

FIGURE 2.3: Trinity concept

*BA Porter, 'Do external auditors have the role of society's corporate watchdogs', paper presented at the Asian–Pacific Conference on International Accounting Issues, Palmerston North New Zealand, November 1992.
Source: BA Porter, 'The audit trinity: The key to securing corporate accountability', *Managerial Auditing Journal* 24(2), 2009, p. 173.

2.3 ISSUES IN GOVERNANCE

This section of the chapter discusses issues of governance and accountability that have a direct impact on the auditor's work.

Governance encompasses a broad range of concepts, structures and functions of an organisation. Governance can be viewed from an internal or an external lens. Internally, governance covers concepts such as leadership, communication and culture of an organisation. Structures and functions may include the accountability structures that demonstrate the reporting lines and responsibilities and functions include the accounting information systems, auditing and other transactional cycles and documentations. On the other hand, externally, aspects such as information privacy, security and cyber-crimes, legal compliance and cross-border arrangements, and indeed economic stability and social accountability, all affect the governance of an organisation. The auditors must be aware of the factors that impact on the internal and external governance of a client organisation. In particular, the auditor has direct involvement with risk management, internal control and financial misstatements.

2.3.1 Risk management and internal control

Effective governance and accountability are based on the effective functioning of internal control and risk management. With respect to internal control and **risk management** systems, companies are now more mindful of engaging internal auditors and relying on their active involvement. With particular reference to the requirements of the US Sarbanes–Oxley Act, the US Securities and Exchange Commission and the ASX corporate governance principles, chief executive officers and chief financial officers are expected to 'certify' the adequacy of internal control and risk management systems. They are therefore more inclined to seek the expertise of internal auditors. The management of large organisations, other companies and public sector organisations have developed different processes to identify and manage risk across the entity. Although there is a considerable amount of information about risk management, no common terminology exists. What is clear, though, is that companies' boards increasingly recognise that corporate risk is broadening, extending to all aspects of the business. Risk management is no longer confined to health, safety and insurance, but now requires a breadth of knowledge that also embraces business continuity, project management, corporate governance, financial performance, intellectual property and fraud. Some companies have appointed chief risk officers to oversee the entire risk management process; others are establishing special risk committees or have included risk management portfolios in the briefs of audit committees. Corporate governance, in particular, is driving the broader risk management agenda.

The more recent risk management standard, AS/NZS ISO 31000:2009 *Risk Management — Principles and Guidelines*, was published jointly by Standards Australia and Standards New Zealand in 2009.[12] Risk is defined as *the effect of uncertainty on objectives and risk management is the coordinated activities to direct and control an organisation with regard to risk.*[13] The AS/NZS ISO 31000:2009 states that a risk management framework, therefore, is a set of components that provide the foundations and organisational arrangements for designing, implementing, monitoring, reviewing and continually improving risk management throughout the organisation. The standard provides a schematic illustration of the relationships between the risk management principles, framework and process.

The Committee of Sponsoring Organizations of the Treadway Commission (COSO), the body that established the framework of internal control, introduced *Enterprise Risk Management — Integrated Framework*. The framework details the essential components of **enterprise risk management** (ERM)[14] and the context in which they are effectively implemented. Key concepts that relate to the effective application of the principles and components are outlined.

This *Integrated Framework* was first established in 1992 and was revised in 2004. Company management and auditors recognise that entities face uncertainty, and the challenge for them is to determine how much uncertainty the entity is prepared to accept. Value is created or added, and decisions are made with an appropriate degree of recognition of risk and opportunity, requiring management and auditors to consider the nature and extent of information to be used, and of the structure and processes to be put in place. Enterprise risk management is defined in the framework as:

> a process, effected by an entity's board of directors, management and other personnel, applied in strategy setting and across the enterprise, designed to identify potential events that may affect the entity, and manage risks to be within its risk appetite, to provide reasonable assurance regarding the achievement of entity objectives.[15]

Figure 2.4 shows a typical risk management system.

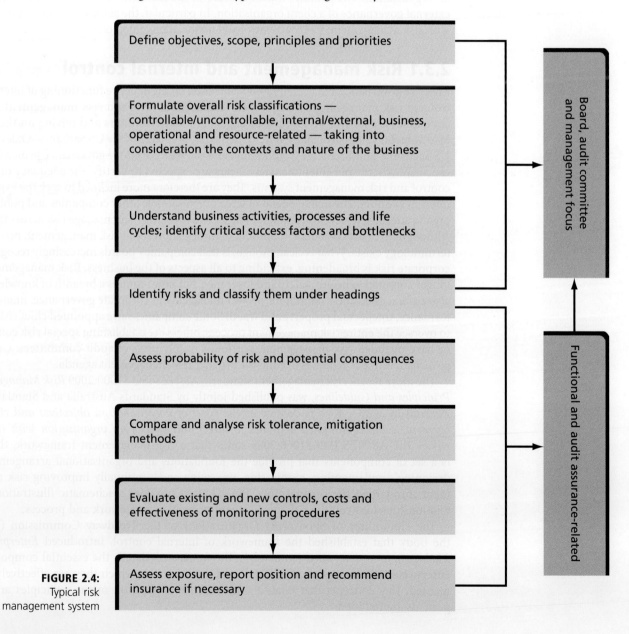

FIGURE 2.4: Typical risk management system

Define objectives, scope, principles and priorities

Formulate overall risk classifications — controllable/uncontrollable, internal/external, business, operational and resource-related — taking into consideration the contexts and nature of the business

Understand business activities, processes and life cycles; identify critical success factors and bottlenecks

Identify risks and classify them under headings

Assess probability of risk and potential consequences

Compare and analyse risk tolerance, mitigation methods

Evaluate existing and new controls, costs and effectiveness of monitoring procedures

Assess exposure, report position and recommend insurance if necessary

Board, audit committee and management focus

Functional and audit assurance-related

ERM consists of eight interrelated components. These processes are derived from the way management runs a business.

1. In the internal environment, management establishes a risk management philosophy (the risk-taking approach) in order to form a risk culture while integrating risk management with related initiatives.

2. Risk objectives are set in four categories — strategic, operations, reporting and compliance. Some organisations include the objective of safeguarding resources. These objectives allow management and the board to focus on separate aspects of risk management.

3. Event identification is a process where both external and internal factors that might affect event occurrence are considered. The identification methodology may use a combination of techniques and tools, looking at both the past and the future.

4. Risk assessment then allows an entity to consider how potential events might affect the achievement of objectives. Two perspectives are determined — likelihood and impact.

5. Risk response options are identified by management, which considers the impact of the event in relation to risk tolerances, evaluates costs and benefits, and designs and implements response options.

6. Control activities are the policies and procedures that ensure risk responses are properly executed throughout the organisation, at all levels and in all functions. Control activities are closely aligned with general and application controls (discussed in chapter 11).

7. Pertinent information and effective communication are required to allow ERM responses to changing conditions in real time. Information can be quantitative, qualitative, internal and external. Communication channels should also ensure personnel can communicate risk-based information across business units, processes or functional areas.

8. Monitoring, a process that assesses both the presence and functioning of the ERM components and the quality of their performance over time, can be done either as an ongoing exercise or as a separate evaluation process.

There is a direct relationship between objectives, components and units. The ERM matrix in figure 2.5 provides an overview.

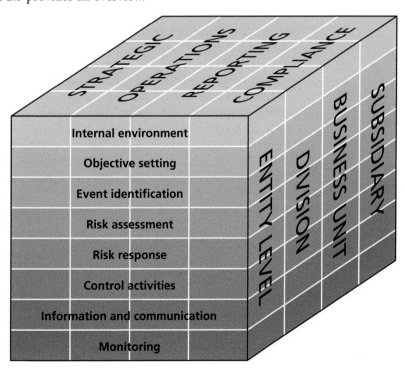

FIGURE 2.5:
Relationship of objectives and components of ERM

Source: Committee of Sponsoring Organizations of the Treadway Commission, *Enterprise Risk Management — Integrated Framework*, 2004, executive summary, p. 5.

Subsequent to the global financial crisis, COSO issued two reports in 2009, *Effective Enterprise Risk Oversight — The Role of the Board of Directors* and *Strengthening Enterprise Risk Management for Strategic Advantage*, and a practice guide in October 2012,[16] that further enforce the importance of applying effective risk management. Risk management oversight is emphasised so that the board of directors should:

- understand the entity's risk philosophy
- concur with the entity's risk appetite
- know the extent to which management has established effective ERM
- review the portfolio of risk
- be apprised of the most significant risks and whether management is responding appropriately.

In 2012, COSO released a Thought Paper dealing with the latest thinking on risk management assessment approaches and techniques.[17] Applying the principles of ERM, the Thought Paper explains risk assessment through event identification, which precedes risk response. Its purpose is to assess how significant the risks are, both individually and collectively, in order to focus management's attention on the most important threats and opportunities, and lay the groundwork for risk response. Dr Patchin claims that the risk assessment process should be practical, sustainable, easy to understand and in the right-size for the enterprise in question.[18] The Thought Paper presents a process that involves (1) developing risk assessment criteria, (2) assessing risks, (3) assessing risk interactions, and (4) prioritising risks.

After several rounds of consultations, COSO has also released *Internal Control-Integrated Framework* in June 2013.[19] The new Update IC-IF will continue to apply the five components of internal control: control environment, risk assessment, control activities, information and communication and monitoring activities. However, it will also provide a codified set of 17 principles. Four of these principles relate to risk assessment: (a) specifies relevant objectives; (b) identifies and analyses risk; (c) assesses fraud risk; and (d) identifies and analyses significant change.

ASA 315 (ISA 315) states that the auditor should obtain sufficient understanding of the internal control structure to plan the audit and develop an effective audit approach. The auditor should use professional judgement to assess audit risk and to design audit procedures to ensure risk is reduced to an acceptably low level. Thus, in assessing the internal control structure, auditors should gain an understanding of whether the internal control structure can ensure that the conduct of the business is orderly, including the ability to prevent and detect fraud, error, non-compliance, and the misappropriation of assets. The auditor should gain an understanding of the business and the company environment to appreciate risks that might be embedded within the nature of the business and the approach undertaken by the management in dealing with such risks. These are inherent risks. Moreover, the auditor in planning the audit will spend time reviewing the internal control of the company in order to assess the likelihood of control failures. Both inherent risks and control risks will be further discussed in chapter 9.

The ERM framework, where objectives can be categorised, can help auditors assess inherent and control risks. Table 2.1 lists the eight components of ERM in the left-hand column. The auditor assessment of inherent risk and control risk is linked with each of the eight components, where each component is then viewed according to the risk objectives at strategic, operational, reporting, compliance and resource management levels. Table 2.1 suggests that some of the components can form the basis of the auditor's determination of inherent risks (I), and others can be used to identify control risks (C).

TABLE 2.1: Possible relationships between audit risk components (inherent and control risks) and the ERM components

Components	Levels				
	Strategic	Operational	Reporting	Compliance	Resources
Internal environment	I	C	C	I, C	I
Risk objectives	I	I	I	I	I
Event identification	I	I, C	C	I, C	I, C
Risk assessment	I	I	I	I	I, C
Response options	I	C	C	C	C
Control activities	n/a	C	C	C	I
Information and communication	I	C	C	I, C	I
ERM monitoring	I	C	C	C	I

I = inherent risks
C = control risks

2.3.2 Financial misstatements — earnings management

Financial statements should be prepared without material misstatements. **Earnings management** occurs when financial statements and transactions are 'managed' in order to achieve a certain outcome and to influence people's perceptions of the performance of the entity. The desirable outcome may not be the direct consequence of the economic substance of the transactions involved. Earnings management is an issue of judgement and may result in the financial report being materially misstated. Extreme cases of aggressive earnings management can amount to fraud.

Incentives for earnings management are inherent in the management structure and can spring from political considerations, executive remuneration, the ambiguity and inability of accounting standards to deal with complex transactions, or situations including financial distress or related party transactions. The capital market may also present incentives where pressure comes from market expectations, analysts' forecasts, management transition and so on.

Many earnings management techniques involve accruals, revenue recognition, restructuring charges, estimation of liabilities, delaying sales, and manipulating research and development write-offs. Researchers have generally used four models to identify earnings management. The most popular method is to decompose the total accruals into normal and abnormal groups (discretionary accruals). Other models consider the components of earnings management, earnings distribution or manipulation of account-specific items. Man and Wong[20] describe the cases of earnings management in four categories, by using:

1. discretionary accruals where managers use accruals to manage earnings in order to meet or beat financial analysts' expectations or other incentives
2. asset turnover and profit margin diagnostic where management exercises the practices of 'smoothing income' or 'taking a bath' to manage earnings downwards
3. classification shifting where, for example, management deliberately misclassifies a core expense as a non-core specific item to create an illusion of an increase in core earnings and to affect share performance
4. restatements of accounts, with the existence of fraudulent account or financial information. Restatements of accounts can include the restatements of financial information as

non-intentional errors or intentional irregularities. Sometimes directors and audit committee members leave firms when there are significant restatements and they may suffer reputational risks.

Auditors should be aware of the possible earning management techniques and maintain professional scepticism in management judgement.

LEARNING 4
objective

Appreciate the roles of internal and operational audits in the governance processes.

2.4 INTERNAL AND OPERATIONAL AUDITING IN THE GOVERNANCE PROCESS

Professional accountants can be engaged in many other audit and assurance services to enhance enterprise governance. This section describes some of the key audit roles performed by professional accountants that provide assurances on the adequacy of conformance and the strategic values of business performance.

2.4.1 Internal auditing

Internal auditing has been regarded as the key audit role in organisations in enhancing governance processes. The Institute of Internal Auditors' *International Professional Practice Framework (IPPF)* defines internal auditing activity as:[21]

> A department, division, team of consultants, or other practitioner(s) that provides independent, objective assurance and consulting services designed to add value and improve an organization's operations. The internal audit activity helps an organization accomplish its objectives by bringing a systematic, disciplined approach to evaluate and improve the effectiveness of governance, risk management and control processes.

Several parts of this definition merit comment.

- 'Internal' indicates that such auditing is carried on within an organisation by employees of the organisation or by personnel contracted for the purpose.
- 'Independent and objective' suggests that internal auditing is an activity carried out without bias or prejudice, with unrestricted access to people, records, facilities and products. In undertaking the function, the internal auditor's judgements are not subordinated to those of management.
- 'Assurance and consulting services designed to add value and improve an organization's operations' notes that the internal auditing function provides a certain level of assurance for subject matters that assist in better management decisions and operations. The activity is wide ranging and includes functions that are advisory or task oriented, the performance of which contributes to the overall value of the business by improving the efficiency of operations and the quality of management decisions.
- 'A systematic, disciplined approach to evaluate and improve the effectiveness of governance, risk management and control processes' refers to the structure and approach of internal auditing. The nature of internal auditing involves a search for facts and a systematic process of evaluating the results of operations, identifying risks, giving risk-reduction advice, assessing the adequacy of controls, implementing improvements in control procedures and ensuring an effective governance structure.

Over the years, internal auditing has evolved into a highly professional activity that extends beyond the appraisal of the efficiency and effectiveness of an entity's operations. Internal auditing has become a function that evaluates and improves an organisation's risk management, control and governance processes to add value to the organisation. These changes affect the efficiency and effectiveness of all phases in an organisation and are a governance process in themselves.

The Institute of Internal Auditors (IIA) was incorporated in New York in 1941 and is now a worldwide organisation, with local chapters in over 100 countries. It is administered through regional groupings. National institutes have also been formed in some countries. In Australia, the first chapter of the IIA was established in Sydney in 1952. A national institute, the Institute of Internal Auditors–Australia, was formed in 1986. It currently has seven chapters and a sub-branch, and is one element in the IIA's South Pacific region, which includes New Zealand, Papua New Guinea and the South Pacific islands. The IIA administered its first certified internal auditor's examination in 1972.

In 2002, the IIA's Board of Regents launched a global research study to define the knowledge, skills and abilities required of a global internal auditor in order to develop a 'common body of knowledge' for the certified internal auditor examination. For the first time in its history, the IIA electronically gathered data via a survey conducted in eight languages. The survey concluded in January 2003 with nearly 2000 responses (40% from North America and 60% from other countries). Nearly two-thirds of respondents held positions of audit manager and above. Respondents also represented all industries and mirrored that of the IIA membership profile. The latest Common Body of Knowledge (CBOK) survey that was published was in 2006 and the results of the survey supported the existing syllabus content with modifications. It identified that the key common body of knowledge for internal auditors is in governance, risk and control. The skills of business analysis, information technology and business management required to effectively conduct internal audit engagements are acknowledged. The syllabuses have been modified based on the findings. The latest CBOK study in 2010 found that the core competencies of an internal auditor include communication skills, problem identification and solution skills, and keeping up to date with industry and regulatory changes and professional standards. Understanding the business was ranked as the most important overall technical skill in both the 2006 and 2010 surveys.

To become a certified internal auditor (CIA), a person must pass the examination and have a minimum of 2 years experience as an internal auditor (or equivalent). Auditing experience in public accounting qualifies as work experience in internal auditing. To retain the CIA certificate, the person must comply with the IIA's standards and code of ethics. IIA Australia has recently launched its graduate certificate in internal auditing and provides learners with a comprehensive set of knowledge and skills for a career in internal auditing.

The objective of internal auditing is to help members of an organisation to effectively discharge their responsibilities. In meeting this objective, internal auditing provides analyses, appraisals, recommendations, counsel and information concerning the activities that have been audited. The objectives of internal auditing include risk management and promotion of effective governance and control throughout the organisation at a reasonable cost.

PROFESSIONAL ENVIRONMENT
New guidance could add teeth to internal audit

Small companies should benefit from revised internal audit standards. They could make the chief audit executive a whole lot more popular, too.

Internal auditors will have a louder voice in their company come January 1, 2013 — that's when new revisions to internal auditor standards drawn up by the Institute of Internal Auditors (IIA) will go into effect.

... The IIA's standards are technically best practices, since the IIA has no regulatory authority to actually enforce them.

Source: K Hoffelder, New guidance could add teeth to internal audit', CFO.com, 24 October 2012.

The scope of internal auditing should encompass the examination and evaluation of (1) the adequacy and effectiveness of the organisation's governance and internal control structure; (2) the quality of performance in carrying out assigned responsibilities; (3) the procedures of risk identification and management; and (4) the mechanisms to ensure regulatory compliance. Internal auditors should:

- review the reliability and integrity of financial and operating information and the means used to identify, measure, classify and report such information
- review the systems established to ensure compliance with those policies, plans, procedures, laws and regulations that could have a significant impact on operations and reports, and determine whether the organisation is in compliance
- assess risks within the business operations and those from outside the business which may affect the ongoing wellbeing of the organisation as a whole
- review the means of minimising risks and help management with risk management processes
- appraise the economy and efficiency with which resources are employed
- review operations or programs to ascertain whether they are being carried out as planned, and whether results are consistent with established objectives and goals.

There is usually a close relationship between internal auditors and an entity's outside independent auditors. The work of internal auditors may supplement, but not substitute for, the work of independent auditors in a financial statement audit. One of the responsibilities of the chief audit executive is to coordinate the work of internal auditors with the work of the external auditor. It is not uncommon for the external auditor to review the internal auditing department's planned work program for the year to minimise duplication of effort or seek direct assistance during a financial statement audit (as explained in chapter 4). ASA 610 *Using the Work of Internal Auditors* (ISA 610) establishes standards and provides guidance to external auditors on obtaining an understanding of the activities of internal auditing and its effect on audit risk.

Although they have a close working relationship, internal and independent auditors have important differences, as outlined in table 2.2.

TABLE 2.2:
Organisational and functional differences between internal and independent auditors

	Internal auditors	Independent auditors
Employer	Companies and government units	Public practice entities
National organisations	Institute of Internal Auditors–Australia	• Institute of Chartered Accountants in Australia (ICAA) • CPA Australia
Certifying authority	Certified internal auditor (CIA) Graduate Certificate in Internal Auditing	• Institute of Chartered Accountants in Australia (ICAA) • CPA Australia
Licence to practise	No	• Certified practising accountant (CPA) • Registered company/independent auditor • Public practising certificate
Primary responsibility	To board of directors	To members
Scope of audits	All activities of an organisation	Mainly financial statements

Independent auditors are contractors. They provide a service for a fee and are independent of the entity they audit. In contrast, internal auditors work in a staff capacity, although they are independent of the rest of the entity. They report to the board of directors directly or its audit committee. Sometimes, the internal audit function is outsourced. Sometimes, concerns are expressed about the independence issue if the same audit practice is conducting both functions, as noted in ASA 610, paragraph 4 (ISA 610.4):

> Irrespective of the degree of autonomy and objectivity of the internal audit function, such function is not independent of the entity as is required of the external auditor when expressing an opinion on the financial report. The external auditor has sole responsibility for the audit opinion expressed, and that responsibility is not reduced by the external auditor's use of the work of the internal auditors.

Following the introduction of CLERP 9 in Australia and the Sarbanes–Oxley Act in the United States, it is now prohibited for external auditors to provide internal audit services for audit clients in order to preserve the appearance of independence. Therefore, an effective and objective relationship between the external auditors and internal auditors should add value as a joint effort to the organisation's corporate governance.

Where external auditors audit a client with an internal audit function, it is common for the external auditor to evaluate the work of the internal auditors, so as to minimise any duplication of audit work where relevant and reliable internal audit work has been performed. The standard also refers to the requirement that the external auditor should obtain a sufficient understanding of internal audit activities to assist in planning the audit and developing an effective audit approach.

Important criteria in assessing the performance of internal auditing by the external auditor are as follows.

- *Organisational status.* Internal auditors should report to the highest level of management and be free of any other operating responsibility. Internal auditors need to be free to communicate with the external auditor.
- *Scope of internal auditing.* The external auditor should consider not only the nature and extent of the internal audit assignments, but also the extent to which management acts on internal audit recommendations.
- *Technical competence.* Internal audit functions should be performed by those with adequate technical training and proficiency.
- *Due professional care.* Internal audits should be properly planned, supervised, reviewed and documented. External auditors should consider the adequacy of audit manuals, work programs and internal audit working papers.

The US Sarbanes–Oxley Act prohibits audit firms from providing internal audit services to their audit clients in order to avoid the self-review threat. The independent auditor focuses mainly on historical information when issuing an opinion on an entity's financial statements. In contrast, there is no limit to the scope of the work of an internal auditor, who is concerned with the economy, efficiency and effectiveness of an entity's operational procedures and activities. The work is future-oriented. However, both independent and internal auditors audit for compliance with (1) the control policies and procedures of an entity, (2) regulations and (3) the procedures necessary to safeguard the entity's assets. In these areas, the independent auditor evaluates the work performed by internal auditors.

Independent auditor's reports have a standard format and audit opinions are expressed in accordance with specified circumstances. They are also widely distributed to members and third parties. In contrast, internal auditor's reports are distributed mainly to the board, management and the audit committee, and their format varies considerably, depending on the nature of the audit being undertaken.

2.4.2 Operational auditing

Operational auditing has been used in the past to evaluate a variety of activities that include management's performance, management's planning and quality control systems, and specific operating activities and departments. As suggested by its name, this type of auditing relates to an entity's non-financial operations. It is the systematic process of gathering evidence to ascertain whether a process or operation is effectively and efficiently run.[22] Internal auditors generally conduct operational audits of non-government units, although independent auditors are sometimes engaged. Operational auditing is sometimes known as value-for-money or performance auditing.

Operational auditing examines the use of resources to evaluate whether these resources are being used in the most efficient and effective ways to fulfil an organisation's objectives. An operational audit may include elements of a compliance audit, a financial audit and an information systems audit. An operational audit involves establishing performance objectives, agreeing the standards and criteria for assessment, and evaluating actual performance against targeted performance. This term is mainly used in the private sector.[23]

The definition of operational auditing encompasses effectiveness and efficiency — the main purpose of operational auditing is to help the management of the audited organisation to improve effectiveness, efficiency and economy. Thus operational auditing focuses on the future, in direct contrast to a financial statement audit, which has a historical focus.

Unlike a financial statement audit, an operational audit does not end with a report on the findings, but extends to making recommendations.

Increased interest in operational auditing has resulted from some highly publicised corporate disasters such as the Gulf of Mexico oil spill in May 2010. The causes of the initial explosion on the drilling platform and the failure of the 'blowout preventer' to deploy on the sea floor were suspected to be systemic problems. This disaster directly relates to the operational risks and effectiveness of the oil drills operated by BP.

Operational audits are seen to be an integral element of internal auditing, and there are different approaches to the performance of operational audits discussed in training sessions and workshops. It is recommended that operational audits are designed with the end results in mind, based on operational goals, objectives and initiatives. Three approaches have been suggested and are briefly described here.

1. The risk-based audit approach identifies the areas of greatest risk, and uses an objective/ risk/controls formula and a matrix to document and analyse an effective audit program. The risk-based approach also distinguishes between control adequacy (what should be) and control effectiveness (what is).
2. The value-for-money audit approach defines attributes of effectiveness and focuses on effectiveness, efficiency and economy of operations from customers' viewpoints.
3. The process audit approach examines the effectiveness of processes and distinguishes value-added from non-value-added activities, building the control framework into the processes.[24]

Typically, there are five phases to an operational audit and each phase must be completed. These phases are (1) preliminary preparation, (2) field survey, (3) program development, (4) audit application and (5) reporting and follow up.

In the *preliminary preparation*, the auditor gains a comprehensive understanding of the organisation's structure, characteristics, history, policies and operations. Documents such as flowcharts are prepared. In the *field survey* phase, problem areas and sensitive issues are identified through probing questions, observations and inspection. Based on the knowledge gained, the auditor then *develops* a detailed audit plan, with objectives and a step-by-step program. The plan should detail outcomes expected so that benchmarks and expectations are assessed. Once the auditor is satisfied with the program, *application* of the program is done through detailed review of problem areas, sensitive activities and crucial operations. The measurement of actual performance of the operations is based on how predetermined criteria such as stated productivity, budgets or externally generated standards are met. Performance is analysed to determine the degree to which such criteria are satisfied. The auditor may use different audit tools such as cause-and-effect analysis to enable recommendations and conclusions to be made. In the *reporting and follow-up* step, the auditor does not use formalised standard language. An operational audit report may include a statement of the objectives and scope of the audit, a description of the work carried out, a summary of the findings, the auditor's discussion and comments about the findings, recommendations for improvement, and follow-up mechanisms. The operational audit report should be sent to senior management and to the audit committee. The auditor should ensure that further discussions on the auditee's responses, future improvements and issues take place so that proper improvements are implemented and monitored.

Based on their expertise and experience, independent auditors are qualified to perform operational audits. An operational audit engagement is a distinct form of management advisory service. The following observations may be made about operational audits.

- Independent accountants are increasingly being asked to provide this service for both private sector and government clients.
- This type of service provides independent evaluation and advice to boards of directors, senior management and elected officials who are being held to high standards of responsibility and stewardship.
- The experience gained in public accounting in the diagnostic and fact-finding aspects of financial auditing and management advisory services provides an excellent background for performing operational audits.

2.4.3 The widening role of internal audit

It is interesting to note that internal auditors typically used a risk-based approach and performed a range of audits of controls over operational effectiveness, compliance with applicable laws and regulations, and the integrity of financial reporting. They provided value to their company by identifying areas of operational improvement as well as opportunities to improve controls and reduce risk. However, following recent corporate collapses and the introduction of the Sarbanes–Oxley Act of 2002, many internal audit practitioners shifted their work dramatically to a compliance-driven controls focus. In the main, sections 404 and 302 of the Sarbanes–Oxley Act translated into detailed auditing standards requirements. Many companies, struggling to find resources to complete the documentation and perform the testing of internal controls, turned to the internal audit function as their section 404 resource. Internal auditors, with the support of the audit committee, accepted this role. The 2013 *State of internal audit profession study* undertaken by PricewaterhouseCoopers covers the following key messages.[25]

- 80% of respondents believed that risks and threats were increasing and yet only 12% think their organisation manages risk well. Across the core attributes, the foundational capabilities of many internal audit functions are not strong enough to add sufficient value in today's areas of risk.
- Internal audit is no longer expected to merely interpret past existing data. They require the skills to go beyond existing data and seek out hypothetical data for analysis.
- There is a lack of alignment in views on the criticality and management of risks between management, the board and the internal audit.

The significance of the PricewaterhouseCoopers report lies with its clear message that internal audit must reach new heights and contribute to the organisation in a more meaningful way. Internal audit must continue to evolve in its focus and improve its performance, or risk losing its relevance as other risk functions become more vital contributors to the organisation's risk management. The PricewaterhouseCoopers report the overwhelming opinions of 1700 chief audit executives participating in its ninth annual *State of internal audit profession study*. Hence, recognising the internal auditor's changing role — from merely a 'checking' function to a significant role in governance — the IIA Research Foundation's 2010[26] global study of the profession, entitled *Common Body of Knowledge* (CBOK), identifies a more forward-looking perspective of internal auditing that existed in the profession. IIA Australia, in conjunction with Protiviti, publishes survey reports on an annual basis, entitled *Achieving High Performance in Internal Audit*. The fifth edition of this survey report published in 2013 identifies the following emerging priorities for chief audit executives (CAEs):[27]

- major project implementations
- strategic risk
- core financial controls
- information technology issues
- fraud.

Thus, internal auditors today require a broad range of technical skills, competencies, and behavioural characteristics to perform a job that is changing constantly in scope and function.[28] As David Salierno states:

> Overall, the results show a healthy, maturing profession with consistent core tenets globally ... Results point to a vibrant, dynamic profession that is valued by its clients and responding well to organizational challenges.[29]

This section has shown that the landscape of auditing, including internal auditing, is changing fast. It highlights the importance of understanding risks, but not at the expense of overlooking compliance. It also provides the context of the widening expectations of what internal auditors should do in relation to business risks and the operational performance of the organisation.

Learning check

Do you know ...

2.1 ☐ Governance generally refers to the authority to manage, control and direct an entity in line with a set of criteria. It is underpinned by transparency and accountability. The OECD's perspective of governance relates to governments of nations, while enterprise governance refers to the governing procedures within entities. Enterprise governance can be applied to both corporations and other firms, including business enterprises in the public sector. Enterprise governance consists of the control processes and accountability mechanisms for ensuring conformance, and the processes and strategies to derive added value in business performance. Auditors can add value by providing assurances for corporate governance processes and by enhancing the integrity of other activities.

2.2 ☐ Assurances provided by the auditor are not confined to financial report audits, but can extend to involve controls, risk management and earnings management.

2.3 ☐ Internal auditing and operational auditing are performed within organisations to enhance the governance processes. Internal auditing is evolving, and operational auditing is often seen as part of an internal audit. In recent years, internal auditors have undertaken a much wider role, emphasising the emerging significance of the internal audit profession.

2.5 ENHANCING ACCOUNTABILITY THROUGH THE AUDIT COMMITTEE

It is not surprising that the concept and functioning of audit committees are now a priority in the aftermath of the corporate collapses of the early 2000s. This section examines the fundamentals of how audit committees enhance effective internal accountability within organisations, in both the private and public sectors. We can also see that the role of the audit committee is being looked at again after the global financial crisis. This is discussed at the end of the section.

Many public entities and government agencies in Australia have recognised the importance of audit committees and are working to develop their effectiveness in response to the challenges posed by globalisation, the increasing complexity of business and the greater accountability requirements placed on directors. An audit committee facilitates the participation of independent directors in the governance process. It provides a forum where directors, management and auditors can discuss and resolve issues relating to management risk and financial reporting obligations. Although external auditors have a responsibility to report to shareholders, their objective views can be of value to the directors' governance process through involvement by the audit committee. On the other hand, internal auditors or chief audit executives should work directly under the audit committee in order to foster objectivity and organisation-wide support.

In August 2007, the Australian Institute of Company Directors, the AUASB and the Institute of Internal Auditors–Australia jointly published the third edition of *Audit Committees: A Guide to Good Practice*. The guide demonstrates the interaction of audit committee and internal and external auditors, among others. The ASX 300 companies, under the ASX corporate governance principles, are now required to have an audit committee which should be chaired by an independent person.

This section sets out the latest developments regarding audit committees, and discusses the key objectives and responsibilities of an audit committee, with specific reference to the relationship of the audit committee with internal and external auditors. Some of the current expectations of audit committees are examined, including their composition, expertise and functions. This section also reviews how the audit committee can enhance the effectiveness of internal accountability.

2.5.1 The role and objectives of the audit committee

The main objectives of an effective audit committee include the following:
- assisting the directors in discharging their responsibilities with due care, diligence and skill; in particular, the audit committee is concerned with:
  - financial reports and other financial and non-financial information
  - the appropriateness of accounting policies used
  - adequacy of financial management policies and procedures
  - adequacy and monitoring of internal control structures
  - proper risk management plans and processes
  - business practices
  - protection of assets, including intellectual property
  - compliance with relevant laws, regulations, standards and best practice guidelines
- improving the credibility and objectivity of the accountability process
- improving the effectiveness of the internal and external audit functions and providing an objective forum for improving communication between the board and the internal and external auditors
- facilitating the independence of the internal and external auditors

- strengthening the role and influence of the non-executive directors
- fostering an ethical culture throughout the organisation.

In January 2003, following the Sarbanes–Oxley Act, the US Securities and Exchange Commission (SEC) proposed new rules requiring national securities exchanges and associations to prohibit the listing of any security whose issuer does not comply with the standards on audit committees established by the Sarbanes–Oxley Act.

Under the proposal, audit committee members of the listed companies must be 'independent'. The definition of 'independent' means that (a) the member may not accept any kind of compensation from the issuer, or its affiliates, other than in the capacity of a member of the board, and (b) the member may not be an affiliated person of the issuer or a subsidiary of the issuer other than in the capacity of a board member. Criterion (a) also extends to indirect payments and to persons related to the audit committee member.

In addition, the SEC proposal requires the audit committee to be directly responsible for the hiring, compensation, retention and oversight of the work of an independent accountant employed to prepare an auditor's report or other audit work. The audit committee has the responsibility of handling complaints and engaging advisers. The names of the audit committee members are required to be disclosed in the annual report.

The UK Financial Reporting Council published the Smith Report in January 2003. The report, commissioned by the government, deals with a set of proposed rules for audit committees for listed companies. Briefly, the Smith Report states that audit committees should:

- have at least three members; all members should be independent non-executive directors
- have at least one member with significant and relevant financial experience
- monitor the integrity of financial statements and review reporting decisions
- review the internal financial control systems and risk management systems
- review the effectiveness of internal audit
- recommend the external auditor for appointment and provide an explanation in the annual report in the event of any disagreement with the board
- review the external auditor's independence, objectivity and effectiveness
- develop policy on taking non-audit services from the external auditor.

Both the SEC and the Smith Report proposals take a more prescriptive approach to enforcing the role of audit committees in internal accountability processes.

The Corporate Governance Council of the Australian Securities Exchange (ASX) published the second edition of *Corporate Governance Principles and Recommendations* in 2007.[30] It recognised that there is no single model of good corporate governance, and the eight core principles are believed to provide a reference point for enhanced structures to minimise problems and achieve the best performance and accountability. Each principle is accompanied by best practice recommendations.

Under ASX Listing Rule 4.10, companies are required to provide a statement in their annual report disclosing the extent to which they have followed these best practice recommendations in the reporting period. Where they have not followed all recommendations, they must identify the recommendations that have not been followed and give reasons for non-compliance (an 'if not, why not' approach).

The requirements apply to the company's first financial year starting after 1 January 2003. With respect to audit committees, specific requirements apply to companies on the S&P/ASX All Ordinaries Index — they are subject to ASX Listing Rule 12.7, whereby an entity included on that index at the beginning of its financial year must have an audit committee during that year. The composition, operation and responsibility of the audit committee must comply with the best practice recommendations set out in Principle 4 by the ASX Corporate Governance Council.

Principle 4 'Safeguard integrity in financial reporting' states that a company should 'have a structure to independently verify and safeguard the integrity of the company's financial reporting'. Such a structure of review and authorisation should be designed to ensure the truthful and factual presentation of the company's financial position through, for example, the audit committee.

The following recommendations are pertinent.

- Recommendation 4.1: The board should establish an audit committee. This is an efficient way to focus on relevant financial reporting issues.
- Recommendation 4.2: The audit committee should be structured so that it (a) consists only of non-executive directors, (b) consists of a majority of independent directors, (c) is chaired by an independent chair, who is not the chair of the board, and (d) has at least three members. This recognises that the audit committee should be of sufficient size, independence and technical expertise to discharge its mandate effectively. The ASX encourages companies to move towards having their audit committees made up of only independent directors. The ASX also comments that the audit committee should include members who are all financially literate, with at least one member with financial expertise and some members who have an understanding of the industry.
- Recommendation 4.3: The audit committee should have a formal charter. A formal charter sets out the role, responsibilities, composition, structure and membership requirements of the audit committee. It should be given sufficient authority to meet its charter, which should include rights of access to management and to internal and external auditors without management present, and rights to seek explanations and additional information. The recommendation refers to the responsibilities provided in *Audit Committees: A Guide to Good Practice*. Audit committees should meet often enough to undertake their role effectively, and minutes should be kept. The audit committee should report to the board on the following matters:
  - assessment of whether external reporting is consistent with information and knowledge available to them and whether it is adequate for shareholders
  - assessment of the reporting processes
  - procedures for the selection and appointment of the external auditor and the rotation of the audit partner
  - recommendations for the appointment or removal of an auditor
  - assessment of the performance and independence of the external auditor, with special consideration if there is the provision of non-audit services
  - assessment of the performance and objectivity of the internal audit function
  - the results of its review of risk management and internal compliance and control systems.
- Recommendation 4.4: Companies should provide the information indicated in the 'Guide to Reporting on Principle 4'. The following materials should be made publicly available:
  - the audit committee charter
  - information on procedures for the selection and appointment of the external auditor, and for the rotation of external audit engagement partners.

Figure 2.6 (overleaf) summarises the matters which demonstrate the audit committee's relationships with both the internal and external auditors, as recommended by the corporate governance principles. It shows the significance of the role of both the auditors and the audit committee in ensuring the integrity of financial reporting, the adequacy of risk management and the reliability of the internal control structures in enhancing accountability. In general, the audit committee is involved in monitoring the audit process, providing support and fostering the integrity of the financial statements.

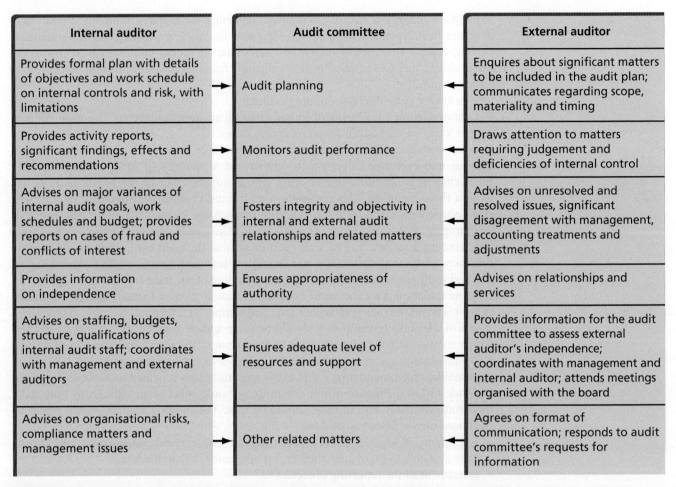

Internal auditor	Audit committee	External auditor
Provides formal plan with details of objectives and work schedule on internal controls and risk, with limitations	→ Audit planning ←	Enquires about significant matters to be included in the audit plan; communicates regarding scope, materiality and timing
Provides activity reports, significant findings, effects and recommendations	→ Monitors audit performance ←	Draws attention to matters requiring judgement and deficiencies of internal control
Advises on major variances of internal audit goals, work schedules and budget; provides reports on cases of fraud and conflicts of interest	→ Fosters integrity and objectivity in internal and external audit relationships and related matters ←	Advises on unresolved and resolved issues, significant disagreement with management, accounting treatments and adjustments
Provides information on independence	→ Ensures appropriateness of authority ←	Advises on relationships and services
Advises on staffing, budgets, structure, qualifications of internal audit staff; coordinates with management and external auditors	→ Ensures adequate level of resources and support ←	Provides information for the audit committee to assess external auditor's independence; coordinates with management and internal auditor; attends meetings organised with the board
Advises on organisational risks, compliance matters and management issues	→ Other related matters ←	Agrees on format of communication; responds to audit committee's requests for information

FIGURE 2.6: Relationships of the audit committee with the internal and external auditors

Following the global financial crisis, PricewaterhouseCoopers issued a report on audit committee outlook. It was discussed that while senior executives have identified new risks and reassessed old ones, they realise they need to broaden the range of risks that they analyse and manage. There is also now a greater focus on continuous disclosure requirements. Although the fundamentals of good audit committees do not change, developing good reporting capabilities, reviewing the cultural aspects of the control environment and regularly testing the risk management tone inside the company with a preparedness for the future are seen to be important parts of the audit committee's work. Effective audit committee practice starts with the quality of the people in the organisation and their interactions.[31]

Further, with the enactment of the Dodd–Frank Wall Street Reform and Consumer Protection (Dodd–Frank) Act in 2010 in the United States, major financial services and professional firms, including internal auditors and audit committee members, are required to review actively revenue-generating products, situations relating to material financial distress, securities, compliance in regards to executive compensation, whistleblower provisions and other governance issues.

In Australia, the ICAA produces a series of audit committee guides. It also recommends a more holistic approach to governance, risk and compliance as a key governance tool for boards and audit/risk committees.

LEARNING ⑥
objective

Describe the nature of governance and the type of audits in the public sector.

2.6 GOVERNANCE IN THE PUBLIC SECTOR

Auditing in the public sector is an expanding area of activity. It extends to all tiers of government (federal, state and local). The principles of auditing theory and practice in the private sector are applicable to auditing in the public sector. However, there are some variations in audit approach that are due mainly to the different environment in which public sector entities operate.

2.6.1 The requirements of public accountability

A knowledge of the parliamentary system is necessary for understanding the process of accountability in the public sector. Figure 2.7 shows a typical structure of a parliamentary system in a democratic state. (The framework for the Australian Parliament is indicated and discussed hereafter, but the principles also apply at the state level.)

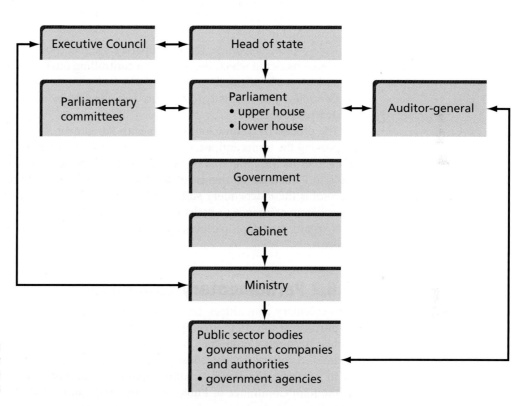

FIGURE 2.7:
Outline of a parliamentary system and the accountability process

The legislature comprises the head of state (the governor-general in Australia) and the two houses of Parliament — the upper house (the Senate) and the lower house (the House of Representatives). To become law, a legislative Bill has to be passed by both houses. It should be noted that the Queensland Parliament is the only unicameral state in Australia, with the Legislative Council (the Upper House) being abolished in 1922.

The party that wins a majority of seats in the lower house performs the role of government. The leader of the majority party is appointed as the prime minister by the head of state. The prime minister chooses elected members of his or her party to serve as ministers. The government is responsible for policy direction and for the acquisition and allocation of public resources to matters of state. Ministers are responsible for a particular government portfolio and have two roles: (1) as Cabinet members, responsible for the administration of their 'ministry', and (2) as members of the Executive Council in an advisory capacity to the head of state.

Government services are provided through agencies, government authorities and companies or other controlled entities.

- *Agencies:* **Agencies** are government departments, parliamentary departments or prescribed agencies. They are established by proclamation of the head of state. Each department has a chief executive who is responsible to a minister. The minister is responsible for the overall formation of the department's policy and administration. Central agencies comprise the Department of the Prime Minister and Cabinet and the Treasury Department. Each agency has extensive responsibility for policy advice and direction.
- *Authorities:* A government authority is a body corporate created for a public purpose by an Act. The authority is independent of other government operations and may be partly self-funding. Each authority has a governing board or committee whose composition is prescribed in the Act.
- *State-owned companies:* These companies are incorporated in accordance with the Corporations Act in which the state has a controlling interest. They provide essential services and are profit-oriented.
- *Controlled entity:* This type of entity is controlled by a government authority or a state-owned company.

The process of accountability starts with Parliament allocating resources to the agencies, approving the terms and use to which these resources are put, and specifying the expected outcomes of the programs or initiatives. The process ends with these agencies reporting back to Parliament on the use of allocated resources, and the results achieved. The auditor-general is the independent auditor who undertakes the audit and reporting function, and provides an assurance to Parliament that public resources have been appropriately used. In this regard, therefore, parliamentary committees play a crucial role in the accountability process.

2.6.2 Parliamentary committees

Parliamentary committees are set up by Parliament or by statute for a particular reason. A purpose of the committee may be to review the expenditure of public finances (e.g. the Public Accounts Committee) or to review agency budgets (e.g. the Senate Estimates Committee). A committee may consist of representatives from both houses of Parliament.

In Australia, the committee that examines the reports of the Australian auditor-general is the Joint Committee of Public Accounts and Audit (JCPAA). This committee comprises members of both houses of Parliament, including the chairperson of the House of Representatives Standing Committee on Expenditure.

The JCPAA owes its existence and authority to the *Public Accounts and Audit Committee Act 1951* (Cwlth) and the Public Accounts Committee Regulations. It is the Australian Parliament's watchdog, helping to ensure that government agencies are held to account for their use of public money. The duties of the committee are to:

- examine the accounts of the receipts and expenditures of the Australian government
- examine the financial affairs of government authorities and intergovernmental bodies
- examine all reports of the auditor-general laid before the houses of Parliament
- report to both houses of Parliament matters relating to accounts, statements and reports which the committee feels should be brought to the attention of the Parliament

- report desirable alterations to the method of keeping public accounts in the mode of receipt, control, issue or payment of public money
- inquire into matters raised by the auditor-general and referred to it by either house of Parliament.

The JCPAA holds public inquiries and examines all the reports of the auditor-general. The auditor-general provides the JCPAA with formal submissions, briefings and information as appropriate. An audit observer (from the Office of the Auditor-General) responsible for the department or body under review is present at all inquiries. The auditor-general (and senior staff) may meet with the committee to discuss the implications of all findings.

2.6.3 The auditor-general and the Australian National Audit Office

The auditor-general (A-G) (in both state and federal spheres) is an independent officer of Parliament who audits and reports to Parliament on the activities and performance of government agencies, authorities, companies and their controlled entities. Independence is an essential attribute, because it lends credibility to the work of the A-G. (Hereafter, we will discuss the federal A-G, although the functions of this office at both federal and state levels are essentially similar.)

The *Auditor-General Act 1997* (Cwlth) provides for the appointment of an A-G for the Commonwealth of Australia and defines the functions of the role. The terms and conditions of the A-G's appointment and the powers prescribed in the Act support independence.

The A-G is appointed by the governor-general on the recommendation of the responsible minister for a term of 10 years. The proposed recommendation is initially referred to the JCPAA. On approval by the JCPAA, the proposal is put to the governor-general. This consultative process enhances the independence of the A-G.

The A-G can be removed from office only under specified conditions. These are:
- if both houses of Parliament in the same parliamentary session request that the governor-general remove the A-G on the grounds of misbehaviour or physical or mental incapacity
- if the A-G becomes bankrupt.

The A-G may resign, however, by giving the governor-general a signed resignation notice.

The A-G has a legislative mandate to audit the financial statements of all entities controlled by the Australian Government, and may also undertake performance audits of all entities other than government business enterprises (GBEs). In the case of GBEs, the A-G may be asked by the JCPAA or the responsible minister to undertake an audit of a GBE.

The A-G's capacity and ability to obtain the required information enhances the independence of the audit. (Information-gathering powers are prescribed by the Act.) The A-G has the power to direct a person in writing to provide any information, to attend and give any evidence before the A-G (or an authorised official), and to produce any document(s) under his or her control or custody. The A-G can obtain information orally, in writing or under oath if necessary. There are significant penalties for providing false and misleading information. The A-G has access to premises occupied by the Australian Government or an Australian Government authority or company, and has free access to any document (or other property) and the right to examine, make copies of, or take extracts from any document.

The A-G's freedom of access to relevant premises and documents and information-gathering powers are not limited by any other law unless expressly stated.

The Australian National Audit Office (ANAO) is a specialist public sector practice, established to provide a full range of audit services to the Parliament and the Australian Government agencies and statutory bodies. It was created by the Auditor-General Act and consists of the auditor-general and staff appointed under the *Public Service Act 1922* (Cwlth). In carrying out the A-G's functions, ANAO staff can be directed only by the A-G or other staff authorised to give such direction. The ANAO audits the financial statements of some 300 government bodies. It provides Parliament with two reports a year on financial statement issues.

The ANAO also does about 50 performance audits each year and tables each report in Parliament. Performance audits comment on the efficiency and effectiveness of public administration, but do not comment on the merits of government policy. The ANAO also produces Better Practice Guides on topics such as audit committees, corporate governance, and preparation of financial statements by public sector entities.

It is worthwhile visiting the ANAO website where some comprehensive discussion papers on corporate governance and independence are posted: www.anao.gov.au.

2.6.4 Audit mandates

Government auditors perform their duties in accordance with **audit mandates**, which specify the type of audit required and what to audit. Audit mandates also state the functions and powers needed to carry out the audit and to report. These mandates are usually embodied in legislation, but in some cases they are determined by arrangement or contract.

The Australian Parliament has passed a number of Acts that provide a legislative framework for the performance, propriety and accountability of Australian Government entities:

- the *Financial Management and Accountability Act 1997* and its regulations, which provide for the proper use and management of public money, public property and other federal resources
- the *Commonwealth Authorities and Companies Act 1997*, which provides regulations for certain aspects of the financial affairs of Australian Government authorities, and stipulates rules for reporting and accountability; it also contains reporting requirements for Australian Government companies in addition to the requirements of the Corporations Act
- the *Auditor-General Act 1997*, which provides for the appointment of the Australian A-G and sets out the functions of the office.

Section 24 of the Auditor-General Act requires the A-G to set auditing standards to be complied with by auditors performing:

- an audit referred to in Division 1 (statement audits), including auditing the financial statements of agencies in accordance with the *Financial Management and Accountability Act 1997*
- an audit referred to Division 2 (performance audits) of Part 4 of the Act, including audits of Australian Government agencies, authorities, companies and their subsidiaries, including general performance audits
- an audit under Division 2 of Part 7 of the Act (Audit of the Australian National Audit Office)
- an audit under s. 56 of the *Financial Management and Accountability Act 1997* (Audit of the Finance Minister's annual financial statements).

Section 24 of the Auditor-General Act authorises the A-G to set relevant auditing standards for the abovementioned audits. These standards, which may be referred to as the ANAO auditing standards, are set by the A-G and express the minimum standard of audit work expected of auditors conducting audits on behalf of the A-G. These standards apply to all audits performed under the authority of the A-G in accordance with Division 1 or 2 of Part 4 or Division 2 of Part 7 of the Auditor-General Act or in accordance with s. 56 of the Financial Management and Accountability Act.

The A-G has also recognised that there is commonality in the auditing standards expected of the reporting entities under the Corporations Act and all Australian Government reporting entities and wishes that they conform to the greatest extent possible with the auditing standards promulgated by the Australian Auditing and Assurance Services Board (AUASB). The Auditing and Assurance Standards (AUSs) and Guidance Statements (AGSs) previously released are applicable as an expression of the minimum standard of audit work expected of auditors for all Australian government reporting entities.[32] Since 2009, the A-G set mandatory standards that must be complied with for all audits reported after the standards are published in the Commonwealth of Australia *Gazette*. This refers to audits of financial statements and performance audits.

The ANAO mandatory auditing standards comprise:

- standards made by the AUASB pursuant to s. 227B(1)(a) of the *Australian Securities and Investments Commission Act 2001* and s. 336 of the *Corporations Act 2001*, that are current from time to time;
- the following standards issued by the AUASB:
  - ASRE 2400 *Review of a Financial Report Performed by an Assurance Practitioner Who is Not the Auditor of the Entity*
  - ASRE 2405 *Review of Historical Financial Information Other than a Financial Report*;
  - ASAE 3000 *Assurance Engagements Other than Audits or Reviews of Historical Financial Information*;
  - ASAE 3100 *Compliance Engagements*;
  - ASAE 3500 *Performance Engagements* and
  - the following standards issued by the Australian Accounting Research Foundation: AUS 804 *The Audit of Prospective Financial Information*; AUS 810 *Special Purpose Reports on the Effectiveness of Control Procedures*; and AUS 904 *Engagements to Perform Agreed-upon Procedures*.

2.6.5 Financial statement audits

Financial statement audits are an independent examination of the financial accounting and reporting of public sector entities. The results of the examination are presented in an audit report, which expresses the auditor's opinion on whether the financial statements as a whole and the information contained therein fairly present each entity's financial position and the results of its operations and cash flows. The accounting treatments and disclosures reflected in the financial statements by the entity are assessed against relevant accounting standards and legislative reporting requirements.[33]

The audit objective is to express an opinion on the financial statements of the entity under examination. The A-G is responsible for financial statement audits of government-controlled entities. The financial statements and the auditor's report are included in the annual report of an entity, which is presented to Parliament. In this way, management is held accountable for the entity's performance.

The A-G must state whether the financial statements have been prepared in accordance with the orders of the Minister for Finance and whether they give a true and fair view of matters required by those orders. Reasons must be provided if the A-G is not of that opinion. The A-G must quantify the financial effect where possible, and disclose if there is non-compliance with the orders of the Minister for Finance.

The A-G must report on an exception basis if:

- all the necessary information and explanations were not obtained, stating the particulars of the shortcomings
- proper accounting records have not been kept

- records have not been retained for at least 7 years
- records have not been made available for inspection.

For consolidated financial statements, the A-G must report:

- the name of a subsidiary for which he or she has not acted as an auditor or audited the financial statements
- whether he or she has not examined those financial statements and the auditor's report on them
- the name of the subsidiary for which the financial statements have been qualified
- the deficiency, if the financial statements were not appropriate for consolidation
- whether there was any deficiency in the procedures and methods used in arriving at amounts for consolidation.

In undertaking financial statement audits, the A-G adopts the standards issued by the AUASB.

Where the engagement is a review engagement (i.e. not an audit), the A-G adopts the relevant assurance or review standards. ASRE 2400 is directed towards the review of the financial report comprising historical financial information and is undertaken by an assurance practitioner who is not the auditor. ASRE 2405, on the other hand, is applicable for reviews of historical financial information that is not in the form of a financial report prepared in accordance with a financial reporting framework designed for fair representation. Examples of such financial information include a single financial statement, such as a balance sheet; a listing of accounts receivable; other information derived from financial records; and financial statements prepared in accordance with a reporting framework that is not designed for fair presentation (e.g. condensed financial statements and internal management accounts).

In regard to the reporting format, the terms of the review engagement will stipulate the nature and reporting requirements of the review. The auditor or the assurance practitioner will plan and perform the engagement so as to provide a report that concludes using either of the following formats:

(a) Based on our review, which is not an audit, nothing has come to our attention that causes us to believe that the XX entity as at XX date is not prepared, in all material respects, in accordance with XX criteria used.

(b) Based on our review, which is not an audit, nothing has come to our attention that causes us to believe that the XX name of the historical financial information of XX entity as at XX date does not present fairly, in all material respects, in accordance with XX criteria used.

2.6.6 Performance auditing

Performance audits involve the independent and objective assessment of the administration of an entity or body's programs, policies, projects or activities. In 2013, the ANAO published a set of guidelines for the conduct of performance audits, highlighting the need for the ANAO to include the consideration of:[34]

- economy (minimising cost)
- efficiency (maximising the ratio of outputs to inputs)
- effectiveness (the extent to which intended outcomes were achieved)
- legislative and policy compliance.

As shown in the definition above, performance auditing captures the economic and compliance aspects of an activity. It is a composite means to identify issues in relation to a key aspect or function. Both quantitative and contextual matters will be considered. Figure 2.8 provides a brief cycle of performance audit that shows the processes of planning, evidence gathering and reporting.

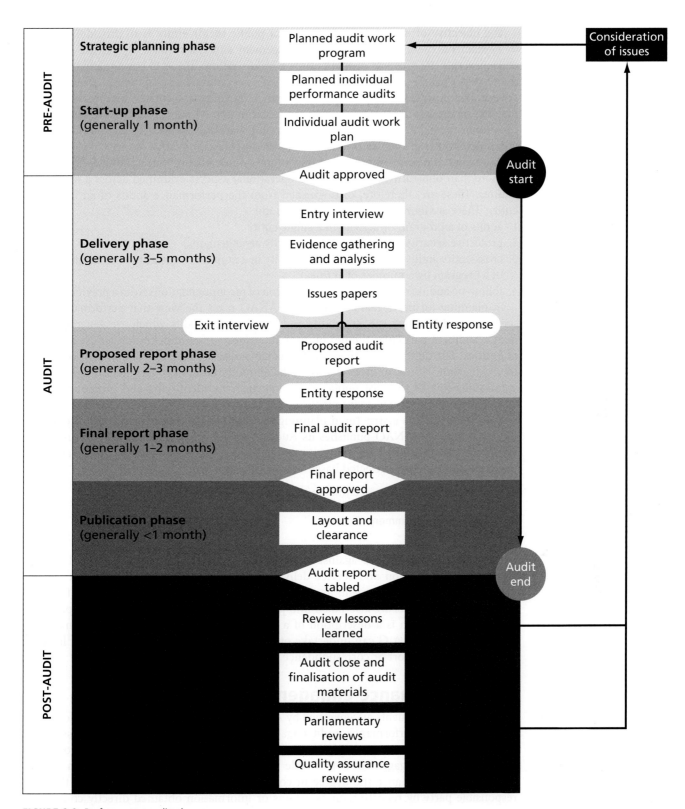

FIGURE 2.8: Performance audit phases

Source: Australian National Audit Office (ANAO), *Guidelines for the Conduct of Performance Audits*, November 2013, p. 5.

The objective of a performance audit of a public sector entity is to provide assurance to Parliament, the executive, boards, management and the community on the economy, efficiency and effectiveness of that entity's administration. The A-G has a mandate to conduct a performance audit of all government agencies, authorities and companies other than government business enterprises. For government business enterprises, performance audits may be undertaken by the A-G where requested by the relevant minister, the Minister for Finance or the JCPAA. General performance audits are concerned with common aspects of administration (e.g. the use of government credit cards, protective security measures, the procurement of resources, and fraud prevention and detection). Such audits are conducted in more than one entity, with particular operational aspects examined across a number of entities. These are, therefore, distinguished from the performance audits of an individual entity. There are four types of performance audit:

1. audits of a program or activity in a single entity
2. protective security audits (examines security arrangements)
3. cross-entity audits (reviews the same activity in a number of entities or the administration of a program by a number of entities)
4. follow-up audits (reviews the implementation of recommendations from a previous audit).

In planning for performance audits, the ANAO takes the view that performance audit services deliver agency-specific audits and cross-agency audits which are general performance audits of particular themes or common aspects of administration across a number of entities. The objectives of these performance audits are twofold. The first is to provide the Parliament with assurance relating to the administration of government programs. The second objective is to assist public sector managers by identifying and promoting better administrative and management practices.

The ANAO adopts a structured planning approach to determine future audit topics. In July each year, the ANAO publishes its Audit Work Program, which is underpinned by a risk-based methodology and aims to provide a broad coverage of areas of public administration. Audit topics are selected based on the following factors:[35]

- portfolio risks and the potential to improve performance
- thematic risks to sound public administration
- parliamentary comment
- ANAO capacity.

Potential topics are rated against criteria such as potential benefits, financial materiality, risks to reputation and service delivery and the extent of previous audit coverage. The priorities of the Parliament, as determined by the JCPAA, and the views of entities and other stakeholders are also taken into account in determining the final work program. The following section is a description of a typical performance audit. In addition to performance audits, the A-G can undertake other assurance activities which may be handled through a formal report or correspondence.

2.6.7 Performance engagements

Performance engagements are governed by ASAE 3500. There are two types of performance engagements: (1) performance audit engagements which provide reasonable assurance; and (2) performance review engagements which provide limited assurance. The objective of a performance engagement is to enable the assurance practitioner to express a conclusion designed to enhance the degree of confidence of the intended users other than the responsible party by reporting on assertions or information obtained directly concerning the economy, efficiency or effectiveness of an activity against identified criteria. The assurance practitioner uses their professional judgement to assess the performance of an activity against these criteria identified in ASAE 3500. ASAE 3500 sets out details of the objective of a performance engagement, the general principles, and the related matters that guide assurance providers in respect of materiality and performance engagement risk, gathering of evidence, communication of deficiencies, representations and documentation. The following provides a summary.

Objective of a performance engagement

In expressing a conclusion ... the assurance practitioner uses professional judgement to assess the performance of an activity against the identified criteria and whether:
- performance is within the tolerances of materiality (that is, the activity has been carried out economically, efficiently or effectively)
- performance is outside the tolerances of materiality (that is, the activity has not been carried out economically, efficiently or effectively).[36]

In the public sector, the conduct of performance engagements ... include the examination of:
- Economy, efficiency or effectiveness:
  - in terms of management systems or an entity's management in order to contribute to improvements
  - of the operations of an entity or an activity of an entity
  - of the internal controls applied by an entity in relation to an activity
  - in the implementation of government policies or programs and the application of government grants
  - in terms of financial prudence in the application of public resources
  - of administrative arrangements.
- The validity and reliability of performance measurement systems and/or statements published by the responsible party in annual reports.
- Compliance with legislation and accompanying instruments and the identification of breaches.
- Intended and unintended impacts of the implementation of government policies or programs and the extent to which community needs and stated objectives of an activity or entity have been met.
- Probity processes and identification of weaknesses.[37]

Para 17 (d) of ASAE 3500 also lists examples of characteristics that form the suitable criteria for a performance engagement. They include relevance, completeness, reliability, neutrality, and understandability. The principles of a performance engagement as explained in ASAE 3500 are described in the following sections.

Ethical requirements

Ethical requirements include adherence to independence and application of the appropriate code of ethics (the professional accounting body's code of ethics).

The assurance practitioner shall comply with the fundamental ethical principles of integrity, objectivity, professional competence and due care, confidentiality and professional behaviour.[38]

Quality control

The assurance practitioner shall implement procedures to address the elements of a proper quality control system. These are the same as the quality control elements of an audit.[39]

Initiation or acceptance

Assurance practitioners should only accept engagements where the activity is the responsibility of a party who is not the sole intended user; the subject matter is identifiable, its performance is capable of consistent measurement against identified and suitable criteria or assertions, and the information about it is capable of being subjected to procedures for gathering sufficient appropriate evidence; and that there are the necessary professional competencies amongst those who conduct the assurance.[40]

Matters to be agreed upon on the terms of engagement

These must be clearly communicated and agreed upon. Any changes must be agreed in writing. The terms and the changes must adhere to the relevant legislation.[41]

Quantitative and qualitative factors

Paragraph 57 of ASAE 3500 lists quantitative and qualitative factors that assurance practitioners must consider when assessing materiality and performance engagement risk, including:

- The importance of the activity to achieving the entity's objectives.
- The financial impact the activity has on the entity as a whole.
- The nature of transactions, for example, high volumes, large dollar values, and complex transactions.
- The extent of interest shown in particular aspects of the activity by, for example, legislature, or other governing body, regulatory authorities or the public.
- The economic, social, political and environmental impact of the activity.
- The extent of management's actions regarding issues raised in the previous performance engagements.
- The diversity, consistency and clarity of the entity's objectives and goals.
- The nature, size and complexity of the activity.
- The complexity and quality of management information and external reporting.
- The effectiveness of internal controls, including the level of coverage by the internal auditors.
- The nature and degree of change in the environment or within the entity that impact on the activity.
- Management's effectiveness in a particular area.[42]

Assurance report content

While most aspects of the performance engagements are similar in approach to that of an audit, the assurance report of a performance engagement, as part of the assurance engagements, shall contain the following elements:

(a) a title that clearly indicates the report is an independent assurance report;
(b) an addressee;
(c) an identification and description of the activity;
(d) identification of the criteria;
(e) where appropriate, a description of any significant, inherent limitation associated with the evaluation or measurement of the activity against the criteria;
(f) . . . a statement restricting the use of the assurance report to those intended users or that purpose [if appropriate];
(g) a statement to identify the responsible party and to describe the responsible party's and the assurance practitioner's responsibilities;
(h) a statement that the performance engagement was conducted in accordance with applicable ASAEs (ASAE 3500 *Performance Engagements*) and the level of assurance provided;
(i) a summary of the work undertaken;
(j) the assurance practitioner's conclusions [which may include the context in which the practitioner's conclusions are to be read; the date of the report; and the name of the practitioner, with specific location].[43]

Reporting findings, recommendations and responsible party comments

The conclusions of the assurance practitioner shall be expressed in positive form where reasonable assurance is provided. A negative form is used where there the practitioner is providing limited assurance. Where both positive and negative forms are expressed, the practitioner shall clearly separate the two types of conclusions.

> The assurance practitioner may expand the assurance report to include other information and explanations that that are not intended to affect their conclusions. Examples include:
> - Disclosure of materiality levels.
> - Findings relating to particular aspects of the performance engagements.
> - Recommendations.
> - Comments received from the responsible party.[44]

Modifications to the assurance report

> Modifications to the assurance report relate to circumstances when the assurance practitioner is unable to express an unqualified conclusion and an assurance report is issued with either:
> (a) a qualified conclusion;
> (b) an adverse conclusion; or
> (c) a disclaimer of conclusion.[45]

Qualified conclusions, adverse conclusions and disclaimers of conclusion

There will be cases whereby, in the opinion of the assurance practitioner, the effect of the matter is or may be material. An example of this would be where 'there is a limitation on the scope of the assurance practitioner's work', and where circumstances or the responsible party prevents, or imposes a restriction that prevents, the 'practitioner from obtaining evidence required'.

In an assertion-based engagement, where it is discovered after the engagement that the activity is not a subject matter appropriate to being subjected to audit or review, the assurance practitioner shall not issue an unqualified conclusion. They shall express 'a qualified or adverse conclusion when the unsuitable criteria or inappropriate subject matter is likely to mislead the intended users; or a qualified conclusion or a disclaimer of conclusion is expressed in other cases'.[46]

PROFESSIONAL ENVIRONMENT
NSW government CFO standards '20 years old'

*T*he NSW auditor-general says minimum standards for chief financial officers in the state government are now 20 years old and need updating to mandate modern professional standards.

In a damning audit report on NSW state finances released on Wednesday which found a $1 billion accounting error, Peter Achterstraat said a Premier's Department circular which set minimum qualifications for CFOs applied only to formal qualifications and newly recruited finance chiefs and did not cover agencies outside departments.

Treasurer Mike Baird said in a statement to *CFO*: 'We agree with the significant weaknesses in financial reporting systems that the Auditor General has identified today, which is why work is already underway to improve these systems.'

'In Opposition we suspected serious weaknesses in financial reporting and on coming to Government we commissioned the Schott Audit which recommended changes that are now underway. Unfortunately improving financial systems does not happen overnight and there is still a long way to go.'

But a month after the present government came to power it rejected a Public Accounts Committee recommendation in October 2010 to mandate CFO qualifications in the Public Finance and Audit Act 1983. The auditor said the government believed this 'could be managed more flexibly through current arrangements'.

The Public Accounts Committee recommendation in part reflected a submission from accounting body CPA Australia that called for the responsibilities and attributes of government CFOs to be spelled out in legislation, as is the case in other states.

Achterstraat said the circular's 'requirements are limited to formal qualifications only and do not address the broad range of skills needed in today's environment,' he said in his report. 'In my opinion, mandating the inclusion of relevant competencies as well as qualifications in all CFO role statements is required.'

In addition, he said of 300 separate legal entities that make up the NSW public sector the circular only formally covered 60 departments.

'Of these 60, about 40 are virtually dormant or exist in legal form only,' Mr Achterstraat said.

'Low rates of attrition across the sector have reduced the circular's effectiveness because it only applied to future recruitment into financial management and accounting roles. The circular allows exemptions for existing officers taking on new roles within the sector.'

Mr Achterstraat said the recent NSW Commission of Audit Interim Report on Public Sector Management (the Schott Report) found CFOs often do not participate in agency leadership groups.

'This is a further indication that existing requirements, which are over 20 years old, do not ensure the current skills and capabilities required,' he said.

'It is crucial CFOs have the proper skills and capabilities to meet the challenges of being part of the leadership group.'

Institute of Chartered Accountants general manager of leadership and quality Yasser El-Ansary said the Auditor-General's views reflected generally accepted standards for private sector CFOs and it is arguable that public sector finance chiefs needed higher standards.

'There is a strong case that those entrusted with the stewardship of public sector finances should meet the highest level of training and competency,' he said.

'Typically when you are talking about public sector finances it does bring with it a degree of accountability that adds a new layer of responsibility on top of that which is faced by those in the private sector.'

Source: S Drummond, NSW government CFO standards '20 years old', *The Australian Financial Review*, 31 October 2012.

Do you know . . .

2.4 ☐ Audit committees perform an important role in corporate governance. They comprise non-executive directors who can provide independent oversight over the financial reporting and auditing function of the organisation.

2.5 ☐ Detailed guidelines of the role of audit committees are contained in the ASX corporate governance principles and all the ASX top 300 companies must have an independent audit committee.

2.6 ☐ The public sector has a tiered system of accountability and governance. Many public sector organisations also apply corporate governance principles and the Australian National Audit Office publishes detailed guidelines on the governance and accountability requirements for the public sector.

2.7 ☐ The auditor-general and the Australian National Audit Office work closely together to ensure proper reporting through audits of financial reports and performance audits carried out to ensure not only compliance but also efficiency and effectiveness.

SUMMARY

Governance is a broad concept that signifies the authority to govern. Such authority is underpinned by transparency and accountability in the way in which such an entity is operated. Enterprise governance encompasses corporate governance and business performance. It promotes significant aspects of governance — conformance and performance — for organisations, and can be applied to business entities, the public sector and not-for-profit organisations. Auditing plays a vital role in enterprise governance, providing assurance for the accountability processes and ensuring certain standards of conformance.

Many auditing and assurance functions are undertaken by internal auditors. Internal auditing, a fast-growing profession that assumes a significant role in the current audit reform, is also undergoing rapid development and change. Internal auditing is now referred to as a key function which combines the roles of internal control, risk management and corporate governance. The accountability of internal auditors is largely through an effective audit committee. Audit committees enhance the effectiveness of corporate and business governance through their link with the board, management and the auditors (both internal and external). The accountability of the public sector, on the other hand, lies with the auditor-general and the work of the Australian National Audit Office. The A-G adopts the AUASB standards. The ANAO also publishes detailed work plans and better audit practice guides.

KEY TERMS

agencies, p. 72

audit mandates, p. 74

audit trinity, p. 53

conformance, p. 48

corporate governance, p. 51

earnings management, p. 59

enterprise governance, p. 48

enterprise risk management, p. 55

governance, p. 47

internal auditing, p. 60

operational auditing, p. 64

performance, p. 48

performance audits, p. 76

risk management, p. 55

MULTIPLE-CHOICE questions

2.1 Which of the following statements is incorrect?
A. Enterprise governance can be applied to both corporations and other business entities, including the public sector.
B. Enterprise governance is a concept of business performance within the organisation with which only the board of directors should comply.
C. Enterprise governance encompasses conformance and performance and is an overall concept that includes corporate governance processes.
D. Internal control and risk management processes are part of enterprise governance.

2.2 The audit trinity concept refers to:
A. Governance, management and audit.
B. Conformance, performance, assurance.
C. Past, current and future approaches.
D. External audit, internal audit, audit committee.

2.3 The auditor-general must report on an exception basis if:
A. Records have not been made available for inspection.
B. Records have been retained for at least 10 years.
C. Proper accounting records have been kept.
D. All the necessary information and explanations were obtained.

2.4 The key benefit to management of an internal audit function is that it:
A. Provides assurance to management that fraudulent activities will be detected.
B. Reduces external audit costs.
C. Aids management in the areas of risk management, control and governance processes.
D. Provides assurance to management that the organisation is complying with its legal requirements.

2.5 The Institute of Internal Auditors states that:
A. Internal auditing provides a disciplined approach to evaluating risks, controls and governance processes.
B. Internal auditing should concentrate on an advisory and consultancy role for management.
C. Internal auditing's role is to support the external audit requirements.
D. All internal audit personnel should be certified internal auditors.

2.6 Which of the following statements best describes the appropriate relationship between internal and external auditors?
A. The internal auditor often competes with the external auditor for audit assignments.
B. The internal auditor's work should supplement the work of the external auditor.
C. There should be proper coordination of the work of the internal and external auditors.
D. There should be complete independence between the work of the internal and the external auditors.

2.7 The approach that has been suggested for operational audits is the:
  (i) Risk-based audit approach
 (ii) Value-for-money audit approach
(iii) Process audit approach.
A. (i) and (ii) only.
B. (i) and (iii) only.
C. (ii) and (iii) only.
D. (i), (ii) and (iii).

2.8 Which of these is a type of public sector performance audit?
  (i) Audit of a program or activity in a single entity
  (ii) Protective security audit
  (iii) Follow-up audit
  A. (i) and (ii) only.
  B. (i) and (iii) only.
  C. (ii) and (iii) only.
  D. (i), (ii) and (iii).

2.9 According to the Sarbanes–Oxley Act and the SEC recommendations, an audit committee should not:
  A. Oversee the hiring and firing of external auditors.
  B. Consist of retired audit partners who had been involved in the client.
  C. Be subject to the recommendations of the Listing Rules.
  D. Meet with the internal auditors without the presence of the CEO.

2.10 The best practice recommendations for audit committees states that the audit committee should consist of:
  A. An independent chairperson who is not chairperson of the board.
  B. Both executive and non-executive directors.
  C. At least one independent director.
  D. At least five members.

REVIEW questions

2.11 Describe the essential components of enterprise risk management (ERM) as put forward by the Committee of Sponsoring Organizations of the Treadway Commission.

2.12 What is meant by earnings management? How do you think the concept of earnings management might have influenced the auditor's role in the audit of financial statements?

2.13 What does the ASX suggest should be the makeup of an audit committee?

2.14 Should the internal auditor report to the chief accountant or the board of directors? Give reasons.

2.15 What are the differences between the independence of an internal auditor and that of an independent auditor? How can an internal auditor be truly independent?

2.16 What are the five phases of an operational audit? Briefly describe each phase.

2.17 Summarise the 'accountability' framework of the public sector.

2.18 What are the duties and powers of the Australian auditor-general?

2.19 When conducting a performance engagement, what are the quantitative and qualitative factors that the assurance practitioner must consider when assessing materiality and performance engagement risk?

2.20 What is meant by economy, efficiency and effectiveness in relation to a performance audit?

PROFESSIONAL application questions

★
BASIC
★★
MODERATE
★★★
CHALLENGING

2.21 Establishing an internal audit department ★★

You are the external auditor of Fringe and Stock Ltd. The CEO, Norbert Fringe, has contacted you because the company is considering setting up an internal audit department for the first time and he is looking for some guidance as to what is required for an effective internal audit department.

Required

Explain the key considerations Norbert Fringe should consider when setting up an internal audit department.

2.22 Response to risk ★

Risk management involves talking appropriate action to risks identified. As part of that process an internal audit department might classify risks based on the probability that an event will occur and the impact of that event if it does occur. This gives four possible classifications:

(i) *High impact, high likelihood*; for example, in a market where there are no significant barriers to entry, new suppliers may easily enter the market place enter the market place reducing the company's market share and profit margins.

(ii) *High impact, low likelihood*; for example, a fire in a company's warehouse destroying inventory.

(iii) *Low impact, low likelihood*; for example, minor damage caused by unlikely weather events.

(iv) *Low impact, high likelihood*; for example, low level theft of the company's inventories from retail stores.

Strategies to deal with these risks include: transfer, reduce, or accept risks.

Required

For each of the examples given above describe how the business might manage the risk.

2.23 Audit committees ★★★

If anyone was made to comment on the audit process, the audit committee, as a subcommittee of the board, has the necessary technical skills and would be the best candidate to provide it.[47]

Required

Discuss the work of the audit committee in enhancing corporate governance.

2.24 Board structure and governance ★★

Stairods Pty Ltd has expanded rapidly over recent years and is now looking to float on the ASX. It is currently undertaking a review of its corporate governance practices and has asked for your assistance in reviewing the composition of the board.

The board of directors consists of six executive directors as follows:

- Rodney Stair   Chairman and Managing Director
- Brendan Carpet   Finance
- Stanley Stair   Operations
- Arthur Cranmer   Sales
- Gemima Strange   Purchasing
- Barbara Stair-Carpet Personnel

Barbara is married to Rodney, is sister to Brendan and mother to Stanley. Brendan is the only director with financial expertise, he is responsible for internal controls and has attempted to introduce both a tightening of internal controls and an internal auditor. These attempts have been unsuccessful as the rapid growth in the business has meant that the board discuss a range of operational issues in their monthly board meetings and the internal control proposals have not been discussed.

Required

Discuss the changes that Stairods Pty Ltd should consider to improve its corporate governance practices.

2.25 Outsourcing internal audit ★★

You have been the in-charge on the audit of Crake Stroom for the last two years and you have built up a good professional relationship with the Finance Director, Cynthia Plant. She has been very happy with the professionalism and efficiency with which you and your firm have carried out the external audit. Cynthia is currently conducting a review of the company's internal audit department and has asked for your thoughts on your firm carrying out this work.

Required

Prepare notes for a meeting with Cynthia Plant which highlight the advantages and disadvantages of the external auditor conducting internal audit work.

2.26 Performance audit ★★

The auditor general has been carrying out a performance audit on the funding provided to agencies dealing with the provision of services to homeless Australians. The period of the review covered the two years ending 30 June 2015 and the aims of the audit were to assess whether:
1. the number of homeless people in Australia had fallen
2. the number of staff employed by the agencies had decreased
3. the total costs or running agencies had decreased.

The findings of the audit show there has been a moderate increase in the number of homeless people in Australia over the two years considered. The review also established that overall the number of staff employed in homelessness agencies had increased and there had been a significant increase in agency operating costs.

Required

Identify the performance audit assertions applicable to each of the aims of the audit and comment on the audit findings.

 ## CASE studies

2.27 Proposed auditing reforms ★★★

The following provides some suggestions of how corporate governance practices could be improved around the globe.[48]

United Kingdom

The Financial Reporting Council (FRC) in the United Kingdom has recommended reforms in auditing that include:

- a greater communication role for audit committees enabling them to provide fuller reports to shareholders.
- disclosure of fees for non-audit services provided by the auditor in the financial reports, enabling 'investors to decide ... whether the auditor's objectivity and independence may have been adversely affected ...' (Hodge et al., 2012, p. 1)

The dominance of the Big-4 in providing audit services is being investigated by the UK Competition Commission (p. 2).

United States

The Public Company Accounting Oversight Board (PCAOB) issued concept releases and proposals to allow discussion 'about potential changes to certain fundamental aspects of auditing' (Hodge et al., 2012, p. 2). Areas include 'the auditor report, audit transparency, and auditor independence, objectivity, and scepticism' (p. 2). In addition, the vexed question of auditor firm rotation has been debated. (See Pozen, 2012, for a summary of the points raised in the debate, with his suggested solution to the rotation issue.)

Reform has been proposed for the audit report with changes being considered in the following area. Included in the report will be a section devoted to auditor discussion and analysis, expanded use of emphasis paragraphs, auditor assurance on other information outside the financial statements, and clarification of language in the standard auditor (report) (p. 1).

Europe

On 30 November 2011, the European Commission (EC) 'published proposals that would bring major changes to the audit market if adopted' (p. 1). The reforms proposed include:

- mandatory rotation of auditing firms
- mandatory tendering of auditors
- prohibition of large firms providing non-audit services to clients (Curry, 2012, pp. 1, 2)

Proposals have also been introduced to promote 'healthy competition in the audit market' (p. 2). The proposals include:

- prohibition on contractual clauses limiting the choice of the auditor to one of the large audit firms (p. 1)
- allowing firms to exercise their profession across Europe (p. 2).

Australia

In Australia, the ASIC is also concerned about competition in the audit market. Doug Niven, Senior Executive Leader of Financial Reporting and Audit at ASIC, stated, '(W)e want to see the mid-tier grow and be credible competitors to the big four. Also, there has to be sufficient competition right throughout' (King, 2012, p. 48).

The reasons for the wish to see increased competition are not stated. It is hoped the desire for increased competition is seen as a means of increasing audit quality and does not lead to competition in the price of the audit as happened in Australia in the 1980s and early 1990s.

Required

Discuss the impact of each of the above proposed changes on the discipline of auditing.

2.28 Madoff's scheme ★★★

Bernard Madoff was operating a simple Ponzi scheme, Harry Markopolos explains. 'He was robbing Peter to pay Paul, so he needed a continual new stream of incoming cash to pay off the old investors', he says. 'Investors who got in early would tell their friends and family how great a money manager Madoff was, so they'd want to invest as well.' The problem is, in a Ponzi scheme there is no underlying investment activity or service provided. It is all, as Markopolos notes, a charade. On the surface, Ponzi schemes offer alluring, steady returns. But the cold, hard truth, as he puts it, is 'those investment returns exist only on the monthly investment statements because they are fiction'. The returns generated by most Ponzi schemes on paper are so good that if you are not a professional investor you would definitely be tempted to invest 100% of your retirement money in them. It takes tremendous discipline and financial knowledge to successfully avoid them.

Madoff enabled his US$65 billion scam by enlisting the apparent complicity of close to 350 'feeder funds' — companies that marketed his Ponzi scheme for him in more than 40 countries and, in effect, fed him with new investors. Those funds all pretended to conduct exhaustive due diligence, such as checking into each manager's background, inspecting his or her operations, verifying the assets, and vetting the strategies. But in reality Madoff paid them handsomely so that they would look the other way. They were accomplices that enabled the scheme to get as large as it did. Madoff alone could not have been able to reach a US$65 billion without their help.

Source: *Internal Auditor*, June 2010, p. 46.

Required

Evaluate the case from an audit point of view, highlighting possible risks for an investor and a fund manager who might be attracted to such a scheme.

RESEARCH question

2.29 Internal audit and audit committee

Discuss in detail the impact on the work of an audit committee in a large organisation which has lost a significant amount in investments owing to the global financial crisis. The management of the company is preparing for a major cut in operations and retrenchments.

2.30 ANAO Better Practice Guide

'Business continuity management is an essential component of good public-sector governance. It is part of an entity's overall approach to effective risk management and should be closely aligned to the entity's incident management, emergency response management and IT disaster recovery. Successful business continuity management requires a commitment from the executive to raising awareness and implementing sound approaches to build resilience. The ANAO published a Better Practice Guide on 4 June 2009 following consultation with Australian Government and private sector entities. The guide provides good references and explores issues within the business continuity environment that have arisen since the previous ANAO publication.'

Source: Australian National Audit Office, 'Better Practice Guides', www.anao.gov.au.

Required

Access the ANAO Better Practice Guide *Business Continuity Management, Building Residence in Public Sector Entities*. Write a synopsis of the efficiency and effectiveness of the ANAO's business continuity management plan.

FURTHER READING

Australian National Audit Office, *Guidelines for the Conduct of Performance Audits*, April 2012.

Australian National Audit Office, *Public Sector Audit Committees, Independent Assurance and Advice for Chief Executives and Boards, Best Practice Guide*, August 2011.

Office of the Auditor General, Western Australia, *Auditing in the Public Interest*, October 2012.

KPMG, *Audit Committee insights — A survey of Australian audit committees*, November 2008.

M Phelps & LLP Phillips, *A roadmap for audit committees in meeting the challenges posed by enhanced regulatory scrutiny under the Dodd-Frank Act*, authored by NR Janis & JA Sincavage, in *Lexology*, The Association of Corporate Counsel, USA, 25 February 2013.

S Kang & K Yong-Shik, 'Does Earnings Management Amplify The Association between corporate governance and firm performance? Evidence from Korea', *International Business and Economics Research Journal*, 10(2), February 2011, pp. 53–66.

R Davidson, J Goodwin-Stewart & P Kent, 'Internal Governance structures and earnings management', *Accounting and Finance*, 45, 2005, pp. 241–67.

C Man & B Wong, 'Corporate Governance and Earnings Management: A survey of literature', *The Journal of Applied Business Research*, March 2013, pp. 391–418.

Y Gendron & J Bedard, 'On the constitution of audit committees', *Accounting, Organisations and Society*, 31(3), April 2006.

IFAC, *Rebuilding Public Confidence in Financial Reporting*, April 2003.

NOTES

1. OECD, 'Glossary of statistical terms: Good governance', www.oecd.org, viewed 28 September 2010.

2. PM Jackson, *The Political Economy of Bureaucracy*, p. 220, Philip Allan, London, 1982.

3. R Gray, D Owen & C Adams, *Accounting & Accountability: Changes and Challenges in Corporate Social and Environmental Reporting*, Prentice Hall, Hertfordshire, 1996.

4. Australian National Audit Office, *Performance Auditing in the Australian National Audit Office*, ANAO, Canberra, 2008, p. 4.

5. A Gray & B Jenkins, 'Codes of accountability in the new public sector', *Accounting, Auditing & Accountability Journal*, 6(3), 1993, pp. 52–67.

6. R Gray op. cit.

7. The Professional Accountants in Business Committee (PAIB) of the International Federation of Accountants (IFAC) was asked by the IFAC Board in October 2002 to explore the new concept of enterprise governance. A particular focus of the project was to consider why corporate governance often fails in companies and, more importantly, what must be done to ensure that things go right. The project was conducted jointly by the Chartered Institute of Management Accountants (CIMA) and IFAC, and a report was published in February 2004. The study provides a framework in which

both corporate governance (conformance) and business governance (performance) are examined with a view to identifying the causes of successes and failures of 27 worldwide cases. The report can be accessed electronically at www.ifac.org.

8. ASX Corporate Governance Council, *Corporate Governance Principles and Recommendations*, www.asx.com.au, was revised in 2010. Changes made include policies concerning reporting on unethical practices, diversity, the establishment of audit committees, risk management and control system requirements.

9. CR Baker & DM Owsen, 'Increasing the role of auditing in corporate governance', *Critical Perspectives on Accounting* 13, 2002, pp. 783–95.

10. BA Porter, 'The audit trinity: The key to securing corporate accountability', *Managerial Auditing Journal* 24(2), 2009, pp. 156–82.

11. ibid., p. 180.

12. AS/NZS ISO 31000:2009, Risk *Management — Principles and Guidelines*, section 2: terms and definitions 2.1 and 2.2, pp. 1–2.

13. AS/NZS 4360:2004, *Risk Management*, Standards Australia, 2004. The standard provides a generic guide for managing risk. It specifies the elements of the risk management process, with a generic and independent approach.

14. Committee of Sponsoring Organizations of the Treadway Commission (COSO), *Enterprise Risk Management — Integrated Framework, Executive Summary*, September 2004, AICPA, available at www.coso.org.

15. ibid., p. 2.

16. Subsequent to the global financial crisis, COSO issued two reports in 2009, *Effective Enterprise Risk Oversight — The Role of the Board of Directors* and *Strengthening Enterprise Risk Management for Strategic Advantage*, and a practice guide in October 2012.

17. Deloitte & Touche LLP, P Curtis & M Carey, 'Risk Assessment in Practice — Thought Leadership in ERM', *COSO*, October 2012.

18. COSO, *COSO Releases ERM Thought Paper Dealing with Latest Thinking on Risk Assessment Approaches and Techniques*, Media Release, 26 October 2012.

19. COSO released an updated *Internal Control-Integrated Framework: 2013* in May 2013. The new IC-IF retains the core definition of internal control and the five components. It continues to emphasise the importance of management judgement in designing, implementing, and conducting internal control, and in assessing the effectiveness of a system of internal control. The fundamental concepts in the original framework have become principles. The new IC-IF has also expanded the financial reporting category of objectives to include other form of reporting, such as non-financial and internal reporting.

20. Man, C & Wong, B, 'Corporate governance and earnings management: A survey of literature', *The Journal of Applied Business Research*, March/April 2013, 29(2), pp. 391–418, www.cluteinstitute.com, viewed 29 March 2013.

21. The Institute of Internal Auditors, *International Standards for the Professional Practice of Internal Auditing (Standards)*, 2012, p. 20, www.theiia.org.

22. Operational auditing does not have an official definition. It is used to describe an audit (assessment, examination) of business operations to determine if management objectives have been achieved. Operational auditing may include compliance, financial, systems auditing, with an aim to evaluate the performance of a business operation. In many ways operational auditing is now regarded as performance auditing. It is considered that operational auditing has been embedded within risk-based auditing and following the Sarbanes–Oxley Act (2002) the concept is somewhat forgotten. The IIA is now reviving its significance through training programs.

23. D Ziegenfuss, 'The rebirth of operational auditing', *New Accountant*, November/December 1998, pp. 21–4.

24. A Cox, 'Incorporating Operational and Performance Auditing into Compliance and Financial Auditing' QFinance, www.qfinance.com, viewed 4 October 2010.

25. *Reaching Greater Heights — Are you prepared for the journey?* was published by PricewaterhouseCoopers in March 2013. The state of the internal audit profession study provides some significant insights about how internal audit's value is perceived by management, namely, that the foundational capabilities of internal audit may not be strong enough to deliver today's work and it continues to struggle in maximising the impact of its contribution.

26. The IIA's *Global Internal Audit Survey* was conducted during the first half of 2010 to understand the current state and future expectations of the internal audit profession, The 2010 survey, which was completed by 13 583 professionals from more than 107 countries, resulted in five reports available as free downloads to IIA members. The reports include *Characteristics of an internal audit activity, core competencies for today's internal auditor, measuring internal auditing's value, what's next for internal auditing and imperatives for change.* Together with the survey reports, a special report on the value of internal auditing from the perspective of stakeholders such as chief executive officers and audit committee members was also published. It was the first time The IIARF administered a survey of stakeholders in the United States.

27. *Achieving High Performance in Internal Audit*, a joint publication by the Institute of Internal Auditors Australia and Protiviti, a Risk & Business Consulting and Internal Audit organisation. The report includes matters on which Audit Committee reports, challenges and trends, internal audit resources, skills enhancements, quality and value.

28. The Common Body of Knowledge (CBOK) study of internal auditing was conducted by a global team of researchers, focusing on the profession in Australasia, North America and Europe. A brief report was also included in the December edition of *Internal Auditor*, December 2007. More details of the study can be found in *Internal Auditor*, 1 December 2001, pp. 38–42.

29. D Salierno, 'In search of greater knowledge: a global study of the profession', *Internal Auditor*, December 2007, pp. 35–7.

30. ASX Corporate Governance Council 2007, *Corporate Governance Principles and Recommendations*, www.asx.com.au, viewed 29 September 2010.

31. PricewaterhouseCoopers, 'Where to from here', *Audit Committee Matters*, March 2010.

32. The Australian National Audit Office auditing standards published by the ANAO on 16 November 2005 were notified in the Commonwealth *Gazette* no. GN45, and replace those in the *Gazette* no. GN17, 1 May 2002.

33. Ian McPhee, Auditor-General for Australia, 'Public sector auditing practices, perspectives, challenges and capacity development', World Bank Seminar, Washington DC, 3–4 May 2006, www.anao.gov.au.

34. Australian National Audit Office, *Guidelines for the Conduct of Performance Audits*, ANAO, Canberra, November 2013.

35. Australian National Audit Office, *Performance Auditing in the Australian National Audit Office*, ANAO, Canberra, 2008.

36. Auditing and Assurance Standards Boards, 'Standard on Assurance Engagements ASAE 3500 Performance Engagements', paragraph 13, AUASB 2008, Melbourne.

37. ibid., paragraph 16.

38. ibid., paragraph 19.

39. ibid., paragraph 23.

40. ibid., paragraph 27.

41. ibid., paragraph 28.

42. ibid., paragraph 57.

43. ibid., paragraph 83.

44. ibid., paragraph 86.

45. ibid., paragraph 88.

46. ibid., paragraph 89.

47. A Ghandar, CPA Australia Policy Adviser, Audit and Assurance, quoted in S Rose, 'Audits called to Account', *The Australian Financial Review*, 27 March 2013, www.afr.com.

48. R Johnson, 'Reforms in these three countries/areas', *Current Affairs in Auditing*, Wiley, June 2012.

Answers to multiple-choice questions

2.1 *B*   2.2 *D*   2.3 *A*   2.4 *C*   2.5 *A*   2.6 *C*   2.7 *D*   2.8 *D*   2.9 *B*   2.10 *A*

chapter 3

Professional ethics, independence and audit quality

OVERVIEW

3.1 The role of the professional accountant

3.2 Professional ethics and the accountant

3.3 Professional independence

3.4 Corporate collapses and reforms

3.5 Audit quality

3.6 Professional discipline

Summary

Key terms

Multiple-choice questions

Review questions

Professional application questions

Case studies

Research question

Further reading

Notes

LEARNING
objectives

After studying this chapter, you should be able to:

1 explain the role and duties of the professional accountant

2 discuss the basic ethical principles for auditors

3 explain the conceptual principles of the *Code of Ethics for Professional Accountants*

4 describe the regulatory and conceptual framework of professional independence and the key guidelines

5 discuss the impact of the Corporate Law Economic Reform Program on audit reform and corporate disclosure

6 state the importance of technical and ethical competence to enhance audit quality

7 describe the essential disciplinary measures for auditors.

PROFESSIONAL STATEMENTS

Australian		International	
ASA 200	*Overall Objectives of the Independent Auditor and the Conduct of an Audit in Accordance with Australian Auditing Standards*	**ISA 200**	*Overall Objectives of the Independent Auditor and the Conduct of an Audit in Accordance with International Standards on Auditing*
ASA 220	*Quality Control for an Audit of a Financial Report and Other Historical Financial Information*	**ISA 220**	*Quality Control for an Audit of Financial Statements*
ASA 700	*Forming an Opinion and Reporting on a Financial Report*	**ISA 700**	*Forming an Opinion and Reporting on Financial Statements*
APES 110	*Code of Ethics for Professional Accountants*	*Code of Ethics for Professional Accountants*	
APES 205	*Conformity with Accounting Standards*		
APES 210	*Conformity with Auditing and Assurance Standards*		
APES 220	*Taxation Services*		
APES 305	*Terms of Engagement*		
APES 315	*Compilation of Financial Information*		
APES 320	*Quality Control for Firms*	**ISQC 1**	*Quality Control for Firms that Perform Audits and Reviews of Financial Statements, and Other Assurance and Related Services Engagements*
ASQC1	*Quality Control for Firms that Perform Audits and Reviews of Financial Reports and Other Financial Information, and Other Assurance Engagements*	**ISQC 1**	*Quality Control for Firms that Perform Audits and Reviews of Financial Statements, and Other Assurance and Related Services Engagements*

SCENE SETTER

Accountants to help tax avoidance?[1]

A scathing United Kingdom parliamentary report into the role of the big four accounting firms in aiding tax avoidance has triggered calls for an Australian-based inquiry.

The report found the firms reaped $16.5 billion globally in helping clients to slash tax bills, but local firms are quick to highlight the differences between the Australian and UK markets and the lack of a similar concern here.

The report of the UK House of Commons Committee of Public Accounts noted that the big four accountancy firms make US$24.7 billion on tax work worldwide each year, of which a half to two-thirds comes from advising companies and individuals on how to minimise their tax.

It concluded there was no clarity over where the firms draw the line between acceptable tax planning and aggressive tax avoidance.

(continued)

Taxing tales
Scale of the big four firms' tax practice, 2011–12 ($m)

	PwC	Deloitte	Ernst & Young	KPMG
Global revenue from tax practice ($US)	7944	5900	6011	4860
Australian revenue from tax practice ($A)	335	n/a	346	212
Portion of Australian turnover %	23	n/a	31	19

Total global revenue from tax practice: $US 24.7bn

Source: UK House of Commons Committee of Public Accountant, Australian Firms.

'The four firms stated that they would no longer engage in some of the schemes they devised 10 years ago, such as cases they have lost in court,' it said.

'We heard about the guidelines that firms have to govern their tax advice, but they are still devising complex schemes that look artificial and their appetite for risk appears high — selling schemes that they consider only have a 50 per cent chance of being upheld in court.'

The big four firms agreed that the international tax rules were out of date and needed updating to reflect the reality of modern business, as well as agreeing that greater transparency was needed.

The Tax Justice Network's Mark Zirnsak said the report sounded a real alarm about firm culture.

'If this is what's being found out in the UK operations, why would we automatically assume that the culture of their Australian operations would be any different?' he asked.

The inquiry found that firms had trouble distinguishing between advising on tax planning and aggressive tax schemes; a finding that disturbed Mr Zirnsak.

'They've been put on notice to really demonstrate that their business is about helping clients tax-plan and not aggressive tax avoidance.'

But Mr Zirnsak said the UK branches admitted the tax rules were inadequate and greater transparency was needed and that was great, and something their Australian counterparts should admit. 'It's interesting given the position here — why is the UK branch happy to accept greater transparency when their Australian counterparts aren't?' he queried.

Mr Zirnsak said he had no doubt the firms were under huge pressure from some clients — those with an appetite for the risk — to minimise tax bills.

'I've got no doubt some of these clients would say, 'If you don't do it, I'll go down the road and find someone who will'.

'An ethical firm needs to say, "Well, go down the road then".'

At the same time, there were companies willing to operate within the law, he added.

Mr Zirnsak said that given the UK findings, 'a similar inquiry here in Australia would not be unwarranted'.

The scope of such an inquiry should include whether the level of confidentiality that applies in Australia, preventing the release of key tax information by the revenue authority, was justified.

This month the UK branch of Ernst & Young released a report on transparency, calling on clients to review their additional reporting and seize the initiative on disclosure.

'We feel that a tipping point has been reached, with many organisations now sensing that greater tax transparency reporting will become expected and more routine,' the report on transparency notes, calling increased transparency 'inevitable'.

'The debate around "fair tax" has raised the bar in terms of the expectations of the level of tax information provided by multinational companies and we expect the response will be a greater degree of disclosure by many organisations.'

Source: K Walsh, 'PwC: Australia not like the UK on tax avoidance', *Australian Financial Review*, 16 May 2013.

One of the distinguishing characteristics of any profession is the existence of a code of professional conduct or ethics for its members. CPA Australia and the Institute of Chartered Accountants in Australia (ICAA) originally established a Joint Code of Professional Conduct in 1997. In February 2006, the professional accounting bodies in Australia set up the Accounting Professional & Ethical Standards Board (APESB), which established the *Code of Ethics for Professional Accountants* (the Code of Ethics), based on the International Federation of Accountants (IFAC) *Code of Ethics for Professional Accountants*, for the implementation of force of law auditing standards on 1 July 2006.[2] The latest amended *Code of Ethics for Professional Accountants* (APES 110) was compiled in December 2011 with an update in May 2013, taking into account revised definitions of the public interest and independence.

Ethical behaviour requires consideration of more than regulatory activities and rules of conduct. The above scene setter shows the subjectivity in judgements where it is impossible to rely solely on rules or regulations. Professional accounting firms offer professional services while at the same time have the duty to protect the public interest. No professional code of ethics or regulatory framework can anticipate all the situations for which personal judgement on ethical behaviour is required. Accordingly, this chapter begins with a brief discussion of the role of professional accountants, and then examines the profession's code, with an emphasis on the organisation of a public accounting practice.

Given its significance, professional **independence** is treated as a stand-alone topic, considered separately from the general discussion on professional ethics. To understand the significance of the ethical values of accountants, the key principles of the Code of Ethics are discussed. The chapter concludes with a discussion of the ethics enforcement procedures (such as investigation and discipline) and quality assurance.

This chapter focuses on a conceptual framework approach in examining threats and safeguards for the compliance of professional ethics as proposed by the APESB and the International Ethics Standards Board for Accountants (IESBA) (formerly the Ethics Committee of IFAC).[3]

Students should study this chapter in conjunction with the detailed provisions of the Code of Ethics. The key principles of **professional ethics** are discussed in this chapter. For the purpose of understanding professional ethics and conduct, the term 'professional accountants' includes auditors and the term 'professional independence' includes the concept of audit independence (unless otherwise stated).

LEARNING objective 1

Explain the role and duties of the professional accountant.

3.1 THE ROLE OF THE PROFESSIONAL ACCOUNTANT

This section describes the role of an accountant as a professional and an individual. First, we discuss the concept of a profession to identify some characteristics and skills that differentiate professionals from non-professionals, and to provide a context for understanding the role of a professional accountant. The fiduciary relationships involved in the performance of professional services (accounting, auditing and assurance) are examined, with the altruistic purpose of benefiting society as a whole. We discuss accountants' duties and examine the significance of the ethical values raised.

3.1.1 The concept of a profession

Much has been written about the professionalism of accountants.[4] To distinguish professional occupations from those that are not, Greenwood[5] outlines five attributes of a profession: (1) a systematic body of theory, (2) authority, (3) community sanction,

(4) ethical codes and (5) a culture. Greenwood stresses, however, that the true difference between a professional and a non-professional is not a qualitative difference but a quantitative one, because non-professionals also possess these five attributes to a lesser degree. The various occupations in society can be said to distribute themselves along a continuum, with the well-organised and undisputed professions at one end displaying these identified attributes to the maximum extent.

The skills that characterise a profession flow from, and are supported by, a body of knowledge that has been organised into systematic theories or propositions that form the basis of and rationalise complex operations. Preparation for a profession requires not only intellectual cultivation, but also practical experience. This preparation takes the form of formal education in an academic setting. In Australia, accounting degrees are accredited by the two professional accounting bodies and satisfy the body of knowledge required for the profession to discharge its social role. However, society in general is subordinate to a professional's expertise, providing the professional with an authority to exercise professional judgement in specific spheres. Under normal circumstances, the professional is subject only to peer scrutiny.

The professional authority expresses itself in the client–professional relationship, although there are ramifications. A profession strives to obtain community approval within certain spheres in the form of a series of powers and privileges, reinforced from time to time by the community's regulatory power. The powers and privileges sanctioned by the community include the profession's control over its accrediting process, its control over its licensing system, and the privileges of confidentiality and a relative immunity from community judgement on technical matters. The profession continues to assure society of its benefits, to maintain its authority and monopoly. A profession's benefit to society is demonstrated by its superior performance in fulfilling a highly competent and sophisticated role in the society.

The monopoly enjoyed by a profession vis-à-vis its clients and the community is fraught with hazards; for example, a monopoly may be abused as a result of self-interest. To counter the hazards, a profession normally has a built-in regulatory code, partly formal and partly informal, to compel ethical behaviour on the part of its members. The formal part is the written code by which the individual usually swears to abide on admission to the profession. Through its ethical code, the profession's commitment to social welfare becomes a matter of **public interest**, thereby helping to ensure the continued confidence of society. **Self-regulatory** codes are characteristic of all occupations. However, a professional code is more explicit, systematic and binding; it possesses altruistic overtones and is more public-service oriented. The specifics of ethical codes are generally described in terms of both client–professional and colleague–colleague relations. Also, a profession generally enforces observation of its ethical code through controlling measures designed to engender self-discipline. Professional associations exercise these controls. In Australia, the ethical requirements for auditors under s. 227A of the *Australian Securities and Investments Commission Act 2001* and s. 336 of the *Corporations Act 2001* — as amended by the *Corporate Law Economic Reform Program (Audit Reform and Corporate Disclosure) Act 2004* (CLERP 9 Act) — have the force of law.

Every profession operates within a framework of formal and informal groups. The formal groups include the organisations within which the profession performs its services (e.g. the professional firms), the organisations that supply the talent and expand the body of knowledge (e.g. the universities and research centres), and the professional bodies that emerge as a focus of common interests and aims. The informal groups are all the other affiliations, selective and specific subgroups and units to which the professional is attached. The interactions of social roles required by these formal and informal groups generate a social configuration unique to the profession — namely, a professional culture. A professional culture distinguishes itself from a non-professional culture through its values, norms and symbols of practice. The professional value is the belief that the profession provides a service to society as a social good which benefits the community. The norms of a professional group form for its members both guides to behaviour in social situations and role definitions. The controlling values, behavioural norms and symbols of practice distinguish the profession from non-professional occupations. IFAC defines a profession's characteristics as:

- mastery of a particular intellectual skill acquired by training and education
- adherence to a common code of values and conduct
- acceptance of a duty to society as a whole.

The concept of a profession thus revolves around the five elements previously discussed. In relation to this concept, Brooks and Dunn[6] identify the duties of a profession as including the maintenance of (1) competence in the field of expertise and knowledge, (2) integrity in client dealings, (3) objectivity in the offering of services, (4) confidentiality in client matters and (5) discipline over members who do not discharge these duties according to public expectations. These duties are vital to the quality of service provided by the professional in maintaining a proper fiduciary relationship with clients. The client, in turn, trusts or relies on the professional's judgement and expertise. The maintenance of such trust or credibility inherent in the fiduciary relationship is fundamental to the role of a professional person.

3.1.2 The duties of a professional accountant

The credibility of an accountant's services is founded on the values, norms and symbols displayed by accountants in the performance of their duties. Such duties involve not only the exercise of competence in the technical aspects of financial services, but also, more importantly, integrity and objectivity in discharging these services.

Consistent with Greenwood's proposition, the accounting profession has features that accord with each of the five attributes he identified. It has an established body of knowledge in financial theories and conceptual framework; it has organised bodies to exercise its authority in the discharge of services to the public; it maintains community approval concerning its control over membership and accreditation; it has a self-regulatory framework through its pronouncements and ethical codes; and it attains a high image in society through its professional culture. A professional accountant, whether engaged in auditing or management, or as an employee or a consultant, is expected to be both an accountant and a professional. That means professional accountants are expected to have special technical expertise associated with accounting and an understanding of related fields (such as law, management, economics, taxation, information technology, systems development and quantitative methods) that exceeds that of the layperson. In addition, they are expected to adhere to the general professional duties and values described above, as well as to those specific standards established by the professional body to which they belong. Sometimes an isolated deviation from these expected norms can result in a lack of credibility for, or confidence in, the entire profession. In the past decade or so, and more so in recent years, the spate of corporate collapses and the considerable number of allegations made against accountants and auditors have resulted in a credibility crisis for the profession, triggering public enquiries into the affairs of the profession in general.

Brooks and Dunn consider that the accounting profession has the duties, rights and values detailed below — each of which is also attributable to a professional accountant.

- Duties to sustain a fiduciary relationship:
  - display behaviour that espouses responsible values
  - pay continual attention to the requirements of clients and other stakeholders

- acquire and maintain the required skills and knowledge
- maintain a credible reputation for the profession
- maintain an acceptable personal reputation.
- Rights allowed:
  - to represent oneself as a professional
  - to be involved in the development of accounting and audit practice
  - to establish entrance standards and examine candidates
  - to require self-regulation and discipline of members of the profession based on specified codes of conduct
  - to have access to certain or all areas of accounting and auditing activity.
- Values required to carry out duties and maintain rights:
  - honesty
  - integrity
  - wish to exercise due care
  - objectivity
  - confidentiality
  - competence
  - a commitment to put the needs of the public, the client, the profession and the employer ahead of any self-interest.

LEARNING 2 objective

Discuss the basic ethical principles for auditors.

3.2 PROFESSIONAL ETHICS AND THE ACCOUNTANT

Ethics is concerned with the evaluation of choices where the options are not clear or where there is no absolute right or wrong answer. The study and practice of ethics are important to enable an accountant to examine critically a situation in which there is a conflict of loyalties and interests, involving issues that relate to roles and responsibilities, both as an individual and a professional. Mintz[7] goes one step further in his perception of ethics. He sees it as a system or code of conduct based on moral duties and obligations that include how one should behave; this code deals with the ability to distinguish right from wrong and the commitment to do what is right. He also defines professionalism as the conduct, aims or qualities that characterise a professional person. The fundamental ethical characteristics required of professional accountants are competence, objectivity and integrity. Although some may regard professional ethics as largely the written code of ethics put forward by a professional body, the practice of ethical behaviour requires:

- an understanding of ethical issues
- a framework within which a responsible decision can be made
- an awareness of the consequences of such decisions.

3.2.1 An understanding of ethics and ethical issues

The word 'ethics' is derived from the Greek word *ethos*, meaning 'character'. Whereas morality focuses on the 'good' and 'bad' of human behaviour, ethics focuses on what is 'right' and 'wrong', and how and why people act in a certain manner. It focuses on a study of choices, standards and behaviour. However, morality and ethics are often used interchangeably, as is the case in this chapter.

One of the ways to achieve a proper understanding of ethics is to consider the kind of issues that ethics can cover. The range of issues is extremely broad. However, there is one question, above all others, which defines the area of concern. This is the question asked by the ancient Greek philosopher Socrates: 'What ought one to do?'

This question not only is practical, but also can relate to every aspect of life. For example, you may be required to make a practical choice, a sensible response, or a justifiable decision. Such a scenario might involve you as assistant accountant discovering that your immediate supervisor has been inflating expense claims, or coming across an accounting treatment which you suspect was adopted to arrive at some misleading income figure. In making your decision, you will need to consider the essential elements of what is right, based on the facts of the scenario, any principles and obligations you have to observe, the consequences of your choice on others, and whether you ultimately feel convinced that it is the right decision. Ethical theories and codes provide the bases for the development and understanding of principles and obligations. Ethicists have also developed ethical decision-making models for analysing situations to help individuals arrive at a responsible decision in a systematic manner.

The following are some of the key ethical theories commonly discussed in social science.

- **Teleology** or consequentialism. Teleology (consequentialism) considers actions or behaviour according to the consequences of that behaviour. An action is right because it produces some specified type of consequence, i.e. welfare, wealth, happiness, pleasure or knowledge. Moral appraisal of an action involves judging how well that behaviour produces the relevant consequences. The most common form of consequentialism is **utilitarianism**, a theory expounded by Jeremy Bentham (1748–1832). Bentham's guiding principle was that the ethically right thing to do is the action that produces more utility (benefits) than other acts. Under utilitarianism, individuals do not merely look to their own pleasure, but are concerned with maximising pleasure for all. John Stuart Mill (1806–1873), Bentham's protégé, modified the theory by recognising different human characteristics rather than placing equal value on 'pleasures' as goals. Modern utilitarianism takes into account stakeholders' interests and preferences, and an ethically right decision gives the maximum amount of benefits which accord with the interests of the greatest number of stakeholders. Utilitarianism is, however, criticised for its oversimplification in recognising and measuring benefits and for its identification of stakeholders.

  Consequentialism identifies the moral worth of conduct in terms of how well that conduct produces some effect. It has a 'forward-looking' rationale in determining what one ought to do. This 'forward-looking' approach contrasts with deontology, as described below.

- **Deontology** or non-consequentialism. Deontology refers to the past or the present. According to deontological ethics, an action is right because of the process, i.e. the intention, rather than its outcome. For example, an action is right because it keeps a promise that one made (backward-looking or past orientation) or because one's duty is to be honest, which is simply the 'right thing to do' (present). Immanuel Kant (1724–1804), a German philosopher, had the view that morality is a matter of doing one's duty, regardless of consequences, and that one must be consistent and carry out one's duties under all circumstances. Morality and rationality are closely connected with logical consistency.

  Kant's 'categorical imperative' contains two key maxims or intentions. The first is 'act only according to that principle by which you can, at the same time, will that it should become a universal law'. The second is 'act so that you treat humanity, whether in your own person or in that of another, always as an end and never as a means only'. Kant's theory of duty is not about following an imposed list of duties, but about being autonomous and rational agents who make choices for which they are responsible. Nor is it about achieving certain satisfactory consequences as in consequentialism. Kant's theory provides an intellectual justification for the golden rule (treat others as you would wish to be treated). His arguments demand universality, consistency and reversibility.

Justice and fairness are also related to deontology. John Rawls[8] argued in 1971 that each person in the same environment has an equal right to the most extensive liberty compatible with any other person. He also stated that inequalities are arbitrary unless it is reasonable to expect that they will produce advantages for everyone, and that the opportunities are accessible by all. Rawls's justice and fairness are the basis of the concepts of corporate social responsibility in modern business. Corporate social responsibility is based on the concept of social contract. Corporations exist with the consent of society; thus they have a responsibility to society, sharing its burdens and benefits, and contributing to continuous mutual existence.

Teleology and deontology are normative ethical theories, i.e. what *ought* to be.

- **Virtue ethics**. Virtue ethics is a concept of ethics which stresses the ability of a person to act morally based on his or her character, rather than having to deal with a problem by consciously and conscientiously applying some moral theories in a systematic or mechanical way. Applying ethical theories is seen as adopting an 'outside-in' approach, whereas a virtue-ethics view sees the process as 'inside-out'. Moral behaviour is a natural result of one's character. One can argue that virtue ethics is the basis of the notion that any code of ethics should be 'owned' by all members of an organisation before it can be effective, i.e. a moral position that emanates from within. Thus ethics is not just a matter of what people do; it is a matter of what people are. Virtue ethics covers human qualities such as courage, honesty and loyalty.

- **Ethical relativism**. Ethical relativism is a view that moral values are relative to a particular environment. Particular moral values are not universal and therefore are not absolute. 'When in Rome, do as the Romans do' — because the Romans are the correct moral judges for behaviour in Rome. Relativism is opposite to universality, but it does not stand as an alternative to utilitarianism or deontology. Ethical relativism is, rather, a view about the domain over which any moral position ranges.

Relativism in business is most often discussed where international business practices are concerned. There is a considerable amount of literature on moral relativism. However, it is important to note that tolerating cultural differences does not mean being indifferent to ethical principles. Although specific rules might differ from culture to culture, those specific rules are, nevertheless, grounded in the same basic principles. Respect for a host culture does not include excuses for inducements, secret commissions and bribes. One test is that people should not be ashamed of their actions, wherever they practise. This concept also explains the existence of company policies about gifts and hospitality. Relativism is not synonymous with ignoring one's own moral values.

Business exists not because it suits certain individuals but because it serves society, and it meets collective and individual needs. Free markets are a matter of choice but, from time to time, societies require regulations and rules to cover matters such as maximum utility, justice and fairness. Corporate social responsibility is now seen to be one of the key factors by which responsible businesses can secure public interest.

Principle 3 of the Australian Securities Exchange (ASX) *Corporate Governance Principles and Recommendations* states that companies should not only comply with their legal obligations, but also consider the reasonable expectations of their stakeholders — shareholders, employees, customers, suppliers, creditors, customers and the broader community in which they operate. It recommends that companies clarify the standards of ethical behaviour required of the board, senior executives and all employees and encourage the observance of those standards.[9] Ethics and governance in business are recognised as key criteria in assessing the performance of organisations. Good ethics is good business.

However, ethics in business is complex. **Ethical issues** are situations where individuals have to make a choice from unclear and complex alternatives, where each alternative may be the right choice according to a specific moral position or viewpoint. As an example, in a case of an assistant accountant who discovers the inflated expenses claim made by the immediate supervisor, the assistant accountant will either 'please' the supervisor by being compliant, thus avoiding trouble, or report the practice to management in order to correct the situation, in pursuit of honesty and professional integrity. The former action derives from self-interest, which is a consequentialist approach; the latter action pursues fairness and justice, a deontological approach. The process of determination involves a careful assessment of facts, alternatives, consequences, principles and one's own moral beliefs. This is an ethical-decision-making process.

Individuals develop their ethical beliefs through a complex process of socialisation in formal and informal groups such as the family, schools, universities and clubs. These are moral communities which have their own values, rules and norms. The moral knowledge acquired while in these communities tends to be intuitive and, as a result, individuals may display inconsistent ethical behaviour and make different decisions under different circumstances. Ethics provide a framework of beliefs and a reasoned and systematic analysis of decisions to help individuals acquire the skills and insights necessary for ethical decision making.

Recent studies have further broadened the concepts of ethics and trust in the accountability structures of organisations through the theory and application of emotional intelligence. In practical terms, this means that high ethical standards should be enacted from the boardroom down. These standards include openness and transparency, with a genuine concern for others and abandonment of the unnecessary culture of secrecy. They are intrinsic to social order within working environments, underlying the emotions of organisations.

Professional bodies in Australia (CPA Australia, the ICAA and the Institute of Public Accountants (IPA)) offer a broad knowledge base in their professional programs in order to cover the expanding role of an accountant and its increasing complexity. In particular, ethics are regarded as the basis for well-founded decisions and responsible behaviour. Thus, ethical-decision-making models play an important part in professional educational programs.

Ethical-decision-making models are systematic procedures designed to help people arrive at well-informed and ethical decisions under different circumstances. Where people face an ethical problem or dilemma, such models will help them tackle issues such as duties, consequences and priorities, and assess alternative actions. The most commonly used ethical-decision-making model was developed by Rockness and Langenderfer, which is also known as the AAA (American Accounting Association) model.[10] This model helps a person consider the facts of the matter, the values and principles; evaluate issues relating to the matter based on one's values and principles; identify and compare alternative courses of action; and responsibly make the decision that aligns with the most important value.

Other examples of ethical-decision-making models appropriate for businesses are as follows.
- Stakeholder impact analysis[11] (introduced by Leonard Brooks) involves identifying and ranking all stakeholder groups and their interests, evaluating the most important ones and assessing the impact of proposed actions with regard to consequences, fairness of treatment, impact on rights, and so on.
- Laura Nash's 12-question model[12] considers the ethical problem from different perspectives, and evaluates all possible causes, loyalties, intentions, stakeholders, timeframe, confidence of decision, impact and exceptional circumstances.

3.2.2 Professional ethics for accountants

Professional ethics extend beyond rules and theories. They include standards of behaviour for a professional person that are designed for both practical and idealistic purposes. In the current environment of **co-regulation**, where the government has intervened in the regulation of accountants and financial reporting matters, such as ensuring auditor independence and standard setting, professional ethics appears to be the foundation that is left in the hands of the profession. A professional accountant acts as both a responsible individual and a person who operates within a set of professional norms and values. A professional code of ethics, therefore, is designed to encourage ideal behaviour and should be both realistic and enforceable.

Students should be aware that both accounting and auditing standards have been 'internationalised'. One of the distinctive features of this book is the discussion of topics based on the latest developments both within Australia and from the IFAC pronouncements, which all member bodies (including CPA Australia, the ICAA and the IPA) have had to comply with since 2005.

The International Ethics Standards Board for Accountants (IESBA) has extended IFAC's principles-based approach to its professional ethics guidelines, covering the needs of accountants both in practice and in business. This resulted in the *Code of Ethics for Professional Accountants* (the IFAC Code), confirmed in June 2005 and revised several times since, the latest revision as *Handbook of the Code of Ethics for Professional Accountants* was published in July 2012.

IFAC's mission is the worldwide development and enhancement of an accountancy profession with harmonised standards able to provide services of consistently high quality in the public interest. The IFAC Code establishes ethical requirements for professional accountants. A member body (such as CPA Australia) or firm may not apply less stringent standards than those stated in the IFAC Code. In July 2006, the APESB of Australia released APES 110 *Code of Ethics for Professional Accountants* (the Code of Ethics) which replaced the Joint Code of Professional Conduct established by CPA Australia and the ICAA. APES 110 has been revised several times to take into account changes in the IFAC Code. The latest revision was made in May 2013 with the amendments being effective in July 2013.

The main features of the APESB Code of Ethics (APES 110) are:
- the numbering system conforms with that of the IFAC Code
- the wording of the IFAC Code has been used for the most part
- where certain paragraphs of the Code of Ethics have no equivalent paragraphs in the IFAC Code, they have been identified as Australian paragraphs by inserting the letters AUST before the paragraph number.

LEARNING 3
objective

Explain the conceptual principles of the Code of Ethics for Professional Accountants.

3.2.3 The *Code of Ethics for Professional Accountants*

In this section, we discuss APES 110 the *Code of Ethics for Professional Accountants* (the Code of Ethics), issued by the APESB.

The Code of Ethics has three parts. Part A (Sections 100–150) provides an introduction and fundamental principles that are applicable to all professional accountants. It also provides a conceptual framework for applying the fundamental principles. Part B (Sections 200–291) applies to professional accountants in public practice. It contains the most important aspect of the ethical requirements for professional accountants in public practice, namely, independence for assurance engagements, discussed in Section 290. Part C (Sections 300–350) applies to professional accountants in business, and looks at cases where potential conflicts arise in business organisations. Parts B and C illustrate how the conceptual framework described in Part A is applied in specific situations. A section on definitions follows the three parts.

The revised Code maintains the principles-based approach supplemented by detailed requirements where necessary, resulting in a Code that is robust but also sufficiently flexible to address the wide-ranging circumstances encountered by professional accountants.[13]

The Code of Ethics provides a conceptual framework of fundamental principles for professional accountants to enable them to identify, evaluate and respond to threats to compliance with such principles. It is believed that a rules-based approach fails to cover all situations and may lead to unquestioning obedience to the letter of a rule while setting definitive lines in legislation that some will try to circumvent.

Fundamental principles applicable to all professional accountants

The accounting profession worldwide is characterised by its intention to achieve a common set of objectives, which establishes high-quality standards of behaviour. The Code of Ethics reiterates the accounting profession's responsibility to act in the public interest. Professional accountants have a responsibility to satisfy not only clients or employers exclusively but in acting in the public interest, a professional accountant should observe and comply with the ethical requirements of the Code of Ethics. The International Federation of Accountants (IFAC) defines the public interest as the net benefits derived for, and procedural rigor employed on behalf of, all society in relation to any action, decision or policy. In the IFAC Policy Position paper 5 the IFAC also advocates that the public includes every aspect of society; that is, investors, consumers, suppliers, citizens and taxpayers, as well as those seeking sustainable living standards and environmental quality, for themselves and future generations.[14] The extent to which any particular group is impacted can vary according to the action, decision or policy taken. To determine the impact, assessments can involve critical examination of cost, benefits, and the adequacy of the process. IFAC considers that the definition and assessment possess relevance to the wider accounting profession for the determination of a number of accounting issues such as the quality of financial reporting, professional standards, regulation, and corporate governance, including licensing of accountants and professional liability reforms.

The Code of Ethics adopts the following approach.

- The public interest is the overriding responsibility. Fundamental principles include integrity, objectivity, professional competence and due care, confidentiality and professional behaviour. All fundamental principles are equally valid for all professional accountants.
- For each fundamental principle, a conceptual framework is used to identify the possible threats and safeguards.
- Threats include self-interest, self-review, advocacy, familiarity and intimidation. Self-interest threats may occur as a result of the financial or other interests of a professional accountant or of an immediate or close family member. Self-review threats may occur when a previous judgement needs to be re-evaluated by the professional accountant responsible for that judgement. Advocacy threats may occur when a professional accountant promotes a position or opinion to the point that subsequent objectivity may be compromised. Familiarity threats may occur when, because of a close relationship, a professional accountant becomes too sympathetic to the interests of others. Intimidation threats may occur when an accountant may be deterred from acting objectively by threats, actual or perceived.
- Safeguards may eliminate or reduce threats to an acceptable level. Safeguards can be those created by the profession, legislation or regulation, and those implemented in the workplace.
- Safeguards created by the profession, legislation or regulation include:
  - educational, training and experience requirements for entry
  - continuing professional development requirements

- corporate or other governance regulations
- professional standards and pronouncements
- the monitoring and disciplinary procedures of professional and other regulatory bodies
- external review by a legal party of the reports and returns or other communications of a professional accountant.

- Professional accountants should consider both quantitative and qualitative factors when determining the significance of any potential threat. If safeguards cannot be implemented, professional accountants should decline or discontinue the specific service involved. Evaluation of any threats should be done as soon as the accountant is aware of the threat or circumstances that might compromise compliance with the fundamental principles.
- The nature of the safeguards to be applied varies with the circumstances in which the threats arise. Professional accountants should exercise professional judgement, i.e. what a reasonable and informed third party, having the knowledge of all relevant factors and the significance of the threats and the safeguards applied, would consider unacceptable.
- Part A's fundamental principles are somewhat repeated in Parts B and C for the purpose of providing examples of circumstances of threats and safeguards for professional accountants in public practice and in business.

A very important aspect of Part A is the inclusion of ethical conflict resolution for all professional accountants. The APESB recognises the possibility of significant ethical issues faced by professional accountants, and recommends that professional accountants should follow established policies of the firm, employing organisation or the national professional body to resolve ethical issues. The APESB also makes use of the concept of an ethical-decision-making model and suggests that an ethical conflict resolution process should include:

- identifying and obtaining all relevant facts and information
- evaluating the ethical issues involved
- assessing the relevant fundamental principles applicable to the situation
- establishing internal procedures
- reviewing alternative courses of action and their consequences
- determining the best course of action that is consistent with the fundamental principles. Where the issue remains unresolved, other appropriate people within the firm or the employing organisation should be approached for help.

The APESB also recommends that if there is a conflict with or within an organisation, professional accountants should meet with the **audit committee** or any party representing the governance body of the organisation. Alternatively, professional accountants may consult the professional body to obtain some ethics guidance without breaching confidentiality. The APESB recommends that the professional bodies should use their best endeavours to provide a basis on which a member's concerns can be discussed, objectively and in confidence. Members may also seek legal advice. In all circumstances, the professional accountant should document the substance of the issue and the details of any relevant discussions held. Professional accountants are advised to consider withdrawing from association with the matter should it remain unresolved.

Threats and safeguards — professional accountants in public practice

Part B of the Code of Ethics for professional accountants in public practice (Sections 200–291) applies the conceptual framework in the form of possible threats to the compliance with fundamental principles, and likely safeguards that can be adopted by professional accountants to reduce or eliminate such threats:

- Section 200 Introduction
- Section 210 Professional Appointment
- Section 220 Conflicts of Interest
- Section 230 Second Opinions
- Section 240 Fees and Other Types of Remuneration
- Section 250 Marketing Professional Services
- Section 260 Gifts and Hospitality
- Section 270 Custody of Client Assets
- Section 280 Objectivity — All Services
- Section 290 Independence — Audit and Review Engagements
- Section 291 Independence — Other Assurance Engagements.

A professional accountant in public practice should not knowingly engage in any business, occupation or activity that impairs or might impair integrity, objectivity or the good reputation of the profession, which as a result would be incompatible with the rendering of professional services. A business or activity is incompatible with the provision of professional services if it creates a conflict of interest with existing clients, or impairs or would impair the integrity, objectivity or (to a material extent) the ability of the accountant to practise or the reputation of the profession.

Table 3.1 (overleaf) summarises the key threats and safeguards as they apply to professional accountants in public practice. Part B of the Code of Ethics examines, with examples, the threats faced by practising accountants and proposes a number of safeguards.

Safeguards that may be used by professional accountants to reduce or eliminate the threats fall into four categories:

1. safeguards created by the profession, by legislation or by regulation
2. safeguards developed by the firm, including:
   - firm leadership that emphasises compliance and ethics
   - quality control and review policies for all client engagements
   - policies and procedures that ensure all relationships or interests are disclosed
   - using different partners and teams with separate reporting lines for the provision of non-assurance services to an assurance client
   - senior management oversight of the safeguarding system
   - disciplinary mechanisms
   - timely communication of policies and procedures to all partners and professional staff
3. safeguards that are engagement-specific, including:
   - professional review by other professional accountants
   - consulting third parties such as the audit committee or a regulatory body
   - partner and senior personnel rotation
   - discussing ethical issues with those in charge of client governance
   - disclosure of fees
   - involving another firm to perform or re-perform part of the engagement
4. safeguards within the client's systems, including:
   - appointment of an independent firm to ratify the engagement
   - competence of employees
   - internal procedures to ensure objective decisions on engagements
   - proper corporate governance structure with appropriate oversight and communications.

TABLE 3.1: Threats to compliance with the Code of Ethics by professional accountants in public practice

Type of threats	Examples
Self-interest	• Financial interest in a client where the result of the professional services may affect the value of that interest • Loans to or from an assurance client • Concern about possibility of losing a recurring client • Potential employment with a client • Inappropriate marketing of professional services • Acceptance of clients with illegal dealings or questionable issues • Accepting an engagement without the necessary competence or specialised knowledge required to carry out the engagement • Temptation to accept gifts offered by client • Conflict of interest such as performing services which are incompatible for the same client • Competing directly with client or having joint ventures with major competitors of client posing objectivity threat
Self-review	• Discovery of a significant error in a re-evaluation • Reporting on systems where the professional accountant has been involved in their design or implementation • A member of the engagement team being or having recently been a director or officer of the client, or employed in an executive position by the client (with direct influence on the assurance matter)
Advocacy	• Promoting shares in a listed audit client • Acting as an advocate on behalf of an assurance client in resolving disputes with third parties
Familiarity	• Close or immediate family relationship with a director or officer of a client or with an employee who has a position of influence over the subject matter of the engagement (applies to any member of the engagement team) • A former partner of the firm being a director or officer of the client, or an employee with direct and significant influence over the subject matter of the assurance engagement • Accepting gifts or preferential treatment, unless the value is clearly insignificant
Intimidation	• Being threatened with dismissal or replacement in a client engagement • Being threatened with litigation • Being pressured to reduce the extent of work required in order to reduce fees • Accepting a gift with the possibility of it subsequently being made public
Public practice behaviour	• Inappropriate marketing of professional services and products • Acceptance of inappropriate clients — client involved in illegal acts, client with questionable issues

Source: Information from APES 110 *Code of Ethics for Professional Accountants*, Part B, Sections 200–291, as at December 2011.

The Code of Ethics also highlights some of the matters which may give rise to a conflict of interest. Professional accountants should evaluate the significance of threats to objectivity before accepting or continuing with specific engagements. Some additional safeguards include clear guidelines for engagement personnel on issues of security and confidentiality and regular review of client engagements. Also, a professional accountant who is asked to replace another professional accountant, or who is considering tendering for an engagement, should determine whether there is any professional or other reason for not accepting the engagement. In changes of professional engagement, there must be direct communication with the existing accountant to establish all relevant facts and circumstances leading to the change. As the existing accountant is bound by confidentiality, the extent to which the client's affairs can be discussed with the proposed accountant depends on the nature of the engagement, and on factors such as whether the client's permission to disclose information has been given, or whether there are any legal or ethical requirements relating to the communication and disclosure.

In some instances, professional accountants are asked to provide a written opinion on the application of accounting principles and standards to a specific circumstance or transaction by or on behalf of a company that is not an existing client. This second opinion or **opinion shopping** may pose threats to professional competence and due care. If the company does not permit the professional accountant to communicate with the existing accountant, he or she should consider whether it is appropriate to provide the opinion sought.

Regarding fees, professional accountants may quote an appropriate fee when entering into negotiations for an engagement. However, a self-interest threat may arise when fees are quoted so low that it is difficult to perform the engagement satisfactorily. Safeguards to be considered include:
- making clients aware of the terms of the engagement and, in particular, the basis on which the fees are charged
- assigning appropriate time and qualified staff to the task.

Threats and safeguards — professional accountants in business

Professional accountants in business include those who are salaried employees, partners, directors (whether executive or non-executive), owner–managers and volunteer workers, regardless of whether they have a legal form of relationship with the employing organisation. The Code of Ethics recognises that the work of a professional accountant in business is relied on by investors, creditors, employers and other sectors of the business community. Professional accountants in business may be solely or jointly responsible for the preparation and reporting of financial and other information. The Code of Ethics does not seek to hinder professional accountants' responsibilities to their employers, but it examines circumstances of possible conflict with their absolute duty to comply with the fundamental principles.

Part C of the Code of Ethics (Sections 300–350) deals with professional accountants in business:
- Section 300 Introduction
- Section 310 Potential Conflicts
- Section 320 Preparation and Reporting of Information
- Section 330 Acting with Sufficient Expertise
- Section 340 Financial Interests
- Section 350 Inducements.

The possible threats identified by Part C of the Code of Ethics as those which may be faced by professional accountants in business are listed in table 3.2 (overleaf).

Other threats that may be faced by professional accountants in business include non-compliance regarding the preparation and reporting of financial information, inability to perform the duties with an appropriate degree of competence and due care because of timing constraints or inadequate resources, receiving offers and inducements to perform an unethical task, and threats to disclose confidential information about the employer.

TABLE 3.2:
Threats to compliance
with the Code of Ethics by
professional accountants in
business

Type of threats	Examples
Self-interest	• Financial interests, loans or guarantees • Incentive schemes entitlements • Concern over the security of the employment • Inappropriate personal use of corporate assets • Commercial pressure from outside the employing organisation
Self-review	• Business decisions or data subject to review or justification by the same person responsible for the decision
Advocacy	• Commenting publicly on future events where outcomes are doubtful or information is incomplete • Acting publicly as an advocate for a position where bias may arise
Familiarity	• A person who can influence financial or non-financial reporting decisions having a relationship with someone who may benefit from the influence • Long association with business contacts influencing decisions • Acceptance of gifts or preferential treatment unless the value is clearly insignificant
Intimidation	• Threats of dismissal or replacement due to disagreement about an accounting treatment • A dominant personality attempting to influence business decisions

Source: Information extracted from APES 110 *Code of Ethics for Professional Accountants*, Part C, Sections 300–350, as at December 2011.

The safeguards proposed by the Code of Ethics are those that are created by the profession, by law or by regulation, and those that are developed within the workplace. The latter include:

- corporate oversight structures
- corporate ethics and conduct programs
- recruitment procedures for high-calibre staff
- strong internal controls and disciplinary processes
- leadership and transparency
- adequate training and education of employees
- procedures and policies to empower staff and encourage communication with senior staff on ethical issues.

Professional accountants in business may also encounter other specific conflicts. They may be under pressure to act contrary to the law, regulations or professional standards, especially where issues relate to financial statements, tax compliance, legal compliance or reports to the securities authorities. Safeguards should be used to reduce such threats by obtaining advice where appropriate, either from within the organisation, from an independent adviser or from the relevant professional body. It is also advisable for the organisation to have a formal dispute resolution process. Legal advice may be sought if necessary.

LEARNING 4
objective
Describe the regulatory and conceptual framework of professional independence and the key guidelines.

3.3 PROFESSIONAL INDEPENDENCE

Independence is the cornerstone of the auditing profession. Ethical situations exist when accountants are faced with situations in which they may compromise their professional integrity in response to outside pressures. An auditor may be pressured by management to compromise his or her objectivity in deciding on an accounting policy, for example, or an accountant may be instructed by a superior to amend financial statements so as to show a profitable return. Many of the ethical situations faced by accountants and auditors involve professional judgement, objectivity and independence.

Without independence, the auditor's opinion is suspect. In relation to auditing and other attestation services, independence has two facets — the fact of independence (also called actual independence) and the appearance of independence (also called perceived independence). The fact of independence depends on the auditor's integrity, objectivity and strength of character, which are defined as follows.

- *Integrity* implies the observance of accepted standards of honesty that must form the basis of all professional decisions and actions.
- *Objectivity* implies that a fair and impartial attitude must be maintained, with bias not being allowed to influence one's judgement.
- *Strength of character* refers to one's ability to withstand pressure and maintain one's integrity and objectivity.

The greatest potential threat to the independence of the auditor is the auditor's relationship with the directors and management. Directors' remuneration, the value of the shares they hold and even their position within the company may all depend on the financial performance of the company. The opinion of the auditor is vital to the credibility of financial statements. Recognising this connection, directors may seek to influence the auditor. Without the strength of character to withstand such pressure, the auditor may be unable to express an independent opinion.

The fact of auditor independence is not always readily visible to those relying on the auditor's opinion; situations in which a reasonable person might consider the auditor's independence to be impaired have been criticised in the past. To ensure independence is more visible, the *Corporations Act 2001* and Part B Section 290 of the Code of Ethics stipulate principles, rules and guidelines that emphasise the need for the appearance of independence. Independence in mind can be assessed using a 'reasonable person' test, whereas independence in appearance is based on specific rules or prohibitions.

3.3.1 Statutory provisions enhancing auditors' independence

Section 307 of the Corporations Act stipulates the overriding principle adopted by the law regarding the role of the auditors. An auditor who conducts an audit of the financial report for a financial year or half-year must form an opinion about whether the financial report is in accordance with the Corporations Act, including compliance with accounting standards and showing a true and fair view of the financial state of affairs of the audited body. As the credibility of the audit opinion lies in the independence of the auditors, independence is the key aspect of the recent audit reform. The Corporations Act was updated by the *Corporate Law Economic Reform Program (Audit Reform and Corporate Disclosure) Act 2004* (CLERP 9 Act) to reflect a set of provisions concerning auditors' independence. Table 3.3 (overleaf) presents the key sections in the Corporations Act regarding the independence of auditors.

It is relevant to note that s. 324CD on conflict-of-interest situations and s. 324CH on relevant relationships are the most detailed statutory provisions regarding independence.

TABLE 3.3:
Key statutory provisions for
auditor independence in the
Corporations Act

Section	Independence provisions
Part 2G s. 250RA	Members are permitted to provide written questions to the auditor within 5 days before the AGM and the auditor is required to prepare a list of questions to the listed company and to attend the AGM.
Part 2M Div 3 s. 307C	Auditor's independence declaration — auditors must give the directors of the disclosing entities a written statement that the requirements of auditors' independence provisions of the Act have not been contravened.
Part 2M Div 6 s. 323A	Auditors have the power to obtain information from controlled entities and the controlled entities must provide information or other assistance to the auditor concerning the consolidated financial statements being audited.
Part 2M.4 Div 3 ss. 324CA, 324CB, 324CC	General requirement for auditor independence for individual auditors, members of audit firms and directors of audit companies. Auditors are required to inform ASIC regarding any conflicts of interest or ensure that such conflicts cease within 7 days of becoming aware of the situation. Detailed situations are listed for each category of auditors (i.e. individual auditors, members of audit firms, directors of audit companies) based on the table in s. 324CD.
Part 2M.4 Div 3A s. 324CD	Conflict-of-interest situations applicable for the above sections where an auditor or a professional member of the audit team becomes incapable of exercising objective and impartial judgement, with regard to the company, the managers or directors currently or formerly involved in the company and the auditor.
Part 2M.4 Div 3B ss. 324CE, 324CF, 324CG	Specific requirements for auditor independence applicable to individual auditors, audit firms and audit companies where the auditor must take all reasonable steps to ensure the audit activity is not continued or inform ASIC within 7 days of becoming aware of the situation if the situation continues. Further details are to be noted in relation to the maximum hours test for non-audit services and the independence test in these sections.
Part 2M.4 Div 3B s. 324CH	Lists the relevant relationships which may be the subject of contravention of ss. 324CE, 324CF and 324CG. These relevant relationships apply to the individual auditor, a professional member of the audit team conducting the audit of the audited body or an immediate family member of a professional member of the audit team.
Part 2M.4 Div 3B ss. 324CI, 324CJ	Special rules for retiring partners of audit firms and retiring directors of audit companies and special rules for retiring professional members of audit companies. There is a 2-year waiting period for such personnel to be engaged as an officer of the audited body.
Part 2M.4 Div 3B s. 324CK	Contravention of independence if at any time during the audit in a financial year where a person who has been or is an auditor or director of the audit company becomes an officer of the audited body, and is aware of a similar occurrence by another auditor or director of the audit company.
Part 2M.4 Div 5 s. 324DA	The limited term for eligibility to play a significant role in audit of listed companies is 5 consecutive years or 5 out of 7 consecutive years where there are 2 years when the auditor did not play a significant role.

Section	Independence provisions
Part 2M.4 Div 5 ss. 324DB, 324DC, 324DD	Rotation obligation required for individual auditors, audit firms and audit companies, in order to ensure s. 324DA is complied with.
Part 2M.4 Div 6 Sub Div A, B, C	Appointment, removal and fees of auditors for companies, including removal and resignation of auditors, fees and expenses.

Source: Various sections of the Corporations Act, available from www.comlaw.gov.au.

A conflict-of-interest situation exists if, because of circumstances:[15]

(a) the auditor, or a professional member of the audit team, is not capable of exercising objective and impartial judgment in relation to the conduct of the audit of the audited body; or

(b) a reasonable person, with full knowledge of all relevant facts and circumstances, would conclude that the auditor, or a professional member of the audit team, is not capable of exercising objective and impartial judgment in relation to the conduct of the audit of the audited body.

Consideration must be given to circumstances arising from any relationship that exists, has existed, or is likely to exist, between, on the one hand, (1) the individual auditor, (2) the audit firm or any current or former member of the firm, or (3) the audit company, any current or former director of the audit company or any person currently or formerly involved in the management of the audit company; and, on the other hand, any of the persons and bodies set out in table 3.4.

TABLE 3.4: Relevant relationships which may give rise to conflict-of-interest situations

Item	If the audited body is …	have regard to any relationship with …
1	a company	the company; or a current or former director of the company; or a person currently or formerly involved in the management of the company.
2	a disclosing entity	the entity; or a current or former director of the entity; or a person currently or formerly involved in the management of the entity.
3	a registered scheme	the responsible entity for the registered scheme; or a current or former director of the responsible entity; or a person currently or formerly involved in the management of the scheme; or a person currently or formerly involved in the management of the responsible entity.

Source: Corporations Act, s. 324CD.

In respect of specific requirements for independence, s. 324CH describes the relationships between a person/firm and the audited body that are relevant for the purposes of ss. 324CE (individual auditors), 324CF (audit firms) and 324CG (audit companies).

Sections 324CE, 324CF and 324CG incorporate the maximum hours test for non-audit services and the independence test where former professional employees are concerned.

Non-audit services providers satisfy the maximum hours test if, during the audit period, the number of hours for which they provide non-audit services to the audited body on behalf of the auditor is not more than 10 hours, and during the 12 months immediately before the beginning of the audit period the number of hours is not more than 10 hours. Any breach of these conditions must be proven by the prosecution.

In relation to a former employee or former owner of an individual auditor's business, that person satisfies the independence test if the person:
- does not influence the operations or financial policies of the accounting and audit practice conducted by the auditor
- does not participate, or appear to participate, in the business or professional activities of the accounting and audit practice conducted by the auditor
- does not have any rights against the auditor in relation to the accounting and audit practice conducted by the auditor in relation to the termination of the person's former employment
- has no financial arrangements with the auditor in relation to the accounting and audit practice conducted by the auditor, other than wage/salary payments which do not depend on the earnings of the auditor
- has no other financial arrangement with the auditor to receive a commission or similar payment.

Where an individual auditor, audit firm or audit company is the defendant in contravention of s. 324, an offence is not committed if the person has reasonable grounds to believe that, at the time of the audit activity, there was a quality control system in place that provided reasonable assurance, taking into account the size and nature of the audit practice, and that the audit firm or audit company and its employees complied with the requirements of the law.

Although shareholders have the responsibility of appointing and removing auditors and setting audit fees, approval of the auditor appointment is often based on the recommendation of the board of directors. The ASX Corporate Governance Principles recommend that the audit committee should oversee the appointment of auditors and their independence.

Although the Corporations Act has incorporated the CLERP 9 Act, it is understandable that not all ethical issues can be covered by law. For example, directors and management may place pressure on auditors to compromise their integrity and objectivity, and influence an auditor's appointment. This may also result in opinion shopping, which puts pressure on the auditor to issue an unqualified auditor's report, so as not to lose the audit to another firm. Another example is when an unrealistically low audit fee is set by an audit firm to gain new clients. This is called **low-balling** and may result in compromised standards of performance. We deal with the professional bodies' pronouncements in the following sections.

3.3.2 Independence of mind and in appearance

Members of assurance teams, firms and, where appropriate, audit companies and **network firms**,[16] must be independent of assurance clients in order to act in the public interest. An assurance engagement is intended to enhance the credibility of information about a subject matter. A professional accountant, in carrying out an assurance engagement, aims to provide a reasonable or limited level of assurance on a broad range of subject matters including financial and non-financial information. The auditor must obtain reasonable assurance as to whether the financial report taken as a whole is free from material misstatement (whether due to fraud or error) when conducting an audit in accordance with auditing standards.

The outcome of the evaluation or measurement of a subject matter is the information that results from applying the criteria to the subject matter, as described in the assurance engagement framework. Audit or review engagements may be assertion-based or direct reporting. In either case, they involve three separate parties: a professional accountant in public practice, a responsible party and intended users. In a financial report audit, which is an assertion-based assurance engagement, the evaluation or measurement of the subject matter is performed by the responsible party, and the subject matter information is in the form of an assertion by the responsible party that is made available to intended users. However, the nature of assurance engagements may differ, and consequently different threats to independence may exist, requiring the application of different safeguards. Section 290[17] of the Code of Ethics provides a detailed conceptual approach to independence. The conceptual approach to independence requires that there is independence of mind and in appearance.

Independence of mind relates to the state of mind that permits the expression of a conclusion without being affected by influences that compromise professional judgement. It requires the professional accountant to exercise scepticism and act with integrity and objectivity. *Independence in appearance* means avoiding situations and facts that are so significant that a reasonable person, knowing all relevant facts and having considered the safeguards in place, would reasonably conclude that a firm's or a professional accountant's integrity and objectivity had been impaired.

Since it is impossible that a person exercising professional judgement will not have any economic, financial or other relationships with other people, Section 290 of the Code of Ethics recommends that the significance of such relationships should be evaluated in the light of what a reasonable and informed third party, with all relevant information, would reasonably conclude as unacceptable.

3.3.3 Independence for audit and review engagements — a conceptual approach

The conceptual approach considers the public interest and requires firms and members of an audit and review engagement team to eliminate threats or to reduce them to an acceptable level by applying appropriate safeguards. The nature of the threats and the applicable safeguards differ according to the characteristics of the engagement.

Independence requirements for audit and review engagements can be summarised as follows.
- Where the engagement is provided for audit clients, the audit team, the firm and network firms must be independent of the audit client.
- Where audit and review engagements are provided for a non-audit assurance client, and the report is not restricted to specific users, the assurance team and firm must be independent of the client.
- Where audit and review engagements are provided for a non-audit assurance client, and the report is restricted to specific users, the assurance team and firm must be independent of the client, and should not have a material direct or indirect financial interest in the client.

Specific threats to audit independence

Some specific threats to an auditor's independence are discussed here. Where appropriate, some benchmarks are discussed by introducing the provisions of the US Sarbanes–Oxley Act. Provisions in the United Kingdom are similar to those in Australia. These threats are detailed in Section 290.102 to Section 290.231 of the Code of Ethics.

Financial interests

A self-interest threat may be created by a financial interest in an audit client. When evaluating whether a financial interest could compromise professional independence, several factors should be considered: the nature of the financial interest, the position of the person with the financial interest, the materiality of the financial interest, and whether it is a direct or indirect financial interest (this is based on the degree of control or influence that can be exercised).

The financial interest allowed by s. 324CH is $5000. Detailed provisions in the Code of Ethics include the various safeguards applicable to all assurance clients (including audit clients). However, if the self-interest threat created is so significant that the only safeguard available to eliminate the threat or to reduce it to an acceptable level would be to dispose of the direct financial interest before the individual becomes a member of the assurance team, then this must be done. When a firm or a member of the audit team holds a direct financial interest or a material indirect financial interest in the audit client as a trustee, such an interest should only be held when the member of the firm is not a beneficiary of the trust, or that the interest held by the trust in the audit client is not material. Where an inadvertent violation of this part of the Code of Ethics occurs, the firm should consider involving an additional professional accountant who did not take part in the engagement to review the work done by the member of the audit team, or excluding the member from any substantive decision making concerning the audit engagements.

Loans and guarantees

A loan or a guarantee of a loan by an audit client that is a financial institution to the firm or network firm does not create a threat to independence provided the loan is made under normal lending procedures, terms and requirements and the loan is immaterial to both the firm, the network firm and the audit client. Where the loan is material, it may be possible to reduce the threat to independence by involving an additional professional accountant from outside the firm or network firm to review the work performed. However, where such a loan is made to a partner, the threat to independence can only be reduced by the repayment of the loan, or termination of the guarantee.

Business, family and personal relationships

A close business relationship between a firm or a member of the audit team and the audit client or its management, or between the firm, a network firm and an audit client, and involves a commercial or common financial interest may create self-interest and intimidation threats. A joint venture or an arrangement to combine one or more services or products of the firm with any part of the audit client's services, are two such examples. Unless the relationship is clearly insignificant, the only possible course of action is to terminate the business relationship or reduce the magnitude of the relationship so that the financial interest is clearly insignificant. Otherwise, the firm should refuse to perform the audit engagement.

In the case of a corporate audit client which is not a small proprietary company for the relevant financial year, if an audit firm appoints as a consultant for reward a director, officer or an employee of the audit client who is in a position to influence the conduct or efficacy of the audit, no safeguards could reduce the threat to an acceptable level and, consequently, the only available course of action is to terminate the consultancy arrangement or refuse to perform the audit engagement.

Where a close family member of a member of the audit team is a director, an officer, or an employee of the audit client in a position to exert direct and significant influence over the subject matter of the audit engagement, threats to independence may be created. The significance of the threats will depend on factors such as the position the close family member holds with the client, and the role of the professional on the audit team. Safeguards include removing the individual from the audit team or structuring the responsibilities of the assurance team so that the professional does not deal with matters that are within the responsibility of the close family member.

Employment relationships

If a member of the assurance team, partner or former partner joins the audit client, the significance of the self-interest, familiarity or intimidation threats is based on the following factors:

- the position of the person at the audit client
- the extent of involvement of the person with the audit team
- the length of time between the involvement and the appointment
- the previous position the person had at the audit firm.

Section 206 of the Sarbanes–Oxley Act prohibits an accounting firm from providing audit services for a company issuing financial statements if the CEO, controller or chief financial officer (CFO) of the company was employed in the audit practice of the accounting firm during the 1-year period before the audit.

In the United Kingdom, the Co-ordinating Group on Audit and Accounting Issues, in its report submitted to the Secretary of State and the Chancellor of the Exchequer on 29 January 2003, recommended a 2-year cooling-off period where the audit partner wishes to join an audit client as director. Similar provisions are now incorporated into the Corporations Act, as described earlier.

If a former partner of the firm becomes an officer or director of a corporate audit client at the same time as another former partner of the firm (who was a partner of the firm at the time the firm undertook an audit of the corporate audit client) is also an officer or director of the corporate audit client, the threat created would be so significant that no safeguard can reduce it. The firm should refuse to become engaged as an auditor of the company involved.

Where an audit client is a public interest entity; that is, it is either a listed company, or an entity defined by regulation or legislation as a public interest entity, the audit has to comply with the independence requirements applicable to listed entities. Familiarity or intimidation threats are created when a key audit partner joins an audit client that is a public interest entity. In this case independence would be deemed to be compromised unless, subsequent to the partner ceasing to be a key audit partner, the public interest entity had issued audited financial statements covering a period of not less than twelve months and the partner was not a member of the audit team with respect to the audit of those financial statements.

An intimidation threat is also created when the audit firm's senior or managing partner joins an audit client that is a public interest entity, either as an employee of significant influence, or as a director or officer of the entity. Independence is deemed to be compromised unless twelve months have passed since the individual was the senior or managing partner of the firm.

Where, as a result of a business combination, the above key audit partner or senior or managing partner is in a position described above, independence is not compromised only when (1) the position was not taken in contemplation of the combination; (2) any benefits or payments due to the former partner from the audit firm have been settled in full; (3) the former partner does not continue to participate or appear to participate in the firm's business or professional activities; and (4) the position held by the former partner with the audit client is discussed with those charged with governance.

Staff assignments, recent service and serving as an officer or director of an audit client

Secondment of staff by an audit firm to an audit client creates a self-review threat. This should only be for a short period and the seconded staff should not be involved in providing non-assurance services to the client or assume management responsibilities. In all circumstances the audit client should be responsible for directing and supervising the seconded staff. The significance of any threat should be evaluated carefully. Examples of safeguards include conducting an additional review of the work performed by the seconded staff, not giving the seconded staff audit responsibility for any function or activity that s/he has performed during the period of the loan assignment, and not including the seconded staff as a member of the audit team.

If, before the period covered by the audit report, a member of the audit team had served as an officer or director of the audit client, or had been an employee in a position to exert influence over the subject matter of the audit engagement, self-interest, self-review and familiarity threats may be created. The significance of the threats will depend on such factors as the position of the individual held with the audit client, the length of time that has passed since the individual left the audit client, and the role the individual plays in the audit team. The safeguards to be considered should include involving an additional professional accountant to review the work performed by the individual, or discussing the issue with those charged with governance of the audit client, such as the audit committee.

A partner or a member of the audit team should not, during the 12 months immediately preceding the period to which the audit relates, have served as an officer or director of the audit client, or have been an employee in a position to exert influence over the subject matter of the audit engagement or the conduct or efficacy of the audit.

A partner or employee of the firm should not serve as an officer or as a director on the board or as a liquidator, provisional liquidator, controller, scheme manager, official manager, or administrator (except in the case of a members' voluntary winding up) of an audit client.

No partner or employee of the audit firm should act in the position of a company secretary of an audit client. A company secretary is deemed as an officer of the company. If such an individual were to accept such a position the only course of action for the audit firm is to refuse to perform or withdraw from the audit engagement. Performing routine administrative services to support a company secretarial function or providing advice in relation to company secretarial administration matters does not constitute threats to independence as long as the audit client is responsible for all decision making.

Long association with an audit client including partner rotation

Using the same senior personnel on an assurance engagement over a long period of time may create a familiarity threat. The significance of the threat will depend on the length of time the individual has been a member of the assurance team, the role of the individual on the assurance team, the structure of the firm and the nature of the assurance engagement. Safeguards include rotating senior personnel, involving an additional professional accountant who is not a member of the assurance team to review the work done by the senior personnel, or having independent internal quality reviews.

For the audit of public interest entities, or listed entities, an individual shall not be the key audit partner for more than seven years. After such time, the individual shall not be a member of the engagement or be a key audit partner for the client for two years. During this period, this individual should not participate in the audit, quality assurance processes, or consult with the audit team or the client regarding technical or industry-specific issues, transactions or events. An exception to this is provided under section 290.152 where, due to unforeseen circumstances, a key audit partner is permitted to be on the audit team for an additional year as long as the threat to independence is eliminated or reduced to an acceptable level.

In the case where the firm has only a few people with the necessary knowledge of the audit client who is a public interest entity, an independent regulator in the relevant jurisdiction may grant an exemption from partner rotation, provided specified safeguards are applied.

Provision of non-assurance services to audit clients

The greater the knowledge of the assurance client's business, the better the assurance team will understand the client's procedures and policies, its controls and risks. Similarly, audit firms traditionally have the skills and expertise which might benefit audit clients. The provision of assurance (including auditing) and non-assurance services to the same client may create perceived and real threats to independence. The significance of any threat created by the provision of such services should be evaluated. Sections 290.156–290.219 specify different circumstances whereby threats to independence may exist. These circumstances include:

- management responsibilities
- preparing accounting records
- valuation services
- taxation services
- internal audit services
- information technology (IT) systems services
- litigation support services
- legal services
- recruiting services
- corporate finance services.

Threats to independence depend on the nature of the services provided, the involvement of the person in the audit engagement team, and the materiality of the matter in relation to the client's financial statements. The following safeguards are suggested:

- policies and procedures to prohibit professional staff from making management decisions for the audit client
- discussing independence issues related to the provision of non-audit services with those charged with governance, such as the audit committee
- identifying responsibility for provision of non-audit services by the firm
- involving an additional professional accountant to advise on the potential impact of the non-audit engagement on the independence of the member of the audit team and the firm
- involving an additional professional accountant to provide assurance on a discrete matter of the assurance engagement outside of the audit engagement
- obtaining the audit client's acknowledgement of responsibility for the results of the work performed by the firm
- making arrangements so that personnel providing non-audit services do not participate in the audit engagement.

With respect to **non-audit services** to audit clients, certain matters (discussed below) should be noted.

Management responsibilities

A management responsibility is dependent on the circumstances and requires the exercise of judgement. Examples of management responsibilities include setting policies and strategic direction of the audit client, directing responsibilities of its employees, taking responsibility for designing, implementing or maintaining internal control, and so on. Where the audit firm assumes a management responsibility, the threat to independence is so significant that no safeguards can reduce such threats. Further, a familiarity threat is also created. Therefore, the firm shall not assume any management responsibility for an audit client.

Preparation of accounting records and financial statements for audit clients

Technical assistance such as input regarding accounting principles, financial statement disclosure, appropriateness of controls, and the methods used to determine the stated amounts of assets and liabilities is an appropriate way of promoting the fair presentation of financial statements, and provision of such advice does not threaten the firm's independence.

Services such as helping clients resolve reconciliation problems, analysing information for regulatory reporting, helping in the preparation of consolidated accounts, drafting disclosure and proposing journal entries are considered to be a normal part of the audit process and do not, under normal circumstances, threaten independence. Where the audit client is a public interest entity, the firm shall not provide accounting or bookkeeping services, including payroll or the preparation of financial statements on which the firm will express an opinion.

In emergency cases the audit firm is asked to assist in the preparation of accounting records and safeguards, such as ensuring the personnel providing the accounting services shall not be in the audit team. The services are provided for a short period only and are not expected to recur and the situation is discussed with those charged with governance.

Valuation services

Valuation services performed for an audit client such as making assumptions regarding future developments or applying certain methodologies in calculating the value of an asset, a liability or a business as a whole may result in a self-review threat. If such valuation services involve matters material to the financial statements and have a significant degree of subjectivity, the firm should withdraw from the audit engagement or refuse to perform the valuation services. An audit firm shall not provide any valuation services to an audit client where the audit client is a public interest entity.

Taxation services

Taxation services such as compliance, planning, provision of formal tax opinions and help with tax disputes are generally not seen to create threats to independence. An audit firm shall not prepare tax calculations of current and deferred tax liabilities for the purpose of preparing accounting entries for an audit client which is a public interest entity.

Providing tax planning and other tax advisory services, where the advice is clearly supported by tax authority or other precedent, by established practice or has a basis in tax law, does not create a threat to independence. The significance of any threat should be evaluated and safeguards applied when necessary. Safeguards include using professionals who are not members of the audit team to perform the service, or having a tax professional who is not involved in providing the tax service, to advise the audit team in respect of the financial statement treatment, or obtaining the service of an external tax professional or obtaining tax clearance from tax authorities. However, if the effectiveness of the tax advice is dependent on an accounting treatment and the audit team has reasonable doubt as to the appropriateness of the related accounting treatment, and the outcome will have a material effect on the financial statements on which the audit firm will express its opinion, the self-review threat is so significant that no safeguards will be available. Therefore, the firm shall not provide such taxation advice to an audit client.

The same principles will apply where the tax services involve a valuation for tax reporting services, or when the audit firm is asked to assist in the resolution of a tax dispute. The significance of the threats shall be evaluated and safeguards put in place. Where the taxation services involve acting as an advocate for an audit client before a public tribunal or court in the resolution of a tax matter and the amounts involved are material to the financial statements on which the firm will express an opinion, the advocacy threat will be so significant that no safeguards will be available. Therefore, the firm shall not perform this type of service for the audit client.

Internal audit services

Performing a significant portion of the audit client's internal audit activities may create a self-review threat. The client should acknowledge its responsibilities for establishing, maintaining and monitoring the system of internal controls. Safeguards should be applied in all circumstances to reduce to an acceptable level any threats created. Services involving an extension of the procedures required to conduct an audit in accordance with the auditing standards would not impair independence with respect to an audit client, provided that the audit firm's personnel do not act in a capacity equivalent to a member of audit client management.

Where an audit firm provides assistance in a client's internal audit activities, or undertakes the outsourcing of some of the activities, any self-review threat created may be reduced to an acceptable level by ensuring that there is a clear separation between the management and control of the internal audit by audit client management and the internal audit activities themselves. Safeguards that should be applied in all circumstances to reduce such threats to an acceptable level include ensuring that the audit client is responsible for internal audit activities and designates a competent employee to be responsible for internal audit activities; the audit client approves the scope, risk and frequency of the internal audit work; and the findings and recommendations resulting from the internal audit are reported appropriately to the audit committee or management.

Where the audit client is a public interest entity, a firm shall not perform internal audit services that relate to a significant part of the internal controls over financial reporting, the financial accounting system, or amounts or disclosures that are, in aggregate, material to the financial statements on which the firm will express its opinion.

IT systems services to audit clients

The provision of services by an audit firm to an audit client that involve the design and implementation of financial information technology systems used to generate the financial statements may create a self-review threat.

The audit client should acknowledge its responsibility, and designate senior management to be responsible for management decisions in respect of the IT systems in question, for evaluating the results and adequacy of the system, and for the operation of the system.

The provision of services in connection with the assessment, design and implementation of internal accounting controls and risk-management controls are not considered to create a threat to independence, provided no management functions are performed.

Where the audit client is a public interest entity, the audit firm shall not provide IT services involving the design or the implementation of IT systems that form a significant part of the internal controls over the financial reporting, or that generate information that is significant to the client's accounting records or financial statements on which the audit firm expresses opinion.

Other services

In respect of litigation support services and legal services a self-review threat may be created. The audit firm shall evaluate such threats based on the nature of the service and the materiality of the matter in relation to the financial statements on which the audit firm expresses its opinion. Sometimes safeguards such as using professionals who are not part of the audit team, or vice versa, is advised. However, the appointment of a partner or an employee of the audit firm as General Counsel for legal affairs of an audit client is significant and no member of the audit firm shall accept such an appointment.

In terms of recruitment services, the audit firm may provide such services as reviewing professional qualifications, being a part of the interview panel and advising on a candidate's competence for financial accounting, administrative or control positions. If the audit client is a public interest entity, the audit firm shall not provide recruiting services with respect to a director or an officer position.

In regard to providing corporate finance services, the significance of any threats shall be evaluated based on the nature of the services and the materiality of the related matter on the financial statements on which the audit firm expresses its opinion.

Fees

An audit firm's economic dependence on an audit client may result in concern about the possibility of losing that client, and thus a self-interest threat exists. The significance of the threat will depend on the structure of the firm and whether the firm is well established or a small, newly formed entity. Where the audit client is a public interest entity, the firm shall disclose to those charged with governance of the audit client the fact that the total of such fees represents more than 15% of the total fees received by the firm, and discuss the appropriate safeguards to be applied. These are:

- an independent member of the audit team shall perform an engagement quality control review prior to the issuance of the second year's financial statements; or
- a professional regulatory body performs a review of that engagement that is equivalent to the engagement quality control review; or
- the above review being performed on the second year's audit after the audit opinion has been issued, and before the issuance of the audit opinion of the third year's financial statements.

When the total fees significantly exceed 15%, the firm shall consider having a pre-issuance review rather than a post-issuance review.

Where the audit fees are overdue, the firm shall consider if such overdue fees constitute a loan. The firm shall determine if an additional independent member is required to advise or review the work performed. It is also appropriate to consider if it should be re-appointed or continue with the audit engagement.

An audit firm shall not enter into any arrangement where a contingent fee is charged, directly or indirectly. Where other contingent fee arrangements by a firm are made for a non-assurance service to an audit client, the existence and significance of any threats will depend on factors such as the range of the possible fee amounts, whether an authority determines the outcomes of the matter, the nature of the service and the effect of the event or transaction on the financial statements.

A firm should not obtain an audit engagement by charging a significantly lower fee than that charged by the predecessor firm. The firm must be able to demonstrate that appropriate time and qualified staff are assigned to the task and all applicable assurance standards, guidelines and quality control procedures are being complied with.

Compensation and evaluation policies

A key audit partner shall not be evaluated on or compensated based on that partner's success in selling non-assurance services to the partner's audit client.

Gifts and hospitality

A firm or a member of the audit team should not accept gifts or hospitality from the audit client unless the value is clearly insignificant.

Actual or threatened litigation

When litigation takes place or is likely between the audit firm or any member thereof and the audit client, self-interest and intimidation threats are created. The relationship must be treated with candour and full disclosure. However, in such circumstances, the firm must evaluate the threats based on the materiality of the litigation, and whether the litigation relates to a prior audit engagement. Safeguards by removing the member of the team involved in the matter or having an independent professional reviewing the work performed are possible. It is also advisable that if the safeguards do not reduce the threats the firm shall withdraw from the engagement.

3.3.4 Other current recommendations for enhancing independence

The Corporations Act, with the amendments from the CLERP 9 Act, incorporated many previous recommendations such as the Ramsay Report (2001), the Joint Committee of Public Accounts and Audit Report (JCPAA) (September 2002), Corporate Governance Principles and Guidelines issued by the Corporate Governance Council of the ASX (with 2010 amendments), and the HIH Royal Commission Report (April 2003).[18]

Independence, a significant aspect of governance in financial reporting, has also been incorporated into the revised ASX Corporate Governance Principles in 2010. For example in Principle 2 the structure of the board shall include the assessing of relationships that might affect the independence status of directors, including the roles of the chair and CEO should not be exercised by the same individual. An audit committee of at least 3 members should be established by the Board (Principle 4) to safeguard the integrity of the financial reporting functions. The audit committee should be structured so that it consists of non-executive directors, a majority of independent directors, and is chaired by an independent person only. Principle 6 'Respect the rights of shareholders' includes a recommendation that the external auditor should attend the annual general meeting and be available to answer shareholder questions about the conduct of the audit and the preparation and content of the auditor's report. Also, the HIH Royal Commission (2003) recommended that all standards of independence, including the legislation and professional standards should consistently define independence:

- An auditor is not independent with respect to an audit client if the auditor might be impaired ... in the auditor's exercise of objective and impartial judgment on all matters arising out of the auditor's engagement.
- A reference to an auditor includes both an individual auditor and an audit firm. In determining whether an auditor or an audit firm is independent, all relevant circumstances should be considered, including all pre-existing relationships between the auditor, the audit firm and the audit client, including its management and directors.

Justice Owen in the HIH case recommended that the board should make an annual statement identifying non-audit services provided by the audit firm and the fees applicable to each category of the work, explaining why those services do not compromise audit independence. This recommendation has been incorporated in the Corporations Act, Chapter 2M.3 on financial reporting.

In summary, professional independence of auditors has been a key debate over the last few years. Major reforms include the revision of the former Professional Statement F.1 to take into account the IFAC 'principles-based' model of threats and safeguards, the subsequent adoption of the IFAC Code by the APESB in Australia with the release of the Code of Ethics, and the Sarbanes–Oxley Act, which is also enforced by the Securities and Exchange Commission (SEC) of the United States.

The reform agenda of the audit profession extends beyond professional independence. The corporate collapses around 2000–03, subsequent regulatory changes in corporate governance and the more recent corporate collapses during the global financial crisis (2008–09) have all had a profound impact on the financial accountability framework and expectations of auditors.

We have discussed how the concepts of ethics and independence have been dealt with using a principles-based approach. The increased amount of legislative requirements, however, raises questions about a rules-based approach which, in turn, may increase the tendency to promote mere compliance rather than ethical conduct.

3.3.5 Monitoring auditor independence

With the enactment of the CLERP 9 Act, the Australian Securities and Investments Commission (ASIC) undertook to carry out its auditor inspection program. Under the Corporations Act, ASIC has responsibility for the surveillance, investigation and enforcement of the new regulatory requirements for auditor independence, and the FRC has responsibility at a policy level to oversee the effective implementation of the new independence regime in Australia. Accordingly, ASIC conducted on-site inspections of the Big Four accounting firms. The Big Four together audit approximately 54 per cent of all entities listed on the ASX and 91 per cent by market capitalisation of the 300 largest entities. ASIC focused on assessing whether the firms had documented and implemented a quality control system that provides reasonable assurance that they comply with the independence requirements in Division 3, Part 2M.4 of the Corporations Act. Although the inspection program was not to benchmark the firms or to make specific recommendations on how to improve the firms' independence, the program considered the following areas:

- culture at the top
- systems and processes
- interests in clients
- non-audit services
- client management.

In brief, the inspections identified that (1) all firms had documented policies that were generally adequate, and (2) no breaches of the Corporations Act were identified in the course of the inspection.

The first inspection results were provided to the FRC as set out under a memorandum of understanding between the two organisations.[19] Detailed observations and findings are provided in Section 1 of the report, which include firms' formal reporting systems under CLERP 9, monitoring compliance, evaluating financial interests in audit clients, perceptions of the provision of any non-audit services as a reasonable person, control procedures at engagement level, documenting approval of non-audit services, training and communication regarding non-compliance.[20] On 23 October 2006, the FRC submitted its first 2005–06 Auditor Independence Report to the Treasurer. Since then, ASIC performs audit inspections and produces a report on its findings every 18 months. The audit inspection program aims to promote high quality external audits of financial reports of listed and other public interest entities in Australia. Audit quality is established by:

- the likelihood of material misstatement
- the likelihood that the audit detects misstatement
- whether the auditor does anything about it.

The latest audit inspection report was published in December 2012, for 2011–12.[21] The key findings of the audit inspection include:

- a lack of improvement in audit quality since 2010
- an increase of instances where necessary audit procedures have not been followed to obtain reasonable assurance that the audit financial report was not materially misstated

- a discovery that in 18% of the 602 key audit areas, across 117 audit files that were inspected, auditors did not obtain sufficient appropriate audit evidence, exercise sufficient scepticism, or otherwise comply with auditing standards in a significant audit area
- a conclusion that some audit firms need to improve their own quality control systems. The areas that required improvements are:
- the sufficiency and appropriateness of audit evidence obtained
- the level of professional scepticism exercised
- the extent of reliance that can be placed on the work of other auditors or experts.

The audit profession is very much aware of the negative publicity regarding the audit inspection report. This has led to some changes within firms. Audit quality is a significant matter in maintaining the relevance of auditing. It will be discussed later in this chapter, together with an understanding of the impact of the corporate collapses over the last decade.

3.4 CORPORATE COLLAPSES AND REFORMS

In this section, we discuss some significant corporate events and consequential changes in the auditing profession over recent years that have had a fundamental effect on the practice of auditing. Firstly, we describe some of the major corporate collapses that have taken place in Australia and the United States in the period 2000–05. These corporate failures, mostly related to **accounting misstatements**, **internal control problems** and poor corporate governance, compounded by the apparent failure of the auditors, caused a major credibility crisis in the accounting and auditing profession. A number of radical reforms were subsequently undertaken by the profession and the regulators. We then consider more recent corporate collapses in Australia. The collapses and the subsequent reforms reinforce the need for the auditors to be particularly vigilant to avoid any further loss of public trust or additional regulation of their activities.

3.4.1 Accounting crises and corporate collapses

The major **corporate collapses** of Enron and HIH have reshaped the auditing profession. Enron, an energy giant in the United States, went into liquidation in October 2001. HIH Insurance, the leading Australian general insurance group, was placed into liquidation in March 2001. These were among a large number of corporate collapses and accounting restatements between 2000 and 2002 that gave rise to a worldwide scrutiny of the accounting profession and the implosion of Arthur Andersen, a global accounting firm and one of the then Big Five accounting firms.

Lynn E Turner, former chief accountant for the SEC, calculated that investors in the United States lost nearly $200 billion in earnings restatements and lost market capitalisation following audit failures in the 6 years leading up to 2002. Between 1997 and 2000, the number of accounts restatements doubled, from 116 to 233.[22] In fact, following the collapse of Enron, which also caused the demise of Arthur Andersen, a record number of accounts were restated in 2002 (2001: 270; 2002: 330). An analysis carried out by Huron Consulting in January 2003 showed the five major accounting issues leading to such restatements (as percentages of 2002 restatements) were revenue recognition (22%), reserves, accruals and contingencies (14%), equity accounting (12%), acquisition accounting (4%), and capitalisation and expense of assets (9%).[23]

Accounting restatements or **earnings management** is a topical area in auditing. Typically this refers to those accounting activities that are performed with the intention of 'managing' the financial statements in order to show a desirable outcome and not the economic reality. This is also referred to as **financial statement fraud**.[24] Financial statement fraud involves deliberately misleading or omitting amounts or disclosures in financial statements, in an attempt to deceive financial statement users, particularly investors and creditors. Such fraud includes activities that have not traditionally been seen as fraudulent in the strict legal sense. Financial statement fraud includes:

- falsification, alteration or manipulation of material financial records
- material intentional omissions or misrepresentations of events, transactions, accounts or other significant information from which financial statements are prepared
- deliberate misapplication of accounting principles, policies and procedures used to measure, recognise, report and disclose economic events and business transactions
- intentional omission of disclosures or presentation of inadequate disclosures regarding accounting principles and policies and related financial information.

Financial statement fraud misleads users and investors. Because of the large number of corporate collapses as a result of these financial statement frauds, the public lost confidence in the integrity of financial reports. The auditors in these cases could have been under management pressure to satisfy certain interests and some might have resolved to compromise their integrity and objectivity. On the other hand, auditors are expected to possess the necessary professional scepticism in order to probe and carry out due investigations to establish the reliability of the financial statements and the internal controls and personnel involved in producing them.

Subsequent to these major corporate failures, ASIC put in place a surveillance (inspection) program that reviewed the financial reporting statements of every Australian listed company. The program targeted areas of accounting abuse, giving priority to risk areas such as capitalised and deferred expenditure, recognition of revenues, and the recognition of controlled entities and assets.

Corporate investigations

Economic events in the United States typically affect worldwide markets. In early 2000, Cendant Corporation paid US$2.83 billion to shareholders after it was revealed that its inflated income was due to fraud and accounting errors, with Ernst & Young paying a $335 million settlement as auditor of CUC International (the company prior to a merger seeing it become Cendant). The fraud had lasted for 17 years. In May 2001, Sunbeam's alleged accounting fraud resulted in Arthur Andersen making a settlement for a shareholder suit of $110 million. A month later, Arthur Andersen agreed to pay a $7 million fine after the SEC charged it with issuing false and misleading reports bolstering Waste Management by more than $1 billion between 1992 and 1996. Arthur Andersen had also paid part of a $229 million settlement to shareholders of Waste Management. However, the year 2001 ended with the massive impact of Enron's bankruptcy in December.

In Australia, ASIC has investigated several cases that involve auditors. For example, the former ABC Learning Centres auditor was found guilty on the charge of failing to obtain sufficient evidence to support the financial report on which he expressed his opinions. He was suspended for 5 years. The former auditor for Centro was suspended based on the findings that he failed to perform his duties as an auditor. Both cases where reported in the enforcement report of ASIC dated 9 April 2013.[25] Both of these cases are further described in a later part of this chapter.

Enron and other corporate collapses in the United States

In the discussion that follows on the collapses of companies in the United States such as Enron and WorldCom and the implosion of the accounting firm, Arthur Andersen, it is important to appreciate that these are seminal events in the history of the accounting profession. These events led directly to the loss of public trust in the accounting profession and the resulting stringent government legislation such as the Sarbanes–Oxley Act. It also led to considerable efforts by IFAC to re-establish trust in the profession. Collapses in Australia at the same time, such as One.Tel and HIH Insurance, also impacted on new government legislation affecting the profession with the proclamation of the CLERP 9 Act.

Enron began as a small oil and gas pipeline company in Texas in 1985 and had expanded into brokering and trading electricity and other energy commodities following the industry's deregulation. It spent time and money in lobbying the US Congress and state legislatures for access to utilities markets and became a major broker profiting from energy commodity sales and purchase prices. In the face of keen competition, it began its aggressive and complex dealings in interest rate margins, price changes and so on. The executive compensation for Enron's then CEO, Ken Lay, topped $53 million in 2000, with exercised stock options of more than $123 million and unexercised options of more than $361 million. In October 2001, the company filed for bankruptcy, with a disclosure that it had recorded a $35 million loss and a $1.2 billion reduction in asset value. By November 2001, Enron had restated its financial statements for 5 years, admitting it had overstated income by $586 million. The SEC began its investigation in late October, examining its accounting practices and the performance of its auditor, Arthur Andersen. The accounting practices being questioned included complex debt-hiding schemes using special purpose entities, manipulation of the Texas power and energy markets, and bribes; its auditor, Arthur Andersen, was alleged to have breached its independence by being involved as internal auditor for the company, and by allowing ex-audit partners to take part in its governance. Arthur Andersen was later charged with a criminal offence for its alleged obstruction of justice by destroying Enron documents. The firm was found guilty of a criminal offence in June 2002, although this was overturned on appeal in 2005 but by then it was too late as the firm had imploded. The evidence available clearly demonstrates that the pursuit of profit rather than the maintenance of independence was evident in the relationship Arthur Andersen had with its major clients such as Enron and WorldCom.

Other major accounting frauds in the United States involved Xerox, Global Crossing and WorldCom. Xerox was alleged to have falsified its accounts for 5 years, and the SEC brought actions against its auditors, KPMG. The suit against KPMG alleged that the misleading accounting scheme had allowed Xerox to claim it met performance expectations of Wall Street analysts, which boosted the company's share price.[26]

Global Crossing, a telecommunications giant, filed for bankruptcy in February 2002. It was the fourth largest bankruptcy in US history, resulting in the loss of 9000 jobs and retirement savings, with the share price falling from a high of $64 to 30 cents before its collapse. The Bermuda-based company listed $22.4 billion in assets (mostly worthless) and $12.3 billion in debt. Like Enron, it involved manipulation of accounting books and the use of accounting services provided by Arthur Andersen as the accountant and management consultant. The company was alleged to have inflated revenues and cash flow figures to boost share prices and to satisfy analysts.

WorldCom was reported to have overstated its cash flow by booking $3.8 billion in operating expenses as capital expenses, and provided its founder with a $400 million off-balance-sheet loan. The company further stunned Wall Street by announcing it found another $3.3 billion in improperly booked funds, and taking a goodwill charge of $50 billion. The former CFO and ex-controller were arrested and charged with criminal activities. WorldCom's auditor was Arthur Andersen.

In Australia, the year 2000 also saw a significant joint public undertaking by the directors of the former Adelaide Steamship Company Limited and its auditors, Deloitte Touche Tohmatsu. A declaration by Deloitte confirmed the firm's intention to apply policies such as refraining from directorships of listed companies for 3 years, rotation of audit partners, audit independence and quality assurance standards, and compliance with accounting standards, with a joint payment of $20 million to the company. The litigation had been started by ASIC in April 1994 with a number of defendants including the directors and the then auditors, Deloitte Touche Tohmatsu.

Among a number of ASIC investigations, HIH is one of the more notable. During 2002, ASIC also successfully brought disciplinary actions against nine auditors and a liquidator as part of its program of surveillance of auditors and liquidators to ensure compliance with the Corporations Act.

HIH Insurance Ltd

In March 2001, HIH Insurance Limited was placed into provisional liquidation by the Supreme Court of New South Wales, following actions taken by ASIC to seek suspension of trading of HIH shares and to start formal investigation into its corporate governance, disclosure and possible insolvent trading activities. The HIH Royal Commission Report, released in April 2003, found that the auditor, Arthur Andersen, yielded to management on controversial accounting issues, breached professional standards and failed to display independence. HIH's accounts overstated profits and understated liabilities, with errors made in the recognition of further tax benefits, capitalisation of information technology costs and acquisition costs, goodwill recognition, provisioning for future claims and the going concern status of the company. Also, three former partners in Arthur Andersen sat on the board of HIH, with various consultancy arrangements and close relationships between the former partners and the audit team. HIH was placed into liquidation with estimated losses of $5 billion.

The HIH Royal Commission Report (three volumes published in April 2003) highlighted the fact that the company was significantly 'under-reserved' for claims and mismanaged by its directors and management, epitomised by a lack of attention to detail, a lack of accountability for performance and a lack of integrity in the company's internal processes and systems.[27] Justice Owen expressed his concern that these features combined led to a series of business decisions that were poorly conceived and even more poorly executed. A cause for serious concern also arose from the group's corporate culture, which, according to Justice Owen, was 'inimical to sound management practices'. The 61 recommendations of the HIH Royal Commission cover corporate governance and financial report, assurance, regulation and insurance changes. Some of these recommendations have been incorporated into the CLERP 9 Act discussed later in this chapter.

Parmalat

Meanwhile, other countries also experienced similar problems. For example, in the Parmalat case in Italy, both auditors and company management were found guilty of fraud. This fraud involved the audited accounts of Bonlat, a subsidiary based in the Cayman Islands. The audited accounts showed cash balances were consolidated by the parent, Parmalat, and used to allay concerns about the high levels of debt the parent had on its balance sheet. The auditor did not question why a group that had so much cash on deposit needed to borrow. There was also much other false paperwork that was aimed at showing how the cash balance was built up, but a forgery was at the core. The scandal involved a forged letter purportedly from the Bank of America, confirming that Bonlat had the cash deposits of 4 billion euros. By rotation, Deloitte & Touche took the audit from Grant Thornton, which seemingly had relied on Parmalat's internal mail to deliver its letters seeking confirmation of balances with the bank. The letters were intercepted and altered, allowing the deception to continue. However, following a sell off of a number of assets and a restructure, the company was able to survive and is still a trading entity.

Akai Holdings

Ernst & Young reached a settlement with the liquidators of Akai Holdings, who agreed to drop a US$1 billion (HK$7.8 billion) negligence suit against the accounting firm related to the collapse Akai in Hong Kong. The size of the settlement was not revealed, but is believed to be substantial.

The implosion of Akai Holdings in 2000 saw US$1.8 billion in assets disappear and was Hong Kong's biggest-ever corporate collapse. James Ting Wai, Akai's former chairman, was sent to jail in 2005 after being found guilty of false accounting, but he was later released after winning an appeal due to errors in the prosecution's case.

The accounting firm suspended one of its partners and began an internal investigation after Akai liquidators charged that key documents related to the firm's audits of the Akai books had been modified to cover up misconduct. The investigation made clear that certain documents produced for the audits in 1998 and 1999 could no longer be relied on due to actions taken by the manager on the Akai audit in 2000.

Lehman Brothers

In more recent times, the global financial crisis saw a further spate of corporate collapses. Lehman Brothers filed for bankruptcy on 15 September 2008, and its demise has become a symbol of the financial crisis. A US court-appointed expert examiner, Anton Valukas, in a scathing report, blamed the collapse of investment bank Lehman Brothers on its top management as well as audit firm Ernst & Young and banks Citigroup and JPMorgan Chase. The Valukas report describes an institution so obsessed with growth that executives and auditors overlooked risks and ignored repeated warnings.

Valukas accused the senior management of balance sheet manipulation and said they oversaw and certified decisions that exacerbated Lehman's woes. The examiner was reported as saying that there was also sufficient evidence to support a possible claim that the firm's auditor, Ernst & Young, had been 'negligent' and that Lehman could pursue claims against the firm for 'professional malpractice'.

More recent cases in Australia

There have been more recent corporate collapses in Australia, but one must be careful in assuming that there was any corresponding negligence on the part of the auditors. In fact it usually takes years after a corporate collapse for cases to go through the courts and more often than not there are out-of-court settlements that do not become part of the public record. ABC Learning's rise and spectacular fall is an example of what happens when a company ignores the fundamentals of sound accounting. At the end of 2006, ABC Learning was trading on the share market at around $8.60 and operated around one in five child care centres in Australia. Less than two years later, the shares were worth around 54 cents and the company was placed in the hands of administrators. It appears that debt, a crisis of liquidity and inflated asset values all led to the collapse of ABC Learning, which went into liquidation with reported debts of $1.5 billion. When it came to the treatment of revenues and earnings in the final accounts, Ernst & Young took a very different view from ABC's previous auditors, who, it appears, were happy to endorse the interpretation provided by the company's management. Whether there was any negligence on the part of the auditors is unknown.

Storm Financial, one of the nation's biggest financial planning networks, was placed in voluntary administration in early 2009, casting doubt over the future of about 13 000 client portfolios. The drama began after hundreds of Storm's highly leveraged clients were found to owe more than the value of their portfolios. The clients had obtained margin loans through a division of the Commonwealth Bank, Colonial Geared Investments, as well as Macquarie Margin Lending and other providers. However by August 2010, the Commonwealth Bank of Australia had reached a negotiated settlement with about 70 per cent of its devastated clients who lost their savings in the collapse of Storm Financial. However, more than 300 Storm clients unhappy with the scheme have joined forces in a class action against the bank, filed by Sydney law firm Levitt Robinson. At this stage there have been no suggestions that the auditors have been at fault.

Auditor PricewaterhouseCoopers (PwC) moved to end its long-term relationship with Centro Properties Group after the shopping centre owner sued the firm in 2009 to help defend itself in a $1 billion shareholder class action. PwC asked the Australian Securities & Investments Commission for permission to resign as Centro's auditor. Under corporations law, an auditor needs regulatory approval to cut its ties with a company, unless it is expressly dismissed by shareholders. Centro Properties and Centro Retail filed the cross-claim against PwC in relation to two class-action claims brought by Maurice Blackburn and Slater & Gordon. PwC, which resigned as Centro's auditor two weeks later, is defending the cross-claim.

3.4.2 The ASIC surveillance program

As part of its ongoing campaign to improve financial reporting, ASIC has made several attempts to tackle accounting and auditing issues through its surveillance program and through a major survey of Australia's top 100 listed companies on the issue of audit independence. The surveillance program reports highlighted matters of concern. These include:

- the amortisation of intangible assets
- revenue recognition
- abnormal items
- provisions for future maintenance
- asset valuations
- disclosure of directors' and officers' emoluments and transactions
- environmental reporting
- negative reserves
- accounting for acquisition of businesses, especially in new-economy business.[28]

Following the Enron collapse, ASIC reported on 18 December 2002 that its comprehensive review of 1000 listed companies, designed to identify Enron-style accounting abuses, found 166 companies were at risk of being insolvent, and 49 had qualified accounts. The financial statements of another 31 companies remained in question. ASIC also considered taking action against the companies' directors and their auditors in 2003 where results of investigations justified this. ASIC's chief accountant said the reasonably high incidence of auditors either qualifying company accounts or highlighting risks through 'emphasis of matter' commentary reflected market conditions and indicated investors were well informed about risks associated with the businesses.[29] In a report published in December 2003, it was found that overall compliance with accounting standards appeared to be high but there were 25 cases where an accounting standard had been breached. The problems identified were misrepresentation of the values of assets, non-recognition of inappropriate value of goodwill, misconstruing revenue and the value of assets, and including expenses as extraordinary items.[30]

Section 1309 of the Corporations Act makes it an offence to give false information to the ASX where the auditor, director or officer involved either knew it was false or misleading, or failed to take reasonable steps to ensure that it was not. An important feature of s. 1309 is that it does not require dishonesty or fraud in order for there to be a successful prosecution. ASIC is able to seek a fine of up to $22 000 per offence, plus a maximum of 5 years imprisonment, or both. Following the enactment of the CLERP 9 Act in 2004, ASIC now focuses more on the quality of the audit process, and an audit inspection program was introduced in 2005 to safeguard the integrity of the financial market and its information.

In 2005, ASIC inspected the Big Four and reported back on independence. In 2006, the inspection extended to cover auditor independence and audit quality, and was carried out on the Big Four as well as six mid-tier firms (BDO, Horwath and PKF in Sydney, Grant Thornton in Perth, Pitcher Partners in Melbourne and RSM Bird Cameron).[31] A further investigation in 2009 found that in one in five audits it examined, ASIC could not find sufficient evidence to verify the auditor's opinion.

The surveillance program has now developed into the audit inspection program. ASIC undertakes an inspection every 18 months for audit undertaken. The latest inspection report has resulted in findings that audit quality has deteriorated. Audit quality is further discussed later in this chapter.

3.4.3 The spate of reforms

There have been a number of reforms proposed by accounting bodies, governments, stock exchange commissions and academics in recent years. We discuss the more notable reforms from the United States and Australia. As new legislation continues to be further amended, the following paragraphs are intended to make reference to some notable reforms of the past decades that affect auditors.

Key reform activities in Australia and the United States during the period include the following.

- The Australian Government commissioned a report into auditor independence by Professor Ian Ramsay of the University of Melbourne, which was released in October 2001. The major recommendations of the report include auditors' declaration of independence, prohibition of non-audit services, and the establishment of audit committees.
- In May 2002, both the ICAA and CPA Australia adopted a new internationally harmonised standard for professional independence. The then new F.1 statement was based on the IFAC code of independence issued in November 2001. The statement also covers some of Professor Ramsay's recommendations, including mandatory rotation of audit partners for listed entities every 7 years, a 2-year waiting period before a retired auditor can become a director of an audit client, and a ban on providing certain non-audit services.
- In May 2002, the Business Roundtable, an elite association of 150 chief executive officers of leading corporations in the United States, released a set of guidelines to increase trust in US companies after the Enron fiasco. These guidelines typically promote internal communications of potential misconduct, strengthen the role of the audit committee, and ensure prompt disclosure of significant matters by the Board.
- The Sarbanes–Oxley Act, enacted by the US Congress and signed into law by then President George W Bush on 23 January 2002, is far-reaching legislation affecting a wide range of financial services, accounting, auditing, financial reporting and the role of professional services firms. It contains stringent rules on auditor independence such as rotation of audit partners, prohibition of conflict-of-interest situations and audit quality control, and requires the auditor to report to the audit committee on significant matters. It also establishes the Public Company Accounting Oversight Board, which oversees audit firms and their procedures and the enforcement of accounting standards.
- In September 2002, the Commonwealth Treasury of Australia issued the proposal for reform, Corporate Law Economic Reform Program Paper No. 9 (CLERP 9), on corporate disclosure. The significant matters dealt with in CLERP 9 are oversight of the auditing profession, the market for audit services, **auditor liability** and independence, accounting standards and disclosure requirements, and shareholder participation. (CLERP 9 is discussed in detail later in this chapter.)

In 2003, the Australian Securities Exchange (ASX) Corporate Governance Council issued its 10 Corporate Governance Principles and their related Best Practice Recommendations. Audit committees became mandatory for the top 300 Standard & Poor's-listed companies, with the task of providing oversight of audit and financial statement matters. Certification by CEOs and CFOs of the adequacy of internal controls and financial statements were included in the ASX's recommendations.

The new Corporate Governance Principles (revised in 2010) are available on the ASX website (www.asx.com.au).

LEARNING 5
objective

Discuss the impact of the Corporate Law Economic Reform Program on audit reform and corporate disclosure.

Corporate Law Economic Reform Program

Announced by the Australian Treasurer in March 1997, the Corporate Law Economic Reform Program (CLERP) is a comprehensive initiative to improve key areas of Australia's business and company regulation as part of the Australian Government's drive to promote business, economic development and employment. The CLERP papers were incorporated into either the *Corporations Act 2001* or the *Financial Services Reform Act 2001* and their subsequent amending Acts are no. 1 on accounting standards, no. 2 on fundraising, no. 3 on directors' duties and corporate governance, no. 4 on takeovers, no. 5 on electronic commerce, no. 6 on financial markets and investment products, and no. 9 on audit reform and corporate disclosure. An up-to-date version of the Corporations Act can be found at www.comlaw.gov.au.

Relevant recommendations of the HIH Royal Commission, the work undertaken by the Joint Committee of Public Accounts and Audit, and overseas developments such as the Sarbanes–Oxley Act in corporate disclosure were also taken into account in the reform.

CLERP 9 Act

The CLERP 9 Act introduced significant changes. Those relating to audit reform can be classified into a number of key areas, described below.

Auditor appointment, independence and rotation

The key changes made by the CLERP 9 Act are found in the expanded Part 2M.4 of the Corporations Act and remain relevant to date. These changes fall into the following categories:

- additional disclosures in the directors' report on the auditor and the audit
- general auditor independence requirements
- specific auditor independence requirements
- restrictions on auditors being employed by an audit client
- auditor rotation for listed companies.

Except in respect of the directors' report disclosures, the changes made to ensure auditor independence are imposed on auditors, audit firms, audit companies and others involved in audit activity, rather than audit clients. With effect from 1 July 2004, directors' reports for disclosing entities must include the name of each officer during the financial year who was formerly a partner or director of an audit firm or audit company that is currently the disclosing entity's auditor, or was a partner or director at a time when the audit firm or audit company conducted the audit of the disclosing entity. In a section of the directors' report headed 'non-audit services', the following information must be included:

- details of the amount paid or payable to the auditor for non-audit services provided by or on behalf of the auditor during the year, including the names of the auditor and the dollar amount for each non-audit service
- a statement whether the directors are satisfied that the provision of non-audit services by the auditor during the year is compatible with the general standard of independence for auditors imposed by s. 300(11B)(b) of the Corporations Act

- a statement of the directors' reasons for being satisfied that the auditor's independence was not compromised.

The statements provided by the directors must be in accordance with advice by the listed company's audit committee if applicable. If the listed company does not have an audit committee, a resolution of the directors is needed. Such advice of the audit committee must also be endorsed by a resolution passed by the members of the audit committee.

Also, the auditor must give the directors of the company, registered scheme or disclosing entity a written declaration regarding audit independence. The written declaration must state:

- that, to the best of the auditor's knowledge and belief, there have been no contraventions of the auditor independence requirements of the Corporations Act and any applicable code of professional conduct in relation to the audit review

  or

- that, to the best of the individual auditor's knowledge and belief, the only contraventions of the point above are those contraventions set out in the declaration (s. 307C).

Failure to give such a declaration is an offence. Although the declaration is inadmissible as evidence against the individual auditor in any criminal proceedings, self-incrimination is no excuse for avoiding the requirement of the s. 307C declaration. The directors' report must include a copy of the auditor's independence declaration.

Division 3 of Part 2M.4 sets out a general standard of auditor independence, as well as specific relationships that might compromise auditor independence. The general auditor independence provisions are as follows.

- The individual auditor or audit company must be aware of a conflict of interest when it arises. The general auditor independence requirements are based on the concept of a conflict of interest that exists in relation to the audited body, and the auditor or audit company must take reasonable steps to ensure that the conflict of interest ceases to exist as soon as possible after it is known. ASIC must be notified regarding the conflict of interest after 7 days should the conflict continue to exist.
- Disclosure made to ASIC cannot be used in criminal proceedings against the individual. If the auditor or audit company fails to become aware of the situation, but would have been aware if a quality control system reasonably capable of making the auditor aware was in place, s. 324CA(2) is contravened.
- A conflict of interest exists if the auditor or a professional member of the audit team is not capable of exercising objective and impartial judgement in relation to the conduct of the audit, with full knowledge of all relevant facts.
- Section 324CH(1) states that, if the individual auditor or a professional member of the audit team falls under any of the following specific relationship categories, auditor independence may be compromised:
  - is related to the audited body as an officer or an audit-critical employee
  - has been an officer or audit-critical employee within the last 12 months before the audit
  - is a former professional employee of the auditor related to the audited body by being an officer or audit-critical employee who can influence the policies of the auditor
  - participates in business or professional activities or receives a commission from the auditor for generating business
  - is a non-audit service provider and has provided more than 10 hours of non-audit services during the period being audited or the 12 months immediately before the audited period, and the non-audit provider has certain investments in the audited body then the auditor in question must stop doing the audit, otherwise s. 324CH(1) is contravened.

- An audit-critical employee refers to, for a company or responsible entity, an employee who is able, because of his or her position, to exercise significant influence over a material aspect of the contents of the financial report being audited, or the conduct of the efficacy of the audit.
- Section 324CJ prohibits a member of an audit firm, or director of an audit company who was a professional member of an audit team, from becoming an officer of an audit client until 2 years from the date of ceasing to be with the audit firm or audit company. Similar rules apply for lead or review auditors.
- Section 324CK prohibits multiple former audit firm partners or audit company directors from becoming officers of an audit client.
- The definition of an officer also includes being an officer of a related body corporate of the audit client. Section 324CK does not apply to small proprietary companies.
- Section 324DA requires a person who plays a significant role in an audit to rotate in 5 out of 7 years. This applies to a lead or review auditor for the audit. Moreover, if members of the audit firm are aware of a case where a s. 324DA situation arises, they must, as soon as possible after becoming aware, ensure that either the firm resigns from the audit or the lead or review auditor ceases to act on the audit; otherwise the person who is aware of the situation will contravene s. 324DC. However, ASIC has the power to modify the number of years for rotation requirements to be applied to a person who has played a significant role in an audit, so that person can rotate in 6 out of 7 years (instead of 5 out of 7). A notice of declaration must be given to the client if this is the case.
- The circumstances where an auditor ceases to hold office have been expanded to now include two cases: (1) where the auditor ceases to be capable of acting because of not being registered as an auditor, and (2) where the auditor fails to give a further notice within 21 days from a first notice stating that a conflict of interest or relationship has ceased.

Auditors and annual general meetings

The CLERP 9 Act made the following changes.
- Shareholders can submit written questions to the auditor before the annual general meeting (AGM) relating to the auditor's report and the conduct of the audit.
- The auditor must attend the AGM (the lead auditor must attend).
- A reasonable opportunity must be allowed for members as a whole to ask questions of the auditor and for the auditor to respond.

Expansion of auditor's duties

An auditor conducting an audit must, within 28 days of awareness, notify ASIC regarding any person who attempts to unduly influence, coerce, manipulate or mislead a person involved in the conduct of the audit or otherwise interfere with the conduct of the audit, or where there are reasonable grounds to suspect that a contravention of the Corporations Act is either significant or not able to be adequately dealt with by the auditor.

The auditor should know the level of penalty provided for the contravention or the effect of the contravention on the overall financial position of the company, in order to assess whether the contravention is significant.

Other audit reforms

Other audit reforms include the following.
- Section 307B requires an auditor to retain working papers for an audit until the end of the 7 years after the date of the audit report.

- Qualified privilege is extended to all individual auditors, to registered company auditors acting on behalf of the audit company, and to all auditors in relation to certain new disclosure requirements.
- The Financial Reporting Council (FRC) has been significantly enhanced to include a broad oversight of the processes for setting not only accounting standards, but also auditing standards. The FRC must monitor and report annually to the Minister on the effectiveness of auditor independence in Australia.
- Auditor qualification requirements have been expanded to include the practical experience requirements for registration by satisfying all the components of auditing competency standards. ASIC will approve the auditing competency standard on application of any professional body or firm, based on the individual's performance, ensuring consistency with the Corporations Act or any Australian law. An auditor who is not a member of a professional body may be required to undertake continuing professional development. An annual statement including the details of the nature and complexity of major audit work undertaken and details of compliance must be lodged by 31 January each year.
- The matters that can be referred to the Companies Auditors and Liquidators Disciplinary Board (CALDB) have been revised to include failing to lodge an annual statement, failing to comply with an ASIC condition of registration, and ceasing to have the practical experience necessary.
- A company can now apply to be an authorised audit company if:
  - each director of the company is a registered company auditor
  - each share in the company is held and beneficially owned by the shareholder
  - a majority of the voting power attaches to shares held by individuals who are registered company auditors
  - ASIC is satisfied that the company has adequate and appropriate professional indemnity insurance for claims that may be made against the company in relation to the audit of companies and registered schemes
  - the company is not externally administered.

LEARNING objective 6

State the importance of technical and ethical competence to enhance audit quality.

3.5 AUDIT QUALITY

Discharging responsibilities with due professional care and adequate competence in the public interest is a characteristic of a professional person. When auditors face pressures (from management or time constraints), the audit quality may be compromised. In this section we reiterate the importance of technical and ethical competence in enhancing audit judgement and quality.

3.5.1 Technical competence

Professional accountants must comply with various accounting standards, auditing standards and standards relating to specific professional services covered by a range of miscellaneous professional statements. Non-compliance represents unacceptable professional conduct.

Accounting concepts and standards

The APESB has released APES 205 *Conformity with Accounting Standards*. All members in Australia must follow APES 205 when they prepare, present, audit, review or compile financial reports. Members involved in or responsible for the preparation or presentation of general purpose financial reports must apply the principles and guidance provided in the statements of accounting concepts and the Australian financial reporting framework, subject to conformity with Australian accounting standards. Members involved in or responsible for preparing, presenting, auditing, reviewing or compiling an entity's special purpose financial report must ensure that the report states clearly that it is a special purpose financial report, its purpose and the significant accounting policies used. A member in public practice who is performing professional work based on an applicable financial reporting framework must ensure that the member of the firm has the requisite professional knowledge and skill, or otherwise engage a suitably qualified external person.

Auditing standards and auditing guidance statements

Section 307A of the Corporations Act requires auditors to comply with the Australian auditing standards. The APESB released APES 210 *Conformity with Auditing and Assurance Standards* in July 2006. The standard states that the auditing and assurance standards contain basic principles and essential procedures, together with related guidance. Auditing and assurance standards are to be applied to all Australian financial report audits, and applied and adapted, where permitted, to all other Australian audit engagements, review engagements and other assurance engagements.

Standards for taxation, insolvency and management consulting services

Standards for taxation, insolvency and management consulting services, which are also mandatory for members, are not directly relevant to the provision of auditing services except insofar as they assist in maintaining the reputation and standing of the profession. It is pertinent, however, that their subject matter is closely related to the fundamental concepts of independence, objectivity, integrity and competence. For example, APES 220 *Taxation Services* emphasises the responsibility of members not to act contrary to the public interest. Objectivity, confidentiality, professional competence and due care are required for this relationship. A member shall not associate him/herself with any arrangement which involves documents or accounting entries that are intended to misrepresent the true nature of a transaction, or which depends upon lack of disclosure for its effectiveness. Also, a member shall not promote, or assist in the promotion of, any schemes or arrangements which have no commercial justification other than the avoidance of tax through exploitation of the revenue laws.

Compliance with standards

Although accounting standards are developed within the AASB's conceptual framework, there is no generally agreed conceptual framework for auditing. This has led to the accusation that auditing standards tend to codify rather than lead practice, so that auditing is what auditors do, rather than what users require. This point was made in the Pacific Acceptance case, in which the auditors were found to have been negligent, despite having followed accepted practices of the day. Research is needed to design a framework that supports the development of more effective auditing standards.

In May 2006 following the issue by IFAC in February 2004 of ISQC 1 *Quality Control for Firms that Perform Audits and Reviews of Financial Statements, and Other Assurance Related Services Engagements*, the APESB issued APES 320 *Quality Control for Firms*.

*T*he major accounting firms have admitted that their auditors are failing to question boards or companies when confronted with incomplete information or gaps in books and records.

The admission of the gap in what is known as professional scepticism comes before an expected crackdown by the corporate regulator.

A confidential review by the Institute of Chartered Accountants (ICAA) of the big four accounting firms and Grant Thornton showed that while 83 per cent of partners rated professional scepticism as the most important skill for an auditor, only 21 per cent believed their teams were exhibiting it strongly.

Only 6 per cent of those surveyed said professional scepticism was a focus at university and only a quarter said it was a focus in their workplace.

'Much more needs to be done to grow and nurture scepticism but it is not a skill [where] you can just sit in front of the whiteboard and come out with a qualification,' ICAA chief executive Lee White said.

The spotlight on auditors follows the collapses of Banksia Securities, ABC Learning Centres, Bill Express, the note-printing scandal at the Reserve Bank of Australia, and a string of high-profile auditing issues including at Lend Lease and Spotless.

While Mr White said that scepticism could not be learned, the institute is looking to bring in psychologists to work with firms to build up the skill.

'This is all about the human tendencies and the skills learned at the school of hard knocks,' said Mr White, a former chief accountant at the Australian Securities and Investments Commission. 'It is a skill that boards, audit committees, CEOs and CFOs need.'

The release of the ICAA review comes just weeks before the results of the Australian Securities and Investments Commission's annual review of the industry and chairman Greg Medcraft has made the performance of gatekeepers such as auditors a hallmark of his tenure.

'I would say the number one thing they should be is sceptical,' Mr Medcraft said on Friday.

'If you are not getting the answers to the questions you ask [as a member of an audit committee], then you should think about being on the board,' Mr Medcraft said.

'And, also to boards, you need to understand that delegation doesn't mean to say that you let go of your accountability. You are still the stewards of the company and you are going to be held accountable.'

ASIC has disciplined 15 company auditors in the past five years, and banned 13 from practising.[32]

Source: P Durkin, 'More sceptical accountants wanted', *Financial Review*, 5 November 2012.

3.5.2 Ethical competence — the significance of ethical values in auditing

Threats to independence are often encountered by auditors and accountants in public practice and are complex issues. Some of the threats are a direct consequence of the audit–client relationship (such as management pressure) and the phenomenon of accountants in public practice providing non-audit services, which may have an impact on the appearance of audit independence. Accountants' and auditors' decisions depend on their ability to identify and rank in importance various conflicting interests and duties while maintaining professional competence and independence. How independent these decisions are in reality often depends on how successfully the auditor deals with issues such as those discussed next.

The environment affecting professional conduct

Auditors often face pressure situations that present them with an ethical dilemma — one in which they have to choose between unclear alternatives, some of which may compromise their integrity. Not all these situations are easily defined and the auditor may need to look beyond the requirements of the Code of Ethics.

Leung and Cooper reported that accountants in public practice have identified issues concerning clients' proposals for tax evasion (73%) and clients' proposals to manipulate financial statements (68%) as the two most common ethical problems, compared with other fields of employment.[33]

In Australia, a study carried out in 1998 showed that the level of auditor fee dependence does not affect auditor propensity to issue unqualified auditor's reports.[34] The issue of independence in mind and in appearance requires a professional accountant to be sceptical while demonstrating his or her ability to withstand pressures. Campbell and Houghton in 2005 discussed a collection of thoughts concerning auditing and ethics from the legal, economic and empirical perspectives.[35] The following comes from the foreword:[36]

> It is inevitable that an auditor will be faced with ethical decisions during the course of their career. It is therefore fundamental that appropriate and professional decision-making protocols and behaviours are ingrained in the culture in which they work.
>
> A strong code of professional and personal ethical guidelines is a critical starting point to embedding ethical behaviour ...

Although accounting and auditing are based on relatively systematic techniques, few allegations of breaches result from methodological errors. Rather, many are cases of judgements about the appropriate use of a technique or standard. Some may be errors of judgement, and others may result from a misinterpretation of the problem, a lack of awareness because of complexity, or a failure to observe the ethical values of honesty, integrity, objectivity, due care, confidentiality and a commitment to the public interest. An accounting treatment in accordance with an accounting standard may be biased, for example, if it is based on inadequate or incomplete information that is wrongly judged to be sufficient to support it. A non-disclosure of an accounting item may not be a question of incompetence but of misplaced loyalty to management, a client or one's self-interest (rather than the public who rely on the information).

Auditing and accounting standards, although a sound basis for professional practice, will not cover every contingency. In complex situations in which the course of action is not clearly prescribed, accountants must be able to maintain integrity and objectivity in making a judgement. When professional accountants find a problem that exceeds their expertise, it is their ethical values that will compel them to recognise such limitations, seek advice, remain objective and disclose the relevant facts. This is necessary to maintain the trust within a fiduciary relationship. There are cases, however, where accounting standards and technical guidelines are insufficient (because of the complexity of business transactions) for providing an objective basis for accounting treatment. Consequently, although technical feasibility may govern short-term solutions, ethical considerations such as the potential consequences of such accounting problems should dominate in the longer term.

Priority of duty and loyalty

Given that the role of professional accountants is to provide fiduciary services to society as a whole, the performance of such services involves choices between the interests of various parties — the client or the employer of such services, the management of the client or employing organisation, the current and prospective investors of the business being examined, other stakeholders, employees and the government. Auditors are appointed by the shareholders or members of the client to examine the financial affairs of the organisation. The underlying principle in this engagement is to protect the interests of the resource providers against the possible pursuit of self-interest by management. To the extent that the stakeholders mentioned are considered to be the 'public', the auditor has a fiduciary relationship with the public that requires the exercise of the same duties and values that would apply in a more direct contractual relationship. The choice of accounting and auditing methods and treatments that maximise a current benefit at the expense of future income would therefore breach the trust required for the fiduciary arrangement with the public. Accordingly, the loyalty to the public should not be less than the loyalty owed to existing shareholders or owners. Defining the legal liability of auditors in this respect has been complex. The establishment of auditors' relationships with various parties has broadened the strict privity of contract in terms of liability (see chapter 5).

Accountants employed within an organisation have no contractual relationship with shareholders or the public. However, in performing their duties to their employers, they are required to adhere to the values expected of a professional person by considering their responsibility to others who may be disadvantaged by an act at the request of the professional's superior. Accountants employed in this capacity need, therefore, to consider the accuracy and reliability of their work for the benefit of the end-user (i.e. the public as the stakeholders). This situation is complex, entailing consideration of such debatable issues as confidentiality to one's employer and the ethical premises for 'whistleblowing' (disclosing unethical deeds to parties outside of an organisation). For example, professional accountants have been given certain privileges to disclose information required by law to third parties such as ASIC. It is also important to note that the CLERP 9 Act included in the Corporations Act offers new protection for whistleblowers in Part 9.4AAA 'Protection for whistleblowers'.

The code of a profession endeavours to provide guidelines to follow in difficult ethical situations, yet accountants often have to rely on personal integrity and values to make the 'right' decision. One viewpoint[37] is that a professional accountant facing a difficult choice should consider that loyalty is owed to affected stakeholders in the following order: the public interest, the profession, the client/employer and, finally, the individual.

Developments for professional competence

The ethical provisions in the Code of Ethics deal mainly with business matters that relate to public accounting, but ethical responsibility also extends to technical competence. Competence is the product of education and experience. Education begins with preparation for entry into the profession and extends to continuing professional education throughout the member's career. Experience involves on-the-job training and the acceptance of increased responsibilities during a member's professional life.

The Code of Ethics states that (1) members have a duty to maintain their level of competence throughout their professional career, and (2) public accountants should undertake only work in which they are competent. Minimum annual hours of continuing professional education are prescribed for all members, affiliates and members holding a certificate of public practice. Compliance with these rules is monitored by requiring members to keep a personal record of time spent on continuing professional education and to certify compliance at the time they pay their annual subscription. IFAC also issues its series of international education standards (IESs) each year. IES 4 *Professional Values, Ethics and Attitudes* requires all prequalifying accounting programs of IFAC member bodies (160 worldwide) to include a number of topics in ethics to form the basis of the development of professional values and ethics in accounting students. A major study on ethics education completed in 2006 also highlighted the profession's focus and commitment in enhancing the ethical conduct of accountants and auditors.[38] There is an increasing emphasis in professional development programs on the topics of developing competence in dealing with ethical conflicts. Reforms also suggested a competency program for auditors, including the international education standard IES 8 issued by IFAC, which stipulates the educational requirements for audit professionals. Also, in Australia in November 2004, CPA Australia and the ICAA jointly issued a set of competency standards applicable to accountants and auditors. The standards were approved by ASIC.[39]

Overall, it is argued that moral cognition may provide the initial determination of an appropriate choice of action, but it is not sufficient to explain or predict behaviour. The extent to which individuals will make a decision and act on it consistent with their personal and professional values depends on how well they can resist the pressure of the work environment or, alternatively, how well the environment will support such actions.

3.5.3 Quality controls in auditing firms

Every profession is concerned about the quality of its services, and the public accounting profession is no exception. Quality audits are essential to ensure that the profession meets its responsibilities to clients, to the general public and to regulators who rely on independent auditors to maintain the credibility of financial information. To help assure quality audits, the profession and the regulators have developed a multilevel regulatory framework. This framework encompasses many of the activities of the private and public sector organisations associated with the profession (described earlier in this chapter). For the purpose of describing the framework, these activities may be organised as follows.

- *Standard setting*: The AUASB issues standards, guidance notes and other guidances to provide clear standards for auditing and assurance services, and for review and other related services. The professional bodies and IFAC issue ethical codes to establish and monitor the performance of professionalism and ethical behaviour of professional accountants.
- *Firm regulation*: Each public practice entity adopts policies and procedures to ensure that practising accountants adhere to professional standards.
- *Self- or peer regulation*: The accounting profession has implemented a comprehensive program of self-regulation (including mandatory continuing professional education) and a program of quality control and practice reviews.
- *Government regulation*: The FRC, ASIC and CALDB, along with the courts, monitor and regulate auditor independence and conduct.

Standard setting

We have already noted the role of the AUASB in setting standards for the various types of auditing and assurance engagements. The APESB was established as an initiative of the ICAA and CPA Australia in February 2006, with the NIA joining subsequently. The APESB issues professional and ethical standards and guidance notes to provide a formal and rigorous forum for the consideration, promulgation and approval of professional and ethical standards. The initial focus of the APESB is to review and re-launch existing professional and ethical standards and guidance notes.

As at January 2008, the APESB had issued the following standards.
- APES 110 *Code of Ethics for Professional Accountants* — a mandatory standard for compliance for all members. APES 110 provides a conceptual framework to help members to identify, evaluate and respond to ethical threats to compliance with the fundamental principles outlined in the standard. This standard has the force of law for members who conduct audits of companies, registered schemes and disclosing entities in accordance

with Chapter 2M, or financial services licensees in accordance with Chapter 7 of the *Corporations Act 2001*.

- APES 205 *Conformity with Accounting Standards* — this replaces the former miscellaneous professional statement APS 1 *Conformity with Accounting Standards*. The objective of the standard is to establish the responsibilities of members to follow accounting standards when they prepare, present, audit, review or compile financial statements that are either general purpose financial statements or special purpose financial statements.
- APES 210 *Conformity with Auditing and Assurance Standards*, in which compliance is mandatory. APES 210 establishes the responsibilities of members in relation to compliance with the auditing and assurance standards, in the conduct of all Australian audit engagements, review engagements and other assurance engagements, and related services.
- APES 220 *Taxation Services* — this replaces the former APS 6 *Statement of Taxation Standards*. The standard relates to the provision of all taxation services and applies to members in business and in practice.
- APES 305 *Terms of Engagement* — this replaces APS 2 *Terms of Engagement*. From 1 July 2008, all members in public practice are required to document and communicate the terms of engagement.
- APES 320 *Quality Control for Firms* — a reissued statement to replace APS 5 *Statement of Quality Control for Firms*. This APES incorporates conforming amendments to ISQC 1. In respect of audits and reviews conducted under the provisions of the *Corporations Act 2001*, auditing standards have the force of law. To the extent that those auditing standards make reference to the quality control requirements for firms issued by a professional accounting body, the requirements of APES 320 have the same level of legal enforceability as the explanatory guidance in which such reference is included.

Quality control standards

The quality of auditing services rendered by a firm depends on auditing standards for each engagement, and on quality control policies and procedures for the firm's auditing practice as a whole. The statement directly relevant to audit practice as a whole is ASA 220 *Quality Control for an Audit of a Financial Report and Other Historical Financial Information* (ISA 220).

ASA 220 (ISA 220) identifies the responsibilities of an engagement partner and the engagement team in an audit engagement. The engagement partner should be responsible on behalf of the firm for the quality control and promotion of a quality-oriented culture on each audit engagement to which that engagement partner is assigned. He or she should set an example regarding audit quality that emphasises professional standards, compliance and ethical requirements. The engagement partner, together with members of the engagement team as appropriate, should document the extent of enquiries and discussions that have taken place concerning ethics. This document should include:

- identified potential threats and safeguards adopted
- the manner in which any issues arising have been resolved
- a conclusion on compliance with ethical requirements.

The elements of quality control are relevant for individual audits, as well as general quality controls applicable to the audit practice as a whole. The general quality controls discussed here are the policies and procedures that should, if adopted by a firm, provide reasonable assurance that all audits conducted by the firm are being carried out in accordance with auditing standards. Table 3.5 (overleaf) shows the quality-control elements as described in APES 320 (ISQC 1).

TABLE 3.5:
Quality control — elements, policies and procedures

Element	Policy	Procedures
Leadership responsibilities	The leadership responsibility should rest with its top management, so that it has an internal quality-oriented culture.	Set good example in compliance, clear and consistent messages at all levels, issue reports that are appropriate, effective training materials and staff appraisal procedures. Firm sets business strategy that recognises that quality overrides commercial considerations.
Ethical requirements	Establish policies to provide reasonable assurance that the firm and its personnel comply with ethical requirements.	Fundamental principles including integrity, objectivity, professional competence and due care, confidentiality and professional behaviour. Independence requirements must be adhered to, with clear communication and evaluation mechanisms.
Acceptance and continuance of client relationships	Policies include obtaining information to establish the integrity of clients.	Consider the integrity of the principal owners, key management and those charged with the governance role, the competence of the engagement team, and whether the firm can comply with the ethical requirements. Consider significant matters that have arisen during the current or previous audit engagement and the implications for continuing the relationship.
Human resources	The engagement partner should be satisfied that the collective team has appropriate capabilities, competence and time to perform the audit engagement in accordance with professional standards and regulatory and legal requirements. Whenever necessary, consultation within or outside the audit firm is to occur with those who have appropriate expertise.	Appropriate capabilities and competence include: an understanding of, and practical experience with, audit engagements of a similar nature and complexity; an understanding of the professional standards; appropriate technical knowledge, including relevant technology, knowledge of the industry, ability to exercise professional judgement and an understanding of the firm's quality control policies and procedures. Identify areas and specialised situations where consultation is required. Inform personnel of the firm's consultation policies. Specify areas of expertise. Maintain proper documentation of consultations to enable an understanding of the issues and the results. Designate individuals as specialists for consulting processes. Specify the extent of documentation for the results of the consultation.

Element	Policy	Procedures
Engagement performance	The engagement partner should take responsibility for the direction, supervision and performance of the audit engagement in compliance with professional standards.	Inform the audit team of their responsibilities, the nature of the entity's business, risk-related issues, problems that may arise, and the detailed approach to the performance of the engagement. Supervise, including tracking performance, considering capabilities, resolving significant issues and identifying matters for consultation. Review responsibilities, documentation and consultation.
Monitoring and quality control review	Monitor the adequacy and effectiveness of quality control policies and procedures. The engagement team should follow the firm's policies for dealing with and resolving differences of opinions. A quality control reviewer should be appointed and significant matters discussed. The report is not issued until the completion of the review.	Note deficiencies in the firm's quality control program. Define the scope and content of the monitoring program. Provide the findings of monitoring to appropriate management levels in the firm. Inform the engagement team that they may bring matters involving differences of opinion to the attention of the engagement partner. The quality control review should include an objective evaluation of the significant judgements made by the engagement team, and the conclusions reached in formulating the auditors' report.

Source: APES 320 *Quality Control for Firms.*

Firm regulation

Firm regulation occurs within the public accounting firm. A prime example is implementing a system of quality control as required by quality control standards discussed in the preceding section. This means that the firm's day-to-day actions must comply with the policies and procedures pertaining to quality control elements. To help staff meet professional standards, for example, firms often provide on-the-job training and require their professionals to participate in continuing professional education courses. Personnel whose work is substandard should be counselled and, if rapid improvement is not forthcoming, their employment should be terminated. (Individuals who perform well are rewarded.) Motivation also results from the desire to avoid the expense and damage to a firm's reputation that accompany litigation and other actions brought against the firm for alleged non-compliance with professional standards. Auditors' exposure to litigation is discussed in chapter 5.

The system of quality control in a firm is described in APES 320 and includes the following.

Leadership responsibilities for quality within a Firm

A Firm shall establish policies and procedures designed to promote an internal culture recognising that quality is essential in performing Engagements. Such policies and procedures shall require the Firm's chief executive officer (or equivalent), or, if appropriate, the Firm's managing board of Partners (or equivalent), to assume ultimate responsibility for the Firm's system of quality control. [paragraph 14]

Relevant Ethical Requirements

A Firm shall establish policies and procedures designed to provide it with Reasonable Assurance that the Firm and its Personnel comply with Relevant Ethical Requirements. [paragraph 19]

Acceptance and continuance of Client relationships and specific Engagements

A Firm shall establish policies and procedures for the acceptance and continuance of Client relationships and specific Engagements, designed to provide the Firm with Reasonable Assurance that it will only undertake or continue relationships and Engagements where the Firm:

(a) Is competent to perform the Engagement and has the capabilities, including time and resources, to do so;

(b) Can comply with Relevant Ethical Requirements; and

(c) Has considered the integrity of the Client and does not have information that would lead it to conclude that the Client lacks integrity. [paragraph 38]

Human resources

A Firm shall establish policies and procedures designed to provide it with Reasonable Assurance that it has sufficient Personnel with the competence, capabilities and commitment to ethical principles necessary to:

(a) Perform Engagements in accordance with Professional Standards and applicable legal and regulatory requirements; and

(b) Enable the Firm or Engagement Partners to issue reports that are appropriate in the circumstances. [paragraph 47]

Engagement performance

A Firm shall establish policies and procedures designed to provide it with Reasonable Assurance that Engagements are performed in accordance with Professional Standards and applicable legal and regulatory requirements, and that the Firm or the Engagement Partner issue reports that are appropriate in the circumstances. Such policies and procedures shall include:

(a) Matters relevant to promoting consistency in the quality of Engagement performance;

(b) Supervision responsibilities; and

(c) Review responsibilities. [paragraph 58]

Monitoring

A Firm shall establish a Monitoring process designed to provide it with Reasonable Assurance that the policies and procedures relating to the system of quality control are relevant, adequate, and operating effectively. This process shall:

(a) Include an ongoing consideration and evaluation of the Firm's system of quality control, including, on a cyclical basis, Inspection of at least one completed Engagement for each Engagement Partner;

(b) Require responsibility for the Monitoring process to be assigned to a Partner or Partners or other persons with sufficient and appropriate experience and authority in the Firm to assume that responsibility; and

(c) Require that those performing the Engagement or the Engagement Quality Control Review are not involved in inspecting the Engagements. [paragraph 106]

Documentation of the system of quality control

A Firm shall establish policies and procedures requiring appropriate documentation to provide evidence of the operation of each element of its system of quality control. [paragraph 124]

APES 320 has important implications for public practitioners. It has the force of law for those performing audits under the Corporations Act. CPA Australia reminded its members that they should also comply with its Risk Management Statement (RMS 1), which was not referred to in APES 320.

Although APES 320 clearly lays down the expectations of quality control procedures in audit firms, it is worthwhile to consider the promotion of ethical behaviour through education. David Satava et al. (2006) recommends the implementation of principle-based ethics. The authors regard audit reforms as primarily rule-based, while it is the principles of ethics that govern the behaviour of individuals. The six recommendations made included:

- mandating the teaching of business ethics to accounting students
- mandating that CPAs (or CAs) be required to complete continuing education courses in ethics
- urging firms to conduct periodic cultural audits of their firms to monitor attitudes about principle-based and rule-based ethics and to provide in-house training
- encouraging the professional bodies to financially support joint research between academics and practitioners regarding audit practices, firm culture, business ethics, corporate governance and related concepts
- urging professional associations, academics and business ethics societies to disseminate information to boards and audit committee members about rule-based and principle-based ethics and the relationship to auditing standards
- increasing the funding of the enforcement division of the SEC (or ASIC or equivalent) with regard to the monitoring of corporate frauds.[40]

Audit Quality Review Board

In February 2006, the Audit Quality Review Board (AQRB) was officially launched by the Honourable Chris Pearce MP, Parliamentary Secretary to the Treasurer. It complemented other review processes undertaken by the professional bodies and the surveillance program of ASIC. The AQRB's role was to review the systems used by major audit firms that are intended to ensure independence and quality standards in relation to the audits of listed companies. Most of the directors of the AQRB have never worked in the auditing profession and are independent of the firms to be reviewed. The Big Four auditing firms voluntarily agreed to provide the AQRB with access to their quality systems, highlighting their continued commitment to the integrity of the auditing process. An important role of the AQRB is self-evaluation, with a summary report of the systems monitored to be made publicly available. It had an initial 3-year term, funded by a levy on participating firms and supported by the St James Ethics Centre, which is available to resolve ethical issues in the AQRB and be involved in dispute resolution. The AQRB finished its term in 2009 and other forms of government regulation have been put in place as follows.

Treasury

On 5 March 2010, the Chairman of the Financial Reporting Council, Mr Jeffrey Lucy AM, released a Treasury consultation paper *Audit Quality in Australia: A Strategic Review*. The Treasury paper identified the key drivers of audit quality in Australia and assessed whether any measures should be taken to address any real or perceived threats to these drivers of audit quality. Treasury has drawn on the experience, research and studies on audit quality undertaken in Australia, in foreign jurisdictions, including the UK and US, and by international bodies. Treasury's paper is designed to facilitate informed debate within Australia with a view to achieving appropriate policy responses to the issues raised in the paper which may provide a blueprint for possible future reforms. Full details can be found at www.treasury.gov.au.

The Treasury paper draws on research findings from an Australian National University-led project about the future of auditing. The Treasury review used the researchers' findings, placing special emphasis on the insights provided into the drivers of audit quality in Australia compared to the US and the UK. This very extensive research project on the future of auditing explored issues within certain major themes including:

- expectations gap/informativeness of the audit opinion
- staffing, skills and social impacts
- public policy implications
- the audit and assurance service.

The researchers concluded that various stakeholders see that the external financial statement audit is valued and that there is no call to reduce or eliminate its mandate. However, the audit expectations gap survives and the researchers are of the view that it is not possible to close this gap completely and that to aim to do so is an unrealistic expectation. In terms of reforms to the regulatory regime in the past several years, some evidence of unintended consequences was noted, such as the audit opinion provided across a whole range of auditees is almost identically worded and this, in and of itself, could have contributed to an undervaluing of the financial statement audit in the market for information. There is also a recognition that audit documentation quality has improved, but at a cost. The researchers also noted that there are many challenges relating to the staffing of suppliers to the audit market. These relate to more junior staff and generation Y issues, as well as the challenges for providing appropriate incentives for more senior staff and the limitations some of the regulatory changes have caused. Finally, the researchers observe that the absence of a call for the reversal or reduction of the audit mandate is a powerful starting point for the future of auditing in Australia.

The Treasury paper observes that the ANU researchers had provided 'a valuable insight into the views of participants in the market for audit services in Australia', and that 'the scale of the project is extensive and Treasury is of the view that the [800-page] report ... and its list of conclusions, policy issues and suggestions on actionable items will contribute over time to the public debate on the future of auditing in Australia.'

Self-regulation

The ICAA and CPA Australia independently undertake quality assurance practice reviews. To continue to hold a Certificate of Public Practice, members have to demonstrate compliance with quality control standards. Members are obliged to give an annual signed assurance that the quality control requirements are being met. Reviewers appointed by the ICAA and CPA Australia visit all practices on a cyclical basis over 5 years. Findings from the reviews are confidential. The reviewed practice is given an assessment by the reviewer. If findings are unsatisfactory, the practitioner is required to take remedial action and is subject to further review within an agreed timeframe. Serious deficiencies are dealt with through disciplinary procedures. The main focus of practice reviews is educational.

Government regulation

The main objective of government regulation is to protect the investing public from sub-standard financial reporting and auditing practice. It is basically punitive in nature.

ASIC

Government regulation is exercised through ASIC's surveillance (inspection) program, which involves the scrutiny of all aspects of the financial statements of listed and some non-listed Australian public companies. The objective of this surveillance process is to ensure compliance with mandatory accounting standards. The surveillance program is supplemented by an auditors' review program and a liquidators' review program.

Where necessary, breaches of the Corporations Act by auditors and liquidators are referred to the CALDB, which can cancel the registration of auditors under powers conferred by the Corporations Act, s. 1292(1). CALDB also monitors the minimum educational and experience requirements and the ethical and professional considerations relevant to the registration of auditors and liquidators.

A significant additional regulatory mechanism occurs through the courts, whereby an accountant may face a lawsuit for negligence and incur costs and damages for failure to comply with the profession's standards of practice. All these forms of regulation are important. They are interrelated and designed to improve the quality of audit practice.

Learning check

Do you know . . .

3.1 ☐ An accountant is regarded as a professional person who possesses knowledge, authority and community approval; complies with an ethical code; and belongs to and practises within the culture and rules of a professional body. Accountants' complex roles involve extensive duties and relationships and distinctive rights under a regulatory framework, and require the practice of certain values.

3.2 ☐ Ethics concerns the study of choices in situations in which there are conflicting duties, rights and interests. Professional ethics examines ethical situations in a professional setting, where accountants are guided by a professional code of ethics and other moral standards and norms.

3.3 ☐ The *Code of Ethics for Professional Accountants* (the Code of Ethics) issued by the Accounting Professional & Ethical Standards Board of Australia aligns with the IFAC *Code of Ethics for Professional Accountants*. It lays down fundamental principles for accountants' roles and a conceptual framework for identifying, evaluating and managing the threats and implementing safeguards to ensure compliance with the fundamental principles.

3.4 ☐ Independence is the cornerstone of auditing. It has two facets — the fact of independence (also called actual independence) which refers to integrity, objectivity and strength of character, and the appearance of independence (also called perceived independence), enhanced by the principles, rules and guidelines of regulatory authorities and professional bodies. The fundamental framework of independence identifies threats and safeguards so that professional accountants can enhance their duty to serve the public interest.

3.5 ☐ To act in the public interest and with due professional care means accountants must maintain a high quality and high standards in their behaviour and the professional services they offer. Accountants and auditors must comply with technical standards and with quality assurance requirements.

LEARNING 7 objective

Describe the essential disciplinary measures for auditors.

3.6 PROFESSIONAL DISCIPLINE

The value of an auditor's opinion is significantly enhanced by the public's recognition of the high standards of practice and professional conduct of the auditor. This recognition comes in three ways:

1. high entry standards for professional membership
2. high standards of performance and conduct required of members
3. the power to discipline and, in extreme cases, to dismiss from membership those whose performance falls short of required standards.

The investigative and disciplinary powers of the ICAA and CPA Australia over their members are contained in the Supplemental Royal Charter and the Articles of Association respectively. Article 26 of CPA Australia's Articles of Association confers on its National Council the right to impose forfeiture of membership, suspension from membership, fines, censure and/or admonishment on any member of CPA Australia who, in the opinion of the Council:

(a) has been guilty of any breach of the memorandum, articles, by-laws or pronouncements of CPA Australia

(b) has been guilty of dishonourable practices or conduct derogatory to the profession of an accountant or conduct that is not in the best interests of CPA Australia or its members

(c) has failed to observe a proper standard of professional care, skill or competence

(d) has become an insolvent under administration.

The Supplemental Royal Charter of the ICAA confers similar powers on that body, with the additional right to discipline any member found by any court to be guilty of a felony, misdemeanour or fraud.

3.6.1 Disciplinary procedures

The Articles of Association of CPA Australia provide for establishing an Investigation Committee and a Disciplinary Committee in each state. Complaints against members are first referred to the Investigation Committee, which interviews the member and obtains information from any source considered necessary. The Investigation Committee then advises the Disciplinary Committee whether there is a case to answer. If there is a case, the Disciplinary Committee requires the member to appear before it, with legal representation if the member so desires. The member also has the right of appeal to an Appeals Committee at a national level. Penalties imposed against the member are made public as appropriate, such as by publication in CPA Australia's journal.

The ICAA has similar procedures. Its investigation committees, which function at the state level, have the authority to consider minor cases. Minor cases are those that do not require, in the opinion of the state investigation committees, the imposition of a sanction greater than (1) a reprimand, (2) an order for the payment of costs associated with the hearing, (3) an order that the member obtain and implement advice on the conduct of his or her practice, (4) a requirement that a member attend specified professional development activity, or (5) a fine not exceeding $5000.

The National Disciplinary Committee of the ICAA has the authority to impose sanctions as for minor cases. Additional punitive measures that it can impose include exclusion from membership, suspension from membership for up to 5 years, cancellation of a certificate of public practice, a declaration that a member is ineligible for a certificate of public practice for up to 5 years, and a fine not exceeding $100 000. There is a right of appeal (except for minor cases) to the National Appeals Committee.

Both the National Disciplinary Committee and the National Appeals Committee comprise senior members of the profession, state or national councillors, Fellows of the ICAA of at least 15 years standing and lay representatives. Thus, the person subject to discipline faces the elders of the profession and members of the public. To ensure the objectivity of deliberations, committee members can serve on only one of these committees at any one time.

In addition to investigation and disciplinary procedures exercised by the profession, the CALDB has the power to cancel or suspend the registration of an auditor who:

- has failed to adequately and properly perform the duties of an auditor
- is not a fit and proper person to remain registered as an auditor (s. 1280 of the Corporations Act).

Do you know ...

3.6 ☐ Auditors need to appreciate the current audit environment, which may present threats to auditors' independence, quality of work and objectivity. The audit environment is complex, and there are many pressures on auditors in their discharge of professional judgement. Auditors must be aware of duty and loyalty priorities when making difficult decisions to uphold their objectivity, integrity and ethical and professional standards. An auditor's decision may affect a number of stakeholders, and the responsibility to serve the public interest should prevail.

3.7 ☐ A characteristic of a profession is the ability to self-regulate. In the current environment of co-regulation, one feature of self-regulation is the establishment and monitoring of disciplinary procedures to ensure that members of a professional body comply with a minimum set standard of behaviour. The investigative and disciplinary powers of the ICAA and CPA Australia are contained in the Supplemental Royal Charter and the Articles of Association respectively. With increasing government regulation of auditors, it is important that the profession demonstrates its commitment to regaining its credibility by strengthening its quality control measures, including disciplinary procedures.

SUMMARY

The foundation of a profession lies with its ethical values. With the increasing complexity of businesses and the significant role of accountants and auditors as moral agents, it is important that students are aware of the ethical issues embedded within accounting and auditing practices.

As part of the reforms, and in line with the direction adopted by the International Federation of Accountants (IFAC), Australia's accounting bodies have adopted the global trend in refining the professional code. In July 2006, the Australian Accounting Professional & Ethical Standards Board released APES 110 *Code of Ethics for Professional Accountants,* which aligns with the IFAC *Code of Ethics for Professional Accountants,* and espouses the basic principles and expectations of behaviour to which members of the profession must adhere. Ethical threats and safeguards are identified, and examples of applications are made accessible to all accountants and auditors. Moreover, detailed independence guidelines are issued to ensure that auditors not only are independent in mind, but also will avoid any circumstances which might compromise perceived independence.

In reviewing professional ethics and independence, it has become clear that quality audits do not just involve technical competence, but require ethical competence and sound judgement.

KEY TERMS

accounting misstatements, p. 125

audit committee, p. 106

auditor liability, p. 131

co-regulation, p. 103

corporate collapses, p. 125

deontology, p. 101

earnings management, p. 125

ethical issues, p. 102

ethical relativism, p. 102

financial statement fraud, p. 125

independence, p. 97

internal control problems, p. 125

low-balling, p. 114

network firms, p. 114

non-audit services, p. 119

opinion shopping, p. 109

professional ethics, p. 97

public interest, p. 98

self-regulatory, p. 98

teleology, p. 101

utilitarianism, p. 101

virtue ethics, p. 102

 MULTIPLE-CHOICE questions

3.1 Which of the following characteristics does not distinguish a profession from other occupations?
A. Ability to command high fees in return for services.
B. Mastery of particular intellectual skills through education and training.
C. A common code of conduct to be practised and monitored by an association.
D. Acceptance of a duty to society as a whole.

3.2 Self-regulation means that a profession has autonomy in the discharge of its services. How have the corporate collapses of the early 2000s affected the self-regulatory regime of the auditing profession?
A. The auditing profession has gained extensive publicity and influence in the stock market.
B. The increased demand for reforms has resulted in the profession losing its self-regulatory power.
C. Auditors have become police for the corporate sector, with their increased role of reporting to ASIC.
D. Auditors are seen to have an important role in corporate management.

3.3 John resigned from an assurance engagement because his independence was impaired. He was concerned that if he did not resign then ASIC would have a case against the firm and its reputation would suffer as a result. This is an example of:
A. Consequentialism.
B. Non-consequentialism.
C. Virtue ethics.
D. Ethical relativism.

3.4 Ethical relativism means:
A. Adopting an international standard of behaviour for organisations.
B. Moral values are relative to a particular environment.
C. Instituting company policies on gifts and hospitality.
D. Developing a system that international businesses can apply anywhere.

3.5 The fundamental ethical characteristics required of professional accountants are:
A. Professionalism, experience and expertise.
B. Authority, community sanction and knowledge.
C. Competence, objectivity and integrity.
D. Self-interest, self-review and familiarity.

3.6 Threats to auditor independence can come from various sources. Which of these is referred to in the Code of Ethics as a self-review threat?
  A. The possibility of potential employment with the audit client.
  B. Preparation of original data used to generate a financial statement that is the subject matter of the audit engagement.
  C. Concern on the part of the auditor about the possibility of losing the engagement.
  D. Pressure to reduce inappropriately the extent of work performed in order to reduce fees.

3.7 The significance of economic, financial or other relationships in determining independence in appearance is evaluated by:
  A. What the auditor general decides is significant.
  B. What the auditor believes is unacceptable.
  C. What the company deems to be unacceptable.
  D. What a reasonable and informed third party would conclude as unacceptable.

3.8 Self-interest or self-review threats may result from the following, except:
  A. Executing authority on behalf of the client on transactions.
  B. Preparing source documents for the client to evidence the occurrence of transactions.
  C. Reporting to the CEO on a system which you helped implement.
  D. Writing a letter to the management to inform them of the discrepancies in the system.

3.9 Using the same senior personnel on an assurance engagement over a long period of time may create what type of threat to audit independence?
  A. Self-interest.
  B. Advocacy.
  C. Familiarity.
  D. Intimidation.

3.10 The Sarbanes–Oxley Act is seen to be different from other reforms because:
  (i) It is rules-based and has extensive prescriptive measures to restrict an auditor's involvements with audit clients.
  (ii) It covers a number of aspects of corporate governance and audit independence issues.
  (iii) It introduces an independent governmental oversight body to effectively eliminate audit self-regulation.
  A. (i) only.
  B. (i) and (ii) only.
  C. (ii) and (iii) only.
  D. (i) and (iii) only.

 ## REVIEW questions

3.11 How does ethics apply to auditors?

3.12 Identify the five types of ethical threats to professional independence and give a specific example of each.

3.13 What are the main ways in which the profession ensures the quality of audit services?

3.14 Describe what is meant by independence in mind and independence in appearance.

3.15 Discuss the safeguards which would eliminate or reduce the threat to independence created by providing non-assurance services.

3.16 Describe the components of the audit expectation gap.

3.17 Why did Arthur Andersen have so many audit failures, leading to its implosion in 2002?

3.18 Is regulation good for the audit profession? Discuss.

3.19 What are the major ways in which audit quality can be assured?

3.20 Why is the auditing profession losing its self-regulation rights?

PROFESSIONAL application questions

3.21 Professionalism ★

Brenda Jones is a newly qualified accountant who is carrying out her first audit as the in-charge auditor for a construction company client that is engaged in a range of long-term contracts. Brenda has little experience of these types of clients and the accounting requirements in relation to long-term contracts. John Bull is the CFO of the client, he is a busy man and has a notorious reputation for being unfriendly to auditors. You are Brenda's supervisor and it has become apparent that she has not got to grips with the accounting issues involved and has avoided asking the necessary questions of John Bull to gain an understanding of the company's transactions and the necessary audit work required to obtain evidence on the long-term contract transactions.

Required

Explain to Brenda the importance of professionalism, using the *Code of Ethics for Professional Accountants* and particularly referring to its guidance on competence and give advice as to how she should proceed.

3.22 Conflicts of interest ★★

Your firm, Earnest, Devoid and Couples, has been the auditor for many years of Barley Gordon Ltd, which operates a large chain of electrical goods retailers across Australia and New Zealand. The electrical goods retailing business is dominated by two major players in the market, Barley's, as they are affectionately known by the buying public, and Duck Guys Ltd, or Duckies as they are known.

The market is very competitive with both companies engaged in significant television advertising, price competition and other marketing activities in order to gain market share, largely by attracting the customers from the other company.

You have recently been approached by the CFO of Duckies to carry out its year-end audit. Duckies was attracted to your firm because of your extensive experience in the industry.

Required

Explain the safeguards that could be put in place in relation to the conflict of interest arising from the above.

3.23 Ethical issues ★

You are Mark Ouse, an audit senior with the firm Pull, Lift, Tug & Co. You are planning the financial report audit of Nestree Ltd, a manufacturer of confectionery. The following issues have arisen.

1. Arthur Stick, the Finance Manager of Nestree, was ill for three months of the year and Eloise Lift, the engagement partner, received a request from Nestree to supply a member of staff on secondment until Arthur was well. Eloise was only too happy to help and Daisy Flute, a member of Pull, Lift, Tug & Co's audit staff was seconded to Nestree for three months. Nestree was happy with this arrangement and Eloise enjoyed the additional fees this created for the firm. As a result of Daisy's secondment and the knowledge she now has

about Nestree, Eloise is suggesting that she will be a valuable member of the audit team for the current financial year's audit.

2. From the review of the draft financials that Mark has received, Nestree appears to take an optimistic approach to its valuation of development expenditure capitalised in intangible assets. Executive remuneration includes a profit-related bonus.

3. Staff of Nestree are entitled to visit the company shop where defective confectionery products or 'seconds' that do not make it past the company's quality control processes are available for purchase at a significant discount to normal retail prices. Nestree has in the past invited the audit team to enjoy this benefit while it is attending the company during its audit visit.

4. You are aware that Nestree's Finance Director, Barbara Polo, plays on the same softball team as Eloise Lift and recently spent a week with the team on a tour of Vanuatu.

Required

Explain the ethical threats above and identify how they might be avoided.

3.24 Ethical issues ★

Steven, a trainee auditor, is undertaking part-time university studies. While auditing the books of Oval Park Health Club, he discovers certain financial and management information that he believes will help him complete one of his university assignments. He copies the information and uses it in his assignment, carefully removing all reference to the name of the club to preserve the client's confidentiality.

Required

Discuss the ethical issues involved in this situation.[41]

3.25 Code of Ethics for Professional Accountants ★★

The following circumstances raise questions about an auditor's ethical conduct.

1. An auditor accepts an engagement knowing that she does not have the specialist knowledge required.
2. A public accounting firm states in a newspaper that it has had fewer lawsuits than its main competitors have had.
3. An auditor discloses confidential information about a client to a successor auditor.
4. A public accountant pays a commission to a solicitor to obtain a client.
5. A public accountant agrees to be the committee chairperson for a local fundraising activity.
6. An auditor accepts a Christmas gift from a client.
7. An auditor accepts a commission from an insurance company for recommending it to one of its audit clients.
8. An auditor has a bank loan with a bank that is an audit client.
9. An auditor retains a client's records as a means of enforcing payment of an overdue audit fee.

Required

(a) Discuss the fundamental principles of the *Code of Ethics for Professional Accountants* in relation to the above.

(b) Indicate in each of the above circumstances whether the effect on professional ethics is (i) a violation, (ii) not a violation or (iii) indeterminate, and explain.

3.26 Independence ★★

Polo Babywear Ltd was formed on 30 August 2013 and its first financial year ended on 30 June 2015. The audit firm of Ross, Young & Partners has tendered for and won the audit for the first financial year. After signing the audit engagement letter, Mr Ross is approached and asked to act as the company secretary for a period of 6 months because the company has had difficulty in obtaining staff. The role would be mainly to sign documents and to satisfy ASIC that the company had a complete set of officers. Mr Ross would have no financial interest in the company through share ownership or otherwise, would receive no salary, would not keep the books, and would not give any advice that is different from what he would normally give in his duties as a public accountant.

Mr Ross decides to accept the offer, conditional on the appointment being definitely completed before the rendering of the audit opinion on the financial statements.

Required

Discuss Mr Ross's acceptance of the dual roles of company secretary and auditor.[42]

3.27 Independence ★★

You are Margaret String, one of the partners in the accounting firm Bader, String, Floss & Co. You have a large client, Drench Ltd, for which your firm has carried out a range of taxation, consultancy, audit and other assurance services. The firm now obtains significant fee income from Drench. An amount still has to be paid for work carried out earlier in the year in relation to consulting advice given to Drench about internal controls around its new purchase ledger system that was implemented during the year.

The planning work for the year end is about to commence and this will be the twelfth year that you have carried out the audit. The relationship between Drench and the audit team is excellent and the same audit staff have been happy to return to carry out the audit for the last five years, this consistency of staffing has been welcomed by Drench's accounting staff who feel this allows the audit to be done quickly and efficiently.

Drench is very happy with the quality of the audit staff, in fact it recently offered the role of Financial Controller to the audit team senior, Sally Bring. Sally accepted and will be starting her new role before the year-end audit visit. Before she leaves the firm, Sally has decided to take the audit team out for dinner, to say goodbye and thank them for their work over the last five years.

Required

Identify the risks to independence arising from the above and suggest how these threats might be mitigated.

3.28 Incompatible duties ★★

Brian Dewy has been asked by an audit client to perform an assurance engagement involving the evaluation of a computer security and control system. The client asks Brian, in reviewing the system, to:

- advise on the potential expansion of current control in respect of its IT system and strategy
- search for and interview new personnel to replace the existing IT manager
- train personnel.

In addition, the client asks Brian, during the 3 months after the review, to:

- comment on the ongoing operation of the system
- monitor client-prepared source documents and make changes in basic computer information system-generated data as he deems necessary without the concurrence of the client.

Brian says that he may perform some of the services requested, but not all of them.

Required

(a) Nominate which of these services Brian may perform.
(b) Before undertaking this engagement, Brian should inform the client of all significant matters related to the engagement. What are these matters?

3.29 Audit quality ★★

You have just started carrying out the fieldwork for the audit of the financial report of Jocular Services Ltd for the year ended 30 June 2015. It has become apparent through your discussions with the client that there was something significantly wrong with last year's audit that was carried out by your firm.

Your discussions with the manager of last year's audit indicate that the audit senior carried out the work on his own as the client is only small. The audit visit was one week and at the end of the Friday of that week the senior handed over the completed audit working papers to the manager. That Friday happened to be the last day of employment for the audit senior who had accepted a job with a circus, as CFO.

It is clear to you that the audit file has recorded work that was not actually carried out. The file includes procedures that refer to documents that the client does not maintain and also includes explanations that do not correspond to what you now know to be the case. You suspect that the audit file from last year is an elaborate fiction. It looks like an audit file should and appears in all regards to be plausible; however, the details do not appear to correspond to the reality of the audit client.

You are discussing with the audit manager how to proceed.

Required
(a) Discuss the significance of audit quality control and identify the likely outcome of the above.
(b) How could the situation described above have been prevented?

 CASE studies

3.30 Ethical issues ★★

Noreen Parke has been working at Tony Young & Associates for 3 years. Noreen and her husband, Tom, are both interested in environmental issues and have participated in community work concerning the environment. During a pharmaceutical company's annual audit for the financial year ended 30 June 2015, Noreen notices the company had recently changed its contractor for waste management to Dumpound Ltd. Noreen happens to know, through her community activities, that Dumpound is being investigated by the local council for the level of toxic waste at one of its sites.

The waste management contract between Dumpound and the pharmaceutical company does not specify damages and has not been signed by Dumpound. The contract is for a substantial amount and is valid for 3 years, and Noreen is concerned about the implications. The local council carries out strict inspections and imposes heavy fines for toxic dumping.

Noreen raises the issue with Tony, the partner in charge of the audit. 'This is reality, Noreen,' Tony says. 'As far as I am concerned, we are responsible for the correctness of its financial report, and nothing else. Besides, you do not have the qualifications to judge whether a company is a good corporate citizen or not. We are not concerned with the business management.' Noreen is told to mind her audit without raising any fuss.

Required
(a) Explain the ethical issues involved here.
(b) Recommend a course of action for Noreen.

3.31 Ethical issues in auditing ★★★

John, a young CPA and one of the audit team members for Moulberg Electrical Appliances Ltd, has developed very good insights into the company's systems in the last 12 months and was asked by his partner, Chandler, to draft a report on the reliability of the internal control at Moulberg for review. The report is to be used as a part of a due diligence assurance engagement for Moulberg's prospectus. Moulberg wants to be listed on the Australian Securities Exchange by next June.

In carrying out the review, John finds a number of matters that concern him. He notices that the controls over inventory requisitions are very poor, leading to numerous complaints from customers about delays and wrong deliveries, and cancellations. Moreover, the inventory records do not show the history or the values of the inventory, so that estimates were used to arrive at the year-end inventory. He also noticed the poor standard of the appliances, with manufacturers' warranties long expired.

John completes his report, with details of the poor internal controls for his partner's review. However, his partner replaces his report with a very brief summary, and a conclusion that the internal control systems are sound and reliable.

John makes an appointment to see Chandler, but is worried as to how he should approach him about Moulberg Electrical Appliances' issues.

Required

Discuss the professional and ethical issues faced by John and provide an analysis which can help him deal with the matter with Chandler.

RESEARCH question

3.32 Auditor independence

The Department of Treasury *Audit Quality in Australia: A Strategic View*, is available from the website www.treasury.gov.au. The 2009 report was completed on behalf of the Financial Reporting Council (FRC). Access the report and discuss the following:

1. Why is auditor independence important and what do you think is the role of the FRC in this regard?
2. If you were an external consultant for the FRC, identify the audit quality issues highlighted in the review and recommend changes to the audit independence regime.
3. Evaluate the system of how the FRC examines auditor independence.

FURTHER READING

ASIC (Australian Securities and Investments Commission), *Audit Inspection Program (Second Report to FRC)*, Report no. 78, August 2006.

Accounting Professional Ethical Standards Board (APESB), *Code of Ethics for Professional Accountants*, Melbourne, 2008.

B Andrews, 'Safeguards for the future', *Business Review Weekly*, 27 October 2005.

T Campbell, 'The ethics of auditing', in *Ethics and Auditing*, edited by T Campbell and K Houghton, ANU Press, 2005.

F Clarke & G Dean, *Indecent Disclosure: Gilding the Corporate Lily*, Cambridge University Press, Melbourne, 2007.

B Cooper, P Leung, S Dellaportas, B Jackling & G Wong, 'Ethics education for accounting students — a toolkit approach', *Accounting Education: An International Journal* 17(4), December 2008.

S Dellaportas, K Gibson, R Alagiah, M Hutchinson, P Leung & D Van Homrigh, *Ethics, Governance and Accountability: A Professional Perspective*, John Wiley & Sons, Brisbane, 2005.

S Franklin, 'Proposals to improve the image of the public accounting profession', *CPA Journal* 76(3), 1 March 2006.

K Houghton, C Jubb, M Kend & J Ng, *The Future of Auditing*, ANU E Press, Canberra, 2009.

International Federation of Accountants (IFAC), *Code of Ethics for Professional Accountants*.

IFAC Task Force on Rebuilding Public Confidence in Financial Reporting, *Rebuilding Public Confidence in Financial Reporting — An International Perspective*, New York, 2003, www.ifac.org.

K Trotman, *Professional Judgement: Are Auditors Being Held to a Higher Standard than Other Professionals?* Institute of Chartered Accountants in Australia, August 2006.

AL Watkins & VM Iyer, 'Expanding ethics education: professionals can participate', *CPA Journal* 76(2), 1 February 2006.

NOTES

1. K Walsh, 'PwC: Australia not like the UK on tax avoidance', *Australian Financial* Review, 16 May 2013.

2. The Institute of Chartered Accountants in Australia (ICAA) and CPA Australia announced on 2 November 2005 the establishment of an independent ethical standards board to set the code of professional conduct and professional statements by which their members are required to abide. The Accounting Professional & Ethical Standards Board (APESB) was said to be formed in the public interest. The two accounting bodies have made an effort in the co-regulatory environment, post CLERP 9, to review self-regulation. The ICAA then CEO, Stephen Harrison, said it was appropriate to move standard setting to a more independent body rather than having the profession set its own standards. The APESB sets its own business plan, and promulgates, reviews and oversees ethical and professional standards. It consists of up to eight members, comprising representatives from the public sector, corporate sector, audit profession, academia, and the general public. Two of these are CPA Australia members and another two are ICAA members.

3. The IFAC Board and the IFAC Ethics Committee, now the International Ethics Standards Board for Accountants (IESBA), have developed a conceptual framework of professional ethics and incorporated the framework as a model on which national ethical guidance is to be based. This represents a conceptual change, and IFAC realises that training is required for all accountants for it to be successfully implemented.

4. The distinctions between a professional and a non-professional are the key issues discussed in A Abbot, 'Professional ethics', *American Journal of Sociology* 88(5), 1988, pp. 855–85. The literature has identified five major characteristics of a professional: theoretical knowledge, authority to practise, the community's sanction in terms of regulation and discipline, an enforceable code of ethics or conduct, and a self-defined culture.

5. E Greenwood, 'Attributes of a profession', *Social Work*, July 1957, pp. 45–55.

6. L Brooks & P Dunn, *Business and Professional Ethics for Directors, Executives & Accountants*, South-Western Publishing, USA, 2009.

7. Steven M Mintz, *Cases in Accounting Ethics and Professionalism*, 2nd edn, McGraw-Hill, New York, 1992.

8. John Rawls, *A Theory of Justice*, Harvard University Press, Cambridge, Mass., 1971.

9. The ASX Corporate Governance Principles and Recommendations were first published in 2003 with ten principles. The principles were revised in 2007. Principle 3 'Promote ethical and responsible decision-making' contains detailed suggestions on companies' codes of conduct.

10. The American Accounting Association (AAA) model originates from HQ Langenderfer & JW Rockness, 'Integrating ethics into the accounting curriculum — issues, problems and solutions', *Issues in Accounting Education* 4, 1989, pp. 58–69. They introduced a seven-step decision-making model. These steps are: (1) determine the facts, (2) define the ethical issue, (3) identify the major principles, rules and values involved, (4) specify alternatives, (5) compare the values and alternatives, and see if a clear decision emerges, (6) assess the consequences, and (7) make a decision.

11. Stakeholder impact analysis is introduced by Leonard Brooks, *see* note 6, pp. 180–7.

12. Laura L Nash, 'Ethics without the sermon', *Harvard Business Review* 59, 1981, pp. 79–90.

13. ibid.

14. IFAC Policy Position 5 was issued in June 2012 with guidance on who the public is and how to assess whether actions, decisions or policies are in the public interest. The assessment involves an assessment of costs and benefits, and an assessment of process. This is detailed in the IFAC Policy Position 5 appendices.

15. *Corporations Act 2001*, s. 324CD, paragraph 1.

16. The International Ethics Standards Board for Accountants (IESBA) has reissued Section 290 of the IFAC Code, which now incorporates a definition of a network firm. In respect of assurance engagements, it is important that the firm performing the assurance role and, when applicable, network firms, are independent of the assurance client. A *network* is defined as a larger structure that is aimed at cooperation and has one or more of the elements such as profit/cost sharing, common shares ownership or management, common quality control or business strategy, common brand name, or use of a significant part of the same professional resources. Professional accounting firms that perform assurance engagements and that have operating agreements or referral networks with other firms will need to evaluate the requirements of the standard and whether they are deemed to be in a network. It is required that the network of firms is independent of the prospective assurance client.

17. The APESB issued ED 03/07 in May 2007 in respect of Section 290 Independence — Assurance Engagements. The ED proposed a clarification of independence regarding network firms. Paragraphs 290.1 to 290.13 remain unchanged. Paragraphs 290.14 to 290.34 remain unchanged but were renumbered as paragraphs 290.27 to 290.47. In the case of an assurance engagement, it is in the public interest and, therefore, required by the Code of Ethics that members of assurance teams, firms and, when applicable, network firms are independent of assurance clients (paragraph 290.1). Also, APES 110 *Code of Ethics for Professional Accountants* was subject to a six-monthly review, the report of which was issued in January 2007. The recommendations contained in the report include:

    - cross-referencing to the Corporations Act to be considered
    - update of terminology
    - independence and definitions of network firms
    - a statement of conformity with the IFAC Code of Ethics to be incorporated
    - the need for a new standard covering issues relating to prospectuses and reports on profit forecasts.

18. The Joint Committee of Public Accounts and Audit (JCPAA) report, *Review of Independent Auditing by Registered Company Auditors*, committee chaired by Bob Charles MP, was released by the Parliament of Australia in September 2002. This is available at www.aph.gov.au. It contains 13 recommendations concerning the legislative requirements of independent auditing.

    Discussion Paper 9, Corporate Law Economic Reform Program (CLERP 9), is concerned with quality disclosure for financial reports and audits. CLERP 9 covers the oversight of the audit profession, the market for audit services, auditor independence, auditor liability, accounting standards, analyst independence, continuous disclosure, disclosure requirements for shares and debentures, enforcement issues and shareholder participation and information. It was released in September 2002 and was subsequently made law in the CLERP 9 Act of 2004, and integrated into the Corporations Act.

    The eight essential corporate governance principles issued by the Corporate Governance Council of the Australian Securities Exchange are available at www.asx.com.au (see note 9).

    The report of the HIH Royal Commission by Mr Justice Neville Owen was delivered to the Governor-General on 4 April, and was released on 16 April 2003. There are three volumes, dealing with the background of the HIH Insurance Company's collapse, and the involvement of the directors and officers, auditors and other parties. The report made 61 Policy Recommendations which cover corporate reporting, Australia's prudential authority's governance arrangements, auditor independence and reports. Copies of the report are available at www.hihroyalcom.gov.au.

19. ASIC Media and Information Release 05–343, 'ASIC reports on the first year of its auditor inspection program', www.asic.gov.au.

20. Auditor independence inspection program, September 2005, Australian Securities and Investments Commission.

21. ASIC report 317 audit inspection program report for 2011–12 covers the findings from an inspection of 20 Australian audit firms substantially undertaken in the 18 months to 30 June 2012.

The key findings include the lack of improvement in audit quality since 2010, an increase in instances where auditors did not perform all of the necessary procedures to obtain reasonable assurance that the audited financial report was not materially misstated.

22. Nanette Byrnes, Mike McNamee, Diane Brady & Louis Lavelle, 'Accounting in crisis', *Business Week*, 28 January 2002, www.businessweek.com.

23. Texas Society of CPAs, 'Huron Consulting Group analyzes leading causes of financial restatements in 2002', 21 January 2003, www.tscpa.org.

24. A description is offered by Jeremy Cooper, Deputy Chairman of ASIC, at the AICD NSW Division Directors' Briefing entitled 'Financial statement fraud corporate crime of the 21st century', at KPMG Centre, Wednesday 8 June 2005.

25. 13-073 Media Release and Enforcement Report of ASIC for the 6 months ended December 2012 include the various enforcement outcomes of ASIC. Enforceable undertakings are reported for the auditors of the former ABC Learning Centres and that of the former Centro group. Details of the findings are recorded in 12-186 MR and 12-288 MR respectively, www.asic.org.au, 9 April 2013.

26. *Reuters*, 'SEC sues KPMG on Xerox accounting', FoxNews.com, 29 January 2003, www.foxnews. com.

27. The HIH Royal Commission Report, *The Failure of HIH, a Critical Assessment*, vol. 1, Australian Treasury, April 2003.

28. Various press releases from ASIC during 1999 to 2002.

29. ASIC, 'ASIC releases stage one results of accounting surveillance', Media Release 02/460, 18 December 2002, www.asic.gov.au.

30. G Costa, 'Accuracy a qualified success', *The Age*, 18 December 2003, www.theage.com.au.

31. The full ASIC report for 2006 is available on the ASIC website and is summarised on the Institute of Chartered Accountants' website, www.charteredaccountants.com.au. The overall observations and findings include that many firms committed resources to develop policies and systems on independence. There were considerable variations between the firms and some firms have been slow to plan and implement a transition to the new regime on independence. Areas for improvement include compliance with independence policies, documentation and approval of non-audit services, and completion of audit documentation.

32. Article published in the *Australian Financial Review* on 5 November 2012 showing the complexity of audit quality, scepticism and the expectations of auditors. This report was followed by ASIC's inspection report that shows the lack of audit quality by many audit firms, www.afr.com, 5 November 2012.

33. P Leung & BJ Cooper, 'Accountants, ethical issues and the corporate governance context', *Australian Accounting Review* 15(1), 2005.

34. A Craswell, D Stokes & J Laughton, 'Auditor independence and fee dependence', *Journal of Accounting and Economics* 33(2), pp. 253–75.

35. T Campbell & K Houghton (eds), *Ethics and Auditing*, ANU Press, Canberra, 2005. The book contains three main parts: Approaches to the critique of auditing, Auditor independence, and Beyond the auditor: the search for solutions.

36. Bill Edge, 'Foreword: Restoring public trust', in *Ethics and Auditing*, ibid., p. xv.

37. Brooks, *see* note 6.

38. An IFAC commissioned study entitled *Ethics Education: Approaches to the Development and Maintenance of Professional Values, Ethics and Attitudes in Accounting Education Programs* was completed by Leung, Cooper, Dellaportas, Jackling & Leslie in 2006, and published on the IFAC website. The IFAC Ethics Education study is sponsored by the IFAC Education Committee and key accounting bodies and accounting firms.

39. CPA Australia & the Institute of Chartered Accountants in Australia, *Auditing Competency Standard for Registered Company Auditors*, 24 November 2004.

40. David Satava, Cam Caldwell & Linda Richards, in 'Ethics and the Auditing Culture: Rethinking the Foundation of Accounting and Auditing', *Journal of Business Ethics* 64, pp. 271–84, 2006.

41. Adapted from Professional Year Programme of the ICAA, 1997, Accounting 2 Module.

42. Adapted from the AICPA.

Answers to multiple-choice questions

3.1 *A*   3.2 *B*   3.3 *A*   3.4 *B*   3.5 *C*   3.6 *B*   3.7 *D*   3.8 *D*   3.9 *C*   3.10 *A*

chapter 4

Other assurance engagements and quality standards

OVERVIEW

4.1 Assurance engagement standards

4.2 Assurance engagements involving historical financial information

4.3 Assurance engagements other than audits or reviews of historical financial information

4.4 Examples of assurance engagements other than those relating to historical financial information

4.5 Quality management and the assurance practitioner

Summary

Key terms

Multiple-choice questions

Review questions

Professional application questions

Case studies

Research question

Further reading

Notes

LEARNING objectives

After studying this chapter, you should be able to:

1 appreciate the framework on assurance engagements other than those relating to general purpose financial report audits

2 discuss assurance engagements for historical financial information other than those relating to general purpose financial report audits

3 discuss the features and extent of other assurance engagements

4 use examples to illustrate the scope of assurance engagements other than those relating to historical financial information

5 appreciate some of the professional quality standards applicable to assurance engagements.

PROFESSIONAL STATEMENTS

Australian		International	
Framework	*The Framework for Assurance Engagements*	**Framework**	*The Framework for Assurance Engagements*
ASA 240	*The Auditor's Responsibilities Relating to Fraud in an Audit of a Financial Report*	**ISA 240**	*The Auditor's Responsibilities Relating to Fraud in an Audit of Financial Statements*
ASA 800	*Special Considerations—Audits of Financial Reports Prepared in Accordance with Special Purpose Frameworks*	**ISA 800**	*Special Considerations—Audits of Financial Statements Prepared in Accordance with Special Purpose Frameworks*
ASA 805	*Special Considerations—Audits of Single Financial Statements and Specific Elements, Accounts or Items of a Financial Statement*	**ISA 805**	*Special Considerations—Audits of Single Financial Statements and Specific Elements, Accounts or Items of a Financial Statement*
ASA 810	*Engagements to Report on Summary Financial Statements*	**ISA 810**	*Engagements to Report on Summary Financial Statements*
ASAE 3000	*Assurance Engagements Other than Audits or Reviews of Historical Financial Information*	**ISAE 3000**	*Assurance Engagements Other than Audits or Reviews of Historical Financial Information*
ASAE 3100	*Compliance Engagements*		
ASAE 3402	*Assurance Reports on Controls at a Service Organisation*		
ASAE 3410	*Assurance Engagements on Greenhouse Gas Statements*	**ISAE 3410**	*Assurance Engagements on Greenhouse Gas Statements*
ASAE 3500	*Performance Engagements*		
		ISAE 3400	*The Examination of Prospective Financial Information*
ASAE 3420	*Assurance Engagements to Report on the Compilation of Pro Forma Historical Financial Information included in a Prospectus or Other Document*	**ISAE 3420**	*Assurance Engagements to Report on the Compilation of Pro Forma Financial Information included in a Prospectus or Other Document*
ASAE 3450	*Assurance Engagements Involving Corporate Fundraisings and/or Prospective Financial Information*		
AUS 810	*Special Purpose Reports on the Effectiveness of Control Procedures*		
AUS 904	*Engagements to Perform Agreed-upon Procedures*	**ISRS 4400**	*Engagements to Perform Agreed-upon Procedures Regarding Financial Information*
ASRE 2400	*Review of a Financial Report Performed by an Assurance Practitioner Who is Not the Auditor of the Entity*	**ISRE 2400**	*Engagements to Review Financial Statements*
ASRE 2405	*Review of Historical Financial Information Other than a Financial Report*	**ISRE 2400**	*Engagements to Review Financial Statements*

Australian		International	
ASRE 2410	Review of a Financial Report Performed by the Independent Auditor of the Entity	ISRE 2410	Review of Interim Financial Information Performed by the Independent Auditor of the Entity
ASRE 2415	Review of a Financial Report—Company Limited by Guarantee		
AGS 1036	The Consideration of Environmental Matters in the Audit of a Financial Report	IAPS 1010	The Consideration of Environmental Matters in the Audit of Financial Statements
APES 110	Code of Ethics for Professional Accountants		International Federation of Accountants Code of Ethics for Professional Accountants

SCENE SETTER

Integrated reporting brings legal worries

Directors believe the fear of being sued could hamper the adoption of integrated reporting in Australia.

A draft global framework for integrated reporting, which aims to improve investor disclosure by including non-financial data in annual reports, was launched by the International Integrated Reporting Council on Tuesday.

Australia Post chairman and former Telstra finance chief John Stanhope said directors feared talking about future strategies and business models — one of the central tenets of integrated reporting — if they can then be sued based on these if they don't come true.

He said there may need to be some form of 'safe harbour' clause introduced, possibly in the continuous disclosure rules.

The draft plan asks companies to report on six 'capitals'. As well as traditional financial and manufactured capital, companies would need to report on social and relationship capital, natural capital, human capital and intellectual capital.

Mr Stanhope, a member of the Financial Reporting Council's integrated reporting taskforce, said the novelty of the concepts and the jargon used in the framework will also need to be explained. 'It is going to depend on how we tell the story,' he said at a panel discussion in Sydney hosted by CPA Australia.

'If you start to talk to Joe Citizen who has 2000 Telstra shares about six capitals, they will get a little lost. So it has to be simply put what we are talking about and how it is relevant to them as a stakeholder.'

Pablo Berutti, head of responsible investment Asia Pacific at Colonial First State Asset Management,

hoped integrated reports will become a source of concise information for analysts.

'Most analysts I work with have enormous volumes of information directed at them,' he said. 'Hopefully in the battle for analysts bandwidth it can displace the less relevant information that is out there.'

The Australian Council of Super Investors urged listed companies to adopt the guidelines. 'The new framework holds great promise for improving the dialogue between companies and investors about the real drivers of long-term performance, risk and value,' said chief executive Ann Byrne.

National Australia Bank, Stockland and bankmecu were among the 85 companies globally that participated in the pilot phase.

Roger Simnett, a professor in the school of accounting at University of NSW, said companies that had adopted integrated reporting in South Africa — the only jurisdiction where regulators prefer such reports — showed investors were reacting favourably, with a small 0.2 per cent drop in companies' cost of capital since it was introduced there two years ago.

Auditors may also have trouble signing off on integrated reports.

'Moving from the assurance process under the current reporting framework to the integrated reporting framework will require a lot of careful consideration on the role of the auditor and the level of assurance that can realistically be provided,' said Pitcher Partners managing director, Carl Millington.

Nick Ridehalgh, an Australian member of the working group that devised the framework, said one of the next steps was to get regulatory approval.

This chapter provides an overview of the latest developments in relation to non-audit assurance engagements. It identifies non-audit assurance services for financial and non-financial information. In particular, examples of these services are discussed with a view to help students appreciate the range of assurance services that are performed by independent practitioners, the principles and skill bases that are applied, and the issues relating to the credibility of such assurance reports. Students should be very much aware of the latest developments in respect of integrated reporting. Integrated reporting is a process that results in communication, most visibly a periodic 'integrated report', about value creation over time. An integrated report is a concise communication about how an organisation's strategy, governance, performance and prospects lead to the creation of value over the short, medium and long term. An integrated report should be prepared in accordance with the International <IR> Framework.[1] In recent times, the profession has been concerned with the development of integrated reporting that combines most non-financial information into the annual report, and the related assurance activities that should be applied.

The chapter also discusses quality standards and how total quality management affects the assurance practitioner.

LEARNING 1 objective

Appreciate the framework on assurance engagements other than those relating to general purpose financial report audits.

4.1 ASSURANCE ENGAGEMENT STANDARDS

A professional accountant may be asked to provide an opinion on a variety of different reports, activities and procedures. The opinion may be designed to give third parties some assurance that the report is fair or that activities and procedures have occurred in line with best practice or regulatory requirements. The variety of work that an accountant might be asked to perform is almost endless. The approach to developing standards to ensure quality is maintained when these activities are carried out has been to establish a framework that applies to all engagements where assurance is being provided and then develop specific standards where necessary to deal with specific types of engagements. The section below looks at the framework for assurance engagements which identifies what an assurance engagement is and gives some general requirements that apply to any assurance engagement. The discussion of the requirements for specific engagements starts in section 4.2.

4.1.1 The assurance engagement framework

The *Framework for Assurance Engagements* (Framework) issued by the Auditing and Assurance Standards Board (AUASB) is based on the International Framework issued by the International Federation of Accountants (IFAC) and it defines and describes the elements and objectives of an assurance engagement. It does not establish standards or provide procedural requirements but instead shows the concepts of an assurance engagement.[2]

What is (and is not) an assurance engagement

An **assurance engagement** is 'an engagement in which an assurance practitioner expresses a conclusion designed to enhance the degree of confidence of the intended users other than the responsible party about the outcome of the evaluation or measurement for a subject matter against criteria'.[3] For example, in an audit of a financial report in Australia the auditor expresses an opinion to the shareholders on whether the financial report, which is an evaluation of the financial position, financial performance and cash flows of the company, has been prepared by the directors in accordance with the requirements of an appropriate financial reporting framework (Australian accounting standards and the *Corporations Act 2001*). The following sections outline the elements of an assurance engagement as specified in the Framework.

A three-party relationship

A responsible party (responsible for the outcome), an intended user (relies on the outcome), and an assurance practitioner (provides an opinion on the outcome to give comfort to the intended user that it has been prepared in accordance with suitable criteria). The responsible party and the intended user(s) need not be separate entities and their relationship should be viewed within the context of the engagement. For example, an entity's board of directors may engage an assurance practitioner to perform an assurance engagement on a particular aspect of the entity's activities that is the direct responsibility of another level of management (although the board of directors has ultimate responsibility).

The subject matter of an assurance engagement

May be in different forms. These include information or data that can be historical, financial, performance-related, or physical; systems or processes; or behaviour such as corporate governance or human resource practices. The subject matter can relate to a particular timeframe, but must be identifiable and capable of evaluation or measurement. In assertion-based engagements, the responsible party provides an **assertion** about the subject matter (subject matter information). In direct reporting engagements, no such assertion is made, and the practitioner reports on the subject matter directly.

Suitable criteria

Refers to the basis on which the information about the subject matter is prepared or standards against which the subject matter can be measured. The suitability of criteria is normally based on:

- relevance — the criteria meet the objective of the engagement and contribute to conclusions being drawn
- completeness — the criteria are sufficient when no factor that might affect the conclusions in the context of the engagement objectives is omitted
- reliability — the criteria can be evaluated and measured with reasonable consistency
- neutrality — the criteria are objective and free from bias
- understandability — the criteria are clear and comprehensive and are not subject to a significant range of interpretation.

Evidence-gathering or engagement process

The assurance practitioner should conduct the engagement with an attitude of professional scepticism to obtain sufficient and appropriate evidence about the outcome. The practitioner evaluates the evidence obtained and exercises professional judgement in order to form conclusions. Evidence gathering normally involves a systematic approach that requires specialised knowledge and skills, and the application of techniques.

A conclusion or an assurance report

The assurance engagement report may be in long or short form. The long form of an assurance engagement report describes the objective(s) in detail, the criteria applied, specific findings and, in some cases, recommendations. The short-form report includes only some basic elements described in appropriate standards on auditing or on assurance engagements.

The above elements can apply to all assurance engagements; an audit of a financial report fits this model as the following sections discuss.

A three-party relationship

The directors are responsible for the preparation of a financial report, the intended users are the shareholders (and potentially other users) who will be relying on the financial report, and the assurance practitioner is the auditor who expresses an opinion to the shareholders.

The subject matter

The financial report comprising the statement of financial position, statement of comprehensive income and cash flow statement prepared by the directors is the outcome (or subject matter information) which provides information about the subject matter, the financial performance, financial position and cash flows of the company.

Suitable criteria

The financial reporting framework used in preparing the outcome which in Australia would be Australian accounting standards and the Corporations Act.

Evidence gathering

The auditor carries out a range of audit procedures identified in Australian auditing standards to ensure sufficient and appropriate evidence has been obtained to support the opinion given in the audit report.

Written assurance report

Audit report to the shareholders expressing an opinion as to whether or not the financial report is in accordance with Australian accounting standards and the Corporations Act and represents a true and fair view of the financial position, financial performance and cash flows of the company.

The above shows how the general principles of what constitutes an assurance engagement can be applied to an audit of a financial report and you will be seeing much more of these types of audits in the coming chapters, but these basic principles apply to any engagement where the five elements are met and therefore the AUASB standards must be applied.

General requirements that apply to all assurance engagements

Assurance practitioners who perform assurance engagements are subject to the broad fundamental ethical principles and APES 110 *Code of Ethics for Professional Accountants* (IFAC *Code of Ethics for Professional Accountants*), revised December 2010. The Code of Ethics formulates the fundamental ethical principles for professional accountants, which are integrity, objectivity, professional competence and due care, confidentiality, professional behaviour and technical standards. Before an assurance engagement is accepted the practitioner must be satisfied that ethical requirements can be satisfied. It is also important to establish that there is a rational purpose for the engagement, the subject matter is appropriate, the criteria are suitable, and sufficient evidence will be available to support the opinion which will be contained in a written report.

There is a wide variety of assurance engagements that a practitioner may be asked to perform, the type of engagement will have an effect on the type of opinion that will be provided and the practitioner will use professional judgement to determine the nature, timing and extent of procedures that will be required to support the opinion. The Framework requires an assurance engagement to be planned and performed with an attitude of professional scepticism to ensure sufficient appropriate evidence is obtained to support the opinion. In particular the practitioner must consider materiality, engagement risk (the risk that the practitioner gives the wrong opinion when material errors exist), and the quantity and quality of available evidence. These factors are interrelated: in a less risky engagement less evidence will be required; if the quality of the evidence is poor then more evidence will be required. High risk engagements lead to lower materiality levels and a requirement for more evidence. Each of the issues mentioned here will be discussed in more detail in chapters 6 to 10, relating to audits of financial reports.

The next section highlights different categories of assurance engagements but it is also necessary to identify the types of services provided by professional accountants that are not assurance services. These services do not have all of the five elements needed to be an assurance engagement and the auditing and assurance standards do not apply. Examples include: agreed-upon engagements (these are covered by Standards on Related Services), compilations (such as preparing financial reports), preparation of tax and other returns where no assurance is given, and consulting services. If a practitioner provides a report on these types of engagements it is important that the report is clearly distinguishable from that of an assurance report to avoid users being misled. Such reports should avoid using words such as 'audit', 'review' or 'assurance' and avoid references to auditing and assurance standards.[4]

4.1.2 Categories of assurance engagements

This section gives an overview of how the wide variety of possible assurance engagements can be categorised. From section 4.2 onwards there is a discussion of the specific requirements for the different categories of engagements.

Assertion-based engagements compared to direct reporting engagements

An **assertion-based engagement** is where the outcome on which the assurance practitioner provides an opinion is not on the subject matter itself but on an assertion made about the subject matter (subject matter information). For example, in an audit of a financial report the subject matter is the financial position, performance, cash flows of the company but the subject matter information is the financial report which contains information in the statement of financial position, the statement of comprehensive income and the cash flow statement. The auditor expresses an opinion on the financial report (the subject matter information), not directly on the subject matter.

In a **direct reporting engagement** the assurance practitioner expresses an opinion on the subject matter itself absent of any subject matter information. Consider an engagement to give an opinion on the effectiveness of a company's internal controls. The effectiveness of the internal controls would be the outcome, the internal controls themselves would be the subject matter and the criteria would be a framework that gives best practice guidance for internal controls such as the Committee of Sponsoring Organizations of the Treadway Commission's Enterprise Risk Management Framework. If the assurance provider is required to provide an opinion on whether or not they believe the internal controls are effective then this would be a direct reporting engagement. If the assurance provider is asked to provide an opinion not on the internal controls directly, but instead on a report produced by management about the effectiveness of the internal controls, this is an assertion-based engagement because the opinion is on the accuracy or fairness of the assertions contained in the report rather than the internal controls themselves.

Reasonable assurance compared to limited assurance

The Framework specifically identifies two types of assurance engagements:
1. reasonable assurance engagements
2. limited assurance engagements.

A reasonable assurance engagement requires the assurance practitioner to reduce engagement risk (the risk of giving the wrong opinion) to an acceptably low level and express a positive form opinion whereas a limited assurance engagement requires the assurance practitioner to reduce engagement risk to a level that is appropriate to the engagement and express a negative form opinion.[5] An assurance practitioner is generally unable to provide absolute (100%) assurance due to factors such as the use of samples for testing, limitations over internal controls, evidence being persuasive rather than conclusive, some items requiring judgement and in some cases the nature of the subject matter. If no opinion is provided then the engagement is not an assurance engagement and would be covered by Australian standards on Related Services.

In a reasonable assurance engagement the assurance practitioner will express an opinion that in all material respects the subject matter (subject matter for a direct reporting engagement or subject matter information for an assertion-based engagement) is in compliance with the criteria — this is the positive form of opinion. There is a clear positive statement that the practitioner believes that the subject matter is free from material errors. In order to be confident of this opinion the practitioner must ensure that the nature, timing and extent of assurance procedures carried out have generated sufficient and appropriate evidence to reduce engagement risk to an acceptably low level. In order to achieve this, the assurance provider has obligations to:
1. obtain an understanding of the engagement
2. assess risks
3. respond to those assessed risks
4. perform procedures such as substantive tests and where necessary tests of the effectiveness of internal controls
5. evaluate the evidence obtained.[6]

An example of an engagement where reasonable assurance would be given through a positive opinion would be an audit of a financial report.

In a limited assurance engagement the assurance provider will express an opinion that nothing has come to their attention to suggest that the outcome is not in compliance with the criteria. This is a negative form of assurance which is not as strong an opinion as the positive form. The negative form in this sense does not refer to an opinion which indicates material errors exist. The wording of the opinion is a double negative giving a soft positive: '*nothing* has come to their attention ... to suggest ... *not* in compliance'; the 'nothing' and the 'not' create a double negative which in turn is a soft, less reliable, positive. The negative form opinion does not require the same level of evidence as required for a positive opinion and therefore the procedures carried out will be deliberately limited compared to a reasonable assurance engagement. Evidence gathering is largely restricted to discussions with management and others and analytical procedures rather than detailed substantive or controls testing, this is why this opinion conveys only limited assurance to the user that material errors do not exist rather than the stronger positive opinion that gives reasonable assurance. An example of an engagement where limited assurance would be given through a negative opinion would be an engagement to review a financial report; the review being much less rigorous than an audit.

Assurance engagements related to historical financial information

A large part of the work of an assurance practitioner will be in giving assurance on historical financial information and this work can be categorised into three main areas:

1. audits of annual general purpose financial reports (covered by ASAs 100 to 799)
2. other audits of historical financial information (covered by ASAs 800, 805 and 810), including:
   (a) financial reports prepared in accordance with special purpose frameworks (ASA 800)
   (b) single financial statements and specific elements, accounts or items of a financial statement (ASA 805). This is an auditing standard not made under the *Corporations Act 2001*
   (c) summary financial information (ASA 810). This is an auditing standard not made under the *Corporations Act 2001*
3. reviews of financial reports and other historical financial information (covered by ASREs 2400 to 2415).

Assurance engagements other than those related to historical financial information

Assurance providers do not restrict themselves to engagements related to historical financial information and practitioners can be asked to give opinions on prospective financial information, internal controls and a wide variety of other non-financial information. The range of assurance engagements is wide and therefore an overarching standard, ASAE 3000 *Assurance Engagements other than Audits or Reviews of Historical Financial Information* (ISAE 3000), gives general requirements for assurance engagements of this kind. Further requirements are included in other assurance standards that relate to specific types of engagements, which include:

- compliance engagements — covered by ASAE 3100 *Compliance Engagements*
- performance engagements — covered by ASAE 3500 *Performance Engagements*
- controls service organisations — covered by ASAE 3402 *Assurance Reports on Controls at a Service Organisation*
- greenhouse gas statements — covered by ASAE 3410 *Assurance Engagements on Greenhouse Gas Statements*
- compilation of pro forma historical financial information included in a prospectus or other document — covered by ASAE 3420 *Assurance Engagements to Report on the Compilation of Pro Forma Historical Financial Information included in a Prospectus or other Document*
- corporate fundraisings and/or prospective financial information — covered by ASAE 3450 *Assurance Engagements involving Corporate Fundraisings and/or Prospective Financial Information.*[7]

In producing standards on assurance and other services the AUASB undertakes to issue the following standards:

- auditing standards (ASAs), developed in the context of financial report audits, to be applied to all audits of historical financial information

- standards on review engagements (ASREs), to be applied to the review of a financial report and to the review of other historical financial information
- standards on assurance engagements (ASAEs), to be applied to assurance engagements dealing with subject matters other than historical financial information
- standards on related services (ASRSs), to be applied to engagements involving agreed-upon procedures for information and other related services engagements as specified by the AUASB.

Figure 4.1 presents Pronouncements of the AUASB.

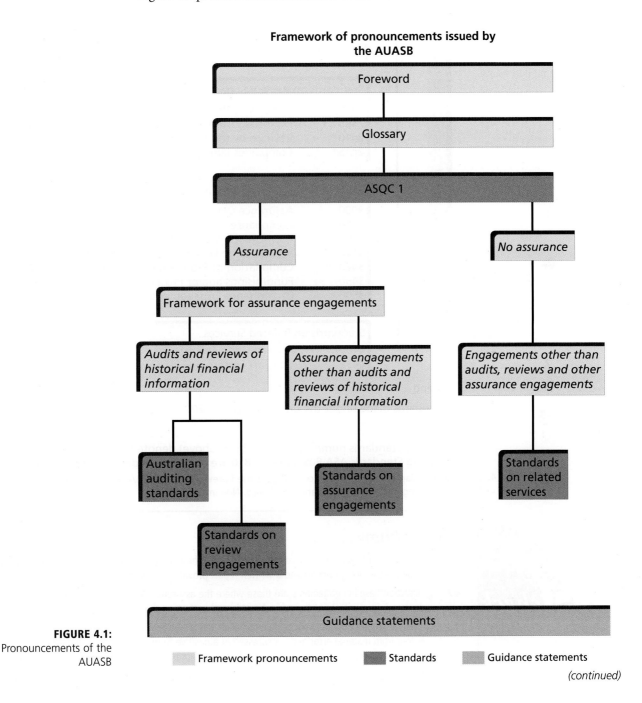

FIGURE 4.1:
Pronouncements of the AUASB

(continued)

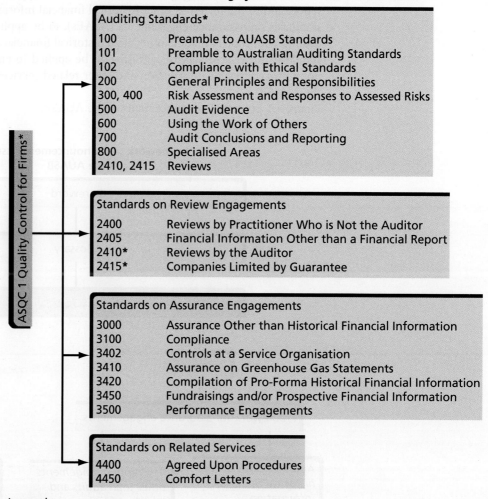

Overview of Numbering System used in AUASB Standards

ASQC 1 Quality Control for Firms*

Auditing Standards*

100	Preamble to AUASB Standards
101	Preamble to Australian Auditing Standards
102	Compliance with Ethical Standards
200	General Principles and Responsibilities
300, 400	Risk Assessment and Responses to Assessed Risks
500	Audit Evidence
600	Using the Work of Others
700	Audit Conclusions and Reporting
800	Specialised Areas
2410, 2415	Reviews

Standards on Review Engagements

2400	Reviews by Practitioner Who is Not the Auditor
2405	Financial Information Other than a Financial Report
2410*	Reviews by the Auditor
2415*	Companies Limited by Guarantee

Standards on Assurance Engagements

3000	Assurance Other than Historical Financial Information
3100	Compliance
3402	Controls at a Service Organisation
3410	Assurance on Greenhouse Gas Statements
3420	Compilation of Pro-Forma Historical Financial Information
3450	Fundraisings and/or Prospective Financial Information
3500	Performance Engagements

Standards on Related Services

4400	Agreed Upon Procedures
4450	Comfort Letters

<u>Legend</u>

*Standards made under the *Corporations Act 2001*

<u>Notes</u>

Auditing Standards numbered 200 to 2415 (above) denote a series of numbers.
Auditing Standards ASA 805 and ASA 810 are not made under the *Corporations Act 2001*.

FIGURE 4.1: ***Source:*** Adapted from appendices 1 & 2 of the Foreword to the AUASB Pronouncements, issued by
(continued) the Auditing and Assurance Standards Board, November 2012.

Learning check

Do you know ...

4.1 ☐ Assurance engagements are those where there is a three party relationship, a subject matter, suitable criteria, evidence gathering and a written report providing an opinion.

4.2 ☐ Assertion-based engagements are those where the assurance provider is giving an opinion on an assertion made about the subject matter rather than on the subject matter directly.

4.3 ☐ There are reasonable assurance opinions which give a high level of assurance that the subject matter is free from material error and is expressed in a positive form, whereas a limited assurance opinion only gives a low level of assurance and is expressed in a negative form.

LEARNING objective 2

Discuss assurance engagements for historical financial information other than those relating to general purpose financial report audits.

4.2 ASSURANCE ENGAGEMENTS INVOLVING HISTORICAL FINANCIAL INFORMATION

In chapters 6 to 18 we will discuss the requirements for audits of a financial report. In this section we discuss the additional requirements where the audit is not of a complete general purpose financial report.

4.2.1 Audits of historical financial information

An auditor may be asked to audit: (1) a special purpose financial report that has been prepared using an alternative financial reporting framework, (2) a part only of a financial report (rather than the full report such as auditing just the statement of financial position), or (3) a summarised financial report. In each of these cases the engagement is an audit of historical financial information and therefore all the normal auditing standards (ASAs 100–799) apply. The specific requirements discussed below refer to additional considerations that must be taken into account when carrying out these special purpose audits.

Audits of financial reports prepared in accordance with special purpose frameworks

A special purpose financial report is distinct from a general purpose financial report. General purpose financial reports are those prepared in order to meet the information needs of a wide range of users; these are the normal annual financial reports produced by companies in accordance with a general purpose framework (Australian accounting standards and the *Corporations Act 2001*) for their shareholders. A special purpose financial report is not prepared to meet the common information needs of a wide range of users but is prepared to meet the needs of specific users. Where these reports are prepared using an alternative to the general purpose framework this is referred to as a special purpose framework. They are typically prepared by an organisation for a particular purpose, such as for the requirements of a securities exchange, loan creditors, or mergers. Examples of special purpose financial reports include financial reports prepared:

- in accordance with the financial reporting provisions of a contract, where a specific reporting framework must be followed in order to meet the requirements of that contract
- in accordance with the tax basis of accounting
- in accordance with the financial reporting provisions of a regulatory authority
- by a non-reporting entity
- by a not-for-profit organisation in accordance with the financial reporting provisions of an applicable State Act.

Additional requirements to the normal auditing standards are given in ASA 800 *Special Considerations — Audits of Financial Reports Prepared in Accordance with Special Purpose Frameworks* (ISA 800) which applies to an audit of a special purpose financial report for a financial year or for a half-year, prepared in accordance with Part 2M.3 of the *Corporations Act 2001*. It also applies to audits of any special purpose financial reports or other historical financial information prepared using a special purpose framework for any other purpose.

When accepting an engagement for the audit of a financial report prepared under a special purpose framework the auditor must consider: (1) the purpose for which the financial report is prepared, (2) the intended users, and (3) the steps taken by management to determine that the applicable financial reporting framework is acceptable in the circumstances (paragraph 8). The auditor must consider the extent to which the application of other auditing standards requires special consideration in relation to the engagement and obtain an understanding of relevant contractual provisions where different interpretations of those provisions could lead to material differences in the financial report (paragraphs 9 and 10).

With regard to the audit report, the auditor must indicate in the audit report the purpose for which the special purpose financial report is prepared and, if necessary, the intended users and an emphasis of matter paragraph should be included to alert users that the financial report is prepared under a special purpose framework and may therefore not be suitable for other purposes. The auditor's report usually contains the following elements:

- a title
- an addressee
- an introductory paragraph that identifies the financial information that was audited, the responsible party and the basis on which the financial report has been prepared
- a statement clearly identifying the responsible party's responsibility for the preparation and presentation of the financial information, the relevant internal controls and ensuring the financial report is free from material misstatement whether due to fraud or error
- a statement of the responsibility of the auditor to follow auditing standards and ethical requirements and to plan and perform the audit to obtain reasonable assurance that the report is free from material error
- a scope paragraph that describes the nature of the audit and the work carried out
- a statement regarding the sufficiency and relevance of the audit evidence obtained
- an opinion on the financial information
- the date of the auditor's report, and the auditor's address and signature.

Where the auditor believes that the scope of their work is limited or the financial report has not been prepared in accordance with the financial reporting framework and this has not been resolved through discussion with management, the auditor should consider qualifying their audit report as necessary to identify the problem. Different types of audit opinions will be discussed in chapter 7.

A measure of uniformity is desirable in audit reports, so, where the auditor has been asked to report in a prescribed format, the auditor should consider the substance and wording of the report and, where necessary, make appropriate changes to conform with the specific requirements of the appropriate auditing standard.

Audits of single financial statements and specific elements, accounts or items of a financial statement

An auditor may be asked to give an audit opinion on only one part of a financial report. This may be a single financial statement, such as a statement of financial position, or on a particular item, such as an audit of accounts receivable, a bonus calculation or a provision for income taxes. These engagements are audits of historical financial information so the normal auditing standards apply and additional requirements are contained in ASA 805 *Special Considerations — Audits of Single Financial Statements and Specific Elements, Accounts or Items of a Financial Statement* (ISA 805). Where the financial statement, element, account or item has been prepared under a special purpose reporting framework the provisions of ASA 800 described in the previous section must also be considered.

There are two important considerations in audits of these kinds: (1) the subject matter information being audited is more limited than a full financial report and there is the possibility that the information provided to users is limited in such a way that prevents them from having a full understanding of the facts, and (2) if the auditor is not also auditing the full financial report it is likely that they have a more limited understanding of the organisation than if they were conducting a full financial report audit, and the auditor should consider the extent to which this limits their ability to effectively carry out the engagement.

The auditor needs to consider the extent to which the normal auditing standards are relevant for the purposes of this audit, where the auditor is only looking at a part of the financial statements some standards are likely to be irrelevant. If the auditor does not have the same detailed knowledge of the organisation that a financial report auditor has, obtaining this knowledge may be disproportionately costly given than only one element of the financial statements is being audited. In these circumstances it may be necessary to discuss with management whether another type of engagement may be more practical. Where an auditor is engaged to audit the financial report and is also engaged to audit either an individual financial statement or an element of a financial statement it is important to ensure that the two engagements are clearly separate. If the single financial statement or element is published together with the financial report it is management's responsibility to ensure that they are clearly distinguishable and the auditor must prepare two clearly distinguishable audit reports.

Audits of summary financial statements

An entity sometimes prepares financial statements which summarise its annual audited financial report for the purpose of informing user groups who are interested in highlights only of the entity's financial position. Requirements in relation to these audits are contained in ASA 810 *Engagements to Report on Summary Financial Statements* (ISA 810). In these engagements the auditor is not expressing an opinion that the summary financial statements are free from material error but that they are consistent in all material respects with the full financial report. It is therefore important that the users of the summary have access to the full financial report should they wish to see it.

The auditor should not report on summary financial statements unless he or she has expressed an opinion on the financial report on which the summary is based. The auditor's report on a summary financial statement should identify the audited financial report from which the summary was derived, a reference to the date of the auditor's report of the full financial report and the type of audit opinion given in that report, a reference to the ethical requirements relating to the audit engagements, an opinion that is consistent with the audit opinion issued for the full financial report, and a statement that indicates that, for a better understanding, the summary financial report should be read in conjunction with the audited financial report and the related auditor's report.

4.2.2 Review engagements relating to financial reports and other historical financial information

An assurance practitioner may be engaged to perform a review of a financial report rather than an audit, and this review may be conducted by a practitioner who has no other dealings with the company or may be conducted by the company's independent auditor. Specific requirements exist for reviews of financial reports which are distinct from those requirements that relate to the reviews of other historical financial information.

For certain types of companies (disclosing entities — largely those listed on the ASX) there is an obligation under the Corporations Act (s. 302) to prepare a half-year financial report (interim financial report) and to have this report either audited or reviewed. The discussion that follows applies to reviews of any financial report; for the most part, however, these engagements will be reviews of half-year (interim) financial reports produced by listed companies.

A review of an **interim financial report** enables the auditor to express a conclusion whether, on the basis of the review, anything has come to light to cause the auditor to believe that the interim financial report is not prepared in accordance with an applicable financial reporting framework. A review differs significantly from an audit in that it does not provide a basis for an opinion to be formed regarding whether the financial report gives a true and fair view, or is presented fairly, in all material aspects, in accordance with the applicable financial reporting framework. A review is not designed to obtain reasonable assurance that the interim financial report is free from material misstatement.

The requirements of ASAs 100–799 do not apply to review engagements, and the review standards to be followed depend on whether the reviewer is also the company's independent auditor expressing an audit opinion on the company's full-year financial report. The distinction needs to be made because a company's independent auditor who is carrying out a review will already have detailed knowledge of the organisation whereas a practitioner who is only employed to review the half-year accounts and has no other experience with the company will need to obtain this information for the purposes of the review. Three AUASB standards exist for these types of reviews.

1. ASRE 2400 *Review of a Financial Report Performed by an Assurance Practitioner Who is Not the Auditor of the Entity* (ISRE 2400). This is a standard issued in March 2013 to be applicable from 1 July 2013. The standard establishes the requirements and provides application and other explanatory material regarding the assurance provider's responsibilities when accepting, conducting and reporting on an engagement to review a financial report or a complete set of financial statements, and the provider is not the auditor of the entity. The objectives are to obtain limited assurance, primarily by performing enquiry and analytical procedures; and to report on the financial report as a whole and communicate as required by the standard.

2. ASRE 2410 *Review of a Financial Report Performed by the Independent Auditor of the Entity* (ISRE 2410). The compiled standard was issued on 1 July 2013. The compilation combines all previous amendments to the standard and is operative from 1 July 2013.

3. ASRE 2415 *Review of a Financial Report — Company Limited by Guarantee or an Entity Reporting under the ACNC Act or Other Applicable Legislation or Regulation*. This standard was approved on 28 March 2013 with an operative date of 1 July 2013.

The main requirements for these standards are basically the same and apply to a review of a financial report prepared in accordance with Part 2M.3 of the Corporations Act or for any other purpose.

The general principles of a review of a financial report include:

- complying with the ethical requirements relevant to the audit of the annual financial report
- implementing quality control procedures that are applicable to the individual engagement
- exercising professional judgement in planning and performing the review, with an attitude of professional scepticism, recognising that circumstances may exist that cause the financial report to require a material adjustment for it to be prepared in accordance with the applicable financial reporting framework.

The review procedures include:

- understanding the entity, including its environment and internal control, in order to identify the types of potential material misstatements and to consider their occurrence
- considering materiality and using professional judgement when determining the nature, timing and extent of review procedures and when evaluating the effect of misstatements
- making enquiries and using analytical and other review procedures such as reading minutes of meetings of those charged with governance; communicating with other auditors who are performing a review of the financial report of the entity's significant components; enquiring of management about changes in accounting principles or in the methods applied, and about any new transactions that have necessitated a new accounting

principle, any known uncorrected misstatements, any unusual or complex situations that may have affected the financial report, any significant assumptions that are relevant to fair value measurements, and so on.

The review practitioner can also perform many of the review procedures before or simultaneously with the entity's preparation of the interim financial report. The review practitioner might also find it practicable to perform some of the audit or review procedures concurrently with the review of the interim financial report — for example, performing audit or review procedures in relation to significant or unusual transactions that occurred during the interim period, including business combinations, restructurings, or significant revenue transactions and opening balances where applicable.

In addition to these review standards, ASRE 2405 *Review of Historical Financial Information Other than a Financial Report* (ISRE 2400) gives specific requirements for other reviews of other historical financial information which are substantially the same as the aforementioned requirements. The main difference arises in the selection of suitable criteria. When reviewing a financial report the suitable criteria refers to a financial reporting framework such as Australian accounting standards and the Corporations Act; for financial information other than a financial report the reviewer must ensure that the criteria against which the information is being compared is appropriate.

The conclusions and opinion from the review must be contained in a written report that is similar in format to any other assurance engagement relating to historical financial information. These reports should include sections to highlight the financial report being reviewed, the management's and the review practitioner's respective responsibilities as well as the opinion itself. It is important to ensure that readers of these opinions are clear that the assurance provided is lower than would be obtained from an audit so the report must include: a statement that the conclusion is based on a review conducted in accordance with the relevant review standard (ASRE), that a review is restricted to enquiries and analytical procedures, and that the review is substantially less in scope than an audit and therefore the auditor is not able to obtain assurance that the review has identified all significant matters that might have been identified during an audit.

LEARNING 3
objective
Discuss the features and extent of other assurance engagements.

4.3 ASSURANCE ENGAGEMENTS OTHER THAN AUDITS OR REVIEWS OF HISTORICAL FINANCIAL INFORMATION

ASAE 3000 (ISAE 3000) establishes the mandatory requirements for undertaking and reporting on assurance engagements other than audits or reviews of historical financial information covered by ASAs or ASREs. ASAE 3000 (ISAE 3000) uses the term

assurance practitioner, which includes a person or an organisation, whether in public practice, industry, commerce or the public sector, involved in the provision of assurance services. The assurance practitioner should also consider the following.

- *Ethical requirements.* Compliance with the fundamental ethical principles of integrity, objectivity, professional competence and due care, confidentiality and professional behaviour is required. The applicable code is APES 110 *Code of Ethics for Professional Accountants* (IFAC *Code of Ethics for Professional Accountants*) and codes of conduct issued by other relevant professional bodies.
- *Quality control.* Procedures need to be implemented to cover the following elements of a quality control system: leadership responsibilities for quality, ethical requirements, acceptance and continuance of client relationships and specific assurance engagements, assignment of assurance teams, assurance engagement performance, and monitoring.
- *Acceptance and continuance.* Assurance engagements should be accepted or continued only if the subject matter is the responsibility of a party other than the intended users; if nothing comes to the attention of the practitioner to indicate that the requirements of the fundamental ethical principles or the ASAEs will not be satisfied; and if the people who will perform the engagement possess the necessary professional competencies.
- *Terms of engagement.* The terms of the assurance engagements must be agreed on in writing with the engaging party. Where the engagement is performed according to legislation, the minimum acceptable assurance engagement terms are those contained in the legislation. Any request for a change in the terms of the engagement cannot be agreed to without reasonable justification. If necessary, the assurance engagement may have to be changed to be a non-assurance engagement and the new terms must be confirmed in writing.
- *Planning and performance.* The planning and performing procedures of the assurance engagement are similar to those applicable to a typical audit engagement. The assurance practitioner plans the assurance engagement so that it will be performed effectively. Such planning involves an overall strategy for the scope, emphasis, timing and conduct of the evidence-gathering procedures. An attitude of professional scepticism is required. Furthermore, the assurance practitioner needs to obtain a full understanding of the subject matter and other circumstances, sufficient to identify and assess the risks of the subject matter information being materially misstated. He or she should also assess the suitability of the criteria to evaluate or measure the subject matter. These criteria should be considered based on their relevance, completeness, reliability, neutrality and understandability.
- *Materiality.* The assurance practitioner must consider the materiality of the risk relating to the assurance engagement with the aim of reducing such risk to an acceptable level. Where the work of an outside expert is used, the assurance practitioner and the expert should, together, possess adequate skill and knowledge regarding the subject matter to determine that sufficient appropriate evidence has been obtained.
- *Evidence.* Sufficient appropriate evidence must be obtained on which to base a conclusion. This may involve the use of selective testing, enquiries, and performing other evidence-gathering procedures. Written representation from the responsible party should be obtained whenever possible. The assurance practitioner should also consider the effect of events up to the date of the assurance report, and their impact on the subject matter. All evidence is documented on a timely basis to provide a basis for the conclusion to be drawn, including the nature and extent of the engagement work performed.
- *Report content.* The assurance report must be in writing and contain a clear expression of the assurance practitioner's conclusion about the subject matter. There is no standardised format for reporting on all assurance engagements. The basic elements are:
  - a title to indicate that the report is an independent assurance report
  - an addressee

- an identification and description of the subject matter information
- a description of any significant inherent limitation associated with the evaluation of measurement of the subject matter against the criteria
- a statement of restriction regarding the criteria being applicable only to the intended users
- a description of the responsible party and responsibilities
- a statement that the assurance engagement was performed in accordance with ASAEs and the level of assurance provided
- a summary of the work performed
- the assurance practitioner's conclusion in accordance with the type of assurance: i.e. a positive assurance for a reasonable assurance engagement and a negative assurance for a limited assurance engagement; where the assurance conclusion is other than unqualified, the report must contain clear reasons
- the report date and the name of the firm or assurance practitioner.

The assurance practitioner can expand the assurance report to include other information and explanations that are not intended to affect the conclusion. These might be the qualification of the assurance practitioner, a disclosure of the materiality levels, findings in relation to a particular aspect of the assurance engagement, and recommendations. The assurance report may require an emphasis of matter, or when the practitioner is unable to express an unqualified conclusion; the opinion will be modified with either (1) a qualified conclusion, (2) an adverse conclusion, or (3) a disclaimer. The principles relating to these modifications are the same as those for the financial report audit. The assurance practitioner also considers other reporting responsibilities, including the appropriateness of communicating relevant matters of governance interest to those charged with governance. Application of ASAE 3000 conforms with ISAE 3000, although ASAE 3000 expands on some parts of the standard such as the explanation of reasonable assurance and documentation of alternative procedures.

Do you know ...

4.6 ☐ Auditors provide a wide range of assurance services that are not related to historical financial information and ASAE 3000 applies to these assurance services.

4.7 ☐ When carrying out an assurance engagement the practitioner should consider: ethical requirements, quality control, acceptance and continuance, terms of engagement, planning and performance, materiality, evidence and report content.

4.8 ☐ Assurance reports may express an unqualified opinion, issue a qualified conclusion or an adverse conclusion, or give a disclaimer of opinion.

LEARNING 4 objective

Use examples to illustrate the scope of assurance engagements other than those relating to historical financial information.

4.4 EXAMPLES OF ASSURANCE ENGAGEMENTS OTHER THAN THOSE RELATING TO HISTORICAL FINANCIAL INFORMATION

In this section, we discuss some of the common types of assurance engagements that do not relate to historical financial information. In each case the assurance engagement will be conducted in accordance with ASAE 3000 (ISAE 3000) referred to above and other appropriate requirements as follows.

4.4.1 Compliance engagements

Organisations may have obligations to follow requirements imposed by law or regulation, by contract or internally imposed through accounting policies and procedures. Compliance engagements provide assurance that regulations, contractual obligations or other requirements have been complied with. An example of this would be reporting on whether an entity has complied with certain aspects of a bank loan agreement relating to interest payments and maintenance of predetermined financial ratios.

In conducting these assurance engagements the practitioner must comply with ASAE 3100 (ISAE 3100). The level of work that the auditor needs to carry out will be to a large extent dependent upon whether the engagement is a reasonable assurance engagement or limited assurance engagement, and specific procedures need to be designed accordingly. Given the variety of possible engagements that could arise, it is important that the auditor ensures that the overall aspects of compliance relate to matters within their scope of professional competence. One of the most significant issues in these engagements is ensuring the suitability of the criteria against which the outcome is to be measured. This may be simple with legislation or contractual provisions where the criteria are clearly stated; in other circumstances, such as compliance with organisational policies and procedures, the suitability of the criteria will need to be carefully considered. The report prepared by the auditor should clearly identify the criteria and the time period covered and state whether, in the auditor's opinion, the entity has complied with its obligations.

4.4.2 Performance engagements

Performance refers to the economy, efficiency and effectiveness of business activities. Effectiveness refers to objectives being met, efficiency refers to maximising output for a given level of input and economy refers to obtaining the appropriate level and quality of inputs while minimising cost. Organisations may wish for any of their processes to be assessed to ensure they are maximising performance.

In conducting these assurance engagements the practitioner must comply with ASAE 3500 (ISAE 3500). Performance engagements may give rise to either reasonable assurance or limited assurance. The difficulties for the auditor in these engagements relate to the appropriateness of the subject matter and the suitability of the criteria. The auditor needs to determine if the activity being tested (the subject matter) is capable of consistent measurement to ensure that procedures can be applied to allow sufficient and appropriate evidence to be obtained. The other issue is the criteria against which the activity is to be measured; it may be difficult to establish what actually constitutes appropriate benchmarks against which to compare the activity. Where regulations exist this may be simple, otherwise there may be published standards of best practice for the industry.

4.4.3 Prospective financial information

Prospective financial information (PFI) refers to information about future events which may or may not occur. This information may be in the form of: (1) forecasts which are best-estimates based on assumptions that management expect to occur, or (2) projections which are hypothetical assumptions. Forecasts are therefore more likely to occur than projections. Given the inherent uncertainties surrounding financial information based on future predictions, assurance engagements in relation to this information would only ever give limited assurance. An example of circumstances where this kind of information would need assurance attached to it is where an organisation has prepared forecast information in support of an application for a bank loan and the assurance provided by the auditor would enhance the credibility of these forecasts.

In a prospective financial information (PFI) engagement, evidence should be obtained that:

- the assumptions used by management in preparing the PFI are appropriate
- the financial information has been prepared in accordance with those assumptions
- the information is properly presented and disclosures are adequate, including making clear whether information is a best-estimate or a hypothetical assumption
- the PFI is prepared on a basis consistent with historical financial statements.

It is not within the scope of the engagement to express an opinion on the truth, fairness or other characteristics of the information. The auditor will express a negative form opinion on the suitability of the assumptions and then give a further opinion about whether the information has been prepared in accordance with those assumptions and an appropriate financial reporting framework. An additional statement will be included which highlights that actual results are likely to be different to the forecast where events do not occur as expected.

4.4.4 Effectiveness of control procedures

Engagements in relation to controls procedures aim to provide a level of assurance in relation to the design and operating effectiveness of internal control procedures. These engagements may be direct reporting engagements where the auditor gives an opinion directly on the internal controls themselves or an assertion-based engagement where management has made assertion(s) (usually in the form of a written report) about the effectiveness of their control procedures and the auditor is providing an opinion on those assertions.

The requirements in Australia in relation to these engagements are contained in the auditing standard AUS 810 *Special Purpose Reports on the Effectiveness of Control Procedures* issued in July 2002 by the old Auditing and Assurance Standards Board. There is no current international equivalent standard. Engagements of this nature may give rise to either reasonable assurance or limited assurance. The main difficulty for the auditor in these engagements relates to the suitability of the criteria against which control procedures will be measured. This may be based on a framework like that contained in the Committee of Sponsoring Organizations of the Treadway Commission's *Enterprise Risk Management Framework*. What constitutes an effective system of internal controls is discussed in detail in chapter 9.

In addition to assurance engagements in relation to internal controls, an accountant may be asked to perform agreed-upon procedures where no assurance is provided. These procedures relate to engagements where the accountant and the client agree procedures to be performed that require a report of factual findings where the practitioner offers no assurance on what has been found but merely reports the findings. Users must draw their own conclusions from the report. The requirements in Australia in relation to these engagements are contained in the auditing standard AUS 904 *Engagements to Perform Agreed-upon Procedures* issued in July 2002 by the old Auditing and Assurance Standards Board. The international equivalent is ISRS 4400 *Engagements to Perform Agreed-upon Procedures Regarding Financial Information* which has not yet been adopted in Australia; however, the requirements of AUS 904 are not inconsistent with ISRS 4400. A proposed new standard to replace AUS 810 on assurance engagements relating to the effectiveness of control procedures is in the process of being finalised.

4.4.5 Sustainability assurance reports

There has been rapid growth in sustainability reporting over the past few years. The first environmental reports were published in the late 1980s by companies from the chemical industry, which had serious image problems. The other group of early reporters were small- and medium-sized enterprises (SMEs) with very advanced environmental management systems. The rapid European development in the 1990s was influenced by environmental management accounting systems (EMAS) and the growing number of EMAS registered organisations. In September 2012, there were 4500 EMAS registered organisations of which 59% were small to medium sized organisations and another 23% were micro organisations.[8] With the inclusion of social issues in companies' environmental reports, sustainability reporting developed. **Sustainability** refers to the notion of conducting business activities with minimal long-term effect on the environment. Sustainability relates to the continuing wellbeing of society, as well as the non-human environment. It implies paying attention to the comprehensive outcomes of events and actions where practicable, and being accountable for such outcomes. This is known as full cost accounting or environmental accounting.

The upward trend of sustainability reporting has largely been a response to stakeholder concerns about the social, economic and environmental performance of business, but it is also increasingly linked to investor interests in risk-related aspects of financial performance. Reporting guidelines have emerged to drive up the quality of reporting and to enable comparability, and for investors to relate non-financial performance to financial performance.

Reporting guidelines include triple bottom line reporting, the Global Reporting Initiative and the AA1000 Assurance Standard. **Triple bottom line reporting** (TBL) focuses on decision making and reporting that explicitly considers an organisation's economic, environmental and social performance. TBL is regarded as an internal management tool as well as an external reporting framework. TBL reports were produced between 2003 and 2005 by the Department of Sustainability and Environment. In 2006, it became the sustainability report. From 2006 onwards, under section 516A of the *Environment Protection and Biodiversity Conservation Act* 1999 (EPBC Act) the Department of Sustainability, Environment, Water, Population and Communities produced annual reports on environmental performance. The CSIRO produced a substantial report entitled *Balancing Act — a Triple Bottom Line Analysis of the Australian Economy* in 2005 (updated in 2011), which also reports on the social, environmental and financial performance of 135 industries.[9]

The discussion paper titled 'Triple Bottom Line Assessment for the ACT Government', published in June 2011, contains summaries of the development of TBL to other sustainability reporting regimes.[10]

However, TBL reporting assurance statements have much variability and ambiguity inherent within the contents of the third-party statements. Extensive research is currently being undertaken by many academics in the area of sustainability and the great variability in the adoption of assurance practices.[11]

The **Global Reporting Initiative** (GRI) was started in 1997 as a multi-stakeholder process and independent initiative to develop and disseminate globally applicable sustainability reporting guidelines. It is a set of official guidelines published by the collaborating centre of the United Nations Environmental Program. The GRI provides a generally accepted framework for reporting an organisation's economic, environmental and social performance. Many sustainability reports nowadays use the GRI as the basis of reporting. Companies may include a GRI index covering strategy, profile and performance indicators, as well as a self-assessment of their GRI application. Sustainability assurance engagements typically will use GRI guidelines as the criteria for reporting.

Some of the Big Four accounting firms offer audits and reviews and advisory services on sustainability reporting. Some also provide assurance on specific data, such as greenhouse gas emissions reported under schemes including the NSW Greenhouse Gas Abatement Scheme. Other assurance services in respect of sustainability may include:
- reports against benchmarks such as the sustainability reporting standards established as the Sustainability Reporting Guidelines of the GRI

- reports against best practice reports for a particular sector
- specific environmental, health, safety, social and economic data against industry data.

Research conducted by CPA Australia and the University of Sydney shows that the majority of the companies that provided sustainability/TBL reporting did not use a recognised framework like the GRI. However, of those that *did* use a framework, all used the GRI.[12] From the study, the following observations emerged.

- Companies operating in areas that are more sensitive to environmental and occupational health and safety issues are more likely to be obliged to report sustainability-type information; companies that are required to report information as a result of regulation or voluntary codes are in a better position to report such information to the public.
- Across the sample of private enterprises, the most commonly reported GRI indicators were environmental incidents and non-compliance fines, standard injury, loss days, absentee rates and greenhouse gas emissions.
- Just over half the companies in the private sector and one in eight government business enterprises had their sustainability reports audited or verified. The majority of these companies, however, included a reference to their discrete report in the annual report. One company reproduced the majority of the information, but for the others it was a single reference. The survey also showed that website disclosures have been both extensive and different from those appearing in the annual report.
- The analyses of the association between sustainability disclosure and financial performance show the following.
  - The higher scores of sustainability disclosures were positively associated with higher levels of operating cash flow to total assets, working capital to total assets, retained earnings to total assets and asset backing per share.
  - Sustainability disclosures, however, were found to be negatively associated with cash position to total assets and price-to-book value. This suggests that companies with higher sustainability disclosures tend to have their shares more conservatively valued.
  - Firms with a higher level of sustainability disclosures tend to have stronger financial performance and lower financial distress ratings.[13]

A research study by Hargroves and Smith[14] identified some common principles of sustainable development, including:

- dealing transparently and systematically with risk, uncertainty and irreversibility
- ensuring appropriate valuation, appreciation and restoration of nature
- integration of environmental, social, human and economic goals in policies and activities
- equal opportunity and community participation
- conservation of biodiversity and ecological integrity
- ensuring intergenerational equity
- recognising the global integration of localities
- a commitment to best practice
- no net loss of human capital or natural capital
- adhering to the principle of continuous improvement
- the need for good governance.

More recent developments have seen the creation of The Prince of Wales' Accounting for Sustainability Project (A4S) which is working with a wide range of stakeholders, including the GRI, to develop practical guidance and tools that allow organisations to embed sustainability into their decision-making and reporting processes. The three areas of work are:

1. reporting: promoting the idea of connected reporting
2. embedding: embedding sustainability into corporate decision making
3. governance structures: what is the best structure to oversee the development of a new connected reporting model.

Various documents have been published, including a practical guide to connected reporting and a comprehensive case study designed to help preparers produce more useful reports. The International Integrated Reporting Committee (IIRC) has been set up to communicate with all stakeholders and develop a new integrated reporting model. Connected reporting aims to provide a more rounded and balanced approach than traditional ideas of corporate reporting, with a focus on the needs of long-term investors and executive management. Reports should address how an organisation's objectives are connected with its risks and opportunities, key resources, governance and reward structures, industry and markets, as well as society more generally. They should also explain how business strategy is connected to the organisation's financial and non-financial performance.

In Australia there is legislation, *The National Greenhouse and Energy Reporting Act 2007*, that requires Australian corporations on the National Greenhouse and Energy Register (NGER) to report annually to the Greenhouse and Energy Data Officer on their greenhouse gas emissions and energy production and consumption. Registration is required where a corporation exceeds one of the thresholds stipulated in relation to: (1) total amount of greenhouse gases emitted (based on equivalent kilotonnes of carbon dioxide), (2) total amount of energy produced (terajoules), or (3) total energy consumed (terajoules). The thresholds were set for financial years commencing in July 2008 at high levels so that only the larger emitters would initially be required to report. For financial years commencing after 2009, a corporation must register where their annual greenhouse gas emissions exceed the equivalent of 50 kilotonnes of carbon dioxide or where their annual energy produced or consumed exceeds 200 terajoules. The reports may include projects to reduce greenhouse gas emissions and the removal or offset of greenhouse gases.

There is no requirement for these reports to be audited; however, where the Greenhouse and Energy Data Officer suspects that a corporation may be in contravention of their obligations, the Officer has the power to appoint an auditor to carry out either an assurance engagement (limited or reasonable assurance) or a verification engagement. These engagements are conducted in accordance with the requirements of the *National Greenhouse and Energy Reporting (Audit) Determination 2009*. An assurance engagement follows the assurance standards discussed in this chapter; a verification engagement differs from an assurance engagement in that the purpose is to verify the matter being audited and give a report of findings rather than an opinion as to the reliability, accuracy and completeness of the matter being audited. ASAE 3410 *Assurance Engagements on Greenhouse Gas Statements* was issued by AUASB on 28 June 2012 with an operative date of 1 July 2012.

As well as offering assurance services in relation to specific data such as greenhouse gas statements, other engagements may include:
- reports against benchmarks such as the sustainability reporting standards established as the sustainability reporting guidelines of the GRI
- reports against best practice reports for a particular sector
- specific environmental, health, safety, social and economic data against industry data.

There is a large and competitive marketplace for provision of these types of services. There is no legal obligation for these services to be provided by a qualified assurance provider and therefore the quality of assurance provided may not be consistent where clear standards are absent. As part of its work plan, the AUASB also aimed to develop a standard on assurance engagements in connection with water accounting reports.

The AA1000 Assurance Standard (AA1000AS) was issued by AccountAbility, an institute of social and ethical accountability in the United Kingdom. AA1000AS is a generally applicable standard for assessing, attesting to and strengthening the credibility and quality of organisations' sustainability reporting, and their underlying processes, systems and competencies. The standard covers the full range of organisational sustainability performance, focuses on the materiality and accuracy of subject matter to stakeholders, assesses the organisation's responsiveness to stakeholders and requires disclosure by assurance providers covering their competencies and relationships with the reporting organisations. Using AA1000AS, three principles must be applied in an assurance process: materiality, completeness and responsiveness.[15] The materiality principle requires the assurance practitioner to state whether information has been included about the organisation's sustainability performance as required by its stakeholders for them to be able to make informed judgements, decisions and actions. The completeness principle requires the assurance practitioner to evaluate the extent to which the reporting organisation can identify and understand material aspects of its sustainability performance. The responsiveness principle requires the assurance practitioner to evaluate whether the reporting organisation has responded to stakeholder concerns, policies and relevant standards, and has adequately communicated these responses in its report.

The latest GRI report *The External Assurance of Sustainability Reporting* provides a set of simple guidelines and reference to ISAE 3000 and AA1000AS.[16]

PROFESSIONAL ENVIRONMENT

Independent reasonable assurance report in relation to Santos Limited's greenhouse gas emissions

*T*o the Directors of Santos Limited

We have carried out a reasonable assurance engagement in order to provide an opinion as to whether the subject matter detailed below, and as presented on page 21 of Santos Limited's ('Santos') Sustainability Report 2012, has been presented, in all material respects, in accordance with the criteria as presented below.

Subject Matter

The subject matter for our assurance engagement comprises scope 1 greenhouse gas emissions from Santos operated assets for the year ended 30 June 2012.

Criteria

The criteria for reporting the subject matter is as set out in the:
• *National Greenhouse and Energy Reporting Act 2007*
• *National Greenhouse and Energy Reporting Regulations 2008*
• *National Greenhouse and Energy Reporting (Measurement) Determination 2008* as amended on 30 June 2011

The Responsibility of Management

Santos' management are responsible for the preparation and fair presentation of the subject matter. This responsibility includes establishing and maintaining internal controls relevant to the preparation and presentation of the subject matter that is free from material misstatement, whether due to fraud or error; selecting and applying appropriate accounting policies; and making estimates that are reasonable in the circumstances.

Assurance Practitioner's Responsibility

Our responsibility is to express an opinion on the subject matter based on our reasonable assurance engagement. We conducted our reasonable assurance engagement in accordance with the International Standard on Assurance Engagements ISAE 3000 *Assurance Engagements other than Audits or Reviews of Historical Financial Information*. This

Auditing Standard requires that we comply with relevant ethical requirements and plan and perform the assurance engagement in order to provide an opinion as to whether the subject matter is presented in all material respects in accordance with the criteria detailed above.

Our procedures included but were not limited to the following:

- Gaining an understanding of the greenhouse gas reporting processes supporting the business activities.
- Conducting interviews and collation of evidence to understand the processes and controls supporting the data.
- Checking that the methodologies have been correctly applied as per the requirements in the *National Greenhouse and Energy Reporting (Measurement) Determination 2008* as amended on 30 June 2011.
- Testing the calculations performed by Santos.
- Undertaking analytical review procedures to support the reasonableness of the data.
- Identifying and testing assumptions supporting the calculations.
- Testing on a sample basis to underlying source information to ensure completeness and accuracy of data.
- Reviewing the appropriateness of the presentation of information.

Our procedures were designed to obtain a reasonable level of assurance on which to base our opinion. The procedures performed depend on the auditor's judgement including the risk of material misstatement of the subject matter, whether due to fraud or error. While we considered the effectiveness of management's internal controls when determining the nature and extent of our procedures, our reasonable assurance engagement was not designed to provide assurance on internal controls. We believe that the evidence we have obtained is sufficient and appropriate to provide a basis for our opinion.

Inherent limitations

There are inherent limitations in performing assurance — for example, assurance engagements are based on selective testing of the information being examined — it is possible that fraud, error or non-compliance may occur and not be detected. An assurance engagement is not designed to detect all instances of non-compliance with the criteria, as an assurance engagement is not performed continuously throughout the period and the procedures performed in respect of compliance with the criteria are undertaken on a test basis. The opinion expressed in this report has been formed on the above basis.

Additionally, non-financial data may be subject to more inherent limitations than financial data, given both its nature and the methods used for determining, calculation and sampling or estimating such data. We specifically note that Santos has used estimates or extrapolated underlying information to calculate certain amounts included within the greenhouse gas information.

Use of our Report

This report has been prepared for the purpose set out above and for distribution to the management and Directors of Santos. We disclaim any assumption of responsibility for any reliance on this assurance report or on the subject matter to which it relates, to any person other than management and Directors of Santos, or for any purpose other than that for which it was prepared.

Independence, Competence and Experience

In conducting our assurance engagement we have met the independence requirements of the APES 110 *Code of Ethics for Professional Accountants*. We have the required competencies and experience to conduct this assurance engagement.

> **Reasonable Assurance Opinion**
> In our opinion, Santos' scope 1 greenhouse gas emissions from Santos operated assets for the year ended 30 June 2012, as presented on page 21 of its Sustainability Report 2012, are presented, in all material respects, in accordance with the criteria detailed above.
>
> Ernst & Young
> Melbourne
> 21 February 2013[17]

While there have been general assurance standards around for some time now, standards relating specifically to sustainability reports are only just starting to be drafted. A new assurance standard ASAE 3410 *Assurance Engagements on Greenhouse Gas Statements* was issued on 28 June 2012, with effective date on 1 July 2012. It applies the general principles of assurance engagements to a greenhouse gas statement, which will include any engagements on those statements prepared in accordance with the NGER. In a greenhouse gas statement, the main focus will be on the quantities of greenhouse gas emissions and how this information is presented and disclosed. The main issue that needs to be considered by a practitioner when considering accepting an engagement is what specialist skills they need to have in order to successfully carry out the engagement. In particular, the assertions made in a greenhouse gas report may be of a technical, chemical or physical nature and whilst a practitioner has extensive assurance skills this may not be enough when dealing with specialised subject matter. The future may see either a refinement in sustainability reporting or a new paradigm in corporate reporting where the financial and non-financial reports are combined. Either way, best practice for reporting and the assurance providers' role is unlikely to remain unchanged and we can therefore expect continuing development in this area.

4.4.6 Forensic auditing engagements

The complexity of the information economy, the reliance of business on technology and the increasing amount of interconnectivity among organisations are a result of and a driver for the current electronic environment. These widespread developments have created opportunities for theft, fraud and other forms of exploitation by offenders both outside and inside organisations.

As businesses grow, their networked systems become increasingly sophisticated and less dependent on human intervention. Monitoring individual behaviour becomes difficult, and vulnerability to electronic crimes (**e-crimes**) grows as organisations are increasingly connected to, and reliant on, individuals and systems outside their control. Most are alert to the risks posed by the different types of electronic viruses (e.g. in May 2000 the 'I love you' virus led to derivative viruses and was estimated to have cost businesses and governments more than US$10 billion).

Denial-of-service attacks, including the launch of viruses, can be perpetrated internally or externally. They disable network and electronic services. These attacks use the large-scale communications bandwidth of an intermediary to overwhelm their victims' systems with meaningless service requests, thereby degrading the service or denying legitimate users any service. But criminals are doing much more — everything from stealing intellectual property and committing fraud to unleashing viruses and committing acts of cyberterrorism in which political groups or unfriendly governments disseminate information. Broadband technology means that the Internet has gone from being the occasional dial-up service to being 'always on', much like the telephone. That concept may be beneficial to some, but it poses a real danger to consumers and users of electronic services.

The incidence of fraud suffered by Australian and New Zealand companies has risen from 174 914 in 2010 to 194 454 in 2012, according to the KPMG survey of fraud, bribery and corruption in Australia and New Zealand 2012.[18] The key issues identified in the survey were the devastating impact of insider fraud, collusion between insiders and third parties, the increase of bribery and corruption cases, and the impact of gambling on the fraudsters. The KPMG Fraud and Misconduct survey 2010 for Australia and New Zealand also reported that the total amount reported as having been lost to fraud increased from $301 million to $345.4 million.[19] Of the largest frauds 65% by number and 98% by value were inside jobs. The finance and insurance sector remains particularly vulnerable to frauds committed by external parties. Finance sector frauds typically involved credit cards, lending fraud and bogus insurance claims.

A **forensic audit** engagement is an effective investigative tool to help combat fraudulent claims, because it investigates the causes and effects of possibly fraudulent activities or system failures that may be the consequences of fraud. The forensic auditor looks for evidence of fraud and documents system failures, and identifies the extent of losses incurred. A forensic audit may be held in response to a claim against a company as a result of intentional or unintentional failures of electronic systems for processing transactions. Forensic audits can also be used by an insurer to evaluate the liability of a claim (e.g. a disability claim through a work-related accident or a system failure claim through a computer crash).

PROFESSIONAL ENVIRONMENT
Profile of the typical fraudster

The following is a description provided in the *KPMG Fraud and Misconduct Survey 2010* of what the typical fraudster looks like in 2010.[20]

By analysing the most common, or 'average', responses to survey questions dealing with major frauds, we have developed a profile of the typical fraudster.

Such an individual will be:
- a male non-management employee of the victim organisation, acting alone and with no known history of dishonesty
- aged 38 years and earning $113 000 p.a.
- employed by the organisation for a period of 5 years and held his current position for 3 years at the time of detection
- motivated by greed and stole on average $229 000
- detected by the organisation's internal controls 12 months after the commencement of the fraud.

When compared with our 2008 survey, our typical fraudster is the same age, will have been in his current position for 1 year less time and will be detected 1 month later. On a more positive note, he will have misappropriated less money.

Source: Excerpt from *KPMG Fraud and Misconduct Survey 2010*, p. 17, www.kpmg.com.

The auditor should be capable of understanding the entire organisation, its culture and its systems and, where the client has an electronic environment, the network systems. Many frauds were allowed to continue because of lack of attention to symptoms. The auditor should look for symptoms using, if appropriate, specially designed programs (e.g. a data analysis program). A forensic audit involving the electronic environment may feature:

- comparing employee emails and addresses, log-on times and messages
- searching for duplicate numbers on payments or receipts
- scanning lists of suppliers, customers and inventory movements
- analysing the sequence of transactions to identify the intervention by unauthorised personnel
- finding users of the same addresses and signalling phantom users.

An active, critical approach to controlling electronically processed transactions is necessary to minimise risks in a forensic assurance engagement. The assurance practitioner may be able to identify suspicious matters in the process, but the skilful evaluation of the results will demand professional judgement, competence and experience.

ASA 240 *The Auditor's Responsibilities Relating to Fraud in an Audit of a Financial Report* (ISA 240) is a contributing factor to the growth of firms turning their attention to forensic services. Most Big Four firms have set up forensic divisions.

The 2012 *KPMG survey of fraud, bribery and corruption in Australia and New Zealand* highlighted the major motivations behind fraud incidents as demonstrated in figure 4.2.

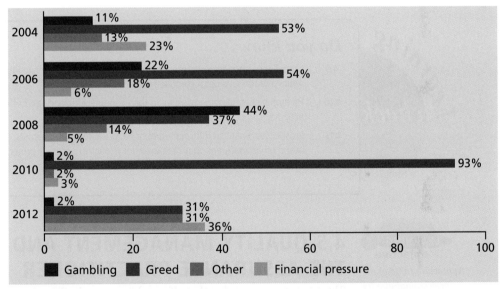

FIGURE 4.2:
Motivation to commit fraud 2004–2012

Source: KPMG Survey of fraud, bribery and corruption in Australia and New Zealand, p. 12.

4.4.7 Continuous audit

The electronic revolution has created a demand for more timely assurance on a broader range of information than that provided by the annual audit of historical financial statements. Companies now release information to interested parties over a short time frame (via their websites) and **continuous auditing** allows auditors' reports on that information to be provided almost immediately. A continuous audit is a process or method that enables independent auditors to provide written assurance on subject matter using a series of auditors' reports issued simultaneously with, or a short time after, the occurrence of events underlying the subject matter. It is conducted on continuous financial and non-financial information made available to users in formats defined by management.[21]

Auditors could be asked to continuously audit and report on:
- financial statements available on demand via a website
- specific financial information in conjunction with a debt covenant agreement
- compliance with published policies and practices regarding e-commerce transactions (e.g. reliance on secure encrypted systems for credit card processing)
- the effectiveness of controls operating in key systems or processes.

A continuous audit presents a number of auditing issues. There is little time for the auditor to gather audit evidence for verifying and substantiating the subject matter(s) concerned. The auditor cannot rely on normal audit procedures such as obtaining independent confirmations and checking material misstatements, so a reliable and well-controlled application system is vital. The auditor must use fully automated audit software such as IDEA or ACL to read, manipulate and generate the information required. Other conditions necessary for ensuring a successful continuous audit are:
- effective communication (and technology) between the client and the auditor
- agreement as to the form, content and scope of the audit
- a sound knowledge by the auditor of the operating systems used by the client.

The previous discussion is more relevant in an electronic environment where strategies and business processes are used to provide value-added performance to users and prospective investors.

Do you know ...

4.9 ☐ Compliance engagements provide assurance that regulations, contractual obligations or other requirements have been complied with.

4.10 ☐ Performance engagements refer to the economy, efficiency and effectiveness of business activities.

4.11 ☐ Prospective financial information may be in the form of forecasts, which are best estimates based on assumptions that management expect to occur, or projections which are hypothetical assumptions.

LEARNING objective 5

Appreciate some of the professional quality standards applicable to assurance engagements.

4.5 QUALITY MANAGEMENT AND THE ASSURANCE PRACTITIONER

There is a strong view that the self-regulatory standards and regulations that ensure the quality of professional services prevail in the profession. These self-regulatory controls include:
- high education entry requirements
- rigorous induction programs
- character checking on entry to the profession
- compulsory public practice induction
- compulsory continuing professional development
- extensive ethical rulings and codes of ethics
- separate public practice registration
- compulsory quality review programs
- compulsory professional indemnity insurance
- adherence to detailed and mandatory auditing standards and auditing pronouncements.

These controls set a minimum list of mechanisms and standards with which professional accountants and auditors must comply. However, as auditors expand their services and as their roles become more complicated, it is expected that they must not only keep abreast of current demands in quality delivery applicable to businesses, but also have the ability to assess the impact of such standards on their own work. This section focuses on some of the **benchmarks** of which auditors, assurance practitioners and professional accountants must be aware.

4.5.1 The ISO standards

The International Organization for Standardization (ISO) is a network of the national standards institutes of over 150 countries, with a Central Secretariat in Geneva, Switzerland, that coordinates the system. The ISO is a non-government organisation — its members are not, as is the case in the United Nations system, delegations of national governments. Nevertheless, the ISO occupies a unique position between the public and private sectors worldwide, owing to its national memberships coming from both sectors and its ability to set up national partnerships of industry associations.

The ISO acts as a bridging organisation in which a consensus can be reached on solutions that meet both the requirements of business and the broader needs of society, including the needs of stakeholder groups such as consumers and users. It began operations officially in February 1947. For the purpose of uniformity, the short form of the organisation's name is always ISO (derived from the Greek word *isos*, meaning 'equal').

International standards provide a common technological language between suppliers and their customers, which facilitates trade and the transfer of technology. The vast majority of ISO standards[22] are highly specific to a particular product, material or process. However, the standards that have earned the ISO 9000 and ISO 14 000 families a worldwide reputation are known as 'generic management system standards'. 'Generic' means that the same standards can be applied to any organisation, whatever its product or service, in any sector of activity, regardless of whether it is a business enterprise, a public administration or a government department. 'Management system' refers to what the organisation does to manage its processes, or activities. 'Generic' also signifies that no matter what the organisation is or does, if it wants to establish a quality management system or an environmental management system, then such a system has a number of essential features that are spelt out in the relevant standards of the ISO 9000 or ISO 14 000 families.

The ISO 9000 and ISO 14 000 families are among the ISO's most widely known and successful standards ever. ISO 9000 has become an international reference for quality requirements in business-to-business dealings, and ISO 14 000 has also achieved wide acceptance by organisations in meeting their environmental challenges.

The ISO 9000 series is concerned with 'quality management' (i.e. what an organisation does to enhance customer satisfaction by meeting applicable regulatory requirements and to continually improve its performance in this regard). The ISO 14 000 series is concerned mainly with 'environmental management' (i.e. what the organisation does to minimise harmful effects on the environment caused by its activities and to continually improve its environmental performance).

The ISO 9000 and ISO 14 000 standards are implemented by some 760 900 organisations in 154 countries. ISO 9000 provides a framework for quality management throughout the processes of producing and delivering products and services for the customer.

ISO 14 000 environmental management systems help organisations of all types to improve their environmental performance and make a positive impact on business results.

ISO 9000

ISO 9000 provides a framework for taking a systematic approach to managing business processes that produce outputs that meet customers' expectations. The original ISO 9001, 9002 and 9003 have been integrated into ISO 9000:2000. ISO 9000:2000 specifies requirements for a quality management system for any organisation that needs to demonstrate its ability to consistently provide product that meets customer and applicable regulatory requirements and aims at enhancing customer satisfaction. The standard is used for certification/registration and contractual purposes by organisations seeking recognition of their quality management system.

Eight quality management principles have been established to reflect best management practices:
1. customer focus
2. leadership
3. involvement of people
4. process approach
5. system approach to management
6. continual improvement
7. factual approach to decision making
8. mutually beneficial supplier relationships.

The quality management system covers the entire activities of an organisation and provides assurance to customers that the quality processes of an organisation are being achieved.

ISO 14 000

The ISO has developed what is called a three-pronged approach to meeting the needs of business, industry, governments and consumers in the area of the environment. First, it provides a wide-ranging portfolio of standardised sampling and testing methods, with the development of numerous international standards for monitoring such aspects as the quality of air, water and soil. Secondly, it developed environmental management system standards that can be implemented in any type of organisation in the public or private sector. The technical committee issued what is collectively known as the ISO 14 000 family. The third part of the approach is the technical reports issued by the technical committee.

ISO 14 000 is a series of international standards on environmental management. It provides a framework for the development of an environmental management system and the supporting audit program and is the cornerstone standard of the ISO 14 000 series. The standard specifies the actual requirements of an environmental management system and it applies to those environmental aspects over which the organisation has control or can be expected to have an influence. ISO 14 001 is the only ISO 14 000 standard against which it is possible to be certified by an external certification authority. The standard is applicable to any organisation that wishes to:
- implement, maintain and improve an environmental management system
- assure itself of its conformance with its own stated environmental policy
- demonstrate conformance
- ensure compliance with environmental laws and regulations
- seek certification of its environmental management system by an external third party organisation
- self-determine conformance.

To date there are many standards in the series that are guidelines for organisations to achieve ISO 14 001 registration. They include:
- ISO 14 004, which provides guidance on the development and implementation of an environmental management system
- ISO 19 011, which provides guidelines for quality and/or environmental management systems auditing — it is expected that by using this standard, organisations can save time, effort and money by:
  - avoiding confusion over the objectives of the environmental or quality audit program
  - securing agreement of the goals for individual audits within an audit program

- reducing duplication of effort when conducting combined environmental/quality audits
- ensuring auditor's reports follow the best format and contain all relevant information
- evaluating the competence of members of an audit team against appropriate criteria.

The work program of the technical committee is delegated to various sub-committees each of which is responsible for establishing guidelines in specific areas such as environmental management systems, environmental auditing, life cycle assessment, greenhouse gas management and environmental performance evaluation.

There are many different approaches to environmental auditing. For an environmental management system (EMS) to be effective, the auditor determines whether an organisation's EMS conforms to ISO specifications and requirements. Some of the corporate culture characteristics required are:

- top management commitment and board level support
- communication of relevant information and standards to all levels of management
- dissemination of knowledge of the industry and the environmental issues to all staff.

The International Auditing and Assurance Standards Board also suggests that environmental management system audits require the auditor to be knowledgeable about the industry and its environmental issues; verification standards and techniques; environmental laws and regulations; and management systems and practices, including the risks and controls safeguards as required.

The Professional Environment below demonstrates the trend of business reporting that combines environmental, social and governance aspects into a composite reporting regime. The auditing profession has embarked towards a framework of integrated reporting, where both financial and non-financial information are to be reported.

PROFESSIONAL ENVIRONMENT

Environmental, social and governance reporting — supporting informed decisions

*T*oday, as organisations flood the market with sustainability information to meet various reporting requirements and demands from stakeholders, the validity and usefulness of this type of information both internally and externally is a front-burner topic in executive suites and boardrooms.

While sustainability reporting remains largely voluntary in most areas, there is increasing pressure for more depth and accuracy in sustainability reporting ...

Therefore, business leaders are increasingly concerned about the accuracy and trustworthiness of the ESG information they release to the public ...

Source: Deloitte, 'Environmental, social and governance reporting — supporting informed decisions', 2010, Deloitte Development LLC.

4.5.2 Total quality management and the assurance practitioner

With auditors becoming increasingly involved in auditing an entire business, ISO 9000 can be very useful in helping auditors to identify and review issues that have an impact on quality management in an organisation. Arguably, the main consideration in **total quality management (TQM)** is its sustainability. Research into this issue (and the applicability of ISO 9000)[23] has led to the design of a tool to audit issues that have a negative impact on sustainability. Based on work carried out in different manufacturing organisations, the sustainability of total quality management was found, for example, to rely on factors such as continual improvement, organisational behaviour, human resources management, industrial relations and the labour process. These factors reflect a variety of perspectives within business operations. The issues found to have an impact on such factors were analyses of strengths, weaknesses, opportunities and threats (SWOT), competitors, quality and performance standards, new technologies, industrial relations, management–worker relationships, policies design, the positioning of quality functions and resources, functional boundaries, communication, job flexibility, the supervisory structure, the improvement infrastructure, and education and training.

In providing various types of assurance reviews, auditors are generally able to help management pinpoint the matters that have a negative impact on the total quality management of an organisation. Furthermore, they may be able to use the standards specified in ISO 9000 as audit tool benchmarks to provide the necessary level of assurance for effectiveness.

An understanding of the total business process is one of the strengths that financial accountants and auditors can build on as they add value for their employers and clients. Most accountants and auditors are good at analysing situations in organisations, constructing detailed work plans, explaining complex situations to clients from a variety of backgrounds and keeping confidences. Auditors can also perform ISO audits or help clients achieve ISO registration/performance.

Undoubtedly, auditing is an important function for the effective deployment of quality systems such as ISO 9000. Not only is it conducted to ensure total compliance with set procedures and agreed standards at all times and at all stages during the productive and organisational process, but it also helps to develop the organisation by providing mechanisms for continual improvement, innovation and the fostering of a problem-solving culture.

Since quality control is seen as a crucial element in regaining and retaining the credibility of the auditing and accounting profession, some large accounting firms have undertaken independent reviews of their own processes and policies in order to provide additional assurance of their quality procedures. One example is the Transparency Report 2009 for Ernst & Young Global.[24] The 19-page report aims to contribute to enhancing investor understanding and confidence in audit quality and discusses the legal and governance structures of Ernst & Young, its internal quality control system, independence practices, education of statutory auditors, financial information and partner remuneration.

Do you know . . .

4.12 ☐ The auditor and other assurance engagement providers must perform the respective assurance services in the most competent, objective and diligent manner. Both technical and ethical competence must be observed.

4.13 ☐ The ISO standards on quality provide a general set of guidelines for quality and environmental matters. Quality reviews are undertaken by the profession regularly.

SUMMARY

In addition to general purpose financial report audits, auditors and accountants are engaged to perform many other assurance services. Assurance engagements are engagements in which an assurance practitioner expresses a conclusion designed to enhance the degree of confidence of the intended users other than the responsible party about the outcome of the evaluation or measurement of a subject matter against a set of criteria. Two types of assurance engagements are performed — reasonable assurance engagements and limited assurance engagements. A reasonable assurance engagement aims at reducing risk to an acceptably low level as a basis for a positive conclusion. Reasonable assurance means a high but not absolute level of assurance. A limited assurance engagement aims at reducing risk to a level that is acceptable in the circumstances but where that risk is greater than for a reasonable assurance engagement as the basis for a negative conclusion. Assurance engagements must consist of an outcome, a set of criteria and a subject matter.

Assurance engagements concerned with financial information may include those performed for special purposes, for example as a requirement of a loan agreement, or for a component of the financial information prepared for a period other than the financial statement period, such as an interim reporting period. Where non-financial information is concerned, an assurance practitioner may be required to perform assurance engagements on various matters such as sustainability performance. The trend continues towards the use of benchmarks such as the Global Reporting Initiative (GRI), and assurance standard AA1000 is used by practitioners to perform assurance engagements for sustainability reports.

Although audit and assurance engagements vary in requirements, it is important for the assurance practitioner to be aware of standards in addition to the auditing standards issued by the AUASB. Standards such as the ISO 9000 and ISO 14 000 series indicate the wide-ranging benchmarks that are in use in commerce and industry.

KEY TERMS

assertion, p. 166

assertion-based engagement, p. 168

assurance engagement, p. 166

assurance practitioner, p. 178

benchmarks, p. 191

continuous auditing, p. 189

direct reporting engagement, p. 168

e-crimes, p. 187

forensic audit, p. 188

Global Reporting Initiative, p. 182

interim financial report, p. 175

sustainability, p. 182

total quality management (TQM), p. 193

triple bottom line reporting, p. 182

MULTIPLE-CHOICE questions

4.1 Which of these is an assurance engagement?
  (i) A performance audit.
  (ii) A consulting engagement to help an organisation meet its tax obligations.
  (iii) A review of historical financial information.
  A. (i) and (ii) only.
  B. (ii) and (iii) only.
  C. (i) and (iii) only.
  D. (i), (ii) and (iii).

4.2 Under the *Framework for Assurance Engagements* which of these is one of the types of assurance engagements?
  (i) Absolute assurance.
  (ii) Reasonable assurance.
  (iii) Partial assurance.
  (iv) No assurance.
  A. (ii) only.
  B. (i) and (ii) only.
  C. (ii) and (iii) only.
  D. (ii), (iii) and (iv) only.

4.3 A special purpose financial report is one that relates to:
  A. Non-financial information.
  B. Reports that must comply with approved accounting standards.
  C. Entities that are not reporting entities.
  D. Entities that are listed on the securities exchange or have borrowed from the public.

4.4 The scope of sustainability assurance varies among organisations. Typically, sustainability assurance does not include:
  A. Financial performance.
  B. Social performance.
  C. Environmental reporting.
  D. Fraud audit.

4.5 AA1000 is a well-recognised assurance standard. It contains principles such as:
  A. Integrity in reporting.
  B. Timeliness of conclusions.
  C. Materiality, completeness and responsiveness requirements.
  D. Total adherence to the standards for all assurance engagements.

4.6 Which of the following statements best describes the relationship between the fraudster and an organisation?
  A. A management team.
  B. A non-management employee.
  C. Audit personnel.
  D. A junior disgruntled staff member.

4.7 In a continuous audit client information is released in a very short timeframe, and auditors' reports on that information follow the release almost immediately. One of the issues for auditors is:
  A. The auditor cannot check the internal control system.
  B. There is enough time for the auditor to gather evidence.
  C. The auditor cannot use fully automated audit software.
  D. The auditor cannot rely on normal audit procedures.

4.8 Quality review should be practised:
A. At all levels of the firm.
B. At managerial level only.
C. During staff performance review.
D. During takeovers only.

4.9 The ISO 9000 series is concerned with:
A. Environmental management.
B. Quality management.
C. Audit requirements of specific businesses.
D. Marketing management.

4.10 Total quality management is a concept applicable to:
A. Non-executive directors only.
B. Independent directors only.
C. Accountants only.
D. All assurance engagement providers.

REVIEW questions

4.11 Discuss why auditors and accountants are engaged in assurance engagements other than financial statement audits.

4.12 What is meant by reasonable and limited assurance engagements? Give an example for each type.

4.13 List and explain the elements of an assurance engagement.

4.14 What is forensic accounting?

4.15 Explain why an organisation might employ an assurance practitioner to perform due diligence before deciding to purchase a new business.

4.16 What are the likely factors that lead to fraud?

4.17 What is meant by the three Es in a performance audit?

4.18 What is meant by the term prospective financial information?

4.19 Discuss the significance of assurance quality.

4.20 Define total audit quality management.

PROFESSIONAL application questions

★
BASIC
★★
MODERATE
★★★
CHALLENGING

4.21 Compilation, review or audit ★

You have been approached by a client who is not sure of the requirements with regard to financial reporting. Your client understands that there are compilations, reviews and audits but is not aware of the differences between them.

Required

Prepare notes for a meeting with your client that discuss the differences between a compilation, a review and an audit. Identify the different levels of assurance that will be given and what form that opinion will take. You should also give brief notes about the kind of procedures that would be involved in each engagement.

4.22 Assertion-based or direct reporting ★★

There are different categories and different types of assurance engagements:
1. Assertion-based engagements and direct reporting engagements.
2. Absolute, reasonable, limited and no assurance engagements.

3. Positive form assurance and negative form assurance.
4. An audit and a review of a financial report.
5. General purpose financial reports and special purpose financial reports.
6. Prospective financial information and historic financial information.
7. Compliance, performance, forensic and continuous auditing.

Required

For each of the above explain in detail the characteristics of each item and the extent to which they differ from one another.

4.23 Assurance services ★★

A firm provides the following service for its clients:

1. Preparation of a report giving advice to a client on the introduction of a new system of internal controls.
2. A report giving an opinion on a school's responses to a questionnaire required by the auditor-general.
3. Preparation of the company's tax returns.
4. A report to management about the success of a marketing campaign.
5. A report to directors in relation to half-year financial report for a listed company.
6. An audit of a management report into the effectiveness of a company's internal control system.
7. A statement of findings to management in relation to the completeness and accuracy of its purchase ledger balances.

Required

For each of the above identify whether assurance services are being provided, give explanations to justify your answer. For each assurance service, identify what level of assurance will be provided and what form the opinion will take.

4.24 Fraudulent expense claims ★★

You have been approached by your client Stan Frank who runs a small plumbing business. Stan's plumbers work on a range of small domestic jobs as well as large jobs on construction sites. It is not unusual for Stan's staff to be required to stay away from home during the week.

Stan has become concerned that the amount he has been paying for travel and accommodation expenses for staff staying away has increased significantly and he recently sacked a member of staff on suspicion of providing a false claim.

Stan has asked to have a meeting with you to discuss the problems he has found. He wants you to carry out an investigation into possible fraudulent expenses claims.

Required

Prepare notes for your meeting with Stan that will allow you to understand the nature of the engagement.

4.25 Forensic audit ★★

Standard Publishing Insurance Co. Ltd provides insurance cover for professional publishers. Australian Online Design Co. Ltd (AODCL) recently filed a claim for the loss it incurred following a breakdown of its computer network, in which its customers' files were lost. AODCL sells business publications (journals, magazines and news reports) to 1000 corporate customers via subscriptions through the Internet. The payment and delivery systems are also linked to the customers' files, held by the master e-commerce system. You are called in to conduct a forensic audit to establish the validity of the claim, and the extent to which it is appropriate.

Required

Explain the key considerations of the forensic audit you will conduct.

4.26 Key performance indicators — social and environmental performance ★★

Upper Crust Pizza Ltd is a profitable business that has been run for many years. The chairman of the board of directors is Simon Strange who built the company from nothing to the successful public company it now is. As he gets close to retirement Simon wants to ensure his legacy includes social and environmental success as well as the financial success that he has enjoyed.

Simon is considering how the organisation can improve the welfare of the staff, better look after customers, and improve how it interacts with the wider community and the environment.

Required

Considering staff, customers, the wider community and the environment suggest Key Performance Indicators that might be used to improve social and environmental performance.

4.27 Business plan ★★

You are the auditor for Blank Space Ltd a design group with several divisions each focusing on a different client group. Melanie Blank is the CEO and is looking for ways to improve the profitability of the group and has decided to focus on the main profit-making divisions. The coming year will therefore see a restructure of the group and Melanie wants to ensure this is done in as controlled a manner as possible and has produced a business plan for the period of the restructure.

Melanie has asked you to provide a report on the business plan for the coming year — you have been provided with the most up-to-date six monthly financials.

You are preparing for a meeting with Melanie initially to discuss the work you might perform on the business plan.

Required

Identify and explain the information you would seek to obtain before accepting appointment to report on the business plan.

4.28 Controls and risks for payments ★★★

You are engaged to write a checklist for Cyber-Sell, a company that buys and sells products over the Internet as a key secondhand market.

Required

Using the following headings, identify the controls and risks you would expect in the Cyber-Sell sales systems regarding:
(a) confidentiality of information
(b) transaction integrity
(c) authorisation of payments
(d) assurance of business credibility.

4.29 IT tender process ★★★

Johnson Brain is a subsidiary in the Franklin Spleen group of companies and is about to implement a new IT solution to manage an important part of its production process.

The Franklin Spleen group has a broad range of detailed group policies and procedures that all companies in the group must follow. The policy around major expenditure requires a tender process to take place as follows.
1. Full detailed project specifications should be produced.
2. Invitations to tender must be advertised publicly.
3. The receipt of tenders submitted must be documented and all submissions opened at the same time.
4. A project team of at least three must review and assess submissions, one of whom must have appropriate expertise in IT project management.

5. Contracts will be awarded based on an assessment matrix which gives a score weighted across various factors of functionality, financial stability of the supplier, track record, price, and future support.

You have been asked to provide assurance on Johnson Brain's new IT solution.

Required

Identify the type of assurance engagement you have been asked to carry out and for each of the five points above suggest procedures that might be carried out to satisfy yourself that the appropriate tender process has been followed.

CASE studies

4.30 Environmental auditing ★★

(a) Explain the meaning of environmental auditing.
(b) List some standards that have been issued in relation to environmental auditing.
(c) Describe the types of tasks that may be involved in environmental auditing.

4.31 Triple bottom line (TBL) assurance ★★★

Go to CPA Australia's website, www.cpaaustralia.com.au, and access the TBL assurance database. Identify the nature and extent of assurance provided for all mining and chemical companies reported in the database. Discuss the findings.

RESEARCH question

4.32 Fraud and accountability

1. Develop a checklist for an organisation you are about to evaluate regarding its level of risk in relation to fraud. Consult the latest KPMG Fraud and Misconduct Survey.
2. Access the website of the AUASB and discuss its role in promoting accountability for audit and assurance providers.

FURTHER READING

AccountAbility, AA1000 *Assurance Principles Standard*, London, 2008, www.accountability.org.uk.
KPMG, *Fraud and Misconduct Survey 2010*, October 2010, www.kpmg.org.au.

NOTES

1. The International Integrated Reporting Council (IIRC) is a global coalition of regulators, investors, companies, standard setters, the accounting profession and NGOs. Together, this coalition shares the view that communication about businesses' value creation should be the next step in the evolution of corporate reporting. The IIRC is chaired by Professor Mervyn King and Paul Druckman is Chief Executive Officer. The mission of the IIRC is to create *the* globally accepted International <IR> Framework that elicits from organisations material information about their strategy, governance, performance and prospects in a clear, concise and comparable format. The Framework will underpin and accelerate the evolution of corporate reporting, reflecting developments in financial, governance, management commentary and sustainability reporting. The IIRC will seek to secure the adoption of <IR> by report preparers and gain the recognition of standard setters and investors.

2. International Federation of Accountants (IFAC), 'Handbook of International Auditing, Assurance and Ethics Pronouncements', 2006 edition, IFAC, New York, pp. 280–303.

3. Auditing and Assurance Standards Board (AUASB), 'AUASB Glossary', October 2009, AUASB, Melbourne.

4. Auditing and Assurance Standards Board (AUASB), 'Framework for Assurance Engagements', April 2010, paragraph 16, AUASB, Melbourne.

5. ibid., paragraph 12.

6. ibid., paragraph 52.

7. This new assurance standard replaces the existing pronouncements, AUS 804 *The Audit of Prospective Financial Information* and AGS 1062 *Reporting in Connection with Proposed Fundraisings*. This is part of the Planned Regulatory Activities from July 2012 to December 2013. Auditing and Assurance Standards Board (AUASB), 'Annual Regulatory Plan 2012–2013', updated December 2012, AUASB, Melbourne.

8. The European Eco-Management and Audit Scheme, 'Statistics', 11 July 2013, EMAS, France, http://ec.europa.eu/environment/emas.

9. Environmental performance reporting in accordance with the EPBC Act section 516A concerns environmental performance on water, population and the communities. The latest report was published for the year of 2010–11.

10. Policy and Cabinet Division, Chief Minister and Cabinet Directorate, 'Triple Bottom Line Assessment for the ACT Government', Discussion Paper, June 2011, Australian Capital Territory, Canberra.

11. P Perego & K Ans, 'Multinationals' Accountability on Sustainability: The Evolution of Third-Party Assurance of Sustainability Reports', *Journal of Business Ethics* 110, 2012, pp. 173–90.

12. Sustainability Reporting: Practices, Performance and Potential, CPA Australia, 2005, www.cpaaustralia.com.au.

13. There are three parts to the Sustainability Report from the research carried out by CPA Australia and the University of Sydney. The report includes a summary of current practices, the portfolio reporters and ethical funds performance, and the association between sustainability disclosure policies and market returns, financial performance and credit risk profiles. The summary and list of documents can be viewed at www.cpaaustralia.com.au.

14. K Hargroves & M Smith (eds), *The Natural Advantage of Nations: Business Opportunities, Innovation and Governance in the 21st Century*, Earthscan/James&James, London, 2003.

15. AccountAbility: AA1000 Assurance Standard, 2003, www.accountability.org.uk.

16. The GRI Research and Development series released 'The External Assurance of Sustainability Reporting' publication in 2013, which provides guidelines on the matters to be reported and the standards to be used. It also explains the concept and use of external assurance of sustainability reporting, describes some of the issues reporters need to consider and the usual components of an external assurance engagement process for sustainability reporting.

17. Santos Limited's Greenhouse Gas Emissions statement, Independent Reasonable Assurance Report by Ernst & Young, 21 February 2013.

18. KPMG, 'A survey of fraud, bribery and corruption in Australia and New Zealand 2012', kpmg.com.au; kpmg.co.nz.

19. KPMG, 'Fraud and Misconduct Survey 2010 — Australia and New Zealand', KPMG, 2010, kpmg.com.au, kpmg.co.nz.

20. Excerpts from *KPMG Fraud and Misconduct Survey 2010* p. 17, www.kpmg.com.

21. ibid.

22. The following summary is adapted from information available on the ISO's website, www.iso.ch.

23. BG Dale, 'Total quality management sustaining audit tool: description and use', *Total Quality Management*, December 1997.

24. Ernst & Young, 'Transparency report 2009', Ernst & Young Global, www.ey.com.

Answers to multiple-choice questions

4.1 *C*   4.2 *A*   4.3 *C*   4.4 *D*   4.5 *C*   4.6 *B*   4.7 *D*   4.8 *A*   4.9 *B*   4.10 *D*

chapter 5

The auditor's legal liability

OVERVIEW

5.1 The legal environment

5.2 Liability to shareholders and auditees

5.3 Liability to third parties

5.4 Competition and consumer legislation

5.5 The global financial crisis (GFC) and potential liabilities for auditors

Summary

Key terms

Multiple-choice questions

Review questions

Professional application questions

Case studies

Research question

Further reading

Notes

LEARNING objectives

After studying this chapter, you should be able to:

1 comprehend the impact of the changing legal environment on professional liability

2 explain the auditor's liabilities to shareholders and auditees

3 describe the concept of due care owed by auditors to those relying on their services

4 explain the circumstances giving rise to negligence in the conduct of an audit and compliance

5 identify the issues and rulings of legal cases with respect to the auditor's liability to third parties

6 enumerate the precautions the auditor should take to avoid litigation.

PROFESSIONAL STATEMENTS

Australian		International	
ASA 210	*Agreeing the Terms of Audit Engagements*	ISA 210	*Agreeing the Terms of Audit Engagements*
ASA 502	*Audit Evidence — Specific Considerations for Litigation and Claim*	ISA 501	*Audit Evidence — Specific Considerations for Selected Items*
AGS 1014	*Privity Letter Requests*		

SCENE SETTER

Auditors need legal defence to act as early warning system

KPMG Australia chairman Peter Nash said company auditors have the ability to act as an early warning system to prevent company collapses and widespread economic turmoil but need greater legal protection in order to so.

Mr Nash told a meeting of Financial Executives International delegates in Sydney that auditors have the ability to comment on the risks to business strategies but there needs to be some form of 'safe harbour' enshrined in law to protect them from being sued.

His comments echo the concerns expressed by directors over the new integrated reporting proposal, which calls for more comment in annual reports on future strategies.

Mr Nash feels that new rules, including mandatory audit firm rotation, introduced in some jurisdictions in the wake of the financial crisis do not address one of the central aims of the changes — to make audits a better tool for preventing major financial meltdowns.

'Auditors essentially do what they did 40 years ago, which is provide assurance over a set of financial statements,' he told the gathering.

'If you want auditors to play a role in preventing a financial collapse, you have to ask them to look forward not backwards.'

A decade ago, auditors probably would not have had the expertise to comment on the risks in business strategies, but they did now, Mr Nash told the *Australian Financial Review*.

Mr Nash said although audit firms had a cap on liability, he felt there would also need to be some form of protection for auditors commenting on the risks to any corporate plans.

This would not be a blanket exemption from legal action, but as long as the auditor had carried out appropriate due diligence and could provide adequate evidence of the basis for their conclusions, it would provide a defence.

He said the push to introduce integrated reporting, which included requirements for board and senior management to give more commentary on their business model, strategy and the risks to that strategy, was providing an opportunity for audit to change as well.

The Australian Securities and Investments Commission's new regulatory guide 247 on board and management commentary at the start of annual reports, expects more comment on strategy and less use of the 'unreasonable prejudice' exemption in the Corporations Act.

However, directors and corporate governance experts also say that without some form of safe harbour from litigation, the extra comments will primarily lead to higher compliance and legal costs.

Source: S Drummond, 'Auditors need legal defence to act as early warning system', *Australian Financial Review*, 15 May 2013.

Auditors are accountable in law for their professional conduct. The historical audit role of providing opinions on financial reports traditionally provided some assurance of a firm's on-going viability for users of financial reports based on the going concern concept used in financial statements. However, where accountability has extended to non-financial matters such as in integrated reports, the role of auditors is being examined as to its relevance. While the responsibility arises under **common law** and statute law, the role of auditors has somewhat been subject to public scrutiny, especially in times of crisis.

Responsibility of the auditor under common law may be via contracts with clients or, in certain circumstances, with third parties to whom a legal duty of care is owed. Also of interest is the extent of liability in terms of:

- the determination of damages awarded by the courts where **negligence** is proven
- defences that may be offered by auditors in full or part mitigation of their responsibility.

We illustrate these issues by referring to decided cases. We also describe the extent of auditors' statutory responsibilities. The vulnerability of the auditing profession to negligence lawsuits has been evident for a number of years, arising from the decided cases discussed in this chapter. It is important to note, however, that we do not discuss cases where auditors have settled any unproven allegations out of court, because of the lack of sufficient publicly available information and evidence. Such cases in fact occur quite often.

LEARNING objective 1

Comprehend the impact of the changing legal environment on professional liability.

5.1 THE LEGAL ENVIRONMENT

In recent years, both the volume and cost of litigation relating to **alleged audit failures** have caused some concern to the profession. This can be attributed, in part, to several widely reported business failures that resulted in significant losses to investors. However, not all business failures can be equated with audit failures. There is a growing concern that too often following a business failure and alleged fraudulent financial reporting, the plaintiffs and their legal representatives prey on the auditor regardless of degree of fault, simply because the auditor may be the only party left with sufficient financial resources to indemnify the plaintiffs' losses. This has been referred to as the **insurance hypothesis**.

The requirement to hold a practising certificate imposes an obligation on auditors to carry **professional indemnity insurance** for possible liability to their clients and members of the public. This source of compensation creates a perception that auditors have 'deep pockets' and, arguably, contributes to the extent of claims filed against them. There is a presumption that the courts, finding this source of compensation to be a means of spreading loss, are easily influenced by the arguments of the plaintiffs' solicitors.

Audit firms have been, traditionally, partnerships that share **joint and several liability** in cases of alleged wrongdoings. Like many countries, Australia has been experiencing a 'hard insurance market', i.e. a market characterised by tougher risk selection by insurers. Moreover, the collapse of HIH Insurance, which held around 35% of the professional indemnity market, corporate and accounting failures such as Harris Scarfe, One.Tel, Enron and WorldCom in the early 2000s, Storm Financial (2007) and ABC Learning (2008) in Australia, and more recent Dynegy (6 July 2012) in the United States,[1] have exacerbated the problem and led to inadequate insurance coverage to meet some of the outstanding claims.[2]

Insurance premiums can vary substantially, depending on the firm's claims, experience and risk profile. Furthermore, the cover that can be obtained often falls well short of meeting the claims. This coverage gap between the potential liability and available insurance cover exposes auditors to the risk of significant personal liability. Many argue that this risk represents a real threat to the viability of the profession.

A further influence on litigation against auditors is the increasing **internationalisation of the profession.** International firms practising in Australia may well be caught up directly in lawsuits originating overseas. Australian auditing firms auditing controlled entities or branches of multinational companies with overseas creditors and ownership interest could find themselves being sued in overseas courts.

However, there have been major changes in the legal environment concerning auditor liability in the last few years. The changes were prompted by the Australian Government's determination to tackle the insurance crisis and, at the same time, provide a consistent approach to professional indemnity across the states. We discuss some of these changes in the following sections.

5.1.1 The litigation crisis

In the past, some major cases have been settled against auditing firms, but in more recent years there has been a tendency to settle out of court — and accordingly such cases are not reported. Examples of major cases that have been settled in Australia include the following.

- KPMG paid $136 million in 1994 over its audit of the failed merchant bank Tricontinental.
- KPMG and Price Waterhouse paid $120 million over the 1991 collapse of the State Bank of South Australia.
- In November 2000, a joint settlement was signed between the parties to the Adsteam litigation and the Australian Securities and Investments Commission (ASIC) that the directors and Deloitte Touche Tohmatsu would pay Residual Assco (formerly known as the Adelaide Steamship Company Ltd or Adsteam) the sum of $20 million in settlement of all proceedings. Deloitte would ensure that it would continue to upgrade its policies and procedures to enhance standards of professional independence and quality assurance in its audit division.[3]
- In April 2002, Andersen settled with Southern Equities (formerly Bond Corporation) $1 billion in damages launched by the liquidator of Alan Bond's former flagship company after 5 months of hearings in Adelaide's Supreme Court and an estimated $30 million in legal costs. Andersen was alleged to have failed in its duty as auditor for the company's 1988 accounts, in which Bond Corporation declared a $321 million profit with no audit qualification, while its profits were generated from several contentious deals that the liquidator alleges were falsely inflated. These false transactions included the purchase and resale of 260 hectares of land near Rome, a put and call option over the former Emu Brewery site in Perth, the purchase of the Hilton hotel in Sydney, and the refinancing of a parcel of shares in UK brewer Allied Lyons.[4]
- Shopping centre giant Centro and its former auditor PricewaterhouseCoopers have agreed to a record $200 million settlement in a marathon legal dispute with shareholders. Two groups of investors, represented by law firms Maurice Blackburn and Slater & Gordon, sued the retail landlord for their losses over its near collapse in late 2007. The outcome of negotiations has resulted in a $200 million global settlement, with PricewaterhouseCoopers to pay about $66 million or one-third of the total. The reputation of PricewaterhouseCoopers has taken a battering during the case over claims it failed to identify the problems in Centro's accounts and to sound the alarm to the group's directors. During the Federal Court hearing PricewaterhouseCoopers admitted negligence, acknowledging it should have considered more carefully the classification of debt between current and non-current obligations.[5]
- In 2009, Babcock & Brown went into liquidation. The directors of Babcock & Brown and the firm's auditor Ernst & Young were sued for at least $160 million in damages following court action by the liquidator.

The potential claims against auditors reporting on entities responsible for many millions of dollars of assets and liabilities may be astronomical. The damages awarded against auditors can be far in excess of their ability to pay, either from their own resources or through their professional indemnity cover. The award is likely to be totally unrelated to the audit fee received for the work performed, as is exemplified by the initial award of $145 million in the case of *Cambridge Credit Corporation Ltd and Anor v. Hutcheson & Ors* (1985) ACLR 545.

The judgement in the Cambridge Credit case provided the momentum for the accounting profession to seek legal reforms that are likely to curb unwarranted litigation. The momentum for reform was accelerated by the comments made by Rogers CJ in *AWA v. Daniels, t/a Deloitte, Haskins & Sells & Ors* (1992) 10 ACLC 933 (at 1022):

The scope for injustice occasioned by solitary liability is self-apparent ... In brief, a well-insured defendant, who may perhaps be responsible for only a minor fault, in comparison with the fault of other persons, may nonetheless be made liable, at least in the first instance, for the entirety of the damage suffered by the plaintiff. The defendant may indeed seek contribution from other persons responsible for the major damage. Why should the whole of the burden of a possibly insolvent wrongdoer fall entirely on a well-insured, or deep-pocketed defendant?

However, auditors continue to be targeted. In more recent times, PricewaterhouseCoopers have had action taken against them over the Centro collapse and in the collapse of Westpoint, auditors have again found themselves the subject of a legal suit, as illustrated in the Professional Environment below.

PROFESSIONAL ENVIRONMENT

Wickham auditor removed from industry

Thursday 27 June 2013

ASIC has cancelled the registration of the auditor of Wickham Securities Limited following the collapse of the $30 million property lender.

Under an enforceable undertaking (EU) with ASIC, Brian Patrick Kingston of Bajaume, Queensland, has agreed to never reapply for registration or perform any duties or functions of an auditor.

'Auditors are important gatekeepers — investors rely on what auditors do and naturally expect their work to be top quality,' ASIC Commissioner John Price said.

'Mr Kingston clearly failed in his job.

'ASIC will not tolerate inferior work and is determined to lift standards within the auditing profession.'

Wickham collapsed on 21 December 2012. On 27 September 2012 Mr Kingston issued an unqualified audit opinion on the financial report of Wickham for the year ended 30 June 2012.

ASIC formed the view that, in respect of the audit, Mr Kingston failed to carry out or perform adequately and properly the duties of an auditor. In particular, ASIC was concerned the audit was not conducted in accordance with the Australian Auditing Standards because:

• sufficient appropriate audit evidence to support material financial balances contained in the 2012 financial report was not obtained

• an unqualified audit opinion was rendered without sufficient appropriate audit evidence supporting the appropriateness of the going concern basis of accounting in the preparation of the 2012 financial report

- an adequate level of professional scepticism was not exercised in auditing the recoverability of loan assets and assessing going concern, and reliance was placed on representations from Wickham management and directors having without having performed appropriate audit procedures to corroborate or confirm those representations, and
- key audit planning, execution and completion procedures were not performed or documented by Mr Kingston.

ASIC's investigation into the collapse of Wickham, and Sherwin Financial Planners Pty Ltd and related entities continues.

Source: ASIC Media Release 13-156, 27 June 2013.

Also, the continuing global financial crisis (GFC) is likely to lead to claims against auditors from liquidators of failed companies, although it is still too early to tell as these actions against auditors usually take years to evolve.

5.1.2 The professional standards legislation

The main concerns for the Australian Government regarding the lack of appropriate insurance are threefold. First, many professionals may be operating without appropriate insurance cover and divorcing themselves from assets through discretionary trusts and the like, leaving clients unable to access appropriate damages in the case of negligence. Second, a contraction of supply of professional services is likely to lead to reduced competition. Third, the withdrawal of professional services, especially in areas critical to the public interest, will adversely affect the wellbeing of the community. It is also likely that most, if not all, of the generally higher costs of professional indemnity insurance will be passed on to clients.

Following much public debate, the federal government's Treasury Legislation Amendment (Professional Standards) Bill 2003 was passed by the Senate on 24 June 2004. The Bill proposed a scheme whereby it adapts the professional standards legislation (PSL) at the state and territory level and applies the arrangement to limit civil liability for misleading and deceptive conduct under the Commonwealth's then *Trade Practices Act 1974* which became the *Competition and Consumer Act 2010*, the *Australian Securities and Investments Commission Act 2001* and the *Corporations Act 2001*. The government recognises there is a constitutional issue that the Commonwealth must observe when it comes to making laws that may be seen to prefer a particular state. The task of selecting a PSL scheme in connection with a Commonwealth law presents some initial challenges. For example, the PSL adopted by New South Wales and Western Australia was different from that adopted by Victoria at the time. The amendments made by the Bill established a structure under which the Commonwealth can support PSL by allowing liability under the relevant Commonwealth legislative provisions dealing with misleading and deceptive conduct to be capped. The Bill also reiterated the reference to 'choice of law rules' which requires consideration of where the tort (i.e. negligent act) occurred, irrespective of where the court action is held.[6] Thus the liability reforms supported by the federal, state and territory governments:

- are a nationally consistent system of PSL
- replace joint and several liability with a national model of **proportionate liability.**

In practice, PSL allows occupational schemes to be registered and, if they are approved by the state government, members of the schemes must comply with certain requirements including a minimum level of professional indemnity insurance cover of $500 000. The state ministers agreed that any legislation and schemes being developed should be flexible enough to meet the concerns of large purchasers of professional services. Subsequently, the *New South Wales Professional Standards Act 1994* and the *Victorian Professional Standards*

Act 2003 (with amendments as at 12 December 2005) were amended to take such flexibility and differences into account. The general thrust of this legislation is as follows.[7]

- The occupational association within the schemes include members of associations that belong to more than one occupational group, and officers and employees of corporations that are members of the occupational association.
- Limitation caps are calculated with reference to a multiple of fees charged. A scheme may also specify a multiple monetary ceiling or minimum cap for the purposes of the scheme by way of a formula.
- Conditions of application include that the person has business assets the net current market value of which is not less than the amount of the monetary ceiling specified in the scheme in relation to the class of person and the kind of work related to the cause of action, and that there is adequate insurance cover.
- The cap does not apply to liability arising from claims for death, personal injury or any conduct involving a breach of trust, fraud or dishonesty (Victoria).
- A minimum cap of $500 000 applies but can vary within and between occupational groups.
- Risk management strategies must be in place, which include codes of practice, codes of ethics and quality management.
- Membership of a professional standards scheme is voluntary but the limitation of liability must be disclosed to a client or potential client.

At the time of revising this section, the government has instituted new regimes for applying for PSL. The Institute of Chartered Accountants in Australia and CPA Australia are in the process of amending the structure of PSL support to their members. Students should consult the professional bodies' webpage and access their advice to members.

5.1.3 The impact of the CLERP 9 Act

One of the reforms introduced by the *Corporate Law Economic Reform Program (Audit Reform and Corporate Disclosure) Act 2004* (CLERP 9 Act) deals with the registration of company auditors. CLERP 9 allowed companies to register as company auditors for the first time. However, before they can be registered, ASIC must be satisfied that they have adequate and appropriate professional indemnity insurance. Audit companies need insurance so they can meet claims reasonably expected to arise from their work. ASIC also issued a guidance paper, *Authorised Audit Companies: Insurance Arrangements*, in June 2004 to solicit awareness and comments.[8] In the main, a company may be registered as an authorised audit company if the following conditions are met:[9]

(a) each of the directors of the company must be a registered company auditor;
(b) each share in the company must be held and beneficially owned by an individual or the legal personal representatives of the individual;
(c) a majority of the votes that may be cast at a general meeting of the company attach to shares in the company that are held and beneficially owned by individuals who are registered company auditors;
(d) the company must not be in external administration ...

ASIC must be satisfied that the company has adequate and appropriate professional indemnity insurance for claims that may be made against it for Corporations Act audits of companies and registered schemes. Such insurance should be enough to cover any claims reasonably expected to arise from such audits of companies and registered schemes, fit for purpose and on usual commercial terms, and reasonably available in the marketplace. The minimum insured amount will depend on the largest audit engagement fee that the directors of the audit company reasonably believe will be charged. To determine the required insured amount, ASIC has a formula that can be used.

Learning check

Do you know …

5.1 ☐ Auditors have faced a litigation crisis following the corporate collapses of the 1980s. This crisis may be a result of the deep-pockets theory, the expectation gap and the possible erosion of audit quality.

5.2 ☐ The legal reforms proposed to limit auditors' liability for negligence include introducing a uniform approach to professional indemnity across all states and territories. The professional standards legislation (PSL) was passed in 2004 with individual PSL Acts introduced in the states and the territories.

5.3 ☐ The PSL introduces a structure in which a flexible capping system is applied at state and territory level through the approval of a registered scheme by occupational associations. Limitation caps are calculated with reference to a multiple of fees charged. A scheme may also specify a multiple, monetary ceiling or minimum cap for the purposes of the scheme by way of a formula.

5.4 ☐ Provisions are made for companies to be registered as authorised audit companies with conditions to be applied for limited professional liability, with a minimum insurance cover.

Explain the auditor's liabilities to shareholders and auditees.

5.2 LIABILITY TO SHAREHOLDERS AND AUDITEES

For audits conducted in accordance with the Corporations Act, the auditor is liable under statute and common law to the company for any negligent performance of statutory duties. These duties cannot be restricted or reduced.

Auditors are also liable in the same manner as any other citizen for cases of fraud or defamation. The Corporations Act stipulates that auditors, in cases of irregularities, are required to report to ASIC if they have 'reasonable grounds to suspect' any contravention of the law. One of the major problems in accepting greater responsibility for reporting suspected fraud to a regulatory body is that the auditor, if he or she is mistaken, may be liable for a defamation action by the party identified by the auditor as perpetrating the fraud. Also, negligence, if proven to be wilful, may constitute a conspiracy with management to defraud the company or other parties. Auditors in the United Kingdom and the United States have found themselves in court on the criminal charge of fraud after issuing unqualified reports on financial statements subsequently found to be misleading.

In the provision of auditing services, an auditor is liable to compensate a plaintiff if:

- a duty of care is owed to the plaintiff
- the audit is negligently performed or the opinion is negligently given
- the plaintiff has suffered a loss as a result of the auditor's negligence (where the causal relationship is reasonably foreseeable)
- the loss is quantifiable.

Describe the concept of due care owed by auditors to those relying on their services.

5.2.1 Due care

We examine the development of the concept of **due care**, as applied to the performance of an auditor's duties, by referring to cases decided in UK and Australian courts. The interpretation of due care and reasonable skills and diligence has changed over time. We consider the relevance of professional standards, namely:

- auditing standards in determining the adequate performance of audit work
- accounting standards in determining the basis for expressing an opinion on fairness of presentation.

The classic statement on the extent of auditor responsibility in examining the accounts to be reported on is contained in the Kingston Cotton Mill Co. case of 1896 (see box overleaf).

Kingston Cotton Mill Co. (No. 2) (1896) 2 Ch. 279

Facts of the case: For several years the manager of the Kingston Cotton Mill had been exaggerating the quantities and values of the company's stock (inventory) so as to fraudulently overstate the company's profits. This came to light when the company was unable to pay its debts and its true financial position was revealed. The auditor relied on a certificate signed by the manager and ensured that the amount appearing in the accounts was consistent with that certificate. The valuation of stock was described in the accounts as being as 'per manager's certificate'. In line with contemporary practice, the auditor did not physically observe stock or attempt to verify the valuation of individual items. Neither did the auditor reconcile stock with the opening balance and purchases and sales during the year, all of which would have put the auditor on notice that something was amiss.

In relation to the auditor's responsibilities in general, but particularly with respect to the detection of fraud, the following points from the judgement of Lopes LJ are important:

It is the duty of an auditor to bring to bear on the work he has to perform that skill, care and caution which a reasonably competent, careful and cautious auditor would use. What is reasonable skill, care and caution must depend on the particular circumstances of each case. An auditor is not bound to be a detective, or, as was said, to approach his work with suspicion or with a foregone conclusion that there is something wrong. He is a watchdog, but not a bloodhound. He is justified in believing tried servants of the company in whom confidence is placed by the company. He is entitled to assume that they are honest, and to rely upon their representations, provided he takes reasonable care. If there is anything calculated to excite suspicion, he should probe it to the bottom but, in the absence of anything of that kind, he is only bound to be reasonably cautious and careful.

The Kingston Cotton Mill case laid down some fundamental auditing principles such as the 'watchdog' role and the notion of taking reasonable skill and care although the acceptability of its practice has eroded over time.

An equally famous case dealing with the auditor's responsibility for reporting on the accounts is the 1895 London and General Bank case.

London and General Bank (No. 2) (1895) 2 Ch. 673

Facts of the case: The bank made loans to customers for which it held inadequate security. Interest due on the loans was accrued but not received, yet dividends were paid out of profits arising from such interest. The auditor made a full report to the directors in respect of the valuation of these loans and the need for a provision for bad debts against both the loan and the accrued interest. However, in his report to the shareholders, the auditor merely qualified his opinion with the following sentence: 'The value of the assets as shown on the balance sheet is dependent upon realisation.'

Judgement: As regards the auditor's responsibility for reporting, Lindley LJ observed:

It is no part of an auditor's duty to give advice either to directors or shareholders as to what they ought to do.

> It is nothing to him whether the business of the company is being conducted prudently or imprudently, profitably or unprofitably; it is nothing to him whether dividends are properly or improperly declared, provided he discharges his own duty to shareholders. His business is to ascertain and state the true financial position of the company at the time of the audit and his duty is confined to that.
>
> He is not an insurer; he does not guarantee that the books do correctly show the true position of the company's affairs; he does not guarantee that the balance-sheet is accurate according to the books of the company. If he did, he would be responsible for an error on his part, even if he were himself deceived, without any want of reasonable care on his part — say, by the fraudulent concealment of a book from him. His obligation is not so onerous as this.
>
> Such I take to be the duty of the auditor: he must be honest — that is, he must not certify what he does not believe to be true, and he must take reasonable care and skill before he believes that what he certifies is true.
>
> The case highlights the honesty and independence requested of auditors.

Implications of the Kingston Cotton Mill Co. case and the London and General Bank case

These two cases have formed the basis for most subsequent decisions as to the determination of auditor negligence. The recognition of auditing as a profession is crucial in both instances. The auditor does not guarantee that the financial statements are fairly presented any more than a solicitor guarantees to win a case or a doctor guarantees to effect a cure. Neither does an auditor guarantee to bring to bear the highest degree of skill in the performance of his or her duties, because there may be more skilful auditors within the profession. Furthermore, the auditor is not necessarily answerable for an error of judgement provided that he or she exercises the skill and care of a reasonably competent and well-informed member of the profession.

Nevertheless, a too-literal interpretation of the Kingston Cotton Mill Co. case has been criticised as retarding the development of improved auditing practices. For 60 years after the case, auditors continued to rely heavily on management representations (such as inventory certificates), notwithstanding developments in auditing techniques (especially in the United States) that enabled the auditor to acquire a significantly higher degree of assurance with relatively little increase in audit effort.

In fraud detection, experience led auditors to expect common frauds and to design audit procedures so as to have a reasonable chance of detecting such frauds; nonetheless, they continued to rely on the Kingston Cotton Mill Co. case judgement in denying any legal responsibility for the detection of fraud in those instances where their suspicions were not aroused.

The developments in the United States arose out of criticisms of auditors contained in the Securities and Exchange Commission's report of 1941 into the McKesson and Robbins fraud. From that date, the evaluation of internal control, attendance at stocktaking and the circularisation of accounts receivable became required procedure in that country.

A comparable advance in Australia, following British case law, came about with the observation of Denning L in *Fomento (Stirling Area) Ltd v. Selsdon Fountain Pen Co. Ltd* (1958) 1 WLR 45 at 61 as to an auditor's approach. This observation was that the auditor:

must come to it with an enquiring mind — not suspicious of dishonesty, I agree — but suspecting that someone may have made a mistake somewhere and that a check must be made to ensure that there has been none.

Auditors hold themselves out as possessing special skills. Consequently, the courts will require a higher standard of care from auditors. Pennyquick J's observation in *Thomas Gerrard & Son Ltd* (1967) 2 All ER 525 at 536 was another advance. He stated:

The real ground on which re Kingston Cotton Mill Co. (No. 2) is, I think, capable of being distinguished is that standards of reasonable care and skill are, on the expert evidence, more exacting today than those which prevailed in 1896. I see considerable force in this contention.

The narrow interpretation of the Kingston Cotton Mill Co. case concerning some audit practices was finally laid to rest by the Pacific Acceptance case (see box on the next page). However, the more exacting auditor responsibility prompted by the Pacific Acceptance case showed the changing expectations in respect of the auditor's responsibility, with the standards of reasonable care also being altered.

Pacific Acceptance Corporation Ltd v. Forsyth (1970) 92 WN (NSW) 29

Facts of the case: A branch manager of Pacific Acceptance made loans to a real estate speculator on the strength of security confirmed by a solicitor introduced by the speculator. In fact, most of the security offered in the form of title deeds, registered charges and mortgages was worthless, being either forged or improperly drawn up. Numerous auditing deficiencies were alleged, such as the assignment of insufficiently experienced audit staff, lack of adequate supervision, excessive reliance on management representations instead of examination of documentary evidence, and a failure to identify irregularities and to follow up those discovered during the audit.

Judgement: In finding the auditor liable, Moffit J had the following to say about the auditor's level of skill and care:

The legal duty, namely, to audit the accounts with reasonable skill and care, remains the same, but reasonableness and skill in auditing must bring to account and be directed towards the changed circumstances referred to. 'Reasonable skill and care' calls for changed standards to meet changed conditions or changed understanding of dangers, and in this sense standards are more exacting today than in 1896. This the audit profession has rightly accepted, and by change in emphasis in their procedures and in some changed procedures has acknowledged that due skill and care calls for some different approaches.

The judgement was wide ranging and covered the following procedures and practices which it was held should exist in a normally competent audit.

• Pay due regard to the possibility of material fraud or error in framing or carrying out audit procedures so the auditor has a reasonable expectation that the fraud or error will be detected.
• Promptly report fraud or warn of suspicion of fraud, whether material or not.
• Closely supervise and review the work of inexperienced staff.
• Properly document audit procedures in a written audit program which is to be amended as necessary as the audit progresses.
• Audit the whole of the year, not just the year-end balances; the duty to audit encompasses the client's financial affairs throughout the period of appointment and is not confined to reporting on the year-end balances as presented in the accounts.
• Carry out proper objective auditing procedures; reliance on independent sources or client personnel is an aid but not a substitute for the auditor's own procedures.
• Do not shirk reporting to shareholders on the pretext that some detriment would arise if the matter were revealed.

One feature of the case was the willingness of the audit staff to allow themselves to be persuaded by the perpetrator of the fraud to accept his representations on matters where corroborative evidence was available, but not sought. This lack of objective independence was also a feature of the Cambridge Credit case. UK Department of Trade inspectors investigating corporate failures have been critical of auditors for failing to stand up to company chairpersons with strong personalities. The Pacific Acceptance case established some of the key features of professional due care expected of an auditor.

HIH Royal Commission report, The Failure of HIH Insurance, April 2003

In terms of due care and independence, Justice Owen highlighted the fiduciary duty and relationship with others in his judgement in the HIH Royal Commission.[10]

There are many situations where the law imposes obligations upon people who face conflicts between their interests and their duties. In determining what I consider to be an appropriate standard of audit independence I have had regard to certain of those situations, namely the imposition of fiduciary obligations, the independence of directors, requirements in respect of related party transactions, and disqualification of members of the judiciary on the grounds of bias or apprehended bias, which are discussed below.

Fiduciary obligations

The primary elements of a fiduciary relationship are that:
• the fiduciary has undertaken to act in the interests of another
• the undertaking gives to the fiduciary the power to affect the interests of the other party
• the person to whom the fiduciary duty is owed is vulnerable to the fiduciary's abuse of his or her position ...

It has been said that there are three purposes of the law of fiduciary obligations, namely:
• the maintenance of high standards of honesty and propriety by those who are under a duty to act in the interests of others
• the confiscation of gains arising from the abuse of a relationship of trust
• the protection of one person's reasonable expectations that the other will act in her or his interests, and not in pursuance of a contrary self interest or conflicting duty [HIH Royal Commission Report, vol. 1, p. 168].

Justice Owen described the auditors' duty as:

The users of the financial statements are not privy to the information that is received by the auditor or the process by which the auditor exercises skill and judgement to reach conclusions on that information. The users of the company, users of the financial reports and regulatory bodies place significant reliance upon the integrity of auditors. Auditors have an obligation to ensure that they are, and are seen to be, maintaining high standards of honesty and probity, acting in the interests of the shareholders of the company to whom they are reporting and exercising independence of mind to ensure that financial reports provide a true and fair view of the financial position and performance of the company [HIH Royal Commission Report, vol. 1, p. 167].

In a case at the New South Wales Court of Appeal, *Stanilite Pacific Ltd & Anor v. Seaton and Ors, t/a Price Waterhouse* (2005) NSWCA 301, the judgement of Hodgson JA referred to an extension of the duty to exercise reasonable skill and care in giving consent for the report to be included in a prospectus, with a view to avoiding exposure of the client to claims for misleading statements in the prospectus. The following quote is relevant:

In particular, it was their duty to exercise reasonable skill and care in conducting the subsequent events review on 18 April 1995, in participating in the Due Diligence Committee and in giving the consent on 3 May 1995. However, the extent of the duty is to

LEARNING 4 objective

Explain the circumstances giving rise to negligence in the conduct of an audit and compliance.

5.2.2 Negligence

Negligence has been defined as any conduct that is careless or unintentional in nature and entails a breach of any contractual duty or duty of care in **tort** owed to another person or persons. The auditor's duty of care to a client arises either in a contract or in the tort of negligence. If the auditor has been negligent, then the client may sue the auditor for breach of an implicit term of the contract to exercise reasonable care and skill, so as to recover any consequential loss suffered. The client may sue the auditor in the tort of negligence to obtain **damages** sufficient to restore the client to its original position. The case of negligence, however, depends on the court's judgement under the circumstances of the case. Compliance with accounting standards, auditing standards and guidelines provides a certain degree of assurance that the auditor has exercised reasonable care and skill.

In making a report, the auditor expresses an opinion as to whether the financial statements fairly present the financial position of the entity and its operations for the period. In most of the cases so far described, the plaintiff has alleged that the auditor's investigation was flawed, thus preventing the auditor from being in a position to express an opinion. There have been very few cases against the auditor solely on the grounds that the financial statements did not present the entity's financial position fairly or, as in the London and General Bank case, that any qualification in the auditor's report was not sufficiently informative as to the extent of the failure of the financial statements to present the financial position fairly. In the 1970s, when high inflation prevailed, it was argued that financial statements based on the historical cost convention were misleading, yet financial statements based on this convention continued to be prepared and reported on by auditors as presenting a true and fair view.

The Corporations Act requires the financial statements to be prepared in accordance with applicable accounting standards and to show a true and fair view of the financial affairs at the reporting date. Auditors must exercise judgement in applying standards to the specific circumstances of the entity on which they are reporting. Judgement must also be exercised in those circumstances where compliance with accounting standards would not give a true and fair view, and where additional information and explanations must be added.

Following the Pacific Acceptance case, the Australian accounting bodies issued more comprehensive and specific auditing standards and practice statements concerning the conduct of the audit. In the 1992 AWA case (see box on p. 218), for example, the court considered whether the auditor had complied with the requirement of paragraph 28 of the former Auditing Practice Statement AUP 12 that 'the auditor should make management aware on a timely basis of material weaknesses which have come to his attention'. In this case, it was held that the auditor had been negligent. With the legal codification of auditing standards, the courts will be expected to be able to determine also whether the auditor has complied with the auditing standards.

On the other hand, auditors are subject to an increasing amount of scrutiny by regulatory bodies such as ASIC. For example, ASIC reported cases such as the following.

• On 17 October 2005, a PKF audit partner was required to give to an enforceable undertaking to ASIC to have a compliance plan that sets out the adequate measures the responsible entity operating under a registered scheme must comply with. The undertaking was given following a review of the audit working papers by ASIC.[12]

be assessed having regard to the circumstance that the accounts for the half year ended 31 December 1994 had been audited and given an unqualified certificate, and that there was no requirement to reaudit those accounts.[11]

- In 2009, ASIC banned three KPMG audit partners from practising as auditors for up to two years after their involvement in the Westpoint collapse in 2006. ASIC claimed that three partners in KPMG's Perth office had breached auditing standards. It announced the trio would not practise as auditors for two years, 18 months and nine months respectively. It said the partners had agreed to enforceable undertakings, which include the bans on working as auditors, the need for 10 hours of additional professional training and a bill for all ASIC investigation and legal costs.[13]

The two examples provided are evidence of ASIC's concern to ensure that auditors discharge their duties with due care and diligence, in compliance with auditing standards and the legislative provisions concerning independence.

In ASIC's audit inspection program report for 2011–12, which was issued in December 2012, ASIC found that in 18% of the 602 key audit areas reviewed across 117 audit files over firms of all sizes, auditors did not obtain sufficient appropriate audit evidence, exercise sufficient professional scepticism, or otherwise comply with auditing standards in at least one significant audit area. ASIC claimed that audit firms should consider ways to improve and maintain audit quality, particularly in relation to audit evidence, professional scepticism, and the use of other auditors and experts.[14]

In addition, ASIC raised areas of future focus for audit firms and inspection, including:

- audit evidence, professional scepticism, and the use of other auditors and experts;
- quality of judgements and decisions made by the auditor; and
- deficiencies in auditor conduct appear to have contributed to insufficient transparency in the financial position and financial performance of an entity leading up to the collapse.[15]

5.2.3 Privity of contract

The term **privity of contract** refers to the contractual relationship that exists between two or more contracting parties. In a typical auditing relationship, an audit (or audit-related service) is assumed to be performed in accordance with professional standards unless the contract (engagement letter) contains specific wording to the contrary.

As a general common law rule, only parties to a contract will have rights or obligations under that contract as shown in figure 5.1.[16]

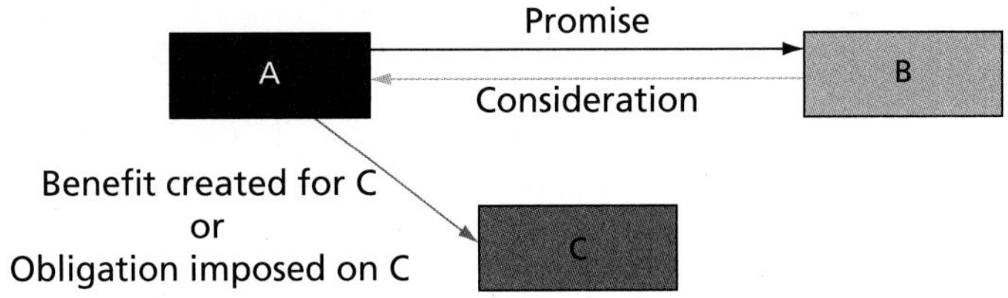

Promise

Consideration

Benefit created for C
or
Obligation imposed on C

FIGURE 5.1:
Privity of contract
demonstration

In the above example if a contract has been agreed upon between A and B, no obligations can be imposed on C, even if the contract is intended to benefit C. However, it can be seen that such strict application of the privity of contract may give rise to unintended results. In the case of *Tweedle v. Atkinson* (1861) the Court found to uphold the privity of contract even though the plaintiff was the intended beneficiary.

In this case, the father of a bride promised the father of the groom to pay the groom (plaintiff) a sum of money upon the marriage. However, before making this payment, the bride's father died and his estate refused to honour his promise. The plaintiff sued for the money but failed on the ground that, although the contract had been made for his benefit, he was not a contracting party.

Scope of the doctrine

The doctrine of privity of contract applies only to contractual rights and obligations; if the contract involved gives rise to non-contractual rights and obligations then it is possible for these to be enforced against, or in favour of, those who are not parties to the contract. For example, if A and B who are parties to a contract that is intended to protect not only A and B but also other third parties, then if B fails to discharge his/her obligations leading to an injury occurred by C, then C may have a claim against B in tort — for negligence.

The privity doctrine in Australia

In *Trident General Insurance Co Ltd v. McNiece Bros Pty Ltd* (1988) 165 CLR 107 the High Court cast doubt upon the extent of the doctrine. Two judges said the doctrine of privity of contract produced injustice where third parties were intended to benefit from the contract and could not enforce it directly. They said it is time to review the laws. The judges allowed the intended beneficiaries in this case to get the benefit, as looking at commercial reality it would have been inequitable for the insurance company to turn its back on the risk. Problems highlighted by some members of the court included the following.

- Often, damages are not suffered by the contracting party. If A breaches contract, B might have suffered no damages compared to C and C can't enforce the contract.
- Although B can enforce the contract for the benefit of C, specific performance is discretionary and may not be granted in these circumstances.
- One way around this situation is to say B entered into the contract as trustee for C — but it's often an inadequate remedy.[17]

There is sometimes misunderstanding regarding the parties to the contract in an audit under the Corporations Act where the auditor's report is addressed to the members. The term 'members' is used collectively and does not indicate responsibility to individual shareholders or others entitled to receive copies of the accounts. Under contract, only the directors (on behalf of the company) or, more commonly, the liquidator or receiver may sue the auditor in respect of losses incurred by the company arising from the auditor's negligence. Monies recovered by way of damages from the auditor are then applied to meet the claims of creditors first; only the residue, if any, is available for the shareholders. Individual shareholders, creditors, employees, directors and others have no claim against the auditor under contract. The issue of auditors' responsibility to existing and future shareholders and creditors is demonstrated in figure 5.2.

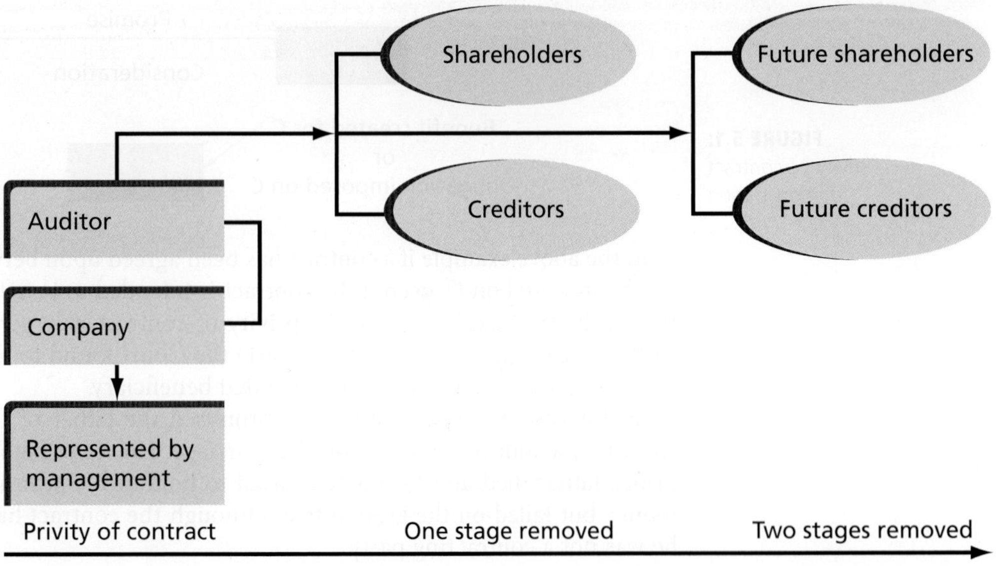

FIGURE 5.2: Liability of auditors at one and two stages removed

| Privity of contract | One stage removed | Two stages removed |

An Australian case brought by a company against its auditors for failing in their contractual duty to the company was that of *WA Chip & Pulp Co. Pty Ltd v. Arthur Young* (1987) 12 ACLR 545. In this case, a senior employee obtained loans from the company that were not properly authorised and eventually became irrecoverable. The auditors were aware of the loans and expressed concern at their size but relied on verbal assurance from the person authorising the loans that he had authority to do so. At no time did the auditors bring their concern to the attention of the general manager of the company because the amounts were not material. It was held that the auditors had been negligent.

In the United States, the highest courts in two states used the doctrine of privity as a basis for their decisions limiting the legal liability of auditors. According to the decisions reached by the California Supreme Court in *Bily v. Arthur Young Co.* and by the New York Court of Appeals in *Security Pacific Business Credit Inc. v. Peat Marwick Main & Co.*, an auditor is not liable to a third party who uses audited financial statements. The resolution of the cases limits claims only to entities that are in direct privity with accounting firms, particularly the accountants' clients. The decisions shed light on the issues of increasing professional liability burdens being exerted on accountants, the unreasonable demands being imposed by users and the potentially destructive effects of unlimited liability.[18]

5.2.4 Causal relationship

A **causal relationship** (illustrated by the two cases in the following boxes) exists between the breach of duty by the defendant and the loss or harm suffered by the plaintiff. This relationship must have been reasonably foreseeable and it must be proven that the loss suffered is attributable to the negligent conduct of the auditor in a negligent case. In *Caparo Industries Pty Ltd v. Dickman & Others* (1990) 1 All ER 568 in the United Kingdom (see box on pp. 225–6), Bridge L stated:

In advising the client who employs him, the professional man owes a duty to exercise that standard of skill and care appropriate to his professional status and will be liable both in contract and in tort for all losses which his client may suffer by reason of any breach of that duty.

Segenhoe Ltd v. Akins & Ors (1990) 8 ACLC 263

Facts of the case: In this Australian case, Segenhoe argued that it, as a separate legal entity and distinct from its shareholders, had suffered loss by wrongly paying an amount to its shareholders that would otherwise not have been paid. It claimed the loss was due to the negligence of the auditor and should be recovered from the auditor.

Judgement: The court held that where an auditor has been negligent and the company has been induced to pay a dividend out of capital — relying on an incorrectly audited profit and loss account — the auditor is liable for the loss incurred. Further, the right of the company to recover from shareholders' dividends paid out of capital is a question of mitigation of loss; the company is not required to undertake complicated litigation against shareholders. The court supported the view that where auditors are negligent, ultimately, they are likely to be liable for the full amount of loss while the corporate veil is retained.

Galoo Ltd v. Bright Graham Murray (1994) BCC 319

Facts of the case: For the purposes of appreciating the development of audit liability, the decision of the English Court of Appeal in the Galoo Ltd v. Bright Graham Murray case has reaffirmed the causation relationship requirement to establish the liability of the auditor. Galoo had incurred losses of approximately $55 million between 1986 and 1990, and had paid a dividend of $1.1 million in 1988. Galoo sued the auditor for breach of its contractual duty to exercise reasonable care and skill, arguing that the trading losses were attributable to the continued existence of the company, which in turn was due to reliance on the allegedly negligent audit opinions.

Judgement: The court of appeal held that there was no causal connection between the alleged negligence and the losses incurred. The financial statements may have allowed the company to continue trading, but the company's existence was not the cause of its losses. The claim against the auditor was struck out.

5.2.5 Contributory negligence

Contributory negligence relates to the failure of the plaintiff to meet certain required standards of care. Together with the defendant's negligence, it contributes to bringing about the loss in question. The judgement in the AWA case (see box below) is the landmark decision on contributory negligence in an auditor–client relationship. Contributory negligence is taken to mean that the court tends to examine all relevant circumstances to judge the likely proportion of liability attributable to respective parties.

AWA Ltd v. Daniels t/a Deloitte Haskins & Sells & Ors (1992) 10 ACLC 933

Facts of the case: This case is a landmark for the principle of contributory negligence. Under the established principle that the auditor's duty has to be evaluated in the light of the standards of today, the auditor was held to have been negligent in failing to warn of the appropriate level of management and to implement follow-up actions to rectify internal control weaknesses discovered during the course of the audit, even though that was not the main purpose of the audit. An important development, however, was that the company was held to be guilty of contributory negligence through not establishing adequate controls in the first place. This reverses a finding of the Pacific Acceptance case in which it was held that the extent of an auditor's responsibility was not diminished by failings of management that contributed to the losses.

Judgement: In the AWA case, the court accepted that the directors have a duty to establish a sound system of internal control to safeguard the company's assets. Their failure to do so was held to be contributory negligence. In the words of the judgement:

the primary complaints of the plaintiff are failure on the part of the auditors to report on the insufficiency and inappropriateness of the plaintiff's internal controls. Now that was not the principal purpose of the audit. It was something that the auditors discovered in the course of preparing to do their audit. I am of

5.2.6 Damages

Where auditors fail in their duty to act with reasonable care and skill, whether under contract or in tort, a plaintiff is entitled to recover any economic loss arising out of such breach of duty. Two issues need to be considered here. Firstly, what is the purpose of statements that may give rise to reliance reasonably being placed on them? Secondly, to what extent may responsibility for any loss be assigned on the one hand to the auditor's negligence and, on the other, to other causes and other parties?

The Cambridge Credit case (1985 and 1987) provides a suitable basis for examining some of these issues. Cambridge Credit Corporation failed in 1974 and it was determined that the audit of the 1971 accounts had been negligently performed. Had the auditor's report been appropriately qualified, the amended view of the company's financial position would have required the trustee for the debenture holders to appoint a receiver. It was alleged that the company, through the auditor's negligence, was allowed to remain in business for a further 3 years, incurring further losses before a receiver was finally appointed in 1974. Damages were claimed in the amount of losses incurred by virtue of the company being liquidated in 1974 instead of 1971.

The law is much clearer on the purpose of accounts than is most accounting theory. Accounts form the basis for the determination of legal relationships between the company and other parties; for instance, where dividends are paid out of capital (contrary to the provisions of the Companies Acts) as a result of an overstatement of profits, the auditors are liable to the extent of such dividends. In the Cambridge Credit case, the debenture trust deed provided that if the company's gearing ratio as per the audited accounts exceeded a given amount, then the debenture trustee would be entitled to appoint a receiver. Due to an overstatement of profits undetected by the auditor, the gearing ratio appeared sufficient to support the level of borrowing. In this case, the receiver sued the auditor for losses arising from the failure to appoint a receiver in 1971.

At this point, we must consider the issue of the extent of loss caused by the auditor's negligence. The original verdict in the 1985 Cambridge Credit case determined damages in an amount based on the losses of the company incurred through its continued trade over a further 3 years. However, the auditor appealed on the grounds that he could not have foreseen the economic downturn that caused the losses to reach the level they did, and that he did not have control over the actions of management (notably, its decisions to expand borrowings and real estate investments when the real estate market was being affected by the economic decline) that may have contributed to the extent of the actual losses. The court of appeal agreed that there was no causal connection between the auditor's negligence and the losses eventually sustained by the company, and upheld the principle that the auditors are not liable for all the consequences of their negligence, only those they cause directly.

---

the view that AWA should be held to have been guilty of contributory negligence ...

Contributory negligence is a plaintiff's failure to meet the standard of care to which it is required to conform for its own protection and which is a legally contributing cause, together with the defendant's default, in bringing about the loss.

In May 1995, the New South Wales Court of Appeal reduced the auditor's share of the damages, placing further responsibility on AWA management. The court upheld the notion of proportionate liability. As a result, AWA management shared 33.3% of the loss, the auditor's liability was reduced from 72% to 66.6%, and the chief executive officer's responsibility was reduced from 8% to zero.

As was explained in the AWA case, damages may also be reduced in the event of contributory negligence by the company. However, that case involved the reporting of internal control weaknesses to management. Where the matter involves the auditor's report on the financial statements issued by the directors (for the purpose of helping members to oversee the directors' conduct), the members, as a class, cannot be held to have contributed to the loss, notwithstanding any negligence by the directors in preparing the report. The judgement in the AWA case does not appear to be in dissent with this view, although courts are now likely to consider the possibility of contributory negligence instead of dismissing it as in the past.

However, in a victory for accounting firms, the New York Court of Appeals in *Continental Casualty Co. v. PricewaterhouseCoopers, LLP,* 15 N.Y.3d 264 (2010) affirmed the dismissal of a fraud claim brought against an accounting firm by investors in a hedge fund who claimed that they were induced to rely on the firm's allegedly fraudulent audits of the fund's financial statements when making their investment. The Court of Appeals held that the fraud claim should be dismissed because the investors could not show any 'direct' damages resulting from the auditor's alleged fraudulent inducement that occurred at the time the investment was made. Rather, the investors' only injuries were 'derivative' damages resulting from their pro-rata share of the hedge fund's losses, which occurred after the date of investment and were sought by a trustee on behalf of the fund in a separate case.

Continental will likely be helpful to accounting firms and other defendants in obtaining dismissal of claims brought by individual investors in hedge funds or other investment vehicles where the fund itself also has asserted or could assert claims. In addition, the decision may be helpful to fraud defendants generally, since the Court took an arguably narrow view of the damages recoverable for fraud in the inducement. The Court made clear that such damages were limited to the plaintiff's 'actual pecuniary loss' calculated at the time the investment was made, rather than a potentially broader scope of damages that could have included damages sustained after the date of investment.[19]

5.3 LIABILITY TO THIRD PARTIES

LEARNING 5 objective

Identify the issues and rulings of legal cases with respect to the auditor's liability to third parties.

Action for damages may also be brought against an auditor under tort, outside of any contractual relationship. In *Donoghue v. Stevenson* (1932) AC 562 it was held that a duty of care is owed to **third parties** in the absence of a contract where the plaintiff has suffered physical injury. The case related to a woman who drank a bottle of ginger ale (bought by her sister) which appeared to have the remains of a snail at the bottom. She was taken ill and later sued Stevenson, the soft-drink manufacturer. Atkins LJ, in defining the limits of when a duty of care is owed, stated:

You must take reasonable care to avoid acts or omissions which you can reasonably foresee would be likely to injure your neighbour. Who, then, in law is my neighbour? The answer seems to be — persons who are so closely and directly affected by my act that I ought reasonably to have them in contemplation as being so affected when I am directing my mind to the acts or omissions which are called in question.

From this case, it became evident that a duty of care can be owed to a third party through negligent acts. Liability to third parties for financial injury is still confused. Since the 1964 Hedley Byrne case, a number of such actions have been brought against auditors, but rarely successfully. The UK House of Lords verdict in the Caparo Industries case makes it doubtful that any third party claim under the Corporations Act (s. 331A) against an auditor in respect of his or her report would succeed.

Prior to the Hedley Byrne case (see box on p. 221), the precedent was derived from such cases as *Ultramares Corporation v. Touche Niven & Co.* (1931) 255 NY in the United States

and *Candler v. Crane Christmas & Co.* (1951) 1 All ER 426 in the United Kingdom. In the Ultramares case, Cardozo CJ found for the defendant accountants on the grounds that:

> If liability for negligence exists, a thoughtless slip or blunder, the failure to detect a theft or forgery beneath the cover of deceptive entries may expose accountants to a liability in an indeterminate amount for an indeterminate time to an indeterminate class.

In adopting Cardozo CJ's view, the courts simply denied liability for negligence in making statements. If the plaintiff suffered an economic loss as a result of statements made by a defendant, then the plaintiff would recover damages only if the defendants had been guilty of fraud, as in *Derry v. Peek* (1889) 14 App Cas 337 and the Candler case.

In the Candler case, it was found that the defendants owed no duty to the plaintiffs in the absence of any contractual relationship and that the negligence claim could not be sustained. Denning LJ, however, passed a dissenting judgement:

> [Accountants] owe a duty, of course, to their employer or client, and also, I think, to any third person to whom they themselves show the accounts, or to whom they know their employer is going to show the accounts so as to induce him to invest money or take some other action on them. I do not think, however, the duty can be extended still further to include strangers of whom they have heard nothing and to whom their employer without their knowledge may choose to show their accounts. Once the accountants have handed their accounts to their employer, they are not, as a rule, responsible for what he does with them without their knowledge or consent ... [This duty] extends, I think, only to those transactions for which the accountants knew their accounts were required.

The UK House of Lords upheld this view in reaching its decision in the Hedley Byrne case. The majority decision in the Candler case was expressly overruled and Denning LJ's dissenting judgement was upheld as correctly stating the law.

Under the Hedley Byrne principle, auditors' liability to third parties to whom they owe a duty of care is no different from their liability to clients in that (1) they must have been negligent in the performance of their duties, (2) the plaintiff must have suffered an economic loss arising directly from that negligence and (3) the loss must be quantifiable. The problem lies in determining to whom that duty of care is owed. The Hedley Byrne case identified a number of relevant factors and emphasised that different factors would have different weights in different types of cases. The issue has come to be known as one of **proximity**. The Pandora's box envisaged by Cardozo CJ in the Ultramares case has not been opened.

The Hedley Byrne case is a landmark case for professional liability to third parties. Readers will often refer to it. It establishes the concepts of foreseeability and due care — both tests are essential elements in establishing auditor liabilities.

Hedley Byrne & Co. Ltd v. Heller & Partners (1963) 2 All ER 575

Facts of the case: The Hedley Byrne case involved not an auditor but a bank. The bank (Heller & Partners) was approached by Hedley Byrne, an advertising agency, for a credit reference on a potential client, Easipower Ltd, which was a customer of the bank. The reference was supplied by the bank without making a careful check of its records. The negligence of the bank in supplying the reference was not disputed. On the strength of the reference, the advertising agency incurred costs on behalf of its client, which went into liquidation before the costs were recovered.

The bank's first defence was that it owed no duty of care to the plaintiff in the absence of any contractual or fiduciary relationship with the advertising agency. The bank's duty of care was owed to its client.

The second defence was the presence of a disclaimer at the foot of the reference supplied.

Judgement: In reaching a decision, the House of Lords upheld the minority judgement of Denning LJ in the Candler case. Reid L, in his judgement, said in relation to the limits of duty:

> I can see no logical stopping place short of all those relationships where it is plain that the party seeking information or advice was trusting the other to exercise such a degree of care as the circumstances required, where it was reasonable for him to do that and where the other gave the information or advice when he knew or ought to have known that the inquirer was relying on him. I say 'ought to have known' because in questions of negligence we now apply the objective standard of what the reasonable man would have done.

The verdict, however, was in favour of the defendant on the grounds that the disclaimer of liability was a good defence, notwithstanding that a duty of care existed.

5.3.1 Proximity

As a result of the reluctance of professional indemnity insurers to allow cases to come to court for reasons explained earlier in this chapter, there have been very few decided Australian cases of significance involving claims by third parties against auditors. There have been only a few such cases overseas, and examination of these cases demonstrates the law's confusion about the matter. Most of these cases involve action being brought by companies relying on audited accounts in making a takeover bid for another company. Proximity is held to arise through the fact that where a company's financial condition is such that it is a likely takeover target, auditors should be aware that potential suitors will rely on the accounts and that a duty of care thus arises. Proximity is generally meant to be interpreted as the person injured physically or financially being within that class that could reasonably be considered as being affected by the act.

The Australian High Court applied the doctrine of negligent misrepresentation in the Evatt case (see box below) in 1968. The expertise of the defendant was crucial to the decision.

However, the decision of the Privy Council in the Evatt case in 1971 was rejected by a majority of the High Court in the Shaddock case in 1981. The issue of proximity has also been highlighted by the Hedley Byrne case.

Mutual Life and Citizens Assurance Co. Ltd v. Evatt (1968) 122 CLR 556

Facts of the case: Evatt was a policyholder in Mutual Life and Citizens Assurance Co. Ltd (MLC Assurance). MLC Assurance was a subsidiary of MLC Ltd. Evatt approached MLC Assurance and sought advice on the financial stability of H.G. Palmer Ltd (Palmer). Palmer was also a subsidiary of MLC Limited. He also enquired whether investment in Palmer was a sound decision. Evatt claimed that he approached MLC because it had a special relationship with Palmer. Acting on that advice, the plaintiff invested in Palmer, which subsequently failed. The plaintiff claimed that MLC's negligent advice had caused his loss.

Judgement: The High Court of Australia held that the defendant did owe the plaintiff a duty to take care in giving advice. It was held that the fact that the defendant was not in the business of giving investment advice did not affect the existence of duty to take reasonable care in giving such advice. Barwick CJ said:

> The elements of special relationship to which I have referred do not require either the actual possession of skill or judgement on the part of the speaker or any profession by him to possess the same. His willingness to proffer the information or advice in the relationship which I have described is, in my opinion, sufficient.

MLC Assurance appealed to the Privy Council (see *Mutual Life and Citizens Assurance Co. Ltd v. Evatt* [1971] AC 793). The Privy Council reversed the decision of the High Court on the basis that MLC Assurance was not in the business of giving investment advice, and nor did it claim expertise in the giving of investment advice.

Thus, the Privy Council accepted that negligent misrepresentation was part of the law of Australia but restricted its application, insofar as advisers are concerned, to situations in which the advice was given by a person who was in the business of giving advice of that nature.

Shaddock & Associates Pty Ltd v. Parramatta City Council (1981) 55 ALIR 713

Facts of the case: Shaddock & Associates was a land developer with an interest in buying a parcel of land in Parramatta. It asked the Parramatta City Council whether there were any proposals for road widening that might affect the property. The Council said that there was not, so Shaddock purchased the land. In fact, the Council did have a proposal to compulsorily acquire a part of the said property for road-widening purposes. The plaintiff (Shaddock) was unable to sue for breach of contract and so sued for tort of negligent misstatement.

Judgement: In summing up the circumstances in which a duty of care will apply, Mason J said:

> Whenever a person gives information or advice to another upon a serious matter in circumstances where the speaker realises, or ought to realise, that he is being trusted to give the best of his information or advice as a basis for action on the part of the other party and it is reasonable in the circumstances for the other party to act on that information or advice, the person giving the information or advice is under a duty to take reasonable care that the information or advice is accurate.

The High Court held that the Council owed a duty of care to the plaintiff. It was further held that the Council had breached its duty and was therefore liable to compensate the plaintiff. This gives a determinative role to reliance as the cornerstone of proximity in cases of negligent misstatements.

In the New Zealand case of *Scott Group Ltd v. McFarlane* (1978) 1 NZLR 553, two out of three appeal court judges held that the auditor owed a duty of care to the plaintiff, but only one judge thought that any loss had been suffered as a result of reliance on the negligently audited accounts, and the amount of loss (if any) could not be determined.

In the JEB Fasteners case, Woolf J held that the auditor owed a duty of care, but that the plaintiff's loss had not arisen out of reliance on the audited accounts.

JEB Fasteners Ltd v. Marks, Bloom & Co. (1981) 2 AER 289

Facts of the case: Marks, Bloom & Co. was the auditor of BG Fasteners. Marks, Bloom & Co. was aware that BG Fasteners was in financial difficulty. A company, JEB Fasteners, previously unknown to the auditor, took over BG Fasteners. Subsequently, JEB Fasteners sued the auditor for negligence on the grounds that inventories of the company were over-stated. It was alleged that JEB Fasteners paid more for the acquisition than it would have, had it known the true facts.

Judgement: The test applied was one of reasonable foreseeability that the company would use the audited accounts to obtain financial support, or be a subject of a takeover. It was held that there was sufficient degree of 'proximity or neighbourhood', thus a duty of care was owed to the plaintiff. No damages were awarded because the plaintiff's purpose for taking over the company was to obtain the services of two directors of BG Fasteners. The causal relationship between the auditor's negligence and economic loss was not established.

In the Twomax case, a third party was successful in recovering losses suffered through reliance on negligently audited accounts. The essential elements in a negligence action that must be proven to the satisfaction of the courts are shown in figure 5.3.

Twomax Ltd v. Dickson, McFarlane & Robinson (1983) Scots Law Times reports 98

Facts of the case: Dickson, McFarlane & Robinson was the auditor of Kintyre Knitwear. Kintyre reported losses of $33 000 and $12 000 for the years ending 31 March 1971 and 1972 respectively. A profit of $20 000 was reported for the 1973 year. Relying on the 1973 audited accounts, Twomax and two other investors acquired a controlling interest in Kintyre. Subsequently, for the year ended 31 March 1975, the audited accounts showed a loss of $88 000. The company went into liquidation and the investors lost their entire investment. It was alleged that the profits reported in 1973 were a myth, and litigation was commenced against the auditor.

Judgement: The precedent set in the JEB Fasteners case was upheld. Stewart J, in his judgement, concentrated on the principle of foreseeability. Given the financial condition of Kintyre, the probability of a takeover was reasonably foreseeable. The potential investors were owed a duty of care. The auditor, however, did not meet the required standard of care: the audit was negligently performed; there were errors in the accounts; overseas commissions were underestimated; and there was underprovision for bad and doubtful debts. The auditor 'made no attempt to circularise any debtors for the 1973 audit or even to go through the list of debtors for bad or doubtful debts'. Lord Stewart awarded damages to the plaintiff.

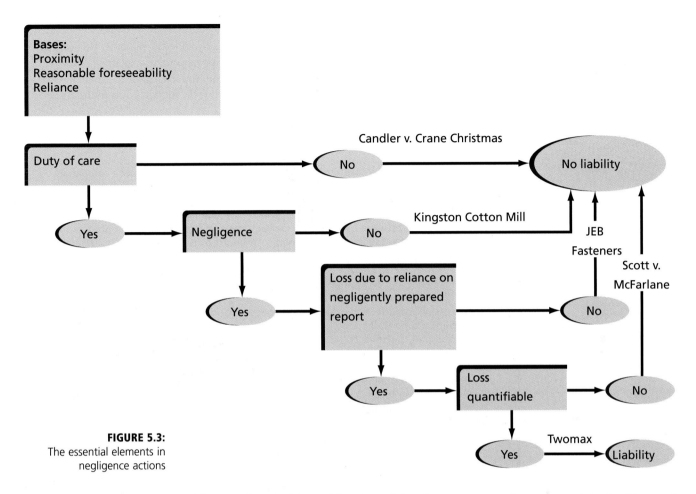

FIGURE 5.3:
The essential elements in negligence actions

The UK Court of Appeal hearing of the Caparo case was later reversed in the House of Lords. In a majority verdict, two of the judges held that a duty of care was owed only to third parties who were existing shareholders that the auditors knew would receive and rely on their report. This reversed the findings in the three previous cases which all held that a duty of care was owed to those relying on the accounts for the purposes of making a take-over bid, regardless of whether they were already shareholders. The third judge upheld the High Court's finding that no duty of care was owed. The Caparo case establishes that the auditor's duty of care is owed to a general body of shareholders as a group, and not to individual shareholders.

Caparo Industries Pty Ltd v. Dickman & Others (1990) 1 All ER 568

Facts of the case: Caparo Industries relied on the audited accounts of Fidelity PLC in making a successful takeover bid for that company. The audited accounts for Fidelity showed a profit for the year ended 31 March 1984 of £1.2 million. After taking Fidelity over, Caparo discovered that the result should have been a loss of over £400 000 and alleged that the auditors had been negligent in auditing the accounts. The trial was of a preliminary issue as to whether the auditors owed a duty of care to the plaintiff. The issue of negligence was not an issue to be determined then.

The High Court judge found that no duty of care was owed to the plaintiff. This verdict was overturned by a majority verdict in the Court of Appeals but, as explained above, on different grounds from that of previous cases. Given the importance of the matter, leave was given for a final appeal to the House of Lords, which is the highest court in the United Kingdom.

Judgement: Their Lordships reached their verdict by identifying the statutory purpose for the audit:

> The structure of the corporate trading entity, at least in the case of public companies whose shares are dealt with on an authorised stock exchange, involves the concept of more or less widely distributed holding of shares rendering the personal involvement of each individual shareholder in the day-to-day management of the enterprise impracticable, with the result that management is necessarily separated from ownership. The management is confided to a board of directors which operates in a fiduciary capacity and is answerable to and removable by the shareholders who can act, if they act at all, only collectively and only through the medium of a general meeting, hence the legislative provisions requiring the board annually to give an account of its stewardship to a general meeting of the shareholders. This is the only occasion in each year on which the general body of shareholders is given the opportunity to consider, to criticise and to comment on the conduct of the board of the company's affairs, to vote on the directors' recommendation as to dividends, to approve or disapprove the directors' remuneration and, if thought desirable, to remove and replace any or all of the directors. It is the auditors' function to ensure, so far as possible, that all the financial information as to the company's affairs prepared by the directors accurately reflects the company's position in order, first to protect the company itself from the consequences of undetected errors or possibly wrongdoing (by, for instance, declaring dividends out of capital) and, second, to provide shareholders with reliable intelligence for the purpose of enabling them to scrutinise the conduct of the company's affairs and to exercise their collective powers to reward or control or remove those to whom that conduct has been confided. (Lord Oliver)

On this basis it was argued that it would be unreasonable:

> to widen the area of responsibility ... and to find a relationship of proximity between the adviser and third parties to whose attention the advice may come in circumstances in which the reliance said to have given rise to the loss is strictly unrelated either to the intended recipient or to the purpose for which the advice was required. (Lord Oliver)

And neither was it the intention of the Act:

> For my part, however, I can see nothing in the statutory duties of a company's auditors to suggest that they were intended by Parliament to protect the interests of investors in the market. (Lord Oliver)

In summary, therefore, the House of Lords argued that the purpose of the financial statement on which auditors express an opinion is to assist the shareholders in their collective function of scrutinising the company's affairs. It would be unreasonable, therefore, to hold the auditors responsible for their use, by shareholders or others, for any other purpose.

Preceding the Caparo case, of the cases in which the courts held that the auditors owed a duty of care to those relying on the accounts in making a takeover bid, in only the Twomax case did the court find that any loss arose from that reliance. In the Scott Group and JEB Fasteners cases, the courts found no direct link between reliance on the accounts and any loss suffered; they recognised not only the limitations of general purpose financial reports as a basis for investment decision making, but also the reliance by investors on many other sources of information.

Reaction to the Caparo case verdict

Reaction to the House of Lords verdict in the Caparo case has generally been unfavourable. The general view of the legal profession is that the verdict appears to treat auditors more favourably than it treats other experts on whom third parties place reliance. There is also concern that it appears to reverse what is seen as a socially desirable development in law of holding experts liable for the consequences of negligent advice.

Even auditors are divided in their reaction. Many accept that audited financial statements provide investors with a reliable source of information. The value of auditors' services are seen, therefore, to be diminished. One response by third party users of financial statements (such as investors, lenders and suppliers of goods and services) has been to request a letter from the auditor in which the auditor acknowledges the user's reliance on the audited financial statements, thereby establishing a relationship with the required **foreseeability** and proximity. Such letters are known as privity or comfort letters. (Auditing Guidance Statement AGS 1014 *Privity Letter Requests* provides guidance to auditors who are asked to provide such a letter.)

In reaching its verdict, the House of Lords implied that it is up to the UK Parliament to introduce legislation whereby auditors' statutory responsibilities could be extended to meet directly the interests of investors.

The Caparo case was followed by a majority verdict of the Victorian Supreme Court in the Lowe Lippmann Figdor & Franck case (see box below).

Lowe Lippman Figdor & Franck v. AGC (Advances) Ltd (1992) 2 VR 671

Facts of the case: AGC (Advances) was a finance company and the main creditor of Lyvetta. Lowe Lippmann Figdor & Franck was the auditor. Lyvetta created a false set of stock sheets, which led to an overstatement of stock as at 30 June 1981 by $228000. This converted what would have been a loss of $205000 for that year into a profit of $23000. Lyvetta's auditor knew of the stock sheets that disclosed the true position, but signed a report on the 1981 accounts which was unqualified. Lyvetta requested an increase in its credit facilities from AGC. Before making advances, AGC wished to examine an audited copy of Lyvetta's financial statements.

An officer of AGC telephoned the auditor and requested the audited accounts 'for review purposes'. The officer also asked the auditor whether the profit was $100000 as had been stated by Lyvetta. The auditor replied that the profit would be a lesser sum.

In this case the auditor failed to detect that the value of closing stock and, thus, profit was overstated in the company's 1981 accounts. Its negligence in this regard was not denied. The company derived a substantial portion of its finance from AGC, which extended its credit on the strength of the company's 1981 audited results. On the subsequent collapse of the company, AGC sued the auditor for its losses on the grounds that it was owed a duty of care.

Judgement: The Supreme Court finding, which was reversed on appeal, held that the test of proximity was satisfied and that the auditor did owe a duty of care in tort to AGC. The main grounds for reaching this verdict were that AGC had made direct contact with the auditor by telephone, indicating its interest in receiving the audited accounts as quickly as possible.

On appeal, however, it was held that the expression of interest by AGC in the audited accounts for the purpose of reviewing its position did not create a special relationship with the auditor. The interest of a major creditor in the audited accounts is only to be expected. The auditor was not aware that the accounts were produced for the special purpose of inducing AGC to act in a certain way, i.e. the lack of intention to induce. As the judgement states:

> The auditor who supplies his report to the company in the usual way cannot be liable unless his purpose, or one of his purposes, in making the statement in question is to induce the plaintiff, or a class which includes the plaintiff, to act on it.

The court referred to the Caparo case, and its acceptance of the limitations of the purpose of an auditor's report delivered under the Companies Act (as it then was) appears to have been influenced by that judgement. The judgement also cites, as precedent, *San Sebastian Pty Ltd v. The Minister* (1986) 162 CLR 340 — an Australian case involving reliance by a property developer on planning scheme documents issued by a local authority.

Post-Caparo case developments

Limits to the applicability of the Caparo case have been established in the UK Court of Appeal case of *Morgan Crucible Co. PLC v. Hill Samuel Bank Ltd and Others* (1991) 1 AER 148. In a contested takeover of First Castle Electronics by Morgan Crucible Co., the directors of First Castle Electronics issued circulars to their shareholders advising them not to accept Morgan Crucible's offer. Consequently, Morgan Crucible increased its offer and was eventually successful. The circulars issued by First Castle Electronics included the results revealed by the most recent audited accounts, as well as interim accounts for the first half of the current financial year and a profit forecast for the year.

In a letter to the directors of First Castle Electronics, the auditor reaffirmed its opinion as to the truth and fairness of the audited accounts and stated that the accounting policies that were adopted in compiling the interim accounts and profit forecast were in accordance with generally accepted accounting practices in the United Kingdom and consistent with those that were normally adopted by the group. The court held that the auditor should have known that its representations, although related to circulars issued by First Castle Electronics, would be relied on by Morgan Crucible in making its offer. By its actions, the auditor established a duty of care to Morgan Crucible by implying the relevance of its representations to the purposes of the takeover bid.

In the Columbia Coffee & Tea case, a purchaser of shares sued the auditor for negligence in respect of the value of the shares. The Supreme Court of New South Wales did not follow the decision in the Caparo case or the Lowe Lippmann Figdor & Franck case.

Rolfe J of the New South Wales Supreme Court focused on the fact that the audit manual of the defendant auditor acknowledged that the persons interested in its reports extended beyond those to whom the reports were addressed. Rolfe J held that this amounted to the auditor assuming responsibility for a class of persons beyond just the company and its shareholders.

Thus, according to Rolfe J, the auditor could owe a duty of care to a purchaser of shares who:

- relied on the audited accounts and auditor's report
- suffered economic loss as a result.

On the facts in the Columbia Coffee case, Rolfe J found that the prospective investor had not actually relied on the audited accounts in any way, so the action failed as a result of a lack of causation.

Esanda Finance Corporation v. Peat Marwick Hungerfords
(1994) 12 ACLC 199

Facts of the case: Peat Marwick Hungerfords was the auditor of Excel for the year ended 30 June 1989. Esanda Finance Corporation alleged that it, relying on the audited accounts, lent money to companies associated with Excel, accepting a guarantee from Excel, and purchased debts from Excel on terms that included an indemnity from Excel against a shortfall. Excel was subsequently placed in receivership. This resulted in a loss to Esanda. In a statement of claim, Esanda did not plead that the auditors intended it to rely on the audited accounts.

Judgement: King CJ outlined (at 201) that since the introduction into law of the concept of legal liability for negligent misstatement in the Hedley Byrne case:

> ... there have been difficulties in defining the circumstances giving rise to a duty of care in relation to statements and the class of persons to whom the duty is owed. The concept of reasonable foreseeability of harm which had served adequately in relation to physical acts was found to be no longer adequate, standing alone, by reason of the spectre of, to use the famous words of Cardozo J in *Ultramares Corporation v. Touche* (1931) 174 NE 441, 'liability in an indeterminate amount for an indeterminate time to an indeterminate class'. This has led to a revival of recognition of the notion of proximity, found in the seminal speech of Lord Atkin in *Donoghue v. Stevenson* (1932) AC 562 at 578 et seq., but rather submerged in subsequent cases, as an essential requirement, together with foreseeability of harm, for the imposition of a duty of care.

It was indicated that the auditor was a member of the Institute of Chartered Accountants in Australia and, as such, bound by the Australian accounting standards. Reference was made to the then APS 1 *Conformity with Accounting Standards and Urgent Issues Group (UIG) Consensus Views*, which, in substance, provides that the Australian accounting standards are mandatory for members and lays down the principles to be followed by members. The failure by a chartered accountant to observe the provisions of APS 1 may be regarded as failure to observe a proper standard of professional care, skill or competence. Specific reference was made to the former Australian Accounting Standard AAS 5 *Materiality in Financial Statements*. The test of materiality requires consideration as to who are likely to be the prime users of financial statements. It was indicated that the present and potential providers of equity or loan capital and creditors are an important group of users of financial statements. This was an attempt to demonstrate that a duty of care was owed to the plaintiff.

King CJ put this matter to rest:

> I am unable to see how membership of the body responsible for the promulgation of those Standards can give rise to a duty of care to persons to whom a duty would not otherwise be owed. Apart from any other consideration, the Standards themselves do not purport to create such a duty. They are not concerned with the legal duty but with the content of financial statements. The concept of materiality is developed for the purpose of determining what should be included in financial statements. The reference to providers of loan capital and creditors as users of financial statements occurs in the context of determining what is material for inclusion in such statements. It does not imply any assumption of legal responsibility to such users to exercise care.

King CJ, referring to the Columbia Coffee & Tea case, stated that the *Auditor's Audit Manual* is not of similar status, purpose and language to the accounting standards. He added that reasoning underlying the Columbia Coffee & Tea case is inconsistent, in his view, in relation to the significance of the accounting standards.

The case was further appealed to the High Court, which ruled in favour of the auditor in an unreported judgement delivered on 18 March 1997. The judgement upheld the earlier decision of the Supreme Court of South Australia.

Brennan CJ stated that it was not possible, based on the facts, for the third party to rely on the report prepared by the auditor. He held that for a third party to succeed in such circumstances, the following would have to be established.

- The report was prepared on the basis that it would be conveyed to a third party.
- The report would be conveyed for a purpose that was likely to be relied on by that party.
- The third party would be likely to act in reliance on that report, thus running the risk of suffering the loss if the statement was negligently prepared.

It was suggested that liability could exist if someone in Esanda's position suffered loss. However, there was nothing to suggest that Esanda was unable to have accountants assess Excel's true financial position on its behalf, as a condition of entering into a financial transaction with Excel. There was nothing to suggest that it was reasonable for Esanda to act on the audited statements without further enquiry.

The outcome in the Esanda Finance case (above) provided some comfort to the auditor. This outcome was the result of an appeal against the decision of Bollen J in *Esanda Finance Corporation v. Peat Marwick Hungerfords* (1993) 11 ACLC 908. The Full Court of the Supreme Court of South Australia held that the defendant did not owe the plaintiff a duty of care. The Court endorsed the approach of the House of Lords in the Caparo case and indicated that the decision in the Columbia Coffee & Tea case was wrong.

Thus, the judgement of the Esanda case appears to support the view of Justice Cardozo in the Ultramares case that to allow third parties to sue in such a case would be to expose auditors to 'liability in an indeterminable amount for an indeterminable time to an indeterminable class of persons'.

The corporate collapses in the late 1990s and early 2000s and the heightened criticism regarding auditors' conduct has, however, provided a certain change in the courts' interpretations. In the case of the *Royal Bank of Scotland PLC v. Bannerman Johnstone Maclay and Others* (2002) TLR 1 August 2002, the Court of Sessions did not accept the auditors' statements that the only intention they had was to carry out their Companies Act duties to audit the accounts. The Court held that the knowledge of the user and the knowledge of the specific use to which the accounts information would be put formed the basis of a duty of care for those making the information or advice available. The auditors therefore owed a duty of care to a bank that had advanced money to APC Limited, the audit client. The bank later had to appoint a receiver to the company, and it thereby suffered loss for which it sought to make the auditors liable.

In Australia, the common law concerning the nature and extent of an auditor's duty of care to third parties remains complex because judgements contain differences of judicial opinion and interpretation. However, the judgement in Esanda was a positive development for auditors because the Court rejected the contention that liability could be based on foreseeability of reliance alone. The High Court found that there had to be circumstances establishing a relationship of proximity between the auditor and the third party before a duty of care could be said to exist. This indicates that the auditor has to come into a real relationship with the third party for liability to arise, rather than just know of the third party's existence as a theoretical possibility.

There have been, therefore, fundamental shifts in the legal liabilities of auditors. An analysis of various cases[20] reveals that case rulings in the later decades of the twentieth century moderated previous decisions that had resulted in an expansion of the scope of auditor liability. There was expansion of auditor liability in the early to middle decades of the twentieth century, then a subsequent reversal in later decades. Although there has been a convergence in approach within Commonwealth nations in respect of auditor liability for negligent misstatements, the current position and court expectations are changing as a result of a continual struggle to balance the respective rights and interests of auditors, investors and the wider community.

LEARNING objective 6

Enumerate the precautions the auditor should take to avoid litigation.

5.3.2 Avoidance of litigation

The following precautions may be taken by auditors wishing to avoid or minimise the consequences of litigation.

- *Use engagement letters for all professional services.* Engagement letters are of particular importance in non-audit engagements where misunderstanding may arise as to the nature of the public accountant's association with the financial statements. They are also important in audit engagements where there may be some misunderstanding as to the extent of an auditor's responsibilities, particularly as to the detection of fraud. ASA 210 *Agreeing the Terms of Audit Engagements* (ISA 210) requires the auditor to record in writing the terms of the audit engagement that are agreed to with the entity. Also, the auditor is required to forward a copy of the terms of the engagement to the entity. The written terms of the engagement should help the auditor minimise any potential risk of exposure which might arise as a result of any misunderstandings as to the auditor's responsibilities. Where relevant, the auditor should include in the engagement letter any arrangements concerning the involvement of other auditors, internal auditors or predecessor auditors and any restriction on the auditor's liability when such possibility exists.

ASA 502 *Audit Evidence — Specific Considerations for Litigation and Claims* (ISA 501):

establishes requirements and provides application and other explanatory material regarding specific considerations by the auditor in obtaining sufficient appropriate audit evidence relating to certain aspects of litigation and claims.

This Auditing Standard:

(a) sets out the procedures the auditor should include when designing and performing audit procedures to identify litigation and claims involving the entity which may give rise to a risk of material misstatement;

(b) requires the auditor to endeavour to communicate in writing with the entity's external legal counsel, if a risk of material misstatement regarding litigation and claims is identified, or where audit procedures performed indicate that other material litigation and claims may exist;

(c) requires the auditor to endeavour to communicate in writing with the entity's internal legal counsel, if in-house legal counsel has the primary responsibility for litigation and claims involving both in-house and external legal counsel;

(d) describes the written representations that the auditor must request from management and, where appropriate, those changed with governance; and

(e) describes the auditor's responsibilities:

(i) when the response from legal counsel contains a material disagreement with management's original evaluation of a particular matter; and

(ii) when management refuses to give the auditor permission to communicate with legal counsel, or legal counsel refuses to respond appropriately and the auditor is unable to obtain sufficient appropriate audit evidence by performing alternative audit procedures.

- *Investigate prospective clients thoroughly*. Establishing a policy on client acceptance is seen as a means of reducing exposure to litigation. Litigation tends to follow corporate collapse. It can be limited by avoiding clients that are in poor financial health or managed by directors whose business ethics or competence are suspect as a result of past association with failed corporations.
- *Comply fully with professional pronouncements*. Strict adherence to the legally enforceable auditing standards is essential. An auditor must be able to justify any material departures from established guidelines.
- *Recognise the limitations of professional pronouncements*. Professional guidelines are not all-encompassing. In addition, it should be recognised that the courts and regulatory agencies will use subjective tests of reasonableness and fairness in judging the auditor's work. The auditor must use sound professional judgement during the audit and in the issue of the auditor's report.
- *Establish and maintain high standards of quality control*. The dominant objective of quality control is the assurance that all the firm's work complies with required professional standards. Recent cases have emphasised the particular importance of:
  - the assignment of appropriately competent staff to engagements and their proper supervision
  - adequate documentation of all audit procedures
  - compliance with independence guidelines, especially in terms of personal relationships with clients.
- *Maintain adequate professional indemnity cover*. Professional indemnity insurance has been the cause of misunderstanding. Some argue that it protects auditors against their legal responsibilities, encouraging a less than desirable standard of care, because any losses can be claimed against insurance. A contradictory view is that the possession of indemnity insurance encourages lawsuits on the grounds that the insurance company will have to pay. It is generally held, however, that responsible public accountants need to carry such insurance for the protection of their clients. Professional indemnity insurance is required to obtain a certificate of public practice.
- *Be prepared to issue a privity letter, on request*. Following the Caparo decision, auditors may be asked to acknowledge the third party's reliance on an audited financial report (the privity letter). The purpose of the letter is to establish a relationship with required foreseeability and proximity, and thus a duty of care by the auditor to the third party. AGS 1014 *Privity Letter Requests* was revised in July 2002 to guide auditors if requested to produce a privity letter. AGS 1014.5 states that a decision to provide such a letter is an individual business risk and management decision. Recently, an AUASB board meeting was held on 29 July 2013 to request the board's approval to revise and reissue AGS 1014 *Privity Letter Request* as a new Guidance Statement, and withdraw AGS 1014.[21]

Following the introduction of professional standards Acts in the Australian states and enactment of the CLERP 9 Act, professional accountants must now ensure that they establish adequate risk strategies. In determining risks and potential exposure, two elements need to be considered: (1) the cause of the exposure, such as failure of compliance, loss of property, injury incurred, and (2) the effect of the exposure, that is, financial impact, impact on staff and other stakeholders, impact on reputation and probity, impact on operational management and impact on the delivery of programs. The most commonly used method of identification is an effective inspection program. An effective inspection program should detect most emerging risk issues.

An inspection program should be flexible and can be a combination of routine and non-routine inspection including:

- routine inspection of all risks
- routine inspection of a particular area of risk
- specific inspections resulting from recommendations, complaints, reports or advice from staff, users, stakeholders and others
- inspections as a result of incidents or accidents.[22]

5.4 COMPETITION AND CONSUMER LEGISLATION

In 2010, the Commonwealth replaced the former *Trade Practices Act* 1974 with the *Competition and Consumer Act* 2010. In addition to the legislative rulings, the *Competition and Consumer Act 2010* and the state fair trading Acts provide further rights for individual investors and shareholders.[23] Section 18 of the Australian Consumer Law (ACL) prohibits misleading and deceptive conduct, and has been used as a basis for several successful actions by investors against promoters of businesses and others in respect of misleading statements. Investors can also make use of the *Competition and Consumer Act 2010* to take actions under common law for deceit and negligence. Similarly, the state fair trading Acts offer a further channel for redress to shareholders and investors. In the Esanda case, in ruling out the claim that 'the auditor's duty to report is statutory, and is merely incidental to the provision of accounting and auditing services for reward, and [does] not give rise to trade or commerce,' Bollen J argued:

> the words 'trade or commerce' are to be given a wide import. The lending of money is surely in trade or commerce. Accountants assist those who lend money. Auditors work for those who lend money. It may be held in the end that an auditor is right in the middle of trade or commerce.

Therefore, the Esanda case is a very important case for the future of auditors' liability to third parties. Note, too, that litigation under the *Competition and Consumer Act 2010* does not require the various factors of foreseeability and proximity as do cases under tort of negligence.

The professional standards legislation (PSL) reform includes the reform to be effected in the *Competition and Consumer Act 2010*. As all professionals are covered by competition laws, partnerships, audit companies or sole practitioners and their associations have become subject to the competition provisions of the *Competition and Consumer Act 2010* and the competition codes. In relation to consumer protection, unincorporated practitioners are covered by state and territory fair trading Acts which substantially mirror the consumer protection provisions of the *Competition and Consumer Act 2010*. The PSL was part of the response of the Commonwealth, states and territories to curb large damages payouts and to ensure adequate protection is in place for those who rely on professional indemnity insurance cover. The trade-off for consumers and the community in capping the liability of professionals is the implementation of statutory schemes that aim at improving professional standards. Improvements in professional standards will be achieved through compulsory insurance cover, risk management strategies, professional education, and complaints and disciplinary mechanisms.

In the fifth monitoring report by the Australian Competition and Consumer Commission for the 12 months to 31 December 2004 (published in August 2005), the average professional indemnity premiums decreased by 4 per cent in the previous year, and the average size of claims for professional indemnity insurance rose by 60 per cent because of a small number of high-cost claims in that year. The report found that most insurers believed that tort reforms had either minimal or no impact on the number and size of professional indemnity claims in 2004. With the reforms implemented by state and territory governments, professional bodies are developing self-regulation schemes that require members to adopt insurance and risk-management schemes that will be approved and monitored under the legislation.[24]

5.5 THE GLOBAL FINANCIAL CRISIS (GFC) AND POTENTIAL LIABILITIES FOR AUDITORS

As the fall-out from the GFC continues, there are potential liability dangers ahead for auditors. The global nature of the financial problems arising from the GFC means that this is arguably the biggest test of the auditing profession since the collapse of Enron. Auditors are already being blamed, at least in part, for not spotting significant financial problems before the crisis. Perhaps this is not fair. In the context of the financial crisis, it is important to look at what auditors are required to do, as opposed to what people might think they do. Nevertheless, many commentators in the press during 2012 and 2013 were asking questions. What tasks or assistance is the auditor prohibited from completing that would impair their independence? Why do auditors ask fraud questions and who will they need to talk with concerning fraud? How do the auditors gain an understanding of specific industry and business? What do the auditors mean by the 'tone at the top'?

There is also the question of whether auditors now have the expertise to audit complex financial institutions. The earlier times of auditing in an industrial era represented by easily measurable tangible physical assets have been eclipsed by complex financial instruments (e.g. derivatives), whose value depends on uncertain future events. For example, investors in the UK have questioned whether the auditors of the collapsed Royal Bank of Scotland, Deloitte, should have spotted problems some time ago. Similar questions have also been asked of KPMG, which audited HBOS, and PricewaterhouseCoopers which audited Lloyds TSB — the other two big banks which were effectively nationalised by the UK government.

In 2009, pictures were beamed around the world of the two PricewaterhouseCoopers partners arrested as part of the police investigations into the alleged massive fraud at Satyam in India. In the same week in London, auditors were grilled by members of parliament about their role in the banking crisis. The joint administrators of Quinn Insurance Ltd (QIL) sued the firm's former auditors, PricewaterhouseCoopers for €1 billion over alleged negligent auditing. Meanwhile in Miami, USA, lawyers were gearing up for a landmark case against BDO, the fifth-biggest accounting firm, over the Bernie Madoff ponzi scheme in the US that cost investors billions of dollars. In New York, Deloitte & Touche agreed to pay $19.9 million to settle claims by investors who lost money in the stock of JPMorgan Chase & Co.'s Bear Stearns unit from 2006 to 2008. In addition, Deloitte & Touche was also sued and was requested to pay $7.6 billion in damages for failing through years of audits to detect massive fraud at a Florida mortgage company. Ernst & Young, in September 2009, reached a multi-million settlement with the liquidators of Akai Holdings, who agreed to drop a US$1 billion (HK$7.8 billion) negligence suit against the accounting giant related to Hong Kong's biggest corporate collapse. The accounting firm suspended one of its partners and suspects another former professional in its Hong Kong offices may have also been involved in the alleged misconduct. Ernst & Young also have been named in a class action case arising from the collapse of Lehman Brothers. Furthermore, mortgage finance company Fannie Mae and accounting firm KPMG agreed to pay $153 million to settle a shareholder lawsuit filed by Ohio pension funds and others accusing the companies of issuing false and misleading financial reports.

Meanwhile in Australia, the administrators of ABC Learning, backed by litigation-funders IMF Australia, are investigating a $1 billion damages claim against the former directors of the collapsed childcare company, including founder Eddy Groves, chairman Sallyanne Atkinson, and auditors Pitcher Partners. Lawyers for Ferrier Hodgson appeared in the Federal Court, where they obtained approval to receive funding from litigant funding firm IMF to conduct a series of public examinations of former ABC directors, auditors Pitcher Partners, members of its banking syndicate and external consultants. Another example is legal action over Centro's 2007 financial accounts. Lawyers for two class actions seeking more than $1 billion in compensation for investors are in progress. Plaintiff law firms Slater and Gordon and Maurice Blackburn filed their suits in the Federal Court in 2008 and in May 2009, Centro filed a cross-claim against PricewaterhouseCoopers. The accounting firm responded in July by filing a defence alleging its auditors were misled and foreshadowing its own cross-claim against Centro's directors.

What the developments above suggest is that there will be significant legal actions against auditors arising out of the GFC. Many actions are settled out of court and details not made publicly available. The impact of these claims on auditing firms is unknown and only time will tell.

Do you know ...

5.5 ☐ Under statute and common law, auditors are liable to the auditee company if the following factors exist: (1) a duty of care is owed to the plaintiff; (2) negligence has been proven; (3) a causal relationship is established for financial or other loss suffered by the plaintiff; and (4) the losses are identifiable and quantifiable.

5.6 ☐ Contributory negligence is applicable where management is found to be liable for a failure of internal control, leading to injury to the plaintiff.

5.7 ☐ An auditor's liability to third parties is established if (1) a duty of care is owed to the party (based on the criteria of proximity, reliance and reasonable foreseeability); (2) negligence has been proven in the performance of the auditor's duties; (3) economic loss has been suffered as a consequence of the negligence; and (4) the loss is quantified.

5.8 ☐ The landmark cases of Caparo and Esanda establish that the duty of care of auditors is owed to a body of shareholders as a whole, unless at the time of the audit the auditor had knowledge of the third party and that there would be reliance on the auditor's report and financial statements.

5.9 ☐ Auditors should avoid litigation by (1) complying with auditing standards; (2) ensuring a clear understanding of the engagement is conveyed through the engagement letter; (3) under certain circumstances, giving consideration to issuing a privity letter; and (4) adhering to proper quality controls.

5.10 ☐ Auditors are subject to the provisions of s. 52 of the Trade Practices Act which prohibits misleading and deceptive conduct in the performance of professional services. The new s. 87AB of the Act allows a PSL scheme to be prescribed and applied to damages claims for misleading and deceptive conduct under s. 52 of the Act.

SUMMARY

Litigation has had a significant impact on the public accounting profession and it seems reasonable to expect that it will continue to do so in the foreseeable future. The changing legal environment concerning auditors has been the result of case law and major corporate collapses. Auditors can be liable for negligence or breach of duties under the Corporations Act and significant legal claims and settlements are complex, leading to the need for legal reforms. The CLERP 9 Act has made it possible for auditors to be registered as authorised audit companies with a liability cap and specific minimum insurance cover. The future effects of the global financial crisis remain to be seen in terms of auditor liability. It is likely that the GFC will lead to claims against auditors from liquidators of failed companies.

Although legal reforms have been implemented, auditors may still be liable for failures in performing their duties. Auditors may be liable to the body of shareholders, to the auditee company, or to third parties. However, certain conditions appear to be necessary from case law before an action can be successfully brought against the auditor. In the main, a relationship must have existed where a duty of care is owed. A number of case decisions over the past few decades have highlighted the importance of the criteria in establishing auditor liability in court — namely, reliance by the plaintiff on the auditor's report, proven breach of negligence by the auditor, a causal relationship between the negligence and the loss suffered by the plaintiff, and the existence of a duty of care.

The concepts of proximity and foreseeability provide some guidance for examining whether a duty of care exists. The courts have also established the concept of contributory negligence (as a result of case law) where the conduct of directors and auditors is found to be 'contributing' to the damage suffered by the plaintiff. However, the issue of auditor liability is very much an unresolved matter. The case law concerning auditors' liability to third parties is inconsistent and the applications of the tests for proximity and reasonable foreseeability have been inconclusive. The AUASB is likely to revise and reissue AGS 1014 *Privity Letter Requests* (issued July 2002) as a new Guidance Statement and withdraw AGS 1014 in the near future.

KEY TERMS

alleged audit failures, p. 204

causal relationships, p. 217

common law, p. 204

contributory negligence, p. 218

damages, p. 214

due care, p. 209

foreseeability, p. 227

insurance hypothesis, p. 204

internationalisation of the profession, p. 205

joint and several liability, p. 204

negligence, p. 204

privity of contract, p. 215

professional indemnity insurance, p. 204

proportionate liability, p. 207

proximity, p. 221

third parties, p. 220

tort, p. 214

5.1 Auditors' liabilities are owed:
A. To shareholders only as auditors are appointed by shareholders.
B. To the company to ensure a corporate veil exists to protect the directors.
C. In respect of their duties specified in the Corporations Act.
D. To both the company and the body of the shareholders as a whole.

5.2 The legal regime relating to auditors' liabilities to third parties for negligence:
A. Has remained substantially the same for the last few decades.
B. Has been relied on to establish auditors' fraudulent activities.
C. Has depended on interpretations of the court.
D. Has changed dramatically because many auditors were found to be fraudulent.

5.3 Martin Loyl is a staff auditor of Penfolk Associates, a medium-sized partnership accounting firm. Recently Martin was found to have been negligent in the performance of his audits of several clients. Under these circumstances, which of the following statements is true?
A. Penfolk is not liable for Martin's work as Martin is an employee only.
B. Penfolk is not liable as long as Martin does not continue auditing the same clients.
C. Martin is personally liable for any loss suffered as a consequence of the negligence.
D. None of the above.

5.4 You are an honorary auditor of a charity association. In carrying out the audit for the financial year ended 30 June 2015, you discover there were no invoices for an expense item of $18 000. The manager tells you that all disbursements are in order and that he expects the association is going to receive a grant from the government, pending the auditor's report. What should you do?
A. Issue an unqualified auditor's report as it is an honorary job and the manager is reliable.
B. Issue a qualified auditor's report making it clear that you disclaim possible liability should it arise from a discrepancy.
C. Further investigate the expense item, and issue a qualified auditor's report if the item is considered material.
D. Notify the manager that you do not wish the report to be sent to the government for obtaining the grant.

5.5 Sheila Bruce is a CPA, and is sued by one of her audit clients who alleges that she failed to satisfy the auditing standards in terms of identifying bad debts as part of her receivables audit. Under these circumstances:
A. Auditing standards are not legislated therefore the client has no right to sue Sheila.
B. Sheila has to prove her audit has been done with reasonable skill, care and diligence.
C. It is quite unreasonable to expect Sheila to be able to identify bad debts.
D. Sheila is liable because the receivables balance is a significant item in all audits.

5.6 What is the term used when a failure on the part of a plaintiff to meet certain required standards of care is a factor leading to a loss by the plaintiff?
A. Negligence.
B. Reasonable foreseeability.
C. Contributory negligence.
D. Damages.

5.7 The term 'privity of contract' refers to:
A. The contractual relationship that exists between two or more contracting parties.
B. The fact that an audit is to be performed in accordance with professional standards.

C. The fact that an auditor appointed to conduct a statutory audit cannot reduce their liability by contract (s. 241).

D. The mandatory requirement that there must be an engagement letter setting out the terms of the audit contract.

5.8 The decision in the Caparo case (1990) reduced the duty of care of auditors to:

A. All users known to the auditor.

B. The shareholders as a group.

C. All users that ought reasonably to have been known to the auditor.

D. All users of the financial statements, except for investors.

5.9 Litigation against auditors under the *Competition and Consumer Act 2010*:

A. Does not require the 'negligence' factors of foreseeability and proximity.

B. Under section 52 requires professional service to be rendered with due care and skill.

C. Has been ruled out by the Esanda judgment.

D. Is specifically excluded.

5.10 Which of the following statements is untrue?

A. The codification of auditing standards means that auditors will have the obligation to comply with all Corporations Act audits.

B. CLERP 9 provides for the registration of authorised audit companies to be legislated.

C. The ACCC assumes a role in the reform of professional indemnity for cases of misleading and deceptive conduct.

D. The Australian Treasury approves the professional standards legislation which overrides state law regarding professional indemnity.

 REVIEW questions

5.11 Discuss the key factors attributable to the increase in professional indemnity insurance, and the impacts this has had.

5.12 Name the elements necessary to be successful in a case of negligence and show how these were applied in the case of *Twomax Ltd v. Dickson, McFarlane & Robinson* (1983).

5.13 How did the key principles of 'due care' develop through the Kingston Cotton Mill Co. case, the London and General Bank case, and the Pacific Acceptance case?

5.14 The Esanda case established the elements that would be necessary for a third party to succeed in an action of negligence against the auditor due to reliance on the audited accounts. Identify what these elements are.

5.15 Why would the courts want to limit the ability of third parties to sue auditors who have been negligent? Are there any arguments that this liability should not be limited?

5.16 List five precautions auditors may take to avoid litigation.

5.17 What are the contributions of (a) the Caparo case (1990), (b) the AGC Advances case (1992), (c) the Columbia Coffee case (1992) and (d) the Esanda Finance case (1994), with respect to the auditor's duty of care to third parties?

5.18 What legal reforms in relation to audit legal liability have been implemented in Australia?

5.19 Explain how engagement letters can be used to avoid litigation.

5.20 What is a privity letter? How should the auditor respond to a request for a privity letter?

5.21 Negligence, duty to detect irregularities ★

In completing the audit of Jonstone Construction Ltd for 30 June 2015, Ben Snowden signed an unmodified audit report. During the course of the audit, certain anomalies were found in the purchases system. It became apparent that a number of invoices from subcontractors by-passed the normal purchase ledger processes and were authorised directly by the Chief Operations Officer (COO). Ben Snowden did not report these issues to management because no material errors were found.

Subsequently, it was found that the COO was engaged in a significant fraud where some subcontractors were encouraged to submit inflated invoices, the COO would authorise them and the COO and the subcontractor shared in the extra amount paid.

Johnston Construction is now seeking to sue Ben Snowden for negligence for not detecting the fraud. Ben Snowden has indicated that it is not his job as auditor to detect fraud, but merely to express an opinion on the financial report and as no material errors were found during the audit then there is no negligence.

Required

Explain the legal implications of these facts as they relate to the role and liability of Ben Snowden in the audit of Jonstone Construction Ltd.

5.22 Due care ★★

As the audit senior for Lockerparts Hardware Ltd, you are happy with the smoothness of the audit for the year ended 30 June 2015. Today, your audit partner tells you that Lockerparts has just gone into liquidation. The financial controller was diverting company funds into a Swiss bank account and has left the country to live in Majorca. The lawyers for the creditors of Lockerparts are taking action against the partner for not performing an appropriate audit. They believe that a properly conducted audit should have detected such a fraud.

The fraud was substantial; however, it was not material from the company's point of view. You explain to the partner that the audit was performed in accordance with all auditing standards and nothing was found to arouse suspicion during the audit. The audit took the same amount of time as last year's, and all appropriate work steps were performed. Your work was reviewed by a manager and the entire file was reviewed by the audit partner.

The audit partner is still concerned. He rings an audit partner in an associated office of your accounting firm and asks her to review the audit file. She agrees and spends a day reviewing the file. After completing her review, she is satisfied that the audit was performed properly.

Required

(a) Explain whether your accounting firm has acted with due care. What do you think will be the court's decision if the case goes to trial?

(b) Even if the partner is convinced he acted with due care, explain why he may offer Lockerparts a substantial settlement amount.

5.23 Negligence ★★

StirMed sells a range of medical products mainly through representatives visiting hospitals and doctors. StirMed has been going through lean times recently and managing day-to-day cash flow has become a challenge.

In spite of the cash flow difficulties, the financial report to 30 June 2015 showed reasonable revenue; however, there were high levels of both receivables and payables and the bank overdraft was getting close to its agreed limit. The auditors, Brent, Date and Co, completed their audit for the year ended 30 June 2015 and gave an unmodified opinion.

Within seven months of the year end, StirMed went into liquidation — unable to pay its debts. As part of the liquidator's investigations, it became apparent that a major fraud had been carried out by two of StirMed's representatives who had created fictitious sales in order to increase their commission. This resulted in both sales and receivables being overstated by material amounts. The liquidator is questioning the conduct of the auditors in not detecting this fraud. Sales and receivables testing was carried out by Francis, the most junior member of the audit team.

Required

Discuss the legal problems and possible liability of Brent, Date and Co as a result of the above facts.

5.24 Negligence, liability to third parties ★★

Sonny Manufacturing Ltd sought a $2 million loan from Bank of Australia. The bank insisted that audited financial statements be submitted before it would extend the credit. Sonny agreed to do this and also agreed to pay the audit fee. An audit was performed by an independent qualified accountant who submitted his report to Sonny to be used solely for the purpose of the loan negotiation with the bank. The bank, after reviewing the audited financial statements, decided not to extend the loan to Sonny. The bank had been using some ratios from the financial statements and decided they were too low. Sonny used the financial statements to obtain a loan from another financial institution. However, it was subsequently discovered that the auditor had failed to detect a significant embezzlement by a senior manager at Sonny.

Required

(a) What are the liabilities, if any, of the auditor? To whom is the auditor liable?
(b) If the auditor did uncover the embezzlement, and noted it in the notes to the financial statement, is he still liable and to whom?
(c) What factors should appropriately be considered before the auditor's liability is confirmed?

5.25 Limiting liability ★★

Brandy, Font and Co. is keen to ensure that it minimises its exposure to liability due to negligence. Dennis Brandy, the senior partner, is aware that some audit firms are setting themselves up as limited liability partnerships and is considering whether this structure will be appropriate for his firm. Dennis has asked you to prepare a report that outlines what the firm should be doing to minimise its liabilities and identifies the advantages and disadvantages of the firm setting up as a Limited Liability Partnership.

Required

Draft the report requested by Dennis Brandy.

5.26 Negligence, liability to third parties ★★

Franche Brown Ltd was a manufacturer of plant and machinery for a range of industries and specialised in large bespoke plant for food manufacturers. The company had large work-in-progress included in the balance sheet relating to various projects across Australia and New Zealand as well as some in South-East Asia. The annual audit for 30 June 2015 was completed by Royston Tring and Co., a firm of chartered accountants. It signed the auditor's report on 25 August 2015. In September 2015, Doitsch Green Ltd made a successful takeover offer for Franche Brown Ltd.

Within a few months of the takeover, it became apparent to the accountants at Doitsch Green Ltd that the work-in-progress value included in the balance sheet of Franche Brown Ltd was significantly overstated and that many of the contracts would make losses due to a mix of poor costing procedures and even poorer implementation.

Doitsch Green Ltd has sued Royston Tring and Co. for negligence. In the subsequent court case, it was found from a review of the audit working papers files that Royston Tring and Co. had placed reliance on management representations with regard to the degree of completion of the contracts in progress as well as expected completion costs and ultimate recoverability of amounts outstanding.

Required

(a) Prepare a case against Royston Tring and Co. to prove it acted negligently.

(b) Explain whether you think Doitsch Green Ltd would win the case.

5.27 Liability to third parties, privity letters ★★★

You have been the auditor of SHF Ltd for several years. The auditor's report for the year ended 30 June 2015 was unqualified. In August 2016, SHF obtained a large loan from a finance company, LRB Ltd, to provide additional working capital. The company experienced severe trading problems and was placed in receivership in May 2017.

LRB is taking action against your firm based on the audit of the 30 June 2015 accounts. It claims that the cause of SHF's failure related to both the inadequate allowance for doubtful debts and a fall in the value of inventories on hand, and that these problems were apparent earlier than June 2015, but had not been adequately dealt with in the financial statements. LRB also claims that it would not have given the loan to SHF had those accounts been qualified.

Required

(a) Outline your defence against the action taken by LRB. Provide specific case references to support your answer.

(b) Explain whether you would change your answer to part (a) if LRB had written to your firm telling you that it intended to make a loan to SHF and was relying on the audited financial statements to assist it in making its decision.[25]

5.28 Negligence, liability to third parties ★★★

Newsday Marketing Ltd's financial statements for the year ended 30 June 2014 were audited by Brian Lung and Partners. The unqualified auditor's report was published alongside the directors' statements on 20 August 2014. Stephen Maine, a tycoon in the publishing industry, put forward a bid to take over Newsday at $2.50 per share, based on the net asset value of the audited accounts (which also showed a net profit for the year of $18 million). The takeover was finalised on 30 September 2014. In October it was leaked to the press that the financial statements of Newsday Marketing had excluded a significant legal liability on a case, for a claim of $5 million. The case was being appealed by Newsday in June 2015. The outcome of the damages claim caused the company's share price to plummet. Stephen Maine was extremely annoyed, partly because he had examined the accounts but overlooked the lawsuit. He decided to sue Brian Lung for negligence and compensation for not including an estimate for the likely damages.

Required

Analyse Brian Lung's legal liability and the likelihood that Stephen Maine may succeed in the action.

CASE studies

5.29 Negligence, contributory negligence ★★★

You are the external auditor of Kiwi Tours Ltd, a company which promotes New Zealand tours to Australia and owns a chain of duty-free shops. You have been auditing the company since it was listed on the Australian Securities Exchange 10 years ago. Although the accounts have never been qualified, you are aware that the company has been making losses for the past 3 years as a result of short-term cash flow difficulties. The company has no long-term loans and the bank overdraft is near its limit at the end of the financial year.

During the financial year, the company upgraded its accounting system to a computer database. A consultant was hired to aid in the correct changeover of files for this system. At year-end, this new system had been in place for 6 months, and the directors report they are happy with the way it is operating. You do not have the expertise to review and evaluate the database management system, so you ask an independent expert to undertake this role. This person concludes that the system appears reliable and that the changeover was correctly carried out. You have never before audited this type of system, so you attend some courses to familiarise yourself with its features. Your firm has a standard work program that you use to test the controls operating within the system.

In your review of the minutes of the board of directors' meetings, you become aware that the New Zealand parent company (which owns 40 per cent of the shares of the company) is considering making an offer for the remaining shares. This is because the company's share price is trading well below its net asset backing.

After your audited 30 June 2015 financial report is published, the takeover offer from the New Zealand parent company proceeds on the basis of an offer price equivalent to the net asset backing of $1.10 per share (as determined from the financial statements). The takeover results in acceptances of 96 per cent of the issued capital, and compulsory acquisition proceedings have been instituted for the other 4 per cent.

While these compulsory acquisition proceedings are being instituted, it is discovered that there were errors in the changeover of the computer system, which resulted in inventory at the duty free stores being materially misstated. After the subsequent write-down of inventory, a new asset backing of $0.70 per share is established. The New Zealand parent company is suing you for alleged negligence for its loss of $0.40 per share.

Required

(a) Decide what major questions must be answered to determine whether you have been negligent. You should support your answer by referring to case law and the auditing standards.

(b) Outline the major issues to be determined to decide whether the company is guilty of contributory negligence.

(c) Assuming you were negligent, explain whether you owe a duty of care to the New Zealand parent company.[26]

5.30 Liability to shareholders and the company ★★★

Maxref Ltd is a new dotcom company specialising in online trading in multimedia items such as DVDs, music, online reports and celebrity commodities. It has been listed on the Australian Securities Exchange since last year. As auditor for Maxref's first year's financial statements for the year ended 30 June 2015, you note that the accounts show a turnover of about $10 million, shareholders' funds of $3 million, and a profit before tax of $ 250 000. During the course of your audit you discover that the balance of the sales ledger control account is $500 000 and that about 80 per cent of the accounts receivable are from new customers who bought items online without full details of the banking particulars. You further discover that all online transactions were reported and executed without proper security checks. Moreover, half of the items listed as stock for sale cannot be located. The share price of the company stands at $1.50. You raise the issue with the director of Maxref and he tells you that this is not uncommon with this type of e-business and that he is concerned only that the Australian Securities Exchange allows it to go on trading. He assures you that nothing major will happen; an unqualified auditor's report is all that is necessary. However, you are worried about your own liability.

Required

Discuss the potential liability of the auditor to:

(a) the shareholders

(b) the company.

You may refer to any relevant case law in your answer.

RESEARCH question

5.31 Auditors' liability

You work in a chartered accounting firm and your partner, Sally Smith, has asked you to do some research and write a report to update her about the potential liability that auditors face as a result of the global financial crisis. The issue arose when a neighbour mentioned to Sally at the weekend that a global accounting firm has had a class action lodged against it over the collapse of Lehman Brothers.

Using the reference materials available on the internet, research the topic and prepare a report for Sally, fully referenced and up to 5000 words.

FURTHER READING

J Baker, R Hanson & J Smith, 'Multidisciplinary practice: big changes brewing for the accounting profession', *CPA Journal*, June 2000, pp. 14–18.

JL Bellovary, DE Giacomino & MD Akers, '*Weighing the public interest: is the going concern opinion still relevant?*', The CPA Journal, January 2006, www.nysscpa.org.

I Dev & D Rushe, 'Auditors: in the palm of the banks? Once again audit failures have raised questions over conflicts of interest', *The Sunday Times*, 25 January 2009.

Directorate General for Internal Market and Services — Consultation on Auditors' Liability Summary Report, January 2007.

Forum on Auditor's Liability, Summary of the meeting of 23 November 2005, European Commission, Brussels, http://europa.au.int.

MJ Garrison & JD Hansen, 'Accounting and auditing update', *Ohio CPA Journal*, July–September 1999, pp. 46–8.

Government of New South Wales, *Professional Standards Act* 1994 (NSW), no. 81.

D Gwilliam, '*The auditor's liability to third parties*', in Current Issues in Auditing, eds Michael Sherer & Stuart Turley, Paul Chapman Publishing, London, 1991, pp. 60–75.

A Hepworth, 'Insurers seek to lower exposure', *Australian Financial Review*, 13 January 2003.

K Houghton, C Jubb, M Kend & J Ng, *The Future of Auditing — Keeping Capital Markets Efficient*, Australian National University Press, Canberra, 2009.

C Humphrey, A Loft & M Woods, 'The global audit profession and the international financial architecture: understanding regulatory relationships at a time of financial crisis', *Accounting Organizations and Society* 34, 2009, pp. 810–25.

J Hughes, 'Global auditors tackle problems of local scandals', *Financial Times*, 28 January 2009.

K Houghton, 'Where auditing should head next', *Australian CPA*, March 2003, Technical Section.

London Economics in association with Professor Ralf Ewert (Goethe University, Frankfurt am Main, Germany), *Study on the Economic Impact of Auditors' Liability Regimes (MARKT/2005/24/F)*, Final Report to EC-DG Internal Market and Services, London Economics, September 2006, http://ec.europa.eu.

Malcolm Maiden, 'Auditing the auditors', *The Age*, 20 April 2002.

Justice Owen, *HIH Royal Commission: The Failure of HIH Insurance*, April 2003.

C Pacini, W Hillison & D Sinason, 'Auditor liability to third parties: an international focus', *Managerial Auditing Journal* 15(8), 2000, pp. 394–406.

C Pacini, MJ Martin & L Hamilton, 'At the interface of law and accounting: an examination of a trend toward a reduction in the scope of auditor liability to third parties in the common law countries', *American Business Law Journal*, Winter 2000, pp. 171–235.

Professional Standards Council, NPSL–Progress So Far, 6 July 2005.

Professions Australia, '*Recommendations for implementation by 1 January 2004 on behalf of Australia's professions*', May 2003.

H Shields, 'Auditors must stand up and be counted', *The Scotsman*, 25 January 2009.

P Sikka, 'Financial crisis and the silence of the auditors', *Accounting, Organizations and Society* 34 (6–7), 2009, pp. 867–73.

P Sikka, S Filling & P Liew, 'The audit crunch: reforming auditing', *Managerial Auditing Journal* 24(2), 2009, pp. 135–55.

NOTES

1. *Reuters*, 'Dynegy Inc files for bankruptcy; will merge with unit', 6 July 2012.

2. A detailed coverage was submitted as part of Part 5 'Auditor Liability' by the Hon. Peter Costello MP, Treasurer, and Senator the Hon. Ian Campbell, Parliamentary Secretary to the Treasurer, in the Commonwealth Treasury report on 'Corporate disclosure: Strengthening the financial reporting framework', Corporate Law Economic Reform Program Discussion Paper 9.

3. From the press release of ASIC, 2 November 2000. The chief allegations made by ASIC included that the profit and loss account of Adsteam did not give a true and fair view of the state of affairs of the company and that the accounts contravened accounting standards and the Companies Code, involved inaccuracies, and allowed dividends to be paid otherwise than out of profits. Deloitte was the auditor at the time.

4. M Drummond, 'Andersen to settle $1 bn Bond claim', *Australian Financial Review*, 26 April 2002.

5. *Australian Financial Review*, 'Centro, PwC take record $200m legal hit', 9 May 2012.

6. There are a number of references which analysed the Bill. The main reference here is from the Department of Parliamentary Services, Bills Digest, 75, 2003–04, Treasury Legislation Amendment (Professional Standards) Bill 2003.

7. Information summarised from details set out by the Professional Standards Council, with details of the professional standards Acts of Victoria and New South Wales, the annual report of the Professional Standards Council of NSW, 2004–05, Lawlink NSW (access www.lawlink.nsw.gov.au), Commonwealth of Australia Law via www.comlaw.gov.au.

8. ASIC Information Release IR 04-23 and Draft Guidance Paper *Authorised Audit Companies: Insurance Arrangements*, June 2004.

9. ibid., p. 3.

10. Justice Owen, HIH Royal Commission Report. The report is in 3 volumes and is available via the Treasury website. Justice Owen has made a number of recommendations to be included in the law regarding the independence of the auditors. See www.hihroyalcom.gov.au.

11. Paragraph 98, in *Stanilite Pacific Ltd. (in liquidation) & Anor v. Seaton and Ors* (2005) New South Wales Court of Appeal, hearing date: 20–24 June 2005, judgement date: 14 September 2005.

12. ASIC, 'PKF Audit Partner gives undertakings to ASIC', Media Release 05-320, 17 October 2005.

13. Australian Securities & Investments Commission (ASIC), 'KPMG partners provide enforceable undertaking not to practice', Media Release 09-146AD, Monday 17 August 2009.

14. ASIC, 'ASIC Report 317, Audit inspection program report for 2011–12', December 2012, pp. 21–3, table 2.

15. ASIC, 'ASIC Report 317, Audit inspection program report for 2011–12', December 2012, p. 26, table 3.

16. Clarke, J, *Privity of contract*, viewed 2 December 2013, www.australiancontractlaw.com/law/scope-privity.html, 2010.

17. Australian Contract Law, 'Privity of contract', www.australiancontractlaw.com/law/scope-privity.html, 2010.

18. The profound influence of Bily v. Arthur Young has been reported in *CPA Journal* by BS Augenbraun, July 1993, and by Gwyn Quillen (partner in Alschuler Grossman Stein & Kahan LLP), 'The profound influence of Bily v. Arthur Young', June 2001, www.alschuler.com.

19. AI Raylesberg, RA Schwinger & E Twiste of Chadbourne & Parke LLP, 'NY Court: Investors cannot pursue fraud claims against accounting firm for purely derivative damages', VCExperts, https://vcexperts.com.

20. C Pacini, W Hillison, R Alaghiah & S Gunz, 'Commonwealth convergence toward a narrower scope of auditor liability to third parties for negligent misstatements', *Abacus*, October 2002, pp. 425–64.

21. AUASB, AUASB Board Meeting Summary Paper, 'Revision to AGS 1014 Privity Letter Requests — Project Plan', 29 July 2013.

22. CPA Australia, 'Identify risk categories', viewed 20 April 2006, www.cpaaustralia.com.au.

23. Australian Competition Law, *Trade Practices Act 1974 (Cth) (consolidated and annotated)*, See australiancompetitionlaw.org/legislation/1974tpa.html, 2011.

24. Address to Western Australian Branch of Professions Australia by Commissioner John Martin, ACCC, 'Trade Practices and the professions — the ACCC's view on the future', 25 October 2005, Perth.

25. Adapted from Professional Year Programme of the ICAA, 1998, Advanced Audit Module.

26. Adapted from Professional Year Programme of the ICAA, 1996, Advanced Audit Module.

Answers to multiple-choice questions

5.1 *D*   5.2 *C*   5.3 *D*   5.4 *C*   5.5 *B*   5.6 *C*   5.7 *A*   5.8 *B*   5.9 *A*   5.10 *D*

part 2

AUDIT PLANNING

6 Overview of the audit of financial reports

7 The auditor's report

8 Client evaluation and planning the audit

9 Audit risk assessment

10 Materiality and audit evidence

chapter 6

Overview of the audit of financial reports

OVERVIEW

6.1 The appointment of an independent auditor

6.2 Duties of an independent auditor

6.3 Auditing standards

6.4 Independent auditor relationships

6.5 Management and the auditor — responsibilities

6.6 Benefits and limitations of an audit

6.7 An overview of the audit process

Summary

Key terms

Multiple-choice questions

Review questions

Professional application questions

Case study

Research question

Further reading

Notes

LEARNING objectives

After studying this chapter, you should be able to:

1 discuss the legal and professional issues in appointing independent auditors

2 state the statutory and other duties of the independent auditor

3 indicate the current auditing standards and their major concepts

4 describe the auditor's relationship with the shareholders, audit committee and other important groups

5 explain the interrelationship between management's and the auditor's responsibilities

6 describe the benefits and limitations of audits of financial reports

7 describe the overall audit process.

PROFESSIONAL STATEMENTS

Australian		International	
ASQC 1	*Quality Control for Firms that Perform Audits and Reviews of Financial Reports and Other Financial Information, and Other Assurance Engagements*	**ISQC 1**	*Quality Control for Firms that Perform Audits and Reviews of Financial Statements and Other Financial Information, and Other Assurance Engagements*
ASA 200	*Overall Objectives of the Independent Auditor and the Conduct of an Audit in Accordance with Australian Auditing Standards*	**ISA 200**	*Overall Objectives of the Independent Auditor, and the Conduct of an Audit in Accordance with International Standards on Auditing*
ASA 210	*Agreeing the Terms of Audit Engagements*	**ISA 210**	*Agreeing the Terms of Audit Engagements*
ASA 240	*The Auditor's Responsibilities Relating to Fraud in an Audit of a Financial Report*	**ISA 240**	*The Auditor's Responsibilities Relating to Fraud in an Audit of Financial Statements*
ASA 560	*Subsequent Events*	**ISA 560**	*Subsequent Events*
ASA 580	*Written Representations*	**ISA 580**	*Written Representations*
ASA 610	*Using the Work of Internal Auditors*	**ISA 610**	*Using the Work of Internal Auditors*
ASA 700	*Forming an Opinion and Reporting on a Financial Report*	**ISA 700**	*Forming an Opinion and Reporting on Financial Statements*
ASA 705	*Modifications to the Opinion in the Independent Auditor's Report*	**ISA 705**	*Modifications to the Opinion in the Independent Auditor's Report*
ASA 706	*Emphasis of Matter Paragraphs and Other Matter Paragraphs in the Independent Auditor's Report*	**ISA 706**	*Emphasis of Matter Paragraphs and Other Matter Paragraphs in the Independent Auditor's Report*
AASB 134	*Interim Financial Reporting*	**IAS 34**	*Interim Financial Reporting*
APES 110	*Code of Ethics for Professional Accountants (Section 290, Independence — Audit and Review Engagements)*	**IFAC**	*Code of Ethics for Professional Accountants (Section 290, Independence — Audit and Review Engagements)*
APES 210	*Conformity with Auditing and Assurance Standards*	**N/A**	

SCENE SETTER

The value of audits

The Association of Chartered Certified Accountants performed a survey to evaluate the value of the financial statement audit to investors in 2010. The responses were quite encouraging given the survey was sent in the wake of the global financial crisis. It was found that 90% of respondents thought that the current audit is of value to them. Further, 80% thought that audited financial statements were very important to them. Reasons cited why they value audit included the following.

- Audit provided an independent impartial opinion on the financial statements of the company.
- Audit played a role in understanding the financial health of the company.
- Audit generated public confidence in the financial statements prepared by management.

Source: The Association of Chartered Certified Accountants, *The Value of Audit: Views from Retail (Private) Investors,* July 2011.

Audits of financial reports play an important role in a free market economy. Chapter 1 introduced some of the fundamental principles of auditing and presented an overview of the audit environment and audit standards. This chapter considers financial report audits in more detail. We will consider the appointment of independent auditors and the duties of independent auditors. These form the basis of the auditor relationship with the client. We also identify the sources and form of the auditing standards that guide the performance of audits. We then consider a number of the auditor's relationships with others (particularly the relationship between the auditor and management) and an associated issue — the interrelationship between accounting and auditing. We also consider some of the benefits and limitations of audits. Finally, we provide an overview of the audit process.

LEARNING 1 objective

Discuss the legal and professional issues in appointing independent auditors.

6.1 THE APPOINTMENT OF AN INDEPENDENT AUDITOR

The *Corporations Act 2001* governs the appointment, removal and resignation of independent auditors. In this section, we outline the basic principles of auditor appointment (as well as the applicable statutory provisions), the procedures for the registration of auditors, and the procedures for the removal and resignation of auditors. The important principles underpinning this process are that the audit is important and that it should be independent. This importance is emphasised by the fact that auditors must be appointed for all companies other than small proprietary companies within one month of incorporation. The aspect of independence is illustrated by the fact that once a relationship between an auditor and company is established, it is not easy to dissolve. This allows the auditor the freedom to speak out without the threat of being easily dismissed by the client.

6.1.1 Principles of the appointment of auditors

As a general rule, the members of a company (i.e. shareholders with voting rights) appoint the auditor. Historically this was done by the management of the company. However, for most companies this is now done by the audit committee on behalf of the shareholders of the company. A company (with the exception of a small proprietary company) must have its financial reports audited in accordance with s. 301 of the Corporations Act. (*Note:* Hereafter, any sections of legislation referred to in this chapter are sections of the Corporations Act unless otherwise specified.)

Directors of public and large proprietary companies are required to appoint an auditor within one month after the company is incorporated, unless the members have appointed one at a general meeting (s. 327A). As a result of changes made by the *First Corporate Law Simplification Act 1995* (Cwlth), small proprietary companies are generally not required to appoint an auditor (s. 301). However, the directors of a small proprietary company are required to appoint an auditor if either the Australian Securities and Investments Commission (ASIC) or shareholders holding at least 5% of the voting shares request the company to prepare audited financial reports for a particular year (s. 293). ASIC has issued Class Order 98/1418 which, under certain circumstances, relieves a company from preparing full audited financial reports when it is a wholly owned entity. The main requirement for meeting this provision is a Deed of Cross Guarantee between the wholly owned entity and the holding entity.

The duration of the first appointment is only until the first annual general meeting, during which the members appoint an auditor (s. 327B). Once an auditor is appointed, the company is liable to pay the auditor's reasonable fees and expenses in carrying out the audit (s. 331). An auditor holds office until his or her death, removal or resignation (s. 327B). The removal or resignation of an auditor (see section 6.1.2) is governed by the Corporations Act. An auditor also ceases to hold office after a company goes into liquidation (s. 330).

A person may be appointed to act as the auditor of a company only if he or she has consented to the appointment in writing before the appointment (s. 328B).

6.1.2 The removal and resignation of auditors

An auditor may be removed from office only by resolution of the company at a general meeting, for which special notice (under s. 329) has been given at least 2 months before the meeting is held. When a company receives special notice of a resolution to remove an auditor, it must send a copy of the notice to the auditor and lodge a copy with ASIC as soon as possible. The auditor is then given 7 days to make representation in writing, with copies of the representation being sent to all members entitled to attend the meeting. The auditor also has the right to be heard at the meeting. When an auditor is removed from office at a general meeting, the company may appoint another auditor at that meeting by a resolution passed by at least a three-quarter majority, or at an adjourned meeting.

These provisions regarding the removal of an auditor have the effect of strengthening the auditor's independence. The auditor can therefore qualify the accounts or argue an accounting position without the potential threat of immediate dismissal by the directors.

For auditors of a company (other than a proprietary company) to resign, they must apply to ASIC for consent to resign, stating their reasons. The company must be notified in writing of the application (s. 329). If ASIC gives its consent, then the auditor may resign after giving written notice to the company. The resignation of an auditor of a proprietary company does not require consent from ASIC. The auditor who resigns also has the protection that such statements made by the auditor in relation to his or her resignation are not admissible in evidence in any proceedings, nor may they be used for any action to be taken against the auditor. The controls over the resignation of auditors are to protect the shareholders of the company being audited. These are to ensure that the auditor cannot easily walk away if there are difficult accounting issues that need to be dealt with or if the company is experiencing financial distress.

If the auditor resigns or is removed, notice of that resignation or removal must be lodged with ASIC within 14 days and a copy of the notice must be sent to the trustee of the company (if one is appointed).

There are also ethical provisions that must be followed by auditors if there is a change of auditor to ensure any inappropriate reasons for the changes come to light (see chapter 8).

6.1.3 The registration of auditors

The Corporations Act requires auditors to be competent. Section 324AF of the Corporations Act states that a registered company auditor must be appointed as the lead auditor to audit a company. To this end, they are required to have a certain level of training and experience. To be suitably qualified to act as an auditor, under s. 1280 the person must:

- be a member of the Institute of Chartered Accountants in Australia (ICAA), CPA Australia, the Institute of Public Accountants or other prescribed body

- hold a degree, diploma or certificate from a university or other prescribed body in Australia, and have passed a course of study in accountancy of not less than 3 years duration and a course of study in commercial law of not less than 2 years duration
- have such practical experience in auditing as prescribed
- be capable of performing the duties of an auditor and be a fit and proper person to be registered as an auditor.

The practical experience required is specified in the Corporations Regulations as:
- work experience in company auditing under the direction of a registered company auditor
- at least one year's experience in the supervision of audits of companies.

Those people who satisfy the above criteria may apply to ASIC to be registered under s. 1279.

The Corporations Act also ensures the independence of the auditor in s. 324CH by some detailed and complex requirements, including the auditor shall not undertake the audit of a company where the auditor, professional member of the audit team, or immediate family member is an officer of the company or audit-critical employee of the audited body. In addition, any auditor or professional member of the audit team cannot be a partner of the company, an employer or employee of an officer of the company, or a partner or employee of an employee of an officer of the company. No auditor, professional member of the audit team or immediate family member can have an asset that is an investment in the audited body. They also cannot be indebted to the audited body unless the debts are incurred in the ordinary course of business on normal business terms. Further details of these specific requirements can be found in s. 324CH.

ASIC maintains a list of registered company auditors for public reference. Registration provides an assurance of the qualification, level of competence and experience of the auditor concerned. Alongside the registration requirements are conditions that require the accounting bodies to maintain and monitor a comprehensive and mandatory code of ethics and other rules, and to continue the professional development of members.

The cancellation and suspension of registration of auditors and liquidators are governed by ss. 1290–1298. Under these provisions, the Companies Auditors and Liquidators Disciplinary Board, on application to ASIC, has the power to hold hearings and decide whether to cancel or suspend the registration of an auditor. It also has the power to impose penalties (including a reprimand) or to require the auditor to undertake or refrain from a certain conduct.

An audit company may also register as an auditor. To be registered as an authorised audit company, a company must meet the following conditions laid down by ASIC.
- The company is registered under the Corporations Act, and is not under external administration.
- Each of the directors of the company:
  - must be a registered company auditor, i.e. registration must be current and not suspended
  - must not be disqualified from managing a corporation.
- All shares in the company are held and beneficially owned by an individual or the legal representatives of an individual.
- The company's constitution does not allow shares to be held by entities other than individuals or the legal representatives of individuals.
- The majority of the votes that may be cast at the annual general meeting of the company are attached to shares that are held and beneficially owned by individuals who are registered company auditors.
- The company holds professional indemnity insurance as required by ASIC.

6.2 DUTIES OF AN INDEPENDENT AUDITOR

When an auditor accepts an appointment, he or she enters into a **contractual relationship** with the company. The audit engagement letter, agreed to and signed by the auditor and the client, details some of the duties of an auditor for a company (ASA 210 *Agreeing the Terms of Audit Engagement* (ISA 210)). There are express or implied terms in such contracts that the auditor will:

- exercise a reasonable degree of care and skill
- be independent of the company
- report to members his or her opinion, based on the audit, as to whether the financial reports are properly drawn up so as to give a true and fair view of the company's financial position, in accordance with the Corporations Act and applicable accounting standards
- comply with auditing standards and other professional standards.

6.2.1 The duty to use reasonable care and skill

The duty to use reasonable care and skill is subject to interpretation of the circumstances of each case. The duty to use reasonable care and skill was established in *London and General Bank* (No. 2) (1895) 2 Ch. 673, which was one of the earliest legal cases to discuss auditors' duties. Lindley LJ said of auditors '[they] must take reasonable care and skill before [they] believe that what [they] certify is true'.

An auditor is under an obligation to use reasonable care and skill at all times in carrying out the audit and forming the audit opinion. The interpretation of 'reasonable care and skill' is a matter of professional judgement, whereby the auditor considers his or her priorities of duties and rights under specific circumstances. However, the ultimate test of what constitutes 'reasonable care and skill' is decided by the courts when legal action is taken against the auditor and was discussed in chapter 5.

6.2.2 The duty to be independent

The Corporations Act reinforces the requirement that the auditor for a company must be independent by disqualifying certain categories of person or firm (s. 324CH) connected with the company. APES 110 *Code of Ethics for Professional Accountants* (the Code of Ethics), the Australian adaptation of the IFAC Code, states principles, rules and guidelines that emphasise that the auditor must not only be independent but also be *seen* to be independent. Auditors are entitled to seek assistance from the company's directors, officers and accountants in carrying out their function. However, they should not rely on information obtained in this manner without exercising reasonable care and diligence, applying their own tests and independent judgement as required. Independence was discussed in more detail in chapter 3.

6.2.3 Statutory duties to report to members and to ASIC

Auditors are required to provide an auditor's report to the members (i.e. shareholders with voting rights) of the company concerning the financial report audit. The format of the auditor's report is governed by ASA 700 *Forming an Opinion and Reporting on a Financial Report* (ISA 700) and the matters on which auditors must express their opinions are specified by statute. Auditors are also required to disclose and report on other regulatory matters under certain circumstances.

The audit opinion

The opinions expressed in an auditor's report must be in accordance with ASA 700. The opinion produced by the auditor was introduced in chapter 1 and is 'whether the financial report is prepared, in all material respects, in accordance with the applicable financial reporting framework'. The audit opinion can be either unmodified or modified. According to ASA 705 *Modifications to the Opinion in the Independent Auditor's Report* (ISA 705), audit opinion modifications are expressed as:

- a qualified opinion
- an adverse opinion
- a disclaimer of opinion.

A further type of modification is where the auditor can decide to issue additional communication through an emphasis of matter or other matter paragraphs under certain circumstances according to ASA 706 *Emphasis of Matter Paragraphs and Other Matter Paragraphs in the Independent Auditor's Report* (ISA 706). The auditor's report is discussed in detail in chapter 7.

The duty to report

An auditor is under a statutory duty to report to members on the company's financial reports for an accounting period and on the accounting records relating to those financial reports (s. 308 of the Corporations Act). A copy of the auditor's report must be laid before the annual general meeting of a public company and must be furnished to the directors in sufficient time to reach members by the earlier of either 21 days before the annual general meeting after the end of the financial year or 4 months after the end of the financial year (s. 315).

Section 308 sets out the matters that must be contained in an auditor's report. The report must state whether, in the auditor's opinion, the financial reports are properly drawn up:

- so as to give a true and fair view of the financial affairs of the company
- in accordance with the Corporations Act
- in accordance with applicable accounting standards and the Corporations Regulations.

Section 308 also requires the report to describe any defect or irregularity in the financial reports. The auditor must report on the following implied conditions if there is any deficiency or failure to comply:

- whether the auditor has obtained all the information, explanation and assistance required
- whether proper financial records have been maintained
- whether other records or registers have been maintained as required by the Corporations Act.

If, in the auditor's opinion, the financial reports are not drawn up in accordance with a particular applicable accounting standard, then the report must give particulars of the qualified financial effect of the non-compliance on the financial reports. The auditor's report must also include any statements or disclosures required by the auditing standards.

Under AASB 134 *Interim Financial Reporting* (IAS 34), reporting requirements for half-year accounts are prescribed. The information disclosed in the half-year accounts is less extensive than that disclosed in the full-year accounts, and the standard requires each half-year to be treated as a discrete reporting period. The disclosing entities that are required under AASB 134 to prepare half-year accounts must also have them audited as required by s. 302 of the Corporations Act. The audit requirements are similar to a normal annual audit and are described in s. 309.

In recent years there have been criticisms of the format of the audit report. The Professional Environment vignette below outlines the reasons for some changes that are currently being considered by the International Auditing and Assurance Standards Board. Further discussion of this new audit report is in chapter 7 of this book.

The duty to report to ASIC

The auditor conducting a financial report audit must notify ASIC as soon as possible if there are reasonable grounds to suspect a contravention of the Corporations Act (s. 311). This is required unless the auditor believes the contravention will be adequately dealt with by commenting on it in the auditor's report or bringing it to the attention of the directors. Another reason to report to ASIC under s. 311 is if there is any attempt to 'influence, coerce, manipulate or mislead a person involved in the conduct of the audit'.

6.2.4 Professional duties

The auditor, as a member of the accounting profession, also has professional responsibilities. Members involved in the audit of a general purpose financial report of a reporting entity are required to take all reasonable steps within their power to ensure that accounting standards, which have the full force of the law under the Corporations Act, are consistently applied in the preparation and presentation of the report. Those involved in audits of financial reports are also required to comply with all auditing standards (APES 210 *Conformity with Auditing and Assurance Standards*, paragraphs 4.1 and 4.2 as well as the Corporations Act) in addition to any ethical and legal requirements (see chapters 3 and 5 respectively).

LEARNING objective 3

Indicate the current auditing standards and their major concepts.

6.3 AUDITING STANDARDS

Auditing standards provide the framework of required and recommended principles and procedures in the conduct of a financial report audit. As introduced in chapter 1, Australian auditors rely on a codified set of auditing standards prepared by the Auditing and Assurance Standards Board (AUASB), which under the CLERP 9 Act of 2004 was incorporated as a board under the government-appointed Financial Reporting Council.

6.3.1 The standard-setting framework

Auditing standards originate from two sources: (1) the AUASB and (2) the International Auditing and Assurance Standards Board (IAASB). The AUASB harmonises Australian standards with international standards and also identifies emerging issues and uses its own resources and those of contractors to initiate and develop the standards. The IAASB, a standing committee of the International Federation of Accountants (IFAC), has the objective of developing and issuing international standards on auditing (ISAs) which provide a degree of uniformity in auditing practice throughout the world. The AUASB's work program therefore integrates the work of the IAASB.

Both the AUASB and the IAASB use an extensive due process in the development of auditing standards. The AUASB has adapted the ISAs to Australian conditions and issues an exposure draft subject to the due process. From 1 July 2006, Australia fully adopted international auditing standards developed by the IAASB, adapted as necessary and issued as Australian standards for auditing (ASAs). The AUASB undertakes to issue the following standards, which are similar to those issued by the IAASB:

- auditing standards (ASAs), developed in the context of financial report audits, to be applied to all audits of historical financial information
- standards on review engagements (ASREs), to be applied to the review of a financial report and to the review of other historical financial information
- standards on assurance engagements (ASAEs), to be applied to assurance engagements dealing with subject matters other than historical financial information
- standards on related services (ASRSs), to be applied to engagements involving agreed-upon procedures for information and other related services engagements as specified by the AUASB.

The AUASB also issues Guidance Statements on audit, review assurance and related services. These statements do not establish new principles but provide guidance on procedural matters.

Figure 6.1 shows the broad AUASB standard-setting framework in Australia.

For the purposes of this chapter, discussion is limited to the Australian adapted international auditing and assurance standards (ASAs) for the audit or review of historical financial information.

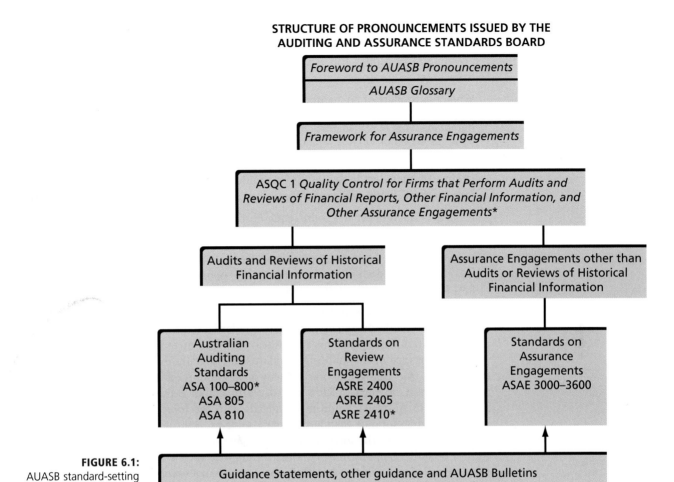

STRUCTURE OF PRONOUNCEMENTS ISSUED BY THE AUDITING AND ASSURANCE STANDARDS BOARD

Foreword to AUASB Pronouncements

AUASB Glossary

Framework for Assurance Engagements

ASQC 1 *Quality Control for Firms that Perform Audits and Reviews of Financial Reports, Other Financial Information, and Other Assurance Engagements**

Audits and Reviews of Historical Financial Information

Assurance Engagements other than Audits or Reviews of Historical Financial Information

Australian Auditing Standards ASA 100–800* ASA 805 ASA 810

Standards on Review Engagements ASRE 2400 ASRE 2405 ASRE 2410*

Standards on Assurance Engagements ASAE 3000–3600

Guidance Statements, other guidance and AUASB Bulletins

FIGURE 6.1:
AUASB standard-setting framework

*Made under section 336 of the *Corporations Act 2001*.

Source: *Foreword to AUASB Pronouncements*, AUASB, 2012, Appendix 1, p. 10.

6.3.2 The development and importance of auditing standards

The ASAs (ISAs) set a minimum standard of technical proficiency in auditing, codifying current best practice. They are applicable to each financial report audit (subject to the exceptional circumstances departure provision) that an independent auditor undertakes, regardless of the size of the entity, the form of business organisation, the type of industry or whether the entity is for profit or not for profit. Shareholders and other users are informed in the 'Scope' section of the auditor's report that the audit has been conducted in accordance with the auditing standards.

APES 210 stipulates that compliance with auditing standards is mandatory — i.e. the standards are enforceable under the Code of Ethics, which stipulates that non-compliance can lead to disciplinary proceedings by the professional body to which the auditor belongs.

Within each auditing standard, the mandatory components are at the front and are to be complied with in the planning, conduct and reporting of audit and audit-related services. The explanatory text and other information provide guidance and practical examples to assist the auditor in the conduct of the audit are located at the end of the standards and shown with an 'A' prefix.

The standards indicate the minimum level of care required in performing an audit. Ultimately, however, the courts determine whether the level of care provided is adequate. As the comments of Moffitt J in *Pacific Acceptance Corporation Ltd v. Forsyth* (1970) 92 WN (NSW) 29 (at 75) indicate:

> When the conduct of an auditor is in question in legal proceedings, it is not the province of the auditing profession itself to determine what is the legal duty of auditors or to determine what reasonable skill and care requires to be done in a particular case, although what others do or what is usually done is relevant to the question of whether there has been a breach of duty.

The courts may decide that auditors should review and update their practices and procedures to meet changing business conditions and expectations. Moffit J (at 74) commented:

> It is not a question of the court requiring higher standards because the profession has adopted higher standards. It is a question of the court applying the law, which by its content expects such reasonable standards as will meet the circumstances of today, including modern conditions of business and knowledge concerning them ... it might be said that the modern procedures call for more sophistication and higher standards on the part of those who perform the work.

It is argued that the standards enhance the reputation of the profession. In constantly updating old standards and issuing new standards, the accounting bodies are seen to be responding to difficult problems and endeavouring to meet the changing needs of society.

The importance of the auditing standards in Australia in recent years has been further enhanced by the changes to make them legally enforceable. These changes were implemented as part of the CLERP 9 initiatives to enhance the credibility of audited financial reports in Australia. Auditing standards with the force of law are now issued by the Auditing and Assurance Standards Board under s. 336 of the Corporations Act, as discussed in chapter 1. The force of law is by virtue of s. 307A where it states, 'the individual auditor or audit company must conduct the audit or review in accordance with the auditing standards'. For many of the standards the main changes were to replace the terms 'should' with 'shall'. This was because of the legal status of the standards the term 'shall' more clearly illustrates the mandatory nature of the requirements. The other main change was to change the title of the auditing standards from AUSs to ASAs. The new force of law auditing standards were applicable from 1 July 2006. It should be noted that these standards still largely conform with international auditing standards. However, change with auditing is a constant and further significant changes have taken place over recent years with the 'Clarity project'.

The background to the Clarity project is discussed in chapter 1. The Clarity project was undertaken by the IAASB and was completed in 2009. Clarity standards are structured with mandatory components first followed by explanatory material (differentiated by an 'A' in front of the section number).

Figure 6.2 provides an overview of the categories of auditing standards, as well as the ASA number sequence used for each category, then in brackets the number of standards in each category.[1]

As can be seen from figure 6.2, the standards provide a guide that takes the auditor through the whole audit process. A number of standards are not surprisingly in the category of 'audit evidence', as obtaining evidence to support an opinion is crucial to the auditor's work. The standards are designed to be applicable to the whole audit process. Specific standards are not written for particular classes of transactions or balances. However, we will consider some of the issues associated with particular transactions and balances in part 4 of this book. Figure 6.5 later in this chapter outlines the overall audit process and the associated discussion provides linkages to chapters throughout the book. Table 6.1 is a current list of the Australian auditing standards.

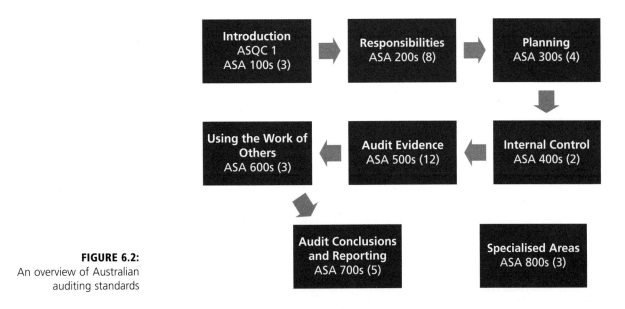

FIGURE 6.2:
An overview of Australian
auditing standards

TABLE 6.1: Australian auditing standards in Clarity format

No.	Title
ASQC 1	*Quality Control for Firms that Perform Audits and Reviews of Financial Reports and Other Financial Information, and Other Assurance Engagements*
ASA 100	*Preamble to AUASB Standards*
ASA 101	*Preamble to Australian Auditing Standards*
ASA 102	*Compliance with Ethical Requirements when Performing Audits, Reviews and Other Assurance Engagements*
ASA 200	*Overall Objectives of the Independent Auditor and the Conduct of an Audit in Accordance with Australian Auditing Standards*
ASA 210	*Agreeing the Terms of Audit Engagements*
ASA 220	*Quality Control for an Audit of a Financial Report and Other Historical Financial Information*
ASA 230	*Audit Documentation*
ASA 240	*The Auditor's Responsibilities Relating to Fraud in an Audit of a Financial Report*
ASA 250	*Consideration of Laws and Regulations in an Audit of a Financial Report*
ASA 260	*Communication with Those Charged with Governance*
ASA 265	*Communicating Deficiencies in Internal Control to Those Charged with Governance and Management*
ASA 300	*Planning an Audit of a Financial Report*
ASA 315	*Identifying and Assessing the Risks of Material Misstatement through Understanding the Entity and Its Environment*
ASA 320	*Materiality in Planning and Performing an Audit*

(continued)

No.	Title
ASA 330	*The Auditor's Responses to Assessed Risks*
ASA 402	*Audit Considerations Relating to an Entity Using a Service Organisation*
ASA 450	*Evaluation of Misstatements Identified during the Audit*
ASA 500	*Audit Evidence*
ASA 501	*Audit Evidence — Specific Considerations for Inventory and Segment Information*
ASA 502	*Audit Evidence — Specific Considerations for Litigation and Claims*
ASA 505	*External Confirmations*
ASA 510	*Initial Audit Engagements — Opening Balances*
ASA 520	*Analytical Procedures*
ASA 530	*Audit Sampling*
ASA 540	*Auditing Accounting Estimates, Including Fair Value Accounting Estimates, and Related Disclosures*
ASA 550	*Related Parties*
ASA 560	*Subsequent Events*
ASA 570	*Going Concern*
ASA 580	*Written Representations*
ASA 600	*Special Considerations — Audits of a Group Financial Report (Including the Work of Component Auditors)*
ASA 610	*Using the Work of Internal Auditors*
ASA 620	*Using the Work of an Auditor's Expert*
ASA 700	*Forming an Opinion and Reporting on a Financial Report*
ASA 705	*Modifications to the Opinion in the Independent Auditor's Report*
ASA 706	*Emphasis of Matter Paragraphs and Other Matter Paragraphs in the Independent Auditor's Report*
ASA 710	*Comparative Information — Corresponding Figures and Comparative Financial Reports*
ASA 720	*The Auditor's Responsibilities Relating to Other Information in Documents Containing an Audited Financial Report*
ASA 800	*Special Considerations — Audits of Financial Reports Prepared in Accordance with Special Purpose Frameworks*
ASA 805	*Special Considerations — Audits of Single Financial Statements and Specific Elements, Accounts or Items of a Financial Statement*
ASA 810	*Engagements to Report on Summary Financial Statements*

Do you know ...

6.1 ☐ The statutory duties of auditors are stipulated in the Corporations Act and the Corporations Regulations. These include the duty to report to members in accordance with legislative requirements and the duty to report to ASIC on certain matters.

6.2 ☐ Auditors also have duties to exercise reasonable care and skill, be independent of the company and comply with professional standards.

6.3 ☐ Auditing standards are set by the AUASB. They are important for maintaining quality service and safeguarding auditors when called on to justify their opinion. Shareholders and other users of auditor's reports can also be assured of the minimum standards used by auditors in arriving at the audit opinion.

LEARNING 4 objective

Describe the auditor's relationship with the shareholders, audit committee and other important groups.

6.4 INDEPENDENT AUDITOR RELATIONSHIPS

In a financial report audit, the auditor maintains professional relationships with four important groups: (1) the shareholders, (2) the board of directors and audit committee, (3) internal auditors, and (4) management.

6.4.1 Shareholders

The shareholders of the company are the main beneficiaries of the audit function — a point that is emphasised in the auditor's report title, which is usually titled 'Independent Auditor's Report', and is addressed to the members (or shareholders). The primary reason for the existence of audits is due to the demand for audited information from shareholders as explained in chapter 1.

Shareholders rely on the audited financial reports for assurance that management has properly discharged its stewardship responsibility. The auditor, therefore, has an important responsibility to shareholders of the company. During the course of an audit engagement, the auditor is unlikely to have direct personal contact with shareholders, who often are not officers, key employees or directors of the entity. Yet the auditor's appointment, removal or resignation are ultimately determined by (or influenced by) the shareholders. In theory, the directors' powers to appoint the auditor are limited; in practice, the shareholders of the company generally accept the recommendations of the directors. Generally, these days the appointment decision is done by the group of non-executive directors that comprise the audit committee.

The relationship with the shareholders is certainly one that tests the auditor's professionalism. They have very little to do with the shareholders, yet that is the group to whom they have primary responsibility. This was seen as an issue in the reforms undertaken as part of CLERP 9. Some changes to try to improve communication between the two were as follows: shareholders can submit written questions to the annual general meeting (AGM) relating to the audit report and the conduct of the audit (s. 250PA); the auditor must attend the AGM (s. 250RA); and a reasonable opportunity must be allowed for members as a whole to ask questions of the auditor and for the auditor to respond (s. 250T). This sort of transparency and accountability to shareholders is relatively unique to the Australian auditing environment.

6.4.2 The board of directors and audit committee

The board of directors of an entity is responsible for ensuring that the entity operates in the best interests of the shareholders. Directors on the board might be executive or non-executive directors. Executive directors are part of the management of the company, whereas non-executive directors are independent in that they are not part of the management of the company. The auditor's relationship with the directors largely depends on the composition of the board. Thus, when the board consists mainly of entity or executive officers, the auditor's relationship with the board may be the same as his or her relationship with management. However, most boards now have number of outside, non-executive or independent directors, which means a different relationship is possible. In fact it is recommended by the ASX that the majority of a board of directors should comprise independent directors.[2] Outside members are not officers or employees of the entity, so the board in such cases — composed exclusively or mainly of outside members — can serve as an intermediary between the auditor and management, and may have oversight responsibilities for the financial reporting and auditing process.

Irrespective of the structure of the board of directors, companies are encouraged to have an **audit committee**. Audit committees can play a key role in helping boards of directors fulfil their corporate governance and oversight responsibilities. Neither the independent auditor nor the internal auditor should be a member of the audit committee. However, both meet with the audit committee to discuss matters pertaining to the audit. The Australian Securities Exchange now requires all listed companies in the Top 300 to have an audit committee. The importance of the audit committee in dealing with external auditors and the difficulties in this relationship are reflected in the below Professional Environment.

Audit committees have an important role in corporate governance. *Audit Committees: A Guide to Good Practice* was developed to assist companies in setting up audit committees. The main objectives of an appropriately established and effective audit committee are wide ranging, however, their responsibilities in relation to the external audit are outlined in figure 6.3.

FIGURE 6.3:
Responsibilities of audit committees in relation to external audit

- Making recommendations to the board on the appointment of the external auditor. The audit committee may agree on the audit fee or make a recommendation to the board. The audit committee needs to be satisfied that a high quality and comprehensive audit can be conducted for the agreed fee.
- Recommending to the board, if appropriate, the extension of the rotation period of the external audit engagement partner subject to certain requirements.
- Carefully examining any recommendations by management that the external auditor needs to be replaced, or that the audit needs to be put out to tender. The audit committee reports to the board on its examination before any decision is made by the board.
- Agreeing on the terms of the audit engagement with the external auditor at the start of each audit.
- Reviewing the independence of the external auditor. The audit committee considers whether the external auditor's relationships and services with the entity and other relevant organisations might impair, or appear to impair, the external auditor's independence. Under the Corporations Act 2001, the audit committee of a listed entity much provide written advice to the board regarding the provision of non-audit services by the external auditor. Some audit committees may establish policies on the extent to which the external auditor can provide other assurance, or non-assurance, services and monitor the application of the policies to consider the possible implications for the auditor's independence.
- Inviting the external auditor to attend audit committee meetings throughout the financial year, as a minimum to coincide with the reporting and audit cycles. For example, meetings to review the external audit plan, including proposed audit strategies, particularly in the areas of identified audit risk, to discuss audit results and to consider the implications of the external audit findings for the control environment.
- Meeting privately with the external auditor, at least once each year without management, to facilitate free and open communication. For example, the audit committee may ask the external audit if there are any significant resolved or unresolved issues arising from the audit or whether senior management imposed any restrictions on the conduct of the audit.
- Evaluating the performance of the external auditor.
- Monitoring the relationship between the internal and external auditors.

Source: Audit Committees: A Guide to Good Practice, 2e, AUASB, AICD, and IIA, 2012.

It is important that the terms of reference of the audit committee are clearly defined in a formal charter, so the committee's role does not overlap that of management's. This charter should ensure that the audit committee has adequate resources and the authority necessary to meet its objectives. The majority of audit committee members should be independent, non-executive directors and at least one member should have significant financial experience. The chairperson of the board of directors should not be the chairperson of the audit committee.

When an effective audit committee is in place, it provides an effective mechanism for the auditor to communicate with management about issues relating to the nature and scope of the audit, and to report significant issues arising from the audit. This process is discussed in more detail in chapter 18.

6.4.3 Internal auditors

An independent auditor often has a close working relationship with the entity's internal auditor. Internal auditing was discussed in chapter 2. From the perspective of the independent auditor, internal auditing is a component of the entity's control environment. As an independent unit within the entity, the internal auditor examines, evaluates and monitors the adequacy and effectiveness of the internal control structure. The work of the internal auditor in conducting tests of control is likely to influence the nature, timing and extent of the independent auditor's audit procedures. ASA 610 *Using the Work of Internal Auditors* (ISA 610) requires the independent auditor to assess the work of the internal auditor for the purpose of planning the audit and developing an effective audit approach.

The internal auditor's work cannot be used as a substitute for the independent auditor's work, but it can be an important complement. ASA 610 requires the independent auditor, in determining the effect of such work on the audit, to consider (1) the organisational status, (2) the scope of work, (3) the technical training and proficiency of internal auditors, and (4) due professional care observed in the work of internal auditors.

6.4.4 Management

The term **management** is a collective reference to individuals who actively plan, coordinate and control the operations and transactions of the entity. In an auditing context, 'management' refers to the entity officers, controllers and key supervisory personnel.

During the course of an audit, there is extensive interaction between the auditor and management. To obtain the evidence needed, the auditor often requires confidential data about the entity, so a relationship based on mutual trust and respect is imperative. An adversarial relationship will be counterproductive. The typical approach of the auditor towards management's assertions may be characterised by professional scepticism. This means the auditor should neither disbelieve management's assertions nor thoughtlessly accept them without concern for their truthfulness. Rather, the auditor should recognise the need to evaluate objectively the conditions observed and evidence obtained during the audit.

ASA 200 states in paragraph 15: 'The auditor shall plan and perform an audit with professional scepticism recognising that circumstances may exist that cause the financial report to be materially misstated.' Past experience of the management being honest does not relieve the auditor to maintain scepticism or allow them to accept less than persuasive audit evidence from management. Increased emphasis on scepticism in an audit is an important current issue for auditors as is highlighted in the professional environment vignette overleaf.

The auditor should also consider ASA 580 *Written Representations* (ISA 580) when considering management representations during an audit. As stated in paragraph 4, 'Although written representations provide necessary audit evidence, they do not provide sufficient appropriate audit evidence on their own about any of the matters with which they deal.' Auditors should ensure that they do not rely on management representations for the sake of convenience when alternative evidence is available.

LEARNING 5
objective

Explain the interrelationship between management's and the auditor's responsibilities.

6.5 MANAGEMENT AND THE AUDITOR — RESPONSIBILITIES

This section describes in more detail the division of responsibility between an entity's management and the auditor in the financial reporting process. An important aspect of this division is the relationship between accounting and auditing.

6.5.1 The relationship between accounting and auditing

There are significant differences in the accounting process by which financial reports are prepared and the audit of these reports. Each process has different objectives and methods, and the parties responsible for each are not the same.

Accounting methods involve identifying the events and transactions that affect the entity, and then measuring, recording, classifying and summarising these items in the accounting records. The outcome of this process is the preparation and distribution of financial reports in accordance with an identified financial reporting framework. The ultimate objective of accounting is the communication of relevant and reliable financial information that will be useful for decision making. An entity's employees are involved in the accounting process and the entity's directors have ultimate responsibility for the financial reports.

The audit of financial reports involves obtaining and evaluating evidence on management's financial report assertions. Auditing culminates in the issue of an auditor's report that contains the auditor's opinion on whether the financial information is presented fairly in accordance with an identified financial reporting framework. The auditor is responsible for adhering to auditing standards both in gathering and evaluating evidence, and in issuing an auditor's report that contains the auditor's conclusion. This conclusion is expressed in the form of an opinion on the financial information. Rather than creating new information, auditing adds credibility to the financial reports prepared by management.

The relationship between accounting and auditing in the financial reporting process is illustrated in figure 6.4.

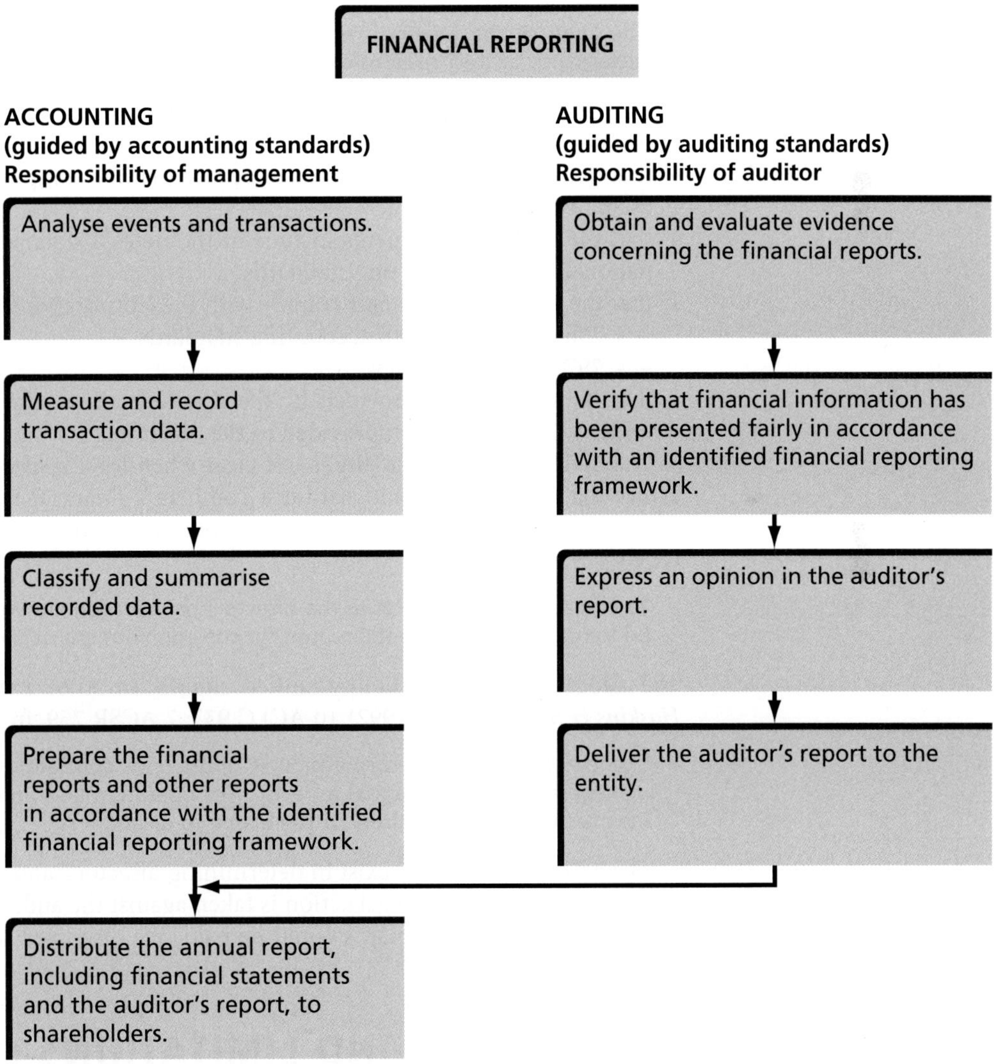

FINANCIAL REPORTING

ACCOUNTING
(guided by accounting standards)
Responsibility of management

Analyse events and transactions.

Measure and record transaction data.

Classify and summarise recorded data.

Prepare the financial reports and other reports in accordance with the identified financial reporting framework.

AUDITING
(guided by auditing standards)
Responsibility of auditor

Obtain and evaluate evidence concerning the financial reports.

Verify that financial information has been presented fairly in accordance with an identified financial reporting framework.

Express an opinion in the auditor's report.

Deliver the auditor's report to the entity.

Distribute the annual report, including financial statements and the auditor's report, to shareholders.

FIGURE 6.4:
Relationship between accounting and auditing

Sometimes an auditor may be asked to help prepare an entity's records; an act which is clearly part of the accounting process. Section 290.171–2 of the Code of Ethics (IFAC Code) prohibits this involvement with public company audit clients, other than in exceptional circumstances. Such involvement is allowed with other clients, provided the need for professional independence is considered, the client accepts responsibility for the records, and the auditor makes no executive decisions.

6.5.2 The division of responsibility

Fundamental to an audit of the financial reports is the division of responsibility between management and the independent auditor. Paragraph 4 of ASA 200 states:

> The financial report subject to audit is that of the entity, prepared by management of the entity with oversight from those charged with governance. Australian Auditing Standards do not impose responsibilities on management or those charged with governance and do not override laws and regulations that govern their responsibilities. However, an audit in accordance with Australian Auditing Standards is conducted on the premise that management and, where appropriate, those charged with governance have acknowledged certain responsibilities that are fundamental to the conduct of the audit. The audit of the financial report does not relieve management or those charged with governance of their responsibilities.

The Corporations Act (s. 295) stipulates that directors must make a signed declaration that states:
- that there are reasonable grounds to believe that the company will be able to pay its debts as and when they fall due
- that the financial statements include in the notes a statement of compliance with international financial reporting standards
- that the financial statements comply with the Corporations Act, including:
  - s. 296 compliance with accounting standards
  - s. 297 true and fair view
- that the declarations provided by the chief executive officer and chief financial officer under s. 295A have been provided to the directors.

The division of responsibility is not clear when legal responsibility is to be allocated for errors that have been found within a company's financial reports. Historically, the view was as outlined by Moffitt J in *Pacific Acceptance Corporation Ltd v. Forysth* (1970) 92 WN (NSW) 29:

> To excuse an auditor because the directors or management were also at fault ... , would be to negate a fundamental reason for the appointment of the auditor.

The allocation of responsibility shifted slightly in *AWA Limited v. Daniels t/a Deloitte Haskins & Sells and Ors* (1992) 10 ACLC 933; 7 ACSR 759, in which Rogers CJ stated:

> I cannot accept that a corporation is entitled to abdicate all responsibility for proper management of the financial aspects of its operation and then, when loss is suffered, to seek to attribute the entirety of the blame to its auditors.

'Shades of grey' will still exist in determining directors' and auditors' respective responsibilities. In practice, most legal action is taken against the auditors because they have greater resources from which damages could be paid. We discussed these issues in more detail in chapter 5.

LEARNING objective 6

Describe the benefits and limitations of audits of financial reports.

6.6 BENEFITS AND LIMITATIONS OF AN AUDIT

To properly understand the value of an audit it is important to know that as well as benefits there are limitations. An understanding of both of these will ensure that the role of auditors is appreciated for what it actually provides and will help to mitigate misunderstandings of this role that in part contribute to the 'audit expectation gap' as discussed in chapter 1.

6.6.1 Benefits

Irrespective of the view held or the dominance of any particular explanatory theory for auditing (discussed in chapter 1), a number of benefits arise from having an audit of the financial reports. These benefits can also create a demand for auditing services. Examples of possible benefits are described below.

Access to capital markets

Public companies must satisfy statutory audit requirements in accordance with the *Corporations Act 2001*. The Australian Securities Exchange imposes its requirements for listing securities. Without audits, companies may be denied access to these capital markets. These requirements are designed to ensure some protection for investors (particularly small investors) in the capital markets. More information is available from the ASIC website (www.asic.gov.au).

The lower cost of capital

Small companies often have financial report audits to obtain bank loans or more favourable borrowing terms. Often, banks require audited financial reports before lending any funds; sometimes, they will also require auditor's reports of compliance with debt covenants.

Given the reduced information risk resulting from audited financial reports, potential creditors may offer low interest rates and potential investors may be willing to accept a lower rate of return on their investment. In short, audited financial reports improve an entity's credibility and therefore reduce risk for investors and creditors.

A deterrent to inefficiency and fraud

Financial report audits can be expected to have a favourable effect on employee efficiency and honesty. Knowledge that an independent audit is to be performed is likely to result in fewer errors in the accounting process and reduce the likelihood of employee misappropriation of assets. Similarly, the auditor's involvement in an entity's financial reporting process is a restraining influence on management. The fact that its financial report assertions are to be verified reduces the likelihood that management will engage in fraudulent financial reporting. Note that an audit is not designed to detect fraud. ASA 240 *The Auditor's Responsibilities Relating to Fraud in an Audit of a Financial Report* (ISA 240) states that the auditor's duty to investigate and report irregularities arises only in circumstances in which suspicions are aroused.

Control and operational improvements

Based on observations made during an audit of the financial reports, the independent auditor can suggest how controls could be improved and how greater operating efficiencies within the entity's organisation may be achieved. This is especially valuable to small and medium-sized entities. Weaknesses in controls and suggestions for improvement are usually outlined in the **management letter** (see chapter 18) prepared by the auditor at the end of the audit.

6.6.2 Limitations

Traditionally, the financial reports have been regarded as being mainly for the benefit of the members of a company. By receiving full and accurate information on the financial affairs of their company, members are able to better assess the performance of management. A financial report audit performed in accordance with **auditing standards** provides an objective assurance of the credibility of the assertions by management. However, the financial report audit is subject to a number of inherent limitations. Some of these limitations are described below.

A time lapse

A common criticism of the audit function (and also of financial accounting reporting practices) is that the lapse of time between the end of the reporting period and the presentation of the auditor's report may be up to 4 months. The auditor is required to undertake a review of subsequent events under ASA 560 *Subsequent Events* (ISA 560), but this does not create full 'up-to-date' financial reports as of the date of the auditor's report. The Enhanced Disclosure Scheme, a result of the *Corporate Law Reform Act 1994* (Cwlth), provides investors with more up-to-date information about a company by requiring the ongoing or continual disclosure of information that a reasonable person could expect would have a material effect on the value of the investment. Also, the scheme requires all disclosing entities to prepare and lodge half-yearly financial reports. It is expected that both financial reporting and auditing will move to become more 'real time' to maintain relevance. In particular, the internet has had a major impact on the timeliness of financial reporting and auditing.

Audit testing on selective samples

Results of audit selective testing may involve either using the scientific sampling method to obtain representative data or exercising an element of judgement based on the auditor's understanding of the business. Audit testing based on selective samples has limitations owing to sampling risk (which is the risk that a sample drawn from a population may not be representative of that population). The advantage of scientific sampling is that this sampling risk can be quantified. Refer to chapter 13 for a more detailed discussion of some of the risks and limitations associated with sampling.

Assessment of materiality

The assessment of **materiality** is a part of the audit process that requires a high degree of **professional judgement**. It requires both quantitative and qualitative considerations. There are no universally agreed-upon guidelines for quantitative measures of materiality. Guidelines that attempt to establish a quantitative threshold are necessarily arbitrary, thereby requiring significant professional judgement. Qualitative considerations of materiality relate to an assessment of the impact of the causes of the misstatements rather than just the amount of the impact. This qualitative assessment also requires a significant degree of professional judgement by the auditor. Refer to chapter 10 for a more detailed discussion on materiality.

Highly specialised areas

Auditors may be required to form a professional judgement in areas that are highly specialised or that are not dealt with adequately by the accounting standards or auditing standards. For example, there are many questions concerning the valuation of intangible assets or environment-related accounting items, and audit judgement can be influenced by a number of factors.[3] Substantial disagreements between auditors and management during the course of an audit often relate to specialised areas or contentious accounting issues.

Report format limitations

Finally, the auditor is required to report within a **standard format of auditor's reports**, as prescribed by ASA 700. The auditor's report and the body of the financial reports are subject to interpretation. The standard format of the auditor's report may not reflect fully the complexities involved in the audit process and the decision of the audit opinion. Despite these limitations, an audit of the financial reports adds credibility to the financial information.

In recent years there has been quite a bit of consideration on changing the audit report. A central issue relates to providing more non-standard information (see chapter 7). It is expected that changes in this area will help to alleviate the historical limitation of the audit report.

Do you know . . .

6.4 ☐ Shareholders of the company are the main reason for the audit function. However, they typically have little contact with the auditor.

6.5 ☐ The independent auditor must retain a degree of professional scepticism when dealing with the management of the organisation, while maintaining objectivity and mutual respect.

6.6 ☐ Management is mainly responsible for the preparation and presentation of financial reports.

6.7 ☐ There are many benefits associated with having a financial report audit — informed access to capital markets, the potentially lower cost of capital, a deterrent to inefficiency and fraud, and a means of improving control and operations.

6.8 ☐ Financial report audits can be limited by such factors as the lapse of time before the audited financial reports are published, the inherent limitations in the audit tests, technical uncertainties and the prescribed format of auditor's reports.

LEARNING 7
objective
Describe the overall audit process.

6.7 AN OVERVIEW OF THE AUDIT PROCESS

In the context of the environment and issues we have discussed so far in this chapter, the auditor undertakes a comprehensive audit process, through a number of phases, before being in the position to express an opinion on a set of financial reports. Figure 6.5 gives an overview of the audit process.

As shown in figure 6.5 (overleaf), it is possible to overview the audit process by looking at it in phases.

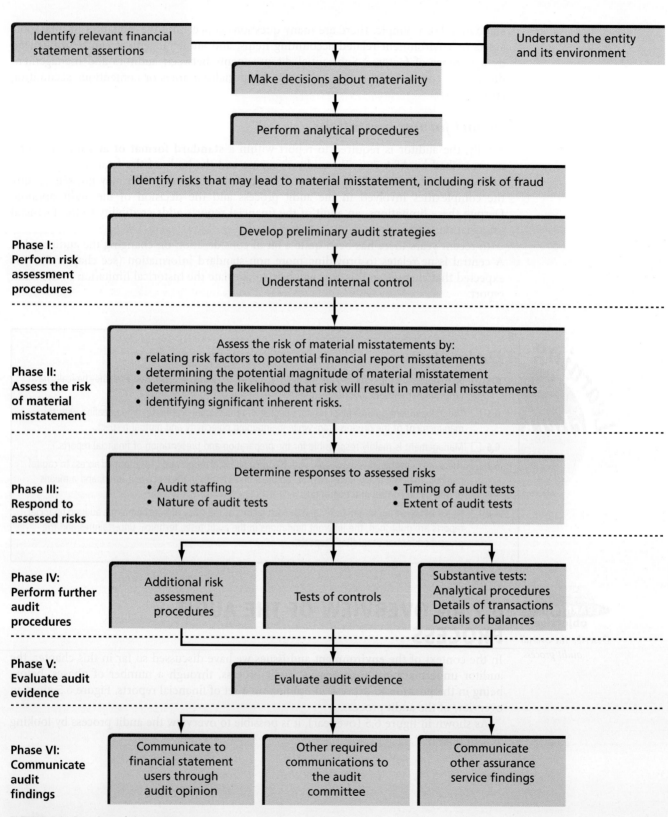

FIGURE 6.5: Overview of the audit process

Phase 1 relates to the performance of risk assessment procedures which include the following.

- *Identifying the relevant financial report assertions.* These assertions relate to existence or occurrence, completeness, rights and obligations, accuracy or valuation and allocation, and presentation and disclosure, and are specifically covered in part 4 of this book. Assertions are important because they help the auditor make decisions about the assessment of risk by considering potential types of misstatements that may occur (e.g. valuation of inventory) and thus design audit procedures that are appropriate to the assertion and the risk assessment.
- *Understanding the entity and its environment.* An understanding of the entity and its environment is fundamental to any audit and includes, for example, industry knowledge and the regulatory environment, the nature of the entity and its accounting policies. These are discussed in detail in chapter 8.
- *Making decisions about materiality.* The concept of materiality guides the auditor in planning the audit and evaluating audit findings. Chapter 10 discusses materiality judgements the auditor has to make and provides practical examples of how auditors make decisions in respect of materiality.
- *Performing analytical procedures.* Analytical procedures involve evaluating financial information by considering plausible relationships among both financial and non-financial data, and are discussed in chapters 8 and 9.
- *Identifying risks* that may result in misstatements and developing audit strategies to overcome them — including evaluation of the internal control system — are part of performing risk assessment procedures that are discussed in chapters 9, 10 and 11.

Phase II in figure 6.5 relates to the assessment of the risk of material misstatement such as a major understatement of expenses or overvaluation of inventory. This area of risk assessment is discussed in chapters 8 and 9. It is also linked to auditing transactions and balances discussed in part 4 of this book.

Phase III considers how the auditor responds to the assessed risks, which determines the nature, timing and extent of audit tests, together with consideration of the underlying inherent risks in the entity being audited. These issues are covered in parts 3 and 4 of this book.

Phase IV relates to the performance of further audit procedures, including tests of controls and substantive testing, covered in chapters 11 and 12 respectively. Phases V and VI relate to the evaluation of evidence and communication of audit findings, which are covered in chapters 7, 10 and 18.

The auditor's task, therefore, is to obtain reasonable assurance that the financial reports being audited are free of material misstatements. It is not feasible to audit every transaction and thus the auditor needs to decide what will be tested. The phases discussed above provide an overview on how the auditor undertakes such a task, while balancing risks, materiality and a range of other factors.

SUMMARY

This chapter explains the important process by which auditors get appointed and the controls to ensure that this process happens as soon as a company begins operations. The Corporations Act outlines many of the requirements as part of this process and also outlines many of the duties and responsibilities of the financial report auditor. Other professional duties, including the duty to use reasonable care and skill (see chapter 5) and the duty to be independent (see chapter 3), are key duties expected of the auditor.

Australian auditing standards (ASAs) provide the main guidance for the auditor in the conduct of an audit, and are prepared by the AUASB based on the international standards issued by the IAASB. Users of financial reports look to the auditors for assurance that the financial information meets the qualitative characteristics of relevance and reliability, and that the financial reports taken as a whole are presented fairly in accordance with an identified financial reporting framework.

In the course of the audit, the auditor maintains professional relationships with four important groups: the shareholders, the entity's board of directors and audit committee, the internal auditors, and the entity's management. The relationship between accounting and auditing in the financial reporting process involves a basic division of responsibilities between the management of an entity and its independent auditors. Management is responsible for preparing the financial reports in accordance with an identified financial reporting framework, and the auditor is responsible for expressing an opinion on the financial reports in an audit performed in accordance with auditing standards.

While the financial report audit is an important part of the corporate governance and reporting mosaic, it is not perfect. We discuss some of the clear benefits of the audit process as well as some of the limitations.

The chapter concludes by presenting an overview of the audit process and explaining how this process will be considered throughout the text.

KEY TERMS

audit committee, p. 262	management letter, p. 267
auditing standards, p. 268	materiality, p. 268
contractual relationship, p. 253	professional judgement, p. 268
management, p. 263	standard format of auditor's reports, p. 269

MULTIPLE-CHOICE questions

6.1 ASIC may grant audit relief, in certain circumstances, to which of the following types of entity?
A. Large proprietary company.
B. Small proprietary company.
C. Public company.
D. Government company.

6.2 The Corporations Act requires that auditors are competent. To be suitably qualified, the person must:
  (i) Be a member of the ICAA, CPA Australia, Institute of Public Accountants or other prescribed body.
  (ii) Hold a degree, diploma or certificate from a university.
  (iii) Be capable of performing the duties of an auditor and be a fit and proper person to be registered as an auditor.
A. (i) and (ii) only.
B. (i) and (iii) only.
C. (ii) and (iii) only.
D. (i), (ii) and (iii).

6.3 The removal and resignation of auditors must be:
  (i) By resolution of the company.
  (ii) Greater than 75% of the shareholders vote in agreement.
  (iii) With special notice to ASIC for its consent.
A. (i) and (ii) only.
B. (i) and (iii) only.
C. (ii) and (iii) only.
D. (i), (ii) and (iii).

6.4 Section 308 of the Corporations Act requires certain implied conditions to be reported on if there is any deficiency or failure to comply. Which of the following is one of those implied conditions?
A. Whether the auditor has obtained all information, explanations and assistance required.
B. Whether an audit has been carried out.
C. Whether the auditor is independent of the company.
D. Whether the financial reports are properly drawn up so as to give a true and fair view of the company's financial affairs.

6.5 Which of the following is *not* a duty of an independent auditor?
A. To be independent.
B. To detect all fraud.
C. To use reasonable care and skill.
D. To report to shareholders.

6.6 The objective of the standard report format is to:
  (i) State clearly the level of assurance provided by the opinion.
  (ii) Differentiate clearly the responsibilities of the auditor and management in the audit.
  (iii) Communicate the work done by the auditor and limitations of the audit.
A. (i) and (ii) only.
B. (i) and (iii) only.
C. (ii) and (iii) only.
D. (i), (ii) and (iii).

6.7 The role of the AUASB in relation to International Standards on Auditing (ISAs) is to:
   A. Apply all ISAs to the Australian environment.
   B. Select ISAs that are appropriate for the Australian environment.
   C. Ignore ISAs and develop Australian auditing standards.
   D. Harmonise Australian auditing standards with ISAs.

6.8 The auditing standards are:
   A. Only mandatory if you are a member of the accounting profession.
   B. A guide on how to conduct an audit.
   C. Legally required to be followed under the Corporations Act.
   D. Necessary for audit committee members to fulfil their responsibilities.

6.9 The internal auditor is:
   A. Appointed by the shareholders.
   B. A substitute for the independent auditor's work.
   C. A component of an entity's control environment.
   D. Always a qualified accountant.

6.10 The auditor should view management with:
   A. Trust.
   B. Scepticism.
   C. Suspicion.
   D. Indifference.

REVIEW questions

6.11 What are the requirements that must be met in order to become a registered auditor?

6.12 What are the main Corporations Act requirements with regard to the appointment, removal and registration of auditors?

6.13 Why is independence crucial for an external auditor?

6.14 Why must auditors follow Australian auditing standards?

6.15 What are some of the benefits of an effective audit committee?

6.16 How does the relationship that independent auditors have with shareholders compare with their relationship with management?

6.17 What are the benefits of a financial report audit?

6.18 What are the main limitations of a financial report audit?

6.19 What are the duties of an independent auditor engaged to perform a financial report audit?

6.20 What are the different phases in the audit process?

PROFESSIONAL application questions

★
BASIC
★★
MODERATE
★★★
CHALLENGING

6.21 Accounting compared to auditing ★

Many companies are not required to have their financial report audited but they still need to employ accountants.

Required

Compare and contrast accounting and auditing.

6.22 Appointment of auditors ★★

Revglow Ltd, a large proprietary company, was incorporated on 1 July 2015. A short time later, one of the non-shareholding directors, Fred Bile, approached his tax agent, Gina Rogers, to ask her to be Revglow's auditor. Ms Rogers is a chartered accountant, but had not performed any audits and was hesitant about accepting the engagement. Mr Bile said the appointment would be only temporary until proper documentation could be prepared and the audit work put out to tender. Ms Rogers said she would accept this arrangement and Mr Bile prepared a letter confirming the appointment on 21 July 2015.

At its first meeting on 1 September 2015, the board decided to confirm Ms Rogers as the auditor of Revglow for a period of 3 years. They were impressed with the recommendation given by Mr Bile and decided that requesting tenders would be a time-consuming and inefficient process.

Required

Discuss whether the requirements of the Corporations Act have been followed in the above scenario.[4]

6.23 Management and auditor responsibilities ★★

You are a newly qualified accountant who works for the audit firm Fulford & Co. You have been approached by a potential new client, Bishopthorpe Electronics Pty Ltd, who is looking for an audit firm to carry out an audit on its annual financial report prepared in accordance with the Corporations Act. The managing director, Bob Fleming, is not sure exactly what an audit involves and what are the responsibilities of the auditor.

Required

Prepare notes for a meeting with Bob Fleming which identifies the responsibilities of the auditor and the responsibilities of management.

Your notes should cover the following points:

- Distribution of the annual report to shareholders.
- Delivery of the audit report to the entity.
- Obtaining and evaluating evidence concerning the financial report.
- Preparation and presentation of the financial report.
- Maintaining adequate internal controls.
- Testing internal control procedures.
- Expressing an opinion on the financial report.
- Selecting appropriate accounting policies.
- Ensuring the financial report is presented in accordance with standards.

6.24 Removal of an auditor ★★

On 31 March 2014, Black and Black (a firm of certified practising accountants) completed the audit of E-Wine Pty Ltd for the year ended 31 December 2013. E-Wine is a wine store that operates solely on the internet. On 15 May 2014, Tom Black (the audit partner responsible for E-Wine) received a phone call from the financial controller of E-Wine, Ms Chong, who was very angry. Ms Chong said that their accounts receivable clerk suddenly resigned a month ago. This sudden departure raised suspicions and, after an investigation of the accounting records, it was discovered that $200 000 was missing. Subsequently, the board met and decided Black and Black was almost entirely to blame. As a result, Ms Chong said the board had decided to dismiss Black and Black as auditors, effective immediately. Black and Black would receive written confirmation in the next week and legal action would probably follow.

Required

(a) Explain whether E-Wine has taken the proper action to remove its auditor.
(b) Explain why restrictions are placed on removing auditors.

6.25 Statutory and professional duties ★★

You are an audit senior working in a Big Four accountancy practice in Australia. It is April and not long until the 'busy' season, which generally starts from about May. A number of audit managers and seniors will come from the United Kingdom on secondment for the Australian busy season.

Your audit partner notes that you do not have much work at the moment and he suggests that you prepare a memo for the new UK arrivals to help their acclimatisation into the Australian audit environment. He wants the following outlined in the memo:

- statutory duties to report, as outlined in the Corporations Act
- a discussion of the purpose of Australian auditing standards.

Required

Prepare the memo as requested by the audit partner.

6.26 Harmonisation of auditing standards ★★

Australia made a decision to harmonise its auditing standards with the ISAs issued by the IAASB. Since 2006, the AUASB has been issuing ASAs based on the ISAs. In relation to the Clarity project where the Clarity format ISAs were used as the underlying auditing standards for the ASAs, the underlying standards could only be amended from the equivalent ISA due to one of three reasons:

1. where the ASA must address Australian legal and/or regulatory requirements
2. where the ASA must comply with Australian legislative instrument requirements
3. where the ASA needs to address 'additional public interest' matters.

Required

Given how closely Australian auditing standards are to ISAs, discuss the pros and cons of setting *separate* Australian auditing standards.

6.27 Audit committees ★★★

You work for a mid-sized audit firm, Green & Co. One of your clients, Wedford Ltd, recently established an audit committee in compliance with the Australian Securities Exchange listing requirements. The committee is made up of Francis Carton, Jo Pashtoon and Charles Digson.

Francis is an executive of the company and has worked his way up from a factory worker through to management. Francis is the chairperson of the audit committee.

Jo is not a member of management and is therefore a non-executive director, but she does serve on a number of other boards. Jo's background is in accounting and before she became a director she was the CFO of a large corporation for many years.

Charles is the chairperson of the board of directors and is an executive of the company. Charles' background is in manufacturing and he has been with Wedford Ltd for 5 years.

The committee has drafted a charter which details its rights and responsibilities. This will include the committee's interactions with the newly formed internal audit department. The board would like to discuss with you the relationship between your firm as external auditors, the internal audit team and the audit committee.

Required

Prepare a report for the board, covering the following matters:
(a) Outline the objectives of an audit committee.
(b) Discuss the interaction between the audit committee and both the internal and external audit functions.
(c) Identify the strengths and weaknesses of Wedford Ltd's audit committee.
(d) Recommend terms of reference for the committee.

6.28 Auditor rotation ★★★

Audit independence has been important issue, particularly over the past ten years. A number of the requirements associated with auditor appointment and removal are to enhance the independence of the audit process. An auditing academic was heard to make the following statement:

> True audit independence can never be achieved! Auditors operate in a commercial environment and need to work to win the audit of a client. The ongoing fees that they receive are then obviously conditional on management's approval. If management is unhappy with the auditor they will find a way to get rid of them — it is as simple as that. Perhaps a solution could be to give the role of appointing auditors to ASIC? They could allocate auditors to the top 300 listed companies and give them a fixed term audit for five years. Then they would reallocate auditors to those companies. Auditors would not have to compromise their independence to win the client or keep the client. It is a brilliant idea — even if I do say so myself!

Required
Discuss the academic's proposal.

 CASE study

6.29   Corporate governance and the audit role   ★★
Outlined below is an extract from the Qantas Corporate Governance Statement issued in 2012:[5]

The Board safeguards the integrity of financial reporting

Audit Committee
The Board has an Audit Committee which:
- has four Members who are Independent Non-Executive Directors
- is chaired by Garry Hounsell, an Independent Non-Executive Director who is a Fellow of The Institute of Chartered Accountants in Australia and a Certified Practising Accountant
- has a written Charter which is available in the Corporate Governance section on the Qantas website
- includes Members who are all financially literate
- is responsible for assisting the Board in fulfilling its corporate governance responsibilities in relation to:
  - the integrity of the Qantas Group's financial reporting
  - compliance with legal and regulatory obligations
  - the effectiveness of the Qantas Group's enterprise-wide risk management and internal control framework
  - oversight of the independence of the external and internal auditors.

The experience and qualifications of Members of the Audit Committee are detailed on pages 12 to 15. Membership of and attendance at 2011/2012 Audit Committee Meetings are detailed on page 37.

The Board and Audit Committee closely monitor the independence of the external auditor. Regular reviews occur of the independence safeguards put in place by the external auditor. As required by section 300(11D)(a) of the Corporations Act and the Audit Committee Charter, the Audit Committee has advised the Board that it is appropriate for the following statement to be included in the 2012 Directors' Report under the heading 'Non-audit Services':

'The Directors are satisfied that:

a.   The non-audit services provided during the 2011/2012 financial year by KPMG as the external auditor were compatible with the general standard of independence for auditors imposed by the Corporations Act 2001

b. Any non-audit services provided during the 2011/2012 financial year by KPMG as the external auditor did not compromise the auditor independence requirements of the Corporations Act 2001 for the following reasons:

- KPMG services have not involved partners or staff acting in a managerial or decision-making capacity within the Qantas Group or being involved in the processing or originating of transactions
- KPMG non-audit services have only been provided where Qantas is satisfied that the related function or process will not have a material bearing on the audit procedures
- KPMG partners and staff involved in the provision of non-audit services have not participated in associated approval or authorisation processes
- A description of all non-audit services undertaken by KPMG and the related fees have been reported to the Board to ensure complete transparency in relation to the services provided
- The declaration required by section 307C of the Corporations Act 2001 confirming independence has been received from KPMG.'

Qantas rotates the lead audit partner every five years and imposes restrictions on the employment of personnel previously employed by the external auditor.

Policies are in place to restrict the type of non-audit services which can be provided by the external auditor and a detailed review of non-audit fees paid to the external auditor is undertaken on a quarterly basis.

At each meeting, the Audit Committee meets privately with Executive Management without the external auditor, and with the internal and external auditors without Executive Management.

Internal Audit

The internal audit function is carried out by Group Audit and Risk and is independent of the external auditor. Group Audit and Risk provides independent, objective assurance and consulting services on Qantas' system of risk management, internal control and governance through:

- maintaining and improving the risk management framework as approved by the Board
- bi-annual risk reporting to the Board
- performing audits and other advisory services to assure risk management throughout the Qantas Group.

Group Audit and Risk adopts a risk-based approach in formulating its audit plan to align audit activities to the key risks across the Qantas Group. The audit plan is approved by the Audit Committee bi-annually and submitted to the Safety, Health, Environment and Security Committee for information and approval where appropriate.

The Audit Committee approves the Group Audit and Risk Internal Audit Charter which provides Group Audit and Risk with full access to Qantas Group functions, records, property and personnel, and establishes independence requirements. The Audit Committee also approves the appointment or replacement of the internal auditor. The internal auditor has a direct reporting line to the Audit Committee and also provides reporting to the Safety, Health, Environment and Security Committee.

In addition to Group Audit and Risk, operationally focussed business units within the Qantas Group have their own internal audit functions to provide assurance to accountable managers on the effectiveness of operational risk management and compliance. The findings from these audit activities, along with the status of audit management actions, are reported through operational safety governance structures and to the Safety, Health, Environment and Security Committee.

Required

Outline seven key strengths of this policy and explain why each one will help the independent auditor do his or her work.

RESEARCH question

6.30 Auditing standards and audit quality

A report by the Institute of Chartered Accountants in England and Wales (ICAEW) made the following statement in relation to the question: 'How do rules affect judgement, integrity and consistency in the conduct of the audit?'[6]

> Behind the view that auditors need more rules on how to do their jobs lies a lack of trust in the use of judgement by auditors and a lack of experience and confidence on the part of some regulators. It will take time to change this but rules do not necessarily reduce, and certainly do not eliminate, the need for judgement and integrity. Nor do rules necessarily promote consistency. In standards that are more rules-based, the role of judgement and the need for integrity are simply transferred, in part, to the application of those rules. Current auditing standards do not require more procedures and less judgement than before, but more procedures and more judgement.

Required
(a) Are Australian auditing standards 'principles-based' or 'rules-based'?
(b) Which of these two approaches will improve audit quality?

FURTHER READING

AUASB, AICD and IIA, *Audit Committees — A Guide to Good Practice*, 2009.

ASX Corporate Governance Principles and Recommendations, September 2007, www.asx.com.au.

FL Clarke, GW Dean & KG Oliver, *Corporate Collapse: Regulatory, Accounting and Ethical Failure*, rev. edn, Cambridge University Press, Melbourne, 2003.

Institute of Chartered Accountants in England and Wales (ICAEW), *Principles-Based Auditing Standards*, ICAEW, London, 2006.

Institute of Chartered Accountants in England and Wales (ICAEW), *Third Parties*, ICAEW, London, 2007.

P Lipton & A Herzberg, *Understanding Company Law*, 11th edn, LBC Information Services, Sydney, 2003.

NOTES

1. The number of standards was based on the number in the *Auditing and Assurance Handbook 2010*.

2. Recommendation 2.1. ASX Corporate Governance Council, *Corporate Governance Principles and Recommendations*, 2nd ed., Sydney, 2007.

3. KT Trotman, *Research Methodology for Judgement and Decision-making Studies in Auditing*, Coopers & Lybrand and the AAANZ, Melbourne, 1996.

4. Adapted from the Professional Year Programme of the ICAA.

5. Qantas, Annual Report 2012, 'Corporate Governance Statement', 2012, pp. 31, 32–3.

6. ICAEW, *Audit Quality. Fundamentals — Principles-based Auditing Standards*, p. 5, 2006.

Answers to multiple-choice questions

6.1 *B*   6.2 *D*   6.3 *B*   6.4 *A*   6.5 *B*   6.6 *D*   6.7 *D*   6.8 *C*   6.9 *C*   6.10 *B*

chapter 7

The auditor's report

OVERVIEW

7.1 Standards of reporting

7.2 The auditor's report and communication with management

7.3 Other reporting considerations for corporate entities

Summary

Key terms

Multiple-choice questions

Review questions

Professional application questions

Case studies

Research question

Further reading

Notes

LEARNING objectives

After studying this chapter, you should be able to:

1 outline the reporting standards for a financial statement audit

2 explain what is stated in the audit opinion of an auditor's report

3 describe the other reporting considerations for corporate entities.

PROFESSIONAL STATEMENTS

Australian		International	
AASB 134	*Interim Financial Reporting*	**IAS 34**	*Interim Financial Reporting*
ASA 200	*Overall Objectives of the Independent Auditor and the Conduct of an Audit in Accordance with Australian Auditing Standards*	**ISA 200**	*Overall Objective of the Independent Auditor and the Conduct of an Audit in Accordance with International Standards on Auditing*
ASA 210	*Agreeing the Terms of Audit Engagements*	**ISA 210**	*Agreeing the Terms of Audit Engagements*
ASA 260	*Communication with Those Charged with Governance*	**ISA 260**	*Communication with Those Charged with Governance*
ASA 450	*Evaluation of Misstatements Identified during the Audit*	**ISA 450**	*Evaluation of Misstatements Identified during the Audit*
ASA 510	*Initial Audit Engagements — Opening Balances*	**ISA 510**	*Initial Audit Engagements — Opening Balances*
ASA 560	*Subsequent Events*	**ISA 560**	*Subsequent Events*
ASA 570	*Going Concern*	**ISA 570**	*Going Concern*
ASA 700	*Forming an Opinion and Reporting on a Financial Report*	**ISA 700**	*Forming an Opinion and Reporting on Financial Statements*
ASA 705	*Modifications to the Opinion in the Independent Auditor's Report*	**ISA 705**	*Modifications to the Opinion in the Independent Auditor's Report*
ASA 706	*Emphasis of Matter Paragraphs and Other Matter Paragraphs in the Independent Auditor's Report*	**ISA 706**	*Emphasis of Matter Paragraphs and Other Matter Paragraphs in the Independent Auditor's Report*
ASA 710	*Comparative Information — Corresponding Figures and Comparative Financial Reports*	**ISA 710**	*Comparative Information — Corresponding Figures and Comparative Financial Statements*
ASA 720	*The Auditor's Responsibilities Relating to Other Information in Documents Containing an Audited Financial Report*	**ISA 720**	*The Auditor's Responsibilities Relating to Other Information in Documents Containing Audited Financial Statements*
ASA 800	*Special Considerations — Audits of Financial Reports Prepared in Accordance with Special Purpose Frameworks*	**ISA 800**	*Special Considerations — Audits of Financial Statements Prepared in Accordance with Special Purpose Frameworks*
ASRE 2410	*Review of a Financial Report Performed by the Independent Auditor of the Entity*	**ISRE 2410**	*Review of Interim Financial Information Performed by the Independent Auditor of the Entity*
GS 001	*Concise Financial Reports*		
GS 006	*Electronic Publication of the Auditor's Report*		
GS 008	*The Auditor's Report on a Remuneration Report Pursuant to Section 300A of the Corporations Act 2001*		

How do users perceive auditor's reports?

The message conveyed in auditor's reports has long been misunderstood by users and has been part of the reason for the audit expectation gap. In recent years standard setters have attempted to change the auditor's report to improve its communicative value. In an Invitation to Comment in 2012, Professor Arnold Schilder [Chairman of the International Auditing and Assurance Standards Board (IAASB)] made the following statements:[1]

More than ever before, however, users of audited financial statements are calling for more pertinent information for their decision-making in today's global business environment with increasingly complex financial reporting requirements.

Further he went on to say:

... the auditor's report should better explain what an auditor does and enable the auditor to shine light on key matters based on the auditor's work.

In 2013, an Exposure Draft was issued by the IAASB that proposed major changes to the way in which auditors report. If these changes go through as expected in late 2014, the IAASB anticipates this new report to be effective for reporting periods ending from 31 December 2016.

Source: International Auditing and Assurance Standards Board (IAASB) 2012, *Invitation to Comment: Improving the Auditor's Report,* New York, International Federation of Accountants, June, p. 1.

The final phase of the auditing process is reporting the findings. The audit report is the key communication tool by the auditor in respect of the auditing process that has been undertaken. The above excerpt demonstrates the diverse usage and perceptions of the audit report. This chapter expands the explanation of the auditor's report provided in chapter 6.

LEARNING 1 objective

Outline the reporting standards for a financial statement audit.

7.1 STANDARDS OF REPORTING

In providing an understanding of the standards required for an auditor's report, we must reiterate the underlying concepts in financial reports. A general purpose financial report means a financial report prepared in accordance with a general purpose framework. A general purpose framework means a financial report framework that is designed to meet the common financial information needs of a wide range of users. The general purpose financial reporting framework may be a **fair presentation framework** or a **compliance framework**.

ASA 700 *Forming an Opinion and Reporting on a Financial Report* (ISA 700) describes a fair presentation framework as a financial reporting framework that, in addition to compliance with the requirements of the framework, includes acknowledgements, explicitly or implicitly, that to achieve fair presentation it may be necessary for management to provide disclosures beyond the required framework. In the case where it is necessary to depart from a requirement of the framework, an explicit acknowledgement is required. On the other hand, a compliance framework is used to refer to a financial report framework that requires compliance with the requirements only, and does not contain any of the above acknowledgements.

The main features of ASA 700 are that it establishes mandatory requirements and provides explanatory guidance on:

- the form and content of the auditor's report on a general purpose financial report prepared in accordance with an applicable financial reporting framework designed to achieve either fair presentation or compliance
- matters the auditor usually considers in forming an opinion on the financial report
- the auditor's reporting on other reporting responsibilities in addition to the auditor's opinion on the financial report
- the auditor's performance and reporting responsibilities when the audit has been conducted in accordance with Australian auditing standards and international auditing standards
- the auditor's responsibilities regarding supplementary information included with the financial report that is not required by the financial reporting framework.

When an entity, in accordance with AASB 101 *Presentation of Financial Statements*, has included in the notes to the financial statements, an explicit and unreserved statement of compliance with international financial reporting standards (IFRSs), and the auditor agrees with the entity's statement of compliance, the auditor shall state that in the auditor's opinion, the financial report complies with IFRSs. ASA 700 provides illustrations of an auditor's opinion in various forms in Appendix 1. This is outlined in table 7.1.

TABLE 7.1:
Examples of an auditor's opinion from ASA 700

Illustration number	Example
1	An auditor's report on a financial report prepared in accordance with a fair presentation framework
1A	An auditor's report on a single entity's financial report prepared in accordance with a fair presentation framework under the *Corporations Act 2001*
2	An auditor's report on a complete set of financial statements prepared in accordance with a compliance framework
3	An auditor's report on a consolidated entity's financial report prepared in accordance with a fair presentation framework
3A	An example of an auditor's report on a consolidated entity's financial report prepared in accordance with a fair presentation framework under the *Corporations Act 2001*.

It should be noted that a financial report is a complete set of general purpose financial statements, including the related notes and an assertion statement by those responsible for the financial report.

7.1.1 Financial statements

The financial statements on which an auditor reports constitute part of a **general purpose external financial report**. The disclosure and presentation requirements for such reports are generally determined by **accounting standards** and statutory and other requirements. The *Corporations Act 2001* outlines the contents of a financial report (s. 295), including:

- the financial statements for the year required by accounting standards such as AASB 101, including:
  - an income statement (in Australian accounting standards, this is also known as a statement of comprehensive income)
  - a balance sheet (known in Australian accounting standards as a statement of financial position)
  - a cash flow statement (called a statement of cash flows in Australian accounting standards)
  - a statement of changes in equity
- notes to the financial statements, including:
  - disclosures required by regulations
  - notes required by accounting standards
  - any other information necessary to give a **true and fair view** (see s. 297)
- the directors' declaration that:
  - the financial statements and notes comply with accounting standards
  - the financial statements and notes give a true and fair view
  - in the directors' opinion, there are reasonable grounds to believe that the company will be able to pay its debts as and when they become due and payable
  - in the directors' opinion, the financial statements and notes are in accordance with the law.

7.1.2 Accounting standards

The auditor is mainly commenting on whether the financial statements are in accordance with accounting standards issued by the Australian Accounting Standards Board (AASB) that have the force of law. The AASB accounting standards are required standards for reporting entities that are companies by virtue of the Corporations Act (s. 334). Australian accounting standards are, as far as possible, compatible with international accounting standards (IASs).

7.1.3 Relevant statutory and other requirements

Where the audit is being conducted in accordance with statutory and other requirements such as the Corporations Act in Australia, the auditor usually has an additional responsibility to report on compliance with relevant sections of the regulations or statutory requirements. Reporting on such matters may be explicit or on an exception basis. The opinion on such requirements may be separated from the opinion on fair presentation in accordance with accounting standards and mandatory professional reporting requirements — that is, the report may be qualified with respect to other requirements, but unqualified as to presentation (or vice versa). Auditors are required to form an opinion on the following requirements:

- the financial statements are in accordance with the law, comply with accounting standards and give a true and fair view
- all information, explanation and assistance necessary for the conduct of the audit have been provided
- the financial records have been kept to enable the preparation and audit of the financial statements
- the records and registers have been kept as required by law.

The financial statements on which the auditor is to report include the directors' declaration (s. 295). In reaching an opinion on the financial statements, the auditor will need to review the contents of this declaration as noted above.

LEARNING 2
objective

Explain what is stated in the audit opinion of an auditor's report.

7.2 THE AUDITOR'S REPORT AND COMMUNICATION WITH MANAGEMENT

The auditor's report is the auditor's formal means of communicating to interested parties a conclusion about the audited financial information. In issuing an audit opinion on a general-purpose financial report, the auditor must comply with ASA 700.

7.2.1 Forming an opinion

The auditor is required to form an opinion on whether the financial report is prepared, in all material aspects, in accordance with the applicable financial reporting framework. The auditor needs to conclude that they have obtained reasonable assurance about the financial report as a whole, and that it is free from material misstatement, either due to error or fraud. The auditor takes into consideration a number of factors, including whether:

- sufficient audit evidence has been obtained, with special reference to the needs to address audit risks
- any uncorrected misstatements are material, either individually or in aggregate
- in all material aspects, that the requirements of an applicable financial reporting framework have been met, with the consideration of the qualitative aspects of accounting practices, including any indicators of management bias
- the financial report adequately discloses the significant accounting policies selected and applied
- the accounting policies applied are consistent with the applicable financial reporting framework and are appropriate
- the estimates made by management are reasonable
- the information presented in the financial report is relevant, reliable, comparable and understandable
- adequate disclosures to enable the intended users to understand the effect of material transactions and events have been conveyed adequately
- the terminology used in the financial report, including the title of each financial statement, is appropriate, including whether the financial report adequately refers to or describes the applicable financial reporting framework.

Where the fair presentation framework is used, the auditor should also ensure the financial report achieves fair presentation by the consideration of the overall presentation, structure, and content of the financial report, and whether the financial report, including the related notes, represents the underlying transactions and events in a manner that achieves fair presentation.

7.2.2 Expression of opinion

As stated in ASA 200 *Overall Objectives of the Independent Auditor and the Conduct of an Audit in Accordance with Australian Auditing Standards* (ISA 200), the overall objectives of an audit of a financial report are:

(a) to obtain reasonable assurance about whether the financial report as a whole is free from material misstatement, whether due to fraud or error, thereby enabling the auditor to express an opinion on whether the financial report is prepared, in all material respects, in accordance with an applicable financial reporting framework

(b) to report on the financial report, and communicate as required by the Australian Auditing Standards, in accordance with the auditor's findings.

The auditor's report must clearly express the auditor's opinion on the financial report in terms of the above. In Australia, the applicable financial reporting framework means the financial reporting framework adopted by management and where appropriate, those charged with governance in the preparation of the financial report, that is acceptable in view of the nature of the entity and the objective of the financial report, or that is required by law or regulation. They can include the fair presentation framework or the compliance framework.

Unless required by law or regulation to use different wording, the auditor's opinion on a general-purpose financial report prepared in accordance with a financial reporting framework that is designed to achieve fair presentation shall state whether the financial report 'gives a true and fair view' or 'presents fairly, in all material respects,' in accordance with the applicable financial reporting framework.

As part of the Clarity framework, the AUASB also produces Guidance Statements. The most recent Guidance Statements, GS 006 *Electronic Publication of the Auditor's Report* and GS 008 *The Auditor's Report on a Remuneration Report Pursuant to Section 300A of the Corporations Act 2001*, have direct relevance to the form and content of the auditor's report. Section 308(3C) of the Corporations Act requires that, if the directors' report for the financial year includes a remuneration report, the auditor must report also to members on whether the auditor is of the opinion that the remuneration report complies with s. 300A of the Act. If not of that opinion, the auditor's report must state why. This requirement to express a distinct opinion on the remuneration report in the directors' report is in addition to the auditor's responsibility to express an opinion on the financial report. This should be reported in a separate paragraph of the auditor's report following the opinion paragraph, in order to clearly distinguish them from the primary responsibility to express an opinion on the financial report.

7.2.3 Unmodified auditor's report

An **unmodified auditor's report** is the most common type of report (opinion) issued. It contains an unmodified (unqualified) opinion that the financial report presents fairly, in all material respects, in accordance with the applicable financial reporting framework; or the financial report gives a true and fair view of the financial position and the results of operations and cash flows of the entity in accordance with the applicable financial reporting framework. Where a compliance framework is used, the financial report is prepared in all material respects, in accordance with the applicable financial reporting framework.

If the reference to the applicable financial reporting framework in the opinion of the auditor is not to the Australian accounting standards, and, where applicable, Australian law or regulation, the auditor's opinion shall identify the jurisdiction of origin of the framework. If the entity has included in the notes to the financial statements an explicit and unreserved statement of compliance with international financial reporting standards (IFRSs) and where the auditor agrees with the statement of compliance, the auditor shall state that in their opinion the financial report complies with IFRSs.

If the auditor addresses other reporting responsibilities in the report that are in addition to the responsibility under the Australian auditing standards, these other reporting responsibilities shall be addressed in a separate section in the report that is subtitled 'Report on Other Legal and Regulatory Requirements', or otherwise as appropriate. Figure 7.1 provides an example of an independent auditor's report for a single company that reports under the Corporations Act.

FIGURE 7.1: Example of an unmodified auditor's report

INDEPENDENT AUDITOR'S REPORT

[Appropriate Addressee]

Report on the financial report*

We have audited the accompanying financial report of ABC Company Ltd, which comprises the statement of financial position as at 30 June 20X1, the statement of comprehensive income, statement of changes in equity and statement of cash flows for the year then ended, notes comprising a summary of significant accounting policies and other explanatory information, and the directors' declaration.

Directors' Responsibility for the Financial Report

The directors of the company [registered scheme/disclosing entity] are responsible for the preparation of the financial report that gives a true and fair view in accordance with Australian Accounting Standards and the *Corporations Act 2001* and for such internal control as the directors determine is necessary to enable the preparation of the financial report that is free from material misstatement, whether due to fraud or error. In Note XX, the directors also state, in accordance with Accounting Standard AASB 101 *Presentation of Financial Statements*, that the financial statements comply with *International Financial Reporting Standards*.**

Auditor's Responsibility

Our responsibility is to express an opinion on the financial report based on our audit. We conducted our audit in accordance with Australian Auditing Standards. Those standards require that we comply with relevant ethical requirements relating to audit engagements and plan and perform the audit to obtain reasonable assurance about whether the financial report is free from material misstatement.

An audit involves performing procedures to obtain audit evidence about the amounts and disclosures in the financial report. The procedures selected depend on the auditor's judgement, including the assessment of the risks of material misstatement of the financial report, whether due to fraud or error. In making those risk assessments, the auditor considers internal control relevant to the entity's preparation of the financial report that gives a true and fair view in order to design audit procedures that are appropriate in the circumstances, but not for the purpose of expressing an opinion on the effectiveness of the entity's internal control. An audit also includes evaluating the appropriateness of accounting policies used and the reasonableness of accounting estimates made by the directors, as well as evaluating the overall presentation of the financial report.

We believe that the audit evidence we have obtained is sufficient and appropriate to provide a basis for our audit opinion.

Independence

In conducting our audit, we have complied with the independence requirements of the *Corporations Act 2001*. We confirm that the independence declaration required by the *Corporations Act 2001*, which has been given to the directors of ABC Company Ltd., would be in the same terms if given to the directors as at the time of this auditor's report.*

---

* The sub-title "Report on the Financial Report" is unnecessary in circumstances when the second sub-title "Report on Other Legal and Regulatory Requirements", or other appropriate sub-title, is not applicable.

** Insert only where the entity has included in the notes to the financial statements an explicit and unreserved statement of compliance with *International Financial Reporting Standards* in accordance with AASB 101.

* Or, alternatively, include statements (a) to the effect that circumstances have changed since the declaration was given to the relevant directors; and (b) setting out how the declaration would differ if it had been given to the relevant directors at the time the auditor's report was made.

(continued)

Opinion

In our opinion:

(a) the financial report of ABC Company Ltd. is in accordance with the *Corporations Act 2001*, including:

   (i) giving a true and fair view of the company's [registered scheme's/disclosing entity's] financial position as at 30 June 20X1 and of its performance for the year ended on that date; and

   (ii) complying with Australian Accounting Standards and the *Corporations Regulations 2001;* and

(b) the financial report also complies with *International Financial Reporting Standards* as disclosed in Note XX.†

Report on the Remuneration Report§

We have audited the Remuneration Report included in [paragraphs a to b or pages x to y] of the directors' report for the year ended 30 June 20X1. The directors of the company are responsible for the preparation and presentation of the Remuneration Report in accordance with section 300A of the *Corporations Act 2001*. Our responsibility is to express an opinion on the Remuneration Report, based on our audit conducted in accordance with Australian Auditing Standards.

Opinion

In our opinion, the Remuneration Report of ABC Company Ltd. for the year [period] ended 30 June 20X1 complies with section 300A of the *Corporations Act 2001*.

[Auditor's signature]**

[Date of the auditor's report]#

[Auditor's address]

---

† Insert only where the entity has included in the notes to the financial statements an explicit and unreserved statement of compliance with *International Financial Reporting Standards* in accordance with AASB 101 and the auditor agrees with the entity's statement. If the auditor does not agree with the statement, the auditor refers to ASA 705.

§ The Report on the Remuneration Report is an example of 'Other Reporting Responsibilities' — refer paragraphs 38 and 39. Any additional 'Other Reporting Responsibilities' that the auditor needs to address will also be included in a separate section of the auditor's report following the opinion paragraph on the financial report. Under paragraph 38, the sub-title "Report on Other Legal and Regulatory Requirements" or other sub-title as appropriate to the section is used.

** The auditor's report needs to be signed in one or more of the following ways: name of the audit firm, the of the audit company or the personal name of the auditor as appropriate.

The date of the auditor's report is the date the auditor signs the report.

Source: ASA 700 *Forming an Opinion and Reporting on a Financial Report,* Example Auditor's Report Single Company — *Corporations Act 2001* (Fair Presentation Framework) pp. 685–6.

PROFESSIONAL ENVIRONMENT
The new auditor's report

*I*n July 2013, the most significant change to auditor's reports in the past 80 years was proposed by the IAASB. The changes are contained within the Exposure Draft titled *Reporting on Audited Financial Statements: Proposed New and Revised International Standards on Auditing.* Within this Exposure Draft are a number of new ISAs. The new ISAs and their main changes are noted below (from the IAASB Explanatory Memorandum):

The proposed ISAs, and the key enhancements to auditor reporting, are:	
Proposed ISA 700 (Revised), *Forming an Opinion and Reporting on Financial Statements*	Revisions to establish new required reporting elements, including a requirement for the auditor to include an explicit statement of auditor independence and disclose the source(s) of relevant ethical requirements, and to illustrate these new elements in example auditor's reports.

The proposed ISAs, and the key enhancements to auditor reporting, are:	
Proposed ISA 701, *Communicating Key Audit Matters in the Independent Auditor's Report*	New standard to establish requirements and guidance for the auditor's determination and communication of key audit matters. Key audit matters, which are selected from matters communicated with those charged with governance, are required to be communicated in auditor's reports for audits of financial statements of listed entities. Auditors of financial statements of entities other than listed entities may also be required, or may decide, to communicate key audit matters in the auditor's report.
Proposed ISA 260 (Revised), *Communication with Those Charged with Governance*	In light of proposed ISA 701, amendments to the required auditor communications with those charged with governance, for example, to include communication about the significant risks identified by the auditor.
Proposed ISA 570 (Revised), *Going Concern*	Amendments to establish auditor reporting requirements relating to going concern, and to illustrate this reporting within the auditor's report in different circumstances.
Proposed ISA 705 (Revised), *Modifications to the Opinion in the Independent Auditor's Report*	Amendments to clarify how the new required reporting elements of proposed ISA 700 (Revised) are affected when the auditor expresses a modified opinion, and to update the illustrative auditor's reports accordingly.
Proposed ISA 706 (Revised), *Emphasis of Matter Paragraphs and Other Matter Paragraphs in the Independent Auditor's Report*	Amendments to clarify the relationship between emphasis of matter paragraphs, other matter paragraphs and the key audit matters section of the auditor's report.
Proposed conforming amendments to other ISAs	Conforming amendments related to communicating key audit matters

Other changes from these proposed amendments are as follows.
- Prominent placement of the auditor's opinion and entity specific information in the auditor's report.
- Disclosure of the name of the engagement partner for audits of listed entities, with a 'harm's way' exemption. (Note: this disclosure has occurred for many years in Australia.)
- Improved description of the responsibilities of the auditor and key features of the audit — with the option of inclusion of an appendix to the auditor's report or reference to a website.

However, it seems clear that the two most significant changes are the introduction of 'key audit matters' and a more explicit statement on going concern.

Key audit matters
Key audit matters — Those matters that, in the auditor's professional judgment, were of most significance in the audit of the financial statements of the current period. Key audit matters are selected from matters communicated with those charged with governance. (Proposed ISA 701, para. 7)

There is some guidance on key audit matter selection in para. 8 of the Proposed ISA 701 as noted below.
(a) Areas identified as significant risks in accordance with ISA 315 or involving significant auditor judgment.
(b) Areas in which the auditor encountered significant difficulty during the audit, including with respect to obtaining sufficient appropriate audit evidence.

(c) Circumstances that required significant modification of the auditor's planned approach to the audit, including as a result of the identification of a significant deficiency in internal control.

The key audit matter should refer to the related disclosure in the financial statements. However, the auditor's report disclosure should not just reiterate what is in the financial statements. It will be necessary for the auditor to explain more about why it was considered to be significant.

The number of key audit matters to be communicated is not specified and it is even possible that it be 'none', although this would need to be explained in the auditor's report. A couple of examples of issues that could be included in key audit matters are shown in the illustrative new auditor's report presented in the Exposure Draft and shown at the end of this Professional Environment.

Going concern

The issue of what assurance auditors do or do not provide on going concern has been a problem for auditors for many years. It has been a significant issue contributing to the audit expectation gap because users think auditors provide more assurance on the company being a going concern than they actually do. Historically, the auditor's report has not addressed going concern unless problems have been identified. However, the new auditor's report will require auditors to report on going concern even when there are no problems, specifically the following should be included in the auditor's report from para. 20 of the Proposed ISA 570.

(a) An explanation of the going concern basis of accounting in the context of the applicable financial reporting framework;

(b) A statement that, as part of the audit of the financial statements, the auditor has concluded that management's use of the going concern basis of accounting in the preparation of the entity's financial statements is appropriate;

(c) A statement that, based on the audit of the financial statements, the auditor has not identified a material uncertainty that may cast significant doubt on the entity's ability to continue as a going concern; and

(d) A statement that neither management nor the auditor can guarantee the entity's ability to continue as a going concern.

An example of what the going concern paragraph might look like is shown in the illustrative new auditor's report.

Outlined below is an illustrative new auditor's report for a listed entity prepared in accordance with a fair presentation framework from the IAASB Exposure Draft (2013).

INDEPENDENT AUDITOR'S REPORT

To the Shareholders of ABC Company [or Other Appropriate Addressee]

Report on the audit of the financial statements

Opinion

In our opinion, the accompanying financial statements present fairly, in all material respects, (or *give a true and fair view of*) the financial position of ABC Company (the Company) as at December 31, 20X1, and (*of*) its financial performance and its cash flows for the year then ended in accordance with International Financial Reporting Standards (IFRSs).

We have audited the financial statements of the Company, which comprise the statement of financial position as at December 31, 20X1, and the statement of comprehensive income, statement of changes in equity and statement of cash flows for the year then ended, and notes to the financial statements, including a summary of significant accounting policies.

Basis for opinion

We conducted our audit in accordance with International Standards on Auditing (ISAs). Our responsibilities under those standards are further described in the *Auditor's Responsibilities for the Audit of the Financial Statements* section of our report. We are independent of the Company within the meaning of [*indicate relevant ethical requirements or applicable law or regulation*] and have fulfilled our other responsibilities under those ethical requirements. We believe that the audit evidence we have obtained is sufficient and appropriate to provide a basis for our opinion.

Key audit matters

Key audit matters are those matters that, in our professional judgment, were of most significance in our audit of the financial statements. Key audit matters are selected from the matters communicated with [*those charged with governance*], but are not intended to represent all matters that were discussed with them. Our audit procedures relating to these matters were designed in the context of our audit of the financial statements as a whole. Our opinion on the financial statements is not modified with respect to any of the key audit matters described below, and we do not express an opinion on these individual matters.

[*The two specific topics and content presented below are purely for illustrative purposes. This section would be tailored to the facts and circumstances of the individual audit engagement and the entity. Accordingly, the IAASB has intentionally drafted these examples in a manner that illustrates that key audit matters will vary in terms of the number and selection of topics addressed and the nature in which they may be described, and are intended to be consistent with the disclosures in the entity's financial statements.*]

Valuation of financial instruments

The Company's disclosures about its structured financial instruments are included in Note 5. The Company's investments in structured financial instruments represent [*x%*] of the total amount of its financial instruments. Because the valuation of the Company's structured financial instruments is not based on quoted prices in active markets, there is significant measurement uncertainty involved in this valuation. As a result, the valuation of these instruments was significant to our audit. The Company has determined it is necessary to use an entity-developed model to value these instruments, due to their unique structure and terms. We challenged management's rationale for using an entity-developed model, and discussed this with [*those charged with governance*], and we concluded the use of such a model was appropriate. Our audit procedures also included, among others, testing management's controls related to the development and calibration of the model and confirming that management had determined it was not necessary to make any adjustments to the output of the model to reflect the assumptions that marketplace participants would use in similar circumstances.

Revenue recognition relating to long-term contracts

The terms and conditions of the Company's long-term contracts in its [*name of segment*] affect the revenue that the Company recognizes in a period, and the revenue from such contracts represents a material amount of the Company's total revenue. The process to measure the amount of revenue to recognize in the [*name of industry*], including the determination of the appropriate timing of recognition, involves significant management judgment. We identified revenue recognition of long-term contracts as a significant risk requiring special audit consideration. This is because side agreements may exist that effectively amend the original contracts, and such side agreements may be inadvertently unrecorded or deliberately concealed and therefore present a risk of material misstatement due to fraud. In addition to testing the controls the Company has put in place over its process to enter into and record long-term contracts and other audit procedures, we considered it necessary to confirm the terms of these contracts directly with customers and testing journal entries made by management related to revenue recognition. Based on the audit procedures performed, we did not find evidence of the existence of side agreements. The Company's disclosures about revenue recognition are included in the summary of significant accounting policies in Note 1, as well as Note 4.

Going concern

The Company's financial statements have been prepared using the going concern basis of accounting. The use of this basis of accounting is appropriate unless management either intends to liquidate the Company or to cease operations, or has no realistic alternative but to do so. As part of our audit of the financial statements, we have concluded that management's use of the going concern basis of accounting in the preparation of the Company's financial statements is appropriate.

Management has not identified a material uncertainty that may cast significant doubt on the entity's ability to continue as a going concern, and accordingly none is disclosed in the financial statements. Based on our audit of the financial statements, we also have not identified such a material uncertainty. However, neither management nor the auditor can guarantee the Company's ability to continue as a going concern.

Other information

[The illustrative wording for this section is subject to the IAASB's finalization of proposed ISA 720 (Revised). The content of this section may include, among other matters: (a) a description of the auditor's responsibilities with respect to other information; (b) identification of the document(s) available at the date of the auditor's report that contain the other information to which the auditor's responsibilities apply; (c) a statement addressing the outcome of the auditor's work on the other information; and (d) a statement that the auditor has not audited or reviewed the other information and, accordingly, does not express an audit opinion or a review conclusion on it.]

Responsibilities of [management and those charged with governance or other appropriate terms] for the financial statements

Management is responsible for the preparation and fair presentation of these financial statements in accordance with IFRSs, and for such internal control as management determines is necessary to enable the preparation of financial statements that are free from material misstatement, whether due to fraud or error. [*Those charged with governance*] are responsible for overseeing the Company's financial reporting process.

Auditor's responsibilities for the audit of the financial statements

The objectives of our audit are to obtain reasonable assurance about whether the financial statements as a whole are free from material misstatement, whether due to fraud or error, and to issue an auditor's report that includes our opinion. Reasonable assurance is a high level of assurance, but is not a guarantee that an audit conducted in accordance with ISAs will always detect a material misstatement when it exists. Misstatements can arise from fraud or error and are considered material if, individually or in the aggregate, they could reasonably be expected to influence the economic decisions of users taken on the basis of these financial statements.

[The shaded material below can be located in an Appendix to the auditor's report (see paragraph 39 of this ISA). When law, regulation or national auditing standards expressly permits, reference can be made to a website of an appropriate authority that contains the description of the auditor's responsibilities, rather than including this material in the auditor's report.]

As part of an audit in accordance with ISAs, we exercise professional judgment and maintain professional skepticism throughout the planning and performance of the audit. We also:

- Identify and assess the risks of material misstatement of the financial statements, whether due to fraud or error, design and perform audit procedures responsive to those risks, and obtain audit evidence that is sufficient and appropriate to provide a basis for our opinion. The risk of not detecting a material misstatement resulting from fraud is higher than for one resulting from error, as fraud may involve collusion, forgery, intentional omissions, misrepresentations, or the override of internal control.

- Obtain an understanding of internal control relevant to the audit in order to design audit procedures that are appropriate in the circumstances, but not for the purpose of expressing an opinion on the effectiveness of the entity's internal control.
- Evaluate the appropriateness of accounting policies used and the reasonableness of accounting estimates and related disclosures made by management.
- Evaluate the overall presentation, structure and content of the financial statements, including the disclosures, and whether the financial statements represent the underlying transactions and events in a manner that achieves fair presentation.

We are required to communicate with [*those charged with governance*] regarding, among other matters, the planned scope and timing of the audit and significant audit findings, including any significant deficiencies in internal control that we identify during our audit.

We are also required to provide [*those charged with governance*] with a statement that we have complied with relevant ethical requirements regarding independence, and to communicate with them all relationships and other matters that may reasonably be thought to bear on our independence, and where applicable, related safeguards.

Report on other legal and regulatory requirements
[*The form and content of this section of the auditor's report would vary depending on the nature of the auditor's other reporting responsibilities prescribed by local law, regulation, or national auditing standards. Depending on the matters addressed by other law, regulation or national auditing standards, national standard setters may choose to combine reporting on these matters with reporting as required by the ISAs (shown in the Report on the Audit of the* Financial Statements section), with wording in the auditor's report that clearly distinguishes between reporting required by the ISAs and other reporting required by law or regulation.]

The engagement partner responsible for the audit resulting in this independent auditor's report is [*name*].

[*Signature in the name of the audit firm, the personal name of the auditor, or both, as appropriate for the particular jurisdiction*]
[*Auditor address*]
[*Date*]

7.2.4 Modified auditor's report

A **modified auditor's report** is issued when the auditor concludes that, based on the audit evidence obtained, the financial report as a whole is not free from material misstatement, or, the auditor is unable to obtain sufficient appropriate audit evidence to conclude that the financial report as a whole is free from material misstatement.

There are three types of modified opinions:
1. a qualified opinion
2. an adverse opinion
3. a disclaimer of opinion.

The decision regarding which type of modified opinion is dependent upon the auditor's judgement as to whether the nature of the matter giving rise to the modification is, or may be, materially misstated or not. The auditor shall take into consideration the pervasiveness of the effects or possible effects of the matter on the financial report. Pervasiveness refers to the fact that, in the auditor's judgement, the effects are not confined to specific elements or items of the financial report; or if so confined, it represents or could represent a substantial proportion of the financial report. If the matter is in relation to disclosures, the auditor regards that the matter is fundamental to users' understanding of the financial report. Figure 7.2 illustrates how the auditor's judgement on these matters affects the type of opinion expressed as shown in ASA 705 *Modifications to the Opinion in the Independent Auditor's Report* (ISA 705).

Nature of Matter Giving Rise to the Modification	Auditor's Judgement about the Pervasiveness of the Effects or Possible Effects on the Financial Report	
	Material but Not Pervasive	Material and Pervasive
Financial report is materially misstated	Qualified opinion	Adverse opinion
Inability to obtain sufficient appropriate audit evidence	Qualified opinion	Disclaimer of opinion

FIGURE 7.2:
Modified opinions

Source: ASA 705 *Modifications to the Opinions in the Independent Auditor's Report*, A1., p. 700.

7.2.5 Circumstances to modify

There are three types of modified opinions. They are: a qualified opinion, an adverse opinion or a disclaimer of opinion. The circumstances leading to each of these are described below.

1. **Qualified opinion** is expressed when the auditor, having obtained sufficient appropriate audit evidence, concludes that misstatements, individually or in the aggregate, are material, but not pervasive, to the financial report; or the auditor is unable to obtain sufficient appropriate audit evidence on which to base the opinion, but the possible effects on the financial report of undetected misstatements, if any, could be material but not pervasive.

2. **Adverse opinion** is expressed when the auditor, having obtained sufficient appropriate audit evidence, concludes that misstatements, individually or in the aggregate, are both material and pervasive to the financial report.

3. **Disclaimer of opinion** is expressed when the auditor is unable to obtain sufficient appropriate audit evidence on which to base the opinion, and the auditor concludes that the possible effects on the financial report of undetected misstatements, if any, could be both material or pervasive. In extreme cases, the auditor may conclude that, even after having obtained sufficient appropriate audit evidence, it is not possible to form an opinion on the financial report due to the potential interaction of multiple uncertainties and their possible cumulative effect on the financial report.

The auditor makes a judgement within the framework of auditing standards and the financial reporting framework in determining whether financial statements are fairly presented. In deciding on the appropriate opinion, the auditor considers whether there are material misstatements or whether circumstances have prevented the auditor from obtaining sufficient appropriate audit evidence that is necessary to judge whether the financial report is free from material misstatements. Material misstatements may be the result of a number of factors, including an inappropriate selection or application of accounting policies that are required by the applicable financial reporting framework, or inadequate disclosures of matters that are required. Auditors may find that they can result in a disagreement with management relating to the financial statements or that the financial report is in conflict between applicable financial reporting frameworks.

Materiality is an important consideration in arriving at an appropriate opinion because an unqualified opinion is appropriate when the matter is immaterial. When the effect is material, a qualified opinion is expressed. When the effect on the financial statements is an extreme case, the auditor is likely to issue a disclaimer or adverse opinion (depending on the circumstances).

Before issuing a qualified opinion of any kind, the auditor should do everything reasonably possible to express an unqualified opinion. Conversely, the auditor should not refrain from issuing a qualified opinion if necessary, particularly when in disagreement with management. As a consequence of the qualification, the format of the auditor's report is modified. A 'qualification' section is inserted, which outlines the reasons for the opinion expressed and quantifies the effect thereof.

We now consider in more detail the circumstances that give rise to a modified audit report.

From the table shown in figure 7.2 there are two main aspects whereby it is appropriate for the auditor to issue a modified audit report. These two aspects are that the financial report is materially misstated, or that the auditor is unable to obtain sufficient appropriate audit evidence. Each of these aspects is now discussed.

Nature of material misstatements

A misstatement is a difference between the amount, classification, presentation, or disclosure of a reported financial report item and the amount, classification, presentation, or disclosure that is required for the item to be in accordance with the applicable financial reporting framework (ASA 450 *Evaluation of Misstatements Identified during the Audit*). A material misstatement of the financial report may arise due to an accounting policy that is inappropriately selected or applied, or when an inadequate disclosure is made.

In relation to accounting policies, management may have selected a policy that is inconsistent with the applicable financial reporting framework; or the financial statements, including the related notes, do not represent the underlying transactions and events in a manner that achieves fair presentation. Where an entity has changed its selection of significant accounting policies, a material misstatement of the financial report may arise when the entity has not complied with the requirements for the accounting and disclosure of such changes. Material misstatement may also arise where the selected accounting policies have not been consistently applied between periods, or to similar transactions and events, or where there is an inappropriate method of application or an error in the application.

Regarding disclosures, material misstatements of the financial report may arise when:
- the financial report does not include all of the disclosures required by the applicable financial reporting framework
- the presentation of the disclosures is not in accordance with the applicable financial reporting framework
- the financial report does not provide the disclosures necessary to achieve fair presentation.

The auditor will determine the type of modification to the auditor's opinion. The auditor will express a qualified opinion when the auditor, having obtained sufficient appropriate audit evidence, concludes that misstatements, individually or in the aggregate, are material, but not pervasive, to the financial report. On the other hand, if the auditor, having obtained sufficient appropriate audit evidence, concludes that misstatements, individually or in the aggregate, are both material and pervasive to the financial report, the auditor shall express an adverse opinion.

Nature of inability to obtain sufficient appropriate audit evidence

There are certain circumstances that may result in the auditor being unable to obtain sufficient appropriate audit evidence. These circumstances may be beyond the control of the entity such as in a fire, where the entity's accounting records have been destroyed, or where a significant component of the accounting records have been seized by government authorities indefinitely. There may be circumstances relating to the timing or the nature of the auditor's work. Examples of these circumstances include:

- the auditor is unable to obtain sufficient appropriate audit evidence about an associated entity, or in relation to its financial information, to evaluate whether the method of accounting has been appropriately applied
- the timing of the auditor's appointment is such that the auditor is unable to evaluate some significant appropriate audit evidence such as the observation of the counting of physical inventories
- the entity's accounting controls are not effective but the auditor decides that the substantive tests or procedures she or he can perform are not sufficient.

On the other hand, a limitation of scope of the audit may result from a limitation placed by management. For example, a limitation of scope will arise where management prevents the auditor from performing an audit procedure such as the observation of the counting of physical inventories, or from obtaining external evidence or confirmation in relation to certain account balances.

In some cases, where a management-imposed limitation may be a matter that the auditor is required to report to ASIC under sections 311 (duty to report contravention of *Corporations Act 2001*), 601HG (duty to report contravention of a compliance plan) or 990K (duty to report contravention in respect of a licensee's legal requirements) of the *Corporations Act 2001*.

Though under section 312 the law requires any officer of the company to assist the auditor in obtaining appropriate audit evidence, the auditor may consider it necessary to withdraw from the audit due to the inability to obtain sufficient appropriate audit evidence. However, in some circumstances the practicality of withdrawing may be dependent upon the stage of completion of the audit at the time management imposes limitations. If the auditor has substantially completed the audit, the auditor may decide to continue to the extent possible, and disclaim an opinion and explain the scope limitation as a basis for disclaimer, prior to withdrawing. Or in other cases where withdrawal is impossible (as required by law for instance) and the auditor needs to continue with the audit (e.g. in public sector entities), the auditor may consider it necessary to include an 'other matter' paragraph in the auditor's report.

Where an auditor decides to withdraw from the audit, it is necessary to consider the professional, legal or regulatory requirements including communicating such matters relating to the withdrawal to regulators or the entity's owners. It should be noted that it is possible for the auditor to express an unmodified opinion on a financial report prepared under a given financial reporting framework, and with the same report, provide the expression of an adverse opinion on the same financial report under a different financial reporting framework.

The auditor shall express a qualified opinion when the auditor is unable to obtain sufficient appropriate audit evidence; however, it is judged that the possible effects on the financial report of undetected misstatements, if any, could be material but not pervasive. However, if the auditor judges that the possible effects on the financial report of undetected misstatements, if any, could be both material and pervasive, then the auditor shall express a disclaimer of opinion.

Where the auditor has to consider multiple uncertainties, a disclaimer of opinion is likely to be used. The reason for a disclaimer is that, while the auditor may be able to obtain sufficient appropriate audit evidence regarding each of these circumstances, it is not possible for the auditor to conclude the possible cumulative effect of the interactions of these circumstances.

7.2.6 Form and content of modifications

Paragraphs 16 to 27 of ASA 705 discuss the form and content required for modifications of opinions. Three matters are to be noted for the modifications. They are: (1) basis for modification paragraph, (2) the opinion paragraph and (3) the description of the auditor's responsibilities. The circumstances leading to each of these are now described.

Basis for modification paragraph

Where the auditor modifies the opinion on the financial report, the auditor must include a paragraph that describes the matter giving rise to the modification, in a paragraph headed either, 'Basis for Qualified Opinion', 'Basis for Adverse Opinion, or 'Basis for Disclaimer of Opinion'. This paragraph should be placed before the opinion paragraph.

The description of the matter leading to the modification of opinion shall include a description of the matter, and any quantifiable financial effects of the misstatement, unless impracticable to do so, in which case the auditor shall so state in the basis for modification paragraph. This may take the form of an effect on income tax, income before taxes, net income and equity if inventory is overstated. Where any narrative disclosures are involved, the auditor shall include an explanation of how the disclosures are misstated. ASA 705 paragraph 19 states that where the matter relates to a non-disclosure of information required to be disclosed, the auditor shall:

(a) discuss the non-disclosure with those charged with governance

    Aus 19.1 request management and/or those charged with governance to correct the non-disclosure in the financial report

(b) describe in the basis for modification paragraph the nature of the omitted information

(c) unless prohibited by law or regulation, include the omitted disclosures, provided it is practicable to do so and that the auditor has obtained sufficient appropriate audit evidence about the omitted information.

If the auditor does not include the omission in the basis for modification paragraph, the auditor shall explain the reasons for the omission. If the modification results from an inability to obtain sufficient appropriate audit evidence, the auditor shall include in the basis for modification paragraph the reasons for that inability.

However, it may not be practicable if the disclosures have not been prepared by management or the disclosures are otherwise not readily available to the auditor; or that in the auditor's judgement, the disclosures would be unduly voluminous in relation to the auditor's report. In some cases, the auditor should consider reporting obligations under the Act.

Even if the auditor has expressed an adverse opinion or has disclaimed an opinion on the financial report, the auditor shall describe in the basis for modification paragraph the reasons for any other matters of which the auditor is aware that would have required a modification to the opinion, and the effects thereof.

The opinion paragraph

The auditor shall use the heading 'Qualified Opinion', 'Adverse Opinion' or 'Disclaimer of Opinion' as appropriate, when the auditor wishes to modify the opinion. The following forms are noted in ASA 705 as per the paragraphs in the standard indicated below:

(23) A qualified opinion. . . . in the auditor's opinion, except for the effects of the matter(s) described in the Basis for qualified opinion paragraph:

    (a) The financial report presents fairly, in all material respects (or gives a true and fair view) in accordance with the applicable financial reporting framework when reporting in accordance with a fair presentation framework; or

(b) The financial report has been prepared, in all material respects, in accordance with the applicable financial reporting framework when reporting in accordance with a compliance framework.

(24) An adverse opinion ... in the auditor's opinion, because of the significance of the matter(s) described in the basis for adverse opinion paragraph:

(a) The financial report does not present fairly (or give a true and fair view) in accordance with the applicable financial reporting framework when reporting in accordance with a fair presentation framework; or

(b) The financial report has not been prepared, in all material respects, in accordance with the applicable financial reporting framework when reporting in accordance with a compliance framework.

(25) A disclaimer of opinion. When the auditor disclaims an opinion due to an ability to obtain sufficient appropriate audit evidence, the auditor shall state in the opinion paragraph, that:

(a) Because of the significance of the matter(s) described in the basis for disclaimer of opinion paragraph, the auditor has not been able to obtain sufficient appropriate audit evidence to provide a basis for an audit opinion; and, accordingly,

(b) The auditor does not express an opinion on the financial report.

The auditor shall ensure that the auditor's responsibility is described appropriately when the auditor expresses a qualified or adverse opinion. The auditor should amend the description of his or her responsibility to state that the auditor believes that the audit evidence they have obtained is sufficient and appropriate to provide a basis for the modified audit opinion.

Where the auditor disclaims an opinion due to an inability to obtain sufficient appropriate audit evidence, they shall amend the introductory paragraph of the auditor's report to state that the auditor was engaged to audit the financial report. The auditor should amend the scope of the audit to state only:

'Our responsibility is to express an opinion on the financial report based on conducting the audit in accordance with Australian Auditing Standards. Because of the matter(s) described in the basis for disclaimer of opinion paragraph, however, we were not able to obtain sufficient appropriate audit evidence to provide a basis for an audit opinion.'

Finally, in all cases where the auditor expects to modify the audit opinion, it is important that the auditor should communicate with those charged with governance the circumstances that led to the expected modification and the proposed wording of the modification. Paragraph A25 of ASA 705 describes the manner with which the auditor is required to consider when communicating with those charged with governance. The auditor should ensure notice is given to those charged with governance in respect of the intended modification, and the auditor should also seek concurrence regarding the facts of the matter that gives rise to the modification, or to confirm matters of disagreement. Those charged with governance should be given the opportunity to respond to the auditor's communication or to furnish more information and explanations in respect of the matter(s) raised.

7.2.7 Emphasis of matter and other matter in the independent auditor's report

The AUASB issues a new ASA 706 *Emphasis of Matter Paragraphs and Other Matter Paragraphs in the Independent Auditor's Report* (ISA 706) in accordance with section 227B of the ASIC Act 2001 and section 336 of the *Corporations Act 2001*.

The auditor in reporting his or her audit opinion, may find it necessary to draw users' attention to a matter or matters presented, or disclosed in the financial report that are of such importance that they are fundamental to users' understanding of the financial report; or such matter or matters, other than those disclosed or presented, that are relevant to users' understanding of the audit, the auditor's responsibilities or the auditor's report.

The objective of the auditor is to draw users' attention when it is judged that such additional communication is necessary. An **emphasis of matter** paragraph means a paragraph included in the auditor's report that refers to a matter appropriately presented or disclosed in the financial report that, in the auditor's judgement, is of such importance that it is fundamental to users' understanding of the financial report. An other matter paragraph means a paragraph included in the auditor's report that refers to a matter, other than that presented or disclosed in the financial report that, in the auditor's judgement, is relevant to users' understanding of the audit, the auditor's responsibilities or the auditor's report.

The emphasis of matter paragraph should satisfy the following criteria:
- it is fundamental to the users' understanding of the financial report
- it is not a modification of opinion
- the auditor has obtained sufficient appropriate audit evidence that the matter is not materially misstated in the financial report
- it is a matter presented or disclosed in the financial report
- it may be a matter required by other auditing standards.

The form of the emphasis of matter paragraph shall:
- be in a paragraph immediately after the opinion paragraph in the auditor's report
- be headed 'Emphasis of Matter' or other appropriate heading
- include a clear reference to the matter being emphasised and to where relevant disclosures that fully describe the matter can be found in the financial report
- indicate that the auditor's opinion is not modified in the respect of the matter emphasised.

ASA 706 also includes specific Australian circumstances that the financial report has been prepared in accordance with Australian accounting standards but additional disclosures have been made in the financial report because the application of a particular accounting standard has resulted in the financial report being potentially misleading; or, in the opinion of those charged with governance, are necessary to present a true and fair view. The auditor in reviewing this matter, is of the opinion that:
- it is likely that users may be misled regarding the financial report
- the additional disclosures contain all, and only relevant and reliable information, and are presented in such a manner as to ensure the financial report as a whole is comparable and understandable in meeting of the objectives of the financial report.

In this case, the auditor shall include in the auditor's report an emphasis of matter paragraph headed 'Application of Australian Accounting Standard AASB', or an appropriate alternative which:
- draws attention to the additional disclosures
- states in the auditor's opinion that the application of the specific Australian accounting standard has, in the circumstance, resulted in the financial report being potentially misleading
- states the reasons why the auditor believes the additional disclosures are necessary to ensure that the financial report, as a whole, is not misleading
- states that in the auditor's opinion, the additional disclosures are relevant and reliable in meeting the objectives of the financial report.

The circumstances in which an emphasis of matter paragraph can be provided are specifically outlined in ASA 706 and include:
- an uncertainty relating to the future outcome of an exceptional litigation, or regulatory action

- an early application, where permitted, of a new accounting standard that has a pervasive effect on the financial report in advance of its effective date
- a major catastrophe that has had, or continues to have, a significant effect on the entity's financial position.

The inclusion of an emphasis of matter paragraph in the auditor's report does not affect the auditor's opinion. The emphasis of matter is not a substitute for a qualified opinion, an adverse opinion or disclaiming an opinion when required by the circumstances of a specific audit engagement; nor is it a substitute for disclosures that the applicable financial reporting framework requires management to make.

Appendix 1 of ASA 706 includes other auditing standards that require the auditor to include an emphasis of matter paragraph. They are ASA 210 *Agreeing the Terms of Audit Engagements* (ISA 210), ASA 560 *Subsequent Events* (ISA 560), ASA 570 *Going Concern* (ISA 570) and ASA 800 *Special Considerations — Audits of Financial Reports Prepared in Accordance with Special Purpose Frameworks* (ISA 800).

Other matter paragraphs

The circumstances in which an other matter paragraph may be necessary are:
- those which are relevant to users' understanding of the audit which include where the auditor is unable to withdraw from an engagement even though the possible effect of an inability to obtain sufficient appropriate audit evidence, due to a limitation on the scope of the audit as imposed by management, is pervasive. The auditor may include an other matter paragraph to explain why it is not possible to withdraw from the engagement.
- those which are relevant to users' understanding of the auditor's responsibilities or the auditor's report, such as those that are required by law, or regulation that the auditor is permitted to elaborate on matters that provide further explanation of the auditor's responsibilities; or such other matters that the auditor has been asked to perform and report on or express an opinion on, but are in addition to the auditor's responsibility under the Australian auditing standards.

The auditor may also include an other matter paragraph referring to the fact that another financial report has been prepared by the same entity in accordance with another general-purpose framework and that the auditor has issued a report on that financial report.

The inclusion of an other matter paragraph does not affect the auditor's opinion. The auditor should consider whether, in the circumstances, it is appropriate to indicate that the auditor's opinion is not modified in respect of the other matter paragraph.

The content of an other matter paragraph reflects only that such other matter is not required to be presented and disclosed in the financial report. An other matter paragraph does not include information that the auditor is prohibited from providing by law, regulation or other professional standards (for example, ethical standards relating to confidentiality of information). An other matter paragraph also does not include information that is required to be provided by management.

The auditor should make those charged with governance aware of the nature of any specific matters that the auditor intends to highlight in the auditor's report, and provide them with an opportunity to obtain further clarification from the auditor where necessary. It is, however, unnecessary to repeat such communication if the specific matter in the other matter paragraph recurs on each successive engagement.

Other auditing standards that contain the requirements for the auditor to include other matter paragraphs are ASA 560, ASA 710 *Comparative Information — Corresponding Figures and Comparative Financial Reports* (ISA 710) and ASA 720 *The Auditor's Responsibilities Relating to Other Information in Documents Containing an Audited Financial Report* (ISA 720). Appendix 3 of ASA 706 includes illustrations of various types of auditors' opinions.

Management letter

A management letter is usually prepared by auditors, detailing recommendations for suggested improvements noticed during the audit. ASA 260 *Communication of Audit Matters with Those Charged with Governance* (ISA 260) provides guidance on the content of management letters (see chapter 18).

LEARNING 3 objective

Describe the other reporting considerations for corporate entities.

7.3 OTHER REPORTING CONSIDERATIONS FOR CORPORATE ENTITIES

This section discusses reporting responsibilities relating to some specific circumstances, including consolidated accounts, comparatives, initial engagements (opening balances), and half-year statements.

7.3.1 Reporting on consolidated statements

When a reporting entity has one or more controlled entities, it may be necessary for more than one auditing firm to participate in the examination. In the case of controlled entities that are companies, the other auditors would be appointed by the directors of the parent entity (as the majority shareholder or through the exercise of such other powers as provide for control over the other entity) and are required to issue a report on the controlled entity's financial statements under the Corporations Act.

The Corporations Act (s. 323B) gives the auditor of a reporting entity for which consolidated statements are required the right to access the accounting records and registers of controlled entities, and the right to require from their officers and auditors such information and explanation as needed. In many cases, auditors build up a continuing formal relationship with other auditors. Such relationships may include inter-firm reviews of compliance with quality control procedures. Evaluation of the work of the other auditor need not be done on each specific engagement. In the case of branches or divisions, the other auditor would be appointed by the principal auditor and thus act as an agent. The other auditor would therefore normally be one with whom the principal auditor has built up a formal relationship. Such relationships also commonly exist between auditors of parent and controlled entities where the parent entity recognises the advantages to itself when appointing auditors of controlled entities.

The opinion expressed on the consolidated financial statements is the sole responsibility of the principal auditor. So that the principal auditor may obtain the necessary assurance as to the accounts of controlled entities not audited by him or her, it is necessary for certain steps to be undertaken with respect to the work of the other auditor. If the auditor concludes that reliance cannot be placed on the work of another auditor and is unable to perform satisfactory alternative procedures, then the auditor's report should be qualified with respect to the limitation of the scope of the audit. If, for example, the auditor of a controlled entity does not cooperate fully with the auditor of a parent entity, then a qualification relating to the failure to receive adequate information and explanations would be required.

7.3.2 Comparatives

Comparatives refer to amounts or disclosures of one or more previous periods presented on a comparative basis with those of the current period. Comparatives form an integral part of the current period's financial statements. As such, reporting standards apply not only to the amounts and disclosures of the current period, but also to comparatives. ASA 710 paragraph 7 states that the auditor shall determine whether the comparatives comply in all material respects with the financial reporting framework applicable to the financial report being audited. Paragraph 8 of ASA 710 states that the auditor is required to:

- evaluate the risk that the comparatives may be materially misstated
- obtain sufficient appropriate audit evidence for that purpose
- ensure the comparatives meet the requirements of the applicable financial reporting framework.

Qualified previous period report

It is possible that a previous period audit opinion was qualified and an unqualified opinion is expressed for the current year. However, the auditor's report for the current year will be qualified if (1) the matter that gave rise to a qualification for the previous period also results in a qualification of the auditor's report in the current period's financial information or (2) the unresolved matter, although not resulting in a qualification of the current period's financial information, is material in relation to amounts and disclosures in the current period.

Subsequent events

A material misstatement may be discovered in previous period financial statements on which the auditor previously expressed an unqualified opinion. In such circumstances, if the statements have been revised and reissued with a new auditor's report, then the auditor should ensure that comparatives agree with the new financial statements. If the previous period statements are not revised, but the comparatives have been properly accounted for and disclosed in accordance with an identified financial reporting framework, then the auditor should express an unqualified opinion.

The auditor should express a qualified opinion if the previous period financial statements are not revised and the misstatement has not been properly accounted for and is material in respect to the current period's amounts.

Change of auditor

Additional reporting requirements must be met when there has been a change of auditors during the period covered by the comparative financial statements. If the incoming auditor is unable to obtain sufficient appropriate audit evidence regarding the comparatives, then the current auditor's report is qualified on the basis of scope limitations. The successor auditor should refer to the predecessor's auditor's report in the 'qualification' section.

Unaudited previous period financial statements

If the previous period statements are unaudited, then the auditor has a responsibility to seek sufficient appropriate audit evidence to assess whether the comparatives are misstated. If there is persuasive evidence that there are no material misstatements, then an unqualified opinion should be expressed. If sufficient appropriate evidence is unavailable, then the incoming auditor should qualify the auditor's report on the basis that the comparatives are unaudited and that no opinion on them is expressed. The auditor should also encourage disclosure in the financial statements that the comparatives are unaudited.

7.3.3 Initial engagements (opening balances)

According to ASA 510 *Initial Audit Engagements — Opening Balances* (ISA 510), in an **initial audit engagement** the auditor needs to obtain sufficient appropriate audit evidence to ensure that:

- opening balances do not contain misstatements that materially affect the current period's financial statements

- the previous period's closing balances have been correctly brought forward or have been restated where appropriate
- appropriate accounting policies are consistently applied or changes in accounting policies have been properly accounted for and adequately disclosed.

7.3.4 Half-year statements

Section 302 of the Corporations Act prescribes that disclosing entities must:
- prepare half-year financial statements and a directors' report
- have the financial statements audited or reviewed, and obtain an auditor's report
- lodge the financial statements, the directors' report and the auditor's report with ASIC.

According to s. 302 of the Corporations Act, the half-year accounts may be either audited or reviewed, although the majority of Australian companies opt for review. If the half-year statements are audited, then the reporting requirements are covered by ASA 700 (ISA 700). If a review engagement is needed, then it should be performed in accordance with ASRE 2410 *Review of an Interim Financial Report Performed by the Independent Auditor of an Entity* (ISRE 2410).

There are no requirements for the auditor's report on half-year statements to be circulated to the entity's members. However, the auditor should encourage distribution of the report to members in the interests of effective communication. AASB 134 *Interim Financial Reporting* (IAS 34) specifies the required disclosures relating to the income statement/statement of comprehensive income, the balance sheet/statement of financial position, the statement of cash flows and the statement of changes in equity. For the purpose of preparing the half-year statements or consolidated statements, each half-year is to be treated as a discrete reporting period.

When a review is conducted instead of an audit, the Corporations Act requires the company's auditor to undertake it. In accordance with ASRE 2410 (ISRE 2410), a review of half-year statements should be based on current knowledge of the entity. In undertaking the review, the auditor should consider aspects of the audit process relevant to the current audit for the forthcoming full-year financial statements.

The review must be conducted in accordance with the auditing standards applicable to review engagements. The limited nature of the review procedures used provides a level of assurance that is less than given in an audit. A disclaimer that no audit opinion is expressed is included because no audit is performed.

Do you know ...

7.4 ☐ There are two types of auditor's reports: unmodified and modified. Unmodified auditor's reports signify a 'clean' opinion. The auditor's report may be modified as a result of (1) a material misstatement in the financial report or (2) the auditor being unable to obtain sufficient appropriate audit evidence to arrive an opinion.

7.5 ☐ The type of modified opinion depends on the magnitude and pervasiveness of the matter(s). The available opinions are:
- a qualified opinion
- a disclaimer of opinion
- an adverse opinion.

7.6 ☐ The circumstances that may result in a qualification are where there is: (1) a scope limitation, (2) a disagreement with management, and (3) a conflict between applicable financial reporting frameworks. Where these matters are both material and pervasive, they become the bases for an adverse opinion or a disclaimer of opinion. An adverse opinion is where the auditor has obtained sufficient appropriate audit evidence but has concluded that the misstatement is both material and pervasive. A disclaimer of opinion is given where the auditor is unable to obtain sufficient appropriate audit evidence and the potential misstatements are pervasive.

7.7 ☐ An 'emphasis of matter' section is not a qualification and may be used only in specific circumstances, which include the need for additional disclosures, inherent uncertainties due to a catastrophe (including going concern) and subsequent events.

7.8 ☐ The opinion expressed on the consolidated statements of a company is the sole responsibility of the principal auditor.

7.9 ☐ For opening balances in initial engagements, an unqualified opinion is expressed if there are no misstatements in opening balances, closing balances of previous periods have been correctly brought forward, and accounting policies are consistently applied.

7.10 ☐ An auditor's report or a review is required for half-year financial statements. It is given to the directors for lodgement with ASIC.

SUMMARY

Reporting the findings is the final phase of an audit of financial statements. The auditor must comply with relevant auditing standards when reporting on audited financial statements. The auditor's conclusion relies heavily on the work performed in completing the audit. Depending on the circumstances, the auditor may issue an unmodified auditor's report, a modified auditor's report that has a qualification and expresses one of three types of opinions (a qualified opinion, an adverse opinion or a disclaimer of opinion), or a report with an emphasis of matter. Given the signal it sends to users of the financial statements, a modified report should be issued only after careful consideration. When expressing a qualified, adverse or disclaimer of opinion, the report must contain a clear statement as to the reasons for the qualification and the effect thereof. There are specific circumstances that allow the issue of an emphasis of matter as part of the auditor's report.

There are special reporting considerations for reporting on consolidated statements, comparative financial statements, initial engagements (opening balances) and half-year statements. The auditor must exercise due care in conducting the audit so as to obtain a reasonable basis for an opinion and to express the opinion justified by the findings.

KEY TERMS

accounting standards, p. 283

adverse opinion, p. 294

comparatives, p. 301

compliance framework, p. 282

disclaimer of opinion, p. 294

emphasis of matter, p. 299

fair presentation framework, p. 282

general purpose external financial report, p. 283

initial audit engagement, p. 302

modified auditor's report, p. 293

qualified opinion, p. 294

true and fair view, p. 284

unmodified auditor's report, p. 286

MULTIPLE-CHOICE questions

7.1 Which statement would not be found in a directors' declaration?
A. That the financial report gives a true and fair view.
B. That the financial report is free from material misstatement whether due to fraud or error.
C. That in the directors' opinion there are reasonable grounds to believe that the company will be able to pay its debts as and when they fall due.
D. That in the directors' opinion the financial report is in accordance with the law.

7.2 The auditor's opinion is expressed in reference to the financial report as a whole. This means that the auditor must:
A. Not be overly concerned about individual amounts on the financial report.
B. Consider whether the firm has made a profit or a loss.
C. Consider whether the report creates an impression that is consistent with the auditor's intimate knowledge of the entity and its financial condition.
D. Decide whether the statements are a complete financial report as required by accounting standards.

7.3 An adverse opinion means:
A. A qualification of the auditor's report does not sufficiently represent the significance of the misstatements that are pervasive in the financial report.
B. The auditor is uncertain about expressing an opinion.
C. The financial report is fairly presented, except for a specific reservation, deficiency or other shortcoming.
D. The financial report is prepared in accordance with a financial reporting framework and are generally acceptable to the auditor.

7.4 Which of these factors could be the cause of a material misstatement?
(i) Selection of inappropriate accounting policies.
(ii) Inadequate disclosure.
(iii) Disagreement with those charged with governance in relation to the financial report.
A. (i) and (ii) only.
B. (i) and (iii) only.
C. (ii) and (iii) only.
D. (i), (ii) and (iii).

7.5 The emphasis of matter paragraph in an audit report would normally refer to the fact that the auditor's opinion is:
A. Qualified in this respect.
B. Not qualified in this respect.
C. A disclaimer of opinion.
D. An adverse opinion.

7.6 When the auditor issues a disclaimer of opinion on a financial report, the audit report should:
A. Be unqualified.
B. Begin with the term 'except for'.
C. Express an adverse opinion.
D. Have a paragraph headed 'disclaimer of opinion'.

7.7 The issue of a 'disclaimer of opinion' by an auditor is most likely because of:
A. The omission of the statement of cash flows.
B. A material departure from applicable accounting standards.

C. Management's refusal to provide written representations.

D. A scope limitation in an extreme case.

7.8 Which of these would be considered a scope limitation?

  (i) The client would not permit confirmation of receivables with their best customers for fear of annoying the customers.

 (ii) The auditor is appointed to the engagement too late to observe the client's counting of the inventory.

(iii) The auditor is forced to call upon an outside expert to properly value antiques that are held in the client's vault as investments.

A. (i) and (ii) only.

B. (i) and (iii) only.

C. (ii) and (iii) only.

D. (i), (ii) and (iii).

7.9 A 'true and fair view' is indicative that:

A. The auditor has obtained a second opinion on the accounts.

B. The auditor is satisfied with the reasonableness of the figures in the financial report.

C. Management's assertions can be relied on.

D. The accounting standards have been consistently applied in the preparation and presentation of the financial report.

7.10 Which of these items does not form part of the financial report, as defined in the Corporations Act (s. 295)?

A. A statement of cash flows for the year.

B. Any additional disclosures necessary to give a true and fair view.

C. The directors' report.

D. Notes required by Accounting Standards.

REVIEW questions

7.11 Outline the contents of a general purpose financial report.

7.12 What are the contents of an unmodified auditor's report? Explain each section.

7.13 What are the different types of modified audit opinions? Explain each type.

7.14 Under what circumstances may the auditor decide to include an 'emphasis of matter' section in the auditor's report?

7.15 What is the difference between an unmodified auditor's opinion and a modified auditor's opinion?

7.16 Is materiality the only consideration for an auditor deciding whether to qualify the audit opinion?

7.17 What does each of the modified types of auditor's opinions mean to users wanting to rely on the financial report?

7.18 What circumstances may give rise to (1) an adverse opinion and (2) a disclaimer of opinion?

7.19 When an auditor is faced with a disagreement, what factors should be considered to determine whether a qualified or an adverse opinion is appropriate?

7.20 What might constitute 'other matters' on which an auditor may be required to report?

BASIC
★★
MODERATE
★★★
CHALLENGING

 PROFESSIONAL application questions

7.21 Effect of circumstances on an audit opinion ★

Assume you are an auditor and you are facing the following separate circumstances; the effects of all the items below are material:

1. The provision for stock is inadequate.
2. A retailer values inventory at sales price less an allowance for sales margin.
3. A manufacturing company is currently negotiating with the bank an extension of a loan facility that is due for repayment shortly after the AGM; without this refinancing the business will not be able to continue operations.
4. A significant proportion of a retailer's sales are on a cash basis and inadequate records have been maintained; there are no audit tests that can be done to satisfy yourself that the cash sales are accurate.
5. Management have excluded from the financial report the necessary disclosures in relation to a contingent liability.
6. The company that runs a dairy farm has prepared the financial report on a going concern basis; shortly after the year end the company's contract with a major supermarket was cancelled. Without this customer you expect the business to cease trading within six months and it is unlikely that the company will be able to secure any new contracts in that time.
7. The directors of a construction company refuse to give you access to reports produced by an independent quantity surveyor in relation to the value of work done on some of their construction projects.
8. A wholesaler has a policy of including all of its buildings in the balance sheet at cost less depreciation. You establish that one of the warehouses included in the balance sheet at a value of $20m has an actual market value of $23m.

Required

Indicate the effect of the above circumstances on your auditor's report if management were to refuse to make any changes you feel necessary in order that the financial report gives a true and fair view.

7.22 Effect of circumstances on audit opinion ★★

Scarborough Hydraulics Ltd contracts with governments to carry out a variety of infrastructure projects including water treatment and desalination plants and other drainage works. It also acts as a contractor to maintain a range of government infrastructure assets. The contracts that it has with its government customers have very strict turnaround times to ensure that, in the event of problems, water services to the public are quickly brought back on-line.

You have completed your audit of Scarborough Hydraulics and the following material events occurred:

1. Scarborough holds a stock of high value drainage components to allow them to be able to respond quickly to their customers' needs. Due to the size and quantity of these items they were stored in a large outdoor space on the outskirts of Sydney. Shortly after the year end a significant amount of this stock was stolen. The security at this site was inadequate and no record of the theft is available.
2. Scarborough has a large manufacturing centre in Melbourne which provides prefabricated concrete for the company's infrastructure projects. The company policy is to include factories in the balance sheet at market value less accumulated depreciation. The Melbourne factory is included in the balance sheet based on a valuation carried out five years ago. The company has not engaged a valuer to revalue the property because the directors believe that market values have remained fairly level over the last five years, so the existing carrying value is not materially different from current value.

3. During the year Scarborough completed a contract to provide drains for a private construction company that was building 500 houses in a new suburb of Brisbane. Shortly before the year end a downpour of rain saw the drainage system fail causing damage to the houses being built. The construction company is suing Scarborough for the costs of rectifying the damage. Scarborough have not provided for any possible payout because they expect their losses to be covered by a claim against one of their sub-contractors that supplied the faulty part that caused the failure.

Required

Discuss each of the above issues, state what effect each would have on the audit opinion and give reasons.

7.23 Going concern? ★★

HomeRus Ltd is a retailer of a range of low cost household products and is listed on the ASX. It is highly geared because it borrowed heavily to finance the purchase of shopping centres around Australia. There has been a squeeze on the prices it can charge for its products due to a dip in the economy creating sluggish demand from customers. There has also been a fall in the value of a large part of its property portfolio. The share price of the company has fallen significantly in recent years and a change in senior management last year has done nothing to turn this around. Market analysts continue to forecast poor performance for the company and have suggested that the low share price puts the company at risk of being taken over by one of its competitors.

There have been some approaches by other companies to take over the company, but all negotiations have come to nothing. Some commentators have indicated that the company is pretty sound with good locations and some minor changes will prepare the company for an improving economy. Others, however, have suggested that a buyer coming in at a cheap price could sell off the more valuable properties to make a profit and close the other parts of the business.

No reference has been made to going concern issues in any recent financial report.

Required

Discuss the problems facing HomeRus Ltd and the auditor when considering disclosures around going concern and possible audit opinions.

7.24 Going-concern issues, audit opinion ★★

Temper Telecommunication Ltd is a listed public company that manufactures communication equipment. Last year the company engaged itself in a contract involving the engineering and infrastructure for a highly complex broadband network in Adelaide. The company has a 30 June year-end, and the statutory accounts are due to be signed one week after the board of directors meeting on 5 August 2015. During the course of the audit, you become aware that the due to the complex negotiations with the Australian Government on broadband networks, and the likely change in government policies, the company was advised that the plan for the broadband network engineering project may be suspended until further notice. Temper Telecommunications had bought sophisticated equipment which was to be paid off through the life of the project over 3 years. It also commenced the architectural planning, employing two highly paid experts in broadband architecture. Temper Telecommunications is now experiencing growing cash flow difficulties (the project was meant to be able to save its business).

It has recently applied for a significant increase to a borrowing facility that is already fully drawn. Management is adamant that the company will continue to be viable. If necessary, it claims it can resort to cutbacks in its other future capital expenditure program, seek additional off-balance-sheet financing and/or reschedule existing debt arrangements.

Required

(a) Explain the concept of going concern. Discuss the reporting options open to an auditor when going concern issues arise.

(b) Discuss the potential auditor's report options in relation to Temper Telecommunications Ltd.

7.25 Preparation of the auditor's report — various circumstances ★★

You are the audit partner of Gerrotown Housing Ltd, which provides social housing to approximately 1000 tenants at below normal market rents. Gerrotown is a reporting entity under the Corporations Act. Consider the impact of the following two situations on your auditor's report for the year ending 30 June 2015.

1. During the year there has been a review of the basis for calculating the lives of the houses owned by the organisation. Previously, these houses were assessed to have a useful life of 30 years, but this has now been changed to 50 years. During your audit work you reviewed the Gerrotown Housing Ltd asset management policy which plans for maintaining and upgrading properties only up to 30 years old. You also found that during the year Gerrotown Housing Ltd demolished a house that it built in 1983.

2. Approximately 700 of the houses that Gerrotown Housing Ltd provides to its clients are leased from the state government. The lease obliges Gerrotown Housing Ltd to sub-let the houses to social housing tenants at low rents calculated using a formula in the lease. The current lease for these houses expires on 31 December 2015 and Gerrotown Housing Ltd is negotiating new lease terms. From your review of the board minutes, it appears that the state government is looking to increase the lease costs that will be charged to Gerrotown Housing Ltd by 20% due to increases in rates and maintenance costs on these houses. The board minutes record that these houses would now not generate any surplus and may put the long-term survival of Gerrotown Housing Ltd in jeopardy. The board are unwilling to sign the new lease as it is currently drafted.

Required

Discuss the impact of the aforementioned events on the auditor's report you intend to issue for Gerrotown Housing Ltd for the year ending 30 June 2015 and in each case provide the wording for any additional paragraphs you may include in your audit report.

7.26 Effect of circumstances on audit opinion ★★★

You are an audit manager finalising your 30 June 2015 audits. The following independent and material matters have come to your attention:

1. The audit of the statutory records of Whale Ltd, a reporting entity, revealed the following problems:
   (a) failure to update the members' register for changes in shareholders
   (b) failure to obtain written consent from directors to act
   (c) no preparation of minutes of directors' meetings in respect of the current year
   (d) failure to hold the annual general meeting in the previous financial year
   (e) the company made no comment in respect of either the failure to keep properly updated statutory registers or the failure to hold an annual general meeting.

2. Shark Ltd, a reporting entity, uses last-in first-out in respect of valuation of closing inventories, which is one of the most significant balance sheet accounts. The difference between first-in first-out and last-in first-out has a material effect on the closing inventory balance.

3. Dugong Ltd is a holding company with a number of wholly owned subsidiaries. One of these, Manatee Ltd, is a self-sustaining foreign subsidiary with manufacturing and distribution facilities throughout South-East Asia. The group accounts of Dugong and its subsidiaries consist of the consolidated statements of Dugong and its subsidiaries and exclude those of Manatee, which are attached separately. The consolidated statements include a note stating

that the directors believe it is misleading to consolidate Manatee because its operations are very different from those of the rest of the group and are carried out under substantially different conditions. The note includes details of intercompany balances and transactions.

Required

Discuss the audit issues to be considered in each of the above circumstances, and their likely impact on the audit opinion to be issued. Justify your answer with references to auditing standards and the Corporations Act, as appropriate.[2]

7.27 Preparation of the auditor's report — various circumstances ★★★

Mike Brady, a registered company auditor, has completed the audit of the financial report of Trueline Ltd for the year ended 30 June 2015. Mike also audited the financial report for Trueline for the previous financial year. He drafted the following report for 30 June 2015:

> We have audited the statement of financial position, income statement, statement of cash flows and statement of changes in equity for Trueline Ltd as of 30 June 2015. Our audit was made in accordance with an applicable financial reporting framework. In our opinion, the above-mentioned financial statements are accurately and fairly presented in accordance with generally accepted accounting principles in effect at 30 June 2015.
>
> Mike Brady, CPA
> 25 August 2015

Other information
1. During the year, Trueline changed its method of accounting for long-term construction contracts. It properly reflected the effects of the change in the current year's financial report and restated the previous year's statements. Mike is satisfied with Trueline's justification for making the change. The change is discussed in Note 24 to the financial statements.
2. Mike was unable to perform normal accounts receivable confirmation procedures, but he used alternative procedures to satisfy himself as to the validity of the receivables.
3. Trueline is the defendant in a litigation case, of which the outcome is highly uncertain. If the case is settled in favour of the plaintiff, Trueline will be required to pay a substantial amount of cash that may require the sale of certain non-current assets. The litigation and possible effects have been properly disclosed in Note 26 to the financial statements.

Required

(a) Consider all the above facts and the pertinent requirements of ASA 700 (ISA 700), and then rewrite the auditor's report in an acceptable and complete format, incorporating any necessary departures from an unmodified report.
(b) Identify any items included in the 'Other information' section that would not affect the auditor's report. Explain why this is the case.[3]

 ## CASE studies

7.28 Standardised audit reports ★★

The report produced by the auditor should be the first thing that a user of a financial report reads. It is only having read the audit report that the user can have any confidence that the contents of the financial report are a reasonable representation of the financial position and performance of the company.

In order to understand what comfort the audit report gives, any user must understand what an audit is, the role of the auditor and the role played by management and the board of directors of the company.

The amount of information included in the auditor's report has increased in recent years in an attempt to reduce the expectation gap.

Required

(a) Discuss the advantages and disadvantages of the standardisation of audit reports.

(b) Explain the following components of an auditor's report and discuss why they are important:

   (i) auditor's and directors' responsibilities.

  (ii) independence.

 (iii) audit opinion.

7.29 Effect of circumstances on audit opinion ★★

You are an audit partner finalising your 30 June 2015 audits. The following independent and material matters have come to your attention.

1. Food Fund Foundation, a charity, is a non-reporting entity. As in previous years, you have performed the audit in accordance with its constitution. The financial report is prepared by another firm of accountants on behalf of Food Fund's board of directors, because Food Fund does not have the in-house expertise to perform this function. During your review of the internal control structure, you noted that the company did not have sufficient controls over the collection of income to enable you to be satisfied that all income received was recorded. However, you have been satisfied that the company has correctly accounted for all income recorded.

2. Telken Ltd is the parent entity of the Telken Group, a reporting entity. Your firm did not act as auditor of either Telfast Ltd or Teldane Ltd — the entities controlled by Telken. You were unable to obtain the auditor's report for Telfast, although you do have a copy of the final draft auditor's report, and the other auditor's verbal assurance that an unqualified auditor's report was issued. In addition, despite receiving a copy of the audited report for Teldane, you do not believe the financial report is suitable for consolidation with the other entities in the group. This is because Teldane operates in Afghanistan, which has a vastly different accounting framework from that used in Australia. You have been able to quantify the financial effect of the required adjustments on the financial report of the Telken Group. However, management has refused to make the adjustments and has consolidated the existing version of Teldane's financial report.

3. Eureka & Co. Pty Ltd, a non-reporting entity, operates a small goldmine, which is run as a family business. The board consists of Mr Lalor and his sister, Ms Lalor, who are also the principal shareholders. As part of the final audit meeting, Ms Lalor tells you: 'I reckon the vein we're currently mining will last 18 months at the most — 14 months at the least. After the gold is extracted, we are shutting up shop; we'll let the license expire and retire to Kalgoorlie.' Ms Lalor then shows you a surveyor's report backing up her assertion regarding the amount of gold in the vein. The financial report does not disclose this information.

4. Prime Trust is a reporting entity. Ms Ford, the finance director, refuses to adopt AASB 124 Related Party Disclosures (IAS 24) on the grounds that it 'requires information to be disclosed to the public that should remain known only to the parties concerned'. This is consistent with her stance in previous years, which resulted in your issuing a qualified auditor's report. You are satisfied that the current financial report is materially correct in all regards, apart from the non-compliance with AASB 124 (IAS 24).

Required

Identify the type of auditor's report to be issued for each of the above situations.[4]

RESEARCH question

7.30 Heart Transplant Pty Ltd

The following is an auditor's report for the Heart Transplant Pty Ltd for the year ended 30 June 2015. The Heart Transplant Pty Ltd is an intermediary consultant which organises the affairs of heart transplant patients with the hospitals, using a fee for service. It also accepts donations and has been active in charitable activities.

The Auditor's Report

Scope

We have audited the attached financial report of Heart Transplant Pty Ltd, for the year ended 30 June 2015. The Committee is responsible for the financial report and has determined that the accounting policies used and described in Note 1 to the financial statements which form part of the financial report are appropriate to meet the requirements of the Corporations Act and are appropriate to meet the needs of the patients. We have conducted an independent audit of this financial report in order to express an opinion on it to the members of the Heart Transplant Pty Ltd. No opinion is expressed as to whether the accounting policies used are appropriate to the needs of the members.

The financial statements have been prepared for the purpose of fulfilling the requirements of the *Corporations Act 2001*. We disclaim any assumption of responsibility for any reliance on this report or on the financial report to which it relates to any person other than the members, or for any purpose other than that for which it was prepared.

Our audit has been conducted in accordance with Australian Auditing Standards. Our procedures included examination, on a test basis, of evidence supporting the amounts and other disclosures in the financial report, and the evaluation of significant accounting estimates. These procedures have been undertaken to form an opinion whether, in all material respects, the financial report is presented fairly in accordance with the accounting policies described in Note 1 so as to present a view that is consistent with our understanding of the company's financial position, and performance as represented by the results of the operations. These policies do not require the application of all Accounting standards and other mandatory professional reporting requirements in Australia. The audit opinion expressed in this report has been formed on the above basis.

Qualification

It is not practicable to establish control over monies received from voluntary revenue, including gifts and donations received prior to entry in the financial records. Accordingly, audit procedures with respect to monies received from voluntary revenue had to be restricted to the amounts recorded in the financial records.

Qualified Audit Opinion

In our opinion, except for the effects of the matters in the Qualifications paragraph, the financial report presents fairly, in accordance with the accounting policies described in Note 1 to the financial statements, the financial position of Heart Transplant Pty Ltd as at 30 June 2015 and the results of its operations for the year then ended.

Signed on: 23 September 2015.

Required

Examine the audit report and the areas whereby the audit report should be amended in accordance with ASA 700, ASA 705 and ASA 706.

FURTHER READING

CJP Chen, 'An emerging market's reaction to initial modified audit opinions: evidence from the Shanghai Stock Exchange', *Contemporary Accounting Research*, Fall 2000, pp. 429–55.

Going Concern Issues in Financial Reporting: A Guide for Companies and Directors, AICD, Australian Government Auditing and Assurance Standards Board, 2009.

NOTES

1. International Auditing and Assurance Standards Board (IAASB) 2012, *Invitation to Comment: Improving the Auditor's Report*, New York, International Federation of Accountants, June, p. 1.

2. Adapted from Professional Year Programme of the ICAA, 1996, Advanced Audit Module.

3. Adapted from AICPA.

4. Adapted from Professional Year Programme of the ICAA, 1998, Advanced Audit Module.

Answers to multiple-choice questions

7.1 *B*   7.2 *C*   7.3 *A*   7.4 *D*   7.5 *B*   7.6 *D*   7.7 *D*   7.8 *A*   7.9 *B*   7.10 *C*

chapter 8

Client evaluation and planning the audit

OVERVIEW

8.1 Acceptance and continuance of client relationships

8.2 Audit engagement letters

8.3 Steps in planning an audit

8.4 Understanding the entity and its environment

8.5 Analytical procedures in planning

8.6 Consideration of fraud risk in planning

8.7 Audit documentation

Summary

Key terms

Appendix 8A: Key financial ratios used in analytical procedures

Multiple-choice questions

Review questions

Professional application questions

Case studies

Research question

Further reading

Notes

LEARNING objectives

After studying this chapter, you should be able to:

1 describe the steps involved in client acceptance and continuance

2 state the purpose and content of an engagement letter

3 explain the steps in planning an audit

4 identify the risks of misstatement through understanding the entity and its environment

5 explain the role of analytical procedures in audit planning

6 describe the requirements to consider the risk of fraud in the audit planning process

7 explain the purpose and function of audit working papers.

PROFESSIONAL STATEMENTS

Australian		International	
ASA 200	Overall Objectives of the Independent Auditor and the Conduct of an Audit in Accordance with Australian Auditing Standards	ISA 200	Overall Objectives of the Independent Auditor and the Conduct of an Audit in Accordance with International Standards on Auditing
ASA 210	Agreeing the Terms of Audit Engagements	ISA 210	Agreeing the Terms of Audit Engagements
ASA 220	Quality Control for an Audit of a Financial Report and Other Historical Financial Information	ISA 220	Quality Control for an Audit of Financial Statements
ASA 230	Audit Documentation	ISA 230	Audit Documentation
ASA 240	The Auditor's Responsibilities Relating to Fraud in an Audit of a Financial Report	ISA 240	The Auditor's Responsibilities Relating to Fraud in an Audit of Financial Statements
ASA 250	Consideration of Laws and Regulations in an Audit of a Financial Report	ISA 250	Consideration of Laws and Regulations in an Audit of Financial Statements
ASA 300	Planning an Audit of a Financial Report	ISA 300	Planning an Audit of Financial Statements
ASA 315	Identifying and Assessing the Risks of Material Misstatement through Understanding the Entity and Its Environment	ISA 315	Identifying and Assessing the Risks of Material Misstatement through Understanding the Entity and Its Environment
ASA 520	Analytical Procedures	ISA 520	Analytical Procedures
ASA 550	Related Parties	ISA 550	Related Parties
ASA 610	Using the Work of Internal Auditors	ISA 610	Using the Work of Internal Auditors
ASA 620	Using the Work of an Auditor's Expert	ISA 620	Using the Work of an Auditor's Expert
ASQC 1	Quality Control for Firms that Perform Audits and Reviews of Financial Reports and Other Financial Information, and Other Assurance Engagements	ISQC 1	Quality Control for Firms that Perform Audits and Reviews of Financial Reports, and Other Financial Information, and Other Assurance Engagements
APES 110	Code of Ethics for Professional Accountants	IFAC	Code of Ethics for Professional Accountants
APES 305	Terms of Engagement		
APES 320	Quality Control for Firms	ISQC 1	Quality Control for Firms that Perform Audits and Reviews of Financial Statements, and Other Assurance and Related Services Engagements

SCENE SETTER

Triangulation of audit evidence in fraud assessments

Regulation internationally has increased the responsibility on auditors for the detection of financial statement fraud. A recent study experimentally examined some of the effects of greater evaluation of fraud as part of an audit. The study examined a scenario where two kinds of management-controlled pieces of audit evidence were contradicted by external evidence. A couple of the major findings from the research were as follows. First, where there is increased emphasis on fraud detection, auditors need to rethink the source of audit evidence to types of evidence that are more difficult to be manipulated by management, such as evidence that comes from outside the organisation. Second, auditors were found to appropriately use evidence on the performance of the client's business model in comparison with the financial statements to evaluate the risk of fraud in the organisation.

Source: K Trotman and W Wright, 'Triangulation of audit evidence in fraud risk assessments', *Accounting, Organizations and Society* 37(1), 2012, pp. 41–53.

Auditors take on a significant risk when they agree to give an audit opinion. To minimise their risk, auditors need to know who and what they are dealing with, and must organise their audit work so that any misstatements that exist in the accounts, whether malicious or accidental, are detected by their audit procedures. As noted in the Scene Setter, considering fraud has also become more important for auditors in the planning process. Good planning should ensure that appropriate attention is devoted to the different areas of the audit, potential problems are identified, work is completed expeditiously, tasks are assigned to appropriate members of the audit team, and the audit team is properly supervised. One of the main objectives of an audit plan is to reduce audit risk to an acceptable level.

The planning stage of an audit should include the following.

- Procedures covering the acceptance of new audit clients or the continuing of existing relationships. These procedures consider the integrity of owners and management, whether the audit team is competent and has the necessary time and resources to perform the work, and whether the firm and the audit team can comply with ethical requirements. Once the audit has been accepted, it is then important to establish and document the terms of engagement.
- Establishing an overall audit strategy that will include determining the relevant characteristics of the engagement (such as the reporting framework used as this will set the scope for the engagement), establishing key dates, determining materiality, and preliminary risk assessment, including internal controls and considering the availability of resources.
- Developing an audit plan to include planned risk assessment procedures and further audit procedures necessary to comply with auditing standards. The plan and any significant changes to it must be documented.

In this and the next two chapters we consider the elements that make up the planning stage of an audit.

This chapter starts by discussing the steps involved in completing the initial phase of an audit (i.e. accepting the engagement or deciding to continue the client relationship). We identify the steps involved in the planning phase of the audit, with particular emphasis on obtaining an understanding of the entity and its environment and the use of analytical procedures as part of this process. Then we describe the need to consider the risk of fraud in the audit planning process — this forms part of understanding the entity but the possible existence of fraud creates its own specific challenges for the auditor. Finally, we explain the importance of documenting all phases of the audit, giving guidance on how to set about preparing working papers and accumulating them into audit files.

Chapter 9 looks in more detail at risk assessment, including internal control risk, and chapter 10 completes our look at planning by discussing materiality and audit evidence.

LEARNING 1
objective

*Describe the steps involved
in client acceptance
and continuance.*

8.1 ACCEPTANCE AND CONTINUANCE OF CLIENT RELATIONSHIPS

The initial phase of a financial statement audit involves a decision to accept the opportunity to become the auditor for a new client or to continue as auditor for an existing client. Two important preconditions for accepting any audit engagement according to ASA 210 *Agreeing the Terms of Audit Engagements* paragraph 6 (ISA 210) are to determine that the financial reporting framework to be applied by the client is acceptable and also to ensure that management agrees and understands its responsibilities.

An auditor is not obliged to perform a financial statement audit for any entity that requests it. In accepting an engagement, an auditor takes on professional responsibilities to the public, the client and other members of the public accounting profession. The client's best interests must be served with competence and professional concern. In relation to other members of the profession, the auditor has a responsibility to enhance the stature of the profession and its ability to serve the public. An auditor wishing to avoid legal liability would not associate with clients that pose a high risk of litigation. Thus, a decision to accept a new client or continue a relationship with an existing client should not be taken lightly.

ASQC 1 *Quality Control for Firms that Perform Audits and Reviews of Financial Reports, and Other Financial Information, and Other Assurance Engagements* (ISQC 1) requires that an audit firm should establish client evaluation and acceptance procedures that ensure that the firm accepts audit engagements only where it has considered the client's integrity and where it is competent and is able to meet the ethical requirements. APES 320 *Quality Control for Firms* also outlines these requirements and is basically the same. The three steps in accepting an audit engagement are shown in figure 8.1. Client evaluation involves mainly a consideration of the integrity of management and the identification of any special circumstances and unusual risks associated with the entity. Ethical considerations relate to whether the audit firm is able to meet independence criteria, complete the engagement with professional competence and perform the audit with due care. There are then legal considerations in ensuring compliance with the requirements of the Corporations Act in the evaluation of independence. Finally, if the audit firm is of the opinion that the audit can be completed in accordance with professional standards, then the firm prepares an engagement letter to confirm the auditor's responsibility (discussed in section 8.2).

CLIENT EVALUATION

| Evaluate integrity of management. |

| Identify special circumstances and unusual risks. |

ETHICAL AND LEGAL CONSIDERATIONS

| Evaluate independence. |

| Assess competence to perform audit. |

| Determine ability to use due care. |

ENGAGEMENT

| Prepare engagement letter. |

FIGURE 8.1:
Steps in accepting an audit engagement

8.1.1 Client evaluation

Client evaluation is an important element of quality control. ASA 220 *Quality Control for an Audit of a Financial Report and Other Historical Financial Information*, (ISA 220.12) places the onus on the engagement partner to ensure that appropriate procedures are in place in relation to the acceptance and continuation of client relationships.

Evaluating the integrity of management

The main role of the auditor is to express an opinion on the financial statements prepared by management. When management lacks integrity, there is a greater likelihood that material errors and irregularities may occur in the accounting process from which the financial statements are prepared. In undertaking a client evaluation, the auditor seeks reasonable assurance that an entity's management can be trusted. For a new client, the **proposed auditor** may obtain information about the integrity of management by communicating with the **predecessor auditor**, if applicable, and by making enquiries of other third parties. For an existing client, the auditor should consider previous experience with the client's management.

Communicating with existing auditors

Section 210.9 of APES 110 *Code of Ethics for Professional Accountants* (IFAC Code, Section 210.9) indicates that an accountant in public practice who is asked to replace another professional accountant in public practice or who is considering tendering for an engagement currently held by another professional accountant should determine whether there are reasons for not accepting the engagement.

Further, specific requirements for audit engagements are outlined in Section AUST210.11.1 of the Code of Ethics (there is no IFAC Code equivalent).

The proposed accountant who is asked to replace the existing auditor must:
- ask the prospective client's permission to communicate with the existing auditor — if refused, the auditor should decline the engagement (unless there are exceptional circumstances)
- if permission is granted, ask the existing auditor (in writing) to supply all information that should be made available to enable the proposed accountant to make a decision as to whether to accept the audit engagement.

Where the proposed accountant cannot reduce threats to compliance with fundamental principles by application of safeguards (such as discussion with the existing accountant) or by other means, the proposed accountant should decline the engagement (Section 210.11 of the Code of Ethics; IFAC Code, Section 210.11).

The previous auditor's working paper files are also a valuable source of information about a new client. The new auditor may, therefore, ask to review these files. The previous auditor is under no obligation to consent to such a review, but many audit firms will consent to a supervised review, given the client's permission.

Making enquiries of other third parties

The auditor may also obtain information about a client management's integrity from knowledgeable people in the community. The proposed auditor may direct enquiries to the prospective client's bankers, legal advisers, investment bankers and others in the financial or business community who may have such knowledge.

Other potential sources of information include news items in the financial press or changes in senior management.

Reviewing previous experience with existing clients

Before making a decision to continue an engagement with an existing audit client, the auditor should carefully consider previous experiences with the entity's management, such as any material errors or irregularities and illegal acts discovered in previous audits. During an audit, the auditor makes enquiries of management about such matters as the existence of contingencies, the completeness of all minutes of board meetings, and compliance with regulatory requirements. The truthfulness of management's responses to such enquiries in previous audits should be carefully considered in the evaluation of the integrity of management.

The auditor should regularly evaluate clients in respect of the occurrence of specified events to determine whether to continue a relationship with that client. These events include:

- the expiration of a period of time — there are now some legal requirements for partner rotation, which may be an appropriate time for a full and objective appraisal of the relationship with the client
- a significant change in the business, such as a change in management, financial condition, litigation status or the nature of the client's business
- the existence of conditions that would lead the auditor to reject a client had those conditions existed at the time of the initial acceptance of the audit engagement.

The auditor should also consider the history of disagreements relating to accounting standards. The importance of the entity's quality of earnings cannot be understated, and if the client has a history of arguing about choice, interpretation or application of accounting standards, then the auditor must consider the client's reasons for such arguments. If it is the auditor's opinion that the client's motivation is to manage earnings, this should be considered in the overall evaluation of the client.

Identifying special circumstances and unusual risks

This step in accepting an engagement includes identifying the intended users of the audited financial statements, making a preliminary assessment of the prospective client's legal and financial stability, and evaluating the entity's audit ability.

Identifying intended users of the audited financial statements

In chapter 5 we noted that the auditor's legal responsibilities in an audit may vary based on the intended users of the financial statements. Thus, the auditor should consider the prospective client's status as a private or public company, any named beneficiaries or foreseen or foreseeable third parties to whom the potential for liability exists under common law, and what, if any, statutes apply in the circumstances. The auditor should also consider whether a general purpose financial report will meet the needs of all intended users or whether any special reports will be required. Added reporting requirements may mean additional competency requirements, add to audit costs and broaden the auditor's legal liability exposure.

For assurance engagements other than a financial statement audit, it may be necessary to restrict the report to specific identified users.

Assessing a prospective client's legal and financial stability

If an entity experiences legal difficulties, and if plaintiffs can find any pretext for claiming reliance on the financial statements, then such litigation will probably also involve the auditors, who are often thought to have 'deep pockets'. Thus, auditors may incur the financial and other costs of defending themselves, no matter how professionally they perform their services.

For this reason, auditors may attempt to identify and reject prospective clients that pose a high risk of litigation. These may include entities whose operations or main products are the subjects of either material lawsuits or investigations by authorities, the outcome of which could adversely affect the viability of the business. Clients to reject may also include entities already known to be experiencing financial instability, such as an inability to meet debt payments or to raise needed capital. The auditor can identify such matters by making enquiries of management, reviewing credit agency reports, and analysing previously issued audited or unaudited financial statements, and, if applicable, previous annual returns with regulatory agencies.

This raises the issue of who will audit risky clients. The possibility of auditors wanting to avoid risky clients provides some support for the legal liability reforms discussed in chapter 5.

However, this concern relates mainly to clients that have not previously been audited. This is because it is very unlikely that the Australian Securities and Investments Commission (ASIC) would accept the resignation of an auditor under s. 329 of the Corporations Act because of a client's poor legal and financial stability.

Evaluating the entity's auditability

Before accepting an engagement, the auditor should evaluate whether other conditions exist that raise questions as to the prospective client's auditability. Such conditions may include the absence or poor condition of important accounting records, management's disregard of its responsibility for maintaining other elements of an adequate internal control structure, or restrictions imposed by the prospective client on the conduct of the audit. In such cases, the auditor should decline the engagement or make clear to the client the possible effects of such conditions on the auditor's report.

8.1.2 Ethical and legal considerations

In conducting an audit, the auditor should comply with the ethical requirements of the profession's auditing standards, legislation and regulations and, where appropriate, the terms of the audit engagement, as specified in ASA 200 *Overall Objectives of the Independent Auditor and the Conduct of an Audit in Accordance with Australian Auditing Standards* (ISA 200).

Evaluating independence

Historically, the profession's ethical requirements were the main determinant of an auditor's evaluation of independence. However, for company auditors, the legal requirements have become more stringent in recent years (see detailed discussion in chapter 3).

In relation to the ethical requirement of independence, Section 290.6 of the Code of Ethics APES 110 (IFAC Code, Section 290.6) sets out the requirement of independence of mind and independence in appearance.

Thus, before accepting a new audit client, the firm must evaluate whether there are any circumstances that would compromise its independence. One procedure is to circulate the name of a prospective client to all professional staff to identify any financial or business relationships inconsistent with independence. If such relationships exist, then they should be discontinued where practicable — such as by sale of the shares — or the engagement should be declined. In addition, the firm should determine that acceptance of the client engagement would not result in any conflict of interest with other clients. For a continuing audit, a professional independence questionnaire may be completed annually for each client to ensure ongoing compliance with the firm's quality control policies and procedures on independence. Some firms require the engagement partner to provide a written representation to this effect.

Another area where the firm should evaluate independence is in the provision of non-assurance services to audit clients. Historically, this was very lucrative for accountants. However, it has also attracted a degree of controversy as some sectors see this as a threat to the independence of the external audit function. In Section 290.158 of the Code of Ethics (IFAC Code, Section 290.158) it states that firms should evaluate the significance of any threat to independence created by the provision of these types of services. The firm should try to eliminate or reduce the threat by applying safeguards and if these safeguards cannot reduce the threat to an appropriate level, one of the services should be refused. In the United States, regulators have placed restrictions on the types of non-audit services that can be provided by auditors. Currently no such regulatory restrictions have been implemented in Australia. However, under s. 300 (11B) of the Corporations Act, the boards of all listed companies must provide details of the amounts paid for non-audit services, as well as a statement that they are satisfied the provision of these services is compatible with the general standard of independence for auditors that is required by the Corporations Act.

A number of other regulatory requirements implemented under the Corporations Act that prescribe certain ethical requirements are discussed in more detail in chapter 3.

The significant requirements relating to independence are summarised below.

- s. 307C — The auditor must give a written declaration to the directors that there have been no contraventions of the auditor independence requirements of the Corporations Act or any applicable code of professional conduct.
- s. 324CA — If the auditor becomes aware of a conflict of interest, he or she should, as soon as possible, take all reasonable steps to ensure the conflict of interest ceases to exist.
- s. 324DA — If an auditor plays a significant role in the audit of a listed company for 5 successive years, he or she is not eligible to play a significant role for at least 2 successive years.

Assessing competence to perform the audit

The quality control policy on the assignment of engagement teams in ASA 220.14 (ISA 220.14) places the onus on the engagement partner to ensure that the team has the competence and ability to perform the audit in accordance with auditing and ethical standards as well as relevant legal requirements.

To be able to comply with this requirement, the firm should have appropriate quality control over human resources (such as hiring, continuing professional development and advancement) to ensure that there are sufficient personnel within the organisation with the necessary capabilities, competence, and commitment to ethical principles.

The typical **audit team** consists of:

- a **partner**, who has both overall and final responsibility for the engagement
- an **audit manager**, who coordinates and supervises the execution of the audit program
- one or more seniors, who may oversee the conduct of the audit with specific responsibility for work in complex areas
- staff assistants, who perform many of the required procedures under the supervision of the seniors.

The team may also need the assistance and guidance of **experts**, such as computer audit specialists. If the audit firm does not have the required skills, it may engage external consultants to provide the necessary expertise.

An auditor is not expected to have the expertise of a person trained for, or qualified to engage in, the practice of another profession or occupation. ASA 620 *Using the Work of an*

Auditor's Expert (ISA 620) recognises that the auditor may use the work of experts to obtain sufficient appropriate audit evidence. Examples are the use of:

- appraisers to provide evidence about the valuation of assets such as property, plant and equipment, works of art and precious stones
- geologists and engineers to determine the quantities of mineral and petroleum reserves and remaining useful life of plant and equipment
- actuaries to determine amounts used in accounting for a superannuation plan
- lawyers to assess the probable outcome of pending litigation, interpretations of agreements, statutes and regulations.

Before using an expert, the auditor should be satisfied as to the professional qualifications, reputation and objectivity of the expert. The auditor should consider, for example, whether the expert has appropriate professional qualifications, relevant experience in the matters in question, adequate standing within the profession, and any relationship with the client that may impair his or her objectivity. The auditor should evaluate that the scope and work performed by the expert is appropriate as audit evidence regarding the assertion being considered.

Determining ability to use due care

Ethical principles require the auditor to exercise due care in performing the audit and preparing the report. The auditor should decline an engagement if due professional care cannot be exercised throughout the audit. Determination of due care may involve a review of both the work done and the judgements exercised by those assisting in the audit. The responsibility for ensuring that this is done on an audit engagement rests with the engagement partner (ASA 220.18; ISA 220.18). This also includes communicating relevant information about the client to the engagement team, as well as ensuring all members of the team understand the objectives of the work that will be performed. The engagement partner is also responsible for ensuring there is appropriate supervision and review on an audit engagement.

Supervision involves tracking the progress of the audit engagement, resolving significant issues that arise, and identifying matters that require more experienced staff. It also involves evaluating the progress of individual members of the engagement team to ensure that they understand what they are doing and have the time to perform their work. Review responsibilities relate to more experienced team members reviewing the work of less experienced team members to ensure that their work has been carried out properly and that sufficient and appropriate evidence has been obtained and documented to support the auditor's report.

When scheduling the audit, consideration should be given to whether the number and levels of staff appropriate to complete the audit with due care will be available. Although the detailed schedule generally would not be prepared until several steps in the audit planning phase have been completed, the firm should have a reasonable idea of the resources needed and timing of the audit.

Preliminary work on a **time budget** for the audit is often done as part of the scheduling considerations. The development of a time budget involves estimating the hours expected to be required at each staff level (partner, manager, senior and so on) for each part of the audit. These time estimates can then be multiplied by the chargeout rates for each staff level to arrive at an estimate of total costs for the engagement.

The fee for the audit is often determined on a fixed basis from a tendering process. The auditor should ensure that the time budget is appropriate to allow for the performance of a quality audit irrespective of the fee that has been quoted to the client. However, in originally quoting the audit fee, the auditor should ensure that the fee is commensurate with the service provided, and reflects the time needed and quality of staff necessary to complete the audit in accordance with auditing standards.

When performing the audit, the auditor should consider the activities of the internal audit function of the client and their effect on the external audit, as outlined in ASA 610 *Using the Work of Internal Auditors* (ISA 610). The work of internal auditors who understand the internal control structure and perform tests of controls and substantive procedures may reduce the extent of independent audit work in certain areas. However, when internal audit work is relied on, the external auditor must evaluate and test that work to ensure that it is adequate to meet the external auditor's obligation of due care.

LEARNING objective 2

State the purpose and content of an engagement letter.

8.2 AUDIT ENGAGEMENT LETTERS

As a final step in the audit acceptance phase, in compliance with auditing standards and good professional practice, it is important to confirm the terms of each engagement in an **engagement letter**, as in figure 8.2, which shows an extract from ASA 210.

The form and content of the letter may vary for different clients, but shall include the following according to ASA 210.10:
- the objective and scope of the audit of the financial report
- the responsibilities of the auditor
- the responsibilities of management
- identification of the applicable financial reporting framework for the preparation of the financial report
- reference to the expected form and content of any reports to be issued by the auditor and a statement that there may be circumstances in which a report may differ from its expected form and content.

FIGURE 8.2:
Auditor's engagement letter as per Appendix 1 of ASA 210

> **To the appropriate representative of management or those charged with governance of ABC Company:[1]**
>
> *[The objective and scope of the audit]*
> You[2] have requested that we audit the financial report of ABC Company which comprises the statement of financial position as at 30 June 20X1 and the statement of comprehensive income, statement of changes in equity and statement of cash flows for the year then ended, and notes comprising a summary of significant accounting policies and other explanatory information, and the directors' declaration. We are pleased to confirm our acceptance and our understanding of this audit engagement by means of this letter. Our audit will be conducted with the objective of our expressing an opinion on the financial report.
>
> *[The responsibilities of the auditor]*
> We will conduct our audit in accordance with Australian Auditing Standards. Those standards require that we comply with ethical requirements and plan and perform the audit to obtain reasonable assurance about whether the financial report is free from material misstatement. An audit involves performing procedures to obtain audit evidence about the amounts and disclosures in the financial report. The procedures selected depend on the auditor's judgement, including the assessment of the risks of material misstatement of the financial report, whether due to fraud or error. An audit also includes evaluating the appropriateness of accounting policies used and the reasonableness of accounting estimates made by management, as well as evaluating the overall presentation of the financial report.
>
> Because of the inherent limitations of an audit, together with the inherent limitations of internal control, there is an unavoidable risk that some material misstatements may not be detected, even though the audit is properly planned and performed in accordance with Australian Auditing Standards.
>
> *(continued)*

In making our risk assessments, we consider internal control relevant to the entity's preparation of the financial report in order to design audit procedures that are appropriate in the circumstances, but not for the purpose of expressing an opinion on the effectiveness of the entity's internal control. However, we will communicate to you in writing concerning any significant deficiencies in internal control relevant to the audit of the financial report that we have identified during the audit.

[The responsibilities of management and identification of the applicable financial reporting framework (for purposes of this example, it is assumed that the auditor has not determined that the law or regulation prescribes those responsibilities in appropriate terms; the descriptions in paragraph 6(b) of this Auditing Standard are therefore used).]

Our audit will be conducted on the basis that [management and, where appropriate, those charged with governance][3] acknowledge and understand that they have responsibility:

(a) For the preparation of the financial report that gives a true and fair view in accordance with the *Corporations Act 2001* and Australian Accounting Standards;[4]

(b) For such internal control as [management] determines is necessary to enable the preparation of the financial report that is free from material misstatement, whether due to fraud or error; and

(c) To provide us with:

   (i) access to all information of which the directors and management are aware that is relevant to the preparation of the financial report such as records, documentation and other matters;

   (ii) additional information that we may request from the directors and management for the purpose of the audit; and

   (iii) unrestricted access to persons within the entity from whom we determine it necessary to obtain audit evidence.

As part of our audit process, we will request from [management and, where appropriate, those charged with governance], written confirmation concerning representations made to us in connection with the audit.

We look forward to full cooperation from your staff during our audit.

[Other relevant information]

[Insert other information, such as fee arrangements, billings and other specific terms, as appropriate.]

[Reporting]

[Insert appropriate reference to the expected form and content of the auditor's report.]
The form and content of our report may need to be amended in the light of our audit findings.

Other matters under the *Corporations Act 2001*

Independence
We confirm that, to the best of our knowledge and belief, we currently meet the independence requirements of the *Corporations Act 2001* in relation to the audit of the financial report. In conducting our audit of the financial report, should we become aware that we have contravened the independence requirements of the *Corporations Act 2001*, we shall notify you on a timely basis. As part of our audit process, we shall also provide you with a written independence declaration as required by the *Corporations Act 2001*.

The *Corporations Act 2001* includes specific restrictions on the employment relationships that can exist between the audited entity and its auditors. To assist us in meeting the independence requirements of the *Corporations Act 2001*, and to the extent permitted by law and regulation, we request you discuss with us:

- the provision of services offered to you by [insert firm name] prior to engaging or accepting the service; and
- the prospective employment opportunities of any current or former partner or professional employee of [insert firm name] prior to the commencement of formal employment discussions with the current or former partner or professional employee.

Annual General Meetings

The *Corporations Act 2001* provides that shareholders can submit written questions to the auditor before an Annual General Meeting provided that they relate to the auditor's report or the conduct of the audit. To assist us in meeting this requirement in the *Corporations Act 2001* relating to Annual General Meetings, we request you provide to us written questions submitted to you by shareholders as soon as practicable after the question(s) is received and no later than five business days before the Annual General Meeting, regardless of whether you believe them to be irrelevant.

Presentation of Audited Financial Report on the internet

It is our understanding that ABC Company intends to publish a hard copy of the audited financial report and auditor's report for members, and to electronically present the audited financial report and auditor's report on its internet website. When information is presented electronically on a website, the security and controls over information on the website should be addressed by the entity to maintain the integrity of the data presented. The examination of the controls over the electronic presentation of audited financial information on the entity's website is beyond the scope of the audit of the financial report. Responsibility for the electronic presentation of the financial report on the entity's website is that of the governing body of the entity.

Please sign and return the attached copy of this letter to indicate your acknowledgement of, and agreement with, the arrangements for our audit of the financial report including our respective responsibilities.

Yours faithfully

....

Partner

XYZ & Co.

Acknowledged and agreed on behalf of ABC Company by (signed)

....

Name and Title

Date

1. The addressees and references in the letter would be those that are appropriate in the circumstances of the engagement, including the relevant jurisdiction. It is important to refer to the appropriate persons — see paragraph A21. For an audit under the *Corporations Act 2001*, the appropriate persons are the Directors.
2. Throughout this letter, references to "you," "we," "us," "management," "those charge with governance" and "auditor" would be used or amended as appropriate in the circumstances.
3. Use terminology as appropriate in the circumstances. For an audit under the *Corporations Act 2001*, the appropriate terminology is "the Directors".
4. Or, for financial reports not prepared under the *Corporations Act 2001*, "For the preparation and fair presentation of the financial report in accordance with Australian Accounting Standards."

To eliminate the need to prepare a new letter each year, the letter normally includes a statement that it continues in force until replaced. A new letter may be appropriate on the occurrence of events such as a change in management, ownership, nature and/or size of the entity's business or legal requirements.

Auditors appointed in accordance with the provisions of the Corporations Act must fulfil their statutory responsibilities. However, they may assume additional responsibilities if desired by both parties. When auditors are appointed by an entity not incorporated under the Corporations Act — such as a partnership or a tertiary education institution — it is even more important to confirm the nature of duties and responsibilities through an engagement letter.

An engagement letter constitutes a legal contract between the auditor and the client. By clearly stating the nature of services to be performed and the responsibilities of the auditor, such letters may help the auditor to avoid involvement in litigation. The letter in figure 8.2 is for use as a guide, in conjunction with the considerations outlined in ASA 210 (ISA 210), and will need to be varied according to individual requirements and circumstances. Note that APES 305 *Terms of Engagement* contains further requirements relating to accountants providing services to their clients. Compliance with ASA 210 will ensure compliance with APES 305.

Do you know ...

8.1 ☐ The decision to accept an audit engagement depends on evaluating the client by asking the existing auditor and other parties about the integrity of management and by identifying special circumstances and unusual risks associated with the entity.

8.2 ☐ The decision to accept an audit also depends on ethical and legal considerations that relate to the firm's ability to meet the independence criteria and to complete the audit with competence and due care. The auditor then needs to prepare an engagement letter.

LEARNING 3
objective

Explain the steps in planning an audit.

8.3 STEPS IN PLANNING AN AUDIT

Once the steps associated with accepting an audit engagement have been completed, the next phase is to develop an audit plan for the conduct and scope of the audit. Proper **audit planning** is crucial. The explanatory material of ASA 300 *Planning an Audit of a Financial Report* (ISA 300) states that the plan should be to conduct the audit in an efficient and timely manner. Note that although efficiency and timeliness are important, the most important consideration is to ensure the audit is done effectively. Thus ASA 300.4 (ISA 300.3) outlines the objective of the auditor which is to 'plan the audit so it will be performed in an effective manner'.

Audit planning involves the development of an overall audit strategy that sets out the general direction and scope of the audit. From this general strategy, a more detailed audit plan is developed that sets out the procedures to be carried out in the audit. Adequate planning helps to ensure that appropriate attention is given to important areas of the audit, that problems are identified properly, and that work is completed expeditiously. It is also necessary for coordinating the work done by other auditors and experts. The audit should be planned with a degree of professional scepticism in relation to matters such as the integrity of management, errors and irregularities, and illegal acts. The amount of planning required in an engagement will vary with the size and the complexity of the entity, and the auditor's knowledge of the business and experience with the entity. Considerably more effort is needed to plan an initial audit than a recurring audit. Note that planning continues throughout the engagement and the audit approach should be amended where events occur during the audit that suggest the original plan is no longer appropriate.

Steps in planning the audit

Planning starts with obtaining an understanding of the entity and its environment and the events, transactions and practices affecting the entity. An important part of obtaining this understanding includes the use of **analytical procedures**. A specific issue that has become more significant in recent years is fraud and therefore an important element of understanding an entity relates to the auditor considering the likelihood of fraud and its possible effects on the financial statements. We will now consider each of these issues.

Planning also involves setting materiality levels, assessing audit risk and its components, obtaining an understanding of the internal control structure, and developing a preliminary audit strategy for significant assertions, as shown in figure 8.3. We explain the first step in this chapter. In all but the smallest engagements, the auditor makes a preliminary visit to the entity, usually before its financial year-end. This visit is referred to as the **interim audit**. During the interim audit, the auditor obtains an understanding of the internal control structure and assesses control risk. (We consider the concepts pertaining to this step in chapter 9.) An audit program is then developed on the basis of a final determination of detection risk for each assertion, consistent with the overall level of audit risk (see chapter 9).

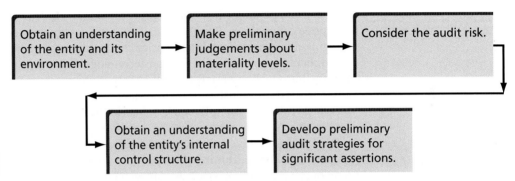

FIGURE 8.3:
Steps in planning the audit

LEARNING 4
objective

Identify the risks of misstatement through understanding the entity and its environment.

8.4 UNDERSTANDING THE ENTITY AND ITS ENVIRONMENT

To plan an audit, the auditor should obtain an understanding of the entity and its environment and the events, transactions and practices that may have a significant effect on the financial statements. This is stated in paragraph 3 of ASA 315 *Identifying and Assessing the Risks of Material Misstatement through Understanding the Entity and Its Environment* (ISA 315.3):

> The objective of the auditor is to identify and assess the risks of material misstatement whether due to fraud or error, at the financial report and assertion levels, through understanding the entity and its environment, including the entity's internal control, thereby providing a basis for designing and implementing responses to the assessed risks of material misstatement.

This understanding provides a framework for planning an overall audit approach that responds to the unique characteristics of the entity. In recurring engagements, the auditor's emphasis is on evaluating new developments in the entity's business and industry. Changes may be gradual or sudden, and may increase the likelihood of errors of audit importance or alleviate audit problems. ASA 315.11 (ISA 315.11) outlines the key issues in understanding the entity and its environment:

- industry, regulatory and other external factors, including the applicable financial reporting framework
- nature of the entity, including its operations and its ownership and governance structures
- selection and application of accounting policies

- objectives and strategies and the related business risks that may result in a material misstatement of the financial statements
- measurement and review of the entity's financial performance.

These are discussed in the following sections of this chapter. Another step suggested by ASA 315.12 (ISA 315.12) in understanding the entity and its environment is to assess internal control. This is discussed further in chapter 9.

Other specific knowledge needed relates to due consideration of the possibility of fraud in the audit planning process and this is discussed separately after consideration of the aforementioned issues.

8.4.1 Industry, regulatory and other external factors

Industry conditions

Understanding industry conditions includes understanding the market for a client's products, the competition, the entity's and competitors' capacity relative to market conditions, and price competition. For example, if an entity has high fixed costs and low contribution margins, and is faced with intense price competition, the auditor should expect some financial difficulties for the entity. In high technology industries, the auditor needs to be aware that the introduction of new technologies by competitors may make the entity's technology obsolete. Certain industries may also have transactions that increase the risks of material misstatements. For example, some industries have long-term contracts that involve significant estimates of revenues and costs that give rise to risks of material misstatements. More generally, if the industry has weak conditions overall, there is more sensitivity from the market to bad news. This increases pressure on management to meet targets and may therefore increase the risk of earnings management.

Information on the industry and economic conditions can be obtained from trade journals, industry statistics compiled by government or private agencies, data accumulated by the audit firm, and professional guidance statements where available.

Regulatory environment

The auditor should also understand the entity's regulatory environment. The regulatory environment can have direct economic consequences and affect accounting and disclosure requirements.

Economic consequences can arise from the government imposing (or taking away) tariffs and other trade barriers that may have a material impact on a company. Economic consequences also arise from regulatory approval or otherwise of certain products. For example, in the pharmaceutical industry, approval or otherwise of products under the *Therapeutic Goods Act 1989* can have significant economic consequences.

ASA 250 *Consideration of Laws and Regulations in an Audit of a Financial Report* (ISA 250) states that the auditor must obtain a general understanding of the legal and regulatory framework applicable to the entity and the industry and the entity's level of compliance.

The impact of regulation on accounting and disclosure requirements for most Australian companies mainly relates to the requirements of the Corporations Act. However, there are also specific regulatory requirements for particular industries that must be considered. For example, the Australian Prudential Regulation Authority (APRA) is prudential regulator of the financial services industry, which includes banks, credit unions, insurance companies and many members of the superannuation industry. The auditor should be aware that non-compliance with relevant laws and regulations may materially affect the financial statements.

Economy-wide factors

The general economy and its effect on the entity's business should also be considered by the auditor. This includes the general level of economic activity, interest rates and the availability of financing, and the level of inflation.

For example, during the global financial crisis (GFC) that began late in 2007, operating cash flow and capital spending deteriorated, and borrowing capacity dwindled. The stock market dropped significantly, adversely affecting investor wealth and making equity capital difficult to obtain. Companies responded by laying off employees and restructuring. These economic conditions create circumstances that require write-offs of receivables, write-downs in the value of inventory, or significant reductions in the value of assets. These conditions increase the inherent risk of misstatements and require close examination by the auditor.

8.4.2 The nature of the entity, including its selection and application of accounting policies

Auditors should also obtain an understanding of the nature of the audit client when planning the audit, including its selection and application of accounting policies. The following discussion covers both what the auditor should understand and how the auditor would use this knowledge in audit planning.

Business operations

Knowledge of the entity's business operations includes understanding such matters as the entity's:
- method of obtaining revenues (e.g. manufacturing, retailing, import–export trading, banking, utility)
- products or services and markets (e.g. major customers and contracts, terms of payment, profit margins, market share, competitors, exports, pricing policies, reputation of products, warranties, back orders, marketing strategy, objectives)
- conduct of operations (e.g. stages and methods of production, business segments, fixed vs variable costs, details of declining or expanding operations)
- location of production facilities, warehouses and offices
- employment (e.g. wages levels, union contracts, superannuation benefits, incentive bonus programs, government regulation relating to employment matters)
- transactions with related parties.

An auditor usually expects differing financial positions, results of operations, and cash flows for manufacturers as opposed to service entities. Companies in the airline or hotel industries, for example, have high fixed costs, and capacity use is an important aspect of the business. The auditor of the airline might focus on the relationship between fuel costs, employee compensation and revenues. This type of information helps the auditor develop a knowledgeable perspective about financial amounts and disclosures that are specific to the entity.

Knowledge of the entity's business operations may influence the selection and application of accounting policies. For example, the terms and conditions of sales made in the normal course of business will influence revenue recognition principles. The extent to which an airline offers frequent flyer benefits influences the application of accounting for frequent flyer liabilities. Finally, the expected product life cycle, which can be very short for some technology companies, will influence the useful life of related manufacturing equipment.

Auditors also use knowledge of the entity's operations to identify significant inherent risks. Auditors of manufacturing companies are usually concerned about the fairness of assertions relating to receivables and inventories, whereas such assertions might not be significant for service companies. A bank auditor might focus on the fairness of the entity's loan loss reserves because of the centrality of business loans to the bank's business operations.

Another important aspect of understanding business operations involves obtaining knowledge of related party transactions. Related party transactions are transactions between a company and its management, principal owners, their immediate family members, and/or affiliated companies. These transactions represent high inherent risks because they may not have the economic substance of an arm's-length transaction between two independent parties. ASA 550 *Related Parties* (ISA 550) describes important audit procedures that should be performed in planning an audit.

It is particularly important to identify the existence of related parties so that transactions with related parties can be identified throughout the audit. For example, the auditor might identify related parties by requesting information from management, reviewing filings with ASIC and other regulatory agencies, reviewing shareholder listings of closely held companies to identify principal shareholders, or reviewing previous years working papers for the names of known related parties.

Investments

Knowledge of the entity's investing activities includes understanding the entity's:
- capital investment activities, including investments in plant and equipment and technology, and any recent or planned changes
- acquisitions, mergers or disposals of business activities (planned or recently executed)
- investments and disposition of securities and loans
- investments in non-consolidated entities, including partnerships, joint ventures and special-purpose entities.

A crucial decision for any business is its investment in productive assets. A forest products company is usually concerned about its investments both in timber and timberlands and manufacturing capacity. The company's ability to generate revenues depends on these investments. Critical investments for technology and pharmaceutical companies are their investments in research and development. Software companies invest in people, and although this human capital cannot be capitalised on the balance sheet/statement of financial position, it is nevertheless important to revenue generation. Understanding the nature of an entity's investments helps the auditor develop expectations of financial statement amounts and disclosures.

In an environment where public companies are under significant pressure to perform, an auditor should understand the relationships between productive assets and a company's revenues and cost. It is essential for auditors to understand the economic drivers of financial results. For example, technology companies might spend very large amounts of money on a manufacturing line for a product that might have a useful life of 18 to 24 months. This understanding is critical for estimating depreciation expense and matching expenses with revenues.

Financing

Knowledge of the entity's financing activities includes understanding the entity's:
- debt structure, including covenants, restrictions, guarantees and off-balance-sheet financing arrangements

- group structure — major subsidiaries and associated entities, including consolidated and non-consolidated structures
- leasing of property, plant and equipment for use in the business
- beneficial owners
- use of derivative financial instruments.

Decisions about the acquisition and financing of productive assets go hand in hand. Many companies now use complex transactions with related companies, along with intricate operating agreements to accomplish both specific financial reporting and operating objectives. The use of special-purpose entities or variable-interest entities to structure the use of assets and keep debt off the balance sheet is a significant inherent risk for auditors of both public and private companies. Sophisticated financing structures may increase the risk of misapplication of applicable accounting standards.

During good economic times, companies might commit to financial guarantees that seem to be only a remote possibility. During an economic downturn, however, the need to make good on guarantees might become a reality. Auditors should be alert to the violation of debt covenants, or events that might trigger guarantees, for such events might raise substantial doubt about an entity's ability to continue as a going concern.

Financial reporting and accounting practices

Knowledge of the entity's financial reporting activities includes understanding such matters as the entity's:
- accounting principles and industry-specific practices
- revenue recognition practices
- accounting for fair values
- inventories (e.g. locations and quantities)
- industry-specific significant accounts and transaction classes (e.g. loans and investments for banks, accounts receivable and inventory for manufacturers, research and developments for pharmaceuticals)
- accounting for unusual or complex transactions, including those in controversial or emerging areas (such as accounting for share-based transactions)
- financial statement presentation and disclosure.

It is important that the auditor should evaluate the accounting policies selected by the entity to ensure that they are appropriate for the business and also consistent with the industry. The airline industry, for example, has specific accounting practices for accounting for the liability associated with frequent flyer benefits. The software industry has specific industry practices associated with the question of when the costs of developing software should be capitalised rather than expensed. This understanding is essential for developing a knowledgeable perspective about the entity's accounting practices and whether they present fairly in accordance with applicable accounting standards.

In obtaining the understanding of accounting policies the auditor should be aware of the methods to account for significant and unusual transactions and also those in areas where there is limited guidance. The auditor should also carefully evaluate any changes proposed to accounting policies.

8.4.3 The entity's objectives, strategies and related business risks

In relation to evaluation of an entity's objectives, strategies and related business risks, ASA 315.11(d) (ISA 315.11(d)) states that the auditor shall obtain an understanding of them in the context of whether they are associated with risks of material misstatement.

These terms are defined as follows.

- An **entity's objectives** are the overall plans for the entity as defined by those charged with governance and management.
- An **entity's strategies** are the operational approaches by which management intends to achieve its objectives.
- **Business risks** result from significant conditions, events, circumstances, actions or inactions that could adversely affect the entity's ability to achieve its objectives and execute its strategies.

Some matters the auditor may consider in the evaluations include:

- industry developments (e.g. a possible business risk may be that in a changing industry the entity may not have the appropriate personnel or expertise to deal with the changes)
- new products and services (e.g. a possible business risk may relate to whether the new products and services are accepted in the market)
- expansion of the business (e.g. a potential business risk might be that the estimated demand associated with the expansion has not been accurately estimated)
- current and prospective financing requirements (e.g. a business risk is loss of financing because of inability to meet debt covenant requirements).

Business risk is broader than simply examining the entity for the risk of material misstatements. However, business risk includes the risk of material misstatements. The requirements on auditors for evaluation of an entity's objectives and strategies and related business risks is only to the extent that these may result in material misstatement of the financial statements. To illustrate this, assume the client expands the business by moving into a new market and this expansion does not lead to the expected sales. This may result in a number of material misstatements that require adjustments — for example, inventory may need to be written down and accounts receivable may need to be written off. There may also be longer term consequences that may not necessarily affect the current period's audit, such as going concern issues arising from an inability to repay loans associated with the expansion. The interrelationship between business risk and audit risk is presented in figure 8.4 below.[1] As can be seen, business risk is broader than audit risk and it *could* lead to a risk of material misstatement.

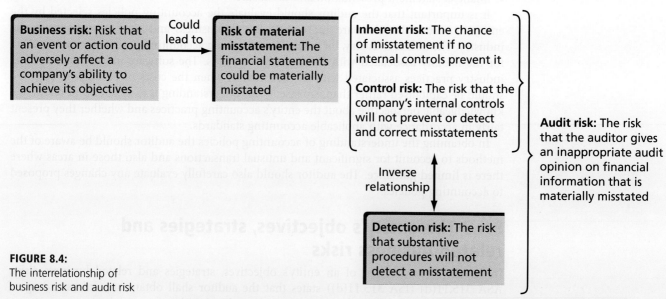

FIGURE 8.4:
The interrelationship of business risk and audit risk

Source: C Richardson, 'Risk: business or audit?', *Student Accountant*, September 2006, p. 46.

8.4.4 Measurement and review of the entity's financial performance

Auditing standards also require auditors to obtain an understanding of the measurement and review of the entity's financial performance, including both internal and external measures. Such measures might include:

- key ratios and operating statistics
- key performance indicators
- employee performance measures and incentive compensation plans
- industry trends
- the use of forecasts, budgets and variance analysis
- analyst reports and credit rating reports.

A company might use a variety of financial and non-financial measures to monitor performance. Today, many companies measure the efficiency of the manufacturing process by comparing the quantity of raw material used to the quantity of finished goods produced, the labour hours involved in producing finished goods, and materials and labour variances. In addition, they might monitor the effectiveness of the manufacturing process using quality control statistics or measures of the amount of rework required to meet standards. This information is essential for developing a knowledgeable perspective about reported amounts for inventory and cost of sales.

Many performance measures are produced by the entity's information system. If management assumes that data used for reviewing the entity's performance are accurate without having a basis for that assumption, errors may exist in the information, potentially leading management (or the auditor using the same information) to incorrect conclusions about performance. If the auditor uses management's performance measures to form an audit conclusion (e.g. in performing analytical procedures), he or she should consider the reliability of the information system that produces the measure and whether the measure is sufficiently precise to detect material misstatements.

Management and auditors use performance measure information in different ways. When reported measures differ from management's expectations, management may take corrective action to improve the entity's performance. For example, poor inventory turnover might cause a company to offer more attractive pricing in order to sell inventory. However, the auditor should consider whether a deviation in performance measures might indicate a risk of misstatement in underlying financial information. A decline in inventory turnover might mean that certain manufacturing costs are being capitalised as part of inventory rather than being expensed. Deviations from expected performance measures are critical when assessing the inherent risk associated with financial statement assertions.

Auditors are required to perform analytical procedures in planning the audit, which will usually involve use of management performance measures. This is discussed in the next section.

LEARNING objective 5

Explain the role of analytical procedures in audit planning.

8.5 ANALYTICAL PROCEDURES IN PLANNING

While the auditor is obtaining an understanding of the entity and its environment, ASA 520 *Analytical Procedures* (ISA 520) requires that auditors apply analytical procedures at the planning stage of the audit to obtain a more detailed understanding and to identify areas of potential risk.

Analytical procedures involve a study and comparison of relationships among data to identify expected or unexpected fluctuations and other unusual items. The common types of analytical procedures involve a comparison of the entity's financial information with:

- comparable information for a previous period or periods
- expected results such as budgets and forecasts
- industry averages.

Analytical procedures also include the study of relationships:

- among elements within the financial statements, such as a study of gross margin percentages
- between financial information and relevant non-financial information, such as a study of payroll costs for a number of employees.

Such procedures are performed during the planning phase to (1) enhance the understanding of the entity's business and (2) identify unexpected fluctuations and unusual relationships.

Unexpected fluctuations and unusual relationships indicate areas of greater risk of misstatements, so the auditor plans to perform extended procedures on these amounts. When results of analytical procedures are as expected, there is less possibility of a misstatement or an irregularity. The auditor may, therefore, reduce the level of substantive tests of details performed in support of these amounts.

Generally, analytical procedures performed during the planning phase use aggregate entity-wide data based on year-to-date or expected annual data. However, for entities with diverse operations, some disaggregation by product line or division may be necessary. In other cases, such as a company with seasonal business, it may be desirable to perform the analysis on monthly or quarterly data rather than on year-to-date or annual data. Appendix 8A to this chapter outlines ten of the most common ratios used in analytical procedures.

Unexplained significant differences are ordinarily viewed as an increased risk of misstatement in the accounts involved. In such cases, the auditor usually plans to perform more substantive tests on details of those accounts. By directing the auditor's attention to areas of greater risk, analytical procedures may help obtain a more effective and efficient audit.

Analytical procedures are also used as a substantive procedure. Their use for this purpose is explained in chapter 12. They are also used in the overall review of the financial statements immediately before the issue of the auditor's report. This use is explained in chapter 18.

LEARNING objective 6

Describe the requirements to consider the risk of fraud in the audit planning process.

8.6 CONSIDERATION OF FRAUD RISK IN PLANNING

The importance of considering **fraud** in the planning of an audit has increased in recent years. This is partially due to the number of high-profile corporate collapses that occurred between 2000 and 2002, which resulted in increased public scrutiny and demands placed on the audit function (discussed earlier in the text). ASA 240.11(a) *The Auditor's Responsibilities Relating to Fraud in an Audit of a Financial Report* (ISA 240) provides a definition of fraud as 'an intentional act by one or more individuals among management, those charged with governance, employees, or third parties, involving the use of deception to obtain an unjust or illegal advantage'.

Where fraud occurs, it is likely that some attempt will be made to cover it up, and so detecting misstatements as a result of fraud can be much more demanding than detecting misstatements as a result of errors. As part of the process of understanding the entity, the auditor should consider the possibility that fraud has occurred and discuss with management their procedures for preventing and detecting fraud. Although the auditor's role is not that of a fraud detector, the audit plan should include an expectation of detecting any material fraud that has occurred.

The fact that fraud is a problem in the Australian environment is clearly illustrated by the levels of fraud reported from the KPMG Fraud Survey 2012 in Australia and New Zealand shown in the Professional Environment box.

Fraud facts

372.7m

**Total value of
fraud experienced
by respondents**

3.08m

**Average loss to fraud
per organisation
experiencing fraud**

82%

increase
in individual **frauds
exceeding $1 million**

43%
**Respondent firms
experiencing fraud**

30%
**Respondent firms detecting
less than 40% of frauds
in their organisation**

47%
**Major frauds occurring
due to deficient
internal controls**

The victims

$322.2m

Fraud loss to respondent **financial services**
organisations

$50.3m

Fraud loss to respondent **non-financial services**
organisations

Respondents experiencing loss by size of organisation

■ Experiencing fraud
☐ Not experiencing fraud

Less than 100	101 – 500	501 – 1,000	1,001 – 10,000	More than 10,000
91%	69%	55%	44%	50%
9%	31%	45%	56%	50%

Number of employees

Source: ©KPMG Australia 2013

The villains

Inside jobs are on the increase, with 75% of major frauds committed by insiders.

2010   2012

| External perpetrator **35%** | Internal perpetrator **65%** | External perpetrator **25%** | Internal perpetrator **75%** |

 Management: **false invoicing**

 Non-management: **theft of cash**

External parties: **Fraudulent tendering**

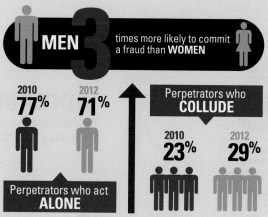

MEN **3** times more likely to commit a fraud than **WOMEN**

2010 **77%**   2012 **71%**

Perpetrators who act ALONE

Perpetrators who COLLUDE

2010 **23%**   2012 **29%**

Collusive fraud is **GROWING**

Most fraudsters don't have a history of dishonesty, earn close to $100k and are motivated by greed/lifestyle or personal financial pressure.

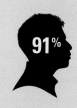 **91%**

 **82%**

 Greed/lifestyle **Personal financial pressure**

Perpetrators with no known history of fraud

Increase in fraudsters earning close to $100k

Most common motivations for fraud

The heroes: prevention and detection

 **Awareness training**

 Internal controls

 **Notification by employees**

 Notification by external parties

Organisations rely on internal controls and employees to detect major fraud, however awareness of fraud reporting remains quite low, particularly among third parties. Other methods of detection have increased, through the use of fraud detection procedures, anonymous reporting and internal audit. With regard to the latter, it is worth noting the revised Institute of Internal Auditors Standard (1220.A1), which now requires internal auditors to consider the probability of significant errors, fraud or non-compliance.

Source: ©KPMG Australia 2013

Source: KPMG Forensic 2013, Fraud, Bribery and Corruption Survey 2012, pp. 4–5, www.kpmg.com.au.

As can be seen in the Professional Environment (pp. 335–6), fraud continues to be a major problem in the Australian and New Zealand environment.

The auditor is required to consider the risks of material misstatements in the financial statements due to fraud.

In paragraph 24 of ASA 240 *The Auditor's Responsibility Relating to Fraud in an Audit of a Financial Report* (ISA 240.24), the following is required:

> The auditor shall evaluate whether the information obtained from the other risk assessment procedures and related activities performed indicates that one or more fraud risk factors are present.

In making the assessment of whether fraud risk factors are present, the auditor should understand the three conditions that are generally present when fraud occurs. These are known as the 'fraud triangle' (as shown in figure 8.5):

1. incentives/pressures
2. opportunity
3. attitudes/rationalisation.

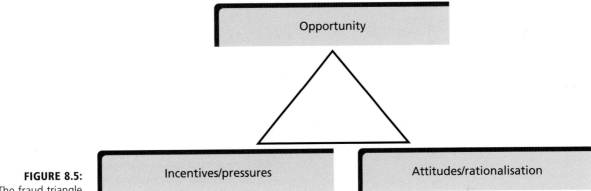

FIGURE 8.5: The fraud triangle

The auditor should be concerned with fraud risk factors that relate to either misstatements resulting from fraudulent financial reporting or from misappropriation of assets. The next two sections of this chapter discuss risk factors that auditors should consider when assessing the risk of fraudulent misstatements. This is followed by some of the specific procedures that auditors should perform to identify these risks.

8.6.1 Fraudulent financial reporting

Fraudulent financial reporting is a serious problem for auditors of public companies and, in some cases, private companies. The incentives to achieve targets and attain bonuses, and the pressures associated with not meeting analysts' estimates, are enormous in public companies. Auditors must be alert for the types of risk factors that are often associated with fraudulent financial reporting. Examples of these factors are presented in table 8.1.

The greatest opportunities for fraudulent financial reporting exist with complex transactions and accounting estimates that are difficult to corroborate. Perhaps the best way to reduce the incentives and opportunity for fraud begins with the board of directors and its audit committee. Effective oversight of the financial reporting process by competent directors with significant financial reporting experience can create a tone at the top of the organisation that expects representational faithfulness in financial reporting. This requires audit committee members who are capable of asking penetrating questions of management and auditors who are capable of identifying and understanding the economic substance of both complex transactions and accounting estimates. The opportunity is also reduced when senior management leads by example in making decisions that reinforce representational faithfulness in financial reporting. However, auditors must recognise that senior management is also in a position to make decisions that may not result in fair presentation in the financial statements, so this aspect of assessing the risk of fraudulent financial reporting needs careful review.

TABLE 8.1:
Risk factors associated with fraudulent financial reporting

Risk factors	Examples of high-risk conditions
Incentives/pressures	Economic, industry and operating conditions • Low barriers to entry, high degree of competition combined with declining margins. • Vulnerability to technological change, product obsolescence or interest rates. • Inability to generate operating cash flows. • Rapid growth in profitability compared with others in the industry. Pressure from third parties • There are optimistic or aggressive expectations regarding profitability, revenues or other targets. • The company is close to debt covenants. Management's personal financial position is threatened by the entity's financial performance • Management has significant financial interests in the entity. • A significant portion of management's compensation is based on bonuses tied to accounting numbers. Senior management places excessive pressure on other managers to meet financial targets.
Opportunity	The nature of the industry or the entity's operations provides opportunities to engage in fraudulent financial reporting that can arise from the following: • significant related-party transactions not in the ordinary course of business or with related entities not audited or audited by another firm • assets, liabilities, revenues or expenses based on significant estimates that involve subjective judgements or uncertainties that are difficult to corroborate • significant, unusual, or highly complex transactions, especially those close to period end that pose difficult 'substance over form' questions. There is ineffective monitoring of management as a result of the following: • domination of management by a single person or small group (in a non-owner-managed business) without compensating controls • ineffective board of directors or audit committee oversight over the financial reporting process.

Risk factors	Examples of high-risk conditions
	There is a complex or unstable organisational structure, as evidenced by the following: • overly complex organisational structure involving unusual legal entities or managerial lines of authority • high turnover of senior management, advisers or board members. Internal control components are deficient as a result of the following: • inadequate monitoring of controls, including automated controls • high turnover rates or employment of ineffective accounting, internal audit, or information technology staff • ineffective accounting and information systems, including situations involving reportable conditions.
Attitudes/ rationalisation	• Management and employees do not place a high priority on the entity's values or ethical standards. • Non-financial management shows excessive participation in, or preoccupation with, the selection of accounting principles or the determination of significant estimates. • Management shows an excessive interest in maintaining or increasing the entity's share price or earnings trend. • Management is concerned about achieving commitments made to analysts, creditors and other third parties regarding aggressive or unrealistic forecasts. • Management places a low priority on correcting known weaknesses in internal controls on a timely basis. • Management attempts to justify marginal or inappropriate accounting on the basis of materiality on a recurring basis.

Finally, auditors should be alert to the signs of management attitudes or rationalisations that permit fraudulent financial reporting. This can reveal itself when non-financial management shows excessive participation in determining accounting results, which may provide a signal that achieving earnings targets is more important than representational faithfulness in reporting results. Frauds rarely start with an original plot to materially misstate financial reports. Rather, there is significant evidence that fraudulent financial reporting begins with a series of immaterial misstatements that eventually result in bigger and bolder steps that lead to material misstated financial statements. When management feels that it is appropriate to justify marginal or inappropriate accounting based on the immateriality of items, it may signal a willingness to use accounting techniques (rather than underlying economic substance) to achieve financial goals. Table 8.1 provides other examples of management attitudes or rationalisations that create situations allowing for fraudulent financial reporting.

Fraudulent financial reporting is an extreme form of 'earnings management' behaviour. Earnings management is defined as situations where managers apply accounting discretion and/or structure transactions to alter the company's financial statements with the intent of either misleading some stakeholders about the company or to influence contracts based on accounting numbers.[2] The examination of whether earnings have been subject to management is an important part of an auditor's role. The determination of what is acceptable and what is not by the auditor requires a good understanding of the entity and its environment. As can be seen from figure 8.6 below, there is a spectrum of earnings management and only at the extreme does it become fraud.[3]

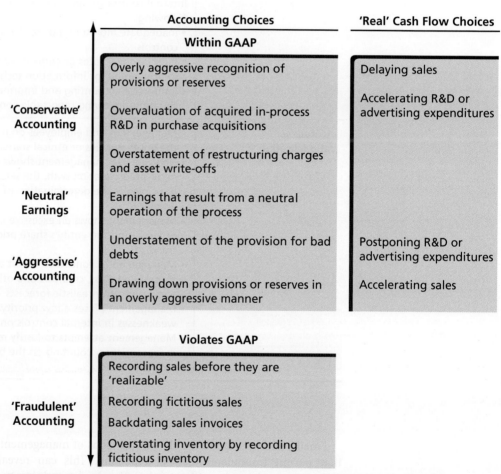

FIGURE 8.6:
The distinction between fraud and earnings management

Source: P Dechow & D Skinner, 'Earnings management: Reconciling the views of accounting academics, practitioners, and regulators', *Accounting Horizons*, vol. 14, no. 2, June 2000, pp. 235–50.

Auditors must approach audits with a sufficient degree of professional scepticism and recognise the types of factors listed in table 8.1. When even one or two of these factors are present, the auditor's knowledgeable perspective should lead to decisions to assess inherent risk or control risk at high levels. Professional scepticism is an important attribute of auditors in this environment where fraud risk evaluation is more important. The Institute of Chartered Accountants in Australia performed a comprehensive survey on audit quality in 2012 and they found that scepticism was a very important attribute, as explained in the Professional Environment opposite.

The must-have skills of an auditor

*T*he Institute of Chartered Accountants in Australia surveyed 1702 partners and staff on drivers of audit quality. Some of the findings are reported in the article that follows.

The importance of scepticism

Significantly, the survey found that auditors placed a great deal of importance on professional scepticism. While audit inspections by regulators in Australia and across the world continue to observe what they see as a lack of scepticism in audits, the Institute findings indicate auditors are aware of the importance of professional scepticism. Indeed, professional scepticism ranks in the top three important skills across all four respondent groups. Partners ranked it as the most important skill, while managers, graduates and staff ranked it as the second most important issue.

So how does one explain the difference between the Institute survey and findings by regulators around the world? The Institute is asking firms to address this. It might flow simply from a difference in the timings of reviews. At the same time, however, the firms need to make sure all their training drives a real scepticism and that it is not simply just a learned mantra. The findings were reassuring in that scepticism appears to be top of mind, however work might need to be done to ensure Australian regulators will in the future find the same thing.

El-Ansary says that the results suggest some work still needs to be done to ensure scepticism is remaining top of mind.

'The professional scepticism piece for us is an area where there is a pretty strong bias towards scepticism in the field work that is carried out day to day,' he says.

'What is apparent is that there is an opportunity, particularly for the younger staff involved in the audit teams, to learn from those who have more experience than them, to bring the appropriate perspective to the work they carry out day to day.'

'We need to focus around opportunities like mentoring and things like appropriate levels of training to help bolster their capacity, to bring that appropriate level of scepticism to the judgement decisions they make day to day.'

'I think that is one of the takeaways for us from this survey, and I think we need to acknowledge this framework around scepticism is robust, but there is most certainly an opportunity to continue to build on their capability in this area.'

'Professional scepticism is actually an issue that permeates right across the business community because it's about asking the tough questions that need to be asked, even when that might make some people uncomfortable.'

'What we have seen over the past five or six years in the marketplace is that it has become apparent that not enough scepticism is brought to bear in a number of instances where ultimately decisions were being made that led to the demise or major failure within large corporate groups, both here in Australia and abroad. I think professional scepticism is a key component of what we need to take away from the GFC as well. It's an issue that's pertinent in the audit space because we need auditors to exercise an appropriate level of scepticism around what they are being told, what they hear and what they see during the ordinary course of an audit.'

Source: L Gettler, 'The must-have skills of an auditor', *Charter*, October 2012, pp. 30–2.

8.6.2 Misappropriation of assets

The vast majority of fraud reported in the KPMGs 2012 fraud survey was misappropriation of assets by vendors (which usually involves collusion with employees), employees or management. Table 8.2 provides examples of the types of risk factors that are often associated with misappropriation of assets.

TABLE 8.2:
Risk factors associated with misappropriation of assets

Risk factors	Examples of high-risk conditions
Incentives/ pressures	Personal financial obligations may create pressure on management or employees with access to cash or other assets susceptible to theft to misappropriate those assets.
	Adverse relationships between the entity and employees with access to cash or other assets susceptible to theft may motivate those employees to misappropriate those assets. For example, adverse relationships may be created by the following: • known or expected future employee layoffs • recent or expected changes to employee compensation or benefit plans • promotions, compensation, or other rewards inconsistent with expectations.
Opportunity	Certain characteristics or circumstances may increase the susceptibility of assets to misappropriation. For example, opportunities to misappropriate assets increase when there are the following: • large amounts of cash on hand or processed • inventory items that are small in size, of high value, or in high demand • easily convertible assets, such as bearer bonds, diamonds, or computer chips.
	Inadequate internal control over assets may increase the susceptibility to misappropriation of those assets. For example, misappropriation of assets may occur because there is the following: • inadequate segregation of duties or independent checks • inadequate record keeping with respect to assets • inadequate system of authorisation and approval of transactions (for example in purchasing) • inadequate physical safeguards over cash, investments, inventory or fixed assets • lack of complete and timely reconciliations of assets.
	Inadequate management understanding of information technology, which enables information technology employees to perpetrate misappropriation such as inadequate access controls over automated records, including controls over and review of computer systems event logs.
Attitudes/ Rationalisation	• Disregard for the need for monitoring or reducing risks related to misappropriation of assets. • Disregard for internal control over misappropriation of assets by overriding existing controls or by failing to correct known internal control deficiencies. • Behaviour indicating displeasure or dissatisfaction with the company or its treatment of the employee. • Changes in behaviour or lifestyle that may indicate assets have been misappropriated.

The incentives and pressures that motivate employees to engage in fraud range from a grudge against management because an expected promotion or bonus was not granted, to benefits or other compensation being lost, or to the uncertainty associated with possible layoff. For example, a loyal bookkeeper denied a $100 monthly raise may find other ways to obtain the raise. Employees may have a variety of motivations that are difficult to identify, such as having to pay bills associated with gambling debts, sending children to private school, covering an investment loss, or living beyond one's means. Alternatively, an employee might invest in a business opportunity, the opportunity goes bust, and the employee makes up the loss by finding a way to embezzle assets from a company. Many of these motivations are not obvious, and the auditor often picks up clues by comments overheard in lunchrooms or in other casual conversations with employees.

Opportunity is the second, and critical, aspect of the fraud triangle. Employees involved in the misappropriation of assets usually have access to cash, inventory or various assets that can be easily converted into cash. When internal controls are seen to be weak, it provides an opportunity for fraud. The 2010 Report to the Nations by the US Association of Certified Fraud Examiners[4] reported 1843 cases of occupational fraud and the reasons that allowed these frauds to occur. A lack of internal controls was cited as the biggest deficiency in thirty-eight per cent of cases, followed by override of internal controls in nineteen per cent of cases. For example, a purchasing agent might exploit weak controls to have assets shipped to a home rather than to the business and have the business pay the invoice. The opportunity for fraud can be reduced by a strong system of internal control. The key aspects of a good system of internal control are discussed in depth in the next chapter but (1) good segregation of duties, (2) appropriate authorisation of transactions, and (3) accurate records that are regularly compared with assets minimise the opportunity for employee fraud.

When assets are misappropriated, individuals usually find ways to rationalise the behaviour by putting their personal wellbeing ahead of their responsibilities to their employers. Sometimes people rationalise their behaviour by believing that they are only doing what others have done. Sometimes people start by believing that the amount is small and they will pay it back. Soon they find that the small amount goes undetected, and they forget about paying it back and find themselves 'hooked' on their new source of cash. In some cases employees feel that their talents have been overlooked, and they see fraud as a form of compensation. A person's ability to rationalise fraudulent behaviour is difficult to detect because an auditor cannot audit someone's thoughts. Auditors should be alert to clues that might show up in people's behaviour, such as not taking holidays so they can continue to cover up their fraudulent activities, or not cooperating in correcting known deficiencies in internal controls.

Finally, auditors should not assume that all three conditions (incentives/pressures, opportunity and rationalisation) must be observed before concluding that there are identified risks of fraud. Incentives and rationalisation may be difficult to observe. Management or employees may actively try to hide some of the risk factors and cover up the existence of fraud. Professional standards are clear that, although the risk of material misstatement because of fraud may be greatest when all three fraud conditions are observed or evidenced, the auditor cannot assume that the inability to observe one or two of these conditions means that the risk of material misstatement because of fraud is low.

8.6.3 Auditing for fraud

Risk assessment procedures

What procedures should auditors perform to support a decision about the risk of material misstatement because of fraud? ASA 240 (ISA 240) suggests that auditors should perform the following procedures to identify the risk of material misstatement due to fraud.

- Make enquiries of management and others within the entity to obtain their views about the risk of fraud and how it is tackled.
- Consider any unusual or unexpected relationships that have been identified in performing analytical procedures in audit planning.
- Consider other information obtained while planning the audit.

Auditors usually make a series of enquiries about management's views regarding the risk of fraud and policies that have been established to reduce those risks. For example, auditors should enquire of management about whether management has knowledge of any fraud, suspected fraud, or allegations of fraud affecting the entity. The auditor should also understand how management communicates to employees its views on business practices and ethical behaviour. Auditors usually begin by making enquiries of management about their awareness of fraud risk and programs that have been put in place to prevent or detect fraud. Auditors should also make direct enquiries of the audit committee (or at least its chair) regarding the audit committee's view of the risk of fraud and the audit committee's oversight in this area. Finally, auditors usually find that it is helpful to conduct discussions with employees with varying levels of authority, including operating personnel not directly involved in the financial reporting process, and employees involved in initiating, recording, or processing complex or unusual transactions (e.g. sales transactions with multiple elements). Responses to enquiries might serve to corroborate management's representations, or they might provide information such as employees describing instances of management override of controls. When the auditor obtains inconsistent responses, he or she should obtain additional information to resolve the inconsistencies.

Analytical procedures performed in audit planning may be helpful in identifying accounts and assertions that are likely to contain misstatements. For example, an increase in gross margins combined with an increase in the number of inventory turnover days may indicate that production costs that should be expensed have been capitalised. These results might also indicate problems with recording fictitious inventory. Furthermore, a comparison of revenues and sales returns by month during the year and shortly after year-end may indicate the existence of undisclosed side agreements with customers that preclude revenue recognition. However, the auditor should also be aware that analytical procedures that compare only financial numbers might be ineffective in finding fraudulent financial reporting. In the case of fraud, the numbers may have been made to look reasonable. As a result, auditors often attempt to compare financial results with non-financial measures of business activity, such as comparing inventory quantities and values with direct labour hours.

Finally, the auditor should consider other information obtained during audit planning. Auditors may, for example, pick up clues about the risk of fraud when performing client acceptance and continuance evaluations, such as concerns about the integrity of management or challenges in recording complex transactions noted by the predecessor auditor. A continuing auditor might review the previous year's management letter to determine whether identified weaknesses in internal control have been corrected. Auditors might find that a company is very close to significant debt covenants when obtaining an understanding of the entity and its environment. Finally, auditors have a professional requirement to understand the entity's system of internal control (discussed in chapter 11). Weak internal controls provide an opportunity for fraud. The auditor should consider all the information acquired while performing risk assessment procedures in order to develop a knowledgeable perspective about the risk of fraud.

Brainstorming session

ASA 240 (ISA 240) requires the audit team members to discuss the risk of fraud as part of audit planning. This brainstorming session has several objectives. It should:

- allow junior members of the audit team to benefit from more senior members' knowledge of the audit client and of how fraud might be perpetrated
- allow more seasoned personnel a fresh set of eyes that might identify risks that otherwise might be overlooked
- allow audit management to set the appropriate tone for the audit and to emphasise the importance of approaching the audit with a 'questioning mind'
- emphasise the possibility that fraud might exist in any audit.

The main goal is to consider audit areas where the entity is most vulnerable to the risk that fraud could result in material misstatements in the financial statements. For example, the audit team might consider pressures faced by management to meet debt covenants or pressures from an owner–manager who expects certain levels of entity performance.

An important goal is to link the risk factors to specific account balances or assertions that are likely to be misstated. For example, one person's discussion with the purchasing agent, and a review of the purchases journal, may indicate that a high volume of business is directed to one vendor. However, another person's discussion with an owner–manager may provide no indication of establishing an exclusive supply relationship with a vendor. If there is a high volume of transactions that can be material to the financial statements, the audit team may want to design procedures to review the reasonableness of prices (the valuation and allocation assertion) in this aspect of the purchases cycle to evaluate the potential for vendor kickbacks to a purchasing agent. All three aspects of the fraud triangle may not be apparent. There may be valid business reasons for the situations. Nevertheless, the auditor needs to respond by assessing inherent or control risk as high, and by designing audit procedures that restrict detection risk to a low level.

Specific risks

Professional standards state that even if the auditor does not identify specific fraud risks, there is a possibility that management override of internal controls could occur. Management is in a unique position to perpetrate fraud because of its ability to, directly or indirectly, manipulate accounting records and prepare fraudulent financial statements. As a result, auditors should perform certain procedures to meet the risk of management override of controls. For example, auditors should examine journal entries and other adjustments for evidence of possible material misstatement because of fraud.

In summary, a significant aspect of developing a knowledge perspective about the risk involves explicit discussion and evaluation of fraud risk factors. Auditors should perform procedures to understand the relevant aspect of the fraud triangle (see figure 8.5 and tables 8.1 and 8.2) so that they can make informed decisions about the risk of material misstatement because of fraud. Once specific risk factors are identified, the auditor should evaluate whether they are high risk and likely to result in material misstatements in the financial statements.

LEARNING objective 7

Explain the purpose and function of audit working papers.

8.7 AUDIT DOCUMENTATION

From planning the audit through to preparing the auditor's report, it is important for auditors to provide sufficient evidence to support their audit opinion, and that evidence collected in support of an audit opinion (such as worksheets and checklists) is documented in the audit **working papers**. The term 'audit working papers' includes all documentation whether it is stored on paper, or in film or electronic media.

8.7.1 The purpose and function of working papers

Working papers are the subject of ASA 230 *Audit Documentation* (ISA 230). Properly prepared working papers demonstrate that the audit was performed in accordance with auditing standards. They show that the audit was properly planned and carried out, that there was adequate supervision, that an appropriate review was made of the audit work undertaken and, most importantly, that the evidence is sufficient and appropriate to support the audit opinion.

Working papers also serve to monitor the progress of the audit, especially where responsibility for separate tasks is allocated to different staff members. Completed working papers also provide a guide to the planning and performance of audits in subsequent periods.

The auditor's working papers should record the nature, timing and extent of the audit procedures performed; the results of the procedures and audit evidence obtained; and significant matters arising during the audit and conclusions reached (ASA 230.8; ISA 230.8).

Working papers should be tailored to meet the needs of the specific audit engagement. ASA 230.A2 (ISA 230.A2) states that the form, content and extent of the working papers are influenced by:

- the size and complexity of the entity
- the nature of the audit procedures to be performed
- the identified risks of material misstatement
- the significance of the audit evidence identified
- the nature and extent of exceptions identified
- the need to document a conclusion or the basis for a conclusion not readily determinable from the documentation of the work performed or audit evidence obtained
- the audit methodology and the tools used.

8.7.2 Working paper files

Working papers are generally filed under one of two categories: (1) a permanent file and (2) a current file.

Permanent file

A **permanent file** contains data expected to be useful to the auditor on many future engagements with the entity. Items typically found in a permanent file are:

- extracts or copies of the replaceable rules — these describe, among other matters, the objectives of the company, the number and types of shares authorised for issue, their price, the rights of shareholders and the duties of directors
- copies of important long-term operating agreements or contracts such as leases, superannuation plans, profit-sharing and bonus agreements, and labour contracts — these documents could significantly affect the future operations of the company so it is important that the auditor review them and keep copies on file
- analysis of accounts that are important to the audit each year (such as shareholder fund accounts and long-term debt)
- analytical review schedules from previous years, including ratios and percentage analyses or trend statements for various items — a review of these schedules enables the auditor to focus on unusual changes in the current year's account balances compared with those for previous periods
- a description of the entity's internal control structure — this may consist of the description of the control environment, control policies and procedures, internal control questionnaires, flowcharts, decision tables, and a chart of accounts and sample forms to help the auditor understand the company's procedures
- information relevant to audit planning, such as the master copy of the audit program, information on accounts (bank accounts or cost centres) or locations (controlled entities or branches) tested on a rotation basis
- copies of significant correspondence between the auditor and the client, such as the management letters sent by the auditor and details of any response from the company to these letters.

Current file

The **current file** contains evidence gathered in the performance of the current year's audit program to support the conclusions reached. This file contains a significant amount of detail of the work performed including (but not limited to) the documentation discussed below.

Working trial balance

A partial working trial balance is illustrated in figure 8.7 (overleaf). Note that columns are provided for the current year's ledger balances (before audit adjustments and reclassifications), adjustments, adjusted balances, reclassifications and final (audited) balances. Including the final (audited) balances for the previous year facilitates the performance of certain analytical procedures.

The working trial balance may be prepared by the entity or the auditor. When it is prepared by the entity, the auditor verifies the trial balance by adding the columns and tracing the account balances to the general ledger. A working trial balance is very important to the conduct of the audit because it:

- provides a basis for controlling all the individual working papers
- serves as a connecting link between the entity's general ledger and the general purpose financial report
- identifies the specific working papers containing the audit evidence for each financial statement item.

Figure 8.7, for example, indicates that the amount reported in the financial statements for marketable securities is based on general ledger account 150 and that the evidence used by the auditor to evaluate management's assertions about marketable securities can be found in a section of the working papers with a reference or index of B. The absence of an account number for cash in figure 8.7 indicates that this financial statement item is the aggregate of several general ledger cash accounts. In such cases, the initial working paper of the section referenced on the working trial balance (A in this case) should contain a group schedule showing which general ledger accounts have been combined for this financial statement item. The link between the cash line item in the working trial balance for Omni Co. Ltd (working paper AA–1) and Omni's balance sheet (statement of financial position) presentation of cash is illustrated in the bottom part of figure 8.8.

Omni Co. Ltd
Working trial balance — Balance sheet
30 June 2014

W/P ref. AA–1

Prepared by: _____ Date: _____
Reviewed by: _____ Date: _____

W/P ref.	Acc. no.	Description	Final balance 30/6/13	Ledger balance 30/6/14	AJE ref.	Adjustments Debit (Credit)	Adjusted balance 30/6/14	RJE ref.	Reclassifications Debit (Credit)	Final balance 30/6/14
		Assets								
A		Current Cash	392 000	427 000	(1)	50 000	477 000			477 000
B	150	Marketable securities	52 200	62 200			62 200			62 200
C		Receivables (net)	1 601 400	1 715 000	(1)	(50 000)	1 665 000	(A)	10 000	1 675 000
D	170	Inventories	2 542 500	2 810 200	(2)	133 000	2 943 200			2 943 200
E		Prepaid expenses	24 900	19 500			19 500			19 500
		Total current	4 613 000	5 033 900		133 000	5 166 900		10 000	5 176 900
F	240	Long-term investments		190 000			190 000			190 000
G		Property, plant and equipment (net)	3 146 500	3 310 900			3 310 900			3 310 900
		Total	7 759 500	8 534 800		133 000	8 667 800		10 000	8 677 800
		Liabilities and equity								
		Current liabilities								
M	400	Notes payable	750 000	825 000			825 000			825 000
N	410	Accounts payable	2 150 400	2 340 300	(2)	(133 000)	2 473 300	(A)	(10 000)	2 483 300
O	420	Accrued payables	210 600	189 000			189 000			189 000
P	430	Income taxes payable	150 000	170 000			170 000			170 000
		Total current	3 261 000	3 524 300		(133 000)	3 657 300		(10 000)	3 667 300
R	500	Debentures payable	1 000 000	1 200 000			1 200 000			1 200 000
S	600	Ordinary shares	2 400 000	2 400 000			2 400 000			2 400 000
T	700	Profit and loss appropriation	1 098 500	1 410 500			1 410 500			1 410 500
		Total	7 759 500	8 534 800		(133 000)	8 667 800		(10 000)	8 677 800

FIGURE 8.7: Partial working of trial balance working paper

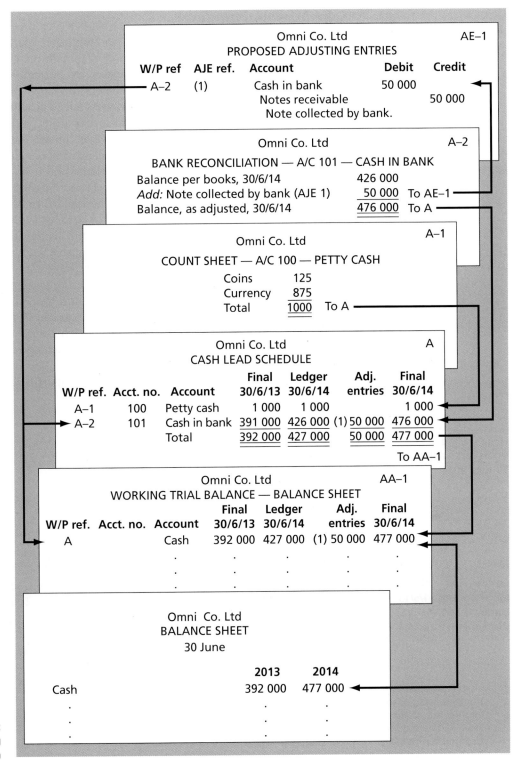

FIGURE 8.8:
Integrated working papers for cash

Schedules and analyses

The terms 'working paper schedule' and 'working paper analysis' are used interchangeably to describe the individual working papers that contain the evidence supporting the items in the working trial balance. Working papers are normally filed by balance sheet item, with a further section for the income statement (or statement of comprehensive income). The first schedule for each item is referred to as a **lead schedule**. This schedule groups the general ledger accounts that are combined for reporting purposes and identifies the individual working paper schedules or analyses that contain the audit evidence obtained for each account comprising the group. The middle part of 8.8 illustrates the use of a cash lead schedule for Omni Co. Ltd (working paper A) and how it is linked both to the cash line of the working trial balance (working paper AA–1) and the supporting working papers for the two general ledger cash accounts listed on the lead schedule (i.e. working paper A–1 for A/C 100 Petty Cash and working paper A–2 for A/C 101 Cash in Bank).

Individual schedules or analyses often show the composition of an account balance at a particular date, as in working paper A–1 of figure 8.8. Other examples include a list of customer balances constituting the accounts receivable control account balance and a list of investments constituting the marketable securities account balance. A working paper schedule may also show the changes in one or more related account balances during the period covered by the financial statements, as illustrated in figure 8.9. In some cases, the auditor uses schedules prepared by the entity, which are indicated by the letters 'PBC' for 'prepared by client'. Such schedules need to be checked against the accounting records to ensure their accuracy. Audit work performed is indicated by the tick marks and related explanations on the working paper, as illustrated in figure 8.9.

| Omni Co. Ltd
Notes receivable and interest
30 June 2014 | | | | | | | | | | | W/P ref. C–4
Prepared by: _____ Date: _____
Reviewed by: _____ Date: _____ |

Accts 160, 161, 450

					Notes receivable				Interest			
Maker	Made	Date due	Interest rate (%)	Face amount	Balance 30/6/13	Debits	Credits	Balance 30/6/14	Accrued 30/6/13	Earned 2014	Collected 2014	Accrued 30/6/14
Coffman Ltd	1/1/13	31/12/13	10	25 000	25 000		25 000 C	—	1250 X	1250 ø	2500 C	—
Morrison Bros.	1/5/13	31/4/14	10	30 000	30 000		30 000 C	—	500 X	2500 ø	3000 C	—
Shirley & Son	1/10/13	30/9/14	12	40 000 ✓	—	40 000 ﹀		40 000	—	3600 ø	—	3 600
Warner Ltd	1/4/14	31/3/15	12	20 000 ✓	—	20 000 ﹀		20 000	—	600 ø	—	600
				55 000 X F	60 000 F	55 000 F	60 000 FF	1250 X F	7950 F	5500 F	4200 ∧ FF	

X   Checked against 30/6/13 working papers.
C   Traced collections to cash receipts and deposit slips.
φ   Verified calculations.
✓   Examined note during cash count.
﹀   Confirmed with maker — no exceptions.
∧   Traced to ledger balance.
F   Footed.
FF   Footed and cross-footed.

FIGURE 8.9: Notes receivable and interest working paper

Schedules are particularly important where evidence is obtained from the examination of a sample. The schedule should indicate the basis of selection and the specific items selected for sampling, enabling performance of the audit to be replicated if any query arises. It is also useful if documents and records sampled by the auditor are marked to establish the proper conduct of the audit in the event of any enquiry.

Audit memoranda and corroborating information

Audit memoranda refer to written data in narrative form prepared by the auditor. Memoranda may include comments on the performance of auditing procedures and conclusions reached from the auditing work performed. Documentation of corroborating information includes extracts of minutes of board meetings, confirmation responses, written representations from management and outside experts, and copies of important contracts.

Proposed adjusting and reclassifying entries

It is important to distinguish between adjusting entries and reclassifying entries. Audit adjusting entries are corrections of entity errors of omission or misapplication of accounting standards. Thus, adjusting entries ultimately deemed to be material (individually or in the aggregate) are expected to be recorded by the entity. In contrast, reclassifying entries are concerned with the proper financial statement presentation of correct account balances. Assume, for example, that the accounts receivable balance includes some customer accounts with credit balances relating to customer advances. Although it is not necessary for the entity to record the reclassifying entry on its books, for reporting purposes an entry should be made on the working trial balance in which accounts receivable is debited to offset the customer advances and a liability account is credited. This is illustrated in figure 8.7, and results in the reclassification being reflected in the financial statement. As with adjusting entries, only reclassifications that have a material effect need be made.

In the working papers, each entry should be shown on (1) the schedule or analysis of the account, (2) the lead schedules, if any, (3) the summary of proposed adjusting or reclassifying entries, and (4) the working trial balance. This is illustrated in figure 8.8.

The summaries of adjusting and reclassifying entries are initially designated as 'proposed' entries because (1) the auditor's final judgement as to which entries must be made may not occur until the end of the audit and (2) the entity must approve them. The disposition of each proposed entry should ultimately be recorded on the working papers. If the entity declines to make adjusting or reclassifying entries that the auditor feels are necessary, then the auditor's report must be appropriately modified.

Audit program

An audit program is a listing of the auditing procedures to be performed. Audit programs are used for the evaluation of internal controls and for substantive procedures. Examples of these audit programs are included throughout this book, particularly in chapters 14–17.

8.7.3 Preparing working papers

A number of basic techniques are used widely in preparing a working paper. These relate to the mechanics of working paper preparation and include the following essential points.

- *Heading.* Each working paper should contain the name of the entity, a descriptive title identifying the content of the working paper (such as 'Bank Reconciliation — National Bank'), and the date of the end of the reporting period or the period covered by the audit.
- *Index numbers.* Each working paper is given an index or reference number — such as A–1, B–2 — for identification purposes. Indexing facilitates the organisation and review

of working papers. Most audit firms have standardised referencing systems so the organisation of audit files is consistent throughout the firm.
- *Cross-referencing.* Data on a working paper that are taken from another working paper or that are carried forward to another working paper should be cross-referenced with the index numbers of those working papers, as illustrated in figure 8.8.
- *Evidence.* The paper should document the evidence examined and the audit procedures applied to that evidence. A common practice is the use of symbols or ticks to identify the different procedures applied. A legend on the working paper should explain the nature and extent of the work represented by each mark. Most firms use standardised marks to indicate common procedures such as adding columns and posting totals to ledgers.

  Where the evidence is in the form of documents and records, it is usual to leave a trail of symbols and ticks on those documents and records. This enables the work of the auditor to be traced back to the evidence if necessary.
- *Conclusion.* The results of audit procedures should be summarised, indicating whether they confirm the particular assertion being tested.
- *Signature and dates.* On completing their respective tasks, both the preparer and reviewer of a working paper should initial and date it. This establishes responsibility for work performed and the review.

The partial working papers in figure 8.8 do not show all these essential elements because that figure was designed mainly to illustrate indexing and cross-referencing. Figure 8.9, however, illustrates the above elements. The quality of audit working papers and appropriate documentation is of crucial importance to auditors as it provides the evidence of their work performed.

8.7.4 Reviewing working papers

There are several levels in the review of working papers within an audit practice. The first-level review is made by the preparer's supervisor, such as a manager. This review occurs when the work on a specific segment of the audit has been completed. The reviewer is interested mainly in the work done, the evidence obtained, the judgement exercised and the conclusions reached by the preparer of the working paper.

The working papers undergo other reviews when the audit has been completed. These reviews are explained in chapter 18.

8.7.5 Ownership and custody of working papers

The property rights of working papers rest with the auditor if he or she is acting as an independent 'contractor'. This was established in *Chantrey Martin & Co. v. Martin* (1953) 3 WLR 459. Working papers prepared at the auditor's request by the entity's staff also belong to the auditor. In certain circumstances, an auditor may be acting as an agent for other auditors. In the absence of any agreement to the contrary, the working papers belong to the principal auditors. In non-audit situations (such as when the auditor is making representations on behalf of the client to the Australian Taxation Office), the auditor owns the audit working papers but not the working papers relating to representations to the Tax Office.

The auditor's ownership rights, however, are subject to constraints imposed by the auditor's own professional standards. The basic principles in Section 140.1 of the Code of Ethics (IFAC Code, Section 100.4(d) outlines similar principles with different wording) include the following:

140.1 The principle of confidentiality imposes an obligation on Members to refrain from:
    (a) Disclosing outside the Firm or employing organisation confidential information acquired as a result of professional and business relationships without proper

and specific authority from the Client or employer or unless there is a legal or professional right or duty to disclose; and

(b) Using confidential information acquired as a result of professional and business relationships to their personal advantage or the advantage of third parties.

A successor auditor may have access to the working papers of the predecessor auditor, with client approval. However, there is no obligation on the part of the predecessor auditor to make working papers available.

Physical custody of the working papers rests with the auditor, who is responsible for their safekeeping. Working papers included in the permanent file are retained indefinitely; current working papers should be retained for as long as they are useful to the auditor in servicing an entity or needed to satisfy legal or professional requirements of record retention. Section 307B of the Corporations Act requires auditors to keep their working papers for 7 years.

Do you know ...

8.7 ☐ Working papers contain the evidence that the auditor collects to help perform the audit and review the work of assistants, to use as a guide to subsequent audits, and to show that the audit was carried out in accordance with auditing standards.

8.8 ☐ Working paper files are classified into permanent or current files. The permanent file contains information of a continuing nature. The current file contains information relevant to the current period's audit.

SUMMARY

Before accepting an audit engagement, the auditor should ensure that it can be completed in accordance with all applicable professional standards, including auditing standards and professional ethics. Important steps in accepting the engagement include evaluating the integrity of management, identifying any special circumstances and unusual risks, assessing competence, evaluating independence, determining that the engagement can be completed with due care, and issuing an engagement letter. In the planning process it is also important that the auditor consider the risk of fraud in the entity.

Proper planning is crucial in performing an efficient, effective audit. Planning steps include obtaining an understanding of the entity and its environment, making preliminary judgements about materiality levels, considering audit risks, obtaining an understanding of the entity's internal control structure, and developing preliminary audit strategies for significant assertions. Chapter 9 looks in detail at procedures to assess risk including risks related to internal controls, and chapter 11 looks at how to test the existence and operation of internal controls. Chapter 10 considers the planning aspects relating to obtaining audit evidence and considerations of materiality, and this is developed further in chapter 12, which discusses the design of substantive procedures and the development of an audit program in order to implement the audit plan.

The procedures performed, the evidence obtained and the auditor's evaluation of that evidence should be fully documented in working papers, which should provide the support for the auditor's report and evidence of the auditor's compliance with auditing standards.

analytical procedures, p. 326

audit manager, p. 321

audit planning, p. 326

audit team, p. 321

business risks, p. 332

current file, p. 347

engagement letter, p. 323

entity's objectives, p. 332

entity's strategies, p. 332

experts, p. 321

fraud, p. 334

interim audit, p. 327

lead schedule, p. 350

partner, p. 321

permanent file, p. 347

predecessor auditor, p. 318

proposed auditor, p. 318

time budget, p. 322

working papers, p. 346

APPENDIX 8A
Key financial ratios used in analytical procedures

Users of general purpose financial reports can obtain valuable insights into a company's financial condition and performance through analysis of key financial ratios. The same analysis performed by auditors provides them with a better understanding of the entity.

Given that auditors already have some knowledge of the entity from other planning procedures, analytical procedures can play a different role in the audit. Using prior knowledge, auditors can gauge whether current-year ratios are expected to differ from those in previous years or from industry norms. When comparisons reveal unexpected fluctuations, or when expected fluctuations do not occur, the auditor will generally investigate whether the aberration is due to the misstatement of one or more variables used in calculating the ratio.

This appendix explains the calculation of ten common ratios and their purpose, and how they are interpreted. The comments on interpretation are general in nature and should be tailored according to a particular entity's circumstances, such as its recent experience and the industry in which it operates.

Ratio	Calculation	Purpose and interpretation
Solvency		
Quick ratio	$\dfrac{\text{Cash} + \text{Accounts receivable} + \text{Current asset investments}}{\text{Current liabilities}}$	To reveal protection afforded by cash or near-cash assets to short-term creditors. The larger the ratio, the greater the liquidity.
Current ratio	$\dfrac{\text{Total current assets}}{\text{Total current liabilities}}$	To measure the degree to which current liabilities are covered by current assets. The higher the ratio, the greater the assurance that current liabilities can be paid in a timely manner.
Debt to equity	$\dfrac{\text{Total liabilities}}{\text{Shareholders equity}}$	To measure the extent to which a company is using its debt financing capacity. In general, this ratio should not exceed 100% because in such cases creditors will have more at stake than owners will.

Times interest earned	$$\frac{\text{Opening profit before interest and tax}}{\text{interest expense}}$$	To measure the number of times a company can meet its fixed interest charges with earnings.

Efficiency

Accounts receivable turnover	$$\frac{\text{Sales}}{\text{Accounts receivable}}$$	To measure the number of times receivables are collected during the period. When used in analytical procedures, some auditors prefer to use the ending receivables balance rather than average receivables, which would make a misstatement more difficult to detect. A variation, *the collection period*, is found by dividing the turnover ratio by 365. This ratio may be useful in evaluating the adequacy of the allowance for doubtful debts.
Inventory turnover	$$\frac{\text{Cost of sales}}{\text{Inventory}}$$	To indicate how rapidly inventory turns over. When using this calculation in analytical procedures, some auditors prefer to use the ending inventory balance rather than average inventories, which would make a misstatement more difficult to detect. Although the ratio varies widely among industries, low values may indicate excessively high inventories and slow-moving items; conversely, extremely high values may reflect insufficient inventories to meet customer demand, resulting in lost sales.
Asset turnover	$$\frac{\text{Sales}}{\text{Total assets}}$$	To measure the efficiency with which a company uses its assets to generate sales. For the reasons noted previously, some auditors prefer using ending rather than average assets to calculate this ratio.

Profitability

Return on sales	$$\frac{\text{Operating profit}}{\text{Sales}}$$	To reveal profits earned per dollar of sales. This ratio indicates ability to earn satisfactory profits for owners, as well as the entity's ability to withstand adverse conditions such as falling prices, rising costs and declining sales.
Return on assets	$$\frac{\text{Operating profit}}{\text{Total assets}}$$	To indicate profitability based on total assets available. Companies efficiently using assets will have a high ratio; less efficient companies will have a low ratio.
Return on shareholders' equity	$$\frac{\text{Operating profit after tax}}{\text{Ordinary shareholders equity}}$$	To reveal management's ability to earn an adequate return on capital invested by owners. Generally, a minimum of 10% is considered desirable to provide funds for dividends and growth.

MULTIPLE-CHOICE questions

8.1 The predecessor auditor firm should tell the successor auditor firm:
  (i) The total cost it incurred in performing the audit of a company in the previous year.
  (ii) Its evaluation of the strength of the company's internal control systems.
  (iii) Its understanding of the reason for the change in auditors.
  A. (ii) only.
  B. (iii) only.
  C. (ii) and (iii) only.
  D. (i) and (iii) only.

8.2 In the investigation of a potential new client, if the client refuses to give permission to inquire of the existing auditor, or if the existing auditor does not respond fully, the prospective auditor should:
  A. Request assistance from ASIC.
  B. Consider the implications in making the acceptance or rejection decision.
  C. Contact the previous auditor and make the necessary enquiries.
  D. Not accept the engagement.

8.3 The exercise of 'due professional care' requires an auditor to:
  A. Examine all available corroborating evidence.
  B. Critically review the judgement exercised at every level on the engagement.
  C. Reduce control risk below the maximum.
  D. Attain the proper balance of professional experience and formal education.

8.4 Engagement letters are widely used in practice for professional engagements of all types. The main purpose of the engagement letter is to:
  A. Remind management that the main responsibility for the financial statements rests with management.
  B. Satisfy the requirements of the auditor's liability insurance policy.
  C. Provide a starting point for the auditor's preparation of the preliminary audit program.
  D. Provide a written record of the agreement with the client as to the services to be provided.

8.5 In the tour of the client's operations, the auditor noted two machines were not operating in the client's factory. This meant that production was 25% lower than normal. The factory manager informed the auditor that this was because the machine was being serviced; however, the auditor saw no evidence of this. How would this affect the audit plan?
  A. It would have no effect. The factory manager's explanation should be accepted.
  B. It would increase the amount of audit work on property, plant and equipment.
  C. It would be necessary to perform a more thorough review of sales for the year and the sales forecasts.
  D. It would be necessary to perform more work on inventory to check for obsolescence.

8.6 The purpose of using analytical procedures in auditing is to:
  A. Test for inefficiencies in operations.
  B. Understand internal controls.
  C. Identify unexpected fluctuations and relationships.
  D. Assess the auditor's competence to perform the audit.

8.7 In performing your analytical review of sales, you find the following for a company with a 30 June year-end:

Monthly gross margin
- April — 25%
- May — 27%
- June — 37%
- July — 21%

How would this affect the audit plan?
A. The cut-off for sales would need to be reviewed carefully.
B. It would be necessary to discuss with management the high level of sales in June.
C. All cash payments in June would need to be reviewed to ensure they have been properly recorded.
D. There is no problem — the gross margin figures all appear to be healthy.

8.8 What is the auditor's responsibility in assessing the risk of fraud in planning?
A. To assess the risk of material misappropriation of assets only.
B. To assess the risk of any fraud that may have occurred in the entity.
C. To assess the risk of any material misstatements in the financial statements due to fraud.
D. To ensure no criminal acts have occurred within the entity in the prior year.

8.9 A high risk condition for the fraud risk factor 'opportunity' would be:
A. Known or expected future layoffs.
B. That the company is close to its debt covenants.
C. Behaviour indicating displeasure or dissatisfaction with the company or its treatment of an employee.
D. Large amounts of cash on hand.

8.10 The auditors have requested the client's accounting staff to prepare some of the schedules and analyses. Who retains the property rights for these working papers?
A. The auditors, as they are the independent contractors.
B. The accounting staff, as they are acting as agents.
C. The company, as it is its staff who performed the work.
D. ASIC, as all working papers must be lodged with it.

REVIEW questions

8.11 List the steps performed by an auditor before accepting a new audit appointment.

8.12 Identify applicable ethical considerations in accepting a new audit engagement.

8.13 What are the benefits of audit planning?

8.14 Discuss the contention that the engagement letter understates the auditor's legal responsibilities so as to discourage litigation.

8.15 Discuss the steps involved in the audit planning process.

8.16 What is the purpose of touring operating facilities and offices?

8.17 Explain the importance of analytical procedures and why auditors may also use non-financial measures in these procedures.

8.18 What are the auditor's responsibilities in relation to fraud?

8.19 Define the term 'working papers' and indicate their main function in auditing.

8.20 Identify the benefits of preparing audit documentation.

BASIC
★
MODERATE
★★
CHALLENGING
★★★

 PROFESSIONAL application questions

8.21 Risk of fraud ★

Following are a number of factors recognised by the auditor as having an effect on the risk of fraud.

1. The company is vulnerable to interest rate fluctuations.
2. Management has significant financial interests in the entity.
3. Employees express dissatisfaction with the company and its treatment of staff.
4. Many asset values are based on significant estimates that involve subjective judgements.
5. Management does not place a high priority on ethical standards.
6. Inadequate systems of authorisation and approval of purchase transactions.
7. Management shows an excessive interest in increasing the entity's share price.
8. There is a high turnover of internal audit and information technology staff.
9. Employees ignore internal controls and do not focus on reducing risks of misappropriations of assets.
10. The entity's industry is highly competitive.
11. Employees anticipate future redundancies.
12. Management attempts to justify marginal or inappropriate accounting on the basis of materiality on a recurring basis.

Required

For each of the foregoing risk factors, use the following codes to identify the risk component that is most directly related to (a) fraudulent financial reporting or misappropriation of assets and (b) incentives/pressures, opportunity or attitude/rationalisation.

FFR = fraudulent financial reporting   I/P = incentives/pressures
MA = misappropriation of assets   O = opportunity
                                          A/R = attitude/rationalisation

8.22 Evaluating independence ★★

Prior to the appointment of Burberry Partners as the auditor of WeCare for the 2015 financial year, some preliminary analysis has identified the following situations.

- One of the accountants intended to be part of the 2015 audit team owns shares in WeCare. The accountant's interest is not material to him.
- Burberry was previously engaged by WeCare to value its intellectual property. The consolidated balance sheet as at 30 June 2015 included intangible assets of $30 million, which were valued by Burberry on 1 March 2015 following WeCare's acquisition of HealthyGlow. The intangibles are considered material to WeCare.

Required

For each situation above:

(a) Identify and explain the potential type of threat to Burberry's independence (your answer should take into consideration the independence of individuals as well as the firm as a whole).
(b) Explain the action that Burberry should take to eliminate the potential threat identified in (a) above.

8.23 Client evaluation ★★

Dinfal Ltd is a company that manufactures a range of products for the electronics industry. You work for a medium-sized firm of accountants, Ejo, Gam & Step. It is now 29 May 2015 and you have been approached by Dennis Launch, one of the directors of Dinfal Ltd, to perform the financial report audit for the year ended 30 June 2015.

From your brief conversation with Dennis you establish the following:

Dinfal Ltd was set up by Dennis and his cousin Berty Drip, who are both directors and each own 50% of the shares. Both Dennis and Berty consider themselves to be entrepreneurs and have a range of experience in different industries. Since creating Dinfal Ltd six years ago, the profits have increased very quickly, sales having nearly doubled each year.

Dennis mentions that they left their previous two auditors due to differences of opinion about accounting policies and accounting treatments for various transactions including research and development expenditure.

Your firm has wide experience of the industry but no previous connection to the company. You have explained to Dennis that there are certain procedures that need to be followed before you can accept appointment as auditors. Dennis has indicated that Dinfal Ltd is seeking additional financing and would like the audit to be completed as soon as possible so that the audited financial report can be provided to the potential financiers to prevent any delay in accessing additional funds.

Required

Highlight the issues that your firm should consider before accepting the appointment as the auditor of Dinfal Ltd.

8.24 Audit engagement letters ★★

You are a partner in an audit firm and your firm has just won the audit for Dezigns Ltd, a company involved in marketing and development of brands for large companies. As per the requirements in ASA 210 *Agreeing the Terms of Audit Engagements* (ISA 210), you prepare an audit engagement letter. It details the objective of the audit, scope and nature of the auditor's responsibilities, a statement that management is responsible for the preparation of the financial statements and safeguarding company assets, and details about the audit fee. The managing director of Dezigns Ltd is not very impressed when he is handed the letter. He states:

'My business is operated on trust and my word is my bond. I am not going to sign this agreement because it is getting our relationship off on the wrong footing. I am particularly offended by all of the details outlining my responsibilities — I think I know what they are. However, I know you have certain business practices so I am prepared to sign a contract outlining your audit fees.'

Required

Write a letter to the managing director answering his concerns and explaining why you need a signed audit engagement letter.

8.25 Planning the audit ★★

Your client is Gateshead Pty Ltd, a large family-owned company which imports and sells computer hardware products. You are planning the 30 June 2015 audit and, from your enquiries of management, have obtained the information below.

1. In January 2015, Gateshead applied for and was granted a new loan. The submission made to the bank stated:
   - the current ratio was 0.90
   - gross profit was up by 25% compared with that at the same time last year
   - the debt-to-equity ratio was 0.40.
2. The bank agreed to the new loan but did enter into a loan covenant with Gateshead. The covenant required that the company should not breach certain ratios, and placed certain restrictions on dividends.

From audits you have conducted in previous years, you are suspicious about the validity of the ratios discussed in the submission. You hear from one of Gateshead's accounting staff that the figures had been 'gently massaged' to obtain the required ratios.

Required

Discuss (referring to specific areas of the audit) the implications of this information on your planning of the audit.

8.26 Planning the audit; analytical review ★★

Tirthe Ltd sells a range of indoor and outdoor furniture by recycling and reinterpreting old furniture and other wood, metal, glass and plastic products obtained from a variety of sources such as derelict buildings, deceased estate auctions and so on. Revenue comes from sales to the general public and businesses such as hotels and restaurants. Some small items are collected by customers but generally goods are delivered by Tirthe Ltd. The directors have reported that it has been another good year for the organisation and that they expect the coming year to be successful.

The draft income statement for 2015 together with audited figures for 2014 are given below:

	30 June 2015 (draft)	30 June 2014 (actual)
Revenue	536 994	617 140
Cost of sales	(322 187)	(302 788)
Gross profit	214 807	314 352
Other income	—	7 186
Operating expenses		
Administration	(95 438)	(92 064)
Selling and distribution	(50 575)	(79 933)
Finance costs	(7 434)	(7 623)
Profit/(loss) before tax	61 360	141 918

Required

You are planning the audit of Tirthe Ltd for the year ended 30 June 2015, discuss the issues to be considered in your audit planning from the information contained in the income statements.

8.27 Fraud risk ★★

Cleanway Ltd is a public company that competes in the highly competitive market for manufactured household products. The company is dominated by Rob Bigbucks, the chairman and chief executive officer, who has guided the company since it was a private company and has extensive influence on all aspects of company operations. Rob is known to have a short temper and in the past has threatened individuals in the accounting department with no pay rise if they failed to help him achieve company goals. Furthermore, the company has extended its influence over customers and has dictated terms of sale to ensure that customers are able to obtain desired quantities of their most popular products. Bonuses based on sales are a significant component of the compensation package for individual product sales managers. Sales managers who do not meet sales targets three quarters in a row are often replaced. The company has performed well up until a recent recession, but now the company is having difficulty moving inventory in most product lines as retailers have difficulty selling in a down economy.

Required

(a) Identify the fraud risk factors that are present in this case.
(b) Identify the accounts and assertions that are most likely to be misstated based on the fraud risk factors noted in the case.

8.28 Planning ★★★

Needles and Glue Ltd is an online retailer of a broad range of art and craft products. You are an audit senior at the firm Naylor Swit & Co and are planning the financial report audit for the year ended 30 June 2015. Needles and Glue is a new client to your firm and this is the first year end since you were appointed. The following information was obtained from a meeting with the CEO, Barbara Wool.

The company has managed to ride a wave of renewed interest by younger people in arts and crafts and the revenue for 2015 is approximately $3.2 million. This continues a trend that has seen revenue increase by between 20% and 30% consistently for the six years since the company was started by Barbara and her tennis partner Sandra Cloth who is the COO. Profits in 2015 are $0.2 million and have not increased significantly in four years despite the increased turnover. In 2016 there are plans to broaden the range of products sold to include bedding, curtains and household furnishings.

Rapid expansion has put pressure on the company's various systems, not least of which is the online sales order system. Needles and Glue do not have their own in-house IT function, relying on Barbara's sister Tabatha who is responsible for accounting, IT, HR, payroll and general office management.

You are aware that in previous years errors had been detected at the audit stage, partly due to IT system errors and partly due to Tabatha's inexperience as an accountant. Barbara and Tabatha are confident that any errors in the financial report will be immaterial and not worth investigating given how busy they are with the growing business.

As part of the growth of the business the company is looking to raise additional bank borrowings to fund more warehouse space and invest in improvements to the IT systems. Barbara has indicated that she needs the audit report signed before 18 September which is when she will be meeting the bank to discuss the details of the loan.

Required

Identify the issues that give rise to risks for the financial report audit you are about to commence.

8.29 Planning the audit ★★★

Alice is an audit senior for the accounting firm of Wong and Partners. In Alice's planning of the audit of Lincoln Traders Ltd for the year ended 30 June 2015, she asked to review the minutes of board of directors meetings for the year to date. From her review, she noted the following information.

Wong and Partners Lincoln Traders Ltd Planning	P–7 Prepared by: Alice Date: 28/5/15
Notes from board of directors meetings for year to May 2015:	
16/8/14	The board agreed to revalue land and buildings in its financial statements in accordance with a property valuation recently undertaken at the company's request. The effect would be to increase their value by 50%.
17/10/14	The company took over one of its major customers during the year. This was not expected to alter its trading relationship.
15/12/14	It was agreed that a new 'bonus scheme' would be implemented. This scheme would award directors a bonus of a percentage of the profits for this year if they could exceed last year's profit figure by 20%.
16/2/15	It was agreed that construction should begin on a new factory for processing tuna. A construction contract was approved and it was expected the work on the new factory would commence before the end of March, at least three months before the end of the financial year.
17/5/15	The board agreed to make a large loan to one of the company's subsidiaries in Fiji one month before the end of the financial year. The loan did not have any security and no interest was charged.

Required

Discuss the effect that each of the five noted items in the minutes of the board of directors meeting will have on specific aspects of the audit plan.

8.30 Working paper review ★★★

You are employed by the accounting firm Round, Flat & Co and you have been asked to perform a review of the file of working papers for the recently completed financial report audit of the client Rhomboid Ltd for the year ended 30 June 2015. You were not involved in the audit and your check is part of the internal quality control processes conducted by the firm.

As part of your review you find the following working paper:

Working paper: Sales Testing

Prepared by   NFP   15/07/2015

Reviewed by

Objective
To check that sales in the ledger are accurate.

Method
Select a sample of 20 sales orders received from customers and agree to the goods despatched note and sales invoice.

Results
Exceptions found were not significant.

Conclusion
There is no indication that the sales are incomplete.

Required

Identify the inadequacies in the working paper.

CASE studies

8.31 Planning the audit ★★★

Moss Green Ltd is a wine grower and producer of medium- to high-quality wines located in Western Australia's Margaret River region. The company has recently listed on the Australian Securities Exchange. After listing, it changed auditors from Tickit Associates to your firm, Watson and Partners. You are an audit supervisor in Watson and Partners and you are planning the audit for 31 December 2015.

The managing director of Moss Green Ltd is Tom Green. He is the founder of the winery and has a very 'hands on' management style. He is a trained winemaker and has always focused more on the wine making and marketing side of the business than the financial side, which he leaves to Wendy Chong, the financial director, in whom he has great faith. He pays her a good base salary and provides an attractive bonus scheme based on growth in net profitability.

The company has been very successful in selling its medium-quality wine to the United Kingdom. This is mainly due to a very large contract with one of the leading supermarket chains there, Safeburys. Part of the success has been due to the low value of the Australian dollar compared with the British pound. However, the company manages its foreign exchange risk through hedging, which is controlled by Wendy. Tom has also been very happy with Wendy's performance in this area as she has made some healthy profits on her hedging contracts.

The wine production manager is Alfred Horndale. From discussions with Alfred, you become aware that the company has significant stock from the 2013 vintage in the Margaret River warehouse and in London (because it was rejected by Safeburys — payment for this stock is currently in dispute).

As is the standard practice, you contacted Tickit Associates before you accepted the engagement at the beginning of the year to see whether there were any matters you should have been aware of before accepting the engagement. They told you that they had only two main concerns. First, they had problems getting Tom Green to have any interest in the financial side of the business, and it was their view that he was not financially literate. Second, there had been a number of disputes over accounting policy with Wendy Chong, particularly over getting her to implement AASB 141 *Agriculture* and AASB 137 *Provisions, Contingent Liabilities and Contingent Assets*.

Required

Prepare a memo to the audit partner outlining potential problem areas and their impact on the audit plan.

8.32 Analytical procedures ★★★

You are the audit manager of a medium-sized firm and have just received a package from Rachel Jones, the financial controller of Telechubbies Ltd, a toy manufacturer. This is your firm's first year as auditor of Telechubbies. The information contained in the statement of financial position and income statement overleaf was prepared for a board meeting and Rachel felt it might be useful to you in preparation of the forthcoming audit for the year ended 31 December 2015.

During a brief telephone call with Rachel, you made the following notes:

1. One of the conditions of the long-term loan is that the company is not to exceed a debt-to-equity ratio of 2:1 at any time. The loan is reviewed each year on 31 December.
2. Provision against inventory obsolescence is provided for at a flat rate of 10%. The amount provided in previous years was 20%. Rachel said that the company believes it has been overly conservative in previous years and 5% is a more realistic level, given the nature of its products.
3. The long-term loan receivable is from a company involved in the development and production of computer software. It is owned by one of the directors.

Required

(a) Suggest possible sources of information that would help you gather sufficient knowledge of the business to perform the audit of Telechubbies Ltd.

(b) Perform preliminary analytical procedures using the information provided. Identify the key areas that would require special attention during the audit of the 31 December 2015 financial statements.

(c) Outline ways in which the analytical procedures performed could be extended using the information collected in (a).

(d) Suggest ways of using analytical procedures as a substantive test during the audit of Telechubbies Ltd.[5]

Statement of financial position	2015 $'000	2014 $'000	2013 $'000
Current assets			
Cash	1 586	1 743	830
Inventory	16 498	11 731	7 197
Trade receivables	12 134	10 700	9 323
Total current assets	30 218	24 174	17 350
Non-current assets			
Property, plant and equipment	14 606	12 840	9 572
Long-term loan receivable	5 200	3 600	3 300
Total non-current assets	19 806	16 440	12 872
Total assets	50 024	40 614	30 222
Current liabilities			
Trade payables	9 012	6 288	2 021
Provisions	4 875	3 821	4 577
Total current liabilities	13 887	10 109	6 598
Non-current liabilities			
Long-term loan payable	20 000	16 000	12 000
Total liabilities	33 887	26 109	18 598
Net assets	16 137	14 505	11 624
Shareholders' equity			
Share capital	2 000	2 000	2 000
Retained earnings	14 137	12 505	9 624
Total shareholders' equity	16 137	14 505	11 624

Income statement	2015 $'000	2014 $'000	2013 $'000
Sales	72 945	74 927	89 735
Cost of sales	51 840	51 765	63 066
Gross profit	21 105	23 162	26 669
Depreciation	5 595	4 332	2 796
Inventory obsolescence	1 650	2 346	1 439
Marketing expense	1 345	1 980	2 548
Administration expense	8 925	8 727	11 516
Interest expense	1 040	1 275	1 140
Total expenses	18 555	18 660	19 439
Profit before tax	2 550	4 502	7 230
Tax expense	918	1 621	2 386
Profit after tax	1 632	2 881	4 844

 RESEARCH question

8.33 Obtaining an understanding

You are an audit senior in an accounting firm. Your firm has recently won an audit for a company that operates within the mining industry; however, your firm does not have any other clients that operate in this industry. Your audit partner is concerned about his lack of knowledge of the mining industry. He is also concerned about the effect of the changes that were proposed to the taxation rate on mining as part of the 2010 Australian Federal Budget. He is aware of the requirement of ASA 315.11(a), which states that the auditor shall obtain an understanding of:

> Relevant industry, regulatory, and other external factors and the applicable financial reporting framework.

Required

(a) Prepare a list of all useful sources that you can use to obtain the required knowledge.

(b) Prepare a memo to the audit partner on the 'state of the mining industry' and associated risk factors.

(c) Outline the possible direct effect that the proposed new tax might have on the audit of mining companies.

FURTHER READING

SK Asare & AM Wright, 'The effectiveness of alternative risk assessment and program planning tools in a fraud setting', *Contemporary Accounting Research*, Summer 2004, pp. 325–52.

JS Hammersley, EM Bamber & TD Carpenter, 'The influence of documentation specificity and priming on auditors' fraud risk assessments and evidence evaluation decisions', *The Accounting Review*, March 2010, pp. 547–71.

P Johnson, 'Fraud detection with Benford's law', *Accountancy Ireland*, August 2005, pp. 16–17.

A Jones III & C Strand Norman, 'Decision making in a public accounting firm: an instructional case in risk evaluation, client continuance, and auditor independence within the context of the Sarbanes–Oxley Act of 2002', *Issues in Accounting Education*, November 2006, pp. 431–47.

TG Kizirian, BW Mayhew & L Dwight Sneathen Jr, 'The impact of management integrity on audit planning and evidence', *Auditing*, November 2005, pp. 49–67.

K-Y Low, 'The effects of industry specialization on audit risk assessments and audit-planning decisions', *Accounting Review*, January 2004, pp. 201–19.

M Nelson, 'A model and literature review of professional scepticism in auditing', *Auditing: A Journal of Practice and Theory*, November 2009, pp. 1–34.

E Patterson & J Noel, 'Audit strategies and multiple fraud opportunities of misreporting and defalcation', *Contemporary Accounting Research*, Fall 2003, pp. 519–49.

TW Singleton & AJ Singleton, 'Why don't we detect more fraud?', *Journal of Corporate Accounting & Finance*, May 2007, pp. 7–10.

TJ Wilks & MF Zimbelman, 'Using game theory and strategic reasoning concepts to prevent and detect fraud', *Accounting Horizons*, September 2004, pp. 173–84.

NOTES

1. C Richardson, 'Risk: business or audit?', *Student Accountant*, September 2006, p. 46.

2. P Healy & J Wahlen, 'A review of the earnings management literature and its implications for standard setting', *Accounting Horizons*, 13(4), 1999, pp. 365–83.

3. P Dechow & D Skinner, 'Earnings management: Reconciling the views of accounting academics, practitioners, and regulators', *Accounting Horizons*, vol. 14, no. 2, June 2000, pp. 235–50.

4. Association of Certified Fraud Examiners, *2010 Report to the Nations*, 2010, www.acfe.com, viewed 21 October 2010.

5. Adapted from Professional Year Programme of the ICAA, 1999, Advanced Audit Module.

Answers to multiple-choice questions

8.1 *B*   8.2 *D*   8.3 *B*   8.4 *D*   8.5 *C*   8.6 *C*   8.7 *A*   8.8 *C*   8.9 *D*   8.10 *A*

chapter 9

Audit risk assessment

OVERVIEW

9.1 Risk assessment and financial statement assertions

9.2 Business risk assessment

9.3 Risk assessment procedures

9.4 Internal control

9.5 Understanding internal control

9.6 Preliminary assessment of control risk

9.7 Audit risk

Summary
Key terms
Multiple-choice questions
Review questions
Professional application questions
Case studies
Research question
Further reading
Notes

LEARNING objectives

After studying this chapter, you should be able to:

1 appreciate the importance of audit risk assessment and why it is linked to financial statement assertions

2 explain the importance of business risks in audit planning

3 describe the procedures performed by an auditor to assess risk

4 appreciate the importance of internal control to an entity and to its independent auditors

5 indicate the procedures for obtaining and documenting an understanding of the entity's internal control

6 explain why and how a preliminary assessment of control risk is made

7 explain the importance of the concept of audit risk and its three components.

PROFESSIONAL STATEMENTS

Australian		International	
ASA 200	*Overall Objectives of the Independent Auditor and the Conduct of an Audit in Accordance with Australian Auditing Standards*	**ISA 200**	*Overall Objective of the Independent Auditor, and the Conduct of an Audit in Accordance with International Standards on Auditing*
ASA 265	*Communicating Deficiencies in Internal Control to Those Charged with Governance and Management*	**ISA 265**	*Communicating Deficiencies in Internal Control to Those Charged with Governance and Management*
ASA 315	*Identifying and Assessing the Risks of Material Misstatement through Understanding the Entity and Its Environment*	**ISA 315**	*Identifying and Assessing the Risks of Material Misstatement through Understanding the Entity and Its Environment*

SCENE SETTER

An expanded role for auditors to consider business models and company risks?

The current role of the auditor is focused on the completed financial statements provided by the Board of Directors and management. The role of audit is primarily guided through the framework of auditing standards.

However, auditors are well positioned to provide insights into disclosures on the longer-term viability of a company. In addition to considering whether the specific requirements of accounting standards are satisfied, auditors could for example consider whether certain limited objectives behind the requirements have been met. This might be achieved by auditors reporting on the audit committee disclosures on the business model(s) of a company and its risks.

Source: Access Economics & The Institute of Chartered Accountants in Australia, *Early warning systems: Can more be done to avert economic and financial crises?*, February 2011, p. 16.

We have considered issues associated with accepting the audit engagement, and taken outlined initial considerations in planning the audit in chapter 8. Before we move on to how to carry out audit testing, let us further explain some of the procedures that need to be carried out at the planning stage. The auditor must assess the risk attached to his or her opinion and the elements that contribute to that risk.

This chapter looks at the auditor's obligations with regard to assessing the risks that the company is exposed to, with particular reference to those risks that will affect the financial statement assertions. In chapter 10 we discuss the nature of audit evidence and materiality that the auditor must consider in tackling the risks identified.

The auditor's responsibility to obtain an understanding of the entity for the purposes of planning the audit is discussed in chapter 8 — we now consider how this influences the auditor's risk assessment. First we consider the nature of business risk, followed by a discussion of the nature of internal control and risks related to internal control, concluding with a discussion on the nature of audit risk.

LEARNING 1
objective

Appreciate the importance of audit risk assessment and why it is linked to financial statement assertions.

9.1 RISK ASSESSMENT AND FINANCIAL STATEMENT ASSERTIONS

In this section we consider why an auditor needs to consider risk with reference to the financial statement assertions.

The overall objective of a financial statement audit as described in paragraph 11 of ASA 200 *Overall Objectives of the Independent Auditor and the Conduct of an Audit in Accordance with Australian Auditing Standards* (ISA 200) is to enable 'the auditor to express an opinion on whether the financial report is prepared, in all material respects, in accordance with an applicable financial reporting framework'. As part of the audit planning stage, according to paragraph 3 of ASA 315 *Identifying and Assessing the Risks of Material Misstatement through Understanding the Entity and Its Environment* (ISA 315.3), the auditor must obtain an understanding of the entity and its environment, including internal controls in order to assess the risk that the financial statements contain material misstatements (the information obtained is not only evidence to support the auditor's risk assessment but also is used to determine the further audit procedures that are required). To meet this objective, it is necessary to identify specific audit objectives for transactions balances and disclosures. In preparing the financial statements, the management of the entity can be said to be making a set of assertions about each transaction class and account balance as well as the way items are presented and disclosed — referred to as **financial statement assertions**.

The auditor formulates an opinion on the financial statements as a whole on the basis of evidence obtained through the verification of assertions related to individual account balances, transaction classes or presentation and disclosure. The objective is to restrict audit risk at the account balance level so, at the conclusion of the audit, the audit risk in expressing an opinion on the financial statements as a whole will be at an appropriately low level. Thus, the overall audit risk is disaggregated to each account balance or transaction class.

9.1.1 Management's financial statement assertions

Management's financial statement assertions are both explicit and implicit. ASA 315 presents a classification of these assertions. ASA 315.A111 (ISA 315.A111) identifies and defines these assertions under three categories — (1) classes of transactions and events (such as purchases and sales), (2) account balances (such as assets and liabilities in the balance sheet/statement of financial position), and (3) how items are presented and disclosed in the financial statements. Table 9.1 gives further details of these assertions.

TABLE 9.1:
Categorisation and definitions
of financial statement
assertions

Assertion	Definition
Assertions about classes of transactions and events	
Occurrence	Transactions and events that have been recorded have occurred and pertain to the entity.
Completeness	All transactions and events that should have been recorded have been recorded.
Accuracy	Amounts and other data relating to recorded transactions and events have been recorded appropriately.
Cut-off	Transactions and events have been recorded in the correct accounting period.
Classification	Transactions and events have been recorded in the proper accounts.
Assertions about account balances	
Existence	Assets, liabilities, and equity interests exist.
Rights and obligations	The entity holds or controls the rights to assets, and liabilities are the obligations of the entity.
Completeness	All assets, liabilities and equity interests that should have been recorded have been recorded.
Valuation and allocation	Assets, liabilities and equity interests are included in the financial report at appropriate amounts, and any resulting valuation or allocation adjustments are appropriately recorded.
Assertions about presentation and disclosure	
Occurrence, rights and obligations	Disclosed events, transactions, and other matters have occurred and pertain to the entity.
Completeness	All disclosures that should have been included in the financial report have been included.
Classification and understandability	Financial information is appropriately presented and described, and disclosures are clearly expressed.
Accuracy and valuation	Financial and other information is disclosed fairly and at appropriate amounts.

For a snapshot understanding of some of these assertions, consider the following balance sheet component:

Current assets:
Cash $2 252 900

In reporting this item, management makes the following explicit assertions.
- Cash exists (existence).
- The correct amount of cash is $2 252 900 (valuation and allocation).

Management also makes the following implicit assertions:
- All cash that should be reported has been included (completeness).
- All the reported cash is owned by the entity (rights and obligations).
- All appropriate disclosures in relation to cash have been made in the financial statement.

If any of these assertions is a misrepresentation, then the financial statements could be misstated.

In the following sections, we classify the assertions into six broad categories, provide examples, and then illustrate specific audit objectives for cash derived from each category of assertion.

Existence or occurrence

Assertions about **existence** or **occurrence** relate to whether the assets or liabilities of the entity exist at a given date and whether recorded transactions or events have occurred during the period.

Existence applies to accounts with physical substance, such as cash and inventories, as well as to accounts without physical substance, such as accounts receivable and accounts payable. In the previous example, this assertion refers to the existence of items included in cash, such as petty cash funds, undeposited receipts and bank accounts. It does not extend to whether $2 252 900 is the correct amount for these items — this relates to the valuation and allocation assertion.

Management also asserts that the revenues and expenses shown in the income statement are the results of transactions and events that occurred during the reporting period, and are properly recognised by the entity. Again, this occurrence assertion extends only to whether transactions and events occurred, not to whether the amounts reported are correct. This assertion would be misrepresented if reported sales transactions were fictitious or occurred after the end of the period, or if reported expenses include personal expenses improperly charged to the entity.

The main concern about this assertion relates to the possible overstatement of balances through the inclusion of items that do not exist, the effects of transactions that did not occur or the improper inclusion of transactions that do not apply to the entity.

Completeness

Assertions about **completeness** relate to whether all transactions, events and accounts that should be presented in the financial statement are included.

For each account balance presented in the financial statement, management implicitly asserts that all related transactions and events have been included. Management asserts, for example, that the cash balance of $2 252 900 includes the effects of all cash transactions and all the cash funds previously mentioned. The completeness assertion for cash would be misrepresented if a bank balance was omitted or cash receipts transactions that occurred were not recorded until the next period.

The auditor's concern about the completeness assertion relates mainly to the possible understatement of financial statement balances through the omission of items that exist or of the effects of transactions that occurred. If omissions are identified, then the issue of the correct dollar amounts at which they should be included relates to the valuation and allocation assertion.

This assertion is the most difficult for the auditor to verify because the starting point of the enquiry is what ought to be recorded, not what is recorded.

Cut-off

Assertions about **cut-off** relate to whether all transactions, events and accounts have been recorded in the correct period.

It is important to ensure that transactions occurring around the year-end are recorded in the correct period. This is particularly important with regards to inventory movements and the corresponding recording of sales and purchases. For example, if an organisation has a 30 June year-end, it is important that any sales made in June are recorded in revenue for the year and receivables at the year-end, and that the items sold are no longer recorded in inventory. Similarly, for any sales in July it is important to ensure that the sales and receivables are not included until the following year and that the goods are included in inventory as at 30 June.

It is possible for organisations to manipulate profits by recorded transactions, particularly those occurring around the year-end, in the wrong period. By testing that the cut-off is correct and that the items are recorded in the correct period, the auditor will have some comfort that profits are not being manipulated.

Rights and obligations

Assertions about **rights and obligations** relate to whether assets are the rights of the entity and liabilities are the obligations of the entity at a given date.

The rights and obligations assertion deals only with assets and liabilities. This assertion refers to rights constituting a degree of control over future economic benefits sufficient for recognition as an asset, and to obligations (legal or constructive) sufficient to require recognition as a liability. Management implicitly asserts, for example, that it controls the cash and other assets reported in the balance sheet and that accounts payable and other liabilities are the obligations of the entity.

Note that although existence or occurrence is relevant in relation to transaction class audit objectives (refer to table 14.1 on pages 572–3), it doesn't necessarily follow that there are corresponding rights and obligations.

Accuracy, classification, valuation and allocation

Assertions about **valuation and allocation** relate to whether asset and liability components have been included in the financial statement at the appropriate amounts. Accuracy and classification relate to whether transactions such as revenue and expenses have been appropriately recorded in the proper accounts.

The reporting of an account balance at an appropriate amount means that the amount has been measured in accordance with applicable accounting standards and is free of mathematical or clerical errors. The determination of amounts in accordance with applicable accounting standards includes the proper measurement of assets, liabilities, revenues and expenses through:
- proper application of valuation principles such as cost, net realisable value, market value or present value
- the reasonableness of management's accounting estimates
- consistency in the application of accounting policies.

Thus, for example, accounts receivable are reported at net realisable value; inventories are reported at lower of cost and net realisable value; and investments, depending on their characteristics, are reported at cost or fair value. Accounting estimates, such as allowances for bad debts and net realisable values of inventory, should be reasonable. Where applicable, the valuation requirements of accounting standards should be consistently applied across periods except when a change is justified.

Mathematical correctness refers to such matters as the clerical accuracy of journal entries, postings to ledger accounts and the determination of account balances. It also applies to the correctness of calculations for such items as accruals and depreciation. Continuing our cash illustration from page 369, mathematical errors in adding the cash receipts or payment journals, or clerical errors made in recording the amount of a transaction or posting the journal totals to the general ledger account for cash would cause a misstatement in the valuation and allocation assertion for cash.

Presentation and disclosure

Assertions about **presentation and disclosure** relate to whether particular components of the financial statements are properly classified, described and disclosed.

In the financial statements, management implicitly asserts that the financial information is properly presented and that accompanying disclosure is adequate. Presentation and disclosure often include the following aspects, which are illustrated by the cash example.

- *Occurrence and rights and obligations.* Disclosed events and transactions relating to cash have occurred and concern the entity.
- *Completeness.* All appropriate disclosures in relating to cash have been included in the financial statement.
- *Classifications and understandability.* Cash is properly classified, which includes whether it is current or non-current and whether it is an asset or liability. The disclosures in relation to cash are appropriately presented and clearly expressed.
- *Accuracy and valuation.* Financial and other information relating to cash is disclosed fairly and at appropriate amounts.

The assertions described above guide the auditor not only at the planning stage of the audit but also when carrying out audit procedures and obtaining audit evidence.

Explain the importance of business risks in audit planning.

9.2 BUSINESS RISK ASSESSMENT

We now discuss what business risk is and why the auditor is interested in it as well as some of the procedures an auditor should consider in obtaining an understanding of the nature of an organisation's risks. In recent years there has been an increased emphasis on auditors obtaining a better understanding of the business risks an organisation is exposed to, and the processes that are implemented to identify and respond to those risks.

ASA 315 paragraph 4(b) (ISA 315.4(b)) states:

> Business risk means a risk resulting from significant conditions, events, circumstances, actions or inactions that could adversely affect an entity's ability to achieve its objectives and execute its strategies, or from the setting of inappropriate objectives and strategies.

Having identified the business risks facing an organisation, the auditor must consider the extent to which these risks could lead to a material misstatement in the financial statements and to what extent the company has implemented controls to reduce these risks. Once it has been established which elements of the financial statements and the assertions described above, are at risk, the auditor can then determine the type of audit testing required. This assessment of business risks and the connection to the design of audit procedures are considered in section 9.7 later in this chapter and also in chapter 10.

A business risk approach allows the auditor to identify the threats that the organisation faces in attempting to achieve its goals and the extent to which these give rise to audit risks. It also recognises that most business risks will eventually have financial consequences and, therefore, an effect on the financial statements. The in-depth understanding of the business that the auditor obtains in taking a business risk approach should increase the chances that the auditor will identify the risks of material misstatement in the financial statements and therefore improve the quality of the audit and the audit opinion. A well-informed auditor is of significant benefit to the company, since he or she is able to provide better quality advice to the company concerning the types of controls that could be implemented to reduce these risks.

Sometimes referred to as a 'top down approach', everything is considered at the highest level when reviewing business risk and then worked down to the lowest level where a material risk might be possible. Using a top down approach leads to a change in focus — rather than starting by looking at the detailed internal controls, a broader higher level discussion initially takes place before going into greater detail. This involves the senior members of the audit team discussing the business with the senior members of the client staff. The whole process is managed and controlled from the top. Initially, an assessment of business risk should be carried out by management to ensure that they meet their own legal responsibilities to manage the business properly.

Business risks can be split into three categories: financial risk, operational risk, and compliance risk.

- *Financial risk.* These are the risks arising from the company's financial activities or the financial consequences of operations. Examples include going concern problems arising from poor performance, overtrading related to a company expanding too quickly, the credit risk of not being able to collect debts, the risk of increased interest rates for companies with large debts, and unknown or unrecorded liabilities.
- *Operational risk.* These are the risks arising from the operations of the business. Examples include stockouts (no stock on hand when customers want to make a purchase) leading to loss of sales, physical disasters that destroy stock or machinery, loss of key staff who have critical knowledge or skills, and poor brand management leading to falling sales.
- *Compliance risk.* These are the risks arising from non-compliance with laws, regulations, policies, procedures and contracts. Examples include breaking stock exchange rules leading to delisting, breaking laws and incurring fines, the risk of being sued by a customer for supplying faulty goods, problems with tax authorities with regard to errors in tax or GST returns, and risks relating to the breach of health and safety requirements, which could lead to the closure of the business.

Understanding an organisation's risk exposure is not confined to the auditor. It is necessary for the directors to ensure that controls are implemented to reduce risk to an acceptable level. In responding to risks, managers need to establish whether they should accept the risk or what controls to implement to reduce or avoid the risk. Once controls have been designed and implemented, managers can satisfy themselves that their systems are working properly by employing internal auditors to perform checks on controls.

LEARNING 3 objective

Describe the procedures performed by an auditor to assess risk.

9.3 RISK ASSESSMENT PROCEDURES

The work the auditor does in obtaining an understanding of the entity, discussed in chapter 8, includes obtaining an understanding of business risks and the company's own risk assessment procedures. These procedures include discussions with management as well as performing analytical procedures, making observations of processes in action and inspecting relevant documents.

9.3.1 Enquiries

When discussing risks with the staff of an organisation, the auditor should not be restricted to discussions with management and those who are involved in preparing financial statements. Much information about the organisation can be obtained by talking to employees at all levels, including those involved in production, logistics, internal audit and so on. Enquiries made of the internal auditors will be useful in highlighting weaknesses in systems, but discussions with production staff or project managers will give a different perspective on the issues and therefore highlight risk areas that a purely financial approach would not consider. Enquiries of those external to the organisation such as the company's bankers or legal advisers may also give a different perspective on events.

9.3.2 Analytical procedures

As discussed in chapter 8, analytical procedures provide a broad indication of the likelihood of possible errors. The auditor establishes expectations about the financial statements from discussions with management and a risk may be indicated where the financial statements do not fit those initial expectations. The analytical review procedures can, at a high level, indicate areas where risks may exist.

9.3.3 Observations and inspections

Observing procedures taking place gives some indication as to how they actually operate. Inspecting a procedures manual and then observing the procedure taking place may indicate that documented procedures are not being followed. Walking around business premises, visiting offices, and visiting business sites all add to an improved understanding of the business and its risks.

Once these assessment procedures have been carried out, the audit team should meet to share opinions about what they have discovered. This allows more senior team members to share their knowledge from past experience with the client. The auditor must now establish which of the risks identified need to be tackled in the audit plan. This process involves considering not only the item in the financial statements that is at risk of being misstated (such as sales or receivables), but also the assertions that are at risk.

This process requires the auditor to:
- identify the risk and any related controls
- consider the account balance, class of transaction or disclosure that is at risk
- link the identified risk to the assertions
- establish whether the risk is material (discussed in chapter 10)
- consider whether it is likely the risk could lead to misstatement of financial statements.

The culmination of this process is the identification of 'significant risks'(see ASA 315 paragraph 27; ISA 315.27). Significant risks are those that require specific audit attention. When establishing the extent to which a risk is a significant risk, the auditor should ignore any controls that may exist. The auditor then separately considers the strength of any controls that are designed to reduce the risk. What constitutes a significant risk is a matter of judgement for the auditor. The factors that may indicate a significant risk include:
- fraud
- unusual or complex transactions or events
- related party transactions
- transactions involving an element of judgement.

Having identified the significant risks above, the auditor should then consider the controls that exist to reduce these risks. The identification of these controls will generally have been done already as part of risk assessment procedures. A key objective here is to ensure that any controls that do exist have been designed effectively and are operating in the way they were designed to.

When the risk assessment process is completed, the auditor will have identified business risks, considered the extent to which these are risks to the audit opinion ('audit risk', discussed later in this chapter), established to what extent these risks are 'significant risks', and identified controls that may exist to reduce the risk. The auditor is now in a position to develop the detailed audit approach and the detailed audit plan. The audit procedures to be carried out on these risks are covered in chapters 11 to 17 and form the major part of the auditor's work.

LEARNING objective 4

Appreciate the importance of internal control to an entity and to its independent auditors.

9.4 INTERNAL CONTROL

We begin by explaining the importance of internal control within an entity, and then describe the nature of an entity's information system and the control activities within that system. These procedures, together with the control environment, make up the internal control structure.

9.4.1 The importance of internal control

As companies have grown in size and complexity, the importance of internal control within those companies has also grown. This is because these factors have made it impossible for managers and those charged with governance to manage the company's risks without appropriate control systems in place. Similarly, the growth in size and complexity of companies has meant that for auditors to provide assurance some reliance on these controls is usually needed.

In implementing this recommendation, the Committee of Sponsoring Organizations (COSO) of the Treadway Commission issued a report in 1992 on control. According to COSO, the two main purposes of its efforts were to:
- establish a common definition of internal control that served the needs of different parties
- provide a standard against which businesses and other entities . . . can assess their control systems and determine how to improve them.

COSO is an organisation that provides thought leadership through development of frameworks and guidance on internal control, enterprise risk management, and fraud deterrence. They released a new report in 2013 titled *Internal Control — Integrated Framework*.

The COSO report (2013) defines **internal control** as:

a process, effected by an entity's board of directors, management, and other personnel, designed to provide reasonable assurance regarding the achievement of objectives relating to operations, reporting, and compliance.

The COSO report especially emphasises the following fundamental concepts that are embodied in the definition.
- Internal control is a *process*. It is a means to an end, not an end in itself. It consists of a series of actions that are pervasive and integrated with, not added onto, an entity's infrastructure.

- Internal control is effected by *people*. It is not achieved merely by having policy manuals and forms, but by the actions and attitudes of people at every level of an organisation, including the board of directors and management.
- Internal control can be expected to provide only *reasonable assurance*, not absolute assurance, for an entity's management and board. This is because limitations are inherent in all internal control systems and because the entity must consider the relative costs and benefits of establishing controls.
- Internal control is geared to the achievement of *objectives* in the categories of operations, reporting, and compliance.

A definition of internal control is provided in ASA 315, paragraph 4(c) (ISA 315.4(c)) that is very similar to the definition provided by COSO.

Management's responsibilities in relation to internal control

Management has the responsibility of maintaining controls within an entity as outlined in the definition of internal control from the COSO report. However, there are currently no requirements for management to make any formal assertions in the financial statements in relation to this responsibility. In 2007, the ASX Corporate Governance Council published the second edition of the *Corporate Governance Principles and Recommendations*. Principle 7 relates to recognising and managing risk and states that entities should establish a sound system of risk oversight and management and internal control. Two of the recommendations to achieve this are quoted below.

> *Recommendation 7.1:* Companies should establish policies for the oversight and management of material business risk and disclose a summary of those policies.

> *Recommendation 7.2:* The board should require management to design and implement the risk management and internal control system to manage the company's material business risks and report to it on whether those risks are being managed effectively. The board should disclose that management has reported to it as to the effectiveness of the company's management of its material business risks.

ASX Listing Rule 4.10.3 states that the following information must be reported by all entities:

> A statement disclosing the extent to which the entity has followed the best practice recommendations set by the ASX Corporate Governance Council during the reporting period.

The corporate governance statement required by the Listing Rules does not form part of the directors' report as required by the Corporations Act nor does it form part of the financial statements. Therefore the auditor does not express an opinion on this information.

Auditors' responsibilities in relation to internal control

Auditors do not have any statutory legal obligations to report on internal control within the entity. The main guidance on auditors' requirements in relation to internal controls is provided by the auditing standards. ASA 315, paragraph 12 (ISA 315.12) states that the auditor must obtain an understanding of internal control relevant to the audit. This understanding also has a significant impact on the audit strategy, as discussed in chapter 10. The auditing standard requirements focus on obtaining the understanding to facilitate the performance of the audit rather than to comment on the controls as part of the audit.

However, if in the course of the audit, the auditor identifies a significant deficiency in internal controls, they are required to communicate this issue in writing to those charged with governance and management on a timely basis (ASA 265, paragraphs 7–11) (ISA 265).

In the United States, s. 404 of the Sarbanes–Oxley Act in 2002 and the Public Company Accounting Oversight Board (PCAOB) Standard No. 2 require management of public companies to assess the adequacy of internal controls over financial reporting, and their auditors must audit both management's assessment of internal controls over financial reporting and the actual effectiveness of the system of internal controls over financial reporting.

9.4.2 Internal control system

Internal control consists of the following components as outlined in ASA 315, paragraph A51 (ISA 315.A51):

- control environment
- risk assessment
- information system
- control activities
- monitoring.

Control environment

The **control environment** means management's overall attitude, awareness and actions regarding internal control and its importance in the entity. Numerous factors constitute the control environment, including:

- integrity and ethical values
- commitment to competence
- participation by those charged with governance
- management's philosophy and operating style
- organisational structure
- assignment of authority and responsibility
- human resource policies and practices.

Integrity and ethical values

Increasingly, employees, customers, suppliers and the public are demanding that business management exhibit integrity and ethical values. Managers of well-run entities are increasingly accepting the view that 'ethics pays' — that is, that ethical behaviour is good business.

To emphasise the importance of integrity and ethical values among all personnel of an organisation, the chief executive officer and other members of top management should:

- *set the tone by example*, by demonstrating integrity and practising ethical behaviour
- *communicate* to all employees, verbally and through written policy statements and codes of conduct, that the same behaviour is expected of them, that each employee has a responsibility to report known or suspected violations to a higher level in the organisation, and that violations will result in penalties
- *reduce or eliminate incentives and temptations* that may lead individuals to engage in dishonest, illegal or unethical acts. Incentives for undesirable negative behaviour include placing undue emphasis on short-term results or on unrealistic performance targets, and offering bonus and profit-sharing plans that may, in the absence of necessary controls, encourage fraudulent financial reporting practices.

Commitment to competence

Personnel at every level in the organisation must possess the knowledge and skills needed to perform their jobs effectively. Meeting financial reporting objectives in a large publicly held company generally requires higher levels of competence on the part of chief financial officers and accounting personnel than are needed for such personnel in a small, privately owned company.

Participation by those charged with governance

An entity's control consciousness is influenced significantly by those charged with governance, which usually means the board of directors and audit committee. Factors that influence the effectiveness of those charged with governance include their independence from management, accounting knowledge, experience and stature of members, the extent of their involvement and scrutiny of management's activities, and the appropriateness of their actions. They should also communicate with internal and external auditors and help to enhance the independence of these audit functions.

Management's philosophy and operating style

Characteristics that form part of a management's philosophy and operating style and that have an impact on the control environment include the management's:
- approach to taking and monitoring business risks
- reliance on informal face-to-face contacts with key managers versus a formal system of written policies, performance indicators and exception reports
- attitudes and actions towards financial reporting
- conservative or aggressive selection of accounting principles from available alternatives
- conscientiousness and conservatism in developing accounting estimates
- attitudes towards information processing and accounting functions and personnel.

The last four characteristics are particularly significant to an assessment of the control environment for financial reporting.

Organisational structure

An organisational structure contributes to an entity's ability to meet its objectives by providing an overall framework for planning, executing, controlling and monitoring the entity's activities. Developing an organisational structure for an entity involves determining the key areas of authority and responsibility and appropriate lines of reporting. The appropriateness of an entity's organisational structure depends, in part, on the size and nature of its activities. An entity's organisational structure is usually depicted in an organisation chart that should accurately reflect lines of authority and reporting relationships.

Assignment of authority and responsibility

The assignment of authority and responsibility is an extension of the development of an organisational structure. It includes the particulars of how and to whom authority and responsibility are assigned, and should enable employees to know:
- how their actions contribute to the achievement of the entity's objectives
- for what they will be held accountable.

It also includes policies relating to appropriate business practices, knowledge and experience of key personnel, and resources provided for carrying out duties. Further, it should include policies and communications to ensure that all personnel understand the entity's objectives and how their actions interrelate and contribute to these objectives, and recognise how and for what they will be held accountable.

Human resource policies and practices

A basic concept of internal control is that it is implemented by people. Thus, for the internal control structure to be effective, human resource policies and practices must ensure that entity personnel possess the expected integrity, ethical values and competence by:
- developing appropriate recruiting policies
- screening prospective employees

- ensuring new personnel are familiar with the entity's culture and operating style
- developing training policies that communicate prospective roles and responsibilities
- exercising disciplinary action for violations of expected behaviour
- evaluating, counselling and promoting people based on periodic performance appraisals
- implementing compensation programs that motivate and reward superior performance and promote ethical behaviour.

Risk assessment

Management's purpose in performing a **risk assessment** is to identify the risks and to put effective controls in operation to control those risks. In a strong risk assessment system, management should consider:
- the entity's business risks and their financial consequences
- the inherent risks of misstatements in financial statement assertions
- the risk of fraud and its financial consequences.

The extent to which management appropriately identifies risks and successfully initiates control activities to reduce those risks will affect the auditor's assessment of inherent and control risks. ASA 315, Appendix 1 (ISA 315, Appendix 1) notes that risks can also change owing to circumstances such as:
- changes in operating environment
- new personnel
- new or revamped information systems
- rapid growth
- new technology
- new business models
- corporate restructurings
- expanded foreign operations
- new accounting pronouncements.

To the extent to which these risks are present, management should put controls in place to control these risks.

Information system

The **information system** (which includes the accounting system) relevant to financial reporting objectives consists of procedures and **records** to initiate, record, process and report entity **transactions** and maintain accountability for the related assets and liabilities.

As noted before, a major focus of the accounting system is on transactions. Transactions consist of exchanges of assets and services between an entity and outside parties, as well as the transfer or use of assets and services within an entity. It follows that a major focus of control policies and procedures related to the accounting system is that transactions are handled in such a way that the financial statements are presented fairly in accordance with accounting standards. Thus, an effective accounting system should:
- identify and record only the valid transactions of the entity that occurred in the current period (existence or occurrence assertion)
- identify and record all valid transactions of the entity that occurred in the current period (completeness assertion)
- ensure that recorded assets and liabilities are the result of transactions that produced entity rights to, or obligations for, those items (rights and obligations assertion)
- measure the value of transactions in a manner that permits recording their proper monetary value in the financial statements (valuation and allocation assertion)

- capture sufficient detail of all transactions to permit their proper presentation in the financial statements, including proper classification and required disclosures (presentation and disclosure assertion).

An effective accounting system should provide a complete audit trail or transaction trail for each transaction. An **audit trail** is a chain of evidence from initiating a transaction to its recording in the general ledger and financial statements provided by coding, cross-reference and documentation connecting account balances and other summary results with original transaction data. Audit trails are essential both to management and to auditors. Management uses the trail in responding to enquiries from customers or suppliers concerning account balances. It is particularly important for management to ensure a clear audit trail in IT systems where documentary evidence may be retained for only a short period of time. Computer systems that use online processing should create a unique transaction number that can be used to establish such a trail. Auditors use the trail in tracing and vouching transactions.

Documents and records represent an aspect of the accounting system that provides important audit evidence. Documents provide evidence of the occurrence of transactions and the price, nature and terms of the transactions. Invoices, cheques, contracts and time tickets are illustrative of common types of documents. When duly signed or stamped, documents also provide a basis for establishing responsibility for executing and recording transactions. Records include employee earnings records, which show cumulative payroll data for each employee, and perpetual inventory records. Another type of record is daily summaries of documents issued, such as sales invoices and cheques. The summaries are then independently compared with the sum of corresponding daily entries to determine whether all transactions have been recorded. In modern accounting systems, records are usually in electronic format, and entities may create printed copies for ease of use.

Control activities

Control activities are detailed policies and procedures that management establishes to help ensure that its directives are carried out. They help ensure that necessary actions are taken to reduce risks that threaten the achievement of the entity's objectives.

Control activities relevant to a financial statement audit may be categorised in many different ways, including as follows:
- information processing controls
  - general controls
  - application controls
- segregation of duties
- physical controls
- performance reviews.
These categories are now explained.

Information processing controls

Of particular relevance to an audit are **information processing controls** that cover risks related to the authorisation, completeness and accuracy of transactions. Most entities, regardless of size, now use computers for information processing in general and for accounting information in particular. Remember that the general principles of control relating to manual and computer systems are the same. However, information processing controls are often further categorised as **general controls** and **application controls**.

General controls

General controls are those controls that apply to **computer information systems** as a whole and include controls related to such matters as data centre organisation, hardware and systems software acquisition and maintenance, and backup and recovery procedures. General controls are evaluated before application controls because weak general controls may allow strong application controls to be compromised. The following five types of general controls are widely recognised.

- **Organisational controls** consider the segregation of duties within the information technology (IT) department and between IT and user departments. A critical component is segregating access to programs from access to data files. Weakness in these controls usually affects all IT applications.
- **Systems development and maintenance controls** relate to review, testing and approval of new systems and program changes, and controls over documentation.
- **Access controls** are designed to prevent unauthorised use of IT equipment, data files and computer programs. The specific controls include a combination of physical, software and procedural safeguards.
- **Data and procedural controls** provide a framework for controlling daily computer operations, minimising the likelihood of processing errors, and assuring the continuity of operations in the event of a physical disaster or computer failure through adequate file backup and other controls.

Figure 9.2 on pages 390–1 lists some of these general controls.

Application controls

The purpose of application controls is to use the power of information technology to control transactions in individual transaction cycles. Hence, application controls will differ for each transaction cycle (e.g. sales versus cash receipts). The following three groups of application controls are widely recognised:

- input controls
- processing controls
- output controls.

These controls are designed to provide reasonable assurance that the recording, processing and reporting of data by IT are properly performed for specific applications. Thus, the auditor must consider these controls separately for each significant accounting application, such as invoicing customers or preparing payroll cheques.

In today's IT environment, application controls execute the function of **independent checks** by (1) using programmed application controls to identify transactions that contain possible misstatements and (2) having people follow up and correct items noted on exception reports. The following discussion explains how programmed controls may be used to identify items that should be included on various exception reports.

Input controls Input controls are program controls designed to detect and report errors in data that are input for processing. They are of vital importance in IT systems because most of the errors occur at this point. Input controls are designed to provide reasonable assurance that data received for processing have been properly authorised and converted into machine-sensible form. These controls also include the people who follow up on the rejection, correction and resubmission of data that were initially incorrect.

Controls over the conversion of data into machine-sensible form are intended to ensure that the data are correctly entered and converted data are valid. Specific controls include the following.

- *Verification controls.* These controls often compare data input for computer processing with information contained on computer master files, or other data independently entered at earlier stages of a transaction.

- *Computer editing.* These are computer routines intended to detect incomplete, incorrect or unreasonable data. They include:
  - *missing data check* to ensure that all required data fields have been completed and no blanks are present
  - *valid character check* to verify that only alphabetical, numerical or other special characters appear as required in data fields
  - *limit (reasonableness)* check to determine that only data falling within predetermined limits are entered (e.g. time cards exceeding a designated number of hours per week may be rejected)
  - *valid sign check* to determine that the sign of the data, if applicable, is correct (e.g. a valid sign test would ensure that the net carrying amount of an asset was positive and that assets are not over-depreciated)
  - *valid code check* to match the classification (i.e. expense account number) or transaction code (i.e. cash receipts entry) against the master list of codes permitted for the type of transaction to be processed
  - *check digit* to determine that an account, employee or other identification number has been correctly entered by applying a specific arithmetic operation to the identification number and comparing the result with a check digit embedded within the number.

The correction and resubmission of incorrect data are vital to the accuracy of the accounting records. If the processing of a valid sales invoice is stopped because of an error, both accounts receivable and sales will be understated until the error is eliminated and the processing completed. Misstatement should be corrected by those responsible for the mistake. Furthermore, strong controls create a log of potential misstatements, and the data control group periodically reviews their disposition.

Processing controls Processing controls are designed to provide reasonable assurance that the computer processing has been performed as intended for the particular application. Thus, these controls should preclude data from being lost, added, duplicated or altered during processing.

Processing controls take many forms, but the most common ones are programmed controls incorporated into the individual applications software. Such controls include the following.

- *Control totals.* Provision for accumulating control totals is written into the computer program to facilitate the balancing of input totals with processing totals for each run. Similarly, run-to-run totals are accumulated to verify processing performed in stages.
- *File identification labels.* External labels are physically attached to magnetic tape or disks to permit visual identification of a file. Internal labels are in machine-sensible form and are matched electronically with specified operator instructions (or commands) that have been incorporated into the computer program before processing can begin or be successfully completed.
- *Limit and reasonableness checks.* A limit or reasonableness test would compare data with an expected limit (e.g. the product of payroll rates times hours worked would be included on an exception report and not processed if it exceeded a predetermined limit).
- *Before-and-after report.* This report shows a summary of the contents of a master file before and after each update.
- *Sequence tests.* If transactions are given identification numbers, the transaction file can be tested for sequence (e.g. an exception report would include missing numbers or duplicate numbers in a sequence of sales invoices).
- *Process tracing data.* This control involves a printout of specific data for visual inspection to determine whether the processing is correct. For evaluating changes in critical data

items, tracing data may include the contents before and after the processing (e.g. information from shipping data with information on sales invoices).

Output controls Output controls are designed to ensure that the processing results are correct and that only authorised personnel receive the output. The accuracy of the processing results includes both updated machine-sensible files and printed output. This objective is met by the following.

- *Reconciliation of totals.* Output totals that are generated by the computer programs are reconciled to input and processing totals by the data control group or by user departments.
- *Comparison with source documents.* Output data are subject to detailed comparison with source documents.
- *Visual scanning.* The output is reviewed for completeness and apparent reasonableness. Actual results may be compared with estimated results.

The data control group usually controls who can have access to data in a database and maintains control over any centrally produced reports for the distribution of output. This group should exercise special care over the access to, or distribution of, confidential output. To facilitate control over the disposition of output, systems documentation should include reports of who has access to various aspects of a database or some form of a report distribution sheet.

An important new way in which companies are using technology is through cloud computing which is performing computing tasks via a network connection to a service provider. This is changing significantly the way in which many businesses use IT and will have significant effects on the work of the auditor as highlighted in the Professional Environment article below.

PROFESSIONAL ENVIRONMENT
Auditing in the cloud: Challenges and opportunities

*E*xternal financial statement auditors should assess the service level agreement between a company and its cloud provider in order to determine the extent of testing they can conduct in-house, versus the level and type of reliance they will need to receive from a third-party assurance provider. This assessment should at least help mitigate some of the audit risks when the client utilises the services of a cloud computing provider. As these services become more complex, however, and companies rely at a maximum on the level of security and controls implemented by a cloud service provider, external auditors may need to develop in-house skills in auditing these systems and the organisational controls that surround their development and continued operation. With so many companies adopting this emerging technology, 'auditing in or through the cloud' will be ingrained in the vocabulary of every auditor not too far in the future.

Source: C Nicolaou, A Nicolaou & G Nicolaou,
'Auditing in the cloud: Challenges and opportunities',
The CPA Journal, January 2012, p. 70.

Segregation of duties

Segregation of duties ensures that individuals do not perform incompatible duties. Duties are considered incompatible when it is possible for a person to commit an error or irregularity and then be in a position to conceal it in the normal course of his or her duties.

A person who processes cash receipts from customers, for example, should not also have authority to approve and record credits to customers' accounts for sales returns and bad debt write-offs. In such cases, the person could steal a cash remittance and cover the theft by recording a fictitious sales return or by writing off the balance.

Such reasoning supports segregation of duties in the following situations.

- *Responsibility for executing a transaction, recording the transaction and maintaining custody of the assets resulting from the transaction should be assigned to different individuals or departments.* For example, purchasing department personnel should initiate purchase orders, goods inward personnel should record the goods received, and storeroom personnel should assume custody of the goods. Before recording the purchase, accounting personnel should ascertain that the purchase was authorised and that the goods ordered were received. The accounting entry, in turn, provides an accountability basis for the goods in the storeroom.
- *The various steps involved in executing a transaction should be assigned to different individuals or departments.* Thus, in executing a sales transaction, the entity should assign responsibility for authorising the sale, filling the order, shipping the goods and invoicing the customer to different individuals.
- *Responsibility for certain accounting operations should be segregated.* In a manual information system, for example, different personnel should maintain the general ledger and the accounts receivable subsidiary ledger, and personnel involved in recording cash receipts and payments should not reconcile the bank accounts.

When duties are segregated such that the work of one individual automatically provides a cross-check on the work of another, the entity has the added benefit of an independent check. Note that whereas an independent check always involves segregating duties, segregating duties does not always involve an independent check. The following are examples of how segregation of duties affects the control risk.

- Separating the custody of assets from the maintenance of the accounting record of assets reduces the risk of theft because the perpetrator will not have an opportunity to cover up the theft by eliminating the record of the assets.
- Segregation of duties for processing cash payment transactions and reconciling the bank accounts reduces the risk of unrecorded payments by cheque. Whereas the cash payment clerk may wish to conceal an error by falsifying the reconciliation, an independent person has no such incentive.
- Segregating responsibility for approving credit from initiating sales orders reduces the risk of bad debts that may result from sales made to bad credit risks to achieve sales targets or to boost commissions.

Physical controls

Physical controls limit access to assets and important records. Such controls may be direct or indirect. Direct controls include initiating measures for the safekeeping of assets, documents and records (such as fireproof safes and locked storerooms) and restricting access to storage areas to authorised personnel only. Indirect controls apply to the preparation or processing of documents (such as sales orders and payment vouchers) that authorise the use or disposition of assets. They involve the use of mechanical and electronic equipment such as cash registers, which help to assure that all cash receipt transactions are rung up and which provide locked-in summaries of daily receipts. To be effective, physical controls must include periodic counts of assets and comparisons with the amounts shown on control records. Examples include petty cash counts and physical inventory checks.

Access controls, both physical and electronic, are particularly important in a computer information system. They should provide assurance that transactions being entered into the computer systems are appropriately authorised and that access to data and programs is restricted to authorised personnel.

Access to computer hardware should be limited to authorised people. Physical safeguards include housing the equipment in an area restricted by security guards, or using keys, badges or other automated security devices.

Access to data files and programs should be designed to prevent unauthorised use of such data. All computer users should have passwords, whether for access to the mainframe computer, to terminals or to a microcomputer system. Each user may have restricted access to specific programs and files. Access may be further designated as 'read only' or 'read and write'. The computer should also be programmed to record the names of all users who access the computer for the purposes of adding, altering or deleting data. If passwords are to provide for the security of data files and programs, they should be changed regularly, not easily guessed, and secured by both the user and the system.

In systems with online entry of data, many users have direct access through remote input devices. Access often extends beyond the entity's employees to customers and suppliers through remote terminals such as automated teller machines or even via the Internet. To provide the necessary control, each user of a remote input device is provided with a key, code or card that identifies the holder as an authorised user.

Security packages can also provide access security. They can define the relationships of different types of users to the programs and data files stored in the computer. The software can detect access violations by logging all abortive access attempts.

Performance reviews

Performance reviews involve managers' participation in the supervision of operations. Frequent performance reviews will give managers a greater chance of detecting errors, and can include management review and analysis of:

- reports that summarise the detail of account balances such as an aged trial balance of accounts receivable or reports of sales activity by region, salesperson or product line
- actual performance compared with budgets, forecasts or previous period amounts
- the relationship of different sets of data such as non-financial operating data and financial data.

This review and analysis by management provides an independent check of the accounting information. The quality of this review may provide good control over the accuracy of transactions and balances. It involves similar activities to how auditors use analytical review for planning purposes.

Monitoring

Monitoring of controls is a process to ensure the quality of internal control performance over time. Effective monitoring activities usually involve (1) ongoing monitoring programs, (2) separate evaluations, and (3) reporting deficiencies to the audit committee.

Ongoing monitoring activities might take a variety of forms. An active internal audit function that regularly performs tests of controls using an integrated test facility or internal auditors may regularly rotate tests of different aspects of the system of internal control. In addition, controls may be designed with various self-monitoring processes. For example, problems with internal control may come to management's attention through complaints received from customers about invoicing errors or from suppliers about payment problems, or from alert managers who receive reports with information that differs significantly from their first-hand knowledge of operations.

Monitoring also occurs through separate periodic evaluations. Management of public companies must perform periodic evaluations of internal controls in order to support an assertion about the effectiveness of the system of internal control. Furthermore, management and the audit committee should be conscious of IT risks and perform separate evaluations of computer general controls because of their pervasive effect on various programmed application controls. The audit committee also might charge internal audit with periodic reviews of IT risks and controls. Finally, management may receive information from the separate evaluation of regulators.

The final element of sound monitoring controls involves the reporting of deficiencies to the audit committee (or full board of directors). Deficiencies that surface through ongoing monitoring programs or separate evaluations should be regularly brought to the audit committee for discussion and decisions about corrective actions.

9.4.3 Limitations of control

One of the basic concepts identified earlier in the chapter is that internal control can provide only reasonable assurance regarding the achievement of an entity's objectives. Reasons for this include the following inherent limitations in an entity's internal control structure.

- *Costs versus benefits.* The cost of an entity's internal control structure should not exceed the benefits that are expected to ensue. Because precise measurement of both costs and benefits is not usually possible, management must make both quantitative and qualitative estimates and judgements in evaluating the cost–benefit relationship.
- *Management override.* Management can overrule prescribed policies or procedures for illegitimate purposes, such as for personal gain or enhanced presentation of an entity's financial condition (such as inflating reported earnings to increase a performance bonus or the market value of the entity's shares). Override practices include making deliberate misrepresentations to auditors and others, such as by issuing false documents to support the recording of fictitious sales transactions.
- *Non-routine transactions.* Internal control systems focus on routine transactions for reasons associated with the costs and benefits of implementation. This means that there will generally be an increased risk associated with non-routine transactions within the entity.
- *Mistakes in judgement.* Occasionally, as a result of inadequate information, time constraints or other pressures, management and other personnel may exercise poor judgement in making business decisions or performing routine duties.
- *Collusion.* Individuals acting together may evade the planned segregation of duties to perpetrate and conceal an irregularity (e.g. collusion among three employees from the personnel, manufacturing and payroll departments to initiate payments to fictitious employees, or 'kickback' schemes arranged between an employee in the purchasing department and a supplier, or between an employee in the sales department and a customer).
- *Breakdowns.* Breakdowns in established controls may occur because personnel misunderstand instructions or make errors as a result of carelessness, distractions or fatigue. Temporary or permanent changes in personnel, systems or procedures may also contribute to breakdowns.
- *Changes in conditions.* Over time, conditions may change that may result in procedures becoming inadequate.

LEARNING 5 objective

Indicate the procedures for obtaining and documenting an understanding of the entity's internal control.

9.5 UNDERSTANDING INTERNAL CONTROL

This section explains how auditors meet their responsibilities for obtaining and documenting an understanding of the entity's internal control.

9.5.1 What to understand about internal control

A sufficient understanding of internal control is essential for an effective audit because it informs the auditor about where misstatements are likely to occur. In order to support an opinion on the financial statements, auditors need a sufficient knowledge of internal control to plan a financial statement audit. This involves performing procedures to:

- understand the policies and procedures related to each component of internal control
- determine whether the policies and procedure are in operation.

The auditor uses this knowledge in three ways. The auditor should know enough to:

- identify the types of potential misstatements that may occur
- understand the factors that affect the risk of material misstatement
- design further audit procedures.

Each of these steps is discussed below.

Identifying the types of potential misstatements that may occur

An important aspect of assessing the risk of material misstatement involves obtaining an understanding of the points at which errors or fraud could occur. Some internal control weaknesses have a pervasive effect on the financial statements. A poor control environment, or weak computer general controls, might increase the risk of material misstatement for most or all assertions in the financial statements. Other weaknesses are assertion-specific. At some stage in the recording of a transaction, the change of information, or the addition of new information, may not be controlled. For example, an entity might record sales when an order is taken from a customer rather than when goods are shipped, resulting in potential cut-off errors. Perhaps a company has designed effective computer controls, but owing to changes in personnel the company has hired someone who does not adequately understand the role that he or she plays in following up on items that appear on exception reports. This lack of knowledge and inappropriate manual follow-up may create potential for error or fraud. As a result, auditors usually consider how errors in each financial statement assertion might occur. Once this potential is understood, the auditor will identify controls that prevent or detect misstatements in each assertion.

Understanding the factors that affect the risk of material misstatement

Once the auditor understands the types of potential misstatements that may occur, the auditor must assess the risk of material misstatement. When considering the factors that affect the risk of material misstatement, the auditor usually considers:

- the magnitude of the misstatement that might occur
- the likelihood of misstatements in the financial statements.

For example, the magnitude of a revenue recognition problem is usually greater than the magnitude of a misstatement in the amortisation of prepaid expenses. In addition, revenue recognition might be a more likely problem for a software company that is selling a group of bundled products and services than for a retailer who delivers goods at the point of sale. Every company might have a risk of a material misstatement if a hacker is able to gain unauthorised access to a company's computer system. The magnitude of potential misstatement might be very significant. However, the auditor must also assess the likelihood of such an event. If a company has good access controls, strong firewalls, and other controls that might detect attempts at unauthorised access to computer systems, the likelihood of unauthorised access is remote.

Designing further audit procedures

The auditor uses the knowledge of internal control in three ways. First, the auditor needs to consider whether the risk assessment procedures are adequate to allow the auditor to assess the risk of material misstatement for each significant financial statement assertion. If the auditor does not have adequate information, the auditor should perform additional risk assessment procedures.

Second, the auditor uses this knowledge to plan tests of controls. The design of tests of controls is discussed extensively later in this chapter. Finally, the auditor needs to know the system of internal control in order to design substantive tests. Knowledge of the audit trail is essential in understanding the potential for error or fraud and for designing effective substantive tests. Chapter 12 discusses the important audit decisions about the design of substantive audit procedures. Note that there are some circumstances where testing of controls is necessary to reduce audit risk to a sufficiently low level, as discussed below.

Risks for which substantive tests alone will not reduce audit risk to a sufficiently low level

In some cases, the client's accounting system is sufficiently automated that substantive tests alone will not reduce audit risk to a sufficiently low level. Many businesses that take orders online or over the phone do not generate a paper trail for the transactions. For example, many airlines take reservations online, record the reservation and transaction in electronic form, and then issue an electronic ticket. Some companies have purchase systems that never generate a paper purchase order, but have only an electronic trail of the transaction and provide the vendor with only an electronic purchase order in a business-to-business e-commerce system. In these cases the only way that the auditor can obtain reasonable assurance about the completeness and accuracy of the transactions in the transaction cycle is to test computer general controls, computer application controls, and manual follow-up procedures. In many charitable organisations, there is no way to ensure the completeness of donations without testing the internal controls over cash receipts. The understanding of the nature of the system of internal controls may dictate a lower assessed level of control risk audit strategy.

9.5.2 Procedures to obtain an understanding

The procedures necessary to obtain an understanding consist of:
- reviewing previous experience with the entity
- enquiring of appropriate management, supervisory and staff personnel
- inspecting documents and records
- observing entity activities and operations.

In a repeat engagement, the previous year's working papers contain a great deal of information relevant to the current year's audit. The auditor can use the previous year's recorded understanding and assessment of control risk as the starting point, making enquiries as to the changes that may have occurred in the current year. The working papers should also contain information about the types and causes of misstatements found in previous audits. The auditor can follow up on this information to determine whether management has taken corrective actions.

The auditor should also inspect relevant documents and records of the entity, such as organisation charts, policy manuals, the chart of accounts, accounting ledgers, journals and source documents. These inspections will inevitably lead to additional enquiries about specific controls and changes in conditions.

To reinforce understanding of the information system and control procedures, the auditor performs a **transaction walk-through review** by tracing one or a few transactions in each major class through the transaction trail to confirm the documented understanding.

9.5.3 Documenting the understanding

Documenting the understanding of the control system is a requirement for all audits. Documentation may take the form of completed questionnaires, flowcharts and/or narrative memoranda. In an audit of a large entity, involving a combination of audit strategies, all three types of documentation may be used for different parts of the understanding. In an audit of a small entity, a single memorandum may suffice to document the auditor's understanding of all the components. In a repeat engagement, it may be necessary only to update documentation from the previous year's working papers. Only those parts of the information system that are relevant to the audit need to be documented.

Questionnaires

An **internal control questionnaire** (ICQ) consists of a series of questions about accounting and control policies and procedures that the auditor considers necessary to prevent material misstatements in the financial statements. The questions are usually phrased in such a way that a 'yes' answer indicates a favourable condition. Space is also provided on the questionnaire for comments such as who performs a control procedure and how often.

Standardised questionnaires are used for many audits. Some firms use quite different questionnaires for large versus small entities or for particular industries.

Excerpts from two questionnaires are illustrated in figures 9.1 and 9.2 (overleaf). These relate to parts of the control environment.

FIGURE 9.1:
Excerpts from an internal control questionnaire — control environment

CLIENT _Amalgamated Products Limited_	END OF THE REPORTING PERIOD _30/6/14_
Completed by: _RSC_ Date: _12/3/14_	Reviewed by: _GEY_ Date: _29/4/14_

Internal control questionnaire component: Control environment

Question	Yes, No, N/A	Comments
Integrity and ethical values		
1. Does management set the 'tone at the top' by demonstrating a commitment to integrity and ethics through both its words and deeds?	Yes	*Management is conscious of setting an example. Entity does not have a formal code of conduct.*
2. Have appropriate entity policies regarding acceptable business practices, conflicts of interest, and codes of conduct been established and adequately communicated?	Yes	*Expectations of employees included in a policy manual distributed to all employees.*
3. Have incentives and temptations that might lead to unethical behaviour been reduced or eliminated?	Yes	*Profit-sharing plan monitored by audit committee.*
Board of directors and audit committee		
1. Are there regular meetings of the board and are minutes prepared on a timely basis?	Yes	*Board has nine inside members, three of whom serve on the audit committee. Considering adding three outside members to the board who would comprise the audit committee.*
2. Do board members have sufficient knowledge, experience and time to serve effectively?	Yes	
3. Is there an audit committee composed of outside directors?	No	

(continued)

FIGURE 9.1:
(continued)

Management's philosophy and operating style

1. Are business risks carefully considered and adequately monitored?	Yes	*Management is conservative about business risks.*
2. Is management's selection of accounting principles and development of accounting estimates consistent with objective and fair reporting?	Yes	
3. Has management demonstrated a willingness to adjust the financial statements for material misstatements?	Yes	*Management has readily accepted all proposed adjustments in previous audits.*

Human resource policies and practices

1. Do existing personnel policies and procedures result in the recruitment or development of competent and trustworthy people needed to support an effective internal control structure?	Yes	*Formal job descriptions are provided for all positions.*
2. Do personnel understand the duties and procedures applicable to their jobs?	Yes	
3. Is the turnover of personnel in key positions at an acceptable level?	Yes	*Normal 'turnover'.*

FIGURE 9.2:

Excerpts from an internal control questionnaire — computer information system (CIS) general controls

CLIENT *Amalgamated Products Limited*	END OF THE REPORTING PERIOD *30/6/14*
Completed by: *RSC* Date: *12/3/14*	Reviewed by: *GEY* Date: *29/4/14*

Internal control questionnaire component: CIS Control environment

Question	Yes, No, N/A	Comments
Organisational controls		
1. Are the following duties segregated within the CIS department?		
(a) Systems design	Yes	
(b) Computer programming	Yes	
(c) Computer operations	Yes	
(d) Data entry	Yes	
(e) Custody of systems documentation, programs and files	Yes	*Good segregation in CIS department.*
(f) Data control	Yes	
2. Are the following duties performed only outside the CIS department?		
(a) Initiation and authorisation of transactions	Yes	
(b) Authorisation of changes in systems, programs and master files	Yes	
(c) Preparation of source documents	Yes	
(d) Correction of errors in source documents	Yes	
(e) Custody of assets	Yes	

Systems development and maintenance controls

1. Is there adequate participation by users and internal auditors in new systems development?	Yes	*Wide consultation.*
2. Is proper authorisation, testing and documentation required for systems and program changes?	Yes	*Strong controls in this area.*
3. Is access to systems software restricted to authorised personnel?	Yes	
4. Are there adequate controls over data files (both master and transaction files) during conversion to prevent unauthorised changes?	Yes	

Access controls

1. Is access to computer facilities restricted to authorised personnel?	No	*Facilities in unlocked area of main office.*
2. Does the librarian restrict access to data files and programs to authorised personnel?	Yes	
3. Are computer-processing activities reviewed by management?	No	*More review by management needed.*

Data and procedural controls

1. Is there a disaster contingency plan to ensure continuity of operations?	Yes	
2. Is there off-site storage of backup files and programs?	Yes	
3. Are sufficient generations of programs, master files and transaction files maintained to facilitate recovery and reconstruction of CIS processing?	Yes	
4. Are there adequate safeguards against fire, water damage, power failure, power fluctuations, theft, loss, and intentional and unintentional destruction?	Yes	

Some auditing firms have automated their internal control questionnaires. The staff auditor enters the responses into a laptop computer as the information is obtained, using software that analyses the pattern of responses across related questions and guides the auditor through subsequent steps in assessing control risk and designing substantive audit procedures.

Some auditing firms also provide special training for staff in the interviewing skills needed to administer questionnaires. By being alert to non-verbal signals given by interviewees (such as hesitation, an apparent lack of familiarity with controls, or undue nervousness during the interview), the auditor can significantly enhance his or her understanding.

As a means of documenting the understanding, questionnaires offer a number of advantages. They are developed by experienced professionals and provide guidance for less experienced staff who may be assigned to obtain the understanding on a particular audit. They are relatively easy to use and reduce the possibility that the auditor may overlook important internal control matters. Their disadvantage is that to cater for the varied types of information systems, they may be long and unwieldy.

Flowcharts

A **flowchart** is a schematic diagram that uses standardised symbols, interconnecting flow lines and annotations to portray the steps involved in processing information through the information system. Flowcharts can depict the processing of individual classes of transactions, such as sales, cash receipts, purchases, cash payments, payroll and manufacturing.

Flowcharts should show:
- all operations performed in processing the class of transactions
- the methods of processing (manual or computerised)
- the extent of segregation of duties (by identifying each operation with a functional area, department or individual)
- the source, flow and disposition of the documents, records and reports involved in processing.

Many accounting firms now use computer packages to produce flowcharts, and this is one of the set-up costs associated with performing a new audit. The flowcharts are usually kept in the permanent file of audit working papers. In subsequent audits, the auditor reviews the system at the planning stage of the audit and amends the flowchart documentation when changes have been made. If the client implements a completely new system, this would require the auditor to prepare new flowcharts to reflect those changes. Outlined below is an example of how a flowchart might be prepared.

Flowcharting is a creative task, making it unlikely that any two people would draw flowcharts exactly alike for a given system. The more commonly used flowcharting symbols are shown in figure 9.3. Some firms supplement these basic symbols with more extensive sets of special purpose symbols.

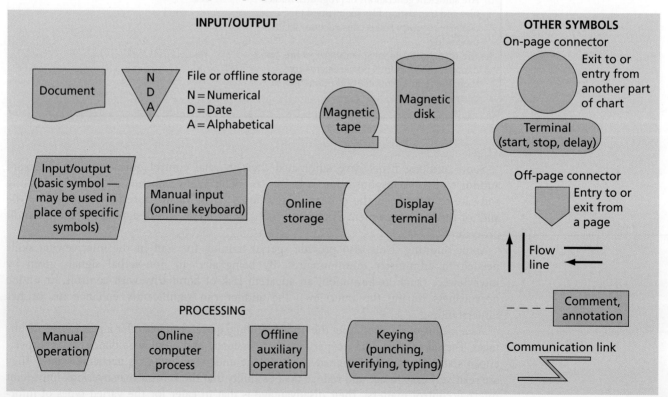

FIGURE 9.3: Flowcharting symbols

In addition to the four essential components of flowcharts listed, the following guidelines are helpful in preparing useful flowcharts.

- Identify the class(es) of transaction to be included in a flowchart.
- Collect information through interviews, observations and the review of documents.
- Visualise an organisational format for the flowchart (e.g. the number and order of columns needed to represent departments, functions or individuals) and prepare a rough sketch.
- Prepare the flowchart, selecting the correct symbols carefully.
- Test the completeness and accuracy of the flowchart by tracing a hypothetical transaction through it.

To illustrate, assume the auditor wishes to prepare a flowchart depicting Hayes Ltd's processing of mail cash receipts. The following description of the processing system is based on information obtained through enquiries of entity personnel, observations and review of documents.

Hayes Ltd — mail cash receipts processing

All receipts from customers are received by mail and are accompanied by a pre-printed remittance advice (the bottom portion of the invoice originally sent to the customer). In the mail room, the cheques and remittance advices are separated. The cheques are restrictively endorsed (For Deposit Only) and a listing (prelist) of the cheques is prepared in triplicate and totalled. The cheques and one copy of the prelist are then forwarded to the cashier. The remittance advices and a copy of the prelist are sent to accounts receivable accounting, and another copy of the prelist is sent to general accounting.

The cashier prepares a bank deposit slip in duplicate and makes the daily bank deposit. The cashier forwards the validated copy of the bank deposit (slip stamped and dated by the bank) to general accounting and files the prelist by date.

In accounts receivable accounting, the remittances are processed on a computer. The accounts receivable clerk keys the remittance data into a cash receipts transaction file via an online terminal. This file is then processed to (1) update the receivables master file and (2) generate an entry in the general ledger transaction file, which is subsequently used to update the general ledger. This processing routine also generates two printed reports. A receivables summary report shows the total credits posted to the receivables master file and is reconciled to the total on the prelist received from the mail room. The remittance advices, prelist and summary report are then filed by date. The general ledger transaction report shows the daily totals for cash, discounts and receivables, and is forwarded to general accounting.

General accounting compares the totals from the prelist received from the mail room, the validated deposit slip received from the cashier and the general ledger transaction report received from accounts receivable accounting, and resolves any discrepancies. The documents are then collated and filed by date.

After considering the information on processing, the auditor devises a flowchart with the following four columns: mail room, cashier, accounts receivable accounting and general accounting. After first preparing a rough sketch, the auditor prepares the flowchart shown in figure 9.4 (overleaf).

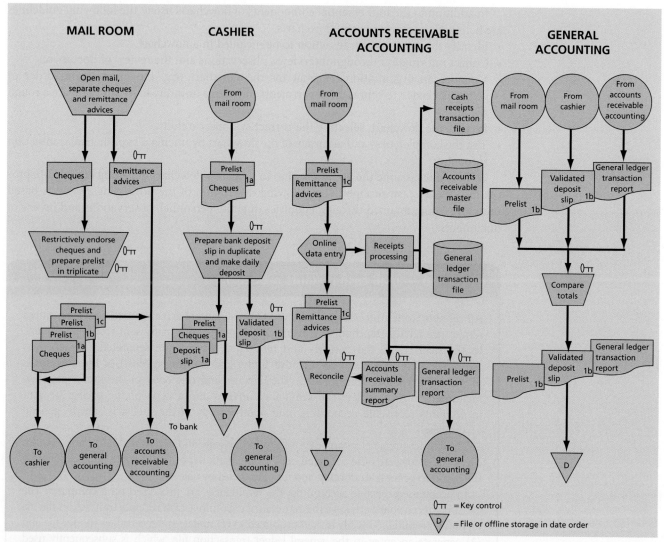

FIGURE 9.4: Flowchart for the processing of mail receipts

A flowchart is a means to an end, not an end in itself. It should enable the auditor to see the relationships that exist among controls and facilitate the identification of key controls related to specific financial statement assertions. From studying the flowchart in figure 9.4, you could observe, for example, the following controls (among others).

- Documents and records:
  - the use of pre-printed remittance advices returned by customers with payments
  - the preparation of a prelist of cash receipts in triplicate for use in subsequent control
  - the retention of a validated (receipted) deposit slip for use in subsequent control
  - the generation of a sales summary report and general ledger transaction report for use in subsequent controls
  - the segregation of handling cash (mail room and cashier) from accounting for cash and receivables (general accounting and accounts receivable accounting).
- Independent checks:
  - the reconciliation of the accounts receivable summary report in accounts receivable accounting with the total on the prelist received from the mail room

- the reconciliation by general accounting of amounts reported on the prelist received from the mail room, the validated deposit slip received from the cashier, and the general ledger transaction report received from accounts receivable accounting.
- Other control activities:
  - the restrictive endorsement of cheques immediately upon receipt
  - the deposit of receipts intact daily.

The auditor may document additional controls by making written notes on a flowchart. In this illustration a note could be added to indicate that an independent monthly reconciliation is made of the bank account. Similarly, annotations about any observed weaknesses could be added to the flowchart.

Narrative memoranda

A **narrative memorandum** may be used to supplement other forms of documentation by summarising the auditor's overall understanding of the information system or specific control policies or procedures. In audits of small entities, a narrative memorandum may serve as the only documentation of the auditor's understanding. Figure 9.5 illustrates this type of documentation for a small company managed by its owner.

CLIENT	_Ownco Pty Ltd_	END OF THE REPORTING PERIOD	_30/6/13_
Completed by: _m/w_ Date: _31/3/13_		Reviewed by: _i/p_ Date: _2/5/13_	
Updated by: _m/w_ Date: _15/3/14_		Reviewed by: _i/p_ Date: _29/4/14_	

Understanding of the control environment

The company manufactures plastic fishing worms at one location and is managed by its sole owner, Ed Jones, who is responsible for marketing, purchasing, hiring and approving major transactions. He has a good understanding of the business and the industry in which it operates. Jones believes that hiring experienced personnel is very important because there are no layers of supervisory personnel and thus, as a result of limited segregation of duties, few independent checks of employees' work. Jones has a moderate-to-conservative attitude to business risks. The business has demonstrated consistent profitability and, because Jones considers lower taxes to be as important as financial results, he has a conservative attitude to accounting estimates.

Jones and Pat Willis, the bookkeeper, consult with our firm on routine accounting questions, including preparation of accounting estimates (tax accrual, inventory obsolescence or bad debts). Our firm also helps assemble the financial statements.

The company's board of directors is composed of family members. The board is not expected to monitor the business or the owner–manager's activities.

Most of the significant accounting functions are performed by Willis, the bookkeeper, and Jones's secretary, Chris Ross. Willis was hired by the company in 2008 and has a working knowledge of accounting fundamentals, and we have no reason to question her competence. Willis regularly consults with our firm on unusual transactions, and past history indicates that it is rare for adjustments to arise from errors in the processing of routine transactions.

Jones purchased a microcomputer and a turnkey accounting software package. The source code is not available for this software. Access to the computer and computer files is limited to Willis, Ross and Jones, who effectively have access to all computer files.

Jones carefully reviews computer-generated financial statements, and monitors the terms of the long-term debt agreement that requires certain ratios and compensating balances.

FIGURE 9.5:
Narrative memorandum documenting understanding of the control environment

Source: Adapted from Audit Guide: Consideration of the Internal Control Structure in a Financial Statement Audit, AICPA, 1990, pp. 117–18.

LEARNING 6
objective

Explain why and how a preliminary assessment of control risk is made.

9.6 PRELIMINARY ASSESSMENT OF CONTROL RISK

In the previous sections we have discussed the ways an auditor obtains an understanding of an organisation's internal controls and documents this information. We now turn our attention to how the auditor uses this information to assess the strengths and weaknesses of those internal controls and the level of control risk. **Control risk** is the risk that a material misstatement could occur in an assertion, either individually or when aggregated with other misstatements, and not be prevented, detected, or corrected on a timely basis by the entity's internal control structure (ASA 200, paragraph 13(n); ISA 200.13(n)). We consider the role of the **preliminary assessment of control risk** and the nature of evidence used in making the assessment. The process of assessing control risk and its role in determining the audit strategy are discussed in chapter 11.

9.6.1 The purpose of the preliminary assessment

Assessment of control risk is conducted in two phases. The preliminary assessment of control risk is designed to obtain a reasonable expectation of controls so as to decide on an appropriate audit strategy to then be able to design a detailed audit program. The preliminary assessment of internal control will normally be high when the entity's internal control system is not expected to be effective or where it is not considered cost effective to evaluate the system as part of the audit. Where the preliminary assessment is determined to be high, no further audit testing of controls is necessary. The second phase occurs on completion of all tests of controls (covered in chapter 11). If these tests do not support the preliminary assessment of control risk, then the auditor must perform additional substantive procedures. In most instances, however, the preliminary assessment is sufficiently reliable (especially for repeat engagements) so that the need to extend substantive procedures after completion of tests of controls rarely arises.

In computer information systems, the use of computer-assisted audit techniques (CAATs) may enable the auditor to perform extensive substantive testing as cheaply as less extensive testing. This applies where all of the testing can be computerised, enabling the auditor to draw conclusions based on exceptions reported by the computer; for example, it may be possible for the auditor to use a computer program to check the pricing of all sales invoices. Assessment of control over invoice pricing is, therefore, unnecessary.

9.6.2 The process of assessing control risk

Assessing control risk is the process of evaluating the effectiveness of the design and operation of an entity's internal controls in preventing or detecting material misstatements in the financial statements.

The first step is to assess the control environment. A weak control environment can undermine the internal control structure. Strong individual control procedures cannot compensate for a weak control environment. Assessment of the control environment is a matter for professional judgement, and is common to all assertions for all transaction classes.

The second step is to assess the design effectiveness of **control procedures** and the ability of such procedures to prevent or correct misstatements. The effectiveness of a control is ultimately limited by its design. Control risk is assessed in terms of individual financial statement assertions. Because the **accounting system** focuses on the processing of transactions, and because many control procedures concern the processing of a particular type of transaction, the auditor commonly begins by assessing control risk for transaction class assertions, such as the occurrence, completeness and allocation assertions for cash receipts and cash payment transactions. It is important to keep in mind that control risk assessments are made for individual assertions, not for the accounting system as a whole.

The final step is to assess whether the controls were effectively applied throughout the period under audit. This stage of tests of controls is normally deferred until after the preliminary assessment and performed only where the auditor adopts a lower assessed level of control risk strategy.

In evaluating design effectiveness in order to make a preliminary assessment of control risk for an assertion, the auditor has to:

- identify potential misstatements that could occur in the entity's assertion
- identify the necessary controls that would be likely to prevent or detect the material misstatements
- evaluate the evidence and make the assessment.

Identifying the potential misstatements

To evaluate the potential misstatements that might occur in the system, the auditor goes back to some of the documentation used in obtaining the understanding of the system. In reviewing these questionnaires, the auditor carefully evaluates the 'no' responses that indicate weakness and therefore potential misstatements that should be considered, as shown in table 9.2. Some auditing firms use computer software to link responses to specific questions in computerised questionnaires to potential misstatements for particular assertions. However, most auditing firms have developed **internal control evaluation checklists** that enumerate the types of potential misstatement that could occur in specific assertions. Using either the computer software aid or checklists and the understanding of the entity's information system, the auditor identifies the potential misstatements applicable to specific assertions, given the entity's circumstances.

Identifying the necessary controls

Whether by using computer software that processes internal control questionnaire responses or by manually analysing checklists, the auditor can identify the necessary controls that would be likely to prevent or detect specific potential misstatements. Table 9.2 outlines some necessary controls in a computerised information system.

TABLE 9.2:
Control risk assessment considerations for application controls in a computerised information system

Potential misstatement/assertion	Necessary controls	Possible tests of controls
Input controls		
Data for unauthorised transactions may be submitted for processing (completeness).	Authorisation and approval of data in user departments, and screening of data by data control group	Examine source documents and batch transmittals for evidence of approval; observe data control group.
Valid data may be incorrectly converted to machine-readable form (occurrence, completeness, accuracy).	Computer editing and use of control totals	Observe data verification procedures; use test data to test edit routines; examine control total reconciliations.
Errors on source documents may not be corrected and resubmitted (occurrence, completeness, accuracy).	Maintenance of error logs; return to user department for correction; follow-up by data control group	Inspect logs and evidence of follow-up by data control group.

(continued)

Potential misstatement/assertion	Necessary controls	Possible tests of controls
Processing controls		
Wrong files may be processed and updated (occurrence).	Use of external and internal file labels	Observe use of external file labels; examine documentation for internal file labels.
Data may be lost, added, duplicated or altered during processing (occurrence, completeness, accuracy).	Use of control totals; limit and reasonableness checks; sequence tests	Examine evidence of control total reconciliations and use of test data.
Output controls		
Output may be incorrect (occurrence, completeness, accuracy).	Reconciliation of totals by data control group and user departments	Examine evidence of reconciliations.
Output may be distributed to unauthorised users.	Use of report distribution control sheets; data control group monitoring	Inspect report distribution control sheets; observe data control group monitoring.

Making the assessment

The auditor can make a preliminary assessment of control risk from the knowledge acquired from (1) procedures to obtain an understanding and (2) the identification of potential misstatements and the necessary controls to prevent or detect those misstatements. The auditor's assessment must also consider the assessment of the control environment and the extent to which the design of the control procedures is likely to be effective. Once control risk is assessed and it is less than high, the auditor must then perform **tests of controls** to obtain evidence to support this assessed level of control risk.

The process of risk assessment and its effect on audit strategy, together with a discussion of the tests of controls that are needed when the auditor plans the audit based on a lower assessed level of control risk approach, are covered in chapter 11.

Learning check

Do you know . . .

9.5 ☐ Internal controls are crucial to ensure that entities are run in an effective and efficient manner.

9.6 ☐ ASA 315 (ISA 315) requires auditors to obtain an understanding of internal controls relevant to the audit.

9.7 ☐ In obtaining an understanding of the entity's internal control, the auditor can consider previous experience with the entity, enquire of entity personnel, inspect documents and records, and observe activities.

9.8 ☐ The auditor documents the understanding through internal control questionnaires, flowcharts and narratives.

9.9 ☐ Having documented the understanding, the auditor makes a preliminary assessment of the strengths and weaknesses of the internal control system.

9.7 AUDIT RISK

Audit risk is the risk that the auditor gives an inappropriate audit opinion when the financial statements are materially misstated (ASA 200, paragraph 13(c); ISA 200.13(c)). The more certain auditors want to be of expressing the correct opinion, the lower will be the audit risk that they are willing to accept. In setting the desired audit risk, auditors seek an appropriate balance between the costs of an incorrect audit opinion and the costs of performing the additional audit procedures necessary to reduce audit risk.

The first step involves obtaining an understanding of the entity (chapter 8) and assessing the level of business risk, discussed earlier in this chapter. Auditors then consider the effect these factors could have on the risk of material misstatements at the financial statement level. If auditors assess an entity as being well managed and financially sound, for example, then they may reduce the overall assessment of audit risk through their assessment of inherent risk.

However, if auditors consider an entity to be in financial difficulty or to have an inadequate internal control structure, then they may assess audit risk as being higher, through their assessment of inherent or control risk respectively. In such cases, a more extensive audit investigation would be required for audit risk to be at an acceptable level.

The risk-based approach is fundamental to auditing as is highlighted in the Professional Environment below.

PROFESSIONAL ENVIRONMENT
The risk-based audit approach

*T*he risk-based approach requires the auditor to first understand the entity and its environment in order to identify risks that may result in material misstatement of the financial report. Next, the auditor performs an assessment of those risks at both the financial report and assertion levels. The assessment involves considering a number of factors such as the nature of the risks, relevant internal controls and the required level of audit evidence.

The result of the assessment effectively categorises the audit into a) areas of significant risk of material misstatement that require specific responses and b) areas of normal risk that can be addressed by standard audit work programs. Having assessed risks, the auditor then designs appropriate audit responses to those risks in order to obtain sufficient appropriate audit evidence on which to conclude. Risk assessment continues throughout the audit and the audit plan and procedures are amended where a reassessment is necessary.

Getting risk right = efficiency and effectiveness

A properly timed and performed risk assessment and response process by the experienced auditor provides the foundation for the entire audit — it focuses the auditor's attention on identifying, assessing and responding to those risks that have the potential to materially affect the financial report. The risk-based audit approach provides the auditor with an approach to conduct the audit as efficiently and effectively as possible, benefiting both the audit team and the entity.

Source: S Fraser, 'The risk-based audit approach', *Charter*, December 2011.

9.7.1 Audit risk components

Audit risk is commonly assessed within three components: inherent risk, control risk and detection risk. Each component is discussed as follows. The auditor specifies an overall audit risk level to be achieved for the financial statements as a whole. In contrast, the assessed levels of inherent and control risk and the acceptable level of detection risk can vary for each account balance and transaction class.

Inherent risk

Inherent risk is the possibility that a material misstatement could occur in an assertion, either individually or when aggregated with other misstatements, assuming there are no related controls (ASA 200, paragraph 13(n); ISA 200.13(n)).

The assessment of inherent risk requires consideration of matters that may have a pervasive effect on the entity as a whole and matters that may affect only specific accounts.

The inherent risk of material misstatement is greater for some industries than for others. Entities operating in the gas and oil exploration or insurance industries, for example, have unique accounting problems compared with merchandising or manufacturing entities. The existence of related parties, foreign exchange dealings and other complicated contracts also presents opportunities for misstatements to occur.

Further, inherent risk may be greater for some accounts or transactions than for others. Cash, for example, is more susceptible to misstatement through misappropriation than are plant assets. Similarly, the valuation of assets held under a finance lease is more susceptible to misstatement (as a result of the complex nature of finance lease calculations) than is the valuation of similar assets owned outright. Auditors cannot change inherent risk; they can only judge the level of risk and design audit procedures in light of that assessment.

As defined by auditing standards, inherent risk is confined to the risk of misstatements. Earlier in this chapter we discussed how an auditor needs to consider the business risks and the entity's risk management procedures for identifying and managing such risks. Not only does this direct auditors' attention to matters that could affect the ability of the entity to survive as a going concern, it also enables auditors to use their risk management skills to alert management of the entity to shortcomings in their approach to risk.

Control risk

We have already identified that control risk is the risk that a material misstatement could occur in an assertion, either individually or when aggregated with other misstatements, and not be prevented, detected, or corrected on a timely basis by the entity's internal control structure (ASA 200, paragraph 13(n); ISA 200.13(n)).

Control risk is a function of the effectiveness of the internal control structure. Effective internal controls reduce control risk. Control risk can never be zero, because internal controls cannot provide complete assurance that all material misstatements will be prevented or detected. Controls may be ineffective, for example, as a result of human failure owing to carelessness or fatigue. Auditors cannot change the level of control risk. They can *influence* control risk by recommending improvements in internal controls, but this influence is more likely to affect future periods, and then only to the extent that the entity's management implements the suggestions.

When an auditor assesses control risk, the procedure is to obtain an understanding of the internal control structure so as to assess its potential effectiveness. The auditor then performs further tests to determine whether the internal control structure is operating effectively. These procedures are explained in detail in chapter 11. Auditors, although unable to control inherent risk and control risk, can assess these risks and design substantive procedures to produce an acceptable level of detection risk, thus reducing audit risk to an acceptable level.

Detection risk

Detection risk is the risk that an auditor's substantive procedures will not detect any material misstatements that exist in an assertion, either individually or when aggregated with other misstatements (ASA 200, paragraph 13(e); ISA 200.13(e)).

Detection risk is a function of the effectiveness of substantive procedures and their application by an auditor. Unlike inherent and control risk, the actual level of detection risk is controllable by the auditor through:
- appropriate planning, direction, supervision and review
- variation in the nature, timing and extent of audit procedures
- effective performance of the audit procedures and evaluation of their results.

Having established an acceptable level of detection risk, the auditor then develops an audit strategy. The audit procedures designed to meet the identified risks must reduce audit risk to an acceptable level (ASA 200, paragraph 17; ISA 200.17) — this is covered in chapters 11 to 17. A summary of the components of audit risk is presented in figure 9.6.

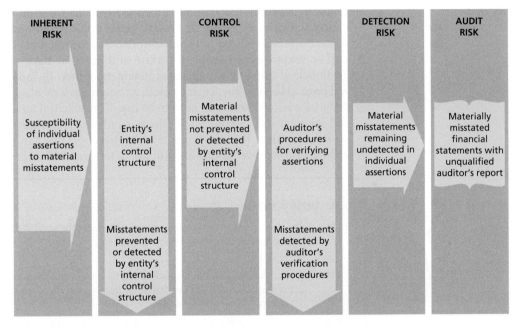

FIGURE 9.6: Summary of audit risk components

9.7.2 The relationships among risk components

Given that an auditor's objective is to achieve an acceptably low level of audit risk as is practicable, and recognising the cost of performing audit procedures, there is an inverse relationship between the assessed levels of inherent and control risks and the level of detection risk that the auditor can accept. Thus, if inherent and control risks are assessed as being low, the auditor can tolerate a higher level of detection risk, enabling a reduction in the extent of substantive procedures that must be undertaken. However, it is important to note that an auditor may tolerate different levels of risks in different audits, depending on the auditor's professional judgement of the perceived consequences of the risks being taken.

The **audit risk model** provides a framework for auditors to follow in responding to these assessed risks through their choice of audit procedures. However, note that the auditing standards are not specific on what is an acceptable level of audit risk, and use of the audit risk model requires a significant degree of judgement by the auditor. In relating the components of audit risk, the auditor generally expresses each component in non-quantitative terms (such as low, medium and high, as shown in figure 9.7).

		Auditor's assessment of control risk is		
		High	**Medium**	**Low**
Auditor's assessment of inherent risk is	**High**	Lowest	Lower	Medium
	Medium	Lower	Medium	Higher
	Low	Medium	Highest	Highest

FIGURE 9.7:
Acceptable detection
risk matrix

Non-quantified audit risk model

Auditors generally use non-quantified expressions for risk, such as the risk components matrix shown in figure 9.7. The matrix demonstrates that the acceptable levels of detection risk are inversely related to the assessments of inherent and control risks.

If an auditor's assessment of control and inherent risks are both high (there is a high likelihood of errors in the financial statements), then the acceptable level of detection risk will have to be very low; i.e. the risk that the auditor's substantive procedures will not detect material misstatements will need to be low. Conversely, if an auditor's assessment of control and inherent risks are both low (there is only a small likelihood of errors in the financial statements), then the acceptable level of detection risk can be high; i.e. the risk that the auditor's substantive procedures will not detect material misstatements can be high.

Do you know ...

9.10 ☐ The auditor's objective in planning and performing the audit is to reduce audit risk to an appropriately low level to support an opinion as to whether the financial statements are fairly presented.

9.11 ☐ Audit risk is the risk that the auditor may give an inappropriate audit opinion when the financial statements are materially misstated. The three components of audit risk are (1) inherent risk, (2) control risk, and (3) detection risk.

9.12 ☐ For a specified level of audit risk, there is an inverse relationship between the assessed levels of inherent and control risks and the level of detection risk that the auditor can accept.

SUMMARY

An auditor must reduce the risk that he gives an incorrect opinion in his audit report. In order for this risk to be managed, the auditor must understand the risks that the organisation is exposed to as well as the controls that are in place to mitigate those risks.

In assessing risk, the auditor can take a top down approach to identifying risks by looking first at high-level issues and then moving to the specific problems that these risks may create. The auditor then establishes which of the risks are considered 'significant risks' to the financial statements, and these are then tackled in the audit plan.

Where there are controls to mitigate the risks identified, the auditor may obtain details of these controls in order to place some reliance on them for the purposes of assessing the risk of material misstatements in the financial statements. Having evaluated the risks and the controls that exist, the auditor determines the level of detailed audit work that will be required to reduce overall audit risk. The detailed procedures and the extent of testing are covered in chapters 10 to 17.

KEY TERMS

access controls, p. 381

accounting system, p. 396

application controls, p. 380

assessing control risk, p. 396

audit risk, p. 399

audit risk model, p. 401

audit trail, p. 380

completeness, p. 370

computer information systems, p. 381

control activities, p. 380

control environment, p. 377

control procedures, p. 396

control risk, p. 396

cut-off, p. 370

data and procedural controls, p. 381

detection risk, p. 401

documenting the understanding, p. 389

documents and records, p. 380

existence, p. 370

financial statement assertions, p. 368

flowchart, p. 392

general controls, p. 380

independent checks, p. 381

information processing controls, p. 380

information system, p. 379

Inherent risk, p. 400

internal control, p. 375

internal control evaluation checklists, p. 397

internal control questionnaire, p. 389

monitoring, p. 385

narrative memorandum, p. 395

occurrence, p. 370

organisational controls, p. 381

performance reviews, p. 385

physical controls, p. 384

preliminary assessment of control risk, p. 396

presentation and disclosure, p. 372

records, p. 379

rights and obligations, p. 371

risk assessment, p. 379

segregation of duties, p. 383

systems development and maintenance controls, p. 381

tests of controls, p. 398

transactions, p. 379

transaction walk-through review, p. 388

valuation and allocation, p. 371

MULTIPLE-CHOICE questions

9.1 Which of the following best describes business risk?
A. The risk that the financial statements contain material errors.
B. The risk that the company will not achieve its objectives.
C. The risk of an auditor getting his or her opinion wrong.
D. Economic factors that may cause cash outflows from an entity.

9.2 Which of the following is correct relating to risk?
A. Understanding business risk is the responsibility of the directors only.
B. Only internal auditors need to understand business risks.
C. External auditors should concern themselves with audit risk only.
D. Auditors should identify significant risks to be covered in their audit work.

9.3 Why is it important to obtain an understanding of the internal control system?
A. Weak internal controls may increase the risk of material misstatement.
B. To determine the level of inherent risk.
C. Because strong internal controls indicate management integrity.
D. The auditor must always carry out tests of controls.

9.4 Restricting the use of the information system to particular authorised personnel by use of passwords is an example of:
A. Organisational controls.
B. Systems development and maintenance controls.
C. Data and procedural controls.
D. Access controls.

9.5 Which of the following identifies the five components of internal control?
A. Control environment, legal environment, information system, control activities, monitoring of controls.
B. Control environment, legal environment, risk assessment, control activities, monitoring of controls.
C. Control environment, risk assessment, information system, control activities, monitoring of controls.
D. Control environment, legal environment, risk assessment, information system, control activities.

9.6 Flowcharts should depict all of the following except:
A. All operations performed in processing the class of transactions.
B. The method of processing.
C. The extent of segregation of duties.
D. The audit procedures conducted.

9.7 The auditor's understanding of internal control is documented to substantiate:
A. The fairness of presentation of the financial statements.
B. Adherence to requirements of management.
C. Compliance with auditing standards.
D. Conformity of the accounting records with any applicable accounting standards.

9.8 For a given assertion, the relationship between the assessed control risk (CR) and inherent risk (IR) and the level of detection risk (DR) is shown correctly in which of the following (assume + means an increase in the risk and – means a decrease):
A. +DR if +CR and +IR.
B. +DR if –CR and –IR.
C. +DR if +CR and –IR.
D. +DR if –CR and +IR.

9.9 For a particular assertion, control risk is the risk that:
  - A. A material misstatement will occur in the accounting process and not be detected on a timely basis by the internal control structure.
  - B. Audit procedures will fail to detect a weak control system.
  - C. Controls will not detect errors that occur.
  - D. The prescribed control procedures will not be applied uniformly.

9.10 Inherent risk could be best described as:
  - A. A function of the effectiveness of the internal control structure.
  - B. The risk that the auditor's substantive procedures will not detect any misstatements that occur and that are not prevented or detected by the internal control structure.
  - C. The possibility that a material misstatement could occur.
  - D. The risk that a material misstatement could occur and not be prevented or detected on a timely basis by the entity's internal control function.

REVIEW questions

9.11 Who is responsible for minimising the business risk of an organisation?

9.12 Describe the auditor's responsibility with regard to business risk and financial statement assertions.

9.13 List the four procedures necessary to obtain an understanding of the entity's internal control.

9.14 What is internal control? Why is it important?

9.15 Internal control can provide only reasonable assurance as there are inherent limitations within an entity's control structure. Identify and describe three of these limitations.

9.16 What are the responsibilities of management and the auditor in relation to internal control?

9.17 Control activities are detailed policies and procedures that management establishes to help ensure that its directives are carried out. List the four different categories of control activities and give an example of each.

9.18 Describe the alternative techniques for documenting the auditor's understanding of internal controls.

9.19 Audit risk is said to be a function of inherent risk, control risk and detection risk. Explain audit risk. Define and differentiate between each of its components.

9.20 If inherent risk and control risk are high why will detection risk be set as low and what effect does this have on the audit strategy?

PROFESSIONAL application questions

★
BASIC
★★
MODERATE
★★★
CHALLENGING

9.21 Assertions ★

In planning the audit of a client's liabilities, an auditor derived the following specific objectives from management's financial statement assertions:

1. Liabilities are not valued below the amount expected to be paid in accordance with an applicable accounting standard.
2. The total of the schedule of purchase ledger balances agrees to the balance on the purchase ledger control account.
3. All liabilities represent obligating events occurring before the year end.

4. Current liabilities include all amounts owed by the company that fall due within 12 months of the year end.
5. All liabilities that were settled before the year end have been excluded from the balance sheet.
6. Liabilities have been properly classified in the balance sheet.
7. All finance lease obligations have been included in liabilities.
8. Details of any mortgages in relation to bank loans have been disclosed in the notes of the financial report.
9. Provisions for staff annual leave have been correctly calculated.
10. Long-term liabilities have been discounted to present value where the discounting amount is material.

Required
For each specific audit objective (items 1–10), identify the management assertion from which it was derived.

9.22 Obtaining an understanding ★
You are an audit senior at the accounting firm of Court & Partners in Sydney. The firm has recently won the audit of a small manufacturing firm located in Bankstown and you have been given the job. The audit partner in the planning meeting tells you not to worry about the controls because the firm is quite small, and based on his experience of firms of this size, controls are mostly poor and it is not even worth looking at them.

Required
(a) Comment on the audit partner's advice.
(b) Discuss any special considerations in evaluating and relying on controls in small firms.

9.23 Control activities and related assertions ★★
This chapter identified several categories of control activity, using the following categorisation:
    A. Information processing controls:
        1. General controls
        2. Application controls (input, processing, output)
    B. Segregation of duties
    C. Physical controls
    D. Performance reviews
The internal controls in relation to payroll for Stent Ltd include the following:
1. Employees are paid fortnightly and must complete an online timesheet; standard hours are 76 per fortnight and any hours in excess of this require a supervisor to log on and approve these hours before the timesheet will be processed.
2. The payroll system takes the hourly rate from each employee's master file and multiplies this by the hours entered to calculate gross pay.
3. Payroll staff process fortnightly pay amounts; Human Resources department controls employee master file information.
4. PAYG and superannuation calculations are performed by the payroll system based on the calculations embedded in the software.
5. Only payroll staff are able to log on to the payroll system and this access is restricted to only those computers in the Payroll department.
6. A supervisor reconciles the payroll to the amount to be paid to staff by electronic funds transfer and approves the payment; the payroll journal is similarly reconciled to the payroll.
7. The payroll journal is processed by the accounting department.
8. Control accounts are maintained and reviewed monthly to ensure amounts paid correspond to the payroll amounts.

Required

Indicate the category of control activity and related financial statement assertion for each of the above.

9.24 Business risk   ★★

The following facts relate to Sporty Pty Ltd:

1. Sporty operates fitness centres across Australia.
2. The company is owned by the five directors who have financed the purchase of shares by taking out personal loans, which are secured on their homes.
3. The directors aim to expand the business and then float the company on the ASX.
4. The strategy involves charging lower prices than their competitors in order to attract new members.
5. The directors are expanding by buying out small independent fitness clubs.
6. The purchase and refurbishment of the new clubs is financed by bank loans.

The managing director wants to maintain good corporate governance and business practices and therefore would like to carry out a review of business risks but does not know anything about it.

Required

Explain the benefits of carrying out a business risk assessment and describe the steps involved in risk management. In your comments, give examples of specific business risks faced by Sporty Pty Ltd.

9.25 Business risk and assertions   ★★

You are a senior auditor working on the audit of HealthyGlow for the year ended 30 June 2015. You are in the planning stage of the audit. It is April 2015 and you discover that HealthyGlow has recently acquired two new, full-body scanning machines, representing the very latest in technology, at a cost of more than $10 million each. The machine enables a full 360 degree scan of the body with the ability to identify tumours, cysts and other abnormal internal growths which currently have a 50% probability of being detected with other scanning devices on the market.

Recent studies have shown there may be potential long-term side effects to patients who are scanned by the new technologically advanced machine. However, given the machine has only just arrived on the market, the results will not be known for many more years. This uncertainty and the potential high risk associated with the machine have caused bad press for both the scanning machine and HealthyGlow.

HealthyGlow charges patients a premium price for the scanning machine due to its advanced technological abilities. As a result of high demand, the hospital has decided to reserve the use of the machine for pre-paid patients only. All scans must be paid for in full by patients at the time of booking. Payments are immediately recognised as revenue by the hospital.

Demand for the scanners has been extremely high and HealthyGlow now has bookings for four months in advance. You note that even though it is only April 2015, the hospital has bookings for July and August 2015.

The Medical Association of NSW is currently reviewing the use of the scanning machines and may ban their use within Australia until the issue is resolved. The decision is expected to be communicated on 1 August 2015. Management have indicated there is an 80% chance the scanners will be given the go ahead.

Required

(a) Assess the main business risks for HealthyGlow.
(b) Identify two key account balances likely to be affected by the above information.
(c) For each account balance identified in (b), identify and explain the key assertion most at risk.[1]

9.26 Business risks and audit risks ★★

Trang Professional Ltd operates business colleges, its customers come from a range of professions such as lawyers, medical practitioners, accountants and others. Trang delivers knowledge update courses that allow its customers to maintain their professional accreditations as well as more generic courses such as supervisory skills, professional writing and so on.

Trang has just invested a significant amount of money in a new integrated IT system that includes customer booking system, inventory control for course material, purchase and sales recording, payroll and HR all linked around a nominal ledger and management reporting module. This new system was funded through bank borrowings. This is the first time the company has borrowed so extensively and it is starting to understand the effects of the terms and conditions applied to the loan that require it to maintain certain interest cover and gearing ratios.

The colleges have classrooms full of customers and therefore have a significant number of people in their buildings. The company is subject to strong health and safety rules as well as fire protection legislation. One of Trang's main costs relates to property rental and one of its key performance measures is to maximise revenue per square metre.

It is clear from feedback from students that the value they place on the organisation is directly linked to the lecturers that Trang employs. Lecturers quickly obtain a reputation in the market place and a good reputation is directly linked to higher class sizes. As a result, Trang seeks to create salary packages that incentivise staff to maximise student numbers.

Required
(a) Identify and explain the business risks above.
(b) Identify and explain the audit risks above.

9.27 Assessment of control risk ★★

Rhapsody Co supplies a wide range of garden and agricultural products to trade and domestic customers. The company has 11 divisions, with each division specialising in the sale of specific products; for example, seeds, garden furniture and agricultural fertilisers. The company has an internal audit department which provides audit reports to the audit committee on each division on a rotational basis.

Products in the seed division are offered for sale to domestic customers via an Internet site. Customers review the product list on the Internet and place orders for packets of seeds using specific product codes, along with their credit card details, onto Rhapsody Co's secure server. Order quantities are normally between one and three packets for each type of seed. Order details are transferred manually onto the company's internal inventory control and sales system, and a two-part packing list is printed in the seed warehouse. Each order and packing list is given a random alphabetical code based on the name of the employee inputting the order, the date, and the products being ordered.

In the seed warehouse, the packets of seeds for each order are taken from specific bins and despatched to the customer with one copy of the packing list. The second copy of the packing list is sent to the accounts department where the inventory and sales computer is updated to show that the order has been despatched. The customer's credit card is then charged by the inventory control and sales computer. Bad debts in Rhapsody Co are currently 3% of total sales.

Finally, the computer system checks that for each charge made to a customer's credit card account, the order details are on file to prove that the charge was made correctly. The order file is marked as completed, confirming that the order has been despatched and payment obtained.

Required:

(a) In respect of sales in the seeds division of Rhapsody Co, prepare a report to be sent to the audit committee of Rhapsody Co which:

  (i) identifies and explains *four* weaknesses in that sales system

  (ii) explains the possible effect of each weakness.

(b) Make an overall assessment of the control risk for this sales system.[2]

9.28 Assessment of control risk ★★★

ErgoOffice Ltd manufactures office furniture. It employs 250 staff at its single factory and its turnover last year was $40 million.

You are an audit senior with a firm of accountants which has held appointment as external auditor to ErgoOffice for a number of years. However, you have not previously been involved with the audit. You are currently reviewing the audit file before planning the audit for the financial year ending 30 June 2015. Last year there were no major audit problems and inherent risk was assessed as relatively low and the control environment was considered satisfactory.

The description of the purchases system as updated in last year's audit file reads as follows.

Requisitioning

Department heads have authority to issue requisitions for non-capital purchases up to $5000. Stock requisitions are automatically issued by the computer when predetermined reorder levels are reached.

Ordering

All requisitions pass through the purchasing office which checks the authority of the requisitioner, identifies suitable suppliers and obtains quotes where necessary. The purchasing office then opens up an order against the supplier which is recorded in the supplier master file on the computer. The computer assigns an order number. A copy of the order is printed out and sent to the supplier.

Goods inward

Deliveries are accepted only at the centralised goods inwards dock. The goods inward clerk accesses the order on the computer and checks that the goods are in agreement with the order and are in good condition. The goods inward clerk then updates the computer record of the order with receiving information.

Recording

Purchase invoices are numbered on receipt. The bought ledger clerk checks the invoice arithmetically and verifies it against the computer record of the order, ensuring that the records confirm receipt of the goods. These checks are evidenced on the invoice together with the account coding specified on the order. Receipt of the invoice is also noted on the order record to prevent accidental acceptance of a duplicate invoice. Invoices are batched daily by the bought ledger clerk for computer processing and a control sheet is prepared for each batch listing the total payable. The assistant accountant approves each invoice before passing the batch to the computer operator.

Payment

At the end of each month the computer prints out cheques for the balance owing to each supplier together with a remittance advice itemising the make-up of the balance. A copy of the remittance advice is also printed out in the form of a bought ledger.

The assistant accountant reconciles the total payable with the daily batch control information, test checks creditors with suppliers' statements, approves the copy remittance advices for payment, has the cheques mechanically signed and passes them directly to the mail room.

You note that your predecessor completed an internal control evaluation checklist and used the results to justify assessing control risk as low for all purchase and payment transaction assertions associated with creditors.

Required

(a) Outline the control procedures operating in the purchasing system of ErgoOffice Ltd.
(b) Comment on the extent to which you can accept your predecessor's assessment of the control environment.
(c) Describe further work you would plan to undertake to assess inherent risk and the control environment during the current year's audit.[3]

9.29 Control system weaknesses ★★★

Jertsy Ltd owns a range of fashion clothing stores in Australian state capitals. Each store manager operates with a degree of autonomy with regard to the types and quantities of clothes that they buy and sell. Head office has established a standard mark-up on cost that local managers must use to arrive at selling prices.

Store staff tend to be younger people who work part time and move on after a year or two; as a result there is a significant staff turnover. This high staff turnover does not affect trade and business is booming having tapped into youth fashion.

Each store maintains its own accounting records and returns are sent to head office reporting purchases, sales and any sundry expenditure incurred locally. These monthly returns are consolidated by the accountant who prepares monthly management reports.

The recent success of the business has allowed senior management to adopt a strategy of growth by opening new stores, but they are worried about maintaining control as the business expands.

Required

Identify the weaknesses in the existing system and suggest improvements that should be included in any new system that senior management might choose to introduce.

9.30 Audit risk, components of audit risk ★★★

Audrey Pearce is an audit partner of Pearce Green, a firm of accountants. She is considering audit risk at the overall financial statement level in planning the audit for the finance company Homes South Ltd (HS) for the year ending 30 June 2015. This risk is influenced by a combination of factors related to management, the industry and the entity. Audrey has gathered the following information concerning HS's environment.

1. HS has been consistently more profitable than the industry average by marketing mortgages on properties in a prosperous rural area, which has experienced considerable growth in recent years. HS packages and sells mortgages to large investment trusts. Despite recent volatility of interest rates, HS has been able to continue selling its mortgages as a source of new lendable funds.
2. HS's board of directors is controlled by George Watson, the majority shareholder, who also acts as the chief executive officer. Management at the company's branch offices has authority for directing and controlling HS's operations, and is compensated according to branch profitability. The internal auditor reports directly to Henry Stevenson, a minority shareholder, who is chairman of the audit committee.
3. The accounting department has experienced little turnover in personnel during the 5 years for which Audrey has audited HS. HS's formula constantly underestimates the allowance for loan losses, but its financial controller has always been receptive to Audrey's suggestions to increase the allowance.

4. During 2014, HS opened a branch office in a metropolitan area 30 kilometres from its principal place of business. Although this branch is not yet profitable (as a result of competition from several well-established banks), management believes it will be profitable by 2016.
5. During 2014, the company increased the efficiency of its operations by installing a new computer system.

Required

Based only on the information provided, indicate the factors that would affect the risk of material misstatement and explain why.

 CASE studies

9.31 Business risk ★★★

Face Paint Ltd sells cosmetics and markets itself on the basis that its products have not been tested on animals, it has ethical policies towards its staff and suppliers, and that it takes corporate responsibility very seriously. The company is associated with an organisation that represents a collective of suppliers and staff, EcoProducts, which holds one ordinary B share in Face Paint (under Face Paint's constitution, this gives EcoProducts significant powers, including a controlling vote on all matters of strategy).

In the financial year to 30 June 2015, Face Paint floated on the Australian Securities Exchange. As part of this float, there was also a restructuring of the shares. In the restructure, 50 000 ordinary A shares were bought back by the company and exchanged for 25 000 ordinary shares. A further 1 200 000 ordinary shares were sold on the securities exchange for $5. The new issue was fully subscribed.

Face Paint's results show an increase on the previous year. Revenue is $26 040 196 (2014: $21 143 992) and profit before tax is $1 713 936 (2014: $819 293). The cash raised by the flotation enabled the company to pay off some long-term debts and improve its short-term liquidity position.

Face Paint has two main product divisions: makeup and gifts. Makeup includes everything that would be expected in a cosmetics line. Gifts include not only handmade soaps and shampoos but also a range of handmade products from developing countries and products made from recycled materials.

The company markets its products in four ways: mail-order catalogue, company website, retail stores and personal selling. In recent years the mail order and personal selling have been falling significantly, but at the same time sales via the company's website have increased substantially.

As part of its commitment to its suppliers, many of whom depend exclusively on Face Paint, the company sometimes pays high prices for its purchases, even when other cheaper but less eco-friendly alternatives exist. Also as part of this commitment, Face Paint sometimes pays suppliers in advance of receiving goods or in some cases even before placing an order. Given that the business is expanding, there has been an increase in the range of products sold and therefore an increase in the number of suppliers from all over the world, resulting in a large increase in the level of advance payments. At 30 June 2015 the amount paid in advance was $1 932 071 (2014: $614 221).

Required

Consider the situation above and highlight the business risks. Then consider the extent to which those risks could have an impact on the financial statements.

9.32 Information systems and internal controls ★★

Balancing Books Ltd runs four private colleges that provide education and training for people in the bookkeeping industry. Its 2-year course includes training in debits and credits and accounting systems. You are conducting the interim audit for the year ended 30 June 2015. The tangible fixed assets of each college are recorded in an asset register which is maintained at each college location by each college manager. The system operates as described below.

1. In order to obtain new assets, a purchase requisition form is completed and approved by the manager at each college.
2. The requisition is sent to head office, where the purchasing officer checks the requisition for approval and completes a purchase order for the new asset.
3. Assets costing more than $5000 are approved by the financial accountant. All assets over $20 000 require board approval.
4. The purchase order is then sent to the supplier and a copy is sent to the central store at the head office location.
5. The asset is received by the central store where the receiving clerk checks that all the asset details agree with those on the receiving report and the copy of the purchase order. The receiving clerk then issues the asset with its computer-generated sequential barcode number. This barcode is fixed to the asset and written on the receiving report and the supplier invoice.
6. The relevant college manager inputs the new asset details into the asset register using a copy of the purchase order, the original requisition and the asset's barcode.
7. For disposal or write-off of an asset, an asset disposal write-off form is completed by the relevant college manager, signed and sent to head office. Disposals and write-offs are approved by the financial accountant. A copy of the form is filed at head office and the approved original returned to the college manager for action. The college manager then updates the fixed asset register for the subsequent disposal.
8. The asset register is maintained on FAST — a tailored fixed-assets computer system — and reconciled to the general ledger by each college manager monthly.
9. The FAST system calculates depreciation automatically each month using the rate input by the college manager at the time the asset was added to the register.

Required
Identify five internal control strengths on which you would rely for your audit.[4]

 RESEARCH question

9.33 Internal control
The current unqualified audit report presented in ASA 700 states the following:

> In making those risk assessments, the auditor considers internal control relevant to the entity's preparation and fair presentation of the financial report in order to design audit procedures that are appropriate for the circumstances, but not for the purposes of expressing an opinion on internal control.

Required
(a) What does this mean? Do you think this is what users believe the auditor does?
(b) What does the research say about what users believe auditors provide in relation to internal control assurance?

FURTHER READING

AD Akresh, 'A risk model to opine on internal control', *Accounting Horizons*, March 2010, pp. 65–78.
JC Bedard, DR Deis, MB Curtis & JG Jenkins, 'Risk monitoring and control in audit firms: a research synthesis', *Auditing: A Journal of Practice and Theory*, May 2008, pp. 187–218.
D Carmichael, 'How new risk standards differ from past practice', *Accounting Today*, September 2006, pp. 14–33.

SL Charles, SM Glover & NY Sharp, 'The association between financial reporting risk and audit fees before and after the historic events surrounding SOX', *Auditing: A Journal of Practice and Theory*, May 2010, pp. 15–39.

HJ Chen, SY Huang & KH Shih, 'An empirical examination of the impact of risk factors on auditor's risk assessment', *International Journal of Management*, September 2006, pp. 515–28.

JR Cohen, G Krishnamoorthy & AM Wright, 'The impact of roles of the board on auditors' risk assessments and program planning decisions', *Auditing*, May 2007, pp. 91–112.

Committee of Sponsoring Organisations of the Treadway Commission (COSO), Internal Control Integrated Framework, AICPA, New York, 1992.

J Doyle, W Ge & S McVay, 'Determinants of weaknesses in internal control over financial reporting', *Journal of Accounting & Economics*, September 2007, pp. 193–223.

WR Knechel, 'The business risk audit: origins, obstacles and opportunities', *Accounting, Organizations & Society*, May 2007, pp. 383–408.

DK McConnell Jr & CHC Schweiger, 'Implementing the new ASB risk assessment audit standards', *CPA Journal*, June 2007, pp. 20–6.

National Commission on Fraudulent Financial Reporting, Report of the National Commission on Fraudulent Financial Reporting, Washington DC, 1987.

MH Sanchez, KF Brown et al., 'Consideration of control environment and fraud risk: a set of instructional exercises', *Journal of Accounting Education*, 2007, pp. 207–21.

M Shatter, 'Learning from the US', *Charter*, September 2005, pp. 50–2.

M Wright, *Audit Guide No. 5: Auditing in an IT Systems Environment*, Australian Accounting Research Foundation, Melbourne, 1999.

NOTES

1. Adapted from the Professional Year Programme of the ICAA, 2008, Audit and Assurance Module Exam.

2. Adapted from the ACAA, 2007, Audit and Internal Review Exam.

3. Adapted from ACCA, Audit Framework (UK stream), June 1999, Module C, Certificate Stage.

4. Adapted from Professional Year Programme of the ICAA, 1996, Accounting 2 Module.

Answers to multiple-choice questions

9.1 *B*   9.2 *D*   9.3 *A*   9.4 *D*   9.5 *C*   9.6 *D*   9.7 *C*   9.8 *B*   9.9 *A*   9.10 *C*

chapter 10

Materiality and audit evidence

OVERVIEW

10.1 Materiality
10.2 Audit strategies
10.3 Audit evidence
10.4 Auditing procedures
Summary
Key terms
Multiple-choice questions

Review questions
Professional application questions
Case studies
Research question
Further reading
Notes

LEARNING objectives

After studying this chapter, you should be able to:

1 define the concept of materiality and its relationship with audit evidence

2 describe alternative audit strategies

3 indicate the factors that affect the sufficiency and appropriateness of audit evidence

4 describe the types and classifications of auditing procedures that may be used in an audit.

PROFESSIONAL STATEMENTS

Australian		International	
ASQC 1	*Quality Control for Firms that Perform Audits and Reviews of Financial Reports and Other Financial Information, and other Assurance Engagements*	**ISQC 1**	*Quality Control for Firms that Perform Audits and Reviews of Financial Reports, and Other Assurance Engagements*
ASA 315	*Identifying and Assessing the Risks of Material Misstatement through Understanding the Entity and its Environment*	**ISA 315**	*Identifying and Assessing the Risks of Material Misstatement through Understanding the Entity and its Environment*
ASA 320	*Materiality in Planning and Performing an Audit*	**ISA 320**	*Materiality in Planning and Performing an Audit*
ASA 330	*The Auditor's Responses to Assessed Risks*	**ISA 330**	*The Auditor's Responses to Assessed Risks*
ASA 500	*Audit Evidence*	**ISA 500**	*Audit Evidence*
ASA 501	*Audit Evidence — Specific Considerations for Inventory and Segment Information*	**ISA 501**	*Audit Evidence — Specific Considerations for Selected Items*
ASA 502	*Audit Evidence — Specific Considerations for Litigation and Claims*	**ISA 501**	*Audit Evidence — Specific Consideration for Selected Items*
ASA 505	*External Confirmations*	**ISA 505**	*External Confirmations*
ASA 580	*Written Representations*	**ISA 580**	*Written Representations*
ASA 610	*Using the Work of Internal Auditors*	**ISA 610**	*Using the Work of Internal Auditors*
ASA 620	*Using the Work of an Auditor's Expert*	**ISA 620**	*Using the Work of an Auditor's Expert*
AASB 1031	*Materiality*		

The importance of audit evidence and scepticism

12-301MR ASIC's audit inspection findings for 2011–12

ASIC Chairman Greg Medcraft has described as 'disappointing' the results of ASIC's audit inspection report which shows a decline in audit quality.

The report for the 18 months to 30 June 2012 covered inspections of 20 Australian audit firms and found 18% of the 602 audit areas reviewed did not perform all of the procedures necessary to obtain reasonable assurance that the audited financial report was not materially misstated. The figure for the previous 18 months was 14%.

While the financial reports audited may not have been materially misstated, the auditor had not obtained reasonable assurance that the financial report as a whole was free of material misstatement.

'Auditors are gatekeepers that play a critical role in ensuring that Australian investors can be confident and informed,' Mr Medcraft said.

'These results are disappointing. Audit firms need to increase their efforts to improve audit quality and the consistency of audit execution.'

ASIC will work with firms and the audit profession more generally on how they can improve audit quality. We will monitor the implementation and execution of any plans to improve audit quality, and their effectiveness.

ASIC has identified three areas needing improvement:
- the sufficiency and appropriateness of audit evidence obtained by the auditor
- the level of professional scepticism exercised by auditors, and
- the extent of reliance that can be placed on the work of other auditors and experts.

Source: Australian Securities and Investments Commission, Media Release, 4 December 2012.

Now that we have considered issues associated with accepting the audit engagement, planning the audit and assessing risk, we explain the nature of the investigation that an auditor undertakes to arrive at an opinion as to the fairness of the financial statements. In this chapter we look at the fundamental issues relating to the audit process:
- the threshold of materiality that the auditor uses in identifying misstatements that could materially affect the decisions and judgements of users relying on the financial statements
- the considerations involved in choosing the appropriate audit strategy
- the types of evidence available to the auditor
- the procedures used by auditors in obtaining the different types of evidence.

We considered in earlier chapters the auditor's approach to planning an audit in order to minimise the risk that he or she will arrive at an unsafe audit opinion. In this chapter we begin by exploring the concept of materiality and why this has a significant effect on the audit plan and the auditor's final assessment of the financial statements before finalising the audit opinion.

Next, the chapter looks at the overall **audit strategy** and links this to the concepts of audit risk that are discussed in chapter 9. This discussion of audit strategy introduces the idea of obtaining audit evidence from substantive procedures or by relying on internal controls. These two issues are taken further when audit testing methodologies are discussed in more depth in chapters 11 and 12.

The final part of the chapter gives an overview of audit evidence by considering the different types of evidence that might be available to auditors to give them confidence that the financial statements are fairly stated, and linking these to the types of audit procedures that auditors might carry out to obtain that evidence. Audit tests for specific account balances are covered in more detail in chapters 14 to 17.

LEARNING 1
objective

Define the concept of materiality and its relationship with audit evidence.

10.1 MATERIALITY

Materiality underlies the application of accounting and auditing standards and thus has a pervasive effect in a financial statement audit. An auditor is able to give an unqualified audit opinion if the financial statements are free from material error. Materiality is particularly important for the auditor at two of the key stages of the audit process: the planning stage, when determining the nature, timing and extent of audit procedures, and at the final stage when evaluating the extent of material misstatements.

As we saw in the previous two chapters, a key aspect of planning an audit is the assessment of risk. This will determine the likelihood of the financial statements containing material errors. In the following sections we consider what materiality is and discuss the issues to consider when establishing materiality levels at the various stages of the audit. We then consider the connection to audit evidence that is explored in more detail later in the chapter.

The Professional Environment below details a recent study which explored how firms consider materiality.

PROFESSIONAL ENVIRONMENT
Materiality guidance in auditing firms

*E*ight of the largest auditing firms in the United States participated in a study to better understand how they assess materiality. Brief summaries of their responses to four questions are presented as follows.

RQ1: What benchmarks do firms use for determining overall materiality?
For public companies seven firms use income before income taxes as the main benchmark. The other firm uses income after income taxes.

RQ2: What percentages are applied to the benchmarks for determining overall materiality?
Six firms use 5 percent of income before tax while one firm allows 5–10 percent. The firm that uses income after tax uses 2–5 percent.

RQ3: How do firms determine tolerable misstatement?
Seven firms use a percentage of materiality that fits into a 50–75 percent range and one allows a range up to 90 percent.

RQ4: What amounts are used to determine what is a clearly trivial misstatement?
Seven firms establish a clearly trivial misstatement to be 3–5 percent of overall materiality. One firm allows up to 8 percent of overall materiality.

Source: Excerpts from Eilifsen, A & Messier W, 'Materiality guidance of the major auditing firms', presented at the International Symposium of Audit Research Conference, June 2013.

10.1.1 The concept of materiality

Paragraph 2 of ASA 320 *Materiality in Planning and Performing an Audit* (ISA 320) describes the concept of materiality as follows:

Misstatements, including omissions, either individually or in aggregate, are considered to be material if it is reasonable to expect that they will influence the economic decisions of users taken on the basis of the financial report.

In auditing, materiality applies to both planning and performing the audit, and in evaluating the effect of identified misstatements on the audit and of uncorrected misstatements, if any, on the financial report and in forming the opinion in the auditor's report. There is an inverse relationship between materiality and audit risk; the auditor should take this relationship into consideration when determining the nature, timing and extent of audit procedures. Where the auditor considers that there is a higher risk of misstatement, materiality will be set at a lower level.

10.1.2 Preliminary judgements about materiality

ASA 320, paragraph 6 states that in planning the audit, the auditor makes judgements about the size of misstatements that will be considered material. These judgements provide a basis for:

(a) Determining the nature, timing and extent of risk assessment procedures;
(b) Identifying and assessing the risks of material misstatement;
(c) Determining the nature, timing and extent of further audit procedures.

It should be noted that the auditor shall evaluate which uncorrected misstatements, individually or in the aggregate, will be immaterial or not. Circumstances may cause the auditor to judge that they are still material.

As discussed in chapter 9, the auditor must assess the risks associated with each client and each audit engagement. We have seen how the auditor might take a business risk assessment approach to identifying risks within an organisation. Note that not all business risks give rise to risks of material misstatement in the financial statements. ASA 315 *Identifying and Assessing the Risks of Material Misstatement through Understanding the Entity and its Environment* paragraph 25 (ISA 315.25) requires that the auditor identify and assess risk of material misstatement at the financial report and assertion levels for classes of transactions, account balances and disclosures. It also requires that the auditor uses professional judgement in determining whether any of the risks identified represent a significant risk. 'Significant risk' means an identified and assessed risk of material misstatement that, in the auditor's judgement, requires special audit consideration.

In planning an audit, the auditor should assess materiality with the following considerations.

- The level of materiality for the financial report as a whole. If in some specific circumstances, there is one or more particular class for transactions, account balances or disclosures for which misstatements of lesser amounts than materiality for the financial report as a whole could reasonably be expected to influence the economic decisions of users. The auditor shall also determine the materiality level or levels to be applied to those particular classes of transactions, account balances or disclosures.
- The auditor shall also determine performance materiality for the purposes of assessing the risks of material misstatement and determining the nature, timing and extent of further audit procedures. Performance materiality is the amount or amounts set by the auditor at a less than material level for the financial report as a whole in order to reduce to an appropriately low level the probability that the aggregate of uncorrected and undetected misstatements exceeds materiality for the financial report as a whole. It can also be applied for particular classes of transactions, account balances or disclosures.
- Include in the documentation the decisions and factors that have been taken into account in arriving at the overall materiality and the performance materiality levels. The auditor should also be revising the levels of materiality as the audit progresses.

10.1.3 Materiality for the financial report as a whole

As mentioned earlier, determining materiality is a matter of professional judgement. The notion of materiality influences whether an item or an aggregate of items is required to be recognised, measured, disclosed or in respect of the audit, further investigated. The level of materiality also guides the margin of error that is acceptable in the amount attributable to an item or an aggregate of items, and the degree of precision required. Both the size and the nature of the omission or misstatement should be evaluated together. The auditor may apply a percentage to a chosen benchmark as a starting point in determining materiality for the financial report as a whole. As per paragraph A3 of ASA 320 (ISA 320), the auditor shall consider a number of factors in his/her choice of the benchmark. These considerations include:

- the elements of the financial report (for example, assets, liabilities, equity, revenue, expenses)
- whether these items on which the attention of the users of the particular entity's financial report tends to be focused (for example, for the purpose of evaluating financial performances users may tend to focus on profit, revenue or net assets)
- the nature of the entity, where the entity is in its life cycle, and the industry and economic environment in which the entity operates
- the entity's ownership structure and the way it is financed
- the relative volatility of the proposed benchmark.

For example, an appropriate benchmark can be categories of reported income such as profit before tax, total revenue, gross profit, total expenses, total equity or net asset value. For profit-oriented entities, profit before tax is often used for continuing operations; otherwise, gross profit may be used if the profit before-tax-figure is volatile. For example, if the auditor judges that there are exceptional circumstances whereby there may be an exceptional decrease or increase in such profit, then the auditor may choose a normalised profit before tax as a more appropriate benchmark. Determining the appropriate percentage as the materiality level also requires professional judgement. There is a relationship between the percentage and the chosen benchmark, such as the percentage applied to profit before tax from continuing operations will normally be higher than a percentage applied to total revenue. For example, five per cent of profit before tax from continuing operations may be appropriate for a manufacturing concern and one per cent of total revenue may be adequate for a not-for-profit organisation.

In the course of an audit many errors will be detected but only those that are material, as opposed to those that are clearly trivial, need to be considered by the auditor. Note that in making a judgement about materiality, the auditor should use the smallest aggregate level of misstatement that is considered to be material to any one of the financial statements. This decision rule is appropriate because the financial statements are interrelated and many audit procedures are applicable to more than one statement. The audit procedure to determine whether year-end credit sales are recorded in the proper period, for example, provides evidence about both accounts receivable (balance sheet/statement of financial position) and sales (income statement).

Materiality judgements involve an assessment of both the amount (quantity) and the nature (quality) of the misstatements. Materiality considerations may be influenced by legal and statutory requirements; for example, disclosures relating to audit fees and directors' remuneration must be made irrespective of the amounts involved.

Quantitative guidelines

In assessing the quantitative importance of a misstatement, the auditor needs to relate the dollar amount of the error to the financial statements under examination. AASB 1031 provides some quantitative threshold guidance to help determine materiality (Note: An exposure draft has been issued to withdraw AASB 1031 *Materiality* — see Professional Environment on page 421.) However, this standard also highlights the importance of professional judgement, characteristics of the entity, and perceptions of the information needs of likely users in making a materiality determination. In this context, and in the absence of evidence or a convincing argument to the contrary, the following guidance is provided:

- an amount that is equal to or greater than 10% of the appropriate base amount is presumed to be material
- an amount that is equal to or less than 5% of the appropriate base amount is presumed not to be material
- logically following from the previous points, whether an amount between 5% and 10% is material is a matter of judgement.

Materiality judgements relating to profit and loss should ordinarily exclude the effect of unusual items or abnormal fluctuations, exceptional events or transactions, and discontinued operations. Therefore, in relation to profit and loss, an amount as referred to above should be an amount after allowing for any income tax effect where the base amount itself has been determined after allowing for any income tax effect.

In determining whether an amount or aggregate of an item is material, the auditor should compare the item with the more appropriate of the base amounts described below:

- *for items relating to the statement of financial position:*
  - equity or the appropriate asset or liability class total
- *for items relating to the statement of comprehensive income:*
  - operating profit or loss and the appropriate income or expense amount for the current reporting period; and
  - average profit or loss and the average of the appropriate income or expense amounts for a number of reporting periods including the current reporting period;
- *for items relating to the statement of cash flows:*
  - net cash from or used in the operating, investing, financing or other activities, as appropriate for the current financial year
  - average net cash flows used in the operating, investing, financing or other activities, as appropriate for a number of reporting periods (including the current reporting period).

Some of the commonly used bases and materiality levels (or thresholds) (expressed as a percentage of that base) used in practice are as follows (notice that each threshold is a range and therefore judgement needs to be applied):

Base	Materiality threshold (%)
Profit before tax	5.0–10.0
Turnover	0.5–1.0
Gross profit	2.0–5.0
Total assets	0.5–1.0
Equity	1.0–3.0

Sometimes auditors use the blended method; i.e. combining the five thresholds listed above with equal weights, and calculating an average of the total. These thresholds used in practice show the importance of profit before tax as a base in determining materiality. This is because the above thresholds are determined by the *normal* relativity between other bases and profit before tax. Therefore for a *normal* company, use of any of the above bases and thresholds should provide a similar materiality figure (i.e. one consistent with a materiality figure based on profit before tax).

Qualitative considerations

In planning the examination, the auditor generally is concerned only with misstatements that are quantitatively material. The errors are not yet known, so their qualitative effect can be considered only as evidence becomes available. Qualitative factors are also applicable to materiality levels for particular classes of transactions, account balances or disclosures. The auditor must consider the nature and other related matters of the items that might give rise to the risk of material misstatements such as:
- the significance of the misstatement to the particular entity
- the pervasiveness of the misstatement
- the effect of misstatement on the financial report as a whole.

Qualitative considerations relate to the causes of misstatements or to misstatements that do not have a quantifiable effect. A misstatement that is quantitatively immaterial may be qualitatively material. This may occur, for instance, when the misstatement is attributable to a control weakness, an irregularity or an illegal act by the entity. Discovery of such an occurrence could lead the auditor to conclude there is a significant risk of additional similar misstatements. Other examples of qualitative misstatements are:
- an inadequate or improper description of an accounting policy
- a failure to disclose a breach of regulatory requirements
- corporate fraud
- a change in accounting method which is likely to materially affect the results of subsequent financial years
- a related party transaction or event requiring disclosure through law, regulation or an applicable financial reporting framework
- the probability of a breach of a financial covenant; e.g. a loan agreement may require the entity to maintain a specified minimum current ratio as at the end of the reporting period and the company may be tempted to overstate current assets or understate current liabilities. For this reason, auditors might choose to use a lower materiality threshold for current assets and current liabilities.

Although it is suggested that auditors should be alert for misstatements that could be qualitatively material, ordinarily it is not practical to design procedures to detect them.

10.1.4 Materiality for particular classes of transactions, account balances or disclosures

Account balance materiality is the minimum misstatement that can exist in an account balance for it to be considered materially misstated. Misstatement up to that level is known as **tolerable misstatement**. The recorded balance of an account generally represents the upper limit on the amount by which an account can be overstated. Thus, accounts with balances smaller than materiality are sometimes said to be immaterial in terms of the risk of overstatement. However, there is no limit on the amount by which an account balance could be understated. Thus, accounts with immaterial balances could still be materially understated.

In making judgements about materiality for particular classes of transactions, at the account balance level or for disclosures, the auditor must plan the audit to detect misstatements that, although immaterial individually, may be material to the financial statements taken as a whole when aggregated with misstatements in other account balances. In evaluating individual misstatements, ASA 320 paragraph A10 (ISA 320) provides guidance (additional to that on qualitative materiality discussed earlier in this chapter) in determining qualitative or quantitative materiality:

- Whether law, regulation or the applicable financial reporting framework affect users' expectations regarding the measurement or disclosure of certain items (for example, related party transactions, and the remuneration of management and those charged with governance).
- The key disclosures in relation to the industry in which the entity operates (for example, research and development costs for a pharmaceutical company).
- Whether attention is focused on a particular aspect of the entity's business that is separately disclosed in the financial report (for example, a newly acquired business).

10.1.5 The relationship between materiality and audit evidence

Materiality, like risk, is a key factor that affects an auditor's judgement about the sufficiency of audit evidence. It is generally correct to say, for example, that the lower the materiality level, the greater the amount of evidence that is needed (an inverse relationship). This is the same as saying that it takes more evidence to obtain reasonable assurance that any misstatement in the recorded inventory balance does not exceed $100 000 than it does to be assured the misstatement does not exceed $200 000. It is also generally correct to say that the larger or more significant an account balance is, the greater the amount of evidence that is needed (a direct relationship). This is the same as saying that more evidence is needed for inventory when it represents 30% of total assets than when it represents 10%.

Using materiality to evaluate audit evidence

If there are misstatements in the accounts, then the auditor may perform additional audit procedures or ask that management correct the errors. If uncorrected errors exceed materiality and management refuses to make adjustments, then the auditor may consider issuing

a qualified audit opinion. The uncorrected aggregated misstatements that the auditor needs to examine when considering whether they misstate the financial statements include:
- specific misstatements identified by the auditor
- the auditor's best estimates of other misstatements that cannot be specifically identified (i.e. projected errors).

The auditor reviews the aggregate of the total misstatements and considers the need to approach management about having these corrected. The auditor may issue a modified auditor's report if aggregated uncorrected misstatements exceed materiality. In this chapter our focus is on planning materiality. Chapter 18 discusses making a final assessment of materiality.

LEARNING 2 objective

Describe alternative audit strategies.

10.2 AUDIT STRATEGIES

The audit strategy significantly affects the detailed work performed in the audit. The interrelationship among evidence, materiality and the components of **audit risk** affects the auditor's decision on the type of strategy chosen. At the two ends of the spectrum are the strategies of a predominantly substantive approach and a lower assessed level of control risk approach. How these two approaches are developed and how they affect the nature, timing and extent of the work performed are discussed on the following pages.

10.2.1 Developing the audit strategy

The process of developing the audit strategy starts with obtaining an understanding of the internal control structure. This is a requirement of all audits (see figure 10.6, p. 441).

If the auditor assesses that appropriate controls do not exist or are likely to be ineffective, then no reliance can be placed on internal controls — **control risk** is assessed at a relatively high level and therefore a **predominantly substantive approach** will be adopted. **Substantive procedures** are those that substantiate the amounts recorded in the financial statements. They are normally costly to perform. A more efficient audit can be performed if controls are judged to be effective enough for reliance to be placed on them (control risk has been assessed to be relatively low) that will enable a reduction in the level of substantive procedures undertaken (see figure 10.1, overleaf). Furthermore, in certain situations, substantive procedures may be unable to provide sufficient evidence and a more effective audit could be performed if the auditor could rely on certain controls. The completeness of cash receipts is an obvious example; unless controls over the receipt of cash are effective, it may be impossible to determine, through the use of substantive procedures, that all cash to which the entity is entitled has been properly recorded.

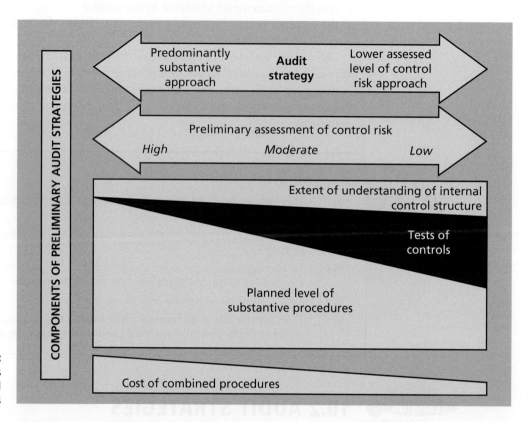

FIGURE 10.1:
Preliminary audit strategies for material financial statement assertions

An audit strategy that relies on internal controls to support the use of a reduced level of substantive procedures is sometimes referred to as a **lower assessed level of control risk approach** (referred to as the 'combined approach' in ASA 330 *The Auditor's Responses to Assessed Risks* (ISA 330)). This is not a single strategy, but a range of strategies determined by the relative effectiveness of applicable control procedures (combined with assessments of inherent risk and materiality). The auditor must make four separate decisions before adopting such a strategy, and each decision (except the first) must be supported by relevant evidence.

1. Is it cost-effective to adopt a lower assessed level of control risk strategy?
2. Are control procedures effectively designed?
3. Are control procedures effectively operated?
4. Do the results of substantive procedures confirm the reliability of controls (the assessment of control risk)?

In many situations it is apparent to the auditor during the course of planning the audit that there is nothing to be achieved by assessing control risk as less than high, such as when:

- the entity is small, such that controls are unlikely to be effective
- the understanding of the internal control structure reveals that controls are inadequate
- previous audits have revealed inadequate controls
- there are few transactions in a **transaction class** or items making up an account balance, such that substantive procedures are unlikely to be costly.

In such situations the auditor plans an audit consisting entirely of substantive procedures. In all other situations the auditor makes a preliminary assessment of the effectiveness of controls (control risk).

In the planning phase the auditor is concerned with the design of control procedures. In evaluating the effectiveness of the design, the auditor identifies the presence of the control procedures that are likely to reduce risk for a particular assertion. Based on this preliminary assessment, the auditor will plan the audit, incorporating both tests of controls and substantive procedures. The tests of controls are designed to verify that control procedures are actually operating as laid down. The level of use of planned tests of controls depends on the assessed effectiveness of internal controls (control risk). The more effective the controls are assessed to be, the lower the assessed level of control risk. Therefore more extensive tests of controls are required to confirm that assessment, and this results in a lower planned level of substantive procedures (as shown in figure 10.1). Note that the total evidence acquired will not change the mix of tests of controls and substantive procedures.

In some respects it may be better if the auditor waits until completing tests of controls before planning substantive procedures. However, experience has shown that the results of tests of controls usually confirm the assessed effectiveness of internal controls (and therefore the level of control risk) and, thus, the planned audit strategy. By designing substantive procedures at this stage, the auditor can start detailed planning of the final audit. Moreover, tests of controls are typically performed during the interim audit simultaneously with substantive tests of details of transactions (sometimes as dual-purpose tests). Given that both tests are applied to the same records, it is more efficient to draft the audit program so as to incorporate all tests to be conducted on the same records simultaneously.

If the tests do not confirm the operation of the control as planned, then the auditor will need to reconsider the audit strategy and increase the level of use of substantive procedures as appropriate.

Procedures used in assessing control risk are explained in chapter 9. These procedures include methods of obtaining an understanding of the internal control structure and of assessing the design effectiveness of controls, the design of tests of controls and the interpretation of the results of tests of controls in making the final assessment of the effectiveness of internal controls (and control risk).

Effect of the assessment of effectiveness of controls on substantive procedures

In considering the effect of the assessment of effectiveness of internal controls on the level of substantive procedures necessary to achieve the desired level of audit risk, the auditor may vary the nature, timing or extent of such procedures.

The nature of substantive procedures may vary between tests of details and analytical procedures. Because they examine individual transactions and items making up an account balance, tests of details are far more persuasive than analytical procedures, which consider only the reasonableness of recorded totals. However, where a relatively high level of detection risk may be tolerated, analytical procedures may be sufficient. In such cases the use of analytical procedures is the preferred option because they are less costly to perform than tests of details, and evidence will have already been obtained through tests of control that support the higher level of detection risk.

The timing of substantive procedures refers to the distinction between those performed at the end of the reporting period and those performed before that date. Performance of procedures before year-end reduces pressure on the auditor and enables the audit to be completed earlier. For example, where controls over inventory records are effective, reliance may be placed on a physical stocktake before year-end updated by transactions in the intervening period. Where controls are particularly effective, attendance at the stocktake alone may be sufficient.

The extent of substantive procedures relates to the number of items or sample size to which a test or procedure is applied. The extent of procedures will need to be greater to achieve a low planned level of detection risk.

Irrespective of the assessed risk of material misstatement, the auditor shall design and perform substantive procedures for each material class of transactions, account balance, and disclosure, taking into account all the relevant factors. This is in part due to limitations in the auditors' assessment of risk and also because there are inherent limitations to internal controls that would preclude solely relying on control testing. The design of substantive procedures is explained in more detail in chapter 12.

10.2.2 The relationship between strategies and transaction classes

The strategies are not intended to characterise the approach to an entire audit. Rather, they represent alternative approaches to auditing individual assertions. Often, however, a common strategy is applied to groups of account balance assertions affected by the same transaction class. The rationale is that many internal controls focus on the processing of a single type of transaction. Double entry means that each transaction class affects two or more account balances. Sales transactions relate to accounts receivable in the balance sheet and to sales in the income statement. Thus, the assessed effectiveness of internal controls for the occurrence assertion for sales transactions will apply to the existence assertion in the audit of both sales and accounts receivable balances. Because the accounts receivable balance is affected by cash receipts and sales adjustment transactions as well as sales transactions, the auditor also considers the assessment of internal controls for all three transaction classes in developing the audit strategies for accounts receivable assertions.

Indicate the factors that affect the sufficiency and appropriateness of audit evidence.

10.3 AUDIT EVIDENCE

In the previous section we established that there are different strategies available to the auditor. Note that whichever strategy is adopted, the auditor must ensure that sufficient and appropriate audit evidence is obtained before a conclusion is made about the opinion to be given in the audit report. This section discusses the nature of audit evidence and what is meant by the terms 'sufficient' and 'appropriate', and looks at the different types of corroborating information the auditor might obtain. In the following section we see how these different types of evidence are linked to the different types of procedures the auditor performs.

10.3.1 Auditor's objectives as responses to assessed risks

In order to arrive at the audit opinion, the objective of the auditor is to obtain sufficient appropriate audit evidence regarding the assessed risks of material misstatement, through designing and implementing appropriate responses to those risks (ASA 330; ISA 330). The auditor is required to determine overall responses to address the assessed risks of material misstatement at the financial report level. Furthermore, the auditor designs and performs audit procedures to respond to the assessed risks of material misstatement at the assertion level. The auditor may test controls and apply substantive procedures for each material class of transaction, account balance and disclosure for the financial report closing process; and identify any significant risks of material misstatements.

Table 10.1 illustrates the derivation of specific audit objectives for cash linked to the appropriate assertions. Specific audit objectives are tailored to fit the circumstances of each audit entity, such as the nature of its economic activity and its accounting policies and practices. From the evidence accumulated, the auditor reaches a conclusion as to whether any of management's assertions are misrepresentations. Subsequently, the auditor combines conclusions about the individual assertions to reach an opinion on the fairness of the financial report as a whole.

TABLE 10.1:
Specific audit objectives —
using cash as an example

Assertion category	Specific audit objective
Assertions about account balances	
Existence	The petty cash funds, undeposited receipts, bank accounts and any other items reported as cash exist at the end of the reporting period.
Rights and obligations	All items included in cash are controlled by the entity at the end of the reporting period.
Completeness	Reported cash includes all petty cash funds, undeposited receipts, and other cash on hand.
	Reported cash includes all bank account balances.
Valuation and allocation	The items constituting cash have been correctly totalled.
	Cash receipts and payments journals are mathematically correct and have been properly posted to the general ledger.
	Cash on hand has been correctly counted. Bank account balances have been properly reconciled.
Assertions about presentation and disclosure	
Occurrence, rights and obligations	All items included in cash are unrestricted and the cash is available for operations.
	All items disclosed pertain to the organisation.
Completeness	All items financial or otherwise requiring disclosure have been disclosed.
Classification and understandability	All financial and other required disclosures are clearly expressed to ensure that they are understandable.
Accuracy and valuation	All financial and other required disclosures have been made at the correct amounts.

10.3.2 The nature of audit evidence

Audit evidence means information used by the auditor in arriving at the conclusions on which the auditor's opinion is based. It is a fundamental concept in auditing by which the auditor achieves the objective of reasonable assurance that none of management's assertions is materially misstated. Audit evidence consists of:

- information contained in the accounting records underlying the financial report
- other information.

Examples of each type of evidence in each category and the relationship of the categories to the auditing standard are shown in figure 10.2 (overleaf). Note that some of this evidence may be available only in an electronic form. Both categories of evidence are required in making an audit in accordance with auditing standards. **Underlying accounting records** include records of initial accounting entries and supporting records, such as cheques and records of electronic fund transfers; invoices; contracts; the general and subsidiary ledgers, journal entries and other adjustments to the financial report that are not reflected in journal entries; and records such as work sheets, spreadsheets supporting allocations, computations, reconciliations and disclosures.

If information to be used as audit evidence has been prepared using the work of an expert appointed by management, the auditor shall evaluate the competence, capabilities and objectivity of that expert; obtain an understanding of the work of that expert; and evaluate the appropriateness of that expert's work as audit evidence for the relevant assertion. When using information produced by the entity, the auditor shall evaluate whether the information is sufficiently reliable for the auditor's purposes, including obtaining audit evidence about the accuracy and completeness of the information; and evaluating whether the information is sufficiently precise and detailed for the auditor's purposes. It is imperative that the auditor obtains supportive or corroborative evidence of the reliability of the financial records. Much of this evidence is available within the entity, but recourse to sources outside the entity (such as customers and independent experts) is also necessary.

Nature of audit evidence	Relationship to auditing standards
Underlying accounting data • Books of original entry (journals) • General and subsidiary ledgers • Related accounting manuals • Informal and memorandum records, such as worksheets, calculations and reconciliations **Corroborating information** • Documents such as cheques, invoices, contracts • Confirmations and other written representations • Information from enquiry, observations, inspection and physical examination • Other information obtained or developed by the auditor	SUFFICIENT AND APPROPRIATE AUDIT EVIDENCE

FIGURE 10.2: Categories and types of audit evidence

The process of identifying specific sources of evidence to meet specific audit objectives for individual account balances is covered extensively in later chapters of this book. In this chapter, we establish a general framework for identifying the types of evidence and the financial statement assertions to which they relate.

10.3.3 The auditing standard applying to evidence

The auditor shall obtain sufficient appropriate audit evidence to be able to draw reasonable conclusions on which to base the auditor's opinion. ASA 500 *Audit Evidence* (ISA 500) describes appropriateness as the measure of the quality of audit evidence, that is, its relevance and its reliability in providing support for the conclusions on which the auditor's opinion is based. Sufficiency is the measure of quantity of audit evidence that is needed by the auditor from the assessment of risks of material misstatement. The standard specifies that 'sufficient' (enough) 'appropriate' (relevant and reliable) audit evidence should be obtained to provide a 'reasonable' (rational) basis for an opinion.

If sufficient appropriate evidence is not available, then the scope of the audit is restricted, which may prevent the auditor from giving an unqualified opinion. The audit evidence required to support an opinion is a matter for the auditor to determine in the exercise of professional judgement after a careful study of the circumstances of the specific audit engagement. Considerations that may influence the auditor's judgement are discussed on the following pages.

Sufficiency of audit evidence

Sufficiency relates to the quantity of audit evidence. Audit evidence is cumulative in nature, and is primarily obtained from audit procedures performed during the course of the audit. Reasonable assurance is obtained when the auditor has obtained sufficient appropriate audit evidence to reduce audit risk — that is, to reduce the risk that the auditor expresses an inappropriate opinion when the financial report is materially misstated — to an acceptably low level. Factors that may affect the auditor's judgement of sufficiency include:

- materiality and risk
- economic factors
- the size and characteristics of the population.

Materiality and risk

In general, more evidence is needed for accounts that are material to the financial statements. Thus, in the audit of a manufacturing company, the quantity of evidence needed in support of the audit objectives for inventories will be greater than the quantity needed for the audit objectives for prepaid expenses.

Similarly, more evidence is normally required for accounts that are likely to be misstated than for accounts that are likely to be correct. Normally, for example, there is a higher risk of error in the valuation of inventory than in the valuation of land used as a factory site. The required degree of assurance (conversely, audit risk) has an impact on the sufficiency of evidence. The auditor will obtain evidence to reduce the level of audit risk to an acceptably low level.

Economic factors

Auditors work within economic limits that dictate that sufficient evidence must be obtained within a reasonable time and at a reasonable cost. Thus, auditors are often faced with a decision as to whether the additional time and cost will produce commensurate benefits in terms of both the quantity and quality of the evidence obtained. To verify the existence of inventory at each of an entity's twenty-five branches, for example, the auditor can visit each branch. A less costly alternative is to visit five of the branches and rely on the reports of the entity's internal auditors for the other twenty.

Population size and characteristics

The size of a population refers to the number of items that constitute the total — for example, the number of credit sales transactions or the number of customer accounts in the accounts receivable ledger. The size of the accounting populations underlying many financial statement items makes sampling a practical necessity in gathering evidence. The nature of audit sampling is explained in chapter 13.

Appropriateness of audit evidence

Appropriateness refers to the quality of audit evidence. For evidence to be appropriate, it must be relevant and reliable.

Relevance

Relevance means that evidence must be sufficient with respect to each of the auditor's objectives. An auditor may determine, for example, the existence of inventory through inspection, but must also perform tests of pricing of inventory to provide evidence for valuation.

Reliability

The reliability of evidence is influenced by factors such as the source and nature of the information, and its timeliness and objectivity. The importance of these factors is illustrated by the examples below.

Source and nature of the information

Evidence may be oral or written and may be created by the auditor, obtained from sources outside the entity or obtained from sources within the entity. The auditor will need to make a professional judgement and consider the following common beliefs (though these assumptions continue to be the subject matter for research).

- Audit evidence from external sources is more reliable than that obtained from the entity's records.
- Audit evidence obtained from the entity's records is more reliable when the related internal control structure operates effectively.
- Evidence obtained directly by the auditor is more reliable than evidence obtained by or from the entity.
- Evidence in the form of documents (whether paper or electronic) and written representations is more reliable than oral representations.
- Original documents are more reliable than photocopies or facsimiles.

Suppose that you, as an auditor, seek evidence concerning the amount of cash on hand and the amount owed by customer X. You conclude that the cash should be counted, but by whom — you or the entity? If you count it, you have direct personal knowledge of the amount on hand; if the entity makes the count and gives you a report, you have indirect knowledge. Clearly, the former provides more appropriate evidence. For the customer's balance, you can examine evidence within the entity (such as the duplicate sales invoice) or ask the customer to confirm the balance owed. In this case, the latter is considered to be the more reliable evidence because the customer is a third party who is independent of the entity.

Timeliness

Timeliness relates to the date to which the evidence is applicable. The timeliness of the evidence is especially important in verifying current asset, current liability and related profit and loss balances. For these accounts, the auditor seeks evidence that the entity has made a proper cut-off of cash, sales and purchase transactions at the end of the reporting period. This task is facilitated when appropriate auditing procedures are applied at or near that date. Similarly, evidence obtained from physical counts at the end of the reporting period provides better evidence of quantities on hand at that date than counts made at other times.

Objectivity

Evidence that is objective in nature is generally considered more reliable than evidence that is subjective. Evidence of the existence of tangible assets, for example, can be ascertained with a substantial degree of conclusiveness through physical inspection.

In contrast, evidence in support of management's estimates of inventory obsolescence and product warranties may be largely subjective. In such cases, the auditor should:
- consider the expertise and integrity of the individual making the estimate
- assess the appropriateness of the processes followed by the entity in arriving at the estimate.

Reasonable basis

The auditor is not expected or required to have an absolute, certain or guaranteed basis for an opinion. In arriving at a professional judgement of reasonable assurance, the auditor is guided by the persuasiveness of the evidence.

Professional judgement

Given that professional judgement is involved, different auditors will not always reach identical conclusions about the quantity and quality of evidence needed to reach an opinion on financial statements. However, several factors contribute to achieving a uniform application of the reasonable basis requirement.

Auditing standards contain many specific requirements about audit evidence and provide guidance about ways to meet these requirements. Auditors are required to justify any departure from the requirements and must consider carefully the desirability of not complying with the guidance.

The practice of auditing involves two counterbalancing forces. On the one hand, the auditing firm is well aware that an inadequate basis for an opinion may result in lawsuits by those harmed by reliance on an incorrect auditor's report. On the other hand, competition tends to make each firm cost- and fee-conscious. Accordingly, the firm is restrained from obtaining an inordinately high degree of assurance in a specific engagement because other firms may be able to perform the audit at a lower cost.

Professional scepticism

Management is responsible for the financial statements and is also in a position to control much of the corroborating evidence and underlying accounting data that support the statements. Professional scepticism is about achieving an appropriate balance between distrusting management and placing complete trust in the integrity of management. In conducting the audit, the auditor must be alert to any suspicious circumstances that may require a greater degree of scepticism than would otherwise be appropriate.

10.3.4 Types of corroborating information

Students should be familiar with the basic components of underlying accounting data identified in figure 10.2 (i.e. journals, ledgers, worksheets, reconciliations). The main types of **corroborating information** are identified and elaborated on here. For each type, its nature, reliability and the categories of assertion to which it is most relevant are considered.

Analytical evidence as a substantive test

Analytical evidence involves comparisons of current period entity data, such as total revenues or return on assets, with expected values. The normal expectation is that the values will be similar to previous period values. Or the auditor may expect current values to be related to budgeted amounts, industry data or specially developed values based on known changes in the period. The comparisons are then used to draw inferences about the fairness of specific financial statement balances in terms of existence, completeness, and valuation and allocation.

When several related financial variables all conform to expectations, the reliability of this type of evidence is enhanced. When recorded sales, cost of sales, gross profit margin, accounts receivable and inventory turnover rates all conform to expectations, for example, the analytical evidence may be viewed as supporting the existence, completeness, and valuation and allocation assertions for sales and cost of sales balances. The existence and effectiveness of controls influence the reliability of analytical evidence. When controls are effective, the auditor has greater confidence in the reliability of the information and therefore the results of analytical procedures.

Confirmations

A **confirmation** is a direct written response made by knowledgeable third parties to specific requests for factual information. Table 10.2 shows the items that are often confirmed.

TABLE 10.2:
Frequently confirmed items
and their sources

Item	Knowledgeable respondent
Cash at bank	Bank
Accounts receivable	Individual customers
Inventory stored in public warehouse	Warehouse custodian
Accounts payable	Creditors
Debentures payable	Trustee
Lease terms	Lessor
Ordinary shares issued	Registrar
Insurance coverage	Insurance company

ASA 505 *External Confirmations* (ISA 505) provides guidance on the use of confirmations that are generally considered to have a high degree of reliability. It is normal practice for the auditor to obtain confirmation evidence for accounts receivable whenever it is practical and reasonable to do so, and it is standard practice to obtain confirmations for bank balances. The use of confirmations in other applications depends on the relative cost and reliability of alternative forms of evidence that may be available to the auditor. However, the effort involved in preparing and sending confirmation requests and in analysing the responses can be quite time-consuming, often making this a costly form of evidence. Confirmations of accounts receivable are covered in chapter 14.

This type of evidence may support any of the assertions, but it is related mainly to the existence or occurrence assertion.

Documentary evidence

Documentary evidence includes documents (printed and electronic) relating to transactions such as invoices and requisitions, and such items as minutes of board meetings, lease agreements and bank statements. Documents, which may be generated externally or internally, are usually contained in entity files and are available for the auditor's inspection on request.

Examples of externally generated documents include customer order forms, suppliers' invoices, tax assessments and bank statements. Externally generated documents are considered to be reliable because they originate from independent third parties. However, they may be altered by an employee at the entity before being shown to the auditor. This risk is particularly high if the auditor is offered a photocopy or facsimile. The reliability of externally generated documents can be enhanced when the auditor obtains copies directly from the external party. Thus, although the copy of the bank statements held by the entity is normally examined, the auditor may ask the entity to have the bank send a statement as of a particular date directly to the auditor for use in verifying cash balances.

Examples of internally generated documents include sales order forms, sales invoices, purchase orders and receiving reports. Given that it is possible for entity employees to create internal documents to support fictitious transactions, the reliability of internally generated documents is enhanced when they bear evidence of having been circulated to external parties before being placed in the entity's files. A delivery note prepared by the entity but signed by the customer to acknowledge receipt of the goods, for example, provides strong evidence that the transaction occurred. Similarly, a deposit slip receipted by the bank provides strong evidence that a deposit was actually made. In contrast, duplicate file copies of sales invoices and purchase requisitions that bear no evidence of external circulation may be less reliable. Figure 10.3 summarises the effects of circulation on the reliability of documentary evidence.

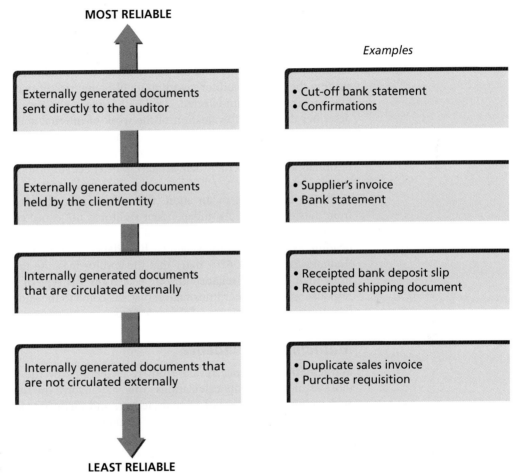

MOST RELIABLE

Examples

Externally generated documents sent directly to the auditor
- Cut-off bank statement
- Confirmations

Externally generated documents held by the client/entity
- Supplier's invoice
- Bank statement

Internally generated documents that are circulated externally
- Receipted bank deposit slip
- Receipted shipping document

Internally generated documents that are not circulated externally
- Duplicate sales invoice
- Purchase requisition

LEAST RELIABLE

FIGURE 10.3:
Effects of circulation on the reliability of documentary evidence

The physical characteristics of documents may also affect their reliability. Special papers, prenumbered documents and machine-imprinted data, for example, are designed to be more difficult to alter or to create phoney documentation.

Documentary evidence is used extensively in auditing and may relate to any of the categories of management assertion. There are two special classes of documentary evidence: (1) confirmations (already discussed), and (2) written representations.

Written representations

Written representations are responses to enquiries by the auditor by responsible and knowledgeable individuals. They may be differentiated from confirmations in two ways: (1) they may originate either from within the entity's organisation or from external sources, and (2) they may contain subjective information or an individual's opinion about a matter, rather than factual information.

ASA 580 *Written Representations* (ISA 580) requires the auditor to obtain certain written representations from management. Commonly presented in the form of a letter, such representations are designed to document management's replies to enquiries made by the auditor during the audit. These representations may reveal information that is not shown in the accounting records, such as the existence of contingencies that may require investigation. The use of a management representation letter is explained in chapter 18. Where the entity has an internal audit function that the external auditor has determined is likely to be relevant to the audit, the objectives of the external auditor are to determine whether to use, and to what extent, specific work of the internal auditors as audit evidence; and if using the specific work of the internal auditors, to determine whether that work is adequate for the purposes of the audit. The work of the internal auditor will be evaluated based on its reliability and relevance; and the external auditor will obtain sufficient audit evidence concerning the internal auditor's work to identify any risk of material misstatements that were not uncorrected or undetected. ASA 610 *Using the Work of Internal Auditors* (ISA 610) describes the basis of evaluation of the work of internal auditors. The evaluation is based on the objectivity of the internal audit function, the technical competence of the internal auditors, whether the work of the internal auditor is likely to be carried out with due professional care and whether there is likely to be effective communication between the internal external auditors.

During the course of an audit, the auditor may also request written representations from outside experts. An independent auditor is not expected to possess the expertise of a geologist in estimating the quantity of ore in a mine or of a lawyer in evaluating litigation pending against the entity. When such evidence is needed, ASA 620 *Using the Work of an Auditor's Expert* (ISA 620) states that the auditor may use the work of a specialist. A relatively high degree of reliance may be placed on this type of evidence, especially when the response validates other information that has come to the auditor's attention. Written representations may refer to any of the assertions.

Mathematical evidence

Mathematical evidence results from recalculations by the auditor and a comparison of those results with entity calculations. This may involve the results of: (1) routine tasks such as checking the additions of journals, ledgers and supporting schedules, and (2) complicated recalculations such as reconciliations. Mathematical evidence generated by the auditor is reliable, has a relatively low cost and contributes to the basis for the auditor's conclusions about valuation and allocation assertions.

Oral evidence

During an audit, an auditor will make frequent oral enquiries of officers and key employees of the entity. **Oral evidence** is rarely reliable by itself. Its main value lies in directing the auditor to other sources of evidence, corroborating other types of evidence and disclosing matters that may merit further investigation and documentation.

When oral evidence plays a key role in an audit decision, the source, nature and date of the evidence should be documented in the working papers. When obtained from management, the auditor may ask that such evidence be reaffirmed in writing in the management's representation letter. Oral evidence may apply to any of the categories of financial statement assertions.

Physical evidence

Physical evidence is obtained from physical inspection of tangible assets. For example, an auditor acquires direct personal knowledge of the existence of undeposited cash receipts or inventories by inspecting them.

Physical evidence is also helpful in determining the quality (or condition) of an asset that may relate to the valuation assertion. In some cases, the auditor may not be qualified to determine quality, condition or value based on the physical evidence, so may engage an expert to examine the physical evidence. The auditor then relies on the expert's written representation, together with the physical evidence (using the work of an auditor's expert is covered by ASA 620).

Electronic evidence

Electronic evidence is any information used by the auditor that is produced or maintained by electronic means. 'Electronic' means the use of computers, scanners, sensors, magnetic media and other electronic devices associated with the creation, manipulation, transmission and reception of electronic data.

When transactions are conducted over computer networks, many traditional accounting documents are eliminated. An entity's computer may be used, for example, to (1) determine when an inventory item needs to be reordered, (2) generate and electronically transmit the order to a supplier's computer, (3) receive shipping and invoicing information directly from the supplier's computer, and (4) initiate the electronic transfer of funds from the entity's bank account to the supplier's bank account to pay for the order.

In such cases, the auditor must use the electronic evidence of the transactions. The reliability of such evidence is a function of the controls over the creation, alteration and completeness of such data, and the competence of the tools (audit software) that the auditor uses to access the electronic evidence.

The impact of technology on other traditional forms of evidence also poses new opportunities and challenges, such as the faxing of confirmations and the emailing of attachments. Again, the auditor must consider controls related to the origin, transmission and receipt of faxed and emailed information in assessing the reliability of the evidence. The improved quality of scanners and printers has also increased the risk of the creation of fraudulent documents.

Electronic evidence may substitute for several of the traditional types of evidence discussed previously and may relate to any of the categories of assertions. However, an overriding concern of the auditor is the risk in relying on electronic evidence.

One example where the auditor needs to be more careful is through the use of email as evidence compared to traditional mail where there was more evidence of the validity of the source, which is particularly important in obtaining confirmations. Another example is through the widespread use of electronic signatures. Auditors need to ensure that there are strong controls over the use of this type of authorisation.

LEARNING 4 objective

Describe the types and classifications of auditing procedures that may be used in an audit.

10.4 AUDITING PROCEDURES

Auditing procedures are methods and techniques used by the auditor to gather and evaluate audit evidence. Each procedure has a particular advantage for obtaining evidence for an assertion. In selecting a procedure, the auditor must take care to balance the potential effectiveness of the procedure in meeting specific objectives against the cost of performing the procedure. Some of these procedures are discussed on the following pages.

10.4.1 Types of auditing procedures

To obtain sufficient appropriate audit evidence, the auditor is required to perform risk assessment procedures and further audit procedures, which comprise tests of controls and substantive procedures (including tests of details and substantive analytical procedures). The nature and timing of the audit procedures to be used may be affected by the fact that some of the accounting data and other information may be available only in electronic form, or only at certain points or periods in time. The auditor may find it necessary, as a result of data retention policies, to request retention of some information for the auditor's review or to perform audit procedures at a time when the information is available. Auditing procedures, inspection, observation, external confirmation, recalculation, re-performance, analytical procedures, and enquiry as well as computer-assisted audit techniques may be used as part of the methodology to obtain evidence for some of these procedures.

Inspection of records, documents or tangible assets

Inspection involves careful scrutiny or detailed examination of an entity's documents and records, and physical examination of tangible resources. This procedure is used extensively in auditing.

Inspecting documents is a way to evaluate documentary evidence. Through inspection the auditor can assess the authenticity of audit evidence or detect alterations or questionable items. Inspection of documents also permits the auditor to determine the precise terms of invoices, contracts and agreements. Inspection may involve *tracing, vouching* or *scanning*. **Scanning** involves the less careful scrutiny of documents and records.

Inspecting tangible resources provides the auditor with direct personal knowledge of their existence and physical condition.

Tracing

Tracing involves inspecting documents created when transactions were executed and determines that information from the documents was properly recorded in the accounting records. The direction of the testing is from the documents to the accounting records, thus tracing the original flow of the data through the accounting system. This procedure provides assurance that data from source documents were ultimately included in the accounts, so it is especially useful for detecting understatements in the accounting records. Thus, it is an important procedure in obtaining evidence relating to completeness assertions.

The effectiveness of tracing is enhanced when the entity uses serially prenumbered documents and the auditor combines this procedure with counting to verify the completeness of the numerical sequence.

Vouching

Vouching involves selecting entries in the accounting records and inspecting the documentation that served as the basis for entries, so as to determine the propriety and validity of the recorded transactions. In vouching, the direction of the testing is opposite to that in tracing.

Vouching is used extensively to detect overstatements in the accounting records. Thus, it is an important procedure in obtaining evidence relating to existence or occurrence assertions. Vouching relates to documentary evidence. Figure 10.4 shows the main differences between vouching and tracing.

Both tracing and vouching provide evidence as to valuation and allocation, and rights and obligations. Valuation and allocation are confirmed by a comparison of the amount on the document with the accounting record. Rights and obligations are confirmed where the information on the document confirms the transaction as creating a right or obligation of the entity.

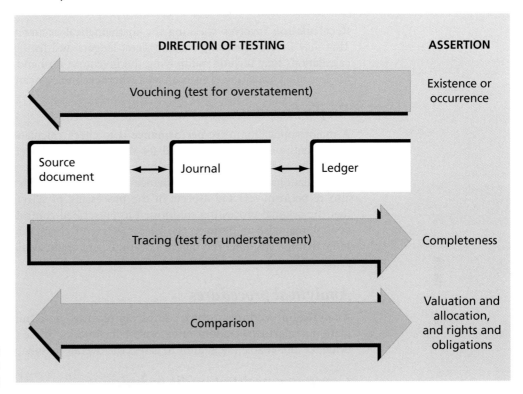

FIGURE 10.4:
Differences between vouching and tracing

Observation

Observation concerns watching or witnessing the performance of some activity or process. The activity may be the manner in which cash is safeguarded or the care taken by the entity in counting inventory. The subject matter of such observation is personnel, procedures and processes. From these observations, the auditor obtains direct personal knowledge of the activities in the form of physical evidence. Observation of procedures provides highly reliable evidence as to their performance at a given time but not necessarily as to their performance at other times. For this reason, auditors often use surprise tactics to perform observation procedures.

Enquiry

Enquiry involves either oral or written questions by the auditor. Such enquiries may be made internally to management or employees, as in the case of questions concerning the obsolescence of inventory items and the collectability of receivables; or externally, as in enquiries to lawyers concerning the probable outcome of litigation. Enquiry produces either oral evidence or evidence in the form of written representations.

Confirmation

Confirmation is a form of enquiry that enables the auditor to obtain information directly from an independent source outside the entity. Normally, the entity makes the request of the outside party in writing, but the auditor controls the mailing of the enquiry. The request should ask the recipient to send the response directly to the auditor. This auditing procedure produces confirmation evidence.

Recalculation

Recalculation involves checking the mathematical accuracy of records and documents. This may involve checking that invoices, ledgers and listings are correctly added. Other calculations may include multiplying the inventory on hand by the cost price to arrive at the inventory valuation. This is an area where technology can be very useful to the auditor.

Re-performance

A major application of **re-performance** is to check calculations and reconciliations made by the entity. Amounts calculated for depreciation and accrued interest may be recalculated. The auditor will usually verify the accuracy of totals on supporting schedules and reconciliations. Mathematical evidence is produced by this procedure. The auditor may also re-perform selected aspects of the processing of selected transactions to determine that the original processing conformed to prescribed control policies and procedures. The auditor may also re-perform the customer credit check for a sales transaction to determine that the customer did indeed have sufficient credit available when the transaction was processed.

Analytical procedures

Analytical procedures involve comparing recorded accounting data with historical information, budget expectations or external benchmarks. These procedures produce analytical evidence and enable the auditor to assess the overall reasonableness of account balances.

Computer-assisted audit techniques

The auditor may also use **computer-assisted audit techniques** in performing several of the procedures described in the preceding sections. The following are examples of how the auditor can use computer audit software to:
- perform the calculations and comparisons used in analytical procedures
- select a sample of accounts receivable for confirmation
- scan a file to determine that all documents in a series have been accounted for
- compare data elements in different files for agreement (such as the prices on sales invoices with a master file containing authorised prices)
- re-perform a variety of calculations, such as totalling the accounts receivable subsidiary ledger or inventory file.

10.4.2 The relationships among auditing procedures, types of evidence and assertions

During the course of an audit, in meeting the numerous specific audit objectives derived from management's financial statement assertions, the auditor will use all the auditing procedures and all the types of evidence described in this chapter. Some examples of the relationships among auditing procedures, types of evidence and assertions are shown in figure 10.5. From this figure we can see that tracing, vouching and inspection involve the use of documentary evidence. The procedure of inspecting may involve the use of physical evidence, as do the procedures of recalculation and observation. Also, the procedure of enquiry may produce either written representations or oral evidence, depending on the nature of the enquiry and the response.

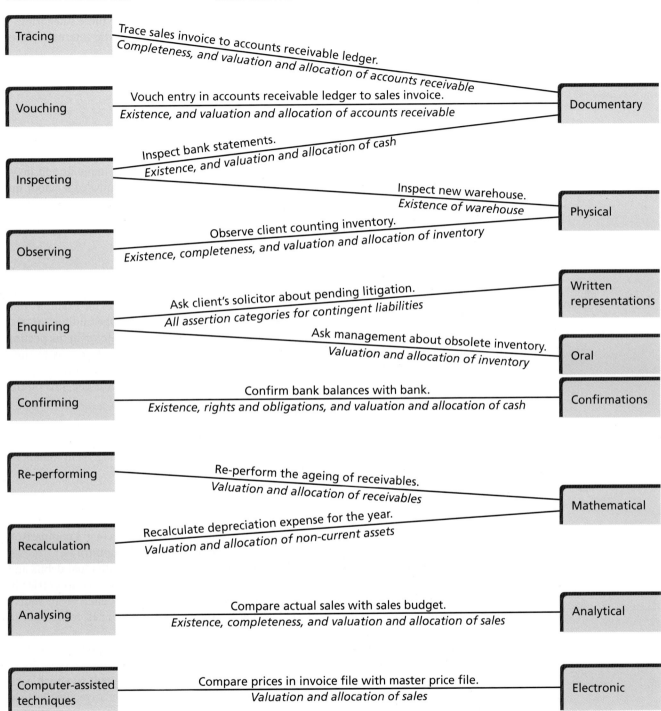

AUDITING PROCEDURE	ILLUSTRATIVE APPLICATION ASSERTION	TYPE OF AUDIT EVIDENCE
Tracing	Trace sales invoice to accounts receivable ledger. *Completeness, and valuation and allocation of accounts receivable*	Documentary
Vouching	Vouch entry in accounts receivable ledger to sales invoice. *Existence, and valuation and allocation of accounts receivable*	Documentary
Inspecting	Inspect bank statements. *Existence, and valuation and allocation of cash*	
	Inspect new warehouse. *Existence of warehouse*	Physical
Observing	Observe client counting inventory. *Existence, completeness, and valuation and allocation of inventory*	
Enquiring	Ask client's solicitor about pending litigation. *All assertion categories for contingent liabilities*	Written representations
	Ask management about obsolete inventory. *Valuation and allocation of inventory*	Oral
Confirming	Confirm bank balances with bank. *Existence, rights and obligations, and valuation and allocation of cash*	Confirmations
Re-performing	Re-perform the ageing of receivables. *Valuation and allocation of receivables*	Mathematical
Recalculation	Recalculate depreciation expense for the year. *Valuation and allocation of non-current assets*	
Analysing	Compare actual sales with sales budget. *Existence, completeness, and valuation and allocation of sales*	Analytical
Computer-assisted techniques	Compare prices in invoice file with master price file. *Valuation and allocation of sales*	Electronic

FIGURE 10.5: Relationships among auditing procedures, types of evidence and specific audit objectives

10.4.3 Classification of auditing procedures

Auditing procedures are usually classified by purpose into the following three categories:
1. procedures to assess risks including obtaining an understanding of the internal control structure
2. tests of controls
3. substantive procedures.

Procedures to obtain an understanding

Auditing standards require the auditor to obtain an understanding of the entity's internal control structure relevant to the audit. To do this, the auditor may enquire of management about internal control policies and procedures, and inspect accounting manuals and flow-charts of the accounting system. In addition, the auditor may obtain knowledge about the internal control structure by observing the entity's activities and operations. In performing these procedures, the auditor is concerned with the design of the entity's internal control structure; that is, how it is supposed to work.

Tests of controls

Tests of controls are made to provide evidence about the effectiveness of the design and operations of internal control structure policies and procedures. Assume, for example, that the control procedure provides for depositing cash in the bank daily. The auditor can test the effectiveness of the control by observing actual deposits being made or by inspecting duplicate deposit slips. Tests of controls also include an enquiry of employees as to their performance of control procedures and a re-performance of control procedures by the auditor. The performance of tests of controls in a financial statement audit depends on the strategy adopted by the auditor.

Substantive procedures

Substantive procedures provide direct evidence as to the fairness of management's financial statement assertions. This category of auditing procedure consists of:
- analytical procedures
- tests of details of transactions
- tests of details of balances.

Analytical procedures involve the use of comparisons to assess fairness (e.g. a comparison of an account balance with the previous year's balance or a budgeted amount).

Tests of details of transactions involve examining support for the individual debits and credits posted to an account (e.g. vouching the debits in accounts receivable to entries in the sales journal and supporting sales invoices). Similarly, tracing the details from source documents to journals and the affected ledger accounts constitutes a test of details of transactions.

Tests of details of balances involve examining support for the closing balance directly (e.g. confirming accounts receivable directly with the customer).

The three types of substantive procedures are complementary. The extent to which each type is used on a given account can vary based on such factors as the relative effectiveness for that account and the cost.

In some cases the auditor may perform tests of transactions to determine that:
- laid-down procedures were followed in processing the transactions (tests of controls)
- the transactions were accurately journalised and posted to the ledger accounts (substantive test of details of transactions).

When both purposes are served by the same test, it is called a **dual-purpose test**.

10.4.4 Evaluation of evidence obtained

To have a reasonable basis for an opinion on the financial statements, the auditor needs a preponderance (i.e. a consensus or majority) of persuasive evidence for all key assertions for each material account. When a reasonable basis for an opinion is lacking, the auditor expresses a disclaimer of opinion. When a reasonable basis for an opinion has been obtained, the auditor should issue either an unqualified, qualified or adverse opinion, depending on the degree of correspondence of the assertions established by the evidence obtained with the concept of fairness.

The process of obtaining and evaluating audit evidence and determining the effects on the auditor's report is summarised in figure 10.6.

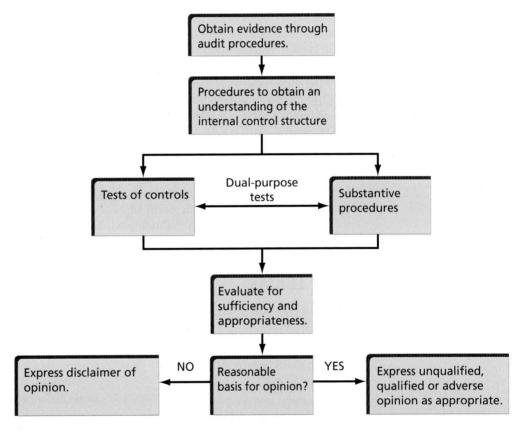

FIGURE 10.6:
Obtaining and evaluating
audit evidence

Do you know . . .

10.6 ☐ Management's financial statement assertions are a useful starting point in developing specific audit objectives for each account balance or class of transactions. If any of these assertions is a misrepresentation, then the financial statements could be materially misstated.

10.7 ☐ Audit evidence comprises underlying accounting data and corroborating information, and it needs to be sufficient and appropriate to afford a reasonable basis for forming an opinion.

10.8 ☐ Audit procedures are the techniques used to obtain evidence. They include analytical procedures, inspection of records, observation, enquiry, confirmation, re-performance and computer-assisted audit techniques

10.9 ☐ Auditing procedures can be classified by their purpose into three categories: (1) procedures to obtain an understanding of the internal control structure; (2) tests of controls; and (3) substantive procedures.

10.10 ☐ Two ends of the spectrum of audit strategies are (1) the predominantly substantive approach and (2) the lower assessed level of control risk approach. The auditor determines the strategy separately for each assertion for each major account balance and transaction class.

SUMMARY

Materiality is considered at both the financial statement and account balance levels, and may be expressed in either quantitative or non-quantitative financial statement terms. There is an inverse relationship between materiality levels and the level of evidence needed.

In conducting the audit, different strategies can be adopted. After understanding the entity and its environment (including its internal control) in order to assess the risks of material misstatement, the audit strategy can be developed. The two ends of the spectrum of audit strategies are the predominantly substantive approach (discussed in chapter 12) and combined approach (lower assessed level of control risk) (discussed in chapter 11).

The auditor achieves the overall objective of rendering an opinion on general purpose financial reports by collecting and evaluating evidence relating to numerous specific audit objectives. These objectives are derived from the management assertions contained in the components of the financial statements. In performing the audit, the auditor exercises professional judgement in selecting from a variety of auditing procedures and types of evidence to meet the numerous specific audit objectives. The auditor also exercises judgement at the conclusion of the audit in evaluating whether sufficient appropriate evidence has been obtained to afford a reasonable basis for the opinion on the financial statements overall.

KEY TERMS

analytical evidence, p. 431

analytical procedures, p. 438

audit evidence, p. 427

auditing procedures, p. 435

audit risk, p. 423

audit strategy, p. 416

computer-assisted audit techniques, p. 438

confirmation, pp. 432, 437

control risk, p. 423

corroborating information, p. 431

documentary evidence, p. 432

dual-purpose test, p. 440

electronic evidence, p. 435

enquiry, p. 437

inspection, p. 436

lower assessed level of control risk approach, p. 424

materiality, p. 417

mathematical evidence, p. 434

observation, p. 437

oral evidence, p. 434

physical evidence, p. 435

predominantly substantive approach, p. 423

recalculation, p. 438

re-performance, p. 438

scanning, p. 436

substantive procedures, p. 423

tests of controls, p. 440

tests of details of balances, p. 440

tests of details of transactions, p. 440

tolerable misstatement, p. 422

tracing, p. 436

transaction class, p. 424

underlying accounting records, p. 428

vouching, p. 436

written representations, p. 433

10.1 In planning the audit, the auditor should assess materiality at two levels:
A. The preliminary level and the final level.
B. The company level and the divisional level.
C. The financial report level and the account balance level.
D. The account balance level and the transaction level.

10.2 Professional standards recognise that a misstatement that is quantitatively immaterial may be qualitatively material. In regard to these items, professional standards require the auditor to:
A. Plan the audit to search for them.
B. Design explicit procedures to detect them.
C. Be on the alert for them.
D. Report them directly to client management.

10.3 In making judgements about materiality at the account balance level, the auditor must consider the relationship between it and materiality at financial report level as a whole. This should lead the auditor to plan the audit to detect misstatements that:
A. Are individually material to the statements taken as a whole.
B. Are individually immaterial to the statements taken as a whole.
C. Bring the cumulative total of known misstatements to the level of materiality established by management.
D. May be immaterial individually, but may aggregate with misstatements in other accounts to a material level.

10.4 Which of the following is true?
A. High business risk always leads to high control risk.
B. Lower control risk leads to higher levels of substantive testing.
C. The auditor designs tests to address all inherent risks identified.
D. High audit risk means low materiality.

10.5 An auditor has obtained an understanding of the internal control structure and has decided that the appropriate controls are ineffective. The most appropriate audit strategy is:
A. The lower assessed level of control risk approach.
B. The predominantly substantive approach.
C. A combination of the lower assessed level of control risk approach and the predominantly substantive approach.
D. The analytical procedures approach.

10.6 Which of these would *not* be considered corroborating information?
A. Oral evidence obtained from client personnel.
B. Confirmation from vendors.
C. Cancelled cheques held by the client
D. The accountant's work sheet.

10.7 In the final analysis, the amount and kinds of evidential matter required to support the auditor's opinion should be determined by:
A. The engagement letter.
B. Auditor judgement.
C. The audit committee.
D. Rigorous statistical analysis.

10.8 The auditor has determined that there is a preponderance of persuasive evidence for each financial statement assertion that is material, and therefore a reasonable basis for their opinion. Which of the following would not be a possible opinion that the auditor could issue?

A. An inability to form an opinion.
B. An unqualified opinion.
C. An 'except for' opinion.
D. An adverse opinion.

10.9 Which of the following would generally be considered the least appropriate form of evidence?

A. The auditor's calculation of earnings per share.
B. Prenumbered sales invoices prepared by the accounts receivable clerk.
C. The auditor's inspection of new machinery acquisitions for the current year where the client is a computer manufacturer.
D. Correspondence from the client's solicitor concerning litigation.

10.10 Which of the following are substantive procedures?

(i) Analytical procedures.
(ii) Tests of detail of balances.
(iii) Tests of controls.

A. (i) and (ii) only.
B. (ii) and (iii) only.
C. (i) and (iii) only.
D. (i), (ii) and (iii).

REVIEW questions

10.11 Under what circumstances would the auditor request the accounts to be adjusted for individually immaterial errors?

10.12 Explain the term 'materiality' in the context of financial reporting.

10.13 List and describe the financial statement assertions in relation to balances.

10.14 What is the significance of materiality in relation to the auditor's objectives when obtaining audit evidence?

10.15 Describe the two main alternative audit strategies that may be adopted in performing an audit.

10.16 What is the difference between how the auditor uses materiality at the planning stage and at the final review stage of the audit?

10.17 Give examples of items that might be included in a management representations letter.

10.18 What is the difference between a test of control and a substantive test?

10.19 What are the factors that affect the reliability of evidence?

10.20 Describe different types of audit procedures that might be used by the auditor in ensuring the assertions for inventory.

PROFESSIONAL application questions

10.21 Audit evidence ★

Corroboratory evidence inspected by an auditor in the course of an audit includes:

1. a letter from a customer directly to the auditor confirming consignment stock held at the year-end

★
BASIC
★★
MODERATE
★★★
CHALLENGING

2. a supplier invoice taken from the company's files
3. a schedule for the calculation of the warranty provision obtained from the company's files
4. delivery notes, sent with goods, receipted by customers, and held in the company's office
5. a contract for the lease of premises signed by one of the directors and the landlord
6. a goods delivery note signed by the warehouse supervisor to indicate goods were received
7. inventory count sheets recording inventory held at the year-end
8. a note on the asset register that the life of a piece of equipment is 10 years.

Required

For each item, comment on its reliability and relevance as audit evidence.

10.22 Types of audit procedures ★

In order to arrive at an audit opinion, auditors must obtain sufficient appropriate audit evidence. ASA 500 identifies the types of auditing procedures that an auditor might carry out in order to obtain audit evidence.

Required

(a) Identify the types of audit procedures that an auditor might use for obtaining audit evidence.
(b) For each type of audit procedure, give an example of a specific procedure that an auditor might perform when auditing the property, plant and machinery balance in the balance sheet/statement of financial position.

10.23 Substantive procedures and audit evidence ★

An auditor may perform the following three types of substantive procedures: (a) tests of details of transactions; (b) tests of details of balances; and (c) analytical procedures. Below are specific audit procedures that fall within one of these categories:

1. Reconcile supplier statements at the year-end with balances in the purchase ledger.
2. Agree a sample of sales invoices to goods despatch records held in the inventory system.
3. Review post year-end receipts from customers to establish the extent of unpaid debts.
4. Calculate gross profit ratios for each branch of a chain of supermarkets and compare month by month and prior year.
5. Obtain schedule of asset disposals in the period and agree to supporting sale documents.
6. Attend the factory on the final day of the year to review work in progress.
7. Agree payment to equipment hire company to a copy of the lease.
8. Calculate expected payroll costs from last year's amount adjusted for staff changes and pay rise in the year.

Required

For each procedure, explain which of the three types it belongs to.

10.24 Materiality ★★

You have just completed audit testing on the 30 June 2015 accounts of JJJ Ltd, a manufacturing firm. Extracts from the draft financial statements are given below.

	$'000
Current assets	12 095
Non-current assets	8 297
Current liabilities	5 630
Non-current liabilities	4 500
Equity	10 262
Operating profit before tax	2 857
Operating profit after tax	2 333

The audit manager has asked you to review the following summary of audit differences working paper to determine whether there are any material errors in the financial report.

Details of errors found	Amount ($)
1. Non-tax-deductible fine incurred because of breaches of safety regulations; not taken up as at 30 June 2015	250 000
2. Incorrect prices on sales invoices issued in June (customers overcharged)	25 000
3. Unrecorded liabilities because of 30 June 2015 stock purchases not being taken up (cut-off error)	71 000
4. Interest receivable on bank deposit not taken up	175 000

Required

(a) Discuss the differences in the purpose, method of calculation and relative use of judgement of:
   (i) materiality as used at the planning stage of the audit
   (ii) materiality as used at the final review stage of the audit.
(b) Outline the materiality guidelines as described in AASB 1031.
(c) Under what circumstances might an error be judged to be material as a result of its nature rather than its amount? Give examples.
(d) Are any of the errors in items 1–4 material? In each case explain how you reached your conclusion.[1]

10.25 Audit risk and audit strategies ★★

Audit procedures may be classified into several categories, including:
1. Procedures designed to obtain an understanding
2. Tests of controls
3. Analytical procedures
4. Substantive testing of transactions
5. Substantive testing of balances.

Required

(a) Describe the relationship between the above five categories and how these need to be considered when designing audit strategies.
(b) How would consideration of the audit risk model affect the audit strategy and therefore the extent to which these types of procedures are performed?

10.26 External confirmations ★★

You are an in-charge auditor discussing audit procedures with members of your team. A new member of staff says that audit evidence should be based on confirmations received from outside the organisation because the company cannot be trusted to tell the truth about its own transactions.

You state that while external confirmations are an excellent form of audit evidence they have their limitations.

Required

Identify four different types of external confirmations, explain why each is a useful source of evidence referring to the financial statement assertion it supports and finally comment on its limitations.

10.27 Audit objectives, procedures and evidence ★★★

You are an audit senior and your firm audits Miningwell Ltd, a large mining company that operates all over Australia. Consider the following situations that have arisen during the audit.

1. Miningwell owns some highly specialised mining tools and equipment held at various remote regions across the country. Your firm has engaged an expert to carry out a physical audit check of these equipment and tools at each location and to perform an independent valuation of each material asset.
2. In reviewing the account receivables of Miningwell, you realise that the majority of Miningwell's customers are in Indonesia and other parts of remote South-East Asia. Because of communication difficulties, direct confirmation of the accounts receivables' balances is unlikely to give satisfactory results.
3. During the audit you also notice that Miningwell owns the majority of shares in related, unlisted companies in Australia.

Required

(a) Identify the key assertion(s) at risk in relation to the balances described in each of these three situations.
(b) Describe the audit procedures you would perform to gather sufficient appropriate audit evidence on each of these assertions.

10.28 Audit evidence ★★★

You are about to complete the planning stage of the audit of Stack Print Ltd and you are considering your approach to several events that have occurred during the year. Stack Print Ltd's revenue for the year is $25 million and profits are $3 million.

A customer has made a claim against Stack Print Ltd for breach of contract. They claim that products were not delivered in accordance with the contract and this led to them having to engage other contractors to carry out the work at great expense. The customer is suing the company for damages of $1 million.

A major customer has not paid Stack Print Ltd for three months and the receivable balance at the year-end for this customer is $120 000. The customer is rumoured to be having significant cash flow difficulties; however, Stack Print Ltd's directors believe they will be paid as the customer is one of long standing and has always paid in the past.

Stack Print Ltd recently purchased new equipment for the factory. This replaced old machinery, which is no longer being used, included in the balance sheet at a net written down value of $2 250 000. The old equipment has not reached the end of its originally expected useful life and remains on the balance sheet and is being depreciated in line with previous years.

Required

Describe substantive procedures that would provide sufficient appropriate evidence in relation to the issues outlined above.

10.29 Auditing procedures and evidence ★★★

Specific auditing procedures for obtaining audit evidence are listed below.
1. Send debtor's confirmation letters to a number of the client's customers.
2. Recalculate depreciation charges.
3. Calculate gross profit rates for the current year and preceding year.
4. Discuss the potential obsolescence of inventory with the management.
5. Examine registration certificates for motor vehicles purchased during the year.
6. Use the computer to scan a file to determine that all documents in a numbered series have been accounted for.
7. Learn about a possible lawsuit in conversation with the financial controller.
8. Obtain a valuation of land held by the company interstate.

9. Observe the year-end inventory count.
10. Select a sample of repairs and maintenance expenses and check whether any should have been capitalised.

Required

Indicate:

(a) the type of evidence obtained by each procedure
(b) the assertion or assertions to which it relates.

10.30 Techniques to obtain evidence ★★★

You are the auditor of Davidson Electronics Ltd a manufacturer of a variety of electronic gadgets for industry and home use. They have a factory where all the products are manufactured and maintain a stock of electronic parts to be used in the manufacturing process.

You are considering the evidence that you will need to obtain to support your audit opinion and are considering using the following techniques to obtain evidence:

1. Analytical review
2. Enquiry
3. Inspection
4. Observation
5. Computation

Required

Explain each of the five techniques referred to and give examples of how they might be applied to the audit of Davidson Electronics.

 CASE studies

10.31 Materiality ★★★

You are nearing completion of the 31 December 2015 audit of ABC Wholesalers Ltd. The figures below have been extracted from the final draft financial report.

	$'000
Operating profit before income tax	5 722
Operating profit after income tax	3 541
Total revenue	718 635
Current assets	253 881
Non-current assets	216 752
Total assets	470 633
Current liabilities	103 333
Non-current liabilities	132 760
Total liabilities	236 093
Equity	234 540

During your review of the audit files, you note the following items recorded on the summary of audit differences.

1. ABC Wholesalers has been involved in a long-running dispute with the taxation authorities in relation to the amount of sales tax payable on certain lines of merchandise. The case was resolved this year in favour of the taxation authorities. The court ruled that ABC Wholesalers, as well as paying the outstanding taxes, must pay a non-tax-deductible fine of $420 000.

2. Sales cut-off at one of ABC Wholesaler's stores was incorrect, resulting in a large sale of inventory made early in January 2015 being recorded in the 31 December 2014 year-end. The cost price of the inventory sold was $250 000. ABC Wholesalers marks up inventory by 40%.
3. Purchases cut-off at the same store was also incorrect, resulting in a large purchase of inventory made in late December not being recorded until January 2015. The invoice price of the inventory purchased was $5 950 000.

You also note that the planning materiality level was set by the audit manager at $200 000.

Required

(a) Consider items 1–3 independently. State whether the amounts involved would be considered material for the purpose of issuing an auditor's report. Give reasons.
(b) Explain the relevance, if any, of the planning materiality level to your decisions in (a).[2]

10.32 Audit evidence and quality ★★★

You are planning the audit of Big Digger Ltd (BD), a company which manufactures gardening equipment. Included in the balance sheet of BD, under non-current assets, is an investment in another company, Get Potted Ltd (GP), which makes garden pots. BD owns 12% of the shares of GP which are valued in BD's balance sheet at the original cost of $125 000.

From your work to gain an understanding of the entity and its environment, you have become aware of a rumour that GP is having financial difficulties and that a recent press report stated that GP was insolvent and had ceased to trade. You are about to start the audit of the investment in GP and have identified that the financial statement assertion at risk with regard to the investment is that of valuation and allocation.

Required

Considering the broad categories of types of auditing procedures below, give examples, where applicable, of specific audit procedures that could be undertaken with regard to the valuation of the investment and discuss the reliability of the evidence received from those procedures. Note that not all the categories below are applicable to this scenario.

1. Analytical procedures
2. Inspection
3. Confirmation
4. Enquiry
5. Recalculation
6. Observation
7. Re-performance
8. Computer-assisted audit techniques

 RESEARCH question

10.33 Materiality

Obtain a set of recently audited financial reports published in Australia.

Required

(a) Describe the factors that might have considered by the auditor in determining the overall materiality of the financial report as a whole.
(b) Identify an asset item and describe the audit evidence and audit objectives that are to be employed by the auditor to ascertain the fairness of its value stated in the financial report.
(c) Discuss what type of audit judgement you used and why.

FURTHER READING

H Chen & K Pany, 'An analysis of the relationship between accounting restatements and quantitative benchmarks of audit planning materiality', *Review of Accounting and Finance* 7(3), 2008, pp. 236–51.

GT Friedlob & LLF Schleifer, 'Fuzzy logic: application for audit risk and uncertainty', *Managerial Auditing Journal* 14(3), 1999, pp. 27–135.

L Gettler, 'Troubles with gatekeepers who sleep on the job', *Sydney Morning Herald Top*, 31 March, 2010, www.smh.com.au.

T B-P Ng, 'Auditors' decisions on audit differences that affect significant earnings thresholds', *Auditing*, May 2007, pp. 71–89.

T DeZoort, P Harrison & M Taylor, 'Accountability and auditors materiality judgments: the effects of differential pressure strength on conservatism, variability, and effort', *Accounting, Organizations & Society*, July/August 2006, pp. 373–90.

SB Law & R Willett, 'The ability of analytical procedures to signal transaction errors', *Managerial Auditing Journal* 19(7) 2004, pp. 869–88.

PBW Miller & PR Bahnson, 'More on users' demands: reliability and materiality', *Accounting Today*, March 2006, pp. 14–15.

MW Nelson & SD Smith & Z-V Palmrose, 'The effect of quantitative materiality approach on auditors' adjustment decisions', *Accounting Review*, July 2005, pp. 897–920.

Y Ohta, 'The role of audit evidence in a strategic audit', *Journal of Accounting and Public Policy* 28(1), 2009, pp. 58–67.

KT Trotman, '*Audit evidence*', *Blackwell Encyclopedic Dictionary of Accounting*, 2005, pp. 59–63.

RR Vanasco, CR Skousen & RL Jenson, 'Audit evidence: the US standards and landmark cases', *Managerial Auditing Journal* 16(4), 2001, pp. 207–14.

SD Vandervelde, 'The importance of account relations when responding to interim audit testing results', *Contemporary Accounting Research*, Fall 2006, pp. 789–821.

TJ Wilks & MF Zimbelman, 'Using game theory and strategic reasoning concepts to prevent and detect fraud', *Accounting Horizons*, September 2004, pp. 173–84.

NOTES

1. Adapted from Professional Year Programme of the ICAA, 1998, Accounting 2 Module.
2. Adapted from Professional Year Programme of the ICAA, 1999, Advanced Audit Module.

Answers to multiple-choice questions

10.1 *C*   10.2 *C*   10.3 *D*   10.4 *D*   10.5 *B*   10.6 *D*   10.7 *B*   10.8 *A*
10.9 *B*   10.10 *A*

part 3

AUDIT TESTING
METHODOLOGY

11   Tests of controls

12   Designing substantive procedures

13   Audit sampling

*I*n the previous section we looked at planning the audit, looking in particular at understanding the entity and its environment and how audit evidence needs to be obtained to meet the risks identified. The nature of the risks identified have an impact on the audit strategy and the detailed audit plan. In this part, we present an overview of the testing methodologies that may be used in obtaining the evidence that the auditor needs to support the audit opinion.

Chapter 11 discusses the nature of tests of controls and is followed by a general discussion of designing substantive testing procedures in **chapter 12**. **Chapter 13** covers issues involved in using sampling as part of audit procedures. Part 4 then looks in detail at specific audit procedures for transactions and balances.

chapter 11

Tests of controls

OVERVIEW

11.1 Control risk assessment and audit strategy

11.2 Tests of controls

11.3 Using internal auditors

11.4 Final assessment of control risk

11.5 Communication of internal control matters

11.6 Types of controls in an information technology environment

11.7 Computer-assisted audit techniques

Summary

Key terms

Multiple-choice questions

Review questions

Professional application questions

Case studies

Research question

Further reading

Notes

LEARNING objectives

After studying this chapter, you should be able to:

1 explain the relationship between control risk assessment and audit strategy

2 describe the purpose of tests of controls and the nature, timing and extent of such tests

3 clarify how the work of internal auditing may be used in tests of controls

4 explain the process of assessing control risk and documenting the conclusion

5 indicate the appropriate communications the auditor makes on internal control matters

6 describe the types of controls you would expect to see in an information technology environment

7 identify the alternative types of computer-assisted audit techniques.

PROFESSIONAL STATEMENTS

Australian		International	
ASA 265	*Communicating Deficiencies in Internal Control to Those Charged with Governance and Management*	**ISA 265**	*Communicating Deficiencies in Internal Control to Those Charged with Governance and Management*
ASA 330	*The Auditor's Responses to Assessed Risks*	**ISA 330**	*The Auditor's Responses to Assessed Risks*
ASA 610	*Using the Work of Internal Auditors*	**ISA 610**	*Using the Work of Internal Auditors*
AUS 810	*Special Purpose Reports on the Effectiveness of Control Procedures*		

SCENE SETTER

SOX requirements to review internal controls

In the United States section 404(b) of the Sarbanes–Oxley Act requires auditors to attest to the effectiveness of internal controls over financial reporting (ICOFR) of their public clients. A review of research was performed by Asare et al. (2013)[1] into this change to auditor's duties. They found that, consistent with the intent of the regulation, external auditor evaluation appears to strengthen a company's ICOFR. Further, the research shows that smaller companies, companies with higher business risk and poor corporate governance are more likely to have material weaknesses in ICOFR.

There has been a decline in the incidence of adverse reports on companies' ICOFR over time — to such an extent that they are now relatively rare. However, Securities and Exchange Commission staff have questioned whether the decline in the number of adverse reports is due to better ICOFR or auditors' missing material weaknesses.

Although in Australia there is no requirement to report on internal controls as there is in the United States as identified in the scene setter, the importance of internal control testing is important for many audits. This chapter discusses tests of controls and links to the risk assessment procedures discussed in chapter 9. We look at how the assessment of control risk has an impact on audit strategy. When controls are evaluated as sufficient to assess control risk as less than high, then auditors must test the controls to support their assessments. This leads to a discussion of tests of controls themselves, and an examination of tests of controls in an information technology (IT) environment.

LEARNING 1
objective

Explain the relationship between control risk assessment and audit strategy.

11.1 CONTROL RISK ASSESSMENT AND AUDIT STRATEGY

In every financial statement audit there is a requirement that the auditor assess the controls operating within the entity that are also relevant to the audit. This is primarily to better assess the risks of material misstatement, which will therefore also affect audit procedures. However, this assessment of controls can also affect the audit strategy, primarily in relation to decisions made on whether to focus more work on testing of controls or substantive audit procedures.

11.1.1 Assessing the control risk

In chapter 9 we discussed the nature of risk assessment and the need for the auditor to understand the entity and its environment in order to assess risk and design an audit strategy to meet these risks. Part of this process is the need to understand the entity's internal control environment and assess the internal control risk. The steps involved in this process are:
1. perform procedures to obtain an understanding of the internal controls
2. identify potential misstatements in the financial statements
3. identify the necessary controls that are likely to prevent or detect potential misstatements.

Having performed the above procedures, the auditor can make a preliminary assessment of control risk, and can then decide on the audit strategy. If the auditor wishes to rely on internal controls for the purposes of supporting the audit opinion, the procedures described above are inadequate. The work done so far will give the auditor knowledge of how the internal controls have been designed and an initial assessment of their strengths and weaknesses. What the auditor has not yet done is determine the extent to which the internal controls established by the entity have actually been implemented during the period that is being audited.

In order to place reliance on the internal controls to support the audit opinion, the auditor must now test these controls to ensure that they have been implemented as they were designed throughout the period under investigation. Therefore, in order to complete the work on internal controls the auditor must carry out two further steps:
1. perform tests of controls
2. evaluate the evidence obtained and assess the level of control risk.

What is clear from the above is that the auditor — having made a preliminary assessment of control risk — might then change this assessment once tests of controls have been completed. After the preliminary assessment, the auditor might have planned the audit approach based on a low control risk, reflecting an effective system of internal controls, but having tested these controls, the auditor might discover that the controls are not operating as they are designed. If this is the case, then the auditor needs to amend the audit approach.

As discussed in chapter 8, planning is an ongoing process. The auditor must be ready to amend the audit plan based on discoveries made during the audit process.

11.1.2 Audit strategy

There are effectively two audit strategies available to an auditor:

1. the predominantly substantive approach, where the auditor relies on substantive procedures for audit evidence
2. the lower assessed level of control risk approach, where the auditor obtains some evidence from testing controls (where the internal controls are considered to be effective) followed by a reduced level of substantive testing.

Figure 11.1 overleaf shows the decisions an auditor must make when following these approaches. The diamond shapes in the figure represent decisions that an auditor must make — these decisions may lead the auditor to change the audit approach in light of new information. A discussion of the two approaches outlined in figure 11.1 follows.

Predominantly substantive approach

Recall from the discussions in chapters 9 and 10 that when an auditor chooses a predominantly substantive approach, he or she should have sufficient knowledge of the system of internal control to understand the potential causes of misstatements and how those misstatements may or may not be controlled. In addition, in some IT-intensive environments, the auditor may be precluded from following a predominantly substantive approach because substantive tests alone do not reduce audit risk to an appropriately low level.

A number of differences may be noted in the part of figure 11.1 labelled 'Assess control risk'. First, as discussed in chapter 9, one component of a predominantly substantive approach for an assertion is a planned assessed level of control risk of high. This is based on the assumption that one of the following applies.

- There are no significant internal controls that relate to the assertion.
- Relevant internal controls are unlikely to be effective.
- It would not be efficient to obtain evidence to evaluate the effectiveness of relevant internal controls.

The decision paths in the 'Predominantly substantive approach' column in figure 11.1 allow for affirmation of, or changes to, these assumptions. Note that the first decision symbol (diamond-shaped) raises the question as to whether any evidence about the effectiveness of the design and operating effectiveness of internal controls was obtained while understanding internal controls. The auditor may have performed a transaction walk-through review, referred to in chapter 9, where a representative transaction from a class of transactions is traced through all the processing steps as a way of confirming the understanding obtained through questionnaires or flowcharts.

If evidence about the effectiveness of the design and operation of internal controls for an assertion is not established while obtaining an understanding, the auditor must assess control risk at the maximum for that assertion and document that conclusion in the working papers. If, however, limited evidence is obtained about the effectiveness of design and operation of internal controls for an assertion, the auditor may make an initial assessment of control risk of slightly less than high. In such a case, the auditor may be sufficiently encouraged to consider changing the audit strategy to a lower assessed level of control risk approach.

AUDIT ACTIVITY	PREDOMINANTLY SUBSTANTIVE APPROACH	LOWER ASSESSED LEVEL OF CONTROL RISK APPROACH

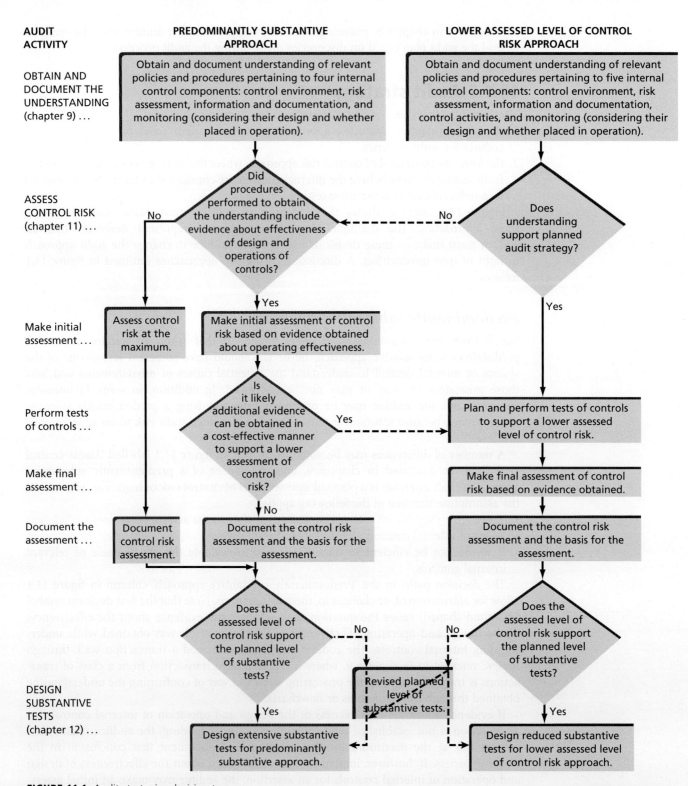

FIGURE 11.1: Audit strategies decision tree

In making the decision about whether to change strategies, consideration should be given to the likelihood that evidence can be obtained in a cost-effective manner to support a lower assessment of control risk such as medium or low. To be cost-effective, the combined costs of performing (1) additional tests of controls and (2) the reduced substantive tests that would be appropriate assuming the lower control risk assessment is supported should be less than the costs of performing the higher level of substantive testing required by the predominantly substantive approach. This decision is reflected in the second decision symbol in the 'Predominantly substantive approach' column where the 'Yes' branch (dotted line extending to the right from that symbol) represents a change in strategy to the lower assessed level of control risk approach. If the decision is made not to change strategies, the assessment of control risk at slightly below the maximum or high, and the basis for that assessment, should be documented.

The final decision symbol in the 'Predominantly substantive approach' column requires the auditor to consider whether the actual assessed level of control risk supports the planned level of substantive tests. For example, the auditor might have originally specified the planned level of control risk as high, resulting in the highest planned level of substantive tests. But if the evidence acquired while obtaining the required understanding supports an actual assessment of control risk as high, revision of the planned level of substantive tests to a lower level will be appropriate. The auditor then proceeds with the detailed design of the appropriate level of substantive tests.

Lower assessed level of control risk approach

In some cases a lower assessed level of control risk approach is planned because the client has effective internal controls and the auditor plans to test those controls, reduce control risk, and modify the nature, timing or extent of substantive tests accordingly. This is often the case with audits of public companies. The auditor sometimes plans a lower assessed level of control risk approach because substantive tests alone will not reduce audit risk to a sufficiently low level.

A more extensive understanding and documentation of relevant internal controls, particularly the control activities component of internal controls, is ordinarily appropriate in order to support the auditor's planned level of control risk of moderate or low for an assertion. Conceivably, the auditor might find that, contrary to expectations, the control appears to be ineffective. In such a case, it is appropriate to change the strategy to a predominantly substantive approach. In figure 11.1, this is reflected in the 'No' branch extending to the left from the first decision symbol in the 'Lower assessed level of control risk approach' column.

If the auditor continues with the lower assessed level of control risk approach, he or she plans and performs the additional tests of controls. The evidence obtained from the tests of controls is then evaluated to make the final or actual assessment of control risk. The final assessment and the basis for that assessment are then documented in the auditor's working papers.

The final decision symbol in the 'Lower assessed level of control risk approach' column in figure 11.1 requires the auditor to consider whether the actual assessed level of control risk supports the planned level of substantive tests and, if not, to revise the planned substantive tests. For example, the auditor might have originally specified a planned low assessed level of control risk, resulting in the lowest planned level of substantive tests. But if evidence from tests of controls leads to an actual assessed level of control risk of medium, revision of the planned substantive tests to support a lower level of detection risk will be appropriate. Or, if contrary to expectations the controls are found to be highly ineffective (control risk is assessed at high or maximum), the auditor would need to revise the planned level of substantive tests to reflect a change to a predominantly substantive approach. This is represented by the dotted line slanting downwards to the left in the revised planned level of substantive tests block near the bottom of figure 11.1. In either case, this figure depicts the repetitive nature of the audit process, and the final step involves designing the detailed substantive tests appropriate for the circumstances.

Do you know . . .

11.1 ☐ Tests of controls are a form of audit evidence. With good results from tests of controls, an auditor may be able to reduce the level of substantive testing of transactions and balances.

11.2 ☐ If the preliminary assessment of internal controls suggests that the controls cannot be relied on, the auditor should go straight to performing substantive testing.

11.3 ☐ Where an auditor decides to use a substantive approach to obtaining evidence, he or she must still obtain an understanding of internal controls to assess the risk of possible financial statement misstatements.

LEARNING ② objective

Describe the purpose of tests of controls and the nature, timing and extent of such tests.

11.2 TESTS OF CONTROLS

Tests of controls are auditing procedures performed to determine the effectiveness of the design and operation of internal controls. The auditor should obtain audit evidence through tests of controls to support any assessment of control risk that is less than high. The lower the assessment of control risk, the more support the auditor should obtain that internal control systems are suitably designed and operating effectively. This is reflected in the requirement of ASA 330 *The Auditor's Responses to Assessed Risks*, paragraph 8 (ISA 330.8), which states that the auditor shall perform tests of controls where the assessment of the risks of material misstatement includes an expectation that controls are operating effectively or where substantive procedures alone cannot provide sufficient appropriate audit evidence.

Tests of controls relating to design are concerned with whether the control is designed to prevent or detect misstatements in a specific financial statement assertion. Tests of controls relating to the **operating effectiveness of the control procedures** are concerned with whether controls are actually working. Tests of operating effectiveness focus on two questions:

1. How was the control applied?
2. Was it applied consistently during the year?

A control is operating effectively when it has been properly and consistently applied during the year by the employee(s) authorised to apply it. In contrast, failure to apply a control properly and consistently, or application of that control by an unauthorised employee, indicates ineffective operation. Such failures are referred to as **deviations**. This terminology is preferable to the term 'error' because a failure in performance indicates only that there may be an error in the accounting records. The failure, for example, of a second employee to verify the accuracy of a sales invoice is a deviation, but the document could still be correct if the first employee prepared it correctly.

Tests of controls are performed to obtain evidence about the design of the effectiveness of the internal control structure as well as the operation of internal controls. Tests of design effectiveness are normally performed when obtaining an understanding (already discussed in this chapter). The focus of the following discussion is on tests of the operation of internal controls, which are performed mainly at the interim audit but also at the final audit.

11.2.1 Designing tests

In designing tests of the operating effectiveness of controls, the auditor must decide their nature, timing and extent.

Nature of tests

The auditor's choices in terms of the nature of tests of controls are:
- *enquiring* of personnel about the performance of their duties
- *observing* personnel perform their duties
- *inspecting* documents and reports indicating performance of controls
- *re-performing* the control.

In performing the tests, the auditor selects the procedure that will provide the most reliable evidence about the effectiveness of the control.

Enquiring is designed to determine:
- employees' understanding of their duties
- how employees perform those duties
- the frequency, cause(s) and disposition of deviations.

Observing employees' performance provides similar evidence. This procedure should be done without the employees' knowledge or on a surprise basis. Enquiring and observing are very useful ways of obtaining evidence about the control procedure of segregation of duties. However, evidence obtained from observation has the following limitations.
- Employees may perform the control differently when not being observed.
- The evidence applies only to the time the observation occurs.

Inspecting documents and records is applicable when there is a transaction trail of signatures and validation stamps that indicate whether the control was performed and by whom. Any document or record that fails to evidence the required performance is a deviation, regardless of whether the document is correct.

Re-performance is a **dual-purpose test** in that it provides evidence as both a test of controls and a substantive test of detail. Where such a test reveals an error, it suggests the failure of controls intended to prevent such errors. Assume, for example, that the control procedure of independent checks requires a second clerk in the invoicing department to check the correctness of unit selling prices on sales invoices by comparing them with an authorised price list. On doing so, the employee initials a copy of the invoice to indicate performance of the independent check. In testing this control procedure, the auditor inspects invoices for the employee's initials and may re-perform the process by comparing selling prices on invoices with the authorised price list. Such a test doubles as both a test of controls and a substantive test of details, because any errors detected provide evidence both of a failure to perform the independent check properly (a deviation) and of monetary errors in the transactions recorded. When this type of testing is done, the auditor should exercise care in designing the tests to ensure that evidence is obtained as to both the effectiveness of controls and the monetary errors in the accounts. The auditor should also be careful in evaluating the evidence obtained.

Timing of tests of controls

The timing of tests of controls refers to the part of the accounting period to which they relate. Planned tests of controls are performed during interim work, which may be several months before the end of the year under audit. These tests, therefore, provide evidence of the effectiveness of controls only from the beginning of the year to the date of the tests. However, the presumption behind assessing the control risk as less than high is that it is an assessment on the controls for the whole period of the audit. So to make that assessment, the auditor must test the controls for the whole period. Thus, for audit efficiency, the auditor should perform the tests of controls as late in the interim period as possible.

The need to perform additional tests of controls later in the year depends on:

- the length of the remaining period
- the occurrence of significant changes in controls subsequent to interim testing, causing the auditor to revise his or her understanding of the internal control system
- the decision to perform substantive tests of details on balances before the year-end (such as confirming accounts receivable one month before year-end), thus requiring assurance that control procedures remained effective in the period between the date of substantive procedures and year-end.

An advantage of performing these tests during interim work is that the auditor can get an early idea as to whether the controls are operating as expected. If they are not, there is sufficient time to change the extent of substantive tests before final audit work.

Extent of tests

More extensive tests of controls provide more evidence of the operating effectiveness of a control. Asking more than one person about the same control procedure, for example, provides more evidence than a single enquiry; similarly, a more extensive inspection of documents for initials or signatures indicating performance of a control procedure provides more evidence than examining fewer documents would.

The extent of tests of controls is determined by the auditor's planned assessed level of control risk. More extensive testing will be needed for a low assessed level of control risk than for a moderate level. This testing by the auditor is only to confirm the preliminary assessment of control risk, which is limited by the control environment and the design of the controls. This means that increasing the extent of the testing cannot cause the auditor to lower the assessed level of control risk.

11.2.2 Audit programs for tests of controls

Documenting work performed and evidence obtained as part of the audit is discussed in chapter 8. The audit testing of controls needs to be documented to provide evidence to support the auditor's reliance on the controls as indicated by the level of control risk assessed. The auditor's decisions regarding the nature, timing and extent of tests of controls should be documented in an audit program and related working papers. A sample audit program for tests of controls of cash payment transactions is illustrated in figure 11.2. This provides details on a number of tests of controls in an IT environment (discussed later in this chapter). The program lists the procedures to be used in performing the tests for indicated assertions. All testing performed by the auditor is linked back to the management assertions.

The audit program also provides columns to indicate:

- cross-references to the working papers in which the test results are documented
- who performed the tests
- the date on which the tests were completed.

Details concerning the extent and timing of the tests may be indicated in the audit program or in the working papers, as assumed in figure 11.2. Further examples of documentation in relation to tests of controls is provided in chapters 14 to 17.

| | | Prepared by: _____ Date: _____ | | |
| | | Reviewed by: _____ Date: _____ | | |

Amalgamated Products, Inc.
Planned Tests of Controls — Cash Distribution Transactions
Year Ending December 31, 20XX

Working paper reference	Assertion/tests of controls	Auditor	Date
	1. Arrange to use the client's computer facilities to test programmed application controls using test data.		
	Occurrence		
	2. Submit test data to ascertain that the program properly identifies exceptions for:		
	a. Transactions where the voucher information does not match with underlying supporting information. (*Note:* This also tests controls over valuation.)		
	b. Transactions that are submitted twice.		
	3. Inspect exception reports issued by the computer in the normal course of business and evaluate the effectiveness of manual follow-up procedures.		
	4. Observe that only authorised personnel are permitted to handle cheques when the computer signs cheques.		
	5. Observe segregation of duties between approving vouchers for payment and the handling of signed cheques.		
	6. Inspect documents to ascertain that payment vouchers and supporting documents are stamped 'paid' when the cheque is issued.		
	Completeness		
	7. Submit test data to ascertain that the program properly identifies exceptions for:		
	a. Breaks in the sequence of prenumbered cheques.		
	b. Mismatches between the sum of checks issued and the total posting to cash disbursements. (*Note:* This also tests controls over valuation.)		
	8. Observe handling and storage of unused cheques.		
	9. Make inquires about any cash disbursements paid by a method other than by cheque.		
	10. Inspect independent bank reconciliations and evaluate the effectiveness of this control. (*Note:* This control also tests controls over existence and occurrence and valuation.)		

FIGURE 11.2: Illustrative partial audit program for tests of controls

Source: Adapted from W Boynton & R Johnson, *Modern Auditing*, John Wiley and Sons, 2007, p. 493.

LEARNING 3
objective

*Clarify how the work of
internal auditing may be
used in tests of controls.*

11.3 USING INTERNAL AUDITORS

Internal audit is generally considered a crucial part of the corporate governance structure of a company. Many companies have internal auditors as full-time employees or contract out the internal audit function to an accounting firm. (We discuss the internal audit, as a distinct audit activity, in chapter 2.) Whenever an entity has an internal audit function, the auditor may coordinate the audit work with that of the internal auditors and/or use the internal auditors to provide direct assistance in the audit.

11.3.1 Coordination with internal auditors

Internal auditors will usually monitor the internal control system in each division or branch as part of their regular duties. The monitoring may include periodic reviews. In such cases, the independent auditor may coordinate work with the internal auditors and reduce the number of entity locations at which they would otherwise perform tests of controls. The auditor must first consider the effectiveness of the internal auditors by:
- considering their organisational status:
  - Do they report to the highest level of management (preferably an audit committee)?
  - Are they free of operating responsibilities?
  - Are they free to communicate fully with the independent auditor?
- determining the scope of their work and, in particular, whether management acts on their recommendations
- evaluating their technical competence
- ensuring that their work is performed with due professional care.

The main focus of internal auditors is usually on the internal control system within the company. Therefore, the reliance (if any) that the external auditor places on the internal auditor's work is in supporting the preliminary assessment of control risk rather than assisting with any of the external auditor's substantive testing. If reliance is to be placed on the internal auditor, ASA 610 *Using the Work of Internal Auditors* (ISA 610) states in paragraph 11 (ISA 610.11) that where the external auditor intends to use the work of the internal auditors, they shall evaluate and perform audit procedures on that work to ensure it is adequate.

Furthermore, ASA 610 (ISA 610) requires the independent auditor to confirm that:
- the work is performed by persons who have adequate technical training and proficiency as internal auditors
- the work of assistants is properly supervised, reviewed and documented
- sufficient appropriate audit evidence is obtained to afford a reasonable basis for the conclusions reached
- the conclusions reached are appropriate in the circumstances
- any reports prepared by internal audit are consistent with the results of the work performed
- any exceptions or unusual matters disclosed by internal auditors are properly resolved.

In coordinating work with internal auditors, the auditor may find it efficient to have periodic meetings with them, review their work schedules, obtain access to their working papers and review internal auditor's reports.

If the external auditor is satisfied that reliance can be placed on the internal audit function, it is potentially a very useful asset in performing the financial statement audit. If the internal auditors are full-time employees of the entity, it means that they are on location all of the time, which puts them in an ideal position to monitor the entity's internal controls. The external auditor cannot efficiently provide the same level of monitoring and is unlikely to be on the client's premises over the course of the year for any more than a few weeks (depending on the size of the client).

LEARNING objective 4

Explain the process of assessing control risk and documenting the conclusion.

11.4 FINAL ASSESSMENT OF CONTROL RISK

The final assessment of control risk for a financial statement assertion is based on evaluating the evidence gained from (1) procedures to obtain an understanding of relevant internal control system components and (2) related tests of controls. When different types of evidence support the same conclusion about the effectiveness of a control, the degree of assurance increases. Conversely, when they support different conclusions, the degree of assurance decreases; for example, the initials of an employee may be consistently present on documents, indicating performance of a control procedure, but the auditor's enquiries of the person initialling the documents may reveal that employee's lack of understanding of the control procedure being applied. The oral evidence reduces the assurance obtained from the inspection of initials on the documents.

The evaluation of evidence involves both quantitative and qualitative considerations. In forming a conclusion about the effectiveness of a control procedure, the auditor often uses guidelines concerning the tolerable frequency of deviations from the proper performance of a control (usually expressed as a percentage). If the results lead the auditor to conclude that the frequency of deviations is less than or equal to the tolerable level, then the operation of the control is considered effective. Before reaching this conclusion, the auditor should also consider the causes of the deviations; for example, the auditor may attach different significance to excessive deviations caused by a temporary staff member than to those caused by an experienced employee. It is also essential in reaching a conclusion about effectiveness to determine whether a deviation is attributable to unintentional errors or to deliberate misrepresentations (irregularities). Evidence of one deviation due to an irregularity may be more important to the auditor than are more frequent deviations caused by errors. When it is concluded that the nature and frequency of deviations exceeds the tolerable level, the preliminary assessed level of control risk is not confirmed. In this case, the auditor must revise the audit program for substantive procedures reflecting either a higher level of control risk than originally planned or the adoption of a predominantly substantive strategy for that particular assertion.

11.4.1 Documenting the assessed level of control risk

The auditor's working papers should include documentation of the control risk. Where control risk is assessed as high, only this conclusion needs to be documented. Where control risk is assessed as less than high, the basis for the assessment must be documented.

A common approach is to use narrative memoranda organised by financial statement assertions. This approach is illustrated in figure 11.3 (overleaf), which documents the control risk assessments for selected sales transaction assertions.

CLIENT _Young Fashions Ltd_   **BALANCE SHEET DATE** _30/6/15_

Completed by: _CRS_   **Date:** _19/2/15_   **Reviewed by:** _RMT_   **Date:** _28/2/15_

Control risk assessment for: Sales transactions

COMPLETENESS

Entity internal control structure policies and procedures relevant to completeness relate primarily to the computer listing of unmatched sales orders, bills of lading, packing slips and sales invoices. Based on discussions with sales ledger personnel on 11/2/14 and with selected shipping personnel at Perth and Adelaide locations on 18/1/14 and 8/2/14, respectively, it normally can take up to two weeks between the placing of a sales order and shipment. It is rare, however, for an unmatched bill of lading or packing slip to remain on the unmatched documents report for more than two days. This was corroborated by examining the unmatched documents report for selected days (see W/P XX–4–2 [not illustrated here]) where the longest period a bill of lading or packing slip was outstanding was two days. Selected transactions on these reports were traced to underlying documents with no exceptions.

    Based on this examination of audit evidence, combined with the results of inquiry of sales ledger and shipping personnel and corroborating observations, control risk is assessed as slightly less than high.

RIGHTS AND OBLIGATIONS

Control risk is assessed as high.

FIGURE 11.3: Partial documentation of control risk assessments

Source: Adapted from Audit Guide: Consideration of the Internal Control Structure in a Financial Statement Audit, AICPA, 1990, p. 145.

LEARNING objective 5

Indicate the appropriate communications the auditor makes on internal control matters.

11.5 COMMUNICATION OF INTERNAL CONTROL MATTERS

Although the auditor has no responsibility to provide any level of assurance on the controls operating within the company as part of the financial statement audit, under ASA 265 _Communicating Deficiencies in Internal Control to Those Charged with Governance and Management_, paragraph 9 (ISA 265.9), there is a duty to communicate in writing significant deficiencies in internal control to those charged with governance.

In terms of determining what is a 'significant deficiency', some possible considerations (summarised from ASA 265, paragraph A6 (ISA 265)) include:

- likelihood of the deficiencies leading to material misstatements in the financial statements in the future
- susceptibility to loss or fraud of the related asset or liability
- subjectivity and complexity of determining estimated amounts, such as fair value accounting estimates
- financial report amounts exposed to the deficiencies
- volume of activity that has occurred or could occur in the account balance or class of transactions exposed to the deficiency or deficiencies
- balance or class of transactions exposed to the deficiency or deficiencies
- the importance of the controls to the financial reporting process.

The auditor shall also communicate this information to management unless there are circumstances which would make it inappropriate to do so. This shall include other deficiencies that are of sufficient importance to merit management's attention. When this communication is made, it is important that the auditor communicates that the purpose of the audit was to express an opinion on the financial report and not on the effectiveness of internal control.

There is no question that management and those charged with governance are more interested than ever in ensuring that controls are operating appropriately within their organisations. Recently, guidance was issued from the International Federation of Accountants on key principles of evaluating and improving internal control that are outlined in the Professional Environment box below.

PROFESSIONAL ENVIRONMENT
Evaluating and improving internal control

These key principles represent good practice for evaluating and improving systems for internal control:

A. Internal control should be used to support the organization in achieving its objectives by managing its risks, while complying with rules, regulations, and organizational policies. The organization should therefore make internal control part of risk management and integrate both in its overall governance system.

B. The organization should determine the various roles and responsibilities with respect to internal control, including the governing body, management at all levels, employees, and internal and external assurance providers, as well as coordinate the collaboration among participants.

C. The governing body and management should foster an organizational culture that motivates members of the organization to act in line with risk management strategy and policies on internal control set by the governing body to achieve the organization's objectives. The tone and action at the top are critical in this respect.

D. The governing body and management should link achievement of the organization's internal control objectives to individual performance objectives. Each person within the organization should be held accountable for the achievement of assigned internal control objectives.

E. The governing body, management, and other participants in the organization's governance system should be sufficiently competent to fulfill the internal control responsibilities associated with their roles.

F. Controls should always be designed, implemented, and applied as a response to specific risks and their causes and consequences.

G. Management should ensure that regular communication regarding the internal control system, as well as the outcomes, takes place at all levels within the organization to make sure that the internal control principles are fully understood and correctly applied by all.

H. Both individual controls as well as the internal control system as a whole should be regularly monitored and evaluated. Identification of unacceptably high levels of risk, control failures, or events that are outside the limits for risk taking could be a sign that an individual control or the internal control system is ineffective and needs to be improved.

I. The governing body, together with management, should periodically report to stakeholders the organization's risk profile as well as the structure and factual performance of the organization's internal control system.

Source: Evaluating and Improving Internal Controls in Organizations: Executive Summary, Copyright © April 2013 by IFAC. All rights reserved.

The importance of internal control is such that the auditor may sometimes be employed by management to give an opinion on the effectiveness of the organisation's internal controls. This is a separate engagement from the work carried out for the purposes of the financial statements audit, and therefore a new engagement letter is required. The specific engagement to give an opinion on the internal controls requires work beyond that needed for the purposes of the financial statement audit, and a specific report is required. These procedures are covered by AUS 810 *Special Purpose Reports on the Effectiveness of Control Procedures*.

See chapter 18 for more detail about communicating to those charged with governance.

Do you know . . .

11.4 ☐ The preliminary assessment of control risk is designed to obtain a reasonable expectation of controls so as to decide on an appropriate audit strategy for designing a detailed audit program.

11.5 ☐ Planned tests of controls are performed where the preliminary assessment of control risk is less than high. The purpose of testing is to provide evidence to support the preliminary assessment of control risk.

11.6 ☐ Tests of controls include enquiring of personnel, observing personnel, inspecting documents and reports, and re-performing the control.

11.7 ☐ The extent of control testing is inversely related to the preliminary assessment of control risk (i.e. low control risk requires extensive testing whereas a high control risk requires no testing).

LEARNING objective 6

Describe the types of controls you would expect to see in an information technology environment.

11.6 TYPES OF CONTROLS IN AN INFORMATION TECHNOLOGY ENVIRONMENT

Information processing controls include both general control procedures and application control procedures. In addition, the auditor should be aware of manual follow-up procedures for the transactions identified by application controls and the possibility of user controls directly relating to an assertion. These procedures are summarised in figure 11.4. This figure helps us understand three important audit strategies for performing tests of controls when accounting and control systems make extensive use of information technology (IT).

The auditor should choose among the following three strategies when assessing control risk:

1. assessing control risk based on user controls
2. planning for a low control risk assessment based on application controls
3. planning for a high control risk assessment based on general controls and manual follow-up. Each strategy is now explained.

User controls

In many cases, the client may design manual procedures to test the completeness and accuracy of transactions processed by the computer. For example, managers who are familiar with transactions that they have authorised may review a list of purchases that have been charged to their responsibility centre. Alternatively, an individual in a user department may compare computer-generated output with source documents supporting the transaction. Although both of these controls may detect and correct misstatements, the latter may be performed with a greater level of detail and may provide a higher level of assurance that misstatements are detected and corrected.

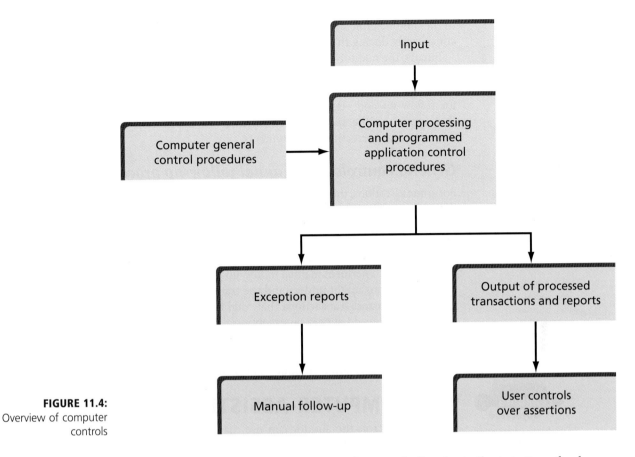

FIGURE 11.4:
Overview of computer controls

If user controls exist, the auditor can test the controls directly, similar to testing other human controls. This is also known as 'auditing around the computer'. The advantage of this strategy for testing controls is that there is no need to test the complexities of computer programs.

Application controls

Many auditors take advantage of automated controls and plan strategies for assessing control risk at a low level based on computer application controls. In order to execute this strategy, the auditor should:

- test the computer application controls
- test computer general controls
- test the manual follow-up of exceptions noted by application controls.

The effectiveness of all three levels of controls is important to a low control risk assessment. First, the auditor should test computer application controls using some form of computer-assisted audit techniques (CAATs). The purpose is to determine that the application control properly identifies exceptions.

Second, computer general controls must also be tested. General controls provide assurance that application controls are properly designed and tested, and any changes are authorised. In essence, they provide increased assurance that application controls function consistently over time. Evidence about strong general controls allows the auditor to test applications at one point in time and believe that they functioned in the same fashion at other times during the audit period. An auditor may test a computer program at a particular point in time to obtain evidence about whether the program executes the control effectively. To improve the timeliness of evidence, the auditor then performs tests of controls relating to the modification and use of that program and whether the programmed control operated consistently during the period (i.e. testing general controls).

Finally, the auditor must also test the effectiveness of manual follow-up procedures. For example, let us assume that computer application controls correctly identify transactions where the amount is wrongly recorded and report these transactions on an exception report for follow-up and correction. If the manual follow-up is ineffective in correcting items that appear on the exception report, then the application control becomes ineffective in detecting and correcting misstatements.

General controls and manual follow-up procedures

For some assertions, the auditor may plan an audit strategy that emphasises tests of details, and the auditor may plan a high control risk assessment for an assertion. When the auditor tests general controls, he or she will usually learn about the effectiveness of the design and testing of application controls. In addition, the auditor may be able to make inferences about the effectiveness of application controls in identifying exceptions through enquiry of knowledgeable individuals who perform manual follow-up procedures. For example, individuals who follow up on exceptions might understand the transaction stream in sufficient detail that they can predict and correct transactions that might otherwise appear on exception reports. When such transactions do appear on exception reports, the auditor may be able to draw an inference about the programmed control. This evidence may be sufficient to allow the auditor to assess control risk at a high level, but the auditor should test programs directly with computer-assisted audit techniques if he or she wants to assess control risk as medium or low.

LEARNING objective 7

Identify the alternative types of computer-assisted audit techniques.

11.7 COMPUTER-ASSISTED AUDIT TECHNIQUES

In testing controls the auditor can use manual audit procedures, computer-assisted audit techniques or a combination of these to obtain the necessary evidence. However, where a computer is used for processing significant applications, it may be difficult to obtain data for testing without computer assistance. This is particularly the case with testing programmed application controls whose performance do not leave a visible trail. In such situations, auditors use of a variety of computer-assisted audit techniques such as test data, integrated test facility and parallel simulation.

11.7.1 Test data

Under the **test data approach**, dummy transactions are prepared by the auditor and processed under auditor control by the entity's software. The test data consist of one transaction for each valid or invalid condition that the auditor wants to test. Payroll test data, for example, may include both a valid and an invalid overtime pay condition. The output from processing the test data is then compared with the auditor's expected output to determine whether the controls are operating effectively. The test data approach has the following advantages.

- It is a way of auditing 'through the computer'.
- It is simple to use.
- There is not much disruption to the client's computer system.

However, the method has the following audit deficiencies:

- The method is a test only of the presence and functioning of controls in the program tested.
- There is no examination of documentation actually processed by the system.
- Computer operators know that test data are being run, which could reduce the validity of the output.
- It is a test at a specific time and therefore does not show how the system operated throughout the period.

11.7.2 Integrated test facility

The **integrated test facility** (ITF) approach overcomes some of the limitations of the use of test data. It requires the creation of a small subsystem (a mini-company) within the regular computer accounting system. This may be accomplished by creating dummy master files or appending dummy master records to existing entity files. Dummy records, specially coded to correspond to the dummy master files, are introduced into the system, together with actual transactions. The dummy records should include all kinds of transaction errors and exceptions that may be encountered. In this manner, the dummy records are subjected to the same programmed controls as are placed on the actual data. A separate set of outputs is produced for the subsystem of dummy files. The results can be compared with those expected by the auditor.

The advantages of the ITF approach are that it allows for ongoing testing of the internal control system and requires minimal disruption to the client. It is a popular approach for internal auditors.

A disadvantage of the ITF approach is the risk that errors could be created in entity data. In addition, the entity's programs may need to be modified to accommodate the dummy data.

11.7.3 Parallel simulation

Parallel simulation involves reprocessing actual entity data using auditor-controlled software. This method is so named because the software is designed to reproduce or simulate the entity's processing of real data. A graphic portrayal of this approach is shown on the left half of figure 11.5. This approach does not corrupt the entity's files and may be conducted at an independent computer facility. It has the following advantages.

- Because real data are used, the auditor can verify transactions by tracing them to source documents and approvals.
- The size of the sample can be greatly expanded at relatively little additional cost.
- The auditor can independently run the test.

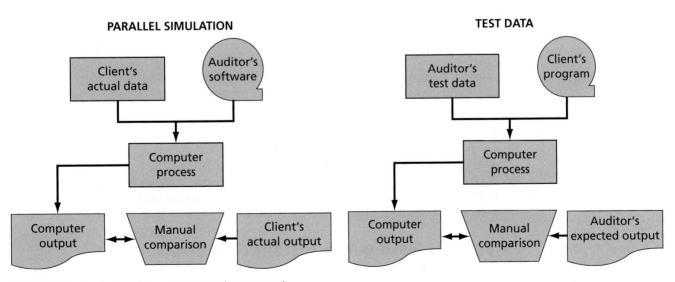

FIGURE 11.5: Parallel simulation versus test data approach

Source: W Boynton & R Johnson, *Modern Auditing*, John Wiley and Sons, 2007, p. 479.

If the auditor decides to use parallel simulation, care must be taken to determine that the data selected for simulation are representative of actual entity transactions and include errors intended to be detected by the application of programmed controls. The auditor must ensure that the input data used for testing are complete. That is, they should not have been subject to corrections or adjustments because of the application of input controls when they were processed in the real system.

A graphic portrayal of both parallel simulation and the test data approach is shown in figure 11.5.

11.7.4 Continuous monitoring of online real-time systems

Test data may be used to test controls in an online entry/online processing system (also known as an online real-time system (OLRT)). However, this approach is not widely used by auditors because of the contamination of file data and the difficulty of reversing the hypothetical data. Parallel simulation may also be used, but the availability of generalised audit software that can be used to simulate OLRT processing is very limited.

In lieu of traditional testing, the auditor often arranges for continuous monitoring of the system. Under this technique, an audit routine is added to the client's processing programs. Transactions entering the system are sampled at random intervals, and the output from the routine is used in testing the controls.

To provide for the integration of audit software into a real-time processing system, audit hook capabilities must be built into the client's computer programs — both the operating systems and application programs — at the time they are created. Audit hooks are points in a program that allow audit modules, or programs, to be integrated into the system's normal processing activities. These audit modules provide the auditor with a means of selecting transactions possessing characteristics of interest to the auditor, such as a transaction of a certain kind or an amount greater or lesser than a given value. Once a particular transaction has been identified as being of interest, a record of it can be retained by one of several methods. Two of these are tagging transactions and a systems control audit review file.

Tagging transactions

The tagging transactions method involves placing an indicator, or tag, on selected transactions. The presence of this tag enables a transaction to be traced through the system as it is being processed. The system must be programmed to provide for the creation of a hardcopy printout of all paths followed by the transaction. Data with which the tagged transaction interacts at designated steps in the processing can be captured as well.

Systems control audit review file

A systems control audit review file (SCARF) (sometimes called an audit log) is a record of certain processing activities. The file is used to record events that meet auditor-specified criteria as they occur at designated points in the system. Identified transactions or events are logged onto a file available only to the auditor. The auditor can later analyse the file and make further tests as appropriate.

11.7.5 Assessing and testing IT controls

Tables 11.1 and 11.2 (overleaf) show representative listings of potential misstatements and necessary controls for general controls and application controls, respectively. Table 11.1 provides a general way of thinking about input, processing and output controls that may facilitate thinking about testing application controls. However, the auditor will normally identify potential misstatements relevant to specific assertions of audit interest, then establish what controls (including application controls) exist, and finally design appropriate tests of controls.

Tests of controls are performed to obtain evidence about the effectiveness of the design or operation of the control. The auditor performs such tests when there is reason to believe that the evidence will permit a further reduction in the assessed level of control risk. The third column in both table 11.1 and 11.2 shows possible tests of controls. Tests of computer-generated controls involve the observations of segregation of duties and inspection of documentation showing that computer general controls were performed. Tests of computer application controls involve some form of computer-assisted audit techniques (CAATs) and testing of manual follow-up procedures.

TABLE 11.1:
Control risk assessment considerations for computer general controls

Potential misstatement	Necessary controls	Tests of controls
Organisational and operational controls		
Computer operators may modify programs to bypass programmed controls.	Segregation of duties within IT for computer programming and computer operations.	Observe segregation of duties within IT.
IT personnel may initiate and process unauthorised transactions.	Segregation of duties between user departments and IT for initiating and processing transactions.	Observe segregation of duties between user departments and IT.
System development and documentation controls		
System design may not meet the needs of user departments or auditors.	Participation of personnel from user departments and internal audit in design and approving new systems.	Enquire about participants involved in designing new systems; examine evidence for approval of new system.
Unauthorised program changes may result in unexpected processing errors.	Internal verification of proper authorisation, testing and documentation of program changes before implementation.	Examine evidence of internal verification; trace selected program changes to supporting documentation.
Hardware and system controls		
Equipment malfunction may result in processing errors.	Built-in hardware and system software controls to detect malfunctions.	Examine hardware and system software specifications.
Unauthorised changes in system software may result in processing errors.	Approval and documentation of all system software changes.	Examine evidence of approval and documentation changes.
Access controls		
Unauthorised users may gain access to IT equipment.	Physical security of IT facilities; management review of use reports.	Inspect security arrangements and use reports.
Data files and programs may be processed or altered by unauthorised users.	Use of library, librarian and logs to restrict access and monitor use.	Inspect facilities and logs.

(continued)

TABLE 11.1:
(continued)

Potential misstatement	Necessary controls	Tests of controls
Data and procedural controls		
Errors may be made in inputting or processing data or distributing output.	Use of data control group responsible for maintaining control over data input, processing and output.	Observe operation of data control group.
Continuity of operations may be disrupted by disaster such as fire or flood.	Contingency plan including arrangements for use of off-premises backup facilities.	Examine contingency plan.
Data files and programs may be damaged or lost.	Storage of backup files and programs off premises; provision for reconstruction of data files.	Examine storage facilities; evaluate file reconstruction capability.

TABLE 11.2:
Control risk assessment considerations for computer application controls

Potential misstatement	Necessary controls	Tests of controls
Input controls		
Data for unauthorised transactions may be submitted for processing.	Authorisation and approval of data in user departments; application controls compares data with previous authorisation.	Examine source documents and batch transmittals for evidence of approval; test application control with CAATs and test manual follow-up.
Valid data may be incorrectly converted to machine-sensible form.	Verification (rekeying); computer editing, control totals.	Observe data verification procedures; use CAATs to test edit routines and test manual follow-up; examine control total reconciliations.
Errors on source documents may not be corrected and resubmitted.	Maintenance of error logs; return to user department for correction; manual follow-up.	Inspect error logs and evidence of follow-up.
Processing controls		
Wrong files may be processed and updated.	Use of external and internal file labels.	Observe use of external file labels; examine documentation for internal file labels.
Data may be lost, added, duplicated or altered during processing.	Use of control totals, limit and reasonableness checks, and sequence tests.	Examine evidence of control total reconciliations; use CAATs to test computer checks and test manual follow-up.
Output control		
Output may be incorrect.	Reconciliation of totals by data control group or user department.	Examine evidence of reconciliations.
Output may be distributed to unauthorised users.	Use of report distribution control sheets; data control group monitoring.	Inspect report distribution control sheets; observe data control group monitoring.

In a computerised system, controls may or may not produce visible evidence. When the computer produces visible evidence to verify that procedures were in operation and to evaluate the propriety of performance, tests of IT controls may include inspection of documentation. However, if such evidence is not generated by the computer, the tests of controls must include CAATs. The Professional Environment box discusses some recent research that evaluated whether control risk assessment and audit firm size influenced the use of CAATs or computer-related audit procedures.

PROFESSIONAL ENVIRONMENT

Factors relating to the use of computer-related audit procedures

*T*his study examines the extent to which computer-related audit procedures are used and whether two factors, control risk assessment and audit firm size, influence computer-related audit procedure use.

Audit firm size may impact the use of computer-related audit procedures given that clients of Big 4 firms are more likely than those of smaller firms to have more complex IT. Previous research has not addressed the extent to which firm size affects the use of computer-related audit procedures. Moreover, recent research suggests that national audit firms have gained market share in the post-Andersen period (Cassell et al. 2007; Krishnan et al. 2008). National firms' clients are likely to have more complex IT than local or regional firms, but less than Big 4 firms. Therefore, an open question is whether national firms' use of computer-related audit procedures resembles that of the Big 4 firms or smaller firms?

We examine computer-related audit procedure use, as well as how control risk assessment and audit firm size influences use, via a field-based instrument. The instrument was completed by 181 auditors representing Big 4, national, regional, and local firms. Results suggest that computer-related audit procedures are generally used when obtaining an understanding of the client systems and business processes and when testing application and general computer controls. Moreover, 42.9 per cent of participants assess control risk less than maximum, which is almost double the rate found in previous research based on a single international audit firm (Waller 1993). In engagements where control risk is assessed at less than maximum, computer-related audit procedures and IT specialists are more likely to be used, than when control risk is assessed at maximum. Findings indicate that in engagements involving Big 4 audit firms, control risk is more likely to be assessed at less than maximum and computer-related audit procedures and IT specialists are more likely to be used than in engagements involving smaller audit firms. Furthermore, while auditors employed by national audit firms are more likely to have control risk assessed below maximum than those working for smaller audit firms, use of computer-related audit procedures is surprisingly similar.

Source: D Janvrin, J Bierstaker & D Jordan Lowe, 'An investigation of factors influencing the use of computer-related audit procedures', *Journal of Information Systems* 23(1), 2009, pp. 97–118.

Do you know ...

11.8 ☐ In order to be satisfied that application controls are operating correctly, the auditor must also test general controls to ensure that application controls are properly designed, tested and any changes authorised.

11.9 ☐ CAATs include parallel simulation, test data, integrated test facility, continuous monitoring of online real-time systems, tagging transactions, and systems control audit review file (SCARF).

11.10 ☐ The procedure for assessing controls applies equally to manual and computer controls, and the outcome of tests of manual, general and application controls needs to be assessed before moving on to substantive testing.

SUMMARY

Internal controls are very important in ensuring that transactions are processed correctly. As such, internal control is something that should be important for all but the very smallest of entities. The importance of internal control to the effective operation of the entity is why the auditor is required to obtain an understanding of the controls relevant to the audit. This is when the auditor makes a preliminary assessment of control risk.

Where the preliminary assessment of control risk is less than high for a particular assertion, the auditor may decide to rely on these controls in performing the audit. As discussed in chapter 9, where reliance is placed on internal controls the auditor can reduce the required level of substantive procedures that would otherwise be performed to obtain the sufficient evidence needed to support the audit opinion (discussed further in chapter 12). However, to be able to do this, the auditor must perform tests of the operating effectiveness of the controls to provide evidence supporting the preliminary assessment of control risk. Further discussion of specific control tests for account balances and transactions cycles is provided in chapters 14 to 17.

KEY TERMS

deviations, p. 460

dual-purpose test, p. 461

integrated test facility, p. 471

operating effectiveness of the control procedures, p. 460

parallel simulation, p. 471

test data approach, p. 470

tests of controls, p. 460

MULTIPLE-CHOICE questions

11.1 The relationship between the required understanding of the internal control structure and the preliminary audit strategy is that:
- A. Normally, greater understanding is required when the lower assessed level of control risk approach is used.
- B. Normally, greater understanding is required when the primarily substantive approach is used.
- C. No understanding is required in the planning stage unless tests of controls are a planned part of the strategy.
- D. Normally, less understanding is required when the lower assessed level of control risk approach is used.

11.2 Where a test of controls reveals some problems, under what circumstances will the auditor still be able to rely on the control system?
- A. The total error found was immaterial to the financial statements.
- B. The error was immaterial and discovered to be an isolated departure.
- C. The circumstance did not lead to a material error in the financial statements.
- D. Substantive procedures indicate that no further errors exist.

11.3 What is the purpose of the preliminary assessment of control risk?
- A. To obtain a reasonable expectation of controls so as to decide on an appropriate audit strategy.
- B. To determine the extent to which internal controls have been implemented.
- C. To obtain the necessary information for developing the flowchart.
- D. To provide management with an opinion on the effectiveness of controls.

11.4 If an auditor has performed tests of controls part-way through a company's year at an interim visit, what further procedures are required at the final audit stage?
- A. Further tests of controls over the whole year.
- B. Management representations that no changes were made to internal controls for the remainder of the year.
- C. No further procedures are required unless the auditor becomes aware of any changes to the internal controls.
- D. Carry out further tests covering the period since the interim audit visit.

11.5 Which of the following would be a test of controls relating to sales?
- A. Checking sales orders to ensure orders over a certain value have been authorised by the credit controller.
- B. Checking that the balance on the list of debtors agrees with the sales ledger control account.
- C. Checking that cash received in the bank account agrees with the correct sales ledger account.
- D. Checking that details on a sales invoice agree with the goods dispatch note.

11.6 What would be an appropriate sample of invoices to gain reasonable assurance that all payments are properly authorised as part of the annual audit?
- A. Randomly pick one month and select every invoice for that month.
- B. Randomly select a sample of 100 invoices from throughout the financial year.
- C. Select all invoices greater than $5000 generated throughout the year.
- D. Any of the above tests would be acceptable.

11.7 What is the best way for an auditor to obtain evidence about the controls in relation to 'segregation of duties'?
- A. Inspect documents and records to ensure an independent check has been performed.
- B. Re-perform the task.
- C. Observe personnel performing their duties.
- D. Discuss the performance of duties within the company with the internal auditor.

11.8 Testing the work of the internal auditors is least likely when the external auditor has decided that:
- A. The internal auditors will be used to directly assist in the conduct of the audit.
- B. The internal auditors have operating responsibilities as well as their auditing role.
- C. The internal auditors are full-time employees of the client.
- D. The reports of the internal auditors are consistent with the results of the work performed.

11.9 In a computer information system control procedures that provide reasonable assurance that the recording, processing and reporting of data are properly performed for specific applications are known as:
- A. General controls.
- B. User controls.
- C. Application controls.
- D. Integrated testing.

11.10 The statement that is accurate concerning audit testing is:
- A. The test data approach is relatively complicated, time consuming and expensive.
- B. The test data approach involves dummy transactions prepared by the client and processed under the control of the auditor.
- C. The test data approach involves dummy transactions prepared by the auditor and processed under the control of the client.
- D. The test data approach involves dummy transactions prepared by and processed under the control of the auditor.

REVIEW questions

11.11 Identify the three steps in a preliminary assessment of risk.

11.12 What audit strategy is the auditor likely to adopt if, at the planning stage, control risk is assessed as less than high?

11.13 Why do auditors want to rely on internal controls wherever possible?

11.14 Identify four different types of procedures that an auditor might use when carrying out tests of controls.

11.15 What is the difference between a walk-through review test and a test of controls?

11.16 Outline the factors that will determine whether the auditor has obtained sufficient appropriate evidence to support a particular risk assessment.

11.17 What factors should be considered when the auditor attempts to coordinate his or her work with the entity's internal auditors?

11.18 What is meant by auditing around the computer and why does this increase audit risk?

11.19 What is the difference between test data and integrated test facility?

11.20 What are the difficulties an auditor might come across in using audit software?

BASIC
★
MODERATE
★★
CHALLENGING
★★★

 PROFESSIONAL application questions

11.21 Assessing control risk ★

An auditor is required to obtain a sufficient understanding of each of the components of an entity's system of internal control to plan the audit of the entity's financial statements and to assess control risk for the assertions embodied in the account balance, transaction class, and disclosure components of the financial statements.

Required

(a) Explain the reasons an auditor may assess control risk at the maximum level for one or more assertions embodied in an account balance.
(b) What must an auditor do to support assessing control risk at less than high when the auditor has determined that controls have been placed in operation?

11.22 Reporting weaknesses ★

Jayne Rydell is the auditor of Big Spanners Ltd. At the planning stage of the audit, the internal controls were documented and the preliminary assessment of internal controls suggested that they were effective. The audit strategy was established and required performing tests of controls followed by reduced substantive testing. When the tests of controls were completed, it became clear that some of the internal controls did not operate during the period in the way that they were recorded, and areas of significant control weakness existed. As a result, the audit strategy needs to be amended to extend substantive testing in those areas where no evidence has been obtained from the tests of controls.

Required

What are Jayne's obligations for reporting detected weaknesses in the internal control system of Big Spanners Ltd?

11.23 Potential misstatements ★★

Your firm has been engaged to audit the financial report of Pellerton Ltd. In obtaining an understanding of internal control relating to purchases, the following questionnaire is used:
1. Are all purchase orders supported by an authorised purchase requisition?
2. Are deliveries received checked to ensure all goods on the delivery have been received in good condition?
3. Is the goods delivery note agreed to the approved order?
4. When goods are received is the inventory system amended to reflect the new delivery?
5. Are purchase invoices agreed to delivery notes?
6. Are mathematical checks performed on purchase invoices before they are processed?
7. Are payments made only after receiving and reconciling supplier statements?
8. Are all payments requested supported by authorised invoices?
9. Are all amendments to purchase ledger accounts authorised by the purchase ledger supervisor?

Required

Identify a potential misstatement that could occur, assuming a *No* answer to each question.

11.24 Using internal auditors ★★

Part A

In determining whether and to what extent to use the work of internal auditors, ASA 610 *Using the Work of Internal Auditors*, paragraph 8 states that the external auditor shall determine:

(a) Whether the work of the internal auditors is likely to be adequate for purposes of the audit; and
(b) If so, the planned effect of the work of the internal auditors on the nature, timing or extent of the external auditor's procedures.

Required

In relation to ASA 610, explain the factors the external auditor will consider when evaluating the work of the internal auditor.

Part B

ZPM is a listed limited-liability company with a year-end of 30 June. ZPM's main activity is selling home improvement or 'do-it-yourself' (DIY) products to the public. Products sold range from nails, paint and tools to doors and showers; some stores also sell garden tools and furniture. Products are purchased from approximately 200 different suppliers. ZPM has 103 stores in 8 different countries.

ZPM has a well-staffed internal audit department, who report on a regular basis to the audit committee. Areas where the internal and external auditors may carry out work include:

1. attending the year-end inventory count in 30 stores annually. All stores are visited on a rotational basis
2. checking the internal controls over the procurement systems (e.g. ensuring a liability is only recorded when the inventory has been received)
3. reviewing the operations of the marketing department.

Required

For each of the above three areas, discuss:
(a) the objectives of the internal auditor
(b) the objectives of the external auditor
(c) whether the external auditor will rely on the internal auditor and, if reliance is required, the extent of that reliance.[2]

11.25 Test data ★★

Jasmine Motor Factors Ltd sells car parts to vehicle repair centres. Customers have a login into Jasmine's parts system which allows them to place orders for parts online. If orders are made on the system before 8 am, Jasmine guarantees same day delivery.

You are planning the financial report audit for Jasmine and are considering how you will be able to use computer-assisted audit techniques to audit the company's purchases system. You know from the previous year's audit that there have been problems with the system accepting invalid inputs from suppliers. You have decided to use test data to check the validity of inputs into the purchase system. You have discussed this approach with Jasmine's staff and they have agreed for you to enter dummy transactions onto the live system.

Required

Identify and explain test data that could be used to gain confidence that Jasmine's purchase system does not accept invalid inputs.

11.26 Tests of controls ★★★

Your firm is the external auditor of Bangers-4-U Ltd, a car hire company. The company has an internal audit department, which you have assessed as being well resourced, and an effective and professional team. You are planning your audit work for the year ended 30 June 2015 and are considering the extent to which you will be able to place reliance on their work as part of your audit.

From your initial discussions with the chief internal auditor you have established that the key areas that they have concerned themselves with during the year are:

1. the sales system and the system for recording invoices for vehicle hire as well as the vehicle scheduling system, which aims to minimise the time that vehicles are sitting idle
2. the vehicle acquisition process and asset register
3. purchase ledger processes for paying suppliers.

Required

Discuss the extent to which you will attempt to rely on the work carried out by the internal audit department.

11.27 Testing a system ★★★

Atlantis Standard Goods (ASG) Co has a year-end of 30 June 2015. ASG is a retailer of kitchen appliances such as washing machines, refrigerators and microwaves. All sales are made via the company's website with despatch and delivery of goods to the customers made using ASG's vehicles. Appliances are purchased from many different manufacturers.

The process of making a sale is as follows.

1. Potential customers visit ASG's website and select the kitchen appliance that they require. The website ordering system accesses the inventory specification file to obtain details of products ASG sells.

2. When the customer chooses an appliance, order information including price, item and quantity required are stored in the 'orders pending' file.

3. Online authorisation of credit card details is obtained from the customer's credit card company automatically by ASG's computer systems.

4. Following authorisation, the sale amount is transferred to the computerised-sales day book. At the end of each day the total from this ledger is transferred to the general ledger.

5. Reimbursement of the sale amount is obtained from each credit card company monthly, less the appropriate commission charged by the credit card company.

6. Following authorisation of the credit card, order details are transferred to a 'goods awaiting despatch' file and allocated a unique order reference code. Order details are automatically transferred to the despatch department's computer system.

7. In the despatch department, goods are obtained from the physical inventory, placed on ASG vehicles and the computerised inventory system updated. Order information is downloaded on a handheld computer with a writable screen.

8. On delivery, the customer signs for the goods on the handheld computer. On return to ASG's warehouse, images of the customer signature are uploaded to the orders file which is then flagged as 'order complete'.

Required

Tabulate the audit tests you should carry out on the sales and despatch system, explaining the reason for each test.[3]

11.28 Reporting on internal controls ★★★

You are the manager of a large auditing firm and have recently finalised the audit of Orico Ltd, a large, publicly-listed company. The audit went smoothly and no major problems were encountered. As in previous years, your firm adopted a controls-based approach to the audit, given the efficient and effective internal control structure that Orico has in place. All of the exceptions that were noted in the testing phase were raised with the appropriate level of management and were not considered serious enough to bring to the attention of the board. All follow-up work as a result of these exceptions has been satisfactorily performed.

The financial controller, Tom DeSouza, has received a request from the overseas parent company that all subsidiaries obtain an opinion on their internal control structure from their external auditors as part of the overall internal audit function of the group. Tom has approached your firm for the opinion and has indicated that the opinion, given that the audit has just been satisfactorily completed, could be prepared and signed with no extra audit time required.

Required

How much reliance can be placed on the results of the audit that has just been completed? Give reasons for your answer.[4]

11.29 Using CAATs to test controls ★★★

Walsh Co. sells motor vehicle fuel, accessories and spare parts to retail customers. The company owns 25 shops.

The company has recently implemented a new computerised wages system. Employees work a standard eight-hour day. Hours are recorded using a magnetic card system; when each employee arrives for work, they hold their card close to the card reader and the reader recognises the magnetic information on the card identifying the employee as being 'at work'. When the employee leaves work at the end of the day the process is reversed, showing that the employee has left work.

Hours worked are calculated each week by the computer system using the magnetic card information. Overtime is calculated as any excess over the standard hours worked. Any overtime over 10% of standard hours is sent on a computer-generated report by email to the financial accountant. If necessary, the accountant overrides overtime payments if the hours worked are incorrect.

Statutory deductions and net pay are also computer calculated with payments being made directly into the employee's bank account. The only other manual check is the financial accountant authorising the net pay from Walsh's bank account, having reviewed the list of wages to be paid.

Required

(a) Using examples from Walsh Co., explain the benefits of using computer-assisted audit techniques to help the auditor to obtain sufficient appropriate audit evidence to be able to draw reasonable conclusions on which to base the audit opinion.
(b) List five examples of audit tests on Walsh's wages system using audit software.
(c) Explain how using test data should help in the audit of Walsh's wages system, noting any problems with this audit technique.[5]

11.30 Assessing and testing IT controls ★★★

Greener Pasture Pty Ltd (Greener Pasture) is a private nursing home.

The table below shows an extract of the audit senior's findings based on a review of controls documentation and interviews with Greener Pasture staff. The revenue system comprises the following.

1. *Billing system* — produces invoices to charge patients for services provided (such as accommodation, medications and medical services). This software includes a complex formula to allow for government subsidies, pensioner benefits and private medical insurance.
2. *Patient database* — a master file containing personal details about each patient as well as the period of stay, services provided and medical insurance details.
3. *Rates database* — a master file of all accommodation billing rates, rebate discounts and government assistance benefits.

The table shows the relevant patient revenue system and the controls in place.

Finding item	Patient revenue system	Type of control	Auditor findings about the control
1.1	Billing system	General IT control	File backup occurs automatically each Sunday at 10 pm so as not to disrupt any billing activities.
2.3	Patient database	Manual application control	Exception reports are produced to show changes to patient address details and insurance company.

Finding item	Patient revenue system	Type of control	Auditor findings about the control
3.4	Billing system	IT application control	The administration officer who creates the patient invoice has complained that she can't override the room charge rate when she thinks a mistake has been made by the system when it calculates the bill.
3.5	All systems	General IT control	All software changes are tested by the programmer and the test results are separately reviewed and approved by the system administrator.
4.6	Rates database	IT application control	The data entry operator can change all data fields providing they have a data change request form signed by the Greener Pasture general manager.

Required

For each of the above items, with reference to the above table and background information, conclude if the control is effective or not. Justify your answer.[6]

 CASE studies

11.31 Introduction — audit firm ★★★

You are an audit senior in Brennon & Co., a firm providing audit and assurance services. At the request of an audit partner, you are preparing the audit program for the income and receivables systems of Seeley Co.

Audit documentation is available from the previous year's audit, including internal control questionnaires and audit programs for the despatch and sales system. The audit approach last year did not involve the use of computer-assisted audit techniques (CAATs); the same approach will be taken this year. As far as you are aware, Seeley's system of internal control has not changed in the last year.

Client background — sales system

Seeley Co. is a wholesaler of electrical goods such as kettles, televisions, MP3 players, etc. The company maintains one large warehouse in a major city. The customers of Seeley are always owners of small retail shops, where electrical goods are sold to members of the public. Seeley only sells to authorised customers; following appropriate credit checks, each customer is given a Seeley identification card to confirm their status. The card must be used to obtain goods from the warehouse.

Despatch and sales system

The despatch and sales system operates as follows.

1. Customers visit Seeley's warehouse and load the goods they require into their vans after showing their Seeley identification card to the despatch staff.
2. A pre-numbered goods despatch note (GDN) is produced and signed by the customer and a member of Seeley's despatch staff confirming goods taken.
3. One copy of the GDN is sent to the accounts department, the second copy is retained in the despatch department.
4. Accounts staff enter goods despatch information onto the computerised sales system. The GDN is signed.

5. The computer system produces the sales invoice, with reference to the inventory master file for product details and prices, maintains the sales day book and also the receivables ledger. The receivables control account is balanced by the computer.
6. Invoices are printed out and sent to each customer in the post with paper copies maintained in the accounts department. Invoices are compared to GDNs by accounts staff and signed.
7. Paper copies of the receivables ledger control account and list of aged receivables are also available.
8. Error reports are produced showing breaks in the GDN sequence.

Required

(a) Explain the steps necessary to check the accuracy of the previous year's internal control questionnaires.
(b) Using information from the scenario, list six tests of control that an auditor would normally carry out on the despatch and sales system at Seeley Co and explain the reason for each test.[7]

11.32 Reliance on internal audit ★★★

Assume you are planning the 31 March 2015 audit of Growth Ltd, a large financial planning association based in Melbourne. Growth has offices in all capital cities of Australia and established an internal audit department late in the previous financial year. As part of the audit planning process, you had a meeting with the head of the department, Ms Tang. Your notes from the meeting are documented below.

1. In the first few months of operation, the department reported to the chief financial officer (CFO), to enable it to gain a good understanding of the systems. Once this set-up phase was completed, the organisational structure of the internal audit department changed. The department now reports to the chief executive officer (CEO), who is also chairman of the board of directors.
2. Ms Tang sets the department's work program after receiving feedback on risk areas from the CFO, the financial controllers of each state and the chair of the board. Over the past year, about 90% of the work program was achieved; only the internal audit of the Perth office was postponed until the next financial year. This was because of a request from the board for the department to allocate resources to investigate a suspected travel claims fraud in Brisbane.
3. Each month, Ms Tang prepares a report for the CEO, outlining the work planned and performed, and a summary of the results achieved. The CEO presents this report at the board's monthly meeting.
4. Ms Tang was appointed chief internal auditor in February 2014 after spending 3 years as the financial controller in Sydney. Previously she was an audit manager at a Big Four firm. She has four staff: two graduates undertaking the ICAA commerce program, an ex-public sector auditor and an assistant who is completing his commerce degree part time.
5. Ms Tang has familiarised herself with the standards set by the Institute of Internal Auditors. Audit programs are being written as each audit is performed; these programs will be revised and updated as the department develops.
6. Some of the financial controllers have been hostile to Ms Tang since the department was established. She suspects this is due to professional jealousy, because they had also applied for the chief internal auditor's position.
7. Two of the six board members have yet to be convinced of the value of the internal audit department. They believe that its focus should be on improving operational efficiency, rather than on dealing with compliance matters. As a compromise, the CEO has agreed to ask Ms Tang to set aside 20% of the department's time to undertake a performance audit of the company's administrative procedures.
8. Ms Tang and her team have visited each office this year (except Perth), examining the systems and carrying out detailed transactions testing. Many minor control breaches were noted,

although none likely to result in major errors or fraud. These breaches were reported in detail to the relevant financial controller.

9. The board has been under enormous pressure over the past 2 months because an offer to buy the business has been received from an international financial planning chain. Accordingly, the internal audit department's reports have received little attention in the monthly board meetings.

At the end of the meeting, Ms Tang suggested to you that it would be advantageous if the internal and external auditors work together more closely. She noted two advantages: firstly, the audit fee may fall and, secondly, the board will appreciate her contribution to reducing Growth's costs.

Required

Prepare a memo to the audit manager, outlining your overall assessment of the internal audit department and your opinion on whether the work of the internal audit department can be relied upon.[8]

RESEARCH question

11.33 Internal controls

The Sarbanes–Oxley Act of 2002 was enacted by the US Congress in response to a number of high-profile corporate failures. The Act brought into sharp focus the internal controls of organisations and placed obligations on both the company directors and their internal and external auditor with regard to ensuring that internal controls are effective in relation to financial reporting.

The cost of compliance with these regulations has been substantial. The Public Company Accounting Oversight Board in the United States introduced Auditing Standard (AS) No. 2, which was replaced by AS 5 (*An Audit of Internal Control over Financial Reporting That Is Integrated with an Audit of Financial Statements*) to refocus attention and ensure that auditors were adding value with the work they were being asked to carry out.

Required

Are companies better off in the post-Sarbanes–Oxley world? What research has been done to establish whether the focus on internal controls has improved internal controls and enhanced corporate governance? To what extent are audit firms duplicating effort and enhancing the fee income without giving real benefits back to the companies they audit and their shareholders?

FURTHER READING

American Institute of Certified Public Accountants (AICPA) Control Risk Audit Guide Task Force, *Audit Guide: Consideration of the Internal Control Structure in a Financial Statement Audit*, New York, 1990.

SK Asare, BC Fitzgerald, LE Graham, JR Joe, EM Negangard & CJ Wolfe, 'Auditors' internal control over financial reporting decisions: Analysis, synthesis, and research directions', *Auditing: A Journal of Practice and Theory*, October 2012, 32 (Supplement 1), pp. 131–66.

D Applegate & T Wills, 'Integrating *COSO*', *Internal Auditor*, December 1999, pp. 60–6.

AF Cohen & DJ Qaimmaqami, 'The US Sarbanes–Oxley Act of 2002: summary and update for non-US issuers', *International Journal of Disclosure and Governance*, February 2005, pp. 81–106.

Committee of Sponsoring Organisations of the Treadway Commission (COSO), *Internal Control Integrated Framework, AICPA*, New York, 1992.

Committee of Sponsoring Organisations of the Treadway Commission (COSO) 2009, *Guidance on Monitoring Internal Control Systems*, pp. 1–2.

C Li, J-H Lim & Q Wang, 'Internal and external influences on IT control governance', *International Journal of Accounting Information Systems*, December 2007, pp. 225–39.

National Commission on Fraudulent Financial Reporting, *Report of the National Commission on Fraudulent Financial Reporting*, Washington DC, 1987.

S Pae & S-W Yoo, 'Strategic interaction in auditing: an analysis of auditors' legal liability, internal control system quality, and audit effort', *The Accounting Review*, July 2001, pp. 333–56.

M Shatter, 'Learning from the US', *Charter*, September 2005, pp. 50–2.

JR Smith, SL Tiras & SS Vichitlekarn, 'The interaction between internal control assessment and substantive testing in audits for fraud', *Contemporary Accounting Research*, Summer 2000, pp. 327–56.

GH Tucker, 'IT and the audit', *Journal of Accountancy*, September 2001, pp. 41–3.

DM Willis & SS Lightle, 'Management reports on internal controls', *Journal of Accountancy*, October 2000, pp. 57–62.

CJ Wolfe, EG Mauldin & MC Diaz 2009, 'Concede or deny: do management persuasion tactics affect auditor evaluation of internal control deviations?', *The Accounting Review*, November, pp. 2013–38.

M Wright, *Audit Guide No. 5: Auditing in an IT Systems Environment*, Australian Accounting Research Foundation, Melbourne, 1999.

NOTES

1. SK Asare, BC Fitzgerald, LE Graham, JR Joe, EM Negangard & CJ Wolfe, 'Auditors' internal control over financial reporting decisions: Analysis, synthesis, and research directions', *Auditing: A Journal of Practice and Theory*, October 2012, 32 (Supplement 1), pp. 131–66.

2. Adapted from the ACCA, June 2006, Audit and Internal Review Exam.

3. Adapted from the ACCA, June 2006, Audit and Internal Review Exam.

4. Adapted from Professional Year Programme of the ICAA, 1999, Advanced Audit Module.

5. Adapted from the ACCA, December 2006, Audit and Internal Review Exam.

6. Adapted from Professional Year Programme of the ICAA, 2008, Audit and Assurance Module.

7. Adapted from the ACCA, June 2008, Audit and Assurance (International) Exam.

8. Adapted from Professional Year Programme of the ICAA, 1999, Advanced Audit Module.

Answers to multiple-choice questions

11.1 *A*   11.2 *B*   11.3 *A*   11.4 *D*   11.5 *A*   11.6 *B*   11.7 *C*   11.8 *B*   11.9 *C*
11.10 *D*

chapter 12

Designing substantive procedures

OVERVIEW

12.1 Assessing the risk of material misstatement

12.2 Determining detection risk

12.3 Designing substantive procedures

12.4 Developing audit programs for substantive procedures

12.5 Special considerations when designing substantive procedures

Summary

Key terms

Multiple-choice questions

Review questions

Professional application questions

Case studies

Research question

Further reading

Notes

LEARNING objectives

After studying this chapter, you should be able to:

1 describe how various risk factors relate to the type of potential misstatement

2 explain the process for determining the appropriate level of substantive procedures based on the assessment of detection risk, inherent risk and control risk

3 explain how the auditor designs substantive procedures for each audit

4 indicate how the nature, timing and extent of substantive procedures are varied to achieve an acceptable level of detection risk

5 explain how computer-assisted audit techniques may be used as substantive procedures

6 describe and apply a general framework for developing audit programs for substantive procedures

7 explain which substantive procedures may normally be included in an audit program

8 indicate special considerations when designing substantive procedures.

PROFESSIONAL STATEMENTS

Australian		International	
ASA 230	Audit Documentation	ISA 230	Audit Documentation
ASA 315	Identifying and Assessing the Risks of Material Misstatement through Understanding the Entity and Its Environment	ISA 315	Identifying and Assessing the Risks of Material Misstatement through Understanding the Entity and Its Environment
ASA 330	The Auditor's Responses to Assessed Risks	ISA 330	The Auditor's Responses to Assessed Risks
ASA 500	Audit Evidence	ISA 500	Audit Evidence
ASA 501	Audit Evidence — Specific Considerations for Inventory and Segment Information	ISA 501	Audit Evidence — Specific Considerations for Selected Items
ASA 502	Audit Evidence — Specific Considerations for Litigation and Claims		
ASA 505	External Confirmations	ISA 505	External Confirmations
ASA 510	Initial Audit Engagements — Opening Balances	ISA 510	Initial Audit Engagements — Opening Balances
ASA 520	Analytical Procedures	ISA 520	Analytical Procedures
ASA 530	Audit Sampling	ISA 530	Audit Sampling
ASA 540	Auditing Accounting Estimates, Including Fair Value Accounting Estimates, and Related Disclosures	ISA 540	Auditing Accounting Estimates, Including Fair Value Accounting Estimates, and Related Disclosures
ASA 550	Related Parties	ISA 550	Related Parties

SCENE SETTER

Accounting board bends rules for deciding asset values

The board that sets US accounting rules voted yesterday to let financial companies report higher values for some troubled assets. The controversial step is likely to increase some banks' reported earnings but may also heighten suspicions that the companies are concealing problems. The Financial Accounting Standards Board (FASB) move was made with unusual speed under intense pressure from Congress and the financial industry, which argued that the old rules exacerbated the financial crisis by forcing banks to overstate expected losses.

But the decision to ease what are known as mark-to-market requirements has raised concerns among some financial experts, who warn that it will become harder for banks and investors to agree on what the troubled assets are actually worth and thus discourage their sale. The ability of financial companies to sell assets to investors is considered essential for an economic revival because this could restore the major source of funding for bank lending to consumers and businesses.

The board also has faced criticism from accounting and investor groups that view yesterday's move as evidence the board lacks the necessary independence and strength to uphold its judgements in the face of pressure. The non-profit board, whose decisions are enforced by the Securities and Exchange Commission, proposed the changes four days after angry Congress

(continued)

members told it to do so. 'I was very disappointed in the process in that the independent agency buckled to the strong-armed tactics of Congress,' said Arthur Levitt, a former SEC chairman. 'This is a step towards the kind of opaqueness that created the economic problems that we're enduring today.'

A FASB spokesman said the board was responding appropriately to an extraordinary economic crisis. The new rules, which will be published next week, broaden an exception to the basic accounting principle that an asset is worth what a buyer is willing to pay. This valuation system is called marking to market, and the result is described as fair value. Companies must disclose in quarterly reports the fair value assets they are willing to sell. When there are no buyers for a particular asset, companies can assign values based on other considerations.

The change made yesterday allows companies to assert the same exception by arguing that prices offered by investors for some securities do not reflect the real value of those assets.

Source: B Appelbaum & Z Goldfarb, 'Accounting board bends rules for deciding asset values', *The Age*, Melbourne, 4 April, 2009.

In chapter 8, we discuss how the auditor needs to obtain an understanding of the entity and its environment, including its internal control, sufficient to identify and assess the risks of material misstatement of the financial statements. Chapters 9 and 10 consider how the auditor might use the audit risk model as a framework to respond to the assessed risks of material misstatements and how these are connected to the concept of audit evidence. In chapter 11, we consider how the auditor might obtain audit evidence by relying on and testing an entity's internal controls.

This chapter explains how the assessment of the risk of material misstatement affects the required level of detection risk, which will affect the design of substantive procedures. The acceptable level of detection risk influences the assessment of the nature, timing and extent of the procedures that need to be performed to gain sufficient appropriate audit evidence to substantiate the earnings and expenditure figures and the values in the balance sheet.

LEARNING ❶
objective

Describe how various risk factors relate to the type of potential misstatement.

12.1 ASSESSING THE RISK OF MATERIAL MISSTATEMENT

To perform the appropriate substantive procedures, the auditor must carefully assess the risk of material misstatement from the knowledge obtained in gaining an understanding of the entity and its environment (ASA 315 *Identifying and Assessing the Risks of Material Misstatement through Understanding the Entity and Its Environment* (ISA 315)). Reaching this conclusion involves three important steps, shown in figure 12.1 and discussed following.

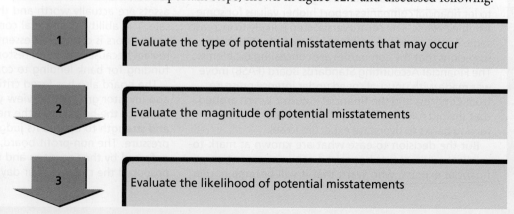

FIGURE 12.1:
Steps for assessing the risk of material misstatement

12.1.1 The type of potential misstatement

The audit process involves recognising risk factors and then linking those to assertions that are likely to be misstated. Risk factors can affect the potential for misstatements in the financial statements in two ways. Some risks have a pervasive effect on the financial statements and influence multiple account balances and assertions (e.g. financial statement level risks). Other risk factors are assertion-specific (e.g. assertion level risks). Table 12.1 provides ten examples of how the auditor would use the knowledge obtained while performing risk assessment procedures to evaluate potential misstatements in the financial statements.

Examples 1, 5, 8 and 10 represent risk factors that may have a pervasive effect on many or all assertions in the financial statements. This should heighten the auditor's concern about the risk of material misstatement throughout the financial statements. Example 10, weak computer general controls, might affect multiple account balances and transaction classes, and the auditor should be alert to problems in either routine or non-routine transactions. Example 5, strong incentives offered by management to meet financial targets, might affect assertions that are associated with non-routine transactions, end-of-period transactions, the choice of new accounting principles, or accounting estimates. In addition, the auditor should also be alert to problems with routine transactions, such as revenue recognition.

TABLE 12.1: Example of risk assessment procedures and the type of potential misstatement that may occur

Risk assessment procedure	Example risk factor	Type of potential misstatement
1. Understand the entity and its environment	The company is in an industry that is experiencing economic difficulty and intense price competition.	Weak industry conditions tend to create sensitivity in capital markets to bad news. This may heighten pressure on management to meet short-term performance indicators (e.g. earnings or revenue growth). This would have a pervasive effect on many financial statement assertions.
2. Understand the entity and its environment	The company has recently changed the nature of its product and is bundling software with other services to customise and implement software and related controls.	The change in business product combined with the bundling of products may create new problems associated with revenue recognition (existence, occurrence and cut-off). It is likely that cash has been received in advance of revenue recognition and the company should record unearned revenues (completeness).
3. Analytical procedures	Analytical procedures for a manufacturer show a significant increase in both profit margins and inventory turnover days.	It is possible that inventory is overstated. The auditor should be alert to problems with the existence or valuation and allocation of inventory.
4. Analytical procedures	Analytical procedures for a retailer show significant decreases in both profit margins and inventory turnover days.	It is possible that the retailer is experiencing problems with inventory shrinkage. This heightens the risk of fraud due to misappropriation of assets (e.g. assets taken from inventory without recording sales).
5. Consider the risk of fraud	Senior management has sent a very strong message, and offered increased incentives, to middle managers to meet financial targets.	Management may have the incentive to engage in fraudulent financial reporting (FFR). Management has the opportunity to use its discretion in a variety of ways and may rationalise FFR to obtain incentives offered to meet targets. Furthermore, the control environment may be weak, which may have a pervasive effect on many assertions.

(continued)

TABLE 12.1: *(continued)*

Risk assessment procedure	Example risk factor	Type of potential misstatement
6. Consider the risk of fraud	An employee in a small to medium- sized business responsible for cash disbursements did not receive an expected promotion and pay increase.	There is an increased risk of employee fraud. An employee may have both the incentive for fraud (not receiving expected promotion and pay increase) and the opportunity to commit fraud with authority to disburse cash. The auditor should be alert for problems with the existence and occurrence of cash disbursements.
7. Consider other inherent risk factors	A construction industry client uses the percentage-of-completion method to recognise revenues and expenses on current projects.	Significant revenues, expenses, assets and liabilities arise from the use of the percentage-of-completion method, which depends on a significant accounting estimate. The auditor should be alert for problems with the valuation and allocation assertion.
8. Consider other inherent risk factors	A company is experiencing working capital and going concern problems.	Potential going concern problems could have a pervasive effect on financial statements. Refer to the scene setter article above in support of the potential for misstatement. The board that sets US accounting rules voted to let financial companies report higher values for some troubled assets. The controversial step is likely to increase the reported earnings of some banks, but may also heighten suspicions that the banks are concealing problems.
9. Understand the entity's system of internal control	The client has a strong control environment and good controls over the existence of inventory.	The risk of misstatement in the existence assertion is minimised by strong internal controls.
10. Understand the entity's system of internal control	The client has weak computer general controls, including poor controls over the approval of system changes.	The risk of unauthorised changes to computer programs, or inadequate testing of new programs, increases the risk that programmed application controls may not function as designed.

Examples 2, 3, 4, 7 and 8 are risk factors that are assertion-specific. Example 2 represents a situation where a software company changes its practices from just selling software licences to bundling software licences with other services to customise and implement new computer programs. The likely types of misstatements are (1) problems with the existence and occurrence assertion and premature revenue recognition, and (2) problems with the completeness assertion and the failure to recognise unearned revenues when cash is received in advance of recognising revenues. An important audit skill is the auditor's ability to recognise risk factors and then link risk factors to specific assertions that might be misstated.

Example 10 presents a situation where the client has strong internal controls, and as a result the likelihood of material misstatement is reduced rather than increased. When these situations are present, the auditor usually performs tests of controls to obtain sufficient, competent evidence that controls operate effectively, which allows the auditor to accept a higher level of detection risk.

12.1.2 The magnitude of potential misstatements

Some potential misstatements are more significant than others. The following are some examples of how the auditor might consider the magnitude of potential misstatement in the financial statements:

- the existence of inventory is more significant for a manufacturer than for a hotel or many other service companies

- inventory is more susceptible to theft for a jeweller than for a timber company
- the depreciation of fixed assets is more significant for a paper manufacturer than for an advertising agency
- the completeness of unearned revenues is more significant for a software company than for a point-of-sale retailer.

Audit time and resources are limited. Auditors need to allocate more audit attention to the assertions that can have a potential material effect, individually or in aggregate, on the financial statements.

12.1.3 The likelihood of material misstatement

Once the auditor has identified risks of possible material misstatements, the auditor must also consider how likely they are. Once the auditor has identified various business risks, inherent risks and fraud risks that might affect the financial statements, he or she should consider the adequacy of the system of internal controls. For example, a retail jewellery store often places highly valuable items in store windows and displays. Because of the increased risk of theft, these items are often displayed in locked showcases during store hours, and are usually put in a safe when the store is closed. Other retailers, with less valuable items in store windows and displays, will leave those items in the store window when the store is closed because of the small risk of theft. The greater the effectiveness of controls a company puts in place, the less the likelihood of material misstatement.

Internal controls are costly, however. Many private companies have few, if any, controls over management's discretion in financial reporting or over financial statement disclosures. Some private companies feel that they are so resource constrained that they hire accounting staff with inadequate skills, and there is a weak control environment. As a result, these entities are often audited with a heavy emphasis on substantive tests because the likelihood of material misstatement is so high.

Public companies may have controls related to most, or all, financial statement assertions, and the auditor will test these controls if he or she decides to place reliance on them in conducting the audit. As a general rule, the higher the likelihood of material misstatement (after considering inherent risk and control risk), the more the auditor should respond with substantive tests to obtain reasonable assurance that he or she is able to detect and correct any material misstatements.

LEARNING objective 2

Explain the process for determining the appropriate level of substantive procedures based on the assessment of detection risk, inherent risk and control risk.

12.2 DETERMINING DETECTION RISK

Detection risk is the risk that the auditor's substantive procedures will not detect a material misstatement. It is therefore directly related to the substantive procedures performed as part of the audit. The relationship between detection risk, inherent risk and control risk can be expressed by the audit risk model, as represented in the equation below:

$$AR = IR \times CR \times DR$$

The model shows that audit risk (AR) is determined by inherent risk (IR), control risk (CR) and detection risk (DR). The auditor normally makes a preliminary assessment of inherent risk and control risk for each financial statement assertion, and having made these assessments the auditor will determine the level of detection risk required in order to achieve an overall acceptable level of audit risk. The auditor ordinarily assesses the level of control risk as high when the entity's internal control structure is ineffective or where evaluating the effectiveness of internal controls would not be efficient. Where the auditor's preliminary assessment of inherent risk and control risk is high, detection risk must be low if the desired level of audit risk is to be attained. A low level of detection risk requires the auditor to adopt a predominantly substantive audit strategy (as explained in chapter 9), whereby evidence obtained through the performance of substantive procedures enables the auditor to minimise the risk of failure to detect such material misstatements as might exist.

Assessing control risk as being less than high means that the auditor is confident that the entity's own procedures reduce the likelihood of material misstatement in that particular financial statement assertion. The auditor needs to obtain less evidence from substantive procedures to achieve the desired level of audit risk, and adopts a lower assessed level of control risk audit strategy, as explained in chapter 11. In such situations, the auditor is said to tolerate a higher level of detection risk. Where tolerable or **planned detection risk** is high, the auditor obtains less evidence from substantive procedures than where planned detection risk is low. The relationship between detection risk and the extent of substantive procedures can initially be confusing. It is reemphasised as follows:

- When the acceptable detection risk is *high*, it means that the auditor is prepared to accept a *high risk* that material errors will not be picked up by substantive audit tests. This means that relatively *less evidence* needs to be collected by substantive audit procedures.
- When the acceptable detection risk is *low*, it means that the auditor requires a *low risk* that material errors will not be picked up by substantive audit tests. This means that relatively *more evidence* needs to be collected by substantive audit procedures.

It is also important to note that the auditor should perform, regardless of the assessed levels of inherent and control risks, some substantive tests for material balances and transactions. The relationships between audit strategy, detection risk and level of substantive procedures that were explained in chapter 9 are summarised in a rain cloud analogy in figure 12.2.

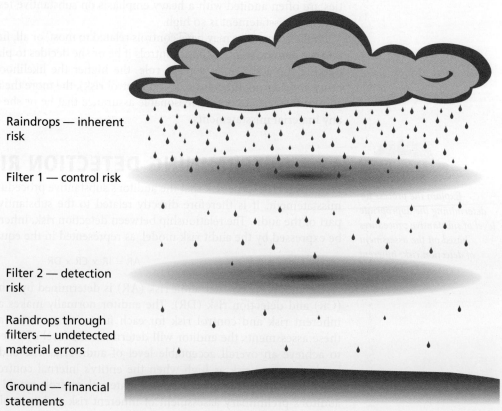

Raindrops — inherent risk

Filter 1 — control risk

Filter 2 — detection risk

Raindrops through filters — undetected material errors

FIGURE 12.2: Rain cloud analogy

Ground — financial statements

The raindrops falling from the cloud represent material errors that occur as a result of the nature of the client's business — this is known as the inherent risk of the client. Filter 1 represents the client's internal control system. The assessment of how effectively this filter stops the raindrops (material errors) is the auditor's assessment of the level of control risk. If this assessment of control risk is low or moderate, and the auditor intends to place some reliance on these controls, then the auditor must perform some tests of controls. Filter 2 represents the substantive audit procedures performed by the auditor. The assessment of how effectively this filter stops the raindrops (material errors) that have passed through Filter 1 (the internal control system) is the level of detection risk. Audit risk is, therefore, the chance that raindrops (material errors) will pass through both filters and reach the ground (material undetected errors).

12.2.1 Predominantly substantive approach

After determination of the risk of material misstatements, the auditor needs to determine the appropriate strategy for the audit. At two ends of the spectrum are the predominantly substantive approach and the lower assessed level of control risk approach. Chapter 11 discusses audit procedures where a lower assessed level of control risk approach is used and this chapter considers procedures where a predominantly substantive approach is used.

The auditor may assess control risk as being high and adopt the predominantly substantive approach where there is reason to suppose that one or more of the following assumptions are appropriate.

- There are no significant control procedures that relate to the assertion.
- Any relevant control procedures are unlikely to be effective.
- It would not be efficient to obtain evidence to evaluate the effectiveness of relevant control policies or procedures.

In making this decision, the auditor considers that the costs of performing the higher level of substantive procedures required by the predominantly substantive approach are less than the combined costs of performing sufficient tests of controls to support a lower assessed level of control risk approach. The auditor also considers the reduced level of substantive procedures that would be appropriate, assuming that a lower control risk assessment is supported.

This may happen more commonly with small audit clients, because small clients may not have adequate resources to implement all appropriate controls, the controls may not be as effective (often as a result of problems due to a lack of segregation of duties) and the size of the entity may make it inefficient for the auditor to rely on these controls in performing the audit.

LEARNING objective 3

Explain how the auditor designs substantive procedures for each audit.

12.3 DESIGNING SUBSTANTIVE PROCEDURES

After the audit strategy has been determined, the auditor will be aware of the **planned level of substantive procedures** required to provide an acceptable level of detection risk to keep audit risk at an acceptable level. The next stage is to design the actual substantive procedures that will be performed during the course of the audit to ultimately provide an audit opinion on the entity's financial statements.

To have a reasonable basis for an opinion on the entity's financial statements, the auditor must obtain sufficient appropriate audit evidence as required by ASA 500 *Audit Evidence* (ISA 500). Substantive procedures either provide evidence that supports the fairness of each significant financial statement assertion or, conversely, reveal monetary errors or misstatements in the recording or reporting of transactions and balances. Designing audit procedures in response to the risks of material misstatements at the assertion level involves the following considerations as discussed in ASA 330 *The Auditor's Responses to Assessed Risks*, paragraph 6 (ISA 330.6):

> The auditor shall design and perform further audit procedures whose nature, timing, and extent are based on and are responsive to the assessed risks of material misstatement at the assertion level.

This requirement applies to both tests of controls and substantive procedures. In this section we explain what the auditor must consider in determining the nature, timing and extent of substantive procedures to be performed as well as in using computer-assisted audit techniques.

12.3.1 Nature

The **nature of substantive procedures** refers to the type and effectiveness of the auditing procedures to be performed. When the planned level of detection risk is low, the auditor must use more effective and usually more costly procedures. When the planned level of detection risk is high, less effective and less costly procedures can be used. As mentioned in chapter 10, the types of substantive procedures are:

- analytical procedures
- tests of details of transactions
- tests of details of balances.

These procedures and their relative effectiveness and cost are discussed below.

Analytical procedures

The use of **analytical procedures** in audit planning to identify areas of greater risk of misstatement is explained in chapter 8. ASA 520 *Analytical Procedures* (ISA 520) suggests that analytical procedures should be used at the planning and overall review stage of the audit. However, it also notes that analytical review may be used at other stages of the audit as a substantive procedure to reduce detection risk. Analytical procedures are usually the least costly to perform. Thus, consideration should be given to the extent to which these procedures can contribute to achieving the planned level of detection risk, thus reducing the extent of tests of details. For most assertions, analytical procedures are considered to be less effective than tests of details, so they are used as a supplement to tests of details.

Despite the fact that analytical procedures are often considered less effective than tests of details, sometimes analytical procedures provide most (if not all) of the required evidence. When the results of the analytical procedures are as expected and the planned level of detection risk for the assertion is high, it may not be necessary to perform tests of details.

In the hotel industry, for example, relatively small amounts of revenue are billed to and collected from many customers each month. Tests of details of these high-volume, low-value revenue transactions would be tedious and costly. But revenues in such cases can often be estimated fairly precisely using independent variables such as the occupancy rate and average room rate. The auditor can multiply the average occupancy rate for each month (probably monthly, given seasonal variations) by the average room rate by the number of rooms to estimate the revenue for every month. The auditor's estimated balance for room revenue can then be compared with the reported balance as part of the evidence used in determining whether revenues are fairly stated. Reasons for substantial differences would need to be discussed with the client to determine whether alternative procedures need to be performed.

In other cases, the auditor may use the expected relationship of one account balance to another. Total sales commission expense, for example, can normally be estimated from total sales revenue, rather than from the details of entries in the sales commissions account.

ASA 520 (ISA 520) indicates that the extent of reliance on analytical procedures depends on:

- *materiality:* other things being equal, the more material a balance is, the less likely it is that the auditor will rely solely on the results of analytical procedures to audit the balance
- *other audit procedures:* if other audit procedures are directed towards the same audit objective and similar results are found, then more reliance can be placed on the analytical procedures
- *accuracy of predicted results:* the more accurate the results that can be predicted, the more reliance that can be placed on the analytical procedures; greater accuracy can be expected, for example, for balances where interrelationships are expected to be constant over time (such as gross profit margin percentages)
- *inherent and control risks:* if these risks are high, then more reliance will be placed on tests of details than on analytical procedures.

The following Professional Environment vignette will help you to determine how analytical review procedures can be used when auditing an income statement.

PROFESSIONAL ENVIRONMENT
Improving communicative value of the audit report

You are auditing the financial statements of Thixen Retail Ltd (TR) for the year ended 30 June 2015. TR owns and operates a number of retail outlets that sell several product lines: newspapers, confectionery, soft toys and stationery. At the planning stage of the audit, you established that TR's internal controls were effectively designed and therefore your audit strategy required the performance of tests of controls followed by a reduced level of substantive testing. The subsequent tests of controls confirmed the original control risk assessment and, as a result, you are now about to perform the reduced level of substantive procedures, which involves an analytical review approach to testing the income statement. Below is an extract from the income statement for the 2 years ended 30 June 2014 and 2015:

	2015 $000	2014 $000
Sales	1549	1146
Cost of sales	932	726
Gross profit	617	420
Expenses		
Wages	324	280
Rent	115	115
Depreciation	23	20
Other expenses	150	130
Profit/(loss) before tax	5	(125)

Your enquiries establish the following further information:

1. Sales summary — analysis of sales across the four business areas:

	Standard gross profit (%)	2015 $000	2014 $000
Newspapers	10%	180	146
Confectionery	25%	520	460
Soft toys	60%	445	290
Stationery	50%	404	250
		1549	1146

2. During 2014 the company employed 5 staff. This was increased to 6 from 1 January 2015. On 1 July 2014, all staff members were given a 5% pay rise.

3. During 2014 the company operated from two shops that were leased at $40 000 and $75 000 p.a. On 1 January 2015 a new shop was opened with a 10-year lease at $60 000 p.a. but the first year was rent-free.

4. In the newly refurbished premises, $65 000 of fixtures were added. The company policy is to depreciate fixtures straight line over 10 years.

How could analytical procedures be used to test the validity of the 2015 figures? Discuss further procedures and information that would be required before concluding that the income statement appears to be fairly stated.

Tests of details of transactions

Tests of details of transactions are tests to obtain evidence of a sample (or all) of the individual debits and credits that make up an account to reach a conclusion about the account balance. These tests mainly involve tracing and vouching. These terms are used to describe the direction (in terms of the accounting system) of the testing. Tracing involves following a transaction from source documents through to the accounting records, whereas vouching involves selecting entries in the accounting records and obtaining the documentation to substantiate the transaction.

The details of transactions may be traced, for example, from source documents (such as sales and suppliers' invoices) to entries in accounting records (such as the sales and purchases journals). Or the details of entries in accounting records (such as the cash payments journal and perpetual inventory records) can be vouched to supporting documents (such as suppliers' invoices). The auditor's focus in performing these tests is on finding monetary errors rather than deviations from controls. As noted in chapter 10, tracing is useful in testing for understatements, and vouching is useful in testing for overstatements.

In tests of details of transactions, the auditor uses evidence obtained about some (a sample) or all of the individual debits and credits in an account to reach a conclusion about the account balance. These tests generally use documents available in entity files, although sometimes documents will be obtained from external sources. The effectiveness of the tests depends on the particular procedure and documents used. Externally generated documents are more reliable than internally generated documents, for example.

Although tests of details of both transactions and balances may be performed in an audit, the former will provide most of the evidence for account balances affected by few transactions during the year, such as property, plant and equipment, or investments. For account balances affected by many transactions, such as cash and accounts receivable, it is more effective to apply tests of details to the balances. Different assertions for the same account may be tested by tests of details of transactions or balances. Often, because the same documentation may be required, tests of details of transactions may be performed in conjunction with tests of controls. This dual-purpose testing increases the cost-efficiency of such tests of details of transactions and is discussed in more detail in chapter 11.

Cut-off tests are a special category of tests of details of transactions that are related more to the closing balance than to transactions. It is much more important at the end of the reporting period to ensure that transactions are recorded on the correct date, given the impact on the financial statements (particularly on the income statement). Although cut-off is important for periodic reports, it is critical only once a year, and control procedures are rarely effective and are usually monitored directly by senior accounting personnel. The purpose of cut-off tests is to ensure (1) completeness (in that all transactions occurring before the end of the reporting period are recorded) and (2) occurrence (in that transactions occurring after the end of the reporting period are excluded). Cut-off errors can significantly affect profit; for example, goods received before the end of the reporting period and included in inventory, but not recorded in purchases until after the year-end, will overstate profit by the amount of the purchases.

Cut-off testing is needed for many accruals that will have a direct impact on profit, including electricity, telephone, gas, wages and advertising. Often, the amount of these accruals is not confirmed until the receipt of an invoice, which may take several weeks (or longer) after the end of the reporting period.

Tests of details of balances

Tests of details of balances focus on obtaining evidence directly about an account balance rather than the individual transactions that are debited and credited to the account. The auditor may, for example, verify amounts owed by individual customers making up the balance on accounts receivable, by requesting confirmation of balances from the customers. The auditor may also inspect plant assets, observe the entity's stocktake and perform pricing tests of the closing inventory.

The effectiveness of these tests also depends on the particular procedure performed and the type of evidence obtained. The information in table 12.2 illustrates how the effectiveness of tests of balances can be tailored to meet different detection risk levels for the completeness assertion for accounts payable.

	Detection risk	Test of details of balances
TABLE 12.2: Test of details of balances	High	Inspect suppliers' statements held by the entity and consider the reasonableness of explanations of differences.
	Low	Confirm the amount owing with the suppliers directly and investigate reported differences.

Tests of details of balances are the main ways of collecting evidence for the balances that make up the balance sheet. From an audit point of view, it is very important that profit is not overstated, which means ensuring that assets are not overstated and liabilities are not understated.

Illustration of the use of substantive procedures

The application of the three types of substantive procedures may be illustrated in the context of the accounts shown in figure 12.3 (overleaf).

Accounts receivable				
Opening balance	20 450			
Credit sales — Company X	5 800			
Credit sales — Company Y	6 000	Collections — Company W		6 750
		Collections — Company X		2 000
		Write-offs — Company T		2 300
		Returns and allowances — Company Y		500
Closing balance	20 700			
Sales revenue				
		Credit sales — Company X		5 800
		Credit sales — Company Y		6 000
		Closing balance		11 800
Commissions expense				
Expense re sales — Company X	290			
Expense re sales — Company Y	300			
Closing balance	590			

FIGURE 12.3:
General ledger accounts illustrating the processing of sales transactions to accounts receivable

Note: In reality, there would be many more transactions than the number shown above.

Accounts receivable

To simplify figure 12.3, only one receivables account is shown; in practice, there would typically be a control account backed up by a subsidiary ledger of customer accounts containing the individual debits and credits for transactions affecting each customer. We will assume the opening balance of accounts receivable is fairly stated based on the previous year's audit. To determine that the closing balance of accounts receivable is fairly stated, the auditor may consider obtaining evidence from any of the following substantive procedures:

- analytical procedures, such as:
  - comparing this year's closing balance in the control account with the previous year's balance, a budgeted amount or other expected value
  - using the closing balance to determine the percentage of accounts receivable to current assets for comparison with the previous year's percentage or industry data
  - using the closing balance to calculate the accounts receivable turnover ratio for comparison with the previous year's ratio, industry data or other expected value
- tests of details of transactions, such as:
  - vouching a sample of the individual debits and credits in customer accounts for the transaction classes indicated to the entries in journals (for example, vouching the debits to the sales journal) and supporting documentation (such as sales invoices)
  - tracing transactions data from source documents (such as remittance advices) and journals (such as the cash receipts journal) to the corresponding entries in the customer accounts for the transaction classes indicated
- tests of details of balances, such as:
  - determining that the closing balances in the individual customer accounts add up to the control account balance
  - confirming the balances for a sample of customer accounts with the customers.

It is important to note that while the processes above have been simplified for illustrative purposes, in practice an accounts receivable ledger on an entity's computerised system could hold hundreds of thousands or even millions of individual accounts. Thus any testing by the auditor as suggested above would be done by using some form of computer-assisted audit techniques, such as generalised audit software.

In the case of accounts receivable, it is common to apply each of the three types of substantive procedures to some extent. However, it must be acknowledged that one of the most important tests is direct confirmation from customers. For other accounts, only one or two of the tests may be performed in obtaining sufficient evidence to meet the planned level of detection risk.

The balance of accounts receivable is, as noted above, generally made up of many customers. In the simplified example in figure 12.3 there are only a few customers. The difference between tests of details of balances and tests of details of transactions can be illustrated by looking at one of the customer balances that makes up the accounts receivable balance in figure 12.3 — Company X, shown in figure 12.4. If the auditor attempts to verify the sale by checking the invoice and delivery records, and the collection by reference to cash receipts (we have assumed the opening balances are fairly stated), these are tests of details of transactions. However, if the auditor confirms the total closing balance with Company X, that is a test of details of balances.

FIGURE 12.4:
Detailed account for Company X

Company X	
Opening balance	5300
Sales	5800
Collection	(2000)
Closing balance	9100

Sales revenue

For simplicity, the sales revenue account in figure 12.3 shows the credits representing the individual sales transactions. In practice, the sales revenue account may show only daily, weekly or monthly totals posted from the sales journal. In either case, to determine that sales revenue is fairly stated, the auditor may obtain evidence from any of the following:
- analytical procedures, such as:
  - comparing the absolute value of the closing balance with the previous year's balance, a budgeted amount or other expected value
  - comparing the closing balance with an independent estimate of the closing balance
- tests of details of transactions, such as:
  - vouching the individual credits to the sales journal and to supporting documentation such as sales invoices, shipping documents and sales orders
  - tracing transactions data from source documents (such as shipping documents) to sales invoices and to the sales journal, and then tracing postings from the sales journal to the sales account
- tests of details of balances (although this type of test is unlikely to be applicable).

In many cases, both analytical procedures and tests of details are applied to the sales revenue account to achieve the acceptable level of detection risk. In some cases, analytical procedures alone may suffice, as is discussed in section 12.5.1.

Commissions expense

The commissions expense account shown in figure 12.3 is a good example of a situation in which analytical procedures alone may be all that is needed to achieve the planned level of detection risk. Examining source documents and recalculating the individual commissions could test the details of the individual debits to the account. However, for this type of account, it may be sufficient simply to obtain evidence by calculating an independent estimate of the total for commission expenses (using an expected relationship with the sales revenue account balance, such as 5%) and then comparing the estimate with the recorded balance for commission expenses.

LEARNING 4 objective

Indicate how the nature, timing and extent of substantive procedures are varied to achieve an acceptable level of detection risk.

12.3.2 Timing

Often, many of a firm's audit clients have similar year-ends. In Australia, a common year-end is 30 June. The result is that the months of July to September are commonly referred to by auditors as the 'busy season', when resources are often stretched to ensure that all audits are completed on a timely basis. To reduce this pressure, auditors try to perform as much work as possible in the 'quieter' time before the audit busy season. This has the dual advantage of (1) putting less pressure on resources during the busy season and (2) helping to complete audits in a timely manner. The level of detection risk has an impact on the extent to which the auditor can alter the **timing of substantive procedures**.

If acceptable detection risk is high, then certain procedures may be performed several months before the end of the year to gain assurance up to the point when the testing occurred. At the end of the year the auditor can conduct **roll-forward testing** to verify the account balance as at the year-end, using analytical procedures or tests of details of transactions applied to transactions in the intervening period. In contrast, when acceptable detection risk for an assertion is low, all substantive procedures relating to account balances will ordinarily be performed at or near the end of the reporting period.

Substantive procedures before the end of the reporting period

Substantive procedures commonly performed before the end of the reporting period are (1) the confirmation of accounts receivable, (2) the observation of physical inventory and (3) the physical inspection of investments.

Performing substantive procedures before the end of the reporting period may be more convenient and cost-effective for the auditor. However, these benefits must be weighed up against the associated increase in audit risk that material misstatements existing in the account at the end of the reporting period will not be detected. This risk becomes greater as the time remaining between the date of the interim audit and the end of the reporting period lengthens.

The potential increased audit risk can be controlled if:

- the internal control structure during the remaining period is effective
- there are no conditions or circumstances that may predispose management to misstate the financial statements in the remaining period
- the year-end balances of the accounts examined at the interim date are reasonably predictable as to amount, relative significance and composition
- the entity's accounting system will provide information concerning significant unusual transactions and significant fluctuations that may occur in the remaining period.

If these conditions do not exist, then the account should be examined at the end of the reporting period. In practice, early substantive testing of account balances is not done unless tests of controls have provided convincing evidence that the internal control structure is operating effectively. Substantive procedures before the end of the reporting period do not completely eliminate the need for substantive procedures at the end of the reporting period. Such procedures (roll-forward testing) ordinarily should include:

- a comparison of the account balances at the two dates and of the totals of transactions making up the difference to identify amounts that appear to be unusual, and the investigation of such amounts

- other analytical procedures or other substantive tests of details to provide a reasonable basis for extending the interim audit conclusions to the end of the reporting period.

When properly planned and executed, the combination of substantive procedures before the end of the reporting period and substantive procedures for the remaining period should provide the auditor with sufficient appropriate audit evidence to have a reasonable basis for an opinion on the entity's financial statements.

12.3.3 Extent

The auditor can vary the amount of evidence obtained by changing the **extent of substantive procedures** performed. 'Extent' means the number of items or sample size to which a particular test or procedure is applied. More evidence is needed to achieve a low planned level of detection risk than a high planned level of detection risk.

The extent will therefore relate to the size of the samples selected by the auditor. Thus, more extensive substantive procedures are being performed when the auditor confirms 2000 accounts receivable rather than 1000 accounts, or vouches 1000 sales journal entries to supporting documents rather than 500 entries. The sample size to which a particular test is applied can be determined by probability theory or professional judgement. No matter what method is chosen, similar factors should be considered to determine sample size. Some of these factors are outlined in Appendix 2 of ASA 530 *Audit Sampling* (ISA 530, Appendix 2). One consideration is that the higher the assessment of inherent risk and control risk, the larger the sample size needs to be because a lower level of detection risk is required. Note, however, that probability theory suggests that once the number of items in the population exceeds 5000, any increase in population size has no significant effect on the size of the sample. This topic is covered in chapter 13.

LEARNING 5 objective

Explain how computer-assisted audit techniques may be used as substantive procedures.

12.3.4 Computer-assisted audit techniques as substantive procedures

In designing substantive audit procedures, the auditor may decide that it is effective and efficient to use computer-assisted audit techniques (CAATs) as an audit tool.

CAATs can be used for tests of controls or substantive tests; the focus of this discussion, however, is the use of CAATs in performing substantive tests. The use of CAATs in tests of controls is discussed in chapter 11. Using CAATs for substantive testing involves analysis of the client's data files (either the master files or transaction files). Some of the types of substantive auditing procedures that can be performed or helped by the use of CAATs include:
- tests of details of transactions and balances, such as the use of audit software for recalculating interest or the extraction of invoices over a certain value from computer records
- analytical procedures, such as identifying inconsistencies or significant fluctuations
- sampling programs to extract data for audit testing
- re-performing calculations performed by the entity's accounting systems.

Three main categories of audit software are used to perform substantive audit testing.
1. *Generalised audit software.* This is the most commonly used audit software in Australia and is also referred to as 'package programs'. It is easy to use, and can be used on many different computers and for different clients. It can be used for many different functions in performing the audit, including performing calculations, selecting samples, identifying records meeting specified criteria, comparing data in different fields, and producing reports. Examples of **generalised audit software** include ACL and IDEA.

2. *Customised audit software.* When the client's computer system is not compatible with the generalised audit software or where the auditor wants to perform a function that the generalised software cannot do, customised audit software must be written (also referred to as 'purpose-written programs'). This will generally cost more than generalised audit software, and must be updated regularly to account for changes in the client's system.

3. *Utility programs.* These programs are generally part of the client's computer system and can perform tasks such as sorting, creating and printing files. They are not specifically designed for audit purposes.

Generalised audit software is the most commonly used audit software; the next section discusses its use.

Generalised audit software

Depending on the application, one or more of the following distinct phases may be involved in using generalised audit software packages:

- identifying the audit objective and the tests to be performed
- determining the feasibility of using a software package with the entity's system
- designing the application, which may include the logic, calculations and form of the output
- processing the application on actual entity file data and reviewing the results.

The use of generalised audit software enables the auditor to deal effectively with large quantities of data. This may permit the accumulation of either the same quantity of evidence at less cost, or more evidence at an economical cost. Often, the main cost is associated with using this type of software on an audit for the first time (i.e. start-up costs). Depending on the client's computer system, the software may be designed to perform many of the auditing procedures that an auditor might perform manually.

Some examples of substantive testing applications are explained in the following sections.

Reconciling detailed audit data with the general ledger

An important first step involves obtaining detailed records from a client and testing the data to make sure that the supporting data match the general ledger. Auditors obtain files such as an accounts receivable file or an inventory file for the client in electronic form. The first step is to ensure that the underlying detail matches the accounting records. Auditors often obtain accounts receivable subsidiary files from a client to prepare confirmations. If the file has a date other than month-end, which does not match the client's month-end general ledger, it is likely that the auditor will send confirmations in wrong amounts. This may result in customers confirming that balances include errors, when they do not. Hence, an important first step involves using generalised audit software to total the detailed information and to compare control totals with the general ledger (at an interim date) or with financial statement amounts (at year-end).

Selecting and printing audit samples

The computer system can be programmed to select audit samples according to criteria specified by the auditor. These samples can be used for a variety of purposes. Individual customer accounts receivable may be selected for confirmation, or the auditor may be interested in obtaining a listing of all items over a certain dollar amount. In the case of confirmation requests, the system may also be used to print the confirmation letter as well as the envelope. A more comprehensive discussion of the use of confirmations in performing substantive tests of accounts receivable is presented in chapter 14. The auditor might also use generalised audit software to sample items that are likely to contain errors. For example, when auditing the cost of manufactured inventory, the auditor might sample costs that have changed by more than 10% from the previous audit. Prices that have changed significantly may have a higher risk of error than prices that are stable.

Testing calculations

Another common use of the computer is to test the accuracy of calculations in data files. Tests of extensions, additions, or other calculations may be performed. Inventory quantities may be extended by a unit cost and the amount of the inventory recalculated. An auditor can use the client's data to recalculate the ageing of accounts receivable. Because of the speed of computer processing, these types of recalculations can easily be performed on an entire audit population.

Testing the entire population

Generalised audit software allows auditors to screen an entire population rather than rely on a sampling procedure. An auditor might test the allowance for doubtful debts by using generalised audit software to develop a payment history for each customer. Generalised audit software allows an auditor to quickly develop a record for time from shipment to receipt of payment for each sales transaction. In a similar fashion, an auditor can scan a perpetual inventory file to search for slow-moving inventory. This type of information can be helpful when testing accounting estimates.

Summarising data and performing analyses

The auditor often wants client data reorganised in a manner that will suit a special purpose. For instance, the auditor may want to determine slow-moving inventory items, debit balances in accounts payable, or past due accounts receivable. Similarly, in performing analytical procedures, the auditor may use the computer to calculate desired ratios, extract non-financial data from the client's database for comparison with financial data, or perform statistical regression analysis and an analytical procedure.

How generalised audit software can be used for substantive testing in the audit of accounts receivable is discussed below, with reference to an example customer file as shown in figure 12.5 (overleaf).

The accounts receivable master file contains records for each customer, similar to the one shown in figure 12.5 for Company X. In using CAATs as an audit tool with generalised audit software (such as ACL or IDEA) the auditor may perform the following tests.

- Test the clerical accuracy of each individual file by recalculating the balance in each category (Fields 4, 5, 6 and 7) and checking that it equals the total (Field 8).
- The totals for each individual accounts receivable file can be added together (Field 8 for each file) to check the overall total for accounts receivable.
- Select all accounts where the balance is over 60 days (from Field 7) to perform tests to ensure payment will be received.
- Select all total balances that are negative (from Field 8) because this is unusual for accounts receivable and should require further audit testing.
- From the master file select a random sample to send confirmation letters. Extract the details from the following fields to print on the confirmation letters: customer number (Field 1); customer name (Field 2); address (Field 3); and total balance (Field 8).
- Select all accounts where the total balance (Field 8) exceeds the balance of the credit limit (Field 9).

- If the company has a copy of the master file from the previous year, a calculation of the percentage of total amounts in each ageing category (Fields 4, 5, 6 and 7 as a proportion of Field 8) in both years can be compared.

Field	Type	Name	Details
1	N	Customer number	0003
2	A	Customer name	Company X
3	A	Address	34 King Edward Road, 8009
4	N	Current balance	5 800
5	N	Balance < 30 days	0
6	N	Balance 30 to < 60 days	2 200
7	N	Balance > 60 days	1 100
8	N	Total balance	9 100
9	N	Credit limit	10 000

FIGURE 12.5:
Example file from accounts receivable master file

12.3.5 Audit risk and choice of substantive procedures

A graphic summary of several important relationships between the audit risk components and the nature, timing and extent of substantive procedures is presented in figure 12.6. As noted earlier, designing substantive procedures involves determining the nature, timing and extent of substantive procedures for significant financial statement assertions. The next section considers how the auditor relates assertions, specific audit objectives and substantive procedures in developing written **audit programs** for substantive procedures.

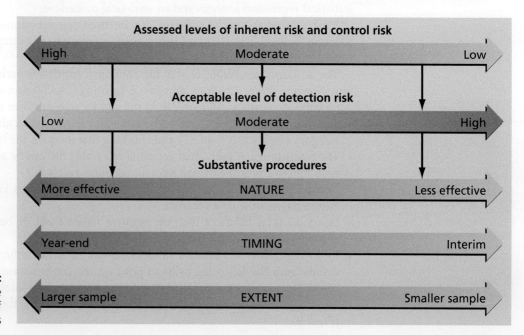

FIGURE 12.6:
Risk components and the nature, time and extent of substantive procedures

Learning check

LEARNING 6 objective

Describe and apply a general framework for developing audit programs for substantive procedures.

12.4 DEVELOPING AUDIT PROGRAMS FOR SUBSTANTIVE PROCEDURES

The overall objective of a financial report audit is the expression of an opinion on whether the entity's financial statements are presented fairly, in all material respects, in accordance with applicable accounting standards. Furthermore, as noted in chapter 10, it is good audit practice to develop numerous specific audit objectives for each account balance, based on each of the financial statement assertions. In designing substantive procedures, the auditor should determine that appropriate procedures have been identified to achieve each of the specific audit objectives relating to each assertion. If this is done for each account, then the overall objective will be met.

12.4.1 Framework for developing audit programs

A framework for developing audit programs for substantive procedures is shown in figure 12.7.

FIGURE 12.7:
General framework for developing audit programs for substantive procedures

GENERAL FRAMEWORK

Complete preliminary planning
1. Develop specific audit objectives for each financial statement assertion relating to closing balances.
2. Assess inherent and control risk and determine the acceptable level of detection risk for each assertion, consistent with the overall level of audit risk and applicable materiality level.
3. From knowledge acquired from procedures to obtain an understanding of the internal control structure, consider the accounting records, supporting documents, accounting process (including the audit trail) and financial reporting process relating to the assertions.
4. Consider options regarding the design of substantive procedures. Alternatives for accommodating varying acceptable levels of detection risk include:
   • nature:
     – analytical procedures
     – tests of details of transactions
     – tests of details of balances

(continued)

- timing: interim versus year-end
- extent: sample size.

5. Consider whether it is effective and efficient to use CAATs.

Specify substantive procedures to be included in audit program

1. Specify initial procedures to:
   (a) trace opening balances to previous year's working papers (if applicable)
   (b) review activity in applicable general ledger accounts and investigate unusual items
   (c) verify totals of supporting records or schedules to be used in subsequent procedures and determine their agreement with general ledger balances, when applicable, to establish the tie-in of detail with control accounts.
2. Specify analytical procedures to be performed.
3. Specify tests of details of transactions to be performed.
4. Specify tests of details of balances (in addition to 1(a), (b) and (c) immediately above) to be performed.
5. Consider whether there are any special requirements or procedures applicable to assertions tested in the circumstances, such as procedures required by auditing standards or by regulatory agencies that have not been included in (3) and (4) immediately above.
6. Specify procedures to determine that disclosure is in accordance with the Corporations Act and applicable accounting standards.

The steps listed in the upper part of figure 12.7 summarise the application of several important concepts and procedures explained in chapters 8–10 and discussed at the beginning of this chapter. Step 1 was explained initially in chapter 8 and is also illustrated in the context of auditing inventory in table 12.3. Steps 2–5 were discussed at the beginning of this chapter and are the preliminary considerations of the auditor before determining actual substantive procedures.

The lower part of figure 12.7 outlines the actual substantive procedures to be performed in the audit. Many of these steps are illustrated in the example audit program for inventory shown in figure 12.8 (overleaf). Step 1 is to ensure that the starting point is correct by checking opening balances with the previous year's records and ensuring that subsidiary records tie in to the general ledger.

The analytical procedures are considered next in step 2. This is because results from these tests may highlight areas of risk that need an increase in the extent of tests of details.

Tests of details of transactions are ordinarily considered next as shown in step 3 because they are usually performed during the interim audit at the same time as tests of controls, often as **dual-purpose tests**. Finally, the program should specify tests of details of balances (step 4), special requirements not previously covered (step 5) and procedures to determine that the disclosures relating to the assertions covered by the program are in accordance with applicable accounting standards (step 6). In specifying the latter procedures, the auditor uses knowledge of relevant business practices and financial reporting disclosure requirements.

The general framework for developing audit programs described in figure 12.7 forms the basis for the numerous illustrations of audit programs for substantive procedures presented in subsequent chapters of this book. The auditor generally adopts a consistent approach in developing audit programs for recurring engagements, but there are some special considerations in developing audit programs for **initial engagements**.

Often, many of the choices in the preliminary planning part of figure 12.7 are input into a computer program designed to help with developing audit programs. The program tailors procedures to the audit engagement based on the information entered, reducing the number of decisions required by the auditor in the second part of figure 12.7, which specifies the substantive procedures.

12.4.2 Audit programs in initial engagements

ASA 510 *Initial Audit Engagements — Opening Balances* (ISA 510) identifies two matters as requiring special consideration during the design of audit programs for initial engagements:
- determining the fairness of the account balances at the beginning of the period being audited
- ascertaining the accounting principles used in the preceding period as a basis for determining the consistency of application of such principles in the current period.

The auditor will need to review the audit working papers of the predecessor auditor to ascertain whether the previous work can be relied on. If this is not possible, the auditor will need to gather information on the opening assets and liabilities as part of the current year's audit. If sufficient evidence cannot be gathered, the auditor may need to qualify the auditor's report based on a limitation of scope.

LEARNING objective 7

Explain which substantive procedures may normally be included in an audit program.

12.4.3 Assertions, audit objectives and substantive procedures

Table 12.3 illustrates the relationships between assertions, specific audit objectives and substantive procedures for the inventories of a manufacturing company. Study of the procedures shown in the second column indicates that there is a mix of analytical procedures and tests of details of both transactions and balances. In some cases, a procedure is listed more than once because the evidence from the procedure relates to more than one specific audit objective or assertion. Table 12.3 is not intended to include a listing of all possible substantive procedures that may be used in auditing inventory, and neither should you infer that all the listed procedures are performed in every audit. How these procedures are incorporated into the audit program is illustrated in the next section.

12.4.4 Illustrative audit program

As required by ASA 230 *Audit Documentation* (ISA 230), the auditor's decisions regarding the design of substantive procedures must be documented in the working papers in the form of written audit programs. An audit program is a list of the audit procedures to be performed. Contrary to the way they are grouped in table 12.3, generally the procedures are not listed by assertion or specific audit objective, so as to avoid the duplication of procedures that apply to more than one assertion or objective.

TABLE 12.3: Relationships between assertions, specific audit objectives and substantive procedures for inventories

Specific audit objective	Examples of substantive procedures
For the existence assertion Inventories included in the balance sheet/statement of financial position physically exist.	Observe and test inventory counts (stocktakes).
	Obtain confirmation of inventories at locations outside the entity.
Inventories represent items held for sale or use in the normal course of business.	Review perpetual inventory records and purchasing records for indications of current activity.
	Compare inventories with a current sales catalogue and subsequent sales and delivery reports.

(continued)

Specific audit objective	Examples of substantive procedures
For the rights and obligations assertion The entity has legal title or similar rights of ownership to the inventories.	Examine paid suppliers' invoices, consignment agreements and contracts.
Inventories exclude items billed to customers or owned by others.	Examine paid suppliers' invoices, consignment agreements and contracts.
	Test shipping and receiving cut-off procedures.
	Compare inventories with a current sales catalogue and subsequent sales and delivery reports.
For the completeness assertion Inventory quantities include all products, materials and supplies on hand.	Observe and test inventory counts.
	Account for all inventory tags and count sheets used in making the inventory counts.
	Analytically review the relationship of inventory balances to recent purchasing and sales activities.
	Test shipping and receiving cut-off procedures.
Inventory quantities include all products, materials and supplies owned by the company stored at outside locations.	Obtain confirmation of inventories at locations outside the entity.
For the valuation and allocation assertion Inventory listings are accurately compiled and the totals are properly included in the inventory accounts.	Trace test counts recorded during the inventory count observation to the inventory listing.
	Test the clerical accuracy of inventory listings.
	Reconcile physical counts to perpetual records and general ledger balances, and investigate significant fluctuations.
Inventories are properly stated at cost (except when net realisable value is lower).	Examine suppliers' invoices.
Slow-moving, excess, defective and obsolete items included in inventories are properly identified.	Enquire of sales personnel concerning possible excess or obsolete inventory items. Examine an analysis of inventory turnover.
	Review industry experience and trends.
	Analytically review the relationship of inventory balances to expected sales volume.
Inventories are reduced, when appropriate, to net realisable value.	Review estimates of realisable values.
For the presentation and disclosure assertions Inventories are properly classified in the balance sheet/statement of financial position as current assets.	Review drafts of the financial statements.
The basis of valuation is adequately disclosed in the financial statements.	Compare the disclosures made in the financial statements with the requirements of the Corporations Act and applicable accounting standards.
The pledge or assignment of any inventories is appropriately disclosed.	Obtain confirmation of inventories pledged under loan agreements.

In addition to listing audit procedures, each audit program should have:
- columns for a cross-reference to other working papers detailing the evidence obtained from each procedure (when applicable)
- the initials of the auditor who performed each procedure
- the date that performance of the procedure was completed.

Figure 12.8 shows an audit program in this format. The procedures in the program are based on those shown in table 12.3, except that each procedure is listed only once, and the procedures are listed in a sequence that is logical for the development of the program and/or performance of the procedures.

FIGURE 12.8: Illustrative audit program for substantive procedures of inventories

Prepared by: _____ Date: _____
Reviewed by: _____ Date: _____

XYZ Co. Ltd
Audit program for substantive procedures of inventories
30 June 2015

Substantive procedures	W/P ref.	Auditor	Date
1. Verify totals and agreement of inventory balances and records that will be subjected to further testing: (a) Trace opening inventory balances to previous year's working papers. (b) Review activity in inventory accounts and investigate unusual items. (c) Verify totals of perpetual records and other inventory schedules and their agreement with closing general ledger balances.			
2. Perform analytical procedures: (a) Review industry experience and trends. (b) Examine an analysis of inventory turnover. (c) Review relationship of inventory balances with recent purchasing and sales activities. (d) Compare inventory balances with expected sales volume.			
3. Test details of inventory transactions: (a) Vouch additions to inventory records and to suppliers' invoices. (b) Trace data from purchases to inventory records. (c) Test cut-off of purchases (receiving) and sales (shipping).			
4. Observe the stocktake: (a) Make test counts. (b) Look for indications of slow-moving, damaged or obsolete inventory. (c) Account for all inventory tags and count sheets used in the stocktake.			
5. Test clerical accuracy of inventory records: (a) Recalculate extensions of quantities times unit prices. (b) Trace test counts to records. (c) Vouch items on inventory listings to inventory tags and count sheets. (d) Reconcile physical counts to perpetual records and general ledger balances.			
6. Test inventory pricing: (a) Examine suppliers' paid invoices for purchased inventory. (b) Obtain market quotations and perform lower of cost and net realisable value test. (c) Review perpetual inventory records and purchasing records for indications of current activity. (d) Compare inventories with current sales catalogue and sales reports. (e) Enquire about slow-moving, excess or obsolete inventories and determine need for write-downs.			
7. Confirm inventories at locations outside the entity.			
8. Examine consignment agreements and contracts.			
9. Confirm agreements for assignment and pledging of inventories.			
10. Review disclosures for inventories in drafts of the financial statements and determine conformity with the Corporations Act and applicable accounting standards.			

Details of procedures are given in outline here. Such an outline forms part of an audit firm's standard documentation to be tailored for each engagement. In a tailored audit program, the details refer to the entity's specific information system and parts of the audit trail applicable to processing the transactions. They also identify the particular documents and records involved, and may specify the extent of each procedure.

Audit programs should be sufficiently detailed to provide an outline of the work to be done; a basis for coordinating, supervising and controlling the audit; and a record of the work performed.

The audit program shown in figure 12.8 illustrates the format of audit programs for substantive procedures and how they can be developed. The application of the substantive procedures shown is explained in chapter 16, which includes the audit of inventories.

LEARNING objective 8

Indicate special considerations when designing substantive procedures.

12.5 SPECIAL CONSIDERATIONS WHEN DESIGNING SUBSTANTIVE PROCEDURES

The foregoing discussions of assessing detection risk, designing substantive procedures and developing audit programs apply to all accounts. This section discusses some special considerations for certain accounts and audit procedures.

12.5.1 Income statement accounts

Traditionally, tests of details of balances have focused more on financial statement assertions that refer to balance sheet/statement of financial position accounts than on income statement accounts. This approach is both efficient and logical because each income statement account is inextricably linked to one or more balance sheet accounts. Figure 12.9 provides some examples.

Balance sheet account	Related income statement account
Accounts receivable	Sales
Inventories	Cost of sales
Prepaid expenses	Various related expenses
Investments	Investment income
Property, plant and equipment	Depreciation expense
Interest-bearing liabilities	Interest expense

FIGURE 12.9:
Tests of details of balances

The assertions for the accounts are linked as well. Evidence that an account receivable does not exist, for example, may indicate that a sale did not occur (although it could also mean the entity failed to record a payment remitted by the customer). Similarly, if interest-bearing liabilities are not complete, then interest expense may not be complete, and so on. Generally, if there is an error or deliberate misstatement in income statement accounts, then there is a higher likelihood that it has occurred towards the end of the year and it will therefore be included in the related balance sheet account.

Given these relationships, evidence obtained through substantive procedures applied to balance sheet accounts also provides much of the evidence required to achieve the desired level of detection risk for income statement account balances. For this reason, analytical procedures are often the only substantive procedures that must be specifically applied in verifying income statement accounts.

Analytical procedures for income statement accounts

Analytical procedures can be a powerful audit tool in obtaining audit evidence about income statement account balances. This type of substantive procedure may be used directly or indirectly. Direct tests occur when a revenue or expense account is compared with other relevant data to determine the reasonableness of its balance. The ratio of sales commissions to sales, for example, can be compared with the ratios for previous years and with budget data for the current year. Comparisons can also be made with non-financial information, as shown in figure 12.10.

Account	Analytical procedure
Hotel room revenue	Number of rooms is × occupancy rate × average room rate
Wages expense	Average number of employees per pay period × average pay per period × number of pay periods

FIGURE 12.10:
Direct tests

Indirect tests occur when evidence concerning income statement account balances can be derived from analytical procedures applied to related balance sheet accounts. Accounts receivable turnover may be used in verifying accounts receivable, for example, and the findings may have an impact on whether bad debts expense and sales are fairly stated.

Tests of details for income statement accounts

When the evidence obtained from analytical procedures and tests of details of related balance sheet accounts does not reduce detection risk to an acceptably low level, direct tests of details of assertions relating to income statement accounts are necessary. This may be the case when:

- inherent risk is high, as in the case of assertions affected by non-routine transactions and management's judgements and estimates
- control risk is high, such as when related internal controls for non-routine and routine transactions are ineffective, and when the auditor elects not to test the internal controls
- analytical procedures reveal unusual relationships and unexpected fluctuations
- the account requires analysis — for example, legal expenses and professional fees, income tax, maintenance and repairs expenses, travel and entertainment expenses, and directors' remuneration.

12.5.2 Accounts involving accounting estimates including fair value accounting estimates and related disclosures

An **accounting estimate** is an approximation of a financial statement item in the absence of exact measurement. Examples of accounting estimates include depreciation, the allowance for bad debts and warranty expense. Management is responsible for making the accounting estimates included in the financial statements. These estimates are balances with a greater risk of misstatement because they are often made in conditions of uncertainty about the outcome of events that have occurred or are likely to occur. Because of the use of judgement and, therefore, the subjective nature of these balances, they are often the ones over which most disputes occur between the auditor and management.

ASA 540 *Auditing Accounting Estimates, Including Fair Value Accounting Estimates, and Related Disclosures* (ISA 540) suggests that one or a combination of the following approaches should be adopted in the audit of accounting estimates to obtain sufficient appropriate audit evidence.

- *Review and test the processes used by management to develop the estimate.* The auditor could review the data and assumptions used by management in preparing the estimate, test the calculations performed, and compare the accuracy of estimates made by management in previous periods.
- *Use an independent estimate for comparison.* The auditor may make an independent estimate of the balance and compare it with management's estimate.
- *Review subsequent events.* A review of subsequent events after the end of the accounting period may provide evidence as to the accuracy of management's estimate.

12.5.3 Fair value accounting estimates and related disclosures

The traditional method of reporting assets and liabilities at cost provides auditors with reliable figures to verify, although it is questionable how relevant some of these figures are to the users of financial statements. To make the financial statements more relevant, there have been moves recently to adopt fair value measurements in some disclosures. Recording of balances in this way may be more relevant but they are generally less reliable and require special considerations by the auditor.

Appendix 1 in ASA 540 (ISA 540) states that the auditor should obtain an understanding of the process of determining the fair value disclosures and the appropriateness of those disclosures under different financial reporting frameworks, which may require certain specific fair value measurements and disclosures. Then, after assessing the inherent risk and the control risk, the auditor should test the fair value measurements and disclosures. In the first instance, published price quotations in an active market are the best evidence of fair value. But sometimes, where there is no active market, the fair value may be based on a discounted cash flow analysis or comparative transaction model, which involve greater uncertainty and often require a number of assumptions by management, which must be evaluated by the auditor.

12.5.4 Related parties

Related party transactions are a risk area for auditors and are covered in ASA 550 *Related Parties* (ISA 550). These transactions have a higher than average risk of irregularities. The auditor should perform the following specific substantive procedures with respect to the related parties, as outlined in ASA 550 (ISA 550).

- *Existence of related parties.* The auditor should review information provided by management identifying related parties and perform audit procedures to ensure that the risk of related parties remaining undetected is low. These procedures may include reviewing previous period working papers, shareholder records and minutes of shareholders and directors meetings.
- *Transactions with related parties.* The auditor should review information provided by management identifying related party transactions and be alert for other material related party transactions. The auditor will need details of all related parties at the beginning of the audit so that any related party transactions encountered can be identified. The auditor also needs to be alert for transactions that have abnormal conditions, lack logical reasons for occurrence, have substance that is different from form, or have been processed in an unusual manner.

12.5.5 Specific considerations for inventory and segment information

The importance of inventory is demonstrated by the fact that it warrants special consideration in the auditing standards. ASA 501 *Audit Evidence — Specific Considerations for Inventory and Segment Information* (ISA 501) outlines some specific requirements, including a requirement to attend the stocktake so the auditor can obtain sufficient appropriate audit evidence regarding the existence and condition of inventory by attendance at physical inventory counting unless impracticable. There is a high risk of misstatement associated with inventory. This risk is due to the often large number of relatively small items that make up the total inventory balance and to the subjectivity associated with the provision for obsolescence. ASA 501 also provides guidance in respect of presentation and disclosure of segment information in accordance with the applicable reporting framework. The audit of inventory is discussed further in chapter 16. An associated auditing standard, ASA 502 *Audit Evidence — Specific Considerations for Litigation and Claims*, specifically looks at the completeness of litigation and claims, and related communication with the entity's legal counsel.

12.5.6 External confirmations

External confirmations are written responses to confirmation requests that the auditor has sent to third parties. The reliability of audit evidence is determined by its source and nature. In this case, the evidence is sourced externally and the nature of the evidence is written, thereby making it a very strong form of audit evidence. However, it is generally expensive and time-consuming to collect. In deciding whether to use external confirmations, the auditor must consider the guidance given in ASA 505 *External Confirmations* (ISA 505). The auditor needs to determine whether the use of external confirmations is necessary to obtain sufficient appropriate audit evidence at the assertion level. In making this determination, the auditor needs to consider the assessed risk of material misstatement at the assertion level and how the audit evidence from other planned audit procedures will reduce the risk of material misstatement at the assertion level to an acceptably low level.

The main areas requiring external confirmations include bank balances, accounts receivable balances, inventory held with third parties and property title deeds. All of these are balances where there is a high risk in ensuring the assertion of existence can be satisfied in the audit testing.

Do you know . . .

12.6 ☐ In developing the audit program, the auditor first identifies the audit objectives, the main evidence available from the information system and the alternative types of substantive procedures.

12.7 ☐ The audit program details substantive procedures required to provide sufficient appropriate audit evidence for each material account balance assertion.

12.8 ☐ Many income statement accounts are inextricably linked to one or more balance sheet/statement of financial position accounts. Thus, much of the evidence obtained through substantive procedures on balance sheet accounts provides evidence for income statement account balances. This allows more extensive use of analytical procedures in these accounts.

12.9 ☐ Because of their nature, a number of accounts and audit procedures are specifically covered by the audit standards.

SUMMARY

After assessing the risk of material misstatement, the auditor must assess how to reduce that risk to an acceptable level by performance of control tests and/or substantive procedures. This chapter has focused on the response to the risk of material misstatements through the design of substantive procedures (i.e. a predominantly substantive audit approach). The acceptable level of detection risk and level of substantive procedures are usually determined by consideration of the audit risk model. The auditor then plans specific substantive procedures to achieve the acceptable level of detection risk by exercising judgements about the nature, timing and extent of such procedures. The auditor also relates the tests to specific audit objectives to ensure that the overall objective of rendering an opinion on the financial statements as a whole is met.

The types of substantive procedures performed on particular account balances and transaction classes are discussed in more detail in the following chapters:

- chapter 14 — Auditing sales and receivables
- chapter 15 — Auditing purchases, payables and payroll
- chapter 16 — Auditing inventories and property, plant and equipment
- chapter 17 — Auditing cash and investments.

The auditor's decisions about the design of substantive procedures are documented in the form of written audit programs, which provide an outline of the work to be done and a way of controlling the audit and recording the work performed. A general framework may be used in developing effective and efficient audit programs for substantive procedures tailored to the entity's circumstances. There are special considerations in designing substantive procedures for selected types of accounts, including profit and loss accounts, accounting estimates and related parties. Ultimately, for most audits, the performance of these substantive tests will constitute a large part of the audit evidence that the auditor uses to form an opinion on the financial statements (discussed in chapter 7).

KEY TERMS

accounting estimate, p. 513

analytical procedures, p. 496

audit programs, p. 506

cut-off tests, p. 499

detection risk, p. 493

dual-purpose tests, p. 508

extent of substantive procedures, p. 503

generalised audit software, p. 503

initial engagements, p. 508

nature of substantive procedures, p. 496

planned detection risk, p. 494

planned level of substantive procedures, p. 495

related party transactions, p. 514

roll-forward testing, p. 502

tests of details of balances, p. 499

tests of details of transactions, p. 498

timing of substantive procedures, p. 502

MULTIPLE-CHOICE questions

12.1 If the predominantly substantive approach preliminary audit strategy is used, planned detection risk will be:
A. Low or very low.
B. Moderate or high.
C. At the higher level.
D. High or very high.

12.2 If the acceptable level of detection risk decreases, the assurance directly provided from:
A. Substantive procedures should increase.
B. Substantive procedures should decrease.
C. Tests of controls should increase.
D. Tests of controls should decrease.

12.3 The auditor assesses control risk because:
A. It includes the aspects of non-sampling risk that are controllable.
B. It indicates where inherent risk may be the greatest.
C. It affects the level of detection risk the auditor may accept.
D. It needs to be reported on in the auditor's report.

12.4 Which of these is not considered a substantive procedure?
A. Analytical procedures.
B. Tests of controls.
C. Tests of details of transactions.
D. Tests of details of balances.

12.5 Which of these would not be considered to be a test of details of balances?
A. Accounts receivable confirmations.
B. Observing the entity's stocktake.
C. Tracing an invoice to the sales journal.
D. Inspecting plant assets.

12.6 Which of these is not compatible with a high level of inherent and control risk?
A. Detection risk is low.
B. A larger sample should be used.
C. Year-end tests are preferable.
D. Substantive procedures are less effective.

12.7 The audit program is basically a list of:
A. Audit procedures to be performed.
B. Detailed audit objectives.
C. Account balances and their related assertions.
D. Control policies and procedures to be tested.

12.8 Extensive tests of details for an income statement account are least likely to be required when:
A. Analytical procedures reveal some unexpected fluctuations.
B. Inherent risk is high.
C. Detection risk is high.
D. Control risk is high.

12.9 What financial statement assertion is most often tested by CAATs?
A. Valuation.
B. Rights and obligations.
C. Measurement.
D. Disclosure.

12.10 Why are related party transactions a risk area for auditors?
- A. They have minimal disclosure requirements.
- B. They have a higher than average risk of irregularities.
- C. They have a direct impact on profit.
- D. They are difficult to assess.

REVIEW questions

12.11 Which components of the audit risk model can be controlled by the auditor? Discuss the interrelationships.

12.12 Identify and explain the three steps in assessing the risk of material misstatement.

12.13 Give three reasons why the predominantly substantive approach can be more suitable to smaller entities.

12.14 Identify the three types of substantive procedures and discuss the effectiveness of each.

12.15 Why are cut-off tests a special category of tests of details of transactions?

12.16 Explain why there is an increased audit risk from conducting procedures before the end of the reporting period and identify two ways in which this increased risk is controlled.

12.17 Why may an auditor decide to perform tests of details on income statement accounts rather than relying on analytical review?

12.18 How can generalised software be used to assist in performing substantive procedures during the audit?

12.19 What steps may the auditor perform in evaluating the reasonableness of accounting estimates?

12.20 Why is the audit of related party transactions a particular risk area for auditors?

PROFESSIONAL application questions

★ BASIC
★★ MODERATE
★★★ CHALLENGING

12.21 Substantive procedures ★

Listed below are fifteen substantive procedures:
1. Select a sample of non-current assets and sight them.
2. Review the income statement for unusual differences in the balances recorded for this year and last year.
3. Select a sample of invoices and ensure that they have been properly recorded in the sales ledger.
4. Review the company-prepared bank reconciliation.
5. Trace the last inventory received before the year-end to the inventory listing.
6. Review the adequacy of the company's allowance for doubtful debts.
7. Obtain the company's depreciation rates from the financial statements and check they have been applied correctly.
8. Perform an accounts receivable circularisation.
9. Review a sample of repairs and maintenance expenditure for the year to ensure that it does not include any items that are capital in nature.
10. Ensure that interest paid on the bank loan is correct by multiplying the interest rate by the outstanding principal for each month of the year.
11. Send a letter to the bank to confirm a loan taken out by the company during the year.
12. Attend the year-end stocktake and perform test counts on a sample of stock items.
13. Ensure that all contingent liabilities have been included in the notes to the accounts.

14. Review all invoices received for one month after the year-end to ensure that they do not relate to the current year.
15. Calculate the accounts receivable turnover and compare with previous year's turnover.

Required

(a) For each test, indicate the type of substantive procedure to which it relates (analytical review, tests of details of balances or tests of details of transactions).
(b) Give one assertion to which each test relates.

12.22 The audit risk model ★★

Angela is an audit manager in a medium-sized firm of chartered accountants. For many years she has carefully considered the audit risk model in her testing. When controls have been good, she has tested them and subsequently reduced her reliance on substantive testing. However, the corporate collapses of recent years have caused her to question this approach. From her reading of the financial press it is her understanding that many of these collapses have resulted from inadequate auditing of items on the income statement. This has made her re-evaluate her audit approach. In future, her audits will be based mainly on substantive testing with a focus on the income statement and her only evaluation of controls will be associated with the requirement to obtain an understanding.

Required

Discuss the appropriateness of this 'new' approach to auditing by the audit manager.

12.23 Potential misstatements ★★

The following are a list of risks to the financial report:
1. Senior management has offered large bonuses to managers to meet financial targets.
2. Analytical procedures for a manufacturer show a significant increase in both profit margins and inventory turnover days.
3. The industry in which the company operates is experiencing economic difficulties.
4. Analytical procedures for a retailer show significant decreases in both profit margins and inventory turnover days.
5. An employee responsible for cash payments did not receive a pay rise due to poor performance.

Required

For each risk identify the potential type of misstatement in the financial report and identify if the misstatement would have a pervasive effect on many or all of the assertions.

12.24 Identifying audit risks ★★

It is March 2015 and you are planning the financial report audit of your client Plush and Plastic Ltd for the year ended 30 June 2015. Plush and Plastic manufacture speciality toys and sell them directly to a range of small and medium sized retailers. You have arranged a meeting with Ted Counter, Plush and Plastic's CFO, to establish any audit risks so that you can complete your audit plan. The following information is provided by Ted in that meeting.

• During the year Plush and Plastic made a significant investment in a new online ordering system so its customers could log on and place orders directly. The intention was to reduce the amount of manual input required and to streamline the goods despatch and warehousing processes. The system has had many problems leading to incorrect goods being delivered and incorrect stock levels being recorded, which in turn has led to poor purchasing decisions being made. This has led to many customer complaints and returns of goods.
• As a result of the implementation of the new online system, the company is in the process of making a significant number of the sales order processing and warehouse staff redundant.
• In order to expand its capacity Plush and Plastic has carried out a major overhaul of some of its equipment and placed an order for new manufacturing equipment which will speed up

production times for its most popular products. The new machinery is expected to be available sometime in the next financial year and will be financed through a bank loan although no agreement has yet been confirmed with its bank.

- Due to the economic downturn some of Plush and Plastics' customers are finding it difficult to pay their bills and are asking for longer payment terms. There is some evidence that order levels from customers are starting to fall. As a result of the strain this has put on cash flows, Plush and Plastic has taken to paying its suppliers after 60 days when this was previously 30 days.

Required

Identify the audit risks for the audit of Plush and Plastic for the year ended 30 June 2015.

12.25 Audit software ★★

Dawson Household Ltd is a wholesaler of household goods including furniture, kitchen appliances, soft furnishings and electronic equipment. Dawson purchases products directly from the manufacturers and sells to a wide range of retailers both large and small. Dawson has around 400 customers.

The terms of agreements between Dawson and its customers vary widely in relation to discounts, credit limits and payment terms. The larger customers have balances of hundreds of thousands of dollars with amounts up to 60 days old whereas smaller customers have balances in the thousands of dollars and generally have payment terms of 30 days.

You are designing your audit testing for the receivables balance at the year end and due to the large number of customers you would like to use CAATs to improve the efficiency of the audit.

Required

Explain specific audit procedures that could be carried out using audit software to test Dawson's receivable balances.

12.26 Analytical review procedures ★★

Draft financial information for Darfield Electronics for the year to 30 June 2015 is as follows:

	2015 Draft $000s	2014 Actual $000s
Revenue	5267	4122
Cost of sales	(2519)	(2290)
Gross profit	**2748**	**1832**
Operating expenses	(1718)	(958)
Profit before interest and tax	**1030**	**874**
Cash	—	527
Trade receivables	931	587
Inventory	481	366
Bank overdraft	206	—
Trade payables	366	275

Required

Analyse the information above, identify audit risks and outline how the auditor should respond to these risks.

12.27 Substantive procedures, accounting estimates ★★

Your client, Sweet Sounds Ltd (SS), manufactures mini hi-fi systems. The company has a year-end of 30 June 2015. In December 2014, SS changed its manufacturing process to make its product more reliable. Because of this increased reliability, the company decided to increase the warranty on its products from 3 years to 5 years in relation to all sales made from 1 January 2015. From management's review of warranty claims relating to the new products, it was noted that claims were down by about 20% compared with the old product. Management made an estimate of the provision for warranty of $4 000 000 for 30 June 2015, up from $3 500 000 for the previous year.

Required

(a) What are the main audit assertions you should consider for this part of the audit for SS? Describe the types of substantive procedures you would perform to cover these assertions.

(b) Discuss any special risks in auditing provisions for warranty (and in auditing SS's provision for warranty in particular).

12.28 Analytical review procedures ★★★

You are an audit senior currently gathering audit evidence on the audit of Regens Ltd, a large listed company. Your manager has asked you to consider the use of analytical procedures in relation to the salaries expense and interest revenue. Materiality for the audit has been set at $250 000.

Salaries expense — $2 210 000

- Salaries are paid monthly to the 40 salaried staff.
- There are three levels of seniority and each level is paid a different rate. There are no pay variations within levels.
- Promotions occur annually at 1 July.
- Turnover is relatively high. Fifteen new staff started work during the year.
- All salaried staff received an increase of 5% on 1 January. There were no other salary increases during the year.
- Both control risk and inherent risk are medium.

Interest revenue — $315 500

- This revenue represents interest earned on bank bills.
- A maximum of five bills are in place at any one time. Bills are always placed for 4-monthly terms and rolled over at maturity.
- Rates vary according to the market.
- Control risk is high and inherent risk is medium.

Required

(a) Explain how you would verify each balance using analytical procedures. Describe the verification work you need to perform on the data used in these procedures.

(b) Using the information given, determine how much reliance you would place on the analytical procedures designed in (a). Explain your decision.

12.29 Impact on substantive procedures ★★★

Westinghome Ltd is a large listed company which specialises in the manufacture of whitegoods and other electrical appliances. It is late April 2015 and you are currently planning the 30 June 2015 audit. The auditor's report is due to be signed on 20 July 2015. During your planning, the following independent and material situations come to your attention.

1. On 1 January 2015, Westinghome signed a 3-year contract with KP Pty Ltd for the supply of cardboard packing boxes for its entire range of products. KP was selected as an exclusive supplier after an exhaustive tender process. One of KP's two directors is Ms M, the wife of one of Westinghome's directors, Mr M. Company minutes reveal that Mr M did not take part in either the preparation of the tender documents or the selection of the successful tenderer. You note that details of this contract were omitted from the preliminary list of related party transactions supplied to you by the financial controller.

2. Westinghome introduced a new system for the control of inventory on 1 January 2014. The company performed extensive testing on this new system and management was convinced that it was operating effectively. This system has a utility that can produce many specialised

reports for internal use by management. The system is a perpetual inventory system; management decided that a year-end stocktake would no longer be required and instead decided to perform monthly cyclical counts to ensure the system was functioning correctly.

3. During the year ended 30 June 2014, Westinghome changed several of its accounting policies. One of the policies changed was accounting for employee entitlements. The effect on the 30 June 2014 financial statements was immaterial and so it was not disclosed, although it was expected to have a material effect in subsequent years. The financial controller is new to the company and appears to be unaware that recent changes have occurred in accounting policies.

4. In 2013, Westinghome introduced a 'budget buster' range of small electrical appliances. The range was introduced to recapture the lower end of the appliance market, which Westinghome was slowly losing to cheaper imported products. Over the last 2 years, Westinghome began receiving reports that some budget buster electric kettles had been giving their users small electric shocks. Some of these kettles are still covered by warranty.

Required

(a) Discuss how your audit plan and audit approach would be affected as a result of each item.

(b) Where possible, relate the effects noted in (a) to specific financial statement assertions.

CASE studies

12.30 Use of computer-assisted audit techniques (CAATs) 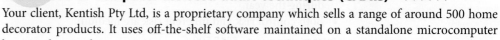★ ★ ★

Your client, Kentish Pty Ltd, is a proprietary company which sells a range of around 500 home decorator products. It uses off-the-shelf software maintained on a standalone microcomputer kept in the warehouse to manage its product lines. The following information is kept in the inventory master file in relation to each product:

1. Item code
2. Item description
3. Location(s)
4. Last movement in (date)
5. Last movement out (date)
6. Quantity on hand
7. Age of quantity on hand (< 1 month, 1–2 months, 2–3 months, > 3 months)
8. Cost per item
9. Total cost.

In addition, Kentish uses a standard stocktake schedule produced by the software for year-end stocktaking purposes. This schedule contains the following details:

1. Item code
2. Item description
3. Location(s)
4. Counted by
5. Checked by.

Kentish's owners and staff are not particularly computer-literate, but they do have a sound accounting knowledge and understand the importance of proper record-keeping. As Kentish is a small business with long-serving staff, employees have free access to the computer any time they need it.

The audit manager decided that a substantive audit approach should be used for inventory.

Required

(a) Assume that you downloaded the stocktaking schedule to your laptop computer and recorded the results of your stock counts electronically. Discuss the implications for the sufficiency and appropriateness of audit evidence as a result of taking this approach.

(b) Using the information on the contents of the inventory master file, outline how CAATs could be used to obtain evidence on the year-end valuation of inventory.

(c) Assume you were planning to use the inventory master file only to perform overall analytical procedures at the end of the audit. Discuss the types of tests that you would perform.

12.31 Substantive testing approach and risk ★★★

The Give for the Kids Foundation has engaged for more than twenty years in a range of fund raising activities in order to provide disadvantaged children with clothes, learning materials and sports equipment for school as well as providing toys and other gifts at Christmas.

The foundation is exempt for income tax purposes, but the rules in this regard are complex and any activity that might be thought as profit-making could be taxable. There is a detailed constitution which sets out the governance structure for the foundation as well as prescribing how the income can be spent, and sets limits on operational expenditure to ensure that the maximum of funds raised can be put to the charitable purpose.

Funds are raised in the following ways.

1. Fundraising events. The foundation receives funding from local government as well as corporate sponsors to cover the cost of running events, the foundation raising funds by charging fees to those attending these events; income also includes the auctioning of donated prizes.
2. Donations of sports equipment, clothing, toys and so on from individuals and companies.
3. Bequests left by generous individuals on their death.
4. Cheques and funds transfers paid directly into the foundation's bank account.
5. Cash collections at shopping centres and other locations.

Funds received to cover the costs of running fundraising events are received on the basis that they will be applied to specific purposes. Reports are required to be presented to the donors identifying how the amounts donated were spent. In some cases these reports must be audited. Cash and other donations may also come with restrictions.

You are planning the audit of the financial report.

Required

(a) Explain why a substantive testing approach is likely to be appropriate for the Give for the Kids Foundation financial report audit.

(b) Identify and explain the inherent risk in the information provided.

 RESEARCH question

12.32 Earnings management

Earnings management is an important issue for auditors. The following findings illustrate this point:

> Results of descriptive analyses indicate that the earnings management attempts in our sample occurred in numerous accounting areas, including revenue recognition, business combinations, intangibles, fixed assets, investments and leases, but by far the most frequently identified attempts involved reserves. Respondents believe that managers' attempts were motivated by a variety of incentives, including the need to meet analysts' estimates and influence the stock market, to reach targets set by compensation contracts or debt covenants, to communicate economic information to stakeholders, and to smooth income or improve future income, as well as by combinations of these incentives. Auditors adjusted 44 percent of the attempts in our sample, 21 percent were not adjusted because the auditor believed the client demonstrated compliance with GAAP, 17 percent because the auditor did not have convincing evidence the client's position was incorrect, and the remaining 18 percent because of some other reason (usually, immateriality).[1]

Required

(a) What is earnings management?

(b) Find evidence in relation to how the audit process affects earnings management.

(c) Discuss the impact of earnings management on the substantive procedures performed during the audit.

FURTHER READING

Australian Accounting Review, 15(3), 2005, pp. 67–74.

M Benis, 'Analytical procedures in auditing', in, *Blackwell Encyclopedia of Management*, vol. 1, *Accounting*, 2nd edn, ed. C Clubb, 2005, pp. 49–55.

SM Glover, DF Prawitt & TJ Wilks, 'Why do auditors over-rely on weak analytical procedures? The role of outcome and precision', *Auditing: A Journal of Practice and Theory*, 2005, pp. 197–220.

EA Gordon, E Henry, TJ Louwers & BJ Reed, 'Auditing related party transactions: a literature overview and research synthesis', *Accounting Horizons*, March 2007, pp. 81–102.

MR Gujarathi & M Kohlbeck, 'Reliance Corporation: inventory write-downs and reversals', *Issues in Accounting Education*, August 2007, pp. 503–14.

NB Hitzig, 'The hidden risk in analytical procedures: what WorldCom revealed', *The CPA Journal* 74(2), 2004, pp. 32–5.

R Tabor & B Bryan, 'Substantive auditing tests', in *Blackwell Encyclopedia of Management*, vol. 1, *Accounting*, 2nd edn, ed. C Clubb, 2005, pp. 406–8.

NOTES

1. Excerpts from MW Nelson, JA Elliott & RL Tarpley, 'Evidence from auditors about managers' and auditors' earnings management decisions', *The Accounting Review*, Supplement 2002, pp. 175–202.

Answers to multiple-choice questions

12.1 *A*   12.2 *A*   12.3 *C*   12.4 *B*   12.5 *C*   12.6 *D*   12.7 *A*   12.8 *C*   12.9 *C*   12.10 *B*

chapter 13

Audit sampling

OVERVIEW

13.1 Basic concepts of sampling

13.2 Use of samples for audit tests

13.3 Statistical sampling techniques

13.4 Non-statistical sampling techniques

Summary

Key terms

Appendix 13A: Non-statistical sampling of substantive test of details

Appendix 13B: Probability-proportional-to-size sampling

Appendix 13C: Test of controls using attribute sampling

Appendix 13D: Variable sampling using the mean-per-unit method

Multiple-choice questions

Review questions

Professional application questions

Case studies

Research question

Further reading

Notes

LEARNING objectives

After studying this chapter, you should be able to:

1 define audit sampling and discuss its applicability

2 distinguish between sampling and non-sampling risks

3 distinguish between statistical and non-statistical sampling

4 explain the steps in planning to select a sample

PROFESSIONAL STATEMENTS

Australian		International	
ASA 500	*Audit Evidence*	**ISA 500**	*Audit Evidence*
ASA 530	*Audit Sampling*	**ISA 530**	*Audit Sampling*

SCENE SETTER

The importance of audit sampling

The objective of the auditor when using audit sampling is to provide a reasonable basis for the auditor to draw conclusions about the population from which the sample is selected.

Source: International Federation of Accountants, ISA 530 *Audit Sampling*, paragraph 4.

Sampling is well established as an audit procedure, but this was not always the case. A textbook published in 1881 contained the following statement:

> A thorough and efficient Audit should embrace an examination of all the transactions of a Company, and an auditor acting on this principle would ascertain that all had been duly entered and discharged.[1]

However, the changing size and complexity of business was causing this to become an unrealistic approach. As early as 1895, Lindley LJ in the London and General Bank case (*Re London and General Bank Ltd* (No. 2) (1895) 2 Ch. 673) accepted sample testing as providing sufficient evidence for audit purposes. He said:

> Where there is nothing to excite suspicion, very little enquiry will be reasonable and quite sufficient; and in practice, I believe, businessmen select a few cases haphazard, see that they are right, and assume that others like them are correct also.

The most recent Australian standard on audit sampling is ASA 530 *Audit Sampling*, based on ISA 530.

In this chapter, we explain the basic concepts of audit sampling and its application in tests of controls and substantive tests of details. The chapter is divided into four sections. The first section explains how evidence obtained from sample testing introduces the risk that the evidence may not be representative of the population from which the sample is taken. This risk is known as sampling risk. The second section describes the process of sampling in audit testing from the planning stage, through the selection and testing of the sample to the evaluation of the results of sample tests. The third section explains the use of statistical sampling techniques and considers the relative merits of the different types. The fourth and final section considers why many practitioners may choose to use non-statistical sampling rather than statistical sampling.

The main body of the chapter does not go into detail about the calculations involved in performing a statistical sample. However, in the appendixes at the end of the chapter, three of the four case studies discuss statistical sampling methods and calculations in more detail. This is because we want to focus on the principles of audit sampling, which are applicable to all the differing types of sampling methods.

LEARNING objective 1

Define audit sampling and discuss its applicability.

13.1 BASIC CONCEPTS OF SAMPLING

Sampling is defined in ASA 530, paragraph 5(a) (ISA 530) as:

> the application of audit procedures to less than 100% of items within a population of audit relevance such that all sampling units have a chance of selection in order to provide the auditor with a reasonable basis on which to draw conclusions about the entire population.

Giving all items in the **population** a chance of selection enables the auditor to obtain audit evidence to help form a conclusion about the population from which the sample is drawn. Not all items must have an equal probability of selection, but all items must have some probability of selection for the selection method to be described as audit sampling.

Sampling may be used in tests of controls or substantive testing. The sampling principles for both are essentially the same. The main difference is at the testing stage where the 'error' relates to control deviations when performing tests of controls or misstatements when performing substantive procedures. An example of sampling in tests of controls is the examination of a sample of purchase invoices to see that they have been initialled by the employee responsible as having been checked against the receiving report. The objective of the test is to confirm compliance with the control procedure laid down. As explained in chapter 11, the proportion of deviations in the sample enables the auditor to draw conclusions as to the effectiveness of the control procedure, contributing to the assessment of control risk.

An example of sampling in substantive tests of details is the checking of a sample of invoices against receiving reports to verify the occurrence of recorded purchase transactions. The incidence of errors in the sample will enable the auditor to draw conclusions as to the occurrence of recorded purchase transactions.

One of the most important issues for the auditor to consider in audit sampling is the risk of drawing an incorrect conclusion from the sample selected. Another important consideration is the distinction between **statistical sampling** and **non-statistical sampling**.

LEARNING 2 objective

Distinguish between sampling and non-sampling risks.

13.1.1 Sampling risk and non-sampling risk

When sampling is used to obtain audit evidence, uncertainties may result from factors associated directly with the use of sampling (**sampling risk**) and from those unrelated to sampling (**non-sampling risk**).

Sampling risk

Sampling risk is defined in ASA 530, paragraph 5(c) (ISA 530) as:

> the risk that the auditor's conclusion based on a sample may be different from the conclusion if the entire population were subjected to the same audit procedure.

The following example illustrates this point. An auditor selects a sample of direct bank payment (or cheque) requisitions to check for appropriate approval as part of tests of controls. The client has a file with 1000 requisitions for the year and 50 of those requisitions are not approved, a fact not known by the auditor. A representative sample of 20 should therefore contain 19 correctly approved requisitions and one that was not approved. Sampling risk is the risk that a randomly selected sample will not be representative (i.e. a sample of 20 will not consist of 19 correctly approved requisitions and one that was not approved). The larger the sample, the more probable it is that it will consist of approved and not-approved requisitions in the same proportion as the population. This probability will increase until the sample size is the same as the size of the population, where sampling risk is reduced to zero.

In performing tests of controls and substantive tests of details, the following types of sampling risk — as outlined in ASA 530, paragraph 5(c)(i)(ii) (ISA 530) — may occur (figure 13.1):

(i) In the case of a test of controls, that controls are more effective than they actually are [risk of overreliance], or in the case of a test of details, that a material misstatement does not exist when in fact it does [risk of incorrect acceptance]. The auditor is primarily concerned with this type of erroneous conclusion because it affects audit effectiveness and is more likely to lead to an inappropriate audit opinion.

(ii) In the case of a test of controls, that controls are less effective than they actually are [risk of under-reliance], or in the case of a test of details, that a material misstatement exists when in fact it does not [risk of incorrect rejection]. This type of erroneous conclusion affects audit efficiency as it would usually lead to additional work to establish that initial conclusions were incorrect.

These risks can have a significant impact on both the effectiveness and efficiency of the audit as shown in figure 13.1 (overleaf).

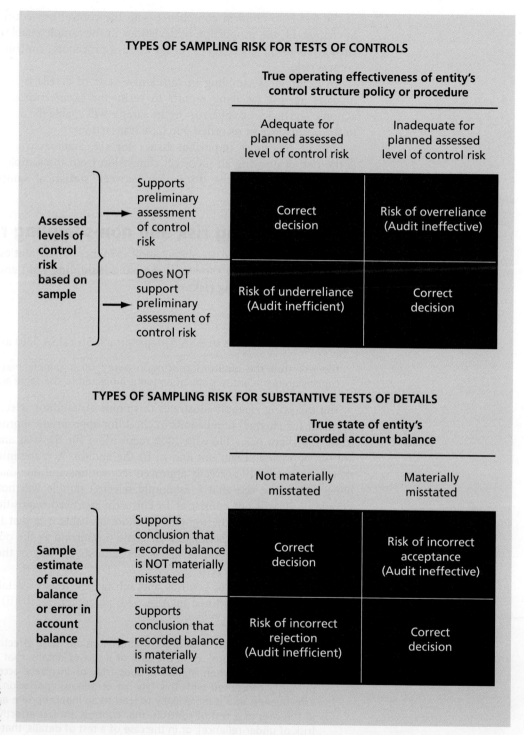

TYPES OF SAMPLING RISK FOR TESTS OF CONTROLS

True operating effectiveness of entity's control structure policy or procedure

		Adequate for planned assessed level of control risk	Inadequate for planned assessed level of control risk
Assessed levels of control risk based on sample	Supports preliminary assessment of control risk	Correct decision	Risk of overreliance (Audit ineffective)
	Does NOT support preliminary assessment of control risk	Risk of underreliance (Audit inefficient)	Correct decision

TYPES OF SAMPLING RISK FOR SUBSTANTIVE TESTS OF DETAILS

True state of entity's recorded account balance

		Not materially misstated	Materially misstated
Sample estimate of account balance or error in account balance	Supports conclusion that recorded balance is NOT materially misstated	Correct decision	Risk of incorrect acceptance (Audit ineffective)
	Supports conclusion that recorded balance is materially misstated	Risk of incorrect rejection (Audit inefficient)	Correct decision

FIGURE 13.1:
Sampling risks for tests of controls and substantive tests of details

The **risk of overreliance** and the **risk of incorrect acceptance** relate to audit effectiveness. When reaching either of these false conclusions, the auditor may find that the combined procedures may be insufficient to detect material misstatements, and that he or she may not have a reasonable basis for an opinion. In contrast, the **risk of underreliance** and the **risk of incorrect rejection** relate to the efficiency of the audit. When reaching either of these wrong conclusions, the auditor will increase substantive procedures unnecessarily. However, such effort will ordinarily lead to a correct conclusion, ultimately, and the audit will nevertheless be effective. The sampling risk associated with audit effectiveness is of much greater concern than the sampling risk associated with audit efficiency because it can lead to an inappropriate audit opinion.

Non-sampling risk

Non-sampling risk is defined in ASA 530 paragraph 5(d) (ISA 530) as:

> the risk that the auditor reaches an erroneous conclusion for any reason not related to sampling risk.

Sources of non-sampling risk include human mistakes (such as failing to recognise errors in documents, applying auditing procedures that are inappropriate to the audit objective, and misinterpreting the results of a sample) and reliance on wrong information received from another party. Non-sampling risk can never be mathematically measured. However, proper planning and supervision and adherence to the quality control standards described earlier can keep this risk to a minimum.

This means that even if the auditor selected 100% of the items within a population for testing, there would still be a risk of drawing an inappropriate conclusion. That is why it is theoretically impossible for auditors to provide an absolute level of assurance on any assurance engagement.

LEARNING 3
objective
Distinguish between statistical and non-statistical sampling.

13.1.2 Statistical and non-statistical sampling

Statistical sampling has the following two characteristics according to ASA 530 paragraph 5(g) (ISA 530):
- **random selection** of the sample items
- the use of probability theory to evaluate sample results, including the measurement of sampling risk.

Statistical sampling does not replace judgement. It provides a decision model within which the auditor's judgements as to the acceptable level of detection risk, testing materiality and other variables are the inputs. Given the acceptable level of both sampling risk and materiality for the audit procedure, the model specifies the sample size and evaluates the sample results in terms of sampling risk and materiality. The interpretation of the results is, therefore, only as reliable as the values placed on the sampling risk and testing materiality.

Non-statistical sampling is a sampling approach that does not have the above characteristics of statistical sampling. In non-statistical sampling the auditor uses judgement directly, both to determine sample size (given the planned level of detection risk and of testing materiality) and to interpret the results against the audit objective. Historically, non-statistical sampling was called judgement sampling; however, as revealed in the preceding discussion, both approaches require a significant amount of judgement. The main difference between the two is that sampling risk can be quantified when using statistical sampling, which requires the use of a random selection method.

The choice of non-statistical or statistical sampling does not affect the selection of auditing procedures to be applied to a sample. Moreover, it does not affect the appropriateness of evidence obtained about individual sample items or the appropriate response by the auditor to errors found in sample items. These matters require the exercise of professional judgement.

Current practice

In Australia, the majority of audit firms use some type of audit sampling for most audit clients. A large number of firms use non-statistical sampling, because it allows the auditor a greater degree of judgement in choosing a sample size and evaluating results based on previous client knowledge. A common approach to sample selection is **haphazard selection** (this method is inappropriate when using statistical sampling). Methods vary between audit firms and within a firm between clients. Statistical sampling is much more likely, for example, for the audit of a financial institution where the audit approach relies heavily on compliance testing. A common statistical sampling computer package used by Australian auditors is ACL. However, for a predominantly substantive audit of a small manufacturing entity, for example, non-statistical sampling is more likely to be used.

There have been very few studies of sampling practices among auditors and no recent studies in the Australian auditing environment, so any assessment of the types of practices used relies mainly on anecdotal evidence. However, Hall, Hunton and Pierce performed a study of sampling practices in the United States in 2002. They found that 85% of sample selection by auditors was non-statistical (i.e. 15% used statistical sample selection), including 74% who used the haphazard method.[2] The Professional Environment activity looks at sample selection.

13.1.3 Types of testing

The auditor can choose to select all items (100% examination) or select specific items.

Selecting all items

The auditor may decide that it is appropriate to examine the entire population of items that make up the account balance or class of transactions. This decision is unlikely in tests of controls but may sometimes occur in substantive testing; for example, in performing the audit of an account balance that is made up of a small number of large-value items, and when inherent and control risks are high, the auditor may find it cost-effective to examine the entire population. This may be a means of reducing sampling risk to zero, but does not constitute audit sampling.

Selecting specific items

Specific items within a population can be tested, based on the auditor's knowledge of the business and the characteristics of the population being tested. ASA 530 paragraph A13 and Appendix 4 (ISA 530) outlines specific ways that items may be selected and is discussed later in this chapter.

Audit evidence choices

There are methods of obtaining audit evidence where audit sampling is rarely used. Most analytical review procedures do not involve audit sampling because they generally involve analysis of large amounts of data in summarised formats, therefore resulting in little need for sampling. The evidence-gathering techniques of enquiry and observation (often used to understand internal controls) are also rarely associated with any form of audit sampling.

You are the supervisor of the audit of Upton Ltd for the year ended 30 June 2015 and one of the assistants has been auditing the debtors, which are shown in the draft balance sheet at a value of $3 745 000. This balance is made up of 2000 accounts receivable (also known as debtors) ledger accounts.

It is noted in the working papers that 80 accounts were selected for checking. The basis of sample selection was as follows:

- the 15 largest accounts were selected
- haphazard sampling of the remainder
- any balances under $500 were regarded as too small to be chosen.

The test performed on those items selected was to ask the customers to confirm in writing what they think the balance outstanding was at year-end (accounts receivable circularisation).

The results of the test show the following:

	Number of items selected	Balance in sales ledger	Balance confirmed by debtor
No errors found (includes the 15 largest accounts)	58	$395 000	$395 000
No confirmation by debtor but confirmed using other audit procedures	5	5 800	5 800
Differences due to goods in transit to customer	4	9 500	6 300
Errors in calculating invoice total	1	1 900	2 100
Invoices posted to incorrect debtors ledger account	3	900	770
Invoice disputes with customer	5	3 100	1 800
Debtor confirmed nil balance outstanding	4	1 200	0
Total	80	$417 400	$411 770

Activities

(a) Discuss the method of sample selection and consider how this could be improved in relation to the different elements within the overall accounts receivable population.

(b) For each of the categories where errors have been identified, discuss the extent to which they should be considered as one-off errors or should be extrapolated to calculate the possible error in the population as a whole.

LEARNING objective 4

Explain the steps in planning to select a sample.

13.2 USE OF SAMPLES FOR AUDIT TESTS

Regardless of whether statistical or non-statistical sampling is used, the auditor undertakes some common steps:

- planning the sample
- selecting and testing the sample
- evaluating the results.

These steps are outlined in more detail in figure 13.2 (overleaf).

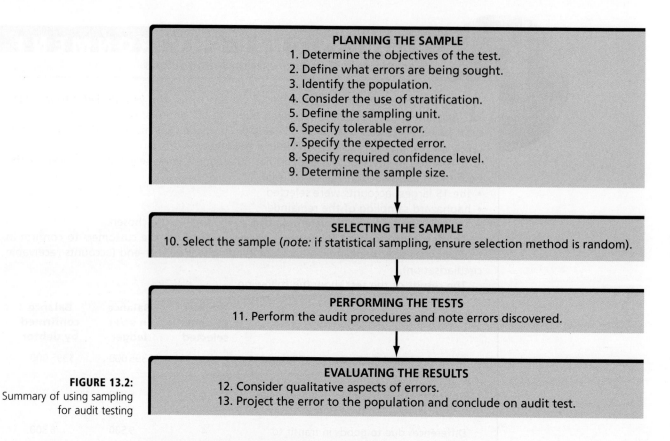

PLANNING THE SAMPLE
1. Determine the objectives of the test.
2. Define what errors are being sought.
3. Identify the population.
4. Consider the use of stratification.
5. Define the sampling unit.
6. Specify tolerable error.
7. Specify the expected error.
8. Specify required confidence level.
9. Determine the sample size.

SELECTING THE SAMPLE
10. Select the sample (*note:* if statistical sampling, ensure selection method is random).

PERFORMING THE TESTS
11. Perform the audit procedures and note errors discovered.

EVALUATING THE RESULTS
12. Consider qualitative aspects of errors.
13. Project the error to the population and conclude on audit test.

FIGURE 13.2:
Summary of using sampling for audit testing

13.2.1 Planning the sample

Once the auditor has decided that examining a sample will yield sufficient evidence on the operation of a control or on the absence of material misstatements in a transaction class or account balance, it is important to plan the sample testing process properly if the results are to be projected to the entire population. Planning the sample involves the following steps:

- determining the objectives of the test
- defining what errors are being sought
- identifying the population and sampling unit
- specifying tolerable error, expected error and required confidence level
- deciding the size of the sample.

Determining the objectives of the test

The auditor needs to consider the specific objectives to be achieved and the combination of audit procedures that is most likely to achieve those objectives. It is important to determine what constitutes an error as well as the appropriate population from which to select the sample. Audit sampling is applicable both for tests of controls and for substantive tests of details. Outlined as follows are summaries of how sampling is used for these testing approaches.

Tests of controls

The overall purpose of tests of controls is to evaluate the effectiveness of the design and operation of internal controls. Sampling is applicable in testing the operation of controls only when there is a trail of documentary or electronic evidence of the performance of control procedures. Such control procedures normally fall into the categories of authorisation procedures, documents and records, and independent checks.

Attribute sampling describes statistical methods of sampling to test the operating effectiveness of controls by measuring the deviation rate. The rate of deviation represents the proportion of transactions tested that have not been processed in accordance with laid-down procedures.

Substantive tests of details

Sampling plans for substantive tests of details may take one of two approaches. The first approach is to obtain evidence that an account balance is not materially misstated (e.g. the carrying amount of accounts receivable). The second approach is to make an independent estimate of some amount (e.g. to value inventory for which no recorded carrying amount exists). Monetary unit sampling is sometimes used in substantive tests of details because it is a statistical technique to estimate the dollar amount of an account balance.

Defining what errors are being sought

The auditor must consider what constitutes an error by referring to the objectives of the test. In tests of controls, the test objective is the identification of 'deviations' from the laid-down control procedure, as discussed in chapter 11. In substantive testing, the test objective is the identification of 'errors or misstatements' in recorded transactions or balances, as discussed in chapter 12. Throughout this chapter, the generic term 'errors' is sometimes used to describe both deviations and misstatements.

The type of error expected will be related to the objective of the test. However, an audit procedure may also reveal errors that were not specifically being sought. When examining purchases invoices to verify that quantities invoiced agree with those on the receiving report, an auditor may also notice some other defect in the invoice, such as errors in posting prices on the invoices. Sample evidence can be interpreted as evidence of the incidence of errors in the population as a whole only for those errors that are being sought. Other errors must be regarded as individual occurrences, which must be separately evaluated. It may be necessary for the auditor to conduct further tests that are designed to determine the extent of such errors; an error must never be neglected simply because it is not what was being verified by a particular test. Cleverly concealed frauds can sometimes be discovered by such chance events.

Identifying the population and sampling unit

The auditor must carefully identify the population and the sampling unit. In particular, the auditor must consider the objective of the audit test to ensure that the population and sampling unit are appropriate. At this stage, the auditor may also consider stratification of the population to increase audit efficiency.

Population

The first stage in planning the sample test is to identify the relevant population. ASA 530 paragraph 5(b) (ISA 530) defines a 'population' as:

> the entire set of data from which a sample is selected and about which the auditor wishes to draw conclusions.

The auditor must ensure that the population is as follows.

- *Appropriate* to the objective of the sampling procedure. When testing for overstatement of accounts payable, for example, the auditor could define the population as the accounts payable listing. However, when testing for understatement of accounts payable, it is inappropriate to use the accounts payable listing; the appropriate population is subsequent payments, unpaid invoices, suppliers' statements and unmatched receiving reports. This is because understatement is about finding out what is not recorded. By looking only at the accounts payable listing, the auditor is simply confirming what has already been recorded.

- *Complete.* Ensuring completeness is important and requires particular care. It is made easier by the use of prenumbering in recording transactions. For the auditor to be able to make appropriate assessments of the level of monetary errors or of the application of a particular control, the population needs to include all relevant items from throughout the period. A complete population is particularly important when the auditor is using computer-assisted audit techniques to perform sample selection — that is, the auditor must use the correct file.

Stratification

A common approach to increasing audit efficiency in sampling is **stratification** of the population. Stratification is defined in ASA 530 paragraph 5(h) (ISA 530) as:

the process of dividing a population into sub-populations, each of which is a group of sampling units that have similar characteristics (often monetary value).

The objective of stratification is to focus greater audit work on areas that are of higher inherent risk or potentially materially misstated. Monetary value is the most common method of stratifying a population, particularly for asset balances. The main risk with asset balances is overstatement, so the auditor will want to place more emphasis on testing items of large dollar values. In a non-current assets register, for example, the assets may be split into three strata:

1. balances greater than $2 000 000
2. balances of $100 000 to $2 000 000
3. balances less than $100 000.

The auditor may choose to perform tests on a random sample of 50% of the items in group 1, twenty items in group 2, and ten items in group 3. When using computer-assisted audit techniques, stratification of the population and sample selection can be performed by most auditing software packages according to whatever criteria are specified by the auditor.

Where individual items are selected for 100% testing on the grounds of materiality, the results of testing such items must be separated from the results of sample testing the remaining items in the population.

Stratification is a means of reducing audit costs while increasing the efficiency of the audit. It is a very popular technique for helping with audit sampling, particularly in the audit areas of accounts receivable; inventory; and property, plant and equipment.

Stratification of the population is consistent with the requirements of 'sampling' because every item in the total population still has a chance of being selected. However, the main difference is that the probability of particular items being selected varies depending on the stratum in which they are located.

Sampling unit

A **sampling unit** means the individual items constituting a population — for example, sales invoices, debtors' balances, non-current assets on a register and a listing of suppliers. The sampling unit can be individual transactions or balances. It will often appear to be self-evident but sometimes requires closer consideration. Accounts payable, for example, may be made up of a population of unpaid invoices or amounts owing to particular suppliers. The auditor will need to consider whether any particular advantage arises out of using a particular sampling unit. Sometimes, customers will be unable to respond to a request for confirmation of the balance owed, but they can confirm individual invoices outstanding; in such cases, the best sampling unit would be the unpaid invoices making up the balance.

When probability-proportional-to-size sampling is used, the sampling unit is an individual dollar (or other monetary unit) contained in the population. This method is discussed in section 13.3.3.

Specify tolerable misstatement

The **tolerable misstatement** is defined in ASA 530 paragraph 5(i) (ISA 530) as:

> the monetary amount set by the auditor in respect of which the auditor seeks to obtain an appropriate level of assurance that the monetary amount set by the auditor is not exceeded by the actual misstatement in the population.

Specify tolerable rate of deviation

The **tolerable rate of deviation** means a rate of deviation from prescribed internal control procedures set by the auditor, in respect of which the auditor seeks to obtain an appropriate level of assurance that the rate of deviation set by the auditor is not exceeded by the actual rate of deviation in the population.

Specify required confidence level

In tests of controls, this is the risk of overreliance, which is the risk that the allowable assessed control risk is lower than it actually is. In substantive testing, this is the risk of incorrect acceptance, which is the risk that testing suggests a material error does not exist when in fact it does. This risk relates to the effectiveness of the audit and is part of sampling risk. The auditor would consider this for both statistical and non-statistical sampling; however, this risk is quantified for statistical sampling.

Deciding the size of the sample

In determining an appropriate sample size, the auditor's main concern is with reducing sampling risk to an acceptably low level. The level of sampling risk that the auditor is willing to accept will have an inverse relationship with the sample size required. The sample size can be determined by the application of a statistically based formula (based on tolerable error and required confidence level) or through the exercise of professional judgement.

Sampling, as an audit procedure, is valid only if the sample selected for testing is representative of the population from which it is drawn, so that the incidence of errors or deviations in the sample closely approximates the incidence of errors or deviations in the population. The larger the sample, the more representative of the population it is likely to be. However, only a 100% sample will be completely representative. Given that the purpose of sampling is to save time and cost, it is pointless to audit a larger sample than necessary. Population size, which is the factor most commonly presumed to be the major influence on sample size, has no effect on sample size for populations over 5000. Table 13.1 (overleaf) outlines factors that influence sample size for tests of controls.

TABLE 13.1:
Factors that influence sample
size for tests of controls

Factor	Effect on sample size
An increase in the extent to which the auditor's risk assessment takes into account relevant controls	Increase
An increase in the tolerable rate of deviation	Decrease
An increase in the expected rate of deviation of the population to be tested	Increase
An increase in the auditor's required level of assurance that the tolerable rate of deviation is not exceeded by the actual rate of deviation in the population	Increase
An increase in the number of sampling units in the population	Negligible effect

Source: ASA 530 Appendix 2 (ISA 530 Appendix 2). Further explanation can be found by reference to ASA 530, Appendix 2.

Table 13.2 outlines factors that influence sample size for substantive procedures.

TABLE 13.2:
Factors that influence
sample size for substantive
procedures

Factor	Effect on sample size
An increase in the auditor's assessment of the risk of material misstatement	Increase
An increase in the use of other substantive procedures directed at the same assertion	Decrease
An increase in the auditor's desired level of assurance that tolerable misstatement is not exceeded by actual misstatement in the population	Increase
An increase in tolerable misstatement	Decrease
An increase in the amount of misstatement the auditor expects to find in the population	Increase
Stratification of the population when appropriate	Decrease
The number of sampling units in the population	Negligible effect

Source: ASA 530 Appendix 3 (ISA 530 Appendix 3). Further explanation can be found by reference to ASA 530 Appendix 3.

The case study in appendix 13A to this chapter provides a formula that can be used to determine sample size based on judgements concerned with required assurance, tolerable misstatement and tolerable rate of deviation.

13.2.2 Selecting and testing the sample

The test objectives and sample size are generally determined during the audit planning and detailed in the audit plan. In the performance of the audit, the staff member responsible then selects the required number of individual members of the population for testing, performs the test and evaluates the results.

Selecting the sample

The basic principle in selecting the sample is that each item in the population must have a chance of being selected, but not necessarily an equal chance. Statistical sampling requires random selection so each sampling unit has a known chance of being selected.

A sample can be selected in a number of ways. The selection approaches suggested in ASA 530 paragraph A13 and Appendix 4 (ISA 530) include:

- random
- systematic
- haphazard.

Another type of selection noted in ASA 530 Appendix 4 is called **block selection**. This is not considered a method of audit sampling because most populations are structured so that items in a sequence can be expected to have similar characteristics. Given this problem, it is difficult to draw valid inferences about the population based on the sample selected. However, this method of selection may be appropriate; for example, if the auditor suspects fraud in accounts payable, then he or she may decide to review all transactions for a particular month.

Random selection

Random selection is generally considered to be the best method of obtaining a sample to evaluate the results statistically. Each item in the population has a known (often equal) chance of selection and a computer program may be used to generate random numbers to test. Alternatively, if computer-assisted audit techniques are being used and the population is on the auditor's computer, most auditing software packages will allow an audit sample to be selected at random. The advantage of this method is that it does not allow auditor bias to affect the selections of the sample, either knowingly or not. Random selection is generally associated with statistical sampling, but is often used in non-statistical sampling as well. Historically, auditors used random number tables to generate random samples. Illustrations of how a random selection might be made using ACL software are shown in figure 13.3(a) and (b). These examples show how the auditor might randomly select 40 invoices from a population of invoices numbered 1 to 10 500. The seed can be any random number and is used to start the random number selection process.

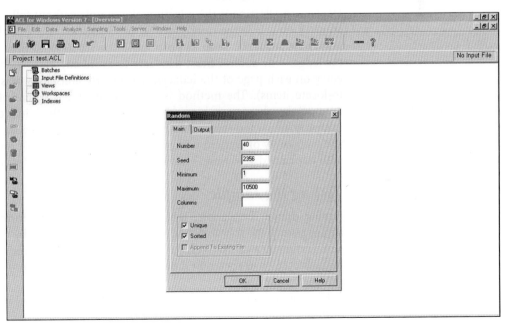

FIGURE 13.3(a):
Random selection using ACL software — selecting options

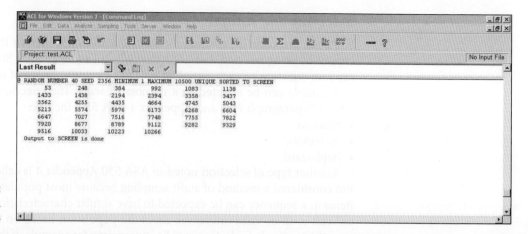

FIGURE 13.3(b):
Random selection using ACL software — results

Systematic selection

Systematic selection is the process of dividing the number of sampling units in the population by the sample size to give a **sampling interval**. The population (say 8200) is divided by the sample size (say 40) to obtain the sampling interval (205 in this case). Every 205th item is then selected, starting from a randomly selected point between 1 and 205. To be able to evaluate the results statistically, the auditor must randomly select the starting point, not use the haphazard method of selection.

The criticism of systematic selection is that the population may have a fixed pattern; for example, employee numbers of supervisors may always end in 0, so that a sampling interval that is a multiple of 10 will result in a sample of supervisors only, or one that excludes supervisors. The auditor should have sufficient knowledge of the population to make sure this does not happen. When this problem could arise, the auditor should use random selection to select the sample.

Haphazard selection

Haphazard selection is the selection of a sample without following a structured technique. Sometimes, this is the only practical method when the population is not ordered in any numerical sequence, such as postings to the repairs and maintenance expense account in the ledger. The auditor must take care to avoid any bias (such as avoiding the first or last entry on each page of the ledger), particularly conscious bias (such as avoiding difficult-to-locate items). The method is not recommended where other methods are available, because the absence of bias cannot be subsequently evidenced. Haphazard selection is inappropriate when statistical sampling is being used because the auditor cannot measure the probability of an item being selected. An illustration of the problem of bias associated with haphazard selection is outlined in the following Professional Environment box.

Testing the sample

Having drawn the sample, the auditor should then perform audit procedures that are appropriate to the test objective on each item selected. In the case of missing documents or similar difficulties encountered in completing the test, the auditor must consider the item to be misstated or to represent a deviation from laid-down controls, and evaluate the sample evidence accordingly.

Once audit procedures have been performed, the errors or deviations discovered need to be evaluated.

*T*he first research study to document selection bias in haphazard samples appeared in 2000 in *Behavioral Research in Accounting* [BRIA] (vol. 12). In this study, individuals selected samples of vouchers and inventory bins using haphazard selection. Analyses of these samples disclosed selection biases in favour of population elements that were larger, conveniently located, brightly coloured, or that had fewer adjacent neighbours. Furthermore, the magnitudes of these selection biases were significant, with some elements selected 57% more often than appropriate for equal probability sampling.

A second study, which appeared in 2001 in *Auditing: A Journal of Practice & Theory* (vol. 20), tested whether doubling the size of an audit sample would reliably eliminate the bias inherent in haphazard sampling. The study used populations of vouchers and inventory bins similar to those employed in the *BRIA* study. Typically, only about 12% of the bias was eliminated, making this approach ineffective as a method for eliminating selection bias in haphazard samples.

The tendency of haphazard sampling to yield biased selections appears to result from subconscious human behaviour in the areas of (1) visual perception and (2) the performance of tasks requiring physical effort. Regarding visual perception, research in psychology has long established that individuals see what they consciously direct their attention to, and they subconsciously see other objects that fall into their field of view. This subconscious visual perception process occurs automatically. For example, some individuals passing through a traffic intersection, once through the intersection, cannot remember looking at the light before proceeding through the intersection. For these individuals, the likelihood is that automatic subconscious processes did see the light, identified it as green, and directed continued movement through the intersection, all without their conscious recognition of the process.

This automatic subconscious visual perception process is thought to play a central role in creating biased haphazard selections via the following mechanism. In haphazard sampling, an auditor attempts to select sample items as randomly as possible. That is, population elements are selected with no specific reason for their inclusion. Procedurally, the auditor scans the population listing (or population) and, because no explicit selection strategy is followed (e.g. random or systematic selection), population elements that stand out and draw attention are selected. Even if the auditor conscientiously tries to avoid noticing any features, automatic subconscious visual processes identity these features, and function to bias the selections in favour of population elements that stand out and draw attention. The result of this process is that haphazard sample selections are likely biased by variations in the degree to which various population elements stand out visually and draw attention to themselves.

A second automatic subconscious behaviour thought to affect haphazard sample selections is the innate tendency (documented by biology research) of individuals to minimise the energy expenditure in carrying out their physical tasks. This energy-conserving tendency suggests that when haphazard sampling is used, population elements that are easier to access are more likely to be selected than elements that are more difficult to access.

Given these principles from psychology and biology, one should expect haphazard samples to be biased in favour of population elements that draw attention and population elements that are conveniently located. Regarding the ability to draw attention, marketing professionals have long recognised that larger items and brightly coloured items are better at attracting attention. Participants in the *BRIA* and *Auditing* studies, even though specifically instructed to choose items haphazardly, demonstrated bias in favour of large vouchers and inventory bins, as well as brightly coloured inventory bins.

Another factor related to the ability to draw attention is the finding from psychology research that objects with few adjacent neighbours tend to stand out and draw attention.

Regarding the impact of a convenient location, most individuals who have worked with four-drawer file cabinets find that accessing contents in the top drawer and the front of each drawer requires less effort, hence the selection bias in favour of these items as reported in the *BRIA* and *Auditing* studies.

Source: Excerpts from TW Hall, TL Herron & BJ Pierce, 'How reliable is haphazard sampling?', *The CPA Journal*, January 2006, pp. 26–8.

13.2.3 Evaluating the results

Each error or deviation discovered will need to be examined for its implications (i.e. its qualitative aspects). Errors or deviations that appear to be consistent with those expected during the procedure's planning can then be projected to consider the effect on the population. Given the planned level of sampling risk, it is assumed that the sample deviation or error rate is representative of the rate of deviation or errors in the population.

Both non-statistical and statistical sampling require the sample results to be projected on the population. The key difference with non-statistical sampling is that sampling risk is not mathematically quantified, but assessed on a more qualitative basis.

Considering the qualitative aspects of errors

In analysing errors, the auditor must consider whether the error has an effect on the whole population or is an isolated or localised occurrence.

An error caused by posting a sales invoice to the wrong customer's account will not affect the total balance of accounts receivable. Similarly, a control deviation properly authorised by management will not affect the assessed level of control risk.

Errors relating to events that can be specifically identified (i.e. payroll errors occurring when the computer broke down and payrolls had to be prepared manually) may be regarded as localised and not affecting the population as a whole.

Projecting the error to the population and concluding an audit test

Where the qualitative analysis identifies errors consistent with the objective of the test, the auditor then draws conclusions about the population, based on the results of testing the sample (of course, in projecting errors to the population it is important that the sample is representative of the population).

Tests of controls

The rate of deviations in the sample is known as the sample deviation rate and, given a representative sample, that rate can be taken to be the rate of deviations in the population or projected error. The auditor must be aware that, because of the sampling risk, the sample deviation rate may not equal the projected error rate. If, in a sample of fifty, two deviations from laid-down control procedures are discovered, then the projected deviation rate for the population can be estimated as 4% ($2 \div 50 = 4\%$). If this is no worse than the tolerable deviation rate (or tolerable error), then it is appropriate to confirm the preliminary assessment of control risk. This assessment does vary, however, depending on whether the auditor uses statistical or non-statistical techniques. In this example, if non-statistical sampling is being used, when comparing the projected deviation rate (4%) to the tolerable deviation rate (e.g. assessed as 8%) the auditor must qualitatively consider the sampling risk that the sample deviation rate exceeds the tolerable deviation rate. The sampling risk is calculated when using statistical sampling. An example of this type of sampling is shown in appendix 13C to this chapter. However, if the deviation rate is much lower than expected, then this cannot be interpreted as justifying a lower assessed level of control risk. This level of risk has been determined from an evaluation of the overall effectiveness of controls.

If the projected deviation rate exceeds the tolerable deviation rate, then the preliminary assessment of control risk is not confirmed. Depending on qualitative considerations of actual deviations or on the existence of compensating controls, the auditor must reassess control risk at a higher level, thus reducing the acceptable detection risk. This means that the auditor has to revise the audit program to increase the level of substantive procedures. This is discussed in chapter 12.

Substantive tests

In substantive testing, to make a decision about the population the auditor will project the sample results onto the population. The most common method of doing this is by the relative differences between the recorded and audited amounts (**difference estimation**) that will give a projected error. When non-statistical sampling is used, the auditor must judgementally consider the sampling risk that the projected error does not equal the actual total misstatement in the population.

Where **projected error** approaches or exceeds tolerable error, the auditor will need to consider carefully whether additional evidence may be necessary. It would normally be appropriate to select a further sample, thus reducing sampling risk. (However, where statistical sampling is used, certain sampling plans do not provide for extension of the existing sample.) If the further sample confirms the projected results, indicating a substantial error, then the auditor will ask management to revise the recorded amount. If the projected error is only slightly greater than the tolerable error and management is unwilling to make any corrections, then the error will be carried forward to the working paper showing aggregate uncorrected misstatements for evaluation at the end of the audit (see chapter 18).

Where a population has been stratified, the projected error must be related to the specific subpopulation. Errors in items singled out for selective testing must be omitted from the errors projected to the population.

When using statistical sampling, the auditor may use the difference estimation method or a method that estimates the population mean called the **mean-per-unit method**. Both methods in a statistical sampling context are discussed later in this chapter and the mean-per-unit method is illustrated in appendix 13D to this chapter.

Do you know . . .

13.1 ☐ Sampling is the testing of a representative sample to obtain evidence about a population. It may be used for tests of controls or substantive testing.

13.2 ☐ Sampling risk is the risk that evidence derived from testing a sample may not reflect characteristics of the whole population.

13.3 ☐ Where sample testing is considered appropriate, some of the main things the auditor must consider include the objectives of the test, the appropriate population from which the sample is to be selected, the errors or deviations being sought, and the size of the sample.

LEARNING objective 5

Describe the main methods of statistical sampling used in auditing.

13.3 STATISTICAL SAMPLING TECHNIQUES

The major statistical sampling techniques used by auditors are:
- attribute sampling plans
- variable sampling plans
- probability-proportional-to-size sampling.

13.3.1 Attribute sampling plans

Attribute sampling plans refer to three different methods of sampling that are used to test the operating effectiveness of controls by estimating the rate of deviation. For all these methods, the auditor must assess the tolerable deviation rate, the expected error rate and the required confidence level; statistically determine the sample size; and ensure that the sample is randomly selected. These plans include the following.

- *Attribute sampling.* This is the most common attribute sampling plan. It is a statistical sampling plan to estimate the proportion of a characteristic in a population. In relation to tests of controls, the auditor determines the effectiveness of a control in terms of deviations from a prescribed internal control policy. An example of this method is shown in appendix 13C to this chapter.
- *Sequential sampling.* **Sequential sampling** is where the auditor may stop testing as soon as enough assurance is obtained to assess that the control being tested is operating effectively. This is to improve audit efficiency when it is expected that there will be relatively few deviations in the population.
- *Discovery sampling.* **Discovery sampling** is used when the expected deviation rate in the population is extremely low and can be set at zero or near zero. The sample is then tested and if no deviations are found the auditor can make a very confident statement about the deviation rate in the population. This type of testing is more often done when the auditor is looking for a very critical characteristic (e.g. fraud).

13.3.2 Variable sampling plans

The main difference between attribute sampling and variable sampling is that the auditor estimates the error in terms of a quantity rather than an occurrence rate. For this reason, variable sampling is generally used in substantive testing to estimate a monetary misstatement in an account balance. For the mean-per-unit method, the auditor must assess the tolerable error rate and the required confidence level, statistically determine the sample size, and ensure that the sample is randomly selected. In using the difference estimation method, the expected error rate must also be calculated. There are a number of different types of variable sampling plans, including the following.

- *Unstratified mean-per-unit.* When using this approach, the auditor estimates a total population amount by calculating the mean for items in the sample and projecting the mean to the number of items in the population. The reason for adopting this approach is to improve audit efficiency. Stratification makes the mean-per-unit method more acceptable because it reduces the required sample sizes.

- *Difference estimation.* In this approach, the auditor calculates the mean difference between audited and recorded amounts of the sample items and projects the mean difference to the population. The estimated population difference between audited values and recorded values is added or subtracted from the total recorded value to produce an estimate of the true population total.

13.3.3 Probability-proportional-to-size sampling

The most commonly used statistical sampling technique for substantive testing is **probability-proportional-to-size (PPS) sampling**. This technique is also known as dollar unit sampling. As previously discussed, attribute sampling is used to reach a conclusion about a population in terms of the rate of occurrence. Variable sampling is generally used to reach conclusions about a population in terms of a monetary (dollar) amount. PPS sampling is a hybrid sampling plan that uses characteristics of both because it uses attribute sampling theory to express a conclusion as a monetary (dollar) amount rather than as a rate of occurrence.

PPS sampling takes each dollar of the population as the sampling unit and tests whether it is correctly stated, incorrectly stated or tainted. Incorrectly stated and tainted dollars are then projected to the number of dollars recorded as the population to estimate the extent of monetary error in the population. Application of this sampling plan is illustrated in the case study in appendix 13B.

13.3.4 Choice of statistical sampling method

If statistical sampling is to be used for tests of controls, then the auditor must use one of the attribute sampling plans. However, if substantive testing is being done, then there is a choice of either PPS sampling or variable sampling. The relative merits and drawbacks of each method are discussed as follows.

PPS sampling

The advantages of PPS sampling over variable sampling are:
- it is not affected by variability and, therefore, it is easy to determine sample size
- it is mathematically simple and, therefore, easy to apply, especially if computer assistance is not available
- it usually enables conclusions to be drawn on the basis of small sample sizes where the auditor expects no or few errors
- individually material items (where they are greater than the dollar sampling interval) are automatically selected for sampling.

The disadvantages of PPS sampling are:
- it is unsuitable for detecting errors of understatement because understated items, being smaller than they ought to be, are less likely to be selected for sampling; special considerations are needed where a PPS sample detects understated items
- if detected errors exceed those expected when the sampling plan is developed, then the auditor is likely to be forced to conclude that the population is materially misstated and to have to conduct further audit work
- as expected error increases, sample size is likely to exceed that required by variable sampling
- the required cumulative addition of the population for the purposes of drawing the sample may not be convenient.

Audit situations in which PPS sampling will produce sufficient evidence using smaller sample sizes are those where:

- few errors are expected
- the auditor is mainly concerned with overstatement
- understatement errors are unlikely
- it is convenient to obtain a cumulatively added listing of the population.

The technique is most useful for verifying the existence of assets and the occurrence of recorded transactions where sampling risk is moderate to low. Many audit tests where sampling is appropriate fall into this category, such as inventory pricing and accounts receivable circularisation.

Variable sampling

Variable sampling is preferable where:

- errors of understatement are expected or are being sought
- the population includes zero and negative balances
- many errors are expected
- it may be necessary to extend the sample to estimate the population value more reliably.

Difference estimation techniques work reliably only where fifty or more errors are found. Where fewer errors are expected, the choice is between PPS sampling and the mean-per-unit methods of variable sampling.

Variable sampling is most likely to be useful in the audit of large computerised accounting systems with the assistance of computer audit software. This will be the case especially when most of the testing can be performed directly on the computer.

In such circumstances, however, the auditor must consider whether the time spent planning and evaluating a sample may be better spent using the computer audit software to perform a 100% test.

Indicate why auditors may use non-statistical sampling.

13.4 NON-STATISTICAL SAMPLING TECHNIQUES

The evidence suggests that non-statistical sampling is much more widely used than statistical sampling, as discussed earlier in section 13.1.2. Given that non-statistical sampling is less rigorous than statistical sampling, why would auditors use non-statistical sampling?

13.4.1 Why use non-statistical sampling?

The rationale for non-statistical sampling is often that it is less costly and less time-consuming but can be just as effective in satisfying audit objectives. This advantage is explained by the following.

- *The lower training costs of non-statistical sampling.* It usually takes less time to learn non-statistical sampling methods.
- *The ease of implementation of non-statistical sampling.* These methods are less complex, which makes them easier and quicker to apply in the field and also reduces the risk that staff will misuse the method.
- *The impracticality of random selection.* In some cases it is impractical to apply random selection — for example, where the population of source documents is large and unnumbered.
- *Proposed adjustment based on qualitative analysis.* The increased precision of a statistical estimate is often not needed because the proposed audit adjustment is based on the auditor's qualitative analysis of sample results rather than a mathematical calculation.[3]

An example of non-statistical sampling of substantive tests of details is illustrated in appendix 13A to this chapter.

13.4.2 Formal and informal non-statistical sampling

A formal non-statistical sampling plan uses a structured approach to determine the sample size and evaluate sample results. The main differences from a statistical sampling plan are that the selection of sample items may be haphazard and the level of sampling risk is not precisely quantified.

An informal approach is an unstructured approach to determining the sample size and evaluating the results. Sample size and results are determined on an entirely qualitative basis, so any conclusions about the population are also qualitative. Disadvantages associated with informal non-statistical sampling include the following.

- *Training difficulties.* There is no systematic way to train staff in this approach, which requires experience and, therefore, is problematic for junior staff.
- *The absence of consistency and uniformity.* Auditors in the same circumstances may reach significantly different judgements about the scope of audit work necessary on an engagement.
- *Peer review exceptions (and potential litigation problems).* There may not be enough documentation to prove that the auditor has complied with auditing standards on sampling.
- *Incorrect evaluation of sampling risk.* The unstructured approach increases the likelihood that the auditor will fail to recognise an unacceptable level of sampling risk.[4]

Learning check

Do you know . . .

13.6 ☐ Statistical sampling techniques relate to sampling for attributes (as in the case of tests of controls) and sampling for variables (as is commonly the case in substantive testing) or probability-proportional-to-size sampling.

13.7 ☐ The advantages of statistical sampling are: samples are determined and evaluated in accordance with probability theory; it provides a uniform framework for making consistent judgements; and it requires explicit consideration of relevant factors such as sampling risk.

13.8 ☐ The advantages of non-statistical sampling are: it has lower training costs; it is easy to implement; sometimes random selection is impractical; and adjustments are often based on qualitative analysis anyway.

SUMMARY

The purpose of sampling is to obtain evidence about an account balance or transaction class without examining each individual item or transaction. The risk is that the sample examined might not be representative of the population from which the sample is drawn (such as transactions from a transaction class, or items making up an account balance). Increasing the size of the sample reduces this risk. Sample size in auditing is a function of:

- the risk the auditor is willing to accept, based on the audit risk model
- the magnitude of control deviations or errors that are considered material
- the level of expectation that deviations or errors do exist in the population.

Statistics tell us much about how to make sure that our sample is sufficiently large to provide the required level of knowledge about the account balance or transaction class. Auditors sometimes use statistical sampling techniques in their sample tests. However, non-statistical sampling is also commonly adopted, often using the principles of statistical theory in the planning of the sample test.

In selecting the sample from the population, the auditor should adopt a technique that provides reasonable assurance that the sample is representative and unaffected by selection bias. Random sampling is required for statistical sampling, but less rigorous techniques may be applied for non-statistical sampling.

In examining the sample, the auditor must remember that it should be representative of the population and that its purpose is to assess the extent to which deviations or errors could be present in the population from which the sample is drawn. The major statistical sampling techniques used by auditors are attribute sampling plans, variable sampling plans and probability-proportional-to-size sampling. Attribute sampling is used for compliance testing, and the other two techniques are used for substantive testing.

Non-statistical sampling is widely used and, if undertaken properly, provides valid evidence. Reasons for its widespread use include its lower training costs, its ease of use and the fact that the auditor often bases adjustments on a qualitative assessment irrespective of the sampling method used.

KEY TERMS

attribute sampling, p. 535	risk of incorrect acceptance, p. 530
block selection, p. 539	risk of incorrect rejection, p. 531
difference estimation, p. 543	risk of overreliance, p. 530
discovery sampling, p. 544	risk of underreliance, p. 530
haphazard selection, p. 532	sampling interval, p. 540
mean-per-unit method, p. 543	sampling risk, p. 529
non-sampling risk, p. 529	sampling unit, p. 536
non-statistical sampling, p. 529	sequential sampling, p. 544
population, p. 528	statistical sampling, p. 529
probability-proportional-to-size (PPS) sampling, p. 545	stratification, p. 536
	systematic selection, p. 540
projected error, p. 543	tolerable misstatement, p. 537
random selection, p. 531	tolerable rate of deviation, p. 537

APPENDIX 13A

Non-statistical sampling of substantive test of details

Facts of the case

Objective	Circularisation of accounts receivable to confirm existence
Population	Accounts receivable (excluding credit balances) $4 250 000
Sampling unit	Account balances 1100
Variability	$100 to $140 000

Judgements

Five accounts over $50 000 totalling $500 000 were considered to be individually material, leaving a population of 1095 accounts with a value of $3 750 000 to be sampled.

Tolerable error	$130 000
Control risk assessment	Moderate
Effect on detection risk of other substantive procedures	Analytical procedures provide moderate assurance. Cut-off test provides moderate assurance.

| *Acceptable level of sampling risk* | Moderate |
| *Expected errors* | Few or none |

Sample size

The formula is:

$$\frac{\text{Population value}}{\text{Tolerable error}} \times \text{Reliability factor}$$

where the reliability factor is determined using the data in table 13A.1. This produces a sample size of:

$$\frac{3\,750\,000}{130\,000} \times 2.3 = 66$$

TABLE 13A.1:
Reliability factors for non-statistical sampling

	Reliability factor	
Required level of assurance	**Few or no errors expected**	**Some errors expected**
Substantial	3.0	6.0
Moderate	2.3	4.0
Little	1.5	3.0

Source: Adapted from AICPA, *Audit and Accounting Guide: Audit Sampling*, p. 59.

Sample selection

The sample was selected systematically from a listing of accounts receivable balances from the accounts receivable ledger, and had been added and checked in total against the balance of the control account in the general ledger.

Sample results

Replies were received from the five large customers and from sixty of those sampled. The accounts of the six customers failing to reply were verified by other tests and found to be correctly stated. The reported errors were considered qualitatively. Those considered to reflect errors in the population are detailed in table 13A.2.

TABLE 13A.2:
Errors considered to reflect errors in the population

	Population	Sample		
	Recorded amount ($)	**Recorded amount ($)**	**Audited amount ($)**	**Overstatement errors ($)**
Material items	500 000	500 000	499 000	1000
Sampled items	3 750 000	180 000	177 000	3000

Projected error

Using the ratio method, the projected error is:

$$\frac{\$3000}{\$180\,000} \times \$3\,750\,000 = \$62\,500$$

Conclusion

The entity corrected the $3000 errors found in the sample, but disputed the $1000 error on the large accounts, resulting in a net projected population error of:

$$\$62\,500 - \$3000 + \$1000 = \$60\,500$$

This is significantly lower than the tolerable error, so the auditor concluded that the recorded existence of accounts receivable is not materially misstated.

APPENDIX 13B
Probability-proportional-to-size sampling

Facts of the case

Objective	To verify that standard costs used in valuing ending inventory have been accurately determined
Population	Inventory, all of which is valued at standard cost, with a recorded value of $1 375 000 and consisting of 320 different items
Sampling unit	Individual dollars of recorded value

Judgements

Tolerable error	$53 500
Internal control	Not assessed because there are no procedures for checking the accuracy of standard costs. Control risk, therefore, is 100%.
Other substantive procedures	The operation of the costing system has been tested (particularly the determination of variances, all of which are immaterial). Analytical procedures confirm that inventory appears to be properly valued. Allowing for reliance on other substantive procedures, detection risk is judged to be 70%.
Inherent risk	Inherent risk, overall, is judged to be low and no material errors have been detected by this test in previous years. Inherent risk is assessed at 70%.
Assurance required	Audit risk is set at 5%. Using the audit risk model, risk for this particular test is determined as being:

$$\frac{\text{Audit risk}}{\text{Inherent risk} \times \text{Control risk} \times \text{Detection risk}}$$

$$\frac{0.05}{0.7 \times 1.0 \times 0.7} = 0.102 \text{ or } 10\%$$

Thus, 90% assurance is required from this particular test.

Expected errors	Two errors are expected on items not individually material.

Sample size

The formula is:

$$\frac{\text{Population value}}{\text{Tolerable error}} \times \text{Reliability factor}$$

where the reliability factor is determined as per the data in table 13B.1. Thus sample size is calculated as being:

$$\frac{1\,375\,000}{53\,500} \times 5.33 = 137$$

The sample interval is $\frac{1\,375\,000}{137} = 10\,036$ (say 10 000).

TABLE 13B.1:
Reliability factors for attribute sampling

Number of sample errors	Confidence level	
	90%	**95%**
0	2.31	3.00
1	3.89	4.75
2	5.33	6.30
3	6.69	7.76
4	8.00	9.16

Note: Based on Poisson distribution.

Sample selection

The sample is selected from inventory listings that have been printed from the computer with a running cumulative total. The listing is test-added to verify its completeness and the sample is selected as shown in table 13B.2 for the first twenty items on the list. A random start below $10 000 is selected (say $4000) and every 10 000th dollar is then systematically selected and used as a hook to catch the inventory item containing that dollar.

As can be seen in table 13B.2, the random sample start of $4000 comes within the range of $2000 to $10 000 on the cumulative value column. Within that range lies inventory number 1101 with a value of $8000, thereby resulting in its selection for testing. The second hook to select an item is $14 000 ($4000 + $10 000), resulting in the selection of inventory number 1103.

TABLE 13B.2:
Details of first twenty items selected

Inventory no.	Qty	Unit cost($)	Total value($)	Cumulative value($)	Hook ($)	Sample ($)
1100	20	100	200	2 000		
1101	400	20	8 000	10 000	4 000	8 000
1102	100	5	500	10 500		
1103	1000	7	7 000	17 500	14 000	7 000
1104	10	50	500	18 000		
1105	300	40	12 000	30 000	24 000	12 000
1200	1500	3	4 500	34 500	34 000	4 500
1201	7	1200	8 400	42 900		
1202	300	20	6 000	48 900	44 000	6 000
1203	20	5	100	49 000		
1204	200	5	1 000	50 000		
1205	30	50	1 500	51 500		
1206	20	75	1 500	53 000		
1207	500	4	2 000	55 000	54 000	2 000
1208	11	1200	13 200	68 200	64 000	13 200
2100	300	4	1 200	69 400		
2101	20	10	200	69 600		
2102	50	5	250	69 850		
2103	100	15	1 500	71 350		
2104	50	10	500	71 850		

Sample results and projected error

Three alternative scenarios will be considered.
1. No errors were found.
2. Two errors were found in items with a recorded value less than the sampling interval.
3. Three errors were found, including one error in an item with a recorded value above the sampling interval.

Scenario 1 — no errors

In this scenario, the monetary precision is better than tolerable error. When determining sample size, the auditor expected two errors and used a reliability factor of 5.33. As it turned out, the auditor could have used a reliability factor of 2.31. The extra sample size enables the auditor to conclude, with 90% assurance, that the maximum possible error in the population is:

Reliability factor × Sampling interval = Upper error limit

which gives

$$2.31 \times \$10\,000 = \$23\,100$$

This figure is known as basic error or basic precision.

Scenario 2 — two errors

The upper error limit is determined as being the basic error plus the projected error plus the precision gap widening. Basic error is the upper error limit if no errors were found (i.e. $23 100 as above). Projected error is based on the assumption that the dollar being sampled is tainted by the extent of any error in the item of which it forms part. Thus, a $200 error in an item with a recorded amount of $1000 taints the dollar being sampled by 20%. This tainting percentage is then projected to all those dollars of which the dollar is a representative sample (i.e. the sampling interval).

Projected error is calculated as follows:

Carrying amount ($) (CA)	Audited value ($) (AV)	Tainting (%) (TP)*	Sample interval ($) (SI)	Projected error ($) TP × SI
1000	800	20	10 000	2000
8000	4000	50	10 000	5000
			Projected error	7000

$$*TP = \frac{(CA - AV)}{CA}$$

For precision gap widening, the projected errors are ranked and the calculation is as follows:

No. of errors	Reliability factor @ 90%	Incremental change (IC)	Projected error ($) (PE)	Precision gap widening ($) (IC × PE) − PE
0	2.31	1.58	5000	2900
1st	3.89	1.44	2000	880
2nd	5.33			3780

The upper error limit can now be calculated.

Basic error	$23 000
Projected error	7 000
Precision gap widening	3 780
	$33 780

If both errors were 100%, then:

Projected error would have been:	$2 \times 100\% \times \$10\,000$	=	$20 000
Precision gap widening would have been:	$\$10\,000 \times 0.58$ plus $\$10\,000 \times 0.44$	=	10 200
Basic error as before:		=	23 100
Upper error limit:	= tolerable error	=	$53 300

In other words, if our worst expectations as to expected errors are confirmed, then our sample size would be just sufficient to provide us with the required level of assurance.

Scenario 3 — three errors

The calculation of projected error and precision gap widening for the two errors in items with recorded values below the sampling interval is exactly the same as for scenario 2. The actual error in the item whose recorded value is above the sampling interval is not subjected to a precision gap widening calculation, and is simply added to the other figures in determining the upper error limit.

If an item with a recorded value of $14 000 were found to be overstated by $3000, then the upper error limit would be:

As previously calculated	$33 780
Error in material item	3 000
Upper error limit	$36 780

Conclusion

The auditor would conclude, with 90% confidence, that the inventory is not overstated as a result of errors in standard costs by more than:
- scenario 1 — $23 100
- scenario 2 — $33 780
- scenario 3 — $36 780.

All of these are below the tolerable error for this particular test. Given assurance from other procedures, the auditor has 95% confidence that the inventory is not materially misstated.

APPENDIX 13C
Test of controls using attribute sampling
Facts of the case

Objective	To test compliance of invoicing procedures, with laid-down controls as a basis for confirming a preliminary assessment of control risk as moderate
Population	8190 credit sale invoices issued in the year

Attributes being tested

1. Authorisation of order
2. Shipment of goods agreed with order
3. Invoices agreed with dispatch note
4. Invoice pricing verified
5. Mathematical accuracy of invoice verified

Judgements

Confidence level	95%
Tolerable deviation	7% (also referred to as the upper rate error limit, or UEL)

Sample size

The auditor can determine sample size in a number of ways.

Sample plan 1

The auditor can estimate the likelihood of deviations being found in the sample. If the auditor expects two deviations, then the required sample size is determined by the formula:

$$\frac{\text{Reliability factor (see table 13B.1)}}{\text{Tolerable deviation rate}} = \frac{6.3}{0.07}$$

$$= 90$$

This approach is complicated by the fact that, without knowing the sample size, it is difficult to estimate how many deviations it is expected to contain.

Sample plan 2

If the auditor is reasonably confident that no deviations will be found, then the minimum sample size possible of $\frac{3}{0.07} = 43$ can be taken, using the same formula as shown in sample plan 1. This approach is also known as discovery sampling.

Sample plan 3

A third approach is to use a standard sample size (say 75) for all tests of controls and determine, retrospectively, what assurance of control effectiveness can be obtained.

Sample selection

Sales invoices for sampling are selected from the sales transaction file on the computer using computer-generated random numbers. The same sample will be used for testing each of the attributes.

Sample results

Two orders not evidenced as being authorised and one invoice not evidenced as being checked for either pricing or mathematical accuracy are found. No other deviations are found.

Projected deviation rate

Sample plan 1

If two deviations are found, the auditor can calculate the upper error limit using the following formula:

$$\frac{\text{Reliability factor}}{\text{Sample size}} = \frac{6.3}{90}$$

$$= 0.07$$

Given that the sample size was determined on the basis that there is a 95% probability, if no more than two deviations are found, that the upper error limit will not exceed 7%, it is hardly surprising, if two deviations are found, that the auditor can conclude that the level of compliance is just acceptable. For the attributes where one deviation was found, the auditor can conclude that the level of compliance is well within the tolerable range.

Sample plan 2

Given that the discovery sample was based on the expectation that no errors would be found, the finding of even one error means that the auditor must conclude that there is a more than 5% probability that the deviation rate could exceed 7%. Using the formula in sample plan 1, there is a 5% probability that the deviation rate could be as high as:

$$\frac{6.3}{43} = 14.65\%$$

The calculation is not necessary because the finding of any deviation means that there is a better than 5% probability that the deviation rate exceeds the tolerable rate. The problem with discovery sampling is that it can lead, unless the auditor is confident that no errors will be found, to underreliance being placed on internal control, with consequent over-auditing in substantive procedures.

Sample plan 3

Using the formula, the auditor, finding two deviations in a sample of 75, can determine with 95% assurance that the upper error limit could be $\frac{6.3}{75} = 8.4\%$. However, this approach is relatively informal, so the auditor may consider whether a 90% assurance that the upper error limit does not exceed $\frac{5.33}{75} = 7.1\%$ would be sufficient to support the preliminary assessed level of control risk, or at least an assessed level higher than planned but still less than high.

Conclusion

With the second and probably the third approaches, the auditor would be required to conclude that the preliminary assessment of control risk used in planning the level of substantive procedures on receivables cannot be supported on the basis of the results of tests of those controls. With the second method, discovery sampling, the sample results do not provide sufficient information to support some higher assessed level of control risk. The auditor could always use judgement as to the importance of orders being approved in the overall context of controls over receivables, and may conclude that the final assessed level of control risk is still sufficient to support the planned program of substantive procedures.

APPENDIX 13D
Variable sampling using the mean-per-unit method
Facts of the case

Objectives	Circularisation of loans receivable by a finance company
Population	Loans receivable $1 340 000
Sampling unit	3000 accounts, all below $500

Judgements

Tolerable error	$60 000
Risk of incorrect rejection	This judgement, which is not necessary in dollar unit sampling, allows the auditor to control the risk that the sample results show the population as being misstated when it is not. The trade-off facing the auditor is of increased sample size against reduced possibility of unnecessary audit work if the sample results in incorrect rejection. This risk is typically set at 5%.
Risk of incorrect acceptance	This is the same as the sampling risk in dollar unit sampling and the same as detection risk. Using the audit risk model, this risk is put at 20%.

Sample size

The above factors were fed into a computer program, which calculated the required sample size as 184. In the process, the computer estimated standard deviation at $100.

Sample selection

The sample was selected from files held on computer by means of a random number generator.

Sample results

The 184 accounts confirmed had a total audited value of $81 328. Details of the audited value of each account confirmed were fed into the computer program. Given that this is a mean-per-unit sample, the auditor was not interested in errors.

Population projection

The computer calculated population value as being $1 326 000 with an achieved allowance for sampling risk of $37 803.

Conclusion

Given that the recorded value lies within the range of $1 326 000 plus or minus $37 803, the auditor may conclude that the recorded value is confirmed by the sample results.

13.1 Which of the following does *not* constitute sampling?
A. Select all payments made during the year greater than $10 000 and ensure they have supporting documentation.
B. Select 50 purchase orders from all purchases made during the year using a random number table.
C. Randomly pick a number of assets from the fixed assets register to sight to ensure existence.
D. Select every tenth payment made during the year from the cash payments journal.

13.2 An advantage of using statistical sampling techniques is that such techniques:
A. Mathematically measure risk.
B. Eliminate the need for judgemental decisions.
C. Define the values of tolerable error and risk of incorrect acceptance required to provide audit satisfaction.
D. Have been established in the courts to be superior to judgemental sampling.

13.3 What would most effectively describe the risk of incorrect rejection in terms of substantive audit testing?
A. The auditor has ascertained that the balance is materially correct when in fact it is not.
B. The auditor has rejected an item from the sample and later found the item was materially incorrect.
C. The auditor concludes that the balance is materially misstated when in fact it is not.
D. The auditor decides to perform a predominantly compliance-based audit due to an evaluation that the controls were effective within the company. Midway through the audit, the auditor realises the controls are not good, and decides to expand substantive testing.

13.4 The critical difference between statistical and non-statistical sampling is the:
A. Added precision attained with statistical sampling.
B. Sampling risk can be quantified in statistical sampling.
C. Elimination of non-sampling risk with statistical sampling.
D. Required use of judgement in non-statistical sampling.

13.5 If all other factors remained constant, changing the tolerable deviation rate from 10% to 8% would mean:
A. The sample size would increase.
B. The sample size would remain the same — there would be no effect on the sample size.
C. The sample size would decrease.
D. The sample size could not be determined without knowing the size of the population.

13.6 Which of the following statements in relation to systematic selection are correct?
(i) It is not possible to measure the probability of an item being selected.
(ii) The results cannot be evaluated statistically.
(iii) It is not appropriate for populations with a fixed pattern.
A. (i) and (ii) only.
B. (i) and (iii) only.
C. (ii) and (iii) only.
D. (i), (ii) and (iii).

13.7 Which of the following would not be considered a method of audit sampling?
A. Systematic selection.
B. Random selection.
C. Block selection.
D. Haphazard selection.

13.8 The sampling unit is:
A. The physical location of the population from which the sample will be drawn.
B. An individual item in the population.
C. The individual control procedure being tested.
D. A population expressed as an attribute of interest.

13.9 Stratification is a way of improving audit efficiency in sampling. Which sampling technique could be said to have a similar effect to stratification?
A. Probability-proportional-to-size sampling.
B. Non-statistical sampling techniques.
C. Attribute sampling plans.
D. Variable sampling plans.

13.10 In evaluating the sample results, the planned control risk will be supported when the projected deviation rate is:
A. Greater than or equal to the expected population deviation rate.
B. Greater than or equal to the tolerable deviation rate.
C. Less than or equal to the expected population deviation rate.
D. Less than or equal to the tolerable deviation rate.

REVIEW questions

13.11 What is meant by tolerable misstatement, tolerable rate of deviation and confidence level?

13.12 What is the difference between sampling risk and non-sampling risk?

13.13 Identify and describe the four types of sampling risk that may occur in audit sampling including how they occur and how they impact an audit.

13.14 Identify the three methods of selecting the sample that are suggested in ASA 530 and explain how each is conducted.

13.15 Discuss the benefits to the auditor from using statistical sampling.

13.16 Explain the difference between selective testing and stratification in selecting items for audit testing.

13.17 For tests of controls and substantive tests, identify the purpose of the test and what errors are being sought.

13.18 Identify the two statistical sampling methods available for substantive testing and list the situations when you would use these methods.

13.19 Explain why an auditor may decide to use non-statistical sampling.

13.20 Explain how the audit considers the qualitative aspects of errors found in a sample and how errors in the sample are extrapolated to the population.

PROFESSIONAL application questions

13.21 Audit testing and sampling ★

Outlined below are some audit tasks performed by an audit assistant:
1. Opened the file of purchase invoices and selected 20 orders as part of tests of controls over occurrence.
2. Performed proof-in-total calculations in relation to the depreciation charge for the year.
3. Discussed with management the contents of the board minutes in relation to the approval of large projects.

4. Selected all large and unusual payments appearing in the bank nominal ledger account.
5. Selected 10 payments made during the year for substantive testing.
6. Selected all material receivables balances for receivables circularisation tests.
7. Selected every hundredth sales invoice and checked to goods despatched note.
8. For a company with a chain of retail shops, calculated the gross profit for each shop for reasonableness checks against prior years and budget.

Required
(a) Are each of the above audit sampling techniques?
(b) If not, are they acceptable audit procedures? Discuss.
(c) If yes, are they random selection methods? Discuss.

13.22 Sampling terminology ★★

Your firm was recently the subject of a routine investigation by a team from ASIC. The investigation largely involved the ASIC team selecting some working paper files in relation to audits the firm had recently carried out and reviewing the contents of those files to ensure that there was sufficient appropriate documented evidence to support the audit opinion.

The result of the ASIC review was very positive and indicated that the firm's audit processes were adequate. One area mentioned in the ASIC report was in relation to the selection of audit samples. While there were no major problems, there was a recommendation that all staff should receive refresher training to ensure that all audit samples selected could be fully justified and are appropriately documented.

Your audit partner has therefore decided to carry out some training for the audit team and you have been asked to contribute a session that covers the following areas:
   (i) Statistical and judgement sampling.
   (ii) A representative sample.
   (iii) Different methods of selecting a representative sample.
   (iv) Tolerable error.
   (v) The extrapolation of errors.

Required
Prepare notes for a presentation that describes each of the items (i) to (v).

13.23 Sampling and internal controls ★

The following procedures are part of the process of testing internal controls to reduce the level of substantive testing:
   (i) Walk-through tests.
   (ii) Audit sampling on internal controls.
   (iii) Responding to deviations arising in the testing of internal controls.

Required
Explain each of the procedures listed above.

13.24 Sample sizes and population selection ★★

During the audit planning of Rainbow Ltd, a manufacturer of miniature water fountains, the audit team highlighted the following matters.
1. The audit partner wishes to place greater reliance on the control structure of non-current assets, arguing that the control risk assessment can be decreased from medium to low if adequate control testing is performed.
2. Your client has warehouses in both Sydney and Melbourne. In the previous year the audit team attended a stocktake at only the Sydney warehouse. One substantive stocktake procedure involved a selection of 50 items from the inventory report. Three errors were identified and projected over the whole population. This year the manager has suggested testing both sites.

3. A number of stock cut-off errors were noted in the previous year. The planning process has identified that this may be an issue this year.

4. Even though the value has remained constant, the number of debtors' accounts has doubled from 800 to 1600 in the last year.

Required

Discuss the effect of each of the above matters on the auditor's selection of sample size and population for testing.[5]

13.25 Use of sampling methods ★★

You are a senior accountant with Da Silva, Chang and Partners (DC), a four-partner firm operating in Perth. DC was formed 2 months ago as a result of a merger between Da Silva Partners and Chang Partners. The only major audit client of the merged firm is Nebraska Ltd, which has 12 outdoor wear stores across Australia and a 30 June year-end.

DC's accounting records show significant write-offs on the Nebraska audit over the past few years, mainly due to the performance of extensive testing. To increase audit efficiency and reduce write-offs, the partners have asked you to review the 2015 planning information and suggest methods of sampling that will reduce the level of work performed without compromising audit effectiveness. The partners have stressed that they still wish to comply fully with audit standards. The 2015 planning notes contain the following information.

1. Trade creditors are handled centrally in Perth. Major purchases of products are made through Perth, but each shop also orders about 20% of its stock. Each shop sends all authorised invoices to Perth for processing and payment on a weekly basis. An alphabetical list of all unpaid invoices is produced each month. There are no individually significant creditors. You need to select a sample of creditors to test for existence and a sample to test for completeness.

2. Fifty per cent of the stock is held in the main warehouse in Perth, which is subject to an annual stocktake and maintains perpetual inventory records. The remainder of the stock is held across the 12 branches, with each holding approximately similar quantities. The branches maintain periodic inventory records and are required to perform a stocktake and send the information to Perth every 6 months. You need to select a sample of stock to test for existence.

3. Although about 70% of total sales are paid for by cash or credit cards, 30% of sales are on account. The Perth head office deals with these accounts and the responsibility for debtor collection. An alphabetical debtors list is produced each month, showing the invoices making up each debtor, payment details and the outstanding balance. The report also shows the ageing details of each debtor. You need to select a sample of debtors to test for existence and a sample to test for valuation.

Required

Describe how you would select the above samples to ensure the audit is performed in an efficient and effective manner.

13.26 Sample techniques ★★

Sally Pearson has just completed testing of the depreciation of property, plant and equipment for her client Happy Grapple Ltd.

Information from the draft financial report of Happy Grapple shows (rounded to $000s):

Profit before tax $2 737
Property, plant and equipment $16 564

In testing depreciation, Sally selected a sample of 35 items with a value of $1 672 000 and had established a tolerable error was 5% of base values.

The result of the tests showed systematic errors in the sample of $72 400 and Sally has concluded that this is an acceptable error and no further audit work is required.

Required

You are Sally's manager and are reviewing her work, do you agree with her conclusions in relation to depreciation? Explain your conclusion.

13.27 Sampling appropriateness ★★

Your client Chicken Supremacy Ltd is a manufacturer of fancy dress costumes. At the planning stage, your preliminary assessment of internal controls in relation to purchases and payables suggested a low control risk. Your audit plan therefore included a combined audit approach in relation to purchases and payables with reliance being placed on internal control procedures followed by a reduction in the level of substantive testing.

You have just completed your tests of controls in relation to the purchases system and the result of the initial testing showed a projected error rate greater than the tolerable error. Your review of the results indicated that the errors were not isolated incidents, the samples were representative of the population as a whole and further testing confirmed the initial results.

Required

(a) Discuss the impact of the results of the tests of controls on purchases and payables.
(b) How would your approach differ if the errors were found to be isolated to a two-week period when the purchase ledger officer was on annual leave.

13.28 Sample selection methods ★★★

Your audit firm is testing accounts receivable and has stratified the population into 5 strata, as outlined in the table below. Probability theory has been used to determine the appropriate sample size for a given level of confidence within each stratum. Different methods of sample selection were used for each stratum.

Dollar value of accounts ($)	No. of accounts in population	Confidence required (%)	No. of accounts sampled	Sample selection method
>1 200 000	10	100	10	—
100 001 to 1 000 000	53	95	10	Used computer-generated random numbers to select.
10 001 to 100 000	110	90	10	Randomly selected the second account, then every eleventh account.
1000 to 10 000	175	80	10	Chose two accounts from every page of a five-page print-out.
<1000	245	50	10	Selected the ten accounts from Tasmania that were all less than $1000.

Required

(a) Define stratification and the benefits that may arise from using this technique.
(b) For each stratum, define the sample selection method used and whether it would be an appropriate sample selection method for statistical sampling.[6]

13.29 Evaluating sample results ★★★

You are the in-charge audit senior on the audit of Socktop Ltd for the year ended 30 June 2015. In the audit plan receivables, inventory and warranty provisions were identified as significant risks and specific audit attention was devoted to these areas. The following is an extract from the draft financial accounts prepared by Socktop Ltd management for the year ended 30 June 2015 and the related provisions as critical audit areas.

	$000s
Receivables	4122
Inventories	3589
Warranty provision	1788
Profit before tax	5097

In testing these areas representative samples were selected and the results of these tests show the following:

	Sample-size $000s	Error $000s	Under/over
Receivables	770	60	overstatement
Inventories	223	8	understatement
Warrant provision	1064	96	overstatement

Required

Discuss the effect of these tests on your conclusions about each area and state the impact on your audit opinion.

 CASE studies

13.30 Sampling — method of selection ★★★

You are currently auditing Krome Ltd, a wholesaler and manufacturer of gardening tools sold in hardware stores. Krome has branch offices in Sydney, Melbourne and Adelaide; and head office is located in Sydney. The company's only factory is also located in Sydney. The audit is administered out of your Sydney office with some work performed by your firm's branch offices.

Your manager has asked you to complete the audit programs for various audit file sections by inserting detailed instructions on sample selection. In order to maintain tight control over costs, the audit manager wants all samples to be selected by the Sydney head office auditors. Branch offices will then simply be given details of the items they are to test.

You have the following information about various account balances of Krome.

1. Krome's fixed assets consist of office furniture and equipment (held at all branches) and factory machinery (held in Sydney). Factory machinery comprises around 50 items totalling 80% of the value of fixed assets. Each branch maintains its own fixed asset register on an off-the-shelf software package.

   You need to select a sample of fixed assets for existence testing.

2. Trade creditors are handled centrally in Sydney. Branches send in authorised invoices with related supporting documents for processing on a weekly basis. Each month, an alphabetical list of creditors is produced showing the invoices outstanding and the total balance owing. Krome uses a wide range of suppliers and accordingly there are no individually significant creditors.

   You need to select a sample of creditors for valuation testing.

3. Each branch processes its own sales invoices using a unique series of invoice numbers (i.e. each branch has a different sequence). A sales listing is produced monthly by each branch, and gives a sequential listing of the invoices used, the customer name and code, date and amount.

   You need to select a sample of sales invoices on which to perform tests of controls to ensure credit limits are complied with.

4. Debtor collections are handled centrally at head office. A consolidated monthly alphabetical debtors listing is produced showing the invoices making up each debtor's balance, the amounts paid that month and the amount outstanding. Ageing details are also provided (current, >30 days, >60 days and >90 days).

   You need to select a sample of debtors for existence testing.

5. To meet reporting deadlines at year-end, each branch handles its own accruals. Once the creditors ledger is closed off, branches track year-end related invoices using a manual listing showing creditor name and cost, invoice amount and accrual amount.

   You need to select a sample of accruals for valuation testing.

6. About 200 of Krome's stock lines carry 12-month 'free replacement' warranties. When a customer in a particular state makes a warranty claim, the item is returned to that branch office. Each branch keeps a list of items returned in product number order, so that trends in warranty claims can be identified by product. At year-end, the warranty provision is calculated by determining the return percentages of major sales items, plus a general allowance for other items.

   You need to select a sample of items to test valuation of the warranty provision.

Required

(a) For each independent situation above:
   (i) describe the steps you would follow to select a sample for testing. Include details of any information you might require from the client's branch offices and assume only manual selection techniques will be used.
   (ii) briefly describe the analytical procedures that could help corroborate the evidence gained from detailed testing of the sampled items.

(b) What action would you take if:
   (i) a sales invoice you selected was subsequently found to be cancelled?
   (ii) your sampling plan for debtors resulted in no debtors from the Melbourne branch being selected?

(c) Give examples of situations where sampling from the recorded population might not be appropriate.[7]

13.31 Sample size ★★★

All 4 You Ltd owns a chain of retail outlets that sell newspapers, books and magazines, snacks and drinks, cigarettes and fancy goods for the tourist trade. There are 85 retail outlets spread throughout Australia.

All 4 You has approximately 100 stock lines ranging in price from less than a dollar to some products designed for the tourist trade, which sell for several hundred dollars. A large amount of stock is retained in three warehouses which are used as distribution centres for the retail outlets. This allows central purchasing processes, reducing purchase costs and managing delivery scheduling to reduce transport costs.

A full stocktake for all warehouses and retail outlets is to be carried out at the year end. The company maintains a stock system that can produce various reports, including:

1. A complete stock listing for each location, showing: stock code; quantity held; cost per unit; and total cost for the stock line.

2. An ageing report of all stock lines, showing: stock code; quantity held; month-by-month quantities sold and purchased over last 3 months.

For the purposes of the stocktake an additional report is produced which, for each location, lists the stock code and description for each item held at the location. Quantities are omitted and should be counted by the stock count team.

Required

You are the auditor planning your audit approach to test the accuracy of the stocktake. How would each of the following affect the sample you would select for testing?

(a) One Melbourne outlet has a higher value of stock held compared with other outlets.

(b) In the central Perth outlet there has been a significant number of stock thefts over the past few months.

(c) No tests of controls were performed in relation to inventories.

(d) The Western Sydney branch historically has shown only insignificant differences between stock counted and the amounts recorded on the stock system.

(e) The staff carrying out the check on the stocktake at the Brisbane warehouse are new to the job.

(f) Of the total of six staff in the South Adelaide outlet, three, including the manager, have been appointed in the last two months.

(g) The Launceston branch has shown an increase in sales margin in recent months that is significantly higher than any other branch.

 RESEARCH question

13.32 Statistical and non-statistical sampling

There is a considerable difference of opinion among auditing practitioners about the most appropriate method of audit sampling. Some believe the only appropriate method is statistical sampling. Others believe that because of the large number of judgements required in statistical sampling, auditors may as well use judgemental sampling. The following comment was made by Donald Schwartz (The CPA Journal, November 1998, p. 50) in relation to this issue:

> Some practitioners question the usefulness of statistical sampling at all, since it certainly does not eliminate, or even reduce, the need for professional judgement. The auditor must still decide on a tolerable misstatement amount, assess related inherent and control risks, and respond appropriately to test results.

Required

(a) What does ASA 530 (ISA 530) say about the respective merits of statistical sampling compared with non-statistical sampling?

(b) Find a research study that evaluates a particular method of sampling (statistical or non-statistical) and summarise the results.

FURTHER READING

RD Allen & RJ Elder, 'A longitudinal investigation of auditor error projection decisions', *Auditing: A Journal of Practice & Theory*, November 2005, pp. 69–84.

American Institute of Certified Public Accountants, *Audit Sampling*, AICPA, New York, 2001.

JL Colbert, 'Audit sampling', *Internal Auditor*, February 2001, pp. 27–9.

PR Gillett & RP Srivastava, 'Attribute sampling: a belief-function approach to statistical audit evidence', *Auditing: A Journal of Practice & Theory*, Spring 2000, pp. 145–55.

TW Hall, TL Herron, BJ Pierce & TJ Witt, 'The effectiveness of increasing sample size to mitigate the influence of population characteristics in haphazard sampling', *Auditing: A Journal of Practice & Theory*, March 2001, pp. 169–85.

TW Hall, JE Hunton & BJ Pierce, 'Sampling practices of auditors in public accounting, industry, and government', *Accounting Horizons*, June 2002, pp. 125–36.

P Johnson, '*Fraud detection with Benford's law*', *Accountancy Ireland*, August 2005, pp. 16–17.

NOTES

1. FW Pixely, *Auditors: Their Duties and Responsibilities*. Effingham Wilson, London, 1881, reprinted by Arno Press. New York, 1976, p. 154.

2. TW Hall, JE Hunton & BJ Pierce, 'Sampling practices of auditors in public accounting, industry, and government', *Accounting Horizons*, June 2002, pp. 125–36.

3. DM Guy, D Carmichael & OR Whittington, *Audit Sampling: An Introduction*, 5th edn, John Wiley & Sons, New York, 2002, p. 222.

4. ibid., p. 224.

5. Adapted from Professional Year Programme of the ICAA, 1996, Accounting 2 Module.

6. Adapted from Professional Year Programme of the ICAA, 1996, Advanced Audit Module.

7. Op cit. Accounting 2 Module.

Answers to multiple-choice questions

13.1 A   13.2 A   13.3 C   13.4 B   13.5 D   13.6 C   13.7 C   13.8 B   13.9 A   13.10 D

part 4

AUDITING TRANSACTIONS AND BALANCES

14 Auditing sales and receivables

15 Auditing purchases, payables and payroll

16 Auditing inventories and property, plant and equipment

17 Auditing cash and investments

*H*aving obtained an understanding of the entity sufficient to develop an audit strategy (as we described in part 2), the auditor is in a position to apply the audit testing procedures (explained in part 3) to specific transactions and balances. The chapters in part 4 are based on the major asset and liability accounts of receivables (**chapter 14**), payables (**chapter 15**), inventory, and property, plant and equipment (**chapter 16**), and cash and investments (**chapter 17**). The first two chapters also consider the transaction classes logically associated with the account balances: sales, sales adjustments and cash receipts in the case of receivables and purchases, cash payments and payroll in the case of payables.

Each chapter starts with a 'Brief summary of audit procedures', which provides the essence of what the auditor is trying to achieve and is useful for both revision and obtaining an understanding of the basics where study time is at a premium. There follows a description of the nature of systems and control procedures that entities commonly use in recording the relevant transaction classes and maintaining the relevant account balances. Then the process of planning the audit approach is covered in depth including understanding the entity, assessing inherent risk and control risk for the relevant transactions and balances, which then leads to the factors the auditor needs to consider in developing the audit strategy and substantive procedures applicable to achieving the planned level of detection risk for each major audit objective.

chapter 14

Auditing sales and receivables

OVERVIEW

14.1 Brief summary of audit procedures
14.2 Audit objectives
14.3 Sales, cash receipts and sales adjustment transactions
14.4 Developing the audit plan
14.5 Substantive procedures
Summary
Key terms

Multiple-choice questions
Review questions
Professional application questions
Case studies
Research question
Further reading
Notes

LEARNING objectives

After studying this chapter, you should be able to:

1 identify the audit objectives applicable to sales and receivables

2 describe the functions and control procedures normally found in information systems for processing sales, cash receipts and sales adjustment transactions

3 apply the concepts of materiality and inherent risk to the audit of sales and receivables

4 discuss considerations relevant to determining the audit strategy for sales and receivables

5 design and execute tests of controls over sales, cash receipts and sales adjustment transactions to assess control risk

6 indicate the factors relevant to determining an acceptable level of detection risk for the audit of sales and receivables

7 design a substantive audit program for sales and receivables

8 explain the procedures for undertaking a confirmation of receivables balances

PROFESSIONAL STATEMENTS

Australian		International	
Framework for Assurance Engagements		*International Framework for Assurance Engagements*	
ASA 315	*Identifying and Assessing the Risks of Material Misstatement through Understanding the Entity and Its Environment*	**ISA 315**	*Identifying and Assessing the Risks of Material Misstatement through Understanding the Entity and Its Environment*
ASA 500	*Audit Evidence*	**ISA 500**	*Audit Evidence*
ASA 505	*External Confirmations*	**ISA 505**	*External Confirmations*
ASA 530	*Audit Sampling*	**ISA 530**	*Audit Sampling*
ASA 540	*Auditing Accounting Estimates, Including Fair Value Accounting Estimates, and Related Disclosures*	**ISA 540**	*Audit of Accounting Estimates, Including Fair Value Accounting Estimates, and Related Disclosures*

SCENE SETTER

Lehman ordered to pay councils millions

The Federal Court has found that the Australian arm of failed Wall Street bank Lehman Brothers breached its fiduciary duty advising a group of local councils and charities, ordering millions of dollars in compensation be paid. In a landmark decision, the Federal Court found the Australian arm of Lehman — previously called Grange Securities — was conflicted in its duty to give sound financials to the councils 'and its own interest in earning very large fees or profits' in its sales of investments known as synthetic collateralised debt obligations. Grange did not disclose to any of the councils, Judge Steven Rares found this afternoon. 'Grange is liable to compensate the councils for their losses incurred as a result of their investments', Justice Rares said in his findings.

The class action involving 72 councils and charities and led by Wingecarribee and Parkes council in NSW as well as Western Australia's City of Swan was brought against the liquidators of Lehman Brothers Australia. All purchased synthetic collateralised debt obligations, or SCDOs, from the Australian arm of the collapsed investment bank. They alleged misleading conduct, breach of contract, breach of fiduciary duty and negligence in the class action seeking $250 million in compensation for losses incurred on synthetic collateralised debt obligations, or CDOs. Justice Rares concluded that Grange 'acted in breach of its fiduciary duties as a financial adviser to each of Parkes and Swan, and in making investments as the agent of Swan and Wingecarribee'.

He also took aim at the high risk nature of the investments describing them as 'not suitable' for risk adverse clients such as councils. 'The (synthetic collateralised debt obligations) did not have a high level of security for the invested capital, were not easily tradeable on an established secondary market or able to be readily liquidated for cash and were not suitable investments for risk averse Councils', Justice Rares said in his judgment. 'I have also found that Grange was negligent in recommending to and advising Parkes and Swan to make those investments.' The investments themselves had exposure to pools of debt comprised of high-risk US mortgages, car loans or credit card debt.

He noted the SCDOs were 'highly complex financial instruments, underpinned by equally complex, and at points arcane, legal documentation to give them effect'. Essentially a SCDO was a 'sophisticated bet'. He also found Grange would often 'target councils' given they had ready access to large sums of money for investment. Justice Rares said the councils were entitled to damages to compensate for their losses, including the capital they invested in the securities. This includes $3 million for the City of Swan, $4 million for Parkes and $9 million for Wingecarribee. They will be entitled to more, but Justice Rares has not calculated the extent of final damages.

Source: Eric Johnston, 'Lehman ordered to pay councils millions', *The Age*, Melbourne, 21 September 2012.

In this and the next three chapters, we apply the procedures explained in the preceding chapters to specific transaction classes and account balances. This chapter examines the audit of the balance in accounts receivable and of the transaction classes of sales, cash receipts and sales adjustments. The chapter covers the following procedures.

1. Identify the audit objectives that apply to the relevant transaction classes and account balances for each of the financial statement assertions explained in chapter 10.
2. Describe (a) the procedures involved in sales, cash receipts and sales adjustment transactions, and (b) the accounting system and control procedures commonly associated with these procedures that will be identified in the course of 'obtaining the understanding' required by ASA 315 *Identifying and Assessing the Risks of Material Misstatement through Understanding the Entity and Its Environment* (ISA 315).
3. Consider factors relevant to developing the audit plan, including determining the appropriate audit strategy and, where appropriate, assessing inherent and control risk, including the use of tests of controls (see chapter 8).
4. Explain the design of substantive procedures, including analytical procedures and tests of details of transactions and balances using the methodology introduced in chapter 12.

14.1 BRIEF SUMMARY OF AUDIT PROCEDURES

In the auditing of sales and receivables, the key issues are to ensure that:

- the sales are genuine and are neither understated nor overstated (these are related to the financial statement assertions of completeness and occurrence respectively, and also accuracy and cut-off)
- the receivables do actually exist and are collectable, and adequate allowances have been made for receivables that have become bad debts or are doubtful in terms of their collectability (these are related to the financial statement assertions of existence and valuation and allocation).

It is also important to ensure, especially in the sale of financial instruments, that the client has made bona fide sales and the receivables created are assets that can be realised and not subject to subsequent legal action, as in the case of Lehman Brothers as described in the scene setter.

As discussed in detail later in this chapter, it is essential to understand the systems and controls in place for processing transactions that result in sales and, when sales are made on credit, the resultant creation and collectability of receivables. Sales can be made either for cash, such as when customers pay for goods with cash in a department store, or on credit, such as when a large food manufacturer buys packaging from a cardboard manufacturer. In the latter case, a receivable is created; a sale (revenue) has occurred and a debt (asset) has to be collected.

The audit of cash sales is linked with the audit of cash receipts. A sample of cash sales transactions (say for a randomly selected week or month) can be examined in detail by reconciling cash sales records to the receipt and banking of cash and checking the pricing with inventory records. To test the reasonableness of cash sales at a macro level, an analysis of (say) weekly cash sales can be made by comparing them with figures for the previous year and by considering the sales figures from the perspective of what would be reasonable for that type of business. For example, one would normally expect cash sales in a department store to be considerably higher in the few weeks preceding Christmas than in the month of October.

With respect to credit sales, the auditor needs to examine a sample of sales invoices and trace the transaction to a customer order or similar document (such as a standing order to supply 1000 items per week) and reconcile the sales order to pricing information, warehouse requisitions, delivery dockets and similar evidence. Because it is a credit sale, the auditor needs to ensure that the receivable is also recorded when the sale is made. Also, as indicated above, a comparative analysis of weekly or monthly credit sales and trends will further help establish the reasonableness of the sales figures.

In auditing sales, auditors need to consider the reasonableness of sales returns and be particularly vigilant of the recording of sales around the end of the reporting period, to ensure that sales and receivables are taken up in the correct period and that inventory movements are properly accounted for. This is generally covered in what is referred to as the audit of 'cut-off' information around the end of the reporting period.

Receivables (generally referred to as accounts receivable) are a balance sheet asset and are created through credit sales transactions. Through the audit of credit sales, the auditor can generally verify that the receivables have been recorded properly. However, because a receivable is an asset, the auditor must be sure that it does actually exist and that it is collectable. Tests of existence are generally done by tracing transactions through the accounts and by independently confirming directly with the customer that it owes the amount recorded in the accounts. Confirmation of accounts receivable involves direct written communication by the auditor with individual customers. This test is often referred to as an accounts receivable circularisation.

However, sometimes the customer does not reply, and when no response has been received after the second (or third) confirmation request, the auditor should perform alternative procedures. The best evidence of existence and collectability is the ultimate receipt of payment from the customer. Before the conclusion of the auditor's examination, the client will receive payments from many customers of amounts owed at the confirmation date. The matching of such cash receipts to unpaid invoices at the confirmation date, evidenced by the remittance advice accompanying the cash receipt, establishes the existence and collectability of the account being tested.

The final issue with receivables is to ensure collectability. This is done by reviewing the client's credit collection policies and procedures and by an analysis of the ageing of the accounts receivable records. This means looking at those accounts that are over 30 days, over 60 days, over 90 days and so on; as the older the debt is, the less likely it is to be collected. Calculations can be compared with previous years, and correspondence with customers can be analysed to determine whether there are difficulties with payments or disputes that will affect collectability. Also, analysis of past years records, subsequent cash receipts and general industry data help determine what debts are, in fact, bad and what level of allowance is required for doubtful debts.

The above briefly summarises the key procedures in the audit of sales and receivables. In practice, the procedures can be more complex and are explained in more detail in the rest of the chapter.

14.2 AUDIT OBJECTIVES

The audit objectives for sales and receivables relate to obtaining sufficient appropriate evidence about each significant assertion for the applicable transactions and balances. The main audit objectives for these transaction classes and account balances are shown in table 14.1. These objectives are those that would apply to most merchandising entities selling on credit; they are not intended to apply to all entity situations.

To achieve each of these specific audit objectives, the auditor uses a combination of tests of controls (as described in chapter 11) and substantive procedures (as described in chapter 12) as determined by the audit strategy adopted (as described in chapter 8). Each audit objective is numbered (**OE1**, **OE2**, **C1**, **AV4** and so on) in table 14.1. Using this numbering system, we can reference specific controls and audit procedures described in this chapter to the applicable audit objective. Some of the assertions for transactions are combined with assertions for balances in the numbering system: occurrence and existence (**OE**), completeness for transactions and completeness for balances (**C**), accuracy and valuation and allocation (**AV**), and classification with presentation and disclosure assertions (**PD**). These combinations reflect the fact that audit evidence obtained in relation to an assertion for transactions will also give some comfort for a balances assertion. For example an audit test that gives some comfort to the auditor that a sales transaction has occurred will also give some comfort that a valid receivable exists, hence occurrence and existence are combined.

Note that table 14.1 summarises assertions for both transaction class audit objectives and account balance audit objectives. Greater detail regarding assertions is provided in paragraph A111 of ASA 315 (ISA 315).

TABLE 14.1:
Selected specific audit objectives for sales and receivables

Transaction objectives	
Occurrence (**OE**)	Sales recorded in the accounts represent goods that were shipped to customers during the period (**OE1**).
	Cash receipts recorded in the accounts represent cash received from customers during the period (**OE2**).
	Sales adjustment transactions recorded in the accounts represent authorised discounts, returns and allowances, and bad debts applicable to the period (**OE3**).
Completeness (**C**)	All goods shipped to customers during the period are recorded in the accounts (**C1**).
	All cash received from customers during the period are recorded as cash receipts in the accounts (**C2**).
	All discounts, returns and allowances, and bad debts arising during the period are recorded as sales adjustments in the accounts (**C3**).
Accuracy (**AV**)	All sales, cash receipts and sales adjustment transactions are properly (accurately) recorded (**AV1**).
Cut-off (**CO**)	Particularly relevant to transactions around the year-end; all sales, cash receipts and sales adjustment transactions arising before the period end are recorded in the current period and those arising after the period end are included in the next accounting period (**CO1**).
Classification (**PD**)	All sales (**PD1**), cash receipts (**PD2**) and sales adjustment transactions are recorded in the correct accounts (**PD3**).
Balance objectives	
Existence (**OE**)	Accounts receivable included in the accounts represent amounts owed by customers at the end of the reporting period (**OE4**).
Rights and obligations (**RO**)	Accounts receivable at the end of the reporting period represent legal claims of the entity on customers for payment (**RO1**).
Completeness (**C**)	All amounts owed by customers at the end of the reporting period are included in accounts receivables in the accounts (**C4**).
Valuation and allocation (**AV**)	Accounts receivable represent gross claims on customers at the end of the reporting period and agree with the sum of the accounts receivable subsidiary ledger (**AV2**).
	The allowance for bad debts represents a reasonable estimate of the difference between gross accounts receivable and their net realisable value (**AV3**).

Presentation and disclosure objectives (PD)	
Occurrence and rights and obligations	Disclosed revenue events have occurred and pertain to the entity (**PD4**).
Completeness	All revenue cycle disclosures that should have been included in the financial report have been included (**PD5**).
Classification and understandability	Sales cycle information is appropriately presented and information disclosed is clearly expressed (**PD6**).
Accuracy and valuation	Sales cycle information is disclosed accurately and at appropriate amounts (**PD7**).

LEARNING 2 objective

Describe the functions and control procedures normally found in information systems for processing sales, cash receipts and sales adjustment transactions.

14.3 SALES, CASH RECEIPTS AND SALES ADJUSTMENT TRANSACTIONS

These transactions arise out of the processes of selling goods and services to customers and collecting the revenue in cash. The three main functions are those of sales, cash receipts and sales adjustments. Figure 14.1 (overleaf) depicts a sales cycle for a business selling goods on credit.

This is a fairly standard example but is relevant to all businesses. The sale process starts when a customer places an order for goods with the company. The sales team will check the credit rating of the customer before agreeing to the sale and a sales order will be produced. The sales order is passed to the warehouse where the goods are picked from inventories and dispatched to the customer together with a dispatch note which records the contents of the delivery, all of which is done electronically once the order is placed. Generally the date of dispatch will be considered the point of sale; at this point a sales invoice is produced from the details of the dispatch note and the inventory price list and may include (trade) discounts where they have been agreed with the customer. The sales invoice is then sent to the customer and will include an expected date for payment and may include a (settlement) discount if paid early. The credit controllers (who may be part of the accounting team) will be responsible for collecting the debt. A statement at the end of each month is normally sent highlighting those invoices which have not yet been paid. Where payment is not forthcoming a reminder letter or email is sent and if it still remains unpaid the debt might be placed in the hands of a debt collection agency. If the debt is not recovered, then an adjustment will need to be made to record the bad debt. Where the customer does pay the amount due, the receipt of funds will normally be by bank transfer and the accounts department will ensure the necessary entries are made in the ledgers. The accounts department will also be responsible for reconciling the list of amounts outstanding to the receivables ledger and to the receivables balance in the general ledger.

The following sections look at sales, cash receipts and sales adjustments in detail, including related information systems and control procedures. Where sales are made on credit, the information system also needs to maintain records of accounts receivable. The discussions here are designed to give an understanding of the sales system; in the later sections of this chapter we will consider how this affects the audit approach. The discussion in this section is based on a company selling goods; however, much of the commentary can easily be adapted to other types of entities.

CREDIT SALES CYCLE

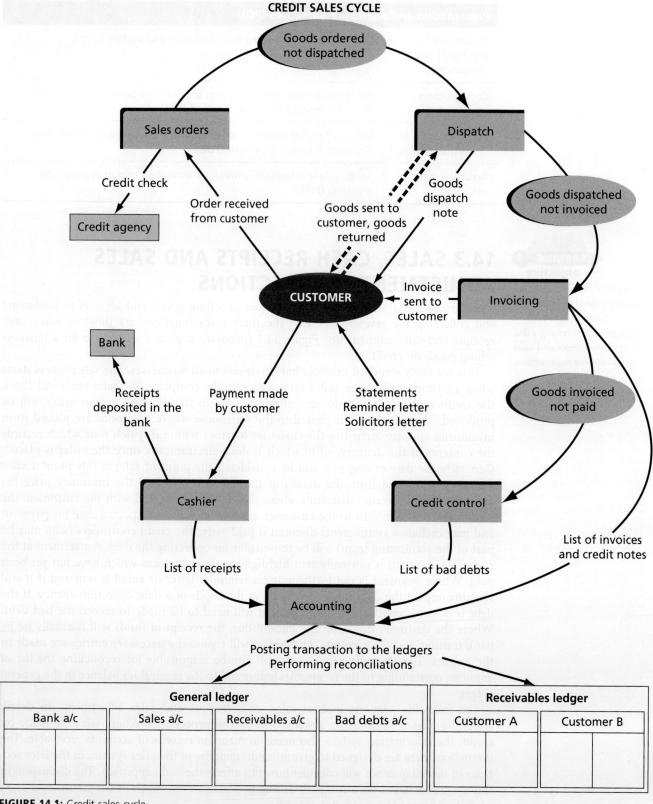

FIGURE 14.1: Credit sales cycle

14.3.1 Credit sales transactions

Sales orders may be taken over the counter, via the telephone, by mail order, through sales representatives, or via the internet. The goods may be picked up by the customer or shipped by the seller. The accounting for sales transactions may be done in real-time or batch processing mode. We begin by identifying the separate functions involved in making credit sales transactions, the documents and records used in processing the transactions, and the control procedures interwoven into each to reduce the risk of misstatements in the financial statements. As we explained in chapter 11, control procedures include information processing controls, physical controls, the segregation of duties and performance reviews. Information processing controls specific to credit sales transactions include, in addition to documents and records, proper authorisation and independent checks.

Functions

The processing of credit sales transactions involves a sequence of steps or credit sales functions as follows:
- accepting customer orders
- approving credit
- filling and dispatching sales orders
- invoicing customers
- recording the sales.

These functions and the applicable control procedures are explained in the following sections.

Accepting customer orders

Sales orders need to be checked for their authenticity, the acceptability of terms and conditions, and the availability of inventory. Orders submitted in writing, by phone or electronically on a **customer order**, provide ready evidence of authenticity. Telephone or email orders from businesses are sometimes authenticated by requiring an order number from the customer. Specification of an order number provides reasonable assurance that the order has been issued in accordance with the customer's purchasing procedures, as is described in chapter 15. Terms and conditions relate to matters such as prices, delivery dates and modifications. Sales clerks accept only orders that meet the entity's normal terms. In some businesses, it is necessary to check the availability of the goods in inventory before accepting an order.

Once accepted, the order is recorded on a multicopy **sales order**, which is a form showing the description of the goods, the quantity ordered and other relevant data and serves as the basis for internal processing of the customer order. Sales orders are commonly prenumbered in case they are mislaid and business is lost as a result. This represents the start of the transaction trail of documentary evidence and confirms the existence of a valid order. It thus relates to audit objective occurrence (OE1) in table 14.1. The independent auditor has little interest in the acceptance of orders. Potential risks are the loss of business and the acceptance of unprofitable business, which are unlikely to lead to misstatements in recorded transactions.

Approving credit

Order acceptance is normally entrusted to the sales department. However, although the sales department is unlikely to accept unprofitable orders because of their adverse effect on departmental performance, the department may accept orders from customers who are poor credit risks. Debt collection is normally an accounting function; bad debt losses are not recognised until months after the sale, and responsibility for the loss is rarely blamed on the sales department. For these reasons, credit approval is separate from sales order acceptance and is the responsibility of an independent credit department. This prevents sales personnel from subjecting the entity to undue credit risks to boost sales.

A credit check is made of any new customer, which may include obtaining a credit report from a rating agency such as Dun & Bradstreet (Australia). The credit supervisor then determines an appropriate credit limit and records this on a newly created customer record. For existing customers, a credit department employee compares the amount of the order with the customer's authorised credit limit and the current balance owed by the customer, although usually this would be done electronically through the entity's computerised information system. Credit approval is normally refused if the order would take the balance over the customer's credit limit or if the account is overdue and this is checked automatically by the computerised information system. To indicate approval (or non-approval) of credit, an authorised credit department employee signs or initials the sales order form and returns it to the sales order department, or does so electronically, following prescribed procedures.

For an auditor, controls over credit approval reduce the risk of a sales transaction being initially recorded in an amount in excess of the amount of cash expected to be realised, and thus contributes to the audit objective of accuracy (**AV1**). The expectations of realising some of these amounts will change over time, resulting in the need for an allowance for bad debts. Controls over credit approval enable management to make a more reliable estimate of the size of the allowance needed (valuation and allocation **AV3**).

Filling and dispatching sales orders

A copy of the approved sales order form, or an electronic notification, is usually sent to the warehouse as authorisation to fill the order and release the goods to the shipping department (or dispatch area). Because the order form constitutes the source of credits to inventory records, the issue of goods by warehouse personnel without such authorisation will result in an apparent inventory shortage for which they are held accountable. Segregation of the custody of inventory from the maintenance of inventory records and the physical check of verifying recorded accountability, reduces the risk of inventory shortages caused by the unrecorded (and possibly unauthorised) release of inventory. Control over inventory is described in chapter 16.

Segregating responsibility for dispatch from responsibility for approving and filling orders prevents dispatch clerks from making unauthorised shipments (**OE1**). In addition, dispatch clerks are normally required to make independent checks to determine that goods received from the warehouse are accompanied by an approved sales order form or electronic authorisation.

The dispatch function involves preparing multi-copy **dispatch notes**. Dispatch notes on pre-numbered forms are usually produced by the computer information system using order information already logged into the system with appropriate delivery data added (such as quantities shipped, carrier details and freight charges). Subsequent checks of the numerical continuity of dispatch notes invoiced ensure completeness (**C1**) of recorded sales transactions. Pre-numbering dispatch notes also helps in establishing cut-off at year-end (**CO**). Gatekeepers are sometimes required to check that drivers of all vehicles leaving the premises possess dispatch notes for the goods in their vehicle, as a double-check against failure to record deliveries.

Dispatch notes provide evidence that goods were shipped and thus of the occurrence (**OE1**) of the credit sale, giving rise to a claim against the customer within accounts receivable. Some entities obtain a copy of the dispatch note, signed by the customer on receipt of the goods, as evidence of the claim on the customer.

Invoicing customers

The invoicing function involves preparing and sending **sales invoices** to customers. Applicable control objectives for invoicing are:

- all deliveries are invoiced to customers
- only actual deliveries are invoiced (and there should be no duplicate invoices or fictitious transactions)
- deliveries are invoiced at authorised prices and the invoice amount is accurately calculated.

Control procedures designed to achieve these objectives are likely to include the following:

- segregating invoicing from the foregoing functions (**OE1, C1**)
- checking the existence of a dispatch note matching the approved sales order before each invoice is prepared (**OE1**)
- using an **authorised price list** in preparing the sales invoices (**AV1**)
- performing independent checks on the pricing and mathematical accuracy of sales invoices (**AV1**)
- comparing control totals for dispatch notes with corresponding totals for sales invoices (**OE1, C1**).

File copies of the sales invoices are usually maintained in the invoicing department.

Recording the sales

The main control objective is to ensure that sales invoices are recorded accurately and in the proper period, which is usually when the goods are shipped.

The recording process involves entering sales invoices in a **sales journal**, posting the invoices to the **accounts receivable subsidiary ledger**, and posting the sales journal totals to the general ledger. It is common practice for invoices to be entered separately in the sales journal and the accounts receivable ledger. The accounts receivable ledger balance is periodically compared with the general ledger control account (**AV2**). Failure of the balances in the accounts receivable ledger to agree in total with the control account in the general ledger indicates that an error has been made. A further control is the use of prelists, whereby the total of invoices entered in the sales journal is checked against the total of sales invoices posted to the accounts receivable ledger (**AV1**). Sales invoices should also be entered in numerical sequence and a check should be made on missing numbers (**C1**). A **monthly customer statement** usually is sent to each customer to give the customer an opportunity to alert the company if the balance does not agree with the customer's records (**OE1**).

As indicated previously, balances in the accounts receivable ledger should be regularly and independently checked against the balance in the control account in the general ledger. Periodic performance reviews by sales executives of sales analysed by product, division, salesperson or region — along with comparisons with budgets — contribute to controls over sales transactions.

As virtually all entities now use online systems, the computer system usually is programmed to validate the customer credit, check inventory availability and issue the necessary instructions to the dispatch department. On delivery of the order, the dispatch department enters the necessary shipping details and the computer information system automatically produces the invoice and updates the **accounts receivable master file**, as well as the related inventory and general ledger files. Additionally, the computer information system maintains a **sales transactions file** or equivalent data within a database system. Important controls in such a system include access controls, programmed application controls and controls over standing data files.

Access controls should permit read-only access to transaction and master files except for authorised individuals. Those people with authority should have prescribed limits to that authority; for example, the credit controller may have the right to override rejections of orders when an order marginally breaches a customer's credit limit; and similarly the sales manager may have the right to amend price or discount rates for individual customers or sales transactions.

Programmed application controls should include checks to ensure that:

- only orders from customers on the accounts receivable master file are accepted
- only orders for goods in the entity's product range are accepted
- the numerical continuity of documents is assured
- transactions are chased at regular intervals
- duplicate document numbers are rejected
- unreasonable quantities, amounts and dates are queried.

The correctness of standing data is of particular significance in a computer information system. Standing data in a sales system include authorised customers, their credit limits and product sales prices. Access controls should ensure that only authorised officers can amend standing data; for example, only the credit controller should be able to add new customers and vary the credit limits of existing customers, and only the sales director should be able to amend selling prices. As an added precaution, standing data should be periodically printed out for approval.

14.3.2 Cash receipts transactions

Cash receipts result from a variety of activities. The scope of this section is limited to the information systems for processing and recording cash receipts from cash sales and collections from customers on credit sales.

Functions

The processing of receipts from cash and credit sales involves the following cash receipts functions:

- receiving cash
- depositing cash in bank
- recording the receipts.

Receiving cash

One risk is that cash paid by customers is stolen before it is recorded. For control purposes, accountability measures must be in place from the moment cash is received, and the cash must be safeguarded. A second risk is the possibility of errors occurring in the subsequent processing of the receipts.

Over-the-counter receipts

For over-the-counter receipts, a cash register or point-of-sale terminal is normally used. These devices provide:

- immediate visual display for the customer of the amount of the cash sale and the cash tendered
- a printed receipt for the customer and an internal record of the transaction on a computer file or a tape locked inside the register
- printed control totals of the day's receipts.

The customer's expectation of a printed receipt and supervisory surveillance of over-the-counter sales transactions helps to ensure that all cash sales are processed through the cash registers or terminals (C2). In addition, there should be an independent check of the agreement of cash on hand with the totals printed by the register or terminal (OE2, C2, AV1). The cash is then forwarded to the cashier's department for deposit in the bank, together with the register or terminal-printed totals.

Many customers pay by credit or debit cards. These payments are processed via online terminals linked to the bank or other card issuer that validates the transaction. Staff need to be properly trained in the use of such terminals and in procedures to be followed where the transaction is refused. Procedures must be in place for reconciling card sales with cash register totals as part of the daily agreement of cash on hand. Amounts due from card issuers also need to be recorded and checked against subsequent payments. The use of credit and debit cards also facilitates the acceptance of mail or telephone orders from customers without the need for creditworthiness checks once the card transaction has been validated. Because no cash handling is involved, such transactions reduce the costs of banking and the risks of misappropriations, and are often preferred despite the commission payable to the card issuer.

Mail receipts and bank transfers

There should always be at least two clerks responsible for mail opening so they would need to be in collusion if they were to misappropriate any cash receipts in the mail. These procedures ensure that mail receipts are not misappropriated (**C2**).

Most cash receipts are attached to or accompanied by a **remittance advice** indicating the payer and the particulars of the payment. Remittance advices (or other details of the payment enclosed with the cash receipt) are forwarded to the accounts receivable department for posting to the accounts receivable ledger.

However, most customers now pay by bank credit transfer. Such payments may be identified as part of the bank reconciliation process (see chapter 17). Because this can lead to delays in recording receipts, entities receiving payments this way usually have online access to their bank account (linked to the accounts receivable master file), which automatically detects credit transfers and updates the accounts receivable records.

Depositing cash in the bank

All cash receipts must be deposited intact daily. This reduces the risk that cash receipts will not be recorded (**C2**) and the resulting bank deposit record establishes the occurrence of the transactions (**OE2**).

When cashiers receive over-the-counter and mail receipts, they should check that the cash agrees with both the accompanying register total and the prelist (**OE2, C2, AV1**). Details of cash receipts are then entered on a daily cash summary and the bank **deposit slip** is prepared in duplicate. The cash is deposited in the bank and the copy of the deposit slip is receipted by the bank and retained by the cashier. The daily cash summary is forwarded to the general accounting department.

Recording the receipts

To ensure that only valid transactions are entered, access to the accounting records or computer programs should be restricted to authorised personnel (**OE2**). The daily cash summary is used to enter the **cash receipts journal**, distinguishing between receipts from cash sales and from credit sale customers. Posting the receipts to the accounts receivable ledger may be done in accounts receivable ledger accounting, based on the remittance advices received or details provided by the bank of receipts by bank transfers (**AV2**).

To ensure the completeness and accuracy of recording mail receipts, independent checks are made of:
- the agreement of the amounts journalised and posted with the amounts shown in the record kept by the mail room
- the agreement of total amounts journalised and posted for over-the-counter and mail receipts and bank transfers with the daily cash summary and receipted deposit slips and bank transfer details retained by the cashier (completeness, accuracy).

In addition, an employee not otherwise involved in executing or recording cash transactions should perform periodic bank reconciliations.

Opportunities for automating accounting for cash receipts involving currency and cheques are limited, which is why many companies now use online banking and direct debit and credit transfer systems. However, the use of point-of-sale cash register terminals provides controls over the pricing of goods sold and over inventory management.

PROFESSIONAL ENVIRONMENT
Point of sale fraud

1. Void sales
The aim of the fraud is to stop the sale from being recorded and to steal the proceeds. If the sale is not recorded, the money will not be missed from the banking of sales receipts.

A real sale of goods with a real customer is required, as someone needs to hand over the money that is stolen. The employee will sell an item to a customer, hand the item to the customer and take the money from the customer, but will either not ring up a sale or ring up a void sale.

That means that a normal receipt for the money received cannot be given to the customer as, according to the business, the sale did not take place. So requiring a receipt to be issued on all sales may limit the opportunity to conduct these frauds, particularly when the receipt is needed for warranty purposes etc.

The customer walks away with the goods, but according to the records of the business, the sale never occurred and the money was never received. It may take some time for the loss of the stock item to be noticed (if it ever is) and then tracing it back to a particular employee and a particular sale may be impossible. This is why retail businesses with a high turnover of common stock items are the most common victims. If the theft needs to be hidden, the fraudster will have to adjust the stock records to record a reduction in the stock item.

2. False returns
The aim of a false return fraud is to process a fake return of goods and to steal the money allegedly paid back to the customer. In most retail businesses, some employees will have the authority to process returns of the goods in certain circumstances.

In a real return of goods, the customer will want the money or a credit after returning the goods, so real returns cannot be used effectively for this fraud. A false return must be created, processed and the money taken. Recording the return updates the bank records for the payment to the false customer, so the reduction in money does not need to be hidden. The problem is that no physical good has been received from the customer. This may or may not be a problem depending on the procedures in place that deal with items returned by customers. Most businesses will want some standard procedure in place to verify the return of any goods, if only to discover the reason and to solve any problems with the item. The employee may use another inventory item as the returned item, even damaging the item to provide a reason why it was returned.

Prevention and detection
Some basic controls
(i) Technology increases controls as smart cash registers are linked into other business systems (particularly stock). The use of technology can install controls with little disruption to customer service.
(ii) Requiring management approval or two signatures to process returns.

(iii) All returns processed without the physical goods attached or identified should be examined.

(iv) Encouraging customers to make sure that they receive a receipt from each sale, or having the sale process dependent upon the scanning or identifying of the item — thus recording the sale at the correct price.

(v) Having each employee sign onto cash registers to process transactions allowing transactions to be tracked back to a particular employee.

(vi) Reporting on credit card numbers that receive refund credits to highlight cards that have had numerous refunds credited to it.[1]

14.3.3 Sales adjustment transactions

Sales adjustment transactions involve the following functions:
- granting cash discounts
- allowing sales returns and allowances
- determining bad debts.

The number and dollar value of these transactions vary significantly among entities. However, where material, the potential for misstatements resulting from errors and irregularities in the processing of these transactions is considerable. Of main concern is the possibility of fictitious sales adjustment transactions being recorded to conceal misappropriations of cash receipts. An employee may, for example, conceal misappropriation of cash received from a customer by writing the customer's account off against the allowance for bad debts, or by overstating cash discounts or sales returns and allowances. Controls useful in reducing the risk of such frauds focus on establishing the validity of such transactions (**OE3**).

Such controls include:
- proper authorisation of all sales adjustment transactions, such as requiring finance office authority for the write-off of bad debts (**OE3**)
- use of appropriate documents and records — in particular, an approved **credit memo** for granting credit for returned or damaged goods, and an approved **write-off-authorisation memo** for writing off bad debts
- segregation of the duties of authorising sales adjustment transactions and of handling and recording cash receipts.

14.4 DEVELOPING THE AUDIT PLAN

In this section, how the auditor develops the audit plan for sales and receivables is explained. This requires an understanding of the client, an assessment of inherent risks and control risks, and the design of auditing procedures to address those risks.
- Firstly, we consider the auditor's approach to understanding the entity and its environment and how this leads to identifying inherent risks.
- Secondly, we describe factors to be considered by the auditor in assessing the control environment within which the information system and control procedures operate.
- Thirdly, we illustrate the inherent risks and control risks using tests of design effectiveness and tests of operating effectiveness.
- Finally, we explain how the procedures result in the development of the detailed audit program (described in chapter 8) used in directing audit staff and controlling their work.

14.4.1 Understanding the entity and the identification of inherent risks

Audit strategy refers to the mix of tests of controls and substantive procedures to be applied in the audit. The main determinants of the mix are the assessed levels of inherent risks and control risks. In order to properly understand these risks, the auditor must understand the nature of the entity being audited. Only then can the auditor identify those risks to be addressed by audit procedures.

Understanding the entity and its environment

Chapter 8 explains the importance for an auditor in understanding the entity and its environment as part of the planning process in order to understand the potential for misstatements on the financial report. In relation to sales and receivables, this will assist the auditor in:

- developing an expectation of total revenues by understanding the company's products, clients, markets and its capacity (maximum sales volume)
- developing an understanding of gross margins by understanding products, market share and competitive advantage
- developing an expectation of receivable levels based on average collection periods for the client and the industry as a whole.

The generation of revenue also drives some costs (i.e. cost of goods sold and selling expense) and, therefore, an understanding of the sales cycle can lead to an understanding of an entity's expenditure cycles and help in assessing the possibility of misstatements in these areas. The auditor can obtain this knowledge through experience with the client entity or other companies in the same industry, through trade associations and reading newspaper or industry articles about the industry (if any articles specifically related to the entity itself).

Analytical review

Analytical procedures are a cost-effective way of identifying areas where there is a potential for misstatement. These procedures at the planning stage are not to give the auditor evidence about financial statement assertions but are instead designed to highlight risky areas where auditing testing is required. Analytical procedures work best when the auditor has in-depth knowledge of the entity and the industry in which it operates and can therefore create expectations of such issues as expected sales levels, gross margins and levels of receivables. Examples of analytical procedures include investigations and comparisons of:

- sales turnover ratio (sales/total assets)
- trends in sales levels — comparison over time, monthly analysis, comparison between business units
- gross margins, particularly where the entity sells a variety of products at different margins
- receivables days (receivables/credit sales) — consider any changes in payment terms or customer mix
- comparison of bad debts to sales revenue and total receivables — any unexplained changes to these levels.

Where the financial statements are different to expectations the auditor may consider this to be a risk and specific procedures should be included in the audit plan to address these risks.

Materiality

Sales transactions are the main source of operating revenue for most business enterprises. The accounts receivable produced by credit sales transactions are material to the balance sheet for all businesses except those transacting most of their sales for cash. Cash balances at the end of a particular reporting period may not be material, but the flow of cash associated with sales transactions is nearly always material. The significance of sales adjustment transactions varies considerably from one entity to another. However, the bad debts expense is often material to the profit and loss of entities that sell to customers on credit. Most of the audit objectives for sales and receivables shown in table 14.1 are important in arriving at an opinion on the financial statements as a whole.

Inherent risks

In assessing inherent risk for financial statement assertions, the auditor should consider pervasive factors that may affect assertions in many transaction classes and account balances, as well as factors that may relate only to specific assertions affecting sales and receivables. These factors include:
- pressure to overstate sales, so as to report that announced sales or profitability targets were achieved when they were not; such reporting includes:
  – recording fictitious sales
  – holding the books open to record sales in the next period in the current year (improper cut-off)
  – shipping unordered goods to customers near the year-end and recording them as sales in the current period only to have them returned in the next period
- pressure to overstate cash and accounts receivable or understate the allowance for bad debts in order to report a higher level of working capital in the face of liquidity problems or going-concern doubts.

Other factors that could contribute to the possibility of misstatements in sales and receivables assertions include:
- the volume of sales, cash receipts and sales adjustment transactions, resulting in numerous opportunities for errors to occur
- contentious issues relating to the timing of revenue recognition, such as the effect of purchasers' rights of return
- susceptibility to misappropriation of liquid assets generated by cash receipts
- the use of sales adjustment transactions to conceal thefts of cash received from customers by overstating discounts, recording fictitious sales returns or writing off customers' balances as uncollectable.

Recognising these risks, management usually adopts extensive internal controls to overcome them. Thus, the auditor needs also to consider the extent to which inherent risks are properly covered by the internal control structure in deciding on the appropriate audit strategy for sales and receivables assertions.

LEARNING objective 4

Discuss considerations relevant to determining the audit strategy for sales and receivables.

Audit strategy

Given the materiality of sales and receivables, the auditor must take care in assessing inherent and control risks, and in determining the audit strategy. As previously discussed, the main inherent risk is that of overstatement of sales revenue and accounts receivable balances. In the audit of transaction classes, this relates to the occurrence and the measurement assertions for sales transactions, and to the completeness assertion for cash receipts and sales adjustments. Internal controls in relation to the sales cycle are discussed in more detail below. In most entities, controls relative to these assertions for sales and cash receipts are effective and the auditor is able to adopt a lower assessed level of control risk strategy for these transaction classes.

Given the variety of sales adjustment transactions in some entities (and their infrequency in others), control risk may be higher for all assertions applicable to such transactions, requiring a predominantly substantive audit strategy.

Although controls over occurrence and completeness assertions of sales transactions are normally effective, this may not extend to the special case of end of the reporting period cut-off because this is of significance only at that particular date. A predominantly substantive approach is, therefore, commonly adopted in verifying cut-off. In the design of substantive audit procedures, the large volume of sales and cash receipt transactions means that it is normally cost-effective to obtain most of the evidence from the application of substantive procedures to the accounts receivable balance.

14.4.2 Internal control components

Internal controls may contain several factors that could potentially reduce several of the inherent risks discussed earlier in this chapter. In chapter 9, we introduced the components of an internal control system, namely: control environment, risk assessment, information system, control activities and monitoring.

The control environment may enhance or negate the effectiveness of other internal control structure elements in controlling the risk of misstatements in sales and receivables assertions. Management's adoption of, and adherence to, high standards of integrity and ethical values is a key control environment factor in reducing the risk of fraudulent financial reporting through the overstatement of sales and accounts receivable. Related aspects include the elimination of incentives for dishonest reporting (i.e. undue emphasis on meeting sales or profit targets) and of temptations (i.e. an indifferent or ineffective board of directors and audit committee).

A number of special personnel policies and practices are often adopted for employees who handle cash receipts. These include having such employees take mandatory annual leave and periodically rotating their duties. The point of these controls is to deter dishonesty by making employees aware that they may not be able to conceal their misdeeds permanently. Some embezzlements from banks and other entities, for example, have been traced to the seemingly dedicated employee who held the same job without taking a holiday for 10 or 20 years, so as not to disrupt the routine of concealment.

In addition to understanding the control environment, the auditor must understand management's risk assessment procedures and evaluate their effectiveness — particularly in relation to new products or markets, new accounting requirements and business expansion. The effect of changes in the business on the information systems, control activities and monitoring procedures also needs to be understood. The assessment of control risk and the testing of the effectiveness of control procedures are covered in the next section.

PROFESSIONAL ENVIRONMENT
Adjustments cause for concern about control environment

Last year, your firm audited a privately owned electrical wholesaler with about $120 million in sales. The client had two locations in Victoria: Melbourne and Bendigo. You stayed in Melbourne to do the audit at the main location and sent a staff assistant to the Bendigo branch for accounts receivable audit work. When the assistant returned a few days later, you were relieved when she said she had not found anything, as the audit was over budget and the audit team was under time pressure.

As you reviewed the customer accounts the assistant had selected for testing, you noticed an unusual one: a $120 000 credit to accounts receivable control, with an offset to the allowance for bad debts. The explanation for the adjustment was noted as 'to adjust the general ledger to the accounts receivable trial balance at the branch'. You asked the assistant why an adjustment that significant was necessary and she repeated the branch manager's explanation that the branch office had some collection problems with several long-term customers, as it had relaxed credit terms and criteria to increase sales.

When planning the audit, you recognised that the manager dominated the branch and could probably override any controls. Later, as you were reviewing the analytical procedures, you noticed that the accounts receivable write-off percentages at the branch in Bendigo were much higher than those of the main store in Melbourne. The explanation in the working papers was that 'according to the branch manager, write-off and return policies were liberalised at the branch in order to attract customers in response to increased competition from a new electrical wholesaler that had recently opened nearby'.

However, you began to sense something was not right. While talking to the financial controller at the main store in Melbourne, you referred to the problems at Bendigo and that they were working out 'because it appears that those credit policy changes you implemented earlier this year helped to attract new customers'. The controller responded, 'Credit policy changes? What are you talking about? The company is a wholesale distributor — it doesn't have the kind of customers you find in a retail store. Most of our customers are major electrical contractors. We have been very sensitive to the economic indicators in that industry and the financial health of our customers. If anything, we have tightened credit'. You now realise that the Bendigo branch manager's explanation had no basis in fact.

You remembered auditing standard ASA 315 *Identifying and Assessing the Risks of Material Misstatement through Understanding the Entity and Its Environment* (ISA 315) and are now convinced something is wrong. What would you do about it?

LEARNING objective 5

Design and execute tests of controls over sales, cash receipts and sales adjustment transactions to assess control risk.

14.4.3 Assessment of control risk

The procedures described in this section are followed only where the process of obtaining the understanding of the internal control structure leads the auditor to believe that it is both possible and cost-effective to assess control risk as being less than high. Where this is not the case, the auditor notes this conclusion in the working papers and obtains the required audit evidence through the performance of a higher level of substantive procedures. This decision is made separately for each financial statement assertion, although the same conclusion tends to apply to most, if not all, assertions.

Sales

This section is concerned with credit sales. The assessment of control risk for cash sales is considered in the next section on cash receipts.

Tests of design effectiveness

Table 14.2 (overleaf) contains a partial listing of possible misstatements, necessary controls, potential tests of the operating effectiveness of controls and the specific transaction class audit objectives for credit sales to which each relates. Using the understanding of the information system, the auditor identifies the presence of necessary controls and makes a preliminary assessment of control risk.

TABLE 14.2: Control risk assessment procedures — credit sales transactions

Function	Potential misstatement	Necessary control	Possible test of operating effectiveness	Relevant transaction class audit objective (from table 14.1)				
				OE1	C1	AV1	CO	PD1
Accepting customer orders	Sales may be made to unauthorised customers.	Determination that customer is on approved customer list	Observe procedure; re-perform.	✓				
		Approved sales order form for each sale	Examine approved sales order forms.	✓				
Approving credit	Sales may be made without credit approval.	Credit department credit check on all new customers	Enquire about procedures for checking credit on new customers.			✓		
		Customer's credit limit check before each sale	Examine evidence of credit limit check before each sale.			✓		
Filling sales orders	Goods may be released from warehouse for unauthorised orders.	Approved sales order for all goods released to dispatch	Observe warehouse personnel filling orders.	✓				
Shipping	Goods dispatched may not agree with goods ordered.	Independent check by dispatch clerks of agreement of goods received from warehouse with approved sales order	Examine evidence of performance of independent check.	✓	✓			
	Unauthorised shipments may be made.	Segregation of duties for filling and dispatching orders	Observe the segregation of duties.	✓				
		Preparation of dispatch note for each shipment	Inspect dispatch notes.	✓				
Invoicing customers	Invoices may be made for fictitious transactions, or duplicate invoices may be made.	Matching of dispatch note and approved sales order for each invoice	Vouch invoices to dispatch notes and approved sales orders.*	✓	✓		✓	
	Some shipments may not be invoiced.	Matching of sales invoice with each dispatch note	Trace dispatch notes to sales invoices.*					
		Periodic accounting for all dispatch notes	Observe procedure; re-perform.		✓		✓	

Function	Potential misstatement	Necessary control	Possible test of operating effectiveness	OE1	C1	AV1	CO	PD1
	Sales invoices may have incorrect prices.	Independent check on pricing of invoices	Inspect copy of invoice for evidence of performance.			✓		
			Re-perform the check on the accuracy of pricing.*			✓		
Recording the sales	Fictitious sales transactions may be recorded.	Requirement of sales invoice and matching documents for all entries	Vouch recorded sales to supporting documents.*	✓		✓	✓	
	Invoices may not be journalised or posted to customer accounts.	Independent check of agreement of sales journal entries and amounts posted to customer accounts with control totals of invoices	Review evidence of independent check; re-perform check; trace sales invoices to sales journal and customer accounts.*		✓	✓	✓	
		Periodic accounting for all sales invoices	Observe procedures; re-perform.*		✓		✓	
	Invoices may be posted to the wrong customer account.	Chart of accounts and supervisory review	Observe procedures; re-perform.*					✓
		Mailing of monthly statements to customers, with independent follow-up of customer complaints	Observe mailing and follow-up procedures.*		✓			

Note: * Sometimes performed as part of dual-purpose tests.

As transactions are processed normally by a computer information system, the auditor also needs to consider the effectiveness of general controls over computer operations.

14.4.4 Tests of operating effectiveness

Tests of controls designed to provide evidence of operating effectiveness involve a variety of procedures, including re-performance of certain control procedures by the auditor. Statistical or non-statistical sampling procedures (see chapter 13) may be applied in the performance of some tests. The auditor needs to remember that the direction of testing should be backwards along the audit trail when the objective is to test controls over the occurrence assertion, and forwards along the audit trail when the objective is to test controls over the completeness assertion. As an example, a sample of invoices from the sales journal would be vouched back to sales orders or shipping documents to test occurrence; to test completeness, a sample of sales orders or shipping documents would be traced to the sales journal to determine that all the transactions were recorded. The auditor must document the tests of controls performed, the evidence obtained and the conclusions reached. A formal audit program that incorporates several of the tests from table 14.2 is presented in figure 14.2.

As explained in chapter 11, certain tests of operating effectiveness simultaneously provide substantive evidence as to the correctness of recorded amounts, and these are known as dual-purpose tests. The auditor must be particularly careful in drawing conclusions from such tests. From substantive tests, it may be concluded that misstatements are significant only if material. However, all misstatements suggest that control procedures have not been properly performed. These deviations from prescribed procedures could have caused misstatements in transactions of any size. Therefore, as a test of controls, it is the number of misstatements that is important, not their size. Detections of misstatements of any size, therefore, may require the assessment of control risk to be revised.

Computer information systems

Tests of the operating effectiveness of controls over a computer information system are usually undertaken by computer-assisted audit techniques (CAATs). The two main categories of CAATs are (1) those that test the operation of programs and related programmed application controls directly and (2) those that test data held on computer files.

In the first category, the most common techniques used for testing controls over the processing of sales transactions are the **test data approach** and the use of embedded audit facilities. Test data are composed of simulated transactions. One batch of data consists of transactions replicating the normal types of transaction processed by the system. A second batch consists of transactions that should activate those programmed application controls of significance to the audit, such as orders exceeding credit limits. Both batches are processed by a copy of the program, and the results are compared with expected results determined manually. Test data are best suited to batch processing systems where the relevant program can be isolated and a copy can be taken for audit purposes. With real-time processing, it is less satisfactory and most such systems incorporate embedded audit facilities. One kind of **embedded audit facility** is the **integrated test facility** (ITF) based on dummy accounts to which test data can be processed on a real-time basis. Another is a **systems control audit review file** (SCARF). This facility enables auditors to specify items of interest, such as orders where credit limits are overridden by the credit controller. The facility will then log all such transactions and record them on a special audit file for subsequent review by the auditors.

FIGURE 14.2: Partial audit program for tests of controls — credit sales

| Prepared by: _____ Date: _____ |
| Reviewed by: _____ Date: _____ |

Amalgamated Products Ltd
Planned tests of controls — Credit sales transactions
Year ending 30 June 2015

Assertion/test of controls	W/P ref.	Auditor	Date
Occurrence 1. Observe procedures, including segregation of duties, for: • approving sales orders • filling sales orders • dispatching sales orders • invoicing customers • mailing monthly statements to customers and following up on customer complaints			

Amalgamated Products Ltd
Planned tests of controls — Credit sales transactions
Year ending 30 June 2015

Assertion/test of controls	W/P ref.	Auditor	Date
2. Select a sample of sales transactions from the sales journal and verify transaction dates, customer names and amounts by vouching entries to the following matching supporting documents: • sales invoices • dispatch notes • approved sales orders.			
Completeness 3. Examine evidence of the use of and accounting for prenumbered sales orders, dispatch notes and sales invoices. Scan the sequence of sales invoice numbers in the sales journal. 4. Select a sample of approved sales orders and trace to matching: • dispatch notes • sales invoices • entries in the sales journal.			
Accuracy 5. For the sample in step 2 above, examine evidence of: • proper credit approval for each transaction • an independent check on proper pricing of invoices • an independent check on the mathematical accuracy of invoices. 6. For sales invoices processed in batches, examine evidence of an independent check on the agreement of totals for sales journal entries and amounts posted to customer accounts with batch totals.			
Cut-off 7. Obtain the number of the last goods dispatch note for the final dispatch of the year, select a sample of dispatch notes before this number and agree: • to sales invoices dated in the current period • entries in sales journal before the period end. 8. Following on from step 7, select a sample of the first dispatch notes after this number and agree: • to sales invoices dated in the next accounting period • sales are not recorded in the sales journal until the following accounting period.			

For tests applied to sales transactions held on computer files, the auditor can use **generalised audit software** for large computer systems and proprietary database packages for smaller, PC-based systems. Both techniques can be used to access data on computer files according to criteria specified by the auditor and to perform a wide range of mathematical functions on that data. For tests involving the inspection of documents, the software can be programmed to select a sample of documents. If statistical sampling techniques are being used (as described in chapter 13), the software can be programmed with the sampling elements, such as the preliminary assessment of inherent and control risk and the tolerable deviation rate. The software selects a suitably random sample and, after testing by the auditor, calculates the achieved deviation rate. For re-performance, the software can be programmed to perform the entire test. In re-performing invoice pricing, for example, the auditor can program the software to select a sample of invoices and compare unit sales prices on those invoices with sales prices held on the price file, and to report differences.

Cash receipts

Table 14.3 illustrates a partial listing of potential misstatements, necessary controls, possible tests of the operating effectiveness of controls, and related transaction class audit objectives for cash receipt transactions. The particulars of the items listed in the table vary among entities, based on such factors as the method of data processing used. As we explained for credit sales, the potential misstatements and necessary controls would be the basis of a checklist used to assess design effectiveness. Similarly, an audit program for tests of the operating effectiveness of controls for cash receipts transactions can be prepared based on the potential tests of controls shown in table 14.3.

TABLE 14.3: Control risk assessment considerations — cash receipts

Function	Potential misstatement	Necessary control	Possible test of operating effectiveness	OE2	C2	AV1	CO	PD2
Receiving cash receipts	Cash sales may not be registered.	Use of cash registers or point-of-sale devices	Observe cash sales procedures.		✓			
		Periodic surveillance of cash sales procedures	Enquire of supervisors about the results of surveillance.		✓			
	Mail receipts may be lost or misappropriated after receipt.	Restrictive endorsement of cheques immediately on receipt — note that payment by cheque is uncommon now. Most payments are by direct bank transfers and so the individual accounts receivable and bank transfers need to be matched	Observe mail opening, including the endorsement of cheques.		✓			
		Immediate preparation of prelist of mail receipts	Observe the preparation of records.	✓	✓	✓		
Depositing cash in the bank	Cash and cheques received for deposit may not agree with the cash count list and prelist.	Independent check of agreement of cash and cheques with register totals and prelist	Examine evidence of independent check.*	✓	✓	✓		

Function	Potential misstatement	Necessary control	Possible test of operating effectiveness	Relevant transaction class audit objective (from table 14.1)				
				OE2	C2	AV1	CO	PD2
	Cash may not be deposited intact daily.	Independent check of agreement of validated deposit slip with daily cash summary	Re-perform independent check.*	✓	✓		✓	
Recording the receipts	Some receipts may not be recorded.	Independent check of agreement of amounts journalised and posted with daily cash summary	Re-perform independent check.*		✓		✓	
	Errors may be made in journalising receipts.	Preparation of periodic independent bank reconciliations	Examine bank reconciliations.*	✓	✓	✓	✓	
	Receipts may be posted to the wrong customer account.	Mailing of monthly statements to customers	Observe mailing of monthly statements.	✓	✓	✓		✓

Note: * Sometimes performed as part of dual-purpose tests.

Sales adjustments

Sales adjustment information systems are more diverse than sales and cash receipt systems, so it is not practicable to illustrate typical potential misstatements and necessary controls. However, tests of controls that are likely to be appropriate include:

- recalculating cash discounts and determining that the payments were received within the discount period
- inspecting credit memoranda for sales returns for indication of proper approval and accompanying receiving reports for evidence of the actual return of goods
- inspecting written authorisations and supporting documentation (i.e. correspondence with the customer or collection agencies) for the write-off of bad debts.

14.4.5 Final assessment

Based on the evidence obtained from the procedures to obtain an understanding of the internal control structure and related tests of controls, the auditor makes a final assessment of inherent risks and control risks. For each significant audit objective where assessment of control risk as being less than high is the basis for adopting a lower assessed level of control risk audit strategy, reasons for this assessment must be documented.

This assessment enables the auditor to plan the level of substantive procedures to be performed. Because many tests of controls are dual-purpose tests, providing evidence of errors in amounts as well as deviations from controls, the auditor usually draws up the detailed audit program based on the preliminary assessment of control risk. This improves audit efficiency in that tests of the operating effectiveness of controls that use sources of evidence on which the substantive tests of details are also based are performed simultaneously with those substantive procedures. The auditor must ensure that control deviations are properly identified and that their implications for the assessment of control risk are properly considered in terms of whether further substantive procedures need to be performed.

Learning check

Do you know ...

14.1 ☐ In determining the correct balance for accounts receivable, procedures for recording sales, cash receipts and sales adjustment transactions the auditor should ensure that (1) goods are delivered only in respect of approved orders, (2) all goods delivered are invoiced, (3) all cash received from customers is recorded, and (4) only genuine sales adjustments are recorded.

14.2 ☐ The reconciliation of accounts receivable ledger balances with the general ledger control account, the sending of monthly statements to customers and the comparison of sales with budgets, are all important independent checks in ensuring the accuracy of the recording of the related transactions and balances.

14.3 ☐ Controls over the completeness of recorded cash receipts are of great importance. For over-the-counter sales, this is achieved by using cash registers; for receipts by mail, it is achieved by segregating the mail opening from the recording of cash receipts and posting to the accounts receivable ledger; for payments by direct bank transfer, it is achieved by reconciling the banking records with the individual accounts receivable accounts.

14.4 ☐ In developing the audit plan, the auditor needs to have (1) obtained an understanding of the information system, control procedures and control environment, (2) assessed inherent risk both for the entity and for the specific transactions and balances, and (3) assessed control risk based on the results of tests of controls.

14.5 ☐ The greatest inherent risks are the overstatement of sales transactions and the accounts receivable balance, and the understatement of cash receipts and the allowance for bad debts. The volume of transactions means that most entities ensure that their internal control structure relating to such matters is effective.

LEARNING 6 objective

Indicate the factors relevant to determining an acceptable level of detection risk for the audit of sales and receivables.

14.5 SUBSTANTIVE PROCEDURES

The main consideration here is the gross amount due from customers on credit sales and the related allowance for bad debts. To design substantive procedures for these accounts, the auditor must first determine the acceptable level of detection risk for each significant related assertion. Given that the verification of accounts receivable requires consideration of sales, sales adjustment and cash receipts transactions, the procedures also contribute to the income statement balance of sales, and to the balance of cash on hand and at bank in the balance sheet.

14.5.1 Determining detection risk

As we explained in chapter 9, for a specified level of audit risk, detection risk is inversely related to the assessed levels of inherent risk and control risk. Thus, the auditor must consider these assessments when determining the acceptable level of detection risk for each accounts receivable assertion. Several pervasive inherent risk and control environment factors that affect sales and receivables transactions and balances were discussed earlier. The combined effects of these factors (especially those contributing to the risk of credit sales being overstated), may result in assessments of inherent risk as being high for:
- the existence and valuation and allocation assertions for accounts receivable
- the valuation and allocation assertion for the related allowance account.

Assessments of inherent risk as being lower may be appropriate for the other assertions. Control risk assessments for accounts receivable assertions depend on the related control risk assessments for the transaction classes (credit sales, cash receipts and sales adjustments) that affect the accounts receivable balance. As we explained in chapter 12, the assessments for transaction class assertions affect the same account balance assertions for accounts affected by the transactions, with the following exception: control risk assessments for the occurrence and completeness assertions for a transaction class that decreases an account balance affect the assessments for the opposite account balance assertions. Thus, because both cash receipts and sales adjustment transactions decrease the accounts receivable balance, the assessment for the occurrence assertion for these transaction classes affects the assessment for the completeness assertion for the accounts receivable balance. Similarly, the assessment for the completeness assertion for these transaction classes affects the assessment for the existence assertion for the accounts receivable balance.

The audit program will be based on the preliminary assessment of control risk. If tests of controls subsequently lead to a revised assessment of control risk, then the design of substantive procedures in terms of their nature, timing or extent will need to be revised. Some auditors use a matrix similar to the one illustrated in table 14.4 to document and correlate the various risk components that must be considered in the design of substantive procedures for each account balance assertion.

The risk levels specified in this matrix are illustrative only and vary based on the entity's circumstances.

TABLE 14.4: Correlation of risk components — accounts receivable

Risk component	Existence or occurrence	Completeness	Rights and obligations	Accuracy or valuation and allocation	Presentation and disclosure
Audit risk	Low	Low	Low	Low	Low
Inherent risk	High	Moderate	Low	High	Moderate
Control risk — sales transactions	Low	Low	Moderate	Moderate	Moderate
Control risk — cash receipts	Low	Low	Low	Low	Low
Control risk — sales adjustments	Moderate	Low	Moderate	High	Moderate
Combined control risk[1]	Low	Moderate	Moderate	High	Moderate
Acceptable detection risk[2]	Moderate	Moderate	High	Low	Moderate

1. This is the most conservative (highest) of transaction class control risk assessments used as the combined risk assessment, as per the method discussed in chapter 12 (section 12.2).
2. Determined from the risk components matrix in figure 9.7 (p. 402), based on the levels of audit risk, inherent risk and combined control risk indicated above for each assertion category.

Consider the following with regard to the existence and occurrence assertions.
- Overall audit risk needs to be low to ensure there is a low risk of giving the wrong audit opinion in relation to existence and occurrence.

- The inherent risk has been assessed as high — the auditor understands the entity and its environment and has concluded that there is a high likelihood that existence or occurrence errors will arise (i.e. a high risk that transactions are recorded in the accounts which do not relate to sales transactions that actually occurred or there are balances included for which no receivable actually exists).
- The combined control risk is low, indicating that the auditor has obtained an understanding of the internal controls related to existence and occurrence and performed tests of controls on their effectiveness, and has concluded that there is a low risk that any errors that do arise (and this is likely given the high inherent risk identified above) will not be detected and corrected by the internal controls.
- The combined control risk for existence and occurrence is made up of the existence and occurrence control risk for sales transactions and the completeness control risk for cash receipts and sales adjustments, all of which are low. The logic for this is as follows (notice all of the following lead to potential existence problems in the balances):
  - an *occurrence* problem with sales transactions (a sale has been included in the accounts but no valid sale was made) leads to an *existence* problem in the receivables balance (the non-existent sale was recorded so a receivable was created that is not valid)
  - for cash receipts, a *completeness* problem (cash has been received but not recorded) leads to an *existence* problem in receivables balance (the receivable does not exist because it has been paid)
  - for sales adjustments, consider bad debts, a *completeness* problem with bad debts (a debt has gone bad but not recorded in the accounts) leads to an *existence* problem in the receivables balance (the receivable does not exist because the debt has gone bad).
- Having assessed inherent risk and control risk, the auditor will now determine the acceptable level of detection risk that will allow the overall audit risk for existence and occurrence to be low. Given inherent risk is high and control risk is low, the auditor has determined that a moderate level of detection risk is appropriate to achieve the required audit risk. This level of detection risk will be used by the auditor to determine the nature, timing and extent of substantive procedures that need to be performed. The level and detail of substantive procedures performed is a matter of professional judgement; the auditor will be performing more than the minimum level of testing (detection risk has not been set high) but the auditor will not be performing the maximum level of testing either (this would be relevant if detection risk was set low).

LEARNING objective 7

Design a substantive audit program for sales and receivables.

14.5.2 Designing substantive procedures

The next step is to finalise the audit program to achieve the specific audit objectives for each account balance assertion. The specific audit objectives covered here are the ones listed in the 'Balance objectives' section of table 14.1. In chapter 12, we introduced a general framework for developing audit programs for substantive procedures. Of the steps listed under the heading 'Complete preliminary planning' in figure 12.7, the application of items 1–4 to accounts receivable has already been considered in this chapter. In this section, we consider the options for designing the substantive procedures for accounts receivable, following the sequence suggested in the lower part of figure 12.7.

Table 14.5 lists possible substantive procedures to be included in an audit program developed on this basis. This table does not represent a formal audit program because it is not tailored to any specific information system, there is no working paper heading, and there are no columns for supporting working paper references, initials and dates. Instead, for instructional purposes, there are columns to indicate the categories of substantive procedure and the specific account balance audit objectives from table 14.1 to which each procedure applies. Several of the procedures apply to more than one audit objective, and each objective is covered by multiple possible procedures. The procedures are explained in the sections that follow, including comments on how some procedures can be tailored, based on the planned level of detection risk to be achieved.

TABLE 14.5: Possible substantive procedures for accounts receivable assertions

Category	Substantive procedure	OE4	RO1	C4	AV no.	PD no.

Initial procedures	1. Perform initial procedures on accounts receivable balances and records that will be subjected to further testing.
	(a) Trace the opening balances for accounts receivable and related allowance to the previous year's working papers.
	(b) Review activity in general ledger accounts for accounts receivable and related allowance, and investigate entries that appear unusual in amount or source.
	(c) Obtain the accounts receivable trial balance and determine that it accurately represents the underlying accounting records by:
	  • adding the trial balance and determining agreement with the total of the subsidiary ledger or accounts receivable master file and the general ledger balance
	  • testing the agreement of customers and balances listed on the trial balance with those included on the subsidiary ledger or master file.
					✓2,3	

Analytical procedures	2. Perform analytical procedures.
	(a) Determine expectations.
	(b) Compare current and previous year balances.
	(c) Calculate significant ratios such as:
	  • gross profit
	  • days sales in accounts receivable.
	(d) Obtain explanations for unexpected changes.
	(e) Corroborate explanations.
		✓		✓	✓2,3	

Tests of details of transactions	3. Vouch a sample of recorded accounts receivable transactions to supporting documentation (see also step 6(c)). (a) Vouch debits to supporting sales invoices, dispatch notes and sales orders. (b) Vouch credits to remittance advices or sales adjustment authorisation for sales returns and allowances or bad debt write-offs.	✓	✓	✓	✓2	
	4. Perform cut-off tests for sales and sales returns. (a) Select a sample of recorded sales transactions from several days before and after year-end, and examine supporting sales invoices and dispatch notes to determine that the sales were recorded in the proper period. (b) Select a sample of credit memos issued after the year-end, examine supporting documentation such as dated goods inwards notes, and determine that the returns were recorded in the proper period. Also, consider whether the volume of sales returns after the year-end suggests the possibility of unauthorised shipments before the year-end.	✓		✓		

(continued)

Category	Substantive procedure	Account balance audit objective (from table 14.1)				
		OE4	RO1	C4	AV no.	PD no.
	5. Perform cash receipts cut-off test. (a) Observe that all cash received before the close of business on the last day of the financial year is included in cash on hand or deposits in transit, and that no receipts of the subsequent period are included. (b) Review documentation such as daily cash summaries, duplicate deposit slips and bank statements covering several days before and after the year-end date to determine the proper cut-off.	✓		✓		

Tests of details of balances	6. Confirm accounts receivable.
	(a) Determine the form, timing and extent of confirmation requests.
	(b) Select and execute a sample and investigate exceptions.
	(c) For positive confirmation requests for which no reply was received, perform alternative follow-up procedures.
	  • Vouch subsequent payments identifiable with items constituting the account balance at the confirmation date to supporting documentation, as in step 3(b).
	  • Vouch items constituting the balance at confirmation date to documentary support, as in step 3(a).
	(d) Summarise the results of confirmation and alternative follow-up procedures.
		✓	✓		✓2	

	7. Evaluate the adequacy of the allowance for bad debts.
	(a) Add and cross-add the aged trial balance of accounts receivable and agree the total with the general ledger.
	(b) Test ageing by vouching amounts in ageing categories for sample of accounts to supporting documentation.
	(c) For past-due accounts:
	  • Examine evidence of collectability, such as correspondence with customers and outside collection agencies, credit reports and customers' financial statements.
	  • Discuss the collectability of accounts with appropriate management personnel.
	(d) Evaluate the adequacy of the allowance component for each ageing category and in total.
					✓3	

Presentation and disclosure	8. Compare the presentation of the financial statements with applicable accounting standards. (a) Determine that debtors are properly classified as to type and expected period of realisation. (b) Determine whether there are credit balances that are significant in the aggregate and should be reclassified as liabilities. (c) Determine the appropriateness of presentation and disclosure and accounting for related party or factored debts.				✓2	✓4,5

Initial procedures

The starting point for verifying accounts receivable and the related allowance account is to trace the current period's opening balances to the closing audited balances in the previous year's working papers (when applicable). Next, the auditor should review the current period's activity in the general ledger control account and related allowance account for significant entries that are unusual in nature or amount and require special investigation.

An **accounts receivable trial balance** (listing all customer balances) is obtained, usually from the entity. To determine that it is an accurate and complete representation of the underlying accounting records, the auditor should add this listing and compare the total with both the total of the subsidiary ledger from which it was prepared and the general ledger control account balance. The auditor should also compare a sample of the customer details and balances shown on the trial balance with those in the subsidiary ledger, and vice versa. The sample can then serve as the physical representation of the population of accounts receivable to be subjected to further substantive procedures.

An example of an **aged trial balance** of an accounts receivable working paper is presented in figure 14.3 (overleaf). This working paper not only provides evidence of performance of the initial procedures just described, but of several of the other substantive procedures discussed in subsequent sections. The initial procedures in verifying the accuracy of the trial balance and determining its agreement with the control account in the general ledger relate mainly to the clerical and mathematical accuracy component of the valuation and allocation assertion.

Computer information systems

The auditor can use computer-assisted audit techniques to perform substantive procedures on information stored on computer files through the use of computer audit software. Both generalised audit software and database packages can be used to print a trial balance directly from the accounts receivable master file, test the ageing of a sample of accounts, and verify the total and its agreement with the control account in the general ledger.

Analytical procedures

Tests of details are usually planned on the basis that the analytical procedures confirm expectations. It is preferable to perform analytical procedures early in the final audit, so any necessary changes to tests of details can be determined before the start of that part of the audit.

The first stage in applying analytical procedures is to review the understanding, of the entity, obtained during the planning phase, as to whether any changes to sales and receivables balances are to be expected.

The second stage is to identify absolute changes in amounts between this year and previous years. This is normally done in the course of preparing the lead schedule for sales and accounts receivable, as explained in chapter 8. On this schedule, previous and current year ledger balances making up the financial statement disclosures are recorded side by side, making any differences readily apparent.

The third stage involves the use of more sophisticated relationships such as ratios and trends. This procedure can be performed on accounting data held on computer files, using computer audit software. Significant ratios are gross profit and average collection period. If gross profit is higher than expected, it could be that sales have been overstated to boost revenue, such as by a deliberate cut-off error. An increase in average collection period indicates potential problems in collecting receivables, with the consequent need for a greater allowance.

Bates Ltd
Aged trial balance — Accounts receivable — Trade
30 June 2015
(PBC)

W/P ref. B-1
Prepared by: A.C.E   Date: 5/7/15
Reviewed by: P.A.R   Date: 20/7/15

Account no. 120

Account name	Past Due Over 90 days	Over 60 days	Over 30 days	Current	Balance per books 30/6/14	Adjustments	Balance per audit 30/6/15	
Ace Engineering		2 529.04	2 016.14	11 875.90	16 421.083✓		16 421.08	
ø Applied Devices			15 938.89 ⬎	27 901.11 ⬎	43 840.003✓		43 840.00	C1
ø Barry Manufacturing	1 088.92 ⬎	743.12 ⬎	3 176.22 ⬎	8 993.01 ⬎	14 001.273✓		14 001.27	C2
ø Brandt Electronics	501.10 ⬎	7 309.50 ⬎	30 948.01 ⬎	24 441.25 ⬎	63 199.863✓		63 199.86	C3
Cermetrics Ltd			3 813.76	8 617.30	12 431.063✓		12 431.06	
ø Columbia Components				4 321.18 ⬎	4 321.183✓		4 321.18	
Drake Manufacturing			739.57	2 953.88	3 693.453✓		3 693.45	
EMC		1 261.01	1 048.23	16 194.76	18 504.003✓		18 504.00	
ø Groton Electric		7 799.36 ⬎	20 006.63 ⬎	89 017.15 ⬎	116 823.143✓		116 823.14	C4
Harvey Industries		1 709.16	6 111.25	18 247.31	26 067.723✓		26 067.72	
ø Jed Ltd	2 615.87 ⬎	12 098.00 ⬎	15 434.46 ⬎	56 536.88 ⬎	86 685.213✓	(9 416.96)	77 268.25	C5
Jericho Electric		1 198.72	13 123.14		14 321.863✓		14 321.86	
.		.	.	.	.	.	.	
.		.	.	.	.	.	.	
.		.	.	.	.	.	.	
W & M Manufacturing Ltd		1 904.65 ⬎	2 166.78 ⬎	28 389.69	32 461.123		32 461.12	C60
Yancey Ltd	814.98	2 861.05	9 874.13	13 561.80	27 111.963		27 111.96	
	10 157.46	56 705.59	160 537.28	392 136.41	619 536.74	(9 416.96)	610 119.78	
	✓	✓	✓	✓	✓ B	✓ B	✓ B	

✓ Added or cross-added
ø Customer name and balance per books checked against subsidiary ledger
⬎ Ageing verified by examining transaction dates of related unpaid sales invoices in subsidiary ledger
C Account selected for confirmation — see W/P B–2

FIGURE 14.3: Aged trial balance working paper

Wherever a change in relationships cannot be readily explained, the auditor must seek an explanation from management and corroborate that explanation, usually by performing more tests of details. For accounts receivable and sales, analytical procedures can provide evidence relating to the existence or occurrence, completeness, and accuracy or valuation and allocation assertions.

Tests of details of transactions

Where balances result from the effects of numerous transactions, it is normally more efficient to concentrate substantive procedures on tests of details of balances, and not tests of details of transactions. The latter are not unimportant, but serve to corroborate tests of details of balances. In the main, the tests of transactions will be performed during the interim audit, commonly in the form of dual-purpose tests. The cut-off tests described in later sections are always performed as part of year-end work and, although they are tests of transactions, serve to verify the recorded balance at the end of the reporting period.

Vouching recorded accounts receivable to supporting transactions

This procedure involves vouching a sample of debits in customers' accounts to supporting sales invoices, and matching documents to provide evidence relevant to the existence, rights and obligations, and accuracy of valuation and allocation assertions. It also involves vouching a sample of credits to remittance advices and sales adjustment authorisations to provide evidence relevant to the completeness assertion for accounts receivable that reductions in customer balances are legitimate.

Performing sales cut-off test

The **sales cut-off test** is designed to obtain reasonable assurance that:
- sales and accounts receivable are recorded in the accounting period in which the transactions occurred
- the corresponding entries for inventories and cost of sales are made in the same period.

The sales cut-off test is made as of the end of the reporting period. Given the greater risk of overstatement, the emphasis is on verifying the occurrence of recorded sales before the year-end. The auditor usually records the number of the last issued dispatch note during attendance at the stocktake and compares it with the cut-off established for inventory purposes. For sales of goods from inventory, the procedure involves comparing a sample of recorded sales from the last few days of the current period with dispatch notes numbered before the cut-off number to determine that the transactions occurred before the end of the reporting period. A smaller number of sales recorded after the end of the reporting period are vouched to dispatch notes numbered after the cut-off, to ensure that none were delivered before the end of the reporting period.

The **sales return cut-off test** is similar and particularly directed towards the possibility that returns made before year-end are not recorded until after year-end, resulting in the overstatement of accounts receivable and sales. The auditor can determine the correct cut-off by examining dated receiving reports for returned merchandise and correspondence with customers. The auditor should also be alert to the possibility that an unusually heavy volume of sales returns shortly after the year-end could signal unauthorised shipments before year-end to inflate recorded sales and accounts receivable.

Performing cash receipts cut-off test

The **cash receipts cut-off test** is designed to obtain reasonable assurance that cash receipts are recorded in the accounting period in which they are received. A proper cut-off at the end of the reporting period is essential to the correct presentation of both cash and accounts receivable. If present at the year-end date, the auditor can observe that all collections including bank transfers received before close of business are included in cash on hand or in deposits in transit, and are credited to accounts receivable. An alternative to personal observation is to review supporting documentation such as the daily cash summary and a validated deposit slip for the last day of the financial year, as well as bank reconciliations at year-end.

Tests of details of balances

As explained above, most of the audit effort on receivables is obtained through tests of details of balances, of which the most important is the confirmation of accounts receivable and related follow-up procedures. Confirmation provides evidence as to existence, rights and valuation. It does not provide evidence of completeness, because customers are unlikely to admit to owing more than their recorded balance. The other major test of details of balances is an evaluation of the adequacy of the allowance for bad debts.

Confirming accounts receivable

Confirmation of accounts receivable involves direct written communication by the auditor with individual customers. The test is often referred to as an accounts receivable circularisation.

Accepted audit procedure

The confirmation of accounts receivable is an accepted audit procedure when they are material and it is reasonable to presume the debtors will respond — ASA 505 *External Confirmations* (ISA 505). Confirmation is usually the most efficient procedure for gaining sufficient appropriate audit evidence to support the existence and rights assertions of accounts receivable. There are circumstances, however, in which the auditor concludes that confirmation is unlikely to be effective and that sufficient appropriate audit evidence can be achieved through the performance of alternative audit procedures. Based on the previous year's audit experience on that engagement, the auditor might expect, for example, that responses will be unreliable in the current year or that the response rates will be inadequate. Also, in some cases, customers may be unable to confirm balances if they use voucher systems that show the amount owed on individual transactions, but not the total amount owed to one creditor. This is often true of government agencies. The auditor may be able to overcome this problem by confirming individual transactions rather than balances.

As written evidence from third parties, responses to confirmation requests constitute highly reliable evidence. Against this, it must be remembered that:

- where customers are small businesses or private individuals, they are less likely to maintain sufficiently accurate accounts payable ledger records to provide a reliable response
- even larger businesses generally maintain less effective controls over the completeness of liabilities recorded in their accounts payable ledger; they often just pay on invoice and may not maintain an accounts payable ledger at all
- customers are unlikely to admit to owing more than is shown on the monthly statement, limiting the evidence to that of existence, rights and, to a lesser extent, valuation
- many trivial differences are likely to be reported as a result of goods and cash in transit
- the non-response rate may be high.

Given that dealings between the entity and its customers are confidential, the entity must authorise its customers to disclose details of the outstanding balance to its auditors. Occasionally, entities have prohibited auditors from confirming certain accounts receivable. The effect of prohibition should be evaluated on the basis of management's reasons, with the auditor determining whether sufficient evidence from other auditing procedures can be obtained. If the auditor regards management's reasons as unacceptable, then there is a limitation on the scope of the audit that might result in a modified auditor's report.

Form of confirmation

There are two forms of confirmation request:

1. the positive form, which requires the debtor to respond that the balance shown is correct or incorrect
2. the negative form, which requires the debtor to respond only when the amount shown is incorrect.

The two forms are illustrated in figures 14.4 and 14.5. The positive confirmation request is usually made in the form of a separate letter on the entity letterhead, but it may also be printed on the customer's monthly statement. The negative request is usually in the form of a request printed on the statement, and as a rule is not used very often. The positive form generally produces statistically valid evidence, providing non-responses are verified by other means. With the negative form, it is impossible to determine whether a lack of response indicates agreement with the balance or simply a failure to reply. The positive form is used when detection risk is low or individual customer balances are relatively large. The negative form should be used only when the following conditions apply:

- detection risk is moderate or high
- there are a large number of small balances in the population
- the auditor has no reason to believe that the respondents are unlikely to give the request due consideration.

**BATES LTD
4 Queensland Road
Eastville**

6 July 2015

Ace Engineering Service
New Road
Westville

Dear Sir or Madam,

This request is being sent to you to enable our independent auditors to confirm the correctness of our records. It is not a request for payment.

Our records on 30 June 2015 showed an amount of $16 421.08 receivable from you. Please confirm whether this agrees with your records on that date by signing this form and returning it directly to our auditors. An addressed envelope is enclosed for this purpose. If you find any difference, please report details to our auditors directly in the space provided below.

Yours faithfully
Controller

The above amount is correct [ ]. The above amount is incorrect for the following reasons:
_____
_____
_____

(Individual or company name)

By:_____

FIGURE 14.4: Positive confirmation request — letter form

Often, a combination of the two forms is used in a single engagement. In the audit of a public utility, for example, the auditor may elect to use the negative form for residential customers and the positive form for commercial customers. When the positive form is used, the auditor should generally follow up with a second and sometimes a third request to those accounts receivable that fail to reply.

Please examine this monthly statement carefully
and advise our auditors

Reddy & Abel
Certified Practising Accountants
465 City Centre Building
Perth

as to any exceptions.

A self-addressed stamped envelope is
enclosed for your convenience.

THIS IS NOT A REQUEST FOR PAYMENT

FIGURE 14.5:
Negative confirmation
request — stamp form

Timing and extent of requests

When the acceptable level of detection risk is low, the auditor ordinarily confirms receivables as at the end of the reporting period. Otherwise, the confirmation date may be one or two months earlier. In such cases, the auditor must:

- perform analytical procedures on entries in the accounts receivable control account in the period between the date of confirmation and the end of the reporting period, and obtain a satisfactory explanation for any unexpected changes
- perform tests of controls in the intervening period to ensure that the assessment of control risk leading to a decision to accept a high level of detection risk continues to apply.

The extent of requests or sample size is determined by the criteria that were described in chapter 13 on audit sampling. Accounts receivable may be divided into distinct populations for sampling. For example, different categories of accounts receivable — such as wholesale and retail — may be subject to different information systems and control procedures and, thus, different control risks. Also, individually material balances are often confirmed directly and the remainder are subdivided into either overdue accounts or other, with a proportionately larger number of the former selected for confirmation as presenting a greater risk of misstatement. Sample size may be determined judgementally or with the aid of a statistical sampling plan. Apart from the exceptions noted, selection of accounts for confirmation should be effectively random, such as through use of a sequential sampling plan.

Control of the requests

The auditor must control every step in the confirmation process. This means:

- before selecting the sample for confirmation, performing the initial procedures described above to ensure the list of balances is complete and accurate
- drawing up a list of selected accounts and verifying that confirmation requests, prepared and signed by entity management at the auditor's request, are in complete agreement with that list
- ascertaining that the amount, name and address on the confirmation agree with the corresponding data in the customer's account
- maintaining custody of the confirmations until they are mailed
- using the audit firm's own return address envelopes for the confirmations
- personally depositing the requests in the mail
- requiring that the replies be sent directly to the auditor.

A working paper should list each account selected for confirmation and the results obtained from each request, cross-referenced to the actual confirmation response (which should also be filed with the working papers). A confirmation control working paper is illustrated in figure 14.6.

Disposition of exceptions

Confirmation responses will inevitably contain some exceptions. Exceptions may be attributable to goods in transit from the entity to the customer, returned goods or payments in transit from the customer to the entity, items in dispute, or errors and irregularities. The auditor should investigate all exceptions and record their resolution in the working papers (as illustrated in figure 14.6).

Bates Ltd
Accounts receivable confirmation control
30 June 2015

W/P ref. ___B-2___
Prepared by: ___A.C.E___ Date: ___28/7/15___
Reviewed by: ___P.A.R___ Date: ___31/7/15___

Account no. 120

Conf. no.	Customer	Book value	Confirmed value	Audited value	(Over) Under statement	Subsequent collections examined to 28/7/15
1	Applied Devices	43 480.00	43 480.00	43 480.00		14 001.273✓
2	Barry Manufacturing	14 001.27	NR	14 001.27		
3	Brandt Electronics	63 199.86	63 199.86	63 199.86		
4	Groton Electric	116 823.14	116 823.14	116 823.14		
5	Jed Ltd 86 685.21	86 685.21	77 268.25	77 268.25	(9 416.96)⊗1	
60	W & M Manufacturing Ltd	32 461.12	NR	32 461.12⌐		4 071.433✓
	Totals	470 847.92	414 968.57	461 430.96	(9 416.96)	

Response recap:	No. of Items	
Value of confirmations mailed	60	$470 847.92
Value of confirmations received	58	$414 968.57
	97%	88%

Summary of results:	No. of Items	
Value of account total	300	$619 536.74
Book value of confirmation sample	60	$470 847.92
Coverage of book value		76%
Audited value of sample	60	$461 430.96
Ratio of audited value to book value of sample		98%

ø   Signed confirmation response attached for confirmed values
NR   No response — alternative procedures performed
✓   Examined entries in cash receipts journal and related remittance advices for total collections indicated
⌐   Examined supporting documentation for portion of book value remaining uncollected as of 28/7/15
⊗1   Credit memo issued 12/7/15 for merchandise returned 28/6/15. Adjusting entry:

    Dr Sales returns   9416.96
       Cr Accounts receivable   9416.96   See W/P B–1 and AE–1

FIGURE 14.6: Confirmation control working paper

Computer information systems

Computer audit software assists the auditor in the process of confirming receivables held on an accounts receivable master file. As explained in our discussion of initial procedures, the software can be programmed to test the completeness and accuracy of receivables listed on the master file. Software can also be used to select accounts on bases as previously discussed print the letters for circularisation and prepare a working paper for recording responses.

Alternative procedures for dealing with non-responses

When no response has been received after the second (or third) positive confirmation request to a customer, the auditor should perform alternative procedures. The two main alternative procedures are examining subsequent collections and vouching unpaid invoices and supporting documentation constituting customer balances.

The best evidence of existence and collectability is the receipt of payment from the customer. Before the conclusion of the auditor's examination, the entity will receive payments from many customers on amounts owed at the confirmation date. The matching of such cash receipts to unpaid invoices at the confirmation date, evidenced by the remittance advice accompanying the cash receipt, establishes the existence and collectability of the accounts.

Vouching open invoices constituting balances is a variation of step 3(a) in table 14.5. Preferably, the unpaid item should be traced to a dispatch note signed by the customer acknowledging receipt of the goods, or to a written order from the customer.

Summary and evaluation of the results

The auditor's working papers should contain a summary of the results of confirming accounts receivable. (The lower part of figure 14.6 illustrates how such data may be presented.) The auditor may use statistical or non-statistical procedures to project misstatements found in the sample to the population. Note though, for a sample test, that it is not sufficient merely to correct errors detected by the confirmation, but that the implications for the entire population of accounts receivable must also be considered.

The auditor evaluates evidence from the confirmations, alternative procedures performed on non-responses, and other tests of details and analytical procedures to determine whether there is sufficient evidence to support management's assertions about accounts receivable.

Evaluating adequacy of the allowance for bad debts

Most entities determine the allowance for bad debts by:

- making a general allowance, such as a percentage of balances overdue by more than a specified period
- making a specific allowance, by identifying customers who are known to be in financial difficulty or who are disputing payment.

The allowance is an estimate that the auditor will verify in accordance with ASA 540 *Auditing Accounting Estimates, Including Fair Value Accounting Estimates, and Related Disclosures* (ISA 540). The auditor will review and test the processes used by management, which involves:

- ascertaining management's procedures, including any internal controls, for determining the estimate and considering their reliability
- ensuring that the procedures have been properly followed and that the estimate has been approved
- identifying the assumptions underlying the estimate and considering their reasonableness
- verifying the reliability of the data (such as the aged analysis of accounts receivable) on which the estimate is based

- checking the calculations (such as the percentages applied to each overdue category) in determining the general allowance
- considering the reliability of previous year's allowances.

When considering the specific allowances, the auditor might obtain an independent estimate or review subsequent events for confirmation of the estimate. In arriving at an independent estimate, the auditor examines correspondence with customers and outside collection agencies, reviews customers' credit reports and financial statements, and discusses the collectability of the account with appropriate management personnel. This review includes a consideration of subsequent events, such as news of a customer's financial difficulties or payment of a disputed amount.

Disclosure

The auditor must be knowledgeable about the disclosure requirements for accounts receivable and sales under the *Corporations Act 2001* or other regulatory frameworks. A review of the accounts receivable trial balance may indicate amounts due from employees, officers, other group entities and related parties that should be specifically identified if material. The same source may reveal credit balances in customer accounts that may warrant classification as current liabilities. There should also be disclosure of the pledging, assigning or factoring of accounts receivable. The auditor should be able to obtain evidence of such activities from a review of the minutes of board meetings and from enquiry of management. As one of the final steps in the audit, the auditor should obtain management's representations on these matters in writing in a representation letter (see chapter 18).

Learning check

Do you know ...

14.6 ☐ The nature, timing and extent of substantive procedures are determined by the planned level of detection risk, which, in turn, is a function of the assessed levels of inherent and control risks.

14.7 ☐ Initial procedures ensure the accuracy of the list of receivables balances used as the basis for tests of the receivables balance.

14.8 ☐ Analytical procedures require the determination of expectations and the comparison of amounts, trends and ratios, particularly the gross profit ratio and the average collection period ratio.

14.9 ☐ Tests of details of transactions are largely dual-purpose tests performed at the interim audit except for cut-off tests of transactions either side of the end of the reporting period. The main test of details of balances is the receivables confirmation, which provides third-party evidence of the balance. The other major test of details of balances is of the reasonableness of the estimated allowance for bad debts.

SUMMARY

Sales and cash receipts from sales are the most important transaction classes for a commercial entity. For businesses selling on credit, maintaining records for the accounts receivable balance is also very important. In auditing these transactions and the accounts receivable balance, the auditor uses techniques explained in chapters 8–12.

In this chapter, we followed the audit approach required by ASA 315 *Identifying and Assessing the Risks of Material Misstatement through Understanding the Entity and Its Environment* (ISA 315). The audit process starts with obtaining an understanding of this system. The auditor also considers issues relating to materiality, inherent risk and the control environment before determining the appropriate audit strategy. For sales and receivables, materiality is invariably high. For audit purposes, the most significant inherent risk is that of overstatement of sales transactions and receivables balances to boost reported profits and assets. For the entity, the greatest inherent risk is that of misappropriation of cash arising from sales transactions. In evaluating the control environment, the auditor considers each of the control environment factors — integrity and ethical values, commitment to competence, management's philosophy and operating style, the assignment of authority and responsibility, and personnel policies and practices — as they relate to sales and receivables.

The next stage of the audit is determining the audit strategy, which, for sales and receivables, is likely to be one based on a lower assessed level of control risk. The first stage in assessing control risk is evaluating design effectiveness. Evaluation checklists are used, which hypothesise potential misstatements for each function in the processing of sales and cash receipt transactions. In assessing design effectiveness, the auditor compares the control procedures in the entity's information system with necessary controls identified by the checklist. At this point, the auditor drafts the audit program based on the preliminary assessment of control risk, identifying both tests of the operating effectiveness of controls and the reduced level of substantive procedures relevant to the assessed level of control risk. The auditor confirms the assessed level of control risk on completion of the tests of operating effectiveness.

The final stage of the audit is performing substantive procedures. It is usually cost-effective to test the balance of receivables rather than the transactions making up that balance. The most important test of transactions is that of cut-off at the year-end. The major test of balances is the confirmation of accounts receivable. Given that customers are third parties, such evidence is highly reliable. There are two ways to request confirmation: (1) the positive form, which requires the debtor to respond that the balance shown is correct or incorrect; and (2) the negative form, which requires the debtor to respond only when the amount shown is incorrect. If no response is received, the auditor performs alternative procedures such as examining subsequent collections and vouching unpaid invoices and supporting documentation constituting customer balances. The auditor must also verify the estimate of the allowance for bad debts.

KEY TERMS

accounts receivable master file, p. 577

accounts receivable subsidiary ledger, p. 577

accounts receivable trial balance, p. 597

aged trial balance, p. 597

authorised price list, p. 577

cash receipts cut-off test, p. 599

cash receipts journal, p. 579

credit memo, p. 581

customer order, p. 575

deposit slip, p. 579

dispatch notes, p. 576

embedded audit facility, p. 588

generalised audit software, p. 589

integrated test facility, p. 588

monthly customer statement, p. 577

remittance advice, p. 579

sales cut-off test, p. 599

sales invoices, p. 577

sales journal, p. 577

sales order, p. 575

sales return cut-off test, p. 599

sales transactions file, p. 577

systems control audit review file, p. 588

test data approach, p. 588

write-off authorisation memo, p. 581

MULTIPLE-CHOICE questions

14.1 Use of an authorised price list in preparing the sales invoices meets primarily the:
   A. Existence or occurrence assertion.
   B. Completeness assertion.
   C. Accuracy, valuation or allocation assertion.
   D. Rights and obligations assertion.

14.2 Accounting for the numerical sequence of dispatch notes used in tracing will primarily meet the:
   A. Existence or occurrence assertion.
   B. Completeness assertion.
   C. Accuracy, valuation or allocation assertion.
   D. Presentation or disclosure assertion.

14.3 To enhance controls in the credit sales area, the warehouse should be instructed not to release goods until:
   A. A faxed copy of the sales requisition is received.
   B. A completed sales invoice is received.
   C. An approved sales order is received.
   D. The shipping department requests the goods.

14.4 A key control environment factor in reducing the risk of fraudulent financial reporting through the overstatement of sales and accounts receivable is:
   (i) Management's adoption and adherence to high standards of integrity and ethical values.
   (ii) Reducing the emphasis on sales targets.
   (iii) Establishing an effective audit committee.
   A. (i) and (ii) only.
   B. (ii) and (iii) only.
   C. (i) and (iii) only.
   D. (i), (ii) and (iii).

14.5 In most credit sales audits, on what is the auditor's concern over sales adjustment transactions based?
   A. The sheer number and value of these transactions.
   B. The lack of proper authorisation for these transactions.
   C. The potential use of these transactions to conceal a theft of cash.
   D. Poor controls normally found over these transactions and the inherent lack of documentation.

14.6 In relation to materiality, which of the following statements is most accurate?
   A. Accounts receivable produced by credit sales transactions are material to the balance sheet for all businesses except those with cash sales.
   B. Cash balances at the end of a particular reporting period will always be material.
   C. The significance of sales adjustment transactions is consistent across entities.
   D. Bad debts expense is sometimes material to the profit and loss of entities that sell on credit.

14.7 Verifying the accuracy of the accounts receivable trial balance relates to the:
   A. Existence or occurrence assertion.
   B. Valuation or measurement assertion.
   C. Completeness assertion.
   D. Rights and obligations assertion.

14.8 When examining sales transactions, which of the following is not possible using generalised audit software?

A. Enquiring about segregation of duties for invoicing customers.

B. Selecting a sample of invoices for inspection.

C. Re-performing invoice pricing and reporting differences.

D. Ensuring the sales journal is correctly totalled.

14.9 Which of the following is a cut-off test?

A. Selecting a sample of delivery notes around the year-end and agreeing to sales invoices to ensure they are included in the appropriate period.

B. Selecting a sample of receivables balances outstanding at the year-end and agreeing to cash received after the year-end.

C. Selecting a sample of bad debts written off after the year-end and agreeing to sales invoices dated before the year-end.

D. Selecting a sample of receivables balances from the list of receivables and agreeing the build-up of the balance to sales invoices.

14.10 In the processing of accounts receivable confirmations the auditor would not normally be expected to:

A. Personally post the requests.

B. Include his/her own return address envelope.

C. Maintain custody of the confirmations until they are mailed.

D. Personally prepare the confirmations.

REVIEW questions

14.11 Identify factors that ought to be considered in the assessment of inherent and control risks specific to sales and accounts receivable.

14.12 Why is the control risk assessment of the completeness of cash receipts and sales adjustment transactions associated with control risk over the existence of the accounts receivable balance?

14.13 Why is the auditor likely to adopt a lower assessed level of control risk approach to the audit of accounts receivable wherever practicable? Why are substantive procedures more likely to be based on the accounts receivable balance than on sales, cash receipts and sales adjustment transactions?

14.14 What are the objectives of the internal controls of a sales system involving the ordering, despatch and invoicing for goods sold?

14.15 If the auditor does not receive a response after sending a letter to confirm a debtor's balance, what alternative audit procedures may be performed?

14.16 There are three stages in applying analytical procedures to sales and receivables in the final audit. Briefly explain each stage.

14.17 Identify situations leading to an inherent risk that an entity may wish to (a) overstate sales revenue and (b) understate sales revenue.

14.18 Confirmations are considered to be the most efficient procedure for obtaining sufficient appropriate audit evidence to support the existence and rights assertions of accounts receivable. However, there are still circumstances under which other procedures may be more effective. List four situations in which confirmations are unlikely to be effective.

14.19 Explain what is meant by 'cut-off' and why it is important to auditors in establishing the fairness of financial statements.

14.20 List the steps involved when the auditor reviews and tests the process used by management to estimate the bad and doubtful debts allowance.

BASIC
★
MODERATE
★★
CHALLENGING
★★★

 PROFESSIONAL application questions

14.21 Cash sales system controls ★

As the internal auditor of the Sellanything Group of companies, you have been asked to investigate the cash sales system of Stationery Ltd, one of the subsidiaries. Stationery sells office supplies in the Melbourne area. Its prices are highly competitive and it offers a same-day delivery service for orders telephoned before noon. Costs are kept down by requiring cash on delivery. Sales are made in the following way.

1. The customer phones through an order to the sales department, which raises a prenumbered multicopy sales order, two of which (the invoice copies) are priced and totalled.
2. The dispatch department makes up the order and gives the goods to the driver with the invoice copies of the order.
3. The driver delivers the goods, collects the cash and receipts the customer's copy of the invoice.
4. The driver returns and hands over the cash and the second copy of the invoice to the cashier.
5. The cashier records and banks the cash.

Required

(a) State any weaknesses in the cash sales system.
(b) Describe any audit tests you would perform to ensure that there was no material error or fraud within the system.

14.22 Sales system testing ★★

Audrey Too Ltd operates a plant hire business. Bookings are received both over the telephone and via email. Audrey Too have a wide range of machines for hire, from chainsaws and lawnmowers through to earthmover equipment; as a consequence customers range from private individuals to small businesses and large corporates. Customers without a credit account must pay via credit card at the time of placing the booking, other customers have negotiated credit terms. These include details in relation to trade discounts, credit levels and payments terms; each agreement is different depending on the negotiating power of the customer.

When bookings are received from credit customers, a check is made to ensure the customer has sufficient credit available; if so the booking is raised. For new customers credit checks are performed before a credit limit is applied. Once the hire takes place an invoice is raised through the sales invoicing system and sent to the customer. Standard rental amounts are charged and the agreed trade discount applied. The invoice is sent either in the post or via email depending on the requirements of the customer.

Required

Describe the tests you would perform to ensure the completeness and accuracy of the sales revenue in Audrey Too's income statement.

14.23 Tests of controls — sales transactions ★★

You have been assigned to perform tests of controls on the sales system at EDB Pty Ltd as part of the 30 June 2015 audit. EDB is a wholesaler of bathroom supplies such as vanity units, toilets, taps and sinks. During testing, you noted the following errors.

1. Invoice no. 54922 issued on 12 December 2014 was entered twice. The error was discovered when the customer rang to complain about being charged double the agreed amount.
2. Invoice no. 51839 issued on 25 September 2014 contained incorrect prices. Three vanity units were charged at $453 each instead of $543, and five sinks were charged at $231 each instead of $321. The error was discovered when the salesperson complained about not receiving the full commission entitlement for the month.

3. No prices were entered on invoice no. 56329 issued on 24 January 2015, resulting in a zero dollar invoice being issued. The error was discovered when accounts receivable staff queried the zero amount appearing on the accounts receivable ledger.

4. Invoice no. 59328 issued on 18 March 2015 matched the customer's order. However, the order was only partially filled because of a lack of stock in the warehouse, meaning items that were never delivered were included in the invoice. The error was discovered when the customer rang to complain about being overcharged.

5. Invoice no. 61348 issued on 7 May 2015 was sent to the wrong address. Apparently, the invoice had the correct address on it, but a typing error occurred on the envelope. The error was discovered when the customer rang to complain about the overdue notice received, stating the invoice had never been received in the first place.

6. Invoice no. 62875 issued on 29 June 2015 was not processed through the usual channels. The details were correct but certain procedures, such as a formal credit check, were not documented. The invoice was a special order for a large building project and amounted to around ten times the value of EDB's average invoices. The sale was personally handled by one of the directors and the invoice was prepared by his assistant.

Required

Treating each of the listed errors independently:

(a) Describe application controls (both manual and via the computer information system) that would have prevented or detected the error.

(b) Describe further work you would perform in relation to each of the errors.

(c) Explain the implications of the errors for your substantive testing of accounts receivable.

(d) Briefly discuss how you would present these matters in your year-end management letter.[2]

14.24 Computer-assisted audit techniques ★★

You are an audit manager at Bling, Tat & Co and you are currently planning the audit of your client PartyFunTime Ltd, an online retailer of a wide range of gifts and party products. PartyFunTime Ltd sells to the public and as a result the business revenue is made up of a large number of relatively low value transactions. Customers place orders through a website and the system verifies stock availability automatically. The customer is required to enter their name, address and credit card details, the system verifies these details automatically and, once confirmed, the order is completed and a despatch request is automatically generated in the central warehouse.

PartyFunTime Ltd's key business risk is a possible IT failure. In order to minimise this risk the company has a contract with Web Tradies Ltd who regularly test the integrity of the system and take action to prevent website downtime.

You have identified a significant risk to the organisation relates to the data input through the website and you would like to employ computer-assisted audit techniques to test input application controls.

Required

Show how test data could be used to test the input controls in relation to the sales of PartyFunTime Ltd.

14.25 Sampling receivables ★★

Flinders Boats Ltd builds a variety of watercraft for a wide range of commercial and private clients. You are engaged in the audit of trade receivables and the audit manager has suggested that monetary unit sampling is an effective way of selecting a sample for carrying out an accounts receivable circularisation.

You have been provided with a trade receivables report from Flinders; this report shows both the balance outstanding from the client as well as the total revenue earned from that client for the year.

Customer No.	Customer Name	Revenue	Balance
1	Dennis Tours	316 789	24 536
2	Mrs Blenkintop	145 364	7 572
3	Ginger Ltd	6 373 821	440 987
4	Fort Grant Pty Ltd	983 542	89 762
5	Arthur Rock	86 627	42 765
6	Coracle Holidays Ltd	6 458 769	286 482
7	Spanish Suitcase	59 319	4 563
8	Mr Jimb	789 746	96 234
9	Class Botham Tours Ltd	3 362 514	(6 453)
10	Needy Seagoon	85 592	6 584
11	Lakeside Excursions Ltd	896 373	324 364
12	Claustra Sub Tours	423 784	33 456
13	Scull and Row Ltd	4 951 648	408 550
14	Trireme Ram Co Ltd	1 750 255	134 635
15	Sandra Blount	603 902	46 454
16	Lord and Lady Damp	307 112	74 851
17	Uphill Sailing Ltd	3 998 636	546 738
18	Keel and Crow Ltd	5 789 352	414 602
19	Mountain Kayak Pty Ltd	73 775	5 675
		37 456 920	2 982 357

Required
(a) Discuss the advantages and disadvantages of using monetary unit sampling to select the debtors to circularise.
(b) Assuming a materiality level of $300 000, select a sample for testing using monetary unit sampling.
(c) Critically discuss the sample selected in part (a) and discuss an alternative method.

14.26 Substantive procedures for bad debt allowance ★★

It is common practice for companies to make two allowances for bad debts.
1. The specific allowance is based on accounts the company has reason to suspect may not be paid.
2. The general allowance relates to accounts as yet unknown but that experience suggests may not be paid. The likelihood of a debt being unpaid is usually assumed to increase the longer it remains unpaid, and many companies determine a general allowance as a percentage of overdue receivables, with an increasing percentage being applied against the longest overdue accounts.

You are aware that ASA 540 (ISA 540) *Auditing Accounting Estimates, Including Fair Value Accounting Estimates, and Related Disclosures* is likely to be relevant to the audit of the allowance for bad debts.

Required

Describe the procedures you would adopt in verifying:

(a) a general allowance for bad debts

(b) a specific allowance for bad debts.

14.27 Substantive audit program for accounts receivable ★★★

Your client is BigC Ltd, a large private firm with offices in all major cities of Australia. BigC Ltd specialises in selling concentrated fruit juices to Australian and overseas buyers. This is the first year your firm will perform the audit. You are currently completing the planning work for the audit of trade debtors for the year ending 30 June 2015, and have gathered the following information.

1. The Melbourne office recently won a large contract to supply an overseas department store chain with concentrated orange juice.
2. For the month of January, the Adelaide office ran a sales promotion that allowed new customers double the normal credit terms of 30 days. Several new large customers took advantage of this offer.
3. The Darwin office has been experiencing a higher than usual level of sales returns owing to a mould growth being discovered in a batch of guava juice.

You have calculated the receivables (or debtors) turnover ratio and receivables to total assets ratio for each of the branch offices, as shown in the tables below.

	Receivables (or debtors) turnover ratio		
Office	8 months to February 2015	12 months to June 2014	12 months to June 2013
Sydney	8.0	9.2	10.1
Melbourne	7.5	9.1	9.2
Hobart	5.2	6.0	7.1
Adelaide	10.1	8.5	9.5
Perth	8.8	9.0	9.0
Darwin	8.5	7.9	7.1
Brisbane	5.9	6.0	6.0

	Receivables to total assets ratio		
Office	8 months to February 2015	12 months to June 2014	12 months to June 2013
Sydney	0.25	0.12	0.10
Melbourne	0.15	0.15	0.15
Hobart	0.18	0.14	0.12
Adelaide	0.15	0.16	0.17
Perth	0.23	0.16	0.20
Darwin	0.17	0.30	0.15
Brisbane	0.19	0.25	0.22

Required

(a) List the questions you would ask of management in relation to the accounts receivable of each of the branch offices.

(b) Describe additional audit work you would perform to satisfy yourself that accounts receivable were fairly stated.[3]

14.28 Accounts receivable circularisation ★★★

Your firm is the external auditor of Southwood Trading Ltd and you are auditing the financial statements for the year ended 30 June 2015. Southwood Trading has a turnover of $25 million and trade debtors at 30 June 2015 were $5.2 million.

The engagement partner has asked you to consider the relative reliability of evidence from third parties and certain matters relating to an accounts receivable circularisation.

In relation to requirement (b)(ii) below, the partner has explained that judgement would be used to select debtors that appear doubtful and those that would not be selected using the dollar unit sampling technique described in requirement (b)(i).

Required

(a) Consider the relative reliability of the following types of evidence from third parties:
  (i) replies to an accounts receivable circularisation to confirm trade debtors
  (ii) suppliers' statements to confirm purchases ledger balances.
(b) In relation to selecting debtors for circularisation:
  (i) explain the use of monetary unit sampling in selecting debtors to circularise
  (ii) consider the criteria you would use to select individual debtors for circularisation using judgement
  (iii) discuss the advantages and disadvantages of using monetary unit sampling (in (b) (i)) as compared with judgement (in (b)(ii)) to select the debtors to circularise. Your answer should consider why it is undesirable to use only judgement to select the debtors for circularisation.
(c) Describe the audit work you would carry out in following up the responses to an accounts receivable circularisation where:

  (i) the debtor disputes the balance and provides a different balance
  (ii) no reply to the circularisation has been received from the debtor, and all attempts at obtaining a reply have failed.[4]

14.29 Analytical review ★★★

High as a Kite Gliding Club is a members-based club for individuals who wish to fly gliders. The club income comes from subscriptions from club members as well as charging for glider rides. In the annual report for the year ended 30 June 2014 it was reported that the club had 160 members.

You are planning the audit for the year ended 30 June 2015 and are considering the completeness of income. From your discussions with the club treasurer you have established the following:

1. Subscriptions are due for the year from July to June and for the 2015 year subscription was set at $500 per member. Of the 2014 members, 11 did not renew their membership.
2. New members are charged a one-off joining fee of $300 plus the annual subscription, 14 new members were signed up from 1 July 2014. In addition to this, 7 new members joined half way through the year, these were each charged the full joining fee but only 50% of the annual subscription during the year.
3. Glider flights are charged at a rate of $20 a flight for members and $100 a flight for non-members. A manual flight book is maintained and this shows that during the year a total of 2320 flights recorded, of which 1670 were members.

Required

Show how analytical procedures can be used to audit revenue.

14.30 Computer-assisted substantive testing for accounts receivable ★★★

Ally McNeil is conducting the audit of a wholesale electrical goods distributor, Electra Pty Ltd. Electra supplies appliances to hundreds of individual customers in the metropolitan area of

Perth. It maintains detailed accounts receivable records on a computer system. The customer account master file is updated at the end of each business day. Each customer record in the master file contains the following data:

- customer account number
- customer address
- open (unpaid) invoices at the beginning of the month, by invoice number and date
- sales during the current month, by invoice number and date
- individual cash receipts during the current month
- date of last sale
- date of last cash receipt.

Ally McNeil is planning to confirm selected accounts receivable as at the end of the current month. She will have available a computer file of the data on the accounts receivable master file on the date on which the company sends monthly statements to its customers. Ally has a generalised software package to help her in this task.

Required

Detail how Ally will be able to use the computer software package and accounts receivable master file to help her in the audit of accounts receivable.[5]

CASE studies

14.31 Audit of sales and accounts receivable ★★★

You have been assigned to audit the sales and accounts receivable balances of Coppero Engineering Ltd, for the year ended 30 June 2015. Coppero Engineering is a major manufacturer of steel parts and fixtures for other manufacturers in the engineering field. The interim work was undertaken in April 2015 and tests indicated that internal controls over sales and accounts receivable are effective and that therefore control risks are acceptable.

You observe that credit sales are made to a group of 2500 active customers, located in Australia and South-East Asia. Approximately 30% of the customers represent 70% of the balances, and although most of these customers are in Australia, a number are also based in Hong Kong, Singapore and Indonesia. The sales made into South-East Asia are invoiced in Australian dollars and you note that the value of the Australian dollar has escalated by 30% in recent months. Total of the accounts receivable balances at 30 June is $95 million and the current allowance for doubtful debts is $500 000.

Sales and receipts are recorded on the company's computerised accounting system, which simultaneously updates the accounts receivable balances and sales and cash receipts transactions journals on a daily basis. On a weekly basis, an aged trial balance is generated, which is reviewed by the credit manager for slow-paying accounts. Follow-up action is then taken as necessary. Sales returns and bad debt write-offs are processed and summarised weekly and any write-offs have to be approved by the chief finance officer, based on the recommendations of the credit manager. Documents to support these write-offs are kept on file.

After the end of the reporting period, the rising Australian dollar and a financial crisis in two of the major Asian markets have caused some concern for the credit manager, who has recently joined the client after a number of years in the retailing industry. Also, the rising trend towards online purchases from overseas and a slowing economy have affected sales growth in the Australian market.

Required

You are asked to prepare an audit program to test Coppero Engineering's year-end accounts receivable. You are required to include in your program specific audit objectives you can test using the audit firm's new generalised audit software package. Your manager is particularly worried about the possible negative effects on the collectability of accounts receivable because of the Asian financial crisis, the rising dollar and the slowing Australian economy.

14.32 Controls over cash receipts ★★★

The head office of Lighttime Ltd, wholesalers of electrical equipment, has asked you to review the system of control over cash collection at the Victorian branch because it suspects that irregularities are taking place. The branch is the largest single outlet of the company and has substantial annual sales invoiced by the branch.

Enquiries reveal the following procedures for invoicing sales and collecting cash. (Cash refers to currency and cheques.)

1. There are two invoice sets that are used for cash sales and credit sales respectively.
2. When payment for cash sales is received by the cashier, one copy of the invoice is stamped as paid and filed alphabetically, and the other is given to the customer.
3. Credit sales invoices are sent to the customers.
4. Mail is opened by the secretary to the credit controller, who passes any cheques to the credit controller for his review, without recording the amounts received.
5. The credit controller gives the cheques to the cashier by depositing them in a tray on the cashier's desk.
6. The cashier then makes a listing of the cheques, which is used by the credit controller for posting to the accounts receivable ledger.
7. The cheques from credit customers and receipts from cash sales are banked daily by the cashier, except for once a week when sufficient currency is retained to reimburse petty cash.
8. The credit controller posts remittances to accounts receivable using a computerised accounting system and verifies the cash discount allowable.
9. The credit controller obtains approval from head office to write off bad debts. Any subsequent remittances received in respect of these accounts are credited to 'sundry income'.

Required
(a) Describe control weaknesses in the accounting for cash receipts.
(b) Suggest improvements in internal control to prevent irregularities in the collection of cash.
(c) Explain substantive audit procedures necessary to determine whether any irregularities have taken place.

RESEARCH question

14.33 Irregularities in accounting

In the early 2000s, many large corporations such as Enron, WorldCom and HIH collapsed because of corporate greed, bad business practices and accounting irregularities. Others, such as Bristol-Myers Squibb, Xerox and Harris Scarfe were forced to restate their earnings, in some cases over a number of years, because of inflation of sales and other accounting irregularities.

Required
Investigate in depth two of the above companies and determine how the irregularities were perpetrated and the reasons behind them. Also determine, to the extent possible, why these irregularities were not found by the auditors during their audits of sales revenue and receivables, and other related areas of the audit.

FURTHER READING

RD Allen & RJ Elder, 'An empirical investigation of the effectiveness of balance and invoice confirmations', *Journal of Forensic Accounting* 11, 2001, pp. 219–36.

CD Bailey & G Ballard, 'Improving response rates to accounts receivable confirmations: an experiment using four techniques', *Auditing: A Journal of Practice & Theory*, Spring, 1986, pp. 77–85.

D Beran & R Evans, 'Auditing for sales adjustment fraud', *Internal Auditor*, February 1990, pp. 51–6.

P Caster, 'The role of confirmations as audit evidence', *Journal of Accountancy*, February 1992, pp. 73–6.

DK McConnell Jr & GY Banks, 'A common peer review problem', *Journal of Accountancy*, June 1998.

C O'Leary, 'Debtors' confirmations — handle with care', *Australian Accountant*, May 1993, pp. 35–7.

JG Swearingen, JA Wilkes & SL Swearingen, 'Confirmation response differences between businesses, clerks and consumers', *CPA Journal*, May 1991, pp. 58–60.

NOTES

1. Extract from Worrells Solvency & Forensic Accountants 2010, 'Point of Sale Fraud — Stealing Cash Receipts', www.worrells.net.au.
2. Adapted from Professional Year Programme of the ICAA, 1999, Accounting 2 Module.
3. Adapted from Professional Year Programme of the ICAA, 1997, Accounting 2 Module.
4. Adapted from ACCA Audit Framework, Paper 6, December 1998.
5. Adapted from an AICPA Audit Framework paper.

Answers to multiple-choice questions

14.1 *C*   14.2 *B*   14.3 *C*   14.4 *D*   14.5 *C*   14.6 *A*   14.7 *B*   14.8 *A*
14.9 *A*   14.10 *D*

chapter 15

Auditing purchases, payables and payroll

OVERVIEW

15.1 Brief summary of audit procedures

15.2 Audit objectives

15.3 Purchase, payment and purchase adjustment transactions

15.4 Payroll transactions

15.5 Developing the audit plan

15.6 Substantive procedures

Summary

Key terms

Multiple-choice questions

Review questions

Professional application questions

Case studies

Research question

Notes

LEARNING objectives

After studying this chapter, you should be able to:

1 identify the audit objectives applicable to purchases, payables and payroll

2 describe the functions and control procedures normally found in information systems for processing purchase, payment and purchase adjustment transactions

3 describe the functions and control procedures normally found in information systems for payroll transactions

4 apply the concepts of materiality and inherent risk to the audit of purchases, payables and payroll

5 discuss considerations relevant to determining the audit strategy for purchases, payables and payroll

6 design and execute tests of controls over purchase, payment and payroll transactions to assess control risk

7 indicate the factors relevant to determining an acceptable level of detection risk for the audit of purchases, payables and payroll

8 design a substantive audit program for purchases, payables and payroll

9 explain the use of suppliers' statements in verifying the completeness of recorded liabilities.

PROFESSIONAL STATEMENTS

Australian	International
Framework for Assurance Engagements	International Framework for Assurance Engagements
ASA 315 Identifying and Assessing the Risks of Material Misstatement through Understanding the Entity and Its Environment	ISA 315 Identifying and Assessing the Risks of Material Misstatement through Understanding the Entity and Its Environment

SCENE SETTER

Top management compensation

Just how big are the incentives for good performance by chief executive officers (CEOs) of large listed companies? A survey of US executives shows that they can be very big indeed. The top paid CEO in the US in 2008, Stephen Schwarzman, was paid a total of US$702.4 million (comprising cash and bonuses, perks, options and equity grants).[1] Most of Schwarzman's pay, US$699.8 million, came from vesting of equity grants he received when the company went public in 2007.

Second on the list was Larry Ellison, boss of Oracle Corp, who was paid US$557 million, up from US$192 million the year before. Once again, a large part of his compensation was related to equity rather than cash — US$543 million came from exercising stock options in the company. Overall, seven US top executives had total compensation of more than US$100 million in 2008, and the survey showed that seven of the 10 highest paid US CEOs were running an oil or natural gas company.[2]

Academic research suggests that auditors need to be aware of the potential effects of incentives related to compensation packages. For example, Healy provided evidence that when top executives are paid a bonus according to a formula with a floor and ceiling, the companies' profits appear to be 'managed' in predictable ways.[3] The floor means that no bonus is earned unless profit exceeds a certain figure, and the ceiling means that no further bonuses are paid once profit reaches a specified high figure. Healy's evidence suggests that if the profit is not likely to reach the floor, managers will take action (through accruals such as closing entries) to reduce profit in the expectation that they can reverse this action next year when profit is above the floor. This action means that managers receive a bonus on the amount that they are able to 'shift'. Managers take the same action to reduce profit if it is likely to be above the ceiling (deferring the profit and bonus to the following year). However, if profit is between the floor and the ceiling, managers will try to increase profit to increase their bonus.

The lesson from the academic research is that if auditors understand how the bonus scheme works, they will be more alert to the type of profit shifting likely to be attempted by managers.

Source: R Moroney, F Campbell & J Hamilton, *Auditing: A Practical Approach*, John Wiley & Sons, 2011, pp. 101–2.

This chapter examines the audit of:
- the account balances of accounts payable and of accruals related to payroll
- the transaction classes of purchases, payments and payroll.

Purchases and payments are for the acquisition of goods and services from outside suppliers, whereas payroll relates to the acquisition of and payment for labour services from employees. Together, they represent the major expenditures of most entities. There are similarities between the two, in that both involve the acquisition of resources and payment to the suppliers. However, the nature of the employment contract between the entity and its employees is such that payroll transactions are always processed separately, including the payment of salaries and wages.

This chapter follows a similar structure to that of the previous chapter on auditing sales and receivables. We begin with a brief summary of audit procedures, which provides the essence of what the auditor is trying to achieve and is useful for both revision and obtaining an understanding of the basics. We then follow with identifying the audit objectives for each of the financial statement assertions that apply to the transaction classes mentioned above and to the accounts payable and accrued payroll liability balances. In the rest of the chapter we follow the audit process — from obtaining an understanding of the internal control structure, through the assessment of the inherent risks and control risks to the design and execution of substantive procedures.

15.1 BRIEF SUMMARY OF AUDIT PROCEDURES

In the auditing of purchases, payables and payroll, the key issues are to ensure that:
- the purchases are all recorded and are not understated (this is related to the financial statement assertions of completeness and also accuracy and cut-off)
- the payables that are derived from the purchases are all fully recorded in the accounts as a liability (this is related to the financial statement assertions of completeness and also valuation and allocation)
- the payroll expense has been properly recorded and the associated deductions for income tax, superannuation and related liabilities are properly recorded as liabilities (these are related to the financial statement assertions related to transactions of completeness, occurrence and accuracy as well as assertions related to balances of completeness, existence and valuation and allocation).

Recorded purchase transactions represent goods and services received during the period under audit and we need to ensure that such purchases are properly recorded in the accounts. Purchase transactions relate to the purchase (from outside entities) of goods such as inventory for manufacturing purposes or resale, plant and equipment, and supplies; and services such as electricity, printing, stationery and rent. The auditor normally takes a sample of purchase transactions for testing (such as a randomly selected week or month, or randomly selected purchases throughout the year) and reviews copies of authorised requisitions and/or purchase orders and receiving reports/delivery dockets (where applicable) for each transaction. These are then matched to suppliers' invoices and prices, quantities and similar. An analytical review of the purchases for the weeks/months is also undertaken to compare totals with the previous year and to look for unusual trends or omissions.

For accounts payable, the auditor traces the opening balance to the previous year's working papers when applicable, reviews activity in the general ledger account for any unusual entries, and obtains a listing of amounts owed at the end of the reporting period. Usually, the listing is prepared for the auditor by the client from the accounts payable ledger. The auditor must verify the mathematical accuracy of the listing by adding the total and verifying that it agrees with the underlying accounting records and the general ledger control account balance. In addition, the auditor selectively compares details of suppliers and amounts on the listing with the underlying records to determine that it is an accurate representation of the records from which the listing was prepared.

Unlike the confirmation of receivables, the confirmation of accounts payable is performed less frequently because a confirmation offers no assurance that unrecorded liabilities will be discovered, and external evidence in the form of invoices and suppliers' monthly statements should be available to substantiate the balances. As documentary evidence originating outside the entity, suppliers' statements provide reliable evidence as to suppliers' balances. However, because they are obtained from the entity, the auditor needs to be cautious that the statements have not been altered, and should not rely on photocopies and faxed statements. Where there is doubt, a copy should be requested directly from the supplier or the balance confirmed directly with the supplier. In the selection of accounts for testing, the criterion should be the volume of business during the year, not the balance shown in the entity's accounts payable listing, because the main concern is that the recorded balance may be understated.

A major concern is identification of unrecorded liabilities, and tests include the examination of the next period's purchase and payment transactions. Analytical procedures may also identify unexpected differences between the current year's and the previous year's expense or liability balances, which could indicate the presence of unrecorded liabilities. An examination of contractual commitments may also alert the auditor to the existence of liabilities not yet provided for, such as progress payments on long-term contracts, or amounts accrued but not yet due, or amounts invoiced under a franchise agreement.

Payroll transactions, as for purchases and payments, have potential for misstatements and tests of the necessary controls are an important part of the audit procedures. Access controls over changes to personnel data on the computer database are important. In the testing of controls, test data can be used to test programmed controls relating to the preparation and recording of payroll, and exception reports can indicate areas that require further follow-up.

The auditor knows that misstatements in payroll may result from unintentional errors or from fraud. Of particular concern is the risk of overstatement of payroll through payments to fictitious employees, payments to actual employees for hours not worked, and payments to actual employees at higher than authorised rates. Audit procedures normally include checks for authorisation of pay rates, procedures for hiring and terminating employees and, in some cases, physical verification that employees actually exist. Analytical reviews of payroll expenses and trends can also provide corroborating evidence for the auditor.

The above briefly summarises the key procedures in the audit of purchases, payables and payroll. In practice, the procedures can be more complex and are detailed in the rest of the chapter.

LEARNING objective 1

Identify the audit objectives applicable to purchases, payables and payroll.

15.2 AUDIT OBJECTIVES

The audit objectives for purchases, payables and payroll relate to obtaining sufficient appropriate evidence about each significant financial statement assertion for the applicable transactions and balances.

Table 15.1 (overleaf) lists the main objectives for each assertion that apply in most audits of these transactions and balances.

TABLE 15.1: Selected specific audit objectives for purchases, payables and payroll

Transaction objectives	
Occurrence (**OE**)	Recorded purchase transactions represent goods and services received during the period under audit (**OE1**).
	Recorded payment transactions represent payments made during the period to suppliers and creditors (**OE2**).
	Recorded payroll expenses relate to employee services received in the period (**OE3**).
Completeness (**C**)	All purchase transactions that occurred during the period and that should have been recorded have been recorded (**C1**).
	All payments that occurred during the period and that should have been recorded have been recorded (**C2**).
	Recorded payroll expenses include all such expenses incurred during the year (**C3**).
Accuracy (**AV**)	Purchase, payment and payroll transactions are properly (accurately) recorded (**AV1**).
Cut-off (**CO**)	Particularly relevant to transactions around the year end; all purchases, cash payments, purchase adjustment and payroll transactions arising before the period end are recorded in the current period and those arising after the period end are included in the next accounting period (**CO1**).
Classification (**PD**)	All purchases (**PD1**), payments (**PD2**) and payroll transactions (**PD3**) are recorded in the correct accounts.
Balances objectives	
Existence (**OE**)	Recorded accounts payable represent amounts owed by the entity at the end of the reporting period (**OE4**).
	Accrued payroll liability balances represent amounts owed at the end of the reporting period (**OE5**).
Rights and obligations (**RO**)	Accounts payable (**RO1**) and accrued payroll liabilities (**RO2**) are liabilities of the entity at the end of the reporting period.
Completeness (**C**)	Accounts payable include all amounts owed by the entity to suppliers of goods and services at the end of the reporting period (**C4**).
	Accrued payroll liabilities include all amounts owed in respect of payroll and deductions therefrom at the end of the reporting period (**C5**).
Valuation and allocation (**AV**)	Accounts payable represent gross amounts due to suppliers and agree with the sum of the accounts payable in the payables subsidiary ledger (**AV2**).
	Accrued payroll liabilities are stated at the appropriate amounts (**AV3**).
	Related expense balances conform to applicable accounting standards (**AV4**).
Presentation and disclosure objectives (PD)	
Occurrence and rights and obligations	Disclosed purchase and payroll events have occurred and pertain to the entity (**PD4**).
Completeness	Accounts payable, accrued payroll liabilities and related expenses are properly identified and classified in the financial statements (**PD5**).
	Disclosures pertaining to commitments, contingent liabilities and related party creditors are adequate (**PD6**).
Classification and understandability	Purchase cycle and payroll information is appropriately presented and information disclosed is clearly expressed (**PD7**).
Accuracy and valuation	Purchase cycle and payroll information is disclosed accurately and at appropriate amounts (**PD8**).

To achieve each audit objective, the auditor uses a combination of tests of controls and substantive procedures (as determined by the audit strategy adopted), following the audit planning and testing methods described in chapters 8–12. The procedures are much the same as those illustrated for sales and receivables in chapter 14.

Each audit objective is numbered (**OE1**, **OE2**, **C1**, **AV4** and so on) in table 15.1. Using this numbering system, we can reference specific controls and audit procedures described in this chapter to the applicable audit objective. Some of the assertions for transactions are combined with assertions for balances in the numbering system: occurrence and existence (**OE**), completeness for transactions and completeness for balances (**C**), accuracy and valuation and allocation (**AV**), and classification with presentation and disclosure assertions (**PD**). These combinations reflect the fact that audit evidence obtained in relation to an assertion for transactions will also give some comfort for a balances assertion. For example, an audit test that gives some comfort to the auditor that a sales transaction has occurred will also give some comfort that a valid receivable exists and hence occurrence and existence are combined.

Note that table 15.1 summarises assertions for both transaction class audit objectives and account balance audit objectives. Greater detail regarding assertions is provided in paragraph A111 of ASA 315 *Identifying and Assessing the Risks of Material Misstatement through Understanding the Entity and Its Environment* (ISA 315).

LEARNING objective 2

Describe the functions and control procedures normally found in information systems for processing purchase, payment and purchase adjustment transactions.

15.3 PURCHASE, PAYMENT AND PURCHASE ADJUSTMENT TRANSACTIONS

This section describes features of internal control structures typically used by entities in processing and recording purchase and payment transactions. The systems in relation to purchase transactions are discussed and figure 15.1 (overleaf) depicts a purchases cycle for a business buying goods or services on credit.

This is a fairly standard example but is relevant to all businesses. The purchases process starts when a department in an organisation requires goods (or services) and completes a requisition for those goods which is given to the organisation's purchasing department. The purchasing department's main roles are to ensure that the requisition has been authorised and then to place an order for goods with suppliers. In many cases the organisation will have a list of preferred suppliers where discounts and other terms of payment have already been agreed. The goods will then be received from the supplier together with a dispatch note which records the contents of the delivery. Generally the date of the receipt of goods will be considered the point at which the purchase has occurred and at this point the organisation is liable to pay for the goods. The purchase invoice, which will include the terms of payment, will subsequently be received from the supplier. This invoice will be posted to the general ledger and payables ledger. A statement at the end of each month is normally received highlighting those invoices which have not yet been paid and these suppliers' statements will be reconciled to the balances in the payables ledger accounts and any discrepancies will be followed up. Once these discrepancies are resolved, the organisation will determine the amount to be paid to each supplier and cheques will be prepared and sent or payments may be made via bank transfers. The payments are then recorded in the general and payables ledgers. The accounts department will be responsible for reconciling a list of payables amounts outstanding to the payables ledger and to the payables balance in the general ledger.

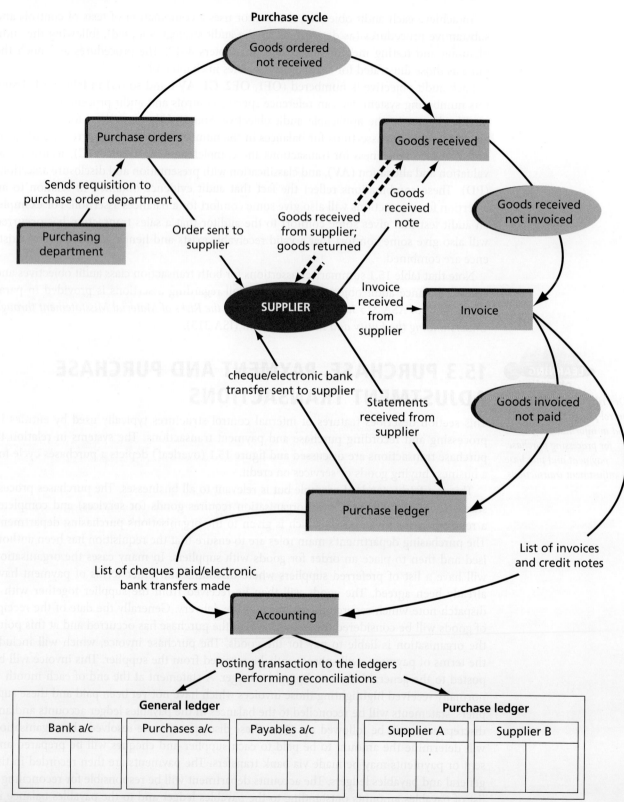

FIGURE 15.1: Credit purchases cycle

The following sections look at purchase transactions and payment transactions in detail, including related information systems and control procedures. Where purchases are made on credit, as is the norm, the information system also needs to maintain records of accounts payable. The discussions here are designed to give an understanding of the purchases system; in the later sections of this chapter we consider how this affects the audit approach. The discussion in this section is based on a company buying goods; however, much of the commentary can easily be adapted to the purchases of services.

15.3.1 Purchase transactions

We begin by identifying the separate functions involved in making purchases, the documents and records that are used in processing the transactions, and the control procedures commonly applied to reduce the risk of fraud or error. Among the control activities considered here are information processing controls, the segregation of duties, physical controls and performance reviews.

Functions

The processing of purchase transactions involves the following functions, a number of which are done electronically:
- requisitioning goods and services
- preparing purchase orders
- receiving the goods
- storing goods received for inventory
- checking and approving the supplier's invoice
- recording the liability.

When practicable, each of these functions should be assigned to a different individual or department. In such cases, the work of one employee or department can provide an independent check on the accuracy of the work of another.

Requisitioning goods and services

Purchase requisitions may originate from stores (the warehouse) for inventory or from any department for other items. For inventory items, computerised inventory records are often programmed to issue requisitions automatically when predetermined reorder levels are reached. For purchases other than inventory replenishment, requisitioning authority is granted to specific people. This authority is usually restricted to the value and types of goods and services applicable to the person's function and level of authority. A stationery clerk may requisition sundry stationery supplies, for example, but only the office manager may requisition a photocopier service contract. Special procedures usually apply for requisitioning plant and equipment or for entering into lease contracts.

Purchase requisition forms are normally generated electronically by authorised employees, or triggered by predetermined criteria programmed into an entity's computer system. The requisition normally indicates the general ledger account coding for the purchase, which the person making the requisition has budgetary responsibility for.

Purchase requisitions are usually prenumbered within each originating department as a control over outstanding requisitions to ensure that goods requisitioned are duly ordered and received. The purchase requisition represents the start of the transaction trail of documentary evidence in support of management's assertion as to the occurrence of purchase transactions. Thus, it provides evidence that relates to the specific audit objective of occurrence (**OE1**) in table 15.1.

Preparing purchase orders

The purchasing department should issue purchase orders only on the receipt of requisitions properly approved by an employee who has appropriate requisitioning authority (except for programmed inventory replenishment). Before placing an order, purchasing department personnel should find the best source of supply and, for major items, obtain competitive bids.

Separating requisitioning from ordering achieves two controls. It restricts the opportunity for those making requisitions to issue fraudulent orders, such as for goods for their own use. Purchasing department personnel are less likely to issue improper orders because they do not normally have access to goods delivered. The second control is improved efficiency through the centralisation of purchasing in a specialised department. The purchasing department is better able to negotiate more favourable terms and prices and, by amalgamating orders, can obtain better volume discounts.

Purchase orders should contain a precise description of the goods and services required, quantities, price, delivery instructions, and the supplier's name and address. Purchase orders should be prenumbered and signed or electronically approved by an authorised purchasing officer. The original is sent to the supplier and copies are distributed internally to the receiving department, the accounting department and the requisitioner.

The purchase orders also become part of the transaction trail of documentary evidence that supports the occurrence assertion for purchase transactions (**OE1**). A file of unfilled purchase orders is generally maintained on the computer or as hard copy. A subsequent independent check on the disposition of purchase orders to determine that the goods and services were received and recorded relates to the completeness assertion for purchase transactions (**C1**).

Receiving the goods

A valid purchase order represents the authorisation for the receiving department to accept goods delivered by suppliers. The quantity ordered is sometimes not displayed to ensure that receiving clerks will make careful counts when the goods are received. Receiving department personnel should compare the goods received with the description of the goods on the purchase order, count the goods and inspect them for damage. Delivery of unordered goods should be refused.

The segregation of receiving from requisitioning and purchase ordering prevents those making requisitions from ordering goods directly from suppliers. It also prevents the purchasing department from gaining access to goods improperly ordered.

A prenumbered **receiving report** (also known as a goods received note) should be prepared for each delivery. The receiving report is an important document in supporting the occurrence assertion for purchase transactions (**OE1**). A copy of the receiving report is forwarded to the accounts department. A subsequent periodic independent check on the sequence of prenumbered receiving reports (to determine that a supplier's invoice has been recorded for each) relates to the completeness assertion (**C1**).

Storing goods received for inventory

On delivery of the goods to stores or other requisitioning department, receiving clerks should obtain a signed receipt on the copy of the receiving report retained by the receiving department. This provides further evidence for the occurrence assertion for the purchase transaction (**OE1**). The signed receipt also establishes subsequent accountability for the purchased goods. The physical safekeeping of inventory and the maintenance of records of inventory quantities are considered in chapter 16.

Checking and approving the supplier's invoice

For goods and services supplied on credit, the supplier is usually instructed by the purchase order to send the invoice directly to the entity's accounting department. Before recording **suppliers' invoices**, the department checks and approves them. Procedures applicable to this function include:

- serially numbering suppliers' invoices on receipt so that subsequent checks of numerical continuity can confirm that all invoices are recorded (**C1**)
- establishing the agreement of the details of suppliers' invoices with the related receiving reports and purchase orders to ensure that all invoices relate to valid purchase transactions (**OE1**)
- determining the mathematical accuracy of the suppliers' invoices (**AV1**)
- coding the account distributions on the suppliers' invoices (i.e. indicating the asset and expense accounts to be debited) (**AV1, PD1**)
- approving invoices for payment by having an authorised person sign the invoices (**OE1**)
- preparing a daily prelist of suppliers' invoices approved for payment (**OE1, C1, AV1**).

A common practice is to stamp a grid on the supplier's invoice. The grid has boxes in which to record the serial numbers of purchase orders and receiving reports, the account codes and the initials of the clerk performing the various checks. Details of the supplier's invoice and subsequent checks for accuracy and validity can all be processed electronically.

Other kinds of supporting documentation (such as copies of contracts) may be required when the invoice relates to certain types of services or to leased assets. In other cases, such as for monthly electricity bills, the supplier's invoice alone may suffice because there is no purchase order and receiving report. Other forms of verification will be required, such as a check of the reasonableness of electricity bills against previous charges.

Unpaid suppliers' invoices and supporting documentation are held in a file in the accounts department pending their subsequent payment. Properly approved suppliers' invoices provide the basis for recording purchase transactions.

Recording the liability

Personnel in the accounts department either send approved suppliers' invoices in batches to the computer department or, more likely, enter the data direct via terminals. Programmed edit checks are made for such matters as valid suppliers and the reasonableness of amounts. When the data for a supplier's invoice are accepted by the computer system, the **accounts payable master file** for that supplier is updated and the invoice is added to the **purchase transactions file**. Additional controls over the accuracy of the data entry process may include the use of batch totals and exception reports (**OE1, C1, AV1**). The purchase transactions file is used to update the inventory and general ledger master files. The update program produces printouts, if required, of the purchases journal and a general ledger summary showing the amounts posted to general ledger accounts.

In the online systems most entities now use, the invoice is entered immediately on receipt, automatically approved by reference to order and receiving details, and coded by reference to information recorded on the order. The accounts payable, inventory and general ledger files are immediately updated. Manual verification is required only if programmed application controls reject the invoice.

Monthly statements received from suppliers should be reconciled with recorded supplier balances. Periodic performance reviews by management — in the form of comparisons of asset, liability and expense balances with budgeted amounts — can provide a means of both controlling expenditures and detecting misstatements in recorded purchase transactions.

For very small purchases, previously paid for out of petty cash, authorised requisitioners may be supplied with credit cards or purchasing cards. Limits placed on such cards provide a sufficient safeguard against material loss.

15.3.2 Payment transactions

In this section, we consider the common documents and records, functions and control procedures for payment transactions.

Functions

The two payments functions are:
- paying the liability
- recording the payments.

The same department or individual should not perform both these functions.

Paying the liability

The accounts department is responsible for ensuring that suppliers' invoices are processed for payment on their due dates. Payment is normally required within 30 days. Where prompt payment discounts are allowed, relevant invoices need to be scheduled for payment within the allowed period.

Payments can be by cheque, or more typically by bank credit transfer for regular suppliers. The computer system can be programmed to extract the payments due on each day from the accounts payable master file, produce the cheques and a **cheque summary** (or a credit transfer list), enter the payment data in a **payment transactions file** and update the accounts payable master file. Before being dispatched, the cheques (and bank credit transfer list) are then reviewed by the accounts department, where they are matched with the supporting documents before being forwarded for signing, although this is now usually done electronically where controls are adequate. The signatory should maintain password control over the electronic signature and scrutinise the list of cheques to be signed. In such systems, cheques must be mailed directly from the computer department and not returned to the accounts department. With online banking, credit transfer details may be electronically transmitted to the bank. Access controls should restrict this function to approved signatories.

Controls over the preparation and signing of cheques and electronic transfers and related specific audit objectives include the following:

- authorised personnel in the finance department who otherwise have no responsibility for initiating or processing purchase transactions should be responsible for signing the cheques or controlling the use of electronic signatures (**OE2**) (see table 15.1)
- authorised cheque signers should determine that each cheque or bank transfer is accompanied by properly approved suppliers' invoices, and that the name of the payee and amount on the payment agree with details on the invoice (**OE2, AV1**)
- the suppliers' invoices and supporting documents should be cancelled to prevent resubmission for duplicate payment (**OE2**)
- the cheque signer should control the mailing of the cheques or initiation of the bank transfers to reduce the risk of theft or alterations (**OE2**)
- where cheques are used, none should be made payable to 'cash' or 'bearer' and no blank cheques should be issued (**OE2**)
- prenumbered cheques should be used (**C2**)
- access to blank cheques and to electronic signatures should be limited to authorised personnel (**C2**).

Cheques generally include a perforated attachment known as a **remittance advice**, which identifies the serial numbers of the invoice(s) being paid. Alternatively, copies of the supplier's statement or remittance advice can be enclosed with the cheques mailed to suppliers, or other identifying details can be used where electronic bank transfers are made.

Recording the payments

The payment transactions file in a computer system is created when cheques or electronic transfers are prepared. The update program produces the cash payments journal and a general ledger summary, and also updates the master files.

Controls over the recording of payments include:

- an independent check by an accounting supervisor of the agreement of the amounts journalised and posted to the accounts payable ledger with the cheque summary received from the treasurer (**OE2, C2, AV1**)
- independently prepared bank reconciliations (**OE2, C2, AV1**).

15.4 PAYROLL TRANSACTIONS

An entity's payroll transactions include salaries, hourly and incentive (piecework) wages, commissions, bonuses and employee benefits (e.g. paid holidays, sick leave). In this section, we focus on employees paid hourly. The payroll transactions also record deductions from payroll in determining net pay. These deductions may be statutory (such as taxation) or by agreement (such as employee contributions to a union). Deductions are recorded as liabilities for payment to the appropriate body. Payroll relates to payment for the services of employees. Most entities have a detailed information system and related internal control procedures for recording labour services (typically in the form of hours worked) and ensuring that payment is made only to current employees in respect of labour services actually provided. Figure 15.2 gives an outline of the process which will be discussed in detail below. The first point to note is the distinction between the personnel department and the payroll function. The personnel department is responsible for recording the personal details of new and existing staff including information such as bank details and pay rates, as well as ensuring staff who leave are removed from the system at the appropriate time. The payroll department is focused on calculating and paying wages and salaries. This segregation of duties plays an important role in preventing dummy employees being created and paid for work that has not been performed. Figure 15.2 assumes that an individual member of staff completes a timesheet that records hours worked, this timesheet goes to their own business department where the timesheet will be approved by a supervisor, and the timesheet is then sent to the payroll department where this is combined with the personnel data such as pay rates and any authorised deductions to calculate the pay due. Part of this calculation will include deductions for tax amounts due (PAYG), superannuation contributions (both employee and employer contributions) as well as other voluntary deductions such as union subscriptions. The staff will then be paid the net amount after deductions either in cash or more likely as a direct transfer into their bank accounts. The amounts deducted and other liabilities such as employer superannuation contributions then need to be paid to the appropriate authority such as the Australian Tax Office, the relevant superannuation fund and the union of which staff are members. The discussion below describes the processes in further detail.

Functions

The relevant functions are those of:
- hiring employees
- authorising payroll changes
- preparing attendance and timekeeping data
- preparing the payroll
- recording the payroll
- paying the payroll and protecting unclaimed wages.

Each function is explained below.

Hiring employees

Employees are hired by the personnel department. Details are documented on a **personnel authorisation form**, which should indicate the job classification, starting wage rate and authorised payroll deductions. In the system, data on new employees are entered in the **personnel data master file**. Access to data entry to this file is restricted by password to authorised individuals in the personnel department. Periodically, a computer-generated log of all changes to the master file is printed and independently checked by a personnel manager not involved in entering the data into the computer. One copy of the personnel authorisation form is placed in the employee's **personnel file** in the personnel department. Another copy is sent to the payroll department.

Payroll cycle

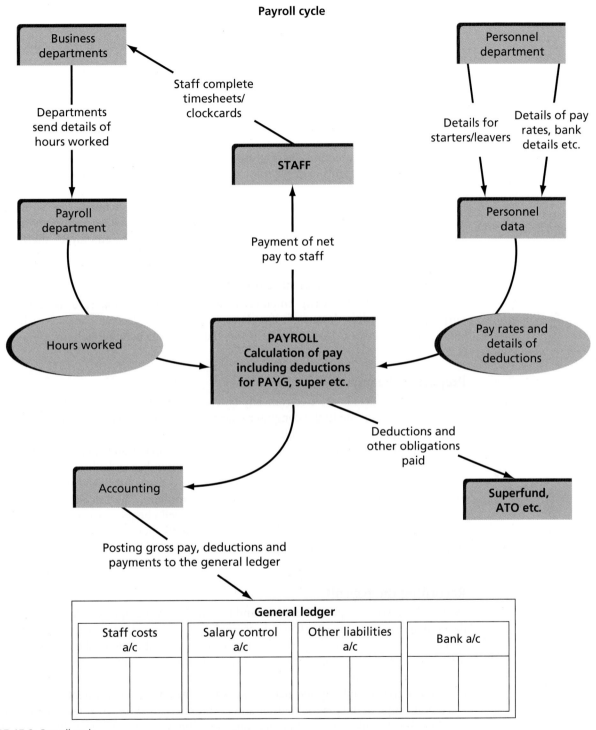

FIGURE 15.2: Payroll cycle

Segregating the functions of personnel and payroll reduces the risk of payments to fictitious employees because only the personnel department may add new employees to the personnel master file and only the payroll department may process the payment of wages (**OE3**, **RO1**). This segregation of functions is also an important control in the next function — authorising payroll changes. Thus, personnel department employees cannot benefit from falsifying personnel records, and payroll department employees can process payroll only for employees listed in the personnel records and at the wage rates specified therein.

Authorising payroll changes

An employee's supervisor may initiate the request for a change in job classification (or a wage rate increase). However, all changes should be authorised in writing by the personnel department before being entered in the personnel data master file. Other controls over entering the changes in the computer and distributing the change forms are the same as those for new employees. These controls over payroll changes help to ensure the accuracy of the payroll (**RO1, AV1**).

The personnel department should also issue a **termination notice** on completion of an individual's employment. It is vital that the payroll department is promptly notified of such terminations to prevent payment continuing to be made to employees after they have left (**OE3**).

Preparing attendance and timekeeping data

In most organisations, each employee's security identification card is used for the purpose of recording hours of attendance at work by electronic means, where such recording is necessary. This control ensures that payment is made only for hours worked (**OE3, RO1**).

Preparing the payroll

Time recording details are electronically entered into the system from employee security cards, which are online to the computer system. The resulting payroll transactions data are then used in preparing the payroll.

The payroll transactions are subjected to supervisory review and approval through an edit check routine, including a check for a valid employee number and a limit or reasonableness check on the hours worked. The output of this run consists of a valid payroll register, an exceptions report and a labour cost distribution summary. The calculation of the payroll and the preparation of the **payroll register** and payroll cheques or electronic bank transfers use data from the valid **payroll transactions file**, the personnel data master file and the **employee earnings master file**(s). This run also records the payroll, as we describe in the next section.

Recording the payroll

Using calculated gross pay, deductions and net pay for each employee, the program updates the employee earnings master file and accumulates totals for the payroll journal entry that is generated and entered in the general ledger master file at the end of the run. The following printed outputs of this run can be produced if required for control purposes:

- an exceptions report
- a copy of the payroll register that is returned to the payroll department
- a second copy of the payroll register and prenumbered payroll cheques or details of electronic direct bank transfers that are sent to the finance office (or pay slips and a cheque for total net pay if wages are paid in cash)
- a general ledger summary that is sent to accounting, showing the payroll entry generated by the payroll program.

Proper review of each of these outputs by the appropriate personnel contributes to control over misstatements (**OE3, C3, AV1**).

It is common practice for a senior accounting officer to approve the payroll details before payroll cheques or bank transfers are prepared. In smaller entities, the authorising officer could verify payroll by reconciling it with the previous period's payroll, allowing for hirings, terminations or changes in hours worked. In any event, the payroll should be independently checked against personnel records at regular intervals.

Paying the payroll and protecting unclaimed wages

In the preceding section we explained that the payroll cheques and a copy of the payroll register are sent to the treasurer's or chief accountant's office where these functions are commonly performed. Applicable controls include the following.

- Finance office personnel should check the agreement of the names and amounts on cheques or bank transfers with payroll register entries (**OE3, C3, AV1**).
- Payroll cheques and bank transfers should be signed or authorised by finance office personnel not involved in preparing or recording the payroll.
- Payroll cheques, where used, should be distributed to employees by finance office personnel not involved in preparing or recording the payroll, who should require proper identification of employees (**OE3, AV1**).
- Any unclaimed payroll cheques should be stored in a safe or vault in the finance office (**OE3, C3**). Another important control over paying the payroll in many large entities is the use of an imprest payroll bank account on which all payroll cheques or electronic transfers are drawn. This account is funded with the amount of net pay. Any errors in preparing payroll cheques or electronic direct bank transfers, or deliberate falsification would soon be detected because the amount paid in would exceed the account balance, causing the bank to refuse acceptance (**OE3, AV3**). It is now common practice for entities to pay wages by direct credit transfer to employee bank accounts, eliminating the need for cheques and the associated risks of their misuse.

PROFESSIONAL ENVIRONMENT

Clive Peeters hit by $20 million employee fraud — how you can avoid getting stung

The mystery surrounding 'accounting discrepancies' at electrical goods retailer Clive Peeters has been solved, with a female payroll officer allegedly admitting to defrauding the company of around $20 million and investing the money in over 40 properties around Australia.

Clive Peeters launched action in the Victorian Supreme Court against employee Sonia Causer on 6 August, claiming the payroll officer falsified entries in the company's payroll accounts, transferred cash from Clive Peeters' bank accounts to her own account and used the money to buy properties worth just under $20 million. The legal action came just days after Clive Peeters suspended its shares from trade on the ASX after warning it had discovered discrepancies in its accounts.

According to court documents, Causer allegedly came clean to Clive Peeters' managing director Greg Smith after the company launched an investigation into the missing money.

'I've stuffed up big time and just want to curl up in a ball and disappear,' Causer allegedly told a colleague. Smith was unavailable for comment prior to publication. Clive Peeters says she has cooperated in the investigation and has agreed to transfer ownership of the properties to Clive Peeters.

The portfolio, which was allegedly built up between November 2007 and June 2009, contains properties in Victoria, Brisbane and Tasmania. Smith has said that the properties, many of which have been generating rental income, will now be sold and with the property sector booming across Australia, there is a fair chance that many will have appreciated in value.

The windfall will be welcomed by Clive Peeters, which has been struggling under the weight of falling consumer spending and high debt, a legacy of its rapid expansion over the past five years. The proceeds of the fraud are almost double the operating profit of $10.3 million that Clive Peeters posted in 2007–08.

While this alleged fraud has had a surprisingly happy ending — most fraudsters simply spend or gamble the proceeds of their crime, rather than actually investing the cash in bricks and mortar — one big question remains: How did Clive Peeters allow this to happen? According to reports, the alleged fraud involved the altering of online transaction details such that many funds destined for creditors (including the Australian Taxation Office) were redirected to the employee's accounts.[5]

Learning check

Do you know . . .

15.1 ☐ Purchasing involves the functions of:
- requisitioning
- ordering
- receiving
- storing goods
- approving the invoice
- recording the liability.

An important control is the segregation of each of these functions.

15.2 ☐ The cheque signatory should verify supporting documents, and reliance may be placed on controls over the existence of liabilities entered in the accounts payable master file. Cheques, where used, are produced by the computer and are generally electronically signed. It is now more common to make payments by electronic bank transfers.

15.3 ☐ Payroll transactions involve the functions of:
- hiring
- authorising changes
- timekeeping
- preparing the payroll
- recording the payroll
- distributing pay.

It is important to segregate the personnel functions of hiring and authorising changes from all other payroll functions.

15.4 ☐ The greatest risk is of payments to fictitious employees, either through the entry of details of fictitious employees in the records or through the failure to remove details of employees who have left.

15.5 DEVELOPING THE AUDIT PLAN

In the previous section, we illustrated features of the internal control structure relating to purchase, payment and payroll transactions typically identified and recorded by the auditor in obtaining the understanding as required by ASA 315 (ISA 315).

In this section, how the auditor develops the audit plan for purchases, payroll and payables is explained. This requires an understanding of the client, an assessment of inherent risks and control risks and the design of auditing procedures to address those risks. Firstly, we consider the auditor's approach to understanding the entity and its environment, and how this leads to identifying inherent risks and the impact on audit strategy. Secondly, there is a brief discussion of factors to be considered by the auditor in assessing the control environment within which the information system and control procedures operate. Thirdly, we illustrate the assessment of control risks and how this assessment is finalised after tests of design effectiveness and tests of operating effectiveness leading to a final assessment of risk (this includes an illustration of an audit program in relation to performing tests of controls for credit purchase transactions.

LEARNING 4 objective

Apply the concepts of materiality and inherent risk to the audit of purchases, payables and payroll.

15.5.1 Understanding the entity and the identification of inherent risks

The auditor must obtain a detailed understanding of the entity and its environment and assess inherent and control risks in order to determine the appropriate level of detection risk. This risk assessment will drive the development of the audit strategy which will direct audit attention to significant risks through a mix of tests of controls and substantive procedures.

Understanding the entity and its environment

As part of the audit planning procedures it is important that the auditor is aware of the risk that misstatements may remain uncorrected in the financial report. This was discussed in detail in chapter 8. With regard to purchases, payroll and payables this will assist the auditor in:

- developing an understanding of cost of sales and gross margins by understanding its products, its market share and its competitive advantage
- developing an understanding of levels of various types of expenses including staff costs
- developing an expectation of payables levels based on average payment periods for the client and the industry as a whole.

The level of expenditure both for cost of goods sold and other costs will to some extent be affected by levels of revenue and therefore an understanding of the sales cycle can lead to an understanding of an entity's expenditure cycles and help in assessing the possibility of misstatements in these areas. The auditor needs to carefully assess the extent to which costs are variable and therefore affected by sales and the extent to which they are fixed or affected by other drivers. Experience with the client entity or other companies in the same industry, through trade associations, reading newspaper or industry articles will allow the auditor to understand the assertions at risk.

Analytical review

Analytical techniques are used at various stages through the audit process. The objective of using these techniques at the planning stage is to help identify high-risk areas for detailed audit testing. Where the auditor has a detailed knowledge of the entity, expectations can be created in relation to things such as income, expenses and asset levels, against which the actual (draft) financial report can be compared. Where the draft report is significantly different to the auditor's expectations, audit attention will be directed to that area of difference. Examples of analytical procedures include investigations and comparisons of:

- gross margins and net margins — give indications of the reasonableness of cost of sales and expense levels
- expected staff costs based on average pay rates and average numbers of staff
- payables days (payables/credit purchases × 365) — consider any changes in payment terms.

The audit strategy and the more detailed audit plan will be amended to address any significant risks identified through analytical procedures.

Materiality

Purchase and payroll transactions account for the major expenses incurred by a business, so are a major component in the determination of profit. They also relate to the acquisition of major classes of asset (notably, inventories and plant and equipment). Moreover, the balance in accounts payable produced by credit purchase transactions is nearly always material to the balance sheet.

Inherent risks

In assessing inherent risk for purchase and payroll assertions, the auditor should consider factors that could motivate management to misstate expenditure. These may include:

- pressures to understate expenses in order to falsely report the achievement of announced profitability targets or industry norms
- pressures to understate payables in order to report a higher level of working capital in the face of liquidity problems or going-concern doubts.

These factors affect mainly the completeness assertion and reduce the acceptable detection risk, particularly in testing for understatement of liabilities. Other factors that may contribute to misstatements include:

- the high volume of transactions, which affects all assertions
- temptations for employees to make unauthorised purchases and payments, or to misappropriate purchased assets, which relate to the occurrence assertion
- contentious accounting issues such as whether a cost should be capitalised or expensed (such as the treatment of repairs and maintenance costs or the classification of a lease as an operating or finance lease), which relate to the valuation assertion
- the complexity of payroll calculations for factory workers whose gross earnings may be based on time and/or productivity, affecting the accuracy of payroll costs.

Payroll fraud is a major concern for the auditor. Employees involved in preparing and paying the payroll may process data for fictitious employees or for employees whose services have already been terminated, and then divert the wages for their own use. This affects the auditor's assessment of risk for the occurrence assertion for payroll.

LEARNING objective 5

Discuss considerations relevant to determining the audit strategy for purchases, payables and payroll.

Audit strategy

The high volume of transactions, combined with the likely existence of effective control procedures over these transactions, means that it is normally appropriate to adopt an approach based on a lower assessed level of control risk, particularly in respect to the occurrence and accuracy assertions. For other assertions, the audit strategy may vary with the preliminary assessment of control risk. The volume of transactions, however, means that the lower assessed level of control risk approach is preferred wherever the assessment of risk can support such a strategy.

15.5.2 Internal control environment

An internal control system is made up of control environment, risk assessment, information system, control activities and monitoring. To be effective, an internal control system should be designed and implemented to prevent, or detect and correct, the inherent risks identified earlier in this chapter.

In most well-established entities, management's own risk assessment procedures will have led it to adopt control procedures to reduce the risk of misstatements occurring in the processing and recording of transactions. However, the existence and effectiveness of controls relating to different transaction class assertions for purchases, payments and payroll can vary considerably among entities and even among assertions for the same entity. Moreover, the auditor must remain mindful of the inherent limitations of internal control — including the possibility of management override, collusion, errors due to fatigue or misunderstanding, and failure to adapt the control structure to changed circumstances.

Factors relating to the control environment that the auditor needs to consider when assessing control risk for purchase, payment and payroll transactions include those described below.

- Integrity and ethical values are important because there are numerous opportunities for employee fraud in processing purchase, payment and payroll transactions, and for fraudulent financial reporting by management of expense account balances.
- Purchasing agents may be subjected to pressures from suppliers, such as offers of 'kickbacks' for transacting more business with those suppliers.
- Management's commitment to competence should be reflected in the assignment and training of personnel involved in processing purchase, payment and payroll transactions. In particular, people involved in payroll functions should be knowledgeable about employment laws and regulations, and the applicable provisions of labour contracts.
- The entity's organisational structure and management's assignment of authority and responsibility over purchase, payment and payroll transactions should be clearly communicated and provide clear lines of authority, responsibility and reporting relationships. For example, purchasing, receiving, and stores or warehousing activities may fall under the duties of the production director; accounting may be the responsibility of the finance director; and payments may be supervised by the treasurer.

Overall responsibility for personnel matters is often assigned to a director or manager of human or personnel resources. Officers' salaries and other forms of compensation are usually set by the board of directors.

LEARNING objective 6

Design and execute tests of controls over purchase, payment and payroll transactions to assess control risk.

15.5.3 Assessment of control risk

Assessment of control risk is normally done in two phases. On obtaining the understanding of the internal control structure, the auditor normally tests the design effectiveness of controls and forms a preliminary assessment.

Where the design effectiveness of control risk is assessed as being less than high, tests of the operating effectiveness of controls are included in the audit program to confirm the preliminary assessment. Tests of controls for each of the three transaction classes are described in the following paragraphs.

Purchase transactions

Table 15.2 (overleaf) contains a partial listing of potential misstatements, necessary controls, potential tests of the operating effectiveness of those controls, and the specific transaction class audit objective for purchases to which each belongs.

TABLE 15.2: Control risk assessment considerations — purchase transactions

Function	Potential misstatement	Necessary control	Possible test of operating effectiveness	Relevant transaction class audit objective (from table 15.1)				
				OE1	C1	AV1	CO	PD1
Requisitioning goods and services	Goods may be requisitioned for unauthorised purposes.	General and specific authorisation procedures	Enquire about procedures.	✓				
Preparing purchase orders	Purchases may be made for unauthorised purposes.	Approved purchase requisition for each order	Examine purchase orders for approved requisitions.	✓				
Receiving goods	Goods received may not have been ordered.	Approved purchase order for each shipment	Examine receiving report for matching purchase order.	✓				
	Incorrect quantities, damaged goods or incorrect items may be received.	Receiving clerks to count, inspect and compare goods received with purchase order	Observe the performance by receiving clerks.	✓				
Storing goods received for inventory	Stores clerks may deny taking custody of purchased goods.	Signed receipt to be obtained on delivery of goods from receiving to stores	Inspect signed receipts.	✓				
Approving the invoice	Invoices may be recorded for goods not ordered.	Matching of purchase order and receiving report with the supplier's invoice	Examine supporting documentation for invoices.*	✓	✓	✓		✓
Recording the liability	Invoices may be recorded incorrectly or not recorded.	Independent check of agreement of prelist with amounts recorded in purchases journal	Examine evidence of independent check; re-perform independent check.*	✓	✓	✓		✓
		Periodic accounting for prenumbered receiving reports and purchase orders	Observe procedure; re-perform.		✓		✓	
		Periodic performance reviews by management of reports, comparing actual asset, payable and expense balances with budgeted amounts	Enquire of management about results of performance reviews; inspect reports.*	✓	✓	✓	✓	✓

* Sometimes performed as a part of dual-purpose tests.

Preliminary assessment — design effectiveness

The potential misstatements and necessary controls listed in table 15.2 form the basis of internal control evaluation checklists. As we explained in chapter 14 on sales and receivables, the auditor applies this checklist to the documented information system and reaches a conclusion as to the effectiveness of controls relative to each potential misstatement. The basis for this conclusion is normally explained in the checklist, which thus forms part of the necessary documentation of the assessment of control risk as being less than high. Where the auditor's understanding of the system is obtained and recorded by means of internal control questionnaires, this process simultaneously assesses and documents control effectiveness. Where controls over a particular assertion are judged to be effective, the auditor incorporates necessary tests of operating effectiveness in drawing up the audit program.

Tests of operating effectiveness

The extent of tests of the operating effectiveness of controls will vary inversely with the auditor's preliminary assessment of control risk. Statistical or non-statistical attribute sampling procedures (see chapter 13) may be applicable to certain tests. Recall that the direction of testing must be compatible with the specific audit objective to which the test relates — vouching for occurrence and tracing for completeness. Evidence applicable to other assertion categories can be obtained from testing in either direction. Also, recall that some tests, particularly those pertaining to checking and approving suppliers' invoices and recording the liability, may be performed as dual-purpose tests. In these tests (marked with an asterisk in table 15.2), evidence is obtained about the effects (measured in dollars) of processing errors on account balances, as well as about the frequency of deviations from controls. Based on the evidence obtained from procedures to obtain an understanding of the internal control structure and related tests of controls, the auditor makes a final assessment of control risk for each significant assertion related to purchase transactions.

A formal audit program that incorporates several of the tests from table 15.2 is presented in figure 15.3 (overleaf).

The auditor normally uses the computer in performing tests of controls, using techniques similar to those described for sales transactions in chapter 14. In particular, tests of effectiveness must be performed for any controls that serve as the basis for a control risk assessment at a reduced level. This includes making enquiries and inspecting documentation concerning general controls over changes to programs and master files used in processing purchase transactions.

Tests of application controls may include the use of test data to determine whether expected results are produced by the entity's program for accepting and recording data for unpaid suppliers' invoices in circumstances such as the following:
- a missing or invalid supplier number
- a missing or invalid account classification code number
- a missing or unreasonable amount
- a missing due date or payment terms
- alphabetical characters in a numerical field.

Examples of other possible computer-assisted audit tests are:
- using generalised audit software or a database program to perform sequence checks and print lists of purchase orders, receiving reports or invoices whose numbers are missing in designated computer files
- designing, selecting and evaluating a sample of receiving reports or unpaid invoices.

Amalgamated Products Ltd
Planned tests of controls — Credit purchases transactions
Year ending 30 June 2015

Assertion/test of controls	W/P ref.	Auditor	Date
Occurrence 1. Observe procedures, including segregation of duties, for: • completing purchase orders from requisitions • receipt of goods • receipt of invoices • reconciliation with supplier statements. 2. Select a sample of purchase transactions from the purchase journal and verify transaction dates, supplier names and amounts by vouching entries to the following matching supporting documents: • purchase invoices • delivery notes • approved purchase orders • approved purchase requisition.			
Completeness 3. Examine evidence of the use of and accounting for prenumbered purchase requisitions, purchase orders, dispatch notes and sales invoices. Scan the sequence of sales invoice numbers in the sales journal. 4. Select a sample of approved purchase requisition and trace to matching: • approved purchase order • delivery notes • purchase invoices • entries in the purchase journal.			
Accuracy 5. For the sample in step 2 above, examine evidence of: • an independent check on proper pricing of invoices • an independent check on the trade discounts received • an independent check on the mathematical accuracy of invoices. 6. For purchase invoices processed in batches, examine evidence of an independent check on the agreement of totals for purchase journal entries and amounts posted to supplier accounts with batch totals.			
Cut-off 7. Obtain the number of the last goods received note for the final goods receipt of the year, select a sample of goods received notes before this number and agree: • to purchase invoice dated in the current period • entries in purchase journal before the period end. 8. Following on from step 7, select a sample of the first goods received notes after this number and agree: • to purchase invoice dated in the next accounting period • the purchase is not recorded in the purchase journal until the following accounting period.			

FIGURE 15.3: Partial audit program for tests of controls — credit purchases

Payment transactions

Table 15.3 contains a partial listing of potential misstatements, necessary controls, possible tests of the operating effectiveness of those controls, and the specific transaction class audit objective for payments to which each belongs. As explained for purchases, the potential misstatements and necessary controls are the basis of a checklist used to assess design effectiveness. Similarly, an audit program for tests of the operating effectiveness of controls for payment transactions can be prepared, based on the potential tests of controls in table 15.3. Possible computer-assisted tests of controls are also similar to those for purchase transactions. Thus, for example, test data can be used to test programmed controls relating to the preparation and recording of cheques or electronic bank transfers to suppliers in payment of liabilities. Computer programs can also be used to design, select and evaluate an attribute sample for payments.

TABLE 15.3: Control risk assessment considerations — payment transactions

Function	Potential misstatement	Necessary control	Possible test of operating effectiveness	OE2	C2	AV1	CO	PD2
Paying the liability	Cheques/bank transfers may be issued for unauthorised purchases.	Cheque/bank transfer signers to review supporting documentation for completeness and approval.	Observe cheque signers performing independent check of supporting documentation.	✓				
	An invoice may be paid twice.	'Paid' stamp or cancelation to be placed on the invoice and supporting documents when a cheque/bank transfer is issued.	Examine paid invoices for 'paid' stamp.	✓				
	A cheque may be altered after being signed (where only cheques used).	Cheque signers to supervise mailing of cheques.	Enquire about mailing procedures; observe mailing		✓			
Recording the payment	A cheque/bank transfer may not be recorded.	Use of, and accounting for, prenumbered cheques/bank transfers.	Examine evidence of use of and accounting for prenumbered cheques/use of bank transfers.		✓	✓		
	Errors may be made in recording cheques/bank transfers.	Independent check of agreement of amounts journalised and posted with the cheque/bank transfer summary.	Observe procedure; re-perform.*	✓	✓	✓	✓	✓
	Cheques/bank transfers may not be recorded promptly.	Periodic independent bank reconciliations	Examine bank reconciliations.*	✓	✓	✓	✓	
		Independent check of dates on cheques/bank transfers with dates recorded	Re-perform independent check*	✓	✓		✓	

* Sometimes performed as a part of dual-purpose tests.

Payroll transactions

The process of assessing the control risk for payroll transactions begins, as for purchases and payments, with identifying potential misstatements and necessary controls (shown in the second and third columns of table 15.4). Possible tests of controls are shown in the fourth column.

TABLE 15.4: Control risk assessment considerations — payroll transactions

Function	Potential misstatement	Necessary control	Possible test of operating effectiveness	OE3	C3	AV1	CO	PD3
Hiring employees	Fictitious employees may be added to the payroll.	Personnel department authorisation for all hiring of new employees	Examine authorisation forms for hiring of new employees.	✓				
Authorising payroll changes	Employees may receive unauthorised rate increases.	Personnel department authorisation for all rate changes	Enquire about procedures for authorising rate changes.			✓		
	Terminated employees may still be on the payroll.	Personnel department notification to payroll department of all terminated employees	Examine termination notices in payroll department.	✓				
Preparing attendance and timekeeping data	Employees may be paid for hours not worked.	Use of electronic recording procedures and supervisory approval of time recorded	Observe time recording procedures; examine supervisory approval procedures.	✓	✓	✓		✓
Preparing the payroll	Payroll data may be lost during submission to computer department.	Batch totals of hours worked prepared by payroll department and verified by data control	Examine evidence of the preparation and use of batch totals where applicable.		✓			
	Payroll transactions file may include incorrectly keyed or invalid data.	Edit checks of data on payroll transactions file	Observe data entry procedures; examine the exceptions and control report.*	✓	✓	✓		✓
Recording the payroll	Processing errors may occur in recording the payroll.	Exceptions and control report to be reviewed by data control	Enquire about the preparation and use of the exceptions and control report.*	✓	✓	✓	✓	✓
	Unauthorised changes may be made to payroll data in computer department.	Payroll department comparison of payroll register with original batch transmittal data	Re-perform comparison.*	✓	✓	✓		✓
Paying the payroll and protecting unclaimed wages	Payroll cheques may be distributed to unauthorised recipients.	Employee identification on distribution	Witness distribution of payroll.	✓	✓	✓		✓

* Sometimes performed as a part of dual-purpose tests.

In computer information systems, access controls over changes to personnel data are important. In the testing of controls, test data can be used to test programmed controls relating to the preparation and recording of payroll. Where time recording is computerised, test data can also be used in testing programmed controls over timekeeping.

The auditor knows that misstatements in payroll may result from unintentional errors or fraud. Of particular concern is the risk of overstatement of payroll through:
- payments to fictitious employees
- payments to actual employees for hours not worked
- payments to actual employees at higher than authorised rates.

The first two risks relate to the occurrence assertion. The third risk relates to the accuracy assertion.

The risk of understatement (the completeness assertion) is of minimal concern because employees will complain when they are underpaid. Accordingly, many tests of payroll controls are directed at controls that prevent or detect overstatements. The direction of testing for these controls is from the recorded payroll data to source documents; for example, the auditor may vouch data for a sample of employees in a payroll register to approved clock card data and authorised pay rates and deductions.

Two tests of controls relating to the control risk for the occurrence assertion are the test for terminated employees and witnessing a payroll distribution. The former represents an exception to the normal direction of testing for payroll, in that the auditor selects a sample of termination notices and scans subsequent payroll registers to determine that the terminated employees did not continue to receive pay cheques. In witnessing the distribution of payroll cheques or envelopes, the auditor observes that:
- segregation of duties exists between the preparation and payment of the payroll
- each employee is identified by a badge or employee identification card
- each employee receives only one cheque or pay envelope
- there is proper control and disposal of unclaimed wages.

Such witnessing of payroll distribution is becoming less common as entities increasingly pay by electronic bank transfers.

15.5.4 Final assessment

Based on the evidence obtained from the procedures to obtain an understanding of the internal control structure and related tests of controls, the auditor makes a final assessment of inherent risk and control risk. For each significant audit objective where assessment of risk as being less than high is used as the basis for adopting a lower assessed level of control risk audit strategy, the auditor must document reasons for this assessment. This assessment enables the auditor to confirm the level of substantive procedures to be performed. The auditor must ensure that control deviations are properly identified and that their implications for the assessment of control risk are properly considered as to whether further substantive procedures need to be performed.

15.6 SUBSTANTIVE PROCEDURES

Accounts payable is usually the largest current liability in a balance sheet and a significant factor in the evaluation of an entity's short-term solvency. Like receivables, it is affected by a high volume of transactions and thus is susceptible to misstatements. However, whereas with receivables the auditor is concerned with overstatement, understatement is the greatest risk with payables. The reason is that management, if motivated to misrepresent payables, is likely to understate them in order to report a more favourable financial position.

Compared with the audit of asset balances, the audit of payables places more emphasis on gathering evidence about the completeness assertion than about the existence assertion. This section focuses on accounts payable arising from purchase transactions, and payroll liabilities arising from payroll transactions.

LEARNING 7 objective

Indicate the factors relevant to determining an acceptable level of detection risk for the audit of purchases, payables and payroll.

15.6.1 Determining detection risk

Accounts payable is affected by purchase transactions that increase the account balance and payment transactions that decrease the balance. Thus, detection risk for creditor assertions is affected by the inherent and control risk factors related to both these transaction classes. The auditor uses the methodology explained in chapter 12 for combining control risk assessments for transaction class assessments to arrive at control risk assessments for payables balance assertions. The auditor then uses this methodology, involving the audit risk model or a risk matrix, to determine acceptable levels of detection risk in planning the audit. The application of this process for accounts payable is summarised in table 15.5. The risk levels specified in this matrix are illustrative only and would vary based on the entity's circumstances. Furthermore, note that the acceptable detection risk levels shown in table 15.5 indicate the need for more persuasive evidence for the completeness assertion and the accuracy or valuation and allocation assertion than for the other assertions.

TABLE 15.5: Correlation of risk components — accounts payable

Risk component	Existence or occurrence	Completeness	Rights and obligations	Accuracy or valuation and allocation	Presentation and disclosure
Audit risk	Low	Low	Low	Low	Low
Inherent risk	Moderate	High	Moderate	High	Low
Control risk — purchase transactions	Low	High	Moderate	High	Moderate
Control risk — payments	Moderate	Low	Low	Low	Low
Combined control risk[1]	Low	High	Moderate	High	Moderate
Acceptable detection risk[2]	High	Low	Moderate	Low	High

1. This is the most conservative (highest) of transaction class control risk assessments used as the combined risk assessment as per the method discussed in chapter 12 (section 12.2).
2. Determined from risk components matrix in figure 9.7 (p. 402), based on the levels of audit risk, inherent risk and combined control risk indicated above for each assertion category.

As noted opposite, payroll is subject to high inherent risks for the completeness and accuracy assertions. For this reason, however, controls are usually effective and control risk is low. Substantive procedures for payroll balances are often limited to the application of analytical procedures to the expense accounts and related accruals, and limited tests of details.

Consider the completeness assertions.

- Overall audit risk needs to be low to ensure there is a low risk of giving the wrong audit opinion in relation to completeness.
- The inherent risk has been assessed as high — the auditor understands the entity and its environment and has concluded that there is a high likelihood that completeness errors will arise (i.e. a high risk that purchase transactions that actually occurred have been omitted from the accounts or there are payable balances that exist that have been omitted).
- The *combined* control risk is high — indicating that the auditor has obtained an understanding of the internal controls related to completeness and performed tests of controls on their effectiveness and has concluded that there is a high risk that any errors that do arise (and this is likely, given the high inherent risk identified above) will not be detected and corrected by the internal controls.
- That the combined control risk for completeness is made up of the completeness control risk for purchase transactions (high) and the existence and occurrence control risk for cash payments (moderate). The logic for this is as follows (notice all of the following lead to potential existence problems in the balances):
  - a *completeness* problem with purchase transactions (a purchase has occurred but not recorded in the accounts) leads to a *completeness* problem in the payables balance (the purchase was not recorded, so the payable was also omitted)
  - for cash payments, an *occurrence* problem (cash payments have been recorded but no payment was made) leads to a *completeness* problem in payables balance (the payable exists but a payment has been recorded to reduce the payable to zero even though no payment was made).
- Having assessed inherent risk and control risk the auditor will now determine the acceptable level of detection risk that will allow the overall audit risk for existence and occurrence to be low. Given inherent risk is high and control risk is high the auditor has determined that a low level of detection risk is appropriate to achieve the required audit risk. This level of detection risk will be used by the auditor to determine the nature timing and extent of substantive procedures that need to be performed. The level and detail of substantive procedures performed is a matter of professional judgement. Detection risk has not been set high so the auditor must perform more than just the minimum substantive testing because detection risk has been set low the auditor will be required to perform extensive substantive testing.

LEARNING objective 8

Design a substantive audit program for purchases, payables and payroll.

15.6.2 Designing substantive procedures

The general framework for developing audit programs for substantive procedures that was explained in chapter 12 and illustrated in chapter 14 for receivables can also be used in designing substantive procedures for payables and payroll liabilities. Table 15.6 (overleaf) lists possible substantive procedures in an audit program developed on this basis. Note that each test in the table is linked to one or more of the specific account balance audit objectives from table 15.1 (p. 622). Also note that multiple procedures are keyed to each account balance audit objective.

The procedures are explained on the following pages, together with comments on how some tests can be tailored based on the acceptable level of detection risk to be achieved.

TABLE 15.6: Possible substantive procedures for payables assertions

Category	Substantive procedure	EO4	C4	RO1	AV2	PD no.
		Account balance audit objective (from table 15.1)				
Initial procedures	1. Perform initial procedures on payables balances and records that will be subjected to further testing. (a) Trace the opening balance for payables to the previous year's working papers. (b) Review activity in the general ledger account for payables, and investigate entries that appear unusual in amount or source. (c) Obtain a listing of accounts payable at the end of the reporting period and determine that it accurately represents the underlying accounting records by: • adding the listing and determining agreement with the total of the subsidiary ledger, or the accounts payable master file and the general ledger control account balance • testing the agreement of suppliers and balances on the listing with those included in the underlying accounting records.				✓	
Analytical procedures	2. Perform analytical procedures. (a) Determine expectations. (b) Compare current and previous year balances. (c) Calculate significant ratios such as: • gross profit • accounts payable turnover. (d) Obtain explanations for unexpected changes. (e) Corroborate explanations.	✓	✓		✓	
Tests of details of transactions	3. Vouch a sample of recorded creditor transactions to supporting documentation. (a) Vouch credits to supporting suppliers' invoices, receiving reports and purchase orders or other supporting documents. (b) Vouch debits to payments.	✓	✓	✓	✓	✓1
	4. Perform purchases cut-off test. (a) Select a sample of recorded purchase transactions from several days before and after the year-end and examine supporting vouchers, suppliers' invoices and receiving reports to determine that purchases were recorded in the proper period. (b) Observe the number of the last receiving report issued on the last business day of the audit period, and trace a sample of lower and higher numbered receiving reports to related purchase documents to determine whether transactions were recorded in the proper period.	✓	✓			

Category	Substantive procedure	Account balance audit objective (from table 15.1)				
		EO4	C4	RO1	AV2	PD no.
	(c) Examine subsequent payments between the end of the reporting period and the end of fieldwork and, when related documentation indicates the payment was for an obligation in existence at the end of the reporting period, trace to the accounts payable listing.	✓	✓			
	(d) Investigate unmatched purchase orders, receiving reports and suppliers' invoices at the year-end.					
	5. Perform payments cut-off test by tracing dates cheques were presented for payment on the subsequent period's bank statement to dates recorded.					
Tests of details of balances	6. Reconcile accounts payable to monthly statements received by the entity from suppliers.	✓	✓		✓	
	(a) Identify major suppliers by reviewing the accounts payable ledger or the accounts payable master file.					
	(b) Investigate and reconcile differences.					
	7. Confirm payables with major suppliers whose monthly statements are unavailable.	✓	✓	✓	✓	✓4
	8. Perform a search for unrecorded liabilities.		✓			
	(a) Investigate differences identified by analytical procedures.					
	(b) Review agreements and long-term contracts requiring periodic payments for evidence of unrecorded liabilities.					
	9. Recalculate accrued payroll liabilities.				✓	
	10. Verify directors' and officers' remuneration.	✓	✓	✓	✓	✓6
Presentation and disclosure	11. Compare financial statement presentation with applicable regulations and accounting standards.				✓	✓4, 7
	(a) Determine that payables are properly identified and classified as to type and expected period of payment.					
	(b) Determine whether there are debit balances that are significant in the aggregate and that should be reclassified.					
	(c) Determine the appropriateness of disclosures pertaining to related party payables.					
	(d) Enquire of management about existence of undisclosed commitments or contingent liabilities.					

Initial procedures

To begin verifying accounts payable:
- trace the opening balance to the previous year's working papers, when applicable
- review activity in the general ledger account for any unusual entries
- obtain a listing of amounts owed at the end of the reporting period.

Usually the listing is prepared by the entity from the accounts payable ledger. The auditor must verify the mathematical accuracy of the listing by adding the total and verifying that it agrees with the underlying accounting records and the general ledger control account balance. In addition, the auditor selectively compares details of suppliers and amounts on the listing with the underlying records to determine that it is an accurate representation of the records from which the listing was prepared.

Analytical procedures

Tests of details are usually planned on the basis that the analytical procedures confirm expectations. It is best to perform analytical procedures early in the final audit so the auditor can determine any changes needed to tests of details before starting that part of the audit.

As explained in the case of receivables in chapter 14, the first stage in applying analytical procedures is to review the understanding of the entity obtained during the planning phase as to whether any changes to payables balances are to be expected. The second stage is to identify absolute changes in amounts between the current year and previous years. This is normally done in the course of preparing the lead schedule for payables and payroll balances, as we explained in chapter 8. The third stage involves the use of more sophisticated relationships such as ratios and trends. As with receivables, the gross profit ratio is important. If it is higher than expected, then one explanation could be an understatement of purchases (such as by a deliberate cut-off error) in order to boost revenues.

Analysis of expense accounts is also important. The auditor usually undertakes this analysis by comparing the ratio of each expense to sales in the current year with that in previous years. In this way, the effect of changes in the level of activity is largely eliminated. An unusually low expense account may indicate unrecorded liabilities through cut-off error; for example, if the final quarter's electricity account has not been paid or allowed for then the current year's electricity expense will appear unusually low compared with that for the previous year. Wherever a change in relationships cannot be readily explained, the auditor must seek an explanation from management and corroborate it, usually by conducting additional tests of details.

Analytical procedures are significant in achieving the desired level of detection risk for payroll balances. Particularly useful ratios are those of the average wages per employee, which should not be dissimilar from previous years, subject only to known wage rises, and payroll expenses as a percentage of sales.

Tests of details of transactions

As explained in chapter 14 in the case of receivables, balances affected by numerous transactions are more efficiently verified by tests of the closing balance and not by tests of the transactions making up that balance. In the main, the auditor performs the tests of details of transactions during the interim audit, commonly in the form of dual-purpose tests. For this reason, no substantive tests of details of payroll transactions are described here, because the tests of controls described earlier also constitute the main sources of substantive evidence for payroll transactions. The cut-off tests now described are always performed as part of year-end work and, although they are tests of transactions, they serve to verify the recorded balance at the end of the reporting period.

Vouching recorded payables to supporting documentation

The emphasis of these tests is on vouching purchase transactions to supporting documentation in the entity's files (such as purchase orders, receiving reports and suppliers' invoices) to verify their occurrence as legitimate transactions. It is equally important, however, to test the numerical continuity of purchase orders and receiving reports, and to trace them to suppliers' invoices and accounts payable to verify completeness.

Performing purchases cut-off test

The **purchases cut-off test** involves determining that purchase transactions occurring near the end of the reporting period are recorded in the proper period. Most entities hold their books open for a certain period to ensure that purchase transactions are recorded in the correct accounting period. When the books are closed, unmatched receiving reports and purchase orders are scrutinised and, if they relate to the current period, they are recorded by way of journal entry. Unlike receivables, it may take several weeks before all transactions occurring before the end of the reporting period are invoiced by the suppliers. Because cut-off is significant only at the end of the reporting period, most entities do not have effective controls to ensure an accurate distinction between the recording of transactions before and after that date. Acceptable detection risk is likely to be low, and extensive tests of details will be performed. The emphasis is on completeness, which is achieved by tracing receiving reports issued in the days immediately before the end of the reporting period to purchases journal entries or to the closing journal entry of purchase accruals. This procedure provides evidence that they are recorded in the current accounting period.

Because many purchases do not result in the issue of a receiving report (such as services), purchases after the end of the reporting period are vouched to supporting documentation to ensure that they do not relate to goods or services received before the end of the reporting period.

Although the emphasis of the test is on completeness, the auditor also traces some receiving reports issued after the year-end to suppliers' invoices, to ensure that they are recorded in the next period's purchase transactions file. In addition, the auditor vouches recorded purchases before the end of the reporting period to receiving reports dated before the end of the reporting period, to ensure that no transactions that occurred after the period are recorded before the end of the reporting period. This provides evidence as to the occurrence assertion. These tests usually cover a period of 5 to 10 business days before the end of the reporting period and as long after as appears necessary. In performing this test, the auditor should determine that a proper cut-off is achieved at the physical inventory count (as explained in chapter 16) as well as in the recording of the purchase transactions. Where inventory is counted other than at the end of the reporting period, the auditor needs to check cut-off for purchases of inventory at the stocktake date as well as at the end of the reporting period.

Performing payments cut-off test

A proper cut-off of payment transactions at the year-end is essential to the correct presentation of cash and accounts payable at the end of the reporting period. The usual method of verifying payments cut-off is to examine the date of presentation of cheques unpresented as at the end of the reporting period. This test is normally performed as part of the test of the bank reconciliation and the use of the next period's bank statement (see chapter 17).

Tests of details of balances

The three tests included in this category for payables are:
1. reconciling payables with monthly statements received by the entity from suppliers
2. confirming accounts payable
3. searching for unrecorded liabilities.

The two tests for payroll balances are:
1. recalculating payroll liabilities
2. verifying directors' and executive officers' remuneration.

LEARNING 9
objective

Explain the use of suppliers' statements in verifying the completeness of recorded liabilities.

Reconciling payables with suppliers' statements

In many cases, suppliers provide monthly statements that are available in entity files. As documentary evidence originating outside the entity, suppliers' statements provide reliable evidence as to suppliers' balances. However, because they are obtained from the entity, the auditor needs to be cautious that the statements have not been altered, and should not rely on photocopies and faxed statements. Where there is doubt, a copy should be requested directly from the supplier or the balance confirmed directly with the supplier.

In the selection of accounts for testing, the criterion should be the volume of business during the year, not the balance shown in the entity's accounts payable listing, because the main concern is that the recorded balance may be understated.

Discrepancies between suppliers' statements and the entity's accounts payable ledger need to be investigated. Most differences are likely to be due to goods and cash in transit and to disputed amounts. This procedure provides evidence as to the existence, completeness and valuation assertions.

Confirming accounts payable

Unlike the confirmation of receivables, the **confirmation of accounts payable** is performed less frequently because:
- confirmation offers no assurance that unrecorded liabilities will be discovered
- external evidence in the form of invoices and suppliers' monthly statements should be available to substantiate the balances.

Confirmation of accounts payable is recommended (1) when detection risk is low and (2) for suppliers with which the entity undertook a substantial level of business during the current or previous years and that do not issue monthly statements, and for suppliers for which the statement at the end of the reporting period is unexpectedly unavailable.

As in the case of confirming receivables, the auditor must control the preparation and mailing of the requests and should receive the responses directly from the supplier. The auditor should use the positive form in making the confirmation request, as illustrated in figure 15.4. Note that the confirmation does not specify the amount due. In confirming a creditor, the auditor prefers to have the creditor indicate the amount due because that is the amount to be reconciled to the entity's records. Information is also requested regarding purchase commitments of the entity and any collateral for the amount due. This test produces evidence for all assertions relating to payables. However, the evidence provided about the completeness assertion is limited, given the possible failure to identify and send confirmation requests to suppliers with which the entity has unrecorded obligations.

Searching for unrecorded liabilities

The major procedure for identifying unrecorded liabilities is the examination of the next period's purchase and payment transactions as described earlier under cut-off tests. Analytical procedures may also identify unexpected differences between the current year's and the previous year's expense or liability balances, which could indicate the presence of unrecorded liabilities. An analysis of rent expense, for example, may indicate that only three quarterly payments have been made, suggesting that the fourth quarter's rent needs to be allowed for. Similarly, a comparison of accruals and prepayments may identify differences arising from the failure to make a closing entry in the current year.

PO Box 1777
Habitat
Homeland

4 July 2015

Supplier Limited
2001 Lakeview Drive
Bigtown

Dear Sir or Madam
Will you please send directly to our auditors, Reddy & Abel, an itemised statement of the amount owed to you by us at the close of business on 30 June 2015. Please also supply the following information:

Amount not yet due $..

Amount past due $..

Amount of purchase commitments $..

Description of any collateral held...

....

....

A business reply envelope addressed to our auditors is enclosed. A prompt reply will be very much appreciated.

Yours faithfully
Controller

FIGURE 15.4:
Accounts payable
confirmation

An examination of contractual commitments may also alert the auditor to the existence of liabilities not yet provided for, such as progress payments on long-term contracts, or amounts accrued but not yet due or invoiced under a franchise agreement.

Chapter 18 describes procedures known as the subsequent-events review and the review for contingent liabilities. Both procedures contribute to the search for unrecorded liabilities.

Recalculating payroll liabilities

It is necessary for many entities to make a variety of accrual entries at the end of the reporting period for amounts owed to officers and employees for salaries and wages, commissions, bonuses, holiday pay and so on, and for amounts owed to government agencies for income tax deductions. Although the auditor's main concern regarding payroll expenses for the year is with overstatement, the main concern regarding the year-end accruals is with understatement. Also of concern is consistency in the methods of calculating the accrued amounts from one period to the next. In obtaining evidence concerning the reasonableness of management's accruals, the auditor should review management's calculations or make independent calculations. Additional evidence can be obtained by examining subsequent payments made for the accruals before the completion of fieldwork. Evidence obtained from these procedures relates mainly to the valuation assertion.

Verifying directors' and executive officers' remuneration

Directors' and executive officers' remuneration is audit-sensitive for the following reasons.

- Directors' remuneration must be disclosed in the financial statements of all companies under the *Corporations Act 2001*.
- Directors and executive officers may be able to override controls and receive salaries, bonuses, share options and other forms of compensation in excess of authorised amounts.

For these reasons, the auditor should compare the authorisations of the board of directors for directors' and executive officers' salaries and other forms of compensation with recorded amounts. This procedure relates to all assertions.

Disclosure

Each major class of creditors and borrowings must be disclosed. These are likely to include bank overdrafts, bank loans, accounts payable, lease liabilities, taxation and employees benefits. In addition, disclosure must be made of the amount of each class of liability secured by a charge and the nature of the security. If accounts payable balances include material advance payments for future goods and services, such amounts should be reported as advances to suppliers and classified under current assets.

Learning check

Do you know . . .

15.5 ☐ The greatest inherent risks are those of fraudulent purchases for private use by an employee, understatement of credit purchase transactions and the payables balance, and payments to fictitious employees. Given the volume of transactions, most entities ensure their internal control structure relating to such matters is effective.

15.6 ☐ Testing the design effectiveness of controls is achieved by evaluating the system with the aid of a list of potential misstatements and suggested control procedures. Possible misstatements include payment for goods not ordered or received and payment to fictitious employees.

15.7 ☐ Analytical procedures require the determination of expectations and the comparison of amounts, trends and ratios, particularly the gross profit ratio and the analysis of expense accounts. For payroll balances, analytical procedures may be sufficient without the need for further tests of details. An important payroll ratio is that of average wages per employee.

15.8 ☐ Test of details of transactions are largely dual-purposes tests performed at the interim audit, except the cut-off tests of transactions either side of the end of the reporting period. Unlike sales, cut-off tests for purchases need to be extended considerably into the next period.

15.9 ☐ The main test of details of balances is the comparison of purchase ledger balances with suppliers' statements. Only if suppliers' statements are unavailable would auditors ordinarily obtain confirmation directly from the supplier.

SUMMARY

Purchase and payroll transactions constitute the major source of expenditure for most entities, and the balances of accounts payable constitutes a major liability. In auditing these transactions and the account balances, the auditor uses techniques that were explained in chapters 8–12. This chapter follows the audit approach required by ASA 315 (ISA 315). The audit process starts with obtaining an understanding of this system. The auditor also considers issues relating to materiality, inherent risk and the control environment before determining the appropriate audit strategy. For purchases and payroll transactions, materiality is invariably high.

For audit purposes, the most significant inherent risk is that of understatement of purchase transactions and accounts payable balances in order to boost reported profits and enhance liquidity. For the entity, the greatest inherent risk is that of improper purchasing and payments to fictitious employees. The auditor considers the control environment factors of integrity and ethical values, commitment to competence, management's philosophy and operating style, assignment of authority and responsibility, and personnel policies and practices as they relate to purchases and payroll.

The next stage of the audit is the determination of an audit strategy, which, for purchases and payroll, is likely to be one based on a lower assessed level of control risk. The first step in assessing control risk is to evaluate design effectiveness. Evaluation checklists are used, which suggest potential misstatements for each function in the processing of purchases, payments and payroll. The auditor compares the control procedures in the entity's information system with necessary controls identified by the checklist in assessing design effectiveness. At this point, the auditor drafts the audit program based on the preliminary assessment of control risk, identifying both tests of the operating effectiveness of controls and the reduced level of substantive procedures relevant to the assessed level of control risk. The assessed level of control risk is confirmed on completion of the tests of operating effectiveness. The final stage of the audit is the performance of substantive procedures. It is usually more cost-effective to test the balance of accounts payable than to test the transaction making up that balance.

The most important test of transactions is that of cut-off at the year-end. The major test of balances is the examination of suppliers' statements. Because these are documentary evidence received from third parties, they are moderately reliable; however, the auditor needs to be alert to the possibility that such statements may be forged or altered by the entity.

Finally, the auditor must also verify directors' and officers' salaries.

KEY TERMS

accounts payable master file, p. 627

cheque summary, p. 629

confirmation of accounts
   payable, p. 650

employee earnings master file, p. 632

payment transactions file, p. 629

payroll register, p. 632

payroll transactions file, p. 632

personnel authorisation form, p. 630

personnel data master file, p. 630

personnel file, p. 630

purchase requisitions, p. 625

purchase transactions file, p. 627

purchases cut-off test, p. 649

receiving report, p. 626

remittance advice, p. 629

suppliers' invoices, p. 627

termination notice, p. 632

MULTIPLE-CHOICE questions

15.1 The specific audit objective 'accounts payable are liabilities of the entity at the end of the reporting period' is derived from the:
A. Completeness assertion.
B. Valuation or measurement assertion.
C. Rights and obligations assertion.
D. Presentation or disclosure assertion.

15.2 The receiving department should be instructed not to accept goods without having on file a properly authorised:
A. Purchase requisition.
B. Invoice.
C. Receiving report.
D. Purchase order.

15.3 Purchase orders become part of the transaction trail of documentary evidence that directly supports which assertion for purchase transactions?
A. Accuracy or valuation assertion.
B. Existence or occurrence assertion.
C. Presentation or disclosure assertion.
D. Rights and obligations assertion.

15.4 Responsibility for determining that unpaid suppliers' invoices are processed for payment on their due dates generally lies with:
A. The chief finance officer's department.
B. The accounts department.
C. The purchasing department.
D. The internal audit department.

15.5 Which of these is not a procedure for identifying unrecorded liabilities?
A. Examination of the subsequent period's purchase and payment transactions.
B. Analytical procedures for expense and liability balances.
C. Examination of contractual commitments.
D. Confirmation of accounts payable balance to invoices.

15.6 Segregation of the functions of payroll and personnel do all of the following, except:
A. Reduce the risk of payments to fictitious employees.
B. Reduce the risk of payments to terminated employees.
C. Restrict the recording of new employee data to the payroll department.
D. Restrict the payment of wages to the payroll department.

15.7 Controls over the recording of cash payments include which of the following?
A. An independent check by the accounting supervisor of the agreement of the amounts journalised and posted to accounts payable with the cheque/bank transfer summary received from the accountant.
B. An independent check of the agreement of the total of cheques issued/bank transfers made with a batch total of the vouchers processed for payment.
C. The cheque signer (where cheques are used) should control the mailing of the cheques.
D. Cheques (where used) should be prenumbered.

15.8 Responsibility for updating of the personnel data master file should rest with authorised employees in the:

A. Personnel department.
B. Payroll department.
C. Controller's department.
D. Employee's operating department.

15.9 A programmed routine in the edit run for payroll lists all employees who worked more than 50 hours during the week for review. This is an example of:

A. A reasonableness test.
B. A validity test.
C. A sequence test.
D. A self-checking test.

15.10 Test data may be used to test application controls over accepting and recording data for unpaid suppliers' invoices. Which of the following conditions would not be relevant?

A. Numerical characters in an alphanumeric field.
B. Missing or invalid supplier numbers.
C. Missing due date or payment terms.
D. Alphabetical characters in a numerical field.

REVIEW questions

15.11 By reference to management assertions, state the main audit objectives for: (1) purchases and payroll transactions and (2) accounts payable balances.

15.12 Explain the importance of segregating the personnel function from wages preparation.

15.13 Describe programmed application controls you would expect to find in a computerised payroll system. Explain the audit procedures for testing those controls.

15.14 Describe computer-assisted audit procedures that can be used in testing controls over purchasing.

15.15 Explain why the assessment of control risk for the occurrence of payment transactions affects the assessed level of control risk for the completeness of the accounts payable balance.

15.16 Describe the performance of the purchases cut-off test.

15.17 It is increasingly common for companies to use online banking to make payments to suppliers. As an auditor, describe controls you would expect to find in place over such a system.

15.18 Explain how analytical review procedures can be applied to the payroll expenses in the income statement.

15.19 Explain the key assertion at risk with regard to payables balances.

15.20 Explain why achieving an accurate cut-off of purchases and sales transactions is of critical importance in assuring the fairness of financial statements. Illustrate your explanation with examples of the effect of cut-off errors.

15.21 Purchase controls   ★★

Your firm is the external auditor of TangleWeb Ltd, which manufactures electrical devices for the airline industry. You have been asked to give advice on the internal controls that should be in place to control payments to suppliers arising from the purchase of components.

The purchase process has five distinct phases: (1) the inventory system flags when new stock is needed and automatically raises a purchase request, (2) the purchasing department place orders with suppliers, (3) the goods are received in the warehouse, (4) the purchase invoices are received by the finance department, (5) the finance department arranges payment of approved invoices.

Required

(a) Describe the procedures that should be in operation in the purchasing department to control the purchase orders and in the warehouse to control receipt of goods.

(b) Describe the controls the finance department should exercise over obtaining authorisation of purchase invoices before posting them to the accounts payable ledger.

15.22 Internal control evaluation — cash payments   ★★

The internal auditor of the Jerry Bowen group of companies is carrying out a review of the internal controls applied by some of the group's subsidiaries in relation to purchases. Work has just been completed in relation to Mangus Opum Pty Ltd, one of the manufacturing businesses and the auditor has provided a summary of her findings:

1. The purchasing department has three staff, one supervisor and two assistants who prepare orders from requisitions issued by the stores department.
2. Orders are placed on prenumbered purchase order forms.
3. A completed copy of the purchase order is sent to the stores department and when goods are received the storeperson sends a copy of the delivery note to the purchasing department, stamped 'Received'.
4. A copy of the purchase order and the delivery note are sent to the finance department to be matched with the invoice.
5. Once invoices are checked they are sent to the operations manager for approval.
6. Signed invoices for payment are returned to the finance department, which prepares a bank EFT file and uploads the file onto the online banking system.
7. A copy of the EFT is emailed to the operations manager who then logs on to the online banking system to authorise the payments.

Required

For each of the payment system procedures listed above, critically evaluate each step in the process identifying strengths and weaknesses in the system and make suggestions for improvements.

15.23 Accounts payable — substantive testing   ★★

You are the audit senior for the audit of Grosse Ltd and have been given the audit file to review. The reporting date is 30 June 2015 and the materiality for the client has been set at $200 000. You obtained the information listed below from your review of the audit file.

1. The balance noted for accounts payable in the general ledger at 30 June 2015 is $158 000, which compares with a balance as at 30 June 2014 of $342 000.
2. The audit assistant noted in the file: 'Because the accounts payable balance is immaterial in the current year, only limited work is necessary.'
3. The only work performed by the audit assistant was to select the three largest payables from the client's detailed purchases ledger (which had been compared with the general ledger) and compare the balances with photocopies of supplier statements.

Required

(a) Outline any queries you would raise with the audit assistant.

(b) Describe the additional audit procedures you believe should be performed to ensure that the accounts payable balance is fairly stated.[6]

15.24 Payroll control and substantive testing ★★

You are reviewing the audit work for Dream Weevel Ltd — a design house with 50 staff in various office locations. Dream Weevel Ltd outsources its payroll process to an online payroll services provider.

Staff are paid fortnightly. At the end of each fortnight each staff member must log on to the online system run by the payroll services provider and record hours worked and leave taken. Each individual is linked to a supervisor who receives an email notification that a member of their staff has completed a time submission. Supervisors must log onto the system to approve their staffs' time records. Once these records are approved they will be available to the payroll service provider's staff to process payroll.

Once the payroll has been processed, various files are made available to the finance team of Dream Weevel Ltd by again logging on to the payroll provider's software. The files include: (1) a report of hours worked and leave taken, (2) a variance report comparing this payroll to the previous fortnight highlighting differences, (3) a full payroll, (4) a general ledger journal, (5) a bank payment file for upload onto online banking.

Once the finance team approves the files a request is sent to the managing director who then logs on and can approve the payroll. The finance manager prints out a copy of the payroll and asks the managing director to sign it. The signed copy is then filed in the finance department.

Your audit assistant performed a month-to-month comparison of salary costs and has found no abnormal trends. The following conclusion was noted on the working paper: 'I have checked that all payroll reports from the period were reviewed and signed by the managing director. This, in conjunction with the results of analytical review, led me to conclude that the payroll expense is fairly stated.'

Required

(a) Outline any queries you would raise with the audit assistant.

(b) Describe the additional audit procedures you believe should be performed to ensure that payroll is fairly stated.

15.25 Payroll system — substantive testing ★★

MO has a high volume of casual staff who work during peak season who are needed to support the increase in workload in the following main areas:

1. distribution: warehouse staff to pack, store and receive goods
2. drivers: to deliver goods to retail stores
3. sales and marketing: MO representatives to operate at the retail stores to sell the range of products and manage the stock
4. administration: data operators and clerical staff to process the purchase orders and sales orders.

Other relevant facts about MO's employee profile include the following.

1. The peak selling periods when casual staff are required represent approximately eight months of the year. For the last three years the average number of casual staff has been 120 per annum.
2. The turnover of permanent staff is approximately 15 per annum. There are currently 75 permanent staff of the payroll. The numbers have risen by 20% in the last two years.

3. There are a variety of industrial awards that support the wage and salary conditions of MO staff, depending on whether they are casual or permanent and whether they work in the warehouse or in the office. Casual staff do not receive annual or long service leave entitlements.

Required:

Your team has identified payroll expense as a high risk area, so for the payroll expense:

(a) Identify two key assertions at risk with respect to the casual employees and provide a brief explanation as to why they are at risk.

(b) For each assertion, describe a specific practical substantive test of detail that would be appropriate to address the risk.

(c) Given the information above, do you consider the use of analytical review to be appropriate and effective in relation to MO' payroll expense? Justify your answer.[7]

15.26 Accounts payable — substantive testing ★★

Your firm is the auditor of JebStone Minter Ltd, and you are planning the audit work you will carry out in verifying accounts payable and accruals at the company's year-end of 30 June 2015. You are aware that 30 June is one of the busiest times of year for the company and while a full stocktake is carried out the company does not stop trading at the year-end.

The company operates from a single site and all raw materials for production are received by the goods inward department. When the materials are received, they are checked for quantity and quality against the delivery note and purchase order, and a multicopy receiving report is made out and signed by the store manager. If there are any problems with the raw materials, then a discrepancy note is raised that gives details of any problems (e.g. incorrect quantities or faulty materials).

The purchases department receives the suppliers' invoices, checks them against the purchase order and receiving report, and posts them to the purchases ledger. At the end of each month, payments are made to suppliers. The purchases ledger is maintained on a microcomputer.

Required

Identify the key assertions at risk and describe audit procedures that you would carry out at the year end to satisfy yourself that the payables and accruals balances are fairly stated.

15.27 Computer information system controls — purchasing and cash payments ★★★

You are the auditor of Sofasellers Ltd, which buys furniture from manufacturers for sale to the public. You have been asked to audit certain aspects of the computerised purchasing and accounts payable system.

The company has a head office, a warehouse and many shops throughout the country. Furniture from manufacturers may be delivered to the warehouse or direct to individual shops. Details of goods received are entered into computer terminals at the warehouse or shop, which are online with the head office main computer.

The computerised purchasing system involves the following six processes.

1. The user department (shop or warehouse) sends a purchase requisition to the buying department at head office.

2. The buying department issues a purchase order, which is sent to the supplier and recorded on the computer.

3. On delivery, the goods are checked by the receiving department in the shop or warehouse and a receiving report is raised, entered into the computer system and allocated against the order.

4. On receipt of the invoice, the head office accounts department sends it to the user department, which authorises it and returns it to the accounts department. Invoice details are then recorded on the computer, which posts it to the accounts payable ledger.

5. The computer system allows payment only if the system has recorded:
    (a) the purchase order
    (b) receipt of the goods.
6. When the purchase invoice is due for payment, the computer prints the cheque and remittance advice.

Cheques are automatically produced, so the partner in charge of the audit has asked you to identify controls over authorising purchase invoices and changing suppliers' details on the computer's standing data file. He has explained that 'application controls' comprise controls exercised by the company's staff and by the computer.

Required

(a) Describe the application controls you would expect to find in operation from raising the purchase requisition to the computer accepting the purchase invoice.
(b) Explain the controls that should be exercised over access to the main computer from terminals in the head office and at the shops.
(c) Describe the application controls that should be exercised over changing supplier details on the standing data file on the computer. You should consider:
    (i) why such controls are important and how a fraud could be perpetrated in the absence of effective controls
    (ii) the controls you would expect to find over changing supplier details and ensuring supplier details are correct. Your answer should include consideration of controls over access to the computer to perform these tasks.[8]

 CASE studies

15.28 Purchases — computer information system control and audit ★★★

You are the audit senior on the MM Ltd audit. MM is a distributor of hair care products including shampoos, conditioners and mousses. MM uses an online computer system. No goods are manufactured in-house; rather, MM maintains a stock of raw materials and subcontracts the manufacture of its products to third parties. Approximately 50 suppliers and subcontractors are used, and all have proven to be reliable. You have made the following notes about the inventory system.

1. Separate systems, staff and warehouses are maintained for both finished goods and raw materials.

Procedures for raw materials
2. Purchase orders are automatically generated by the computer when stocks of any raw material fall below 70% of the previous month's usage. The purchase orders contain the date, the supplier's name and address, and the raw materials needed. Three copies are produced and distributed to:
    • the warehouse to enable follow-up of late orders
    • the accounts clerk for filing by date order
    • the supplier.
3. When raw materials stock is received, the barcode attached to the delivery boxes by the supplier is scanned into the system. A two-part receiving report is produced that is:
    • matched to the warehouse copy of the order by stores staff
    • filed by the accounts clerk.
4. The scanning process is aborted if the codes do not match those on the master file.

Procedures for finished goods

5. Purchase orders are automatically generated when finished goods fall below 60% of the previous month's sales. The production orders contain the date, the subcontractor's name, the raw materials required and the finished goods needed. Two copies are produced and distributed to:
   - the raw materials store for use as a picking slip, and then packed with the goods and sent to the subcontractor
   - the production controller to be filed in date order.
6. When the finished goods stocks are received, the barcodes attached to the delivery boxes by the subcontractor are scanned into the system. A two-part receiving report is produced that is:
   - matched to the production controller's copy of the order
   - filed by the accounts clerk.
7. The scanning process is aborted if the codes do not match those on the master file.

General notes

8. The computer automatically selects the supplier/subcontractor of both raw materials and finished goods based on the latest price (as per their most recent invoice) and their delivery times (based on the number of days between the date on which the purchase/production order is raised and the date on which the goods are scanned by the warehouse).
   Password access is as follows:

Stores staff (raw materials)	Purchase order printing for raw materials only
	Receiving report printing for raw materials
Stores staff (finished goods)	Receiving report printing for finished goods
Production controller	Production order printing; master file amendments
Accounts clerk	Master file amendments

Master file amendments

9. The stock master file contains details of existing stock items, including the code and warehouse location, and approved suppliers and subcontractors.
10. Orders will be generated only to the suppliers and subcontractors recorded on the master file.
11. Master file changes are made by the production controller for both the raw materials inventory and the finished goods inventory. A master file amendment form is completed by the production controller as a record of the changes made.

Required

(a) Identify any weaknesses in the internal controls described. Discuss the implications of each weakness you identify.
(b) Assume your computer information system audit division is to perform testing of controls for the inventory systems described. Identify key controls that you would recommend for testing.
(c) Assuming the use of generalised audit software, list the procedures/reports you would ask the computer information system auditors to run to help you test the valuation of inventory.[9]

15.29 Accounts payable — substantive testing ★★★

You are the audit senior in charge of the audit of Black Ltd, and you are auditing the company's trade creditors at 30 June 2015. A junior member of the audit team has been checking suppliers' statements against the balances in the purchases ledger. He is unable to reconcile a material balance relating to White Ltd, and has asked for your help and suggestions on the audit work that should be carried out on the differences. The balance of White Ltd in Black's purchases ledger is shown opposite.

Supplier: White Ltd

Date	Type	Reference	Status	Dr	Cr	Balance
10.4	Invoice	6004	Paid 1		2130	
18.4	Invoice	6042	Paid 1		1525	
23.4	Invoice	6057	Paid 1		2634	
4.5	Invoice	6080	Paid 2		3572	
15.5	Invoice	6107	Paid 2		1632	
26.5	Invoice	6154	Paid 2		924	
31.5	Payment	Cheque	Alloc. 1	6163		
	Discount		Alloc. 1	126		
14.6	Invoice	6285			2156	
21.6	Invoice	6328			3824	
30.6	Payment	Cheque	Alloc. 2	6005		
	Discount		Alloc. 2	123		
30.6	Balance					5980

Below are the details on White's suppliers' statement.

Customer: Black Ltd

Date	Type	Reference	Status	Dr	Cr	Balance
7.4	Invoice	6004	Paid 1	2130		
16.4	Invoice	6042	Paid 1	1525		
22.4	Invoice	6057	Paid 1	2634		
2.5	Invoice	6080	Paid 2	3752		
13.5	Invoice	6107	Paid 2	1632		
22.5	Invoice	6154	Paid 2	924		
10.6	Receipt	Cheque	Alloc. 1		6163	
4.6	Invoice	6210	Alloc. 1	4735		
12.6	Invoice	6285		2156		
18.6	Invoice	6328	Alloc. 2	3824		
28.6	Invoice	6355	Alloc. 2	6298		
30.6	Balance					23 447

White's terms of trade with Black allow a 2% cash discount on invoices where White receives a cheque from the customer by the end of the month following the date of the invoice (i.e. a 2% discount will be given on May invoices paid by 30 June).

On Black's purchase ledger, under 'Status', the cash and discount marked 'Alloc. 1' pay invoices marked 'Paid 1' (similarly for 'Alloc. 2' and 'Paid 2'). Black's receiving department checks the goods when they arrive and issues a receiving report. A copy of the report is sent to the purchases accounting department.

Required

(a) Prepare a statement reconciling the balance on Black's purchases ledger to the balance on White's supplier's statement.

(b) Describe the audit work you will carry out on each of the reconciling items you have determined in your answer to (a) to determine the balance that should be included in the financial statements.

(c) In relation to verifying trade creditors:
  (i) consider the basis you will use for selecting suppliers' statements to check against the balances on the purchase ledger
  (ii) describe what action you will take if you find there is no supplier's statement for a material balance on the purchase ledger.[10]

RESEARCH question

15.30 Earnings management

A generally accepted definition of earnings management is the planned timing of revenues, expenses, gains and losses to smooth out earnings over a number of accounting periods. Generally speaking, earnings management is used to increase income in the current year at the expense of income in future years by, for example, prematurely recognising sales before they are complete in order to boost profits. However, earnings management can also be used to decrease current earnings, so as to increase income in the future, a practice often referred to as 'cookie jar' accounting. For example, WorldCom Inc., one of the greatest US corporate bankruptcies, used so-called cookie jar accounting to inflate provisions for expected expenses and later reversed them to boost earnings.

Required

Consider the issues that lead to earnings management and, in particular, the reasons for companies adopting 'cookie jar' accounting practices. How might auditors overcome such practices? In your discussion, make reference to widely publicised corporate collapses such as WorldCom and HIH, which have used earnings management techniques.

NOTES

1. 'Blackstone's Schwarzman tops US CEO payroll', *The Age*, 14 August 2009, www.theage.com.au.
2. ibid.
3. Healy, P, 'The effect of bonus schemes on accounting decisions', *Journal of Accounting and Economics 7*, April 1985, pp. 85–107.
4. Suite101.com, 'Be wary of fake invoice fraud', www.suite101.com, viewed 17 December 2010.
5. Smart Company, 'Clive Peeters hit by $20 million employee fraud — how you can avoid getting stung', www.smartcompany.com.au, viewed 17 December 2010.
6. Adapted from Professional Year Programme of the ICAA, 1999, Accounting 2 Module.

7. Adapted from Professional Year Programme of the ICAA, 1997, Accounting 2 Module.
8. Adapted from ACCA Audit Framework, Paper 6, December 1994.
9. Adapted from Professional Year Programme of the ICAA, 1999, Advanced Audit Module.
10. Adapted from ACCA Audit Framework, Paper 6, June 1996.

Answers to multiple-choice questions

15.1 *C*   15.2 *D*   15.3 *B*   15.4 *B*   15.5 *D*   15.6 *C*   15.7 *A*   15.8 *A*
15.9 *A*   15.10 *D*

chapter 16

Auditing inventories and property, plant and equipment

OVERVIEW

16.1 Brief summary of audit procedures

16.2 Inventory

16.3 Property, plant and equipment

Summary

Key terms

Multiple-choice questions

Review questions

Professional application questions

Case studies

Research question

Further reading

Notes

LEARNING objectives

After studying this chapter, you should be able to:

1 identify the audit objectives applicable to inventories

2 explain the nature of inventory records

3 describe procedures to be followed at an inventory count

4 discuss considerations relevant to determining the audit strategy for inventories

5 describe procedures to be followed when observing an inventory count

6 explain the audit procedures for verifying inventory pricing

7 identify the audit objectives applicable to property, plant and equipment

8 discuss considerations relevant to determining the audit strategy for property, plant and equipment

9 design a substantive audit program for property, plant and equipment.

PROFESSIONAL STATEMENTS

Australian		International	
ASA 315	*Identifying and Assessing the Risks of Material Misstatement through Understanding the Entity and Its Environment*	ISA 315	*Identifying and Assessing the Risks of Material Misstatement through Understanding the Entity and Its Environment*
ASA 501	*Audit Evidence — Specific Considerations for Inventory and Segment Information*	ISA 501	*Audit Evidence — Specific Considerations for Selected Items*
ASA 510	*Initial Audit Engagements — Opening Balances*	ISA 510	*Initial Audit Engagements — Opening Balances*
ASA 540	*Auditing Accounting Estimates, Including Fair Value Accounting Estimates, and Related Disclosures*	ISA 540	*Auditing Accounting Estimates, Including Fair Value Accounting Estimates, and Related Disclosures*
ASA 600	*Special Considerations — Audits of a Group Financial Report (Including the Work of Component Auditors)*	ISA 600	*Special Considerations — Audits of Group Financial Statements (Including the Work of Component Auditors)*
ASA 610	*Using the Work of Internal Auditors*	ISA 610	*Using the Work of Internal Auditors*
ASA 620	*Using the Work of an Auditor's Expert*	ISA 620	*Using the Work of an Auditor's Expert*
AASB 102	*Inventories*	IAS 2	*Inventories*
AASB 116	*Property, Plant and Equipment*	IAS 16	*Property, Plant and Equipment*
AASB 117	*Leases*	IAS 17	*Leases*
AASB 136	*Impairment of Assets*	IAS 36	*Impairment of Assets*

SCENE SETTER

Sims shares slashed after $60m British inventory fraud

Sims Metal Management has launched an investigation into potential fraudulent conduct after finding the value of its British inventory had been 'materially overstated', resulting in adjustments of about $60 million.

Investors punished the world's biggest listed metal recycler following the news, sending its shares 5.01 per cent lower on the Australian market yesterday to close at $9.48.

The company said the inventory in question was predominantly associated with the company's recycling solutions business at Long Marston near Birmingham in England and Newport near Cardiff in Wales. The businesses recycle electronics, including computers and televisions.

Sims said it expected the inventory adjustment to be about $60m and that it related to both changes in the assessment of the new realisable value of certain stock and to physical adjustments.

'The preliminary findings indicate the situation has arisen in the context of control failures and potential fraudulent conduct by local and regional plant management responsible for technology and downstream processing systems in the UK,' the company said.

Sims said it had set up a special committee of the board to run the investigation, headed by chairman Geoff Brunsdon and assisted by external auditor PricewaterhouseCoopers and legal advisers Baker & McKenzie.

Source: S Tasker, 'Sims shares slashed after $60m British inventory fraud', *The Australian*, 22 January 2013.

The first half of this chapter deals with the audit of inventories and the second half considers the audit of property, plant and equipment. Audit considerations of the internal control structures of the main transaction classes affecting both account balances have already been described: purchases in the case of inventories and property, plant and equipment assets, and sales in the case of inventories. For this reason, the organisation of the chapter differs from that of the two previous chapters. There is no separate section describing the functions and control procedures for inventory or property, plant and equipment transactions. For inventory, there is a section describing functions and control procedures associated with the custody of inventory and the maintenance of inventory records. In the section on developing the audit plan, the significance of assessing the effectiveness of controls over inventory records is discussed in the context of determining the audit strategy.

For property, plant and equipment, the auditor adopts a predominantly substantive approach to the audit and rarely considers it necessary to examine controls over non-current asset records. The nature of such records is described in the section on developing the audit plan, but there is no assessment of control. The explanation of the audit of property, plant and equipment then proceeds to the design and execution of substantive audit procedures. Given the complex nature of intangible non-current assets, their audit is not dealt with in this text. The audit of non-current investments is the subject of chapter 17.

A feature of both classes of assets is the inherent risk as to their valuation. Thus, verification of the valuation and allocation assertion for these assets receives special consideration.

16.1 BRIEF SUMMARY OF AUDIT PROCEDURES

In the auditing of inventories and property plant and equipment, the key issues are to ensure that:

- the inventories actually exist, are owned and are properly valued
- the property, plant and equipment actually exist, are owned and are properly valued with adequate provision for depreciation.

For entities that rely entirely on a physical inventory count at or near the end of the reporting period, the auditor will adopt a predominantly substantive approach in obtaining evidence as to the existence and completeness of the inventory.

In large entities that maintain comprehensive inventory records, these records may be used as the basis for determining both the quantity and value of inventory at the end of the reporting period. To obtain sufficient audit evidence in such cases, the auditor must perform extensive tests of controls over the recording of inventory transactions and the maintenance of inventory records. However, some physical observation and counting of inventory will still generally be necessary.

Inventory to be counted must be properly identified. This is a particular problem with specialised items or work in process. With work in process, the problem is with identifying the stage of completion, which determines the costs accumulated against the items. Observation of the inventory count is now required by the auditing standards whenever inventories are material to an entity's financial statements and observation is not impracticable. The observation of the count may prove to be inconvenient, time-consuming and difficult for the auditor, but it is seldom impracticable. When it is impracticable for an auditor to observe the count, he or she may perform alternative procedures, such as verifying sales transactions after the inventory count. However, such procedures may not provide the auditor with sufficient appropriate audit evidence as to applicable assertions.

Testing inventory pricing involves verifying the cost of inventory and the net realisable value of the items that management has determined need to be written down. It also involves considering whether other items, whose net realisable value may be below cost, need to be written down. This is a very important procedure as any under- or over-valuation of inventory at the end of the reporting period directly affects the profit (or loss) figure. There are also cut-off procedures to be done by the auditor to ensure there is no inadvertent double counting of inventory and sales. Other tests include inventory turnover, which gives an indication of any obsolescence in the inventory on hand.

Property, plant and equipment are non-current tangible assets intended to be retained for use in the entity's operations. This category of assets includes land and buildings, plant and equipment, and the related accumulated depreciation. Land and buildings may be freehold or leasehold, and plant and equipment may include assets held under finance leases. The main related income statement accounts are depreciation expense, repairs expense, finance charges on finance leases, and rent on operating leases.

In the audit of property, plant and equipment, the opening balances are verified through the preceding year's audit, and changes in the balances are usually relatively few. This contrasts with the audit of current assets, which are subject to numerous transactions and for which the audit effort is concentrated on the closing balance. The auditor relies on the inspection of documentary evidence in verifying additions and disposals, and on mathematical evidence in verifying depreciation. Special attention needs to be given to calculations such as profits and losses on disposals, as these have a direct impact on the income statement. Also, the adequacy of the depreciation charge needs to be checked against the estimated useful life of the asset.

The above briefly summarises the key procedures in the audit of inventory and property, plant and equipment. In practice, the procedures can be more complex and are detailed in the rest of the chapter.

16.2 INVENTORY

In a merchandising entity, inventory consists of goods acquired for resale. In a manufacturing entity, inventory can be in one of three stages:
1. **raw materials** awaiting processing
2. partly manufactured items known as **work in process**
3. **finished goods** awaiting sale.

Smaller entities, particularly those not engaged in manufacturing, may not maintain inventory records. Instead, inventory is determined at or near the end of the reporting period by a count known as a **stocktake** or **physical inventory count**. The main audit procedure in such cases is observation of the count. At the other extreme, large manufacturing entities maintain comprehensive inventory records, with subsidiary inventory ledgers integrated with the general ledger. These records may be used as the basis for determining both the quantity and value of inventory at the end of the reporting period. To obtain sufficient audit evidence in such cases, the auditor must perform extensive tests of controls over the recording of inventory transactions and the maintenance of inventory records.

Obtaining evidence of the existence of inventory through observation is a required audit procedure. The auditor may meet this requirement by observing a number of cyclical counts that the entity undertakes during the year as part of its control procedures over the maintenance of inventory records. Alternatively, where the entity determines inventory by stocktake at or close to year-end, the auditor meets the requirement by attendance at that count.

Verifying the valuation and allocation assertion for inventory is also an important audit procedure. This involves verifying both cost and net realisable value and the judgement by management as to which basis is relevant for each item of inventory.

16.2.1 Audit objectives

Table 16.1 lists the main audit objectives for each assertion, referencing them to specific controls and audit procedures. More detail about assertions specific to transactions and account balances can be found in paragraph A111 of ASA 315 *Identifying and Assessing the Risks of Material Misstatement through Understanding the Entity and Its Environment* (ISA 315).

Note that, for occurrence and completeness, transfer transactions apply only to multi-location entities and manufacturing entities that distinguish between raw materials, work in process and finished goods.

TABLE 16.1:
Selected specific audit objectives for inventory

Transaction objectives	
Occurrence (OE)	Recorded purchases transactions represent inventories acquired during the period (OE1).
	Recorded transfers represent inventories transferred between locations or categories during the period (OE2).
	Recorded sales transactions represent inventories sold during the period (OE3).
Completeness (C)	All inventory receipts during the period have been recorded as purchases (C1).
	All transfers of inventories between locations or categories during the period have been recorded (C2).
	All inventory dispatched during the period have been recorded as sales (C3).
Accuracy (AV)	Inventory transactions are properly (accurately) recorded (AV1).
Cut-off (CO)	Inventories received before the period-end are recorded as purchases in the current period and those received after the period end are included in the next accounting period (CO1).
	Inventories dispatched before the period-end are recorded as sales in the current period and those dispatched after the period-end are included in the next accounting period (CO2).
Classification (PD)	Inventory transactions are recorded in the correct accounts (PD1).
Balances objectives	
Existence (OE)	Inventories recorded represent items on hand at the end of the reporting period (OE4).
Rights and obligations (RO)	The entity has rights to the inventories included in the balance sheet (RO1).
Completeness (C)	Inventories include all materials, products and supplies on hand at the end of the reporting period (C4).
Valuation and allocation (AV)	Inventories are properly stated at the lower of cost and net realisable value, determined in accordance with applicable accounting standards (AV2).

Presentation and disclosure objectives (PD)	
Occurrence and rights and obligations	Disclosed inventories have occurred and pertain to the entity (**PD2**).
Completeness	All inventory disclosures that should have been included in the financial report have been included (**PD3**).
Classification and understandability	Inventories are properly identified and classified in the financial statements (**PD4**).
	Inventories are appropriately presented and information disclosed is clearly expressed (**PD5**).
Accuracy and valuation	Inventories are disclosed accurately and at appropriate amounts (**PD5**).

LEARNING 2 objective

Explain the nature of inventory records.

16.2.2 Recording inventory transactions

The process of obtaining evidence relating to purchases and sales transactions was described in the previous two chapters. For entities that rely entirely on a physical inventory count at or near the end of the reporting period, the auditor will adopt a predominantly substantive approach in obtaining evidence as to the existence and completeness assertions. Where perpetual inventory records are used wholly or partly in determining inventory at the end of the reporting period, it is necessary for the auditor to obtain an understanding of the accounting and internal control systems relating to such records. For non-manufacturing entities, the auditor can rely on records of purchase transactions in obtaining sufficient evidence as to accuracy or valuation and allocation. For manufacturing entities, even where perpetual inventory records are not maintained, the auditor needs to obtain an understanding of the procedures for determining and recording costs of production.

Maintaining inventory records

The use of computer information systems has made it much easier for entities to maintain **perpetual inventory records**, and systems can maintain inventory records by quantity and value, which are fully integrated with the accounting records in an **inventory master file**. For merchandising entities, a single inventory record is required, although this may be subdivided by location. Manufacturing entities need to record separate inventories of raw materials, work in process and finished goods, and to establish procedures for recording the movement of goods through production.

An important control over maintaining inventory records is the segregation of this function from the physical custody of the inventory. The custodian then has no opportunity to conceal an inventory shortage by manipulating the inventory records.

The separate functions are:
- recording the movement of goods into inventory
- recording the movement of goods from inventory
- recording transfers of inventory
- physically comparing inventory with inventory records.

Movement of goods into inventory

In all cases, the initial entry into inventory is through the purchasing system (see chapter 15). The warehouse person acknowledges receipt of the goods by initialling a copy of the receiving report or approving with an electronic signature. The receiving report then provides the source of the quantity and cost entries on the appropriate inventory record. These procedures relate mainly to the occurrence and completeness assertions (**OE1, C1**).

Movement of goods from inventory

When merchandise inventories or finished goods are sold, the dispatch note serves as the basis for authorisation of the release of the goods from inventory, and for the entry in inventory records reducing the quantity on hand. In retail stores, barcodes or security tags scanned at the cash register provide data for reducing recorded inventory. Control procedures as to the occurrence and completeness of sales transactions (see chapter 14) also relate to the occurrence and completeness of recorded inventory movements (**OE3, C3**).

Transfers of inventory

Further procedures are necessary where goods are transferred from one inventory location to another. In manufacturing entities, **inventory transfer requisitions** control the movement of goods from raw materials through work in process to finished goods. These pre-numbered documents are issued by production control and represent authorisation to issue raw materials and to apply direct labour to process materials to produce the finished goods. Each transfer requisition consists of records identifying the specific material and labour requirements for the goods to be produced. Initialled copies of tickets represent acknowledgement, by inventory custodians, of the receipt of goods, or evidence of their proper delivery. They also provide the basis for accounting entries, relieving one inventory location and charging the other. Similar procedures, on a less elaborate scale, are required in retailing entities to record and control internal transfers. All the movements mentioned above are normally tracked electronically through purpose-developed computer programs. These procedures relate to the occurrence and completeness assertions for internal inventory movements (**OE2, C2**).

Physical comparison of inventory with inventory records

Perpetual inventory records need to be compared with actual inventory at regular intervals. The two functions involved are:

- an inventory count (stocktake)
- a comparison with records.

Inventory count

Procedures for an inventory count are similar whether the purpose is to determine inventory at the end of the reporting period or to compare inventory with inventory records at an intermediate date. This section describes procedures applicable to a full inventory count. Procedures for **cyclical inventory counts** may be less thorough and involve counting only a portion of inventory items. The sample selected for counting may be organised systematically, through different sections of the warehouse or different types of inventory, or by random sampling. Another approach is to count items at the reorder point when inventory levels are low, thus reducing both the cost of the count and the likelihood of count errors.

The procedures for an inventory count involve:

- assigning and communicating responsibility
- preparation
- identification
- counting
- checking

- clearing
- recording
- cut-off.

These procedures are described as follows.

- *Assigning and communicating responsibility.* Overall responsibility for the count should be assigned to a person who has no responsibility for either the custody of inventory or the maintenance of inventory records. People involved in the count should also be suitably independent, although warehouse staff may be involved if supervised. The area containing inventory should be subdivided, with count teams assigned to specific sections. Instructions should be drawn up and responsibilities clearly explained to each person involved.

- *Preparation.* Before the count, areas such as the warehouse and shop floor should be tidied, with inventory neatly stacked and items not to be counted (such as scrap or goods held for third parties) removed or clearly marked. Arrangements need to be made to cease production, if possible, and receiving and shipping departments need to be alerted so as to avoid movement of goods to or from those departments during the count. In this way, cut-off errors can be avoided. If an accurate cut-off is not achieved, the physical count may include, for example, goods for which the purchase or production cost is not recorded by the information system until after the count. This could result in an over-statement of inventory.

- *Identification.* Inventory to be counted must be properly identified. This is a particular problem with specialised items or work in process. With work in process, the problem is with identifying the stage of completion, which determines the costs accumulated against the items. Either the goods must be tagged in advance or count teams knowledgeable in the inventory must be assigned to the count in appropriate sections.

- *Counting.* Count teams usually work in pairs where any lifting or moving of items is necessary to ascertain the quantity. Forklift trucks and weighing scales may also need to be available. Instructions should ensure that count teams understand the unit of measurement (e.g. 25-kilogram bags). The degree of thoroughness also needs to be considered — such as whether cartons need to be opened at random or weighed to verify that they are full and the contents are as described.

- *Checking.* Sometimes all counts are double-checked and all discrepancies are re-counted. Where errors are unlikely, only spot checks need to be performed and only counts by those count teams making errors need to be double-checked.

- *Clearing.* As each item is counted, the count team should leave a mark to avoid duplicating the count. On completion of a section, a supervisor should tour the area to ensure no items appear to be uncounted.

- *Recording.* Control over count sheets is particularly important. Three systems are commonly used. Where inventory items are standardised, pre-printed **inventory count sheets** containing descriptions are issued to the count teams, who then complete the sheets by entering the quantity. Another system is to issue blank, prenumbered count sheets. The serial numbers issued to each count team must be noted and checked on completion to ensure that no sheets are missing. Half-filled sheets should be ruled off, and unused sheets should be identified as such to prevent items being added after the count. The third method involves attaching prenumbered, three-part **inventory tags** to each inventory item before the count. The count team enters the description and quantity on the first part of the tag and removes it. The checkers do likewise with the second part, which is compared with the first part. The third part, the stub of the tag, remains attached to the item to enable the supervisor to verify completeness of the count. Again, serial numbers should be fully accounted for. In each case, counters and checkers should be required to sign or initial each count sheet or tag.

- *Cut-off.* Serial numbers of the last prenumbered receiving report, dispatch notes and inventory transfer requisitions issued before the inventory count need to be recorded to ensure that the count is compared with inventory records based on the same documents.

Comparison with records

Comparison with records is of greater importance for cyclical counts, where the aims are to ensure the reliability of the inventory records and to ascertain the effectiveness of procedures designed to ensure accountability for custodianship and record-keeping. With counts undertaken at or near the end of the reporting period, comparison with the records helps identify any major errors in quantities ascertained by the count.

Procedures should require a re-count of material differences. If the difference remains, further investigation is required to ascertain whether the inventory records are in error and why. A record should be maintained of differences and the cause (if known), and the inventory records should be adjusted to agree with the count. This list of errors provides evidence as to the reliability of the records and the possibility of reliance on inventory records in determining inventory at year-end, without the need for a further count.

These procedures relate mainly to the existence assertion (**OE4**) but also contribute to the completeness assertion (**C4**).

Determining and recording inventory costs

For merchandise inventory, procedures relating to measurement in the recording of purchase transactions ensure that proper costs are recorded in inventory records. On sales, the cost of sales should be determined in accordance with the appropriate cost flow assumption, which would normally be either first-in first-out or weighted average. Entities recording cost of sales on a continuing basis will usually rely on computer information systems, which should be programmed to determine the appropriate cost.

Costing of manufactured inventory is far more complex. Procedures are required to:
- determine the cost of materials entered into raw materials
- determine the cost of raw materials transferred to work in process at first-in first-out or weighted average cost
- record costs of direct labour applied to work in process
- identify abnormal waste or spoilage in the production process
- identify manufacturing overhead costs and apportion costs to production departments
- assign overhead costs to work in process using an appropriate absorption rate
- apportion costs to by-products
- relieve work in process and charge finished goods on completion of manufacturing, based on costing procedures such as batch or process costing
- relieve finished goods with the cost of sales at first-in first-out or weighted average.

Some entities record inventory at standard cost and identify differences between standard and actual costs as variances.

In obtaining the understanding of the accounting system, the auditor needs to identify the entity's accounting policy and ascertain the procedures for ensuring that costs are recorded in accordance with that policy. It is also necessary for the auditor to ensure that the policy is consistent with the requirements of AASB 102 *Inventories* (IAS 2). These procedures relate to the accuracy (**AV1**) and valuation and allocation assertion (**AV2**), and contribute to the presentation and disclosure assertion (**PD5**).

16.2.3 Developing the audit plan

The selected approach to the audit of inventory depends on the availability and reliability of inventory records. Consideration of the internal control structure relating to inventory records, described in the previous section, is necessary only where such records exist. In all audits, consideration of the determination of cost records is important.

Materiality and risk

In a manufacturing entity, inventories and cost of sales are usually significant to both the entity's financial position and the results of its operations. Moreover, numerous factors contribute to the risk of misstatements in the assertions for these accounts, including those described below.

- The volume of purchase, manufacturing and sale transactions that affect these accounts is generally high, increasing the opportunities for misstatements to occur.
- There are often contentious valuation and allocation issues such as:
  - the identification, measurement and allocation of indirect materials, labour and manufacturing overhead
  - joint product costs
  - the disposition of cost variances
  - accounting for scrap and wastage.
- Special procedures are sometimes required to determine inventory quantity or value, such as geometric volume measurements of stockpiles using aerial photography, and estimation of value by experts.
- Inventories are often stored at multiple sites, leading to difficulties in maintaining physical control over theft and damage, and in accounting for goods in transit between sites.
- Inventories are vulnerable to spoilage, obsolescence and general economic conditions that may affect demand and saleability, and thus their valuation.
- Inventories may be sold subject to right of return and repurchase agreements.

In planning the audit, the auditor will be aware that the inherent risks are greater with respect to the existence assertion and the valuation and allocation assertion. Management has a greater incentive to overstate inventory, being an asset, than to understate it. It may do so by either inflating the quantity or overstating its value. There are numerous instances of such frauds discovered (and not discovered) by auditors. A lack of third-party evidence means it is also often easier to overstate inventories than assets such as cash or debtors. Further, inventory is subject to theft both by employees and by outsiders. The depletion of inventory as a consequence of shoplifting is well known.

LEARNING objective 4

Discuss considerations relevant to determining the audit strategy for inventories.

Audit strategy

In verifying the existence (and completeness) assertions, the auditor has the choice of three audit strategies — a choice that depends on the entity's own policy for determining inventory quantity. The options are as follows.

- Determine inventory quantity by perpetual inventory records where the entity does not intend to count inventory at or close to the end of the reporting period. The audit strategy requires assessing the control risk over inventory records as being low.
- Determine inventory quantities by a physical count near the end of the reporting period, adjusted to balance sheet quantities by reference to perpetual inventory records. This strategy requires assessing the control risk over inventory records, or of purchases and sales, as being less than high.
- Determine inventory quantities by a physical count at or within a few days of the end of the reporting period. This is a predominantly substantive approach in which the auditor does not test control over inventory records, which may not even exist.

A single entity may use all three methods for different categories of inventory or for inventory at different locations. A manufacturing entity may, for example, determine the quantity of raw materials and finished goods at a year-end inventory count, but rely on perpetual records in determining the work-in-process inventory.

In developing the audit plan, the auditor needs to discuss the approach management intends to take. If management intends to rely solely on inventory records, then more extensive tests of controls will be necessary to confirm the required assessment of control risk. Moreover, this assessment must be completed before the end of the reporting period in the event that tests of controls fail to confirm the assessment of control risk as being low, and the auditor is required to advise management to undertake an inventory count at or near the end of the reporting period.

Specialised inventories may require the assistance of experts in determining either the quantity (as in the case of aerial measurement of stockpiles) or value (as in the case of antiques). In accordance with ASA 620 *Using the Work of an Auditor's Expert* (ISA 620), the type of expertise required will vary with different circumstances so the nature and scope of the work needs to be clearly agreed between the expert and the auditor. The auditor must also ensure that they obtain sufficient understanding of the field of expertise to be able to evaluate the adequacy of the work performed; this includes an assessment of the expert's capabilities and objectivity.

For merchandise inventory, a predominantly substantive approach is usually more efficient in verifying the valuation and allocation assertion. For manufacturing entities, it is usually necessary for the auditor to have assessed control risk over the maintenance of costing records (used as the basis for costing closing inventory) as being less than high. This is an area that often receives insufficient audit attention owing to a reluctance to unravel the complexities of the costing system.

PROFESSIONAL ENVIRONMENT
Inventory record frauds

*I*nventory can be the target of fraud. It is usually the largest dollar value asset of retail businesses and a large portion of the asset value of manufacturing businesses. Most non-service businesses have at least some level of inventory or supplies on hand.

The theft of physical assets is common. The most common of these thefts involve inventory items, as inventory items can be numerous; can be of small value; may be easily accessible and removable; may not be well protected; and may not be immediately missed, if missed at all. Having few, large-value inventory items (like cars in a car yard) is no guarantee of protection from such frauds. The loss is from the theft of business assets.

How is the fraud done?
Actually stealing inventory items can be easy. The lack of physical security is a major contributor to theft of inventory, from both employees and non-employees. If items are openly available to any employee, without authorisation or requisition, inventory will be susceptible to theft. In most retail businesses, these items need to be freely available to salespeople, so that they can do their job. Manufacturing businesses need easy access to materials to work efficiently.

Hiding the theft of inventory in the business records is the fraud. If the theft is a one-time event, it is unlikely that the employee will even attempt to hide the theft. They will leave the loss to be noticed at the next stocktake. If the employee wishes to continue the thefts over a period, they probably need to hide the losses. How the loss is hidden specifies which type of fraud has been committed.

Once inventory has been stolen, the loss should show up in the perpetual inventory records during the next stocktake. The records must be altered to hide the loss. Hence, the theft becomes a fraud. Inventory record frauds rely on the theft of the item being hidden in the inventory records. They include:
- false write-off schemes
- false stocktakes
- perpetual record schemes
- false receiving documentation.

A word on physical security
Having inventory items or other assets left unsecured during and after business hours leaves the opportunity for theft. Physical security limits these losses, or at the very least makes them more noticeable. It will also limit the types of fraud that can be committed. If the employees cannot physically remove inventory items, the avenues for losses from fraud are limited.

One major problem is access to the business premises after hours. This is the perfect time to steal things. Most trusted employees are also the hard workers and have access to the work place on weekends and after hours. This access may include access to inventory or other assets. This access provides the opportunity for fraudsters not only to take assets, but also an opportunity and the time to manipulate the business records to hide the loss.[1]

Assessment of control risk

Assessment of control risk over inventory records is important where the entity does not intend to undertake an inventory count at or close to year-end. In this case, a satisfactory assessment is vital. Assessment of control risk over the cost of inventory is always important for manufacturing entities.

Control risk over inventory records

Table 16.2 (overleaf) contains a partial listing of potential misstatements, necessary controls, possible tests of the operating effectiveness of those controls, and the specific audit objective to which each belongs. As explained previously, the auditor assesses control risk over perpetual inventory records only where they are used in determining inventory at the end of the reporting period. If the preliminary assessment based on the design effectiveness of controls is that control risk is likely to be high, then the auditor would advise management not to rely on the records in determining inventory at the end of the reporting period.

If the preliminary assessment supports management's intended reliance on inventory records, then the auditor would draw up an audit program incorporating possible tests of the operating effectiveness of controls such as those identified in table 16.2.

Many of these tests are in the form of dual-purpose tests. It is important to remember that ASA 501 *Audit Evidence—Specific Considerations for Inventory and Segment Information* (ISA 501) requires the auditor, where reliance is placed entirely on perpetual inventory records in determining inventory at the end of the reporting period, to perform procedures to ensure that changes in inventory between a count date and the period-end are properly recorded. This includes procedures to ensure:

- the design, implementation and maintenance of internal controls over the recording of changes in inventory are effective
- that significant differences between the physical count and the perpetual inventory records are properly adjusted.

TABLE 16.2: Control risk assessment considerations

Function	Potential misstatement	Necessary control	Possible test of operating effectiveness	Relevant audit objective (from table 16.1)				
				OE no.	C no.	AV no.	CO no.	PD no.
Recording movement of goods into inventory	Failure to record goods	Use of prenumbered receiving reports and inventory transfer requisitions	Re-perform test of numerical continuity.		✓1, 2		✓1	
		Independent reconciliation of inventory records with control account in general ledger	Re-perform.*	✓ 1, 2, 3	✓ 1, 2, 3	✓1	✓1, 2	
Recording movement of goods from inventory	Unauthorised removal of goods	Custodian required to acknowledge responsibility for receipt of goods into store	Inspect receiving reports and inventory transfer requisitions for custodian's initials or electronic authorisation.	✓1, 2			✓1	
		Custodian required to obtain receipt for all deliveries from store	Vouch recorded removals with properly authorised dispatch notes and inventory transfer requisitions.*	✓2, 3			✓2	
		Physical comparison of inventory with inventory records	Observe. Re-perform.*	✓ 1, 2, 3	✓ 1, 2, 3		✓1, 2	

Function	Potential misstatement	Necessary control	Possible test of operating effectiveness	Relevant audit objective (from table 16.1)				
				OE no.	C no.	AV no.	CO no.	PD no.
Physical comparison of inventory with inventory records	Unreliable count procedures	Responsibility independent from maintenance of inventory records and custodianship of inventory	Observe.	✓4	✓4			
		Adequate instructions properly issued and followed	Observe. Re-perform.*	✓4	✓4			
	Inadequate investigation and correction	Proper record maintained of differences and their correction	Inspect. Re-perform.*	✓4	✓4			
	Insufficient extent of comparison	Prescribed procedures for systematic counts	Inspect.	✓4	✓4			
Determining inventory costs	Inappropriate basis	Approved by finance director	Enquire. Compare with accounting standards.			✓1, 2		✓1, 4
	Improper calculation	Consistent with engineering specification	Inspect. Re-perform.*			✓1, 2 ✓1, 2		
		Program controls	Use test data.*					

Note: * Usually performed as part of dual-purpose tests.

Close to the end of the reporting period, the auditor needs to consider the extent of test counts relative to total inventory, and to review the recorded differences between test counts and inventory records over the year and the explanations of those differences. If the auditor is not satisfied that results of test counts support an assessment of control risk as low, then the auditor must discuss with management the need for a complete inventory count.

Control risk over inventory cost

In a manufacturing entity, assessment of the reliability of the costing system to provide accurate costs of production that are correctly determined in accordance with acceptable accounting standards can constitute a substantial component of the interim audit.

Manufacturing costs are nearly always determined through the computer information system, and test data can be used to test the accuracy of processing and recording cost information. Where standard costs are intended to be used as the basis for valuing inventories, the tests must extend to the procedures used in developing standards from the engineering specifications as to:

- the quantities of labour and material required
- the determination of standard prices for labour and materials.

16.2.4 Substantive procedures for inventories

Except where perpetual records are used as the basis for determining inventory at the end of the reporting period, and for costing records in manufacturing entities, the audit is based mainly on substantive procedures applied to the account balance at the end of the reporting period.

The emphasis is on the assertions of existence and valuation, because the inherent risk of their misstatement is always high. Acceptable detection risk for these two assertions is usually assessed as low, with detection risk for other assertions being low to moderate.

Designing substantive procedures

Table 16.3 lists possible substantive procedures to be included in the audit program, with each test referenced to the audit objectives shown in table 16.1.

TABLE 16.3: Possible substantive procedures for tests of inventory assertions

Category	Substantive procedure	OE4	C4	RO1	AV2	CO	PD no.
		Relevant audit objective (from table 16.1)					
Initial procedures	1. Perform initial procedures on inventory balances and records that will be subjected to further testing. (a) Trace opening inventory balances to the previous year's working papers. (b) Review activity in inventory accounts and investigate entries that appear unusual in amount or source. (c) Verify totals of perpetual inventory records and their agreement with closing general ledger balances.				✓		
Analytical procedures	2. Perform analytical procedures. (a) Review industry experience and trends. (b) Examine an analysis of inventory turnover and gross profit. (c) Review relationships of inventory balances to recent purchasing, production and sales activities.	✓	✓		✓	✓	
Tests of details of transactions	3. Test entries in inventory records to and from supporting documentation. 4. Test the cut-off of purchases, inventory transfers and sales.	✓ ✓	✓ ✓	✓	✓	✓ ✓	
Tests of details of balances	5. Observe the entity's physical inventory count. (a) Evaluate the adequacy of the entity's inventory-taking plans. (b) Observe physical inventory count and test compliance with prescribed procedures. (c) Make test counts. (d) Look for indications of slow-moving, damaged or obsolete inventory.	✓	✓	✓	✓	✓	

Category	Substantive procedure	Relevant audit objective (from table 16.1)					
		OE4	C4	RO1	AV2	CO	PD no.
	(e) Account for all inventory tags and count sheets used in the physical count.						
	(f) Record cut-off data.						
	6. Test the clerical accuracy of inventory listings.	✓	✓		✓		
	(a) Recalculate totals and extensions of quantities times unit prices.						
	(b) Trace test counts (from item 5(c)) to listings.						
	(c) Vouch items on listings to and from count sheets and inventory tags.						
	(d) Compare physical counts with perpetual inventory records.						
	(e) Verify the adjustment of amounts for movements between the date of the physical count and the end of the reporting period.						
	7. Test inventory pricing.				✓		
	(a) Examine suppliers' invoices for purchased inventories.						
	(b) Examine the propriety of costing information, standard costs and the disposition of variances relating to manufactured inventories.						
	(c) Perform a lower of cost and net realisable value test.						
	8. Confirm inventories at locations outside the entity.	✓	✓	✓			
	9. Examine consignment agreements and contracts.			✓			3
Disclosure	10. Compare statement presentation with applicable accounting standards.						✓2–6
	(a) Confirm agreements for assignment and pledging of inventories.						
	(b) Review disclosures for inventories in drafts of the financial statements and determine conformity with applicable accounting standards.						

Initial procedures

In tracing opening inventory balances to working papers for the previous year, the auditor should make certain that any audit adjustments, agreed on in the previous year, were recorded. In addition, where perpetual inventory records are maintained, entries in the control accounts in the general ledger should be scanned to identify any postings that are unusual in amount or nature and thus require special investigation. Where perpetual inventory records are to be used as the basis for determining inventory at the end of the reporting period, the inventory listing must be test-checked to and from the records, added, and compared with the balance in the control account. Additional work on inventory listings is discussed in a later section on the tests of details of balances.

Analytical procedures

The application of analytical procedures to inventories is often extensive. A review of industry experience and trends may be essential in developing expectations to be used in evaluating analytical data for the entity. Knowledge of an industry-wide fall in turnover, for example, will enable the auditor to expect a fall in the entity's inventory turnover ratio. If the ratio does not show the expected fall, then the auditor may suspect errors as to the existence or occurrence of the inventory balance, or in the completeness of the balance used in calculating the ratio. A review of relationships of inventory balances with recent purchasing, production and sales activities should also help the auditor understand changes in inventory levels. An increase in the reported level of finished goods inventory when purchasing, production and sales levels have remained steady, for example, could indicate misstatements relating to the existence or valuation of the finished goods inventory.

Important ratios are those of inventory turnover and gross profit. We previously explained the use of the gross profit ratio with respect to the audits of sales and purchases. An unexpectedly high inventory turnover ratio, or an unexpectedly low gross profit ratio, might be caused by an overstatement of cost of sales and a corresponding understatement of inventories. Conversely, conformity of these ratios with expectations provides assurance of the fairness of the data used in the calculations.

Where the physical inventory count is other than at the year-end, the auditor should analyse totals of transactions in the intervening period for reasonableness.

Tests of details of transactions

With the exception of cut-off tests, tests of details of transactions are performed only where inventory at the end of the reporting period is determined wholly or partly from perpetual inventory records.

Testing entries in inventory records

Where inventory at the end of the reporting period is determined wholly by reference to perpetual inventory records, the tests of details of inventory transactions will be those described in table 16.2 as dual-purpose tests. Where inventory at the end of the reporting period is determined by a count other than at the year-end and adjusted by reference to inventory records in the intervening period, such tests of details of transactions may be confined to the period between the date of the physical count and the year-end.

Testing cut-off of purchases, manufacturing and sales transactions

The purpose and nature of sales and purchases cut-off tests were explained in chapters 14 and 15, respectively, in connection with the audit of accounts receivable and accounts payable balances. Both tests are important in establishing that transactions occurring near the end of the year are recorded in the correct accounting period. Purchases in transit at year-end, for example, should be excluded from inventory and payables, and inventory in transit to customers at year-end should be included in sales and excluded from inventory. In a manufacturing entity, it must also be determined that entries are recorded in the proper period for the allocation of labour and overhead costs to work in process, and for goods moved between raw materials, work in process and finished goods.

In each case, the auditor must ascertain, through inspection of documents and observation, that the paperwork cut-off and the cut-off for the physical inventory count are coordinated. If it is determined, for example, that an entry transferring the cost of the final completed batch of the period to finished goods has been recorded, then the auditor should determine that the goods, even if in transit, were included in the physical count of finished goods only — that is, that they were neither counted as part of work in process, nor double-counted, nor missed altogether. When attending the count, the auditor should note details of documentation relating to the movement of goods at the date of the count. Where the count is at a date other than at the end of the reporting period, the auditor must also check cut-off at the date of the count to ensure that movements between that date and the end of the reporting period exclude transactions before the count. Evidence from these cut-off tests relates to the occurrence, completeness and accuracy assertions for inventory balances.

LEARNING objective 5

Describe procedures to be followed when observing an inventory count.

Tests of details of balances

As previously explained, the auditor reduces audit risk to the desired level mainly through the performance of substantive tests of details of balances.

Observing the entity's inventory count

In observing the inventory count, the auditor is not responsible for supervising the process. From this procedure, the auditor obtains direct knowledge of the reliability of management's inventory-counting procedures and, thus, the reliance that may be placed on management's assertions as to the quantities and physical condition of the inventories. In some cases, the entity may hire outside inventory specialists to do the count. Where the outside inventory specialists have no particular expertise in the type of inventory being counted, the auditor must be present to observe their counts too because, from an auditing standpoint, they are basically the same as entity employees. Where the specialists are experts in the particular type of inventory (such as precious stones), the auditor may be in a position to place a degree of reliance on the work of the expert in accordance with ASA 620 (ISA 620).

As has been explained, the timing of the inventory count is negotiated with management in accordance with the entity's inventory system and the assessment of control risk. Except where reliance is placed wholly on perpetual inventory records, quantities are determined by physical count as of a specific date. The date should be at or near the end of the reporting period, and the auditor should be present on the specific date. For a multi-site entity, the auditor may vary locations attended each year, so long as the sample of inventory observed each year is of sufficient size. In such cases, the auditor may consider relying on internal audit for attendance at locations not visited, subject to the requirements of ASA 610 *Using the Work of Internal Auditors* (ISA 610). Such reliance, however, does not replace the requirement for the auditor to undertake sufficient personal observation of inventory counts. Other firms of auditors may also be engaged to observe an inventory count, for example where another auditor is responsible for the audit of a subsidiary in a group, subject to the requirements of ASA 600 *Special Considerations — Audits of a Group Financial Report (Including the Work of Component Auditors)* (ISA 600).

Attendance at an inventory count involves the performance of tests of controls over entity procedures and of substantive procedures applied directly by the auditor. Because both procedures are performed simultaneously, both types of procedure are usually included within the program of substantive procedures. Moreover, because there is no alternative audit strategy if the entity's inventory count procedures are found to be inadequate, the auditor should review and evaluate the entity's inventory count plans well in advance of the counting date. With ample lead time, the entity should be able to respond favourably to suggested modifications in the plans before the count begins. It is common for the auditor to help design a count plan that will facilitate both taking and observing the count.

Procedures are the same as for test counts in respect of perpetual inventory records, except that the count is of all inventory, not just a sample.

In observing the inventory count to ensure prescribed procedures are being properly followed, the auditor should:

- observe entity employees performing their prescribed procedures
- determine that prenumbered count sheets or inventory tags are properly controlled
- be alert to the existence of empty containers and hollow squares (empty spaces) that may exist when goods are stacked in solid formations
- observe that cut-off procedures are being followed and that the movement of goods, if any, is properly controlled
- see that all goods are marked as having been counted.

In addition, the auditor should perform substantive procedures, including:

- making test counts and comparing quantities with the entity's count
- recording details of serial numbers of count sheets or tags used and unused (or taking copies of all used count sheets)
- appraising the general condition of the inventory, noting damaged, obsolete and slow-moving items
- ensuring partly-used count sheets are ruled off to prevent additional entries being made
- identifying and noting the last receiving, production and dispatch documents used, and determining that goods received during the count are properly segregated.

The extent of the auditor's test counts partly depends on the nature and composition of the inventory. Before the inventory count, the auditor identifies high-value items for test counting in addition to counting a representative sample of other items. In making test counts, the auditor should record the count and give a complete and accurate description of the item (identification number, unit of measurement, location and so on) in the working papers, as shown in figure 16.1. Such data are essential for the auditor's comparison of the test counts with the entity's counts, and for the subsequent tracing of the counts to inventory summary sheets and perpetual inventory records.

Highlight Ltd Raw materials test counts 30/6/15				Prepared by: L.R.S. Date: 30/6/15 Reviewed by: B.E.M. Date: 7/7/15		
Tag no.	Inventory sheet no.	Inventory		Count		
		Number	Description	Company	Auditor	Difference
6531	15	1-42-003	Back plate	125 ✓	125	
8340	18	1-83-012	5 mm copper plate	93 ✓	93	
1483	24	2-11-004	Single-end wire	1321 m ✓	1325 m	4 m
4486	26	2-28-811	Copper tubing	220 m ✓	220 m	
3334	48	4-26-204	Side plate	424 ✓	424	
8502	64	7-44-310	10 mm copper wire	276 m ✓	276 m	
8844	68	7-72-460	20 mm copper wire	419 m ✓	419 m	
6285	92	3-48-260	Front plate	96 ✓	69	27

Each difference was corrected by the company and the net effect of the corrections was to increase inventory by $840. Total inventory values for which test counts were made and traced to inventory summaries without exception = $210 460 or 22% of the total. In my opinion errors were immaterial.

✓ = Traced to company's inventory summary sheets (F–4), noting corrections for all differences.

FIGURE 16.1: Inventory test counts working paper

On conclusion of the observation procedure, a designated member of the audit team should prepare a working paper detailing such matters as listed below before reaching a conclusion as to the reliability of the count:

- departures from the entity's inventory count
- the extent of test counts and any material discrepancies resulting therefrom
- conclusions on the accuracy of the counts
- the general condition of the inventory.

In the initial audit of an established entity, it is clearly impracticable for the auditor to have observed the physical inventory at the previous year-end that established the opening inventory. ASA 510 *Initial Engagements — Opening Balances* (ISA 510) permits the auditor to verify the inventories by other auditing procedures. When the entity has been audited by another firm of auditors in the previous period, the auditor may review working papers of the predecessor audit firm and consider its competence and independence. If the entity has not been audited previously, the auditor may be able to obtain audit satisfaction by testing transactions from the previous period, reviewing the records of previous counts or applying analytical procedures.

When sufficient evidence has not been obtained as to the existence of opening inventories, or when the auditor is unable to observe the taking of closing inventory counts or to obtain sufficient evidence from alternative procedures, the auditor cannot issue an unmodified auditor's report. We consider the specific effects on the auditor's report in chapter 7. Like the confirmation of accounts receivable, the observation of the entity's inventory count applies to many assertions. This procedure is the main source of evidence that the inventory exists. In addition, this procedure relates to the assertions detailed in table 16.4.

TABLE 16.4:
Assertions for which attendance at an inventory count provides evidence

Assertion	Application
Completeness	Procedures provide assurance that no items were omitted from the count.
Accuracy or valuation and allocation	Observation of the condition of goods as being damaged, obsolete or apparently slow-moving provides evidence as to goods that may need to be valued at net realisable value.
Rights and obligations	Possession of goods on entity premises provides some evidence as to ownership.

Testing clerical accuracy of inventory listings

After the inventory count, the entity uses the count sheets or inventory tags to prepare a listing of all items counted. The inventory items are then priced to arrive at the total value of the inventory. Because this listing serves as the basis for the recorded inventory balance, the auditor must perform procedures to ensure that the listing is clerically accurate and that it accurately represents the results of the physical count.

To determine that the list accurately represents the results of the count, the auditor:

- compares his or her own test counts with the inventory listings
- identifies count sheets or tags used in the count according to records made by the auditor at the time of attendance, and tests items on those count sheets or tags to and from the listings
- compares the count, on a test basis, with amounts per perpetual records, when applicable, and enquires into any differences noted
- tests the clerical accuracy by recalculating the extensions of quantities times unit prices on a test basis, as well as the totals shown on the inventory listings.

PROFESSIONAL ENVIRONMENT
Counting the bikkies

You are planning the audit of Bikkies Ltd, a manufacturing company that supplies biscuits and snack foods to a large number of retailers nationally. You have turned your attention to the audit of inventory and have obtained the following information from client staff.

1. Year-end inventory is expected to be as follows:

Raw materials	$1 850 000
Work in process	1 525 000
Finished goods	2 005 000
	$5 380 000

This represents 20% of total assets.

2. The company uses standard costing to value its inventory, which consists of approximately 150 product lines. At year-end, the relatively equal inventory value of each of these lines will be held.
3. The inventory is stored in approximately 50 warehouses nationally. The company has a policy of taking out short-term leases on unused warehouse space (to minimise rental costs), so the number of warehouses in use varies over time.
4. Goods are manufactured centrally at the Camperdown factory and then shipped out to the warehouses.
5. The recent launch of a new biscuit, Smoothie Bix, resulted in poorer than expected sales. Consequently, the company has excess inventory in finished goods, amounting to $400 000. Their use-by date is 6 weeks after the end of the reporting period.
6. A new work-in-process system was successfully introduced 2 months after the previous year-end. Staff have commented on how this system is a great improvement.
7. Raw materials largely comprise bulk inventories of flour, rice and potatoes. These are held in large storage bins at the Camperdown factory.
8. Work in process largely comprises biscuit dough, which is stored in several locations throughout the Camperdown factory — both in large sealed vats awaiting processing and in mixing bowls attached to the 10 different production lines.
9. As in previous years, all warehouses and the Camperdown factory will be closed at the end of the reporting period to allow a full stocktake. A perpetual inventory system is used.
10. From your experience in previous years, you know that the company has a highly accurate budgeting system. Final figures rarely vary more than 3% from budget.
    (a) Identify the key financial statement assertions for the audit of inventory at Bikkies Ltd.
    (b) Identify and discuss specific issues to be considered in relation to the audit for the existence assertion and valuation and allocation assertion for Bikkies' inventory balance. Describe the audit procedures required to cover these issues.

LEARNING objective 6

Explain the audit procedures for verifying inventory pricing.

Testing inventory pricing

This procedure involves verifying the cost of inventory and the net realisable value of those items that management has determined need to be written down. It also involves considering whether other items, whose net realisable value may be below cost, need to be written down. Thus, it relates to the valuation and allocation assertion.

Inventory at cost. For merchandise inventory and raw materials valued on a first-in first-out basis, this test involves examining suppliers' invoices covering the quantity in inventory.

For work in process and finished goods inventories, the auditor must test cost against costing records. The entity's costing system should have been evaluated during the interim audit, and controls over the determination of product cost assessed. Dual-purpose tests (table 16.2 on pp. 676–7), serving as both tests of controls and substantive procedures, should provide sufficient evidence as to the reliability of product cost data. The auditor then vouches the costs that are applied to inventory to the costing records.

Where inventory is costed at standard cost, variances for the year need to be analysed. When a variance account has a large balance, the auditor must consider whether fair presentation requires a pro rata allocation of the variance to inventories and to cost of sales, instead of charging the entire variance to cost of sales. A large adverse material price variance, for example, may indicate that the true cost of inventory is greater than the standard cost. If the variance is written off, then the cost of inventory is understated.

Inventory at net realisable value. AASB 102 *Inventories* (IAS 2) requires inventory to be written down to net realisable value where below cost. The write-down constitutes an accounting estimate and the auditor must follow the procedures in ASA 540 *Auditing Accounting Estimates, Including Fair Value Accounting Estimates, and Related Disclosures* (ISA 540).

This requires the auditor to review and test the process used by management, use an independent estimate, and review subsequent events.

For items priced at net realisable value, the auditor must verify the basis for arriving at that value. In some cases, it will be the actual, current or contracted selling price less an estimate of costs to be incurred in completion and selling. In other cases, a formula may be used, taking into account the age, past movement and expected future movement of the inventory items. The auditor must examine the data and assumptions on which the estimates are based, check the calculations, consider previous period experience, and see that the estimates are properly approved by management.

In view of the inherent risk of understatement of the required write-down, the auditor should also carry out substantive procedures to identify the need for further write-downs. AASB 102 (IAS 2) specifically identifies the following situations in which a write-down may be necessary:

- a fall in selling price
- physical deterioration of inventories
- obsolescence
- a decision to sell at a loss
- purchasing or production errors.

Specific procedures normally adopted by the auditor include:

- review of sales after the end of the reporting period
- observation of deterioration or obsolescence during the auditor's attendance at the physical count
- analysis of inventory holdings relative to recent or future budgeted turnover to identify excessive holdings; this is often performed with the use of generalised audit software
- enquiry of management and of sales and production personnel
- review of the minutes of the board of directors and executive committees.

Use of an expert. When entity assertions about the value of the inventory relate to highly technical matters, the auditor may require the assistance of an outside expert. This may occur, for example, in an oil company with different grades of petrol and motor oil, or in a jewellery shop with diamonds of varying quality. As explained in chapter 6, the auditor may use the work of an expert as an auditing procedure to obtain sufficient appropriate audit evidence when the auditor is satisfied as to the qualifications and independence of the expert.

Confirming inventories at locations outside the entity

When inventories are stored in public warehouses or with other third parties, the auditor should obtain evidence as to the existence of the inventory by direct communication with the custodian. This type of evidence is deemed sufficient except when the amounts involved represent a significant proportion of current or total assets. When this is the case, the auditor should apply procedures that include:

- considering the integrity and independence of the third party
- observing (or arranging for another auditor to observe) physical counts of the goods
- obtaining another auditor's report on the warehouse's control procedures relevant to physical counting and to custody of goods
- confirming with lenders the pertinent details of pledged receipts (if warehouse receipts have been pledged as collateral).

Confirmation of inventories at outside locations also provides evidence about the rights and obligations assertion. In addition, it results in evidence as to the completeness assertion if the custodian confirms more goods on hand than stated in the confirmation request. It does not provide any evidence about the value of the inventory because the custodian is not asked to report on the condition of the goods stored in the warehouse.

Examining consignment agreements and contracts

Goods on hand may be held for customers, at their request, after a sale has occurred, and goods belonging to others may be held on consignment. A consignment 'sale' is one made on a sale-or-return basis. Payment for the goods is required only on subsequent sale to a third party. For accounting purposes, such goods are included in the 'seller's' inventory. Thus, management is requested to segregate goods not owned during the physical count. In addition, the auditor usually requests a written assertion on ownership of inventories in the representation letter (see chapter 18).

The auditor should also enquire as to whether any of the entity's own goods are held on consignment and included in inventory. If so, the auditor should review the documentation or, if the goods are material, confirm the existence of such goods directly with the other party.

Goods may also be assigned or pledged, usually as security for loans. The auditor must enquire of management as to the existence of such agreements and the appropriate disclosure should be checked in the financial statements. The auditor must also consider the possibility of window dressing. Substantial sales immediately before year-end to an unlikely customer of goods that are not required to be delivered may, in reality, be a loan by the 'customer', secured by the transfer of title to specified goods. Such a 'transaction' enables the entity to reduce its inventories and increase its cash, thus enhancing the quick (or acid test) ratio. Further enquiry may reveal an agreement, by the entity, to repurchase the goods after the year-end. Such a transaction should be accounted for in accordance with its substance — a loan secured by inventory.

Evidence obtained from this procedure relates to the rights and obligations assertion and the disclosure assertion.

Disclosure

It is appropriate to identify the major inventory categories in the balance sheet. In addition, there should be disclosure of the inventory costing method(s) used, the pledging of inventories and the existence of major purchase commitments.

Enquiry of management is used to determine the existence of binding contracts for future purchases of goods. When such commitments exist, the auditor should examine the terms of the contracts and evaluate the fairness of the entity's accounting and reporting. When material losses exist on purchase commitments, they should be recognised in the financial statements, together with a disclosure of the attendant circumstances as noted in the discussion of accounts payable in chapter 15.

The substantive procedures described above provide evidence as to financial statement disclosure. Further evidence may be obtained, as needed, from a review of the minutes of board meetings and from enquiries of management. Based on the evidence, and on a comparison of the entity's financial statement with the Corporations Act (or other regulatory frameworks) and with applicable accounting standards, the auditor determines the fairness of the disclosures.

Learning check

Do you know . . .

16.1 ☐ The most important test of controls is evaluation of the design effectiveness of test counts of physical inventory and comparison with the records. The extent and results of such test counts performed by the entity are important to the assessment of control risk. Where perpetual inventory records are used to determine inventory at the end of the reporting period, the auditor needs to obtain an understanding of the internal control structure and perform tests of controls.

16.2 ☐ For manufacturing entities, the auditor needs to assess cost accumulation procedures and their reliability as a basis for determining inventory cost.

16.3 ☐ The main inherent risks are those of existence and valuation.

• Management has an incentive to overstate the quantity and/or value of inventories.

• Inventory is subject to theft.

• Valuation of inventory involves judgement, estimation and contentious accounting treatments.

16.4 ☐ Physical observation of the inventory count is a required audit procedure whether by attendance at cyclical counts of perpetual inventory records or at a year-end count, and involves:

• considering the adequacy of management plans

• observing compliance with prescribed procedures

• performing substantive procedures in the form of inspecting and test-counting inventory, noting the use of count sheets and obtaining cut-off information

16.5 ☐ Testing of the pricing of inventory involves testing against costing records, verifying write-downs to net realisable value, and considering the need for further write-downs to net realisable value.

16.3 PROPERTY, PLANT AND EQUIPMENT

There are various classes of property, plant and equipment but all are tangible, non-current assets which are held to be used by the entity or to be rented out to others. Property includes:

• land and buildings — which may be freehold or leasehold

• plant and equipment — includes machinery, vehicles, furniture and equipment and may include items held under finance leases.

The main issues that need to be addressed in the audit of property, plant and equipment relate to the transactions for purchasing new and disposing of old assets, including profits or losses on sale. In addition, consideration is required in relation to depreciation charges, the treatment of leased assets and asset revaluations.

Identify the audit objectives applicable to property, plant and equipment.

16.3.1 Audit objectives

The relevant audit objectives are presented in table 16.5.

Note that, as discussed after table 16.1, further detail on these assertions is provided in ASA 315 (ISA 315).

TABLE 16.5:
Selected specific audit objectives for property, plant and equipment

Transaction objectives	
Occurrence (**OE**)	Recorded additions represent property, plant and equipment acquired during the period under audit (**OE1**). Recorded disposals represent property, plant and equipment sold or scrapped during the period under audit (**OE2**).
Completeness (**C**)	All additions that occurred during the period have been recorded (**C1**). All disposals that occurred during the period have been recorded (**C2**).
Accuracy (**AV**)	Additions are correctly journalised and posted (**AV1**).Disposals are correctly journalised and posted (**AV2**).
Cut-off (**CO**)	Additions and disposals of property, plant and equipment before the period end are recorded in the current period and those after the period end are included in the next accounting period (**CO1**).
Classification (**PD**)	Additions and disposals of property, plant and equipment are recorded in the correct accounts (**PD1**).
Balances objectives	
Existence (**OE**)	Recorded property, plant and equipment assets represent productive assets that are in use at the end of the reporting period (**OE3**).
Rights and obligations (**RO**)	The entity owns or has rights to all recorded property, plant and equipment assets at the end of the reporting period (**RO1**).
Completeness (**C**)	Non-current asset balances include all applicable assets used in operations at the end of the reporting period (**C3**).
Valuation and allocation (**AV**)	Property, plant and equipment are stated at cost or a valuation less accumulated depreciation (**AV3**).
Presentation and disclosure objectives (PD)	
Occurrence and rights and obligations	Disclosed property, plant and equipment transactions have occurred and pertain to the entity (**PD2**).
Completeness	• Disclosures as to: cost or valuation • depreciation methods and useful lives of each major class • the pledging as collateral • the major terms of finance lease contracts of property, plant and equipment assets are adequate (**PD3**).
Classification and understandability	The details of additions and disposals of property, plant and equipment support their classification and disclosure in the financial statements (**PD4**).
Accuracy and valuation	Property, plant and equipment transactions are disclosed accurately and at appropriate amounts (**PD5**).

16.3.2 Developing the audit plan

Because transactions relating to property, plant and equipment are few and usually individually material, assessment of control risk relating to these transactions is rarely necessary. This section considers materiality and inherent risk and the development of an appropriate audit strategy. Additionally, the use of a plant register is explained. Although the auditor rarely assesses controls over recording fixed asset transactions in the register, the existence of the register is a source of evidence used in substantive procedures.

Materiality

Property, plant and equipment often represent the largest category of assets on the balance sheet, and expenses associated with property, plant and equipment are material factors in the determination of profit.

Inherent risk

There may be significant variations in the inherent risk assessments for assertions relating to different property, plant and equipment accounts. Inherent risk for the existence assertion may be low in a merchandising entity, for example, because the plant and equipment are not normally vulnerable to theft. However, it may be moderate or high in a manufacturing entity because scrapped or retired machinery may not be written off the books, or small tools and equipment used in production may be stolen. Similarly, the inherent risk in the accuracy or valuation and allocation assertions may be low when equipment items are purchased for cash, but high when items are acquired under finance leases. In the same way, the inherent risk may be high for the rights and obligations assertion and disclosure assertion for plant and equipment acquired under finance leases.

LEARNING 8
objective

Discuss considerations relevant to determining the audit strategy for property, plant and equipment.

Audit strategy

Although material, the verification of property, plant and equipment typically involves significantly less time and cost than the verification of current assets. Unlike receivables or cash balances, control risk assessments for non-current asset balances are usually less dependent on controls over major transaction classes.

The only transaction class with a significant effect on non-current asset balances is that of purchases, which we considered in chapter 15. When expenditures for smaller items (such as furniture, fixtures and equipment) are processed as routine purchase transactions, the auditor may elect to use a lower assessed level of control risk approach. In such cases, the auditor's tests of controls of purchase transactions should include a sample of such assets. In assessing control risk for the plant and equipment assertions, the control risk assessments for purchase transactions are applicable. Other expenditures for land, buildings and major capital improvements tend to occur infrequently and are not subject to the routine purchasing controls. These transactions may be subject to separate controls, including capital budgeting and specific authorisation by the board of directors. Because such transactions are often individually material, a predominantly substantive approach is often adopted for the property, plant and equipment assets, resulting in the specification of low acceptable levels of detection risk.

In determining detection risk for the valuation and allocation assertion for depreciation expense and accumulated depreciation, note that inherent risk is affected by both the degree of difficulty in estimating useful lives and residual values, and the complexity of the depreciation methods used. Control risk may be affected by the effectiveness of any controls related to these estimates and calculations.

Plant register

Entities often maintain a **plant register** as a subsidiary ledger detailing individual items of plant and equipment. The register records the cost of each asset and of any additions or alterations, and the accumulated depreciation charged against it. Balances in the register reconcile with the written-down value of the plant and equipment account in the general ledger. The register also contains additional information, such as serial number, supplier or manufacturer, insurance cover, maintenance record and location, as well as other information relevant to management of the portfolio of plant and equipment. From time to time, the entity may carry out an inventory of plant and equipment, mainly to identify the unrecorded disposals of fully depreciated items.

Control over maintenance of the register is only of audit significance for assets that are vulnerable to misappropriation. Regular checking of such assets provides evidence of their existence and the auditor may not need to inspect such assets physically at the end of the reporting period. Procedures for understanding the internal control structure and assessment of control risk are similar to those for perpetual inventory records described in the first part of this chapter.

LEARNING 9
objective

Design a substantive audit program for property, plant and equipment.

16.3.3 Substantive procedures for property, plant and equipment

As we explained earlier, the performance of substantive procedures achieves the required reduction in audit risk of misstatements in property, plant and equipment balances, with inherent risk assessed as being moderate to high, and control risk not assessed at all (and thus taken as being high). Substantive procedures must, therefore, be designed and performed so as to achieve the desired low level of detection risk.

Designing substantive procedures

In the first audit, evidence must be obtained as to the fairness of the opening balances and the ownership of the assets making up the balances. When the entity has previously been audited by another firm of auditors, this evidence may be obtained from a review of the predecessor auditor's working papers. If the entity has not been previously audited, the auditor must undertake an investigation of the opening balances. Information concerning opening balances obtained in the initial audit is usually recorded in the permanent audit file. This record is updated annually to record changes in the major assets, particularly property, including details of title deeds and registered charges such as mortgages.

In a recurring engagement, the auditor concentrates on the current year's transactions. The opening balances are verified through the preceding year's audit, and changes in the balance are usually few. This contrasts with the audit of current assets, which are subject to numerous transactions and for which the audit effort is concentrated on the closing balance. The auditor relies on the inspection of documentary evidence in verifying additions and disposals, and on mathematical evidence in verifying depreciation.

Possible substantive procedures for property, plant and equipment balances, and the specific account balance audit objectives to which the tests relate, are shown in table 16.6. Risk considerations usually result in greater emphasis being placed on the existence or occurrence and the accuracy or valuation and allocation assertions. We explain each substantive procedure in a later section.

TABLE 16.6: Possible substantive procedures for property, plant and equipment assertions

Category	Substantive procedure	Account balance audit objective (from table 16.5) OE3	C3	RO1	AV3	PD no.
Initial procedures	1. Perform initial procedures on non-current asset balances and records that will be subjected to further testing. (a) Trace opening balances for plant assets and related accumulated depreciation accounts to and from the previous year's working papers. (b) Review activity in the general ledger, accumulated depreciation and depreciation expense accounts, and investigate entries that appear unusual in amount or source. (c) Obtain entity-prepared schedules of additions and disposals and determine that they accurately represent the underlying accounting records by: • adding and cross-adding the schedules and reconciling the totals with increases or decreases in the related general ledger balances during the period • testing the agreement of items on schedules with entries in related general ledger accounts.	✓	✓	✓	✓	✓1, 2
Analytical procedures	2. Perform analytical procedures. (a) Calculate ratios. (b) Analyse ratio results relative to expectations based on previous year's results, industry data, budgeted amounts or other data.	✓	✓		✓	
Tests of details of transactions	3. Compare asset additions with supporting documentation.	✓	✓	✓	✓	✓1
	4. Compare asset disposals with supporting documentation.	✓	✓	✓	✓	✓2
	5. Review repairs and maintenance and rental expense.		✓			
Tests of details of balances	6. Examine title documents and contracts.	✓		✓		
	7. Review provisions for depreciation.				✓	
	8. Consider the possibility of impairment.				✓	✓3
	9. Enquire into the valuation of property, plant and equipment.				✓	✓3
Presentation and disclosure	10. Compare the statement presentation with applicable accounting standards. (a) Determine that property, plant and equipment assets and related expenses, gains and losses are properly identified and classified in the financial statements. (b) Determine the appropriateness of disclosures pertaining to the cost, value, depreciation methods and useful lives of major classes of asset, the pledging of assets as collateral and the terms of lease contracts.					✓2–5

Initial procedures

Before performing any of the other steps in the audit program, the auditor determines that the opening general ledger balances agree with the previous period's audit working papers. Among other functions, this comparison will confirm that any adjustments determined to be necessary at the conclusion of the previous audit and reflected in the previous period's published financial statements were also properly recorded and carried forward. Next, the auditor should test the mathematical accuracy of entity-prepared schedules of additions and disposals, and reconcile the totals with changes in the related general ledger balances for property, plant and equipment during the period. In addition, the auditor should test the schedules by vouching items on the schedules to entries in the ledger accounts, and tracing ledger entries to the schedules to determine that they are an accurate representation of the accounting records from which they were prepared. The schedules may then be used as the basis for several other audit procedures. Figure 16.2 illustrates an auditor's lead schedule for property, plant and equipment and accumulated depreciation.

Highlight Ltd
Property, plant and equipment and accumulated depreciation
Lead schedule
30 June 2015

W/P ref. __G__
Prepared by: __C.J.G.__ Date: __4/8/15__
Reviewed by: __R.C.P.__ Date: __12/8/15__

W/P ref.	Acct no.	Account title	Asset cost Balance 30/6/14	Additions	Disposals	Adjustments Dr/(Cr)	Balance 30/6/151	Accumulated depreciation Balance 30/6/14	Provisions	Disposals	Adjustments (Dr)/Cr	Balance 30/6/15
G–1	301	Land	450 000 ↘				450 000					
G–1	302	Buildings	2 108 000 ↘	125 000		㉑(25 000)	2 208 000	379 440 ↘	84 320		㉑(1000)	462 760
G–3	303	Mach. and equip.	3 757 250 ↘	980 000	370 000	㉑ 25 000	4 392 250	1 074 210 ↘	352 910	172 500	㉑ 1000	1 255 620
G–4	304	Fern. and fixtures	853 400 ↘	144 000	110 000		887 400	217 450 ↘	43 250	21 000		239 700
			7 168 650 ↘	1 249 000	480 000	0	7 937 650	1 671 100 ↘	480 480	193 500	0	1 958 080
			F	F	F	F	FF	F	F	F	F	FF

↘ Traced to general ledger and 30/6/15 working papers
F Footed
FF Cross-footed and footed
Note: This type of analysis would normally be done on an Excel spreadsheet or customised audit software.
To reclassify cost and related accumulated depreciation for purchased addition recorded in Buildings account that should have been recorded in Machinery and Equipment account. See adjusting entry no. 21 on W/P AE–4.

FIGURE 16.2: Property, plant and equipment asset and accumulated depreciation lead schedule

Analytical procedures

Analytical procedures are less useful as a source of evidence as to property, plant and equipment balances than they are for current assets and liabilities. This is because the balances can vary substantially as the result of relatively few transactions of which the auditor is already likely to be aware. A comparison of the annual depreciation charge with the cost or written-down value of the relevant class of assets should yield a measure comparable to the depreciation rate. Such evidence could provide some of the required evidence as to the valuation assertion. Comparison of repairs and maintenance expense with that for previous years or with net sales may indicate the possibility that some maintenance expenditures have not been recorded or that they have been capitalised in error.

Tests of details of transactions

These substantive procedures cover three types of transactions related to property, plant and equipment: additions, disposals, and repairs and maintenance.

Substantiating additions

The auditor first needs to ascertain management's policy with regard to the distinction between capital and revenue expenditure. Most entities specify a cut-off value below which purchases are expensed regardless of their nature. A consistent policy also needs to be followed in distinguishing between improvements (which prolong the life or enhance the usefulness of existing assets) and repairs and maintenance (which are necessary for the asset to continue to function over its expected useful life). The auditor must ensure that additions are properly capitalised and that a consistent policy is followed.

The recorded amounts should be vouched to supporting documentation in the form of authorisations in the minutes, suppliers' invoices and contracts. If there are numerous transactions, the vouching may be done on a test basis. In performing this test, the auditor ascertains that the amount capitalised includes installation, freight and similar costs, but excludes expenses included on the supplier's invoice, such as a year's maintenance charge.

For construction in progress, the auditor may review the contract and documentation in support of construction costs. The auditor should physically inspect major items, ensuring that details of the asset inspected (such as its description and the manufacturer's serial number) agree with the documentation.

The auditor also needs to enquire about leases for property, plant and equipment entered into during the period. Lease agreements convey, to a lessee, the right to use assets, usually for a specified period of time. For accounting purposes, leases may be classified as either finance leases or operating leases. The auditor should read the lease agreement to determine its proper accounting classification in accordance with AASB 117 *Leases* (IAS 17). When a finance lease exists, both an asset and a liability should be recognised in the accounts and financial statements. The cost of the asset and the related liability should be recorded at the present value of the future minimum lease payments. The auditor should do some recalculations to verify the accuracy of the entity's determination of the present value of the lease liability.

The vouching of additions provides evidence about the occurrence, rights and obligations, and accuracy assertions. In addition, the examination of lease contracts relates to the presentation and disclosure assertion, because of the disclosures that are required under AASB 117 (IAS 17).

Substantiating disposals

Evidence of sales, disposals and trade-ins should be available to the auditor in the form of cash remittance advices, written authorisations and sales agreements. Such documentation should be carefully examined to determine the accuracy and propriety of the accounting records, including the recognition of gain or loss, if any.

The following procedures may also be useful to the auditor in determining whether all disposals have been recorded:

- analysing the miscellaneous revenue account for proceeds from sales of property, plant and equipment
- investigating the disposition of facilities associated with discontinued product lines and operations
- tracing disposal work orders and authorisations for disposals to the accounting records
- reviewing insurance policies for termination or reductions of coverage
- enquiring of management as to disposals.

Inspection of the results of any inventory count of plant and machinery undertaken by the entity provides further evidence that all disposals have been recorded.

Evidence that all disposals or retirements have been properly recorded relates to the occurrence, rights and obligations, and accuracy assertions. Evidence supporting the validity of transactions that reduce property, plant and equipment relates to the completeness assertion.

Reviewing repairs and maintenance and rental expenses

The auditor's objective in reviewing repairs and maintenance expenses is to determine the propriety and consistency of the charges to this expense. The auditor should scan the individual charges in excess of the entity's cut-off value for capitalisation to ensure that they are properly expensed. This procedure is related to the examination of additions to ensure that they are properly capitalised.

This substantive procedure provides important evidence concerning the completeness assertion for property, plant and equipment because it reveals expenditures that should be capitalised. In addition, the analysis may reveal misclassifications in the accounts that relate to the presentation and disclosure assertion.

Rental expenses are reviewed to ensure that such rents relate to assets under operating leases. Documentary evidence needs to be tested for evidence of leases that should be accounted for as finance leases. This procedure provides evidence as to the completeness assertion in that all assets acquired under finance leases are properly accounted for as additions to property, plant and equipment.

Tests of details of balances

The auditor usually concludes that the closing balance is correctly stated — with respect to the assertions of existence, completeness, and rights and obligations — after having tested the opening balance with the previous year's working papers, and verified additions and disposals. However, the auditor may examine documentary evidence as to the existence and rights and obligations assertions of the recorded balance.

The main tests of balances relate to valuation and disclosure. These test the accumulated depreciation, the need for provision for impairment, and the appropriateness of any revaluation.

Examining title documents and contracts

The auditor may establish ownership of vehicles by examining registration certificates and insurance policies. For plant and equipment, the 'paid' invoice may be the best evidence of ownership. Evidence of ownership of freehold property is found in title deeds, property rates bills, mortgage payment receipts and fire insurance policies. The auditor can also verify ownership of freehold property by reviewing public records. When this form of additional evidence is desired, the auditor may seek the help of a solicitor. The examination of ownership documents contributes to the existence assertion and rights and obligations assertion for property, plant and equipment.

Reviewing accumulated depreciation

In this test, the auditor seeks evidence as to the reasonableness, consistency and accuracy of depreciation charges.
- *Reasonableness.* The auditor determines the reasonableness of accumulated depreciation by considering such factors as the entity's past history in estimating useful lives and the remaining useful lives of existing assets. The auditor must also ensure that management has reviewed the depreciation rates during the year and adjusted the rates as necessary in accordance with AASB 116 *Property, Plant and Equipment* (IAS 16).
- *Consistency.* The auditor can ascertain the depreciation methods used by reviewing depreciation schedules prepared by the entity and enquiring of management. The auditor

must then determine whether the methods in use are consistent with those used in the preceding year. On a recurring audit, this can be established by a review of the previous year's working papers.

- *Accuracy.* The auditor verifies accuracy through recalculation. Ordinarily, the auditor does this on a selective basis by recalculating the depreciation on major assets and testing depreciation taken on additions and disposals during the year.

These substantive procedures provide evidence about the valuation assertion.

Considering the possibility of impairment

The auditor must be satisfied that the carrying value of property, plant and equipment does not exceed the greater of their realisable value or value in use in accordance with AASB 136 *Impairment of Assets* (IAS 36).

The auditor may derive evidence of overvalued assets by observing obsolete or damaged units during a tour of the plant, identifying assets associated with discontinued activities but not yet disposed of, and enquiring of management as to budgets and forecasts for specific activities in relation to the carrying value of assets associated with those activities.

Where amounts have been written off the carrying value of any property, plant or equipment asset, the auditor must be satisfied, by enquiring of management as to future plans, that the write-down is reasonable.

Enquiring into the valuation

Management may also choose to revalue property, plant and equipment so as to reflect more fairly their value to the business. AASB 116 (IAS 16) requires that any revaluation must be applied to a class of assets, not to individual assets within a class. Full valuations must be made or reviewed by an independent valuer. Interim valuations may be made by an internal valuer. The auditor would need to be satisfied as to the skill, competence and objectivity of the valuer, whether that valuer is independent or an employee of the entity. In particular, it would be necessary for the auditor to:

- sight a copy of the valuer's report
- pay regard to the basis of valuation stated therein
- consider its appropriateness as the basis for determining the carrying amount of that class of assets in the financial statements.

This substantive procedure provides evidence about the valuation assertion and the disclosure assertion.

Presentation and disclosure

The financial statement presentation requirements for property, plant and equipment are extensive. The financial statements should show, for example, the depreciation expense for the year, the carrying value for major classes of property, plant and equipment; and the depreciation method(s) used. For assets carried other than at cost, information that must be disclosed includes (1) the name and qualifications of the valuer and whether they are internal or independent, (2) the basis of valuation and (3) the date and amounts of the valuation. The auditor acquires evidence concerning these matters through the substantive procedures described in the preceding sections.

Property pledged as security for loans should be disclosed. The auditor may obtain information on pledging by reviewing the minutes, the register of charges and long-term contractual agreements; by confirming debt agreements; and by making enquiries of management. The auditor can determine the appropriateness of the entity's disclosures relating to assets under lease by referring to the authoritative accounting pronouncements and the related lease agreements.

Learning check

Do you know ...

16.6 ☐ Transactions involving property, plant and equipment are infrequent and, where material, are usually subject to special treatment. For this reason, auditors rarely test controls over non-current asset transactions or the plant register, preferring to adopt a predominantly substantive approach.

16.7 ☐ The main inherent risks are those for existence and valuation assertions, namely:
- that management has an incentive to overstate the existence and/or value of property, plant and equipment
- that valuation requires considerable estimation and judgement.

16.8 ☐ Because property, plant and equipment transactions are few and the make-up of the balance is relatively constant, the auditor's substantive procedures concentrate on verifying transactions that reconcile the opening balance with the closing balance.

16.9 ☐ Valuation requires:
- a consideration of the reasonableness, consistency and accuracy of the year's accumulated depreciation
- a consideration of the need for an impairment provision
- verification of revaluations.

SUMMARY

Inventories and property, plant and equipment are the major non-monetary assets in most entities' financial statements. Misstatements in these balances are often a major cause of audit failure. There are many similarities in the audit of these balances, but also some significant differences. For both balances, the main inherent risks are misstatements in the existence or occurrence assertion and the accuracy or valuation and allocation assertions. In verifying the existence of inventories, the auditor relies on physical inspection, whether through observation of cyclical counts verifying perpetual inventory records or through attendance at annual inventory counts.

However, in verifying property, plant and equipment, the auditor relies on verifying changes in the recorded balance, including an inspection of additions. The auditor rarely inspects assets making up the balance, reflecting the incidence of transactions that are frequent for inventories, being a current asset, but infrequent for property, plant and equipment.

Given that inventory and property, plant and equipment are non-monetary assets, valuation of both is determined by the application of accounting procedures involving a high degree of judgement. For inventories, the auditor needs to understand the costing system to determine its appropriateness and its accuracy in accumulating cost data. For property, plant and equipment, the main judgements involve estimating useful economic lives, residual value and the basis of depreciation. Again, the auditor needs to determine the appropriateness of the judgements made and the accuracy of the resulting calculations. In both cases, the auditor needs to ensure that the accounting basis adopted complies with applicable accounting standards and that required disclosures are properly made in the financial statements.

KEY TERMS

cyclical inventory counts, p. 670

finished goods, p. 667

inventory count sheets, p. 671

inventory master file, p. 669

inventory tags, p. 671

inventory transfer requisitions, p. 670

perpetual inventory records, p. 669

plant register, p. 690

raw materials, p. 667

stocktake/physical inventory count, p. 667

work in process, p. 667

MULTIPLE-CHOICE questions

16.1 Ensuring inventories include all materials, products and supplies on hand at the end of the reporting period derives from the audit assertion of:
A. Valuation and allocation.
B. Completeness.
C. Existence.
D. Rights and obligations.

16.2 Which of the following audit strategies would be most appropriate when an auditor has assessed that a predominantly substantive approach is necessary to determine inventory quantity?
A. Inventory quantities determined by physical count at or within a few days of the end of the reporting period.
B. Inventory quantities determined by physical count near the end of the reporting period, adjusted by reference to perpetual records.
C. Inventory quantities determined by reference to perpetual records, without a physical count at or near the end of the reporting period.
D. Inventory quantities determined by reference to perpetual records, with a sample of inventory items counted at each month end throughout the period reporting period.

16.3 If preliminary assessment of control risk supports management's intended reliance on inventory records, the auditor is most likely to:
A. Design an audit program to exclude testing the operating effectiveness of those controls.
B. Design an audit program to include testing the operating effectiveness of those controls.
C. Design an audit program testing only inventory transactions and tests of details of the inventory balance.
D. Design an audit program testing only inventory transactions and excluding tests of details of the inventory balance.

16.4 During the observation of the inventory count, the auditor has responsibility to:
  (i) Watch for damaged and obsolete inventory items.
 (ii) Make some test counts of inventory quantities.
(iii) Supervise the taking of the inventory.
A. (i) and (ii) only.
B. (ii) and (iii) only.
C. (i) and (iii) only.
D. (i), (ii) and (iii).

16.5 When the client engages an inventory specialist to take the inventory, the impact on the audit in this area is:
A. To eliminate the need to perform test counts.
B. To eliminate the need to observe the inventory.
C. Minimal because the specialists are considered independent auditors.
D. Minimal because the specialists are considered audit employees.

16.6 The auditor identifies the specific audit objective: 'determine that property, plant and equipment assets are in productive use at the end of the reporting period'. This objective is derived from:
A. The existence or occurrence assertion.
B. The completeness assertion.
C. The presentation and disclosure assertion.
D. The rights and obligations assertion.

16.7 When reviewing accumulated depreciation, the auditor seeks evidence as to the reasonableness, consistency and accuracy of depreciation charges. The substantive procedures performed seek to provide evidence for which assertion?
A. Completeness.
B. Rights and obligations.
C. Valuation.
D. Presentation and disclosure.

16.8 Which of the following statements about inherent risk assessments for property, plant and equipment is inaccurate?
A. Normally low for the presentation and disclosure assertion for plant assets acquired under finance leases.
B. Normally low for the existence or occurrence assertion in a merchandising entity because plant assets are not generally vulnerable to theft.
C. Normally moderate to high for the existence or occurrence assertion in a manufacturing entity because scrapped or retired plant assets may not be written off the books.
D. Normally low for the accuracy or valuation and allocation assertions when plant assets are purchased for cash.

16.9 Analytical procedures are not widely used in the audit of property, plant and equipment. Which of the following are valid comments about the use of analytical procedures in the audit of PPE?
  (i) Compare the annual depreciation charge with the cost of an asset to approximate the depreciation rate.
 (ii) A substantial asset balance variation can be caused by one or a few transactions of which the auditor is likely to already be aware.
(iii) Comparison of repairs expense with prior years may indicate capitalisation in error.
A. (i) and (ii) only.
B. (ii) and (iii) only.
C. (i) and (iii) only.
D. (i), (ii) and (iii).

REVIEW questions

16.10 Which of the following represent an existence test for property, plant and equipment?
A. Select a sample of items of machinery in the factory and agree that they are correctly recorded in the machinery general ledger account.
B. Review entries in the repairs and maintenance expense account for items of a capital nature.
C. Obtain details of material asset disposals during the period and ensure that they are not included on the non-current assets register at the period end.
D. Select a sample of invoices relating to motor vehicle purchases and ensure they are correctly recorded on the non-current assets register.

16.11 Describe the alternative methods by which entities determine their inventory at the end of the reporting period and the possible effect of each method on audit strategy.

16.12 List the procedures that should be adopted in a physical inventory count.

16.13 What are the three audit strategy options that an auditor has for verifying the existence (and completeness) of inventories and what is the implication of each strategy for control risk?

16.14 Many companies use standard costing as the basis for inventory costing. What audit procedures may be appropriate for establishing the fairness of the standard costs, for testing the maintenance of the standard cost records and for determining the disposition of variances?

16.15 How would an auditor test inventory cut-off at the year end?

16.16 When performing tests of details of balances for property, plant and equipment, it is necessary for the auditor to review accumulated depreciation. Discuss what this review entails.

16.17 Why does the auditor usually adopt a predominantly substantive audit strategy for property, plant and equipment assertions?

16.18 Discuss procedures that would be useful in ensuring that all disposals of property, plant and equipment have been recorded.

16.19 Consider the problems confronting the auditor in verifying both the rate and method of depreciation.

16.20 When conducting tests of details of transactions for property, plant and equipment, there are three types of transactions that need to be substantiated. These transactions are additions, disposals and repairs and maintenance. Briefly describe what is involved with substantiating each of these types of transactions.

PROFESSIONAL application questions

BASIC ★
MODERATE ★★
CHALLENGING ★★★

16.21 Inventory — stocktake ★★

You attended the inventory count of your client Davis Hydraulics Ltd. You observed the following during the count.

1. Warehouse staff counted specific areas of the stock as determined by the warehouse supervisor; staff members, including the warehouse supervisor, were allocated their own area to count.
2. Several blank paper sheets were issued to count staff for recording stock counted.
3. Staff were instructed to write down the stock description and number counted.
4. Staff were told to write the stock quantities in pencil on the sheets to ensure errors can be corrected.
5. Any staff that completed a section early were allocated to another area to help out one of the other staff.
6. The supervisor collected all sheets at the end of the count to finalise the stock count.

Required

Identify the weaknesses in the stocktake procedures above and identify how they could be improved.

16.22 Physical inventory — substantive procedures ★★

Stenton Toys Pty Ltd is a toy retailer with shops in each of the Australian state capitals. Stenton has a head office and a central warehouse in Brisbane. All stock purchases are made centrally and are held in the Brisbane warehouse; they are then despatched around the country as needed by each of the shops. Details of stock movements are recorded on a perpetual inventory system and Stenton carries out year-end stocktakes at all locations.

You are the auditor of Stenton and are planning the audit of the stocktake that is about to take place; you have established the following from your planning procedures.

1. An inventory report will be produced from the inventory system for each shop and the warehouse. The report gives details of inventory code, stock description, units held and unit

selling price. The report also gives a breakdown of where inventory items are held and the total value of items held at each location.

2. A sales movement report is also produced which gives details of: inventory code, unit descriptions, units purchased for the period and their cost price, units sold in the period.
3. The largest shop is in Melbourne and 35% of all stock is held there.
4. The Perth shop has suffered significant levels of stock shrinkage recently.
5. To facilitate the stocktake an additional report is produced which includes only the inventory code and description. Stock counters use this report to indicate the units of stock held at the time of the count.

Required

Describe how you would select samples to test the existence and completeness of inventory units. Indicate how the sample sizes used in the Melbourne and Perth shops would differ.

16.23 Physical inventory — substantive procedures ★★

Your firm is responsible for auditing the financial statements of Hucknall Manufacturing Ltd for the year ended 31 May 2015. The company operates from a single site. Its sales are $5 million and the profit before tax is $110 000. There are no inventory records, so the inventory counts at year-end will be used to value the inventory in the financial statements. Because Monday 31 May is a normal working day, it has been decided that the inventory count should take place on Sunday 30 May when there is no movement of inventory.

The company has produced the following schedule to determine the value of inventory at 31 May 2015 from that counted on 30 May 2015.

		$	$
Value of inventory counted at 30/5/15			583 247
Add	Cost of goods received on 31/5/15	10 969	
	Production labour on 31/5/15	3 260	
	Overheads relating to labour at 120%	3 260	18 141
Less	Cost of sales on 31/5/15		(36 740)
Value of inventory at 31/5/15			564 648

The company keeps basic accounting records on a microcomputer, using a standard software package. The following accounting procedures are used for sales, purchases and wages.

1. The shipping department raises dispatch notes when the goods are sent to customers. Sales invoices are produced from the dispatch notes. Sales invoices are input into the computer, which posts them to the accounts receivable ledger and the general ledger.
2. When goods are received, a receiving report is prepared. Purchase invoices are matched with the receiving reports and purchase orders, and authorised by the chief executive officer. After the purchase invoices have been authorised, they are input into the computer, which posts them to the accounts payable ledger and the general ledger.
3. For the wages system, the hours worked for each employee are input into the computer, which calculates the gross wage and deductions (e.g. for tax) and the net pay. All employees are paid weekly.

Required

(a) Describe the audit procedures you should perform to verify the accuracy of the inventory count:
  (i) before the inventory count
  (ii) on the day of the inventory count.
  Include details of the matters you should record in your working papers for follow-up at the final audit.

(b) Explain the substantive procedures you should perform to check the company's schedule (as shown above) that adjust the value of inventory at 30 May to that at the company's year-end of 31 May 2015. (You are required to verify only the total value of inventory of $564 648 at 31 May 2015. You are not required to describe the procedures necessary to verify the accuracy of the individual values of raw materials, work in progress and finished goods.)

(c) Describe the substantive procedures you should perform to check purchases cut-off at the year-end.[2]

16.24 Inventory — net realisable value ★★

You are the auditor of John Benson Ltd, a manufacturer of a variety of paper and cardboard stationery products. Product lines range from the everyday items that are low value but high volume as well as more expensive and specialised items that are produced for more niche markets. Closing inventory includes finished goods, work in process and raw materials.

You have completed the stocktake procedures and are happy that the stock quantities are correct. You are also happy that the cost of each product line has been correctly calculated. You are now focussed on assessing the net realisable value to establish if there is any need for a stock write-down. You have assessed a possible risk attached to the net realisable value of work in process and finished goods.

Required

Discuss the procedures that you should carry out to satisfy yourself that the provision for stock write-down to net realisable value is adequate.

16.25 Property valuation — reliance on experts ★★

Your client, FNP Ltd, engaged the services of Z & Co., a firm of real estate valuers, to perform a valuation of all real estate held by the company. As a result of this revaluation, property values on the balance sheet were significantly increased, leading to a material increase in net asset backing per share.

Required

(a) Describe the audit procedures that would be required with respect to the valuations performed by Z & Co.

(b) Explain whether the procedures identified in (a) would change if employees of FNP had performed the valuations.

(c) Assume that you are not satisfied with the results of procedures performed. Explain what alternative procedures could be performed.[3]

16.26 Inventory valuation — reliance on experts ★★

Your client is Estate Jewellers Pty Ltd, a proprietary company that specialises in estate jewellery. Estate Jewellers purchases pieces at auction, cleans and remodels them, and then sells them to the general public. This is the first year your firm has conducted the audit.

At year-end, Estate Jewellers expects to have around 2000 pieces of jewellery on hand, ranging from small items worth $50 to more expensive items worth over $10 000. No two items of jewellery are the same. Because of the complex nature of inventory, the audit partner has decided to engage an expert to provide a year-end valuation report. The expert is to use the client's (unpriced) inventory list and append his or her estimate of the (lower of cost and net realisable) value of each item. The partner intends to place full reliance on the expert's report to reach an opinion on Estate Jewellers' inventory balance. Year-end stocktake attendance by audit staff is not planned.

Required

(a) When an auditor decides it is appropriate to rely on an expert's report in lieu of stocktake attendance, explain what should be documented in the audit working papers in relation to this decision.

(b) Outline the arguments for and against relying on the expert's report in lieu of attendance at the stocktake.

(c) Explain what difference it would make to the level of reliance you would place on the expert's report if the scope of the expert's work was set by your firm and the expert's fee was paid by:
  (i) the audit firm
  (ii) the client.

(d) It is now after the end of the reporting period and you have arranged a meeting with the expert to discuss his report on the inventory. Give examples of questions to ask the expert in this meeting to satisfy yourself that the report is appropriate for your purposes.[4]

16.27 Property, plant and equipment — substantive procedures ★★

Your firm is the auditor of GreenBrown Ltd, a manufacturer. You have obtained a summary of the property, plant and equipment for the year ended 30 June 2015, which identifies cost and accumulated depreciation brought forward, additions and disposals in the year and depreciation charges.

A review of the management letter from the previous year's audit shows that there were some problems in relation to making a distinction between capital and revenue expenditure; some items were capitalised when they should have been expensed and other capital items were included in repairs and maintenance in the income statement.

Another risk identified from prior years relates to depreciation calculations; there is a range of depreciation rates within categories and there has been concern that the rates applied to some assets have been too low. The depreciation policy disclosed in the financial report shows:
- buildings: 2–4% straight line
- plant and machinery: 5–10% straight line
- fixtures fittings and equipment: 5–20% straight line.

Required
Describe audit procedures to ensure:
(a) the accuracy of the summary of property, plant and equipment
(b) all items of a capital expenditure are included in additions for the year and that no revenue expenditure has been capitalised
(c) the depreciation rates are calculated appropriately.

16.28 Property, plant and equipment — substantive procedures ★★

Your firm is the auditor of Daybrook Insurance Brokers Ltd, which operates from a number of branches and provides insurance for the general public and businesses. The company obtains insurance from large insurance companies and takes a commission for its services. You have been asked to audit certain aspects of the company's property, plant and equipment for the year ended 30 June 2015.

The company's main property, plant and equipment include:
- freehold land and buildings
- microcomputers, printers and related equipment, which are used by staff
- cars, which are provided to directors and salespeople who visit customers.

The company has been operating for a number of years, and it maintains details of its office equipment and cars on a computerised non-current asset register. The company uses the following depreciation rates:
- buildings (2% per year on cost)
- office equipment (including computers) (10% per year on cost)
- cars (25% per year on cost).

You are concerned that the depreciation rate for the computers may be inadequate.

Required

(a) Describe how you would verify the ownership of freehold land and buildings, computers and cars.

(b) Explain how you would determine that the depreciation rate on the various assets is adequate.[5]

 CASE studies

16.29 Property, plant and equipment — substantive procedures

Your firm is auditing the financial statements of Newthorpe Manufacturing Ltd for the year ended 30 June 2015. You have been assigned to the audit of the company's property, plant and equipment, which includes freehold land and buildings, plant and machinery, fixtures and fittings and motor vehicles.

The freehold land and buildings were purchased 12 years earlier (in July 2003) for $2 million. At the date of purchase, a valuer estimated that both the land and the buildings each had a value of $1 million. Depreciation has been charged since 2003 on the buildings at 2% per year on cost. At 30 June 2015 the accumulated depreciation is $200 000 before the revaluation.

A qualified valuer, who is not an employee of the company, valued the land and buildings at $5 million ($2.9 million for the land and $2.1 million for the buildings). These values will be incorporated into the financial statements as at 30 June 2015.

The partner in charge of the audit is concerned at the large increase in the value of the land and buildings since they were purchased. She has asked you to check the reliability and accuracy of the valuation. She suggested that ASA 620 *Using the Work of an Auditor's Expert* (ISA 620) could help you when carrying out this work.

In addition, you have been asked to verify the existence and completeness of plant and machinery recorded in the company's computerised non-current asset register, which records the description of each non-current asset, the original cost, the depreciation charge and the accumulated depreciation.

Required

(a) Describe the audit work you will carry out to check whether the valuer has provided an accurate and independent valuation of the land and buildings.

(b) Describe the audit work you will carry out to check the existence and completeness of plant and machinery, as recorded in the company's non-current asset register.[6]

16.30 Property, plant and equipment — audit objectives

Wear Wraith (WW) Co's main activity is the extraction and supply of building materials including sand, gravel, cement and similar aggregates. The company's year-end is 30 June and your firm has audited WW for a number of years. The main asset on the statement of financial position relates to non-current assets. A draft non-current asset note for the financial statements has been prepared. The note has not been reviewed by the senior accountant and so may contain errors.

	Land and buildings	Plant and machinery	Motor vehicles	Railway trucks	Total
COST	$	$	$	$	$
1 July 2014	100 000	875 000	1 500 000	–	2 475 000
Additions	10 000	125 000	525 000	995 000	1 655 000
Disposals	–	(100 000)	(325 000)	–	(425 000)
30 June 2015	110 000	900 000	1 700 000	995 000	3 705 000

Depreciation					
1 July 2014	60 000	550 000	750 000	–	1 360 000
Charge	2 200	180 000	425 000	199 000	806 200
Disposals	–	(120 000)	(325 000)	–	(445 000)
30 June 2015	62 200	610 000	850 000	199 000	1 721 200
Net book value					
30 June 2015	47 800	290 000	850 000	796 000	1 983 800
Net book value					
30 June 2014	40 000	325 000	750 000	–	1 115 000

- Land and buildings relate to company offices and land for those offices.
- Plant and machinery includes extraction equipment such as diggers and dumper trucks used to extract sand and gravel etc.
- Motor vehicles include large trucks to transport the sand, gravel etc.
- Railway trucks relate to containers used to transport sand and gravel over long distances on the railway network.

Depreciation rates stated in the financial statements are all based on cost and calculated using the straight line basis. The rates are:
- land and buildings (2%)
- plant and machinery (20%)
- motor vehicles (33%)
- railway trucks (20%).

Disposals in the motor vehicles category relates to vehicles which were 5 years old.

Required
(a) List the audit work you should perform on railway trucks.
(b) You have just completed your analytical procedures of the non-current assets note.
   (i) Excluding railway trucks, identify and explain any issues with the non-current asset note to raise with management.
   (ii) Explain how each issue could be resolved.[7]

 ## RESEARCH question

16.31 Inventory manipulation
Consider the following statement:

> The audit of inventory is one of the most risky areas of the audit. Management can manipulate the value of inventory through a variety of methods, such as through varying the provision for obsolescence or the method of valuation. It is therefore an area that can be 'massaged' by management to achieve its required profit level.

Required
(a) Evaluate the statement and illustrate by researching the Harris Scarfe corporate collapse, where inventory manipulation allowed the company to report 'profits' for a number of years.
(b) Consider AASB 102 *Inventories* (IAS 2) and the complementary auditing standard ASA 501 (ISA 501). How is the issue of 'estimation' in the recording of inventory considered and what audit procedures should have prevented the Harris Scarfe manipulation of inventory figures?

FURTHER READING

T Crabb, 'What's in store?', *Australian CPA*, October 2001.

L Sarasohn & M Luehlfing, 'Fixed assets don't squeak', *Management Accounting*, November 1996, pp. 29–36.

NOTES

1. Adapted from Worrells Solvency & Forensic Accountants, Fraud Awareness section, 'Stock fraud — inventory record frauds: description of inventory record frauds', 8 May 2006, www.worrells.net.au.

2. Adapted from ACCA Audit Framework, Paper 6, December 1998.

3. Adapted from Professional Year Programme of the ICAA, 1999, Advanced Audit Module.

4. Adapted from Professional Year Programme of the ICAA, 1999, Accounting 2 Module.

5. ibid.

6. Adapted from ACCA Audit Framework, Paper 6, June 1997.

7. Adapted from ACCA Audit and Internal Review, June 2006.

Answers to multiple-choice questions

16.1 *B*   16.2 *A*   16.3 *B*   16.4 *A*   16.5 *D*   16.6 *B*   16.7 *C*   16.8 *A*   16.9 *D*
16.10 *C*

chapter 17

Auditing cash and investments

OVERVIEW

17.1 Brief summary of audit procedures
17.2 Cash
17.3 Investments
Summary
Key terms
Multiple-choice questions

Review questions
Professional application questions
Case studies
Research question
Further reading
Notes

LEARNING objectives

After studying this chapter, you should be able to:

1 identify the audit objectives applicable to cash

2 discuss considerations relevant to determining the audit strategy for cash

3 design and execute an audit program for cash balances

4 explain procedures for confirming bank balances

5 describe the irregularity known as 'lapping' and how the auditor can detect it

6 identify the audit objectives applicable to investments

7 describe control procedures applicable to investments

8 design and execute an audit program for investments

9 explain the special considerations applicable to the audit of investments in subsidiaries, associates and joint ventures.

PROFESSIONAL STATEMENTS

Australian		International	
ASA 315	Identifying and Assessing the Risks of Material Misstatement through Understanding the Entity and Its Environment	ISA 315	Identifying and Assessing the Risks of Material Misstatement through Understanding the Entity and Its Environment
ASA 540	Auditing Accounting Estimates, Including Fair Value Accounting Estimates, and Related Disclosures	ISA 540	Auditing Accounting Estimates, Including Fair Value Accounting Estimates, and Related Disclosures
ASA 600	Special Considerations — Audits of a Group Financial Report (Including the Work of Component Auditors)	ISA 600	Special Considerations — Audits of Group Financial Statements (Including the Work of Component Auditors)
AGS 1030	Auditing Derivative Financial Instruments	IAPS 1012	Auditing Derivative Financial Instruments
GS 015	Audit Implications of Accounting for Investments in Associates		
GS 016	Bank Confirmation Requests		
AASB 3	Business Combinations	IFRS 3	Business Combinations
AASB 107	Statement of Cash Flows	IAS 7	Statement of Cash Flows
AASB 121	The Effects of Changes in Foreign Exchange Rates	IAS 21	The Effects of Changes in Foreign Exchange Rates
AASB 124	Related Party Disclosures	IAS 24	Related Party Disclosures
AASB 127	Consolidated and Separate Financial Statements	IAS 27	Consolidated and Separate Financial Statements
AASB 128	Investments in Associates	IAS 28	Investments in Associates
AASB 131	Interests in Joint Ventures	IAS 31	Interests in Joint Ventures

SCENE SETTER

Skimming

Skimming is a type of embezzlement which has several forms but is most likely to occur when staff handle cash and have direct contact with the customer. Where sales staff use a cash register, it may be possible for them to steal the cash received and select 'no-sale' on the till; it will appear that staff are using the till but a sale has not been recorded so the receipt can be pocketed — however, the cash in the till at the end of the day will still reconcile to the sales recorded. For cash sales where a till is not used, staff could accept cash from a customer without issuing a receipt, again pocketing the cash and not recording any sale. Where the person handling the cash also has access to inventory or receivables records it may be possible to cover their tracks even if the sale has been recorded. Detecting these types of fraud can be difficult particularly where no sale has been recorded. Segregation of duties between staff handling cash and those recording transactions, whether sales, inventories or receivables, is the single most effective preventative control. Other controls include disabling the no-sale button on cash registers and senior staff opening the post and recording cash receipts to ensure cheques are not embezzled.

The internal control structures for transactions affecting both cash and investment assets in connection with the audits of sales and purchases were described in chapters 14 and 15. This chapter is concerned mainly with the application of substantive audit procedures aimed at verifying these account balances, but also considers control procedures over the safekeeping of these assets: (1) the use of bank reconciliations in the case of cash and (2) the maintenance of an investment register.

For each of these account balances, this chapter:

- identifies the audit objectives
- describes controls over safekeeping
- discusses considerations relating to the audit plan
- explains applicable substantive procedures.

Special consideration is given, in the audit of cash, to procedures designed to detect a fraud known as 'lapping' and to the audit of petty cash balances and imprest bank accounts.

A particular feature of the audit of investments is the special disclosure requirement for investments in subsidiaries, associates and joint ventures. It is usually in the form of consolidated financial statements. This chapter also explains the additional audit responsibilities in verifying investments in group entities, and the responsibilities for the consolidated financial statements.

17.1 BRIEF SUMMARY OF AUDIT PROCEDURES

In the auditing of cash and investments, the key issues are to ensure that:

- the cash exists and is owned by the client and that all cash transactions at the end of the reporting period are complete and properly disclosed
- the investments exist, are owned, properly recorded (including profits or losses on any sales) and disclosed, and are properly valued at the end of the reporting period.

Cash normally comprises cash balances at the bank or similar institutions and cash on hand. In some cases, cash can, in fact, be a negative balance and thus a liability — such as when an entity is operating a bank overdraft facility. The starting point for verifying cash balances is to trace the current period's opening balances to the closing audited balances in the previous year's working papers. Next, the auditor should review the current period's activity in the general ledger cash accounts for any significant entries that are unusual in nature or amount and that may require investigation. The auditor then obtains any schedules that have been prepared by the entity showing reconciliations of bank accounts with the entity's records, including details of any undeposited receipts, unpresented cheques or direct bank transfers at the end of the reporting period. These schedules, usually referred to as bank reconciliation statements, are then mathematically checked and all movements during the period of the audit accounted for.

The auditor normally confirms the bank balance directly with the bank through a bank confirmation request. This letter is sent to all banks with whom the auditor is aware that the client has a relationship. The form requests information about account balances, securities, treasury management instruments, documents and other related information held by the bank on behalf of the entity. The auditor also requests copies of bank statements for a period of, say, up to 2 weeks after year-end, to ensure that all reconciling items of undeposited receipts, unpresented cheques and direct bank transfers at the end of the reporting period are genuine. Where the entity operates a number of bank accounts, an interbank transfer schedule is prepared to ensure all movements around year-end are properly accounted for and included in the bank reconciliation schedules.

Other cash balances, such as office petty cash, imprest bank accounts and cash balances in, for example, the cash tills in a department store, will often also be checked, although such balances are normally immaterial to the operations of the entity. Checking of these balances is usually a way of ensuring procedures are operating properly and that risks of fraud are minimised.

In the case of cash, there is normally no valuation problem because cash is cash. However, if the entity holds cash in foreign currencies, exchange risks have to be looked at. Other problems could occur where there are restrictions on the transfer of cash, such as in some foreign countries where an entity may operate. Finally, because cash balances do not normally show a stable or predictable relationship with other current or historical financial or operating data, the auditor will normally not perform any analytical review procedures in this part of the audit.

In the audit of investments, there are many similarities to the audit of cash but also some important differences. As with cash, the auditor starts with verifying the opening investment balances with audited amounts in the previous year's working papers. Next, the auditor reviews the activity in investment-related accounts to identify entries that are unusual in nature or amount and that should be investigated. Then the auditor checks entity-prepared schedules of investment additions and disposals in the period, for both mathematical accuracy and agreement with the underlying accounting records. In this analysis, the auditor is concerned with tracing evidence of sales and purchases of investments (by, for example, viewing original statements from share brokers and authorisations in the board meeting minutes if the transactions are large), and ensuring that any profits or losses on sales are properly calculated and included in the income statement. At this stage, the auditor can also vouch dividend and interest receipts to remittance advices or other notifications accompanying the payments.

Securities that confirm investment balances held at the entity's own premises should be inspected and counted at the same time as the count of cash and other negotiable instruments. For securities stored for safekeeping in bank safety deposit boxes, the banks will generally seal the boxes on the nominated date of the count at the entity's request and will confirm to the auditor that there was no access to the box, other than by the auditor, until all locations have been counted. Securities held by outsiders for safekeeping must be confirmed as of the date on which securities held by the entity are checked. Where the securities relate to listed companies, there will be no paper certificate confirming legal title. The legal title is usually registered on an Australian Securities Exchange database or something similar, in which case procedures specific to the situation will be necessary to obtain the verification required. The steps in the confirmation process for securities are identical to those for confirming receivables. Thus, the auditor must control the mailings and receive the responses directly from the custodian. The data confirmed are the same as the data that should be noted when the auditor is able to inspect the securities.

It is usually not possible to obtain much evidence from the application of analytical procedures to investment balance sheet accounts. Current asset investments do not tend to have any predictable relationship with other balances, and non-current investments are subject to so few transactions that it is easier to proceed directly to tests of details. Analytical procedures can, however, be applied in comparing interest and dividend revenues with investment balances. It is also important to note that the value of investments, such as investments in shares in listed companies, can change in value on a daily basis. Thus, confirmation of valuations of investments at the end of the reporting period is an important audit procedure.

This section briefly summarised the key procedures in the audit of cash and investments. In practice, the procedures can be more complex and are detailed in the rest of the chapter. Note also that additional procedures are required when an entity controls a number of subsidiaries and consolidated financial statements must be prepared and audited.

17.2 CASH

Cash balances include cash on hand and at bank or on deposit at similar financial institutions. Cash on hand includes undeposited receipts and petty cash. Cash at bank includes cash held in current and savings accounts and in imprest accounts, such as payroll bank accounts, that is available on demand. AASB 107 *Statement of Cash Flows* (IAS 7) has an intermediate category of investments referred to as cash equivalents. Cash equivalents are highly liquid investments readily convertible to known amounts of cash within 3 months. These are included with cash in the statement of cash flows and may be included with cash in the balance sheet (also known as the statement of financial position).

Other balances at bank that are not readily available and do not meet the definition of cash equivalents (i.e. debenture sinking fund cash and other accounts that have restrictions on their use) should ordinarily be classified as investments, rather than as part of cash balances. Unlike any other balance sheet account balances, cash may be either an asset or a liability. The latter arises where the bank or other institution with which the entity holds an account grants the entity an overdraft (i.e. the entity is allowed to write cheques or transfer funds in excess of the balance in the account up to an agreed limit).

LEARNING 1 objective

Identify the audit objectives applicable to cash.

17.2.1 Audit objectives

Internal control considerations and the related audit objectives for cash receipts and payments are covered in chapters 14 and 15. Table 17.1 shows the account balance audit objectives. Assertions about presentation and disclosure in respect of account balance audit objectives include occurrence, rights and obligations, completeness, classification and understandability, and accuracy and valuation. Refer to paragraph A111 of ASA 315 *Identifying and Assessing the Risks of Material Misstatement through Understanding the Entity and Its Environment* (ISA 315).

TABLE 17.1:
Selected specific audit objectives for cash balances

Transaction objectives	
Occurrence (**OE**)	Recorded receipt and payment transactions represent cash inflows and outflows during the period (**OE1**).
Completeness (**C**)	All cash inflows and outflows made during the period have been recorded (**C1**).
Accuracy (**AV**)	Payments and receipts are properly (accurately) recorded (**AV1**).
Cut-off (**CO**)	Year-end transfers of cash between banks are recorded in the proper period (**CO**).
Classification (**PD**)	Payments and receipts are recorded in the correct accounts (**PD1**).

Balances objectives	
Existence (OE)	Recorded cash balances exist at the end of the reporting period (OE2).
Rights and obligations (RO)	The entity has legal title to all cash balances shown at the end of the reporting period (RO1).
Completeness (C)	Recorded cash balances include the effects of all cash transactions that have occurred (C2).
Valuation and allocation (AV)	Recorded cash balances are realisable at the amounts stated on the balance sheet and agree with supporting schedules (AV2).
Presentation and disclosure objectives (PD)	
Occurrence and rights and obligations	Lines of credit, loan guarantees and other restrictions on cash balances are appropriately disclosed (PD2).
Completeness	Cash balances are properly identified and classified in the balance sheet (PD3).
Classification and understandability	Cash balances are appropriately presented and information disclosed is clearly expressed (PD4).
Accuracy and valuation	Cash balances are disclosed accurately and at appropriate amounts (PD5).

LEARNING objective 2

Discuss considerations relevant to determining the audit strategy for cash.

17.2.2 Developing the audit plan

Before planning the audit, it is necessary to consider the effectiveness of control procedures that are designed to ensure the correctness of the recorded balance by way of regular bank reconciliations and the use of imprest accounts. We then consider materiality and risk, before identifying factors that are applicable to determining an effective strategy for the audit of cash.

Safekeeping of cash

Although the auditor adopts a predominantly substantive approach to the audit of cash balances, an understanding of procedures for maintaining accountability over cash is necessary in designing the substantive tests of details. The main procedures are:
- independently performed bank reconciliations
- the use of imprest accounts.

Bank reconciliations

In the audit of cash receipts (see chapter 14) and cash payments (see chapter 15), the auditor will have obtained an understanding of **bank reconciliations** and tested controls relating to their preparation and use. This is a major internal control that relates to the audit of cash. This involves an independent comparison of the balance shown on the bank statement and the balance recorded in the entity's records. The difference between the two is reconciled by listing outstanding deposits and unpresented cheques. Verifying the reconciliation of the bank account at the end of the reporting period is an important substantive procedure.

Imprest accounts

An **imprest petty cash fund** is established by transferring a specified amount of cash, such as $500 or $750, to a petty cash box. When cash is paid out of the fund, an authorised voucher is placed in the petty cash box in its place. This voucher could be a supplier's invoice or a special petty cash voucher authorised by a responsible official. When the cash gets low, the vouchers are used as support for a cheque requisition to replenish the fund. On replenishment, the cash in the petty cash box is restored to its imprest level. The following internal control features apply to the management of an imprest petty cash fund.

- The fund should be maintained at the imprest level; that is, cash in the fund plus vouchers for payments should always equal the imprest amount.
- The fund should be in the custody of one person.
- The fund should be kept secure and stored in the safe when not in use.
- Payments from the fund should be for small amounts, and documentation should support each payment.
- The fund should not be mingled with other cash.
- Replenishment of the fund should be based on a review of supporting documentation.
- Upon payment, supporting documents should be stamped 'paid' to prevent their reuse.

Certain bank accounts — typically payroll and dividend bank accounts — are sometimes also set up on an imprest basis. The **imprest bank account** is opened or replenished with the net payroll, dividend, and so on. When all cheques written on the account have been presented, the balance will be zero. Until such time, reconciliation can be achieved by comparing the balance as per the bank statement with unpresented cheques. Internal controls over an imprest bank account include the following.

- One person, such as a paymaster or the accountant, should be authorised to sign cheques drawn on the account.
- Only payroll cheques, dividend cheques, and so on should be written against the account.
- Each pay/dividend period, a cheque for the total net amount payable should be deposited in the imprest bank account.
- The imprest bank account should be independently reconciled each month.

Materiality and risk

For many entities, cash balances represent only a small proportion of assets. However, the amount of cash flowing through the accounts over a period of time is usually greater than for any other account in the financial statements. Moreover, cash is vital to the survival of the business as a going concern. The inability of an entity to pay its debts as they fall due because it has a shortage of cash can render a company insolvent, despite the profitability of its operations. Cash has a materiality that is greater (relative to its balance) than any other account balance. The cash balance is, therefore, material in a qualitative way, even though it may not always be material in a quantitative way. Figure 17.1 illustrates the effect of the different transaction cycles on the cash balance, which shows that the cash account is affected by all of the business processes and therefore many accounting transactions affect the cash account.

The high volume of transactions contributes to a significant level of inherent risk for cash balance assertions, particularly existence and completeness. In addition, the nature of cash balances makes them susceptible to theft, as evidenced by numerous kinds of fraudulent schemes involving cash. In contrast to receivables or inventories, however, the risks pertaining to the rights and obligations assertion and the valuation and disclosure assertions for cash are minimal, given the absence of complexities involving these assertions.

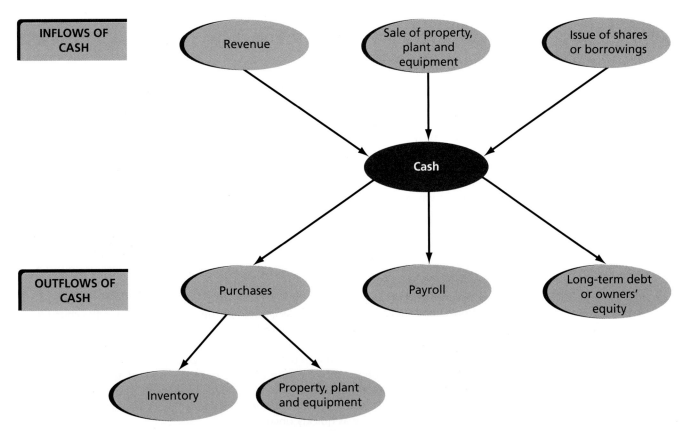

FIGURE 17.1: The effects of major accounting transactions on cash

Audit strategy

Given the large volume of cash transactions tested in other cycles and the often small account balance, the audit strategy is invariably to concentrate on verifying the account balance. The approach is therefore usually substantive. The main procedures for cash balances are to audit the bank reconciliation and reconcile that balance to the confirmation from the bank. The auditor should thus be able to verify the balance exactly because no judgement is needed in determining the figure. Therefore, any differences found will almost always be considered material because of the ease in which the auditor should be able to verify the final balance and the materiality of the transactions that affect this balance.

In auditing the cash balance, the auditor should also be aware of the possibility of fraud. Cash is an area that is more susceptible to fraud than some other areas, so this increases the inherent risk of this part of the audit. This risk is one of the reasons even a small discrepancy in the audit of cash should be followed up. The following Professional Environment article outlines a fraud in a large church at the hands of an unscrupulous bookkeeper.

As previously discussed, liquidity is crucial to the company's survival. The cash adequacy and the flows of cash should be reviewed carefully by the auditor. These issues are considered in more detail in chapter 18.

17.2.3 Substantive procedures for cash balances

Procedures described in this section exclude those for petty cash and imprest bank accounts. The audit of these two accounts is considered separately (see pp. 731–2).

*T*he most commonly occurring fraud within corporations is asset misappropriation. According to the Association of Certified Fraud Examiners, more than 91% of all internal fraud schemes involved an asset misappropriation element, and the median loss from an asset misappropriation was $150 000. Asset misappropriations include the misuse or theft of assets belonging to a company.

These are the white collar crimes we think about most, probably because they are so commonplace in terms of the number of cases that occur. Furthermore, they are the kinds of cases we most commonly hear about in the press.

In the real world

Cash receipts fraud

A large church suffered a significant cash fraud at the hands of an unscrupulous bookkeeper. Controls were in place to guard against theft. A group of volunteers counted the weekly cash collections together, overseeing one another. A sheet documenting the cash collections was prepared and submitted to the bookkeeper along with the cash.

The bookkeeper never deposited the cash, but kept the documentation in the church's files. The documentation was never compared against the bank deposits, so for more than two years, the bookkeeper stole nearly all cash collections without detection.

The fraud was detected when the bookkeeper took a sick day and another employee received the bank statement. Although she did not normally look at the bank statements, the envelope was already open so she decided to examine the contents. She immediately found checks made payable to the bookkeeper. An investigation ensued, and the larger theft of cash was quickly uncovered.

Asset misappropriations are commonly detected through employee monitoring, either via direct supervision by managers, or through indirect methods such as internal controls like segregation of duties, account reconciliation, and independent verification of data.

Many instances of errors and fraud can be detected through normal control activities (like account reconciliation) in conjunction with analytical review of accounts (such as ratio analysis). Additional things such as analysis of computerised data with specialised software can aid in detecting asset misappropriation.[1]

Determining detection risk

As explained previously, the significance of cash to the entity's liquidity and the fact that the balance is relatively small mean that the acceptable level of detection risk in verifying cash balances is invariably set as low.

LEARNING **3**
objective

Design and execute an audit program for cash balances.

Designing substantive procedures

Table 17.2 lists possible substantive procedures to achieve the specific audit objectives for cash balances. The list is organised in accordance with the general framework for developing audit programs for substantive procedures, which was explained in chapter 12. Note that several of the tests apply to more than one audit objective and that each objective is covered by multiple possible procedures. Not all of the procedures will be performed in every audit. Each procedure is explained as follows and includes comments on when certain of the tests could be omitted and on how some tests can be tailored based on applicable risk factors.

TABLE 17.2: Possible substantive procedures for cash balance assertions

Category	Substantive procedure	Cash balance audit objective (from table 17.1)					
		OE2	C2	R02	AV2	CO	PD no.
Initial procedures	1. Perform initial procedures on cash balances and records that will be subjected to further testing. (a) Trace opening balances for cash on hand and in bank to previous year's working papers. (b) Review activity in general ledger accounts for cash and investigate entries that appear unusual in amount or source. (c) Obtain entity-prepared summaries of cash on hand and in bank, verify mathematical accuracy, and determine agreement with general ledger.				✓		
Analytical procedures	2. Perform analytical procedures by comparing cash balances with expected amounts.	✓	✓		✓		
Tests of details of transactions	3. Perform cash cut-off tests. (Note: These tests may have been performed as part of the audit programs for accounts receivable and accounts payable.) (a) Observe that all cash received by the close of business on the last day of the financial year is included in cash and that no receipts of the subsequent period are included, or (b) Review documentation such as daily cash summaries, duplicate deposit slips, and bank statements covering several days before and after the year-end date to determine proper cut-off. (c) Observe the last cheque issued and mailed on the last day of the financial year and trace to the accounting records to determine the accuracy of the cash payments cut-off, or (d) Compare dates on cheques issued for several days before and after the year-end date to the dates on which the cheques were recorded to determine proper cut-off.					✓	
	4. Trace bank transfers before and after the end of the reporting period to determine that each transfer is properly recorded as a payment and a receipt in the same accounting period.					✓	
Tests of details of balances	5. Confirm bank balances.	✓	✓	✓	✓		
	6. Confirm other arrangements with banks.	✓	✓	✓	✓		
	7. Verify reconciliations as appropriate.	✓	✓	✓	✓		✓2
	8. Obtain and use the subsequent period's statements to verify bank reconciliation items and look for evidence of window dressing.	✓	✓	✓	✓		
	9. Count undeposited cash on hand.	✓	✓	✓	✓		

(continued)

Category	Substantive procedure	Cash balance audit objective (from table 17.1)					
		OE2	C2	R02	AV2	CO	PD no.
Presentation and disclosure	10. Compare statement presentation with applicable accounting standards. (a) Determine that cash balances are properly identified and classified. (b) Determine that bank overdrafts are reclassified as current liabilities. (c) Make enquiries of management, review correspondence with banks, and review minutes of board meetings to determine matters requiring disclosure, such as lines of credit, loan guarantees, compensating balance agreements, or other restrictions on cash balances.						✓3–5 ✓3–5 ✓2

Initial procedures

The starting point for verifying cash balances is to trace the current period's opening balances to the closing audited balances in the previous year's working papers. Next, the auditor should review the current period's activity in the general ledger cash accounts for any significant entries that are unusual in nature or amount and that may require investigation.

In addition, the auditor obtains any schedules that might have been prepared by the entity showing summaries of undeposited cash receipts at different locations and/or summaries of bank balances. The auditor should determine the mathematical accuracy of such schedules and check their agreement with related cash balances in the general ledger. This test provides evidence about the valuation assertion. The auditor should also obtain copies of all bank reconciliations for the year.

Analytical procedures

Cash balances do not normally show a stable or predictable relationship with other current or historical financial or operating data. As a result, the auditor will often not perform any analytical review procedures in this part of the audit. If the auditor does decide to perform some analytical review procedures, they are usually limited to comparisons with previous year's cash balances or with budgeted amounts.

Tests of details of transactions

Tests of details of cash receipt and cash payment transactions were discussed in chapters 14 and 15. The audit procedures discussed in these chapters give the auditor comfort in relation to the assertions in relation to cash transactions; this chapter looks at tests of transactions around the end of the reporting period (cut-off) that help verify the balance as at that year-end date.

Cash cut-off tests

A proper cut-off of cash receipts and cash payments at the end of the year is essential to the proper statement of cash at the end of the reporting period. Two **cash cut-off tests** are performed:

- a cash receipts cut-off test (see chapter 14)
- a cash payments cut-off test (see chapter 15).

The use of the subsequent period's bank statement (described below) is also helpful in determining whether a proper cash cut-off has been made. Cash cut-off tests are directed mainly at the financial statement assertions of existence and completeness.

Tracing bank transfers

Many entities maintain accounts with more than one bank. A company with multiple bank accounts may transfer money between bank accounts. Money may be transferred, for example, from a general bank account to a payroll bank account for payroll cheques (or for direct transfers to employees) that are to be distributed on the next pay day. When a bank transfer occurs, several days will elapse before the cheque clears the bank on which it is drawn. Thus, cash on deposit as per bank records will be overstated during this period because the cheque will be included in the balance of the bank in which it is deposited and will not be deducted from the bank on which it is drawn. Bank transfers may also result in a misstatement of the bank balance as per books if the payment and receipt are not recorded in the same accounting period.

Intentionally recording a transfer as a deposit in the receiving bank while failing to show a deduction from the account on which the transfer cheque is drawn is an irregularity known as **kiting**. Kiting may be used to conceal a cash shortage or overstate cash at bank at the end of the reporting period.

The auditor identifies bank transfers by analysing the cash book for a few days either side of the end of the reporting period, then enters these into a **bank transfer schedule**. The schedule is then completed by determining, from applicable bank statements, the dates on which the bank recorded the transfers, as illustrated in table 17.3.

TABLE 17.3: Bank transfer schedule

Cheque number or direct bank transfer reference	Bank accounts		Amount of cheque ($) or direct bank transfer	Payment date		Receipt date	
	From	To		Per books	Per bank	Per books	Per bank
4100	General	Payroll	50 000	30/6	3/7	30/6	2/7
4275	General	Branch 1	10 000	30/6	4/7	2/7	2/7
4280	General	Branch 2	20 000	2/7	2/7	30/6	30/6
B403	Branch 4	General	5 000	2/7	3/7	3/7	30/6

If we assume all cheques are dated and issued on 30 June, cheque 4100 in table 17.3 has been handled properly because both book entries were made in June and both bank entries occurred in July. This cheque would be listed as an unpresented cheque in reconciling the general bank account at 30 June and as a deposit in transit in reconciling the payroll bank account. Cheque 4275 illustrates a transfer cheque in transit at the closing date. Cash per books is understated by $10 000 because the cheque has been deducted from the balance per books by the issuer in June, but has not been added to the Branch 1 account per books by the depositor until July. Thus, an adjusting entry is required at 30 June to increase the branch balance per books.

Cheques/direct bank transfer 4280 and B403 illustrate the likelihood of kiting because these June cheques were not recorded as payments per books until July, even though they were deposited in the receiving banks in June. Cheque 4280 results in a $20 000 overstatement of cash at bank because the receipt per books occurred in June, but the corresponding book deduction was not made until July. Cheque B403 may illustrate an attempt to conceal a cash shortage because the bank deposit occurred in June, presumably to permit the reconciliation of bank and book balances, and all other entries were made in July. Similar issues can apply when transfers are done electronically, although this is much less likely because transactions are often completed on the same day — thus the timing issues that relate to cheques around the end of the reporting period would seldom apply.

Kiting is possible when weaknesses in internal controls allow one person to issue and record cheques (i.e. improper segregation of duties) or when there is collusion between the people responsible for the two functions. In addition to tracing bank transfers, the auditor may detect kiting by:

- obtaining and using a subsequent period's bank statement because the kited cheque clearing in July will not appear on the list of unpresented cheques for June
- performing a cash cut-off test, because the last cheque issued in June will not be recorded in the cheque register.

The tracing of bank transfers provides reliable evidence concerning the existence and completeness assertions.

Tests of balances

There are five commonly used substantive tests for cash balances in this category:

1. confirming bank balances
2. confirming other arrangements with banks
3. verifying bank reconciliations
4. obtaining and using the subsequent period's bank statement
5. counting cash on hand.

LEARNING objective 4

Explain procedures for confirming bank balances.

Confirming bank balances

The auditor normally confirms the bank balance directly with the bank through a **bank confirmation** request. This letter is sent to all banks with whom the auditor is aware that the client has a relationship. The form requests information about account balances, securities, treasury management instruments, documents and other related information held by the bank on behalf of the entity.

The procedures for performing bank confirmation requests are outlined in GS 016 *Bank Confirmation Requests* (there is no international equivalent). An example is shown in figure 17.2 for Bates Ltd.

GS 016 states that the auditor would send bank confirmation requests when the entity's banking operations are significant, complex or unusual, or there are deficiencies in the control environment that impact on assertion and disclosures regarding the entity's activities. In reality, however, the accepted practice is that these requests are sent on every audit and it would be considered highly unusual not to send one. The client must sign a letter of authorisation to the bank requesting completion of the form. The auditor (in consultation with the client) fills in the shaded areas of the form. The bank is then responsible for completing the information requested in the unshaded areas of the form.

The confirming of cash on deposit provides evidence mainly of the existence of cash at bank (because there is written acknowledgement that the balance exists) and of rights and obligations (because the balances are in the name of the entity). The response from the bank also provides some evidence for the valuation assertion for cash at bank, in that the confirmed balance is used in arriving at the correct cash balance at the end of the reporting period. Furthermore, it contributes to the completeness assertion; however, it cannot be relied on entirely because the bank confirmation contains a disclaimer in favour of the bank. The bank cannot be held liable if the information supplied is incomplete or inaccurate.

FIGURE 17.2: Bank confirmation request form

Bank confirmation — audit request

Instructions

Auditor

(a) Complete all known details in shaded areas before forwarding to the bank, including all known account names and the corresponding BSB and account names.

(b) If the space provided on the form is inadequate, attach a separate request giving the full details of the information required.

Bank

(a) Confirm that the details provided in the shaded areas are correct as at the confirmation date, and highlight any variation/s. Also add any relevant information that may have been omitted by the customer/auditor.

(b) Complete unshaded areas in sections 1–10.

(c) Sign the completed form and return the original to the auditor, and in duplicate to the customer, in the stamped addressed envelopes provided. A copy may be retained by the bank.

Bank (Name & Address) **Big City Bank**	Customer/Entity (Name & Address) **Bates Ltd**		
Auditor (Name & Address) **Big 4 Auditor 1 High Street Anytown** Contact Name: **Anne O'Ditor** Telephone Number: **91234567** Fax Number: **97654321** Email Address: **anneoditor@big4.com**	Confirmation Date: **30 June 2015**		
	Authority to Disclose Information attached	Yes ☐ No ☐	
	Third Party Authority attached	Yes ☐ No ☐ Not applicable ☐	
Date of Audit Request: **1 June 2015**	Request for acknowledgement attached	Yes ☐ No ☐	

1. CREDIT ACCOUNT BALANCES

Provide details of all account balances in favour of the bank customer as at the confirmation date, in respect of current accounts, interest bearing deposits, foreign currency accounts, convertible certificates of deposit, money market deposits, cash management trusts and any other credit balances. Provide details for the accounts listed below and for any other accounts not listed.

Provide details of any account or balance that is subject to any restriction(s) whatsoever and indicate the nature and extent of the restriction (e.g. garnishee order).

Account Name	BSB Number	Account Number	Currency	Balance
Bates Ltd	123-456	12345678	Bank to complete unshaded areas	
Bank to provide information on other accounts not identified by auditor/customer				

(continued)

2. DEBIT ACCOUNT BALANCES

Provide details of all account balances owed to the bank by the bank customer as at the confirmation date, in respect of overdraft accounts, bank loans, term loans, credit cards and any other debit balances.

Provide details of any account or balance that is subject to any restriction(s) whatsoever and indicate the nature and extent of the restriction (e.g. garnishee order).

Account Name	BSB Number	Account Number	Currency	Balance
—	—	—	Bank to complete unshaded areas	
Bank to provide information on other accounts not identified by auditor/customer				

3. PROMISSORY NOTES/BILLS OF EXCHANGE HELD FOR COLLECTION ON BEHALF OF THE CUSTOMER
(Bank to complete)

Marker/Acceptor	Due Date	Balance
—	—	—

4. CUSTOMER'S OTHER LIABILITIES TO THE BANK (Bank to complete)

Provide details of the following as at the confirmation date:

(a) Acceptances, bills discounted with recourse to the customer or any subsidiary or related party of the customer, endorsed drafts/notes, forward exchange contracts, letters of credit, liability in respect of shipping documents where customer's account not yet debited.

(b) Bonds, guarantees, indemnities or other undertakings given to the bank by the customer in favour of third parties (including separately any such items in favour of any subsidiary or related party of the customer). Give details of the parties in favour of whom guarantees or undertakings have been given, whether such guarantees or undertakings are written or oral, and their nature.

(c) Bonds guarantees, indemnities or other undertakings given by you, on your customer's behalf, stating whether there is recourse to your customer and/or any other related entity.

(d) Other liabilities — give details.

Name of Liability	Terms of Liability	Currency	Name of Beneficiary	Balance
—	—	—	—	—

5. ITEMS HELD AS SECURITY FOR CUSTOMER'S LIABILITIES TO THE BANK (Bank to complete)

With respect to items held as security for customer's liabilities to the bank, indicate whether the security:

(a) relates to particular borrowings or liabilities to the bank and whether it is lodged in the customer's name or by a third party (if lodged by a third party, that party's authority to disclose details must be attached)

(b) is formally charged (provide details of date, ownership and type of charge)

(c) supports facilities granted by the bank to the customer or to another party

(d) is limited in amount or to a specific borrowing or, if to your knowledge, there is a prior, equal or subordinate charge.

Provide details of any arrangements for set-off of balances or compensating balances (e.g. back-to-back loans). Include details of date, type of document and account covered, any acknowledgement of set-off, whether given by specific letter of set-off or incorporated in some other document. Provide details of any negative pledge arrangements that exist. Provide details here:

—			

6. LEASES (Bank to complete)
Provide details of all known finance leasing commitments:

Leased Item	Restrictions / Special Arrangements	Lease Term	Currency	Implicit Interest Rate	Repayment Terms	Balance
—	—	—	—	—	—	—

7. ACCOUNTS OPENED/CLOSED (Bank to complete)
List details of any accounts opened or closed during the twelve months prior to confirmation date.

Account Name	BSB Number	Account Number	Open or Closed?	Date opened/closed
—	—	—	—	—

8. UNUSED LIMITS/FACILITIES (Bank to complete)
Please confirm details of all available unused limits/facilities at confirmation date.

Types of Facility	Facility Limit	Unused Facility	Terms of Facility Use
—	—	—	—

9. DEFAULTS AND BREACHES (Bank to complete)
With reference to the customer's accounts with the bank, provide details of any defaults or breaches during the period and full details of such defaults and breaches. Include details, for example, of:
   (a) loans payable in default at the confirmation date and whether they have since been re-negotiated
   (b) bank covenants breached during the twelve months up to the confirmation date and whether the breach was remedied.
Provide details here:

—

10. OTHER INFORMATION
Please confirm (see shaded area below) and/or provide any other details (unshaded area) relating to any financial relationships not dealt with under sections to 1–9 above.

Auditor/customer to complete known details in shaded area
Bank to provide other information not identified by customer
—

11. BANK AUTHORISATION (Bank to complete)
This certificate has been completed from our records at .... (bank details). The Bank and its staff are unable to warrant the correctness of that information and accordingly hereby disclaim all liability in respect of the same. The information contained herein is confidential and provided for private use in confirmation of our customer accounts for audit purpose only. It may not be used for any other purpose or by any other persons. In particular this is not a credit reference.

Signature: B Teller	Other authorised details (where applicable)
Name (print name): B. Teller Title: Manager Telephone Number: 93456789 Email Address: b.teller@bigcitybank.com Date completed: 6 July 2015	

The confirming of overdraft and loan balances provides evidence of:

- existence, because there is written acknowledgement that the loan balance exists
- rights and obligations, because the loan is a debt of the entity
- valuation, because the response indicates the amount of the loan balance.

This test also contributes to the completeness assertion in the same manner as for confirming deposit balances.

Confirming other arrangements with banks

The bank confirmation form also requests information as to other arrangements with the bank, such as bills of exchange held by the bank for collection, bills discounted with recourse, guarantees of loans to third parties and unused facilities.

The auditor enters details of such arrangements as are believed to exist. The auditor's request for other information does not require the branch holding the account to make a detailed search of all of the bank's records, and the response must be interpreted in the light of the bank's disclaimer of responsibility. Nevertheless, the confirmation of other arrangements with banks is especially helpful in meeting the disclosure assertion. It also provides evidence for each of the other assertions. However, the evidence for the completeness assertion is limited to information known by the branch officer who is completing the confirmation.

Where the auditor believes there may be material accounts, agreements or transactions that he or she is unaware of, the auditor should contact the bank and request further information.

Verifying bank reconciliations

Testing of a client's bank reconciliation is central to the audit of cash balances. This testing verifies that the balance confirmed with the bank agrees with the bank balance per the client's records. Follow the steps below by referring to the reconciliation shown in figure 17.3.

1. Check the mathematical accuracy (✗) and compare with the general ledger (✗).
2. Verify the bank balance per the bank confirmation with the bank balance per the reconciliation (↖).
3. Trace unpresented cheques on the bank reconciliation to the subsequent period's bank statement (✓).
4. Trace deposits in transit on the bank reconciliation to the subsequent period's bank statement (✓).
5. Verify any bank charges or errors on the reconciliation with the bank statement or other supporting documentation (φ).

In some situations, the auditor may perform the bank reconciliation, such as when:

- the client has not prepared one
- the client's reconciliation has some significant unreconciled items
- there is a lack of segregation of duties in the preparation of the bank reconciliation.

This situation is not ideal, and the auditor should consider control risks as high in this area and strongly recommend improvements in the management letter prepared at the end of the audit.

However, the possible problems of the auditor performing this accounting task (e.g. objectivity issues) are outweighed by the significant problems created by any of the above scenarios for issuing an unqualified audit opinion.

Testing or preparing a bank reconciliation establishes the correct cash at bank balance at the end of the reporting period. Thus, it is a primary source of evidence for the valuation assertion. This test also provides evidence for the existence, completeness, and rights and obligations assertions.

Bates Ltd
Bank reconciliation — City Bank
30/6/15
(PBC)

Prepared by : <u>C.J.W.</u>   Date: <u>15/7/15</u>
Reviewed by: <u>A.C.E.</u>   Date: <u>18/7/15</u>

Account no. 110 30/6/15
Bank acc. no. 12345-642

		Per books	Per bank		
Balance per bank					120 262.47 ﹨
Deposits in transit:		29/6	2/7	8 425.15 ✓	
		30/6	7/7	17 844.79 ✓	26 269.94 ﹨
Unpresented cheques:			1047	225.94 ✓	
			1429	21 600.00 ✓	
			1435	47.25 ✓	
			1436	1 428.14 ✓	
			1437	1 000.00 ✓	
			1440	832.08 ✓	
			1441	41.08 ✓	(25 174.49) ✗
Add NSF cheque — ZIM 28/6					200.00 ϕ
Balance per books					121 557.92 ✗
Adjusting entry — AJE4					200.00
Balance as adjusted					121 357.92
					To A ✗

Adjusting entry

Dr Accounts receivable ZIM	200	
Cr Cash in bank		200
NSF cheque charged by bank 29/6.		

﹨ Verified with bank statement and bank confirmation
✓ Traced to January bank statement
✗ Footed (added)
ϕ Traced to statement and debit memoranda
✗ Traced to general ledger

FIGURE 17.3:
Review of entity-prepared bank reconciliation

Obtaining and using the subsequent period's bank statement

The **subsequent period's bank statement** is normally issued at the end of the month following the entity's financial year-end. In most situations this timeframe will be sufficient. However, if the audit deadline does not permit waiting for the issue of this statement, then a special statement can be requested. The date should be at a point in time that will permit most of the year-end unpresented cheques to clear the bank — usually 7 to 10 business days following the end of the entity's financial year. On receipt of the subsequent period's bank statement, the auditor should:

- trace all cheques and bank transfers dated but not cleared in the previous financial year to the unpresented cheques and bank transfers listed on the bank reconciliation
- trace deposits or bank transfers in transit on the bank reconciliation to deposits on the statement
- scan the statement for unusual items such as large transfers close to year-end.

The tracing of cheques is designed to verify the list of unpresented cheques. In this step, the auditor may also find that a cheque dated in the previous period which is not on the list of unpresented cheques has cleared the bank and that some of the cheques listed as unpresented have not cleared the bank. The former may be indicative of the irregularity known as kiting, which we explained earlier in connection with bank transfers (see pp. 719–20); the latter may be due to delays in the entity mailing the cheques or in the payees depositing the cheques. The auditor should investigate any unusual circumstances.

When the aggregate effect of uncleared cheques is material, it may indicate an irregularity known as **window dressing**. This is a deliberate attempt to enhance a company's apparent short-term solvency. (Assume that the entity's balances at the end of the reporting period show current assets of $800 000 and current liabilities of $400 000. If $100 000 of cheques or direct bank transfer payments to short-term creditors have been prematurely entered, then the correct totals are current assets of $900 000 and current liabilities of $500 000, which results in a 1.8:1 current ratio instead of the reported 2:1.) Window dressing is normally perpetrated by writing cheques on the last day of the financial year but not mailing them until several weeks later, when cleared funds are available at the bank to meet those cheques. If none of a sequence of cheques is presented for payment on the bank statement for more than 2 weeks after the end of the reporting period, then the auditor should make enquiries of the treasurer. Recipients do not usually delay banking cheques once received, and it is normal for most cheques to clear the bank statement within a week of issue. Where the evidence is clear that the company has engaged in material window dressing, the auditor should recommend appropriate adjustments to cash at bank and creditors.

The tracing of deposits in transit to the subsequent period's bank statement is normally a relatively simple matter because the first deposit on that statement should be the deposit in transit shown on the reconciliation. When this is not the case, the auditor should determine the underlying circumstances for the time lag from the accountant, and corroborate his or her explanations. Delays in depositing cash receipts could indicate the practice of a fraud known as lapping (see p. 728). Generally, deposits in transit would be expected to be minimal because of the use of electronic transfers and the speed of processing.

In scanning the subsequent period's statement for unusual items, the auditor should be alert for such items as unrecorded bank debits and credits, and bank errors and corrections. Figure 17.3 illustrates a deposit made before the year-end returned by the drawer's bank after the year-end, marked 'not sufficient funds' (NSF) and requiring adjustment.

Counting cash on hand

Cash on hand consists of undeposited cash receipts and change funds. To perform **cash counts** properly, the auditor should:

- control all cash and negotiable instruments held until all funds have been counted
- insist that the custodian of the cash is present throughout the count
- obtain a signed receipt from the custodian on return of the funds
- ascertain that all undeposited cheques are payable to the order of the entity, either directly or through endorsement.

The control of all funds is designed to prevent transfers by entity personnel of counted funds to uncounted funds. The sealing of funds and the use of additional auditors are often required when cash is held in many locations. Having the custodian present and requiring his or her signature on return of the funds minimises the possibility, in the event of a shortage, of the custodian claiming that all cash was intact when released to the auditor for counting.

This procedure provides evidence of each of the financial statement assertions except disclosure. Note that the evidence about rights is weak because the custodian of the fund may have substituted personal cash to cover a shortage.

Companies generally try to keep cash on hand to a minimum and therefore this amount is often very immaterial. As a result, in many audits this procedure is not performed, although this should be reassessed when there are circumstances indicating a higher risk of fraud associated with cash.

PROFESSIONAL ENVIRONMENT
Cash sales system

B-Star is a theme park based on a popular series of children's books. Customers pay a fixed fee to enter the park, where they can participate in a variety of activities such as riding roller-coasters, playing on slides and purchasing themed souvenirs from gift shops.

The park is open all year and has been in operation for the last 7 years. It is located in a country which has very little rainfall — the park is open-air so poor weather such as rain results in a significant fall in the number of customers for that day (normally by 50%). During the last 7 years there have been, on average, 30 days each year with rain. B-Star is now very successful; customer numbers are increasing at approximately 15% each year.

Ticket sales

Customers purchase tickets to enter the theme park from ticket offices located outside the park. Tickets are only valid on the day of purchase. Adults and children are charged the same price for admission to the park. Tickets are preprinted and stored in each ticket office. Tickets are purchased using either cash or credit cards. Each ticket has a number comprising of two elements — two digits relating to the ticket office followed by six digits to identify the ticket. The last six digits are in ascending sequential order.

Cash sales

1. All ticket sales are recorded on a computer showing the amount of each sale and the number of tickets issued. This information is transferred electronically to the accounts office.
2. Cash is collected regularly from each ticket office by 2 security guards. The cash is then counted by 2 accounts clerks and banked on a daily basis.
3. The total cash from each ticket office is agreed to the sales information that has been transferred from each office.
4. Total cash received is then recorded in the cash book, and then the general ledger.

Credit card sales

1. Payments by credit cards are authorised online as the customers purchase their tickets.
2. Computers in each ticket office record the sales information which is transferred electronically to the accounts office.
3. Credit card sales are recorded for each credit card company in a receivables ledger.
4. When payment is received from the credit card companies, the accounts clerks agree the total sales values to the amounts received from the credit card companies, less the commission payable to those companies. The receivables ledger is updated with the payments received.

You are now commencing the planning of the annual audit of B-Star. The date is 3 June 2015 and B-Star's year-end is 30 June 2015.

Required:
(a) For the cash sales system of B-Star, identify the risks that could affect the assertion of completeness of sales and cash receipts.
(b) Discuss the extent to which tests of controls and substantive procedures could be used to confirm the assertion of completeness of income in B-Star.
(c) List the substantive analytical procedures that may be used to give assurance on the total income from ticket sales for 1 day in B-Star.[2]

Disclosure

Cash should be correctly identified and classified in the balance sheet. Cash on deposit, for example, is a current asset, but a fixed-term deposit may be a long-term investment. In addition, there should be appropriate disclosure of arrangements with banks, such as lines of credit, compensating balances and contingent liabilities. Responses to questions 3 and 4 in the bank confirmation request illustrated in figure 17.2 are matters that may require disclosure as contingent liabilities. A bank overdraft is normally reported as a current liability.

The auditor determines the appropriateness of the statement presentation from a review of the draft of the entity's financial statements and the evidence obtained from the foregoing substantive procedures. In addition, the auditor should review the minutes of board meetings and enquire of management for evidence of restrictions on the use of cash balances.

17.2.4 Other issues

This section covers three topics: (1) testing to detect an irregularity known as lapping (or teeming and lading), (2) auditing imprest petty cash funds, and (3) auditing imprest bank accounts.

Describe the irregularity known as 'lapping' and how the auditor can detect it.

Detecting lapping

Lapping is an irregularity that results in the deliberate misappropriation of cash receipts, either temporarily or permanently, for the personal use of the individual perpetrating the unauthorised act. Lapping is usually associated with collections from customers, but it may also involve other types of cash receipts. Conditions conducive to lapping exist when the same person handles cash receipts and maintains the accounts receivable ledger. The auditor should assess the likelihood of lapping in obtaining an understanding about the segregation of duties in the receiving and recording of collections from customers.

An example of lapping

Assume on a given day that cash register receipts totalled $600 and mail receipts opened by the defrauder consisted of one payment on account by cheque for $200 from customer A (total actual receipts = $800). The lapper would steal $200 in cash and destroy all evidence of the mail receipt, except for the customer's cheque. The cash receipts journal entry would agree with the register ($600), and the deposit slip would show cash of $400 and customer A's cheque for $200. These facts can be tabulated as shown in figure 17.4.

Actual receipts			Documentation		Cash receipts journal entry		Bank deposit slip	
Cash		$600	Cash tape	$600	Cash sales	$600	Cash	$400
Customer A's cheque		200		—		—	Customer A's cheque	200
		$800		$600		$600		$600

FIGURE 17.4: Sample cash receipts journal entry

To conceal the shortage, the defrauder usually attempts to keep bank and book amounts in daily agreement so a bank reconciliation will not detect the irregularity. The defrauder will also need to ensure that customer A's account is correct. This can be done by allocating some of the payment received from another customer (customer B) to customer A's account. As shown in figure 17.5, a cheque for $300 is received from customer B, enabling the defrauder to steal another $100 and cover the amount missing from customer A's account. The total shortage is now $300 — $200 from the first example plus $100 from the second example.

There will, of course, now be a shortfall in customer B's account that will eventually be covered by a cheque from someone else. To enable this to continue, the same person must always deal with cash receipts. Thus, when the person involved with cash receipts never takes holidays, the auditor needs to take extra care.

Actual receipts		Documentation		Cash receipts journal entry		Bank deposit slip	
Cash	$500	Cash tape	$500	Cash sales	$500	Cash	$400
Customer B's cheque	300	Customer A's	200	Customer A's cheque	200	Customer B's cheque	300
	$800	cheque	$700		$700		$700

FIGURE 17.5: Sample cash receipts journal entry

A greater risk of fraud occurs when the person in cash receipts is able to make adjustments to the accounts receivable subsidiary ledger. In this situation, the defrauder can take cash as described above, but does not need to cover up because it is a simple matter to record a credit note against the customer's balance. (This may be queried by the customer when a detailed statement is sent at the end of the month, as it would show a credit note reducing an amount owing rather than a payment made.)

Auditing procedures

Tests to detect lapping are performed only when the control risk for cash receipts transactions is moderate or high. There are three procedures that should detect lapping.

1. *Confirm accounts receivable on a surprise basis at an interim date.* Confirming at this time will prevent the person engaged in lapping from bringing the 'lapped' accounts up to date. Confirmation at the end of the reporting period may be ineffective because the 'defrauder' may anticipate this procedure and adjust the 'lapped' accounts to their correct balances at this date.
2. *Make a surprise cash count.* The cash count will include coin, currency and customer cheques on hand. The auditor should oversee the deposit of these funds. Subsequently, the auditor should compare the details of the deposit shown on the duplicate deposit slip with cash receipts journal entries and postings to the customers' accounts.
3. *Compare details of cash receipts journal entries with the details of corresponding daily deposits.* This procedure should uncover discrepancies in the details such as those shown in the above two examples.

As has been outlined so far in this chapter, cash at bank is an area where the risk of fraud is higher than in some other parts of the audit. This is particularly the case where cash registers and actual cash are involved.

The following Professional Environment box provides tips for prevention of cash register fraud.

PROFESSIONAL ENVIRONMENT

How safe is your money? Top 10 tips to prevent cash register fraud and theft

*I*f you are in the retail business you undoubtedly use cash registers (shop tills) to process customer payments and transactions. Due to the storage of large sums of cash and the fact that cash registers sit prominently on the shop counter, cash registers are at risk of theft and fraud from both members of the public and your own staff.

How do members of the public steal from cash registers? Members of the public can steal cash straight from your shop cash register cash drawer by leaning across (when staff are absent) and pressing the cash drawer release key. The cash drawer opens automatically revealing the cash inside.

Meanwhile, it is not unknown for people to steal the entire cash register. The cash registers are rarely secured to the counter top and as some are smaller and more light-weight than others, they can simply be lifted off the counter.

How do staff steal from cash registers?

Cash registers are vulnerable to dishonest staff who steal from cash registers by taking money straight out of the cash drawer and keeping it. Alternatively they may only scan so many items for people who they know, letting them take the rest of the goods without payment.

Every year retail profits are affected adversely by cash register theft and fraud. The good news is that there are ways to prevent it.

Ten tips to preventing cash register fraud and theft

1. *CCTV cameras.* CCTV cameras can be positioned on the ceiling above the cash register with the view showing the employee and the customer. Signage is very important when using CCTV and in itself can often be a deterrent.
2. *Staff log-in and out codes (clerk codes).* All staff should have their own cash register security code which they must use at all times to log on and off the system. Not all cash registers allow for this, but many of the higher priced cash registers do. It is very important to be able to know who is doing what with your shop till. If money has gone missing often the error or theft can be traced back to the exact member of staff but only if they use their clerk codes when operating the cash register.
3. *Secure the cash register.* Fixing the cash register to the counter top will prevent the cash register from being easily lifted off the counter top by would-be thieves.
4. *Remove large sums of notes regularly.* Regularly remove large sums of notes from the cash drawer and place it in a *secure* safe. This ensures that the cash registers do not contain large amounts of money at any one time, preventing large-scale theft. Make it known that the shop cash register never holds large amounts of money via signage.
5. *Safety in numbers.* If possible always have at least two members of staff working on the tills. They can then *observe* each other preventing employee theft as well as acting as a deterrent for thieves.
6. *Train staff to be alert.* Staff should be alert at all times when operating the cash register and always use their own codes for logging in and out of the machine. This is for their benefit as much as it is for yours.
7. *Identify when someone approaches an unattended till.* You can buy various motion point detectors (such as pressure-switch mats) which can be used to alert you to

someone approaching an unattended cash register. Ensure that there are no large racks etc. blocking the view of the cash register.

8. *Open only when necessary*. *Ensure* cash register drawers can only be opened for the purpose of taking customer payment and not for any other reason. This includes giving change for customer parking etc.

9. *Empty your cash drawer*. Always empty your cash drawer and leave it open in full view of the shop window so that would be thieves can see that there is nothing to gain by breaking in and taking the cash register.

10. *Label your equipment*. Ensure all equipment is marked with an identification number so that if the equipment is stolen and recovered, it can be returned to you.

Don't let your profits sink with inefficient cash register security. Implement these cost effective measures, keep your money safe![3]

Auditing imprest petty cash funds

The balance of petty cash is rarely material and for this reason the majority of audits do not involve an audit of petty cash. Generally, the only time this part of the audit is performed is when the company expects or requests petty cash to be audited. If the auditor does happen to audit petty cash, it is often a good 'litmus test' for the controls that operate throughout the entity. For this reason, the auditor may sometimes document the controls that operate over petty cash, particularly for small clients. If substantive testing of petty cash is done, the following procedures are performed.

Substantive procedures

In auditing petty cash, the auditor performs tests of details of transactions and tests of balances. The auditor tests a number of replenishing transactions, including reviewing supporting documentation, accounting for all prenumbered receipts, and determining that the reimbursement cheque/transfer was for the correct amount. The test of balances involves counting the fund. The count is usually made on a surprise basis at an interim date rather than at the end of the reporting period. The auditor may also count the fund at the end of the reporting period, along with all other cash funds, to avoid the possibility that petty cash may be used to conceal a shortage elsewhere.

Auditing imprest bank accounts

An entity may use an imprest bank account for payroll and dividends.

Substantive procedures

The tests should include confirming the balance with the bank, reviewing the reconciliation prepared by the entity, and using the subsequent period's bank statement. The adjusted or true cash balance at the end of the reporting period should be the imprest amount. The only reconciling items on the bank statement will be unpresented payroll or dividend cheques. Employees usually cash their pay cheques promptly, so all the unpresented cheques should clear the bank on the subsequent period's bank statement. Unpaid dividends are more likely to be a problem. However, larger entities with quoted share capital (which are more likely to experience unpresented dividend cheques) usually employ an independent share registrar, one of whose functions is to distribute dividends. In such cases, the entity pays the total dividend to the registrar in a single cheque, and it is the registrar's responsibility to pay individual dividends and to maintain records of unpresented dividend cheques.

Do you know ...

17.1 ☐ A high volume of cash transactions results in a high inherent risk but controls over cash transactions are usually strong and are tested in connection with the audits of sales and purchases.

17.2 ☐ Regular bank reconciliations are an important control over the prevention and detection of fraud and error.

17.3 ☐ Cash balances are usually relatively small but significant, given their importance for liquidity, and auditors tend to adopt a predominantly substantive approach to the audit of cash balances.

17.4 ☐ The main substantive audit procedures applied to balances are:
- confirming balances with banks
- testing the closing bank reconciliation.

17.5 ☐ Lapping is the concealment of the misappropriation of cash by the use of subsequent receipts, which is facilitated where one individual handles cash and maintains the accounts receivable ledger.

17.3 INVESTMENTS

Entities commonly invest in other entities. These investments take a variety of forms — equity securities such as preference or ordinary shares, or debt securities such as corporate debentures or government bonds. Investments may be held for a variety of reasons:
- to hold surplus funds or funds earmarked for a future purpose
- to secure a long-term relationship with the other party.

A special category of this latter type of investment is investment for the purpose of acquiring influence or control over the activities of the other entity. Such entities may be classified as subsidiaries, associates or joint ventures, and are regarded as part of the economic entity. The financial statements of the investing or 'parent' entity are required to include appropriate balances relating to these other entities, so as to present a consolidated picture of the group or reporting entity. The audit of such investments extends to the verification of the balances in group entity financial statements, which are consolidated with the parent entity's accounts.

Investment transactions involve cash receipts, such as dividends and interest received on investments, and proceeds on their disposal. Control structure considerations for cash receipts were discussed in chapter 14. Investment transactions also involve cash payments for the purchase of investments. Control structure considerations for payment transactions were discussed in chapter 15. This chapter considers additional controls applicable to investing transactions only. We discuss these controls in the course of discussing the development of the audit plan.

LEARNING 6
objective

Identify the audit objectives applicable to investments.

17.3.1 Audit objectives

For the five categories of financial statement assertion, table 17.4 lists specific account balance audit objectives relating to accounts affected by investing transactions. The following sections explain considerations and procedures relevant to meeting these objectives.

TABLE 17.4:
Selected specific audit
objectives for investments

Transaction objectives	
Occurrence (**OE**)	Investment revenues, gains and losses resulted from transactions and events that occurred during the period (**OE1**).
Completeness (**C**)	All purchases of investments during the period have been recorded as additions (**C1**). All sales of investments during the period have been recorded as disposals (**C2**).
Accuracy (**AV**)	Investment revenues, gains and losses are reported at proper amounts (**AV1**).
Cut-off (**CO**)	Investment transactions are recorded in the proper period (**CO**).
Classification (**PD**)	Investment transactions are recorded in the correct accounts (**PD1**).
Balances objectives	
Existence (**OE**)	Recorded investment balances represent investments that exist at the end of the reporting period (**OE2**).
Rights and obligations (**RO**)	All recorded investments are owned by the reporting entity (**RO1**)
Completeness (**C**)	The income statement includes the effects of all investment transactions and events during the period (**C3**).
Valuation and allocation (**AV**)	Recorded cash balances are realisable at the amounts stated on the balance sheet and agree with supporting schedules (**AV2**).
Presentation and disclosure objectives (PD)	
Occurrence and rights and obligations	Disclosed investment pertains to the entity (**PD2**).
Completeness	Appropriate disclosures are made concerning (1) related party investments, (2) the bases for valuing investments, and (3) the pledging of investments as collateral (**PD3**).
Classification and understandability	Investment balances are properly identified and classified in the financial statements (**PD4**).
Accuracy and valuation	Investments are disclosed accurately and at appropriate amounts (**PD5**).

17.3.2 Developing the audit plan

Before planning the audit, it is necessary to consider the effectiveness of control structure components designed to ensure that investment transactions are properly supervised and that the investments are subject to adequate safeguards against misappropriation. We then consider materiality and risk before identifying factors applicable to determining a strategy for the audit of investments.

Safekeeping of investments

Because the purchase and sale of investments are often processed separately from other purchases and sales, entities holding substantial investment portfolios usually adopt specific control procedures over investments.

Control environment

The understanding of several control environment factors is relevant to the audit of the investments. The authority and responsibility for investing transactions, for example, should be assigned to a company officer such as the treasurer. This individual should be a person of integrity, with appropriate knowledge and skills, who realises the importance of observing all prescribed control procedures and can help other participating members of management make initial and ongoing assessments of the risks associated with individual investments.

The information system must include provision for capturing the data required for each method of accounting for the various categories of investment in equity and debt securities, both at acquisition date and at the end of subsequent reporting periods. Accounting personnel must be familiar with these requirements and capable of implementing them.

In addition, internal auditors and the audit committee of the board of directors should closely monitor the effectiveness of controls over investing activities.

Common documents and records

The majority of listed company shares now exist only in electronic format, and transfer or register of title is done through a computer system called the **Clearing House Electronic Subregister System (CHESS)**. CHESS has two main functions, according to the Australian Securities Exchange website, www.asx.com.au.

- It provides a clearing house (i.e. a system to facilitate the settlement or clearing of trades and securities).
- It provides an electronic subregister for securities in ASX-listed companies.

Shareholders can register their legal title to CHESS-approved securities either on the CHESS subregister, which is maintained by CHESS, or on issuer-sponsored subregisters, which are maintained by the company that issues the securities.

The audit evidence in relation to shareholdings using this system is by a review of CHESS holding statements issued to the company. However, in some instances where it is considered sufficiently material, the auditor may want to obtain written evidence of confirmation of shareholdings from the share registry where the legal title is held.

Unlisted shares are still kept in a physical format. Where titles to investments are evidenced by a physical document such as a share or debenture certificate, arrangements need to be made to ensure their safe custody. They may be held in a bank safe deposit box or directly by the bank or other financial institution as nominees for the entity.

Where substantial investments are held, a separate **investment subsidiary ledger** or **investment register** may be maintained. This records details of acquisitions and disposals, the receipt of interest and dividends, and market values.

Functions and related controls

Activities in the investing cycle include the following investing functions and related controls.

- Purchases and sales should be made in accordance with management's authorisations. The purchase and sale of investments intended to be retained as non-current assets normally require board approval.

- Dividend and interest cheques must be promptly deposited intact, and the completeness of recorded investment income must be independently verified.
- Transactions should be recorded on the basis of appropriate supporting documentation, and the duties of recording of transactions and custody of the securities should be segregated.
- Securities should be stored in safes or vaults, with access restricted to authorised personnel. Periodically, relevant documents should be independently compared with recorded balances.
- Changes in value and in circumstances relating to the appropriate classification of investments should be periodically analysed.
- Management should undertake performance reviews to detect poor investment performance and/or incorrect reporting.
- Periodically, the classification of individual investments should be reviewed.

The auditor should obtain an understanding of the entity's prescribed procedures to identify potential misstatements that could occur in investment balances and to design substantive procedures accordingly. If investment certificates are kept in the entity's safe and not independently verified, for example, then the audit program must call for physical inspection at or close to the end of the reporting period.

Materiality, risk and audit strategy

Securities held as short-term investments may be material to an entity's short-term solvency, but income from such securities is seldom significant to the results of operations of entities outside the financial services sector. Securities held as non-current investments may be material to both the balance sheet and the income statement.

There are inherent risks for the auditor in relation to how investments are accounted for and, associated with this, the determination of their market value.

One reason for difficulties in accounting for investments relates to accounting variations between short-term and long-term investments. If the investment is short term, it should be reported at the lower of cost and net realisable value. If the investment is long term, the method of accounting depends on how many shares are held. If the company does not have 'significant influence', the method of accounting is the same as it is for a short-term investment.

The most important audit risk where the investment is short term or there is no significant influence is in relation to ensuring that the market value has been properly assessed. This is not a problem for investments that relate to shares listed on the stock exchange, as there is an active market. When the shares are in unlisted companies, more judgement is required by the auditor and there is a higher level of inherent risk, particularly in relation to the valuation assertion. Where the assessment of market value is below cost, an adjustment may not be warranted if management can provide good reasons for believing the carrying amount of the investment will eventually be recovered. If management does make this assertion, the auditor needs to assess the reasonableness of the assertion.

However, if the company does have 'significant influence', the investment should be accounted for using the equity method of accounting. Where the company has 'control', which means it can dominate (directly or indirectly), the decision-making processes of another company in relation to its financial and operating policies, the company must consolidate the investment into its accounts.

Another difficulty for the auditor is that there are judgements associated with assessing 'significant influence' and 'control' and sometimes the company may be unwilling to adopt a certain treatment because of the effect that it may have on its accounts.

Where the company is defined as having a significant influence but not control over the investment, it is defined as an associate. GS 015 *Audit Implications of Accounting for*

Investments in Associates (there is no international equivalent) outlines guidance about how to ensure that these relationships are represented fairly to users.

Closely related to investments are specialised financial instruments such as options, swaps and forward contacts. These are often called 'derivatives' because their value is derived from market-determined prices such as security prices, foreign exchange rates and commodity prices. They are often used to manage exposure to risks associated with such markets. AGS 1030 *Auditing Derivative Financial Instruments* (IAPS 1012) outlines guidance for auditors in performing the audit of derivatives, and some reasons that derivative financial instruments often have greater inherent risks than other financial instruments. According to AGS 1030, paragraph .07 (IAPS 1012.7):

(a) Little or no cash outflows/inflows are required until maturity of the transactions;
(b) No principal balance or other fixed amount is paid or received;
(c) Potential risks and rewards can be substantially greater than the current outlays; and
(d) The value of an entity's asset or liability may exceed the amount, if any, of the derivative that is recognised in the financial report, especially in entities whose financial reporting frameworks do not require derivatives to be recorded at fair market value in the financial report.

For most companies, the volume of investing transactions is quite low. For this reason it is generally more efficient to use the predominantly substantive approach in the audit of investment balances. That is the approach discussed in this chapter. As with any transaction cycle, of course, the auditor should still obtain an understanding of the internal control structure applicable to investments.

Because of the complexity of accounting for some investments, there is also a heightened risk of fraud in this area, which the auditor should take into consideration when planning the audit.

Another risk arising from investments that affects the overall audit strategy is that associated with related party transactions when these investments meet the definition of related parties in accordance with AASB 124 *Related Party Disclosures* (IAS 24). The auditor should ensure that all transactions between related parties and the company are at arm's length and that all other requirements of AASB 124 (IAS 24) are complied with.

17.3.3 Substantive procedures for investments

For most entities, investment transactions are infrequent, but individual transactions are usually for substantial amounts. Investment transactions rarely present cut-off problems so the auditor may perform many substantive procedures before or after the end of the reporting period. Income statement account balances relating to investments are usually verified at the same time.

Determining detection risk

Design and execute an audit program for investments.

Relevant inherent risk and control risk assessments can vary widely, owing to the various types of investments and circumstances across entities. However, the small number of transactions means that it is not usually cost-effective to test controls. Acceptable detection risk is usually set as being low, and most evidence is obtained through the performance of substantive procedures.

Designing substantive procedures

Table 17.5 lists possible substantive procedures for investment balances and the specific audit objectives to which they relate. Procedures are explained as follows.

TABLE 17.5: Possible substantive procedures for investment balance assertions

Category	Substantive procedure	Investment balance audit objective (from table 17.4)					
		OE no.	C no.	RO1	AV no.	CO	PD no.
Initial procedures	1. Perform initial procedures on investment balances and records that will be subjected to further testing. (a) Trace opening balances for investment accounts to previous year's working papers. (b) Review activity in all investment-related balance sheet and income statement accounts, and investigate entries that appear unusual in amount or source. (c) Obtain entity-prepared schedules of investments and determine that they accurately represent the underlying accounting records from which they are prepared by: • adding and cross-adding the schedules and reconciling the totals with the related subsidiary and general ledger balances • testing the agreement of items on schedules with entries in related subsidiary and general ledger accounts.				✓1, 2		
Analytical procedures	2. Perform analytical procedures by analysing interest and dividend yields relative to expectations.	✓1, 2	✓1–3		✓1, 2		
Tests of details of transactions	3. Vouch entries in investment and related income and equity accounts.	✓1, 2	✓1–3	✓	✓1, 2	✓	✓1, 2, 5
Tests of details of balances	4. Inspect and count securities on hand. (Note: The majority will be held with registries.) 5. Confirm securities held by others (e.g. share registries). 6. Recalculate investment revenue earned. 7. Review documentation concerning fair values.	✓2 ✓2 ✓1	✓3 ✓3 ✓1, 2	✓ ✓	 ✓1 ✓1, 2	✓	✓1, 2, 5
Presentation and disclosure	8. Compare statement presentation with the Corporations Act and applicable accounting standards. (a) Determine that investment balances are properly identified and classified in the financial statements. (b) Determine the appropriateness of disclosures concerning the valuation bases for investments, realised and unrealised gains or losses, related party investments, and pledged investments.					✓4 ✓2, 3	

Initial procedures

Firstly, the auditor verifies the agreement of opening investment balances with audited amounts in the previous year's working papers. Next, the auditor reviews the activity in investment-related accounts to identify entries that are unusual in nature or amount and that should be investigated. Then the auditor checks entity-prepared schedules of investment additions and disposals in the period for mathematical accuracy and agreement with the underlying accounting records. This procedure includes determining that schedules and subsidiary investment ledgers agree with related general ledger control account balances. The schedules can then serve as the basis for additional substantive procedures.

Analytical procedures

It is rarely possible to obtain much evidence from the application of analytical procedures to investment balance sheet accounts. Current asset investments tend not to have any predictable relationship with other balances, and non-current investments are subject to so few transactions that it is easier to proceed directly to tests of details. Analytical procedures can be applied in comparing interest and dividend revenues with investment balances. Unexpected differences in interest or dividend yields may indicate misstatements; for example, a higher-than-expected rate of return may be found to have been caused by erroneously recording the unrealised gain from an increase in the value of non-current securities in the income statement rather than as a revaluation reserve.

Tests of details of transactions

Auditors usually vouch purchases and sales of investments by examining brokers' advices and evidence of appropriate approval. Purchases and sales of non-current investments, for example, should be vouched to authorisations in the minutes of directors meetings. These tests provide evidence about the occurrence of transactions, the transfer of ownership of securities, and the valuation of the securities at the transaction date.

Evidence as to the completeness of recorded purchases is determined through verification of purchase and payment transactions, as described in chapter 15. Evidence as to the completeness of sales of investments is determined through verification of the existence of recorded investment assets as one of the tests of details of balances.

The auditor can vouch dividend and interest receipts to remittance advices accompanying the payment. A problem often arises as to completeness. Receipt of dividends cannot always be foreseen, and the misrecording or even misappropriation of a dividend payment may not be readily detected by the information system. Interest can normally be verified by analytical procedures. Dividends paid by listed companies can normally be checked against reference works recording dividend payments. For substantial investments in unlisted companies, the auditor may need to verify dividends received against copies of the companies' financial statements.

Tests of details of balances

Tests of details of balances involve inspecting or confirming recorded investments, verifying income from investments and checking their market value. The work done will depend on whether the securities are listed or unlisted. If they are listed the following will apply.

Inspecting and confirming CHESS records

Where the securities relate to listed companies, there will be no paper certificate confirming legal title. The legal title is registered either on the CHESS subregister or on the issuer-sponsor subregister (the company that issued the securities). CHESS does not issue routine statements for holdings, but holding statements are issued to the investor on initial purchase of shareholdings and on any subsequent changes in those holdings. The auditor may inspect these holding statements to provide evidence on the existence and the rights and obligations assertions. However, depending on the materiality of the shareholdings, the auditor may obtain a confirmation statement from the CHESS sponsor or share registry at the end of the financial year. This provides evidence on the existence, completeness, rights and obligations, and presentation and disclosure assertions.

Inspecting and counting securities on hand

Securities held at the entity's own premises should be inspected and counted at the same time as the count of cash and other negotiable instruments. In performing the test, the custodian of the securities should be present throughout the count, a receipt should be obtained from the custodian when the securities are returned, and the auditor should control all securities until the count is completed.

For securities stored for safekeeping in bank safety deposit boxes, the banks will generally seal the boxes on the nominated date of the count at the entity's request and will confirm to the auditor that there was no access to the box, other than by the auditor, until all locations have been counted. When the count is not made at the end of the reporting period, the auditor should prepare a reconciliation from the date of the count to the year-end date by reviewing any intervening security transactions.

In inspecting securities, the auditor should observe such matters as:
- the certificate number on the document
- the name of the owner (which should be the entity, either directly or through endorsement)
- the description of the security
- the number of shares (or debentures)
- the value of the shares (or debentures)
- the name of the issuer.

These data should be recorded as part of the auditor's analysis of the investment account. All securities should be checked against the records in the investment register and, for securities purchased in previous years, the details should be compared with those shown on the previous year's working papers. A lack of agreement between the certificate numbers may indicate unauthorised transactions for those securities.

This substantive procedure provides evidence about the existence, completeness, rights and obligations, and presentation and disclosure assertions.

Confirming securities held by others

Securities held by outsiders for safekeeping must be confirmed as of the date on which securities held by the entity are checked. The steps in the confirmation process for securities are identical to those for confirming receivables. Thus, the auditor must control the mailings and receive the responses directly from the custodian. The data confirmed are the same as the data that should be noted when the auditor is able to inspect the securities.

Securities may also be held by creditors as collateral against loans. In such cases, the confirmation should be sent to the indicated custodian. The confirmation of securities held by third parties provides evidence as to the existence or occurrence and the rights and obligations assertions. It also furnishes evidence about the completeness assertion if the confirmation response indicates more securities on hand than recorded.

Recalculating investment revenue earned

The auditor verifies income from investments by use of documentary evidence and recalculation. Dividends on all shares listed on stock exchanges and many others are included in dividend record books published by investment services. The auditor can independently verify the dividend revenue by referring to the declaration date, amount and payment date as shown in the record book. The verification of dividend income is usually incorporated into the schedule of investments.

The auditor can verify the interest earned in relation to debentures by examining the interest rates and payment dates indicated on the debenture certificate. This substantive procedure is directed mainly at the valuation and completeness assertions for interest revenue. However, it also provides evidence about the existence assertion for interest receivable.

Reviewing documentation concerning market values

Where they are held as current assets, quoted equity securities and marketable debt securities (i.e. ordinary shares, government bonds and corporate debentures) are normally valued at the lower of aggregate cost and market value. Investments held as non-current assets are usually stated at the lower of cost and impaired value, but may be carried at valuation. In any event, disclosure is also required of the valuation of quoted securities. The auditor should verify market quotations by referring to published security prices on stock exchanges. For infrequently traded securities, the auditor may need to seek advice from an independent broker as to the estimated market value at the end of the reporting period. When market quotations are based on a reasonably broad and active market, they ordinarily constitute sufficient appropriate audit evidence as to the current market value of the securities.

Audited financial statements of the entity in which investments are held help in the valuation of unquoted shares, debentures and similar debt obligations.

Presentation and disclosure

To conform to the requirements of the Corporations Act and accounting standards, the presentation of investments in securities in the financial statements requires the following:

- an analysis of investments as either current or non-current
- a classification of investments into government and semi-government bonds, debentures, shares and share options
- a recognition of dividends, interest and realised gains and losses in the income statement
- a recognition of impairment write-offs in the income statement
- disclosure of the basis and methods of accounting
- disclosure of the market value of quoted investments
- disclosure of any liens.

The foregoing substantive procedures should provide evidence of the first four of the above items. Inspection of the minutes, loan agreements and register of charges should reveal the existence of liens. In addition, the auditor should enquire of management as to its intent in holding the securities. On the basis of the evidence obtained, the auditor then determines whether the proposed presentations and disclosures are appropriate.

LEARNING 9
objective
Explain the special considerations applicable to the audit of investments in subsidiaries, associates and joint ventures.

17.3.4 Substantive procedures for consolidated financial statements

Where a company (or other entity) controls another company (or other entity), consolidated financial statements must be prepared for the economic entity. The economic entity comprises both the parent company and the controlled entities (unless the company or entity is itself a controlled entity) (AASB 127 *Consolidated and Separate Financial Statements*;

IAS 27). The auditor is required to report on the consolidated financial statements. To do so, the auditor must identify the controlled companies (or other entities) constituting the reporting entity, verify the amounts pertaining to the other companies (or entities) to be consolidated, and verify the accuracy of the preparation of the consolidated financial statements.

Similar but less extensive disclosure requirements apply in respect of investments in associates (AASB 128 *Investments in Associates*; IAS 28) and in joint ventures (AASB 131 *Interests in Joint Ventures*; IAS 31). The same audit procedures with respect to subsidiaries also apply to investments in associates and joint ventures. The parent entity and its subsidiaries, associates and joint ventures are referred to collectively as group entities.

Specific guidance for the audit of investments in associates is given in GS 015 (no international equivalent). GS 015, paragraph 10 suggests that auditors pay particular attention when gathering sufficient appropriate audit evidence in the following areas:
- representations made by those charged with governance of the investor as to the existence and ownership of the investment, and the existence or otherwise of significant influence
- the appropriateness of the carrying amount of an investment
- the appropriateness of adjustments to the carrying amount of an investment
- the adequacy of financial report disclosure
- the appropriateness of other equity accounting adjustments such as adjustments for dissimilar accounting policies and elimination of unrealised profits and losses.

Some of this guidance is also relevant to the audit of subsidiaries and joint ventures.

Determining detection risk

It is difficult to make generalisations about the level of inherent risk for related account balance assertions. Sometimes the investment will be very passive and very low risk. However, there will also be instances where the relationship is very complex and high risk. This may give rise to uncertainty as to the existence of control over the related entities, in which case the inherent risk for the completeness assertion may be high. Sometimes, too, the consolidation adjustments may be particularly complex and involve a significant degree of management estimation. This can happen with the consolidation of foreign group entities whose financial statements may be prepared on accounting bases different from those appropriate to the parent entity, or with new acquisitions requiring determination of the fair value of their net assets at the acquisition date. In such cases, the inherent risk as to the valuation or measurement assertion may be moderate or high.

Another reason related account balances can be risky is where the investor company does not closely monitor the actions of the subsidiary or associate but provides guarantees over its activities. There have been many examples where the unchecked activities of subsidiaries or associates have resulted not only in their own failure but also in the failure of the investor company.

Given the materiality of the amounts involved, the audit approach will be predominantly substantive. Little or no reliance will be placed on controls, which are unlikely to be strong. Detection risk will, therefore, be inversely related to the relevant inherent risk assessments.

Sometimes there will be an additional risk in the audit of investments in associates or subsidiaries, because the audit may be performed by another auditor. In these situations, the auditor should consider the requirements of ASA 600 *Special Considerations — Audits of a Group Financial Report (Including the Work of Component Auditors)* (ISA 600). As part of the review of the other auditor's work, the head office auditor may sometimes send a very detailed questionnaire to the other auditor for completion.

Outlined below are some of the substantive procedures involved in performing an audit of consolidated financial statements.

Designing substantive procedures

Table 17.6 shows a list of possible substantive procedures for the consolidated financial statements, together with the assertions to which each test relates.

TABLE 17.6:
Possible substantive tests of consolidated financial statement assertions

Substantive procedure	Assertions					
	OE	C	RO	AV	CO	PD
Identify the reporting entity.	✓	✓	✓			
Verify the financial statements of other group entities.	✓	✓		✓		
Verify the consolidating adjustments.				✓	✓	
Compare the statement presentation with applicable accounting standards.						✓

Identifying the reporting entity

Where an entity has investments in entities that it controls, and where that entity is a reporting entity, it must prepare consolidated financial statements of the economic entity comprising the parent entity and its subsidiaries. The auditor ensures that all entities included in the consolidated financial statements are properly recognised as subsidiaries and that no such entities are excluded.

The auditor must make an assessment as to whether the entity's investment in other entities constitutes control, thereby requiring consolidation. AASB 127 (IAS 27) provides a definition of control as follows:

> Control is the power to govern the financial and operating policies of an entity so as to obtain benefits from its activities.

The auditor needs, therefore, to exercise judgement on the appropriateness of management's assertions about control (or lack thereof) of other entities.

The auditor also investigates the possibility that cumulative investments by the entity and its subsidiaries enable the economic entity to exercise control over other entities. If, for example, the parent holds 15% of the shares of another entity and one of its subsidiaries holds 40%, then that other entity is controlled by the group and is to be accounted for as a subsidiary. In obtaining an understanding of the business in the planning stage and in reviewing related party transactions, the auditor should be alert for evidence of the existence of control over other entities other than through ownership of voting rights. The auditor will need to obtain and verify an explanation as to why such entities are excluded from the consolidation.

This procedure provides evidence as to the existence assertion and the rights and obligations assertion with respect to entities consolidated as controlled entities, and as to the completeness assertion that all controlled entities are included in the consolidation.

Verifying the financial statements of other group entities

To verify the amounts included in the consolidated financial statements, the auditor must obtain and verify the financial statements of each group entity. Where the auditor is not also the auditor of another group entity, consideration must be given to the extent of reliance that may be placed on the work of the other auditor. ASA 600 (ISA 600) recommends that the principal auditor should:

- obtain information regarding the professional competence of the other auditor
- advise the other auditor of the independence requirements and obtain representation as to the other auditor's compliance
- advise the other auditor of the reliance to be placed on his or her work and of any special requirements, such as identification of intercompany transactions
- advise the other auditor as to applicable accounting and auditing requirements and obtain representation as to the other auditor's compliance
- consider the findings of the other auditor.

Where the principal auditor is unable to rely on the work of the other auditor, the principal auditor has the statutory right of access, under the Corporations Act, to the accounting and other records of any entity controlled by the parent entity. The principal auditor can command any information and explanations necessary to report on the consolidated financial statements from any officer or auditor of that entity.

This procedure provides evidence as to the existence assertion and the completeness assertion with respect to assets, liabilities and transactions with entities consolidated with those of the parent entity.

Verifying the consolidating adjustments

Consolidation adjustments fall into four categories: (1) acquisitions and disposals, (2) the elimination of inter-entity balances and transactions, (3) the standardisation of accounting policies, and (4) the translation of foreign currencies.

Acquisitions and disposals

On the acquisition of an interest in an associate or subsidiary, its assets are consolidated (directly or by way of equity accounting) in the group accounts at their fair value at the acquisition date (AASB 3 *Business Combinations*; IFRS 3). The difference between the fair value of the parent entity's ownership interest in the net assets and the consideration paid constitutes purchased goodwill. It is important that the auditor verifies the amounts recorded as fair value. ASA 540 *Auditing Accounting Estimates, Including Fair Value Accounting Estimates, and Related Disclosures* (ISA 540) provides some guidance for auditors in this area. The auditor should test the entity's fair value measurements and disclosures and, where applicable, evaluate whether the assumptions used by management provide a reasonable basis for the fair value measurements. This involves testing management estimates and evaluating the work of experts. Of particular concern are valuations placed on intangibles not recorded in the books of the controlled entity. Adjustments on the disposal of a controlling interest must be verified against the carrying amount of the controlled entity's net assets immediately before disposal.

Elimination of inter-entity balances and transactions

In the course of auditing each group entity, the auditor ensures that inter-entity transactions are properly identified and recorded. Where group entities are audited by other auditors, they must be asked to ensure that all such transactions are properly accounted for. At year-end, the auditor obtains an analysis of inter-entity balances, verifies their reconciliation to one another and ensures that they are properly eliminated. Inter-entity transactions that require particular scrutiny by auditors are those that occur around the year-end. The auditor should also ensure that any inter-entity profit in assets held by any of the group entities is properly identified and eliminated on consolidation.

Standardisation of accounting policies

Where the financial statements of group entities have been prepared using accounting policies inconsistent with those of the reporting entity, appropriate adjustments must be made on consolidation. When auditing group entities or when communicating with other auditors of group entities, the auditor must identify any accounting policies inconsistent with those of the reporting entity, and verify the consolidating adjustment.

Translation of foreign currencies

Where a group entity's financial statements are prepared in a foreign currency, they must be translated for purposes of consolidation. The auditor must verify the exchange rates used, check the translations and ensure that the accounting treatment conforms to the requirements of AASB 121 *The Effects of Changes in Foreign Exchange Rates* (IAS 21).

These substantive procedures provide evidence as to the existence, completeness and valuation assertions.

Comparison of statement presentation with applicable accounting standards

The auditor should ensure that the disclosures in the consolidated financial statements conform to the requirements of applicable accounting standards and the Corporations Act. Particular requirements are explanations as to why control exists over entities in which the parent entity's ownership interest is 50% or less, and why control does not exist over entities in which the ownership interest is greater than 50%.

Do you know ...

17.6 ☐ Inherent risks in investments include the proper classification of securities depending on management intent.

17.7 ☐ The infrequency of investment transactions leads to a predominantly substantive approach to their audit, which should include:
- confirmation of securities in safekeeping with registries
- verification of investment income
- verification of market values.

17.8 ☐ In performing substantive procedures on shares in listed companies, auditors should be aware of CHESS, which registers ownership of legal title by electronic means only.

17.9 ☐ The auditor is responsible for reporting on the consolidated financial statements, including:
- identifying group entities
- determining the reliability of group entity financial statements, especially where audited by other auditors, for the purpose of including them in the consolidated financial statements
- verifying consolidation adjustments.

SUMMARY

The verification of cash balances is an important part of a financial statement audit. Even though the balances at the end of the reporting period may appear immaterial relative to other assets, the amount of cash flowing through the accounts during the audit period can be very material. Cash is susceptible to misappropriation and is involved in many fraudulent schemes, including kiting and lapping. Thus, several types of substantive procedures to test cash balances are performed during most audits, including conducting cash cut-off tests, tracing bank transfers, counting cash on hand, confirming certain balances and other arrangements with banks, reviewing bank reconciliations, obtaining and using subsequent period bank statements, and determining the adequacy of management's disclosures for cash balances.

Investing transactions occur infrequently and internal control over the processing of transactions is generally good. However, because transactions are infrequent and usually individually significant, it is common for the auditor to use a predominantly substantive approach. Important among audit procedures is the physical inspection of certificates of title of investments, or their confirmation with independent custodians and registers. The auditor also uses a predominantly substantive approach in verifying the consolidation of investments in group entities in the consolidated financial statements of the economic entity.

KEY TERMS

bank confirmation, p. 720

bank reconciliations, p. 713

bank transfer schedule, p. 719

cash counts, p. 726

cash cut-off tests, p. 718

Clearing House Electronic Subregister System (CHESS), p. 734

imprest bank account, p. 714

imprest petty cash fund, p. 714

investment register, p. 734

investment subsidiary ledger, p. 734

kiting, p. 719

lapping, p. 728

subsequent period's bank statement, p. 725

window dressing, p. 726

17.1 Initial substantive procedures for cash balance assertions may include which of the following:

   (i) Trace opening balances for cash on hand and in bank to the previous year's working papers.

   (ii) Review activity in general ledger accounts for cash and investigate entries that appear unusual in amount or source.

   (iii) Obtain entity-prepared summaries of cash on hand and in bank, verify mathematical accuracy and determine agreement with general ledger.

   A. (i) and (ii) only.

   B. (i) and (iii) only.

   C. (ii) and (iii) only.

   D. (i), (ii) and (iii).

17.2 The main evidence regarding year-end bank balances is documented in:

   A. The bank deposit schedule.

   B. The interbank transfer schedule.

   C. The bank reconciliation.

   D. The standard bank confirmation.

17.3 In reviewing the bank reconciliation prepared by the client, the auditor finds a 'miscellaneous reconciling item'. From discussion with the client, the auditor is told that this relates to foreign exchange fluctuations. What should the auditor do?

   A. Accept the client's explanation.

   B. Accept the client's explanation — provided it is also noted in the management representation letter.

   C. Ask the client to provide a detailed schedule of the amounts that make up this variance for subsequent review.

   D. Try to find what constitutes the difference personally.

17.4 In working with the bank reconciliation and the subsequent period bank statement, the auditor finds that many of the cheques on the outstanding cheque list did not clear during the cut-off period. This may be an indication of:

   A. Lapping.

   B. Kiting.

   C. Window dressing.

   D. An attempt to conceal a cash shortage.

17.5 What is the assertion that is the 'highest risk' for an auditor in auditing investments?

   A. Valuation.

   B. Existence.

   C. Completeness.

   D. Presentation and disclosures.

17.6 The correct statement concerning the materiality of securities is:

   A. Short-term investments may be immaterial to the solvency position but material to the income statement.

   B. Short-term investments may be material to the solvency position but immaterial to the income statement.

   C. Long-term investments may be immaterial to the financial position but material to the income statement.

   D. Long-term investments may be immaterial to both the financial position and the income statement.

17.7 The predominantly substantive approach is generally used for investing transactions because of:
A. Infrequent transactions.
B. High volume of transactions.
C. Ineffective controls.
D. Effective controls.

17.8 An auditor testing the reasonableness of long-term investments would ordinarily use analytical procedures to ascertain the reasonableness of:
A. The existence of unrealised gains or losses in the portfolio.
B. The completeness of recorded investment income.
C. The classification of current and non-current portfolios.
D. The valuation of marketable equity securities.

17.9 If a client is not deemed to have 'significant influence' in an investee company, what should the auditor do to obtain audit evidence to verify the investment balance?
A. Review the audited accounts of the investee company.
B. Get an independent valuation of the assets and liabilities of the investee company.
C. Perform the audit of the investee company.
D. Obtain the market value of the investee company's shares.

17.10 In the audit of group entities, where the auditor is not also the auditor of another group entity, the principal auditor may:
A. Be able to rely on the work of the other auditor.
B. Ask the other auditor about the independence requirements, and offer representations as to compliance.
C. Send a detailed questionnaire to the other auditor.
D. Ignore the findings of the other auditor.

REVIEW questions

17.11 Name and describe the two main procedures for internal control of cash and bank amounts.

17.12 Why is detection risk for verifying cash balances invariably low? Why does the auditor not often use analytical procedures for the audit of cash balances?

17.13 What is the purpose of 'window dressing'? How would it be perpetrated? What is the main indicator of window dressing, and why does the indicator work?

17.14 Describe the procedures for counting cash on hand.

17.15 Outline the procedures involved in verifying the bank reconciliation.

17.16 Explain lapping. Describe appropriate audit procedures to perform where it is suspected.

17.17 What substantive tests apply to the existence and valuation assertions for investment balances?

17.18 Why is the predominantly substantive approach used for most entities in the audit of investment balances? Why is it rarely possible to obtain much evidence from analytical procedures in the audit of investment balances?

17.19 Explain the financial reporting principle underlying the audit verification of the existence and completeness assertions with respect to entities consolidated into the group financial statements.

17.20 Describe procedures to be undertaken where group entities are audited by other auditors.

 PROFESSIONAL application questions

17.21 Substantive procedures for bank balances ★

You are the auditor of Bottlenose Ltd and planning the audit for the year ended 30 June 2015. The company has various bank accounts for which bank reconciliations are prepared monthly. The company has recently borrowed money from the bank to finance a new asset acquisition.

Required

Explain the audit procedures that will be carried out on the bank and loan amounts and describe the procedures to be followed in obtaining a bank letter.

17.22 Bank reconciliation errors ★★

You have spent 2 years working as an auditor. In that time you have come across a number of errors in performing bank reconciliations. Outlined below are some of them.

1. An unreconciled item of $340 was on the final bank reconciliation of the client and was deemed by the client to be immaterial.
2. Two deposits totalling $4070 relating to accounts receivable were collected on 2 July (30 June year-end) but recorded as cash receipts on 30 June.
3. An amount from an associated company of $40 000 was banked 2 days before the end of the year in the client's bank account and then paid back 1 week after the end of the year.
4. A cheque for $6000 was omitted from the outstanding cheque list on the bank reconciliation at 30 June. It cleared the bank on 14 August.
5. A bank transfer of $20 000 was included as a deposit in transit at 30 June in the accounting records.

Required

(a) What control could be implemented to reduce the likelihood of each of the above?
(b) What is an audit procedure to detect each of the above?

17.23 Cash control system ★★

Drental Ltd operates a chain of household goods retail stores in various towns and cities. Accounting for each shop is carried out at Head Office but the relevant shop manager is responsible for petty cash held in each location. The client's notes on the petty cash system are as follows.

1. Petty cash is kept in a lockable tin in the manager's desk.
2. Petty cash levels are maintained at $1000 at each store.
3. The monthly spend on petty cash ranges from $400 to $1100.
4. Petty cash transactions range from just a few dollars to several hundred dollars.
5. A petty cash book is maintained by one of the assistants in each shop and each item of expenditure is supported by a receipt and a petty cash voucher signed by the person who spent the money.
6. When more cash is needed a request is sent to Head Office, signed by the store manager, the amount requested will be sufficient cash to bring the balance back up to $1000.
7. The cheques are raised by the accountant at Head Office and are signed by two of the normal bank authorities.

Required

Identify the weaknesses in the petty cash system of Drental Ltd and suggest an internal control that could be implemented.

17.24 Charity income ★★

Roof and Walls is a charity that provides accommodation for people who are in hardship or from disadvantaged backgrounds. The constitution of Roof and Walls stipulates how funds can be spent. Revenue to cover this expenditure comes from a variety of sources, including:

- limited government grants
- legacies and donations received either by EFT into the charity's account or cheques received in the mail
- cash collected by volunteers from the public
- fundraising events, such as charity auctions and a summer ball.

The amounts of the legacies and donations received can range from a few dollars to several thousands of dollars. In some instances the legacies and donations are required to be spent on specific projects, or are received on the basis that the funds are invested and the income is used for a specific purpose.

The government grants are for specific projects, in some cases for the purchase of specific assets.

Required

Identify the inherent risk in relation to revenue for Roof and Walls and indicate the impact on your audit approach.

17.25 Substantive procedures for investments ★★

Ingrid Cox, an audit senior, was given the task of auditing Apple Ltd, an investment company. Her firm had not performed the audit before; however, from a discussion with the previous year's auditors, she found out that the following transactions occurred during the previous year:

- payment of debenture interest
- accrual of debenture interest, payable at the year-end
- redemption of outstanding debentures
- purchase of a portfolio of shares.

Ingrid has been asked to detail audit procedures for this year's audit based on the assumptions that similar transactions will occur.

Required

(a) Identify a substantive procedure that Ingrid would need to perform to verify each of the above transactions, and the assertion to which each relates.
(b) Indicate the type of evidence obtained from each of the procedures noted in (a).

17.26 Audit of consolidated financial statements ★★

Oxford Ltd is a reporting entity of which your firm of accountants is the auditor. Oxford's consolidated financial statements incorporate the financial statements of its four subsidiaries. Three subsidiaries are incorporated in Australia and audited by your firm. The fourth subsidiary is located in another country and audited by another firm of professional accountants.

Required

(a) Explain how you would verify the intercompany balances.
(b) Describe other audit adjustments you would expect to find and explain how you would verify each of them:
  (i) where the subsidiary had been acquired before the financial year under audit
  (ii) where the subsidiary had been acquired during the financial year under audit.
(c) Describe the procedures necessary to determine the level of reliance to be placed on the audited financial statements of the foreign subsidiary.

17.27 Audit of investments ★★

You are working on the audit team of Wringer Ltd and you have been given the responsibility of auditing the investments auditor. You have been provided with the following information.

1. During the year some shares were sold at a profit of $182 900 and the proceeds were reinvested in shares of other companies.

2. There were no purchases or sales of fixed-interest investments in the year ended 30 June 2015. In the year ended 30 June 2014, some of the fixed-interest investments were sold and others were purchased using the proceeds of sale.
3. Extracts from the draft financial report for 30 June 2015 are shown below.

Income account for year ended 30 June		
	2015	2014
Income	$	$
From fixed interest investments	44 200	41 900
From shares in listed companies	123 900	123 500
	168 100	165 400

Extract from balance sheet as at 30 June		
Cost of investments	$	$
Fixed-interest investments	511 200	511 200
Shares in listed companies	1 445 600	1 262 700
	1 956 800	1 773 900

Required

Describe the audit work you would carry out:

(a) to verify income from investments — your audit tests should verify that all the income from the investments has been received by the charity and included in the financial statements, including dividends from the shares in listed investments bought and sold during the year

(b) to verify the ownership of the fixed interest investments and shares in listed companies.[4]

17.28 Other auditors of subsidiaries ★★

You are currently performing the year-end audit of South Seas Ltd, a large corporation with operations in Australia and the South Pacific region. The company's head office is located in Melbourne. As part of the planning process, other offices of your firm and other non-associated overseas firms were engaged to conduct the audit of various branches and subsidiaries of South Seas Ltd. The deadline for all work to be completed by those other auditors was last Friday. It is now Monday and the company requires audit clearance by the end of the week.

You have been assigned the task of reviewing the work that has been performed by those other auditors and have noted the following.

1. Bluewater Ltd is a subsidiary located in Fiji. No results have been received as yet from the other audit firm involved. You have just spoken to the audit partner in Fiji who has told you that, although the work has not yet been completed, no major problems have been encountered. Bluewater contributes 12% of total sales and 8% of net assets in the consolidated accounts.
2. When reviewing work performed by the New Zealand office, you find the stocktake, which should have been performed on 30 June, actually took place on 2 July. The other auditor's explanation for this was that instructions had not been received in sufficient time for them to allocate staff.
3. The Cairns office, which performed the audit of Sugar Supplies Pty Ltd (a subsidiary in which South Seas owns 80% of the issued capital), established its own materiality on the basis of the year-end amounts recorded in Sugar Supplies' books and found no material errors or misstatements.

Required

(a) Discuss the issues your firm would need to consider when relying on the work of the other auditors.

(b) Identify the specific issues you would raise in relation to the work performed by the other auditors to date.

(c) Outline the action you would take in relation to those issues identified in (b).[5]

17.29 Substantive procedures for investments ★★★

You are performing the audit of Toledo Ltd for the financial year ended 30 June 2015. Under the terms of a major loan contract, Toledo is required to maintain certain financial ratios. If the ratios are breached, then the loan is immediately due for repayment. This would create significant cash flow problems. To comply with the loan covenant and maintain the ratios, Toledo must continue to hold its 100% shareholding in Granada Ltd as a long-term investment.

You have obtained a management representation letter from the client, which says in part: 'Toledo Ltd warrants for the period 1 July 2015 to 30 June 2016 that it intends to retain ownership of its entire parcel of ordinary shares in Granada Ltd. Toledo has not entered into any discussions with any party, directly or indirectly, regarding the sale of these shares.'

On 24 July 2015, you noted an article in the financial press which described the rumoured sale of the business assets of Granada to a foreign investor.

Required

(a) Does the management representation letter from Toledo regarding its shareholding in Granada constitute sufficient appropriate audit evidence? Give reasons for your answer.

(b) Describe the procedures you need to perform in relation to this situation before signing the auditor's report.[6]

 CASE studies

17.30 Performing a bank reconciliation ★★★

Your firm is the auditor of Thai Textiles Ltd and you are auditing the financial statements for the year ended 30 June 2015. The company has a turnover of $2.5 million and a profit before tax of $150 000. The company has supplied you with the following bank reconciliation at year-end. You have entered the 'date cleared' on the bank statement (the date on which the cheques and deposits appeared on July's bank statement).

			$	$
Balance per bank statement at 30 June 2015				(9 865)
Add: deposits not credited				
CJ date	Type	Date cleared		
30 June	ARL	4 July	11 364	
24 June	CS	4 July	653	
27 June	CS	5 July	235	
28 June	CS	6 July	315	
29 June	CS	7 July	426	
30 June	CS	8 July	714	
30 June	CS	11 July	362	14 069

(continued)

				$	$
Balance per bank statement at 30 June 2015 *(continued)*					(9 865)

Less: uncleared cheques

CJ date	Cheque no.	Type	Date cleared		
29 June	2163	CP	4 July	1 216	
30 June	2164	APL	18 July	10 312	
30 June	2165	APL	19 July	11 264	
30 June	2166	APL	18 July	9 732	
30 June	2167	APL	20 July	15 311	
30 June	2168	APL	21 July	8 671	
30 June	2169	APL	19 July	12 869	
30 June	2170	APL	21 July	9 342	
30 June	2171	CP	4 July	964	(79 681)
Balance per cash journal at 30 June 2015					(75 477)

Notes
- 'CJ date' is the date on which the transaction was entered into the cash journal.
- Type of transaction: ARL (accounts receivable receipt); CS (receipt from cash sales); APL (accounts payable payment); CP (cheque payment [for other expenses]).
- All cheques for accounts payable payments are written out at the end of the month.

Required

(a) List the matters that cause you concern on the client's bank reconciliation. Describe the investigations that you will carry out on these items.

(b) Explain what adjustments to the financial statements would be required from (a).[7]

17.31 Substantive procedures for cash balances ★★★

You have been asked by the financial controller, Harry Rowling, of Potter Ltd to carry out an investigation of a suspected fraud by the company's cashier. The cashier, Alfred Blyton, has left the firm without notice.

Potter Ltd is a small company, and there were few controls and checks over Alfred's work because the company had employed him for a number of years. You are aware that the auditor found a discrepancy in the bank reconciliation for the company's year end of 30 June 2015, and that Alfred left the day on which it was discovered. Harry has asked you to carry out the investigation, rather than the company's auditor. He is not happy with the auditor because he believes he should have found the fraud earlier or at least warned that there were control weaknesses.

Harry says that Alfred was responsible for:
1. receiving cash from customers for both credit and cash sales
2. making all payments, including purchase ledger payments and sundry payments
3. drawing the cash for wages
4. recording all receipts and payments in the cash book and preparing a bank reconciliation
5. making and approving petty cash payments and recording these transactions in the petty cash book.

The computerised sales and purchase ledgers are maintained by the staff in the sales and purchases accounting departments who post all transactions to these ledgers. Alfred used to send the sales ledger clerk a schedule showing the cash he had received. The remittance advices from customers were attached to this schedule, and they showed the invoices that were being paid.

The purchases ledger controller would inform Alfred of the payments he wished to make, and Alfred would then prepare the cheques, which Harry signed. A remittance advice was attached to the payment that was sent to the supplier. Alfred would prepare the purchases and sales ledger control accounts each month and the reconciliation of these balances to the total balances on the respective ledgers.

For cash sales, the sales department raises a sales order, which is sent to the dispatch department which, in turn, raises a dispatch note. The first copy of the dispatch note is given to the customer, the second copy is sent to the sales accounting department and the third copy is retained in the dispatch department. The sales accounting department then prices the invoice. The customer would pay the cash to Alfred, who retained a copy of the invoice for his records. Alfred would record the sales details in his analysed cash book, and the month's cash sales were posted from the total in the cash book to the nominal ledger.

The payroll department calculates the wages. Alfred would draw the cheque to pay the wages and receive the cash. The payroll department makes up the wage packets and pays the wages to employees. Alfred would retain any wages not given to employees.

Harry is the authorised signatory for cheques; however, Alfred was the signatory when Harry was on holiday.

Required

Describe what checks you would conduct to (a) determine whether a fraud has actually taken place and (b) quantify the loss. Consider:
 (i) bank reconciliations
 (ii) cash receipts
 (iii) cash payments
 (iv) petty cash.[8]

RESEARCH question

17.32 Short-term investments and foreign currency transactions

The audit of short-term investments can be a high-risk area for auditors. The case of *AWA Ltd v. Daniels t/a Deloitte Haskins & Sells & Ors* (1992) 10 ACLC 933 found the auditors negligent for failing to report weaknesses in the foreign exchange trading to an adequate level of management. The collapse of the Barings Bank in Singapore also focused questions on whether adequate attention was paid to reviewing internal controls over foreign currency transactions. Consider, for example, the following extract:

> The refusal of Coopers & Lybrand's Singapore partnership to cooperate with the inquiry into the collapse of Barings Bank has left gaping holes in the explanation of the auditors' role in the affair. The inquiry by the Board of Banking Supervision concluded that the collapse could be attributed to concealed and unauthorised trading by Nick Leeson, which the bank's management and the external auditors and regulators failed to notice.
>
> Crucial from the auditors' point of view is why they failed to notice the 'absolute failure' of Barings' internal controls. Some indication of the crisis was picked up by Barings' internal auditors in 1994, but their recommendations were never implemented, and the external auditors subsequently ruled the company's controls acceptable.[9]

Required

(a) For one of the above two cases mentioned, research the alleged/actual deficiencies of the work performed by the auditor.
(b) What are specific issues of importance in performing an audit of short-term investments?

FURTHER READING

AB Doppelt, 'The telltale signs of money laundering', *Journal of Accountancy*, March 1990, pp. 31–3.

KM Head, 'Cash counts do count', Internal Auditor, April 2000, pp. 71–3.

JM Jacka, 'Discarded cash', Internal Auditor, August 2000, pp. 81–3.

C Locke, 'Auditing issues — bank confirmation requests', Charter, March 1998, pp. 76–7.

J Mills, 'Controlling cash in casinos', Management Accounting (US), May 1996, pp. 38–40.

GF Patterson, Jr, 'New guide on auditing investments', *Journal of Accountancy*, February 1997.

JT Wells, 'Control cash-register thievery', *Journal of Accountancy*, June 2002, pp. 88–92.

JT Wells, 'Money laundering: ring around the white collar', *Journal of Accountancy*, June 2003, pp. 49–51.

NOTES

1. Adapted from Sequence Inc., 'Asset Misappropriation', 2009, www.fraudessentials.com, viewed 31 August 2010.

2. Adapted from ACCA Audit and Assurance (International) Paper F8 question 1 June 2009, www.accaglobal.com/students/acca/exams/f8/past_papers.

3. Barry Fish, 'How safe is your money? Top 10 tips to prevent cash register fraud and theft', *Articlesbase*, 2009, www.articlesbase.com, viewed 1 September 2010.

4. Adapted from ACCA Audit Framework, Paper 6, December 1996.

5. Adapted from Professional Year Programme of the ICAA, 1999, Advanced Audit Module.

6. Adapted from Professional Year Programme of the ICAA, 1997, Advanced Audit Module.

7. Adapted from ACCA Audit Framework, Paper 6Y, December 1997.

8. Adapted from ACCA Audit Framework, Paper 3.4, December 1991.

9. Extract from 'Auditors' silence leaves questions unanswered', *Accountancy* 116(1224), August 1995, p. 11.

Answers to multiple-choice questions

17.1 *D*   17.2 *D*   17.3 *C*   17.4 *C*   17.5 *A*   17.6 *B*   17.7 *A*   17.8 *B*   17.9 *D*
17.10 *C*

part 5

COMPLETING THE AUDIT

18   Completing the audit

*T*he final part of this book captures the significant aspects of the audit. **Chapter 18** discusses how auditors bring together all material aspects of the audit work, including the formulation of an overall audit judgement regarding the sufficiency of audit evidence, the materiality of any misstatements and whether there are any factors that may prevent the auditor from providing an unqualified opinion. Detailed finalisation procedures, including the required form of communication with the client and its governing body, are described so that the auditor can derive their opinion as to the truth and fairness of the financial report.

chapter 18

Completing the audit

OVERVIEW

18.1 Completing the fieldwork

18.2 Evaluating the findings

18.3 Communicating with the entity

Summary

Key terms

Multiple-choice questions

Review questions

Professional application questions

Case studies

Research question

Further reading

Notes

LEARNING objectives

After studying this chapter, you should be able to:

1   describe the auditor's responsibilities with respect to events occurring after the end of the financial year

2   explain the different types of accounting treatments for events occurring after the end of the financial year

3   explain the procedures in ensuring that the going concern basis is appropriate

4   explain the procedures in ensuring that all contingent liabilities have been properly identified and disclosed

5   describe and state the purpose of a management representation letter

6   indicate why analytical procedures are important in undertaking the overall review of the financial statements

7   identify the steps in evaluating audit findings

8   indicate the appropriate communication with the entity at the conclusion of the audit

PROFESSIONAL STATEMENTS

Australian		International	
ASA 260	Communication with Those Charged with Governance	ISA 260	Communication with Those Charged with Governance
ASA 320	Materiality in Planning and Performing an Audit	ISA 320	Materiality in Planning and Performing an Audit
ASA 450	Evaluation of Misstatements Identified during the Audit	ISA 450	Evaluation of Misstatements Identified during the Audit
ASA 502	Audit Evidence — Specific Considerations for Litigation and Claims	ISA 501	Audit Evidence — Specific Considerations for Selected Items
ASA 520	Analytical Procedures	ISA 520	Analytical Procedures
ASA 540	Auditing Accounting Estimates, Including Fair Value Accounting Estimates, and Related Disclosures	ISA 540	Auditing Accounting Estimates, Including Fair Value Accounting Estimates, and Related Disclosures
ASA 550	Related Parties	ISA 550	Related Parties
ASA 560	Subsequent Events	ISA 560	Subsequent Events
ASA 570	Going Concern	ISA 570	Going Concern
ASA 580	Written Representations	ISA 580	Written Representations
ASA 700	Forming an Opinion and Reporting on a Financial Report	ISA 700	Forming an Opinion and Reporting on Financial Statements
ASA 705	Modifications to the Opinion in the Independent Auditor's Report	ISA 705	Modifications to the Opinion in the Independent Auditor's Report
AASB 110	Events after the Reporting Period	IAS 10	Events after the Reporting Period
AASB 137	Provisions, Contingent Liabilities and Contingent Assets	IAS 37	Provisions, Contingent Liabilities and Contingent Assets

SCENE SETTER

IAASB shake-up has auditors on the hop

It is head-down, bum-up season for company auditors in Australia.

That's not the best time to contemplate wholesale changes to how they do what they do.

But that's never stopped the International Auditing and Assurance Standards Board. Last week, it tabled proposed changes to audit rules which some say will fundamentally alter the scope of audits.

Instead of validating the accuracy of a company's financial accounts, auditors will be asked to comment on risks and going concerns, blurring the lines between the role of auditors, management and governance committees. Others fear it will make auditors and the big-six audit firms — PwC, EY, KPMG, Deloitte, BDO and Grant Thornton — bigger targets for lawsuits in the case of corporate collapse.

All agree it will increase the audit costs and play merry hell with timetables — two things the profession can ill afford. Price competition is already rampant. And the dire shortage of young auditors has ranked, for the past five years, as the profession's greatest threat: Gen Y hates the long hours and intense pressure of audit season.

(continued)

Under proposed reporting guidelines, the IAASB wants auditors to communicate in their report matters that are of most significance in the audit of the financial statements. It also wants auditors to include specific statements about going concerns in their reports.

'It gives more information that lawyers could nit-pick in the event of a corporate collapse,' warns Liz Stamford, head of audit policy for the Institute of Chartered Accountants.

'It gives lawyers a bigger target because it details where it [an auditor and management] focused its audit energy,' she said.

The IAASB also wants auditors to make an explicit statement about the auditor's independence from the audited entity and, for listed entities, to disclose the name of the engagement partner in the auditor's report.

Changes represent a big shift
The proposed changes, if implemented holus-bolus, represent a 'reasonably big shift' for the global audit profession, CPA Australia head of audit Amir Ghandar said.

As a big-six audit firm, Grant Thornton fears the changes will become too expensive. They expose to public scrutiny previously private deliberations between auditors and management.

'While these things [going-concern judgments and determination of key audit matters] are currently contemplated and discussed, putting this commentary in the public domain increases the sensitivity around exact words and descriptions used.'

'There will be a lot more conversations around that between the auditor and management. How does that happen at an appropriate cost?' said Grant Thornton national head of audit Andrew Archer.

BDO Australia auditor and head of professional standards Tim Sydenham said he's argued back and forth with a client for a whole day over the use of the word 'significant'.

In addition to cost blowouts, Mr Sydenham is concerned about the impact on reporting timetables.

He expects some elements will become boilerplate.

Teasing out more company-specific information
The IAASB is desperate to avoid this. IAASB technical director James Gunn said the intended outcome of the changes is 'unique' information that is 'more specific to the audited entity'.

Despite concerns — and there are a few — audit firms unanimously support a new format. Most, including PwC, Deloitte, BDO and Grant Thornton, will start 'field testing' the proposed standards during the completion of June 30, 2013 listed-company audits.

'Testing these changes in reality is the only way to explore the benefits and expose unintended consequences well in advance of changes in the standard,' PwC head of assurance, Peter Van Dongen said.

Deloitte head of assurance and advisory Cindy Hook said the firm will discuss the potential impact with clients, including 'matters that would likely be disclosed if the [changes] were effective today'.

The IAASB wants the 'enhancements' to take effect as soon as possible. It has asked the audit community if changes could be integrated into financial statements for periods ending on or after December 15, 2015, (that is, for December 31, 2015 reporting periods) if final standards were issued in by December 2014.[1]

Source: A King, IAASB shake-up has auditors on the hop', *The Australian Financial Review*, 1 August 2013, www.afr.com.

We discussed aspects of interim and year-end audit testing in previous chapters. In this chapter we are concerned with two important additional areas of activity in completing the financial statement audit:

1. completing the audit fieldwork, which relates to all transactions and events up until the date on which the auditor's report is signed
2. evaluating the audit findings and communicating with the entity.

The procedures performed in completing the audit fieldwork have a number of distinctive characteristics:

- they do not relate to specific transaction cycles or accounts
- they involve many subjective judgements by the auditor
- they often involve issues that are potentially of high risk to the auditor.

For these reasons they are usually performed by audit managers or other senior members of the audit team (and closely reviewed by audit partners) who have extensive audit experience with the entity.

Significant importance is also given to evaluating the findings and communicating with the entity. The manager and audit partner on the engagement are actively involved in this process, because it is important to ensure that the work is completed properly and that significant matters are considered in formulating the audit opinion. The communication with the entity also provides an important source of evidence that the auditor has appropriately performed the work.

The adage 'last but not least' applies to completing the audit. The decisions made by the auditor in this last stage are usually crucial to the ultimate outcome of the audit. Moreover, the conclusions reached by the auditor in completing the audit often have a direct impact on the opinion to be expressed on the entity's financial statements.

In completing the audit, the auditor often works under tight time constraints, because entities usually seek the earliest possible date for the issue of the auditor's report. Despite potential problems with tight deadlines, the auditor must take the time to make sound professional judgements and to express the opinion appropriate in the circumstances. Figure 18.1 is a summary of the auditor's responsibilities in completing the audit. These include completing the fieldwork, evaluating the findings and communicating with the client.

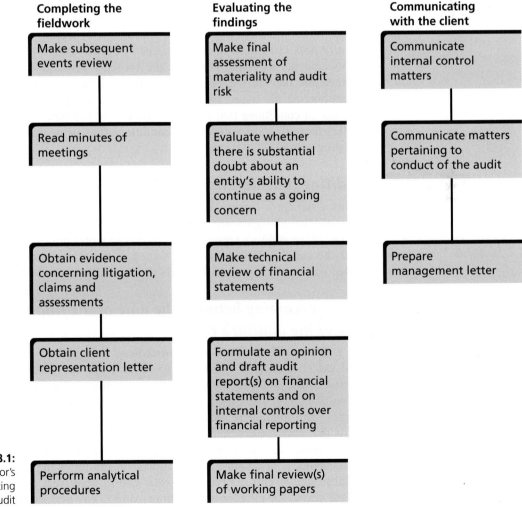

FIGURE 18.1:
Summary of an auditor's responsibilities in completing the audit

Completing the fieldwork	Evaluating the findings	Communicating with the client
Make subsequent events review	Make final assessment of materiality and audit risk	Communicate internal control matters
Read minutes of meetings	Evaluate whether there is substantial doubt about an entity's ability to continue as a going concern	Communicate matters pertaining to conduct of the audit
Obtain evidence concerning litigation, claims and assessments	Make technical review of financial statements	Prepare management letter
Obtain client representation letter	Formulate an opinion and draft audit report(s) on financial statements and on internal controls over financial reporting	
Perform analytical procedures	Make final review(s) of working papers	

18.1 COMPLETING THE FIELDWORK

In completing the fieldwork, the auditor performs specific auditing procedures to obtain additional audit evidence. The specific audit evidence relates to reviewing for **subsequent events** that may have an effect on the financial statements, considering factors that may have an impact on going concern assumptions, reviewing for contingent liabilities, obtaining the **management representation letter** and performing analytical procedures. These procedures are performed at the end of the audit, not necessarily in the following sequence.

18.1.1 Undertaking a review of subsequent events

The auditor is responsible for designing specific procedures to identify subsequent events that may have an impact on the financial statements before the auditor's report is signed, as discussed in ASA 560 *Subsequent Events* (ISA 560). Subsequent events, as described in the standard, are events occurring between the end of the reporting period and the date of the auditor's report, and facts that become known to the auditor after the date of the auditor's report.

In identifying subsequent events, the auditor needs to consider two separate issues. First, the auditor must assess whether it is an event on which he or she has a responsibility to act (ASA 560; ISA 560). Second, if the auditor does have a responsibility to take action, he or she must consider the appropriate reporting treatment for the subsequent event (AASB 110 *Events after the Reporting Period*; IAS 10). AASB 110 (IAS 10) defines events after the reporting period as those events, favourable or unfavourable, that occur between the date of the reporting period and the date when the financial statements are authorised for issue. Two types of events can be identified: (1) those that provide evidence of conditions that existed at the end of the reporting period (adjusting events), and (2) those that are indicative of conditions that arose after the reporting period (non-adjusting events).

LEARNING objective 1

Describe the auditor's responsibilities with respect to events occurring after the end of the financial year.

Auditing considerations of subsequent events

Auditing standards require the auditor to apply procedures designed to provide reasonable assurance that all significant events occurring between the date of the financial report and the date of the auditor's report are identified (ASA 560, paragraphs 4; ISA 560, paragraph 4). After the auditor's report has been signed, it is not the auditor's responsibility to detect subsequent events. Figure 18.2 depicts the time dimension for subsequent events.

Events occurring between the date of the financial report and the date of the auditor's report

The auditor shall perform audit procedures designed to obtain sufficient appropriate audit evidence that all events occurring between the date of the financial report and the date of the auditor's report have been identified. The auditor shall take into account the auditor's risk assessment in determining the nature and extent of such audit procedures. The auditor is required to perform procedures to identify and evaluate all events that may require adjustment or disclosure in the financial statements up until the date on which the auditor's report is signed (identified by period 1 in figure 18.2). This responsibility is discharged by the auditor in the following two ways: (1) by being alert for subsequent events in performing year-end substantive procedures (such as cut-off tests and the search for unrecorded liabilities), and (2) by performing the auditing procedures specified in ASA 560, paragraph 7 (ISA 560, paragraph 7) at or near the completion of the examination, which include:

- obtaining an understanding of any procedures management has established to ensure that subsequent events are identified.
- enquiring of management and, where appropriate, those charged with governance, as to whether any subsequent events have occurred which might affect the financial report.
- reading minutes, if any, of the meetings, of the entity's owners, management and those charged with governance, that have been held after the date of the financial report and enquiring about matters discussed at any such meetings for which minutes are not yet available.
- reading the entity's latest subsequent interim financial report, if any.

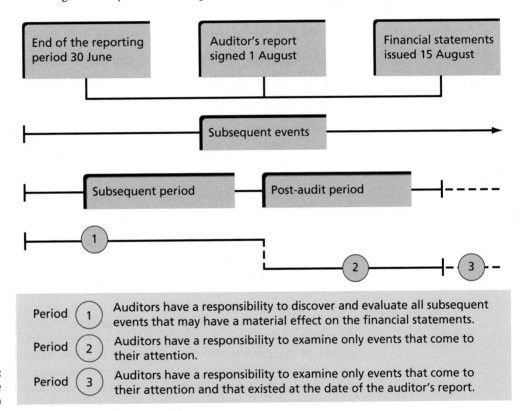

FIGURE 18.2:
Subsequent events time dimension

As part of the subsequent events review, the auditor will usually want to obtain a written representation letter to the legal counsel and a management representation letter to gain some level of assurance on certain items. Subsequent events may also raise going concern issues that the auditor needs to consider. These issues are discussed later in this chapter.

If the audit procedures identify events that could affect the financial statements, the auditor should carry out further procedures to assess whether such events are appropriately reflected in the financial statements. At this point the auditor needs to consider the appropriate accounting treatment of the event.

Subsequent events are often issues that may cause a conflict between the management of the company and the auditor, probably because subsequent events of most interest to the auditor are usually events that have a negative impact on the financial statements. Where management does not amend the financial statements when the auditor believes amendment to be necessary, the auditor should, in accordance with ASA 705 *Modifications to the Opinion in the Independent Auditor's Report* (ISA 705), issue a modified auditor's report (see chapter 7).

Post-audit responsibilities for subsequent events

After the auditor's report has been signed, the auditor has no responsibility to perform procedures to detect subsequent events or to make any enquiry regarding the financial statements. This is one of the main reasons that the date on the auditor's report is important. However, if the auditor becomes aware of a fact after the auditor's report has been signed, it may be appropriate to take some type of action, depending on whether the fact is discovered after the date of the auditor's report but *before* the financial statements have been issued or *after* the financial statements have been issued (shown as periods 2 and 3 respectively in figure 18.2).

Events occurring after the date of the auditor's report but before the financial statements are issued

The period after the date of the auditor's report but before the financial statements are issued is shown as period 2 in figure 18.2. It is not uncommon for this period to comprise several weeks, because the auditor does not have much control over when the financial statements are issued. The auditor has no responsibility to make an enquiry or to perform auditing procedures during this time to discover any material events occurring after the end of the reporting period. However, during this period, management is responsible for informing the auditor of any events that may affect the financial statements. The events may relate to conditions existing at or after the end of the reporting period (see the next page). The auditor should consider the need to amend the financial statements, conferring with management.

If the financial statements are amended, the auditor must carry out any necessary auditing procedures, including extending the review of events after the reporting period, and reissue the auditor's report at the date of approval of the amended financial statements. If management does not amend the financial statements where the auditor believes they should be amended, and the auditor's report has not been released to the entity, then the auditor should issue a qualified opinion or adverse opinion in accordance with ASA 705 (ISA 705). If the financial statements have been released to the entity and management refuses to make the required amendments, then the auditor should act to prevent reliance on the auditor's report. This can be done, for example, by exercising the auditor's right to be heard at the general meeting at which the audited financial statements are presented to members.

Facts discovered after the financial statements are issued

An auditor has no responsibility to make an ongoing enquiry on the financial statements after they have been issued (the period shown as period 3 in figure 18.2). This responsibility is essentially the same as that in period 2, when action by the auditor is required only if he or she becomes aware of an event. The key difference is that the only event that concerns the auditor in period 3 is something that was *missed* before signing the auditor's report and that has now come to light. This is in contrast to period 2 when the auditor must consider whether to take action in relation to *any* event of which he or she becomes aware. This limitation in period 3 ensures that there is an end point to the auditor's responsibilities in relation to a company's financial statements for a particular year.

The main issue to consider in assessing the impact of an event of this type is to determine whether the auditor would have qualified the auditor's report if the event had been known at the date of the report. If this is the case, then the auditor should consider whether the financial statements need revision. If management does not agree to the revision, then the people ultimately responsible for the overall direction of the entity should be notified that the auditor will act to prevent future reliance on the auditor's report.

The preferred result is the preparation of revised financial statements by the client and the issue of a revised auditor's report as soon as practicable. Again, before a revised auditor's report is issued, the auditor should extend the review of subsequent events up to the date of the issue of the revised report. The new report should include an 'emphasis of matter' paragraph referring to a note in the financial statements that explains the revision of the previously issued financial statements and the earlier auditor's report (see chapter 7).

The new report should be dated not earlier than the date on which the revised financial statements are approved. If the issue of the following period's financial statements is imminent, then the revised financial statements may not be issued. However, in these circumstances, appropriate disclosures are required in the following period's statements.

LEARNING 2 objective

Explain the different types of accounting treatments for events occurring after the end of the financial year.

Accounting considerations

AASB 110 (IAS 10) refers to events occurring after the end of the reporting period but before the time of completion. The time of completion is the date of the directors' statement or the date on which the financial statements are approved. In auditing, the time of completion is extended to the date on which the auditor's report is signed, although the directors' statement and the auditor's report are usually signed on the same date.

The accounting issue that needs to be considered in determining the appropriate disclosure is whether the event relates to a condition existing at the end of the reporting period (adjusting event) or whether it relates to a condition occurring after the end of the reporting period (non-adjusting event). The appropriate treatment for these events is outlined in AASB 110 (IAS 10) and discussed in the following sections.

Conditions existing at the end of the reporting period (adjusting events)

The balance sheet/statement of financial position and income statement/statement of comprehensive income must be prepared on the basis of conditions existing at the end of the reporting period. AASB 110 (IAS 10) states that the financial statements must reflect the financial effect of an event occurring after the end of the reporting period that provides additional evidence of conditions that existed at the end of the reporting period (adjusting events after the reporting period).

Estimates made in accounting are a common example of where evidence that comes to light after the end of the financial year may provide further information about the amount of the balance. Examples include the selling price of inventories after the end of the financial year, which provides evidence about the net realisable value at the end of the reporting period, or the settlement of recorded year-end estimated liabilities relating to litigation. Other examples are:

- bankruptcy of a customer after the end of the reporting period, which usually confirms that the trade receivable was not collectable at the end of the reporting period — therefore the entity should adjust the carrying amount of the trade receivable
- determination after the end of the reporting period of the proceeds of assets sold or the cost of assets purchased
- the discovery of fraud or errors that show the financial statements are incorrect.

ASA 540 *Auditing Accounting Estimates, Including Fair Value Accounting Estimates, and Related Disclosures* (ISA 540) requires the auditor to obtain an understanding of the entity and its environment for the identification and assessment of risks of material misstatement for accounting estimates, perform audit procedures and further substantive tests whenever needed to respond to the assessed risks, and evaluate the reasonableness of the accounting estimates and the disclosures in the financial report with respect to any subsequent events relating to them. It is also common practice that auditors obtain written representation from management about the reasonableness of significant assumptions used when making accounting estimates.

Conditions arising after the end of the reporting period (non-adjusting events)

Where an event occurring after the end of the reporting period provides new information that does not relate to conditions existing at year-end, the information should be disclosed by way of a note to the accounts (non-adjusting event) if non-disclosure has the potential to adversely affect decisions made by users of the financial statements. This type of event does not give rise to adjustments to assets and liabilities because it does not relate to conditions that existed at the end of the reporting period.

Examples of these types of events are:

- a fire or flood after the end of the reporting period
- a major currency realignment after the end of the reporting period
- the raising of additional share or loan capital
- mergers or acquisitions after the end of the reporting period.

Example of the difference between conditions existing at and arising after the end of the reporting period

Assume that a major customer becomes bankrupt on 1 August 2010. Also assume that the entity considered the customer's balance to be fully collectable in making its estimate of potentially uncollectable accounts in its 30 June 2010 financial statements. If, on review of the subsequent event, the auditor determines that the bankruptcy was attributable to the customer's deteriorating financial position (which existed, but was unknown to the entity, at the end of the reporting period), then the entity should be asked to adjust the 30 June 2010 financial statements for the loss. If the auditor determines instead that the customer was financially sound at 30 June and that the bankruptcy resulted from a fire or similar catastrophe that occurred after the end of the reporting period, then only disclosure in the notes to the 30 June financial statements is needed.

LEARNING **3**
objective

Explain the procedures in ensuring that the going concern basis is appropriate.

18.1.2 Considering the appropriateness of the going concern assumption

ASA 570 *Going Concern* (ISA 570) addresses material uncertainty in the context of both a fair presentation financial reporting framework and a compliance framework where the financial statement should not mislead readers in respect of the entity's going concern. Financial statements are prepared on a **going concern basis**. An entity is viewed as continuing in business for the foreseeable future. A general-purpose financial report is prepared on a going concern basis, unless management either intends to liquidate the entity or to cease operations, or has no realistic alternative but to do so. When the use of the going concern assumption is appropriate, assets and liabilities are recorded on the basis that the entity will be able to realise its assets and discharge its liabilities in the normal course of business. The auditor must consider whether applying this basis is appropriate in the valuation and allocation of items appearing in the financial statements and in the support of the directors' assertion as to solvency in the directors' declaration. ASA 570 (ISA 570) requires the auditor to assess the risk of going concern problems at the planning stage and again during the final review. The auditor is required to determine whether management has performed a preliminary assessment of going concern and discuss any such assessment with them. Appropriate disclosure in the financial report of a material uncertainty is necessary for the financial report to be presented fairly for a fair presentation framework, or not misleading for a compliance framework.

Indications that continuance as a going concern should be questioned may be financial (i.e. material operating losses), operational (i.e. the loss of key management personnel) or other (i.e. changes in legislation). The period to be considered by such an assessment extends to the expected date of the auditor's report for the succeeding financial statement period. This period is known as the 'relevant period'.

Auditors who identify events or conditions that may cast significant doubt on the entity's going concern status are required to have more detailed communications with those charged with governance when they are separate from management, including discussing the adequacy of financial report disclosures. There are additional procedures required to be performed where there is a significant delay in the approval of the financial report.

Where, at the planning stage, the risk of going concern problems is assessed as being remote, no additional procedures are necessary to test for the existence of such problems. When a question arises regarding the going concern basis, whether at the planning stage or subsequently, additional procedures may be necessary. The auditor performs most of these procedures during the period of completion of the audit (ASA 570, paragraph 16; ISA 570), such as:

(a) Where management has not yet performed an assessment of the entity's ability to continue as a going concern, requesting management to make its assessment.
(b) Evaluating management's plans for future actions in relation to its going concern assessment, whether the outcome of these plans is likely to improve the situation and whether management's plans are feasible in the circumstances.
(c) Where the entity has prepared a cash flow forecast, and analysis of the forecast is a significant factor in considering the future outcome of events or conditions in the evaluation of management's plans for future action:
   (i) Evaluating the reliability of the underlying data generated to prepare the forecast; and
   (ii) Determining whether there is adequate support for the assumptions underlying the forecast.
(d) Considering whether any additional facts or information have become available since the date on which management made its assessment.
(e) Requesting written representations from management and, where appropriate, those charged with governance, regarding their plans for future action and the feasibility of these plans.[2]

Where a going concern problem is identified, the auditor will need to discuss with management its plans for alleviating the problem, such as raising additional finance, disposing of surplus assets or selling loss-making business operations. The auditor will need to obtain written representation concerning such plans and should consider their feasibility by analysing their effect on cash flow or other relevant forecasts.

Unless all those charged with governance are involved in managing the entity, the auditor shall communicate with those charged with governance about events or conditions identified that may cast significant doubt on the entity's ability to continue as a going concern.

Such communication with those charged with governance shall include whether the events or conditions constitute a material uncertainty, whether the use of the going concern assumption in the financial report is appropriate and whether the financial report has adequately disclosed the matter concerned. Where appropriate, the auditor will need to obtain written confirmation from third parties, such as banks or creditors, as to the existence of:

- their commitment to additional lending or to a scheme of reconstruction
- their willingness to be identified in the statements as having entered into such arrangements.

The auditor may modify the auditor's report of an entity in response to going concern problems. The types of reporting options available to the auditor are discussed in chapter 7. AASB 110 states that the preparation of the financial report using the going concern basis is inappropriate if management determines after the end of the reporting period that:

- it intends to liquidate the entity
- it intends to cease trading
- it has no realistic alternative but to liquidate the entity
- it has no realistic alternative but to cease trading.

LEARNING objective 4

Explain the procedures in ensuring that all contingent liabilities have been properly identified and disclosed.

18.1.3 Reviewing for contingent liabilities

A contingency is an existing condition, situation or set of circumstances that involves uncertainty as to possible gain (contingent asset) or loss (**contingent liability**) that will be resolved when one (or more) future event(s) occurs or fails to occur. Contingent liabilities are the most common and are the subject of the rest of this section. AASB 137 *Provisions, Contingent Liabilities and Contingent Assets* (IAS 37) defines a contingent liability as either:

(a) a possible obligation that arises from past events and whose existence will be confirmed only by the occurrence or non-occurrence of one or more uncertain future events not wholly within the control of the entity; or

(b) a present obligation that arises from past events but is not recognised because:
  (i) it is not probable that an outflow of resources embodying economic benefits will be required to settle the obligation; or
  (ii) the amount of the obligation cannot be measured with sufficient reliability.

When the conditional event meets the recognition criteria of reliability of measurement and probability of occurrence, the obligation should be recognised as a liability in the financial statements and thus is no longer a 'conditional' liability. When the conditional event does not meet the criteria for recognition, it may still meet the disclosure requirements as a contingent liability. Irrespective of whether conditional liabilities should be recognised as liabilities or otherwise described in the notes, they are of relevance to the auditor because they are unlikely to be recorded in the accounting records until the occurrence of the uncertain future event. Therefore, there is a risk that they will not be completely and properly disclosed. These obligations include potential liabilities from income tax disputes, product warranties, guarantees of obligations of others, and litigation and claims.

The auditor's concerns about contingent liabilities are not limited to completing the audit. However, the review will often be towards the end of the audit because the auditor needs the most complete information set available. During audit testing, and particularly in searching for unrecorded liabilities (see chapter 15), the auditor should be alert to the possibility of contingent liabilities. Moreover, in reading the minutes of board meetings and in reviewing contracts, the auditor should look for circumstances that may indicate contingencies that should be investigated. Contingencies that are often the highest risk to auditors are associated with litigation. The most appropriate audit procedure in relation to this type of contingency is enquiry of the entity's lawyer(s) by means of a representation letter to a lawyer.

Communication with the entity's legal counsel

Direct communication with the entity's external legal counsel may help the auditor in obtaining sufficient appropriate audit evidence as to whether potential material litigation and claims are known and management's estimates of the financial implications, including costs, are reasonable. A **letter of general enquiry** may be used. The external legal counsel is asked to inform the auditor directly of any litigation and claims that the counsel is aware of, together with an assessment of the outcome of the litigation and claims, and an estimate of the financial implications, including costs. If this is not possible, the auditor may then seek direct communication through a letter of specific enquiry. This letter includes a list of litigation and claims, management's assessment of the outcome for each identified litigation and claim, the financial implications and costs, with a request that the legal counsel confirms the reasonableness of management's assessments (ASA 502, paragraphs A5–A7). Making appropriate enquiries about litigation and claims is an important part of completing the audit. These matters may have a material effect on the financial statements and thus may be required to be disclosed and/or provided for in the financial statements. ASA 502 *Audit Evidence — Specific Considerations for Litigation and Claims* (ISA 501) states in paragraph 2 that the auditor 'is to obtain sufficient appropriate audit evidence regarding the completeness of litigation and claims involving the entity'. ISA 501 *Audit Evidence — Specific Considerations for Selected Items* has similar although less detailed requirements to the above.

The auditor should also review board minutes and correspondence with the entity's lawyers, examine legal expense accounts, and consider any other information obtained as part of the performance of the audit, including discussions with any in-house legal department. An example of a letter of specific enquiry to external legal counsel (for an audit client) is shown in figure 18.3 (p. 770). (*Note:* The example is based on the appendix in ASA 502.) It should be prepared by management and sent by the auditor to each counsel identified as having handled legal matters during the year. As shown in figure 18.3, the letter should ask the lawyer to respond directly to the auditor.

If the response from the legal counsel contains a material disagreement with management's original evaluation of a matter, then the auditor should seek discussions with management and the legal counsel. If the disagreement is not resolved, then the auditor needs to consider its effect on the auditor's report.

If no response is received from the legal counsel, then the auditor should ask management to contact the counsel asking for a completion of the request or an explanation for the lack of response to be sent to the auditor. If the auditor assesses the reasons given by the counsel as unacceptable, or if no response is obtained, then the auditor should consider alternative audit procedures to gain sufficient appropriate audit evidence. Where significant appropriate audit evidence cannot be obtained, the lack or limitation of response would be considered a limitation on the scope of the auditor's work and the auditor would need to consider whether a qualified opinion or a disclaimer of opinion should be expressed (ASA 705; ISA 705).

In some cases, the legal counsel's response may indicate significant uncertainty about the likelihood of a favourable outcome of litigation or claims, or the amount or range of potential loss. The matter may be in only the initial stage of litigation, for example, and there may be no historical experience of the entity in similar litigation. In this situation, the auditor may conclude that the financial statements are affected by an inherent uncertainty that is not susceptible to reasonable estimation at the end of the reporting period. If the uncertainty is adequately disclosed in the financial statements, then the auditor's report should contain an unqualified opinion with an emphasis of matter section. If, in the auditor's opinion, the disclosure of the uncertainty is inadequate or unreliable, then the auditor would express a qualified opinion or an adverse opinion on the basis of a disagreement with those charged with governance (ASA 705; ISA 705). The various reports are discussed in chapter 7.

CLIENT COMPANY LTD
Letterhead

[Date]
[Name and Address of external legal counsel]

Dear ....

In connection with the preparation and audit of the financial report of the company (and the following subsidiaries and/or divisions) for the reporting period ended [date] we request that you provide to this company, at our cost, the following information.

1. Confirmation that you are acting for the company (and the above-named subsidiaries and/or divisions) in relation to the matters mentioned below and that the directors' description and estimates of the amounts of the financial settlement (including costs and disbursements) which might arise in relation to those matters are in your opinion reasonable.

Name of Company (subsidiary or division)	Directors' Description of Matter (including current status)	Directors' Estimate of the Financial Settlement (inclusive of costs and disbursements)

2. Should you disagree with any of the information included in 1 above, please comment on the nature of your disagreement.
3. In addition to the above, a list of open files that you maintain in relation to the company (and the above-mentioned subsidiaries and/or divisions).
4. In relation to the matters identified under 2 and 3 above, we authorise you to discuss these matters with our auditor [name and address], if requested, and at our cost.

It is understood that:
(a) the company (and the above-named subsidiaries and/or divisions) may have used other external legal counsels in certain matters;
(b) the information sought relates only to information relating to legal matters referred to your firm (including branches or subsidiaries) which were current at any time during the above-mentioned reporting period, or have arisen since the end of the reporting period and up to the date of your response;
(c) unless separately requested in writing, you are not responsible for keeping the auditors advised of any changes after the date of your reply;
(d) you are only required to respond on matters referred to you as external legal counsels for the company (and the above-mentioned subsidiaries and/or divisions), not on those within your knowledge solely because of the holding of any office as director, secretary or otherwise of the company (and the above-mentioned subsidiaries and/or divisions) by a consultant, partner or employee of your firm; and
(e) your reply is sought solely for the information of, and assistance to, this company in connection with the audit of, and report with respect to, the financial report of the company (and the above-mentioned subsidiaries and/or divisions) and will not be quoted or otherwise referred to in any financial report or related documents of the company (and the above-mentioned subsidiaries and/or divisions) nor will it be furnished to any governmental agency or other person, subject to specific legislative requirements, without the prior written consent of your firm.

Your prompt assistance in this matter will be appreciated. If you are unable to confirm or provide the information requested above, please advise us and our auditor the reasons for any limitation or impediment to fulfilling this request.

Would you please forward a signed copy of your reply directly to our auditors, [name] at [address], by [date].

Yours faithfully,
[Signature of client]

FIGURE 18.3: Letter of specific enquiry to an external legal counsel

Source: Based on example letter in Appendix 1 of ASA 502 *Audit Evidence — Specific Considerations for Litigation and Claims.*

18.1.4 Written representations

ASA 580 *Written Representations* (ISA 580) requires the auditor to obtain **written representations** from management and, where appropriate, those charged with governance in an audit of a financial report. The objectives of the auditor to obtain a written representation are to:

- confirm with management and those charged with governance that they have fulfilled their responsibility for the preparation of the financial report and for the completeness of the information provided to the auditor
- support other audit evidence relevant to the financial report or specific assertions in the financial report.

The auditor shall request written representations about management's responsibilities regarding the following matters:

- the preparation of the financial report has been in accordance with the applicable financial reporting framework, including where relevant their fair presentation, as set out in the audit engagement
- all relevant information and access as agreed in the terms of the audit engagement has been provided to the auditor
- all transactions have been recorded and are reflected in the financial report.

The description of management's responsibilities in the written representations shall be the same as described in the terms of the audit engagement.

The management representation letter may complement other auditing procedures (e.g. in connection with (1) the completeness of identified contingent liabilities and related party transactions or (2) the existence of mitigating factors in the presence of going concern problems). In some cases, however, a representation letter may be the main source of audit evidence. When a client plans to discontinue a line of business, for example, the auditor may be unable to corroborate this event through other auditing procedures.

Early legal judgements (e.g. *Kingston Cotton Mill Co.* (No. 2) (1896) 2 Ch. 279) allowed the auditor greater reliance on representations than is the case today. However, the Pacific Acceptance case clearly gave a warning to auditors on the degree to which they may place reliance on management representations:

> Prima facie the auditor's job is to check material matters for himself from available documents and he does not ordinarily do his job or 'audit' if he merely seeks the assurance of another as to the check that other has made or as to his views as to the effect of documents [Moffitt J, *Pacific Acceptance Corporation Ltd v. Forsyth & Ors*, 1970: 67].

The auditing standards do suggest that management representations are acceptable where other sufficient appropriate audit evidence cannot reasonably be expected to exist. As the issue of the acceptability of management representations has not recently been tested in the courts, the treatment of management representations as supporting rather than primary evidence is a prudent approach.

The auditor can take some comfort in the fact that some of the representations requested will overlap with Corporations Act requirements under s. 295A to produce a directors' declaration and s. 298 to produce a directors' report. Both of these are produced before the auditor signs the auditor's report. The following auditing standards require subject-matter specific written representations. The list is not a substitute for considering the requirements in the standards (ASA 580, Appendix 1).

- ASA 240 *The Auditor's Responsibilities Relating to Fraud in an Audit of a Financial Report* — paragraph 39
- ASA 250 *Consideration of Laws and Regulations in an Audit of a Financial Report* — paragraph 16
- ASA 450 *Evaluation of Misstatements Identified during the Audit* — paragraph 14

- ASA 502 *Audit Evidence — Specific Considerations for Litigation and Claims — paragraph 6*
- ASA 540 *Auditing Accounting Estimates, Including Fair Value Accounting Estimates, and Related Disclosures — paragraph 22*
- ASA 550 *Related Parties — paragraph 26*
- ASA 560 *Subsequent Events — paragraph 9*
- ASA 570 *Going Concern — paragraph 16(e)*
- ASA 710 *Comparative Information — Corresponding Figures and Comparative Financial Reports — paragraph 9.*

Contents of the written representation from management

Written representations from management, where they relate to financial statement amounts directly, should be limited to matters that are either individually or collectively considered to be material to the financial statements. Representation letters should be prepared on the entity's stationery, addressed to the auditor, signed by appropriate officers (usually the senior executive officer and the senior financial officer), and dated the same as the auditor's report (or as near as practicable). In many audits, the auditor will draft the representations, which subsequently become the responsibility of the officers who sign the letter. A written representation is illustrated in figure 18.4.

FIGURE 18.4: Written representation letter

CLIENT COMPANY LTD
(Entity Letterhead)

(To Auditor)   (Date)

This representation letter is provided in connection with your audit of the financial report of ABC Entity for the year ended 30 June 20XX[11] [or period covered by the auditor's report] for the purpose of the expressing an opinion as to whether the financial report is presented fairly, in all materials respects, (or gives a true and fair view) in accordance with the Australian Accounting Standards and the *Corporations Act 2001*.

We confirm that *(to the best of our knowledge and belief, having made such enquiries as we considered necessary for the purpose of appropriately informing ourselves):*

Financial Report
- We have fulfilled our responsibilities, as set out in the terms of the audit engagement dated [insert date], for the preparation of the financial report in the accordance with Australian Accounting Standards and the *Corporations Act 2001*; in particular the financial report in fairly presented (or gives a true and fair view) in accordance therewith.
- Significant assumptions used by us in making accounting estimates, including those measured at fair value, are reasonable. (ASA 540)
- Related party relationship and transactions have been appropriately accounted for and disclosed in accordance with the requirements of Australians Accounting Standards. (ASA 550)
- All events subsequent to the date of the financial report and for which Australian Accounting Standards require adjustment or disclosure have been adjusted or disclosed. (ASA 560)
- All effects of uncorrected misstatements are immaterial, both individually and in the aggregate, to the financial report as a whole. A list of the uncorrected misstatements is attached to the representation letter. (ASA 450)
- [Any other matters that the auditor may consider appropriate (see paragraph A10 of this Auditing Standard).]

Information Provided
- We have provided you with:
  - Access to all information of which we aware that is relevant to the preparation of the financial report such as records, documentation and other matters;
  - Additional information that you have requested from us for the purpose of the audit; and
  - Unrestricted access to persons within the entity from whom you determined it necessary to obtain audit evidence.
- All transactions have been recorded in the accounting records and are reflected in the financial report.

- We have disclosed to you the results of our assessment of the risk that the financial report may be materially misstated as a result of fraud. (ASA 240)
- We have disclosed to you all information in relation to fraud or suspected fraud that we are aware of and that affects the entity and involves:
  - Management;
  - Employees who have significant roles in internet control; or
  - Others where the fraud could have a material effect on the financial report. (ASA 240)
- We have disclosed to you all information in relation to allegations of fraud, or suspected fraud, affecting the entity's financial report communicated by employees, former employees, analysts, regulators or others. (ASA 240)
- We have disclosed to you all known instances of non-compliance or suspected non-compliance with laws and regulations whose effects should be considered when preparing the financial report. (ASA 250)
- We have disclosed to you all known actual or possible litigation and claims whose effects should be considered when preparing the financial report; and accounted for and disclosed in accordance with [the applicable financial reporting framework]. (ASA 502)
- We have disclosed to you the identity of the entity's related parties and all the related party relationships and transactions of which we are aware. (ASA 550)
- [Any other matters that the auditor may consider necessary (see paragraph A11 of this ASA 580).]
- Aus   We have provided you with all requested information, explanations and assistance for the purposes of audit.*
- Aus   We have provided you with all information required by the *Corporations Act 2001* [where applicable].#

Management   Management

11[Footnote deleted by the AUASB as not applicable in Australia.]
*There may be a regulatory requirement for particular information to be provided. For example, see section 312 of the *Corporations Act 2001.*
#See, for example, sections 300A and 295A of the *Corporations Act 2001.*

Source: Based on example letter in Appendix 2 to ASA 580 *Written Representations*.

Effects on the auditor's report

A management representation letter is not a substitute for any auditing procedures necessary to provide a reasonable basis for an opinion on the financial statements. This evidence is judged to have relatively low reliability. However, the refusal of management to furnish a written representation does constitute a limitation on the scope of the auditor's examination. In such circumstances, the auditor must express a qualified opinion or a disclaimer of opinion (ASA 705; ISA 705). Where management refuses to provide a written representation letter, the auditor may draw management's attention to the statutory requirements under the Corporations Act. Under s. 310 the auditor has rights of access to the books of the company and may require any officer to give the auditor information and explanations or other assistance for the purposes of the audit. Further, s. 307(b) requires the auditor to form an opinion as to whether all information, explanations and assistance necessary for the conduct of the audit have been given, and in accordance with s. 308(3)(b) the auditor must state in the auditor's report whether there have been any shortcomings in these matters. It is important that the auditor assesses the reliability of the written representation or the impact of the financial report if a written representation is not given. Under the following circumstances, the auditor should undertake further actions or adjust the auditor's report.

- The auditor has concerns about the competence, integrity, ethical values or diligence of management, or about its commitment to, or enforcement of these. This will have an impact on the reliability of the audit evidence in general.
- Where the written representation is not consistent with other audit evidence, the auditor shall perform audit procedures to attempt to resolve the matter. The auditor shall reassess the competence and integrity of the management if the matters were not resolved, and shall determine the effect this may have on the audit evidence in general.

- Where the auditor concludes that the written representation is not reliable, the auditor shall take appropriate actions, including determining the possible effect on the opinion in the auditor's report.
- If one or more of the requested written representations are not provided, the auditor shall discuss with management, re-evaluate its integrity, and take appropriate actions including determining the possible effect on the opinion in the auditor's report.

The auditor shall disclaim an opinion of the financial report in accordance with ASA 705 (ISA 705) if the auditor concludes that there is sufficient doubt about the integrity of management such that the written representation provided is not reliable, or management does not provide the written representation in accordance with ASA 580 (ISA 580).

LEARNING 6 objective

Indicate why analytical procedures are important in undertaking the overall review of the financial statements.

18.1.5 Performing analytical procedures

Analytical procedures are an important part of the completion of the audit. As stated in ASA 520 *Analytical Procedures* (ISA 520), paragraph 6:

> The auditor shall design and perform analytical procedures near the end of the audit that assist the auditor when forming an overall conclusion as to whether the financial report is consistent with the auditor's understanding of the entity.

In earlier chapters, we explained and illustrated the application of analytical procedures in planning an audit, in risk assessment and performing year-end substantive procedures. The auditor designs and performs analytical procedures near the end of the audit in order to arrive at an overall conclusion as to whether the financial report is consistent with the auditor's understanding of the entity. 'Analytical procedures' refers to evaluations of financial information through analysis of plausible relationships among both financial and non-financial data. Analytical procedures encompass any investigation that is deemed necessary when there are identified fluctuations or relationships that are inconsistent with other relevant information, or that differ from expectations. Analytical procedures involve the use of ratios and other comparative techniques. The reason for using analytical review in the overall review is to corroborate conclusions formed during the audit on individual elements of financial information and to assist in arriving at the overall conclusion that the financial information as a whole is consistent with the knowledge of the entity's business. Applying analytical review procedures at the end of the audit is also a useful way of gaining assurance that the company will remain a going concern for the relevant period.

A variety of analytical procedures may be used. The procedures should be:
- applied to critical audit areas identified during the audit
- based on financial statement data after all audit adjustments and reclassifications have been recognised.

As in earlier applications of analytical procedures, entity data may be compared with expected entity results, available industry data and relevant non-financial data such as units produced or sold and the number of employees.

In carrying out an overall review, the auditor (often the audit senior in the first instance) reads the financial statements and accompanying notes. In so doing, the auditor considers the adequacy of the evidence gathered for unusual or unexpected balances and relationships that have been either anticipated in planning or identified during the audit through substantive procedures. Analytical procedures are then applied to the financial statements to determine whether any other unusual or unexpected relationships exist. If such relationships exist, then the auditor should perform additional auditing procedures in completing the audit. The auditor is usually in a good position to critically evaluate the results of analytical procedures at the end of the audit, given the knowledge gained over the course of the audit.

However, there is a risk that the auditor who has been responsible for a large amount of the audit fieldwork may be 'too close' to the audit work performed and may miss an unusual or unexpected relationship that would be recognised by someone who has not been so directly involved with the audit. For this reason, and because this review is so important, the partner or manager on the engagement also reviews the analytical procedures. This partner should have a comprehensive knowledge of the entity's business and, as another advantage, would not have been directly involved with the audit fieldwork. Often, partners or managers pick up inconsistencies or problems because they have extensive business knowledge and because they can look at the figures more objectively than can someone who has done most of the fieldwork.

PROFESSIONAL ENVIRONMENT
Linking the auditor's going concern considerations with types of audit opinions

Difficult or uncertain economic conditions, as they relate to going concern, present challenges for:
- company directors (directors) — particularly those of listed companies, who will need to ensure that they prepare thoroughly for their assessment of going concern and make appropriate financial report disclosures
- independent auditors (auditors) — who will need to ensure that they adequately evaluate directors' going concern assessments and only refer to going concern in their audit opinions when appropriate
- users of financial reports — who will need to carefully consider the potential implications of these conditions in market announcements and financial reports. Such users include the investment community, finance lenders, suppliers, customers and employees.

The AUASB and the Australian Institute of Company Directors published a comprehensive guide for directors regarding going concerns. The publication includes a diagram showing the flow of actions that link the auditor's going concern considerations with types of audit opinions. While the audit opinions were based on ASA 701, there are no major differences in the principles used in the information produced as per ASA 705.

The going concern assessment is likely to include a high level of judgement by directors and subsequently by the auditor, depending on the circumstances of the company. Directors are required to consider the solvency of the company as determined by comparing the company's assets and liabilities, along with its ability to meet liabilities as and when they fall due. Professional advice should be sought if the directors are unable to state that the going concern basis of financial reporting is appropriate.

The auditor is required by Australian auditing standards to review the directors' going concern assumption and to determine if, in the auditor's judgement, there are events or conditions which cast significant doubt on the company's ability to continue as a going concern. In this respect, the auditor must understand the contexts of the company and the risks that are embedded within the company's functions and business. The auditor is also required to obtain sufficient and appropriate audit evidence in order to arrive at an opinion regarding the impact of such risks.

The diagram on the next page depicts the flow of considerations regarding going concern when the auditor conducts the final review of the audit.

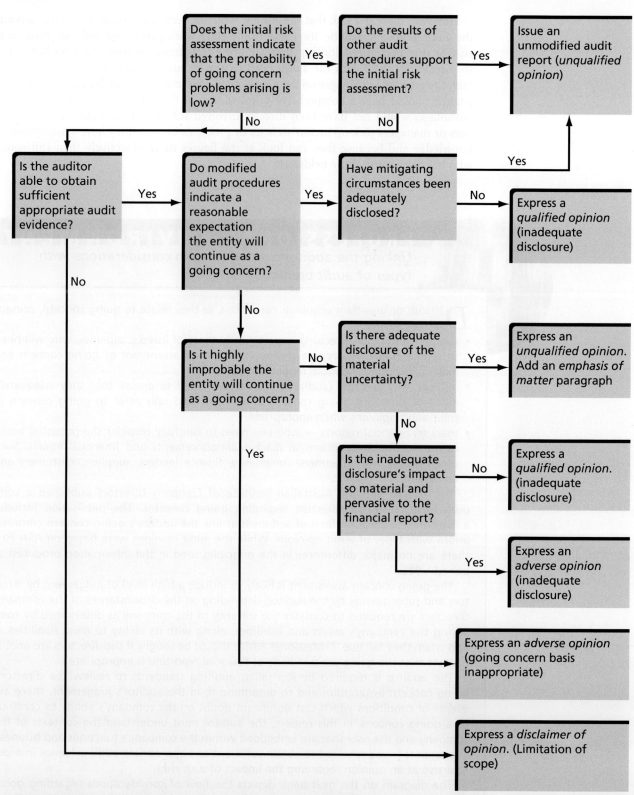

Source: Extract from 'Going concern issues in financial reporting: A guide for companies and directors', Auditing and Assurance Standards Board and Australian Institute of Company Directors, 2009.

Do you know ...

18.1 ☐ The auditor is required to identify and evaluate events occurring up to the date of the auditor's report. These events may relate to conditions that existed at the end of the reporting period (adjusting events) that may require an adjustment to the accounts or conditions that arose after the end of the reporting period (non-adjusting events) that could only result in disclosure by way of a note to the accounts.

18.2 ☐ The auditor should assess the appropriateness of the going concern assumption during the final review. Additional audit procedures must be performed if there are any questions about the going concern assumption.

18.3 ☐ Contingencies are existing situations that involve uncertainty about a possible gain or loss. Legal disputes are the main source of contingencies; for this reason, a lawyer's representation letter is often obtained from the entity's external legal counsel to corroborate management's assertions in relation to the status of litigation or claims.

18.4 ☐ A written representation letter acknowledges that management, and where appropriate, those charged with governance, has the main responsibility for the financial statements. It may be the main source of audit evidence, where appropriate audit evidence cannot reasonably be expected to exist.

18.5 ☐ Analytical procedures performed in completing the audit help the auditor to conclude that the financial information as a whole is consistent with his or her knowledge of the entity's business.

Identify the steps in evaluating audit findings.

18.2 EVALUATING THE FINDINGS

In evaluating the findings, the auditor has the following objectives: (1) to ensure that the audit process has complied with auditing standards, and (2) to determine the type of audit opinion to be expressed (which is discussed in more detail in chapter 7). To meet these objectives, the auditor completes the following steps:

- makes the final assessment of materiality and audit risk
- undertakes the **technical review** of the financial statements
- undertakes the final review(s) of working papers
- formulates an opinion and drafts the auditor's report.

18.2.1 Making the final assessment of materiality and audit risk

In formulating an opinion on the financial statements, the auditor should assimilate all the evidence gathered during the examination. An essential prerequisite in deciding on the opinion to express is a final assessment of materiality and audit risk. ASA 450 *Evaluation of Misstatements Identified during the Audit* (ISA 450) requires the auditor to evaluate the effect of identified misstatements on the audit and the effect of uncorrected misstatements, if any, on the financial report.

Misstatement means a difference between the amount, classification, presentation, or disclosure of a reported financial report item and the amount, classification, presentation, or disclosure that is required for the item to be in accordance with the applicable financial reporting framework.

The definition of misstatements is provided in paragraph A1 of ASA 450:

Misstatements may result from:
(a) An inaccuracy in gathering or processing data from which the financial report is prepared;
(b) An omission of an amount, a disclosure;
(c) An incorrect accounting estimate arising from overlooking, or clear misinterpretation of facts;
(d) Judgements of management concerning accounting estimates that the auditor considers unreasonable or the selection and application of accounting policies that the auditor considers inappropriate.

Misstatements can arise from error or fraud and can include those adjustments of amounts, classifications, presentation, or disclosures that, in the auditor's judgement, are necessary for the financial report to be presented fairly, in all material aspects, or to give a true and fair view. Uncorrected misstatements are misstatements that the auditor has accumulated during the audit and that have not been corrected.

It is required that the auditor shall:

- accumulate misstatements identified during the audit, other than those which are clearly trivial
- consider if the overall audit plan needs to be revised if the circumstances of the occurrence indicate that other misstatements may exist and when aggregated, could be material
- consider the aggregate of misstatements if they approach the threshold of materiality determined at the time of the audit planning stage
- communicate on a timely basis all misstatements accumulated and request management to correct those misstatements
- evaluate the effect of any uncorrected misstatements following a review and reassessment of the materiality level
- communicate with those charged with governance uncorrected misstatements and the likely effect, both individually and in aggregate, they may have on the opinion of the auditor's report, unless prohibited by law or regulation. Any uncorrected misstatements related to prior periods on the relevant classes of transactions, account balances or disclosures, and the financial report as a whole
- obtain a written representation from the management and, where appropriate, from those charged with governance, whether they believe the effects of uncorrected misstatements are immaterial, individually or in aggregate, to the financial report as a whole.

The auditor should maintain proper documentations that include:

- the amount below which misstatements would be regarded as clearly trivial
- all misstatements accumulated during the audit and whether they are corrected
- the auditor's conclusion as to whether uncorrected misstatements are material, individually or in aggregate, and the basis for that conclusion.

The auditor should assess whether the aggregate of the uncorrected misstatements identified during the audit is material. Normally the aggregate of uncorrected misstatements will be recorded on a summary schedule at the front of the audit file. The data that have been accumulated on the summary schedule are then compared with the auditor's preliminary judgements concerning materiality. Any adjustments in planning materiality that have been made during the course of the examination should be included in this assessment. If the aggregate level of uncorrected misstatements is material, then the auditor needs to consider reducing audit risk by extending audit procedures or requesting management to adjust the financial statements.

In planning the audit, the auditor specifies an acceptable level of audit risk. As the aggregate level of uncorrected misstatement increases, the risk that the financial statements may be materially misstated will also increase. When audit risk is at an acceptable level, the auditor can proceed to formulate the opinion supported by the findings. However, if audit risk is not acceptable, then the auditor should either perform additional substantive procedures or convince management to make the adjustments necessary to reduce the risk of material misstatement to an acceptable level. If management does not make the adjustments as required by the auditor, then the auditor may decide to issue a qualified auditor's report.

To assist the auditor in evaluating the effect of misstatements accumulated during the audit and in communicating with those charged with governance, it is important to distinguish between factual misstatements, judgemental misstatements and projected misstatements. Paragraph A3 of ASA 450 refers to the following definitions:

- Factual misstatements are misstatements about which there is no doubt.
- Judgemental misstatements are differences arising from the judgements of management concerning accounting estimates that the auditor considers unreasonable, or the selection or application of accounting policies that the auditor considers inappropriate.
- Projected misstatements are the auditor's best estimate of misstatements in populations, involving the projection of misstatements identified in audit samples to the entire populations from which the samples were drawn. Guidance on the determination of projected misstatements and evaluation of the results is set out in ASA 530.

18.2.2 Undertaking the technical review of the financial statements

This is a very important part of the audit and requires a high degree of technical knowledge, given the large number of professional and legislative requirements and the constantly changing nature of these requirements. The technical review includes matters relating to the form and content of each of the basic financial statements, in accordance with:

- the requirements of applicable accounting standards and other required disclosures
- other matters as required by the Corporations Act
- the official listing requirements of the Australian Securities Exchange (where these apply).

To assist in this process, many public accounting firms have detailed financial statement checklists, which are completed by the auditor who performs the initial review of the financial statements. Once completed, the checklist and financial statements are reviewed by the manager and partner in charge of the engagement. The completed checklist and the findings of the reviewers should be included in the working papers. Before the release of the auditor's report on a publicly listed client, there may also be a technical review by a partner who was not a member of the audit team. This serves as a double-check on the quality of the financial statement presentation and disclosure.

If there are any problems with disclosure, they should be discussed with management. Usually, management will act on the auditor's advice in relation to technical aspects of disclosure. (Often, they will *seek* the auditor's advice in this area). Inevitably there will be disagreements, particularly associated with sensitive disclosure requirements such as directors' remuneration and related parties. If a disagreement about disclosure between management and the auditor cannot be resolved, then the auditor should consider issuing a qualified auditor's report (discussed in chapter 7).

18.2.3 Undertaking the final review(s) of working papers

In chapter 8 we discussed the first-level review of working papers by a supervisor. The review is made to evaluate the work done, the evidence obtained and the conclusions reached by the person preparing the working paper. It is also conducted to ensure that the audit work meets an appropriate level of quality. The work performed undergoes more comprehensive reviews at the end of the audit fieldwork.

Often, the audit manager will review all the audit working papers (including those reviewed by the audit senior) to ensure that the work has been performed properly. The manager will also sign all the working papers reviewed to provide evidence of the review. The manager's review of the working papers is designed to obtain assurance that:

- the work done by subordinates has been accurate and thorough
- the judgements exercised by subordinates were reasonable and appropriate in the circumstances
- the audit engagement has been completed in accordance with the conditions and terms specified in the engagement letter
- all significant accounting, auditing and reporting questions raised during the audit have been properly resolved
- the working papers support the auditor's opinion
- the audit process has complied with the auditing standards and the firm's quality control policies and procedures.

Detailed checklists covering the above matters are commonly used in performing the review of working papers. The manager will also list queries raised while performing the review. The queries are generally resolved by the person who undertook the work and must be cleared by the manager before the audit is completed.

The review by the partner has similar objectives to the review performed by the manager. The extent of the partner review will depend on the partner, the type of engagement and the partner's confidence in the audit manager. Generally, the partner will not review all working papers, but will focus on sections of the audit perceived to be high risk. This assessment may come from the partner's knowledge of the client or from the final analytical review performed on the client.

In the preparation and review of the audit working papers, it is important that they 'stand alone'. That is, when they are finally signed off, another auditor should be able to review the working papers and be comfortable that they provide sufficient and appropriate audit evidence without any further explanation from the preparer of the working papers.

As a further quality control, some firms require a **second partner review** of the working papers by a partner who did not participate in the audit, so that the objectivity of the reviewer may challenge matters approved by earlier reviewers. Thus, the review provides additional assurance that all auditing standards and the firm's quality control standards have been met in the engagement.

18.2.4 Formulating an opinion and drafting the auditor's report

During the course of an audit engagement, a number of auditors perform a variety of audit tests. (The number of auditors will vary according to the size of the company being audited.) As the tests for each section of the audit are completed, the auditor is expected to summarise the findings. This summary should include any proposed audit adjustments, any weaknesses in the system or problems that should be passed on to management, and a conclusion on the section of the audit completed. In completing the audit, the separate findings of each of the sections need to be summarised and evaluated so as to express an opinion on the financial statements as a whole. The ultimate responsibility for these steps rests with the partner in charge of the engagement. In some cases, the audit manager makes the initial determinations, which are then carefully reviewed by the partner.

Before reaching a final decision on the audit opinion, the auditor should meet with management. At this meeting, the auditor reports the findings orally and provides a reason for proposed adjustments and/or additional disclosures that have not been resolved. Management may try to defend its position. Agreement is generally reached on the changes to be made, and the auditor can issue an unqualified opinion. The potential threat of a qualified auditor's report and the negative signal it sends to investors is usually enough to ensure that management agrees with the auditor's opinion. However, when such an agreement is not obtained, the auditor may have to issue a qualified opinion. The auditor's opinion is communicated through an auditor's report. (The various types of auditor's reports are discussed in chapter 7.)

18.3 COMMUNICATING WITH THE ENTITY

Communication with the entity is an important part of the audit. It highlights the problems found, suggests improvements in the client's system, and gives some evidence on the extent of work performed. ASA 260 *Communication with Those Charged with Governance* (ISA 260) discusses the requirement for the auditor to communicate with those charged with governance. According to the definition in ASA 260, 'governance' is the term used to describe the role of people entrusted with the oversight, control and direction of the entity. The auditor determines the relevant people who are charged with governance. Usually the audit committee or governing board is responsible for the oversight function, and senior executives are responsible for the management function.

18.3.1 Communication of audit matters with those charged with governance

The AUASB recognises the importance of an effective two-way communication in an audit of a financial report. Paragraph 9 of ASA 260 (ISA 260) focuses of the following objectives of the auditor:

(a) to communicate clearly with those charged with governance the responsibilities of the auditor in relation to the financial report audit, and an overview of the planned scope and timing of the audit
(b) to obtain from those charged with governance information relevant to the audit
(c) to provide those charged with governance with timely observations arising from the audit that are significant and relevant to their responsibility to oversee the financial reporting process
(d) to promote effective two-way communication between the auditor and those charged with governance.

'Those charged with governance' refers to the persons or organisations with responsibility for overseeing the strategic direction of the entity and obligations related to the accountability of the entity. The oversight duties include the financial reporting process. For some entities, those charged with governance may include management personnel. On the other hand, management means those persons with executive responsibility for the conduct of the entity's operations. For some entities, management may include some or all of those charged with governance, for example, executive members of a governance board. The auditor is required to determine the appropriate persons within the governance structure with whom to communicate.

The matters to be communicated include the following.
- The auditor's responsibilities in relation to the financial report audit; for example, for the forming and expressing of an opinion on the financial report prepared by management. The audit of the financial report does not relieve management or those charged with governance of their responsibilities.

- The planned scope and timing of the audit.
- Significant findings of the financial report audit, including significant qualitative aspects of the entity's accounting practices, significant difficulties encountered during the audit, significant matters discussed with management, any written representations requested, and any other matters of the audit that, in the auditor's professional judgement, are significant to the oversight of the financial reporting process.
- Audit independence which includes statements that the engagement teams (and other related firms) have complied with relevant ethical requirements, all matters that may reasonably be thought to bear on independence (including total fees received) and safeguards that have been applied to eliminate identified threats to independence or reduce them to an acceptable level. In the case of entities audited in accordance with the *Corporations Act 2001*, the auditor shall include a statement that the engagement team and others in the firm, as appropriate, have complied with the independence requirements of s. 307C of the Corporations Act.

Appendix 2 of ASA 260 (ISA 260) provides examples of significant qualitative aspects of the entity's accounting practices that the auditor may consider providing their views on to those charged with governance. These matters include accounting policies, accounting estimates, financial report disclosures and related matters. Other matters that the auditor may consider to include in the communication with those charged with governance are:

- the general approach and overall scope of the audit
- the selection of, or changes in, significant accounting policies and practices that have, or could have, a material effect on the entity's financial report
- the potential effect of any significant risks and exposures
- audit adjustments
- material uncertainties that may cast doubt on the entity's ability to continue as a going concern
- disagreements with management
- expected modifications to the auditor's report
- any other matters agreed on in the terms of the audit engagement.

However, the auditor has no duty to design audit procedures for identifying matters that may be appropriate to report to those charged with governance (i.e. detection of fraud is not part of the requirements of a normal financial statement audit). Sometimes, those charged with governance may want the auditor to review certain parts of the accounting system or perform certain other procedures. These tasks are not considered part of the financial statement audit; instead, they come under the category of 'assurance services'.

The extent and nature of communication with management has been considered in a number of legal cases (before the concept of 'those charged with governance' was introduced). The case of *WA Chip & Pulp Co. Pty Limited v. Arthur Young & Co.* (1987) SACLC looked at the issue of whether detected irregularities immaterial to the audit need to be brought to management's attention. The court found that not only should items material to the audit be reported to management, but also the auditor should consider warning and informing management of any matters that come to the auditor's attention that may be a cause for concern.

The AWA case (*AWA v. Daniels t/a Deloitte, Haskins & Sells & Ors* (1992) IOACLC 933) considered the issue of to whom auditors should report matters. In this case, it was found that weaknesses discovered in the control system must be reported to management promptly and that significant matters must be reported not just to management but to an *appropriate level* of management. This principle is reflected in ASA 260 (ISA 260) in its discussion of reporting to 'those charged with governance'.

The auditor shall communicate with those charged with governance the form, timing and expected general content of the communications. The auditor shall communicate in writing regarding significant findings from the audit if oral communication is considered inappropriate. The auditor shall endeavour to ensure all members of the governance body are appropriately informed of the contents of a written communication with those charged with governance.

The audit plan should contain a separate section on communication with management and those charged with governance. Where feasible, the plan should indicate areas of the entity's operations and controls that may be included in the communications. As the audit progresses, matters that are relevant to be communicated should be noted in the audit working papers to ensure they are not overlooked. Subsequently, the working papers should provide adequate documentation of the comments contained in the written report to management and to those charged with governance. Communication with those charged with governance should be carefully prepared, well organised and written in a constructive tone. The auditor usually discusses the contents of the draft letter with the person responsible for the accounting system (usually the financial controller). In particular, the practicality of implementing the suggested changes to the existing system should be discussed. However, absence of agreement should not inhibit the inclusion of recommendations that the auditor considers desirable. To avoid misunderstanding, written communications should contain a paragraph advising management that the auditor's examination is made to form an opinion on the financial statements and that the written communication should not be regarded as a statement of all matters of concern that may exist.

Prompt communication with management and with those charged with governance on completion of the audit creates a favourable impression and may encourage both an early and a positive response to matters raised from the audit. Where the interim audit reveals material weaknesses in internal control, it may be desirable to issue an interim letter on completion of that phase of the audit as well as on completion of the final audit.

The communication should request a written reply indicating the action taken or intended to be taken on the matters raised. If no response is received, then the auditor should consider whether to raise the matter directly with the audit committee. In any event, if management takes no action, then the auditor should consider raising the matter again in subsequent communications.

18.3.2 Communicating matters with the audit committee

The audit committee is part of the corporate governance structure to improve the credibility and objectivity of the accountability process. It also facilitates communication between the external auditor and the board of directors. External auditors have a number of special responsibilities in their relations with audit committees.

The Auditing Standard ASA 260 *Communication with Those Charged with Governance* provides an overview of the external auditors' duties in communicating with those officers and members of the companies who have a governing duty. These officers include audit committee members, CEOs, CFOs, board members and so on. The 2012 publication by the Auditing and Assurance Standards Board, Australian Institute of Company Directors and The Institute of Internal Auditors — Australia *Audit Committees — A Guide to Good Practice* (2nd edition) provides a comprehensive guide on the role of the audit committee and its relationships with the board, external and internal auditors.[3]

The key requirements for communicating with the audit committee include:
- promoting an effective and constructive two-way communication on relevant matters
- establishing whether any preconditions for an audit are present and how they are communicated to and acknowledged by management so that the audit is carried out properly
- reaching agreement on the terms of the audit engagement and ensuring that the auditor's responsibilities are communicated clearly
- establishing and maintaining independence through identifying and communicating any relationships that might have a bearing on the auditor's independence, including the provision of other assurance
- notifying the audit committee of any contraventions to the auditor's independence requirements and communicating the safeguards applied to any threats to independence
- discussing overall audit strategy, scope and timing, including any limitations and the assessment of materiality, risk areas and plans to examine the effectiveness of internal controls
- discussing any proposed coordination with the internal audit activity, including any planned use of their work
- Discussing the nature, extent and business rationale of any significant related party relationships and transactions including those involving any conflicts of interest
- enquiring into any knowledge and actions regarding actual or suspected or alleged fraud affecting the entity
- communicating significant findings from the audit, including any significant qualitative aspects of the accounting practices, difficulties encountered, any disagreement with management, whether resolved or not resolved, that relate to the financial report
- communicating significant deficiencies in the internal control, identified fraud, weaknesses, any non-compliance with laws and regulations, misstatements, any significant business conditions that may have an impact on the company's going concern, any expected modifications to the auditors' report
- any other matters of governance interest that arose during the course of the audit that are relevant to the oversight of financial reporting, including material risks and exposures, external factors, and material inconsistencies in the information accompanying the audited financial report.

The guide is designed for directors and audit committee members. Auditors, risk and compliance managers and internal auditors will also find it a useful resource. It establishes the expectations between audit committees and other key parties in audit and management.

An effective audit committee should be considered in the auditor's assessment of the client's control structure. The auditor should also use the committee as much as possible in ensuring that the requirements of the financial report audit are properly and objectively fulfilled.

While it is important for the auditor to communicate with the audit committee in finalising the audit and in reviewing matters that may impact on the final audit opinion, the auditor must be able to assess the impact of any other external factors that may provide threats to the validity of the assumptions and presentations of the financial report being audited. At this stage of the audit, the auditor is required to be particularly vigilant in observing internal and external matters, and in maintaining independence in the final decision of the audit opinion. The Professional Environment box following is an essay provided by CPA Australia during the global financial crisis experienced by business, to guide the auditor.

CPA Australia, with the assistance of PwC [PricewaterhouseCoopers] partner Valerie Clifford, has developed the following tips to assist members conducting audits in the current economic environment. The tips should assist auditors in dealing with the greater risks presented by the global financial crisis (GFC) as it impacts on all entities to some degree.

The tips are not meant to be exhaustive and auditors should refer to the auditing standards applicable in their jurisdiction when conducting audits. For matters not covered by the tips, it is expected that auditors will use their professional judgement appropriate to the audit. The tips have general applicability to all audits of financial reports, including audits of self-managed superannuation funds.

1. *Risk of material misstatement.* The risks of material misstatement in financial reports are significantly higher than in previous years.
2. *Communicating with clients.* It is important to advise your client as soon as possible that the risks of material misstatement are higher than in previous years because of the GFC. Therefore you may need to change aspects of the audit of the client's financial report, including:
   - overall decisions regarding client continuance
   - staffing of the audit and the extent of supervision of staff
   - the nature, timing and extent of audit procedures.

   You should also advise those charged with the governance of the client (see also ISA 260/ASA 260 *Communication with those Charged with Governance*) when you become aware of the following:
   - a material weakness in the design or implementation of internal controls which may give rise to a possible material misstatement in the financial report
   - fraud
   - you have doubts about your client's ability to continue as a going concern.
3. *Planning.* Planning the overall audit strategy is more important than ever because of the increased risks in the current climate. It is therefore important in planning the audit that you:
   - consult and plan early
   - think unconventionally to ensure that all possible issues are at least considered
   - thoroughly understand the client's business and its viability
   - challenge the business model
   - consider the need to assign more experienced staff to the audit and to have greater partner involvement
   - consider performing substantive procedures closer to, or at, period end (particularly in critical audit areas).
4. *Training of your audit staff.* Some audit staff may not have had sufficient experience of auditing in a difficult economic environment. Accordingly, they may need training in advance of an audit to show them the things that should now be done differently.
5. *Knowledge sharing and subject matter experts.* Given the increased risks, your audit team should discuss any potentially difficult or contentious matters among themselves and with other professionals or experts within or outside your firm.
6. *Materiality.* When planning the audit, you should consider what would cause the financial report to be materially misstated. In the current environment, there

may be circumstances that affect your determination of materiality, such as the following:

- net income may be nominal during the GFC or significantly different from previous periods
- misstatements that may exist in balances representing opening equity may contribute to a material misstatement during the GFC
- the expectations of users of the financial report, including what they would consider to be material misstatement, may differ significantly from what they were in previous periods
- your own assessment of the risks that may lead to material misstatements in the financial report.

Your overall assessment of materiality remains based on your professional judgement, but it should include qualitative and quantitative considerations.

7. *Risk areas.* Areas of increased risk include:

- management bias (with or without fraudulent intent):
  - i. there is a natural temptation to bias judgements and disclosures toward the most favourable end
  - ii. management may take the GFC as an opportunity to overestimate certain balances (e.g. write-down of assets).
- fraud. Fraud can occur because
  - iii. financial stability or profitability is threatened
  - iv. there is excessive pressure on management
  - v. staff resources have been reduced in critical risk management areas
  - vi. managers may seek to override controls
- asset measurements and valuations. Evaluating the assumptions and data used by management should be a major focus of your response to the increased risk of material misstatement associated with fair value measurements and accounting estimates.

Given these and other risks, you may need to reassess:

- the nature, extent and timing of risk assessment procedures
- the effectiveness of the internal controls that are designed to prevent, or detect and correct material misstatements
- those risks that require special audit consideration (estimates and disclosures)
- whether further audit procedures, as well as those that are usually performed, are required (i.e. do the present tests of controls and substantive procedures take account of the higher risk of material misstatement?)
- your response to the possibility of fraud (i.e. maintain your professional skepticism; focus the engagement team's discussion on the possibility of material misstatements due to fraud; and understand the business rationale for significant transactions).

8. *Going concern.* The critical issues that you need to consider in assessing 'going concern' are:

- the appropriateness of management's assumption that the firm is a going concern
- the disclosure of any material uncertainties about the entity's ability to continue as a going concern
- the appropriateness of management's assumption that the entity is a going concern, even if the financial reporting framework used in the preparation of the financial report does not include an explicit requirement for management to make that assumption
- the actual period for which management is assessing the entity's ability to continue as a going concern

- entities that have not previously needed to prepare a detailed analysis in support of the going concern assumption may need to give the matter further consideration. Both you and the entity should benefit from early discussions regarding the need to give this matter further consideration.

9. *Pearls of wisdom*. The following are some final pearls of wisdom for auditors to consider in the current economic environment:
   - think unconventionally
   - maintain your professional skepticism
   - reassess risks. Identify the most significant client exposures
   - consult early and regularly with those charged with governance; and with management, audit committees and experts
   - raise awareness. Make sure that partners, staff and clients understand the ramifications of the GFC. Formal training may be necessary.
   - keep informed. Monitor the guidance issued by standard setters and regulators in response to the GFC.

Source: CPA Australia 2010, *Toolkit*, 'Tips for auditors in the global financial crisis'.

Do you know . . .

18.6 ☐ The purposes of the auditor's final assessment of materiality and risk are to determine whether (1) the auditor's preliminary judgements concerning materiality have been met and (2) audit risk is at an acceptable level to warrant the expression of an unqualified opinion.

18.7 ☐ The technical review of the financial statements includes a review of matters relating to the form and content of the financial statements, in accordance with the requirements of applicable accounting standards and other required disclosures.

18.8 ☐ At the end of the audit, the audit manager performs a comprehensive review of the working papers to ensure the work has been performed properly. The partner also reviews high-risk sections of the audit and may decide to look at the entire audit working papers as well.

18.9 ☐ In completing the audit, the auditor needs to summarise and evaluate the separate findings of each of the sections to express an opinion on the financial statements as a whole. The type of audit opinion to be expressed is determined by the partner in charge of the engagement.

18.10 ☐ Significant matters identified as a result of audit procedures should be reported to those charged with governance.

SUMMARY

This chapter describes several key responsibilities of the auditor in completing an audit of financial report. The two main differences in completing the audit from the work discussed in previous chapters is that completion does not apply to a specific account balance or transaction class and that it has a high level of involvement of senior audit staff on the engagement. Steps performed in completing the fieldwork include performing the review of subsequent events; considering the applicability of the going concern basis; obtaining evidence concerning contingent liabilities such as litigations and other claims; and obtaining written representations and other forms of communications with management, those charged with governance and outside parties such as external legal counsel, and performing analytical procedures. Steps involved in evaluating the auditor's findings include making a final assessment of materiality and audit risk, making a technical review of the financial statements, making a final review of the working papers, and formulating an opinion and drafting the auditor's report. The auditor is also required to communicate audit matters of governance interest noted during the audit process to those charged with governance.

The process of completing the audit, evaluating the findings and communicating with the entity is one of the most important stages of the audit process. Many of the successful legal cases against auditors related to deficiencies that occurred at this stage of the audit. It is therefore important that the partner and manager have significant involvement during this process. It is also crucial that this process is completed carefully and properly despite the fact that reporting deadlines will often impose significant time pressures.

KEY TERMS

contingent liability, p. 768

going concern basis, p. 766

letter of general enquiry, p. 769

management representation letter, p. 762

second partner review, p. 780

subsequent events, p. 762

technical review, p. 777

written representations, p. 771

MULTIPLE-CHOICE questions

18.1 After the auditor's report has been signed, the auditor:
   A. Does not have a responsibility to detect subsequent events.
   B. Has a responsibility to detect subsequent events only if they will have a material effect on the financial statements.
   C. Has provided absolute assurance that all significant events occurring up to that date have been identified.
   D. Has responsibility to detect subsequent events only if they have a negative impact on the financial statements.

18.2 Which of the following would an auditor ordinarily perform during the review of events after the end of the reporting period?
   A. Analyse related party transactions to discover possible irregularities.
   B. Investigate control weaknesses previously reported to management.
   C. Enquire of the entity's external legal counsel concerning litigation.
   D. Review the bank statements for the period after the year-end.

18.3 The auditor is concerned with completing various phases of the examination after the end of the reporting period. This period extends to:
   A. The audit manager's sign-off of the audit working papers.
   B. The date of the auditor's report.
   C. One month after the balance sheet date.
   D. Five months after the client's year-end.

18.4 The following matters came to the attention of the auditor before the audit fieldwork was completed. Which one would require an adjustment to be made to the financial statements?
   A. A discussion by management to change the main operations of the company.
   B. A major lawsuit against the company, with proceedings commencing after the end of the financial year.
   C. The bankruptcy of a major customer of the client.
   D. The application for a government export grant.

18.5 The representation letter to a lawyer provides the auditor with:
   A. Initial information about litigation and claims.
   B. Corroboration of the information on litigation and claims provided by the auditor's solicitors.
   C. Corroboration of the information on litigation and claims provided by management.
   D. Corroboration of the information on litigation and claims provided by the other party to the matter.

18.6 A client's refusal to provide a management representation letter to the auditor will normally require the auditor to:
   A. Issue a qualified opinion or a disclaimer of opinion.
   B. Contact the audit committee for the relevant information.
   C. Issue an unqualified opinion with an 'emphasis of matter' paragraph.
   D. Issue an adverse opinion.

18.7 Six months after issuing an unqualified opinion on a set of financial statements, the audit partner discovered that the engagement personnel on the audit failed to confirm several of the client's material accounts receivable balances. The audit partner should first:
   A. Enquire whether there are persons currently relying, or likely to rely, on the unqualified opinion.

B. Assess the importance of the omitted procedures to the auditor's ability to support the previously expressed opinion.

C. Perform alternative procedures to provide a satisfactory basis for the unqualified opinion.

D. Request permission of the client to undertake the confirmation of accounts receivable.

18.8 When a question arises regarding the going-concern basis additional procedures may be necessary. Which of the following procedures is an example of a valid additional procedure?

  (i) Consider the effect of unfilled customer orders.

 (ii) Review the terms of debenture and loan agreements.

(iii) Analyse the final financial report.

A. (ii) only.

B. (iii) only.

C. (ii) and (iii) only.

D. (i), (ii) and (iii).

18.9 What is the main purpose of an analytical review at the completion of the audit?

A. To ensure the financial viability of the company.

B. As a final evaluation to confirm the initial risk assessments made by the auditor.

C. To ensure that the earnings per share and asset ratios are correct.

D. To corroborate conclusions formed in performing the audit.

18.10 Professional standards require the auditor to communicate certain matters pertaining to the audit to those charged with governance. This communication would normally include all of the following except:

A. Disagreements with management.

B. Audit adjustments.

C. Material uncertainties that may cast doubt on the entity's ability to continue as a going concern.

D. Specific audit procedures performed.

REVIEW questions

18.11 Identify the audit procedures normally associated with subsequent events.

18.12 Can facts discovered after the issue of the financial statements have an impact on the auditor's report? Discuss.

18.13 How would you define the two types of events that occur after the reporting period? What are the potential accounting effects of each type?

18.14 What procedures should the auditor perform when a question arises regarding going concern?

18.15 What are the objectives of the management representation letter? Under what circumstances are management representations considered acceptable audit evidence?

18.16 Explain the purpose of the performance of analytical procedures at the end of the audit.

18.17 Identify the items that should be included on all working papers.

18.18 What should the auditor do when aggregate uncorrected misstatements are material?

18.19 Contrast the roles of audit managers and audit partners in the final review stage of the audit. Why would a firm require a second partner review?

18.20 Give examples of items that might be reported by the auditor to those charged with governance.

PROFESSIONAL application questions

18.21 Subsequent events ★

You are an audit assistant allocated to perform the audit of Topporene Ltd for the year ended 30 June 2015. The managing director of Topporene is interested in the audit responsibilities for identifying subsequent events. The audit partner would like you to document these responsibilities in a memo to the managing director. The detailed audit work is expected to be completed by 31 August 2015. It is planned that:

- the auditor's report will be signed on 15 September 2015
- the financial statements will be sent to shareholders on 30 September 2015.

Required

(a) In your memo, explain the auditor's responsibilities for identifying subsequent events in the following periods:
  - 30 June 2015 to 31 August 2015
  - 1 September 2015 to 15 September 2015
  - 18 September 2015 to 30 September 2015
  - 1 October 2015 onwards.

(b) Discuss the procedures involved in identifying subsequent events.

18.22 Subsequent events ★★

Tanners Ltd is a wholesaler of packaging products and you are about to complete the financial report audit for the year end 30 June 2015. Before you finalise your audit opinion you are considering some significant events that have recently occurred in Tanners Ltd.

Denners Ltd and Minners Ltd

Denners Ltd, a customer of Tanners, is suing the company due to being sold faulty packaging. Denners is a food manufacturer and has claimed that as a result of unhygienic packaging supplied by Tanners it had to re-supply some products to its customers, pay them compensation for their losses and dispose of other products that were now unfit for sale. Denners has made a claim against Tanners for $450 000, which Tanners is disputing because the fault lay with a new machine recently purchased from Minners Ltd. The board of Tanners have indicated they do not intend to provide for any amounts payable to Denners as these will be recouped from Minners.

Factory fire

There was a fire at one of Tanners' factories in late July 2015. Some machinery, raw materials and finished products were damaged in the fire. The insurance company was informed and an investigation showed that the factory supervisor was at fault by not following safety procedures, as a result the insurance company have refused to accept the claim.

Jonners Ltd

In August 2015, Tanners was informed by one of its long-standing customers, Jonners Ltd, that it was having going concern problems and that paying the amount owed to Tanners was going to be difficult. No amount has been received from Jonners since June. The directors of Tanners believe that it is not necessary to adjust the receivable balance at 30 June 2015 as Jonners has always paid them in the past.

Required

For each of the issues above describe how they should be treated in the financial report and identify any further information you required to arrive at a conclusion as to the appropriate treatment.

18.23 Subsequent events/post-audit discovery of facts ★★

The financial year of Hadrian Ltd ended on 30 June 2015. Your auditor's report was signed on 25 August and the financial statements were issued on 10 September. Listed below are events that occurred or were discovered after the end of the financial year. Assume that each has a material effect on the financial statements.

1. *1 August* — A lawsuit was filed against Hadrian for damages that allegedly occurred before 30 June. In the opinion of Hadrian's lawyers, there is a danger of a significant loss.
2. *15 August* — You discovered that MacTavish, a debtor of Hadrian went bankrupt on 10 August. The most recent sale had taken place on 25 May and no transactions had occurred since that date.
3. *1 September* — You discovered that a legal action commenced against Hadrian in relation to a faulty product sold in May 2015.
4. *15 September* — A fire burnt down one of Hadrian's warehouses, resulting in a loss of 30% of the inventory that was on hand at that date.
5. *30 September* — You discovered that Sporran, a debtor of Hadrian, went bankrupt on 15 July. Sales to Sporran were all made before the end of the year.
6. *30 September* — You discovered that Haggis, a debtor of Hadrian, went bankrupt on 25 September. The sale had taken place before the end of the year, but the amount had appeared collectable at the date on which the auditor's report was signed.

Required

(a) Indicate your responsibilities for each of the above events.
(b) Indicate the type of disclosure (if any) you would recommend in relation to each of the six events.

18.24 Representation letter ★★

You are the manager for the annual audit of Dishliskers Ltd, a company that develops new technologies to help improve the performance of racing greyhounds. There are some material issues still outstanding that need to be addressed before you can finalise the audit.

1. Dishlickers is developing a new type of training pool specifically designed for training greyhounds. The pool aids recovery from injury quicker by exercising the dog's muscles, but with much lower impact than running. There have been various problems with the technology but Wolf Hund, Dishlickers' Chief Innovations Officer, has provided various technical reports produced by external experts indicating that the problems will be overcome and testing has shown the product will work well. Market research reports indicate that there is significant demand for new technologies of this kind and selling prices will be high. Felix Miao, the in-charge auditor, has noted on the file that he believes that the cost of developing the pool should be written off as an expense until it becomes clearer whether future sales will occur.
2. From the review of Board meeting minutes, it was found that Dishlickers is being sued by a client, BlueHound, who claim that the new dog food formula it purchased from Dishlickers made some of its dogs sick and one dog die as a result of consuming the food. Mutt Barking, Dishliskers' CEO, has said that the claims are nonsense and extensive research has shown the new formula to be completely safe as well as nutritious and delicious. A review of correspondence from the solicitors has shown that there is no evidence available yet to indicate if the formula affected the dogs of BlueHound.
3. Over the last few years Dishlickers has expanded rapidly following the success of various products in the market. However, its accounting system development has not kept pace with the growth in the organisation and internal controls are very weak. The audit identified areas where not only financial records could be manipulated, but where there were opportunities for fraud. The audit relied heavily on substantive procedures; no significant issues relating to fraud or errors were found.

Required

For each of the above explain whether a paragraph is required in the representation letter and give an example of the representation wording required.

18.25 Communicating matters to management ★★

You have completed your audit of Egral Ltd, a large listed company. Your main day-to-day contact during the audit was Ms Poon, the accountant, although you also had some dealings with the finance director, Mr Sullivan, and the audit committee.

As part of completion procedures, your assistant has prepared the following draft management letter for your consideration.

Ms Poon, Accountant
Egral Ltd
333 Any Street
Erehwon NSW 2314

Dear Ms Poon

Re: Statutory audit of Egral Ltd

As stated in our engagement letter dated 2 February 2011, the purpose of our audit is to provide reasonable assurance as to whether the financial statements are free of material misstatement. In carrying out this work, we agreed to report to you any major weaknesses in the internal control structure that came to our attention. We note that it is not our responsibility to perform detailed tests of internal controls and that the responsibility for maintaining the internal control system lies with management.

During our testing on trade receivables, we noted that the ledger reconciliation was often performed up to a fortnight past close-off, making it difficult for audit staff to meet the auditor's reporting deadline. Also, some reconciling items appeared for up to 3 months before they were cleared.

In relation to cash payments, we noted that two cheques for transfers to the company's payroll account were signed by only one signatory, Mr Sullivan. Apparently, other signatories were not available on those days and so the payments were processed in order to meet wage obligations.

During our petty cash count at the Parramatta branch, we noted that there were no supporting vouchers for $927.56 of expenditure. This may place the related tax deductions at risk as the expenses are unsubstantiated. Also, it casts suspicion on the petty cash officer who may be taking money from petty cash.

Would you please respond in writing regarding the action you intend to take regarding the above matters? We remind you that these are only the matters we found during our testing; there could be many other undiscovered weaknesses in the internal control structure. Also we remind you that this letter is solely for the use of Egral Ltd and should not be disclosed to third parties without our permission.

ABC Chartered Accountants

Required

(a) Critically analyse the draft management letter and outline suggestions for improvement.
(b) Assume you found some minor errors during the audit (such as an accrual not taken up) that were rectified by the time the financial statements were issued. Would you include these in the management letter? Why or why not?[4]

18.26 Going concern ★★

Aeneid Systems Ltd provides a range of IT services to clients from advice in helping identifying system weaknesses to helping procure new IT solutions to project managing new systems development and implementation. Recently Dido Carthage, Senior Project Manager, left the organisation to set up her own IT advisory business. Aeneid employed Ron Remus as her replacement.

There have been two very complex projects which have proved difficult for Aeneid to control and, as a result, the two clients involved sued Aeneid for breach of contract in failing to manage the projects successfully, resulting in the delivery of systems that were unable to perform the functions that were required. In both cases Aeneid has been found to be at fault and the clients have been awarded substantial damages. The adverse publicity in the industry, the amount of time Aeneid's management have spent fighting the cases and Ron Remus's inability to attract new clients has seen a substantial fall in revenue and cash flows. The budget for the coming year indicates additional bank financing will be required to keep the business operational.

Required

You are just about to complete the financial report audit of Aeneid Ltd.

(a) Identify the procedures you would carry out to determine if Aeneid was a going concern.

(b) What procedures are required to be performed if it is concluded that Aeneid is not a going concern?

18.27 Going concern indicators ★★

Ulysses Polytropos Ltd is an Australian company which manufactures travel products including suitcases, backpacks, wallets, hiking gear, clothing and other sundry travel related items. The market for these products is characterised by fashion conscious customers, innovation in design, high levels of competition and product costs pressure from cheaper but high quality products from a variety of manufacturers around Asia. The market continues to grow which creates new opportunities but also attracts new entrants into the market. Ulysses Polytropos operates at the high quality, and high price, end of the market and has in recent years seen a decline in demand for its products despite the overall buoyant market. This has been attributed to demand for cheaper products as well as domestic customers buying online from around the world. In order to address this decline, the company has tried to change its research and development division but has struggled to attract employees with the vision to take the company forward.

In order to reduce production costs the organisation invested in new manufacturing plant and reorganised the factory layout to create more efficient processes. This required a significant investment, only some of which was able to be financed by long-term bank loans. Ulysses Polytropos has fully drawn down on its bank overdraft facility, the banks are unwilling to provide further funds and in order to manage cash flows creditor payment days have extended, leading to difficult relations with some key suppliers who will no longer do business with the company.

The forecast for the coming 12 months shows the cash position worsening so additional funds will be required to allow the company to continue meeting its obligations. The directors believe that it will take another 18 to 24 months to turn the business around and move back into profitability. The bank overdraft is being reviewed in two months' time and the directors are confident that additional funds will be made available to allow the company to continue to trade for the next two years and then they will see the business become successful again.

Required

Identify and explain any indicators that there are doubts about Ulysses Polytropos Ltd's ability to continue as a going concern.

18.28 Analytical review ★★

You are the audit manager of Jenstone Ltd, a furniture maker, and are preparing a final review of the financial report for the year ended 30 June 2015. You know from your discussions with the client that it has been having a difficult time of it recently after a customer went into liquidation.

This created cash flow problems that resulted in Jenstone being late in making the most recent repayment against the bank loan. This was the second time it had breached the terms of its loan agreement in the last four months.

Below are some extracts from the financial report for the year ended 30 June:

	2015 $m	2014 $m
Income statement		
Revenue	18.6	19.7
Gross Profit	7.4	9.3
Profit before tax	0.4	2.6
Non-Current assets		
Property, plant and equipment	11.8	8.7
Current Assets		
Inventory	2.7	1.2
Trade receivables	1.4	0.8
Cash	–	0.4
Current Liabilities		
Overdraft	0.7	–
Trade payables	1.9	0.9
Bank loan	4.8	0.2

Required

Discuss the above extract from the financial report in light of the difficulties referred to above.

18.29 Final assessment of materiality/effect on auditor's report ★★★

You are nearing completion of the 30 June 2015 audit of Goodies Ltd, a wholesaler of breakfast foods and bakery supplies. Your manager has completed the working paper review and has compiled the following list of errors.

1. Sales cut-off at Melbourne branch was incorrect. Three invoices dated 1 July 2015 were processed with 30 June 2015 sales. These amounted to $5600. Additional audit procedures confirmed there were no other cut-off errors. Mark-up is a standard 70% on cost price.
2. Year-end stocktake procedures revealed one stock line worth $11 250 was counted twice. The error was discovered and corrected by the client's accounting staff.
3. In order to carry out the debtors circularisation, the debtors ledger was divided into two parts:
   (i) All balances over $8000. All these balances were circularised. The total value of the part was $41 800.
   (ii) All other balances. A random sample of 15 of these balances was circularised. The total value of these balances was $52 650.

Audit procedures revealed $2510 of overstatement errors in part (i). These errors were due to customers being invoiced for goods they didn't order. Mark-up is a standard 70 per cent on cost price. Audit procedures also revealed $2080 of overstatement errors in part (ii). The errors in part (ii) resulted from customers being billed twice. (The corresponding entry to inventory was correctly recorded only once.)

4. The loan confirmation from the bank revealed that interest payable for the month of June was $5200. The client has recorded an accrual of only $4200.
5. Audit procedures performed on related parties revealed one director-related transaction for $1200 was not disclosed in the draft notes to the financial statements.
6. A clerical error resulted in the June rent accrual of $5600 was mistakenly recorded as a noncurrent rather than a current liability.

You also have the following balances from the draft financial statements:

Sales	$1 437 300	Other creditors	$51 850
Accounts receivable	257 500	Cost of sales	840 700
Inventory	146 290	Total interest payable for year	61 400

The manager has asked you to review the errors and prepare a summary workpaper that will enable her to assess whether the financial statements are materially misstated.

Required

(a) What do the auditing standards require in relation to estimating the final dollar error in the financial statements before the signing of the audit opinion?
(b) Using the above information, prepare a summary of audit differences workpaper for the audit manager.

				Adjustment required to ...				
Description	$ error in financial statements (A)	Projected error (B)	Total estimated error (A+B)	Current assets dr/(cr)	Current liabilities dr/(cr)	Non-current assets dr/(cr)	Non-current liabilities dr/(cr)	Profit dr/(cr)

(c) Discuss how you would use the summary of audit differences workpaper in determining whether the financial statements are materially misstated.[5]

 CASE studies

18.30 Subsequent events ★★★

Your client is Queenscorp Ltd, a diversified business operating throughout Australia. Year-end was 30 June 2015, the auditor's report was signed on 31 July 2015 and the financial statements were mailed to shareholders on 14 August 2015.

During your subsequent events review, you noted the following independent and material items.

1. Queenscorp has been involved in a legal dispute with a competitor for a number of years. The dispute relates to alleged breaches of copyright by Queenscorp. On 27 July, you discovered that Queenscorp had settled the legal action out of court on terms more favourable than expected.
2. As for (1) above, except that the legal action was settled on 5 August.
3. On 10 July, one of Queenscorp's major product lines developed a fault that rendered the product unusable. Queenscorp became aware of the fault on 30 July. Although the fault posed

no safety risks to consumers, Queenscorp decided to launch a full product recall on the following day.

4. On 30 July 2015, the Bureau of Meteorology issued a cyclone warning for parts of Far North Queensland. Queenscorp has a large sugar cane plantation in this area. On 2 August, the cyclone hit, wiping out about 90% of the crop.

5. Queenscorp has invested significant funds in developing a new type of cholesterol-reducing margarine. On 7 July, Queenscorp applied for a patent for the margarine, only to discover that a competitor had lodged a similar application on 28 June. The granting of Queenscorp's application is now in doubt.

6. Queenscorp's bank loan is conditional upon certain ratios being maintained at all times. On 20 August, you discovered that one of the ratios was breached for a 24-hour period on 18 August.

7. Queenscorp has large landholdings on the outskirts of Sydney. On 20 July, Queenscorp received preliminary notice from the federal government informing the company that, should the new Sydney airport proceed, about 30% of this land will be forcibly acquired. Queenscorp has no legal right to challenge the acquisition.

8. In early June, one of Queenscorp's largest debtors informed Queenscorp that it was experiencing serious financial difficulties. On 5 July, Queenscorp was informed that the debtor had gone into receivership. Preliminary reports suggest Queenscorp will recover only 10 cents in the dollar of the outstanding debt.

Required

(a) Outline the key additional audit procedures you should have performed in relation to each of the above events.

(b) What action should you have recommended to management in relation to each of the above events?[6]

18.31 Subsequent events ★★★

You are the supervisor on the audit of Golden Pokie Club, a large suburban club in New South Wales. As well as the usual club facilities such as poker machines, bars and a bistro, the club also operates a large gymnasium, an indoor heated pool and a restaurant.

The following dates are relevant to the current audit engagement:

End of the reporting period	30 June 2015
Financial statements signed	15 August 2015
Auditor's report signed	15 August 2015
Annual report mailed to members	22 August 2015

You are aware that the following independent and material events have occurred.

1. On 5 August 2015, the financial controller informed you that the board has recently received a letter from the assistant general manager, Mr T. The letter contains a confession: Mr T has been lodging fraudulent expense claims over the past 5 years, amounting to some $40 000. The financial controller's preliminary estimates indicate that this figure is materially correct; however, he believes it will take at least another 2 months before the exact figure is known. The police have been informed of the fraud and are searching for Mr T, who appears to have left the country.

2. On 8 July 2015, the federal government announced that it intends to introduce legislation sometime in September removing the current tax concessions enjoyed by clubs such as Golden Pokie Club. The changes will result in Golden Pokie Club being subject to the same tax rules that apply to companies. At present, the tax laws are such that Golden Pokie Club pays taxes only on net income from non-members, which represents about 10% of total

net income. The club's board of management, in conjunction with other clubs in the state, intends to lobby the government to reverse its decision. The board is confident the club's tax concessions will remain in place.

3. On 17 August 2015, the financial controller informed you that on the previous day a participant in one of the club's aerobics classes, Ms P, injured herself after slipping on the gym floor. Ms P is the spouse of one of the state's leading barristers. A preliminary letter has already been received from Mr P, stating that Ms P intends to take legal action to recover the cost of medical treatment, plus damages, from the club.

4. On 18 August 2015, the financial controller informed you that a serious fire occurred in one of the club's kitchens during the football celebrations. Although covered by insurance, the fire caused extensive damage to the bistro area and the adjacent bar. Both the bistro and bar are expected to remain unserviceable until at least mid-September, resulting in an expected fall in revenue of around 7%.

5. On 1 August 2015, you read the minutes of a board meeting held on 15 July 2015. The minutes note that merger discussions with the nearby bowling club are progressing smoothly and the matter will be put to a vote of members on 30 October 2015. Costs associated with putting the issue to a vote (currently not included in the 30 June 2015 financial statements) are approximately $50 000.

6. On 23 August 2015, the general manager informed you that on 18 August 2015 the board decided to sell land it was holding as a long-term investment. It seems that a very generous offer was made by an overseas buyer. The contract is due to be signed on 25 August 2015.

7. On 10 August 2015, the board signed a contract for the upgrade of the club's air conditioning system. The upgrade is necessary to ensure compliance with workers compensation regulations. The first payment of $100 000 is due on 1 September 2015. Work will be completed (and the final contract payment made) by 30 June 2015.

8. On 31 July 2015, the board decided that the club's restaurant will close permanently on 31 September 2015. Although relatively well patronised, the restaurant has been losing around $10 000 per month and the board feels it can no longer justify keeping it open.

Required

(a) Explain what further evidence you would seek in relation to each of these matters.
(b) Describe the action, if any, you would recommend to management in relation to the accounting treatment of each of these items.[7]

18.32 Analytical procedures and going concern ★★★

You have just completed preliminary analytical procedures of your client Indonesia On-Line Ltd (IOL) which has a 31 March year-end. IOL is involved in the development and design of new computer programs specifically for use on the Internet. The company was formed 5 years ago by a young entrepreneur, Mr Tinta, with equity provided by his parents and a few friends. Mr Tinta designed a program that was one of the first of its kind to assist users in the design of personalised web pages. The program was user-friendly and cheaper than its competitors and therefore became very successful. The company has subsequently launched other Internet-related programs onto the market which have attracted, at best, moderate attention. Mr Tinta has told you that he is in the final stages of a new program that will help users in purchasing products over the Internet. The product has involved substantial research and development over the past 3 years. He is extremely excited about this new product and believes that sales will reverse any past trading problems they have had. He has also told you that he has raised sufficient finance to enable finalisation and launch of the product within 6 months.

During the initial years where the company experienced rapid growth, all profits were reinvested to further research and development and to purchase an office block as the corporate headquarters. Office space not required by the company is rented out to tenants on normal commercial terms. Three small retail sites were also purchased that are used as outlets for the company's products as well as other computer software products. Mr Tinta believes that the market values are far in excess of the current carrying values.

The results of the ratio analysis undertaken as part of the analytical procedures were:

Ratios	2015	2014	2013
Average collection period	*45 days*	*33 days*	*28 days*
Current ratio	0.62	0.73	1.01
Debt–equity ratio	2.03	1.94	1.72
Gross profit ratio	0.20	0.28	0.32
Profit after tax ratio	–0.05	–0.04	–0.02
Net assets per share	$2.87	$2.99	$3.25

Required

(a) Discuss IOL's overall financial position with reference to the ratio analysis undertaken as part of the analytical procedures.
(b) Nominate other factors listed above that may indicate that the company has going concern problems.
(c) List factors that may help IOL resolve this going concern problem. Outline the information that you would need in relation to each factor identified.[8]

 RESEARCH question

18.33 Earnings management and completing the audit

Earnings management is now a very common term in financial reporting. It refers to some of the management practices whereby accounting items are presented in a manner to achieve a certain economic outcome. The treatment of such accounts may or may not be in accordance with all relevant accounting principles and standards. It is believed that the auditor should have a role in detecting earnings management and in determining the extent of the 'manipulation' in arriving at an appropriate audit conclusion.

Required

1. Discuss the meaning of earnings management and how it affects the final stages of a financial report audit.
2. Identify means whereby the auditor may reduce earnings management.

You should undertake research on earnings management and its relationship with the role of the auditor. Refer to published articles including those listed in the Further Reading section below.

FURTHER READING

AUASB, AICD and The Institute of Internal Auditors in Australia, *Audit Committee A Guide to Good Practice*, February 2008, NSW.
AUASB, AICD, *Going Concern Issues in Financial Reporting: A Guide for Companies and Directors*, Australia, 2009.
AUASB, *An Overview of the Revised and Redrafted Australian Auditing Standards*, June 2010.
CPA Australia, 2010 'Tips for auditors in the Global Financial Crisis', Australia.
KA Houghton, C Jubb, M & J Kend Ng, 'The Future of Auditing' keeping Capital Markets Efficient, 2009, ANU, Australia.

Martin, R D, 2000, 'Going Concern Uncertainty Disclosures and Conditions: A comparison of French, German, and U.S. Practices', *Journal of International Accounting, Auditing and Taxation* 9(2), pp. 137–58.

KPMG, 'Audit committee insights — a survey of Australian audit committees', 2008.

KPMG International, 'The convergence challenge Global Survey into the integration of governance, risk and compliance', February 2010.

KPMG LLP, 2007, 'Accounting judgements, estimates, and restatements — implications for audit committee oversight', UK.

NOTES

1. King, A 2013 'IAASB shake-up has auditors on the hop', *Australian Financial Review*, 1 August.

2. ASA 570 *Going Concern (Compiled)*, paragraph 16, 'Additional Audit Procedures When Events or Conditions Are Identified', 1 July 2013.

3. Extracts from *Audit Committees: A Guide to Good Practice*, 2nd edition, AUASB and Australian Institute of Company Directors and the Institute of Internal Auditors 2012, pp. 30–4.

4. Adapted from Professional Year Programme of the ICAA, 2000, Accounting 2 Module.

5. Adapted from Professional Year Programme of the ICAA, 1999, Advanced Audit Module.

6. Adapted from Professional Year Programme of the ICAA, 2000, Accounting 2 Module.

7. Adapted from Professional Year Programme of the ICAA, 1999, Advanced Audit Module.

8. Adapted from Professional Year Programme of the ICAA, 1999, Advanced Audit Module.

Answers to multiple-choice questions

18.1 *A*   18.2 *C*   18.3 *B*   18.4 *C*   18.5 *C*   18.6 *A*   18.7 *B*   18.8 *D*
18.9 *D*   18.10 *D*

Access controls Controls designed to prevent unauthorised use of IT equipment, data files and computer programs (p. 381).

Accountability The responsibility of an entity to report on its use of resources allocated for a specific purpose. This accountability is determined through independent examination (p. 13).

Accounting estimate An approximation of a financial statement item in the absence of exact measurement (p. 513).

Accounting misstatements Occur when an accounting item is not expressed to show its objective and truthful economic value. Include understatements and overstatements, through the use of inappropriate accounting treatment or disclosure policy (p. 125).

Accounting standards Set as generally accepted accounting methods for specific accounting items (p. 283).

Accounting system The series of tasks and records of an entity by which transactions are processed as a means of maintaining financial records (p. 396).

Accounts payable master file A computer file containing details of suppliers, details of transactions with suppliers, and the balance owed (p. 627).

Accounts receivable master file A computer file containing details of customers, details of transactions with customers, and the balance owed (p. 577).

Accounts receivable subsidiary ledger A ledger recording details of transactions by customer and showing the balance owed (p. 577).

Accounts receivable trial balance A listing of individual customer balances at a particular date on the accounts receivable master file or accounts receivable subsidiary ledger (p. 597).

Adverse opinion An opinion expressed when the effect of a disagreement or a conflict between applicable financial reporting frameworks is an extreme case and the auditor concludes that a qualification of the auditor's report is not adequate to disclose the misleading or incomplete nature of the financial report (p. 294).

Aged trial balance An accounts receivable trial balance in which customer balances are analysed by the period since each sales transaction was entered (p. 597).

Agencies A term commonly used to refer collectively to government departments or prescribed agencies (p. 72).

Agency theory A theory that presupposes that when investors entrust their resources to managers (as agents), all parties involved in the relationship will act rationally and attempt to maximise their benefits. The agent is the source of the demand for the audit. This theory is also known as the 'stewardship monitoring hypothesis'. Agency theory assumes that agents are self-interested individuals and that there is information asymmetry between the agent and the principals. Information asymmetry refers to the fact that agents have control over the information regarding resources whereas the principals do not. Self-interested agents will pursue self-interest which, in turn, will result in agency costs to the principals (p. 9).

Alleged audit failures Allegations where the auditor appears to have failed in performing audit functions leading to business failures (p. 204).

Analytical evidence Audit evidence obtained through applying analytical procedures. This involves considering or comparing relationships that exist in the entity's financial information (p. 431).

Analytical procedures Procedures that involve the study and comparison of relationships among data (pp. 438, 496, 326).

Application controls Controls that apply to the processing of specific types of transactions, such as invoicing customers, paying suppliers and preparing payroll. For computerised information system activities, application controls refer to control procedures that provide reasonable assurance that the recording, processing and reporting of data are properly performed for specific applications (p. 380).

Assertion Statement made by management in financial statements that relates to economic actions and events (pp. 7, 166).

Assertion-based engagement Where the outcome on which the assurance practitioner provides an opinion is not on the subject matter itself absent of any subject matter information (p. 168).

Assessing control risk The process of evaluating the effectiveness of the design and operation of an entity's internal controls in preventing or detecting material misstatements in the financial statements (p. 396).

Assurance The provision of confidence and credibility regarding the integrity of a subject matter (p. 6).

Assurance engagement An engagement performed by a professional accountant with the intention of enhancing the credibility of information about a subject matter (pp. 14, 166).

Assurance practitioner A person or organisation, whether in public or the private sector, providing assurance services (p. 178).

Attribute sampling A sampling approach to determine the proportion of the population exhibiting a particular attribute, such as items in a transaction class whose processing deviates from laid-down control procedures (p. 535).

Audit A service where the auditor provides a high level of assurance through (1) the issue of a positive expression of an opinion that enhances the credibility of a written assertion about an accountability matter, and (2) the provision of relevant and reliable information and a positive expression of opinion about an accountability matter where the party responsible for the matter does not make a written assertion (p. 6).

Audit committee A committee of non-executive directors responsible for overseeing financial reporting functions (p. 106).

Audit evidence Information obtained by the auditor in arriving at the conclusions on which the audit opinion is based (p. 427).

Audit expectation gap The gap that exists between what users expect of an auditor and the service auditors provide. This gap is due, in part, to the unreasonable expectations of users (which often exceed acceptable standards) and, in part, to the inadequate performance of auditors (p. 6).

Audit manager Staff member in charge of an audit. The audit manager coordinates and supervises the execution of the audit work program and is responsible for client liaison (p. 321).

Audit mandates An authority to undertake an audit and provide a report. The mandate may prescribe the nature of the audit and the type of report expected (p. 74).

Audit planning The preparation of an overall audit strategy for the expected conduct and scope of the audit (p. 326).

Audit programs A detailed description of tests of controls and substantive procedures that are planned to be performed (p. 506).

Audit quality The means by which all relevant auditing standards are adhered to, demonstrating the appropriate level of care, diligence, competence and professionalism that are required of the auditor (p. 19).

Audit risk The risk that an auditor may give an inappropriate opinion on the financial information that is materially misstated (pp. 399, 423).

Audit risk model A model that expresses the relationships among audit risk components. It simply states that audit risk = inherent risk ì control risk ì detection risk (p. 401).

Audit strategy Defining the overall approach of an audit, taking into account all types of risks relevant to the organisation (p. 416).

Audit team A group of people responsible for an audit, comprising a partner, a manager, an audit senior and staff assistants (p. 321).

Audit trail A chain of evidence provided by coding, cross-references and documentation that connects account balances and other summary results with original transaction data (p. 380).

Audit trinity The key three aspects of audit that contribute to effective corporate governance. They are the external audit, the internal audit and the audit committee (p. 53).

Auditing An independent examination of financial or non-financial information for the purpose of providing an assurance on the credibility of that information to intended users (p. 6).

Auditing procedures Methods and techniques used by the auditor to gather and evaluate audit evidence (p. 435).

Auditing standards Standards that contain the basic principles and essential procedures, together with related guidance, promulgated by the profession for the practice of auditing (pp. 6, 268).

Auditor liability The liability of an auditor for breaching a duty or for not fulfilling a contract (p. 131).

Authorised price list A list of selling prices for each product approved by the responsible official (p. 577).

Bank confirmation Written confirmation of the balance at bank and other matters received directly by the auditor from the entity's bank (p. 720).

Bank reconciliations Schedules agreeing the balance of cash at bank per the entity's records with the balance shown on the statement of accounts received from the bank. The most common reconciling items are outstanding deposits and unpresented cheques (p. 713).

Bank transfer schedule Schedule prepared by the auditor listing bank transfers for a few days either side of the end of the reporting period, and the dates recorded in the records and the bank statements (p. 719).

Benchmarks Well-founded bases or similar cases against which critical comparisons are made (p. 191).

Big Four The largest four international accounting firms in the world — KPMG, PricewaterhouseCoopers, Ernst & Young, and Deloitte Touche Tohmatsu (p. 17).

Block selection Selection of sampling units from a population by random or haphazard selection of characteristics held by clusters of sampling units, such as the initial letter of customers' names or the date at which the transaction occurred (p. 539).

Bond A sum of money posted to provide security for fraudulent or other inappropriate behaviour to protect the principal's capital (p. 10).

Business risk The risk that the entity will not achieve its objectives or execute its strategies (p. 332).

Case law Law established by judicial decisions in particular cases, instead of by legislation (p. 18).

Cash counts Audit procedure of counting cash on hand and agreeing the balance with the records (p. 726).

Cash cut-off tests Audit procedure verifying the agreement of cash receipts recorded in the accounting records at close of business with the physical movement of cash (p. 718).

Cash receipts cut-off test A substantive procedure designed to obtain reasonable assurance that cash receipts are recorded in the accounting period in which they are received (p. 599).

Cash receipts journal A journal recording cash receipt transactions for posting to the ledgers (p. 579).

Causal relationship A relationship where one matter causes another to happen (p. 217).

Cheque summary A computer-produced listing of cheques (p. 629).

Clearing House Electronic Subregister System (CHESS) The computer system that transfers the title or legal ownership of securities between sellers and buyers on the Australian Securities Exchange (p. 734).

Common law Unwritten law formulated, developed and administered by the courts (p. 204).

Comparatives Amounts or disclosures of one or more previous periods that are presented on a comparative basis with those of the current period (p. 301).

Completeness An assertion relating to financial information that all transactions and accounts have been presented in the financial statements (p. 370).

Compliance framework A general purpose financial reporting framework that is adopted by the financial report in strict compliance with all the legislative and professional requirements only (p. 282).

Computer-assisted audit techniques Techniques that involve using the computer in performing auditing procedures (p. 438).

Computer information systems Where a computer of any type or size is involved in the processing of transactions and other events in the entity's information system (p. 381).

Confirmation A form of enquiry that enables the auditor to obtain information directly from an independent source outside the entity (pp. 432, 437).

Confirmation of accounts payable Written enquiry of suppliers, requesting confirmation of the balance owed at confirmation date (p. 650).

Conformance The auditor's function in ensuring that the organisation conforms to policies, procedures and statutory matters (p. 48)

Contingent liability A potential liability that becomes an actual liability when one or more future event(s) occurs or fails to occur (p. 768).

Continuous auditing Auditing activities that provide an ongoing level of assurance on a subject matter (p. 189).

Contractual relationship A relationship between two contracting parties (p. 253).

Contributory negligence The failure of the plaintiff to meet certain required standards of care (p. 218).

Control activities Policies and procedures that management establishes to help ensure that its directives are carried out (p. 380).

Control environment The overall attitude, awareness and actions of management regarding internal control and its importance in the entity (p. 377).

Control procedures Those policies and procedures, in addition to the control environment, that management has established to ensure that, as far as possible, specific entity objectives will be achieved (p. 396).

Control risk A risk that a material misstatement will not be prevented or detected on a timely basis by an entity's internal control structure (pp. 396, 423).

Co-regulation The environment within which both the government and the auditing profession exert active controls (p. 103).

Corporate collapses Corporate failures of large companies (such as HIH Insurance, Enron, WorldCom) that caused a major credibility crisis in the accounting and auditing profession (pp. 12, 125).

Corporate governance The framework and system whereby an entity controls and directs, including the effectiveness of the network of relationships between principals, agents and stakeholders. The framework comprises structures such as board structures, incentive schemes and other internal control environments and activities (pp. 6, 51).

Corroborating information Evidence obtained by an auditor in support of transactions recorded in the accounting records of an entity (p. 431).

Credibility (of information) An assurance on the relevance and reliability of information (p. 7).

Credit memo A form for granting credit to customers for returned or damaged goods (p. 581).

Current file A file that contains corroborating information relating to the execution of the current year's audit program (p. 347).

Customer order An official purchase order issued by a customer (p. 575).

Cut-off An assertion that relates to whether all transactions, events and accounts have been recorded in the correct period (p. 370).

Cut-off tests Tests performed on transactions around year-end to ensure the completeness and occurrence of transactions (p. 499).

Cyclical inventory counts Periodic inventory counts that count, over a year, all or most inventory items (p. 670).

Damages An amount awarded as compensation for the losses suffered by plaintiff(s) in a legal action (p. 214).

Data and procedural controls A framework for controlling daily computer operations, minimising the likelihood of processing errors, and assuring the continuity of operations in the event of a physical disaster or computer failure (p. 381).

Deontology A doctrine that holds that actions and motivations are inspired by a sense of moral obligation (p. 101).

Deposit slip A listing of bank notes, coins and individual cheques for deposit with the bank, a copy of which is receipted by the bank teller and retained by the entity (p. 579).

Detection risk A risk that the auditor's substantive procedures will collectively fail to detect a material misstatement (pp. 401, 493).

Deviations The failure to apply a control properly and consistently, or its application by an unauthorised employee (p. 460).

Difference estimation A sampling approach where the amount being estimated is the absolute value of the difference between the recorded and the audited amount (p. 543).

Direct reporting engagement A compliance engagement where the assurance practitioner directly evaluates an entity's compliance with requirements as measured by the suitable criteria and expresses a conclusion to the intended users in a compliance report (in the context of ASAE 3100); Performance engagements where the assurance practitioner directly undertakes the evaluation or measurement of the activity to report on the economy, efficiency or effectiveness of the activity (in the context of ASAE 3500) (p. 168).

Disclaimer of opinion Expressed when the possible effect of a limitation on scope is an extreme case and the auditor has not been able to obtain sufficient appropriate audit evidence and accordingly is unable to express an opinion on the financial report (p. 294).

Discovery sampling A type of attribute sampling that is used to determine a specified probability of finding at least one example of an occurrence in a population (p. 544).

Dispatch notes Forms authorising the release of goods from store and their delivery to the customer (p. 576).

Documentary evidence Information about financial transactions contained in documents such as source documents, agreements, contracts, various types of forms, invoices and statements (p. 432).

Documenting the understanding Documenting a description of the internal control structure in the form of completed internal control questionnaires, flowcharts or narrative memoranda (p. 389).

Documents and records Documents provide evidence on specific transactions that have occurred, and records are summaries of transactions that have occurred (p. 380).

Dual-purpose test A test that serves as both a test of controls and a test of details of transactions (pp. 440, 461, 508).

Due care Not being negligent — that is, planning and performing an audit and issuing an audit opinion with skill and competence, having regard to the needs of users (p. 209)

Earnings management The measures applied to accounts and financial information in order to express a certain desirable outcome for the entity's financial position (pp. 59, 125).

E-crimes Criminal or fraudulent activities carried out via the Internet (p. 187).

Electronic evidence Any information produced or maintained by electronic means that an auditor uses to form an opinion about an assertion (p. 435).

Embedded audit facility Procedures written directly into the program of specific computer applications enabling auditor intervention to capture or process data for audit purposes (p. 588). *See* **Integrated test facility** and **Systems control audit review file**.

Emphasis of matter A paragraph highlighting a matter in an unqualified auditor's report following an audit opinion in specified circumstances, such as uncertainty over the question of the entity's going concern status (p. 299).

Employee earnings master file Computer file containing details of wage payments, including a cumulative record of wages paid (p. 632).

Engagement letter A letter (contract) stating the scope and terms of the audit engagement (p. 323).

Enquiry Either oral or written questions by the auditor (p. 437).

Enterprise governance The framework that combines both corporate governance and business performance (p. 48).

Enterprise risk management A process applied in strategy setting and across the entity designed to identify potential events that may affect the entity, and manage risks to be within its risk appetite, to provide reasonable assurance regarding the achievement of entity objectives (p. 55).

Entity's objectives The overall plans for the entity as defined by those charged with governance and management (p. 332).

Entity's strategies The operational approaches by which management intends to achieve its objectives (p. 332).

Ethical issues Situations where individuals have to make a choice from unclear and complex alternatives, where each alternative may be the right choice according to a specific moral position or viewpoint (p. 102).

Ethical relativism A view that moral values are relative to a particular environment, and that they vary according to circumstances (p. 102).

Evidence Information gathered by the auditor which is used when forming an opinion on the truth and fairness of a client's financial report (p. 7).

Existence An assertion relating to financial statements that assets or liabilities exist at a given date (p. 370).

Experts Specialists in areas other than auditing who may be consulted or called on to assist in the audit (p. 321).

Extent of substantive procedures The number of items or sample size to which a particular test or procedure is applied (p. 503).

External auditors Individual practitioners or members of public accounting firms who render professional auditing services to clients (p. 13).

Fair presentation framework A general purpose financial reporting framework that is adopted by the financial report so that there are other matters of disclosure or accounts which are provided in order to achieve a fair presentation of the financial status of the entity, in addition to complying with the compliance matters which are required (p. 282).

Financial statement assertions *See* **Assertion**.

Financial report audit An audit that enables an auditor to express an opinion as to whether the financial report is prepared, in all material respects, in accordance with an identified financial reporting framework (p. 6).

Financial statement fraud Dishonest activities that result in misleading financial statements (p. 125).

Finished goods Manufactured inventory that is available for sale (p. 667).

Flowchart A schematic diagram using standardised symbols, interconnecting flow lines and annotations that portray the steps involved in processing information through the information system (p. 392).

Forensic audit Auditing activities that involve the investigation of fraud and fraudulent activities (p. 188).

Foreseeability The reasonable occurrence of an event that will have an impact on a person's decision (p. 227).

Fraud An intentional act of dishonesty or moral lapse (pp. 18, 334).

General controls Controls that apply to computer information systems as a whole. They include controls relating to such matters as data centre organisation, hardware and systems software acquisition and maintenance, and backup and recovery procedures. These controls are sometimes referred to as environmental controls (p. 380).

Generalised audit software Audit software that auditors use under a variety of data organisation and processing methods (pp. 503, 589).

General purpose external financial report A general purpose financial report prepared for a wide range of users external to the entity (p. 283).

Global Reporting Initiative An independent initiative started in 1997 to develop and disseminate globally applicable sustainability reporting guidelines. It provides a generally accepted framework for reporting an organisation's economic, environmental and social performance (p. 182).

Going concern basis An assumption that an entity will continue in the future unless evidence is available to the contrary (p. 766).

Governance It is the authority that ensures decisions are made and implemented so that an entity's economic and functional matters are properly conducted and in accordance with relevant laws and standards. Governance is underpinned by a structure of accountability and its processes (p. 47).

Haphazard selection Selection of sampling units from a population by observation (p. 532).

Imprest bank account Bank account funded with a sum sufficient to meet the payment of special-purpose cheques such as wages or dividends (p. 714).

Imprest petty cash fund Petty cash fund maintained at a constant level via replenishment with the value of vouchers paid out of the fund (p. 714).

Independence Ability to withstand pressure from management influence when conducting an audit or providing audit-related services, such that one's professional integrity is not compromised (pp. 14, 97).

Independent checks The verification of work previously performed by other individuals or departments, or the proper valuation of recorded amounts (p. 381).

Information asymmetry Occurs when there are differences in the degree of control and understanding of information between parties (p. 9).

Information hypothesis A hypothesis that posits that the demand for auditing is a result of investors wanting reliable information that can be used effectively in decision making. Unlike the agency theory, the emphasis is not so much on the agent as on the reliability of the information (p. 11).

Information processing controls Controls that cover risks related to the authorisation, completeness and accuracy of transactions (p. 380).

Information system The information system relevant to financial reporting objectives consists of the procedures and records established to initiate, record, process and report entity transactions (as well as events and conditions) and to maintain accountability for the related assets, liabilities and equity (p. 379).

Inherent risk A material misstatement that could occur in the absence of internal controls (p. 400).

Initial audit engagement The first audit of an entity by the particular audit firm (p. 302).

Initial engagements *See* **Initial audit engagement**.

Inspection Careful scrutiny or detailed examination of documents and records, and the physical examination of tangible resources (p. 436).

Insurance hypothesis A view that posits that managers and professional participants in financial activities seek to use an auditor as a means of insurance — that is, as a means of shifting financial responsibility if any losses are expected from litigation (pp. 12, 204).

Integrated test facility A type of test of controls that requires using a fictitious entity and entering fictitious transactions for that entity with the regular transactions, and then comparing the result with the expected output (pp. 471, 588).

Interim audit Audit work performed before the end of the reporting period. Typically, this involves performing tests of controls and tests of details of transactions (p. 327).

Interim financial report A set of half-yearly statements, including an income statement, a balance sheet/statement of financial position, a statement of cash flows and selected explanatory notes, to be prepared by a disclosing entity (p. 175).

Internal auditing A type of auditing that is performed within the organisation to govern the adequacy of internal controls, the management of risks and quality assurance. The Institute of Internal Auditors defines internal auditing as an independent, objective assurance and consulting activity designed to add value and improve an organisation's operations. It helps an organisation accomplish its objectives

Internal auditing (continued)
by bringing a systematic, disciplined approach to evaluate and improve the effectiveness of risk management, control and governance processes (p. 60).

Internal control Management's philosophy and operating style and all the policies and procedures adopted by management to assist in achieving the entity's objectives, including the safeguarding of assets, the prevention and detection of fraud and error, the accuracy and completeness of the accounting records, and the timely preparation of reliable financial information (pp. 31, 375).

Internal control evaluation checklists Lists that enumerate the types of potential misstatement that could occur in specific assertions (p. 397).

Internal control problems Where there are discrepancies in the internal system that result in control failures (p. 125).

Internal control questionnaire A series of questions about accounting and control policies and procedures that the auditor considers necessary to prevent material misstatements in the financial statements (p. 389).

Internationalisation of the profession The increasing acceptance by the accounting profession of international standards, and the growing support across countries for the elimination of barriers to the practice of accountancy (p. 205).

Inventory count sheets Pre-prepared sheets for recording inventory description and quantity as counted. These are usually prenumbered (p. 671).

Inventory master file A computer file containing details of inventory items, their movement and the quantity on hand (p. 669).

Inventory tags Three-part, tie-on tags for recording the inventory count of each item (p. 671).

Inventory transfer requisition Document authorising the requisitioning of materials and labour for the purpose of manufacturing (p. 670).

Investment register Subsidiary ledger recording individual investments in shares and debentures. Entries show purchases and sales, the cost of each bundle purchased, and the quantity and cost of the balance owned (p. 734).

Investment subsidiary ledger Another name for an investment register (p. 734).

Joint and several liability An obligation of two or more persons. Each is liable severally and all are liable jointly. A plaintiff may sue one or more jointly or severally (p. 204).

Kiting An irregularity overstating the cash balance by intentionally recording a bank transfer as a deposit in the receiving bank while failing to show a deduction from the bank account on which the transfer cheque is drawn (p. 719).

Lapping An irregularity concealing the misappropriation of cash by using subsequent cash receipts to conceal the original misappropriation (p. 728).

Lead schedule A summary working sheet that is supported by individual working papers (p. 350).

Letter of general enquiry A letter sent by the auditor to the entity's legal counsel asking the legal counsel to provide information directly to the auditor regarding any litigation, claims and other liabilities that the legal counsel is aware of, including any costs and an estimate of the financial implications (p. 769).

Low-balling A practice whereby a bid price of an audit service is quoted at an unreasonably low level so as to win the bid, with any 'losses' subsequently recovered through other means (p. 114).

Lower assessed level of control risk approach An audit strategy based on the assumption that control risk is medium to low for an assertion (p. 424).

Management The individuals who control and are responsible for the resources invested within an entity (p. 263).

Management letter A letter written to the management of an entity by an auditor. It contains recommendations for improving the efficiency and effectiveness of significant matters that were noticed during the course of an audit (p. 267).

Management representation letter A letter that contains representations from management to an auditor (p. 762).

Materiality In respect of accounting information, an omission, misstatement or non-disclosure that could adversely affect the decisions of the user in given circumstances (p. 268).

Mathematical evidence Audit evidence that results from recalculations by the auditor and comparisons of those results with client calculations (p. 434).

Mean-per-unit method A sampling method where the amount being estimated is the average value of each sampling unit (p. 543).

Modified auditor's report Issued when the audit opinion is qualified or when it is appropriate for the auditor to draw attention to or emphasise a matter that is relevant to users (p. 293).

Monitoring In relation to controls, involves assessing the design and operation of controls on a timely basis and taking necessary corrective action (p. 385).

Monthly customer statement A listing of transactions with each customer that have occurred since the date of the previous statement, which shows the closing balance due. This statement is sent to the customer (p. 577).

Narrative memorandum Written comments concerning the auditor's consideration of the internal control structure (p. 395).

Nature of substantive procedures The type and effectiveness of the auditing procedures to be performed. The types of substantive procedure are analytical procedures, tests of details of transactions and tests of details of balances (p. 496).

Negligence Not exercising due care (p. 204).

Network firm A firm that is associated or affiliated with another firm under the same management or ownership (p. 114).

Non-audit services Services that are not audit related. Examples are accounting, management consulting, and insolvency and business recovery (pp. 19, 119).

Non-sampling risk The component of audit risk that is not due to examining only a portion of the data, such as through the use of inappropriate procedures or the misinterpretation of evidence (p. 529).

Non-statistical sampling The use of judgement to determine sample size and to interpret the results (p. 529).

Observation The act of watching or witnessing the performance of some activity or process (p. 437).

Occurrence An assertion relating to financial information that transactions did occur (p. 370).

Operating effectiveness of the control procedures The extent to which laid-down control procedures are being complied with (p. 460).

Operational auditing A systematic process of evaluating an organisation's effectiveness, efficiency and economy of operations under management's control, and then reporting to appropriate persons the results of the evaluation (p. 64).

Opinion shopping A practice whereby an audit client invites another firm of accountants to offer a second opinion on a disagreement the client's management has with the auditor over a proposed accounting treatment. This action can pressure the auditor to issue an unqualified auditor's report so as not to lose the audit to the second firm (p. 109).

Oral evidence Responses to oral enquiries of officers and key employees of the entity (p. 434).

Organisational controls Ensure segregation of duties within the information technology department (IT) and between IT and user departments (p. 381).

Parallel simulation A method of testing controls that simulates the entity's processing of real data. Actual entity data are processed using auditor-controlled software. The output is then compared with the entity's actual output (p. 471).

Partner A member of a partnership of public practitioners. A partner has the overall and final responsibility of an audit engagement (p. 321).

Payment transactions file A computer file containing details of payments made (p. 629).

Payroll register A journal recording details of the calculation and amount of wages paid to each employee (p. 632).

Payroll transactions file A computer file recording details of wage payments to employees (p. 632).

Performance The achievement of business objectives (p. 48).

Performance audit An independent and systematic examination of the organisation, program or function for the purpose of (1) forming an opinion on whether it is being managed in an economical, efficient and effective manner, and (2) determining whether the internal procedures for promoting and monitoring economy, efficiency and effectiveness are adequate (p. 76).

Performance reviews Management review and analysis of reports that summarise the detail of account balances, such as reports of sales activity, and of actual performance compared with budgets, forecasts or previous period amounts (p. 385).

Permanent file A permanent file that contains data useful in an audit on many future engagements (p. 347).

Perpetual inventory records Records of the movement of inventory items and of the quantity on hand (p. 669).

Personnel authorisation form A form issued by the personnel department indicating the job classification, wage rate and authorised payroll deductions for each employee (p. 630).

Personnel data master file A computer file containing details of employees, such as wage rate and date of hiring (p. 630).

Personnel file A record maintained by the personnel department recording details of employees such as wage rates and date of hiring (p. 630).

Physical controls Controls that limit access to assets and important records (p. 384).

Physical evidence Audit evidence obtained from physical examination or inspection of tangible assets (p. 435).

Physical inventory count *See* **Stocktake**.

Planned detection risk A detection risk that is considered tolerable (p. 494).

Planned level of substantive procedures Substantive procedures necessary to achieve the planned detection risk (p. 495).

Plant register A record of plant and equipment items containing such information as description, supplier, serial number and location, as well as cost and depreciation charges that reconcile with the control account in the general ledger (p. 690).

Population Transactions in a transaction class or items making up an account balance that the auditor believes to be consistent as far as the likelihood of deviation or misstatement of the type being sought is concerned (p. 528).

Predecessor auditor An auditor who has since been replaced by a current auditor (p. 318).

Predominantly substantive approach A preliminary audit strategy based on the assumption that the assessed level of control risk for an assertion is high (p. 423).

Preliminary assessment of control risk An assessment for the purpose of obtaining a reasonable expectation as to the effectiveness of controls such that the detailed audit program can be designed under the appropriate audit strategy (p. 396).

Presentation and disclosure An assertion that components of financial statements are presented and disclosed in accordance with a financial reporting framework (p. 372).

Presents fairly *See* **True and fair view**.

Privity of contract The contractual relationship that exists between two or more contracting parties (p. 215).

Probability-proportional-to-size (PPS) sampling A statistical sampling plan based on attribute sampling which identifies dollars making up the population as the sampling unit. It is also known as 'dollar unit sampling' (p. 545).

Professional ethics The written code of ethics put forward by a professional body (p. 97).

Professional indemnity insurance An insurance taken by a professional person to indemnify the assured against loss resulting from the proven negligence of the professional person (p. 204).

Professional judgement An exercise of an opinion by an accountant or auditor that is based on the assumption that he or she has the professional skills and expertise to exercise due professional care and to be objective in providing advice or opinions on matters presented to him or her (p. 268).

Projected error Population error based on the projection of the error rate in the sample tested (p. 548).

Proportionate liability An arrangement whereby the plaintiff's loss is divided among the defendants according to their share of responsibility (p. 207).

Proposed auditor The incoming auditor who is appointed to replace the existing auditor (p. 318).

Proximity Closeness in space, time or relationships, where the occurrence of events is foreseeable. It applies within an expected range of relationships (p. 221).

Public interest In the interest of the community or the people as a whole (pp. 26, 98).

Purchase requisitions Forms issued by authorised personnel in user departments detailing goods and services required (p. 625).

Purchase transactions file A computer file listing details of all purchase transactions (p. 627).

Purchases cut-off test A substantive test of details of transactions designed to obtain reasonable assurance that purchase transactions occurring near the end of the reporting period are recorded in the accounting period in which the transactions occurred and that the corresponding entries for inventories are made in the same period (p. 649).

Qualified opinion Expressed when the auditor concludes that an unqualified opinion cannot be expressed but that the effect of any scope limitation, disagreement with those charged with governance, or a conflict between applicable financial reporting frameworks is material but not extreme (p. 294).

Quality control Mechanisms that are instituted by the profession and the firms to govern audit quality. Quality control mechanisms include processes that protect the integrity of how audits are managed and performed (p. 20).

Random selection Selection of sampling units from a population by the use of random number tables or computer-generated random numbers (p. 531).

Raw materials Materials purchased from suppliers to be used in the manufacture of finished goods (p. 667).

Reasonable assurance Assurance engagement performed to provide a reasonable level of confidence in the subject matter (p. 8).

Reasonable skill and care Professionalism or due professional care and competence reasonably expected of a professional person (as opposed to a layperson) under the circumstances of the case. The professional is expected to have considered all facts (and their reliability) to arrive at a responsible and well-informed opinion on the matter (p. 18).

Recalculation Checking the mathematical accuracy of records and documents (p. 438).

Receiving report A form issued by the receiving department detailing the description and quantity of the goods delivered by a supplier (p. 626).

Records The main accounting records of an entity, in the form of journals and ledgers (p. 379).

Regulations The framework that provides the support and control of the market with the authority of either the government or the profession (p. 6).

Related party transactions Transactions consummated by related parties (that is, by parties who are involved in an economic action or event to the extent that 'arm's length' bargaining of terms is not possible) (p. 514).

Reliability Information has the quality of reliability when it is free from material error and bias and can be depended upon by users to represent faithfully that which it either purports to represent or could reasonably be expected to represent (p. 7).

Remittance advice A form accompanying cash or cheques paid by a customer, indicating the customer's details and the items being paid (pp. 579, 629).

Re-performance Recalculating or reconciling financial data. This process also involves redoing certain aspects of the processing of selected transactions (p. 438).

Rights and obligations An assertion that the entity holds or controls the rights to assets and that liabilities are the obligations of the entity (p. 371).

Risk assessment A process whereby management identifies risks pertaining to the entity in order to put effective controls into operation to control those risks (p. 376).

Risk management The entire culture, process and system established to manage opportunities and minimise or control risks (p. 55).

Risk of incorrect acceptance Risk that arises when the sample in a substantive test of details supports the conclusion that the recorded account balance is not materially misstated when it is materially misstated (p. 531).

Risk of incorrect rejection Risk that arises when the sample in a substantive test of details supports the conclusion that the recorded account balance is materially misstated when it is not materially misstated (p. 531).

Risk of overreliance The risk of assessing control risk as being too low (p. 530).

Risk of underreliance The risk of assessing control risk as being too high (p. 530).

Roll-forward testing Analytical procedures or tests of details of transactions performed on transactions that occur between the date of testing (when testing is done before the end of the year) and the end of the reporting period (p. 502).

Sales cut-off test A substantive procedure designed to obtain reasonable assurance that sales and accounts receivable are recorded in the accounting period in which the transactions occurred, and that the corresponding entries for inventories and cost of sales are made in the same period (p. 599).

Sales invoice Form detailing goods or services supplied to a customer and the amount owed (p. 577).

Sales journal A journal listing completed sales transactions (p. 577).

Sales order A form showing the description of the goods, the quantity ordered and other relevant data. The order is signed by the clerk accepting the order (p. 575).

Sales return cut-off test A substantive procedure designed to obtain reasonable assurance that sales returns are accounted for in the period in which the original sales transaction occurred (p. 599).

Sales transactions file A computer file listing details of all sales transactions (p. 577).

Sampling interval The interval between successive sampling units selected for testing where systematic selection is being applied (p. 540).

Sampling risk The possibility that a properly drawn sample may, by chance, not be representative of the population (p. 529).

Sampling unit Items making up a transaction class or account balance out of which the sample is to be selected for testing (p. 536).

Scanning The auditor performs a brief viewing of the items instead of going through the items in detail (p. 436).

Second partner review A review of working papers by an audit partner who did not participate in the audit (p. 780).

Segregation of duties Procedures that ensure individuals do not perform incompatible duties (p. 383).

Self-regulatory The characteristic of an organisation or profession that governs its behaviour through self-imposed codes and regulations (p. 98).

Sequential sampling A type of attribute sampling that permits a halt to sampling if a certain number of occurrences are observed (p. 544).

Standard format of auditor's reports The prescribed format, principles and wording of an auditor's report in accordance with auditing standards (p. 269).

Statistical sampling Sampling that uses probability theory to determine sample size and to interpret the results (p. 529).

Stocktake The process of ascertaining inventory quantities by count, weight or measurement (p. 667).

Stratification Subdivision of a population, such as by monetary value. The subpopulations need to be defined so sampling units can belong only to one stratum (p. 536).

Subsequent events Events occurring between the period end and the date of the auditor's report, and facts discovered after the date of the auditor's report (p. 762).

Subsequent period's bank statement The first bank statement issued after the end of the reporting period that is used by the auditor to verify the existence of outstanding deposits and unpresented cheques listed on the bank reconciliation as at end of the reporting period (p. 725).

Substantive procedures Procedures that provide evidence as to the substance of management's financial statement assertions (p. 423).

Suppliers' invoices Forms issued by the supplier detailing goods or services supplied and the amount owed (p. 627).

Sustainability The notion of conducting business activities with minimal long-term effect on the environment (p. 182).

Systematic selection Selection of sampling units from a population at regular intervals known as the sampling interval (p. 540).

Systems control audit review file An embedded audit facility that enables auditors to specify parameters of interest, such as transactions meeting specified criteria, which are then recorded on a special audit file for subsequent review by the auditors (p. 588).

Systems development and maintenance controls Controls over the review, testing and approval of new systems and program changes (p. 381).

Technical review A review by a partner or manager to ensure that the form and content of the financial statements are in accordance with accounting standards, the Corporations Act and Australian Securities Exchange requirements (where applicable) (p. 777).

Teleology A doctrine that holds that actions are right or wrong only in terms of their ability to bring about desired ends (p. 101).

Termination notice A form issued by the personnel department on an employee's termination of employment (p. 632).

Test data approach A method of testing controls in a computerised information systems environment. The auditor prepares fictitious transactions and has these tested using the

Test data approach (*continued*) entity's software. The output from processing test data is then compared with the expected output (pp. 470, 588).

Tests of controls Audit tests performed to provide evidence about the effectiveness of the design and operations of internal controls (pp. 398, 440, 460).

Tests of details of balances Substantive procedures to obtain evidence directly about an account balance rather than about the individual transactions that are debited and credited to the account (pp. 440, 499).

Tests of details of transactions Tests to obtain evidence of a sample or all of the individual debits or credits in an account, to reach a conclusion about the account balance (pp. 440, 498).

Third parties Parties other than a contracting party (p. 220).

Time budget The estimated amount of time required at each staff level (partner, manager, senior and staff assistants) to complete each part of the audit (p. 322).

Timing of substantive procedures The time at which substantive procedures are performed relative to the end of the reporting period (pp. 502, 537).

Tolerable misstatement The maximum misstatement in the population that the auditor can accept as being consistent with the conclusion that sample results confirm achievement of the audit objective. The auditor should consider how much monetary misstatement may exist in the related account balance or class of transactions without causing the financial statements to be materially misstated. (pp. 422, 537).

Tolerable rate of deviation The maximum rate of deviation from an internal control that will allow the auditor to place the planned reliance on that control (p. 537).

Tort A breach of duty other than under contract, leading to liability for damages (or compensation) (p. 214).

Total quality management (TQM) A management tool that oversees the entire operation and identifies wherever efficiency can be enhanced (p. 193).

Tracing Following through a transaction from source documents to accounting records (p. 436).

Transaction class A group of transactions that are of similar nature and can be aggregated within a category of accounts (p. 424).

Transaction walk-through review Tracing one or a few transactions within each major class of transaction through the transaction trail to identify and observe the related control policies and procedures (p. 388).

Transactions Exchanges of assets and services between an entity and outside parties, as well as the transfer or use of assets and services within an entity (p. 379).

Triple bottom line reporting A reporting system that reports the economic, environmental and social performance of a business (p. 182).

True and fair view A term that is synonymous with 'fairly presented'. It is used when expressing a fair opinion on financial statements when required by the Corporations Act (pp. 8, 284).

Underlying accounting records The information that is contained in the accounting records that support the final balances and accounting entries (p. 428).

Unmodified auditor's report An auditor's opinion on a general purpose financial report prepared in accordance with a financial reporting framework designed to achieve fair presentation that states that the financial report 'gives a true and fair view' or 'presents fairly, in all material respects', in accordance with the applicable financial reporting framework (p. 286).

Utilitarianism A doctrine that holds that actions should be directed towards providing the greatest good for the greatest number of people (p. 101).

Valuation and allocation An assertion that assets, liabilities and equity interests are included in the financial report at appropriate amounts and any resulting valuation or allocation adjustments are appropriately recorded (p. 371).

Virtue ethics A concept of ethics that stresses the ability of a person to act morally based on his or her character; i.e. moral behaviour is a natural result of one's character (p. 102).

Vouching Selecting entries in the accounting records, and obtaining and inspecting the documentation that served as the basis for entries (p. 436).

Window dressing A deliberate attempt to enhance some aspect of a company's apparent short-term solvency, such as by misstating the cut-off of cash receipts or payments (p. 726).

Work in process Part-manufactured products consisting of materials, direct labour and overhead applied to the stage of completion (p. 667).

Working papers Documentation stored on paper, film or in electronic media containing audit evidence in support of the audit opinion (p. 346).

Write-off authorisation memo A form signed by an appropriate official authorising the write-off of bad debts (p. 581).

Written representations Signed statements by responsible and knowledgeable individuals that have a bearing on one or more of management's assertions (pp. 433, 771).

12-question model   103

A

AA 1000 Assurance Standard   182, 184–5
AAA model   103
AARF   24
AAS 5   229
AASB 3 (IFRS 3)   709, 743
AASB 101   283
AASB 102 (IAS 2)   665, 672, 685
AASB 107 (IAS 7)   709, 712
AASB 110 (IAS 10)   759, 762, 765, 768
AASB 116 (IAS 16)   665, 694, 695
AASB 117 (IAS 17)   665, 693
AASB 121 (IAS 21)   744
AASB 124 (ISA 24)   709, 736
AASB 127 (ISA 27)   709, 742
AASB 128 (IAS 28)   709
AASB 131 (IAS 31)   709
AASB 134 (IAS 34)   249, 254, 281, 303
AASB 136 (IAS 36)   665, 695
AASB 137 (IAS 37)   759, 768–70
AASB 1031   415, 419–20, 421
ABC Learning   12, 126, 129, 137, 204,
    234–5
access controls   381
AccountAbility   184
accountability See also public
    accountability
  in integrated reports   204
  public expectation of   13
accountants See professional accountants
accounting's relationship with
    auditing   264–6
Accounting and Auditing Enforcement
    Releases (AAERs)   29
accounting estimates substantive
    procedures   513
accounting firms   17 See also Big Four
    accounting firms
accounting misstatements   125
accounting profession   15–17
  attributes of   97–8
  informal and formal groups   98–9
  regulation of   16
  safeguards   105–6, 107–9
Accounting Professional & Ethical
    Standards Board (APESB)   135–6,
    140–1
  Code of Ethics for Professional
    Accountants (Code of Ethics)   97,
    104–10
accounting restatements   125 See also
    earnings management
accounting standards   135–6, 283–4
accounting systems   379–80, 396

accounts payable
  analytical procedures   648
  audit procedures   620–1
  confirmations   621, 650, 651
  correlation of risk components   644
  detection risks   644–5
  disclosure requirements   652
  initial procedures   648
  purchases and payments cut-off
    tests   649
  recalculating payroll liabilities   651
  reconciling suppliers' statements   650
  substantive procedures   643–52
  tests of details of balances   650
  tests of details of transactions   648–9
  unrecorded liabilities   621, 650–1
  verifying executive remuneration   652
  vouching   649
accounts payable master files   627
accounts receivable
  analytical procedures   595, 597–8
  cash receipts cut-off tests   599
  confirmations   600–4
  correlation of risk components   593–4
  disclosure requirements   605
  initial procedures   595, 597
  presentation and disclosure   596
  sales cut-off tests   599
  substantive procedures   500–1, 595–6
  tests of details of balances   596
    599–605
  tests of details of transactions   595–6
  using generalised audit software   506
  vouching   598
accounts receivable
    circularisation   571, 600
accounts receivable master files
    577, 597
accounts receivable subsidiary ledgers   577
accounts receivable trial balance   597
Achieving High Performance in Internal
    Audit   66
ACL   190, 503, 505, 532, 539–40
acquisitions and disposals for group
    entities   743
actual independence   111
Adelaide Society of Accountants   15–17
Adelaide Steamship Company Limited
    127–8, 205 See also Residual Assco
adjusting entries   351
adjusting events   765–6
Adsteam See Residual Assco
adverse conclusion   81
adverse opinion   294, 295, 296
  form and content of   298
advocacy threats   105, 108, 110

aged trial balance   597
  working papers   598
agencies   72
agency relationships   10
agency theory   9–11
  overlaps with information
    hypothesis   11–12
agency-specific audits   78
agents   47
AGS 1014   203, 227, 232
AGS 1030 (IAPS 1012)   709, 736
AGS 1036 (IAPS 1010)   164
airline industry's operations   329, 331
Akai Holdings   129, 234
Allied Lyons   205
American Accounting Association,
    Committee on Basic Auditing
    Concepts   7
American Accounting Association (AAA)
    model   103
American Institute of Certified Public
    Accountants' (AICPA) Auditing
    Standards Board (ASB)   32
analytical evidence   431–2
analytical procedures
  accounts payable   648
  accounts receivable   500, 595, 597–8
  audit planning   326–7, 333–4, 344
  auditing procedures   438, 440
  cash balances   718
  completion of audit   774–6
  financial ratios used in   354–5
  generalised audit software
    505–6
  hotel industry   496–7
  income statement accounts   513
  inventory transactions   679–80
  investments   738
  property, plant and equipment   692
  purchases, payables and payroll   621,
    635–6
  risk assessments   374
  sales and receivables   582
  sales transactions   501
  substantive procedures   496–8
annual general meetings (AGMs) and
    regulations regarding   22, 134
APC Limited   230
APES 110   95, 104–10, 140–1, 164, 167,
    178, 249, 253, 315, 318, 320–1
  revisions to   97, 104
APES 205   95, 135, 141
APES 210   95, 136, 141, 249, 256, 257
APES 220   95, 136, 141
APES 305   95, 141, 315, 326
APES 315   95

APES 320   95, 136, 141, 143–5, 315, 317
  See also ISQC 1
APESB *See* Accounting Professional &
  Ethical Standards Board (APESB)
application controls   380, 381–3, 468,
  469–70, 578
  assessing and testing   474
APRA   12, 328
APS 1   141, 229
APS 2   141
APS 5   141
AQRB   145
Arthur Andersen   17, 19, 21, 125, 127,
  128, 205
  settlement and fines paid by   126
Articles of Association   148
ASA 100   170, 259
ASA 101   259
ASA 102   259
ASA 200 (ISA 200)   5, 45, 49–50, 95, 249,
  259, 263, 266, 281, 283, 286, 315, 320,
  367, 368
ASA 210 (ISA 210)   203, 231, 249, 253,
  259, 281, 300, 315, 317
  Appendix 1   323–5
ASA 220 (ISA 220)   95, 141, 318, 321
ASA 230 (ISA 230)   259, 346, 489, 509
ASA 240 (ISA 240)   31, 163, 189, 249,
  259, 267, 315, 334, 337, 344, 771
ASA 250 (ISA 250)   45, 50, 259, 315,
  328, 771
ASA 260 (ISA 260)   45, 50, 259, 281, 301,
  759, 781, 783
  Appendix 2   782
ASA 265 (ISA 265)   45, 50, 259, 367,
  455, 466
ASA 300 (ISA 300)   259, 315, 326
ASA 315 (ISA 315)   5, 50, 58, 259, 315,
  327–8, 331, 367, 368, 372–3, 376, 415,
  418, 489, 569, 570, 619, 665, 668, 688,
  709, 712
  Appendix 1   379
ASA 320 (ISA 320)   259, 415, 417–18,
  422, 759
ASA 330 (ISA 330)   45, 50, 260, 415, 424,
  455, 489, 496
ASA 402   260
ASA 450 (ISA 450)   260, 281, 295, 759,
  771, 777–8, 779
ASA 500   527, 569
ASA 500 (ISA 500)   260, 415, 428
  489, 495
ASA 501 (ISA 501)   260, 415, 489, 515,
  665, 675
ASA 502 (ISA 501)   203, 231–2, 260, 415,
  489, 515, 759, 769, 772

ASA 505 (ISA 505)   260, 415, 432, 489,
  515, 569, 600
ASA 510   260, 281, 302–3, 489, 665, 683
ASA 520 (ISA 520)   260, 315, 333–4, 489,
  497, 759, 774
ASA 530 (ISA 530)   260, 489, 527, 528,
  529, 531, 535, 536, 569
  Appendix 2   503
  Appendix 4   532, 539
ASA 540 (ISA 540)   260, 489, 514, 569,
  604, 665, 685, 709, 743, 759, 766, 772
ASA 550 (ISA 550)   260, 315, 330, 489,
  514, 759, 772
ASA 560 (ISA 560)   249, 260, 268, 281,
  300, 759, 762, 772
ASA 570 (ISA 570)   260, 281, 300, 759,
  766–7, 772
ASA 580 (ISA 580)   249, 260, 263–4, 415,
  434, 759, 771
ASA 600 (ISA 600)   260, 665, 681, 709,
  741, 743
ASA 610 (ISA 610)   45, 62, 63, 249, 260,
  263, 315, 323, 415, 434, 455, 464,
  665, 681
ASA 620 (ISA 620)   260, 315, 321–2, 415,
  434, 665, 674, 681
ASA 700 (ISA 700)   5, 8   53, 95, 249,
  253, 260, 281, 282, 303, 759
ASA 705 (ISA 705)   249, 254, 260, 281,
  294, 297–8, 759, 764, 774
ASA 706 (ISA 706)   249, 254, 260, 281,
  298–300
  Appendix 1 and 3   300
ASA 710 (ISA 710)   260, 281, 300, 302, 772
ASA 720 (ISA 720)   260, 281, 300
ASA 800 (ISA 800)   163, 172, 173, 260,
  281, 300
ASA 805 (ISA 805)   163, 172, 174, 260
ASA 810 (ISA 810)   163, 172, 260
ASB   32
ASAE 3000 (ISAE 3000)   75, 163, 170,
  177–8, 179
ASAE 3100   75, 170, 180
ASAE 3402   163, 170
ASAE 3410 (ISAE 3410)   163, 170,
  184, 187
ASAE 3420 (ISAE 3420)   163, 170
ASAE 3450   163, 170
ASAE 3500   45, 75, 78, 79–80, 163,
  170, 180
Asare   455
ASIC *See* Australian Securities and
  Investments Commission (ASIC)
AS/NZ ISO 31000:2009   55
ASQC 1 (ISQC 1)   95, 249, 259, 315,
  317, 415

ASRE 2400 (ISRE 2400)   75, 76, 163,
  172, 176
ASRE 2405 (ISRE 2400)   75, 76, 163,
  172, 177
ASRE 2410 (ISRE 2410)   164, 176, 281, 303
ASRE 2415   164, 176
ASREs   27
ASRS   27, 169, 171
assertion-based audit engagements   114,
  166, 168–9, 181
assertion-based review engagements   114
assertions   7
assertion-specific risk   491, 492
asset misappropriations   716
associates   732
  acquisitions and disposals   743
  disclosure requirements   741
Association of Certified Fraud
  Examiners   343, 716
Association of Chartered Certified
  Accountants   249
assurance   14–15
  relationship with auditing   15
assurance engagement standards
  165–72
assurance engagements   14–15, 114–15
  categories of   168–72
  definitions of   166–7
  effectiveness of control procedures   181
  framework for   165–8
  general requirements applicable   167–8
  involving historical financial
    information   173–7
  other than audits/reviews of historical
    financial information   177–9
  other than those relating to historical
    financial information   179–90
  process for   166
  related to historical financial
    information   170
  related to specific engagements   170–2
  reports   167
  single and specific financial
    statements   174–5
assurance practitioners   178–9
assurance reports
  basic elements of   178–9
  modifying   81
  performance engagements   80
assurance services   51, 52
ASX *See* Australian Securities Exchange
  (ASX)
ASX 300 audit committee
  requirements   67, 262
ASX All Ordinaries Index, audit
  committee requirements   68

ASX Corporate Governance
Council 23, 114
*Corporate Governance Principles and
Recommendations* 51, 68, 102, 132
ASX Listing Rules 23, 68, 223, 376
attribute sampling 535, 544
projected deviation rates 554–5
reliability factors 551
tests of controls 553–5
AUASB *See* Australian Auditing and
Assurance Standards Board (AUASB)
audit committees 49, 106, 781
appointment of auditors 114, 250
matters for communication with
783–4
relationship with independent
auditors 262–3
relationship with internal and external
auditors 70
responsibilities in external audits 262
role and objectives of 45–6, 67–70
role in corporate governance
53, 54, 262
role in fraud risk assessment 344
*Audit Committees: A Guide to Good
Practice* (2nd ed) 67, 69, 262, 783
audit documentation *See* working papers
audit engagements
approaches to independence 115–23
assessing competence 321–2
clients to decline 320
compensation and evaluation
policies 122
ethical and legal considerations
320–3
litigation 122–3
steps in accepting new 317
audit evidence 7, 426–35
applying auditing standards
428–31
appropriateness of 430–1, 495
categories and types of 428
corroborating information 431–5
evaluating 441
impact of technology on 435
inability to obtain relevant 295–6
nature of 427–8
obtaining and evaluating 441
relationship between materiality and
422–3
sampling 532
specific audit objectives 427
sufficiency factors related to 429
timeliness 430
triangulation in fraud
assessments 315–16

audit expectation gap 6, 30–3, 282
areas for improvement 32, 255
audit expectation-performance gap 30–1
audit fees 114 *See also* low-balling
determining 322
threats and safeguards for 122
audit hooks 472
audit independence 14, 21
financial interest threats 115–16
long association with client threats 118
non-assurance services threats and
safeguards 119–23
relationships threats 116–17
staff and secondment threats 117–18
statutory provisions for 111–14
Audit Investigation Group 45
audit log 472
audit managers 321
audit memoranda 351
audit observers 73
audit opinions 283
forming 285–6
modifying 254
audit planning
analytical procedures 326–7, 333–4
cash balances 713–15
communications for 783
detecting fraud 315–16
fraud brainstorm sessions 345
fraud risk considerations 334–45
inventory transactions 672–8
investments 733–6
property, plant and equipment
689–90
steps in 326–7
working papers 346–51
audit procedures
cash and investments 710–12
CAAT 470–5
credit sales 570–1
inventories 666–7
purchases, payables and payroll 620–1
sales and receivables 570
audit programs 351, 506
credit purchases 640
framework for 507–8
initial engagements 508, 509
substantive procedures 507–12
substantive procedures
(inventories) 511
tests of controls 462–3
audit quality 124, 135–47
decline in 5, 416
definitions of 19
ethical competence 137–40
evaluating 30

ICAA survey 2012 341
problems in European system 20
technical competence 135–6
*Audit Quality in Australia: A Strategic
Review* 145
Audit Quality Review Board (AQRB) 145
audit reforms 19–20
audit reports
criticisms about value of 32, 255
current work on updating 32
external users 46
important elements in 8
improving value of 497–8
limitations of standard format of 269
requirements 254
timeliness and relevance 268
users of 28–9
audit risk 399–402
components of 400–1
final assessments 778–9
interrelationship with business
risk 332
relationships among risk
components 401–2
audit risk models 401–2, 493, 644
audit software 438, 501, 503–6 *See also*
generalised audit software
audit strategies 416
control risk assessments and 456–60
decision tree for 458
developing 423–6
inventory transactions 673–4
property, plant and equipment
689–90
purchases, payables and payroll 636
relationships between transaction classes
and 426
strategies for material financial
statement assertions 424
types of 457–60
audit teams 321, 345
audit trail 380, 388, 587
audit trinity 53–9
Audit Work Program 78
auditing
ethical values in 137–40
high-profile scandals 137
relationship between accounting
and 264–6
relationship with assurance 15
value adding services 52
*Auditing: A Journal of Practice &
Theory* 541
Auditing and Assurance Standards
(AUSs) 75
auditing environment 15–17, 18

auditing firms
  impact of internationalisation 205
  key drivers in audit quality 145–6
  lawsuits against 234
  materiality guides for 417
  preferred sampling methods 532
  quality control in 140–7
  reviews measures for 145
  shared liabilities 204
  standards setting for 140–1
auditing guidance statements 136
Auditing Guidance Statements *See*
  individual AGS
auditing procedures 435–41
  classification of 440
  lapping 729
  relationships among evidence and
    assertions 438–9
  types of 436–8
auditing profession
  internationalisation of 205
  litigation crises in 12
Auditing Standard No. 16, Communications
  with Audit Committees 33
auditing standards 24–8, 136, 256–60, 268
  applicability to audit evidence 258,
    428–31
  Australian 25–7
  Clarity Project format 259–60
  framework for 256–7
  international 27
  legal enforceability of 258
  oversight structure in Australia 24
  overview of 259
Auditing Standards Board (ASB) 32
auditor independence
  declaration of 133
  general auditor provisions 133–4
  monitoring programs 124–5
  threats to 133–4
Auditor Independence Reports 124
auditor liability 131
  fundamental shifts in extent of 230–1
  landmark cases 221–2
  PSL reforms 207–8
  shareholders, creditor and
    auditees 209–20
  third party liability cases 230–1
auditor negligence 211, 214–20
  causal relationships 217–18
  contributory 218–19
  damages 219–20
  elements in negligence actions 225
  landmark cases 218–19
  liability to third parties 220–31
  negligence cases 217–18

Auditor-General Act 1997 (Cwlth) 73, 74
auditor-generals (A-G) 72
  financial statements reporting 75–6
  opinion on standards of CFOs 81–2
  responsibilities of 75
  role of 73–4
auditors *See also* external auditors;
  independent auditors; internal
  auditors
  change-over considerations 302
  common areas of dispute with
    management 513, 763–4
  communicating with
    management 285–301
  continuing professional
    development 140
  disciplinary procedures 147–8
  duties of 213
  environments that affect conduct 138
  expansion of roles 367
  extent of liabilities 204
  fiduciary relationships 139, 213
  High Court rulings in favour of 230–1
  independence from clients 21
  interactions with those in
    governance 50
  key roles of 6
  legal action resulting from GFC 234–5
  legal penalties against 206–7
  legal protection from litigation 203
  litigation crises in 205–6
  overall objectives 49–50
  predecessor 318
  professional duties 134, 255–6
  proposed 318
  qualification requirements 135
  reasonable care and skill duties 253
  registration process 14, 251–2
  relationship with shareholders and
    management 46
  reporting duties 253–5
  resignation process 251, 252
  responsibilities 8, 376–7, 761
  role in enterprise governance 50–1
  rotation of 21, 134
  stakeholder expectations of 52
Auditor's Audit Manual 230
auditor's opinion 8
auditor's reports
  circumstances for adjusting 773–4
  emphasis of matter and other
    matter 298–300
  expression of opinion 286
  forming opinions 285–6
  formulating opinion and drafting 780–1
  IAASB's proposed revisions to 288–93

  modified 293–4
  proposed improvements to 282
  reasons for issuing revised 765
  unmodified 286–8
audits
  analytical procedures at
    completion 774–6
  assessing value of 29–30
  benefits of 267
  definitions of 6–7
  failures in 204
  historical perspective 9–10
  limitations of 268–9
  overview of processes 269–71
  reasons for demand 8–13
  structure of 7
  users of 28–9
  See also interim audits
AUS 804 75
AUS 810 75, 163, 181, 455, 468
AUS 904 (ISRS 4400) 75, 163, 181
Australia
  auditing standards 25–7
  auditing standards in Clarity
    format 259–60
  corporate collapses 12–13, 19, 127–8,
    129, 204
  incidence of fraud in 188
  key reform activities 131–5
  KPMG fraud survey 2012 335–6
  negligence cases 217
  privity of contract 216–17
  proximity cases 222–3
  sampling practices in 532
  standard-setting framework 257
  standards oversight structure 24
  sustainability legislative framework 184
Australian Accounting Research
  Foundation (AARF) 24
Australian Auditing and Assurance
  Standards Board (AUASB) 21–2, 24,
  140, 184, 193, 775
  adapting ISAs to Australian
    standards 256–7
  Framework for Assurance Engagements
    (Framework) 165
  Guidance Statements 75, 256
  numbering system used by 172
  primary role of 26–7
  pronouncements by 171
  proposals to withdraw AASB 1031 421
  revisions based on Clarity ASAs 27
Australian Competition and Consumer
  Commission 233
Australian Consumer Law (ACL) 233
Australian Council of Super Investors 164

Australian Institute of Company
Directors 775
Australian National Audit Office (ANAO)
Audit Work Program 78
auditing standards 74, 75
Better Practice Guides 74
performance guidelines 76
Australian Parliament 22
Australian Prudential Regulation Authority
(APRA) 12, 328
Australian Securities and Investments
Commission Act 2001 (ASIC
Act) 22, 75, 98, 207
Australian Securities and Investments
Commission (ASIC) 12
audit inspection findings 5, 25, 124–5,
131, 215, 416
audit inspection/surveillance
programs 124, 126, 130–1, 146–7
Authorised Audit Companies: Insurance
Arrangements 208
Class Order 98/1418 250
litigation cases 128
objectives of 22
penalties for negligence 214–15
register of company auditors 252
regulatory guide on commentary 203
Australian Securities Exchange (ASX) 23
See also ASX Corporate Governance
Council; ASX Listing Rules
Australian Society of Accountants 17
Australian Society of Certified
Practising Accountants 17
Australian Standards of Related Services
(ASRSs) 169, 171
authorised audit companies 135
professional indemnity insurance 208
registration process 252
authorised price list 577
authorities 72
automated audit software *See also* ACL;
IDEA 190
AWA v. Daniels, t/a Deloitte, Haskins
& Sells & Ors (1992) 10 ACLC
933 206, 214, 218–19, 266, 782

B

Babcock & Brown 205
bad debts 604–5
bad debts expense 583
Baker & McKenzie 665
Balancing Act — a Triple Bottom Line
Analysis of the Australian Economy
(2005) 182
bank confirmation requests 710, 720,
721–3

Bank of America 128
bank reconciliation statements 710
bank reconciliations 713–14, 718
entity-prepared 725
verifying 724
bank transfer schedules 719
bank transfers, tracing 719–20
bankmecu 164
Banksia Securities 137, 264
batch processing methods 575
BDO 17, 131, 234, 760
Bear Stearns 234
Behavioural Research in Accounting 541
Better Practice Guides 74
bias in sampling 540
Big Four accounting firms 17
aiding tax avoidance 95–6
AQRB's access to systems 145
audit inspections 124, 131
reviews of services 46
sustainability assurance reports 182
Bill Express 137
Bily v. Arthur Young Co. 217
blended method 420
board of directors 47, 58, 261–3, 781
bond posts by agents 10–11
Bond Corporation 205
Bonlat 128
BP 64
business, family and personal relationships
threats 116
business governance
and auditing and assurance
services 52–3
role of accountants and auditors in 53
See also performance concepts
business risk 332
business risk assessments 372–3

C

CAAT *See* computer-assisted audit
techniques (CAAT)
CALDB *See* Companies Auditors and
Liquidators Disciplinary Board
(CALDB)
Cambridge Credit Corporation Ltd and
Anor v. Hutcheson & Ors (1985)
ACLR 545 206, 213, 219, 225
Candler v. Crane Christmas & Co (1951)
AII ER 426 221
Caparo Industries Pty Ltd v. Dickman &
Others (1990) 1 AII ER 568 28, 217,
220, 225–6
limits of applicability of 228
reactions to verdict in 227
case law and influence in auditing 18

cash
audit objectives 712–13
audit planning 713–715
audit procedures 710–12
cut-off tests 718–19
detection risks 716
other issues associated with 728–31
substantive procedures 715–28
tests of balances 720–27
tests of details of transactions 718–20
cash at bank 712
cash balances 712–32
analytical procedures 718
audit objectives 712–13
audit procedures 711
auditing imprest petty cash funds 731
bank reconciliations control
procedures 713–14, 724–5
cash register fraud 730–1
confirming bank balances 720–2
confirming other agreements with
banks 724
confirming overdraft and loan
balances 724
detection risks 716
disclosure requirements 728
effects of major accounting transactions
on 715
imprest accounts control
procedures 714
materiality and risk in 714–15
obtaining subsequent period's bank
statements 725
substantive procedures 715–28
tests for lapping 728–30
tests of details of transactions
718–20
cash counts 716
cash equivalents 712
cash on hand 712, 726
cash receipts cut-off tests 599
cash receipts journals 579
cash receipts transactions 578–81
control risk assessments 590–1
depositing cash 579
fraud 716
receiving cash 578–9
recording receipts 579–80
cash sales system for theme park 727
causal relationships 217–18
Cendant Corporation 126
Centro Properties Group 12, 126, 130,
205, 235
Centro Retail 130
Certificate of Public Practice 146
certified internal auditors (CIA) 61

Chartered Institute of Management
Accountants (CIMA), *Enterprise
Governance: Getting the Balance
Right* 48
cheque summary 629
cheques 725–6
CHESS *See* Clearing House Electronic
Subregister System (CHESS)
chief financial officers, minimum standards
for state governments 81–2
chief risk officers 55
Citigroup 129
Clarity Project 6, 27–8, 258
Clearing House Electronic Subregister
System (CHESS) 734
tests of details of balances 738–9
CLERP 9 *See* Corporate Law Economic
Reform Program (CLERP 9)
client confidentiality 109
client relationships 317–23
client evaluation process 318–19
evaluating independence 320–1
identifying special circumstances and
unusual risks 319–20
Clive Peeters and employee fraud
633–4
cloud computing 383
Code of Ethics *See Code of Ethics for
Professional Accountants*
Code of Ethics for Professional Accountants
(Code of Ethics) 97, 104–10, 111,
115, 116, 118, 139–40
audit engagements 318
confidentiality 352–3
threats and safeguards for
business 109–10
threats and safeguards for public
practice 106–9
collusion 386, 579
Colonial First State Asset
Management 164
Colonial Geared Investments 130
Columbia Coffee & Tea case 228, 230
combined approach 424
comfort letters 227
commissions expense, substantive
procedures 501–2
Committee of Sponsoring Organizations
of the Treadway Commission
(COSO) 168, 375–6
*Effective Enterprise Risk Oversight–The
Role of the Board of Directors* 58
*Enterprise Risk Management–Integrated
Framework* 55, 181
*Internal Control–Integrated
Framework* 58, 375

*Strengthening Enterprise Risk
Management for Strategic
Advantage* 58
Thought Paper 58
Common Body of Knowledge (CBOK)
survey 61, 66
common law 204, 230–1
*Commonwealth Authorities and Companies
Act 1997* 74
Commonwealth Bank 130
Commonwealth Treasury of Australia 131
communication
between audit committees and
auditors 33
internal control matters 466–8
legal cases concerning management
and 782
with audit committees 783–4
with those in governance 781–3
Companies Act 1862 (UK) 13
Companies Auditors and Liquidators
Disciplinary Board (CALDB) 22–3,
135, 252
disciplinary powers of 147, 148
comparatives 301–2
Competition and Consumer Act 2010,
207, 233
Competition Commission (UK) 45–6
completeness assertions 185, 370
accounts payable 645
cash balances 720
inventory transactions 670
substantive procedures 510
completeness problems 594, 645
compliance engagements 180
compliance frameworks 282, 286
compliance risk 373
computer editing 382
computer information systems
access controls 384–5, 643
control activities 381–3
control risk assessments 397–8
ICQ for general controls 390–1
tests of operating effectiveness 588–9
use in confirmations 604
user controls 468–9
computer-assisted audit techniques
(CAAT) 438, 469, 470–5, 501
purchase transactions 639
substantive procedures 503–6
tests of operating effectiveness 588
conceptual approaches to review and audit
engagements 115–23
confirmation control working
paper 603

confirmations 432 *See also* external
confirmations
accounts payable 621, 650, 651
accounts receivable 600–4
auditing procedures 437–8
control of requests 602–3
disposition of exceptions 603
forms of request 600–3
sales and receivables 571
timing and extent of 602
written 767
conflicts of interest 108–9, 113, 321
conformance concepts 48, 50–2 *See also*
corporate governance
consequentialism 101, 103
consolidated financial statements 710
assertions applicable to 742
comparing statement presentation with
accounting standards 744
detection risks 741–2
identifying reporting entities 742
public sector 76
standardisation of accounting
policies 744
substantive procedures 740–4
verifying consolidating
adjustments 743–4
verifying financial statements of other
group entities 742–3
consolidating adjustments 743–4
construction in progress 693
Consumer Protection (Dodd–Frank)
Act 70
*Continental Casualty Co. v.
PricewaterhouseCoopers, LLP* 15
N.Y.3d 264 (2010) 220
contingent fees 122
contingent liabilities reviews 768–70
continuous auditing 189–90
contractual relationships 253
contributory negligence 218–19
control activities 57, 380–5
application controls 381–3
flowcharts 395
general controls 381
control environment 377–9
control procedures 396
control risk assessments
audit strategies 456–60
cash receipts transactions 590–1
credit sales transactions 586–7
final 465–6
inventory transactions 675–8
IT general controls 473–4
payment transactions 641
payroll transactions 642–3

preliminary assessments of 396–8
purchase transactions 637–40
purchases, payables and payroll 637–43
sales and receivables 585–7
control risks 400, 423
computer information systems 397–8
documenting level of 465–6
IT environments 468–70
relationships between ERM and 59
segregation of duties, effect on 384
tests of controls 398
controlled entities 72, 75, 740
Co-ordinating Group on Audit and
Accounting Issues (UK) 117
corporate collapses 12
impact on auditing 19–20
impact on courts' interpretations of
auditor conduct 230–1
investigations into 126
legislative reform as a result of 125–35
corporate environmental disasters 64
corporate governance 6, 46–7
and auditing functions 51–2
legal developments 51
role of accountants and auditors 53
role of audit committees 262
weaknesses 48
*Corporate Governance and the Financial
Crisis* 48
*Corporate Governance Principles and
Recommendations* 51
audit committees 68–9
ethical behaviour 102
independence provisions 123
*Corporate Law Economic Reform Program
(Audit Reform and Corporate
Disclosure) Act 2004* 21, 51, 98, 111,
132–5, 208, 268
Corporate Law Economic Reform
Program
(CLERP 9) 19, 21, 131, 132–5
corporate social responsibility 102
Corporations Act 2001 26, 132,136, 207
auditor registration 14
ethical provisions 75, 98
financial report contents 284
half-year financial statements 303
independence provisions 112–13, 114,
124, 133–4, 250–2, 298–300, 321
management-imposed limitations 296
misinformation provisions 130–1
financial reports and other historical
information 173, 176
qualified accountant definition 16
requirements for access to company
information 773

requirements for financial reports 254,
286, 301
responsibilities of auditors and
management 266
revisions to 111, 123, 134
working paper timeframe 353
corroborating information 351, 431–5
COSO *See* Committee of Sponsoring
Organizations of the Treadway
Commission (COSO)
CPA Australia 82, 103
adoption of internationalised
standards 131
Articles of Association 148
competency standards 140
disciplinary powers of 148
Joint Code of Professional Conduct 97,
104
membership base 17
post-GFC working tips 785–7
PSL structure amendments 208
publications 17
Risk Management Statement
(RMS 1) 145
sustainability reporting study 183
credit memos 581
credit purchases cycle 624
credit ratings agencies 576
credit sales cycle 574
credit sales transactions 575–8
access controls for 577–8
audit procedures 570–1
control risk assessments 586–7
credit approvals 576
credit checks 575–6
filling and dispatching orders 576
invoicing 577
recording sales 577–8
segregation of duties 576
tests of controls 588–9
tests of design effectiveness 585, 587
tests of operating effectiveness
587–91
understanding sales system 573
credit transfer systems 580, 629
cross-agency audits 78
CSIRO's, *Balancing Act — a Triple Bottom
Line Analysis of the Australian
Economy* (2005) 182
CUC International 126
current file (working papers) 347–9
customer orders 575
customised audit software 504
cut-off assertions 370–1
cut-off errors 499, 648
cut-off tests 499, 599, 648–9

cyberterrorism 187
cyclical inventory counts 670–1, 672

D

Damages 214, 219–20 *See also Cambridge
Credit Corporation Ltd and Anor v.
Hutcheson & Ors (1985) ACLR* 545
data, standing 578
data and procedural controls 381
debt collection 575–6
Deed of Cross Guarantee 250
Deloitte 17, 234
Deloitte & Touche 234
Deloitte Touche Tohmatsu 127–8
litigation settlements 205
denial-of-service attacks 187
deontology *See also* non-
consequentialism 101–2, 103
Department of Sustainability,
Environment, Water, Population and
Communities 182
Department of Trade (UK) 213
deposit slips 579
depreciation (accumulated) 694–5
derivatives 736
Derry v. Peek (1889) 14 App Cas 337 221
detection risks 401
acceptable risk matrix 402
accounts payable 644–5
cash balances 716
consolidated financial statements 741–2
determining 493–5
investments 736
property, plant and equipment
depreciation 689–90
rain cloud analogy 494–5
relationship between substantive
procedures and 494
sales and receivables 592–4
deviations 460, 461
proportion in sampling 528–9, 537
rate of 535, 542–3
tolerable levels 465, 537, 544
difference estimation method 543, 545
direct debits 580
direct reporting audit engagements 114,
166, 168–9, 181
direct reporting review engagements 114
direct tests 513
Directorate for Financial and Enterprise
Affairs 48
director's declarations 771
directors' reports 132, 771
disclaimer of conclusion 81
disclaimer of opinion 294, 296, 441
form and content of 298

discovery sampling 544, 555
dispatch notes 576, 599
dividends
  analytical procedures 711
  audit procedures 735
  test of details of transactions 738
  unpaid 731–2
  verifying 740
documentary evidence 432–3
  effects of circulation on reliability
    of 433
documents and records 380
  externally generated 432
  flowcharts 394
  for internal control 389–95
  internally generated 433
  pre-numbered 433, 575, 625, 626, 671
Dodd–Frank Wall Street Reform 70
dollar unit sampling 545
Donoghue v. Stevenson (1932) AC 562 220
dual-purpose tests 440, 461, 499, 508,
  599, 639, 648
due care concepts 209–14
  in audit engagements 322–3
  criticisms about auditors' level of
    care 211–13
  third party liabilities 220–31
due diligence audits 52
dummy records 471
dummy transactions 470
Dun & Bradstreet 576
duty of care
  determining adequate levels 258
  landmark cases 221–2, 225–6
  third parties liabilities extent
    220–31
Dynegy 204

E

earnings management 59–60, 125, 340
Easipower Ltd 221
e-crimes 187
*Effective Enterprise Risk Oversight — The
  Role of the Board of Directors* 58
efficiency ratios 355
electronic evidence 435
electronic signatures 435
electronic trails of transactions 388
emails as evidence 435
EMAS 182
embedded audit facility 588
emphasis of matter paragraphs 299–300,
  765
employee earnings master files 632
employment relationships threats 117
EMS 193

Emu Brewery 205
engagement letters 231, 253, 317
  form and content of 323–6
engagement partners 321
  responsibilities 141
  review of analytical procedures 775
  review of working papers 780
Enhanced Disclosure Scheme 268
enquiries
  in auditing procedures 437, 438
  risk assessments 373–4
  tests of controls 461
Enron 19, 125, 126–7, 204
enterprise governance 48–9, 50–1
*Enterprise Governance: Getting the Balance
  Right* 48
*Enterprise Risk Management — Integrated
  Framework* 55–6, 181
enterprise risk management (ERM) 55–9
  interrelated components and objectives
    of 57
  relationships between audit risk
    components and 59
entities 327–33
  audit procedures for contingent
    liabilities 768
  communication of audit matters with
    those in governance 781–3
  communication with legal
    counsels 769–70
  economy-wide factors 329
  evaluating objectives, strategies and
    business risks 331–2
  industry conditions 328
  knowledge of business operations
    329–30
  knowledge of financial reporting and
    accounting policies 331
  knowledge of financing activities
    330–1
  knowledge of investing activities 330
  measuring and reviewing financial
    performance 333
  regulatory environment of 328
entity-prepared bank reconciliations 725
entity-prepared schedules 692, 718
*Environment Protection and Biodiversity
  Conservation Act 1999* (EPBC
  Act) 182
environmental accounting 182
environmental management accounting
  systems (EMAS) 182
environmental management principles *See
  also* ISO 14000 191, 192–3
environmental management systems
  (EMS) 193

environmental reports *See* sustainability
  assurance reports
equity method of accounting 735
ERM *See* enterprise risk management
  (ERM)
Ernst & Young 17, 96, 126, 205
  settlements by 129, 234
  sustainability reports 185–7
Ernst & Young Global's Transparency
  Report 2009 194
errors 460 *See also* deviations
  projecting deviation rates 542–3
  qualitative aspects of 542
  rates in sampling population 542
  sampling selection 533, 535
*Esanda Finance Corporation v. Peat
  Marwick Hungerfords* (1994) 12
  ACLC 199 229–30, 233
ethical decision-making models
  103, 106
ethical relativism 102
ethics 100–3 *See also* professional ethics
  ethical issues 102–3
  theories for 101–2
Ethics Committee of IFAC 97
Europe's audit system problems 20
European Commission 20
event identification process 57
evidence *See* audit evidence
evidence gathering process 166
  assurance engagements 178
  limited assurance engagements 169–70
  standards for 258
exception basis reporting 75–6
executive compensation 127, 619
executive directors 261
existence assertions 370
  consolidated financial statements 742
  substantive procedures 509
experts 321
  evaluating work of 428
  for specialised inventories 674, 685–6
explicit assertions 369
external auditors 13–14 *See also*
  independent auditors
  assessing work of internal
    auditors 63, 323
  cloud computing 383
  communicating with audit
    committees 783
  main roles of 51
  role in corporate governance 53, 54
external confirmations, substantive
  procedures 515
external governance issues 55
external legal counsels 769–70

F

fact of independence   111
factual misstatements   779
fair presentation frameworks   282, 285–6
fair value accounting estimates, substantive
  procedures   514
false returns   580
familiarity threats   105, 108, 110, 118, 119
Fannie Mae   234
federal government's liability reforms   207
Ferrier Hodgson   235
fiduciary relationships   139, 213
  breach of   569
fieldwork   762–76
  finalising procedures for   760
  reviewing subsequent events   762–6
finance leases   693
Financial Accounting Standards Board
  (FASB)   489–90
financial interest threats   115–16
*Financial Management and Accountability
  Act 1997*   74
financial report audits   15, 114–15
  objective of   6
  provision of   13–14
  value of audits   249
financial reporting
  comparatives   301–2
  consolidated statements   301
  frameworks adopted by
    management   286
  initial engagements (opening
    balances)   302–3
  levels of materiality   419–20
  standards of   282–4
  statutory requirements   284
Financial Reporting Council (FRC)   19,
    21, 24, 256
  Auditor Independence Report   124
  independence frameworks   124
  primary role of   25, 135
Financial Reporting Council's (UK) Smith
    Report   68
financial risk   373
Financial Services Reform Act 2001   132
financial statement assertions
  audit strategies for material   424
  categories and definitions   369
  completeness   370
  cut-off   370–1
  existence/occurrence   370
  management   368–72
  presentation and disclosure   372
  rights and obligations   371
  valuation and allocation   371–2

financial statement fraud   125–6
financial statements
  public sector   75–6
  reliability of   7
  technical review   777, 779
finished goods   667, 685
firm regulation framework   140, 143–6
First Castle Electronics   228
First Corporate Law Simplification Act 1995
    (Cwlth)   250
flowcharts   392–5
  guidelines   393
  processing of receipts   394
*Fomento (Stirling Area) Ltd v. Selsdon
    Fountain Pen Co. Ltd* (1958) I WLR
    45   211
forecasts   180
foreign currencies   711, 744
forensic and probity audits   52
forensic auditing engagements   187–9
foreseeability   227
forward-looking approaches in ethical
    theories   101
Framework *See Framework for Assurance
    Engagements* (Framework)
Framework for Assurance Engagements
    (Framework)   165–8
fraud
  asset misappropriation   716
  cash receipts   716
  cash register   730–1
  corporate   19–20
  detecting   18, 210–11
  compared with earnings
    management   340
  employee   633–4
  evidence triangulation   315–16
  fake invoices   628
  financial statement   125–6
  incidence of   188–9
  inventory   665, 674–5
  lapping   710, 726
  material   31
  motivations to commit   189
  occupational   343
  payroll   636
  point-of-sale   580–1
  profile of typical   188
  reasons for   343
  risk factors for misappropriation of
    assets   342–3
  susceptibility of cash to   715
fraud risk   334–45
  assessments procedures   344–5
  brainstorming sessions   345
  financial reporting   337–41

financial reporting risk factors   338–9
  identifying specific risk factors   345
fraud triangle   337, 343
full cost accounting   182

G

Galoo Ltd v. Bright Graham Murray (1994)
    BCC 319   218
general controls   380, 381, 468, 469–70
  assessing and testing   473–4
general purpose financial reports   173
  external   283–4
  frameworks for   282
  going concern basis   766
  limitations of   226–7
generalised audit software *See also* ACL;
    IDEA   503
  analytical procedures   505–6
  substantive procedures   504–6
  tests of operating effectiveness   589
  trial balances   597
generic management system
    standards   191–3
gifts and hospitality   122
Global Crossing   127
global financial crisis (GFC)
  factors in development of   48
  impact on accountability
    frameworks   123–4
  impact on audit reforms   19–20
  impact on businesses   329
  impact on potential liabilities for
    auditors   234–5
  tips for working in post-GFC
    environment   785–7
Global Reporting Initiative (GRI)   182–5
  *The External Assurance of Sustainability
    Reporting*   185
going concern
  evaluating appropriateness of   32, 766–8
  proposed revisions   289
  types of audit opinions for   775–6
going concern basis   766
goods received notes   626
governance *See also* corporate governance;
    enterprise governance   47–9
  impact on control environment   378
  internal   49
  internal auditing processes   60–3
  operational auditing processes   64–5
  in public sector   71–82
  risk management and internal control
    issues   55–9
government business enterprises
    (GBEs)   73, 78
government regulation   146

Grange Securities 569
Grant Thornton 128, 131, 137, 264, 760
   acquisitions 17
gross profit ratio 597, 680
group entities 741
GS 001 281
GS 006 281, 286
GS 008 281, 286
GS 015 709, 735–6, 741
GS 016 709, 720
guidance papers 208
Guidance Statements 75
Gulf of Mexico oil spill 64

H

half-year financial reports 175–6 *See also*
   interim financial reports,
   reporting requirements 254
half-year financial statements 303
Handbook of the Code of Ethics for
   Professional Accountants 104
haphazard selection 540
   bias in 541–2
Harris Scarfe 12, 204
HBOS 234
Hedley Byrne & Co. Ltd v Heller & Partners
   (1963) 2 AII ER 575 220, 221–2
High Court's rulings in favour of
   auditors 230–1
HIH Insurance Ltd 12, 19, 21, 125,
   128, 204
HIH Royal Commission 12, 19, 21, 32,
   123, 213–14
historical financial information
   assurance engagements 170
   audits of financial statements
      summary 175
   audits of single and specific financial
      statements 174–5
   audits using special purpose
      framework 173–5
   review engagements 175–7
Horwath 131
hotel industry business operations 329,
   496–7
House of Representatives Standing
   Committee on Expenditure 72
human resource policies and
   practices 378–9
Huron Consulting 125

I

IAASB *See* International Auditing and
   Assurance Standards Board (IAASB)
IAPS 1010 164
IAS 2 665

IAS 7 709
IAS 10 759
IAS 16 665
IAS 17 665
IAS 24 709
IAS 27 709
IAS 31 709
IAS 34 249, 281
IAS 36 665
IAS 37 759
IAS 38 709
IBM 21
ICAA *See* Institute of Chartered
   Accountants (ICAA)
ICOFR 455
ICQ 389–91
IDEA 190, 503, 505
IES 4 139–40
IES 8 140
IESBA 97, 104
IFAC *See* International Federation of
   Accountants (IFAC)
IFRS 3 709
IMF Australia 234, 235
implicit assertions 369, 372
imprest bank accounts 714
   substantive procedures 731–2
imprest petty cash funds 714
   auditing procedures 731
   substantive procedures 731
income statement accounts
   analytical procedures 513
   substantive procedures 512–13
independence *See also* audit independence;
      professional independence
   legislative recommendations 123–4
   facets of 110–11
   tests for 111, 114
   threats to 111
independence of appearance
   111, 115, 138
independence of mind 115, 138
independent auditors 13, 47
   appointment process 250–2
   criteria for assessment of internal
      auditors 63
   differences between internal auditors
      and 62–3
   duties of 253–6
   operational audits 65
   in public sector 72
   registration of 14
   relationship with board of directors and
      audit committees 261–3
   relationship with internal auditors 263
   relationship with management 263–4

   relationships with shareholders 261
   responsibilities in financial reporting
      process 266
   revisions to reports 290–3
independent auditor's reports, emphasis of
      matter and other matter in 298–300
independent checks 381
   flowcharts 394–5
independent directors 262
indirect tests 513
Industrial Revolution and audit
      demand 9–10
information
   credibility of 7
   source and nature of 430
information asymmetry 9
information hypothesis, overlaps with
      agency theory 11–12
information processing controls 380–3,
      468
information system *See also* computer
      information systems 379–80, 381
information technology (IT)
   assessing and testing application
      controls 474
   assessing and testing controls 472–5
   assessing and testing general
      controls 473–4
   audit strategies 457
   control activities 381–3
   controls in 468–70
   general controls and manual follow-up
      procedures 470
   monitoring activities 385–6
   user controls 468–9
inherent risks 400
   property, plant and equipment 689
   purchases, payables and payroll 636
   relationships between ERM and 59
   sales and receivables 583
initial engagements audit programs 508,
      509
initial engagements (opening
      balances) 302–3
initial procedures
   accounts payable 648
   accounts receivable 595, 597
   cash balances 718
   computer information systems 597
   inventory transactions 679
   investments 738
   property, plant and equipment 692
initiation or acceptance, performance
      engagements 79–80
input controls 381–2
   computer information systems 397

Institute of Chartered Accountants
(ICAA)
Charter 16
Members' Handbook 16
membership base 16–17
strategic plans 17
insolvency standards 136
inspections
auditing procedures 438
documentation 436
procedures 374
Institute of Chartered Accountants
(ICAA) 103
adoption of internationalised standards
for independence 131
audit committee guides 70
audit quality survey 2012 341
competency standards 140
disciplinary powers of 148
'Financial report audit: Meeting the
market expectations,' 31
Joint Code of Professional
Conduct 97, 104
National Disciplinary Committee 148
PSL structure amendments 208
review of Big Four firms 137, 264
Supplemental Royal Charter 16, 148
Institute of Internal Auditors (IIA)
Board of Regents 61
Common Body of Knowledge (CBOK)
survey 61, 66
*International Professional Practice
Framework* (IPPF) 60
Institute of Internal Auditors–
Australia 61, 66
Institute of Public Accountants
(IPA) 103
membership base 17
insurance hypothesis 12–13, 204
integrated reporting 184
directors' concerns regarding 203
EMS 193
varied professional views towards
164–5
integrated test facility (ITF) 471, 588
integrated working papers 349
inter-entity transactions 743
interim audits 327
tests of controls 425, 461
tests of details of transactions 508,
599, 648
interim financial reports 175–6
reporting requirements 254
internal auditing 60–3
scope of 62
threats and safeguards 121

internal auditors *See also* certified internal
auditors (CIA) 49
broadening role of 65–6
core competencies 61
differences between independent
auditors and 62–3
enquiries to 373–4
relationship with independent
auditors 263
role in corporate governance 53, 54
in tests of controls 464–5
internal control 375–86
audit procedures 387–8
auditor's responsibilities 376–7
cash balances 713–14
components of 377–86
control activities 380–5
control environment 377–9
documentation system for 389–95
evaluation checklists 397
flowcharts 392–5
ICQ for general controls 390–1
IFAC guidance for evaluation of 467
importance of 375–7
identifying types of misstatements and
risks involved 387
information system 379–80
internal controls over financial reporting
(ICOFR) 455
limitations of 386
management's responsibilities 376
monitoring activities 385–6
narrative memorandum 395
performance reviews 385
physical controls 384–5
procedures to obtain understanding
388
purchases, payables and payroll
636–7
risk assessments 379
sales and receivables 584
segregation of duties 383–4
substantive tests and level of risk 388
for transaction classes 426
understanding 386–8
internal control frameworks 55
assessing structures 58
factors in occupational fraud 343
internal control matters 466–8
internal control questionnaire
(ICQ) 389–91
internal control reporting 31
Internal Control-Integrated Framework 375
internal governance issues 55
International Accounting Standards Board
(IASB), *Conceptual Framework* 421

International Auditing and Assurance
Standards Board (IAASB) 27, 32 *See
also* Clarity Project
audit expectation gap consultation
paper 255
Exposure Drafts 282, 287–93
International Auditing Practice
Statements 27
International Standards on Assurance
Engagements 27
International Standards on Auditing
(ISAs) 27
International Standards on Quality
Control 27
International Standards on Related
Services 27
proposed improvements to auditor's
reports 282
proposed revisions to reporting
rules 759–60
*Reporting on Audited Financial
Statements: Proposed New and Revised
International Standards on Auditing*
(Exposure Draft) 287–93
role of 27
International Auditing Practice
Statements 27
International Education Standards
(IESs) 139
International Ethics Standards Board for
Accountants (IESBA) 97, 104
International Federation of Accountants
(IFAC) 27
accounting profession definitions 99
Code of Ethics for Professional
Accountants (Code of Ethics) 97,
104, 249, 265, 315
*Enterprise Governance: Getting the
Balance Right* 48
guidance on internal control
evaluation 467
*Handbook of the Code of Ethics for
Professional Accountants* 104
International Education Standards
(IESs) 139
International Framework 165–8
ISAs 256
Policy Position paper 5 105
*International Framework for Assurance
Engagements* 51
International Integrated Reporting
Committee (IIRC) 184
International Integrated Reporting
Council 164
International Organization for
Standardization (ISO) 191–3

International Professional Practice Framework (IPPF) 60
International Standards on Assurance Engagements (ISAEs) 27
International Standards on Auditing (ISAs) 27
International Standards on Quality Control 27
International Standards on Related Services (ISRS) 27
internet, and e-crimes 187–8
intimidation threats 105, 108, 110, 117
inventories 667–87
  audit objectives 668–9
  audit procedures 666–7
  fraud 665, 674–5
  substantive procedures 509–11, 515
inventory count 670–1, 681–3
  assertions applicable to 683
  substantive procedures 682
  testing accuracy of listings 683
  working papers 682–3
inventory count sheets 671, 683
inventory fraud 674–5
inventory master files 669
inventory tags 671, 683
inventory transactions 669–72
  analytical procedures 679–80
  at cost testing 685
  audit planning 672–8
  audit strategies 673–4
  comparing inventory with records 672
  confirming inventories located outside entity's 686
  control risk assessments 675–8
  control risk over inventory costs 677–8
  control risk over inventory records 675–7
  cut-off tests 680–1
  disclosure requirements 686–7
  examining consignment contracts 686
  initial procedures 679
  inventory count procedures 670–2
  materiality and risk factors 673
  merchandising and manufactured inventory costing 672
  movement of goods into inventory 669–70
  movement of goods out from inventory 670
  at net realisable value testing 685
  predominantly substantive approaches 674
  substantive procedures 678–87
  testing entries in inventory records 680
  testing inventory listing 683

testing inventory pricing 684–6
tests of details of balances 681–6
tests of details of transactions 680–1
transfers of 670
write-downs 685
inventory transfer requisitions 670
inventory turnover ratio 680
investment registers 734
investment subsidiary ledgers 734
investments 732–44 *See also* derivatives
  analytical procedures 738
  audit objectives 732–3
  audit procedures 710–12
  checking securities on hand and held by others 739
  control environment factors 734
  detection risks 736
  documents and records control procedures 734
  initial procedures 738
  investing functions and related controls 734–5
  predominantly substantive approaches 736
  presentation and disclosure requirements 740
  recalculating investment revenue earned 739–40
  reviewing market values documentation 740
  short and long term materiality risks 735–6
  substantive procedures 736–40
  tests of details of transactions 738
ISA 200 5, 45, 49–50, 95, 249, 281, 315, 367
ISA 210 203, 249, 281, 315
ISA 220 95
ISA 230 315, 489
ISA 240 31, 163, 249, 315
ISA 250 45, 50, 315
ISA 260 45, 50, 289, 759
ISA 265 45, 50, 367, 455
ISA 300 315
ISA 315 45, 50, 315, 367, 415, 489, 569, 619 665, 709
ISA 320 415, 759
ISA 330 45, 50, 415, 489
ISA 450 281, 759
ISA 500 415, 489, 527, 569
ISA 501 203, 415, 489, 665, 769
ISA 505 489, 569
ISA 510 281, 489, 665
ISA 520 315, 489, 759
ISA 530 489, 527, 569

ISA 540 489, 569, 665, 709, 759
ISA 550 489, 759
ISA 560 249, 281, 759
ISA 570 281, 289, 759
ISA 580 249, 415, 759
ISA 600 665, 709
ISA 610 45, 249, 315, 415, 455, 665
ISA 620 315, 415, 665
ISA 700 5, 95, 249, 281, 288, 759
ISA 701 289
ISA 705 249, 281, 289, 759
ISA 706 249, 281, 289
ISA 720 281
ISA 800 281
ISA330 455
ISAE 3000 163, 177–8, 179, 180, 185–6
ISAE 3100 163
ISAE 3410 163
ISAE 3420 163
ISAE 3500 180
ISO 14 0001 192
ISO 14 004 192
ISO 19 011 192–3
ISO 9000 191–2, 193–4
ISO 9000:2000 191–2
ISO 14000 192–3
ISQC 1 95, 136, 141, 249, 315, 415
ISRE 2400 163, 176, 177
ISRE 2410 164, 176, 281
ISRS 4400 163, 181
IT systems threats and safeguards 121

J

JCPAA 72–3, 78, 123
JEB Fasteners Ltd v. Marks, Bloom & Co. (1981) 2 AER 289 224, 226
Joint Code of Professional Conduct 97
Joint Committee of Public Accounts and Audit (JCPAA) 72–3, 78, 123
Joint Stock Companies Registration and Regulation Act (UK) 13
joint ventures 732
  disclosure requirements 741
JPMorgan Chase 129
judgemental misstatements 779

K

Kingston Cotton Mill Co. (1896) 2 Ch. 279 18, 209, 210, 771
kiting 719, 720, 725–6
KPMG 17, 127, 215, 234
  Fraud and Misconduct survey 2010 188
  litigation settlements 205
  Survey of fraud, bribery and corruption in Australia and New Zealand 2012, 189, 335–6

L

lapping 710, 726
  auditing procedures 729
  cash receipts journals 728–9
  tests of controls 728–30
lead schedule 350
legal environment 204–8
legal titles
  physical inspections of 735
  registrations 711, 738–9
Legislative Council 71
Lehman Brothers 129, 234
Lehman Brothers Australia 569
Lend Lease 137
letter of general enquiry 769
letter of specific enquiry 769, 770
Levitt Robinson 130
liability, joint and several 204
limitation of scope 296, 509, 600, 769, 773
limited assurance
  compared with reasonable
    assurance 169–70
  performance engagements 78, 81, 180
litigation
  audit procedures for entities
    undergoing 768
  communicating with entity's legal
    counsel 769–70
  crises 205–6
  increasing rate in auditing profession 12
  strategies to minimise 231–3
Lloyds TSB 234
loans and guarantees threats 116
London and General Bank (No. 2) (1895) 2
  Ch 673 210–11, 214, 253, 528
long form assurance engagement
  reports 167
low-balling 114
Lowe Lippmann Figdor & Franck v.
  AGC (Advances) Ltd (1992) 2 VR
  671 227–8
lower assessed level of control risk
  approach 424–5, 457, 459–60,
  494, 495
  decision tree for 458
Lyvetta 227

M

Macquarie Margin Lending 130
management 47, 263–4
  accounting estimates 513
  common areas of dispute with
    auditors 513, 763–4
  communicating audit findings to 761
  evaluating integrity of 318–19, 377

executive compensation and profit
  shifting 619
factors for earnings management
  339–40
financial statement assertions 368–72
impact on control environment 378
imposed limitations by 296
relationship with shareholders and
  auditors 46
responsibilities in financial reporting
  process 266
responsibilities in internal control 376
review of analytical procedures 775
review of working papers 780
role in fraud risk assessment 344
threats and safeguards for 119
management assertions tests of
  controls 462
management consulting services
  standards 136
management letters 267, 301
management representation letter 762,
  763, 771
  contents of 772–3
manufacturing industry
  audit procedures 684
  control risk over inventory costs
    677–8
  inventory risk factors 673
mark-to-market valuation system
  489–90
material misstatements 490–3
  cash balances 714–15
  detection risks 493
  factors that affect risk 387
  final assessments 777–9
  investments 735–6
  levels of 327
  nature of 295
  in property, plant and equipment 689
  professional judgement 268, 294–5
  purchases, payables and payroll 636
  relationship between audit evidence
    and 422–3
  risk assessments and
    corresponding 491–2
  sales transactions 582–3
  steps in assessing risk of 490
  types in internal control 387
  uncorrected aggregated 423
materiality 185, 417–23
  account balances or disclosures 422
  assessing 418
  benchmarks for 419
  commonly used bases for 420
  concepts of 417–18

evaluating audit evidence 422–3
  judgements 420
  qualitative guidelines 421–2
  quantitative guidelines 419–20
mathematical accuracy of entity-prepared
  schedules 692
mathematical correctness 371–2
mathematical evidence 434
matters to be agreed upon (terms of
  engagements) 80
Maurice Blackburn 130, 205, 235
McKesson and Robbins fraud 211
mean-per-unit method 544
  in variable sampling 555–6
mid-tier accounting 17, 131
misappropriation of assets risk
  factors 342–3
misstatements *See also* material
  misstatements
  accounting 125
  factual 779
  financial 59–60
  tolerable 422, 537
  uncorrected 778
MLC Assurance 222–3
modified auditor's reports 293–4, 600
modified opinion 293–6
  form and content of 297–8
  types of 294–5
modified opinions 423
monetary unit sampling 535
monitoring process 385–6
  ERM 57
  online real-time systems 472
monthly customer statements 577
Moore Stephens 17
morality 100, 101
Morgan Crucible Co. PLC v. Hill Samuel
  Bank Ltd and Other (1991) 1 AER
  148 228
Mutual Life and Citizens Assurance Co. Ltd
  v. Evatt (1968) 122 CLR 556 222–3

N

narrative memorandum 395, 466
National Australia Bank 164
National Disciplinary Committee 148
National Greenhouse and Energy Register
  (NGER) 184, 187
National Greenhouse and Energy Reporting
  (Audit) Determination 2009 184
negative form confirmation
  600, 601, 602
negligence, lawsuits 204
New South Wales Professional Standards
  Act 1994 207

New Zealand
  incidence of fraud in   188
  KPMG fraud survey 2012   335–6
  proximity cases   223
Nexia   17
non-adjusting events   766
non-assurance services
  evaluating independence in   321
  safeguards to independence
    threats   119
  threats to audit independence   119–23
non-audit assurances, integrated
  reporting and inherent legal
  problems   164–5
non-audit fees   19
non-audit services   19, 21
  information to be included in   132–3
  threats and safeguards for   119–22
non-consequentialism   101
non-qualified audit risk model   402
non-sampling risk   529, 531
non-statistical sampling   529, 531–2, 546–7
  formal and informal   547
  projected errors   549–50
  projecting deviation rates   542
  random selection in   539
  reliability factors   549
  substantive test of details   548–50
normative ethical theories   101–2
NSW Commission of Audit Interim
  Report on Public Sector
  Management   82
NSW Greenhouse Gas Abatement
  Scheme   182

O

objectivity of audit evidence   430–1
observations
  auditing procedures   437
  inventory count   666, 667, 681–3
  of procedures   374
  tests of controls   461
occurrence assertions   370
  tests of controls   643, 670
occurrence problems   594, 645
OECD See Organisation for Economic
  Co-operation and Development
  (OECD)
OECD Principles of Corporate Governance
  (2004)   48, 52
Ohio   234
One.Tel   12, 127, 204
online banking   580
online real-time systems (OLRT)   472
operating effectiveness of the control
  procedures   460–2

operational auditing   64–5 See also
  performance auditing; value-for-
  money auditing
operational risk   373
opinion shopping   109, 114
Oracle Corp   619
oral evidence   434, 437
Organisation for Economic Co-operation
  and Development (OECD)   47
  corporate governance revisions   51–2
  OECD Principles of Corporate
    Governance (2004)   48
  Steering Group   48
organisational controls   381
organisational structures   378
output controls   383, 398
oversight bodies   22–3
over-the-counter receipts   578–9

P

Pacific Acceptance Corporation v. Forsyth
  (1970) 92 WN NSW (29)   18, 136,
  212, 214, 258, 266, 771
parallel simulation   471–2
  compared with test data approach   471
Parliament
  accountability framework   74–5
  parliamentary committees   72–3
  structure of   71–2
Parmalat   128
payment transactions   628–9
  access controls   629
  control risk assessments   641
  paying liabilities   628–9
  recording payments   629
payment transactions files   629
payments cut-off tests   649
payroll fraud   636
payroll registers   632
payroll transactions   630–4
  access controls   643
  attendance and timekeeping data   632
  audit procedures   621
  authorising changes to   632
  control risk assessments   642–3
  hiring employees   630–2
  payroll cycle   631
  preparing payroll   632
  recording payroll   632–3
  segregation of duties   630
  unclaimed wages controls   633
payroll transactions files   632
PCAOB See Public Company Accounting
  Oversight Board (PCAOB)
peer regulation frameworks   140
perceived independence   111

performance auditing   52, 64
  objectives in   78
  phases in   77
  public sector   73, 74, 76–8
  types of   78
performance concepts   48, 51
performance engagements   78–81, 180
  assurance report content   80
  objective of   79–80
  quantitative and qualitative factors   80
  reporting findings, recommendations
    and comments   81
  types of   78
  types of conclusions   81
performance measures and
  information   333
performance reviews   385
periodic performance reviews   577, 627
permanent files   347, 353, 392
perpetual inventory records   669, 670,
  673, 675–6
personnel, competence levels of   377
personnel authorisation forms   630
personnel data master files   630
personnel files   630
physical controls   384–5
physical evidence   435
physical inventory   666
physical inventory count   667, 673
Pitcher Partners   17, 131, 164, 235
PKF   17, 131, 214
planned detection risk   494
planned level of substantive
  procedures   495
plant registers   689, 690
point-of-sale fraud   580–1
Ponzi scheme fraud   234
population   535–7
  stratification of   535–6
population sampling   528
positive form confirmation   600, 601
PPS See probability-proportional-to-size
  (PPS) sampling
predominantly substantive
  approaches   423, 457–9, 495
  consolidated financial statements   741
  decision tree for   458
  inventory transactions   673, 674
  investments   736
  property, plant and equipment   666
  sales and receivables   584
preliminary assessment of control
  risk   396, 456
prepared by client (PBC) schedules   350
prescriptive approaches for accountability
  process   68

presentation and disclosure assertions 372
    accounts receivable 596
    specific audit objectives 427
    substantive procedures 510
'presents fairly' assessments 8
PricewaterhouseCoopers 17, 21, 234,
        665, 760
    audit committee outlook report 70
    cross-claim cases 130, 235
    litigation cases against 205, 206
    *State of internal audit profession study
        2013* 65–6
    tips for working in post-GFC
        environment 785–7
principal auditors 301, 743
principles-based approaches 21
    ethics 104, 105, 145
    professional independence 123–4
private companies' material
    misstatements 493
privity letters 227, 232
privity of contract 215–17
Privy Council decisions 222–31
probability ratios 355
probability-proportional-to-size (PPS)
        sampling 537, 545–6, 550–3
    projected errors 552–3
process audit approaches 64
processing controls 382–3
    computer information systems 398
professional accountants
    common ethical problems 138
    continuing professional
        development 140
    duties of 99–100
    fundamental principles for 105–6
    loyalty and duties of 138–9
    professional codes 98
    professional culture 99
    professional ethics 100–10
    role of 97–100
    threats and safeguards in
        business 109–10
    threats and safeguards in public
        practice 106–9
professional accounting
        associations 16–17
    history of formation 15–16
    influence in audit development 16
professional associations 98
professional duties 255–6
professional ethics 97
    assurance engagements 177
    in audit engagements 320–2
    co-regulation environment 103–4
    ethical decision-making models 103

for professional accountants 103–4
    performance engagements 79
    theories for 101–2
    top-down approaches 103
    values of management 377
professional indemnity insurance 204,
        208, 232, 233–4
professional independence 97, 110–25
    client relationships 320
    legislative reform for 123–4
professional judgement
    assessing audit evidence 429, 430
    assessing financial reports 25–6
    assessing materiality 268, 419, 420, 735
    ethical decision making 106
    independence 115
    in level of substantive procedures 594
    in performance engagements 78–9
    reasonable assurance 431
    risk assessments 58
    sampling 531
professional scepticism 60, 126
    audit planning 326
    audit quality 341
    audits of financial reports 25–6
    earnings management 340
    independence 115
    lack of 137, 264
    management assertions 263
    reasonable assurance 431
professional standards legislation
        (PSL) 207–8, 233
professionalism characteristics 100
profit shifting 619
projected deviation rate 554–5
projected errors 543, 549–50, 552–3
projected misstatements 779
projections 180
property, plant and equipment 687–95
    analytical procedures 692
    assets and accumulation lead
        schedule 692
    audit objectives 688
    audit planning 689–90
    audit procedures 666–7
    audit strategies 689–90
    depreciation 689–90
    inherent risks in 689
    initial procedures 692
    materiality related to 689
    predominantly substantive
        approaches 666
    presentation and disclosure
        requirements 695
    revaluations of 695
    substantive procedures 690–5

tests of details of balances 694–5
    tests of details of transactions 693–4
proportionate liability reforms 207
prospective financial information
        (PFI) 180–1
Proviti 66
proximity 221
    cases 222–31
    elements in negligence actions 225
    landmark cases 225–6, 227–8
PSL 207–8, 233
public accountability 71–2
public accounting regulation
        framework 143–6
*Public Accounts and Audit Committee Act
        1951* (Cwlth) 72
Public Accounts Committee
        Regulations 72, 82
public companies
    audit strategies 459
    material misstatements in 493
    statutory audit requirements 267
Public Company Accounting Oversight
        Board (PCAOB) 20, 30, 33, 131, 377
public interest 26, 98
    IFAC's position on 105
public sector governance 71–82
    agency-specific audits 78
    audit mandates 74–5
    consolidated financial statements 76
    cross-agency audits 78
    exception basis reporting 75–6
    financial statement audits 75–6
    parliamentary accountability process 71
    parliamentary committees 72–3
    performance auditing 76–8
    performance engagements 78–81
    state government CFOs 81–2
Public Service Act 1922 (Cwlth) 74
purchase orders 626
purchase requisitions 625
purchase transactions 625–7
    audit procedures 620
    CAAT 639
    credit 640
    checking suppliers' invoices 627
    control risk assessments 637–40
    fake invoices fraud 628
    preliminary assessment of control
        risk 639
    purchase order controls 626
    receiving goods 626
    recording liabilities 627
    requisitioning goods and services 625
    storing goods received for inventory 626
    tests of operating effectiveness 639

purchase transactions files 627
purchases, payables and payroll
adjustment transactions 623–9
analytical procedures 621, 635–6
audit objectives for 621–3
audit plans 634–43
audit procedures 620–1
audit strategies 636
control risk assessments 637–43
credit purchases cycle 624
cut-off tests 680–1
final assessments 643
inherent risks 636
internal control 636–7
material misstatements 636
understanding entity and its
environment 635
purchases cut-off tests 649
purpose-written programs 504

Q

qualified accountants 16
qualified conclusion 81
qualified opinion 294, 296, 302
form and content of 297–8
qualitative misstatements 421–2
quality control
assurance engagements 178
in auditing firms 140–7
client evaluation 318–20
elements, policies and
procedures 142–3
maintenance of 232
performance engagements 79
standards for auditing firms 141–3
quality management principles
191–2
quantitative misstatements 419–20
Queensland Parliament 71
questionnaires 389–91
Quinn Insurance Ltd (QIL) 234

R

Ramsay Report 21, 123
random sampling 531, 539–40
inventory counts 670
rationality concepts 101
raw materials 667
real-time methods 575
reasonable assurance 8, 18, 114, 441
audit evidence 431
compared with limited assurance
169–70
performance engagements 180
sustainability reports for greenhouse
emissions 185–7

reasonable assurance performance
engagements 78, 81
reasonable person test 111
reasonable skill and care 18
recalculation, in auditing procedures 438
receiving reports 626
reclassifying entries 351
regulations 13
audit independence 21
audit quality changes 21–2
co-regulation environment 103–4
multilevel framework 140
sources for 22
regulatory bodies 22–3
related party transactions 330, 736
substantive procedures 514
relevance of evidence 430
reliability of evidence 430
remittance advice 579, 629
remuneration reports 286
rental expenses 694
re-performance *See also* dual-purpose tests
audit software 590
auditing procedures 438
tests of controls 461
*Reporting on Audited Financial Statements:
Proposed New and Revised
International Standards on Auditing*
(Exposure Draft) 287–93
Reserve Bank of Australia 137
Residual Assco 205
responsiveness principle 185
review engagements
assertion-based 114
AUASB standards 176
compensation and evaluation
policies 122
financial reports and other historical
financial information 175–7
general principles of 176
half-year financial statements 303
independence approaches 115–23
procedures of 176–7
public sector 76
rights and obligations assertions 371
consolidated financial statements 742
inventory transactions 686
substantive procedures 510
vouching 437
risk assessments 57
analytical procedures 374
business 372–3
control risks 465–6
financial statement assertions 368–72
for internal control 379
material misstatements 491–2

procedures of 270, 373–4
Thought Paper 58
risk management standards 55
risk management systems
internal control and adequacy of
55–9
typical 56
risk matrix 644
risk objectives 57
risk of incorrect acceptance 530
risk of incorrect rejection 531
risk of overreliance 530, 537
risk of underreliance 530–1
risk response options 57
risk strategies, inspection programs
232–3
risk-based audit approaches 64, 65, 78,
399
roll-forward testing 502
rotation of auditors 21
Royal Bank of Scotland 234
*Royal Bank of Scotland PLC v. Bannerman
Johnstone Maclay and Others* (2002)
TLR 1 230
Royal Charter 16
RSM Bird Cameron 17, 131
rules-based approaches 21

S

sales adjustment transactions 581
materiality concerns 584–5
tests of controls 591
sales and receivables
audit objectives 571–3
audit procedures 570–1
audit strategies 583–4
balance transactions 572
confirmations for 571
control risk assessments 585–7
disclosure requirements 605
final control risk assessments 591
inherent risks 583
internal control components 584
predominantly substantive
approaches 584
presentation and disclosure
objectives 573
substantive procedures 592–605
transaction objectives 572
understanding entity and its
environment 582–4
sales cut-off tests 599
sales invoices 577
sales journals 577
sales orders 575
sales return cut-off tests 599

sales transactions
    materiality in   582–3
    processes in   573
    substantive procedures   501
sales transactions files   577
sample deviation rate   542–3
sampling
    accounts receivable   602
    audit tests   533–43
    basic concepts of   528–33
    bias in   540
    evaluating error rates in   542
    extrapolating errors from   533
    population   528
    selection for   539–40
    sequential   544
    size of   537–8
    subconscious behaviour in   541–2
    substantive procedures   538
    substantive tests   543
    testing   532, 540
    tests of controls   528–9, 538
    tests of details of balances   535
sampling interval   540
sampling risk   528, 529–31
    substantive procedures   530
    tests of controls   530
    types of   529–30
sampling units   536–7
San Sebastian Pty Ltd v. The Minister
    (1986) 162 CLR 340   228
Santos Limited's Sustainability Report
    2012   185–7
Sarbanes-Oxley Act (2002)   21, 123, 131
    corporate responsibility
        requirements   65
    independence requirements   63, 117
    internal control safeguards   19–20, 65
Satyam   234
scanning   436
Schott Report   82
Scott Group Ltd v. McFarlane (1978) 1
    NZLR 553   223, 226
second partner reviews   780
second-tier accounting firms   17, 131
securities
    audit procedures   711, 735
    materiality of   735
Securities Exchange Commission (SEC)
    (US)   33, 68, 123, 211
    investigations into corporate
        collapses   127
securities held by others   739
securities on hand   739
Security Pacific Business Credit Inc. v. Peat
    Marwick Main & Co.   217

Segenhoe Ltd v. Akins & Ors (1990) 8
    ACLC 263   217
segregation of duties   383–4
    cash transactions   709
    credit sales transactions   576
    effect on control risk   384
    inventory transactions   669
    payroll transactions   630, 631–2
    sales adjustment transactions   581
selection bias in haphazard
    selection   541–2
self-interest threats   105, 108, 109, 110, 122
self-regulation frameworks   140, 146
    controls for   190–4
self-regulatory codes   98
self-review threats   63, 105, 108, 110, 115,
    117–18, 120, 121
Shaddock & Associates Pty Ltd v.
    Parramatta City Council (1981) 55
    ALIR 713   223
shareholders
    relationship with auditors and
        management   46
    relationship with independent
        auditors   261
    as users of audit reports   28–9
Sherwin Financial Planners Pty Ltd
    206–7
short form assurance engagement
    reports   167
significant risks   374, 418
Sims Metal Management   665
skimming   709
Slater & Gordon   130, 205, 235
Smith Report 2003 (UK)   68
social auditing   52
solvency ratios   354–5
South Africa's adoption of integrated
    reporting   165
Southern Equities   205
special-purpose financial reports   173–4
special-purpose entities   331
Spotless   137
St James Ethics Centre   145
staff assignment and secondment
    threats   117–18
stakeholder expectations of auditors   52,
    139
stakeholder impact analysis   103
stakeholder theory   47
Standard & Poor's company audit
    committee requirements   68, 132
standard setting benchmarks   182–5,
    191–4
Standards Australia   55
Standards New Zealand   55

Standards of Assurance Engagements
    (ASAEs) See individual ASAEs
Standards on Related Services (ASRs)   27
Standards on Review Engagements
    (ASREs)   27
standing data   578
Stanilite Pacific Ltd & Anor v. Seaton and
    Ors, t/a Price Waterhouse (2005)
    NSWCA 301   214
state and territory governments' liability
    reforms   207–8
State of internal audit profession study
    2013, 65–6
state-owned companies   72
statistical sampling   529, 531–2, 539, 545
    audit software   589
    rate of errors in   542
    techniques   544–5
statute law   204
statutory bodies   22–3
Stockland   164
stocktakes   667
Storm Financial   129–30, 204
stratification of population   535–6, 545
Strengthening Enterprise Risk Management
    for Strategic Advantage   58
subsequent events   302
    accounting considerations   765–6
    adjusting events   765–6
    adjustments and disclosures before issue
        of financial statements   764
    adjustments and disclosures leading up
        to date of report   762–4
    difference between conditions existing
        at and after reporting period   766
    facts discovered after issue of financial
        statements   764–5
    non-adjusting events   766
    post-audit responsibilities   764–5
    reviewing   762–6
subsequent legal action court case   569
subsequent period's bank statement   725
subsidiaries   732, 742
    acquisitions and disposals   743
substantiating additions   693
substantiating disposals   693–4, 693
substantive procedures   388, 423–4, 425
    accounting estimates   513–14
    accounts payable   643–52
    analytical procedures   496–8
    audit program framework   507–8
    auditing procedures   440
    before end of reporting period
        502–3
    CAAT   503–6
    cash balances   715–28

substantive procedures (*continued*)
    considerations for design 495–506, 512–15
    consolidated financial statements 740–4
    corroborating information 431–2
    developing audit programs for 507–12
    effectiveness of controls on 425–6
    extent of 503
    factors influencing sample size for 538
    fair value accounting estimates 514
    generalised audit software 504–6
    imprest petty cash funds 731
    inventory transactions 509–10, 515, 678–87
    investments 736–40
    nature of 496–502
    processing sales transactions to accounts receivable 500–2
    property, plant and equipment 690–5
    related party transactions 514
    relationships between audit risk components and 506
    relationships between detection risk and 494
    sales and receivables 592–605
    sampling 528, 529, 543
    sampling, non-statistical 548–50
    sampling risk 530
    sampling, variable 544–5
    timing of 502–6
Sunbeam 126
Supplemental Royal Charter 16, 148
suppliers' invoices 627
sustainability 182, 183
sustainability assurance reports 181–5
    greenhouse emissions 185–7
    reporting guidelines 182
synthetic collaterised debt obligations (SCDOs) 569
systematic selection 540
systems control audit review file (SCARF) 472, 588
systems development and maintenance controls 381

T

tagging transactions method 472
Tax Justice Network 96
taxation services 120, 136
technical review of financial statements 777, 779
technology's impact on forms of evidence 435
teleology 101 *See also* consequentialism
termination notice 632
terms of assurance engagements 178

test data 588
test data approaches 470, 588, 639
    compared with parallel simulation 471
tests of controls 398
    attribute sampling 553–5
    audit programs 462–3
    in auditing procedures 440
    credit sales transactions 588–9
    extent of 462
    interim audits 425
    nature of 461
    operating effectiveness of the control procedures 460
    sample size 537–8
    sampling 528–9, 534–5
    sampling risk 530
    timing of 461–2
    using CAAT 503
    using internal auditors 464–5
tests of design effectiveness, credit sales transactions 460–1
    credit sales transactions 585, 587
tests of details of balances 499
    accounts payable 650
    accounts receivable 500, 596, 599–605
    auditing procedures 440
    CHESS 738–9
    income statement accounts 512, 513
    inventory transactions 681–6
    investments 738–40
    property, plant and equipment 694–5
    sales transactions 501
tests of details of transactions 440
    accounts payable 648–9
    accounts receivable 500, 595–6, 598–9
    cash balances 718–20
    inventory transactions 680–1
    investments 738
    property, plant and equipment 693–4
    sales transactions 501
tests of operating effectiveness
    cash receipts transactions 590–1
    credit sales transactions 587–91
    purchase transactions 639
The External Assurance of Sustainability Reporting 185
The National Greenhouse and Energy Reporting Act 2007 184
The Prince of Wales' Accounting for Sustainability Project (A4S) 183
theme park cash sales system 727
Therapeutic Goods Act 1989 328
third parties
    client evaluation enquiries 318
    confirmations 432

Thomas Gerrard & Son Ltd (1967) 2 ALL ER 525 212
three-party relationships 166, 167
time budget 322
tolerable detection risk 494
tolerable deviations 537, 542
tolerable misstatement 422, 537
tort of negligence 214
total quality management (TQM) 193–4
tracing 498
    in auditing procedures 440
    bank transfers 719–20
    cheques 725–6
    compared with vouching 437
    deposits 726
    documentation 436
    property, plant and equipment 692
Trade Practices Act 1974 207, 233
transaction classes 424, 426
transaction walk-through review 388, 457
transactions 379
Treasury's Legislation Amendment (Professional Standards) Bill 2003 207
Tricontinental 205
Trident General Insurance Co Ltd v. McNiece Bros Pty Ltd (1988) 165 CLR 107 216
triple bottom line reporting (TBL) 182
'true and fair view' assessments 8, 284
Tweedle v. Atkinson (1861) 215
Twomax Ltd v. Dickson, Mc Farlane & Robinson (1983) Scots Law Times 224, 226

U

Ultramares Corporation v. Touche Niven & Co. (1931) 255 NY 220–1, 230
underlying accounting records 428
United Kingdom
    audit committee compliance 68
    auditor reviews 45–6
    Big Four firms' role in tax avoidance 95–6
    early accounting associations 15–16
    independence provisions 117
    landmark cases 226–7
    negligence cases 218
    proximity cases 224
    sustainability assurance framework 184
United Nations Environmental Program 182
United States
    adoption of new communication standards 33
    audit fees 29

compliance rules for audit
    committee   68
corporate collapses   19, 126–7, 129
governance regulation revisions   70
high-profile frauds   211
ICOFR   455
independence provisions   117
internal control assessments   377
key reforms   131
privity of contract cases   217
sampling practices in   532
University of Sydney sustainability
    study   183
unlisted shares   734
unmodified auditor's reports   286–8
unmodified opinion   286–8
unqualified opinion   302, 769–70 *See also*
    unmodified opinion
unstratified mean-per-unit method   544–5
user controls   468–9
utilitarianism   101
utility programs   504

V

valuation and allocation assertions   371–2
    cash balances   718
    inventory transactions   667, 683
    property, plant and equipment   694
    substantive procedures   510
    vouching   436–7
valuation services   120
value-for-money auditing   64
Valukas report (US)   129

variable sampling   544–5, 546
    mean-per-unit method   555–6
variable-interest entities   331
verification controls   381
Victorian Professional Standards Act
    2003   207–8
virtue ethics   102
void sales   580
vouching   498
    accounts payable   649
    accounts receivable   599, 604
    compared with tracing   437
    dividends   711
    documentation   436–7
    investments   738
    property, plant and equipment
    692, 693

W

WA Chip & Pulp Cp. Pty Ltd v. Arthur
    Young (1987) 12 ACLR 545   217, 782
Waste Management   126
Westpoint Corporation   12, 206, 215
whistleblower protection   139
WHK   17
Wickham Securities Limited   206–7
window dressing   726
work in process   667, 685
working papers
    accounts receivable   604
    aged trial balance   598
    audit memoranda and corroborating
    information   351

audit programs   351
communication with management   783
confirmation control   603
control risk documentation   465–6
documenting oral evidence   434
final reviews for   779–80
integrated   349
internal control   392
inventory count   682–3
notes receivable and interest   350
ownership and custodianship
    352–3
preparing   351–2
purpose and function of   346
repeat engagements   388
reviewing   352
schedules and analyses   350–1
trial balance   347–8
types of   347–9, 353
written audit programs   509
WorldCom   19, 126–7, 204
write-off authorisation memos   581
written assurance reports   167
written declarations   133
written representations   433–4, 437, 763,
    771–4
    management   772–3
    procedures when management doesn't
    provide   773–4
    subject-matter specific   771

X

Xerox   127